ELEMENTS OF
Literature

FIRST COURSE

ELEMENTS OF
Literature
FIRST COURSE

These are the stories
that never, never die,
that are carried like seed
into a new country,
are told to you and me
and make in us
new and lasting strengths.

—from *Nancy Hanks of Wilderness Road:
A Story of Lincoln's Mother*
by Meridel Le Sueur

HOLT, RINEHART AND WINSTON
A Harcourt Education Company

Austin • Orlando • Chicago • New York • Toronto • London • San Diego

Credits

EDITORIAL

Project Director: Kathleen Daniel

Managing Editors: Richard Sime, Bill Wahlgren

Project Editor: Fannie Safier

Book Editors: Laura Baci, Susan Joseph, Marc Ottaviani

Editorial Staff: Steven Fechter, Abigail Winograd, Daniela Guggenheim, Julie Brye, Susan Kent Cakars, Dorothy M. Coe, Edward S. Cohen, Lanie Lee, Christine de Lignières, Ron Ottaviano, Michael Zakhar, and Jan Collins; David Knaggs and Sharon Churchin; Vicky Aeschbacher, Jane Archer-Feinstein, Roger Boylan, James Decker, Eric Estlund, Peggy Ferrin, Emily Gavin, Mikki Gibson, Annie Hartnett, Sean Henry, Julie Hoover, Eileen Joyce, Marcia Kelley, Linda Miller, Chi Nguyen, Carla Robinson, Deanna Roy, Tressa Sanders, Errol Smith, Suzanne Thompson, and Stephen Wesson

Editorial Support Staff: Mark Koenig, Danielle Greer, Dan Hunter, Laurie Muir, David Smith, Leila Jamal, Elizabeth Butler, Ruth Hooker, Kelly Keeley, Marie Price, Margaret Sanchez

Permissions: Tamara Blanken, Sacha Frey, Mark Hughs

Research and Development: Joan Burditt

PRODUCTION AND DESIGN

Text Design: Preface, Inc.

Electronic Files: Preface, Inc., H&S Graphics, Inc.

Production and Manufacturing: Athena Blackorby

Marketing Design: Bob Bretz

COVER

Cover Artist: Greg Geisler

Photo Credits: Front cover: (frog), K. Griffiths/APL/Corbis and Leo Meier/APL/Corbis; (crown), image copyright © 2001 PhotoDisc, Inc./HRW; (lily pond), Steve Hix/FPG International; (sky), Corbis Images/HRW; (grasses), Russell Dian/HRW; (moon), Chad Ehlers/Tony Stone Images; (grassy knoll), Corbis Images/HRW. Back cover: (detail, pair of frogs), Asian Art Museum of San Francisco/The Avery Brundage Collection/B60 B1082/1083.

Quotation on Cover: Meridel Le Sueur (p. 591), courtesy of Holy Cow! Press

Printed in the United States of America

ISBN 0-03-067306-2

3 4 5 6 048 03 02

Program Authors

Kylene Beers wrote the Reading Matters section of the book and developed the accompanying *Reading Skills and Strategies* component. A former middle school teacher, Dr. Beers has turned her commitment to helping readers having difficulty into the major focus of her research, writing, speaking, and teaching. A clinical associate professor at the University of Houston, Dr. Beers is also currently the editor of the National Council of Teachers of English journal *Voices from the Middle*. She is the author of *When Kids Can't Read: The Reading Handbook for Teachers Grades 6–12* and co-editor of *Into Focus: Understanding and Creating Middle School Readers*. She has served on the review boards of the *English Journal* and *The ALAN Review*. Dr. Beers is a recipient of the NCTE Richard W. Halle Award. She currently serves on the board of directors of the International Reading Association's Special Interest Group on Adolescent Literature.

Robert E. Probst established the pedagogical framework for the 1997, 2000, and current editions of *Elements of Literature*. Dr. Probst is Professor of English Education at Georgia State University. He has taught English in Maryland and been Supervisor of English for the Norfolk, Virginia, Public Schools. He is the author of *Response and Analysis: Teaching Literature in Junior and Senior High School* and has contributed chapters to such books as *Literature Instruction: A Focus on Student Response; Reader Response in the Classroom; Handbook of Research on Teaching the English Language Arts; Transactions with Literature;* and *For Louise M. Rosenblatt.* Dr. Probst has worked on the National Council of Teachers of English Committee on Research, the Commission on Reading, and the Commission on Curriculum. He has also served on the board of directors of the Adolescent Literature Assembly and is a member of the National Conference on Research in Language and Literacy.

Robert Anderson wrote the Elements of Literature essay on drama and contributed to the instructional materials for *Brian's Song.* Mr. Anderson is a playwright, novelist, screenwriter, and teacher. His plays include *Tea and Sympathy; Silent Night, Lonely Night; You Know I Can't Hear You When the Water's Running;* and *I Never Sang for My Father.* His screenplays include *The Nun's Story* and *The Sand Pebbles.* Mr. Anderson has taught at the Writers' Workshop at the University of Iowa, the American Theater Wing Professional Training Program, and the Salzburg Seminar in American Studies. He is a past president of the Dramatists' Guild, past vice president of the Authors' League of America, and a member of the Theater Hall of Fame.

John Malcolm Brinnin wrote the Elements of Literature essays on poetry, and contributed to the instructional materials on poetry. Mr. Brinnin is the author of six volumes of poetry, which received many prizes and awards. He was a member of the American Academy and Institute of Arts and Letters. He was also a critic of poetry and a biographer of poets and was for a number of years director of New York's famous Poetry Center. His teaching career, begun at Vassar College, included long terms at the University of Connecticut and Boston University, where he succeeded Robert Lowell as Professor of Creative Writing and Contemporary Letters. Mr. Brinnin's books include *Dylan Thomas in America: An Intimate Journal* and *Sextet: T. S. Eliot & Truman Capote & Others.*

John Leggett wrote the Elements of Literature essays on the short story and contributed to the instructional materials on short stories. Mr. Leggett is a novelist, a biographer, and a former teacher. He went to the Writers' Workshop at the University of Iowa in the spring of 1969, expecting to work there for a single semester. In 1970, he assumed temporary charge of the program, and for the next seventeen years he was its director. Mr. Leggett's novels include *Wilder Stone; The Gloucester Branch; Who Took the Gold Away?; Gulliver House;* and *Making Believe.* He also wrote the highly acclaimed biography *Ross and Tom: Two American Tragedies.*

Judith L. Irvin established the conceptual basis for the vocabulary and reading strands and developed the Reading Skills and Strategies exercises for grades 6–8. Dr. Irvin teaches courses in curriculum, middle school education, and educational leadership at Florida State University. She was chair of the Research Committee of the National Middle School Association and was the editor of *Research in Middle Level Education* for five years. She taught middle school for eight years before seeking her doctorate in Reading–Language Arts. Dr. Irvin writes a column, "What Research Says to the Middle Level Practitioner," for the *Middle School Journal.* Her many books include *Reading and the Middle School Student: Strategies to Enhance Literacy* and *What Current Research Says to the Middle Level Practitioner.*

Special Contributors

Virginia Hamilton wrote the Elements of Literature essays on fables and folk tales and the commentaries on Aesop's fables. Ms. Hamilton is one of America's most highly acclaimed writers of books for children and young adults. She has received many awards, including the Newbery Award for *M. C. Higgins, the Great;* the Newbery Honor Award for *In the Beginning: Creation Stories from Around the World;* the Coretta Scott King Award for *Sweet Whispers, Brother Rush;* and the Edgar Allan Poe Award for *The House of Dies Drear.* Among her collections of folk tales are *The People Could Fly* and *The Dark Way: Stories from the Spirit World.* The *All Jahdu Storybook* is a collection of Hamilton's own tales about a trickster hero who was born in an oven between two loaves of bread. In 1990, Hamilton received an honorary doctorate from the Bank Street College of Education in New York City. In 1995, she received a MacArthur Fellowship. In 1998, Kent State University established the Virginia Hamilton Literary Award for excellence in multicultural literature for children and young adults.

David Adams Leeming wrote the Elements of Literature essay on Greek and Roman myths. Dr. Leeming was a Professor of English and Comparative Literature at the University of Connecticut for many years. He is the author of several books on mythology, including *Mythology: The Voyage of the Hero; The World of Myth;* and *Encyclopedia of Creation Myths.* For several years he taught English at Robert College in Istanbul, Turkey. He also served as secretary and assistant to the writer James Baldwin in New York and Istanbul. He is the author of the biographies *James Baldwin* and *Amazing Grace: A Biography of Beauford Delaney.*

Naomi Shihab Nye wrote the Elements of Literature essay "Nonfiction: Encountering Our Lives." Ms. Nye writes poems, essays, and children's books. Her collections of poems include *Words Under the Words: Selected Poems* and *Red Suitcase.* Her picture books include *Benito's Dream Bottle,* a School Library Journal "Best Book," and *Sitti's Secrets,* recipient of the Jane Addams Children's Book Award. She edited the prize-winning *This Same Sky,* a collection of poems from around the world, and *The Tree Is Older Than You Are,* bilingual poems and stories from Mexico, both for young readers. Ms. Nye has been a visiting writer in elementary and high schools, universities, and communities across the country throughout her working life.

Writers

The writers prepared instructional materials for the text under the supervision of Dr. Probst and the editorial staff.

Lynn Hovland
Former Teacher
Educational Writer and Editor
Berkeley, California

Erin Hurley
Former Faculty Member
Brown University
Providence, Rhode Island

Julith Jedamus
Educational Writer and Editor
Pacific Palisades, California

William Kaufman
Former Teacher
Educational Writer and Editor
Hempstead, New York

David Pence
Former Teacher
Educational Writer and Editor
Brooklyn, New York

Margaret Pickett
Wellesley Middle School
Wellesley, Massachusetts

David Snyder
Wellesley Middle School
Wellesley, Massachusetts

Reviewers and Consultants

Reviewers assisted in choosing selections and evaluated instructional materials. Consultants assisted in securing student active-reading models and provided advice on current pedagogy.

Jody Alexander
Madison School District
Phoenix, Arizona

Joyce Black-Carson
Montera Junior High School
Oakland, California

Alfee Enciso
Palms Middle School
Los Angeles, California

Cheryl Greenwood
Washington Park Middle School
Washington, Pennsylvania

Carleen Hemric
Pershing Junior High School
San Diego, California

Martha Lince
JMF Ctr. for Educational Services
Indianapolis, Indiana

Jan Meeks
Fairmont Junior High School
Boise, Idaho

Pamela Moore
Milford Junior High School
Milford, Ohio

Phil Simcox
Carmody Middle School
Lakewood, Colorado

Nan Worch
Kennedy-King Middle School
Gary, Indiana

Acknowledgments

For permission to reprint copyrighted material in the Annotated Teacher's Edition, grateful acknowledgment is made to the following sources:

Arthur C. Clarke and the author's agents, Scovil, Chichak, Galen Literary Agency, Inc.: From "Space Flight: Imagination and Reality" by Sir Arthur C. Clarke from *The Planets,* edited by Byron Preiss. Copyright © 1985 by Arthur C. Clarke. Published by Bantam Books, a division of Random House, Inc.

Columbia TriStar Television: From *Brian's Song* by William Blinn. Copyright © 1971 by Screen Gems, a division of Columbia Pictures.

The Continuum Publishing Company: From Foreword by Bruno Bettelheim from *German Fairy Tales: Jakob and Wilhelm Grimm and Others,* German Library Series, vol. 29, edited by Helmut Brackert and Volkmar Sander. Foreword copyright © 1985 by Bruno Bettelheim.

The Gale Group: From "Jean Fritz" from *Contemporary Authors,* vol. 5, edited by Ann Evory. Copyright © 1962, 1963, 1964, 1965, 1966, 1968, 1969, 1970, 1971, 1973, 1974, 1975, 1977, 1978, 1982 by Gale Research Company. All rights reserved. From "Joseph Bruchac" from *Contemporary Authors,* vol. 13, edited by Linda Metzger. Copyright © 1984 by Gale Research Company. All rights reserved. From "Ai-Ling Louie" from *Contemporary Authors,* vol. 112, edited by Hal May. Copyright © 1985 by Gale Research Company. All rights reserved. From "Mildred D. Taylor" from *Something About the Author,* vol. 15, edited by Anne Commire. Copyright © 1979 by Gale Research Company. All rights reserved.

Harvard University Press: From *i: Six Nonlectures* by E. E. Cummings. Copyright © 1953 and renewed © 1981 by the E. E. Cummings Trust.

Estate of Evelyn Tooley Hunt: From "Mama Is a Sunrise" by Evelyn Tooley Hunt from *The Lyric,* 1972.

Patricia Lauber: Comment on the curiosity of children.

Liveright Publishing Corporation: From "maggie and milly and molly and may" from *Complete Poems: 1904–1962* by E. E. Cummings, edited by George J. Firmage. Copyright © 1956, 1984, 1991 by the Trustees for the E. E. Cummings Trust.

Ashley Deal Matin: From "Antaeus" by Borden Deal. Copyright © 1961 by Southern Methodist University Press.

Anne McCaffrey and agent, Virginia Kidd: From "Anne McCaffrey" from *Something About the Author,* vol. 8, edited by Anne Commire. Published by Gale Research Company.

Orchard Books, New York: From *But I'll Be Back Again* by Cynthia Rylant. Copyright © 1989 by Cynthia Rylant.

SALON.com: From "The Spirit Within: The SALON Interview/Amy Tan" by Andrew Ross. The article first appeared in SALON.com at http://www.salon.com. An on-line version remains in the SALON archives.

Scholastic Inc.: From Foreword from *A Fire in My Hands* by Gary Soto. Copyright © 1990 by Scholastic Inc.

Anna Lee Walters: From "I Am of the Earth" by Anna Lee Walters from *Voices of the Rainbow: Contemporary Poetry by American Indians,* edited by Kenneth Rosen. Copyright © 1975 by Anna Lee Walters.

A. P. Watt Ltd on behalf of The National Trust for Places of Historic Interest or Natural Beauty: From *O Beloved Kids* by Rudyard Kipling. Copyright © 1983 by The National Trust for Places of Historic Interest or Natural Beauty.

SOURCES CITED

Quote by Ann Beattie from "Sandra Cisneros" from *Chicano Writers, Second Series,* edited by Francisco A. Lomeli and Carl R. Shirley. Published by Gale Research Inc., Farmington Hills, MI, 1992.

From "Anne McCaffrey" from *Contemporary Authors,* vol. 55. Published by Gale Research Inc., Farmington Hills, MI.

Quote by Clarissa Pinkola Estés from "Clarissa Explains It All" by Gene Stone from *Playboy,* vol. 41, no. 7, July 1994. Published by Playboy Enterprises, Inc., Chicago.

From Preface from *A. B. Guthrie, Jr.* by Thomas W. Ford. Published by Twayne Publishers, a division of G. K. Hall & Co., Boston, MA, 1981.

From letter to Adelaide Kuntz from Marsden Hartley, December 5, 1932. Available on microfilm at the Archives of American Art, Elizabeth McCausland Papers, Marsden Hartley Letters to Adelaide Kunzt: 1929–1940, Reel X3.

From "Cinderella in China" by R. D. Jameson from *Cinderella: A Folklore Casebook* by Alan Dundes. Published by Garland Press, New York, NY, 1982.

From "Mildred D. Taylor" by Christine McDonnell from *Twentieth-Century Children's Writers,* 2nd Edition, edited by D. L. Kirkpatrick. Published by St. Martin's Press, New York, 1983.

Quote by Jim Murphy from "Jim Murphy" from *Something About the Author,* vol. 77. Published by Gale Research Inc., Farmington Hills, MI.

From "An American Childhood in China" (review of *Homesick* by Jean Fritz) by Katherine Paterson from "Book World" from *The Washington Post,* November 7, 1982.

From Introduction by Anne Pellowski from *Fourteen Hundred Cowries and Other African Tales,* collected by Abayomi Fuja. Published by Lothrop, Lee & Shepard Company, New York, 1971 (US edition).

CONTENTS IN BRIEF

CONTENTS

Collection One

Out Here on My Own
COLLECTION PLANNING GUIDE T1A–T1D

COMMUNICATIONS WORKSHOPS

Collection Two

Who Am I?

**COLLECTION PLANNING
GUIDE T101A–T101D**

COMMUNICATIONS WORKSHOPS

**Language /
Grammar Links**

- Shades of Meaning—
  Denotations and
  Connotations **120**

- Making the Most of
  Comparing Adjectives
  133

- Using Precise
  Adjectives **143**

- Don't Leave Your
  Modifiers Dangling **151**

- All Modifiers! Places,
  Please! **167**

Collection Three

Do the Right Thing

**COLLECTION PLANNING
GUIDE T189A–T189D**

COMMUNICATIONS WORKSHOPS

**Language /
Grammar Links**

Collection Four

We Rookies Have to Stick Together

COLLECTION PLANNING GUIDE T267A–T267D

Language / Grammar Link

• Transitions Make the Right Connection **324**

Collection Five

Living in the Heart

COLLECTION PLANNING GUIDE T335A–T335D

COMMUNICATIONS WORKSHOPS

**Language /
Grammar Links**

Collection Six

This Old Earth

COLLECTION PLANNING GUIDE T417A–T417D

COMMUNICATIONS WORKSHOPS

**Language /
Grammar Links**

Collection Seven

Our Classical Heritage

**COLLECTION PLANNING
GUIDE T493A–T493D**

COMMUNICATIONS WORKSHOPS

**Language /
Grammar Links**

Collection Eight

900 Cinderellas: Our World Heritage in Folklore

COLLECTION PLANNING GUIDE T589A–T589D

COMMUNICATIONS WORKSHOPS

**Language /
Grammar Links**

- *All Right, A Lot, Should
  Have,* and *Would Have*
  606
- *Two, To,* and *Too* **624**
- *They're, Their, There*
  637
- Using Specific Words
  648
- Oral Storytelling **661**

Resource Center

Elements of Literature on the Internet

TO THE STUDENT

Discover more about the stories, poems, and essays in *Elements of Literature* by logging on to the Internet. At **go.hrw.com** we help you complete your homework assignments, learn more about your favorite writers, and find facts that support your ideas and inspire you with new ones. Here's how to log on:

1. Start your Web browser and enter **go.hrw.com** in the location field.

2. Note the keyword in your textbook.

go.hrw.com
_____
LE0 7-1

3. In your Web browser, enter the keyword and click on GO.

Now that you've arrived, you can peek into the palaces and museums of the world, listen to stories of exploration and discovery, or view fires burning on the ocean floor. As you move through *Elements of Literature,* use the best online resources at **go.hrw.com.**

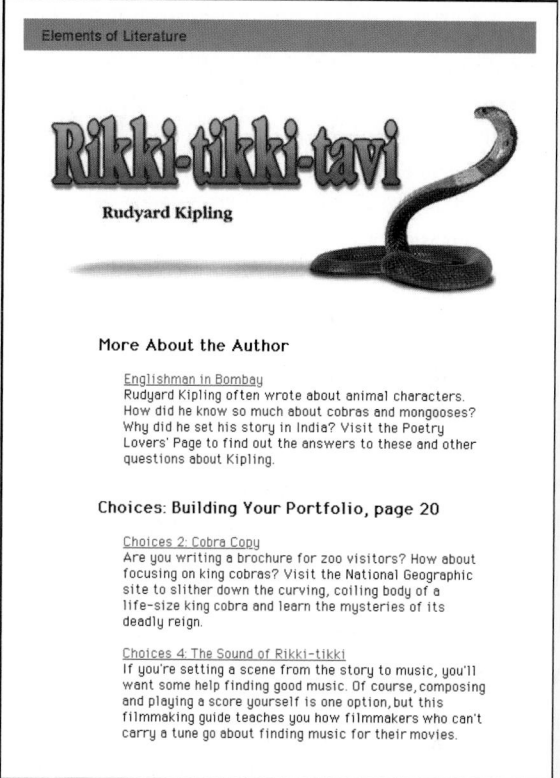

Enjoy the Internet, but be critical of the information you find there. Always evaluate your sources for credibility, accuracy, timeliness, and possible bias.

Web sites accessed through **go.hrw.com** are reviewed regularly. However, online materials change continually and without notice. Holt, Rinehart and Winston cannot ensure the accuracy or appropriateness of materials other than our own. Students, teachers, and guardians should assume responsibility for checking all online materials. A full description of Terms of Use can be found at **go.hrw.com.**

SELECTIONS BY GENRE

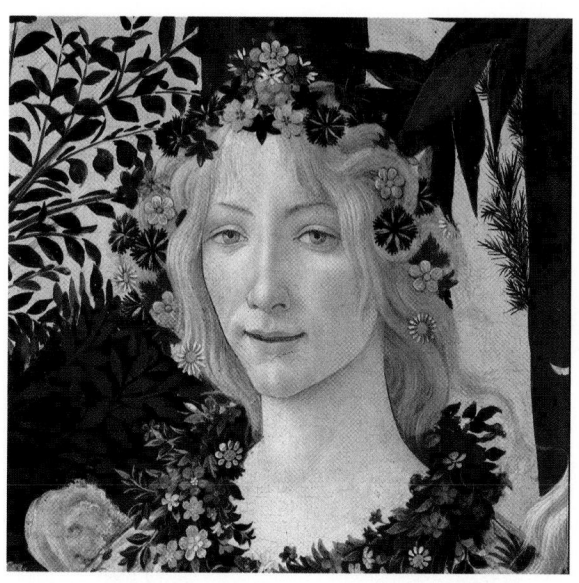

Myth, Folk Tale, and Fable

Myth

Folk Tale/Urban Legend

Fable

Drama

Stage Play

Teleplay

Song

FEATURES

Elements of Literature

Across the Curriculum

Student Models

No Questions Asked

Writer's Workshops

Reading for Life

Learning for Life

Connections

SKILLS

Vocabulary / Spelling Skills

Speaking and Listening Workshops

Sentence Workshops

Assessment

ELEMENTS OF *Literature*

©2003

Building a Foundation for Success in Literature and Reading

Time-tested and a favorite *of teachers around the nation,* **Elements of Literature** *has proven itself as the literature and language arts program that gets results and forges strong connections between students' lives and the literature teachers love to teach. Designed to get students actively involved in literature and learning, this unique program combines a student-centered approach to the study of literature with a sharp focus on the development of practical reading, writing, and life skills.*

GRAMMAR, LANGUAGE, AND WRITING RESOURCES

DAILY ORAL GRAMMAR TRANSPARENCIES AND WORKSHEETS

include exercises that review sentence construction, usage, and mechanics skills in the context of literary selections found in the *Student Edition.*

GRAMMAR AND LANGUAGE LINKS WORKSHEETS provide reinforcement,

practice, and extension of the grammar and language skills presented in the *Student Edition.*

AUTHENTIC AUTHORSHIP THAT SPEAKS TO STUDENTS

The success of *Elements of Literature* is due in large part to the team of authors that shaped it. Robert Anderson, John Malcolm Brinnan, and John Leggett, authors since the program's inception, have established the literary framework and have brought to the program a unique, motivational approach to instruction. Dr. Robert Probst has infused the program with a student-centered pedagogy, encouraging students to make the study of literature relevant to their lives and experiences. Renowned reading expert Dr. Kylene Beers has helped to integrate the reading strand in the *Student Edition* with creative, effective ways to reach struggling and reluctant readers. In addition, literacy expert Dr. Richard Vacca has helped to develop the conceptual framework of the reading strand, bringing to the program its strong emphasis on reading skills.

STUDENT EDITION THAT INVITES INVOLVEMENT

Frequent opportunities for skill building, personal and critical response, and writing practice prepare and motivate your students. Activities on **go.hrw.com** help students build literary and life skills. The **Test Smarts** section helps students prepare for standardized tests. The **Reading Matters** section, developed by reading expert Dr. Kylene Beers, helps students build a strong foundation in reading and master state and national standards.

ANNOTATED TEACHER'S EDITION THAT OPTIMIZES LESSONS

The *Annotated Teacher's Edition* helps you make the best use of the textbook with planning charts at point-of-use and references to the *One-Stop Planner® CD-ROM with Test Generator.* Helpful, creative suggestions for addressing the different kinds of learners in your classroom are annotated throughout the book.

ORGANIZATION THAT ENCOURAGES SUCCESS

- **Grades 6, 7, and 8** are organized by genres centered around themes.
- **Grades 9 and 10** include the study of genres in collections organized by theme.
- **Grades 11 and 12** present selections chronologically and focus on themes emerging naturally from each literary period.
- **Grade 11,** *Literature of the United States with Literature of the Americas,* is available in two volumes.

LANGUAGE HANDBOOK WORKSHEETS

include tests at the end of each section that can be used either for assessment or for review.

WORKSHOP RESOURCES: TRANSPARENCIES AND WORKSHEETS

provide additional practice with the language skills presented in the **Writer's Workshop, Sentence Workshop,** and **Language Workshop** features of the *Student Edition.*

SPANISH RESOURCES

SPANISH RESOURCES help your Spanish-speaking students explore literature with translations of the **Before You Read** feature in the *Student Edition* and the *Graphic Organizers for Active Reading* teaching resource. This package also includes Spanish summaries of the literature selections, reading check questions in Spanish, and the *Visual Connections Videocassette Program* with Spanish soundtrack.

The Building Blocks of Solid Reading Skills

ELEMENTS OF

Literature *helps students become lifelong readers by building skills in reading comprehension, literary response and analysis, and vocabulary development. The cornerstone of the program, this strong emphasis on reading skills is integrated throughout the* **Student Edition** *and in highly effective resource and technology materials.*

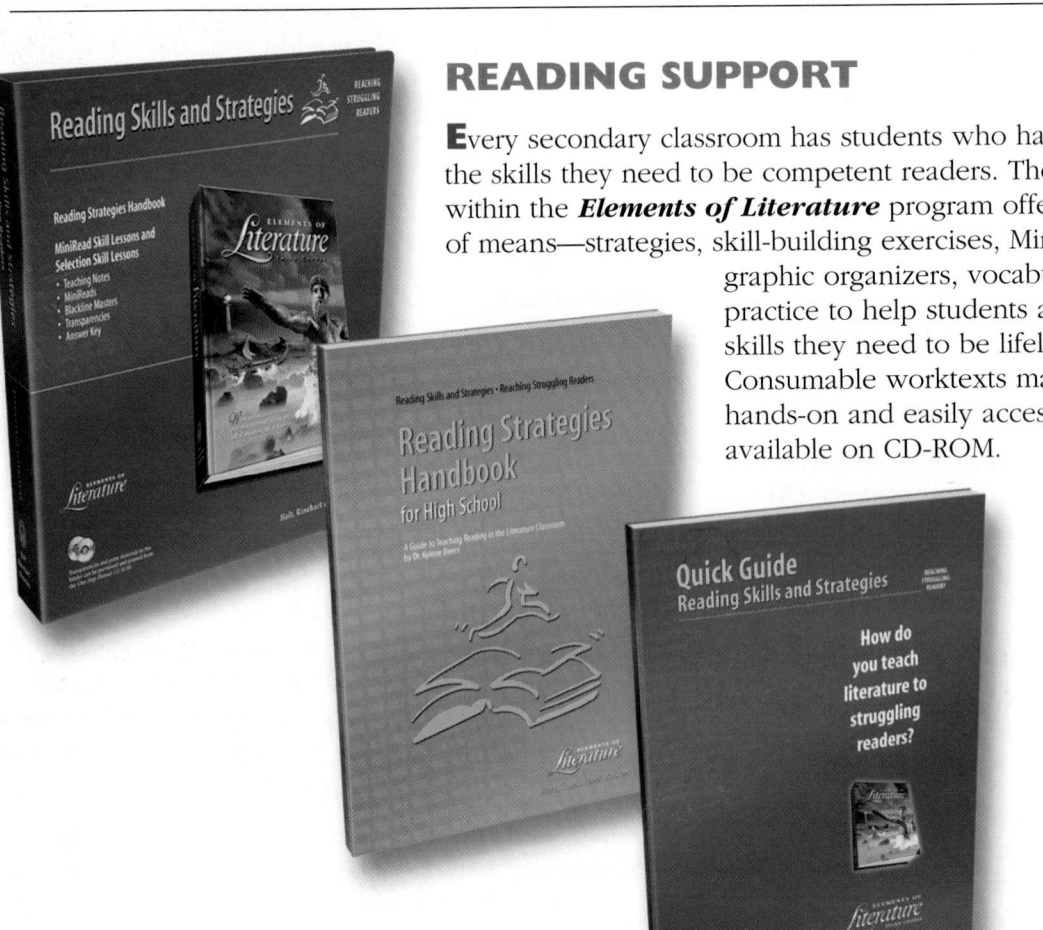

READING SUPPORT

Every secondary classroom has students who haven't mastered the skills they need to be competent readers. The resources within the **_Elements of Literature_** program offer a multitude of means—strategies, skill-building exercises, MiniReads,™ graphic organizers, vocabulary and test practice to help students acquire the skills they need to be lifelong readers. Consumable worktexts make the lessons hands-on and easily accessible. Also available on CD-ROM.

HRW LIBRARY

This diverse collection of award-winning **HRW Library** titles builds students' independence and confidence as they become life-long readers. Each full-length work includes **Connections,** related readings such as poems, short stories, essays, memoirs, and interviews that extend themes into other genres, places, and times.

STUDY GUIDES

- background information and historical, cultural, and literary context
- reproducible masters for reading skills, vocabulary activities, and literary elements study
- more information at **www.hrw.com**

CONTENT AREA READERS

- reading selections in the context of the social sciences, science, and mathematics
- informational materials such as newspaper articles, biographies, and excerpts from nonfiction books

ADDITIONAL READING SUPPORT

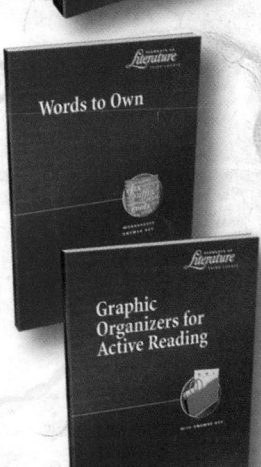

AUDIO CD LIBRARY

helps struggling readers and auditory learners build comprehension skills with dramatic readings of the literary selections in *Elements of Literature.* In this extensive collection of audio CDs, professional actors read poems, plays, short stories, and essays.

WORDS TO OWN WORKSHEETS build

vocabulary skill and help students make words their own.

GRAPHIC ORGANIZERS FOR ACTIVE READING allow

students to respond to literature visually while mastering program content.

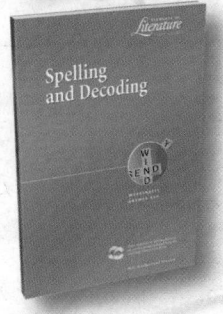

LITERARY ELEMENTS TRANSPARENCIES AND WORKSHEETS

include graphic organizers that help students identify and learn the literary terms presented in the *Student Editions*.

SPELLING AND DECODING WORKSHEETS

(GRADES 6–8) allow students to practice spelling (using words taken from literary selections) and explore sound correspondences and structure patterns.

Solidify Instruction with Planning and Assessment Resources

TEST PREP TOOL KIT

Comprehensive and flexible, the ***Test Prep Tool Kit*** features high-interest activities that keep students involved. The kit consists of 39 activity cards, correlated to state standards, that address the reading and writing objectives typically measured by standardized tests. The cards let students work at their own pace, allowing them to monitor their performance as they work to master a variety of reading and writing skills.

ONE-STOP PLANNER® CD-ROM WITH TEST GENERATOR

With editable lesson plans and an easy-to-use test generator, this convenient planning tool includes all the teaching resources for ***Elements of Literature***. Also included are previews of all teaching resources, of the ***Visual Connections Videocassette Program,*** and of transparencies and worksheets linked to features in the ***Student Edition.*** Point-and-click menu formats make accessing information on the ***One-Stop Planner*** fast and easy in both Macintosh® and Windows® platforms.

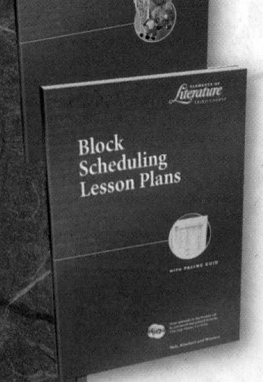

MORE FOR PLANNING

LESSON PLANS, INCLUDING STRATEGIES FOR ENGLISH-LANGUAGE LEARNERS include
resource checklists, ideas for teaching literature selections, and strategies for motivating students who are developing English proficiency.

CROSS-CURRICULAR ACTIVITIES engage students
with lessons that encompass literature, science, music, history, geography, and technology.

BLOCK SCHEDULING LESSON PLANS WITH PACING GUIDE help you
manage and pace block-scheduling instruction and activities.

MORE FOR ASSESSMENT

FORMAL ASSESSMENT includes literary-
element tests, reading-application tests, genre tests, and English-language tests.

PORTFOLIO MANAGEMENT SYSTEM
offers ideas for implementing portfolios in the classroom and blackline masters for assessing portfolios and performance on activities from the ***Student Edition.***

STANDARDIZED TEST PREPARATION includes practice tests for
reading along with blackline masters and transparencies for four writing modes.

PREPARATION FOR COLLEGE ADMISSION EXAMS prepares high school
juniors and seniors for college admission exams with a collection of practice tests.

Reinforce Learning with Internet Resources

ONLINE RESOURCES

GO.HRW.COM

Internet references throughout the *Student Edition* direct you and your students to a Web site dedicated exclusively to content in *Elements of Literature.* From biographical information about authors to help with textbook activities and writing assignments, from historical background to cross-curricular support, this Web site allows your students to link instantly to well-researched resources that support the selections they are studying.

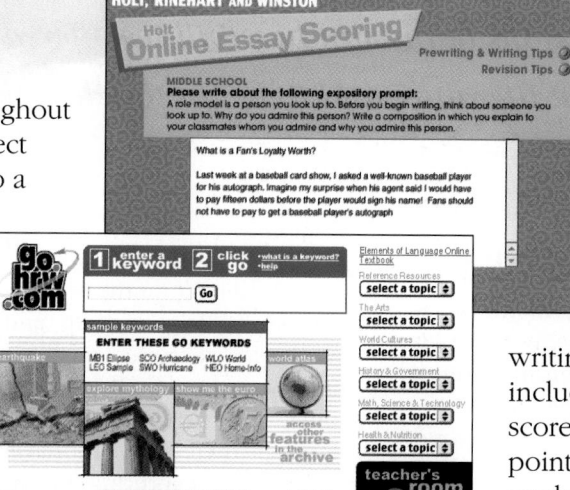

HOLT ONLINE ESSAY SCORING

Help your students improve their writing skills and give them practice with the kinds of prompts typically seen on state writing assessments. The site includes writing prompts, scores based on a four- or six-point holistic scale, and explanations of the scoring criteria.

MORE TECHNOLOGY

AUDIO CD LIBRARY helps struggling readers and auditory learners build comprehension skills with dramatic readings of the literary selections in *Elements of Literature.* In this extensive collection of audio CDs, professional actors read poems, plays, short stories, and essays.

VISUAL CONNECTIONS VIDEOCASSETTE PROGRAM features biographies, interviews, historical summaries, and cross-curricular connections that enrich and extend instruction. Available with Spanish and English soundtracks.

THE HOLT READER: AN INTERACTIVE WORKTEXT CD-ROM includes literary and informational selections and graphic organizers that guide students to participate actively in reading. This CD-ROM is a convenient alternative to *The Holt Reader: An Interactive WorkText* booklet.

WRITER'S WORKSHOP I AND 2 INTERACTIVE MULTIMEDIA CD-ROMS include a variety of writing assignments featuring step-by-step guidance—from prewriting to publishing—and the ability to share work online. These interactive CD-ROMs also include built-in word processing, a spell checker, and advanced writing tools.

LANGUAGE WORKSHOP INTERACTIVE MULTIMEDIA CD-ROM SOFTWARE reinforces and extends the grammar and writing lessons in *Elements of Literature* with a complete, interactive course in grammar, usage, and mechanics. (Grades 6–12)

Literature
AN INVITATION TO A DIALOGUE

Dr. Robert Probst, *Georgia State University*

The classroom is the place for students to learn to read and reflect on visions of human possibilities offered them by the great literature and to begin to tell their own visions and stories.

LITERATURE AND LIFE

Surely, of all the arts, literature is most immediately implicated with life itself. The very medium through which the author shapes the text— language—is grounded in the shared lives of human beings. Language is the bloodstream of a common culture, a common history.
— LOUISE ROSENBLATT

Mathematicians, scientists, and engineers build bridges and send people to the moon, statisticians calculate our insurance premiums and life expectancies, and accountants figure our taxes and amortize our house payments, but the poets, dramatists, novelists, and story-writers have nonetheless remained at the center of life. They bind us together as a society, and they define us as individuals within that society.

When we're very young we need stories almost as much as we need food and protection. Stories entertain us and help us sleep, but they also teach us how to get through the world. They tell us there are pots of gold waiting for us at the end of the rainbow, and they warn us about the trolls hiding under the bridges. They teach us about hope, fear, courage, and all the other elements of our lives. As we grow out of childhood, the great stories, poems, and plays of the world's literature encourage us to reflect on the issues that have intrigued men and women for centuries, inviting us into a continuing dialogue about human experience. When we're older, our own stories represent what we've done, capturing for us what we've made of our lives. Some we'll tell happily, some we'll tell with great pain, and some we may not tell at all, but they're all important because they are a way of making sense of our lives.

If literature is the ongoing dialogue about what it means to be human, then the language arts classroom is society's invitation to students to join that conversation. The texts we use represent the reflections of the world's cultures on the nature of human experience, and the writings we elicit from our students are their first efforts to join in that reflection. The classroom is the place for students to learn to read and reflect on visions of human possibilities offered them by the great literature and to begin to tell their own stories.

Literature offers an invitation to reflect, but it doesn't offer formulas to memorize or answers to write dutifully in notes so that later on, when life presents us with problems, we can pull out our tattered old notebooks and find our path sketched out for us. Literature is an invitation to a dialogue.

That, perhaps more than any other reason, is why it's so important that we teach literature and writing well. It's too easy to avoid the responsible thought demanded by the significant issues, too tempting to accept someone else's formulation of the truth. "Life imitates art," Richard Peck said in a speech in New Orleans in 1974, "especially bad art." By that he meant, I think, that we may too often give in to tempting laziness and allow our lives to be governed by visions of human possibilities that we take from film, television, or graffiti. The problem for teachers, of course, is to lead students not simply to absorb unthinkingly what art offers, but to reflect on it.

This textbook series tries to support teachers' efforts to lead students to think, to feel, and to take responsibility for themselves. It will have much in common with other textbooks. After all, we'd miss "The Raven" if he didn't land croaking on our windowsill one morning just before homeroom, and twelfth grade wouldn't be the same without an evening or two around the hearth with Beowulf. But if this series has much in common with other textbooks, it will also have much that differs—including new authors, perhaps authors we haven't met before, exploring lives and circumstances that previously may not have been well represented in the pages of school texts. Similarly, there will be familiar approaches to teaching—perhaps specific activities—that we've all come to rely upon, but there will be other suggestions that emphasize aspects of literary experience, writing, and discussion that may not have been prominent in other books.

PRINCIPLES OF THE PROGRAM

❶ First among the principles of the program is that *the subject matter of the language arts classroom is human experience comprehended and expressed in language.* The classroom invites the student into the dialogue about the big issues of human experience. The content of literature is the content of our days, and we think and feel about these issues before we enter the classroom and open the text.

When we do finally come to the text, it offers students an opportunity to begin to make sense of experience and to see it captured in the literature.

❷ Implicit in this vision of the language arts is a second principle, that *learning in the English classroom is a creative act,* requiring students to make things with language. Reading literature is a process of engaging the text, weighing it against the experiences readers bring to it.

Similarly, writing isn't simply a matter of learning and applying the rules of grammar and usage or of memorizing the structure and strategies of narratives, descriptions, and arguments.

> **Literature offers us access to hidden experiences and perceptions.**

❸ The third principle focuses on *the encounter between student and content.* It doesn't focus exclusively on the information and skills that have at times provided the framework for our instruction.

Nor, on the other hand, is teaching planned with thought only for the student's interests, needs, and desires, and thus organized around whatever concerns happen to predominate at the moment. It is, to borrow Rosenblatt's term, transactional.

❹ For this series, *the integration of the several aspects of the English language arts program* is the fourth governing principle. Literature can't be taught effectively without work in composition. Writing, without the inspiration offered by good literature, remains shallow and undeveloped. Oral language has to be acquired in the context of groups working collaboratively. These texts will suggest ways of interrelating instruction in literature, writing, and language.

WORKING WITH THE SERIES

You will find, as you work with selections in this textbook, that students have immediate responses to what they've read. That may be the place to start. The students' responses are very likely to lead you back to the issues you would have wanted to discuss anyway, and so the questions we've suggested might be addressed naturally during the flow of the discussion. Look for the potential in students' reactions and their questions even before turning to the questions in the "First Thoughts" section. Then, the questions in the text can extend or expand the discussion.

The same might be said about the writing. The series has been designed so that experiences with literature, with writing, and with group processes will often be interconnected. We hope that the literature will inspire and shape the students' writing, that their writing will lead back to further reading, and that the discussions and group activities suggested will build a supportive community in which all this work can take place.

The objective in all of this is for students to be able to draw upon their literary heritage and their developing skill with written and spoken language so that, as humane and reasoning people, they may be responsibly engaged with the world around them. If the language arts class helps to achieve that goal, we should be well satisfied with our labors.

> **The subject matter of the language arts classroom is human experience comprehended and expressed in language.**

Becoming a Strategic Reader

Dr. Judith Irvin, *Florida State University*

In the past, reading was viewed as a simple task of decoding words. Educators generally emphasized the strategies of sounding out words, recognizing words out of context by sight, and reproducing content by answering comprehension questions. Research has led to a new conceptualization of the reading process—that reading is a complex learning process. In this new view, readers construct meaning from a text, not simply by decoding words but by using reading strategies that incorporate and expand their prior knowledge. Prior knowledge includes not only readers' knowledge of the definition of a word, but also their responses to the context of the word—the entire text. Careful reading of a text using strategies like those explained in the following pages will allow readers to use their prior knowledge to create meaning and to extend their understanding of a text. As students become more involved in developing and reflecting on their reading and learning processes, meaning may now be defined as "something that is actively created rather than passively received" (Buehl, 1995, p. 8).

As will be explained, the process of constructing meaning is not linear, but recursive and interactive and helps to create a richer, more productive reading experience.

THE READER

Former models of reading focused on whether or not students had acquired specific skills. Recent models of reading allow that students come to learning with previous information about particular topics, with definite attitudes about reading, writing, and school in general, and with varying motivations for reading and learning. It is the interaction of what is in readers' minds with what is on the page within a particular context that helps them to comprehend what they read.

SCHEMA THEORY

It is impossible for readers to learn anything new without making connections to their prior knowledge or schemata. The schemata are like the components of an elaborate filing system inside every reader's head. If the reader's mind is the filing system, the schemata, then, are the ideas contained in the file folders within the system. For example, you probably have a schema for a computer, a mental picture of what a computer is and what it does. You probably also bring to that basic picture many other associations, ideas, and feelings. If you use computers regularly, your schema may include positive feelings about their limitless applications. If the computer revolution has left you yearning for the days of yellow note pads and typewriters, then you may have feelings of anxiety as you approach a computer manual. For teachers, it is important to remember that readers encountering new ideas must often be shown how the new material fits into their existing filing system.

THE TEXT

The content, format, and organization of a text are factors that make a text easy or difficult for students to understand. If students' schemata tell them that a particular assignment will be difficult or unrelated to their personal experiences, they will probably be reluctant to read it and will most likely not make much meaning of it. The students know with one look that they will read and respond to a poem differently from the way they will respond to a chapter in a science book. Proficient readers recognize a variety of types of texts and adjust their reading accordingly.

> **It is the interaction of what is in readers' minds with what is on the page ... that helps them to comprehend what they read.**

THE CONTEXT

Readers approach texts differently, and they also vary their reading according to their purposes. If they are reading for pleasure, students may skip over a difficult word or read an exciting passage more than once. But if they are reading for class, skipping a word might mean not understanding an important concept needed in class the next day. A reader's purpose for reading also dictates how attentive he or she is to details and how much effort will be put into remembering what is read. Similarly, when and where the reading is done affects the reading process. Readers will make less meaning from texts they read on the bus or with thoughts of a sick relative in the backs of their minds than they might make if they had a quiet space and clear thoughts.

STRATEGIC LEARNING

Suppose that during a racquetball game you hit a straight shot down the right side of the court, and your opponent misses the ball. The point is yours. This well-placed shot may have been a lucky one, or it may have been the result of a strategy. Before you hit the ball, you may have noticed that your opponent was standing in the middle of the court, and you remembered that she is left-handed with a weak backhand. You hit the ball to exactly the right spot deliberately and strategically. The analogy of planning your shots in a game can be applied to learning.

Strategic learning involves analyzing the reading task, establishing a purpose for reading, and then selecting strategies for making meaning. A strategy is a conscious effort by the reader to attend to comprehension while reading. Weinstein explains that "learning strategies include any thoughts or behaviors that help us to acquire new information in such a way that the new information is integrated with our existing knowledge" (Weinstein, p. 590). Strategies occur before reading when readers activate prior knowledge by thinking and discussing the title and topic and by identifying a purpose for reading. They also occur during reading as readers use context to figure out unknown words and monitor their understanding, and beyond the reading when readers summarize or evaluate the main ideas of the text.

METACOGNITION

Reading is often referred to as a cognitive event. It is also a metacognitive event. Cognition refers to a person's using the knowledge and skills he or she possesses; metacognition refers to a person's awareness and understanding of that knowledge and conscious control over those skills. It is, essentially, thinking about one's way of thinking. Metacognition, then, is knowing how and when to use strategies to solve problems in understanding. It develops as a reader matures, usually during adolescence, but it can be taught and strengthened by explicit instruction and practice.

Becoming a proficient reader and writer is a lifelong process. Accepting the premise that meaning is constructed in the mind of the learner implies that metacognitive abilities must be operational for learning to occur. Young adolescents are just beginning to be able to consider their own thinking in relation to the thoughts of others. The middle level years are an ideal time to develop the metacognitive abilities that will serve them throughout life.

STRATEGIC READING IN THIS PROGRAM

Good readers are strategic, and being strategic involves the metacognitive abilities to think, plan, and evaluate their understanding of a text.

Early adolescence is partially characterized by a new capacity for thought. Students are moving from the concrete stage (able to think logically about real experiences) to the formal stage (able to consider "what if's," think reflectively, and reason abstractly). This intellectual change is gradual and may occur in different contexts at different times for different students.

Because formal thinking is just developing during the middle school years, concrete examples and step-by-step modeling are necessary to move students to the more abstract metacognitive thinking. The full-page Reading Skills and Strategies feature in *Elements of Literature* (Introductory, First, and Second Courses) helps students and teachers focus on reading strategies by addressing the following concepts:

- activating schema (prior knowledge) and building background information
- predicting and confirming
- organizing information
- drawing conclusions
- making inferences
- text differences
- retelling/summarizing

Before students read, they are invited to use their prior knowledge by making predictions about the content of a selection, to establish a clear purpose for reading, and to think about reading strategies they might use as they read. During the reading process, students are guided to use context, to connect what they are reading with what they already know, and to continue to monitor and evaluate their comprehension. And, after completing their reading, students have opportunities to review their reading through peer discussion, class discussion, review of reading notes, and use of graphic organizers.

New research and practice in literacy learning reflect a more holistic view of understanding text. *Elements of Literature* provides students with opportunities to apply reading strategies to a variety of texts in a meaningful manner.

REFERENCES

Buehl, D. *Classroom Strategies for Interactive Learning.* Schofield, WI: Wisconsin State Reading Association, 1995.
Weinstein, C. E. "Fostering Learning Autonomy Through the Use of Learning Strategies." *Journal of Reading* 30 (1987): 590–595.

Reaching Struggling Readers

AN INTERVIEW WITH DR. KYLENE BEERS

Dr. Kylene Beers

from the Editor's Desk

As we have listened to teachers over the past few years, one dominant issue has emerged: How do we teach literature to struggling readers? In our search for an answer, we read the research, attended workshops, and interviewed teachers and students. It was obvious that fill-in-the-blank drill worksheets weren't the answer. It was time for a change, but nothing we encountered seemed to offer a real solution to the problem of teaching literature to struggling readers.

Finally, one day Dr. Robert Probst suggested we contact Dr. Kylene Beers. He told us she knew a great deal about reading and might be the person with the answers. During our first meeting with Dr. Beers, she explained the link between reading skills and strategies and discussed the difference she had seen strategies make in the lives of struggling readers. She made a lot of sense to those of us who can recite whole sections of the *Iliad* but had never heard the words *reading* and *strategy* in the same sentence. A year and a half later we see the results of that first meeting: the *Reading Skills and Strategies: Reaching Struggling Readers* binder. This wasn't the easiest project in the history of publishing. Drill worksheets would have been easier to produce, but it was time for a change—time to turn struggling readers into successful ones.

Here are some of the questions we asked Dr. Beers during the course of this project.

The curriculum demands on English teachers are enormous. Teachers often ask us why they should add reading skills and strategies to an already loaded course.

" I used to ask myself the same thing. Twenty years ago, when I began teaching, I expected that I'd carefully guide excited students through the prose and poetry of literary giants like Whitman, Emerson, Dickinson, Thoreau, Kipling, Joyce, Márquez, Angelou, and, well, you know the names. I expected that students would arrive early for literature class and leave late for their next class. I expected I'd never have to worry about teaching someone to read—that was for the elementary teachers. I was going to teach *Literature*. Those expectations changed quickly. First, I didn't have students who loved literature. Most of my students didn't even like literature. Second, I didn't have students who could already read. When I didn't get the students I expected, I didn't know what to do.

Twenty years later, I'm still not getting what I expected when it comes to teaching. But I've learned that if I understand students' strengths and have some ideas about how to address their weaknesses, then they'll often give me more than I ever expected.

I've spent the past twenty years learning how to help these secondary students who can't read and don't like to read become better readers. I've worked with students at all grade levels and all ability levels. I've gone back to school to study how to teach reading, and now I see myself as a reading/literature teacher. The teaching of literature and the teaching of reading are integral to one another, so interconnected that separating them seems an abomination. "

How can a teacher use a literature anthology with the increasing number of students who have serious difficulty reading any text?

" After many years of working with all types of readers, but especially struggling and reluctant readers, I've learned some things that have helped me reach those students. I've found that struggling readers have difficulty reading for a myriad of reasons. Often they don't know a lot of words, so limited vocabulary keeps them from understanding what they've read. Sometimes they lack decoding ability, so they don't know how to get through big words. Other times, they can call words well, but they don't know how to make sense of what they've read. And sometimes, their distaste for reading makes them think reading is meaningless, so they see no reason for putting any effort into it. As I work with students and address those issues, I keep what I call the ABCDE rules in mind. A look at the diagram below will quickly show you what these rules are. "

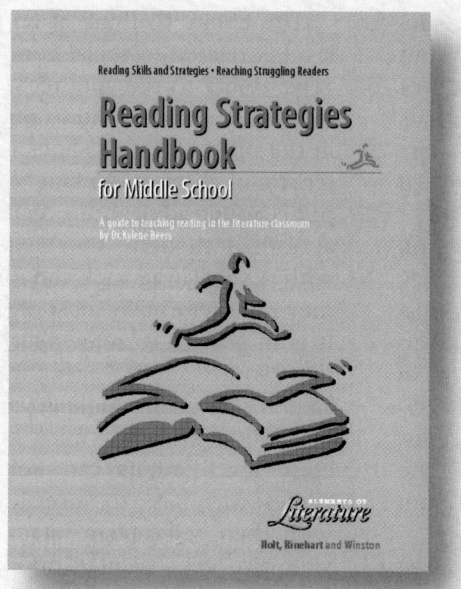

To help provide this **ABCDE** rule for struggling readers, what should a literature program include?

" A literature program should help teachers with each of those areas, particularly A, B, C, and E. If publishers want to help, they will have to develop specialized materials that complement the basal text. Here's what we did with the *Reading Skills and Strategies* binder for *Elements of Literature*:

❶ Easier selections provide practice for skills and strategies.

We hired a group of professional writers to write easy fiction and nonfiction pieces. These short selections, or MiniReads®, are written at an easier level than the selections in the literature book. The purpose of the MiniReads is to give students the opportunity to practice decoding skills, comprehension strategies, and vocabulary strategies with a text that is not only easier but engaging as well.

 ❷ Our MiniRead lessons include modeling.

Each MiniRead includes a complete lesson plan that provides modeling of the skill and strategy. Transparencies help teachers focus students on the strategies. Blackline masters give students a chance to practice the strategies before applying them to selections in the *Student Edition*.

❸ Reading skills and strategies are connected to the selections in *Elements of Literature*.

All skills and strategies are *applied* to selections in the anthology. The detailed lesson plans can be used not only with struggling readers but with all readers.

❹ The *Handbook* provides a thorough explanation of the research.

Without research to back them up, the lessons would have no foundation. The *Reading Strategies Handbook* includes transcripts from classrooms in which the strategies have been tested with struggling readers. The handbook *shows* rather than just *tells* how to initiate specific strategies, what pitfalls to avoid, and how to document progress. Articles about each of the strategies help teachers become more comfortable with using the strategies with any selection. "

DR. KYLENE BEERS   39

Young Adolescent Learning

Dr. Judith Irvin, *Florida State University*

Young adolescents (ages 10–14) experience more changes physically, emotionally, socially, and cognitively during this period than during any other time of life. Children of all ages deserve "developmentally appropriate" school programs and practices; early adolescence, however, is a time when values are formed, self-esteem is enhanced or denied, and decisions with long-term implications are made. For many youth "early adolescence offers opportunities to choose a path toward a productive and fulfilling life. For many others, it represents their last best chance to avoid a diminished future" (Carnegie Council on Adolescent Development, p. 8).

Physically, young adolescents experience growth spurts in which there is a marked increase in height, weight, heart rate, lung capacity, and muscular strength. Bone grows faster than muscle, which may leave bones unprotected by muscles and tendons. Middle level students often have problems with coordination as a result of this rapid growth; thus, they are often characterized as awkward. Although all young adolescents experience this growth spurt, girls (10–11) tend to undergo these changes approximately two years earlier than boys (12–13). Being "off-time" with respect to maturation is what generally causes concern for young adolescents (Rice, 1990).

Socially, peers and social relationships are extremely important to young adolescents. Friendships are vital at this age, especially same-sex relationships. Feeling comfortable and secure with peers of the same sex at ages 10 to 12 helps young adolescents progress toward opposite sex relationships which come later. Because rejection by peers represents a major crisis, students at this age spend much of their time trying to figure out ways to win acceptance by their peers. The trying out of social situations is all a part of social learning and facilitates cognitive development. Some experiences are fleeting, some agonizing, and some thoughtful.

Emotionally, young adolescents begin the important task of forming a positive self-identity, which naturally brings on behavior characteristic of "trying things out." Some experts view early adolescence as a time of emotional turbulence and disruption, but it seems that the small percentage of students who exhibit signs of serious disturbance cause some adults to conclude that this period is one of turmoil and stress for all (Scales, 1991).

Emotions, both happy and sad, run high at this age. A teacher may observe the same girl happy and giggling at one minute, and sad and tearful the next minute. These extremes in emotion are normal experiences and are heightened by young adolescents' feelings of confusion about the changes within themselves and about their place within the social group.

Cognitive development is the least noticed but most profound. This age is characterized by a new capacity for thought. Students are moving from the concrete stage (able to think logically about real experiences) to the formal stage (able to consider "what if's," think reflectively, and reason abstractly). This intellectual change is gradual and may occur in different contexts at different times for different students.

The emerging formal thinker is able to consider the thoughts of others for the first time. Social interaction with peers helps young adolescents move beyond egocentrism. As students discuss issues that are important to them and resolve conflicting viewpoints, they are forced to re-examine their own views in light of the views of others. This process of social interaction enables young adolescents to mature both socially and intellectually.

The ability to think at an abstract level is related to social competence. "The ability to see another's point of view, to empathize, and to put oneself in the other person's shoes is characteristic of abstract thinking" (Milgram, p. 24). Young adolescents do not arrive at formal thought; they experiment with it, vacillating back and forth until they reason formally most of the time. It is important to remember, though, that some adults never reach an abstract level of thinking and some students consistently think on a concrete level. Adults can help young adolescents pass to formal thinking with their self-esteem intact by providing success-oriented opportunities to practice formal thinking.

IMPLICATIONS FOR THE CLASSROOM

Physically, middle level students need to move and change activities frequently. Socially, learning must include positive social interaction with peers and adults. Students must come to realize that others may think differently or hold differing points of view. A positive learning environment, one of acceptance on the part of the teacher and other students, is essential. Emotionally, students need to feel competent, and they need to achieve. They need to participate in school and classroom decisions, but they also require structure and clear limits. A positive self-identity is formed by meaningful interactions with learning activities and positive relationships with peers and adults.

Curriculum and instruction for young adolescents must be different from that of younger or older students. The middle level years are a time when students need to learn and experiment with learning how to learn and learning how to think. During this time of transition, material should be presented concretely, yet opportunities should be provided for progression to more abstract thought. Students need an opportunity to experiment with formal reasoning in a gradual and success-oriented way.

Efforts in middle level schools to break down the subject matter barriers, encourage student choice, minimize the comparison of students on the basis of ability, and provide more authentic assessment are consistent with enhancing cognitive, social, and emotional growth for young adolescents. In addition, efforts to integrate the language arts and integrate the content areas around themes are further attempts to design a curriculum that is responsive to the nature and needs of students in the middle grades.

An understanding of the developmental tasks of young adolescence is prerequisite to making informed decisions about appropriate school environments and learning experiences. Behaviors such as defiance signal a move toward autonomy, and egocen-trism signals more abstract thinking. While these behaviors are not inherently desirable, they are indicative of normal growth and development. The more middle level educators understand and facilitate the developmental tasks of early adolescence, the better they can design a curriculum that meets the needs of their students.

Physically, young adolescents need

- opportunities to move and change activities
- flexibility of space, which may vary in size
- sturdy things, since adolescents are awkward and clumsy
- times of quiet and rest
- opportunities to test the limits of their physical ability
- an environment that downplays the differences in size and ability
- healthy food and especially healthy snacks as they need them
- adults to understand the changes they face
- sex education, information about growth and development

Socially, young adolescents need

- the opportunity to work in same- and opposite-sex groups
- an opportunity to relate to a close group of peers and a larger group of peers
- social activities—fun nights, carnivals they can work on
- free time to socialize
- opportunities to learn and practice social skills
- opportunities to explore values and beliefs

Emotionally, young adolescents therefore need

- an emotionally safe, supportive environment where students are free to risk and learn from failure as well as success
- successful experiences, which help students feel better about themselves as learners
- tolerance for mood swings
- help in understanding their bodies and emotional ups and downs
- an environment that fosters security and affection, a sense of belonging, self-confidence, and self-competence
- recognition and reward
- fun and adventure (educational and recreational)
- participation in school and classroom decisions
- structure and clear limits

Cognitively, young adolescents need

- a vehicle for connecting new information to what is already known, thus helping students to feel more confident about learning new material
- experiences in abstract thinking that may help students move gradually from the concrete to the abstract levels of reasoning
- opportunities to experiment with formal thought such as in cooperative learning groups
- discussions, debates
- learning strategies that help students develop their metacognitive abilities
- learning strategies that help students build background knowledge, activate what they know, and organize information
- time, discussion, prodding

REFERENCES

Carnegie Council on Adolescent Development. *Turning Points; Preparing Youth for the 21st Century.* Washington, DC: Author, 1989.

Milgram, J. "A Portrait of Diversity: The Middle Level Student." *Transforming Middle Level Education: Prospectives and Possibilities.* Ed. J. L. Irvin. Boston: Allyn and Bacon, 1992.

Rice, F. P. *The Adolescent: Development, Relationships, and Culture.* 6th ed. Boston: Allyn and Bacon, 1990.

Scales, P. *A Portrait of Young Adolescents in the 1900s.* Carrboro, NC: Center for Early Adolescence, 1991.

The Integration of Assessment and Instruction

Dr. Roger Farr, *Indiana University*

Assessment of student reading and writing has been important to educators and the public at large since the beginning of this century. Educators have needed some way to determine whether they are meeting their goals and objectives, and the public has wanted some means of making schools accountable for the considerable investment needed to maintain them. The development of large, standardized, very-short-answer tests has been one answer to these demands. They report normed scores that can be compared to a large national sample of students. Similar tests have been developed in most states as criterion-referenced measures that require a student to respond to an arbitrated number of particular educational objectives.

However, at the same time, emerging theory has persuasively described how language abilities actually develop, leading to new emphasis on teaching and measuring language performance as a process—not with the short-answer response typical of most tests used as accountability measures.

Writing tests have been around since 1915 and are now used in at least 35 states. There is new emphasis on writing on college entrance exams. Across all grades reading, writing, and thinking are being integrated in classroom instruction as a combined process.

Teachers have not defensively closed their ears to the critics' and general public's concern for accountability in the schools, however. They have been the primary constructors of city and state criterion-referenced measures attempting to measure and reflect the curricula they also helped structure. Through these tests, they have sought to raise their students' performances and scores on standardized tests and have analyzed the results for their implications for teaching.

What could more solidly assure that assessment reflect and measure instructional goals than to make it a part of instruction?

Meanwhile, teachers have continued to use a variety of daily classroom assessments to inform their teaching. These include observation and a host of other informal techniques and assessments accompanying the texts they use. Teachers have tended to react to the increased instructional time that testing consumes by making their classroom assessment a valid learning experience for the student and an instructional opportunity. What could more solidly assure that assessment reflect and measure instructional goals than to make it a part of instruction?

This dynamic trend in school assessment goes far beyond merely using test results as indicators of what needs to be taught or retaught. It assesses student progress on an ongoing basis as youngsters use language to construct meaning by reading, writing, and thinking every day! The teacher assesses both by observing the process and by analyzing the product.

Often this effort involves having their students keep portfolios that include many types of writing. Much of this writing reacts to and applies information from different texts that the students have read. Frequently included, too, in student portfolios are one or more of a variety of journals. These portfolios are of two general types:

- The *working portfolio* contains all the drafts of a particular piece of writing and ideas for future writing and intentions for future reading. It has records (logs) of reading and writing and journal entries or brief descriptions, observations, or sketches that can be expanded or used in other ways. It is like an artist's studio full of works in progress and works finished.

- The *show portfolio* can be designed to serve numerous purposes: It can be a selection of pieces to demonstrate to parents and/or administrators how a student's language use is developing. It can introduce a student to a new teacher or school. It is like a show that an artist mounts from the works kept in his or her studio.

Teachers are learning that there is a host of ways that portfolios and publishing efforts can be analyzed to assess their students' progress as language users. Most of these projects involve rewriting and provide drafts leading to the more finished product, a set that reveals both language product and the process that leads to it.

Language-processing experiences can culminate in some sort of publishing to communicate with peers and other audiences. Classroom newsletters, creative writing magazines, and other publications develop audience awareness and a keen sense of purpose for writing. Frequently these experiences involve the interaction of students reacting to and editing each other's work as ongoing and interactive assessment. Since all this hinges on the belief that the best way to learn to read, write, and think is to do as much of it as possible, just noting the quantity and fluency of student production is highly revealing.

There are many other observations and analyses that teachers can make that systemize this kind of assessment to a degree that supports its use in reporting progress to parents and other educators. Almost all portfolios include logs of what students read. Teachers are now encouraged to set up opportunities for their students to keep such records. These include notes on their reaction to numerous texts, and writing/thinking efforts in which they apply the meaning they have constructed by reading. This basic language/thinking process often involves both synthesis of texts and critical reaction to them. More often than not, it promotes an appreciation of and critical reaction to literature as well as the use of good writing as a model and as the ignition to an original student effort.

Of course, good teachers have long used these kinds of activities. What is new, it appears, is the emphasis on integrating language/thinking processing and on assessing while instructing! Publishers have come to a similar

understanding about language use and assessment. They have developed interactive performance assessments that use text as prompts for student writing. These are usually presented with a prescribed writing task that identifies a believable audience and that is designed to seem highly valid to the student. Most often these prompts present several pieces of writing that may represent several genres. The student's thinking abilities are engaged by a task that calls for synthesis of and critical reaction to the texts in order to recommend some solution to an authentic problem.

In order to help the teacher analyze the student's performance on these interactive performance assessments, they are accompanied by a rubric that describes several ranks (or scores) for student responses for each of several key factors. For example, a student's response may be ranked from 3 (high) to 1 (low) on its indication (a) of how well the student has comprehended the text or texts, (b) of how well the student has written the response, and (c) of how well comprehension and writing have been integrated to accomplish the assigned task. Each rank for each factor may be described according to several subfactors: In writing, for example, the response may be ranked after considering organization, diction, and mechanics.

A second guide to scoring is even more helpful than the rubric. These assessments are given to a large and varied sample of students at the grade level for which each is created. Then a team of teachers or other specialists selects several sample or anchor papers to demonstrate each score of the ranking system for each factor. These are presented with analytical comments in a booklet with the rubric and are made available to teachers who use the assessment.

Some teachers and groups of teachers are developing these integrated performance assessments on their own. Some of them use published assessments as their models. Although the process is not easy, teachers who have done it remark on how much the

experience teaches them about their instructional values and goals.

The ranked results of performance assessments can be reported to parents, administrators, critics of education, and the public at large. The model or anchor papers and rubrics stand as a clear and revealing explication of what the ranks mean if those who would rely on them make the effort to understand the data being used. Thus, integrated performance assessment can serve to inform accountability interests along with scores from standardized and criterion-referenced assessment.

Most importantly, portfolios and performance assessment develop the habit of self-assessing so that students go through life interested in personal development as readers, writers, and thinkers. This awareness can occur only when the student believes that the goals and objectives against which progress is being measured are real, interesting, and empowering.

Portfolios do that in the extreme if the student is allowed to maintain an important degree of control over the collection. Equally important to the success of the portfolio in developing self-assessment is regular student-teacher conferencing to discuss the portfolio contents, analyze progress, and set new goals.

Integrated performance assessments can achieve this if they are built around interesting prompts and if the tasks seem valid. The results of these student efforts, which usually include drafts that can be analyzed for process, can be studied and discussed by the student and the teacher in conference; and their appropriateness for student self-analysis is emphasized when a student is encouraged to include the set in his or her portfolio.

While legislators and educators together struggle with attempts to create assessments that can report on educational progress and accountability, teachers have been demonstrating dynamic new emphases in integrating language and thinking processes while turning assessment into highly effective instruction.

READING MATTERS

Reading Matters consists of five Strategy Lessons. The lessons have been designed specifically because "reading *does* matter." Here you'll find strategies that students can use to help them master reading informational and literary texts. Each lesson offers a particular strategy that you can use as a preteaching, reteaching, or review tool.

Students should view the information in Reading Matters much as they would view the information in a handbook; it can be accessed at any point, read in any order, and revisited as many times as needed. That's the underlying philosophy of Reading Matters. As you look through these lessons, you'll find that strategies presented in each lesson can be used with various stories in *Elements of Literature.* Furthermore, these lessons can help students read various materials, not only the materials in this book.

Building a Foundation for Success in Literature

BUILDING A FOUNDATION FOR SUCCESS IN LITERATURE **xxix**

TEST SMARTS

Preparing for Multiple-Choice Tests

Use the sample test items to help students prepare for multiple-choice tests. The items test students' ability to decipher unknown words using the context of the passage. The items also emphasize identification of explicitly stated facts and literal meaning, important skills for reading and applying complex, multistep instructions. Students are also asked to infer the main idea, to predict, and to summarize.

Preparing for Writing Tests

The writing lessons help prepare students for taking a variety of writing tests. Each lesson provides a writing prompt and sample responses based on that prompt. The strategies presented in each lesson can also be used to help students complete various Writer's Workshops in *Elements of Literature*.

Reading Matters

As you look through Reading Matters, note that each lesson is addressed directly to your students. Students can turn to this section on an as-needed basis. That means you should

- preview Reading Matters with students early in the year
- make sure students understand that part of being proficient readers means knowing how to get through difficult reading on their own
- remind students often that these lessons can help them with all types of texts, informational texts as well as literary texts

Strategy Lesson 1

Summarizing the Plot
Retelling

"**I**s this a plot?" Manuel asked as he pointed to the first paragraph of a story. He didn't understand that plot isn't a single thing he can point to in the story. He didn't know that **plot** is the "what happens" in the story—all the related events that move from the story's beginning to its end.

The first part of a plot is called its **basic situation.** Here you meet the **characters,** learn what they **want,** and discover the **problems** they face getting what they want. The major part of the plot involves a series of events in which **complications** develop as the characters struggle to resolve their conflicts. The plot then moves to a **climax**—the most emotional and suspenseful part of the story, when the character's problem is solved. In the **resolution** all the loose ends of the plot are tied up, and the story is over.

Retelling Summary Sheet

Keeping up with all the information in a story can be difficult. A strategy called **retelling** can help you identify the elements of a plot and keep all the information about a plot straight in your mind. With this strategy you practice telling the plot of the story using a **retelling summary sheet.** You use the retelling summary sheet as a guide, to be sure you've included all the events in the plot.

Retelling Summary Sheet			
Rating of Coverage			
0	1	2	3
No coverage	A little	Some	A lot

1. Introduction
2. Characters
3. Conflict
4. Complications
5. Climax
6. Resolution

PRACTICE

Retell a short story (or even a movie or TV show), using a retelling summary sheet to help you remember and organize the bare bones of the plot. Score your own retelling. (Zero means you didn't tell about an event at all, and 3 means you did a good job covering the plot.) The sample on the opposite page gives you tips on how to fill out a summary sheet.

Retelling Summary Sheet

Rating of Coverage			
0	1	2	3
No coverage	A little	Some	A lot

1. Introduction Begin with the **title** and **author** of the story. Then, tell where and when the story is **set**—if that's important.

Some people use the terms **protagonist** and **antagonist.** The protagonist is the hero, and the antagonist works against the hero. Luke Skywalker is a protagonist, and Darth Vader is his antagonist.

2. Characters Tell the **characters'** names, and explain how the characters are related or connected to one another. Tell what the main character **wants.**

Strategy Tip
If it's hard to keep events in **chrono-logical,** or time, order, think about how each event caused another event to happen. Use words such as *because of, since, as a result of.*

3. Conflict What is the main character's problem, or **conflict**—that is, who or what is keeping the main character from getting what he or she wants?

Strategy Tip
This is the moment when you know you are finally about to find out how the protagonist will overcome the con-flict (or be defeated).

4. Complications Tell the **main events**—what happens as the character tries to solve the conflict.

5. Climax Describe the **climax,** the most suspenseful moment in the story, when you discover at last how the con-flict ends.

Strategy Tip
Avoid linking the events with a string of *and*'s. Here are some good time-order words to use: *first; second; third; next; eventually; later; afterward; finally; in conclusion.*

6. Resolution Finally, tell what happens after the **climax.** How does the story end?

SUMMARIZING THE PLOT **xxxi**

Understanding
How Character Affects Plot
If . . . Then . . .

What would happen in *Star Wars* if Darth Vader suddenly became afraid of Luke Skywalker? How would the cartoon *Scooby Doo* be different if Scooby became brave? What would happen to *The Flintstones* if Fred suddenly got smart?

In each of those situations, the outcome of the plot would certainly change if the characters changed. In other words, if a character acts one way, then the plot proceeds in a certain way. If a character acts in a different way, the outcome of the plot changes also.

Imagine what would have happened in *How the Grinch Stole Christmas* if the Grinch had not been mean and stingy. Probably he would never have tried to stop Christmas from coming. Think about what would have happened in "Sleeping Beauty" if the princess hadn't been curious. Most likely she wouldn't have wandered into the one room that had the spinning wheel that was to put her and the whole kingdom to sleep for one hundred years.

We All Have Traits

To understand how character affects plot, you've first got to be able to identify the main character's qualities. A character's qualities, or traits, can be flaws or strengths. We all have character traits. We may be ambitious, shy, generous, fearless, kind, selfish—the possibilities are almost endless.

You discover the traits of a character you meet in a story the same way you discover the traits of real people. You think about how the character acts, how the character looks, and what he or she says. You think about how other people respond to the character. In fact, you think about all the ways writers develop a character.

Techniques for Creating Character

Writer uses dialogue to tell what the character **says.**

Writer tells how the character **acts.**

Writer reveals the character's **thoughts** and **feelings.**

Writer describes the character's **appearance.**

Writer shows **what others think** about the character.

Here are some adjectives you can use to describe character traits.

Character Traits

strong/weak	wise/foolish	truthful/sneaky
kind/mean	selfish/unselfish	dependable/unreliable
brave/cowardly	good/bad	generous/stingy
honest/dishonest	clever/silly	
bold/shy	modern/old-fashioned	

If . . . Then . . .

When you're trying to figure out how character affects plot, think of what would happen if the character acted differently—or were a different kind of person. Think **If . . . Then . . .** *If* the character is like this, *then* what would happen in the story? On the other hand, *if* the character is like *that, then* what would happen?

PRACTICE

1. When you read "The Smallest Dragonboy" (page 47), decide which word in each of the following pairs describes Keevan.
   a. brave/cowardly
   b. truthful/sneaky
   c. strong/weak
   Next, decide how the story would change if you were to choose the other word in each pair. If you think Keevan is brave, then how would the story change if he were cowardly? Would he go to the hatching? Would he Impress with the bronze dragon? If you think he is strong, then what would happen if he were weak? Would he stay in bed? Would he find his dragon?

2. When you read "A Day's Wait" (page 81), think about Schatz. Decide which word in each of the following pairs best describes him.
   a. stoic/agitated
   b. brave/cowardly
   c. considerate/selfish
   Now, choose the other word to describe Schatz, and predict how the plot and its resolution would change.

3. In "Rikki-tikki-tavi" (page 3), think about Rikki. Decide which word in each of the following pairs best describes Rikki.
   a. brave/shy
   b. strong/weak
   c. determined/lazy
   Predict how the story would progress and how it would end if Rikki were the opposite of whichever word you chose.

PRACTICE
Possible Answers

1. **a.** Keevan is brave. *If* Keevan had been cowardly, *then* he would not have stood up to Berterli.
   b. Keevan is truthful. *If* Keevan had been sneaky, *then* he would have tattled on Berterli to keep him out of the Hatching.
   c. Keevan is strong. *If* Keevan had been weak, *then* he would not have fought so hard to get to the Hatching.

2. **a.** Schatz is stoic. *If* Schatz had been agitated, *then* he would have expressed his fear of dying and would not have had to wait a full day to find out that he would live.
   b. Schatz is brave. *If* Schatz had been cowardly, *then* he would have let other people into his room. He might have expressed his fear of dying to someone other than his father or the doctor.
   c. Schatz is considerate. *If* Schatz had been selfish, *then* he would have complained about being sick and his father might have asked him earlier what was troubling him.

3. **a.** Rikki is brave. *If* Rikki had been shy, *then* he would not have made friends so easily with the family. He might not have been so determined to protect the family from danger.
   b. Rikki is strong. *If* Rikki had been weak, *then* he would not have fought so hard to defeat the cobras. The cobras and their babies might have taken over the garden, putting the family in great danger.
   c. Rikki is determined. *If* Rikki had been lazy, *then* he would not have been so determined to protect the family from danger. He might have become just a pet to the family rather than a protector.

Uncovering Theme
Most Important Word

Has your teacher ever asked you that dreaded theme question—the one that begins "What is the theme of . . . ?" What do you do when you hear that question? A group of seventh-graders all immediately started turning the pages of their books when their teacher asked them. "Why are you doing that?" she asked. "I'm looking for the theme," one student replied. "Yeah," another said, "I sure hope the writer remembered to include it."

What Is Theme?

Well, the writer did include it, but not in the way the students were hoping. Writers don't end (or begin) their stories with a nice note to the reader that says, "And the theme of the story is . . ." No, instead writers let their readers meet the characters and share an experience with them. At the end of the experience, the reader, along with the characters, has discovered something about human experience. It might be something the reader already knows but rediscovers under new circumstances. It might be something new. The **theme,** then, is a truth about life or people that we discover as we share the characters' experiences.

When you write or state a theme, remember that a theme isn't a word or a phrase—it's at least one sentence!

Most Important Word

If you need help writing a theme statement, try a strategy called **Most Important Word.** After you've read a selection, skim through it again looking for the word in the text you think is most important. Here are comments three students made after reading a poem called "The Secret Heart" by Robert P. Tristram Coffin. In this poem a father checks on his son, who is sleeping.

"I say **heart** is the most important word, because it's used a lot and is in the title and because the boy thinks his dad's hands look like they are making a heart, and that's the image the boy always remembers."

"I think the most important word is **father,** because it is the father who is checking on his son when he is sleeping at night."

"I think the most important word is **love,** because if the father didn't love his son, he wouldn't have been checking on him at night, wanting to protect him."

What's the most important word and why?

After deciding on the most important word and coming up with reasons for your choice, think about how that word could be related to the theme. Since different readers can pull different themes from the same selection, statements of themes usually differ from reader to reader. Look at the following three themes those three students stated, and match them to the comments above.

1. A parent's love for a child is never-ending—it goes on day and night.

2. Children remember their parents' simple acts of love.

3. A father is his child's protector.

PRACTICE

Read this short, short poem by Langston Hughes. Select what you think is its most important word (or words—there could be more than one). Write down reasons for your choice. Then, think of how that word could point to the theme of the poem. Try stating, in a sentence, the theme that you have discovered. Be sure to compare your themes in class.

> O God of dust and rainbows help us see
> That without dust the rainbows would not be.
> —Langston Hughes

MOST IMPORTANT WORD

1. The theme in this sentence matches the comments in the third box and the most important word, *love.*

2. The theme in this sentence matches the comments in the first box and the most important word, *heart.*

3. The theme in this sentence matches the comments in the second box and the most important word, *father.*

PRACTICE

Possible Answers

The most important word is *without,* because rainbows cannot exist without dust.

Theme: You cannot appreciate good without having experienced bad.

Analyzing Point of View
Somebody Wanted But So

Is this glass half empty or half full? The very thirsty child would complain that it's half empty. The mom, who doesn't want the child drinking so much soda anyway, would say it's half full. What you're seeing in this situation is the effect of point of view.

It's half empty!

It's half full

When we talk about **point of view** in stories, we are talking about who is telling the story. Here are the three main points of view:

First-Person Point of View. The story is told by "I," a character in the story.

Omniscient Point of View. The story is told by an all-knowing narrator who is not a character in the story. This narrator can tell everything about everyone in the story. This narrator can even tell the future.

Third-Person Limited Point of View. The story is told by a narrator who is not in the story. This narrator zooms in on only one character and tells the story through that character's eyes and emotions.

Writers are especially aware of point of view, and they experiment with it all the time. Skilled readers also think about how a story would be changed if it were told from a different viewpoint. Try experimenting with point of view by using a strategy called **Somebody Wanted But So (SWBS).**

Somebody Wanted But So

This simple strategy helps you summarize a story; it can also help you think about the story from various characters' perspectives—or points of view. Here's how the strategy works:

On a sheet of paper, jot down the words *Somebody Wanted But So.* Now, think about a story you've just read. For right now, let's think about "Cinderella," a fairy tale you probably know. First, decide which character in the story you want to think about. Here are some choices: Cinderella, the stepmother, the stepsisters, the prince, maybe even the fairy godmother. Now, write your choice under the heading "Somebody," like this:

Somebody	Wanted	But	So
The prince			

With a focus on the prince, next think about what the prince wanted. "But" means he faced a problem getting what he wanted. "So" tells what the outcome is. Once you think through all of this, you have an SWBS chart that looks like this:

Somebody	Wanted	But	So
The prince	to find the young woman he met at the ball,	she left the ball without telling him who she was,	he traveled far and wide until he found her and married her.

You've just thought about the story from the prince's point of view. Now, try thinking about it from Cinderella's point of view. You might come up with a statement like this:

Somebody	Wanted	But	So
Cinderella	to escape the kitchen and a cruel family; she also wanted to go to the prince's ball,	her cruel stepmother would not let her get a dress for the ball,	a fairy godmother visited Cinderella and magically granted her wish.

Notice that as you change the character under the "Somebody" heading, you are shifting focus. If the prince tells the story or if a storyteller tells the story zooming in on the prince, you will not hear about Cinderella and her sad, ragged state until later. You will hear the prince telling you that he has fallen in love with a mysterious, beautiful young woman wearing the most fantastic gown, who left a tiny glass slipper on the palace steps.

PRACTICE

Look at "After Twenty Years" (page 193).

1. Create SWBS charts for Jimmy, Bob, and the plainclothes policeman.

2. Be ready to discuss how the story would change if the point of view were narrowed to what only one of these characters knows and sees.

Somebody	Wanted	But	So
Jimmy	to keep an appointment with Bob that was made twenty years earlier,	when he arrived, he realized that his old friend Bob was a wanted criminal,	he called another police officer to arrest his friend so that he would not have to do it himself.
Bob	to keep an appointment with Jimmy that was made twenty years earlier,	he realized that the man who met him on the street was a police officer posing as Jimmy,	he was arrested for the crimes he committed in Chicago.
The plainclothes policeman	to arrest the criminal known as "Silky" Bob,	he could not identify Bob by himself,	he posed as Jimmy in order to arrest "Silky" Bob.

5 Identifying Cause and Effect

Here are three situations:

- You punch the right button on your stereo, and music starts to play.
- Someone tells you your clothes are cool, and you feel good about yourself.
- Your brother barges into your room without knocking, and you get angry.

In each of those situations, something has happened (an **effect**) because of something else (a **cause**). Look at this chart, and you can see which part of each sentence is the cause and which is the effect:

Cause	→	Effect
punching the stereo's right button	→	music starting to play
hearing your clothes are cool	→	feeling good about yourself
brother barging into your room	→	getting angry

Finding the Cause and Its Effect

If writers showed us cause-and-effect relationships (sometimes called **causal relationships**) by using charts like the one to the left, then finding causes and effects would be easy. Most of the time, information isn't delivered in chart format, so you've got to find causes and effects on your own. Here are some tips for doing that:

1. **Change the words.** Think of *cause* as "source" or "reason" and *effect* as "result" or "outcome."

2. **Check out the question.** If a question in your history book or science book (even in this book!) asks you to identify causes and effects, look carefully at the question. The question itself often lets you know if you are hunting for the cause or the effect.

- **What are three causes of the Civil War?** In this question you see that you are looking for the causes of (reasons for) the Civil War (outcome or effect).

- **What are three effects of poor nutrition?** This time you've got the cause (poor nutrition), and you're looking to see what the effects or results of poor nutrition are.

- **Why is George Washington called the father of our country?** With this question you are given the effect, or outcome: Washington came to be called the father of our country. Now you've got to find the reason or reasons why, so you are looking for the causes.

3. **Be on the lookout for signal words.** Certain words can signal that a reason for something or a cause of something is about to be mentioned. Other words can signal that a result or an effect is being described.

Words That Signal Causes		Words That Signal Effects	
because	since	therefore	thus
due to	were caused by	consequently	so
given that	results from	as a result	for that reason
as		then	why

Graphic Organizers to Show Causes and Effects

Some causes have more than one effect. For example, unhealthful eating habits can cause many health problems. Some effects, such as the Civil War, have more than one cause. You can show these cause-and-effect relationships by using graphic organizers like the following.

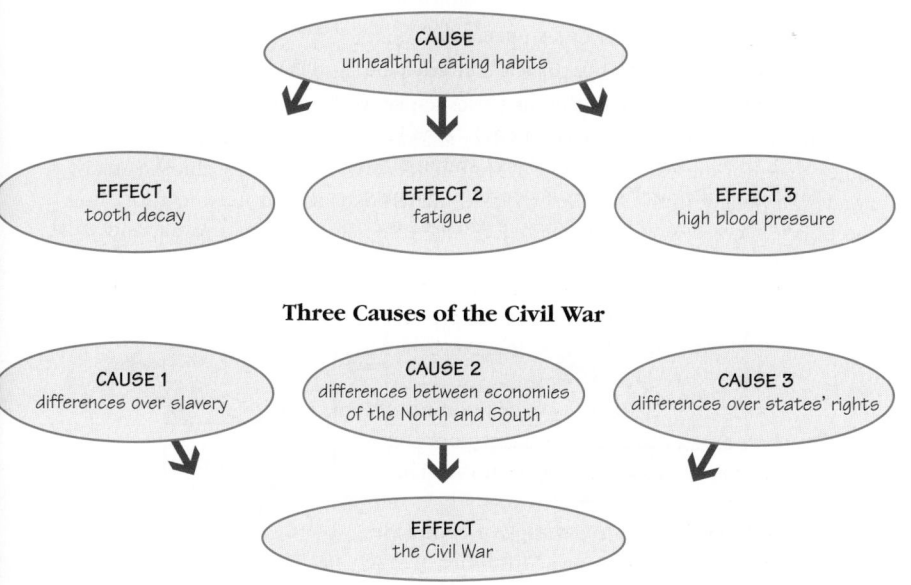

Three Effects of Unhealthful Eating Habits

CAUSE
unhealthful eating habits

EFFECT 1
tooth decay

EFFECT 2
fatigue

EFFECT 3
high blood pressure

Three Causes of the Civil War

CAUSE 1
differences over slavery

CAUSE 2
differences between economies
of the North and South

CAUSE 3
differences over states' rights

EFFECT
the Civil War

PRACTICE 1

Cause	→	Effect
People moved to California in search of gold.	→	The California population grew.
Most people rushing to find gold arrived in 1849, the height of the gold rush.	→	People were called forty-niners.
The mining towns that sprung up had no sheriffs.	→	The towns were unsafe.
Many people came quickly to California looking for gold.	→	By 1850, much of the easily found surface gold was already gone.
California has a wonderful climate and good farmland.	→	Many thousands of people decided to stay in California.

PRACTICE 2
Possible Answers

Country club has racist admission policy.

The team forfeits the tournament rather than play without Dondré.

The state legislature proclaims a Dondré Green Day.

Legislation is passed permitting lawsuits against private facilities that bar team members because of race.

● **PRACTICE 1**

Read the sentences that follow, and make a cause-and-effect chart like the one on page xxxviii. Decide which part of each sentence goes under the "Cause" heading and which part goes under the "Effect" heading. Look for signal words that help you spot causes and effects.

1. The California population grew from about 114,000 in 1848 to about 750,000 in 1852 as people moved to California in search of gold.
2. People rushing to California to find gold were called forty-niners because most of them arrived in 1849, the height of the gold rush.
3. Many of the mining towns that sprang up quickly were unsafe because they had no sheriffs.
4. Because so many people came so quickly to California looking for gold, by 1850, much of the easily found surface gold was already gone.
5. Although most people who went to California did not become rich from mining gold, many thousands decided to stay because of the wonderful climate and good farmland.

PRACTICE 2

Read "A Mason-Dixon Memory" on page 205. Then, read the following sentences and identify the cause-and-effect signal words in each.

- "Why did she look and sound so nervous?"
- "You mean I can't go to the park," I stuttered, "because I'm a Negro?"
- "'They don't allow Negroes in the park,' he said, 'so I'm staying with Clifton.'"

Next, read the following cause-and-effect chain. Then, make a second cause-and-effect chain for the experiences of Dondré Green. Write "Country club has racist admission policy" in the first box. Add as many boxes as you need to show how the policy affected Dondré, what actions his teammates took as a result, and what other effects the incident had.

Test Smarts

Strategies for Taking Multiple-Choice Tests

If you have ever watched a quiz show on TV, you know how multiple-choice tests work. You get a question and (usually) four choices. Your job is to pick the correct one. Taking multiple-choice tests will get much easier when you apply these Test Smarts:

T rack your time.

E xpect success.

S tudy the directions.

T ake it all in.

S pot those numbers.

M aster the questions.

A nticipate the answers.

R ely on 50/50.

T ry. Try. Try.

S earch for skips and smudges.

Track Your Time

You race through a test for fear you won't finish, or you realize you have only five minutes left to complete eleven zillion questions. Sound familiar? You can avoid both problems if you take a few minutes before you start to estimate how much time you have for each question. Using all the time you are given can help you avoid making errors. Follow these tips to set **checkpoints:**

- How many questions should be completed when one quarter of the time is gone?
- What should the clock read when you are halfway through the questions?
- If you find yourself behind your checkpoints, you can speed up.
- If you are ahead, you can—and should— slow down.

Expect Success

Top athletes know that attitude affects performance. They learn to deal with their negative thoughts. So can you! Do you compare yourself with others? Most top athletes will tell you that they compete against only one person: themselves. They know they cannot change another person's performance. Instead, they study their own performance and find ways to improve it. That makes sense for you, too. Review your last scores. Figure out just what you need to do to top them. You can!

What if you get anxious? It's OK if you do. A little nervousness will help you focus. Of course, if you're so nervous that you think you might get sick or faint, take time to relax for a few minutes. Calm bodies breathe slowly. You can fool yours into feeling calmer and thinking more clearly by taking a few deep breaths—five slow counts in, five out.

Study the Directions

You're ready to go, go, go, but first it's wait, wait, wait. Pencils. Paper. Answer sheets. Lots of directions. Listen! In order to follow directions, you have to know them. Read all test directions as if they contained the key to lifetime happiness and several years' allowance. Then, read them again. Study the answer sheet. Does it look like this?

1

2

3

4

or like this?

1   2   3   4

What about answer choices? Are they arranged

A   B   C   D

or

A   B   A   C

C   D   or   B   D

Directions count. Be very, very sure you know exactly what to do and how to do it before you make your first mark.

Take It All In

When you finally hear the words "You may begin," briefly **preview the test** to get a mental map of your tasks:

- Know how many questions you have to complete.
- Know where to stop.
- Set your time checkpoints.
- Do the easy sections first; easy questions are worth just as many points as hard ones.

Spot Those Numbers

"I got off by one and spent all my time trying to fix my answer sheet." *Oops.* Make it a habit to

- match the number of each question to the numbered space on the answer sheet every time
- leave the answer space blank if you skip a question
- keep a list of your blank spaces on scratch paper or somewhere else—but *not* on your answer sheet. The less you have to erase on your answer sheet, the better.

Master the Questions

Be sure—very sure—that you **know what a question is asking you.** Read the question at least twice before reading the answer choices. Approach it as you would a mystery story or a riddle. Look for clues. Watch especially for words like *not* and *except*—they tell you to look for the choice that is false or different from the other choices or opposite in some way. For a reading-comprehension test, read the selection, master all the questions, and then reread the selection. The answers will be likely to pop out the second time around. Remember: A test isn't trying to trick you; it's trying to test your knowledge and your ability to think clearly.

Anticipate the Answers

Before you read the answer choices, **answer the question yourself. Then, read the choices.** If the answer you gave is among the choices listed, it is probably correct.

Rely on 50/50

"I . . . have . . . no . . . clue." You understand the question. You have an answer, but your answer is not listed, or perhaps you drew a complete blank. It happens. Time to **make an educated guess**—not a *wild* guess, but an *educated* guess. Think about quiz shows again, and you'll know the value of the 50/50 play. When two answers are eliminated, the contestant has a 50/50 chance of choosing the correct one. You can use elimination, too.

Always read every choice carefully. **Watch out for distracters**—choices that may be true but are too broad, too narrow, or not relevant to the question. Eliminate the least likely choice. Then, eliminate the next, and so on until you find the best one. If two choices seem equally correct, look to see if "All of the above" is an option. If it is, that might be your choice. If no choice seems correct, look for "None of the above."

Try. Try. Try.

Don't give up. You might be surprised by how many students do give up. Think of tests as a kind of marathon. Just as in any marathon, people get bored, tired, hungry, thirsty, hot, discouraged. They may begin to feel sick or develop aches and pains. They decide the test doesn't matter.

Remember: The last question is worth just as much as the first question, and the questions on a test don't always get harder as you go. If the question you just finished was really hard, an easier one is probably coming up. Take a deep breath, and give it your all, all the way to the finish.

Search for Skips and Smudges

"Hey! I got that one right, and the machine marked it wrong!" If you have ever—ever—had this experience, pay attention! When this happens in class, your teacher can give you the extra point. On a machine-scored test, however, you would lose the point and never know why. So, listen up: All machine-scored answer sheets have a series of lines marching down the side. The machine stops at the first line and scans across it for your answer, stops at the second line, scans, stops at the third line, scans, and so on, all the way to the end. The machine is looking for a dark, heavy mark. If it finds one where it should be, you get the point. If you leave a question blank or accidentally mark two answers instead of one, you lose a point. If your marks are not very dark, the machine sees blank spaces, and you'll lose more points.

To avoid losing points, take time at the end of the test to make sure you

* did not skip any answers
* gave one answer for each question
* made the marks heavy and dark and within the lines

Correct: ▬   ⬤

Incorrect: ⊠   ▨   ▢   ▭
             ⊙   ☑

Get rid of smudges. Make sure there are no stray pencil marks on your answer sheet. Cleanly erase those places where you changed your mind. Check for little stray marks from pencil tapping.

Reading Comprehension

Many tests have a section called **reading comprehension.** The good news is that you do not have to study for this part of the test. Taking a reading-comprehension test is a bit like playing ball. You don't know where the ball will land, so you have to stay alert to all possibilities. However, just as the ball can come at you in only a few ways, there are only a few kinds of questions on reading-comprehension tests. This discussion will help you identify the most common ones. Two kinds of texts are used here. The first one is an informational text. The second is an updated fairy tale.

DIRECTIONS: Read the following selection. Then, choose the best answer for each question. Mark each answer on your answer sheet in the square provided.

Night Lights on the High Seas

For centuries, lighthouses have been used to alert sailors that land is near, to point out dangerous rocks and reefs, and to cast a bright light into the night to guide ships on their way. Seafarers have relied on these structures since the days of ancient Egypt. The lighthouse built in 300 B.C. on Pharos, an island near Alexandria, was regarded as one of the Seven Wonders of the World.

Lighthouses help to guide ships at night by giving off an intense beam that flashes every few seconds. Until the eighteenth century, the source of light was an oak-log fire. Coal fire was used for many years after that, until electricity became common in the early twentieth century. Some modern lighthouses also send out radio signals to help ships find their way in foggy weather. Even in their modern form, lighthouses serve their ancient purpose as guiding lights, flashing specks of civilization in the dark, lonely waters of night.

ITEM I asks for vocabulary knowledge.

1. In the first paragraph, the word *seafarers* means —

    A oceans   C fish

    B sailors   D ships

Answer: Look at the surrounding sentences, or **context,** to see which definition fits.

A is incorrect. The word *ocean* is another word for "sea," but oceans do not rely on lighthouses.

B is the best answer. In the context of the passage, it makes sense that *sailors* have relied on lighthouses for centuries.

C is incorrect. Fish live and travel in the sea, but nothing in the passage indicates that they depend on lighthouses.

D is incorrect. The safety of ships on the ocean depends on lighthouses. However, it is the *sailors* on the ships who have "relied on these structures for centuries."

ITEM 2 asks for close reading. Read carefully to see if the answer is stated directly in the text.

2. What was used to produce the light in lighthouses before the eighteenth century?

    F Wood   H Gas

    G Coal   J Electricity

Answer: Read the passage carefully to find the answer.

F is the correct answer. The second sentence of the second paragraph indicates that "until the eighteenth century, the source of light was an oak-log fire." The words *oak* and *log* clearly indicate that "wood" is the right choice.

ITEM 3 asks for an inference.

3. What is the main idea of this passage?

   A Working in a lighthouse is a dangerous job.

   B Modern lighthouses are very different from those of long ago.

   C The first lighthouse was built in 300 b.c. on the island of Pharos.

   D Lighthouses have helped guide ships for thousands of years.

Answer: Think about which statement covers the passage as a whole.

A is incorrect. The passage does not provide an explanation of working in a lighthouse.

B is incorrect. It does not explain the purpose of lighthouses over the years.

C is incorrect. It is only one detail in the passage.

D is the best answer. It covers most of the details in the passage.

ITEM 4 asks you to recognize an opinion.

5. Which is an **opinion** expressed in the passage?

   F The beam from a lighthouse flashes every few seconds.

   G Modern lighthouses send out radio signals.

   H Pharos is an island near Alexandria.

   J The ocean waters are lonely at night.

Answer: A **fact** can be proved true or false. An **opinion,** a personal feeling or belief, cannot be proved true or false. **F, G,** and **H** are facts that can be proved true or false. **J is correct** because it is the only opinion.

ITEM 5 asks you to decide why the author wrote the passage.

6. What is the author's main **purpose** for writing this passage?

   A To entertain readers with an exciting story

   B To inform readers about the history of lighthouses

   C To persuade readers to visit a lighthouse

   D To describe what life in a lighthouse is like

Answer: Look at the information given in the passage, and decide what the writer's purpose was in writing.

A is incorrect. The writer does not tell a story.

B is the best answer. The writer presents information about the function of lighthouses over time.

C is incorrect. The writer's purpose is not to persuade readers to visit a lighthouse.

D is incorrect. The writer never tells what it's like to live in a lighthouse.

DIRECTIONS: Read the following selection. Then, choose the best answer for each question. Mark each answer on your answer sheet in the space provided.

A Technologically Correct Fairy Tale: Jack and the Beanstalk

There once was a poor widow who lived in a small cottage with her son, Jack. Jack was a good-hearted fellow who <u>devoted</u> all his time to a mega-computer game. Since Jack did not have a paying job, he and his widowed mother were very poor.

The day arrived when the widow had sold all her possessions via the Internet, except for an elderly cow. Jack was to sell the cow at the market since his mother was too <u>frail</u> to make the trip.

"Get a good price for her," the widow instructed.

"Yes, Mother," Jack answered.

Off he went with the cow in tow.

Out on the highway, Jack was stopped by a man who offered to trade him a handful of oddly shaped, brightly colored beans for the cow. "These are turbo-beans," the man whispered. While Jack didn't know exactly what that meant, he did know that the word *turbo* made the beans sound special, so he agreed to the trade. When he got home, he proudly handed the beans to his mother. She promptly tossed them out the window, declaring she didn't know what he could have been thinking. . . .

ITEM 1 is a vocabulary question. To answer it, go back to the fairy tale, and consider the surrounding words, or context, to identify the best definition.

1. In the first paragraph the underlined word *devoted* means —

    A donated

    B avoided

    C captured

    D dedicated

A is incorrect. *Donated* means "gave someone something of value." It doesn't fit in this context.

B is incorrect. It doesn't fit the context, which shows what Jack did with his time, not what he didn't do.

C is incorrect. It doesn't fit in the context.

D is the best answer. In this context, *devoted* means "dedicated" or "gave one's time to a particular pursuit."

ITEM 2 is another vocabulary question.

2. In the second paragraph of the fairy tale, *frail* means —

    F proud

    G weak

    H stubborn

    J forceful

The best answer is G, since it offers the only reason why the widow would not be able to make the trip herself.

ITEM 3 is a factual question. Reread the fairy tale, and you'll find the answer.

3. How did the widow sell all of her possessions, except for the old cow?

    A She sold them via the Internet.

    B She set up a shop on the highway.

    C She sold them to her neighbors.

    D She sold them to the man with the beans.

A is the answer. The fairy tale clearly states that she sold her possessions on the Internet.

B is incorrect. Jack met the man with the beans on the main highway. The widow did not go there.

C is incorrect. Neighbors are not mentioned in the selection.

D is incorrect. Jack, not the widow, traded the cow for the beans.

ITEM 4 asks you to analyze a cause-and-effect relationship. Don't worry, though. The answer is in the text.

4. Because Jack didn't have a paying job, he and his mother were —

    F supported by an uncle

    G very poor

    H reduced to stealing

    J very angry

F is incorrect. An uncle is not mentioned in the story.

G is the best answer. The fairy tale says that they were poor.

H is incorrect. Stealing is not mentioned in the story.

J is incorrect. Anger is not mentioned in the story.

ITEM 5 requires that you make an inference based on the text.

5. Jack's mother didn't think beans for a cow was a good trade. How do you know this?

    A She explains that a cow is worth more than a handful of beans.

    B Jack was supposed to sell the cow.

    C The man cheated Jack.

    D She tossed the beans out the window.

A is incorrect. Jack's mother doesn't say this in the story.

B is incorrect. This is true, but it doesn't explain why his mother didn't think it was a good trade.

C is incorrect. This may be true, but it doesn't tell us how we know what Jack's mother thought of the trade.

D is the best answer. Her actions show what she thought of the trade.

ITEM 6 asks you to use your **prior knowledge** to predict the outcome.

6. If this story ended like a typical fairy tale, which of the following predictions would you make?

    F The beans do, indeed, prove worthless.

    G The beans become the key to lifelong happiness for Jack and his mother.

    H The beans end up in a stew.

    J The cow comes home.

F is incorrect. The fairy tale cannot have its "happily ever after" ending if the beans are worthless.

G is the best answer. In fairy tales, magical gifts from strangers often bring great rewards in the end.

H is incorrect. This is too ordinary an ending for a fairy tale.

J is incorrect. This ending is also too ordinary for a fairy tale.

Strategies for Taking Writing Tests
Writing a Fictional or Autobiographical Narrative

Some tests may include writing prompts that ask you to write a narrative, or story. The following steps will help you write a **fictional** or **autobiographical narrative.** The responses are based on this prompt.

> **Prompt**
> Write a short fictional narrative. The story should include major and minor characters, a thoroughly developed plot, and a definite setting.

Thinking It Through: Writing a Fictional or Autobiographical Narrative

■ **STEP 1 Read the prompt carefully.** Does the prompt ask you to write a fictional story (a made-up story) or an **autobiographical story** (a story of something that really happened to you)?

The word "fictional" tells me that the prompt is asking for a made-up story.

STEP 2 Outline the plot of your narrative. Explain conflict, climax, resolution.

Conflict—the main character, Sue, wants to win the fencing tournament. Climax—Sue fences against the champion. Resolution—Sue wins but feels bad when she sees her opponent crying.

STEP 3 Identify the major and minor characters. What do they look and act like? How do they sound when they speak?

Major character—Sue is tall and lanky; she is shy; she is very competitive. Minor character—Sue's competitor, Tory, is tall; she is confident and sometimes rude.

STEP 4 Identify the setting of your narrative. Where and when does your story take place?

The story takes place in January during the state fencing championships in a gymnasium.

STEP 5 Draft your narrative, adding dialogue, suspense, and sensory details.

I plan to create suspense by drawing out the moment when Sue must decide what to do when she sees Tory crying. I will use sensory details to describe how she feels. I will also include dialogue of her conversation with Tory.

STEP 6 Revise and proofread your narrative. Make sure that you have organized the events in your story in a logical order. Add transitions that show time, such as *earlier, afterward, at the same time,* and *later.*

Writing a Summary

Some tests include writing prompts like the one to the right.

To write a **summary** of a passage, you rewrite in your own words the passage's main idea and significant details. The summary should both paraphrase and condense the original. A summary of a short passage should be about one-third as long. For a longer selection, a summary should include no more than one sentence for each paragraph.

Prompt
Read the essay "Fish Cheeks," and then summarize it. In your summary, include the main idea and significant details of the article.

The following steps will help you write an effective summary in response to a prompt. The student responses are based on the reading selection "Fish Cheeks" on pages 135–137.

Thinking It Through: Writing a Summary

■ **STEP 1 Read the passage carefully. Identify the main idea, and restate it in your own words.** What is the most important point the writer is making about the topic? How would *you* say it?

Main idea: The narrator learns that she can fit in with American teens but she should be proud of her Chinese heritage.

STEP 2 Identify significant details to include in the summary. Which details directly support the main idea? List at least one key idea or detail from each paragraph.

Significant details: The narrator is Chinese American; she has a crush on the minister's son, who is white; the narrator is embarrassed by the Chinese food her mother prepares and by her relatives' table manners; her mother gives her a miniskirt.

STEP 3 Write the main idea and most significant details in a paragraph, using your own words. Give details in the same order they are presented in the passage.

The narrator is a Chinese American teenager struggling to fit in with her friends. When her parents invite the minister and his family to Christmas Eve dinner, the narrator is embarrassed by the food her mother prepares and by the table manners of her relatives. Her mother gives her a miniskirt and tells her that she can look like a typical American girl on the outside but she should always be proud of her Chinese heritage.

Writing a Response to Literature

On a writing test, you may be asked to write a **literary response.** Often on such tests, you will be given a literary selection to read and a prompt such as the one on the right.

The following steps and the partial student responses will help you respond to a prompt like the one above. The short story "A Day's Wait" can be found on pages 81–83.

> **Prompt**
> What sort of character is Schatz from the short story "A Day's Wait"? Analyze his thoughts, actions, and words.

Thinking It Through: Writing a Response to Literature

■ **STEP 1 Read the prompt carefully, noting key words.** Key words might include a verb—such as *analyze, identify,* or *explain*—and a literary element—such as *plot, character, setting,* or *theme.*

> The key words are "analyze" and "character."

STEP 2 Read the selection at least twice. Read first for the overall meaning of the work. Then, read the selection a second time, keeping the key words from the prompt in mind.

STEP 3 Write a main idea statement. Your main idea statement should give the title and author of the work and should directly address the prompt.

> Schatz, the little boy in "A Day's Wait" by Ernest Hemingway, is similar to my little brother; both hide their feelings.

STEP 4 Find specific examples and details from the selection to support your main idea. If you include quotations from the literary work, remember to enclose them in quotation marks.

> When Schatz's father asked Schatz how he was feeling, he replied, "Just the same, so far," although he feared he was dying.

STEP 5 Draft, revise, and proofread your response. To create coherence, use transitions between ideas, such as *for example, however,* and *finally.* When you have written your draft, re-read it to make sure you have presented your ideas clearly. Also, check to see that you have fully addressed all the key words in the prompt. Finally, proofread to correct mistakes in spelling, punctuation, and capitalization.

Using the T.H.E.M.E.S. Strategy on a Writing Test

Writing tests often ask you to write a **persuasive essay** in response to a prompt. Most of these prompts give you a topic, but you must identify your position and generate support for your position. Thinking of what to say in a limited amount of time is one of the most difficult parts of such a test.

Use the T.H.E.M.E.S. strategy, explained in the steps below, to generate support for a position quickly. The student responses are based on this prompt.

> **Prompt**
> The city council is considering building a parking garage or a park on an empty lot. Write an essay that takes a position on the issue and defends the position with relevant support.

Thinking It Through: Using the T.H.E.M.E.S. Strategy on a Writing Test

■ **Each letter in T.H.E.M.E.S. stands for a category you could use to trigger ideas for supporting your position in a persuasive essay.**

T = Time
H = Health
E = Education
M = Money
E = Environment
S = Safety

STEP 1 Identify your position on the topic given in the prompt.

The city council should build a park.

STEP 2 Use T.H.E.M.E.S. to list benefits for your position.

T = A park would take less <u>time</u> to build than a garage. H = People could use the park to exercise and remain <u>healthy.</u> E = People might become more aware, or <u>educated,</u> about the wildlife and plants that occupy the area. M = The city would save <u>money</u> because constructing playscapes and jogging trails is less expensive than clearing the land and building a garage. E = The <u>environment</u> would benefit because the trees and homes of animals are not destroyed. S = Without a garage, fewer cars may drive in the area, reducing the <u>safety</u> hazard of automobile accidents.

STEP 3 Identify the three strongest reasons you developed using T.H.E.M.E.S. Your strongest reasons will be those for which you have the most evidence and those that address readers' concerns about the topic.

My three strongest reasons for building a park are health benefits, reduced costs, and environmental benefits. These are the issues that I think concern my readers the most.

Collection One

Out Here on My Own

Theme

Facing Challenges *Confronting a crisis alone can be a frightening ordeal for anyone. Sometimes, however, a crisis summons qualities that we never knew we had—courage, determination, and self-sacrifice.*

Reading the Anthology

Reaching Struggling Readers

The *Reading Skills and Strategies: Reaching Struggling Readers* binder provides materials coordinated with the Pupil's Edition (see the Collection Planner, p. T1C) to help students who have difficulty reading and comprehending text, or students who are reluctant readers. The binder for seventh grade is organized around eleven individual skill areas and offers the following options:

- 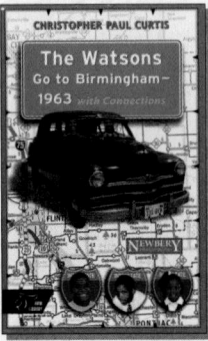 MiniReads are short, easy texts that give students a chance to practice a particular skill and strategy before reading selections in the Pupil's Edition. Each MiniRead Skill Lesson can be taught independently or used in conjunction with a Selection Skill Lesson.

- **Selection Skill Lessons** Selection Skill Lessons allow students to apply skills introduced in the MiniReads. Each Selection Skill Lesson provides reading instruction and practice specific to a particular piece of literature in the Pupil's Edition.

Reading Beyond the Anthology

Read On

Collection One includes an annotated bibliography of books suitable for extended reading. The suggested books are related to works in this collection by theme, by author, or by subject. To preview the Read On for Collection One, please turn to p. T93.

HRW Library

The *HRW Library* offers novels, plays, and short-story collections for extended reading. Each book in the Library includes one or more major works and thematically or topically related Connections. The Connections are magazine articles, poems, or other pieces of literature. Each book in the *HRW Library* is also accompanied by a Study Guide that provides teaching suggestions and worksheets. For Collection One, the following titles are recommended.

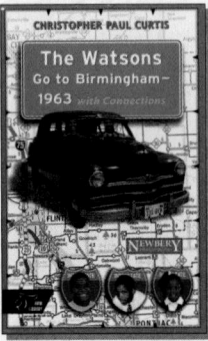

THE WATSONS GO TO BIRMINGHAM
Christopher Paul Curtis
Curtis's alternately funny, poignant, and sobering novel depicts a family rallying together in the wake of the Birmingham bombings of 1963.

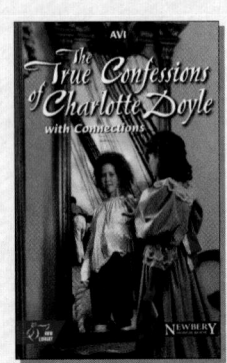

THE TRUE CONFESSIONS OF CHARLOTTE DOYLE
Avi
In the 1830s, a well-bred young lady must overcome her proper social training when she finds herself caught up in a ship's mutiny.

Skills Focus

Selection or Feature	Reading Skills and Strategies	Elements of Literature	Language/ Grammar	Vocabulary/ Spelling	Writing	Listening/ Speaking	Viewing/ Representing
Rikki-tikki-tavi (p. 2) Rudyard Kipling	Dialogue with the Text, pp. 2, 19	Conflict, pp. 2, 19	Specific Verbs, p. 21	Words in Context, p. 21	Collect Story Ideas, p. 20	Create a Sequel, p. 20 Create a Sound-track, p. 20	Make a Science Brochure on Cobras, p. 20
Elements of Literature (p. 22)		Plot, pp. 22–23 • Basic Situation • Conflict • Complication • Climax • Resolution Theme, p. 23					
The Runaway (p. 24) Robert Frost	Form Mental Images, p. 27	Symbol, pp. 24, 27			Use Memories for a Story, p. 27 Rewrite the Poem from the Colt's Point of View, p. 27	Perform a Choral Reading, p. 27	
Song of the Trees (p. 28) Mildred D. Taylor	Make General-izations, pp. 28, 43 Create a Story Map, p. 42	Theme, pp. 28, 43 Plot, p. 42	Subject-Verb Agreement, p. 44	Connotation, p. 44 Denotation, p. 44	Create a Character, p. 43 State a Theme, p. 43	Select a Sound-track, p. 43	Illustrate a Fact-sheet on Trees, p. 43
Reading Skills and Strategies: Metacog-nition: Thinking About Thinking (p. 45)	Metacognition, p. 45 • Preview • Question • Reread • Record • Reflect						
The Smallest Dragonboy (p. 46) Anne McCaffrey	Metacognition, pp. 46, 61	Image, p. 61 Conflict, p. 61 Climax, p. 61	Consistent Verb Tense, p. 63	Glossary of Invented Words, p. 62 Words in Context, p. 63	Start a Plot, p. 62 Write a Science Report, p. 62 Write a Song, p. 62	Perform a Song, p. 62	Use a Chart to Record Data, p. 61
Three Skeleton Key (p. 64) George G. Toudouze	Make Predictions, pp. 64, 77 Record Key Events in a Log, p. 77	Suspense, pp. 64, 77 Foreshadowing, pp. 64, 77 Dialogue, p. 78	Irregular Verb Tenses, p. 79	Use New Words, p. 79	Ideas for Setting, p. 78 Radio Script, p. 78 Write a Help-Wanted Ad, p. 78	Perform and Record a Radio Script, p. 78	Design a Help-Wanted Ad, p. 78
A Day's Wait (p. 80) Ernest Hemingway	Make Infer-ences, p. 80 Make a Story Map, p. 85	Character, pp. 80, 85 Title, p. 85	Irregular Verbs, p. 87	Workplace Vocabulary, p. 87	Journal from a Charac-ter's Point of View, p. 86 Character Sketch, p. 86		Metric System, p. 86
No Questions Asked: The Last Dinosaur (p. 88) Jim Murphy	The **No Questions Asked** feature provides students with an unstructured opportunity to practice reading strategies using a selection that extends the theme of the collection.			Word Roots, p. 90			
Writer's Workshop: Story (p. 94)		Plot, p. 96 Conflict, p. 96 Dialogue, p. 96			Narrative Writing: Short Story, pp. 94–98		
Sentence Workshop: Sentence Fragments (p. 99)			Identify Fragments, p. 99		Revise Sentence Fragments, p. 99		
Reading for Life: Using Text Organizers (p. 100)	Use Text Orga-nizers to Locate Information, p. 100						Use Graphics to Find Information, p. 100
Learning for Life: Making a Presentation (p. 101)		Analyze Courage as a Character Trait, p. 101			Write a Public-Service Announcement, p. 101	Role-Play a Speech, p. 101	Design Visual Symbols, p. 101

Skills Focus

Collection One Out Here on My Own

Resources for this Collection

Note: All resources for this collection are available for preview on the *One-Stop Planner CD-ROM 1 with Test Generator.* All worksheets and blackline masters may be printed from the CD-ROM.

Selection or Feature	Reading and Literary Skills	Language and Grammar

Rikki-tikki-tavi (p. 2)
Rudyard Kipling
Connections: The Dinner Party (p. 17)
retold by Mona Gardner
	• *Reading Skills and Strategies: Reaching Struggling Readers*
	  • MiniRead Skill Lesson, p. 1
	  • Selection Skill Lesson, p. 7
	• *Graphic Organizers for Active Reading*, Worksheet p. 1
	• *Literary Elements:*
	  Transparency 1; Worksheet p. 4
		• *Grammar and Language Links:*
		  Specific Verbs, Worksheet p. 1
		• *Language Workshop CD-ROM,* Verbs
		• *Daily Oral Grammar,*
		  Transparency 1

Elements of Literature: **The Short Story** (p. 22)	• *Literary Elements,* Transparency 1	
The Runaway (p. 24) Robert Frost	• *Graphic Organizers for Active Reading*, Worksheet p. 2	

Song of the Trees (p. 28)
Mildred D. Taylor
	• *Reading Skills and Strategies: Reaching Struggling Readers*
	  • MiniRead Skill Lesson, p. 23
	  • Selection Skill Lesson, p. 30
	• *Graphic Organizers for Active Reading*, Worksheet p. 3
		• *Grammar and Language Links:*
		  Subject-Verb Agreement, Worksheet p. 3
		• *Language Workshop CD-ROM,*
		  Subject-Verb Agreement
		• *Daily Oral Grammar,*
		  Transparency 2

The Smallest Dragonboy (p. 46)
Anne McCaffrey
	• *Graphic Organizers for Active Reading*, Worksheet p. 4	• *Grammar and Language Links:*
		  Consistent Verb Tenses, Worksheet p. 5
		• *Language Workshop CD-ROM,*
		  Verb Tenses
		• *Daily Oral Grammar,*
		  Transparency 3

Three Skeleton Key (p. 64)
George G. Toudouze
	• *Reading Skills and Strategies: Reaching Struggling Readers*
	  • MiniRead Skill Lesson, p. 47
	  • Selection Skill Lesson, p. 53
	• *Graphic Organizers for Active Reading*, Worksheet p. 5
		• *Grammar and Language Links:*
		  Troublesome Verbs, Worksheet p. 7
		• *Language Workshop CD-ROM,*
		  Irregular Verbs
		• *Daily Oral Grammar,*
		  Transparency 4

A Day's Wait (p. 80)
Ernest Hemingway
	• *Reading Skills and Strategies: Reaching Struggling Readers*
	  • Selection Skill Lesson, p. 34
	• *Graphic Organizers for Active Reading*, Worksheet p. 6
		• *Grammar and Language Links:*
		  Irregular Verbs, Worksheet p. 9
		• *Language Workshop CD-ROM,*
		  Irregular Verbs
		• *Daily Oral Grammar,*
		  Transparency 5

No Questions Asked: The Last Dinosaur (p. 88) Jim Murphy	The **No Questions Asked** feature provides students with an unstructured opportunity to practice reading strategies using a selection that extends the theme of the collection.	• *Daily Oral Grammar,* Transparency 6
Writer's Workshop: Story (p. 94)		
Sentence Workshop: Sentence Fragments (p. 99)		• *Workshop Resources,* p. 37 • *Language Workshop CD-ROM,* Sentence Fragments
Learning for Life: Making a Presentation (p. 101)		

Collection Planner

Collection Resources

- *Cross-Curricular Activities*, p. 1
- *Portfolio Management System:*
  Introduction to Portfolio Assessment, p. 1;
  Parent/Guardian Letters, p. 87
- *Formal Assessment,*
  Reading Application Test, p. 14
- *Test Generator,* Collection Test 🔘

Collection Planner

Vocabulary, Spelling, and Decoding	Writing	Listening and Speaking, Viewing and Representing	Assessment
• *Words to Own*, Worksheet p. 1 • *Spelling and Decoding,* Worksheet p. 1	• *Portfolio Management System,* Rubrics for Choices, p. 105	• *Visual Connections,* Videocassette A, Segment 1 📼 • *Audio CD Library,* Disc 1, Tracks 2, 3 🎧 • *Portfolio Management System,* Rubrics for Choices, p. 105	• *Formal Assessment,* Selection Test, p. 1 • *Standardized Test Preparation,* p. 10 • *Test Generator* (One-Stop Planner CD-ROM) 🔘
			• *Formal Assessment,* Literary Elements Test, p. 12
	• *Portfolio Management System,* Rubrics for Choices, p. 106	• *Audio CD Library,* Disc 2, Track 2 🎧 • *Portfolio Management System,* Rubrics for Choices, p. 106	• *Formal Assessment,* Selection Test, p. 3 • *Test Generator* (One-Stop Planner CD-ROM) 🔘
• Words to Own, Worksheet p. 2 • *Spelling and Decoding,* Worksheet p. 2	• *Portfolio Management System,* Rubrics for Choices, p. 107	• *Audio CD Library,* Disc 2, Track 3 🎧 • *Portfolio Management System,* Rubrics for Choices, p. 107	• *Formal Assessment,* Selection Test, p. 4 • *Standardized Test Preparation,* p. 12 • *Test Generator* (One-Stop Planner CD-ROM) 🔘
• Words to Own, Worksheet p. 3 • *Spelling and Decoding,* Worksheet p. 3	• *Portfolio Management System,* Rubrics for Choices, p. 108	• *Audio CD Library,* Disc 3, Track 2 🎧 • *Viewing and Representing:* Fine Art Transparencies 1, 2 Worksheet pp. 4, 8 • *Portfolio Management System,* Rubrics for Choices, p. 108	• *Formal Assessment,* Selection Test, p. 6 • *Standardized Test Preparation,* p. 14 • *Test Generator* (One-Stop Planner CD-ROM) 🔘
• Words to Own, Worksheet p. 4 • *Spelling and Decoding,* Worksheet p. 4	• *Portfolio Management System,* Rubrics for Choices, p. 109	• *Audio CD Library,* Disc 3, Track 3 🎧 • *Viewing and Representing:* Fine Art Transparency 3 Worksheet p. 12 • *Portfolio Management System,* Rubrics for Choices, p. 109	• *Formal Assessment,* Selection Test, p. 8 • *Standardized Test Preparation,* pp. 16, 18 • *Test Generator* (One-Stop Planner CD-ROM) 🔘
• Words to Own, Worksheet p. 5 • *Spelling and Decoding,* Worksheet p. 5	• *Portfolio Management System,* Rubrics for Choices, p. 110	• *Audio CD Library,* Disc 4, Track 2 🎧 • *Portfolio Management System,* Rubrics for Choices, p. 110	• *Formal Assessment,* Selection Test, p. 10 • *Standardized Test Preparation,* p. 20 • *Test Generator* (One-Stop Planner CD-ROM) 🔘
		• *Audio CD Library,* Disc 4, Track 3 🎧	
	• *Workshop Resources,* p. 1 • *Writer's Workshop 1* CD-ROM, Story 🔘		• *Portfolio Management System* • Prewriting, p. 111 • Peer Editing, p. 112 • Assessment Rubric, p. 113
		• *Viewing and Representing,* HRW Multimedia Presentation Maker	• *Portfolio Management System,* Rubrics, p. 114

 Transparency   CD-ROM   Video   Audio CD

T1D

OBJECTIVES

1. Read literature in different genres on the theme "Out Here on My Own"
2. Interpret literary elements used in the literature, with special emphasis on the short story
3. Apply a variety of reading strategies, particularly metacognition
4. Respond to the literature in a variety of modes
5. Learn and use new words
6. Develop skill in storytelling
7. Plan, draft, revise, proof, and publish a story
8. Identify and revise sentence fragments
9. Demonstrate the ability to read a textbook
10. Explore, through a variety of projects, the personal qualities that make people courageous

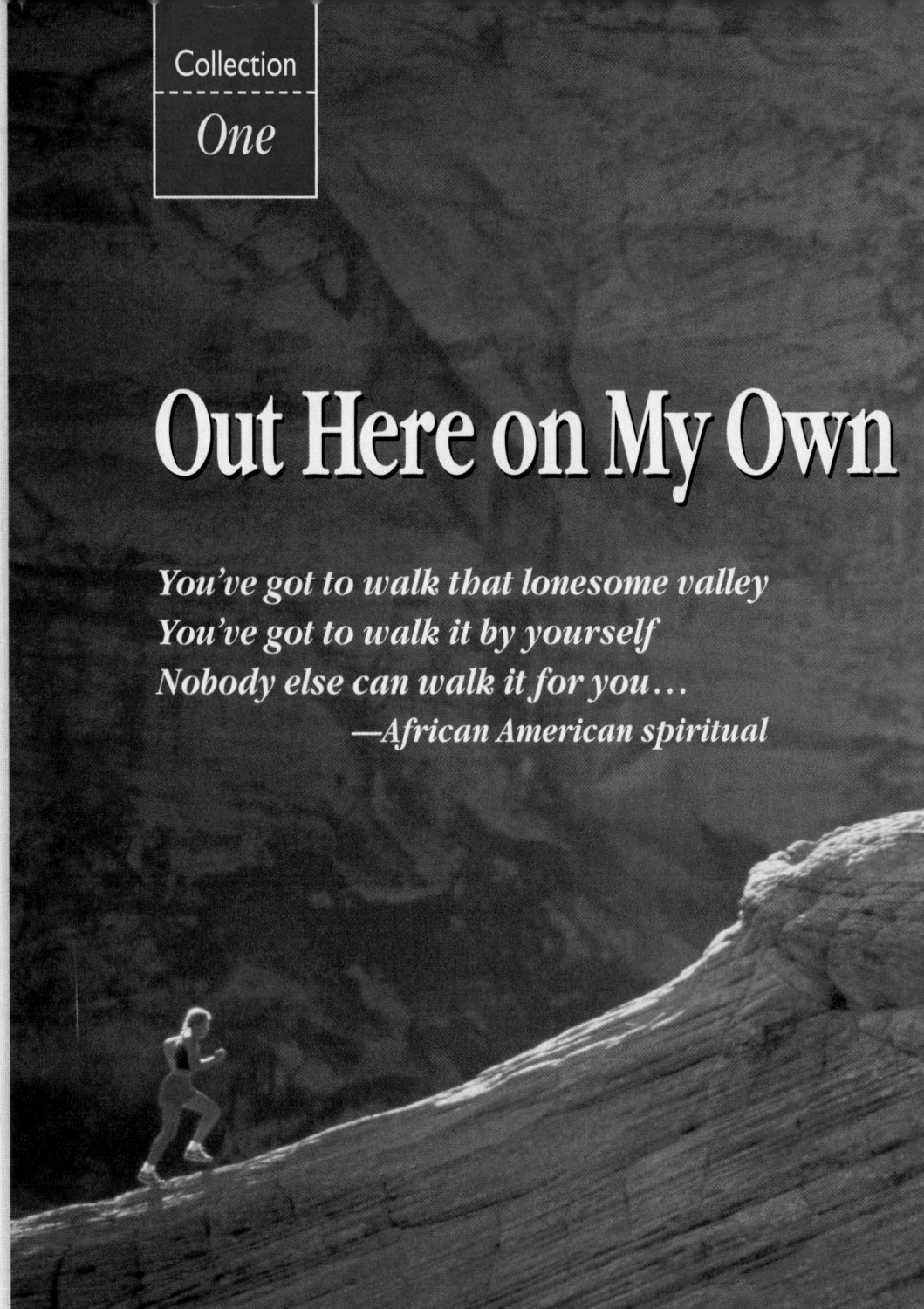

Out Here on My Own

You've got to walk that lonesome valley
You've got to walk it by yourself
Nobody else can walk it for you…
— *African American spiritual*

Introducing the Theme

Briefly describe the scene in *The Lion King* in which the young lion leaves the safety of his home to face new challenges. Or, choose a movie or children's story that has a similar theme. Then, ask students to think of how the main character feels at first. Tell the class that the characters found in this collection will also have to solve problems by themselves, and ask students if they can recall any situations in which someone they knew had to face a challenge alone.

Responding to the Quotation

? What do you think the statement "Nobody else can walk it for you" means? [Possible responses: You have to figure things out for yourself; you are responsible for your own actions.]

WORK IN PROGRESS

Writing Focus: Story

The following **Work in Progress** assignments build to a culminating **Writer's Workshop** at the end of Collection 1.

Writer's Notebook

Have students make a list in their journals of types of challenges that people face in their daily lives or on their jobs. Point out that people with sight, hearing, or other physical impairments struggle against challenges every day, and people such as police officers, fire fighters, and doctors often need to deal with life-threatening challenges. Ask students to come up with a class list of ten people who have overcome serious physical or occupational challenges to become examples of determination and perseverance.

Resources ———

Portfolio Management System
- Introduction to Portfolio Assessment, p. 1
- Parent/Guardian Letters, p. 87

Formal Assessment
- Reading Application Test, p. 14

Test Generator
- Collection Test

Cross-Curricular Activities
- Teaching Notes, p. 1

Selection Readability

This Annotated Teacher's Edition provides a summary of each selection in the student book. Following each Summary heading, you will find one, two or three small icons. These icons indicate, in an approximate sense, the reading level of the selection.

■ One icon indicates that the selection is easy.

■■ Two icons indicate that the selection is on an intermediate reading level.

■■■ Three icons indicate that the selection is challenging.

OBJECTIVES
1. Read and interpret the story
2. Analyze conflict
3. Dialogue with the Text
4. Express understanding through narrative and expository writing, speaking and listening, or storytelling/music
5. Identify vivid verbs and use such verbs in writing
6. Understand and use new words

SKILLS
Literary
• Analyze conflict
Reading
• Dialogue with the Text
Writing
• Use a visual prompt
• Write a science brochure
Speaking/Listening
• Narrate a sequel
Grammar/Language
• Use specific verbs
Vocabulary
• Use new words
Music
• Create a soundtrack
Viewing/Representing
• Describe a picture (ATE)

Planning

• **Block Schedule**
Block Scheduling Lesson Plans with Pacing Guide

• **Traditional Schedule**
Lesson Plans Including Strategies for English-Language Learners

• **One-Stop Planner**
CD-ROM with Test Generator

Before You Read

RIKKI-TIKKI-TAVI

Make the Connection

It's a Wild World

People face difficult situations in all kinds of ways. The expressions "Pick yourself up, dust yourself off, and start all over again," "Run for your life," and "Circle the wagons" suggest different strategies for dealing with tough situations.

What Would You Do?

If you were facing a bully, would you

• run the other way?

• get help from your family and friends?

• face your opponent and fight?

• try to use logic and reasoning to reach an agreement?

• use a strategy other than the ones listed above? (What would it be?)

Talk about your response with a partner or a group.

Elements of Literature

Conflict: "Clash" Action

Conflict is what gives any story its energy. When you can't wait to find out what happens next and you care about who wins out in a story, you're reacting to conflict.

Conflict is a struggle or clash between opposing characters or opposing forces.

For more on Conflict, see pages 22–23 and the Handbook of Literary Terms.

As the first two paragraphs of "Rikki-tikki-tavi" tell us, this is a story about a "great war" that is fought by a brave little mongoose. Does this bold little creature's conflict with a deadly enemy keep you turning those pages?

Reading Skills and Strategies

Dialogue with the Text

When you read a story actively, a great deal goes on in your head:

• You connect what you read with your own experience.

• You ask yourself questions and make predictions about what will happen next.

• You challenge the text.

• You reflect on its meaning.

As you read, you create your own meaning from the text. No two readers will interpret a text in exactly the same way. Your way of reading is unique.

Jotting down notes as you read will help you become aware of yourself as a reader. Try keeping a sheet of paper beside each page so that you can note your thoughts next to the passage you're responding to. One reader's comments appear on the first pages of "Rikki-tikki-tavi" as an example.

 go.hrw.com
LEO 7-1

2 OUT HERE ON MY OWN

Preteaching Vocabulary

Words to Own

You might want to use the following exercises to preteach the words defined in this story at point of use.

1. Describe a time when you or someone you know was **immensely** proud.

2. Draw a picture of a dog that **cowered** before a kitten.

3. Draw pictures suggested by the words **gait** and **gate** to help you remember their meanings. Use the letters of the words in your pictures.

4. Name three people in the world who are **valiant.**

5. Describe a time you gave someone **consolation.**

Rikki-tikki-tavi

Rudyard Kipling

Inch by inch rose up the big black cobra . . .

Summary ■ ■

In this famous "monster-slaying" story, a little mongoose is taken in by a British family living in India, around 1900. His name, Rikki-tikki-tavi, comes from the sound he makes, which Kipling calls his "war cry." When the mongoose learns from other animals that two cobras, Nag and his wife, Nagaina, live in the family garden, he knows he must kill them, and thus the conflict begins. After overhearing the cobras' plans to kill the family, Rikki ambushes and kills Nag in the bunga-low bathroom. To prevent a new gen-eration of cobras from settling in the garden, Rikki destroys all but one of the cobra eggs. He uses the last egg to lure Nagaina away from Teddy, the fam-ily's little son. Nagaina quickly snatches the egg and disappears underground. Rikki bravely follows. At the story's climax, the little hero emerges trium-phant. He has killed the last cobra and the garden is once again at peace.

Background

This story and the Connections piece, "The Dinner Party," take place in colo-nial India, which was governed by Great Britain from 1858 to 1947. Many British military officers and civil ser-vants came with their families to live in India.

Resources

Viewing and Representing
Videocassette A, Segment 1
The *Visual Connections* segment "Snakes: Friends or Foes?" presents dramatic information about snakes, including facts about cobras and mon-gooses. For complete lesson plans, see *The Visual Connections Teacher's Manual.*

Resources: Print and Media

Reading
- *Reading Skills and Strategies*
  MiniRead Skill Lesson, p. 1
  Selection Skill Lesson, p. 7
- *Graphic Organizers for Active Reading*, p. 1
- *Words to Own*, p. 1
- *Spelling and Decoding*
  Worksheet, p. 1
- *Audio CD Library*
  Disc 1, Track 2

Elements of Literature
- *Literary Elements*
  Transparency 1
  Worksheet, p. 4

Writing and Language
- *Daily Oral Grammar*
  Transparency 1
- *Grammar and Language Links*
  Worksheet, p. 1
- *Language Workshop CD-ROM*

Viewing and Representing
- *Visual Connections*
  Videocassette A, Segment 1

Assessment
- *Formal Assessment*, p. 1
- *Portfolio Management System*, p. 105
- *Standardized Test Preparation*, p. 10
- *Test Generator (One-Stop Planner CD-ROM)*

Internet
- go.hrw.com (keyword: LE0 7-1)

Resources

Listening
Audio CD Library
A lively recording of this story is provided in the *Audio CD Library:*
• Disc I, Track I

Selection Assessment
Formal Assessment
• Selection Test, p. I

Test Generator
• Selection Test

Elements of Literature
For additional instruction on conflict, see *Literary Elements:*
• Transparency I
• Worksheet, p. 4

FROM THE EDITOR'S DESK

This story is always a sure-fire success with middle-school students. In every survey done on reading preferences, this story scores in the highest category. Perhaps it is because we are all hooked by suspense—especially when the action involves a tiny challenger against a powerful and dangerous bully. (However, some students come out on the side of the snake. Be warned.)

This is the story of the great war that Rikki-tikki-tavi fought single-handed, through the bathrooms of the big bungalow[1] in Segowlee cantonment.[2] Darzee, the tailorbird, helped him, and Chuchundra, the muskrat, who never comes out into the middle of the floor but always creeps round by the wall, gave him advice; but Rikki-tikki did the real fighting.

He was a mongoose, rather like a little cat in his fur and his tail but quite like a weasel in his head and his habits. His eyes and the end of his

1. **bungalow:** in India, low, one-storied house, named after a type of house found in Bengal, a region of South Asia.
2. **Segowlee** (sē·gou′lē) **cantonment:** British army post in Segowlee (now Segauli), India.

4 OUT HERE ON MY OWN

Dialogue with the Text

What kind of name is Rikki-tikki-tavi?

I wonder what kind of war is fought in the bathrooms of a bungalow. What are these animals fighting about?

What purpose do Darzee and Chuchundra have in the story? Are they Rikki-tikki-tavi's friends?

These Indian names are very interesting! They are different from the names around here.

Reaching All Students

Struggling Readers
Dialogue with the Text was introduced on p. 2. For a lesson directly tied to this selection that teaches students to monitor comprehension by using a strategy called Think-Aloud, see the *Reading Skills and Strategies* binder:
• MiniRead Skill Lesson, p. I
• Selection Skill Lesson, p. 7

English Language Learners
One approach to engaging English language learners is to ask them to listen to the recording of the selection in the *Audio CD Library.* For additional strategies to supplement instruction, see
• *Lesson Plans Including Strategies for English-Language Learners*

Advanced Learners
Ask students to compare the story with other monster-slaying stories from mythology, fairy tales, movies, and cartoons. Have students note the similarities: the poor or orphaned hero, the quest or mission to slay a monster threatening the kingdom, helpers who assist the hero, the descent into the underworld, the final victory, and the return of peace to the kingdom. Heroes whom Rikki resembles include Hercules, Superman, Beowulf, Gilgamesh, and King Arthur.

restless nose were pink; he could scratch himself anywhere he pleased with any leg, front or back, that he chose to use; he could fluff up his tail till it looked like a bottlebrush, and his war cry as he scuttled through the long grass was *Rikk-tikk-tikki-tikki-tchk!*

One day, a high summer flood washed him out of the burrow where he lived with his father and mother and carried him, kicking and clucking, down a roadside ditch. He found a little wisp of grass floating there and clung to it till he lost his senses. When he revived, he was lying in the hot sun in the middle of a garden path, very draggled[3] indeed, and a small boy was saying: "Here's a dead mongoose. Let's have a funeral."

"No," said his mother; "let's take him in and dry him. Perhaps he isn't really dead."

They took him into the house, and a big man picked him up between his finger and thumb and said he was not dead but half choked; so they wrapped him in cotton wool and warmed him over a little fire, and he opened his eyes and sneezed.

"Now," said the big man (he was an Englishman who had just moved into the bungalow), "don't frighten him, and we'll see what he'll do."

It is the hardest thing in the world to frighten a mongoose, because he is eaten up from nose to tail with curiosity. The motto of all the mongoose family is "Run and find out," and Rikki-tikki was a true mongoose. He looked at the cotton wool, decided that it was not good to eat, ran all round the table, sat up and put his fur in order, scratched himself, and jumped on the small boy's shoulder.

"Don't be frightened, Teddy," said his father. "That's his way of making friends."

"Ouch! He's tickling under my chin," said Teddy.

3. **draggled:** wet and muddy, as if from being dragged around.

Dialogue with the Text

Rikki-tikki-tavi reminds me of my cat, Charlie. Charlie can scratch himself anywhere he pleases, and when he's scared, his tail also looks like a bottlebrush. That's a good description of how it looks.

I think it is neat that Rikki got his name from the sound he makes.

I wonder where Rikki-tikki-tavi's mother and father ended up after the flood?

The mother must be an animal lover because she wants to save the mongoose.
I wonder what they are going to do with Rikki-tikki-tavi, and I wonder what purpose this family will serve later on in the story?

Rikki-tikki-tavi must be very tiny if the big man picked him up between his thumb and finger.

Is the big man the father? He is also kind to animals.
I think I would also try to save a cute little animal that was dying. I hope I would know what to do.

Rebecca Irizarry

—Rebecca Irizarry
Maplewood Middle School
Maplewood, New Jersey

A Elements of Literature
Conflict
❓ What is the first conflict that Rikki faces in the story? [A summer flood washes him out of his burrow.]

B Reading Skills and Strategies
Dialogue with the Text
Ask students if they, like Rebecca Irizarry, wonder what happened to Rikki's parents. Tell them that if any passage in the story puzzles or surprises them, they should make a note about it in their journals. Urge them to read through Rebecca Irizarry's response to the opening passages of the story to get an idea of this process.

C Reading Skills and Strategies
Making Inferences
❓ From the humans' reactions to Rikki, what inferences can you make about their characters? [Possible responses: They are not afraid of animals; they are kind; they are intelligent enough to know that a mongoose is a good thing to have around the bungalow.]

D English Language Learners
Interpreting Idiom
Explain to students that the expression "eaten up from nose to tail with curiosity" means that Rikki's curiosity is total. He is constantly running around the garden, asking questions and poking his nose into everything.

Using Students' Strengths

Kinesthetic Learners
If you are reading the story aloud in class or listening to the recording on the *Audio CD Library,* ask volunteers to create sound effects at certain points in the story. They can tap on their desks during the suspenseful moments, such as when Rikki waits to attack Nag, or they can imitate bird sounds at appropriate moments or make the high-pitched hiss that Nagaina makes when she strikes out at her enemies.

Visual Learners
As visual learners read the story, they might benefit by filling in the graphic organizer on p. 1 in the *Graphic Organizers for Active Reading.*

Interpersonal Learners
Have students select a passage to read aloud to partners. The student who is listening should offer advice to improve the oral reading of his or her partner.

A Reading Skills and Strategies

Dialogue with the Text

❓ What is your reaction to the fact that Rikki talks? [Possible responses: Some students may be surprised because they expect this to be a nature story; others may not be surprised because animals talk in stories all the time.] Ask students for examples of popular books, comics, television shows, or movies in which animals talk. [Possible responses: *The Lion King, Watership Down.*]

B Elements of Literature

Foreshadowing

Point out that this is the first time Rikki is mentioned in conjunction with snakes, and the remark creates a sense of dread in the reader. Ask students to guess what will happen later in the story. [Students may guess that Rikki will fight snakes.]

C Vocabulary Note

Context Clues

Point out to students that the word *tailorbird* is a compound noun. Ask them to guess what a tailorbird is by looking at the meaning of each part of the compound. Then, have them read the rest of the paragraph to see if their definitions match the narrator's explanation of how tailorbirds stitch their nests together in the way that tailors sew clothes.

D Reading Skills and Strategies

Making Predictions

Have students write predictions in their journals about who Nag might be. Then, ask what clues in the story led them to their predictions. [The fact that Nag ate a baby bird is one clue. Students may also remember the father's ominous remark about snakes.]

Rikki-tikki looked down between the boy's collar and neck, snuffed at his ear, and climbed down to the floor, where he sat rubbing his nose.

"Good gracious," said Teddy's mother, "and that's a wild creature! I suppose he's so tame because we've been kind to him."

"All mongooses are like that," said her husband. "If Teddy doesn't pick him up by the tail or try to put him in a cage, he'll run in and out of the house all day long. Let's give him something to eat."

They gave him a little piece of raw meat. Rikki-tikki liked it <u>immensely</u>, and when it was finished, he went out into the veranda[4] and sat in the sunshine and fluffed up his fur to make it dry to the roots. Then he felt better.

"There are more things to find out about in this house," he said to himself, "than all my family could find out in all their lives. I shall certainly stay and find out."

He spent all that day roaming over the house. He nearly drowned himself in the bathtubs, put his nose into the ink on a writing table, and burnt it on the end of the big man's cigar, for he climbed up in the big man's lap to see how writing was done. At nightfall he ran into Teddy's nursery to watch how kerosene lamps were lighted, and when Teddy went to bed, Rikki-tikki climbed up too; but he was a restless companion, because he had to get up and attend to every noise all through the night and find out what made it. Teddy's mother and father came in, the last thing, to look at their boy, and Rikki-tikki was awake on the pillow. "I don't like that," said Teddy's mother; "he may bite the child." "He'll do no such thing," said the father. "Teddy's safer with that little beast than if he had a bloodhound to watch him. If a snake came into the nursery now——"

But Teddy's mother wouldn't think of anything so awful.

4. **veranda:** open porch covered by a roof, running along the outside of a building.

Early in the morning, Rikki-tikki came to early breakfast in the veranda riding on Teddy's shoulder, and they gave him banana and some boiled egg; and he sat on all their laps one after the other, because every well-brought-up mongoose always hopes to be a house mongoose someday and have rooms to run about in; and Rikki-tikki's mother (she used to live in the General's house at Segowlee) had carefully told Rikki what to do if ever he came across white men.

Then Rikki-tikki went out into the garden to see what was to be seen. It was a large garden, only half cultivated, with bushes, as big as summerhouses, of Marshal Niel roses; lime and orange trees; clumps of bamboos; and thickets of high grass. Rikki-tikki licked his lips. "This is a splendid hunting ground," he said, and his tail grew bottlebrushy at the thought of it, and he scuttled up and down the garden, snuffing here and there till he heard very sorrowful voices in a thorn bush. It was Darzee, the tailorbird, and his wife. They had made a beautiful nest by pulling two big leaves together and stitching them up the edges with fibers and had filled the hollow with cotton and downy fluff. The nest swayed to and fro as they sat on the rim and cried.

"What is the matter?" asked Rikki-tikki.

"We are very miserable," said Darzee. "One of our babies fell out of the nest yesterday and Nag ate him."

"H'm!" said Rikki-tikki, "that is very sad—but I am a stranger here. Who is Nag?"

Darzee and his wife only <u>cowered</u> down in the nest without answering, for from the thick grass at the foot of the bush there came a low hiss—a horrid, cold sound that made Rikki-tikki jump back two clear feet. Then inch by inch out of the grass rose up the head and

WORDS TO OWN
immensely (im·mens′lē) *adv.:* enormously.
cowered (kou′ərd) *v.:* crouched and trembled in fear.

Using the Glossary to Find Pronunciations

Words to Own are useful words from selections that will help students expand their vocabulary and knowledge base. Pronunciations for these words are often given on the bottom of the page, along with the definitions of the words. If students have trouble pronouncing a particular word, they should turn to the guide to pronunciation symbols that appears at the bottom of each right-hand Glossary page, starting on page 789. The guide contains words and symbols that will help students decode unfamiliar words.

spread hood of Nag, the big black cobra, and he was five feet long from tongue to tail. When he had lifted one third of himself clear of the ground, he stayed balancing to and fro exactly as a dandelion tuft balances in the wind, and he looked at Rikki-tikki with the wicked snake's eyes that never change their expression, whatever the snake may be thinking of.

"Who is Nag," said he. "*I* am Nag. The great God Brahm[5] put his mark upon all our people, when the first cobra spread his hood to keep the sun off Brahm as he slept. Look, and be afraid!"

He spread out his hood more than ever, and Rikki-tikki saw the spectacle mark on the back of it that looks exactly like the eye part of a hook-and-eye fastening. He was afraid for the minute; but it is impossible for a mongoose to stay frightened for any length of time, and though Rikki-tikki had never met a live cobra before, his mother had fed him on dead ones, and he

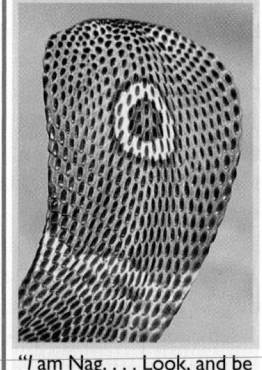

"*I* am Nag. . . . Look, and be afraid!"

knew that all a grown mongoose's business in life was to fight and eat snakes. Nag knew that too, and at the bottom of his cold heart, he was afraid.

"Well," said Rikki-tikki, and his tail began to fluff up again, "marks or no marks, do you think it is right for you to eat fledglings out of a nest?"

Nag was thinking to himself and watching the least little movement in the grass behind Rikki-tikki. He knew that mongooses in the garden meant death sooner or later for him and his family, but he wanted to get Rikki-tikki off

5. **Brahm** (bräm): in the Hindu religion, the creator (also called Brahma).

his guard. So he dropped his head a little and put it on one side.

"Let us talk," he said. "You eat eggs. Why should not I eat birds?"

"Behind you! Look behind you!" sang Darzee.

Rikki-tikki knew better than to waste time in staring. He jumped up in the air as high as he could go, and just under him whizzed by the head of Nagaina, Nag's wicked wife. She had crept up behind him as he was talking, to make an end of him; and he heard her savage hiss as the stroke missed. He came down almost across her back, and if he had been an old mongoose, he would have known that then was the time to break her back with one bite; but he was afraid of the terrible lashing return stroke of the cobra. He bit, indeed, but did not bite long enough, and he jumped clear of the whisking tail, leaving Nagaina torn and angry.

"Wicked, wicked Darzee!" said Nag, lashing up as high as he could reach toward the nest in the thorn bush; but Darzee had built it out of reach of snakes, and it only swayed to and fro.

Rikki-tikki felt his eyes growing red and hot (when a mongoose's eyes grow red, he is angry), and he sat back on his tail and hind legs like a little kangaroo, and looked all round him, and chattered with rage. But Nag and Nagaina had disappeared into the grass. When a snake misses its stroke, it never says anything or gives any sign of what it means to do next. Rikki-tikki did not care to follow them, for he did not feel sure that he could manage two snakes at once. So he trotted off to the gravel path near the house and sat down to think. It was a serious matter for him. If you read the old books of natural history, you will find they say that when the mongoose fights the snake and happens to get bitten, he runs off and eats some herb that cures him. That is not true. The victory is only a matter of quickness of eye and quickness of foot—snake's blow against the mongoose's jump—and as no eye can follow the motion of

A Elements of Literature

Conflict

❓ Point out that Kipling involves Rikki in a second conflict, a battle with Karait. How does the tension build when the narrator explains that Rikki does not realize he is in great danger? [Possible response: Readers want to warn Rikki that Karait is quick, agile, and highly poisonous.]

B Appreciating Language

Action Verbs

Ask students to picture the battle between Rikki and Karait as a scene in an action movie. Tell students that when mongooses fight snakes, they flip and somersault like action heroes. Have students notice Kipling's use of vivid verbs such as *jumped* and *lashed* to build the action. Students will learn how to use action verbs in the Language Link on p. 21.

C Struggling Readers

Breaking Down Difficult Text

To help these students comprehend and visualize this complex scene, read the passage aloud. With the group, break the scene down into a numbered list of actions in the order in which they occur in the story:
1. Teddy shouted
2. Teddy's mother screamed
3. Karait lunged
and so on. Make sure students note that, while the words "... father ran out with a stick" precede the words "Karait had lunged," in the actual chain of events, Teddy's father appears *after* Rikki has already killed Karait.

---

a snake's head when it strikes, this makes things much more wonderful than any magic herb. Rikki-tikki knew he was a young mongoose, and it made him all the more pleased to think that he had managed to escape a blow from behind. It gave him confidence in himself, and when Teddy came running down the path, Rikki-tikki was ready to be petted. But just as Teddy was stooping, something wriggled a little in the dust and a tiny voice said: "Be careful. I am Death!" It was Karait, the dusty brown snakeling that lies for choice on the dusty earth; and his bite is as dangerous as the cobra's. But he is so small that nobody thinks of him, and so he does the more harm to people.

Rikki-tikki's eyes grew red again, and he danced up to Karait with the peculiar rocking, swaying motion that he had inherited from his family. It looks very funny, but it is so perfectly balanced a gait that you can fly off from it at any angle you please; and in dealing with snakes this is an advantage. If Rikki-tikki had only known, he was doing a much more dangerous thing

"Be careful. I am Death!" It was Karait. . . .

A than fighting Nag, for Karait is so small and can turn so quickly that unless Rikki bit him close to the back of the head, he would get the return stroke in his eye or his lip. But Rikki did not know; his eyes were all red, and he rocked back and forth, looking for a good place to hold. Karait struck out, Rikki jumped sideways and tried to run in, but the wicked little dusty **B** gray head lashed within a fraction of his shoulder, and he had to jump over the body, and the head followed his heels close.

Teddy shouted to the house: "Oh, look here! Our mongoose is killing a snake," and Rikki-tikki heard a scream from Teddy's mother. His father ran out with a stick, but by the time he came up, Karait had lunged out once too far, **C** and Rikki-tikki had sprung, jumped on the snake's back, dropped his head far between his forelegs, bitten as high up the back as he could get hold, and rolled away. That bite paralyzed Karait, and Rikki-tikki was just going to eat him up from the tail, after the custom of his family at dinner, when he remembered that a full meal makes a slow mongoose, and if he wanted all his strength and quickness ready, he must keep himself thin. He went away for a dust bath under the castor-oil bushes, while Teddy's father beat the dead Karait. "What is the use of that?" thought Rikki-tikki; "I have settled it all"; and then Teddy's mother picked him up from the dust and hugged him, crying that he had saved Teddy from death, and Teddy's father said that he was a providence,[6] and Teddy looked on with big, scared eyes. Rikki-tikki was rather amused at all the fuss, which, of course, he did not understand. Teddy's mother might just as well have petted Teddy for playing in the dust. Rikki was thoroughly enjoying himself.

That night at dinner, walking to and fro among the wineglasses on the table, he might have stuffed himself three times over with nice things; but he remembered Nag and Nagaina, and though it was very pleasant to be patted and petted by Teddy's mother and to sit on Teddy's shoulder, his eyes would get red from time to time, and he would go off into his long war cry of *Rikk-tikk-tikki-tikki-tchk!*

Teddy carried him off to bed and insisted on Rikki-tikki's sleeping under his chin. Rikki-tikki was too well bred to bite or scratch, but as soon as Teddy was asleep, he went off for his

---

6. **providence:** favor or gift from God or nature.

WORDS TO OWN

gait *n.:* way of walking or running.

---

8 OUT HERE ON MY OWN

Getting Students Involved

Cooperative Learning

Snakes on Trial. Suggest to students that the snake population of a neighboring garden has decided to have the snakes in this story arrested and tried for attempted murder. Ask students how the snakes would plead—Guilty? Self-defense? Divide the class in half. Have one half work on a plan to prosecute the snakes, and have the other half decide how best to defend them.

Other characters should be brought in to give evidence for both sides. When students have completed their plans, divide each team in half and set up two courtrooms in the classroom, each with a prosecution section and a defense section. Have students play the roles of the lawyers and the characters. You and another teacher may play the roles of judges.

Enrichment Activity

Rewriting in the First Person. Have students work in groups of four to list details in the story that would be different if the story were told by a first-person narrator (except Rikki). Assign each group one of the other characters in the story, and have students choose a short passage from the story to rewrite in the voice of their assigned character. Have a member of each group read the rewritten passage aloud.

T8

nightly walk round the house, and in the dark he ran up against Chuchundra, the muskrat, creeping round by the wall. Chuchundra is a brokenhearted little beast. He whimpers and cheeps all night, trying to make up his mind to run into the middle of the room; but he never gets there.

Chuchundra, a brokenhearted little beast.

"Don't kill me," said Chuchundra, almost weeping. "Rikki-tikki, don't kill me!"

"Do you think a snake killer kills muskrats?" said Rikki-tikki scornfully.

"Those who kill snakes get killed by snakes," said Chuchundra, more sorrowfully than ever. "And how am I to be sure that Nag won't mistake me for you some dark night?"

"There's not the least danger," said Rikki-tikki, "but Nag is in the garden, and I know you don't go there."

"My cousin Chua, the rat, told me——" said Chuchundra, and then he stopped.

"Told you what?"

"H'sh! Nag is everywhere, Rikki-tikki. You should have talked to Chua in the garden."

"I didn't—so you must tell me. Quick, Chuchundra, or I'll bite you!"

Chuchundra sat down and cried till the tears rolled off his whiskers. "I am a very poor man," he sobbed. "I never had spirit enough to run out into the middle of the room. H'sh! I mustn't tell you anything. Can't you *hear*, Rikki-tikki?"

Rikki-tikki listened. The house was as still as still, but he thought he could just catch the faintest *scratch-scratch* in the world—a noise as faint as that of a wasp walking on a windowpane—the dry scratch of a snake's scales on brickwork.

"That's Nag or Nagaina," he said to himself, "and he is crawling into the bathroom sluice.[7] You're right, Chuchundra; I should have talked to Chua."

He stole off to Teddy's bathroom, but there was nothing there, and then to Teddy's mother's bathroom. At the bottom of the smooth plaster wall there was a brick pulled out to make a sluice for the bathwater, and as Rikki-tikki stole in by the masonry[8] curb where the bath is put, he heard Nag and Nagaina whispering together outside in the moonlight.

"When the house is emptied of people," said Nagaina to her husband, "*he* will have to go away, and then the garden will be our own again. Go in quietly, and remember that the big man who killed Karait is the first one to bite. Then come out and tell me, and we will hunt for Rikki-tikki together."

"But are you sure that there is anything to be gained by killing the people?" said Nag.

"Everything. When there were no people in the bungalow, did we have any mongoose in the garden? So long as the bungalow is empty, we are king and queen of the garden; and remember that as soon as our eggs in the melon bed hatch (as they may tomorrow), our children will need room and quiet."

"I had not thought of that," said Nag. "I will go, but there is no need that we should hunt for Rikki-tikki afterward. I will kill the big man and his wife, and the child if I can, and come away quietly. Then the bungalow will be empty, and Rikki-tikki will go."

Rikki-tikki tingled all over with rage and hatred at this, and then Nag's head came through the sluice, and his five feet of cold body followed it. Angry as he was, Rikki-tikki was very frightened as he saw the size of the big cobra. Nag coiled himself up, raised his head, and looked into the bathroom in the dark, and Rikki could see his eyes glitter.

7. **sluice** (slo͞os): drain.
8. **masonry**: built of stone or brick.

D Reading Skills and Strategies
Dialogue with the Text
❓ What did you think of Rikki's comment to Chuchundra? [Possible responses: Rikki is rightfully proud of his accomplishments and should look down on Chuchundra as a weakling; Rikki is behaving arrogantly.] Ask students to record in their journals any comments or questions that this scene raises in their minds. Remind them to be aware of their reactions to scenes as they read.

E Elements of Literature
Character
Ask students what role the character Chuchundra plays in the story. [Possible responses: The cowardly, pessimistic Chuchundra serves as a contrast, or foil, to the brave Rikki. His remark that snake killers get killed by snakes serves to heighten the suspense.]

F Elements of Literature
Conflict
Nag and Nagaina's plan introduces a new twist or conflict to the plot. Ask students to describe the snakes' strategy for getting rid of Rikki. [Possible response: The snakes plan to kill Teddy's father and then the other family members because they think Rikki will leave if the people disappear.]

G Critical Thinking
Expressing an Opinion
❓ Based on what you know about Rikki, do you think that this plan is the best possible solution that the snakes could have come up with? [Possible responses: It is a good plan because it poses the least possible risk for the snakes; the plan is flawed because a fight between Rikki and the snakes is inevitable.]

"Now, if I kill him here, Nagaina will know; and if I fight him on the open floor, the odds are in his favor. What am I to do?" said Rikki-tikki-tavi.

Nag waved to and fro, and then Rikki-tikki heard him drinking from the biggest water jar that was used to fill the bath. "That is good," said the snake. "Now, when Karait was killed, the big man had a stick. He may have that stick still, but when he comes in to bathe in the morning, he will not have a stick. I shall wait here till he comes. Nagaina—do you hear me?—I shall wait here in the cool till daytime."

There was no answer from outside, so Rikki-tikki knew Nagaina had gone away. Nag coiled himself down, coil by coil, round the bulge at the bottom of the water jar, and Rikki-tikki stayed still as death. After an hour he began to move, muscle by muscle, toward the jar. Nag was asleep, and Rikki-tikki looked at his big back, wondering which would be the best place for a good hold. "If I don't break his back at the first jump," said Rikki, "he can still fight; and if he fights—O Rikki!" He looked at the thickness of the neck below the hood, but that was too much for him; and a bite near the tail would only make Nag savage.

"It must be the head," he said at last, "the head above the hood; and when I am once there, I must not let go."

Then he jumped. The head was lying a little clear of the water jar, under the curve of it; and as his teeth met, Rikki braced his back against the bulge of the red earthenware to hold down the head. This gave him just one second's purchase,[9] and he made the most of it. Then he was battered to and fro as a rat is shaken by a dog—to and fro on the floor, up and down, and round in great circles, but his eyes were red and he held on as the body cartwhipped over the floor, upsetting the tin dipper and the soap dish and the flesh brush, and banged against

9. **purchase:** firm hold.

the tin side of the bath. As he held, he closed his jaws tighter and tighter, for he made sure[10] he would be banged to death, and for the honor of his family, he preferred to be found with his teeth locked. He was dizzy, aching, and felt shaken to pieces, when something went off like a thunderclap just behind him; a hot wind knocked him senseless and red fire singed his fur. The big man had been wakened by the noise and had fired both barrels of a shotgun into Nag just behind the hood.

Rikki-tikki held on with his eyes shut, for now he was quite sure he was dead; but the head did not move, and the big man picked him up and said: "It's the mongoose again, Alice; the little chap has saved *our* lives now." Then Teddy's mother came in with a very white face and saw what was left of Nag, and Rikki-tikki dragged himself to Teddy's bedroom and spent half the rest of the night shaking himself tenderly to find out whether he really was broken into forty pieces, as he fancied.

When morning came, he was very stiff but well pleased with his doings. "Now I have Nagaina to settle with, and she will be worse than five Nags, and there's no knowing when the eggs she spoke of will hatch. Goodness! I must go and see Darzee," he said.

Without waiting for breakfast, Rikki-tikki ran to the thorn bush, where Darzee was singing a song of triumph at the top of his voice. The news of Nag's death was all over the garden, for the sweeper had thrown the body on the rubbish heap.

"Oh, you stupid tuft of feathers!" said Rikki-tikki angrily. "Is this the time to sing?"

"Nag is dead—is dead—is dead!" sang Darzee. "The <u>valiant</u> Rikki-tikki caught him by the head and held fast. The big man brought

10. **made sure:** here, felt sure.

WORDS TO OWN

valiant (val′yənt) *adj.*: brave and determined.

Skill Link

Identifying Verbs

You might want to use the following exercise before you teach the Language Link on specific verbs, p. 21. This exercise will help you assess your students' skill in identifying verbs.

Activity

Identify the verb in each of the following sentences. Some sentences may have more than one verb. For a review of verbs, see pp. 714–715 in the Language Handbook.

1. Darzee <u>sang</u> a song of triumph.
2. Rikki <u>ran</u> to the thorn bush.
3. "Oh, you stupid tuft of feathers!" <u>said</u> Rikki-tikki angrily.
4. The valiant Rikki <u>caught</u> him by the head and <u>held</u> fast.
5. The sweeper <u>had</u> <u>thrown</u> the body on the rubbish heap.
6. "Goodness! I <u>must</u> <u>go</u> and <u>see</u> Darzee," he <u>said</u>.

7. "Nag <u>is</u> dead—<u>is</u> dead—<u>is</u> dead!" <u>sang</u> Darzee.
8. When morning <u>came</u>, he <u>was</u> very stiff but well pleased with his doings.
9. "The big man <u>brought</u> the bang-stick, and Nag <u>fell</u> in two pieces!"
10. "He <u>will</u> never <u>eat</u> my babies again."

Snake Patrol

Mongooses are very rare in North America, so you've probably never seen one. Mongooses look a bit like weasels or ferrets. They're found in southern Asia and many parts of Africa. They are usually about sixteen inches long and have stiff, brownish-gray hair.

Mongooses are so destructive of other animals that in the United States it's illegal to keep one as a pet. In other countries, such as India, the mongoose is prized for its ability to kill mice, rats, and snakes.

The mongoose's fierceness, lightning-quick movements, and sharp eyes enable it to kill even poisonous snakes, such as cobras, without being bitten.

Although ferocious in combat, the mongoose can be tamed. A mongoose may become loyal enough to its human family to defend it bravely, as Rikki-tikki does in this story.

LITERATURE AND SCIENCE

Ask students to create charts like the ones below, comparing and contrasting Kipling's description of Rikki with the scientific description of mongooses in the Literature and Science feature.

Similarities

[Both are fierce, quick snake killers with sharp eyes]
[Both can become loyal to a human family]

Differences

Rikki-tikki-tavi	Real mongoose
[Doesn't kill small rodents and birds]	[Eats birds and small rodents]

D Appreciating Language
Made-up Words

❓ What is the stick Darzee refers to, what does he call it, and why would he come up with that name for the object? [The stick is the man's gun; Darzee calls it a bang-stick because it is shaped like a stick and makes a banging noise when it goes off.]

E Appreciating Language
Epithets

Point out how Darzee describes Rikki in his song. Tell students that descriptive phrases such as "Killer of the terrible Nag" and "Rikki-tikki with the white teeth" are part of the epic tradition, in which heroic characters are described in terms of their appearance or their deeds. (For more examples of epithets, see Darzee's song on p. 15.)

---

the bang-stick, and Nag fell in two pieces! He will never eat my babies again."

"All that's true enough, but where's Nagaina?" said Rikki-tikki, looking carefully round him.

"Nagaina came to the bathroom sluice and called for Nag," Darzee went on; "and Nag came out on the end of a stick—the sweeper picked him up on the end of a stick and threw him upon the rubbish heap. Let us sing about the great, the red-eyed Rikki-tikki!" and Darzee filled his throat and sang.

"If I could get up to your nest, I'd roll your babies out!" said Rikki-tikki. "You don't know when to do the right thing at the right time."

D "You're safe enough in your nest there, but it's war for me down here. Stop singing a minute, Darzee."

"For the great, beautiful Rikki-tikki's sake I will stop," said Darzee. "What is it, O Killer of the terrible Nag?"

"Where is Nagaina, for the third time?"

"On the rubbish heap by the stables, mourning for Nag. Great is Rikki-tikki with the white teeth."

"Bother[11] my white teeth! Have you ever heard where she keeps her eggs?"

"In the melon bed, on the end nearest the

11. **bother:** here, never mind.

RIKKI-TIKKI-TAVI 11

Crossing the Curriculum

Science/Social Studies

To appreciate the story, students need to know that a cobra is a highly poisonous snake whose bite can kill a person in fifteen minutes. The cobra's venom attacks the nervous system, causing dizziness, blurred vision, and pain. Cobras are particularly dangerous when guarding their eggs. In fact, in India, villages have been evacuated when cobra eggs were found. Ask students to record interesting details about cobras as they read the story.

In the late 1800s, mongooses were imported into the sugar-cane-producing islands of the Caribbean to kill rats. Unfortunately, with no natural enemies, the mongoose bred wildly. Today mongooses living on the islands eat small pets, threaten endangered species, and spread rabies. Ask students what steps they think the governments of these islands should take to solve this problem.

Place students of differing abilities into groups of three or four and ask them to research some aspect of the mongoose, such as its feeding habits, its life cycle, its physical characteristics, its normal habitat, or its fighting techniques. Have students create mongoose-shaped bookmarks and write on them the important facts they discover.

A Critical Thinking

Interpreting

❓ Why is Darzee concerned that Rikki might be planning to eat the cobra eggs? Do you think he is being sympathetic, short-sighted, or both? Why? [Possible response: Darzee is being sympathetic because his children are born from eggs too. However, he is also being shortsighted because cobra eggs soon become cobras. His wife is more practical.]

B Critical Thinking

Interpreting

❓ Why do you think that the narrator says that Darzee is very much like a man? [Possible response: The narrator probably means that humans are foolish and lack foresight.]

C English Language Learners

Interpreting Idioms

Explain to students learning English that when Nagaina says, ". . . I shall settle accounts with the boy," the phrase "settle accounts" means "get even with" or "get back at."

D Reading Skills and Strategies

Making Predictions

❓ What do you think Rikki means to do with the last egg? [Possible responses: He plans to destroy it later; Rikki will use the egg to bargain with the cobra.]

---

wall, where the sun strikes nearly all day. She hid them there weeks ago."

"And you never thought it worthwhile to tell me? The end nearest the wall, you said?"

A "Rikki-tikki, you are not going to eat her eggs?"

"Not eat exactly; no. Darzee, if you have a grain of sense, you will fly off to the stables and pretend that your wing is broken and let Nagaina chase you away to this bush. I must get to the melon bed, and if I went there now, she'd see me."

Darzee was a featherbrained little fellow who could never hold more than one idea at a time in his head, and just because he knew that Nagaina's children were born in eggs like his own, he didn't think at first that it was fair to kill them. But his wife was a sensible bird, and she knew that cobra's eggs meant

Darzee, a featherbrained little fellow.

young cobras later on; so she flew off from the nest and left Darzee to keep the babies warm and continue his song about the death of Nag. **B** Darzee was very like a man in some ways.

She fluttered in front of Nagaina by the rubbish heap and cried out, "Oh, my wing is broken! The boy in the house threw a stone at me and broke it." Then she fluttered more desperately than ever.

Nagaina lifted up her head and hissed, "You warned Rikki-tikki when I would have killed him. Indeed and truly, you've chosen a bad place to be lame in." And she moved toward Darzee's wife, slipping along over the dust.

"The boy broke it with a stone!" shrieked Darzee's wife.

"Well! It may be some <u>consolation</u> to you

C when you're dead to know that I shall settle accounts with the boy. My husband lies on the rubbish heap this morning, but before night the boy in the house will lie very still. What is the use of running away? I am sure to catch you. Little fool, look at me!"

Darzee's wife knew better than to do *that*, for a bird who looks at a snake's eyes gets so frightened that she cannot move. Darzee's wife fluttered on, piping sorrowfully and never leaving the ground, and Nagaina quickened her pace.

Rikki-tikki heard them going up the path from the stables, and he raced for the end of the melon patch near the wall. There, in the warm litter above the melons, very cunningly hidden, he found twenty-five eggs about the size of a bantam's[12] eggs but with whitish skins instead of shells.

"I was not a day too soon," he said, for he could see the baby cobras curled up inside the skin, and he knew that the minute they were hatched, they could each kill a man or a mongoose. He bit off the tops of the eggs as fast as he could, taking care to crush the young cobras, and turned over the litter from time to time to see whether he had missed any. At last there were only three eggs left, and Rikki-tikki began to chuckle to himself, when he heard Darzee's wife screaming:

"Rikki-tikki, I led Nagaina toward the house, and she has gone into the veranda, and—oh, come quickly—she means killing!"

D Rikki-tikki smashed two eggs, and tumbled backward down the melon bed with the third egg in his mouth, and scuttled to the veranda as hard as he could put foot to the ground. Teddy and his mother and father were there at early

---

12. **bantam's:** small chicken's.

WORDS TO OWN
consolation (kän′sə·lā′shən) *n.:* comfort.

Listening to Music

Peter and the Wolf by Sergei Prokofiev

In *Peter and the Wolf*, the Russian composer Sergei Prokofiev (1891–1953) presents vivid melodic portraits of animals and people. Each character is represented by a musical motif played by a particular instrument. Peter is represented by the violins' carefree theme; the wolf, by the ominous rumble of horns; the bird, by a trilling flute; the duck, by a mournful oboe; and so on.

These motifs can also describe characters in "Rikki-tikki-tavi."

Activities

• Have the music playing (without the narration) as students enter the classroom. On the board, display the following instruction: *As you listen to the music, write what animal or human personalities you think it seems to be about.*

• After students read the selection, play several of the musical motifs. Have students, either individually or in groups, identify which motifs could describe different characters in "Rikki-tikki-tavi."

breakfast, but Rikki-tikki saw that they were not eating anything. They sat stone still, and their faces were white. Nagaina was coiled up on the matting by Teddy's chair, within easy striking distance of Teddy's bare leg, and she was swaying to and fro, singing a song of triumph.

"Son of the big man that killed Nag," she hissed, "stay still. I am not ready yet. Wait a little. Keep very still, all you three! If you move, I strike, and if you do not move, I strike. Oh, foolish people, who killed my Nag!"

Teddy's eyes were fixed on his father, and all his father could do was to whisper, "Sit still, Teddy. You mustn't move. Teddy, keep still."

Then Rikki-tikki came up and cried: "Turn round, Nagaina; turn and fight!"

"All in good time," said she, without moving her eyes. "I will settle my account with *you* presently. Look at your friends, Rikki-tikki. They are still and white. They are afraid. They dare not move, and if you come a step nearer, I strike."

"Look at your eggs," said Rikki-tikki, "in the melon bed near the wall. Go and look, Nagaina!"

The big snake turned half round and saw the egg on the veranda. "Ah-h! Give it to me," she said.

Rikki-tikki put his paws one on each side of the egg, and his eyes were blood-red. "What price for a snake's egg? For a young cobra? For a young king cobra? For the last—the very last of the brood? The ants are eating all the others down by the melon bed."

Nagaina spun clear round, forgetting everything for the sake of the one egg; and Rikki-tikki saw Teddy's father shoot out a big hand, catch Teddy by the shoulder, and drag him across the little table with the teacups, safe and out of reach of Nagaina.

"Tricked! Tricked! Tricked! *Rikk-tck-tck!*" chuckled Rikki-tikki. "The boy is safe, and it was I—I—I—that caught Nag by the hood last night in the bathroom." Then he began to jump up and down, all four feet together, his head close to the floor. "He threw me to and fro, but he could not shake me off. He was dead before the big man blew him in two. I did it! *Rikki-tikki-tck-tck!* Come then, Nagaina. Come and fight with me. You shall not be a widow long."

Nagaina saw that she had lost her chance of killing Teddy, and the egg lay between Rikki-tikki's paws. "Give me the egg, Rikki-tikki. Give me the last of my eggs, and I will go away and never come back," she said, lowering her hood.

"Yes, you will go away, and you will never come back; for you will go to the rubbish heap with Nag. Fight, widow! The big man has gone for his gun! Fight!"

Rikki-tikki was bounding all round Nagaina, keeping just out of reach of her stroke, his little eyes like hot coals. Nagaina gathered herself together and flung out at him. Rikki-tikki jumped up and backwards. Again and again and again she struck, and each time her head came with a whack on the matting of the veranda and she gathered herself together like a watch spring. Then Rikki-tikki danced in a circle to get behind her, and Nagaina spun round to keep her head to his head, so that the rustle of her tail on the matting sounded like dry leaves blown along by the wind.

He had forgotten the egg. It still lay on the veranda, and Nagaina came nearer and nearer to it, till at last, while Rikki-tikki was drawing breath, she caught it in her mouth, turned to the veranda steps, and flew like an arrow down the path, with Rikki-tikki behind her. When the cobra runs for her life, she goes like a whiplash flicked across a horse's neck. Rikki-tikki knew that he must catch her or all the trouble would begin again. She headed straight for the long grass by the thorn bush, and as he was running, Rikki-tikki heard Darzee still singing his foolish little song of triumph. But Darzee's wife was wiser. She flew off her nest as Nagaina came along and flapped her wings about Nagaina's head. If Darzee had helped, they might

E Elements of Literature

Conflict

❓ Although everyone seems frozen in time, what dramatic conflict is going on in this scene? [Possible response: Rikki uses the egg to distract Nagaina, who is threatening to strike Teddy. The two are fighting a battle of wills.]

F Critical Thinking

Analyzing Character

❓ Why does Rikki tell Nagaina that he killed Nag? [Possible responses: to make her angry enough to fight him; to boast of his deed; to torment her as she tormented Teddy.] Tell students that Rikki is showing a little arrogance here, in the tradition of the Greek epic heroes Achilles and Odysseus, who taunted their enemies.

G Reading Skills and Strategies

Dialogue with the Text

❓ How do you feel about Nagaina? Does she deserve any sympathy? Explain your responses in your journal or reading notes. [Possible responses: Yes, her husband and babies have been killed; yes, she is a snake and is only acting as a snake would act; no, she's a cold-blooded killer.]

H Elements of Literature

Conflict

❓ In this fight scene, Rikki and Nagaina circle each other like boxers in a ring. How is the action building to a peak? [Possible responses: Only Nagaina and Rikki are left; Rikki is ready to fight, and so is Nagaina.]

Skill Link

Decoding: Silent Letters

Have students compare these three words from pp. 13 and 14: *must, dust, rustle.* Point out that the word *rustle* begins with the word *rust,* so it's logical to think that the beginning of *rustle* would sound like *rust* and rhyme with *must* and *dust.* But it doesn't. In *rustle,* the *t* is silent. Use the word pairs below to show that *-le* after the consonant blend *st* always has the effect of making the *t* silent.

cast/castle   grist/gristle

nest/nestle   whist/whistle

Warn students that *-le* is tricky and doesn't always behave in the same way—that is, it doesn't always make letters silent. Then explore with students the effect of *-le* on another consonant blend: *mb.* When a word ends with *mb,* the *b* is always silent: *crumb, plumb, limb.* But when *mb* is followed by *-le,* the *b* is not silent. Compare *crumb* and *crumble.* The sound of *b* is heard in words with *mble: stumble, tumble,* and so on.

Activity

Write the following items on the board. Ask a volunteer to read an item aloud and then call on a classmate to explain why each underlined word sounds the way it does.

1. The cobras' eggs are nestled in the shade.
2. Darzee trembles as he whistles his song.
3. Nag's victims are struck dumb with terror.
4. Rikki's home is his castle.
5. If you hear a rustle, don't move a limb.

A Elements of Literature

Character

Ask students what character traits Rikki shows by following Nagaina into her hole. [Possible responses: He shows bravery; he shows foolhardiness; he seems determined to finish things once and for all.]

B Reading Skills and Strategies

Making Predictions

❓ Do you believe, as Darzee does, that Rikki will be killed? Why or why not? [Possible responses: no, because Rikki has been successful and lucky in past battles; yes, because even wise mongooses don't follow cobras into their holes.]

C Reading Skills and Strategies

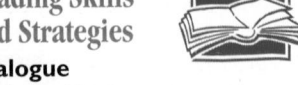

Dialogue with the Text

❓ What was your first reaction when Rikki emerged from the hole? Record your answer in your journal. [Most students will say they were happy; others might be sorry Nagaina is dead.]

have turned her, but Nagaina only lowered her hood and went on. Still, the instant's delay brought Rikki-tikki up to her, and as she plunged into the rat hole where she and Nag used to live, his little white teeth were clenched on her tail and he went down with her—and very few mongooses, however wise and old they may be, care to follow a cobra into its hole. It was dark in the hole, and Rikki-tikki never knew when it might open out and give Nagaina room to turn and strike at him. He held on savagely and stuck out his feet to act as brakes on the dark slope of the hot, moist earth. Then the grass by the mouth of the hole stopped waving, and Darzee said: "It is all over with Rikki-tikki! We must sing his death song. Valiant Rikki-tikki is dead! For Nagaina will surely kill him underground."

So he sang a very mournful song that he made up on the spur of the minute, and just as he got to the most touching part, the grass quivered again, and Rikki-tikki, covered with dirt, dragged himself out of the hole leg by leg, licking his whiskers. Darzee stopped with a little shout. Rikki-tikki shook some of the dust out of his fur and sneezed. "It is all over," he said. "The widow will never come out again." And the red ants that live between the grass stems heard him and began to troop down one after another to see if he had spoken the truth.

Rikki-tikki curled himself up in the grass and slept where he was—slept and slept till it was late in the afternoon, for he had done a hard day's work.

"Now," he said, when he awoke, "I will go back to the house. Tell the Coppersmith, Darzee, and he will tell the garden that Nagaina is dead."

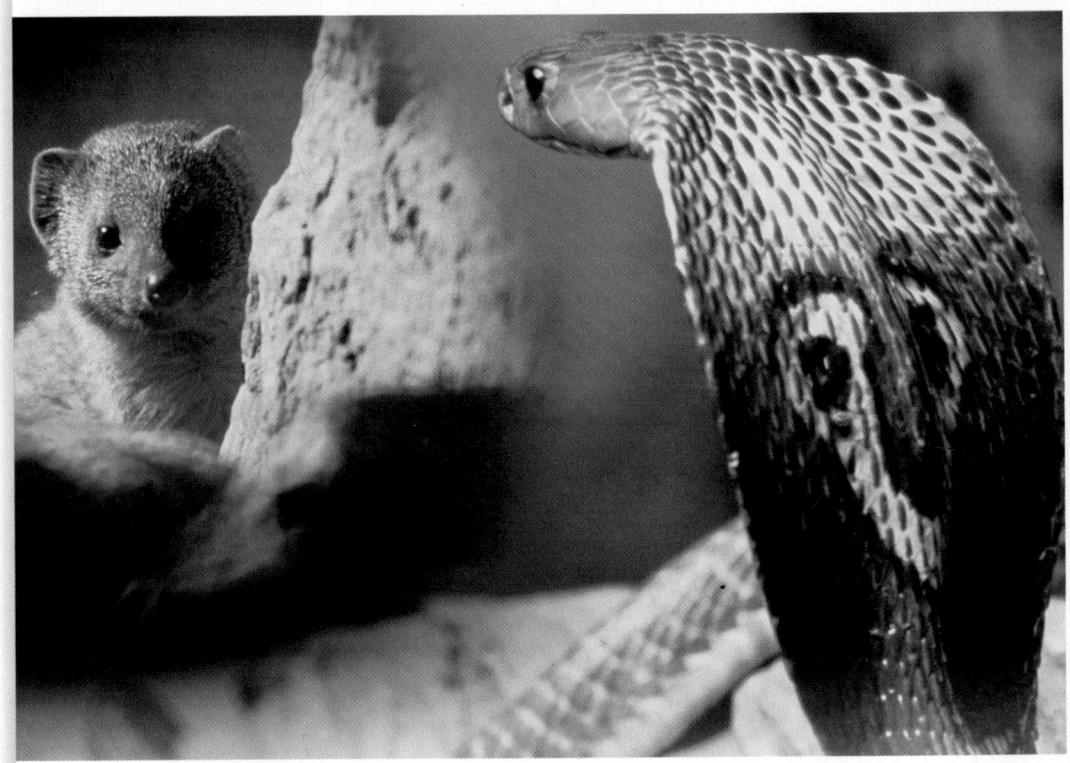

14 OUT HERE ON MY OWN

Making the Connections

Connecting to the Theme: "Out Here on My Own"

When students have finished the story, be sure to talk about the theme. The title of this collection stresses the necessity of acting alone in certain crises. The theme suggests the individual standing up against oppression or injustice. Rikki takes upon himself the challenge of defending the animals' garden and the people in the bungalow.

Though he is aided by other animals, Rikki faces the toughest challenge alone: the descent into the tunnel to fight Nagaina to the death. Ask students to suggest other heroes, in stories and TV shows, who face challenges alone. Who are the enemies? What or who helps the hero? Do the heroes ever lose?

Cultural Connections

Refer students to the *Panchatantra*, a collection of animal fables that dates back to the Indian classical period (ca. 100 B.C.). Like many European folk tales, these fables entertain while they teach a lesson. By discussing how to win or lose friends, how to win and lose money, or how to handle sticky political situations, these fables are instructive. Have students read assorted tales and discuss whether the values they teach are still relevant today.

The Coppersmith is a bird who makes a noise exactly like the beating of a little hammer on a copper pot; and the reason he is always

The Coppersmith, the town crier.

making it is because he is the town crier to every Indian garden and tells all the news to everybody who cares to listen. As Rikki-tikki went up the path, he heard his "attention" notes like a tiny dinner gong and then the steady "*Ding-dong-tock!* Nag is dead—*dong!* Nagaina is dead! *Ding-dong-tock!*" That set all the birds in the garden singing and the frogs croaking, for Nag and Nagaina used to eat frogs as well as little birds.

When Rikki got to the house, Teddy and Teddy's mother (she looked very white still, for she had been fainting) and Teddy's father came out and almost cried over him; and that night he ate all that was given him till he could eat no more and went to bed on Teddy's shoulder, where Teddy's mother saw him when she came to look late at night.

"He saved our lives and Teddy's life," she said to her husband. "Just think, he saved all our lives."

Rikki-tikki woke up with a jump, for the mongooses are light sleepers.

"Oh, it's you," said he. "What are you bothering for? All the cobras are dead; and if they weren't, I'm here."

Rikki-tikki had a right to be proud of himself, but he did not grow too proud, and he kept

that garden as a mongoose should keep it, with tooth and jump and spring and bite, till never a cobra dared show its head inside the walls.

Darzee's Chant
Sung in honor of Rikki-tikki-tavi

Singer and tailor am I—
    Doubled the joys that I know—
Proud of my lilt[13] to the sky,
    Proud of the house that I sew.
Over and under, so weave I my music—
    so weave I the house that I sew.

Sing to your fledglings again,
    Mother, O lift up your head!
Evil that plagued us is slain,
    Death in the garden lies dead.
Terror that hid in the roses is impotent[14]—
    flung on the dunghill and dead!

Who has delivered us, who?
    Tell me his nest and his name.
Rikki, the valiant, the true,
    Tikki, with eyeballs of flame—
Rikk-tikki-tikki, the ivory-fanged,
    the hunter with eyeballs of flame!

Give him the Thanks of the Birds,
    Bowing with tail feathers spread,
Praise him with nightingale words—
    Nay, I will praise him instead.
Hear! I will sing you the praise of the bottle-
    tailed Rikki with eyeballs of red!

(*Here Rikki-tikki interrupted, so the rest of the song is lost.*)

13. **lilt:** light, graceful way of singing or speaking.
14. **impotent** (im′pə·tənt): powerless.

RIKKI-TIKKI-TAVI 15

D Elements of Literature
Conflict
❓ How have the conflicts in the garden been settled? [Possible response: Rikki has made the garden safe for the animals and humans. No cobras dare enter his domain.]

E Advanced Learners
After reading Darzee's chant in praise of Rikki, ask students to work together to produce a graphic aid such as a chart that shows how "Rikki-tikki-tavi" measures up as a heroic "monster-slaying" story.

F Critical Thinking
Interpreting
❓ Knowing what you know about Rikki and about Darzee, why do you think Rikki interrupts Darzee's song? [Possible responses: Rikki does not think of himself as a hero, so he wants Darzee to stop; maybe Darzee is singing while Rikki is trying to sleep; maybe Kipling is trying to end the story on a humorous note, suggesting that Darzee would never shut up unless he were interrupted.]

Speaking and Listening: Appreciating Spoken Language and Analyzing Oral Interpretation
Play the recording of "Darzee's Chant" from the recording of this classic story (Disc 1, Track 1, in the *Audio CD Library*). After students have listened to the reader's interpretation, ask them what effects the interpretation had on them as listeners. Ask them if the reader's pacing and tone, for example, changed the way they imagined Darzee.

Assessing Learning

Check Test: True-False
1. The mongoose Rikki-tikki-tavi is an animal that is dangerous to humans. [False]
2. The mongoose and the snake are natural enemies. [True]
3. Rikki's eyes turn bright red when he is pleased. [False]

4. Nag and Nagaina's plan is to kill Rikki because he killed their young. [False]
5. It is dangerous for a mongoose to follow a cobra into its hole, but Rikki does it anyway. [True]

Standardized Test Preparation
For practice with standardized test format specific to this selection, see
• *Standardized Test Preparation,* p. 10
For practice in proofreading and editing, see
• *Daily Oral Grammar,* Transparency 1

MEET THE WRITER

On His Own

India, the setting of "Rikki-tikki-tavi," is a place **Joseph Rudyard Kipling** (1865–1936) knew well. His father was a professor of art in Bombay, and Kipling was born in that city when India was still under British rule. India was a fascinating place, and young Kipling loved it.

When he was six, his parents shipped Kipling and his sister off to a boardinghouse in England. Throughout his life he called this place "the House of Desolation." Feeling very much on his own in England, he made a discovery:

66 [Books] were among the most important affairs in the world . . . I could read as much as I chose and ask the meaning of things from anyone I met. I had found out, too, that one could take pen and set down what one thought, and that nobody accused one of 'showing off' by doing so. 99

The Cat That Walked by Himself: Illustration by Rudyard Kipling for the first edition of his *Just So Stories,* published in 1902.

The Granger Collection, New York.

When he was seventeen, Kipling returned to India and took a job as an editor with an English-language newspaper. He was fascinated by the lives of British colonials in India and the vivid contrast they made with the Indian people they ruled. Soon the paper was printing Kipling's poems and tales about the life he saw around him. Other newspapers reprinted them, and readers clamored for more. Kipling's fame grew; over the next half century he wrote dozens of books, and in 1907, he won the Nobel Prize in literature. Although he later lived in many places around the world, including Brattleboro, Vermont, India always remained close to his heart.

More Stories by Kipling

You can read more of Kipling's animal stories in *Just So Stories* (Bantam) and *The Jungle Book* (Bantam). *The Jungle Book* is about a boy named Mowgli who is raised by wolves. *Kim* (Penguin), Kipling's best-known novel, traces the adventures of an Irish orphan who is raised as an Indian and eventually becomes a British spy.

The Dinner Party

retold by **Mona Gardner**

I first heard this story in India, where it is told as if true—though any naturalist[1] would know it couldn't be. Later I learned that a magazine version of it appeared shortly before World War I. This account, and its author, I have never been able to track down.

The country is India. A colonial official and his wife are giving a large dinner party. They are seated with their guests—army officers and government attachés[2] and their wives, and a visiting American naturalist—in their spacious dining room, which has a bare marble floor, open rafters, and wide glass doors opening onto a veranda.

A spirited discussion springs up between a young girl who insists that women have outgrown the jumping-on-a-chair-at-the-sight-of-a-mouse era and a colonel who says that they haven't.

"A woman's unfailing reaction in any crisis," the colonel says, "is to scream. And while a man may feel like it, he has that ounce more of nerve control than a woman has. And that last ounce is what counts."

The American does not join in the argument but watches the other guests. As he looks, he sees a strange expression come over the face of the hostess. She is staring straight ahead, her muscles contracting slightly. With a slight gesture she summons the native boy standing behind her chair and whispers to him. The boy's eyes widen; he quickly leaves the room.

Of the guests, none except the American notices this or sees the boy place a bowl of milk on the veranda just outside the open doors.

1. **naturalist:** person who studies nature by observing animals and plants.
2. **attachés** (at'ə·shāz'): diplomatic officials.

(continued on next page)

17

Summary ■ ■

At a large dinner party given by a colonial official and his wife, two of the guests have a discussion centering on the question of nerve control. A colonel insists that in a crisis women invariably lose their nerve and scream, whereas men always control themselves. Another guest, a naturalist, notices a change in the hostess's expression. She sends a native boy out of the room for a bowl of milk. Realizing that there must be a cobra in the room, the naturalist orders everyone to freeze. The cobra emerges from under the table and heads for the milk on the veranda. Only then do we learn that the hostess knew a cobra was in the room because it was crawling across her foot.

Connections

Ⓐ Critical Thinking
Speculating
❓ Why do you think the storyteller presents these details? [Possible responses: She is carefully setting the scene. Something mysterious may be about to happen.]

Ⓑ Critical Thinking
Evaluating an Argument
Ask students to explain the flaw in the colonel's argument. Challenge them to think of examples of women responding to emergencies in a calm and effective manner.

Ⓒ Critical Thinking
Speculating
❓ What do you think has just happened? [Answers will vary. Students may suggest that she is astonished by the colonel's argument or that she has just remembered something.]

Resources

Listening
Audio CD Library
A recording of this short, short story is provided in the *Audio CD Library:*
• Disc 1, Track 3

A Reading Skills and Strategies

Connecting with the Text

❓ What would you do if you were in the American's place? [Some students may say that they would run away. Others may say that they would remain calm.]

B Critical Thinking

Analyzing Ironic Situations
Tell students that this is an excellent example of **situational irony,** a contrast between what is expected to happen and what really does happen. The hostess disproves the colonel's theory about women's reactions in a crisis. The colonel thinks that the American's calm response proves his theory, but it is the hostess who remains calm and quietly takes action to remove the cobra from the room. She does exactly the opposite of what the colonel expects a woman to do.

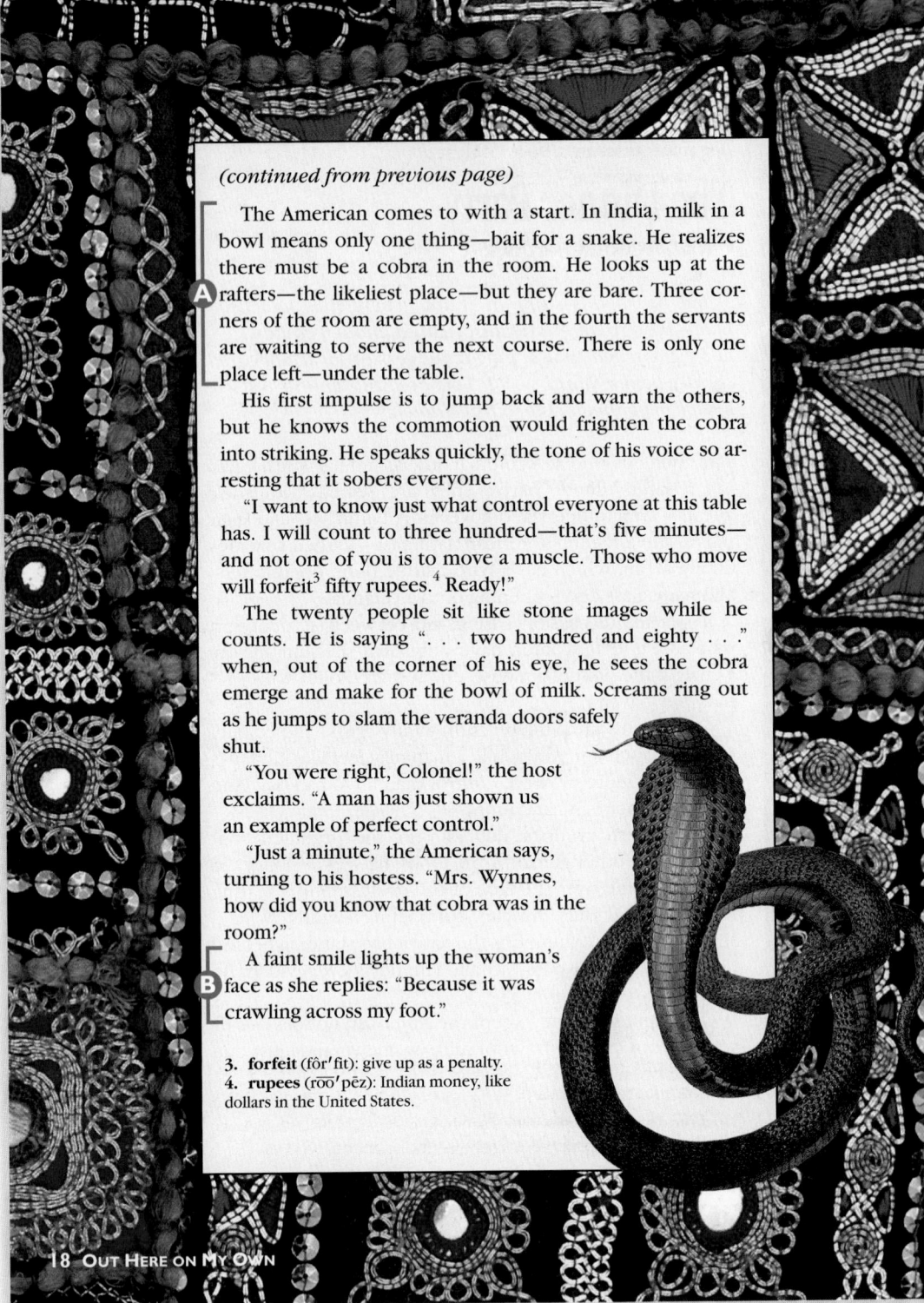

(continued from previous page)

The American comes to with a start. In India, milk in a bowl means only one thing—bait for a snake. He realizes there must be a cobra in the room. He looks up at the rafters—the likeliest place—but they are bare. Three corners of the room are empty, and in the fourth the servants are waiting to serve the next course. There is only one place left—under the table.

His first impulse is to jump back and warn the others, but he knows the commotion would frighten the cobra into striking. He speaks quickly, the tone of his voice so arresting that it sobers everyone.

"I want to know just what control everyone at this table has. I will count to three hundred—that's five minutes—and not one of you is to move a muscle. Those who move will forfeit[3] fifty rupees.[4] Ready!"

The twenty people sit like stone images while he counts. He is saying ". . . two hundred and eighty . . ." when, out of the corner of his eye, he sees the cobra emerge and make for the bowl of milk. Screams ring out as he jumps to slam the veranda doors safely shut.

"You were right, Colonel!" the host exclaims. "A man has just shown us an example of perfect control."

"Just a minute," the American says, turning to his hostess. "Mrs. Wynnes, how did you know that cobra was in the room?"

A faint smile lights up the woman's face as she replies: "Because it was crawling across my foot."

3. **forfeit** (fôr′fit): give up as a penalty.
4. **rupees** (roo′pēz): Indian money, like dollars in the United States.

Connecting Across Texts

Connecting with "Rikki-tikki-tavi"
Be sure to have students discuss how this famous short short story connects with Kipling's tale. Ask: How are the heroes in each story "out there on their own"? [In his descent into the underworld, Rikki is utterly alone. In this story the woman is completely alone in dealing with a cobra that has crawled over her feet. On her own, she cleverly and coolly lures it away.]

You might suggest some research to find out why Mona Gardner says that any naturalist would know the story can't be true. [Cobras usually don't drink milk.]

MAKING MEANINGS

MAKING MEANINGS

First Thoughts

[respond]

1. Respond to "Rikki-tikki-tavi" by completing these sentences. Look back at your Dialogue with the Text notes for ideas.

   • I thought this story was . . .

   • I was frightened for Rikki-tikki when . . .

   • The scene I liked best was . . .

Shaping Interpretations

[analyze]

2. Describe three **conflicts** that Rikki-tikki faces. Which conflict do you think is his greatest challenge, and why?

[interpret]

3. Like all great heroes, Rikki is celebrated by the society he saves. How does Darzee's chant make Rikki into a superhero? What kind of music would you set the song to?

[infer]

4. "The Dinner Party" (see *Connections* on page 17) is another story about an encounter with a snake. How does the hostess deal with *her* snake problem?

Connecting with the Text

[connect]

5. Did Rikki-tikki's conflicts with the deadly garden bullies remind you of your own experiences? For ideas, think back to what you said about bullies before you read the story. You might also check your reading notes.

Extending the Text

[extend]

6. The animal world of "Rikki-tikki-tavi" is filled with conflict and danger. What causes the war in this animal story? What causes most wars among people?

Challenging the Text

[evaluate]

7. Is Kipling fair to the snakes in this story? What could you say in defense of Nag and Nagaina?

[evaluate]

8. The animals in this story talk and think as if they were human. How do you feel about stories like this? Do you like them, or do you prefer to read about real animals without human characteristics? Use examples from the story to help explain your feelings about animal stories.

RIKKI-TIKKI-TAVI 19

Reading Check

a. Explain how Rikki-tikki comes to Teddy's home.

b. Why is it "the hardest thing in the world to frighten a mongoose"?

c. Whom does Rikki-tikki fight in the "great war"? Why does he fight?

d. Rikki-tikki fights alone, but he gets a little help from his friends. Who are they? How do they help him?

e. What does Rikki-tikki do with Nagaina's eggs?

First Thoughts

1. Possible answers:
   • I thought this story was scary.
   • I was frightened for Rikki-tikki when Nag slid into the dark bathroom.
   • The scene I liked best was the one in which Rikki confronted Nagaina.

Shaping Interpretations

2. The three conflicts that Rikki has are with Nag, Karait, and then Nagaina. This last conflict is Rikki's greatest challenge, because Rikki must face the cobra alone in her dark tunnel.

3. Darzee's chant makes Rikki sound larger than life, a savior. The chant should be set to dramatic, perhaps martial, music with lots of trumpets and drums.

4. The hostess quietly asks a servant to place a bowl of milk on the veranda, and the cobra slides away to get the milk.

Connecting with the Text

5. Students may recall instances in which they faced physical bullies or students who were intimidating because they were smarter, faster, wittier, and so on.

Extending the Text

6. Rikki has a natural instinct to hunt and kill snakes. Snakes must kill to stay alive. This begins the conflict. Students might mention differences of opinion, prejudice, conflicts over money or power, or misunderstandings as causes of human war.

Challenging the Text

7. Students may point out that snakes are natural predators who must kill to survive. Kipling makes them evil, but in actual life they are no more evil than the predators who eat their eggs.

8. Students may say they enjoyed animal stories more when they were younger. Some may say they now think stories that personify animals are unrealistic.

Reading Check

a. A flood washes Rikki out of his burrow. The family rescues him and allows him the run of the house and garden.

b. It is hard to frighten mongooses because they are very curious.

c. He fights Nag, Nagaina, and Karait. First, he fights Nag because Nag ate one of the tailorbird's babies. Then, he fights Karait, who threatened Teddy. Rikki fights both Nag and Nagaina because they plan to kill his human friends.

d. Darzee, the tailorbird, warns Rikki when Nagaina tries to catch him and tells Rikki where Nagaina's eggs are hidden. Chuchundra, the muskrat, alerts Rikki to the cobras' planned attack. Darzee's wife lures Nagaina away from her eggs and warns Rikki that Nagaina is threatening the human family.

e. He bites off the tops of the eggs and crushes the young cobras. He smashes two and leaves the last one as bait for Nagaina.

Grading Timesaver

Rubrics for each Choices assignment appear on p. 105 in the *Portfolio Management System*.

CHOICES:
Building Your Portfolio

1. **Writer's Notebook** With each selection, a Writer's Notebook activity appears as the first option in the Choices section. These brief, work-in-progress assignments build toward the writing assignment presented in the Writer's Workshop at the end of the collection. If students save their Writer's Notebook activities as they move throughout the collection, they should be able to use some of them as starting points for the workshop.

2. **Expository Writing/Science** Direct students first to encyclopedias or the Internet to find information on cobras. Also, local animal resource people might speak to your class.

3. **Speaking and Listening** Write the first bulleted list from Before You Read (p. 2) on the chalkboard to help students think about the direction their story might take. Remind students to use action and dialogue where possible and to respond quickly after the previous student has spoken.

4. **Storytelling/Music** Focus on another type of sound in this story—**onomatopoeia,** a term for words that sound like what they describe. For example, Rikki-tikki-tavi's name imitates the *rikk tchk* sound that he makes as a war cry. Have students think of similar examples, such as naming a canary *Tweety* or a dog *Ruff.* Discuss some of the onomatopoeic words in this story. Then, suggest that students add these sounds to their recordings.

CHOICES: Building Your Portfolio

Writer's Notebook

1. Collecting Ideas for a Story

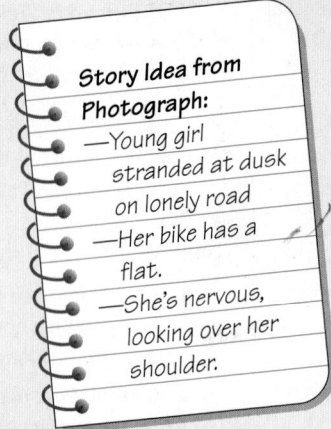

Writers get ideas for stories from all kinds of places. Some writers find stories in photographs or paintings. Look at the picture on page 14, or pick another in this book that grabs your attention. Jot down ideas about the following:

- what you see in the picture
- what you think will happen next
- what you think the character should do
- conflicts the character might face that aren't shown in the picture

Story Idea from Photograph:
—*Young girl stranded at dusk on lonely road*
—*Her bike has a flat.*
—*She's nervous, looking over her shoulder.*

Expository Writing/Science

2. Cobra Copy

Create a brochure that will inform zoo visitors about cobras. Before you do research, decide on the questions you'd like to answer. Here are some possibilities:

- How many kinds of cobras exist?
- Where do they live, and what do they eat?
- How dangerous are they?
- Can cobras hypnotize their prey?

Make a brochure by folding a sheet of notebook paper into thirds and presenting your information on it. You may want to include photographs or artwork.

Speaking and Listening

3. Rikki-tikki-2

Suppose that Nagaina's last egg was left on the veranda during the battle and lay there until it hatched. With a group of classmates, create a sequel to the story. Tell the story of the baby cobra in a "talk-around." Form a circle with three or four classmates; then, have someone start with this sentence: "The baby cobra wriggled into the sunlight." Go around the circle, with each person adding a sentence or two to develop the story. Consider how Rikki-tikki might respond by referring to the choices listed under What Would You Do? on page 2.

Storytelling/Music

4. The Sound of Rikki-tikki

Get together with three or four music-loving classmates. With the group, choose one key scene from the story for each person; then, find music to use as background for your scene. Record the different pieces of music on one tape to create a "soundtrack." Perform a dramatic reading of the scenes with your group, weaving the soundtrack into the performance.

LANGUAGE LINK   MINI-LESSON

Style: Choosing Specific Verbs

Language Handbook HELP

See Action Verbs, page 714.

Technology HELP

See Language Workshop CD-ROM. Key word entry: verbs.

SOME OF KIPLING'S VERBS

creep
cower
roam
trot
scuttle
dance

This story moves at a fast pace, in part because Kipling uses strong, vivid verbs to help us see all the action in the cobra wars. Chuchundra doesn't just walk; he *creeps.* Darzee and his wife don't just sit; they *cower.* Rikki-tikki himself *roams, trots, scuttles,* and *dances.* Consider this sentence about a scene from the story:

> Darzee moved along the branch, his eye on Nag.

How did Darzee move? Replace *moved* with *hopped, strolled,* and *stormed.* How does each verb change what you see? What does each verb tell you about Darzee's feelings and plans?

Go back to Kipling's story and find verbs you can add to the list on the left. Keep a verb bank like this one in your notebook for reference when you revise your own writing.

Try It Out

➤ Rewrite the sentences below, replacing each tame verb with a more specific (and more interesting) verb.

1. That night, Nag went into the bungalow.

2. Rikki-tikki gave a warning.

3. Teddy's parents stood and looked at the cobra.

➤ Be a verb spotter. Choose a piece of your own writing.

• Underline all the verbs.

• Replace at least three verbs with ones that are sharper, more vivid, and more specific.

• Get together with a partner, and explain why you chose the verbs you did—what do you want the reader to see?

Cover for *The Jungle Book* by Rudyard Kipling.
Rare Books and Manuscripts Division. The New York Public Library. Astor, Lenox and Tilden Foundations.

VOCABULARY   HOW TO OWN A WORD

WORD BANK	You've Been There
immensely	1. Describe a time when you or someone you know was <u>immensely</u> proud.
cowered	2. Describe how a large dog would look if it <u>cowered</u> before a kitten.
gait	3. Draw pictures suggested by the words <u>gait</u> and <u>gate</u> to help you remember their meanings. Use the letters of the words in your pictures.
valiant	4. Name three people in the world who are <u>valiant</u>.
consolation	5. What <u>consolation</u> could you offer a friend who didn't make the team?

RIKKI-TIKKI-TAVI 21

LANGUAGE LINK

Students may use their piece for the Writer's Workshop at the end of the collection for the second part of Try It Out. Tell them to look for all the forms of the verb "to be" as the most obvious candidates for change. Also, ask them to think of two possible replacements for each verb and to have a partner choose the best one.

Try It Out
Possible Answers
1. Slithered, sneaked, crawled
2. Screamed, shouted, shrieked
3. Froze and stared

VOCABULARY
Possible Answers
1. I was immensely proud when I won first place in the science fair.
2. Drawings should demonstrate the meaning of *cowered.* The best will show a dog hovering close to the ground, its tail between its legs.
3. Students' drawings should demonstrate that they know that *gait* means a way of walking or running and that a *gate* is a large door or entrance.
4. I made a valiant attempt to get on the Junior Olympics team in soccer by practicing day and night. My parents were valiant in putting up with me.
5. When my sister broke her arm, I offered her consolation by saying that she would feel better in a short time.

Resources

Language
• *Grammar and Language Links,* p. 1
Vocabulary
• *Words to Own,* p. 1
Spelling
For related instruction, see
• *Spelling and Decoding,* p. 1

Language Link Quick Check

Write three descriptive verbs to replace each of the underscored words in the following sentences, and be prepared to explain your choices.

1. The dinner guests <u>ran</u> to the door. [Possible answers: flew, raced, dashed]

2. Mrs. Wynnes <u>said</u> something to her chef. [Possible answers: whispered, yelled, mumbled]

3. The dinner guests <u>ate</u> the scrumptious meal. [Possible answers: munched, gobbled, nibbled]

4. The colonel <u>wrote</u> something in his notebook. [Possible answers: scribbled, scrawled, marked]

5. The boy <u>walked</u> to the veranda. [Possible answers: limped, wandered, marched]

OBJECTIVES
1. To understand the cause-and-effect structure of a plot
2. To recognize elements of suspense, conflict, complication, climax, and resolution
3. To distinguish theme from plot
4. To identify the theme of a story

Resources

Elements of Literature
Plot and Theme
For additional instruction, see *Literary Elements:*
• Transparency 1

Elements of Literature
This feature focuses on the elements of plot and theme as the building blocks of the short story. The discussion of plot includes basic situation, types of conflict, complications, climax, and resolution. The discussion of theme includes steps readers can take to identify the theme of a story.

Mini-Lesson:
The Short Story
Ask what runs through students' minds when they experience suspense in a movie. Review the four parts of a plot with the class. Have students brainstorm a list of external and internal conflicts in popular TV programs and films.

THE SHORT STORY: A Story's Building Blocks

Plot: "What Happens?"

Plot is what happens in a story. Plot consists of a series of related episodes, one growing out of another. These episodes create **suspense,** a feeling of anxious curiosity. Suspense is what keeps us reading: It keeps us glued to the story because we are curious to find out what happens next. In fact, the real power of a story lies in its ability to create suspense. A good storyteller makes us worry about those campers cooking their trout over the campfire by letting us see the bear watching from the trees nearby.

A plot has four parts, which are like building blocks.

1. The first part of a plot tells us about the story's **basic situation:** Who are the characters, and what do they want? This is usually where we find out about the conflict in a story. A **conflict** is a struggle between opposing characters or opposing forces. In an **external conflict** a character struggles with another person, with a group of people, or with a force of nature (a tornado, a bear, an icy mountain path). An **internal conflict** takes place in a character's mind (he suffers from shyness; she struggles to accept a loss). Here is the introduction to a new version of a tale you know well. A hungry wolf provides the external conflict.

"Hi there, Red," said a wolf to a little girl in a red velvet hood. "How'd ya like a ride on my motorcycle?"

"Thank you, sir, but I can't," replied Little Red Riding Hood. "As you can see, I'm carrying this basket of ginger cookies to my grandmother, and I mustn't be late."

"Tell you what, Red. You just hop on the back, and I'll run you over to Granny's in five seconds flat."

"My grandmother lives way out at the end of Lonely Road," Red protested. "It's miles and miles."

"This here motorcycle eats miles. We'll be there before you can say 'ginger cookies.' "

"No, thank you," said Little Red Riding Hood. "I've made up my mind." She began to walk faster.

2. In the second part of a plot, one or more of the characters act to resolve the conflict. Now **complications** develop.

"Suit yourself," chuckled the wolf, who had conceived a wicked plan. He would go alone to the end of Lonely Road, eat Red's grandma, and then, when the delicious little girl turned up, he would eat her and her delicious ginger cookies, too.

3. Now comes the **climax,** the story's most emotional or suspenseful moment. This is the point where the conflict is decided one way or another.

It was nearly dark when Red arrived, but as she approached her grandma's bed, she sensed something was wrong.

"Are you all right, Granny?" Red asked. "Your eyes look bloodshot."

Getting Students Involved

Cooperative Learning
Have the class form several groups. Let each group choose one TV program or film. Then, have members of the group work together to complete this cluster.

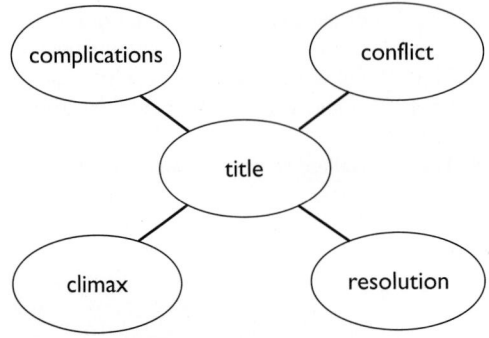

Use the chalkboard or a transparency to have the class view the completed clusters. Ask students to evaluate each group's work.

"All the better to see you with," replied the wolf.

"And your teeth. Suddenly they look like fangs."

"All the better to eat—" the wolf began, but he stopped at the sound of his motorcycle engine thundering in the front yard. "Wait right there, Red," said the wolf, bounding from the bed.

The wolf was startled to find Grandma Riding Hood astride the motorcycle.

"Hey!" he shouted. "Stop fooling with my bike." As he lunged for her, Grandma found the gearshift and the cycle leaped forward, catching the wolf up on its handlebars and hurling him into a giant thornbush—which is where the police found him when they arrived.

4. The last part of a story is its **resolution.** This is where the loose ends of the story are tied up and the story is closed.

Little Red and her grandma let the police make a cap of the wolf's fur. And they all lived happily ever after.

Theme: The Story's Main Idea

All good stories have **themes.** This is the main idea of the story, the discovery about life that we take away from it. Here are some steps to take to identify a story's theme.

1. Think about how the main character has changed in the course of the story and what the character has learned. Sometimes what the character has learned can be stated as the theme. ("If you are self-centered, you can hurt yourself as well as others.")

2. Think about the title of the story and its meaning.

3. Identify some important passages in the story and think about what they suggest to you about our lives.

Sharing Feelings

There is no better mark of a well-told story than the sense of special understanding it creates between the writer

and the reader. Whether the story is about a teenage romance, revenge among criminals, or a dog who rescues a rancher's child, each reader will approach it differently and respond to it in a unique way. If the story moved us deeply, we can hardly wait to talk about our feelings with someone else. That sense of unique communication between writer and reader—and between reader and reader—is the true joy of reading.

A Writer on the Short Story

"Of all the writing forms, I've always been partial to the short story. It suits my temperament. It makes a modest appeal for attention, allowing me to slip up alongside the reader on her/his blind side and grab'm."

—Toni Cade Bambara

Applying the Element

Have students outline the plot of "Rikki-tikki-tavi" by filling in the episodes for each element of the triangle.

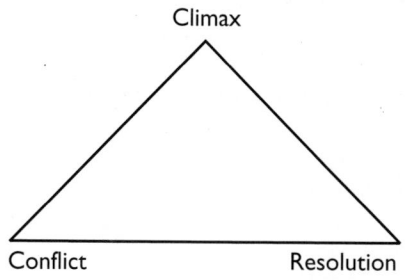

Climax

Conflict   Resolution

Resources ————

Assessment

Formal Assessment

• Literary Elements Test, p. 12

OBJECTIVES

1. Read and interpret the poem
2. Recognize and interpret a symbol
3. Express understanding through narrative and creative writing or choral reading

SKILLS

Literary
- Recognize and interpret a symbol

Writing
- Write from another point of view

Speaking/Listening
- Perform a choral reading

Planning

- **Block Schedule**
  Block Scheduling Lesson Plans with Pacing Guide
- **Traditional Schedule**
  Lesson Plans Including Strategies for English-Language Learners
- **One-Stop Planner**
  CD-ROM with Test Generator

THE RUNAWAY

Make the Connection

Not Just Horsing Around

In "The Runaway," Robert Frost introduces us to a colt who's never seen snow before. Even if the only horses you've met are in the movies, you can probably identify with the colt in this poem. Find a partner and talk about some of the things that children have to learn in life as they grow to adulthood.

Quickwrite

Freewrite about a time when you learned something important about life. Who helped you?

Elements of Literature

Symbol: What Does It Stand For?

A **symbol** is a person, place, or thing that has meaning in itself and stands for something else as well.

Many symbols are traditional. We easily understand them because people have agreed on their meaning. A dove, for example, often symbolizes peace. The image of Uncle Sam is a symbol of the United States.

Writers sometimes create their own symbols. On one level, Frost's "The Runaway" is a simple story about some people who take a walk in a snowstorm and come across a colt who is seeing snow for the first time. On another level the poem may be seen as symbolic. What do you sense the frightened little colt stands for?

> **A** symbol is a person, place, or thing that has meaning in itself and stands for something beyond itself as well.
>
> *For more on Symbol, see the Handbook of Literary Terms.*

Background

Literature and Science

The subject of "The Runaway" is a Morgan colt. Morgans are a breed of swift, strong horses named for Justin Morgan (1747–1798), a Vermont schoolteacher who owned the stallion that founded the line. Morgans are small, sturdy horses that excel at weight-pulling contests. Today they are used mostly for riding and in herding cattle.

 go.hrw.com
LE0 7-1

24 OUT HERE ON MY OWN

 Resources: Print and Media

Reading
- *Graphic Organizers for Active Reading*, p. 2
- *Audio CD Library*
  Disc 2, Track 2

Assessment
- *Formal Assessment*, p. 3
- *Portfolio Management System*, p. 106
- *Test Generator (One-Stop Planner CD-ROM)*

Internet
- go.hrw.com (keyword: LE0 7-1)

The Runaway

Robert Frost

Once when the snow of the year was beginning to fall,
We stopped by a mountain pasture to say, "Whose colt?"
A little Morgan had one forefoot on the wall,
The other curled at his breast. He dipped his head
5 And snorted at us. And then he had to bolt.
We heard the miniature thunder where he fled,
And we saw him, or thought we saw him, dim and gray,
Like a shadow against the curtain of falling flakes.
"I think the little fellow's afraid of the snow.
10 He isn't winter-broken. It isn't play
With the little fellow at all. He's running away.
I doubt if even his mother could tell him, 'Sakes,
It's only weather.' He'd think she didn't know!
Where is his mother? He can't be out alone." **(A)**
15 And now he comes again with clatter of stone,
And mounts the wall again with whited eyes
And all his tail that isn't hair up straight.
He shudders his coat as if to throw off flies.
"Whoever it is that leaves him out so late,
20 When other creatures have gone to stall and bin, **(B)**
Ought to be told to come and take him in."

THE RUNAWAY **25**

Summary ■

The speaker of the poem, along with his unnamed companion, encounters a Morgan colt out alone in a mountain pasture during the first snowfall of the year. At first the speaker thinks the colt is playing in the snow. Soon, however, he realizes that the colt is terrified and trying to run away from the snow. The worried, angry speaker comments to his companion that the owner of the colt ought to be told to bring him in.

Resources ————

Listening
Audio CD Library
For a recording of this poem, see the *Audio CD Library:*
• Disc 2, Track 2

Ⓐ Elements of Literature
Symbol
❓ What details in ll. 12–14 liken the colt to a human child? [Possible responses: The speaker wonders where the colt's mother is and says that even if the mother were to say reassuring words to the colt right now, he might not believe her.]

Ⓑ Reading Skills and Strategies
Responding to the Text
❓ What word best describes the speaker's mood at the end of the poem? [Possible responses: upset; angry; disapproving.] Point out that the speaker's mood and the poem's tone change when the speaker realizes that the colt is afraid and running away, rather than playing.

Reaching All Students

English Language Learners
Some students may not realize how a horse behaves when it's upset. It blows hard through its nose, rolls its eyes, and trembles. Be sure students know that a stall is an enclosure in a stable where an animal is kept and a bin is a container for storing food, especially oats.

Advanced Learners
Have students decide how they could capture the shifting mood of the poem on film or videotape, using such techniques as musical cues and changes in camera angles, setting, and voices.

MEET THE WRITER

A Poem "Begins as a Lump in the Throat"

While in high school in Lawrence, Massachusetts, **Robert Frost** (1874–1963) decided to become a poet. Not only did he succeed, but he became for a time America's most celebrated living poet.

"Rob" Frost lived most of his life on farms in Vermont and New Hampshire. There, he grew corn, edited a local newspaper, taught, and raised a family. Frost filled his poems with images of the people of New England and their hay barns, farmhouses, pastures, apple orchards, and woods. His work speaks to people everywhere because it springs from intense feelings.

Frost says this about poetry: A poem "begins as a lump in the throat, a sense of wrong, a homesickness, a loneliness." The feeling then "finds the thought and the thought finds the words." Frost felt that "it is most important of all to reach the heart of the reader."

MAKING MEANINGS

First Thoughts

[respond]

1. How would you complete each of these sentences?
   - As he faced his first snowfall alone, the colt felt . . .
   - As I read about him, I felt . . .

Shaping Interpretations

[interpret]

2. To break a colt is to get him used to being ridden. What do you think the expression *winter-broken* (line 10) means?

[infer]

3. How do you think the speaker feels about the person who has left the colt alone in the pasture?

[infer]

4. Why do you think Frost called the poem "The Runaway"? (What is the colt running away from?)

26 OUT HERE ON MY OWN

MAKING MEANINGS

First Thoughts

1. Students may say the colt felt scared, terrified, lonely, or abandoned. They may say they felt concerned, sad, or alarmed.

Shaping Interpretations

2. It probably means "used to winter weather."
3. Possible responses: angry, disapproving.
4. The title might refer to the colt running away from the speaker or its attempt to run away from the snow.
5. Students who agree that the horse symbolizes a young child may cite the speaker's description of him as a "little fellow" (l. 9), and the speaker's attribution of human words and feelings to the colt and his mother in ll. 12–14.

Assessing Learning

Check Test: Short Answer

1. What question does the speaker have about the colt? [The speaker asks, "Whose colt?"]
2. How is the colt behaving? [The colt is acting excitedly; it is racing around the pasture, trying to climb the fence, and snorting.]
3. What does the speaker think is the colt's problem? [The speaker decides that the colt is afraid of snow because it has never seen snow before.]
4. What does the speaker imagine about the colt's mother? [The speaker imagines that the colt's mother is speaking to the colt and trying to explain the concept of weather.]
5. What does the speaker think should be done for the colt? [The speaker thinks that the colt's owner should come and take him in.]

[evaluate]
5. Some people think that the colt **symbolizes** a lost child or someone who is too young or too innocent to understand what he or she is experiencing. Do you agree with this interpretation, or do you have another one? Support your interpretation with details from the poem.

[compare]
6. When you read, you form **mental images** of people, settings, and events. Describe what you see as you read (and reread) this poem. Compare your mental images with those of your classmates.

Extending the Text

[connect]
7. Reread the last three lines of "The Runaway." What other situations in life do you think these lines could be applied to? Explain.

[apply]
8. *Runaway* can refer to people, too. What other "runaways" are found in our world? What lines from the poem could apply to them?

CHOICES: Building Your Portfolio

Writer's Notebook

1. Collecting Ideas for a Story

Robert Frost said that a poem begins with a feeling. That's true of stories, too. To find a feeling that you want to write about, go through some of your souvenirs—photographs, ticket stubs, score cards. When you find an item that stirs a strong memory, start jotting down notes. Record as many details of the memory as you can. Describe what you felt. You might find some ideas in your notes for the Quickwrite on page 24.

Creative Writing

2. Straight from the Horse's Mouth

Throughout "The Runaway" the observers guess what the colt is thinking and feeling. Do you think they're right? In poetry or prose, rewrite "The Runaway" from the colt's point of view. Have him share his feelings about the weather, about his mother—and about the people watching him. If you write a poem, you could present it in the following form, with the first letters of the lines spelling out the word *runaway*.

R _____
U _____
N _____
A _____
W _____
A _____
Y _____

Performance

3. Choral Reading

With several classmates, prepare a group reading of "The Runaway." Decide which lines you will assign to a chorus and which lines you'll assign to a single voice. Practice reading aloud so that the poet's use of normal speech rhythms comes through.

THE RUNAWAY 27

---

6. Answers will vary. Among the details of the colt's behavior that students may visualize are the whited eyes, the tail straight up, the forefoot on the wall, the dipped, snorting head, or the shadow against a curtain of snow.

Extending the Text

7. Answers will vary. Students might mention their own experience of taking care of their pets or younger siblings or people's abandonment of their pets or neglect of other responsibilities.

8. Answers will vary. Students may mention teenage runaways who leave home to go out into the world "alone" or other children who are neglected or abandoned. Lines 14 and 19–21 could apply.

Grading Timesaver

Rubrics for each Choices assignment appear on p. 106 in the *Portfolio Management System*.

CHOICES: Building Your Portfolio

1. **Writer's Notebook** Remind students to save their work. They may use it as prewriting for the Writer's Workshop on pp. 94–99.
2. **Creative Writing** Students may wish to work in groups and then choose the best lines for a composite poem.
3. **Performance** Students might look for appropriate background music to play while they recite the poem.

Using Students' Strengths

Musical/Auditory Learners
Invite interested students to adapt their choral readings of the poem (Choice 3) to include sound effects suitable for presenting the poem on the radio. Effects might include background music plus the sounds of the colt's snorts and clattering hooves. Have students tape-record their performances and play them for the class.

Interpersonal Learners
Ask these students to take on the role of the speaker and write a diary entry that he or she might have made after the encounter with the colt. Students might invent a reason or a story to explain why the speaker was particularly touched by the plight of the young colt. Or, they might muse about the vulnerability of young creatures and their need for experience, nurturing, and guidance.

SONG OF THE TREES

Make the Connection

Agree? Disagree?

disagree 0 1 2 3 4 agree

1. People gain self-respect by standing up for their beliefs.

2. Given the chance, most people will never take advantage of another person.

3. Some people are treated unfairly because of the color of their skin.

4. Nobody owns the earth.

Rate each of the statements above with a number from 0 to 4. (Zero means that you completely disagree; 4 means you completely agree.)

Quickwrite

Which statement do you agree or disagree with most strongly? Explain very briefly what you think about that statement and why. You might want to jot down notes on an experience that shaped your opinion. Share your Quickwrite with a partner; then, discuss these issues with the rest of the class.

Elements of Literature

Theme: A Revelation About Life

Have you ever asked after reading a story: "What does it *mean?*" What you are asking about is the story's theme. **Theme** is what a story reveals about people and life. It is the meaning that we take away from the story. Stories like "Song of the Trees" often have several themes, but one usually stands out from the others.

> **Theme** is the idea about life revealed in a piece of literature.
>
> *For more on Theme, see pages 22–23 and the Handbook of Literary Terms.*

Reading Skills and Strategies

Making Generalizations: Putting It All Together

A **generalization** is a broad statement that tells about something "in general." A statement about a story's theme is a kind of generalization. From specific evidence in the story you make a broad, universal statement about life. To make a statement about the theme of "Song of the Trees," you have to

• think about the main events and conflicts in the story

• decide what the characters have learned by the end of the story

• think about how the story relates to your experiences

Background

Literature and Social Studies

The depression referred to in this story is the Great Depression, the severe economic decline that lasted from 1929 to 1942 in the United States. During the Depression many banks and businesses closed. People lost their jobs, their savings, and their homes, and many had barely enough to eat. This was also a time when the segregation of African Americans was still a sad reality in parts of the United States.

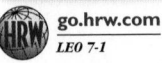
go.hrw.com
LEO 7-1

Preteaching Vocabulary

Words to Own

Have student partners first read the definitions of the Words to Own listed at the bottom of the selection pages and then quiz each other about the meanings of the words. After you are sure they understand the words, have the partners work together on the following exercises.

1. Use body language and facial expressions to pantomime the meanings of **ambled,** **delved, finicky, incredulously,** and **sentries.** Have your partner guess which word you are pantomiming.

2. Role-play a **dispute.** One of you will speak **curtly** and the other will chatter.

3. Draw pictures that show an animal trying to **elude** its hunter, a motorcycle **skirting** an obstacle, and a person with an **ashen** complexion.

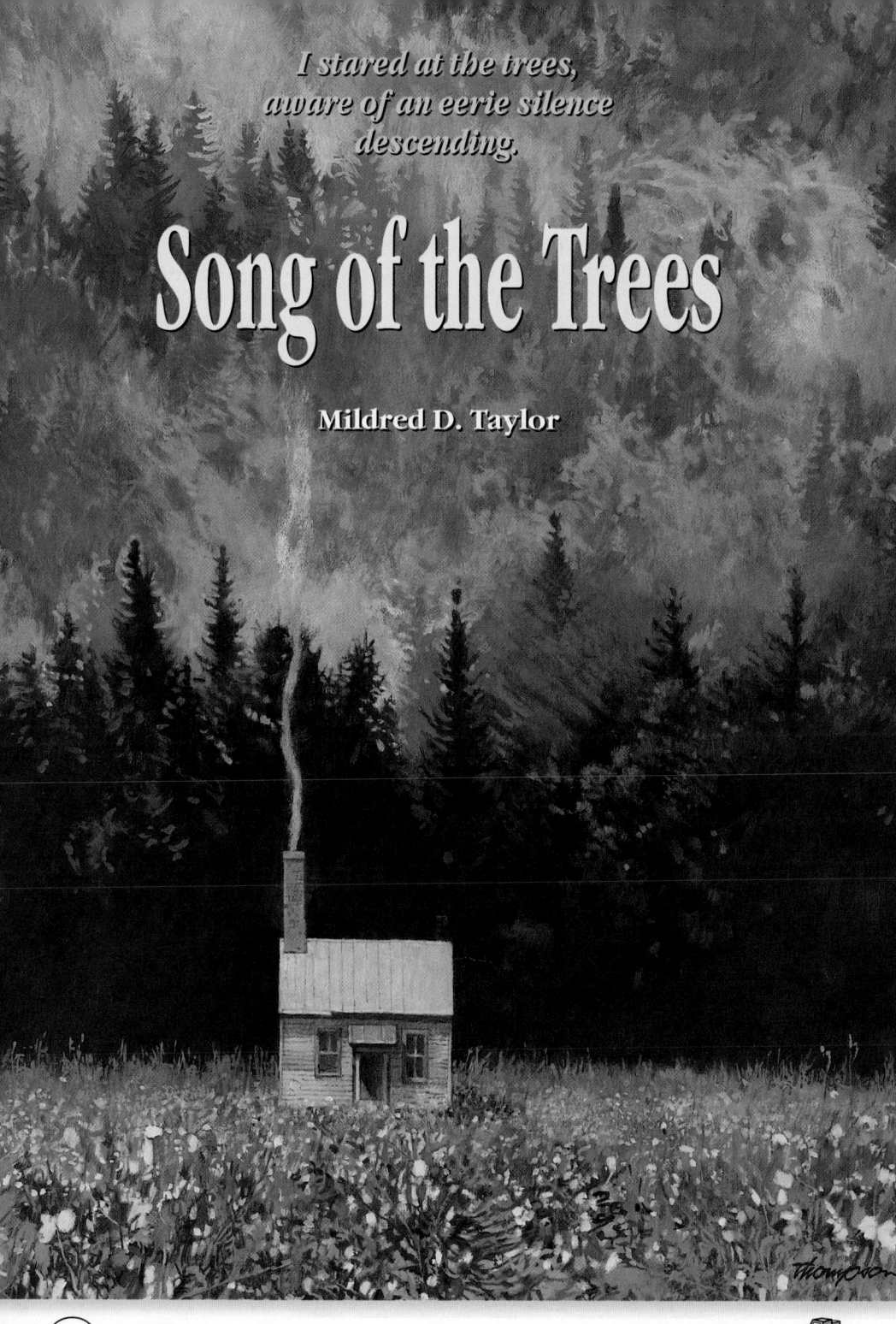

*I stared at the trees,
aware of an eerie silence
descending.*

Song of the Trees

Mildred D. Taylor

Summary ■ ■

This poignant story is set in Mississippi during the Great Depression. Its first-person narrator, eight-year-old Cassie Logan, describes her close-knit African American family's struggle to survive. She also describes her joy in the family's forest, where the trees "sing" to her. While playing in the woods with her three brothers, Cassie learns that Mr. Andersen, an unscrupulous businessman, plans to pay the Logans a small fee for the forest and then cut down all the trees and sell the lumber for his own profit. The eldest brother, Stacey, rides off to bring Papa, who has had to leave home to find work. Papa returns and wires the trees with dynamite, threatening to blow up the whole forest unless Mr. Andersen leaves immediately. Realizing that Papa is willing to risk his own life to defend his family and his trees, Mr. Andersen backs off and leaves the forest.

Background

To make the Great Depression real for students, display photographs taken during the period by such photographers as Dorothea Lange, Walker Evans, and Eudora Welty. Find out if your library has one of these noted collections: *You Have Seen Their Faces*, by Erskine Caldwell and Margaret Bourke-White; *Twelve Million Black Voices*, by Richard Wright; and *One Time, One Place*, by Eudora Welty. Encourage students to share whatever they may have learned about the Depression from family members or friends.

Resources ———

Listening
Audio CD Library
A recording of this story is provided in the *Audio CD Library*:
- Disc 2, Track 3

Selection Assessment
Formal Assessment
- Selection Test, p. 4

Test Generator
- Selection Test

Resources: Print and Media

Reading
- *Reading Skills and Strategies*
  MiniRead Skill Lesson, p. 23
  Selection Skill Lesson, p. 30
- *Graphic Organizers for Active Reading*, p. 3
- *Words to Own*, p. 2
- *Spelling and Decoding*, Worksheet, p. 2
- *Audio CD Library*, Disc 2, Track 3

Writing and Language
- *Daily Oral Grammar*
  Transparency 2

- *Grammar and Language Links*
  Worksheet, p. 3
- *Language Workshop CD-ROM*

Assessment
- *Formal Assessment*, p. 4
- *Portfolio Management System*, p. 107
- *Standardized Test Preparation*, p. 12
- *Test Generator (One-Stop Planner CD-ROM)*

Internet
- go.hrw.com (keyword: LE0 7-1)

A Cultural Connections

"Big Ma" and "Mama" are Cassie's names for her grandmother and mother, respectively. Ask students if they use similar names for their grandparents or older family members or friends. Ask students where the names come from. Some names may be non-English words; some may be made-up childhood names. Stress the playfulness of the names that students have for their relatives.

B Reading Skills and Strategies

Making Generalizations

❓ What lesson is Mama teaching Christopher-John? State the lesson in broad, general terms. [Possible responses: When times are hard, family members must share and make sacrifices for each other; being greedy is wrong.]

C Vocabulary Note

Multiple Meanings

Point out that the word *depression* has several meanings. It can be used to describe an emotional state of sadness and gloom. Capitalized as the Depression, it refers to a specific period in American history (described on the Before You Read page). Ask students how these two senses of the word *depression* are related. [Possible response: When times are tough, as during a depressed economy, people are often sad and gloomy.] Call on a volunteer to suggest another meaning of *depression.* [a hollow]

A "Cassie. Cassie, child, wake up now," Big Ma called gently as the new sun peeked over the horizon.

I looked sleepily at my grandmother and closed my eyes again.

"Cassie! Get up, girl!" This time the voice was not so gentle.

I jumped out of the deep, feathery bed as Big Ma climbed from the other side. The room was still dark, and I stubbed my toe while stumbling sleepily about looking for my clothes.

"Shoot! Darn ole chair," I fussed, rubbing my injured foot.

"Hush, Cassie, and open them curtains if you can't see," Big Ma said. "Prop that window open, too, and let some of that fresh morning air in here."

I opened the window and looked outside. The earth was draped in a cloak of gray mist as the sun chased the night away. The cotton stalks, which in another hour would glisten greenly toward the sun, were gray. The ripening corn, wrapped in jackets of emerald and gold, was gray. Even the rich brown Mississippi earth was gray.

Only the trees of the forest were not gray. They stood dark, almost black, across the dusty road, still holding the night. A soft breeze stirred, and their voices whispered down to me in a song of morning greeting.

"Cassie, girl, I said open that window, not stand there gazing out all morning. Now, get moving before I take something to you," Big Ma threatened.

I dashed to my clothes. Before Big Ma had unwoven her long braid of gray hair, my pants and shirt were on and I was hurrying into the kitchen.

A small kerosene lamp was burning in a corner as I entered. Its light reflected on seven-year-old Christopher-John, short, pudgy, and a year younger than me, sitting sleepily upon a side bench drinking a large glass of clabber milk.[1] Mama's back was to me. She was dipping flour from a near-empty canister, while my older brother, Stacey, built a fire in the huge iron-bellied stove.

"I don't know what I'm going to do with you, Christopher-John," Mama scolded. "Getting up in the middle of the night and eating all that cornbread. Didn't you have enough to eat before you went to bed?"

"Yes'm," Christopher-John murmured.

B "Lord knows I don't want any of my babies going hungry, but times are hard, honey. Don't you know folks all around here in Mississippi are struggling? Children crying cause they got no food to eat, and their daddies crying cause they can't get jobs so they can feed their babies? And you getting up in the middle of the night, stuffing yourself with cornbread!"

C Her voice softened as she looked at the sleepy little boy. "Baby, we're in a depression. Why do you think Papa's way down in Louisiana laying tracks on the railroad? So his children can eat—but only when they're hungry. You understand?"

"Yes'm," Christopher-John murmured again, as his eyes slid blissfully shut.

"Morning, Mama," I chimed.

"Morning, baby," Mama said. "You wash up yet?"

"No'm."

"Then go wash up and call Little Man again. Tell him he's not dressing to meet President Roosevelt[2] this morning. Hurry up, now, cause I want you to set the table."

---

1. **clabber milk:** thickly curdled sour milk.
2. **President Roosevelt:** Franklin Delano Roosevelt (1882–1945) was president of the United States from 1933 to 1945.

30 OUT HERE ON MY OWN

Reaching All Students

Struggling Readers

Making Generalizations was introduced on p. 28. For a lesson directly tied to this selection that teaches students to make generalizations by using a strategy called It says . . . I Say, see the *Reading Skills and Strategies* binder:
• MiniRead Skill lesson, p. 23
• Selection Skill Lesson, p. 30

English Language Learners

Explain that the writer is re-creating the way many blacks in Mississippi in the 1930s talked. Translate dialect such as "Darn ole chair" into "Darn old chair," "No'm" into "No ma'am," "them trees ain't singing" into "those trees aren't singing," etc. For additional strategies to supplement instruction for these students, see
• *Lesson Plans Including Strategies for English-Language Learners*

Advanced Learners

Cultural Connections. This story, set during the Depression, was written by contemporary writer Mildred Taylor. Students may enjoy reading Taylor's novel *Roll of Thunder, Hear My Cry,* which deals with the same period. The story "Marigolds," by Eugenia Collier, may be recommended for mature readers.

T30

Little Man, a very small six-year-old and a most finicky dresser, was brushing his hair when I entered the room he shared with Stacey and Christopher-John. His blue pants were faded, but except for a small grass stain on one knee, they were clean. Outside of his Sunday pants, these were the only pants he had, and he was always careful to keep them in the best condition possible. But one look at him and I knew that he was far from pleased with their condition this morning. He frowned down at the spot for a moment, then continued brushing.

"Man, hurry up and get dressed," I called. "Mama said you ain't dressing to meet the president."

"See there," he said, pointing at the stain. "You did that."

"I did no such thing. You fell all by yourself."

"You tripped me!"

"Didn't!"

"Did, too!"

"Hey, cut it out, you two!" ordered Stacey, entering the room. "You fought over that stupid stain yesterday. Now get moving, both of you. We gotta go pick blackberries before the sun gets too high. Little Man, you go gather the eggs while Christopher-John and me milk the cows."

Little Man and I decided to settle our dispute later when Stacey wasn't around. With Papa away, eleven-year-old Stacey thought of himself as the man of the house, and Mama had instructed Little Man, Christopher-John, and me to mind him. So, like it or not, we humored him. Besides, he was bigger than we were.

I ran to the back porch to wash. When I returned to the kitchen, Mama was talking to Big Ma.

"We got about enough flour for two more meals," Mama said, cutting the biscuit dough. "Our salt and sugar are practically down to nothing and——" She stopped when she saw me. "Cassie, baby, go gather the eggs for Mama."

"Little Man's gathering the eggs."

"Then go help him."

"But I ain't set the table yet."

"Set it when you come back."

I knew that I was not wanted in the kitchen. I looked suspiciously at my mother and grandmother, then went to the back porch to get a basket.

Big Ma's voice drifted through the open window. "Mary, you oughta write David and tell him somebody done opened his letter and stole that ten dollars he sent," she said.

"No, Mama. David's got enough on his mind. Besides, there's enough garden foods so we won't go hungry."

"But what 'bout your medicine? You're all out of it and the doctor told you good to——"

"Shhhh!" Mama stared at the window. "Cassie, I thought I told you to go gather those eggs!"

"I had to get a basket, Mama!" I hurried off the porch and ran to the barn.

After breakfast, when the sun was streaking red across the sky, my brothers and I ambled into the coolness of the forest, leading our three cows and their calves down the narrow cow path to the pond. The morning was already muggy, but the trees closed out the heat as their leaves waved restlessly, high above our heads.

"Good morning, Mr. Trees," I shouted. They answered me with a soft, swooshing sound. "Hear 'em, Stacey? Hear 'em singing?"

"Ah, cut that out, Cassie. Them trees ain't singing. How many times I gotta tell you that's just the wind?" He stopped at a sweet alligator gum, pulled out his knife, and scraped off a glob of gum that had seeped through its cracked bark. He handed me half.

WORDS TO OWN

finicky (fin′ik·ē) *adj.*: fussy and extremely careful.
dispute (di·spyo͞ot′) *n.*: argument.
ambled (am′bəld) *v.*: walked easily, without hurrying.

D Critical Thinking
Challenging the Text
? What do these details suggest about Little Man's character? [Possible response: His neatness and fussiness about his patched clothes suggest that Little Man is proud.] Does this character seem true to life? [Possible response: No, a finicky six-year-old boy is not true to life; yes, some young children are careful about their appearance.]

E Elements of Literature
Theme
? What does the dialogue between Big Ma and Mama reveal about the relationships between the family members? [Possible response: They are protective of each other. Mama is facing serious problems, yet she is careful not to add to David's worries. Mama tries to shield the children from the fact of her illness.]

F Struggling Readers
Reading Aloud
Read this dialogue aloud for students to make sure they don't miss the important information revealed here: The family does not have enough food or extra money; their father is away from home; Mama does not want the children to know she is sick; Cassie has overheard the conversation and knows all of this information.

G Reading Skills and Strategies

Making Generalizations
Point out that the reactions of Cassie and Stacey to the trees represent two different ways that people generally respond to nature. Ask students to make a generalization about these two ways of responding. [Possible response: Some people may respond emotionally and imaginatively to nature, while others respond in a logical, literal, and matter-of-fact way.]

Listening to Music

"Trees" by Joyce Kilmer
Joyce Kilmer's poem "Trees" (1914), once very popular, was set to music by Oscar Rasbach.

I think that I shall never see
A poem lovely as a tree.

A tree whose hungry mouth is prest
Against the earth's sweet flowing breast;

A tree that looks at God all day,
And lifts her leafy arms to pray;

A tree that may in summer wear
A nest of robins in her hair;

Upon whose bosom snow has lain;
Who intimately lives with rain.

Poems are made by fools like me,
But only God can make a tree.

Activity
Have students read the lyrics and listen to the music for "Trees." Ask them to relate the sentiments expressed in the song to Cassie's thoughts and feelings in "Song of the Trees."

A. Appreciating Language
Word Choice

Contrast the sentence *I put the gum into my mouth* with *I stuffed the gooey wad into my mouth* from the story. Discuss why one sentence conveys only information while the other paints a vivid picture. [Students may mention the vivid action verb *stuffed*, the adjective *gooey*, which suggests the sticky feel of the gum, and the noun *wad*, which describes a large mass. They may say that the story sentence appeals to the sense of touch.]

B. Reading Skills and Strategies

Making Generalizations

Point out that in large families, the children often assume different roles with each other. Have students discuss the relationships they have observed among the Logan children and then ask them to make generalizations about the different roles siblings may assume. [Possible responses: One child is often the leader, as is Stacey. Others, like Christopher-John and Little Man, play the "kid brother" role.]

C. English Language Learners
Idioms

Some students may be unfamiliar with the idiom *Last one to it's a rotten egg*. Tell them that children use this phrase to challenge others to a race. Also point out the expression *You're it!*, which tells whose turn it is to chase others in a game of tag. Have students share special phrases from their own childhood games.

D. Elements of Literature
Theme

❓ What do the trees mean to Cassie? [Possible responses: She feels a close connection with the trees, as if they were human; or she loves them and sees them as her protectors and friends.]

E. Reading Skills and Strategies
Drawing Conclusions

❓ Why does the sudden silence in the forest worry Cassie? [Possible responses: She likes to imagine that the trees respond to her. Usually, when she is in the woods, the trees "sing" to her and seem to echo her own happy mood. The silence suggests to her that something is wrong.]

A As I stuffed the gooey wad into my mouth, I patted the tree and whispered, "Thank you, Mr. Gum Tree."

Stacey frowned at me, then looked back at Christopher-John and Little Man walking far behind us, munching on their breakfast biscuits.

"Man! Christopher-John! Come on, now," he yelled. "If we finish the berry picking early, we can go wading before we go back."

Christopher-John and Little Man ran to catch up with us. Then, resuming their leisurely pace, they soon fell behind again.

B A large gray squirrel scurried across our path and up a walnut tree. I watched until it was settled amidst the tree's featherlike leaves; then, poking one of the calves, I said, "Stacey, is Mama sick?"

"Sick? Why you say that?"

"'Cause I heard Big Ma asking her 'bout some medicine she's supposed to have."

Stacey stopped, a worried look on his face. "If she's sick, she ain't bad sick," he decided. "If she was bad sick, she'd been in bed."

We left the cows at the pond and, taking our berry baskets, <u>delved</u> deeper into the forest looking for the wild blackberry bushes.

"I see one!" I shouted.

"Where?" cried Christopher-John, eager for the sweet berries.

"Over there! Last one to it's a rotten egg!" I yelled, and off I ran.

Stacey and Little Man followed at my heels. But Christopher-John puffed far behind. "Hey, wait for me," he cried.

"Let's hide from Christopher-John," Stacey suggested.

C The three of us ran in different directions. I plunged behind a giant old pine and hugged its warm trunk as I waited for Christopher-John.

Christopher-John puffed to a stop, then, looking all around, called, "Hey, Stacey! Cassie! Hey, Man! Y'all cut that out!"

I giggled and Christopher-John heard me.

"I see you, Cassie!" he shouted, starting toward me as fast as his chubby legs would carry him. "You're it!"

"Not 'til you tag me," I laughed. As I waited for him to get closer, I glanced up into the boughs of my wintry-smelling hiding tree, expecting a song of laughter. But the old pine only tapped me gently with one of its long, low branches. I turned from the tree and dashed away.

"You can't, you can't, you can't catch me," I **D** taunted, dodging from one beloved tree to the next. Around shaggy-bark hickories and sharp-needled pines, past blue-gray beeches and sturdy black walnuts I sailed, while my laughter resounded through the ancient forest, filling every chink. Overhead, the boughs of the giant trees hovered protectively, but they did not join in my laughter.

Deeper into the forest I plunged.

Christopher-John, unable to keep up, plopped on the ground in a pant. Little Man and Stacey, emerging from their hiding places, ran up to him.

"Ain't you caught her yet?" Little Man demanded, more than a little annoyed.

"He can't catch the champ," I boasted, stopping to rest against a hickory tree. I slid my back down the tree's shaggy trunk and looked up at its long branches, heavy with sweet nuts and slender green leaves, perfectly still. I looked around at the leaves of the other trees. They were still also. I stared at the trees, aware **E** of an eerie silence descending over the forest.

Stacey walked toward me. "What's the matter with you, Cassie?" he asked.

"The trees, Stacey," I said softly, "they ain't singing no more."

"Is that all?" He looked up at the sky. "Come on, y'all. It's get-

---

WORDS TO OWN
delved (delvd') *v.*: searched.

32 OUT HERE ON MY OWN

Crossing the Curriculum

History

This story is set in Mississippi during the Great Depression, but it was written by contemporary author Mildred Taylor. Have students work in pairs to research an African American writer who worked during the years of the Depression. Some well-known figures include Arna Bontemps, Zora Neale Hurston, Langston Hughes, and Margaret Walker. One of the students in each pair should write a brief overview of the writer's life to read to the class; the other should read a poem, story, or section of a longer work by the writer and give a brief summary of it to the class. Ask students to discuss briefly how these writers' depictions of African American life during the Depression compare with the depiction in Mildred Taylor's story.

ting late. We'd better go pick them berries." He turned and walked on.

"But, Stacey, listen. Little Man, Christopher-John, listen."

The forest echoed an uneasy silence.

"The wind just stopped blowing, that's all," said Stacey. "Now stop fooling around and come on."

I jumped up to follow Stacey, then cried, "Stacey, look!" On a black oak a few yards away was a huge white X. "How did that get there?" I exclaimed, running to the tree.

"There's another one!" Little Man screamed.

"I see one too!" shouted Christopher-John.

Stacey said nothing as Christopher-John, Little Man, and I ran wildly through the forest counting the ghostlike marks.

"Stacey, they're on practically all of them," I said when he called us back. "Why?"

Stacey studied the trees, then suddenly pushed us down.

"My clothes!" Little Man wailed indignantly.

"Hush, Man, and stay down," Stacey warned. "Somebody's coming."

Two white men emerged. We looked at each other. We knew to be silent.

"You mark them all down here?" one of the men asked.

"Not the younger ones, Mr. Andersen."

"We might need them, too," said Mr. Andersen, counting the X's. "But don't worry 'bout marking them now, Tom. We'll get them later. Also them trees up past the pond toward the house."

"The old woman agree to you cutting these trees?"

"I ain't been down there yet," Mr. Andersen said.

"Mr. Andersen . . ." Tom hesitated a moment, looked up at the silent trees, then back at Mr. Andersen. "Maybe you should go easy with them," he cautioned. "You know that David can be as mean as an ole jackass when he wanna be."

SONG OF THE TREES 33

F Reading Skills and Strategies
Making Predictions
Have students read up to this point. Then ask if they can tell what the X's on the trees might mean. [Many students will suspect that the X's indicate trees that are to be cut down.] Have students read on to confirm their predictions.

G Elements of Literature
Conflict
This passage introduces the conflict that will be the central struggle in the rest of the story. Ask students to describe the opposing forces in the conflict. [Possible responses: Mr. Andersen wants to cut down the trees that belong to Cassie's family. The conflict is between a dishonest logger and Cassie's family.]

Using Students' Strengths

Naturalist Learners
Ask students to think about the natural sounds of a place that they love. When they are in this special place, what noises do they hear? Whether the sounds are of ice cracking or of sand shifting with the tide, how do these noises create a song in their mind? Encourage them to create a tape recording of the sounds they hear.

Visual Learners
As visual learners read the story, they might benefit by filling in the graphic organizer on p. 3 in the *Graphic Organizers for Active Reading*.

A Reading Skills and Strategies

Making Generalizations

Remind students of the generalizations they made earlier in the story about the ways people respond to nature. Then, ask students what generalization they can make about the responses of people like Mr. Andersen. [Possible response: Some people see nature only as something to be exploited for profit.]

B Reading Skills and Strategies

Making Predictions

❓ What do you think Stacey's plan is? [Possible responses: to run and tell Mama; to get help from somewhere.]

C Elements of Literature

Conflict

Antagonists are the characters in stories who are involved in conflicts with the **protagonists**, or main characters. Mr. Andersen is the antagonist in this story, particularly in this scene. Point out to students how Mr. Andersen speaks to the women and threatens David's safety.

"He's talking about Papa," I whispered.

"Shhhh!" Stacey hissed.

Mr. Andersen looked uneasy. "What's that gotta do with anything?"

"Well, he just don't take much to any dealings with white folks." Again, Tom looked up at the trees. "He ain't afraid like some."

Mr. Andersen laughed weakly. "Don't worry 'bout that, Tom. The land belongs to his mama. He don't have no say in it. Besides, I guess I oughta know how to handle David Logan. After all, there are ways. . . .

"Now, you get on back to my place and get some boys and start chopping down these trees," Mr. Andersen said. "I'll go talk to the old woman." He looked up at the sky. "We can almost get a full day's work in if we hurry."

A Mr. Andersen turned to walk away, but Tom stopped him. "Mr. Andersen, you really gonna chop all the trees?"

"If I need to. These folks ain't got no call for them. I do. I got me a good contract for these trees and I aim to fulfill it."

Tom watched Mr. Andersen walk away; then, looking sorrowfully up at the trees, he shook his head and disappeared into the depths of the forest.

"What we gonna do, Stacey?" I asked anxiously. "They can't just cut down our trees, can they?"

"I don't know. Papa's gone. . . ." Stacey muttered to himself, trying to decide what we should do next.

"Boy, if Papa was here, them ole white men wouldn't be messing with our trees," Little Man declared.

"Yeah!" Christopher-John agreed. "Just let Papa get hold of 'em and he gonna turn 'em every which way but loose."

34 OUT HERE ON MY OWN

"Christopher-John, Man," Stacey said finally, "go get the cows and take them home."

"But we just brought them down here," Little Man protested.

"And we gotta pick the berries for dinner," said Christopher-John mournfully.

B "No time for that now. Hurry up. And stay clear of them white men. Cassie, you come with me."

We ran, brown legs and feet flying high through the still forest.

By the time Stacey and I arrived at the house, Mr. Andersen's car was already parked in the dusty drive. Mr. Andersen himself was seated comfortably in Papa's rocker on the front porch. Big Ma was seated too, but Mama was standing.

Stacey and I eased quietly to the side of the porch, unnoticed.

C "Sixty-five dollars. That's an awful lot of money in these hard times, Aunt Caroline," Mr. Andersen was saying to Big Ma.

I could see Mama's thin face harden.

"You know," Mr. Andersen said, rocking familiarly in Papa's chair, "that's more than David can send home in two months."

"We do quite well on what David sends home," Mama said coldly.

Mr. Andersen stopped rocking. "I suggest you encourage Aunt Caroline to sell them trees, Mary. You know, David might not always be able to work so good. He could possibly have . . . an accident."

Big Ma's soft brown eyes clouded over with fear as she looked first at Mr. Andersen, then at Mama. But Mama clenched her fists and said, "In Mississippi, black men do not have accidents."

"Hush, child, hush," Big Ma said hurriedly. "How many trees for the sixty-five dollars, Mr. Andersen?"

Taking a Second Look

Review: Drawing Conclusions

Remind students that drawing conclusions involves collecting evidence, much as a detective does, to figure out things in a story that are not stated directly. Readers connect clues in the story with their own knowledge of life to make a judgment about what is going on.

Activities

1. Have students work in small groups to identify passages that offer clues to the kinds of people Cassie, Mr. Andersen, Mama, and Papa really are. Have each group make a chart showing the evidence they found and the conclusions they drew from it.

2. Have students find points in the story where the author does not reveal exactly what is

going on. Ask students to point out clues they used to draw their own conclusions about events.

3. After students have read the story, call on volunteers to give examples of how their own prior knowledge and experience helped them to draw conclusions about the characters.

"Enough 'til I figure I got my sixty-five dollars' worth."

"And how many would that be?" Mama persisted.

Mr. Andersen looked haughtily at Mama. "I said I'd be the judge of that, Mary."

"I think not," Mama said.

Mr. Andersen stared at Mama. And Mama stared back at him. I knew Mr. Andersen didn't like that, but Mama did it anyway. Mr. Andersen soon grew uneasy under that piercing gaze, and when his eyes swiftly shifted from Mama to Big Ma, his face was beet red.

"Caroline," he said, his voice low and menacing, "you're the head of this family and you've got a decision to make. Now, I need them trees and I mean to have them. I've offered you a good price for them and I ain't gonna haggle over it. I know y'all can use the money. Doc Thomas tells me that Mary's not well." He hesitated a moment, then hissed venomously, "And if something should happen to David . . ."

"All right," Big Ma said, her voice trembling. "All right, Mr. Andersen."

"No, Big Ma!" I cried, leaping onto the porch. "You can't let him cut our trees!"

Mr. Andersen grasped the arms of the rocker, his knuckles chalk white. "You certainly ain't taught none of your younguns how to behave, Caroline," he said curtly.

"You children go on to the back," Mama said, shooing us away.

"No, Mama," Stacey said. "He's gonna cut them all down. Me and Cassie heard him say so in the woods."

"I won't let him cut them," I threatened. "I won't let him! The trees are my friends and ain't no mean ole white man gonna touch my trees——"

Mama's hands went roughly around my body as she carried me off to my room.

"Now, hush," she said, her dark eyes flashing wildly. "I've told you how dangerous it is . . ."

She broke off in midsentence. She stared at me a moment, then hugged me tightly and went back to the porch.

Stacey joined me a few seconds later, and we sat there in the heat of the quiet room, listening miserably as the first whack of an ax echoed against the trees.

That night I was awakened by soft sounds outside my window. I reached for Big Ma, but she wasn't there. Hurrying to the window, I saw Mama and Big Ma standing in the yard in their nightclothes and Stacey, fully dressed, sitting atop Lady, our golden mare. By the time I got outside, Stacey was gone.

"Mama, where's Stacey?" I cried.

"Be quiet, Cassie. You'll wake Christopher-John and Little Man."

"But where's he going?"

"He's going to get Papa," Mama said. "Now be quiet."

"Go on, Stacey, boy," I whispered. "Ride for me, too."

As the dust billowed after him, Mama said, "I should've gone myself. He's so young."

Big Ma put her arm around Mama. "Now, Mary, you know you couldn't've gone. Mr. Andersen would miss you if he come by and see you ain't here. You done right, now. Don't worry, that boy'll be just fine."

Three days passed, hot and windless.

Mama forbade any of us to go into the forest, so Christopher-John, Little Man, and I spent the slow, restless days hovering as close to the dusty road as we dared, listening to the foreign sounds of steel against the trees and the thunderous roar of those ancient loved ones as they crashed upon the earth. Sometimes Mama would scold us and tell us to come back to the house, but even she could not ignore the continuous pounding of the axes against the trees.

WORDS TO OWN

curtly (kurt'lē) *adv.*: rudely and with few words.

D **Elements of Literature**
Theme
? Why is Mama standing up to Mr. Andersen? [Possible responses: She wants him to know that she won't give in to his threats and bullying. She is telling him that she won't let him cheat her family.]

E **Reading Skills and Strategies**
Drawing Conclusions
? What kind of person is Mr. Andersen? What evidence did you use to draw your conclusion? [Possible responses: Mr. Andersen is greedy, racially prejudiced, and potentially violent. He threatens David in order to scare the family into giving him what he wants—the right to cut down and sell their trees for profit.]

F **Struggling Readers**
Summarizing
Read aloud this important scene in which Stacey is sent off to bring his father home. Have students visualize the scene as you read. Then, have them summarize what has just taken place. [Possible summary: Cassie wakes up when she hears voices outside in the night. She sees her mother and grandmother outside in their nightclothes and Stacey mounted on a horse. She goes outside to find out what is going on and learns that Stacey is being sent secretly to bring their father home.]

Drawing Conclusions

? Notice Mama's warm response to Cassie's worried questions. What conclusions can you draw about their relationship based on their conversation and your own knowledge? [Possible responses: They have a close, nurturing relationship. They show concern for each other.]

B Elements of Literature

Theme

? Cassie feels that the trees had once made her "feel safe and secure," not only because of their strength but also because of their age. What scenes from the past does she connect with the trees? How did the trees offer comfort to other people? [Possible response: She associates the trees with other groups of "outsiders"—people who have lost their lands. She imagines Native Americans sitting around fires, telling happy tales of their past, and fugitive slaves hiding in the forest, thinking of their faraway homelands.]

C Appreciating language

Subject-Verb Agreement

Explain to students that the dialogue reflects the way people of that place and time actually spoke and is not grammatical. Point out, for example, the ungrammatical use of *me and Christopher-John* and the spelling of *wanna* that shows how Little Big Man pronounced *want to*. Then ask students to explain why *"You and Cassie was in the forest"* is not grammatically correct. [The singular verb *was* does not agree with its plural subject, *You and Cassie*.]

Or the sight of the loaded lumber wagons rolling out of the forest. In the middle of washing or ironing or hoeing, she would look up sorrowfully and listen, then turn toward the road, searching for some sign of Papa and Stacey.

On the fourth day, before the sun had risen, bringing its cloak of miserable heat, I saw her walking alone toward the woods. I ran after her.

She did not send me back.

"Mama," I said. "How sick are you?"

Mama took my hand. "Remember when you had the flu and felt so sick?"

"Yes'm."

"And when I gave you some medicine, you got well soon afterward?"

"Yes'm."

"Well, that's how sick I am. As soon as I get my medicine, I'll be all well again. And that'll be soon, now that Papa's coming home," she said, giving my hand a gentle little squeeze.

The quiet surrounded us as we entered the forest. Mama clicked on the flashlight, and we walked silently along the cow path to the pond. There, just beyond the pond, pockets of open space loomed before us.

"Mama!"

"I know, baby, I know."

On the ground lay countless trees. Trees that had once been such strong, tall things. So strong that I could fling my arms partially around one of them and feel safe and secure. So tall and leafy green that their boughs had formed a forest temple.

And old.

So old that Indians had once built fires at their feet and had sung happy songs of happy days. So old they had hidden fleeing black men in the night and listened to their sad tales of a foreign land.

In the cold of winter, when the ground lay frozen, they had sung their frosty ballads of years gone by. Or on a muggy, sweat-drenched day, their leaves had rippled softly, lazily, like restless green fingers strumming at a guitar, echoing their epic tales.

But now they would sing no more. They lay forever silent upon the ground.

Those trees that remained standing were like defeated warriors mourning their fallen dead. But soon they, too, would fall, for the white X's had been placed on nearly every one.

"Oh, dear, dear trees," I cried as the gray light of the rising sun fell in ghostly shadows over the land. The tears rolled hot down my cheeks. Mama held me close, and when I felt her body tremble, I knew she was crying too.

When our tears eased, we turned sadly toward the house. As we emerged from the forest, we could see two small figures waiting impatiently on the other side of the road. As soon as they spied us, they hurried across to meet us.

"Mama! You and Cassie was in the forest," Little Man accused. "Big Ma told us!"

"How was it?" asked Christopher-John, rubbing the sleep from his eyes. "Was it spooky?"

"Spooky and empty," I said listlessly.

"Mama, me and Christopher-John wanna see too," Little Man declared.

"No, baby," Mama said softly as we crossed the road. "The men'll be done there soon, and I don't want y'all underfoot."

"But, Mama——" Little Man started to protest.

"When Papa comes home and the men are gone, then you can go. But until then, you stay out of there. You hear me, Little Man Logan?"

"Yes'm," Little Man reluctantly replied.

But the sun had been up only an hour when Little Man decided that he could not wait for Papa to return.

"Mama said we wasn't to go down there," Christopher-John warned.

"Cassie did," Little Man cried.

"But she was with Mama. Wasn't you, Cassie?"

"Well, I'm going too," said Little Man. "Every-

Skill Link

Identifying Subjects and Verbs

You might want to use the following exercise before you teach the Language Link exercise on subject-verb agreement on p. 44. This exercise will help you assess your students' skill in identifying subjects and their verbs.

Activity

Identify the subject and the verb in each of the following sentences.

1. The song of the trees sounds beautiful to Cassie.
2. Cassie and her brothers play in the woods.
3. Neither Cassie nor Little Man wants to stay out of the woods.
4. Neither Cassie nor her parents want the trees to be cut down.
5. One of the lumbermen tries to help the children.

RESPONDING TO THE ART

Use this illustration to teach students how artists create the illusion of distance and depth by means of perspective.

Activity. Have students describe what they see in this illustration. How does the artist emphasize the fallen trees? Then, ask students to compare the details in the illustration with the descriptions in the story. Have them evaluate the artist's success in capturing the powerful emotional effect of the scene on p. 36.

A Appreciating Language
Compound Words
Point out that *lumbermen* is a compound word formed from the two words *lumber* and *men*. Traditionally, the word *man* or *men* added to the end of another word has indicated the meaning "a person involved with or engaged in the business of." Explain that today, given that men and women share all kinds of work, the ending *-man* is being replaced by other endings or by words that do not suggest male or female roles. The word *lumbermen,* for instance is being replaced by *loggers*.

B Reading Skills and Strategies

Making Generalizations
❓ Cassie defends Little Man and Christopher-John defends Cassie. What do their actions say about close, loving families in general? [Possible responses: Brothers and sisters will defend each other at any cost. Family members pull together when an outsider threatens one of them.]

C Reading Skills and Strategies
Responding to the Text
❓ What do you think of Tom? [Possible responses: He has a sense of humor; he probably doesn't like or respect Mr. Andersen.] Ask students to go back and find other details about Tom that show him to be sympathetic to the Logans.

D Elements of Literature
Theme
❓ Why do Cassie and Christopher-John risk being hurt, even though they probably know they can't win against grown men? [Possible responses: They will take any risk to try to protect a member of the family; they know they are in the right and the men are unwelcome intruders on the family's property.]

---

body's always going someplace 'cepting me." And off he went.

Christopher-John and I ran after him. Down the narrow cow path and around the pond we chased. But neither of us was fast enough to **A** overtake Little Man before he reached the lumbermen.

"Hey, you kids, get away from here," Mr. Andersen shouted when he saw us. "Now, y'all go on back home," he said, stopping in front of Little Man.

"We are home," I said. "You're the one who's on our land."

"Claude," Mr. Andersen said to one of the black lumbermen, "take these kids home." Then he pushed Little Man out of his way. Little Man pushed back. Mr. Andersen looked down, startled that a little black boy would do such a thing. He shoved Little Man a second time, and Little Man fell into the dirt.

Little Man looked down at his clothing covered with sawdust and dirt and wailed, "You got my clothes dirty!"

I rushed toward Mr. Andersen, my fist in a mighty hammer, shouting, "You ain't got no right to push on Little Man. Why don't you push on somebody your own size—like me, you ole——"

The man called Claude put his hand over my mouth and carried me away. Christopher-John trailed behind us, tugging on the man's shirt.

"Put her down. Hey, mister, put Cassie down."

The man carried me all the way to the pond. "Now," he said, "you and your brothers get on home before y'all get hurt. Go on, get!"

As the man walked away, I looked around. **B** "Where's Little Man?"

Christopher-John looked around too.

"I don't know," he said. "I thought he was behind me."

Back we ran toward the lumbermen.

We found Little Man's clothing first, folded neatly by a tree. Then we saw Little Man, drag-

38 OUT HERE ON MY OWN

---

ging a huge stick and headed straight for Mr. Andersen.

"Little Man, come back here," I called.

But Little Man did not stop.

Mr. Andersen stood alone, barking orders, unaware of the oncoming Little Man.

"Little Man! Oh, Little Man, don't!"

It was too late.

Little Man swung the stick as hard as he could against Mr. Andersen's leg.

Mr. Andersen let out a howl and reached to where he thought Little Man's collar was. But, of course, Little Man had no collar.

"Run, Man!" Christopher-John and I shouted. "Run!"

"Why, you little . . ." Mr. Andersen cried, grabbing at Little Man. But Little Man was too **C** quick for him. He slid right through Mr. Andersen's legs. Tom stood nearby, his face crinkling into an amused grin.

"Hey, y'all!" Mr. Andersen yelled to the lumbermen. "Claude! Get that kid!"

But sure-footed Little Man dodged the groping hands of the lumbermen as easily as if he were <u>skirting</u> mud puddles. Over tree stumps, around legs, and through legs he dashed. But in the end, there were too many lumbermen for him, and he was handed over to Mr. Andersen.

For the second time, Christopher-John and I went to Little Man's rescue.

"Put him down!" we ordered, charging the lumbermen.

I was captured much too quickly, though not **D** before I had landed several stinging blows. But Christopher-John, furious at seeing Little Man handled so roughly by Mr. Andersen, managed to <u>elude</u> the clutches of the lumbermen until he was fully upon Mr. Andersen. Then, with his mightiest thrust, he kicked Mr. Andersen

---

WORDS TO OWN
skirting *v.:* narrowly avoiding.
elude (ē·lōōd′) *v.:* escape by quickness or cleverness.

Getting Students Involved

Cooperative Learning
Tableaux. Dramatic moments in the story lend themselves to the creation of frozen scenes, or tableaux. Possible scenes include Mr. Andersen approaching Big Ma and Mama about buying the forest; Little Man being captured; the children waiting to be whipped.

Activity
Choose students to play the parts for each scene. Have them "set" the scene and freeze in position until a leader taps one of them. That person must speak "in character," telling what he or she is thinking at that moment. Continue until each character has had a chance to speak.

Crossing the Curriculum

Local History
Research. Point out to students how Cassie draws together the trees and the history of the peoples who have lived in the forest (p. 36). She paints a vivid picture of Native Americans celebrating beneath the trees, and later, of African Americans seeking safety under their cover. Have students research the history of their own town or neighborhood and write a brief imaginative description of the place at one point in the past.

solidly in the shins, not once, but twice, before the lumbermen pulled him away.

Mr. Andersen was fuming. He slowly took off his wide leather belt. Christopher-John, Little Man, and I looked woefully at the belt, then at each other. Little Man and Christopher-John fought to escape, but I closed my eyes and awaited the whining of the heavy belt and its painful bite against my skin.

What was he waiting for? I started to open my eyes, but then the zinging whirl of the belt began and I tensed, awaiting its fearful sting. But just as the leather tip lashed into my leg, a deep, familiar voice said, "Put the belt down, Andersen."

I opened my eyes.

"Papa!"

"Let the children go," Papa said. He was standing on a nearby ridge with a strange black box in his hands. Stacey was behind him, holding the reins to Lady.

The chopping stopped as all eyes turned to Papa.

"They been right meddlesome," Mr. Andersen said. "They need teaching how to act."

"Any teaching, I'll do it. Now, let them go."

Mr. Andersen looked down at Little Man struggling to get away. Smiling broadly, he motioned our release. "Okay, David," he said.

As we ran up the ridge to Papa, Mr. Andersen said, "It's good to have you home, boy."

Papa said nothing until we were safely behind him. "Take them home, Stacey."

"But, Papa——"

"Do like I say, son."

Stacey herded us away from the men. When we were far enough away so Papa couldn't see us, Stacey stopped and handed me Lady's reins.

"Y'all go on home now," he said. "I gotta go help Papa."

"Papa don't need no help," I said. "He told you to come with us."

"But you don't know what he's gonna do."

"What?" I asked.

"He's gonna blow up the forest if they don't get out of here. So go on home where y'all be safe."

"How's he gonna do that?" asked Little Man.

"We been setting sticks of dynamite since the middle of the night. We ain't even been up to the house cause Papa wanted the sticks planted and covered over before the men came. Now, Cassie, take them on back to the house. Do like I tell you for once, will ya?" Then, without waiting for another word, he was gone.

"I wanna see," Little Man announced.

"I don't," protested Christopher-John.

"Come on," I said.

We tied the mare to a tree, then belly-crawled back to where we could see Papa and joined Stacey in the brush.

"Cassie, I told you . . ."

"What's Papa doing?"

The black box was now set upon a sawed-off tree stump, and Papa's hands were tightly grasping a T-shaped instrument which went into it.

"What's that thing?" asked Little Man.

"It's a plunger," Stacey whispered. "If Papa presses down on it, the whole forest will go *pffffff*!"

Our mouths went dry and our eyes went wide. Mr. Andersen's eyes were wide, too.

"You're bluffing, David," he said. "You ain't gonna push that plunger."

"One thing you can't seem to understand, Andersen," Papa said, "is that a black man's always gotta be ready to die. And it don't make me any difference if I die today or tomorrow. Just as long as I die right."

E **Reading Skills and Strategies**
Making Predictions
Have students predict what the "strange black box" is and how Papa might be planning to use it to save the trees.

F **Struggling Readers**
Finding Details
Ask students to find details suggesting that Mr. Andersen is afraid of Papa but considers himself superior to Papa. [Possible response: Mr. Andersen obeys Papa's demand to let the children go, but then he addresses Papa as "boy," a glaring insult to a grown man.]

G **Elements of Literature**
Conflict
❓ What advantage does Papa have in his conflict with Mr. Andersen? [Possible responses: Papa is holding the plunger, and seems ready to carry out his threat to destroy the forest and the people in it; Mr. Andersen can't be sure that David is bluffing.]

H **Elements of Literature**
Theme
❓ What do you think David means by "Just as long as I die right"? [Possible responses: He means that he can accept death if it comes as the result of his doing the right thing and defending something he loves. He means that he will not let himself back down out of fear and cowardice.]

Responding to the Text

? Knowing what you know about Papa and his family, do you think that he is "crazy"? Explain why you feel the way you do. [Possible responses: Papa seems intelligent, courageous and calm; he seems willing to do anything to protect his family's land and honor. David must be crazy to take such an extreme risk; if he dies, his family will be without a breadwinner.]

B Elements of Literature

Theme

? How has David won his self-respect? [Possible responses: He has not crumbled under Mr. Andersen's threats but has stood up to him; he has defended his family and property.]

C Reading Skills and Strategies

Responding to the Text

? Does it surprise you that Papa knows about the singing trees? [Possible response: Yes, only moments before, he was prepared to blow up the forest in order to defend his family and his land. This gentleness and sensitivity is unexpected. Papa must be a complex character.]

Mr. Andersen laughed uneasily. The lumbermen moved nervously away.

"I mean what I say," Papa said. "Ask anyone. I always mean what I say."

"He sure do, Mr. Andersen," Claude said, eyeing the black box. "He always do."

"Shut up!" Mr. Andersen snapped. "And the rest of y'all stay put." Then turning back to Papa, he smiled cunningly. "I'm sure you and me can work something out, David."

"Ain't nothing to be worked out," said Papa.

"Now, look here, David, your mama and me, we got us a contract. . . ."

"There ain't no more contract," Papa replied coldly. "Now, either you get out or I blow it up. That's it."

A "He means it, Mr. Andersen," another frightened lumberman ventured. "He's crazy and he sure 'nough means it."

"You know what could happen to you, boy?" Mr. Andersen exploded, his face beet red again. "Threatening a white man like this?"

Papa said nothing. He just stood there, his hands firmly on the plunger, staring down at Mr. Andersen.

Mr. Andersen could not bear the stare. He turned away, cursing Papa. "You're a fool, David. A crazy fool." Then he looked around at the lumbermen. They shifted their eyes and would not look at him.

"Maybe we better leave, Mr. Andersen," Tom said quietly.

Mr. Andersen glanced at Tom, then turned back to Papa and said as lightly as he could, "All **C** right, David, all right. It's your land. We'll just take the logs we got cut and get out." He motioned to the men. "Hey, let's get moving and get these logs out of here before this crazy fool gets us all killed."

"No," Papa said.

Mr. Andersen stopped, knowing that he could not have heard correctly. "What you say?"

"You ain't taking one more stick out of this forest."

"Now, look here——"

"You heard me."

"But you can't sell all these logs, David," Mr. Andersen exclaimed incredulously.

Papa said nothing. Just cast that piercing look on Mr. Andersen.

"Look, I'm a fair man. I tell you what I'll do. I'll give you another thirty-five dollars. An even hundred dollars. Now, that's fair, ain't it?"

"I'll see them rot first."

"But——"

B "That's my last word," Papa said, tightening his grip on the plunger.

Mr. Andersen swallowed hard. "You won't always have that black box, David," he warned. "You know that, don't you?"

"That may be. But it won't matter none. Cause I'll always have my self-respect."

Mr. Andersen opened his mouth to speak, but no sound came. Tom and the lumbermen were quietly moving away, putting their gear in the empty lumber wagons. Mr. Andersen looked again at the black box. Finally, his face ashen, he too walked away.

Papa stood unmoving until the wagons and the men were gone. Then, when the sound of the last wagon rolling over the dry leaves could no longer be heard and a hollow silence filled the air, he slowly removed his hands from the plunger and looked up at the remaining trees standing like lonely sentries in the morning.

"Dear, dear old trees," I heard him call softly, "will you ever sing again?"

I waited. But the trees gave no answer.

WORDS TO OWN

incredulously (in·krej′oo·ləs·lē) *adv.*: unbelievingly.
ashen (ash′ən) *adj.*: pale.
sentries (sen′trēz) *n.*: guards.

Assessing Learning

Check Test: Short Answer

1. Why does Mama scold Christopher-John at the beginning of the story? [He has eaten all the cornbread during the night.]

2. What is Mama hiding from the children? [She is sick and needs medicine.]

3. How do the children know that something is wrong in the forest? [Cassie suspects something because the trees stop "singing." Then they see that the trees are marked with mysterious white X's.]

4. What does Mr. Andersen want with the trees? [To cut them down and sell them.]

5. How does Papa save the forest? [He threatens to blow it up with dynamite.]

Standardized Test Preparation

For practice with standardized test format specific to this selection, see
- *Standardized Test Preparation,* p. 12

For practice in proofreading and editing, see
- *Daily Oral Grammar,* Transparency 2

MEET THE WRITER

"We Were Somebody..."

Mildred D. Taylor (1943–   ) grew up in Toledo, Ohio. In high school she was an honor student, a newspaper editor, and a class officer—but, she says, she wasn't able to do what she really wanted: be a cheerleader.

Every summer she and her family visited Mississippi relatives, and she listened to their stories. By the time she was nine or ten, she knew that she wanted to write.

66 I wanted to show a Black family united in love and pride, of which the reader would like to be a part. 99

Her first effort, *Song of the Trees*, introduced the Logan family and won first prize in the African American category of a competition for children's books. In 1977, when she accepted the Newbery Award for her second work about the Logan family, *Roll of Thunder, Hear My Cry*, Taylor talked about her father:

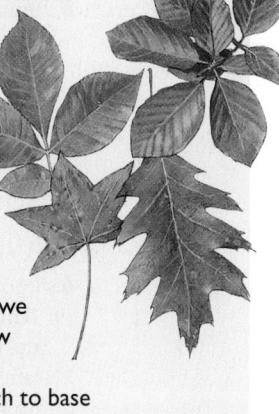

66 Throughout my childhood he impressed upon my sister and me that we were somebody, that we were important and could do anything we set our minds to do or be. He was not the kind of father who demanded A's on our report cards. He was more concerned about how we carried ourselves, how we respected ourselves and others, and how we pursued the principles upon which he hoped we would build our lives. He was constantly reminding us that how we saw ourselves was far more important than how others saw us. . . .

If the Logans seem real, it is because I had my own family upon which to base characterizations. Through David Logan have come the words of my father, and through the Logan family the love of my own family. If people are touched by the warmth of the Logans, it is because I had the warmth of my own youthful years from which to draw. And if people believe the book to be biographical, it is because I have tried to distill the essence of Black life, so familiar to most Black families, to make the Logans an embodiment of that spiritual heritage. 99

More of Mildred Taylor's Heritage

You can rejoin Cassie Logan and her family in the novels *Let the Circle Be Unbroken* (Bantam) and *The Road to Memphis* (Puffin).

BROWSING IN THE FILES

A Critic's Comment. Christine McDonnell comments, "Through these books, Taylor draws us into the circle of an inspiring Black family, nourishes us with their strength and love, and shows us their sustaining traditions, heritage, and community. Writing simply and directly, with graceful, fluid descriptions and sharp dialogue, Taylor gives us much that is needed in these times: hard truth, deep love, dignity in the face of oppression, and warmth and humor rooted in compassion."

Writers on Writing. Many authors choose personal lessons as the subjects for their work. Mildred Taylor is no exception. "From as far back as I can remember," she says, "my father taught me a different history from the one I learned in school. . . . There was often humor in his stories, sometimes pathos, and frequently tragedy; but always the people were graced with a simple dignity that elevated them from the ordinary to the heroic." Discuss how parents and other relatives can provide valuable lessons from their own experience.

MAKING MEANINGS

First Thoughts

1. Possible responses: Papa's confrontation with Mr. Andersen; Papa's appearing just in time to save the children from Mr. Andersen; Little Man's attack on Mr. Andersen; Cassie's view of the ruined forest.

Shaping Interpretations

2. Sample passages: Cassie and her mother going to see the damage to the forest (p. 36), and the end of the story, when Papa speaks to the trees (p. 40). Cassie loves the trees because they are beautiful and old. She thinks of them as friends.
3. Possible responses: Mama, because she must raise the children and cope with daily problems without her husband's help. Papa, because he stands alone against Mr. Andersen. Both respond to the challenge with courage, pride, and dignity.
4. "Hissed venomously" suggests that he is like a snake. Students might feel he is evil or dangerous and express dislike or anger toward him.
5. Answers will vary. Since Cassie's father was away from home, he would not have firsthand knowledge of many of the events Cassie describes. However, the reader would know more about the father's inner thoughts and feelings.

Connecting with the Text

6. Answers may vary. Students should point to the scene on the porch in which Mr. Andersen has his first confrontation with the family members. The family does not have the means to obtain legal help. Mr. Andersen is a wealthy and influential person. When Papa resolves to blow up the trees rather than let them be destroyed by the loggers, Mr. Andersen withdraws his offer and leaves the property alone.
7. Answers will vary. Students may describe their homes, places they moved from, or foreign homelands.
8. Answers will vary. Students may change their opinions of statement 1 because of David's behavior, of 2 and 3 because of Mr. Andersen's behavior and words, of 4 because of Cassie's musings about the trees.
9. Students may base their decision on how badly they needed the money. If their family needed medical care to survive, for example, they might sacrifice the land.

T42

MAKING MEANINGS

First Thoughts

[respond]

1. What scene from the story do you remember most vividly?

Shaping Interpretations

[infer]

2. Cassie gives the trees human characteristics, describing them as if they could talk and sing. Find two passages in the story where the trees seem human. Why do you think Cassie loves her trees so much?

[analyze]

3. Which character in this story is "out there on his or her own"? How does this person deal with the problem confronting him or her?

[infer]

4. When you read on page 35 that Mr. Andersen "hissed venomously," what are you reminded of? How do you feel about Mr. Andersen's behavior?

[speculate]

5. "Song of the Trees" is told by Cassie. How would the story be different if it were told by her father?

Connecting with the Text

[analyze]

6. Look at the story map that you made for the Reading Check on this page. **Analyze** the **plot** by thinking about its major parts. At what point does the main conflict begin, and who is involved in the struggle? What problems make it difficult for Cassie and her family to resolve the conflict? How do they finally solve their problems?

[connect]

7. Have you ever felt as strongly about a place as Cassie feels about her forest? Describe that special place.

[evaluate]

8. Go back to the statements you rated on page 28. Individually and with the class, rate the four statements again, using the same scale. Have any of your opinions changed now that you've read the story?

[connect]

9. Suppose you needed money but the only valuable thing you owned was a beautiful piece of land that had been home to your family for generations. Would you sell this land to be more comfortable for a time? Why or why not?

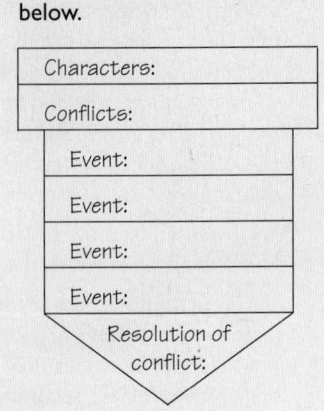

Reading Check

Create a story map for the **plot** of "Song of the Trees." Copy and fill in the diagram below.

| Characters: |
| Conflicts: |
| Event: |
| Event: |
| Event: |
| Event: |
| Resolution of conflict: |

Reading Check

The following is an example. Answers will vary.

- **Characters:** Papa, Cassie, Big Ma, Mama, Stacey, Christopher-John, Little Man, Mr. Andersen.
- **Conflict:** The Logans versus Mr. Andersen.
- **Event:** The Logan children see trees marked with X's.
- **Event:** Mr. Andersen offers sixty-five dollars to Big Ma.
- **Event:** Stacey goes to get Papa.
- **Event:** Papa threatens to blow up the forest.
- **Resolution of Conflict:** Mr. Andersen backs off and leaves.

CHOICES: Building Your Portfolio

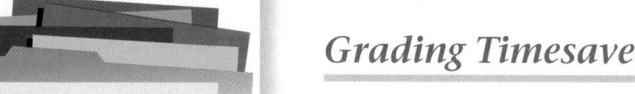

Writer's Notebook

1. Collecting Ideas for a Story

Taylor says that in writing "Song of the Trees," she "drew upon people and places I had known all my life." In creating the character of Cassie, for example, she drew on the personalities of her sister and an aunt. Do you know anyone about whom you could write a story? Create a character based partly on a real person (or on a combination of people). Then, think of a problem, real or imaginary, for your character to solve.

> **Name:** Martita
> **Age:** 13
> **Personality:** reliable, shy, softhearted
> **Problem:** Her dad died. She wants to convince her mom to let her adopt a skinny stray cat.

Stating a Theme

2. What Did the Main Characters Learn?

Theme, as you learned earlier (pages 23 and 28), is the *meaning* of a story. Theme points to what the main characters learned in the story, and to what *you* learned as you shared their experiences.

In a paragraph, state what you think the theme of this story is. Remember that no two statements of theme will be alike. Share your ideas on theme with the class.

Music

3. Sound Decisions

A movie's soundtrack does more than just fill the time between conversations. It establishes a mood and, with repeated hearings, may even remind moviegoers of a movie's theme. If you were creating the soundtrack for a film version of Taylor's work, what music would you use for the song of the trees that Cassie hears: an African American folk song or spiritual? a popular song of the 1930s? classical music that suggests the beauty of nature? Play a recording of the music you select, and explain to the class why you think it sings the song of the trees.

Science/Art

4. Trees' Company

Cassie Logan plays among "shaggy-bark hickories and sharp-needled pines, . . . blue-gray beeches and sturdy black walnuts." Imagine taking a class hike through Cassie's forest. With three or four classmates, research some of the trees you might expect to see. (Leaves from several kinds of trees mentioned in the story are used as illustrations.) Using heavy paper, make a fact sheet for each kind of tree. Show a picture of the tree, its leaves, and its seeds, and give hikers some information about it. Post your fact sheets around the room and lead an in-class "nature hike."

SONG OF THE TREES

SONG OF THE TREES 43

Grading Timesaver

Rubrics for each choices assignment appear on p. 107 in the *Portfolio Management System*.

CHOICES: Building Your Portfolio

1. **Writer's Notebook** Remind students to save their work. They may use it as prewriting for the Writer's Workshop on pp. 94–99.
2. **Stating a Theme** Before students begin writing their paragraphs, suggest they jot down what Cassie might have learned from the events described in the story. Then, have students jot down notes on what they themselves learned from Cassie's experience.
3. **Music** Read the passage about the song of the trees on p. 31, and then model the activity by playing a music selection of your choice. While listening to each recording, students should jot down a few notes about how the music makes them feel and what it makes them think of. Students should share their responses.
4. **Science/Art** Students can find more information about trees and tree preservation by searching the World Wide Web, using a directory or search engine and the key word *forestry*. Preview any Internet activity that you suggest to students. Because these resources are sometimes public forums, their content can be unpredictable.

SONG OF THE TREES 43

SONG OF THE TREES 43

GRAMMAR LINK

Have students choose a piece of writing from their portfolios. Ask them to write *S* for singular and *P* for plural above all subjects and verbs. If they find any subjects and verbs that do not agree, they should look up the rule that applies to the situation.

Try It Out
Answers

The most important moments in this story *come* when Papa and Mr. Andersen meet along the ridge. Mr. Andersen tries to scare and bribe Cassie's father, but neither threats nor the promise of money *moves* Papa. Mr. Andersen, in front of his workers, *backs* down and *leaves*.

VOCABULARY

1. *Finicky* is more extreme than *careful; finicky* implies excess.
2. A *dispute* and a *brawl* are both arguments, but a *brawl* is noisier.
3. *Ambled* means "walked unhurriedly."
4. *Delved* suggests diligent search.
5. *Curtly* implies rudeness.
6. *Skirting* suggests avoidance.
7. To *elude* is to escape in a clever way.
8. *Incredulously* implies disbelief; *doubtfully* refers to uncertainty.
9. *Creamy* implies health; *ashen* suggests sickliness.
10. *Sentries* are guards or soldiers.

Resources ————

Grammar
• *Grammar and Language Links,* p. 3

Vocabulary
• *Words to Own,* p. 2

Spelling
For related instruction, see
• *Spelling and Decoding,* p. 2

Using Reference Aids to Clarify Usage
Students who need help in distinguishing the shades of meaning of these vocabulary words may find clues to their usage in a dictionary, thesaurus, or synonym finder. Students should turn to p. 701 for an example of the way synonyms are listed in a dictionary.

GRAMMAR LINK MINI-LESSON

Subject-Verb Agreement Is Unanimous!

Language Handbook HELP

See Problems in Agreement, page 721.

Technology HELP

See Language Workshop CD-ROM. Key word entry: subject-verb agreement.

Probably the most common error people make in writing (and in speaking) is in subject-verb agreement. The rule is simple: Subjects and their verbs must always agree—that is, a singular subject takes a singular verb, and a plural subject takes a plural verb. The problem comes with identifying the subject and deciding whether it's singular or plural.

EXAMPLES

1. Either Cassie or her brother has/have entered the woods. [Singular subjects joined by *or* or *nor* take a singular verb.]

2. Neither Mr. Andersen nor his workers know/knows what to do with Little Man. [When a singular and a plural subject are joined by *or* or *nor*, the verb agrees with the subject closer to the verb.]

3. The pounding of axes echo/echoes sadly through their woods. [The number of the subject is not changed by a phrase following the subject.]

Try It Out

As the editor of the paragraph below, rewrite the text to correct errors in subject-verb agreement.

The most important moments in this story comes when Papa and Mr. Andersen meet along the ridge. Mr. Andersen tries to scare and bribe Cassie's father, but neither threats nor the promise of money move Papa. Mr. Andersen, in front of his workers, back down and leave.

VOCABULARY HOW TO OWN A WORD

WORD BANK

finicky
dispute
ambled
delved
curtly
skirting
elude
incredulously
ashen
sentries

Connotations: What's the Difference Between . . .

Would you rather be described as *curious* or *nosy*? The two words have the same basic meaning, or **denotation,** but different connotations. **Connotations** are the feelings and associations that have come to be attached to certain words. Most people wouldn't mind being called curious, but *nosy* suggests putting your nose into other people's business.

Test your skills at recognizing shades of meaning. What's the difference between . . .

1. *finicky* and *careful*?
2. a *dispute* and a *brawl*?
3. *ambled* and *walked*?
4. *delved* and *looked for*?
5. *matter-of-factly* and *curtly*?

6. *passing* and *skirting*?
7. *escape* and *elude*?
8. *incredulously* and *doubtfully*?
9. *creamy* and *ashen*?
10. *watchers* and *sentries*?

Grammar Link Quick Check

Choose the correct verb form.
1. "Song of the Trees" was/were Mildred D. Taylor's first short story. [was]
2. My sister and I travel/travels to Mississippi every summer. [travel]
3. Neither Cassie nor her brothers see/sees the trees being cut. [see]
4. According to Cassie, the trees sing/sings to her. [sing]
5. Either Mama or Big Ma make/makes the cornbread. [makes]

Reading Skills and Strategies

Booking space on the Net: Used booksellers take a page from other on-line readers

OBJECTIVES
1. Understand metacognition as a thinking process
2. Monitor reactions to a text before, during, and after reading

METACOGNITION: THINKING ABOUT THINKING

What do readers do when they read a story? Here are some responses:

- "I always count the pages to see how long it is."

- "I sort of look through the story to see whether the words are hard or easy to read. If they're hard, I know I'll have to spend a little more time reading it."

- "Sometimes if I don't understand something, I just keep reading to see if the rest of the story explains it. Other times I just ask someone."

The readers are engaged in a process called **metacognition**. This word comes from Greek and Latin roots: *Meta-* is a prefix that comes from Greek and means "along with" or "beyond," and *cognition* comes from the Latin word for "knowing." So *metacognition* just means "thinking about thinking." Here are a few study strategies to help you practice metacognition.

Before Reading: Preview

Flip through the pages of the story, and look at the illustrations. Then, ask yourself these questions:

- What does the story seem to be about?

- Do I see any difficult words as I look through the story?

During Reading: Question, Reread, and Record

Be aware of your reactions to the story as you are reading. Strike up a dialogue with the text by asking questions and making observations along the way.

- Ask yourself if you understand everything that has happened so far. If your answer is no, reread the sections you found difficult or talk about what's happening with a friend who's also reading the story.

- Are you bothered by anything in the story? Does a particular event or statement seem especially meaningful to you? Record

ideas and details that seem important.

After Reading: Reflect

Take a few minutes to think about your reactions to the story.

- Decide how you feel about the story. Did you like it as much as you thought you would? Did you like it better?

- Were you asked to complete an assignment after reading the story? Which of your responses and reflections can help with the assignment?

There. You are now using metacognition.

Hmmm

Apply the strategy on the next page. ➤

Reading Skills and Strategies

This feature focuses on metacognition, a strategy used by readers to examine how they think. Students will have the opportunity to practice this strategy while they read the next selection, "The Smallest Dragonboy."

Mini-Lesson: Metacognition

To give students a different perspective on the strategy of metacognition, ask them to think about how they or their parents choose a videotape. Do they look at the cover only, or do they read the description that is found on the back? What do they do while watching the tape? Do they stop it and talk about some scenes, or do they watch it straight through? Do they replay any scenes? After the film, do they talk about what they liked? Point out to students that prereading a story is very similar to choosing a video, and tell them that some of the same things they do during and after watching the film can be applied to reading a short story. Have the class preview the next selection in this collection together.

Reaching All Students

Struggling Readers

Use peer response groups of three or four to help students summarize ideas. Have them create a Spider Webbing graph by listing (when they read the story) elements from "The Smallest Dragonboy," on pp. 47–59, that are puzzling, confusing, or interesting. Then, they should rephrase each idea as a question. Each group should choose the question that is most important to it and write that question at the center of a large sheet of paper. Students should write

answers and more questions around the original question—building a web around it. Groups should share their webs.

Advanced Learners

First, ask students to analyze the page and to try to find a general purpose for each of the three reading phases. Example:
- Before: Preview subject, reading level
- During: Keep track of plot, reactions, words
- After: Summarize plot, reactions, goals

Then, have students work independently to create one more strategy (like the ones on the page) for each of the three phases (before, during, after). Ask them to have partners evaluate and rate their strategies (great, good, or just OK).

T45

OBJECTIVES
1. Read and interpret the story
2. Use metacognition to monitor one's own reading
3. Express understanding through narrative and creative writing, science, speaking and listening, or music
4. Identify and use consistent verb tenses
5. Understand and use new words

SKILLS
Reading
- Use metacognition

Writing
- Create character and conflict

Grammar/Language
- Use consistent verb tenses

Vocabulary
- Understand and use new words

Music
- Write and perform a song

Science/Speaking and Listening
- Research and present science facts

Viewing/Representing
- Relate details in a painting to a story (ATE)
- Evaluate an artist's depiction of characters (ATE)

Planning

- **Block Schedule**
  Block Scheduling Lesson Plans with Pacing Guide
- **Traditional Schedule**
  Lesson Plans Including Strategies for English-Language Learners
- **One-Stop Planner**
  CD-ROM with Test Generator

Before You Read

THE SMALLEST DRAGONBOY

Make the Connection

Underdogs

If anyone can say "I'm out here on my own," it's an underdog. An underdog is supposed to be a loser—so when an underdog unexpectedly wins, say, in football, sportscasters and fans make a big fuss. In fact, most of us love to see underdogs win—maybe because in some ways we identify with them.

Quickwrite

Anne McCaffrey's brother Kevin was the inspiration for "The Smallest Dragonboy." As a twelve-year-old, Kevin suffered from a painful bone disease. He seemed to be marked as an underdog, but his courage made him the model for Keevan in the story. Quickwrite about someone you know who was an underdog but unexpectedly triumphed.

Reading Skills and Strategies

Metacognition: Thinking About Your Thinking

When you read "The Smallest Dragonboy," you'll enter the imaginary world of Pern. As you explore this new world, ask yourself questions and make observations. Jot down your thoughts as they occur to you.

When you finish the story, reconsider your questions and observations. What new questions come to mind that did not occur to you earlier, as you were reading? Take a moment to reflect on what you've read and what you're thinking.

For other hints on making reading a thought-provoking process, see page 45.

Background

Literature and Science

"The Smallest Dragonboy" takes place on the planet Pern, an imaginary world somewhere in outer space. Pern is threatened by the dangerous Red Star, which rains deadly threadlike plant spores on the planet every two hundred years or so. If the hungry Thread falls on Pern soil and grows there, it will devour every living thing.

To protect their planet, colonists on Pern have bioengineered a race of great winged dragons. When fed a special rock called firestone, the dragons breathe flames that char Thread to ashes. During Threadfall the dragons and their dragonriders charge into battle in midair while the other colonists hide safely in their cave towns. During periods of Threadfall, the protectors of Pern live inside the cones of old volcanoes in cave colonies called Weyrs.

As the story opens, young candidates for dragonrider in Benden Weyr, a colony in the Benden Mountains, await the hatching of a clutch of dragon eggs. According to custom, each newborn dragon will choose its own rider—and lifelong partner—through a kind of telepathic communication called Impression.

go.hrw.com
LEO 7-1

Preteaching Vocabulary

Words to Own

Have students read the definitions of the Words to Own listed at the bottom of the selection pages. Ask volunteers to mime the meaning of **goaded**, **perturbed**, and **confrontation**. Then, have students reinforce their understanding of the words with these exercises:

1. Write a sentence that includes the words **goaded** and **confrontation**.

2. Write a sentence that includes the words **imminent** and **perturbed**.

3. Write a sentence that includes the word **alleviate** and one other vocabulary word.

4. On a new sheet of paper, copy your sentences but leave blanks for the vocabulary words. Exchange papers with a partner and fill in the blanks on each other's papers with the missing vocabulary words. Check your partner's work.

The Smallest Dragonboy

Anne McCaffrey

Keevan was constantly working, twice as hard as any other boy his age, to prove himself...

Summary ■ ■ ■

This science-fiction fantasy takes place on the planet Pern, an imaginary world where dragons help protect the inhabitants. Each year, when new dragon eggs are about to hatch, new dragonriders are selected from the eligible young people on the planet. Each newborn dragon selects its own rider through a form of telepathic communication called Impression. The hero of the story is Keevan, a boy who is facing his first Impression ceremony. Small for his age, Keevan must work twice as hard as the other boys and endure their taunts and teasing, especially those of the bully Beterli. Goaded into a fight with Beterli, Keevan is badly injured, and it seems he will not be able to participate in the Hatching. However, he uses all his courage and determination to hobble his way to the Hatching, where he is chosen by the bronze dragon, the highest honor a dragonrider can achieve.

Background

McCaffrey conceived the planet Pern as a former colony of Earth that had lost much of its knowledge of science and history. In this world, according to critic Debra Rae Cohen, "social structure, tensions, legends, and traditions are all based on the fundamental ecological battle" against the Thread "and on the empathetic kinship between dragon and rider" who together fight the Thread. The Impression ceremony on which this story focuses is thus the most important event in Pern society.

THE SMALLEST DRAGONBOY **47**

Resources: Print and Media

Reading
- *Graphic Organizers for Active Reading*, p. 4
- *Words to Own*, p. 3
- *Spelling and Decoding*
  Worksheet, p. 3
- *Audio CD Library*
  Disc 3, Track 2

Writing and Language
- *Daily Oral Grammar*
  Transparency 3

- *Grammar and Language Links*
  Worksheet, p. 5
- *Language Workshop CD-ROM*

Viewing and Representing
- *Viewing and Representing*
  Fine Art Transparencies 1, 2
  Fine Art Worksheets, pp. 4, 8

Assessment
- *Formal Assessment*, p. 6
- *Portfolio Management System*, p. 108
- *Standardized Test Preparation*, p. 14
- *Test Generator (One-Stop Planner CD-ROM)*

Internet
- go.hrw.com (keyword: LE0 7-1)

A Reading Skills and Strategies
Metacognition
Have students reflect on words in this passage that were invented just for this story. [*dragonboy, tail fork-end, wingsecond, dragonriders, Hatching Ground, Weyrleader, Weyr*] Ask students what they can do if they have difficulty figuring out what the words mean. [Possible responses: look at the surrounding context, reread the passage; read on to see if the meaning becomes clear; ask classmates their opinions.]

B Struggling Readers:
Breaking Down Difficult Text
Struggling readers may find the story's long sentences and invented words challenging. Write the sentence beginning "On the height . . ." on the board, and ask students to identify the sentence's subject and verb. [*watch dragon, stretched*] Then have them break the text down into short sentences. [On the height, the blue watch dragon stretched the great transparent pinions. His rider was mounted on his neck. His pinions carried him on the winds of Pern to fight the evil Thread. The Thread fell at certain times from the skies.] Encourage students to visualize the scene while you read the original passage aloud.

C Elements of Literature
Conflict
? What do you think will be the main conflict in this story? [Possible responses: Keevan will try to prove himself; Keevan and Beterli will compete to be dragonriders.]

Although Keevan lengthened his walking stride as far as his legs would stretch, he couldn't quite keep up with the other candidates. He knew he would be teased again.

A Just as he knew many other things that his foster mother told him he ought not to know, Keevan knew that Beterli, the most senior of the boys, set that spanking pace just to embarrass him, the smallest dragonboy. Keevan would arrive, tail fork-end of the group, breathless, chest heaving, and maybe get a stern look from the instructing wingsecond.

Dragonriders, even if they were still only hopeful candidates for the glowing eggs which were hardening on the hot sands of the Hatching Ground cavern, were expected to be punctual and prepared. Sloth was not tolerated by the Weyrleader of Benden Weyr. A good record was especially important now. It was very near hatching time, when the baby dragons would crack their mottled shells and stagger forth to choose their lifetime companions. The very thought of that glorious moment made Keevan's breath catch in his throat. To be chosen—to be a dragonrider! To sit astride the neck of a winged beast with jeweled eyes; to be his friend, in telepathic communion[1] with him for life; to be his companion in good times and fighting extremes; to fly effortlessly over the lands of Pern! Or, thrillingly, *between* to any point anywhere on the world! Flying *between* was done on dragonback or not at all, and it was dangerous.

Keevan glanced upward, past the black mouths of the Weyr caves, in which grown dragons and their chosen riders lived, toward the Star Stones that crowned the ridge of the old volcano that was Benden Weyr. On the height, the blue watch dragon, his rider **B** mounted on his neck, stretched the great transparent pinions[2] that carried him on the winds of Pern to fight the evil Thread that fell at certain times from the skies. The many-faceted rainbow jewels of his eyes glistened fleetingly in the greeny sun. He folded his great wings to his back, and the watch pair resumed their statuelike pose of alertness.

Then the enticing view was obscured as Keevan passed into the Hatching Ground cavern. The sands underfoot were hot, even through heavy wher-hide boots. How the boot maker had protested having to sew so small! Keevan was forced to wonder why being small was reprehensible. People were always calling him "babe" and shooing him away as being **C** "too small" or "too young" for this or that. Keevan was constantly working, twice as hard as any other boy his age, to prove himself capable. What if his muscles weren't as big as Beterli's? They were just as hard. And if he couldn't overpower anyone in a wrestling match, he could outdistance everyone in a footrace.

"Maybe if you run fast enough," Beterli had jeered on the occasion when Keevan had been goaded to boast of his swiftness, "you could catch a dragon. That's the only way you'll make a dragonrider!"

> *"Maybe if you run fast enough, you could catch a dragon . . ."*

---

2. **pinions** (pin′yənz): wings.

WORDS TO OWN
goaded (gōd′id) *v*.: pushed or driven. A goad is a stick with a sharp point used to herd oxen.

---

1. **telepathic communion:** communication of thoughts without speaking.

Reaching All Students

English Language Learners
Students who lack proficiency in English may need special help with the invented vocabulary in the story. Have them go through a section of the story to list unfamiliar or invented words. They should then create definitions for the words based on their context in the story. For additional strategies to supplement instruction for these students, see
• *Lesson Plans Including Strategies for English-Language Learners*

Advanced Learners
Give students a list of some well-known fantasy writers, such as C. S. Lewis, J. R. R. Tolkien, and Ursula LeGuin. Ask each student to read one of the writers' short stories or an excerpt (comparable in length to "The Smallest Dragonboy") from a longer work. Have students write essays comparing their chosen works with "The Smallest Dragonboy." Suggest that they begin by comparing the fantastic elements, invented vocabularies, or unusual creatures in both works.

"You just wait and see, Beterli, you just wait," Keevan had replied. He would have liked to wipe the contemptuous smile from Beterli's face, but the guy didn't fight fair even when a wingsecond was watching. "No one knows what Impresses a dragon!"

"They've got to be able to *find* you first, babe!"

Yes, being the smallest candidate was not an enviable position. It was therefore imperative that Keevan Impress a dragon in his first hatching. That would wipe the smile off every face in the cavern and accord him the respect due any dragonrider, even the smallest one.

Besides, no one knew exactly what Impressed the baby dragons as they struggled from their shells in search of their lifetime partners.

"I like to believe that dragons see into a man's heart," Keevan's foster mother, Mende, told him. "If they find goodness, honesty, a flexible mind, patience, courage—and you've got that in quantity, dear Keevan—that's what dragons look for. I've seen many a well-grown lad left standing on the sands, Hatching Day, in favor of someone not so strong or tall or handsome. And if my memory serves me"—which it usually did: Mende knew every word of every Harper's tale worth telling, although Keevan did not interrupt her to say so—"I don't believe that F'lar, our Weyrleader, was all that tall when bronze Mnementh chose him. And Mnementh was the only bronze dragon of that hatching."

Dreams of Impressing a bronze were beyond Keevan's boldest reflections, although that goal dominated the thoughts of every other hopeful candidate. Green dragons were small and fast and more numerous. There was more prestige to Impressing a blue or brown than a green. Being practical, Keevan seldom dreamed as high as a big fighting brown, like Canth, F'nor's fine fellow, the biggest brown on all Pern. But to fly a bronze? Bronzes were

almost as big as the queen, and only they took the air when a queen flew at mating time. A bronze rider could aspire to become Weyrleader! Well, Keevan would console himself, brown riders could aspire to become wingseconds, and that wasn't bad. He'd even settle for a green dragon; they were small, but so was he. No matter! He simply had to Impress a dragon his first time in the Hatching Ground. Then no one in the Weyr would taunt him anymore for being so small.

Shells, Keevan thought now, but the sands are hot!

"Impression time is imminent, candidates," the wingsecond was saying as everyone crowded respectfully close to him. "See the extent of the striations on this promising egg." The stretch marks *were* larger than yesterday.

Everyone leaned forward and nodded thoughtfully. That particular egg was the one Beterli had marked as his own, and no other candidate dared, on pain of being beaten by Beterli at his first opportunity, to approach it. The egg was marked by a large yellowish splotch in the shape of a dragon backwinging to land, talons outstretched to grasp rock. Everyone knew that bronze eggs bore distinctive markings. And naturally, Beterli, who'd been presented at eight Impressions already and was the biggest of the candidates, had chosen it.

"I'd say that the great opening day is almost upon us," the wingsecond went on, and then his face assumed a grave expression. "As we well know, there are only forty eggs and seventy-two candidates. Some of you may be disappointed on the great day. That doesn't necessarily mean you aren't dragonrider material, just that *the* dragon for you hasn't been shelled. You'll have other hatchings, and it's no

---

WORDS TO OWN

imminent (im′ə·nənt) *adj.*: about to happen.

THE SMALLEST DRAGONBOY 49

Taking a Second Look

A Reading Skills and Strategies

Metacognition

Have students ask themselves whether they think this information about Keevan's secretly touching Beterli's egg might turn out to be important in the story. Ask students to jot down their ideas and save them so they can check later to see if they are right.

B Critical Thinking

Analyzing

? What advantages does Beterli have in his conflict with Keevan? [Possible response: Beterli is bigger and stronger.] What advantages do you think Keevan has? [Possible responses: Keevan seems smarter and more levelheaded. Because Keevan is younger, he still has many chances to Impress a dragon, while Beterli is facing his last chance and may feel desperate.]

C Advanced Learners

Making Connections

The scene of the dragonriders gathering for a meal and an exchange of tales may remind students of similar scenes from literature, television, movies, or real life. Ask students to provide examples and to describe the mood of this kind of scene.

---

disgrace to be left behind an Impression or two. Or more."

Keevan was positive that the wingsecond's eyes rested on Beterli, who'd been stood off at so many Impressions already. Keevan tried to squinch down so the wingsecond wouldn't notice him. Keevan had been reminded too often that he was eligible to be a candidate by one day only. He, of all the hopefuls, was most likely to be left standing on the great day. One more reason why he simply had to Impress at his first hatching.

"Now move about among the eggs," the wingsecond said. "Touch them. We don't know that it does any good, but it certainly doesn't do any harm."

A Some of the boys laughed nervously, but everyone immediately began to circulate among the eggs. Beterli stepped up officiously to "his" egg, daring anyone to come near it. Keevan smiled, because he had already touched it—every inspection day, when the others were leaving the Hatching Ground and no one could see him crouch to stroke it.

Keevan had an egg he concentrated on, too, one drawn slightly to the far side of the others. The shell had a soft greenish blue tinge with a faint creamy swirl design. The consensus was that this egg contained a mere green, so Keevan was rarely bothered by rivals. He was somewhat <u>perturbed</u>, then, to see Beterli wandering over to him.

B "I don't know why you're allowed in this Impression, Keevan. There are enough of us without a babe," Beterli said, shaking his head.

"I'm of age." Keevan kept his voice level, telling himself not to be bothered by mere words.

"Yah!" Beterli made a show of standing on his toe tips. "You can't even see over an egg; Hatching Day, you better get in front or the dragons won't see you at all. 'Course, you could get run down that way in the mad scramble. Oh, I forget, you can run fast, can't you?"

50 OUT HERE ON MY OWN

"You'd better make sure a dragon sees *you* this time, Beterli," Keevan replied. "You're almost overage, aren't you?"

Beterli flushed and took a step forward, hand half raised. Keevan stood his ground, but if Beterli advanced one more step, he would call the wingsecond. No one fought on the Hatching Ground. Surely Beterli knew that much.

Fortunately, at that moment, the wingsecond called the boys together and led them from the Hatching Ground to start on evening chores. There were "glows" to be replenished in the main kitchen caverns and sleeping cubicles, the major hallways, and the queen's apartment. Firestone sacks had to be filled against Thread attack, and black rock brought to the kitchen hearths. The boys fell to their chores, tantalized by the odors of roasting meat. The population of the Weyr began to assemble for the evening meal, and the dragonriders came in from the Feeding Ground on their sweep checks.

C It was the time of day Keevan liked best: Once the chores were done but before dinner was served, a fellow could often get close enough to the dragonriders to hear their talk. Tonight, Keevan's father, K'last, was at the main dragonrider table. It puzzled Keevan how his father, a brown rider and a tall man, could *be* his father—because he, Keevan, was so small. It obviously puzzled K'last, too, when he deigned to notice his small son: "In a few more Turns, you'll be as tall as I am—or taller!"

K'last was pouring Benden wine all around the table. The dragonriders were relaxing. There'd be no Thread attack for three more days, and they'd be in the mood to tell tall tales, better than Harper yarns, about impossible

----

WORDS TO OWN

perturbed (pər·turbd′) *v.* used as *adj.*: disturbed; troubled.

Using Students' Strengths

Visual Learners

As visual learners read the story, they might benefit by filling in the graphic organizer on p. 4 in the *Graphic Organizers for Active Reading.*

Interpersonal Learners

After students have read the story, have them work in groups of three to complete the statements below. Then, have members role-play a conflict-resolution session with the Weyrleader acting as a mediator between Keevan and Beterli.

Keevan/Beterli

1. My greatest desire is _____.
2. My fears are _____.

3. What I would say to Beterli/Keevan is _____.

Weyrleader

1. The situation between the boys is _____.
2. Possible solutions are _____.
3. The best way to solve the conflict is _____.

Appreciating Language

Invite students to explore how the author's use of invented language helps to create a fantasy setting that seems real, though it exists only in the imagination. Ask students to consider the following questions and report to the class:

- Do the concepts that the invented words express exist in our world?
- How do the invented words make the setting seem like a real place?
- How is Pernspeak related to English?

RESPONDING TO THE ART

Have students locate the passage in the story that the artist has chosen to illustrate. Ask them to examine the painting and to relate the visual details to those in the story. Let them describe what they see in the foreground and in the background of the picture.

Activity. Do students agree with the artist's interpretation of the characters and the setting? If they were to create their own representation of Pern, what would it look like? Would they use different colors or a different medium, for example, pen and ink, paper cutouts, collage? Students can try their hand at their own artistic representations of this scene or of another one in the story.

A Elements of Literature

Conflict

? What inner struggle with his emotions does Keevan experience as he listens to the dragonriders talk? [Possible responses: He is worried he'll never be able to remember everything he needs to know to be a dragonrider, but he's afraid to tell anyone about his worries because such an admission might reinforce the idea that he's too young to be a dragonrider. He longs to be a dragonrider, but he fears he's not good enough.]

B Reading Skills and Strategies

Finding the Main Idea

Have students paraphrase the main idea expressed by each speaker in this passage. [Possible responses: First speaker—L'vel—There are too many eligible boys for the Hatching. The youngest ones, who aren't ready to be trained yet anyway should be dropped. Second speaker—K'last—The army doesn't need dragonriders right away, so the youngest riders will be ready in plenty of time and should have a chance. Third speaker—The oldest boys should be dropped because they've already had plenty of chances to be chosen by a dragon.]

C Vocabulary Note

Word Origins

Tell students that the adjective *heretical* is derived from the noun *heresy*. A heresy is an opinion that goes against generally accepted beliefs, especially religious beliefs. Based on this definition, have students define the adjective *heretical* ["contrary to accepted beliefs"] and the noun *heretic* ["one who expresses opinions contrary to accepted beliefs"].

---

maneuvers they'd done a-dragonback. When Thread attack was closer, their talk would change to a discussion of tactics of evasion, of going *between,* how long to suspend there until the burning but fragile Thread would freeze and crack and fall harmlessly off dragon and man. They would dispute the exact moment to feed firestone to the dragon so he'd have the best flame ready to sear Thread midair and render it harmless to ground—and man—below. There was such a lot to know and understand about being a dragonrider that sometimes Keevan was overwhelmed. How would he ever be able to remember everything he ought to know at the right moment? He couldn't dare ask such a question; this would only have given additional weight to the notion that he was too young yet to be a dragonrider.

"Having older candidates makes good sense," L'vel was saying as Keevan settled down near the table. "Why waste four to five years of a dragon's fighting prime until his rider grows up enough to stand the rigors?" L'vel had Impressed a blue of Ramoth's first clutch. Most of the candidates thought L'vel was marvelous because he spoke up in front of the older riders, who awed them. "That was well enough in the Interval when you didn't need to mount the full Weyr complement to fight Thread. But not now. Not with more eligible candidates than ever. Let the babes wait."

"Any boy who is over twelve Turns has the right to stand in the Hatching Ground," K'last replied, a slight smile on his face. He never argued or got angry. Keevan wished he were more like his father. And oh, how he wished he were a brown rider! "Only a dragon—each particular dragon—knows what he wants in a

"Any boy who is over twelve Turns has the right to stand in the Hatching Ground . . ."

rider. We certainly can't tell. Time and again, the theorists," K'last's smile deepened as his eyes swept those at the table, "are surprised by dragon choice. *They* never seem to make mistakes, however."

"Now, K'last, just look at the roster this Impression. Seventy-two boys and only forty eggs. Drop off the twelve youngest, and there's still a good field for the hatchlings to choose from. Shells! There are a couple of Weyrlings unable to see over a wher egg, much less a dragon! And years before they can ride Thread."

"True enough, but the Weyr is scarcely under fighting strength, and if the youngest Impress, they'll be old enough to fight when the oldest of our current dragons go *between* from senility."

"Half the Weyr-bred lads have already been through several Impressions," one of the bronze riders said then. "I'd say drop some of *them* off this time. Give the untried a chance."

"There's nothing wrong in presenting a clutch with as wide a choice as possible," said the Weyrleader, who had joined the table with Lessa, the Weyrwoman.

"Has there ever been a case," she said, smiling in her odd way at the riders, "where a hatchling didn't choose?"

Her suggestion was almost heretical and drew astonished gasps from everyone, including the boys.

F'lar laughed. "You say the most outrageous things, Lessa."

"Well, *has* there ever been a case where a dragon didn't choose?"

"Can't say as I recall one," K'last replied.

"Then we continue in this tradition," Lessa said firmly, as if that ended the matter.

52 OUT HERE ON MY OWN

Getting Students Involved

Cooperative Learning

Travel Tips. Have students work in groups of four to create illustrated travel brochures that might be useful to a tourist interested in visiting Pern. They should address the tourist's concerns about safety, as well as explore attractions and unusual features of Pern. Here are some topics students might include:

- Dragons: Are they dangerous creatures? How are they controlled? Why are they different colors?
- Threads: Should visitors worry about them? What is done to prevent an attack?
- The Weyr: Do the people of Pern really live in caves? What will the tourists' accommodations be like?
- Pern Society: Who's the boss?

Encourage students to use details from the story and their imagination to prepare the brochure. To help students get started, give them a sample travel brochure with information about an actual exotic travel destination.

But it didn't. The argument ranged from one table to the other all through dinner, with some favoring a weeding out of the candidates to the most likely, lopping off those who were very young or who had had multiple opportunities to Impress. All the candidates were in a swivet,[3] though such a departure from tradition would be to the advantage of many. As the evening progressed, more riders were favoring eliminating the youngest and those who'd passed four or more Impressions unchosen. Keevan felt he could bear such a dictum[4] only if Beterli were also eliminated. But this seemed less likely than that Keevan would be turfed out,[5] since the Weyr's need was for fighting dragons and riders.

By the time the evening meal was over, no decision had been reached, although the Weyrleader had promised to give the matter due consideration.

He might have slept on the problem, but few of the candidates did. Tempers were uncertain in the sleeping caverns next morning as the boys were routed out of their beds to carry water and black rock and cover the "glows." Twice Mende had to call Keevan to order for clumsiness.

"Whatever is the matter with you, boy?" she demanded in exasperation when he tipped black rock short of the bin and sooted up the hearth.

"They're going to keep me from this Impression."

"What?" Mende stared at him. "Who?"

"You heard them talking at dinner last night. They're going to turf the babes from the hatching."

Mende regarded him a moment longer before touching his arm gently. "There's lots of talk around a supper table, Keevan. And it cools as soon as the supper. I've heard the

3. **in a swivet:** frustrated and annoyed.
4. **dictum:** pronouncement or judgment.
5. **turfed out:** British expression meaning "removed; expelled."

same nonsense before every hatching, but nothing is ever changed."

"There's always a first time," Keevan answered, copying one of her own phrases.

"That'll be enough of that, Keevan. Finish your job. If the clutch does hatch today, we'll need full rock bins for the feast, and you won't be around to do the filling. All my fosterlings make dragonriders."

"The first time?" Keevan was bold enough to ask as he scooted off with the rockbarrow.

Perhaps, Keevan thought later, if he hadn't been on that chore just when Beterli was also fetching black rock, things might have turned out differently. But he had dutifully trundled the barrow to the outdoor bunker for another load just as Beterli arrived on a similar errand.

"Heard the news, babe?" Beterli asked. He was grinning from ear to ear, and he put an unnecessary emphasis on the final insulting word.

"The eggs are cracking?" Keevan all but dropped the loaded shovel. Several anxieties flicked through his mind then: He was black with rock dust—would he have time to wash before donning the white tunic of candidacy? And if the eggs were hatching, why hadn't the candidates been recalled by the wingsecond?

"Naw! Guess again!" Beterli was much too pleased with himself.

With a sinking heart, Keevan knew what the news must be, and he could only stare with intense desolation at the older boy.

"C'mon! Guess, babe!"

"I've no time for guessing games," Keevan managed to say with indifference. He began to shovel black rock into the barrow as fast as he could.

"I said, guess." Beterli grabbed the shovel.

"And I said I have no time for guessing games."

Beterli wrenched the shovel from Keevan's hands. "Guess!"

"I'll have that shovel back, Beterli." Keevan

THE SMALLEST DRAGONBOY 53

Getting Students Involved

Cooperative Learning

Story Mapping. After they have finished reading the story, divide students with different learning styles into groups of four. Group members can assume the roles of storyteller, recorder, reader and checker, and illustrator. Have the storyteller retell the story while the recorder lists the main events in order. The reader should check that this version of the story is correct. Then, provide students with art supplies, and have them illustrate or describe in a few sentences the story's main events, placing each event on a separate sheet of paper. Students should create a display of their illustrations that clearly follows the sequence of events in the story. All group members should be involved in deciding on a mapping strategy. For example, students may place their illustrations in a linear design, connected by arrows, or they may stack them one on top of the other to form a booklet. Have each group share its story map with the class.

D Vocabulary Note

Synonyms

Tell the students that this passage describes the continuing arguments about whether certain boys should be kept out of or removed from the Impression, or Hatching. Have students find four synonyms for *removed* or *removing* in the passage. [Synonyms include *weeding out, loping off, eliminating* and *eliminated,* and *turfed out.*]

E English Language Learners

Idioms

Tell students that the idiom "to sleep on" something means to delay a decision overnight and wait until the next morning, when one has had time to weigh all the possibilities and think clearly about the best solution. Ask how the speakers of another language might express the same idea.

F Reading Skills and Strategies

Metacognition

? Ask students what thoughts went through their minds as they read this passage. How could they tell that something bad might be about to happen? [Possible response: This passage takes the reader forward in the story to a point at which Keevan feels regret for something the reader does not yet know about. The clause "Perhaps . . . things might have turned out differently" suggests that something bad is about to happen because Keevan is in the wrong place at the wrong time. Students might express feeling a sense of dread, suspense, anticipation, or curiosity as they read the passage.]

G Reading Skills and Strategies

Drawing Conclusions

? What do you think Keevan imagines Beterli's news to be? [Possible response: Keevan probably imagines that Beterli has heard that the youngest candidates are to be dropped from this hatching.]

A Appreciating Language
Keeping Verb Tenses Consistent

Have students locate the verbs in this passage and identify the tense of each verb. [Verbs include *yanked, tried, clung, jerked, rammed, felt.* All are in the past tense.]

B Reading Skills and Strategies
Metacognition

Ask students if they understand what must have happened before this abrupt change in scene. Have them tell what they might do to figure things out if they were confused. [Possible responses: Reread the previous paragraph and ask themselves what might have happened; read on to see if events are explained.] Call on a volunteer to explain the events. [Keevan was knocked unconscious in his fight with Beterli and was then carried home, where he later regained consciousness.]

C Elements of Literature
Conflict

? What internal conflict does Keevan face when the adults ask him how he was injured? [Possible response: Keevan would probably like to get even with the bully Beterli, but Keevan's sense of honor and fair play prevents him from tattling and thus keeping Beterli out of the Hatching.]

D Reading Skills and Strategies
Drawing Conclusions

? What "old gag" is Lessa referring to? [Possible response: She is referring to the trick Beterli played on Keevan—the kind of trick in which a tormentor withholds information so that his victim will think something terrible has happened.]

---

straightened up, but he didn't come to Beterli's bulky shoulder. From somewhere, other boys appeared, some with barrows, some mysteriously alerted to the prospect of a <u>confrontation</u> among their numbers.

"Babes don't give orders to candidates around here, babe!"

Someone sniggered, and Keevan, incredulous, knew that he must've been dropped from the candidacy.

A He yanked the shovel from Beterli's loosened grasp. Snarling, the older boy tried to regain possession, but Keevan clung with all his strength to the handle, dragged back and forth as the stronger boy jerked the shovel about. With a sudden, unexpected movement, Beterli rammed the handle into Keevan's chest, knocking him over the barrow handles. Keevan felt a sharp, painful jab behind his left ear, an unbearable pain in his left shin, and then a painless nothingness.

B Mende's angry voice roused him, and, startled, he tried to throw back the covers, thinking he'd overslept. But he couldn't move, so firmly was he tucked into his bed. And then the constriction of a bandage on his head and the dull sickishness in his leg brought back recent occurrences.

"Hatching?" he cried.

"No, lovey," Mende said in a kind voice. Her hand was cool and gentle on his forehead. "Though there's some as won't be at any hatching again." Her voice took on a stern edge.

Keevan looked beyond her to see the Weyrwoman, who was frowning with irritation.

"Keevan, will you tell me what occurred at the black-rock bunker?" asked Lessa in an even voice.

C He remembered Beterli now and the quarrel over the shovel and . . . what had Mende said about some not being at any hatching? Much as he hated Beterli, he couldn't bring himself to tattle on Beterli and force him out of candidacy.

"Come, lad," and a note of impatience crept into the Weyrwoman's voice. "I merely want to know what happened from you, too. Mende said she sent you for black rock. Beterli—and every Weyrling in the cavern—seems to have been on the same errand. What happened?"

"Beterli took my shovel. I hadn't finished with it."

"There's more than one shovel. What did he *say* to you?"

"He'd heard the news."

"What news?" The Weyrwoman was suddenly amused.

"That . . . that . . . there'd been changes."

"Is that what he said?"

"Not exactly."

"What did he say? C'mon, lad, I've heard from everyone else, you know."

"He said for me to guess the news."

D "And you fell for that old gag?" The Weyrwoman's irritation returned.

"Consider all the talk last night at supper, Lessa," Mende said. "Of course the boy would think he'd been eliminated."

"In effect, he is, with a broken skull and leg." Lessa touched his arm in a rare gesture of sympathy. "Be that as it may, Keevan, you'll have other Impressions. Beterli will not. There are certain rules that must be observed by all candidates, and his conduct proves him unacceptable to the Weyr."

She smiled at Mende and then left.

"I'm still a candidate?" Keevan asked urgently.

"Well, you are and you aren't, lovey," his foster mother said. "Is the numbweed working?" she asked, and when he nodded, she said, "You just rest. I'll bring you some nice broth."

At any other time in his life, Keevan would

WORDS TO OWN

confrontation (kän′frən·tā′shən) *n.*: face-to-face meeting between opposing sides.

Skill Link

Identifying Verb Tenses

You might want to use the following exercise before you teach the Grammar Link exercise on p. 63. This exercise will help you assess your students' skills in identifying verb tenses.

Activity

Identify each underlined verb as either present tense or past tense. For a review of verb tenses, see pp. 730–733 in the Language Handbook.

1. Everyone <u>agreed</u> that dragons <u>are</u> fascinating mythical creatures. [past, present]
2. People in Europe <u>told</u> the story of how St. George <u>killed</u> the Dragon. [past, past]
3. Dragons <u>play</u> an important part in Chinese New Year celebrations. [present]
4. Fairy tales often <u>include</u> a fire-breathing dragon. [present]
5. When I <u>was</u> younger, I <u>believed</u> that dragons <u>were</u> real. [all past]

Professional Notes

Anne McCaffrey's Use of Science

A number of critics have pointed out Anne McCaffrey's knowledge of science. Although the Dragonrider books are generally classified as fantasy, some readers feel that a more accurate description of her work would be "science fantasy." This comment appears in an article in Contemporary Authors: "Although Pern is inhabited by flying dragons and dominated by a near-feudal society, elements native to fantasy worlds, McCaffrey's creation is based on solid scientific principles. The author in fact took supplementary courses in physics in order to create credible science fiction. The focus of the Dragonriders series—on Pern's society and on the relationship between dragon and rider—puts the science in the background, unlike many science fiction novels."

A Critical Thinking

Determining Author's Purpose

❓ What is the author's purpose in taking the reader inside Keevan's mind? [Possible responses: She wants the reader to identify with Keevan, to experience events from his point of view, and to share the anxiety he feels. She wishes to heighten the suspense about what will happen next.]

B Reading Skills and Strategies

Metacognition

❓ What ideas do you have about what Keevan might do? [Possible responses: Keevan is giving up; he is about to find a way to get to the Hatching.] What evidence from the story are you basing your prediction on? [Possible response: Keevan's sense of determination and his urgent desire to prove himself]

C Elements of Literature

Suspense

❓ How do the details in this passage increase interest in what will happen next? [Possible responses: The growing loudness and speed of the humming suggest that the eggs are about to hatch. Keevan's struggle to get down the ramp safely and quickly creates a feeling of suspense.]

---

have relished such cosseting, but now he just lay there worrying. Beterli had been dismissed. **A** Would the others think it was his fault? But everyone was there! Beterli provoked that fight. His worry increased, because although he heard excited comings and goings in the passageway, no one tweaked back the curtain across the sleeping alcove he shared with five other boys. Surely one of them would have to come in sometime. No, they were all avoiding him. And something else was wrong. Only he didn't know what.

Mende returned with broth and beachberry bread.

"Why doesn't anyone come see me, Mende? I haven't done anything wrong, have I? I didn't ask to have Beterli turfed out."

Mende soothed him, saying everyone was busy with noontime chores and no one was angry with him. They were giving him a chance to rest in quiet. The numbweed made him drowsy, and her words were fair enough. He permitted his fears to dissipate. Until he heard a hum. Actually he felt it first, in the broken shinbone and his sore head. The hum began to grow. Two things registered suddenly in Keevan's groggy mind: The only white candidate's robe still on the pegs in the chamber was his, and the dragons hummed when a clutch was being laid or being hatched. Impression! And he was flat abed.

Bitter, bitter disappointment turned the warm broth sour in his belly. Even the small voice telling him that he'd have other opportunities failed to <u>alleviate</u> his crushing depression. **B** *This* was the Impression that mattered! This was his chance to show *everyone*, from Mende to K'last to L'vel and even the Weyrleader, that he, Keevan, was worthy of being a dragonrider.

He twisted in bed, fighting against the tears that threatened to choke him. Dragonmen don't cry! Dragonmen learn to live with pain.

Pain? The leg didn't actually pain him as he rolled about on his bedding. His head felt sort of stiff from the tightness of the bandage. He sat up, an effort in itself since the numbweed made exertion difficult. He touched the splinted leg; the knee was unhampered. He had no feeling in his bone, really. He swung himself carefully to the side of his bed and stood slowly. The room wanted to swim about him. He closed his eyes, which made the dizziness worse, and he had to clutch the wall.

Gingerly, he took a step. The broken leg dragged. It hurt in spite of the numbweed, but what was pain to a dragonman?

No one had said he couldn't go to the Impression. "You are and you aren't" were Mende's exact words.

Clinging to the wall, he jerked off his bed shirt. Stretching his arm to the utmost, he jerked his white candidate's tunic from the peg. Jamming first one arm and then the other into the holes, he pulled it over his head. Too bad about the belt. He couldn't wait. He hobbled to the door and hung on to the curtain to steady himself. The weight on his leg was unwieldy. He wouldn't get very far without something to lean on. Down by the bathing pool was one of the long crook-necked poles used to retrieve clothes from the hot washing troughs. But it was down there, and he was on the level above. And there was no one nearby to come to his aid; everyone would be in the Hatching Ground right now, eagerly waiting for the first egg to crack.

C The humming increased in volume and tempo, an urgency to which Keevan responded, knowing that his time was all too limited if he was to join the ranks of the hopeful boys standing around the cracking eggs. But if he hurried down the ramp, he'd fall flat on his face.

He could, of course, go flat on his rear end,

WORDS TO OWN
alleviate (ə·lē′vē·āt′) *v*.: relieve; reduce.

---

56 OUT HERE ON MY OWN

Crossing the Curriculum

Art
Each of the dragon eggshells mentioned in the story has a unique pattern on its surface. Provide students with art materials, and have them design and draw their own dragon eggshells. After they have finished, have them show the drawings to a partner, who will then write a brief description of the dragon that he or she imagines will emerge from the egg.

Geography
Have students create a map of the system of caves beneath the surface of planet Pern. The map should show the chambers and passages mentioned in the story, as well as areas that the students imagine, such as the dragons' quarters, a schoolroom, and so on. Make a place in the classroom for displaying the maps.

Science
Suggest that students work in pairs to make up their own scientific explanations for the planet Pern's appearance and unique features (the green sunlight, the firestone, the Thread). Students may speculate on the nature of Pern's atmosphere; its placement in its solar system; and its landscape, minerals and vegetation.

the way crawling children did. He sat down, sending a jarring stab of pain through his leg and up to the wound on the back of his head. Gritting his teeth and blinking away tears, Keevan scrabbled down the ramp. He had to wait a moment at the bottom to catch his breath. He got to one knee, the injured leg straight out in front of him. Somehow, he managed to push himself erect, though the room seemed about to tip over his ears. It wasn't far to the crooked stick, but it seemed an age before he had it in his hand.

Then the humming stopped!

Keevan cried out and began to hobble frantically across the cavern, out to the bowl of the Weyr. Never had the distance between living caverns and the Hatching Ground seemed so great. Never had the Weyr been so breathlessly silent. It was as if the multitude of people and dragons watching the hatching held every breath in suspense. Not even the wind muttered down the steep sides of the bowl. The only sounds to break the stillness were Keevan's ragged gasps and the thump-thud of his stick on the hard-packed ground. Sometimes he had to hop twice on his good leg to maintain his balance. Twice he fell into the sand and had to pull himself up on the stick, his white tunic no longer spotless. Once he jarred himself so badly he couldn't get up immediately.

Then he heard the first exhalation of the crowd, the oohs, the muted cheer, the susurrus⁶ of excited whispers. An egg had cracked, and the dragon had chosen his rider. Desperation increased Keevan's hobble. Would

6. **susurrus** (sə·sur'əs): rustling sound.

he never reach the arching mouth of the Hatching Ground?

Another cheer and an excited spate of applause spurred Keevan to greater effort. If he didn't get there in moments, there'd be no unpaired hatchling left. Then he was actually staggering into the Hatching Ground, the sands hot on his bare feet.

No one noticed his entrance or his halting progress. And Keevan could see nothing but the backs of the white-robed candidates, seventy of them ringing the area around the eggs. Then one side would surge forward or back and there'd be a cheer. Another dragon had been Impressed. Suddenly a large gap appeared in the white human wall, and Keevan had his first sight of the eggs. There didn't seem to be *any* left uncracked, and he could see the lucky boys standing beside wobble-legged dragons. He could hear the unmistakable plaintive crooning of hatchlings and their squawks of protest as they'd fall awkwardly in the sand.

Suddenly he wished that he hadn't left his bed, that he'd stayed away from the Hatching Ground. Now everyone would see his ignominious failure. So he scrambled as desperately to reach the shadowy walls of the Hatching Ground as he had struggled to cross the bowl. He mustn't be seen.

He didn't notice, therefore, that the shifting group of boys remaining had begun to drift in his direction. The hard pace he had set himself and his cruel disappointment took their double toll of Keevan. He tripped and collapsed, sobbing, to the warm sands. He didn't see the consternation in the watching Weyrfolk above the Hatching Ground, nor did he hear the excited whispers of speculation. He didn't know that

If he didn't get there in moments, there'd be no unpaired hatchling left.

D **Reading Skills and Strategies**
Visualizing
Have students close their eyes as you read this passage aloud. Encourage them to visualize the scene as a "movie in their minds." Ask if the scene reminds them of scenes they have actually seen in movies.

E **Appreciating Language**
Onomatopoeia
Point out that both *susurrus* and *whispers* are examples of onomatopoeia. The sounds in the words reinforce meaning. The rustling sound is conveyed by the sibilant consonant *s*.

F **Struggling Readers**
Summarizing
Have students read this passage carefully and summarize what is happening. Explain that because the story is written from Keevan's point of view, the reader shares in Keevan's confusion. (See p. T47)

Assessing Learning

Informal Assessment

Allow students to work in pairs when they answer the Making Meanings questions on p. 61. Suggest that students first read through the questions and agree on exactly what the question is asking. Then, have each student prepare an answer that includes supporting evidence from the story. Partners may exchange their answers and review each other's work. Students should then write a new response that combines information from both answers. These collaborative answers may then be submitted to you for additional evaluation.

Making the Connections

Cultural Connections

Dragons are featured in both European and Asian folklore. In the European tradition, dragons are typically cruel creatures that represent the evil of the world. Slaying the dragon brings reward to the brave hero. In Asian folklore, however, dragons are seen as friendly creatures that bring good luck. Display or distribute several pictures of dragons from a variety of cultures and have students discuss them. You might, for example, have them compare works from Western and Eastern traditions. You might use a painting of Saint George and the Dragon (see Fine Art Transparency 2) and a photograph of a dragon costume from a Chinese New Year celebration. Ask students to discuss which dragon seems more ferocious and whether one is more appealing that the other. Then have students draw dragons of their own and caption their drawings with descriptions of the dragons' unique qualities.

the Weyrleader and Weyrwoman had dropped to the arena and were making their way toward the knot of boys slowly moving in the direction of the entrance.

"Never seen anything like it," the Weyrleader was saying. "Only thirty-nine riders chosen. And the bronze trying to leave the Hatching Ground without making Impression."

"A case in point of what I said last night," the Weyrwoman replied, "where a hatchling makes no choice because the right boy isn't there."

"There's only Beterli and K'last's young one missing. And there's a full wing of likely boys to choose from. . . ."

"None acceptable, apparently. Where is the creature going? He's not heading for the entrance after all. Oh, what have we there, in the shadows?"

Keevan heard with dismay the sound of voices nearing him. He tried to burrow into the sand. The mere thought of how he would be teased and taunted now was unbearable.

Don't worry! Please don't worry! The thought was urgent, but not his own.

Someone kicked sand over Keevan and butted roughly against him.

"Go away. Leave me alone!" he cried.

Why? was the injured-sounding question inserted into his mind. There was no voice, no tone, but the question was there, perfectly clear, in his head.

Incredulous, Keevan lifted his head and stared into the glowing jeweled eyes of a small bronze dragon. His wings were wet, the tips drooping in the sand. And he sagged in the middle on his unsteady legs, although he was making a great effort to keep erect.

Keevan dragged himself to his knees, oblivious of the pain in his leg. He wasn't even aware that he was ringed by the boys passed over, while thirty-one pairs of resentful eyes watched him Impress the dragon. The Weyrmen looked on, amused and surprised at the

draconic[7] choice, which could not be forced. Could not be questioned. Could not be changed.

Why? asked the dragon again. *Don't you like me?* His eyes whirled with anxiety, and his tone was so piteous that Keevan staggered forward and threw his arms around the dragon's neck, stroking his eye ridges, patting the damp, soft hide, opening the fragile-looking wings to dry them, and wordlessly assuring the hatchling over and over again that he was the most perfect, most beautiful, most beloved dragon in the Weyr, in all the Weyrs of Pern.

"What's his name, K'van?" asked Lessa, smiling warmly at the new dragonrider. K'van stared up at her for a long moment. Lessa would know as soon as he did. Lessa was the only person who could "receive" from all dragons, not only her own Ramoth. Then he gave her a radiant smile, recognizing the traditional shortening of his name that raised him forever to the rank of dragonrider.

My name is Heth, the dragon thought mildly, then hiccuped in sudden urgency. *I'm hungry.*

"Dragons are born hungry," said Lessa, laughing. "F'lar, give the boy a hand. He can barely manage his own legs, much less a dragon's."

K'van remembered his stick and drew himself up. "We'll be just fine, thank you."

"You may be the smallest dragonrider ever, young K'van," F'lar said, "but you're one of the bravest!"

And Heth agreed! Pride and joy so leaped in both chests that K'van wondered if his heart would burst right out of his body. He looped an arm around Heth's neck, and the pair, the smallest dragonboy and the hatchling who wouldn't choose anybody else, walked out of the Hatching Ground together forever.

---

7. **draconic** (drə·kän′ik): of a dragon. *Drakōn* is the Greek word for "dragon."

THE SMALLEST DRAGONBOY 59

A Reading Skills and Strategies

Metacognition

❓ Could you tell who was speaking to Keevan in this passage? What clues did you use to help you figure it out? [Possible response: The speaker might be the dragon. The words are in italics, not quotation marks, so maybe they aren't actually spoken. Earlier in the story we were told that the dragons could communicate with their riders through telepathy.]

B Critical Thinking

Making Connections

Look back at Mende's beliefs about dragons, described on p. 49. How accurate did her description of dragons' inner qualities turn out to be? [Possible response: Her description was accurate because Keevan's dragon seems to have looked into Keevan's heart and based his selection of a rider on Keevan's goodness, honesty, and courage, rather than on his size.]

C Reading Skills and Strategies

Metacognition

❓ How did you react to the story's ending? Do you like "happy endings" like this one? Why or why not? [Students' reactions may vary widely, depending on their tastes and their feelings about this particular story.]

Making the Connections

Connecting to the Theme: "Out Here on My Own"

When students have finished the story, be sure to talk about the theme. Point out that Keevan feels isolated because he is small for his age and because he has to work hard to prove himself and fend off bullies. In the end, he must rely on his own courage and determination to get to the Hatching so that he may be chosen by the bronze dragon. It should be pointed out that

Keevan does have a father and a foster mother and is a member of a tightknit, supportive community. Discuss with students Keevan's self-reliance and his role in the community. Ask students if they think Keevan's feelings of isolation are accurate, or if he simply fails to ask for help from supportive adults.

Cultural Connections

Coming-of-Age Rituals. Tell students that being Impressed by a dragon is a step toward assuming adult responsibilities in Pern society. Ask students to describe milestones or rituals that are used to mark the passage into adulthood in our own society or in a particular ethnic or religious community.

Student to Student

Ⓐ Critical Thinking

Expressing an Opinion

❓ What is your opinion of the speaker? [Possible responses: He's a jerk; he brags too much; he's conceited.]

Ⓑ Reading Skills and Strategies

Metacognition

❓ How did you respond to the ending of the poem? [Possible responses: I was surprised, because I didn't realize that the speaker was daydreaming; I was pleased that the speaker got his comeuppance because his claims of greatness were so ridiculously exaggerated.]

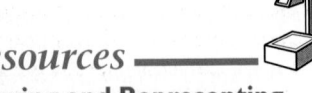

Resources

Viewing and Representing

Fine Art Transparency

St. George Killing the Dragon by Bernardo Martorell accompanies "Sir Kensley the Brave" by Megan Washam.

• Fine Art Transparency 2
• Worksheet, p. 8

MEET THE WRITER

"I Can't NOT Write"

Anne McCaffrey (1926–) is known to her many readers as "the Dragon lady." When asked why she defends dragons, McCaffrey said, "Dragons have always had bad press. And I liked the thought of them being so big, and controlled by a bond of love."

Anne McCaffrey grew up in Essex County, New Jersey. As a "lonely tomboy," she decided on two things she most wanted. "When I was a very young girl, I promised myself fervently (usually after I'd lost another battle with one of my brothers) that I would become a famous author and I'd own my own horse." McCaffrey's books are now known all over the world and have been translated into many languages. Since she moved to County Wicklow in Ireland, she has owned her own horse—a large dapple-gray Irish hunter she calls Horseface. McCaffrey lives and works in Ireland at her home, called Dragonhold. Fans of her books rejoice in McCaffrey's promise: "I shall continue to write—I can't NOT write—until I am too frail to touch the keys of my word processor." When asked how she writes stories, McCaffrey responds:

❝ First I find interesting people to write about (I have written an anthology series, *Crystal Singer*, because I wanted to name a feminine character Killeshandra), and then I find something for them to argue about or fight for or against. Or I think about an interesting concept—the dragons of Pern—telepathic, huge, flame-throwing dragons who fly because they 'think' they can. Aerodynamically, they can't. I like to write better than anything else, including riding Horseface. And I write because I can't always get the kind of story I like to read on library shelves. ❞

The Worlds of Anne McCaffrey

If you want to continue riding with the dragon-riders, read *Dragonsong* (Bantam), *Dragonsinger* (Bantam), and *Dragondrums* (Bantam), a series of science fantasy novels about the dragons of Pern.

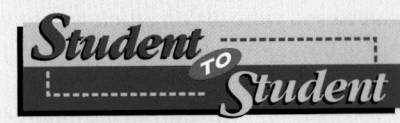

Sir Kensley the Brave

Ⓐ
My name is Sir Kensley the Brave,
A mighty, prestigious knight.
I have no fears nor weaknesses;
Foes tremble at my sight.

5   I do not care for dragons,
And they don't care for me.
For every time I duel with them,
It ends in victory.

The maidens all adore me
10 And attend my every need.
Their love for me increases
With my every knightly deed.

Oh no, my master approaches me
And bellows with much rage,
15 Ⓑ "Get up, daydreaming imbecile,
You lowly servant page!"

—Megan Washam
Pinehurst Elementary School
Alexandria, Virginia

Armor of George Clifford, third earl of Cumberland, made in the royal workshops in Greenwich, England (c. 1580–1585) (69½" high).

The Metropolitan Museum of Art, Munsey Fund, 1932. (32.130.6) Photograph ©1991 The Metropolitan Museum of Art.

Assessing Learning

Check Test: Short Answer

1. Who is the smallest dragonboy? [Keevan]
2. What is the great event that Keevan and the other boys are waiting for? [the hatching of the dragons who will choose their partners]
3. What is an Impression? [It is the meeting and matching up of riders with their dragons.]
4. What happens to Beterli after he bullies and fights Keevan? [Beterli is disqualified from the Impression.]

5. Whom does the bronze dragon choose? [Keevan]

Standardized Test Preparation

For practice with standardized test format specific to this selection, see

• *Standardized Test Preparation*, p. 14

For practice in proofreading and editing, see

• *Daily Oral Grammar*, Transparency 3

First Thoughts

[respond]

1. Describe or draw three vivid **images** that you remember from this story. Compare your pictures with your classmates'. Are any of your images the same as theirs?

Shaping Interpretations

[analyze]

2. Make a chart showing all the **conflicts** Keevan faced. Which conflict do you think was the hardest one for Keevan?

External Conflicts	Internal Conflicts

[analyze]

3. What is the **climax** of this story—its most emotional moment? How did you feel at this point in the story?

[predict]

4. When the Impression is over, Lessa calls Keevan K'van. What do you think this change of name will mean for Keevan's future?

[infer]

5. Why do you think Beterli never Impressed a dragon?

Connecting with the Text

[connect]

6. Describe what you imagine is going on in Keevan's mind as Heth makes his choice. When has something wonderful like this happened to you?

Extending the Text

[connect]

7. How does it feel to be an underdog—to be teased about your looks or height or age? How should people like Keevan handle such teasing?

Challenging the Text

[evaluate]

8. List all the women in this story. Do you think they have powerful positions in Pern society, or do only men hold power? If you were writing about Pern, what roles and responsibilities would you give to men and women?

[respond]

 9. Think back to how you responded to this story as you read it. Did you find some passages confusing? Were all your questions eventually answered? Discuss your reading experiences in class.

THE SMALLEST DRAGONBOY 61

Reading Check

a. What does Keevan want as the story opens? Why does he fear he won't get it?

b. How are dragonriders chosen? Why does Keevan fear he'll be kept from this Impression?

c. How does the bully Beterli try to ruin Keevan's chances on Hatching Day?

d. Describe Keevan's struggle to reach the Hatching Ground.

e. What happens to Keevan at the Impression, just when he is most unhappy and discouraged?

Reading Check

a. He wants to be chosen as a dragonrider. He fears he is too small.

b. Baby dragons break out of their shells and choose dragonriders. Keevan has heard that the number of boys who participate may be reduced.

c. Beterli tricks Keevan into fighting and injures him.

d. Keevan hobbles toward the scene and falls twice.

e. The bronze dragon chooses him.

Connecting Across Texts

Connecting with "The Smallest Dragonboy"

Ask students to compare and contrast the speaker of the poem "Sir Kensley the Brave" with Keevan in "The Smallest Dragonboy."
[Similarities: Both dream of dragons. Differences: Keevan is modest and anxious about his ability to be a dragonrider; the speaker of the poem is arrogantly sure of himself.]

First Thoughts

1. Possible images: Keevan hobbling to the Hatching, Keevan being chosen by Heth, the fight scene between Keevan and Beterli, the dragonriders gathering for dinner.

Shaping Interpretations

2. External conflicts: dealing with Beterli's taunts and teasing, fighting Beterli, getting to the Hatching Ground while injured. Internal conflicts: anxiety about Impressing a dragon, worries about his size, fears of being excluded from the Hatching.

3. The climax is the point at which the bronze dragon chooses Keevan. Students might say that they felt happy, relieved, surprised, or satisfied.

4. Possible responses: K'van will be a dragonrider. Being known as a dragonrider will change the way people think about him and the way he thinks about himself. He may become Weyrleader.

5. Beterli did not have the characteristics that dragons look for—goodness, honesty, mental flexibility, patience, and courage.

Connecting with the Text

6. Possible responses: Once Keevan realizes that the voice is telepathic and coming from a dragon, he is thrilled. Students may cite similar experiences, such as being chosen for a team or the cast in a play, receiving an academic honor, or gaining the respect of someone they admire.

Extending the Text

7. Students will probably respond that teasing can be painful. Students may suggest that a victim ignore teasing or fight back verbally.

Challenging the Text

8. The only women are Mende, Keevan's foster mother, and Lessa, the Weyrwoman. Students may say the women have powerful positions because the foster mothers bring up the boys who will be dragonriders, and Lessa is the only person who can "receive" from all dragons. Lessa rides the Queen dragon.

9. Responses will vary. Some students may be confused by the meaning of the Thread; some students may have questions about the setting or characters.

CHOICES: Building Your Portfolio

1. **Writer's Notebook**   Remind students to save their work. They may use it as prewriting for the Writer's Workshop at the end of the collection.

2. **Science/Speaking and Listening**   If your city has a science museum, invite a guest speaker from the institution to visit your classroom. Another source might be a garden club member who specializes in herbs. Interested students could interview this person.

3. **Language and Vocabulary/ Writing**   Remind students that their glossaries should
   - present words in alphabetical order
   - give pronunciation symbols
   - identify each word's part of speech
   - give a clear, concise definition of each word

4. **Creative Writing/Music**   Play a recording of a familiar song, and write the lyrics on the chalkboard. Have students brainstorm in order to substitute words about K'van and Heth in the song's first line. Encourage students to complete this song about K'van and Heth's adventures or to start from the beginning with another melody. A list of simple, familiar songs might be helpful to some students.

CHOICES: Building Your Portfolio

Writer's Notebook

1. Collecting Ideas for a Story

Anne McCaffrey says she hatches a plot by creating fascinating characters and then finding something for them to fight for or against. Go back to your notes for the Quickwrite on page 46, and use McCaffrey's technique to expand your notes into the beginning of a story. Ask yourself,

- Who is my main character?
- Why is my main character an underdog?
- What is he or she fighting to get or to get away from?

> **Name: Lydia**
> —a girl struggling to be a dancer
> —has hearing loss
> —concentrates on sensing vibrations of music through floor as she dances

Science/ Speaking and Listening

2. Weyr Science

Although dragons are traditionally creatures of fantasy, Pern's dragons are products of bioengineering. What other references to science do you find in the story?

With one classmate or more, choose and research a scientific topic suggested by the text. You might explore one of these:

- animals that use warm sand to incubate their eggs
- weeds and herbs used as medicine
- the formation of volcanic cones

Present your findings to the class. Use charts, drawings, and other visual aids to illustrate your report.

Language and Vocabulary/Writing

3. What's the Word?

To describe life on Pern, Anne McCaffrey has invented new words, like *Weyr* and *Weyrling,* and new compound words, like *dragonboy* and *wingsecond.* You won't find any of these words in a dictionary, so you must guess their meanings from context clues or from what you already know about parts of the words. Help other readers by creating a "Pern glossary" of invented words

from the story. Besides giving definitions and pronunciations, you may want to illustrate some of the words.

Creative Writing/ Music

4. Dragonballads (Working on Your Scales)

On Pern, Harpers compose songs about brave dragons and their riders. Alone or with a partner, write a song about an adventure shared by K'van and Heth. Use the melody of a familiar song, or create your own tune. Work with other students to perform your song in a Pernian concert.

GRAMMAR LINK   MINI-LESSON

Keeping Verb Tenses Consistent

Language Handbook HELP

See *Consistency of Tense, page 731.*

Technology HELP

See *Language Workshop CD-ROM. Key word entry: verb tenses.*

In "The Smallest Dragonboy," Anne McCaffrey relies on verbs to tell readers *what* happened and on verb tenses to tell *when* it happened. Verb tenses help show the sequence of events in a plot; if the writer jumps from one tense to another, the order of events becomes unclear.

When writing about events that take place in the present, use verbs that are in the present tense.

EXAMPLE

"'I don't know why you're allowed in this Impression, Keevan. There are enough of us without a babe.'"

When writing about events that occurred in the past, use verbs that are in the past tense.

EXAMPLE

"Someone kicked sand over Keevan and butted roughly against him."

Be careful not to shift tenses unnecessarily. Unless you want to show a shift in time, be consistent—use one tense.

INCONSISTENT | An egg cracks, and the dragon had chosen his rider.

CONSISTENT | "An egg had cracked, and the dragon had chosen his rider."

Try It Out

➤ Make the verb tenses in each sentence consistent.

1. Keevan watches as the blue dragon stretched its wings.

2. Keevan drops his cane and fell to his knees.

3. Do all the dragons choose, or was one waiting for him?

➤ Keeping your tenses consistent can be difficult. Double-check your "tense sense" by asking a peer reviewer to go over a piece of writing with you. Circle all your verbs; their tenses should all be the same—unless, of course, you are writing about events that take place at different times.

VOCABULARY   HOW TO OWN A WORD

WORD BANK	Write About It and Own It
goaded imminent perturbed confrontation alleviate	1. Write a line of dialogue for Mende, using the word *goaded*. 2. Use the word *imminent* to describe a danger to Pern. 3. Write a line of dialogue for K'van, using the word *perturbed*. 4. Use the word *confrontation* in a description of Beterli. 5. Use the word *alleviate* to describe what Heth wants.

THE SMALLEST DRAGONBOY 63

GRAMMAR LINK

For the second part of Try It Out, have students choose a piece of writing from their portfolios. Ask them to underline each verb and to identify its tense. Then, tell them to exchange papers for their classmates to check. Students should revise any sentences with verb tenses that are awkward or out of sequence.

Try It Out
Possible Answers
1. Keevan watches as the blue dragon stretches its wings. [or *watched, stretched*]
2. Keevan drops his cane and falls to his knees. [or *dropped, fell*]
3. Did all the dragons choose, or did one wait for him? [or *Have* all the dragons *chosen*, or *is* one *waiting* for him?]

VOCABULARY
Possible Answers
1. "I think Beterli should be punished because he goaded Keevan into a fight."
2. Pern was in imminent danger of a Thread attack.
3. "When I heard that younger boys might not be candidates at the Impression, I became very perturbed."
4. In his confrontation with Keevan, Beterli behaved like an aggressive bully.
5. Only Keevan's approval could alleviate Heth's anxiety about his choice of dragonrider.

Resources
Grammar
• *Grammar and Language Links*, p. 5

Vocabulary
• *Words to Own*, p. 3

Spelling
For related instruction, see
• *Spelling and Decoding*, p. 3

Grammar Link Quick Check

Make the verb tenses in each sentence consistent.

1. Beterli teased Keevan and picks a fight with him. [teased, picked or teases, picks]

2. Keevan tries harder than the other boys because he was so small for his age. [tries, is or tried, was]

3. Keevan grits his teeth and blinked away tears as he hobbles to the Impression. [grits, blinks, hobbles, or gritted, blinked, hobbled]

4. In the end, Keevan is chosen by a bronze dragon and became a dragonrider. [is chosen, becomes or was chosen, became]

OBJECTIVES
1. Read and interpret the story
2. Analyze suspense and foreshadowing
3. Make predictions
4. Express understanding through narrative and creative writing, science, speaking, or design
5. Identify and use troublesome verbs correctly
6. Understand and use new words

SKILLS
Literary
• Analyze suspense and foreshadowing
Reading
• Make predictions
Writing
• Describe a story's setting
• Write a radio script
• Write a job listing
Grammar/Language
• Use troublesome verbs correctly
Vocabulary
• Use new words
Science/Speaking
• Research facts and present conclusions about rats
Art
• Design a job listing
Viewing/Representing
• Assess title of fine art (ATE)

Planning

Before You Read

THREE SKELETON KEY

Make the Connection

A Living Nightmare

Movies, TV, and books are full of horror tales. You might think that horror stories are something new, but since ancient times, storytellers have scared people with tales that make them want to check under their beds or behind the rocks in the back of their caves.

Quickwrite

If you were writing a horror story or directing a horror movie, what details would you use to create a scary setting? Freewrite your ideas.

Elements of Literature

Suspense and Foreshadowing: It Was a Dark and Stormy Night

Like many storytellers, the writer of this story hooks our interest with his very first words: "My most terrifying experience?" Once a question like this is asked in a story, we want to know the answer. We want to know what happens next. This feeling of anxious curiosity is called **suspense.**

Writers often intensify suspense by dropping hints that suggest what will happen later in the story. This use of clues is called **foreshadowing.**

Suspense is the uncertainty or anxiety that we feel about what will happen next in a story. **Foreshadowing** is the use of clues to suggest events that will happen later in the story. Foreshadowing often heightens suspense.

For more on Foreshadowing and Suspense, see pages 22–23 and the Handbook of Literary Terms.

Reading Skills and Strategies

Making Predictions: What Will Happen Next?

Part of the fun of reading is trying to guess what will happen next. This process is called **making predictions.** Here is how you make predictions:

• Look for clues that foreshadow what will happen.

• As the suspense builds, predict possible outcomes. See if you can guess where the writer is leading you.

• Ask yourself questions while you read. Revise your predictions as you go.

• Draw on your own experiences and knowledge in making your predictions.

Remember: A good writer always surprises you.

Background

Literature and Geography

The title of this story is the name of a key, or low-lying island, off the coast of French Guiana (gē·an′ə), in South America. At the time the story was written, French Guiana was a colony of France. Cayenne (kī·en′), the capital, was the site of one of several prison camps maintained by France in French Guiana until 1945.

For more information, see the map on page 76.

go.hrw.com
LEO 7-1

Preteaching Vocabulary

Words to Own

Direct pairs of students to take turns reading aloud the definitions of the Words to Own, listed at the bottom of the selection pages: **hordes, suffice, receding, edible,** and **derisive.** Then pair students to fill in the vocabulary words that are missing from the following ministory:

1. "Look out!" said the worker at Burger-Rama. "_____ of hungry teenagers just got off that bus and are heading this way." [hordes]

2. "I hope burgers alone will _____ to keep them happy," moaned the cook. [suffice]

3. Soon the first teenager in the line made a _____ remark about the poor quality of the food. "Don't you have anything _____ here?" he complained. [derisive, edible]

4. At last, all of the teenagers were served, and the crowd began _____. "Whew! I never thought we'd make it through that rush," the cook said. [receding]

Three Skeleton Key

George G. Toudouze

I did not give the warnings of the old-timers a second thought.

My most terrifying experience? Well, one does have a few in thirty-five years of service in the Lights, although it's mostly monotonous, routine work—keeping the light in order, making out the reports.

When I was a young man, not very long in the service, there was an opening in a lighthouse newly built off the coast of Guiana, on a small rock twenty miles or so from the mainland. The pay was high, so in order to reach the sum I had set out to save before I married, I volunteered for service in the new light.

Three Skeleton Key, the small rock on which the light stood, bore a bad reputation. It earned its name from the story of the three convicts who, escaping from Cayenne in a stolen dugout

Summary ■ ■

"Three Skeleton Key" is a horror story set in a lighthouse twenty-odd miles off the coast of South America. The nightmare begins when the three lighthouse keepers realize that a derelict sailing ship heading for their tiny, rocky island is filled with thousands of giant rats. When the ship crashes, the famished rats scramble onto the island and, in time, break into the lighthouse. The men struggle to stay alive and keep from going mad. To draw the attention of people on the mainland, they do not light their lamp one night, signaling that something must be wrong in the lighthouse. When a rescue ship appears, it is at first driven away by the rats. Later, a barge loaded with meat is towed near the lighthouse. The rats board the barge, the barge is set on fire, and the rats are burned or are finished off by sharks.

Resources

Listening
Audio CD Library
Students will appreciate the suspense in this horror tale as they listen to the recording in the *Audio CD Library*:
• Disc 3, Track 3

A Reading Skills and Strategies
Making Predictions

? Based on the text and illustrations on this page, what do you predict the story will be about? [Possible responses: It will be a terrifying story set in an isolated lighthouse with a scary name and a bad reputation. It will have something to do with rats.]

Resources: Print and Media

Reading
• *Reading Skills and Strategies*
  MiniRead Skill Lesson, p. 47
  Selection Skill Lesson, p. 53
• *Graphic Organizers for Active Reading*, p. 5
• *Words to Own*, p. 4
• *Spelling and Decoding*
  Worksheet, p. 4
• *Audio CD Library*
  Disc 3, Track 3

Writing and Language
• *Daily Oral Grammar*
  Transparency 4
• *Grammar and Language Links*
  Worksheet, p. 7
• *Language Workshop CD-ROM*

Viewing and Representing
• *Viewing and Representing*
  Fine Art Transparency 3
  Fine Art Worksheet, p. 12

Assessment
• *Formal Assessment*, p. 8
• *Portfolio Management System*, p. 109
• *Standardized Test Preparation*, pp. 16, 18
• *Test Generator (One-Stop Planner CD-ROM)*

Internet
• go.hrw.com (keyword: LE0 7-1)

A **Elements of Literature**

Foreshadowing

❓ Do you think the story of the three convicts is a hint about what's going to happen? Why or why not? [Possible responses: No, the three convicts died long ago, and the story of the dancing convicts is just superstition. Yes, because their deaths suggest the danger of trying to survive on an isolated island.]

B **Struggling Readers**

Summarizing

Help students summarize what they have learned about the narrator up to this point in the story. [The narrator spent thirty-five years in the lighthouse service; he had a terrifying experience when he was young; he did not believe the superstitions about the island; as a young man, he had planned to save money for marriage.]

C **English Language Learners**

Idioms

Tell students that the word *odd* is used after a number to show that the speaker does not know the exact distance and is making an estimate: The distance was somewhere between twenty and thirty miles.

D **Critical Thinking**

Making Judgments

❓ How does life on the lighthouse island sound to you? [Possible response: It seems confining, lonely, and depressing.]

E **Critical Thinking**

Interpreting

❓ What do you think of a narrator who is "greatly satisfied" with this life? [Possible responses: He must be a loner and an oddball; he must have very low expectations and be easy to please; he must enjoy the quiet and privacy.]

A canoe, were wrecked on the rock during the night, managed to escape the sea, but eventually died of hunger and thirst. When they were discovered, nothing remained but three heaps of bones, picked clean by the birds. The story was that the three skeletons, gleaming with phosphorescent[1] light, danced over the small rock, screaming. . . .

B But there are many such stories and I did not give the warnings of the old-timers at the *Île-de-Seine*[2] a second thought. I signed up, boarded ship, and in a month I was installed at the light.

> **The story was that the three skeletons, gleaming with phosphorescent light, danced over the small rock, screaming . . .**

C Picture a gray, tapering cylinder,[3] welded to the solid black rock by iron rods and concrete, rising from a small island twenty-odd miles from land. It lay in the midst of the sea, this island, a small, bare piece of stone, about one hundred fifty feet long, perhaps forty wide. Small, barely large enough for a man to walk about and stretch his legs at low tide.

This is an advantage one doesn't find in all lights, however, for some of them rise sheer from the waves, with no room for one to move save within the light itself. Still, on our island, one must be careful, for the rocks were treacherously smooth. One misstep and down you would fall into the sea—not that the risk of

drowning was so great, but the waters about our island swarmed with huge sharks, who kept an eternal patrol around the base of the light.

Still, it was a nice life there. We had enough provisions to last for months, in the event that the sea should become too rough for the supply ship to reach us on schedule. During the day we would work about the light, cleaning the rooms, polishing the metalwork and the **D** lens and reflector of the light itself, and at night we would sit on the gallery and watch our light, a twenty-thousand-candlepower lantern, swinging its strong white bar of light over the sea from the top of its hundred-twenty-foot tower. Some days, when the air would be very clear, we could see the land, a threadlike line to the west. To the east, north, and south stretched the ocean. Landsmen, perhaps, would soon have tired of that kind of life, perched on a small island off the coast of South America for eighteen weeks until one's turn for leave ashore came around. But we liked it there, my two fellow tenders and myself—so much so that for twenty-two months on end, **E** with the exception of shore leaves, I was greatly satisfied with the life on Three Skeleton Key.

I had just returned from my leave at the end of June, that is to say, midwinter in that latitude, and had settled down to the routine with my two fellow keepers, a Breton[4] by the name of Le Gleo and the head keeper, Itchoua, a Basque[5] some dozen years or so older than either of us.

Eight days went by as usual; then on the ninth night after my return, Itchoua, who was on night duty, called Le Gleo and me, sleeping in our rooms in the middle of the tower, at two in the morning. We rose immediately and,

---

1. **phosphorescent** (fäs′fə·res′ənt): glowing.
2. **Île-de-Seine** (ēl′ də sen′).
3. **tapering cylinder:** tube shape that gradually narrows toward one end, in this case toward the top.

4. **Breton** (bret′′n): person from Brittany, a region of northern France.
5. **Basque** (bask): Basques are people living in the Pyrenees, a mountain range in France and Spain.

Reaching All Students

Struggling Readers

Making Predictions was introduced on p. 64. For a lesson directly tied to this selection that teaches students to make predictions by using a strategy called Story Impressions, see the *Reading Skills and Strategies* binder:
- MiniRead Skill Lesson, p. 47
- Selection Skill Lesson, p. 53

English Language Learners

Setting plays a vital role in this story. To help students visualize events, display pictures of lighthouses and sailing ships. Then, assign these students to tutors who are proficient in English. Instruct the tutors to read the story aloud and capture the growing suspense, while the other students follow along in the book. For additional strategies, see
- *Lesson Plans Including Strategies for English-Language Learners*

Advanced Learners

The setting is not only a lighthouse but a lighthouse in the southern hemisphere. Ask students to explain to classmates why June would be midwinter in the latitude of Three Skeleton Rock.

Le Séducteur by René Magritte. Oil on canvas (19" × 23").

Virginia Museum of Fine Arts, Richmond, Virginia. Collection of Mr. and Mrs. Paul Mellon. Photograph by Ron Jennings.
©2000 Virginia Museum of Fine Arts. ©1998 C. Herscovici, Brussels/Artists Rights Society (ARS), New York.

climbing the thirty or so steps that led to the gallery, stood beside our chief.

Itchoua pointed, and following his finger, we saw a big three-master, with all sail set, heading straight for the light. A queer course, for the vessel must have seen us; our light lit her with the glare of day each time it passed over her. **F**

Now, ships were a rare sight in our waters, for our light was a warning of treacherous reefs, barely hidden under the surface and running far out to sea. Consequently we were always given a wide berth, especially by sailing vessels, which cannot maneuver as readily as steamers.

No wonder that we were surprised at seeing this three-master heading dead for us in the gloom of early morning. I had immediately recognized her lines, for she stood out plainly, even at the distance of a mile, when our light shone on her. **G**

She was a beautiful ship of some four thousand tons, a fast sailer that had carried cargoes to every part of the world, plowing the seas unceasingly. By her lines she was identified as Dutch built, which was understandable, as

THREE SKELETON KEY 67

F Reading Skills and Strategies
Making Predictions

? Why might the ship be sailing so close to the lighthouse? [Possible responses: The crew could be having trouble; the ship might be out of control; the ship may bear a message for the men in the lighthouse.]

G Elements of Literature
Suspense

? What words in this paragraph create a sense of danger and a feeling of anxiety about what will happen next? [Possible response: The words "heading dead for us" and "in the gloom of early morning" create a feeling that something bad is about to happen.]

Taking a Second Look

Review: Metacognition

Remind students that *metacognition* means "being aware of one's own responses while reading." Explain that such "thinking about thinking" can help them enjoy the suspense in a thrilling story. Use the following activities when students have completed "Three Skeleton Key."

Activities

1. Have volunteers tell how they previewed the story. For example, did they flip through the pages, check out the illustrations, draw an inference from the title?
2. On the board, write the following observations.
   • Why would anyone take a job like that?
   • Oh, no, the rats are going to get in!
   • Wait! I don't quite understand what happened. I'll have to read that paragraph again.

   • I don't want to turn the page. I don't want to know what's going to happen next.
   • Eww! That was creepy, but good.
   Ask students if they had similar thoughts w[...] reading and at what point in the story t[...] thoughts occurred to them. Encour[...] to discuss their responses.

Sea Legend

There are many legends connected with the sea. One well-known legend is that of the Flying Dutchman, a mariner who is doomed to sail the world's oceans until Judgment Day. According to some versions of the tale, his ship was cursed because of the captain's cruelty to slaves he was transporting from Africa or because he had lost a bet with the devil. The ghostly ship, also known as the *Flying Dutchman*, was considered an evil omen by sailors.

B Critical Thinking

Analyzing Character

? What do their reactions to the mysterious ship tell you about differences in Le Gleo's and Itchoua's characters? [Possible responses: Le Gleo is easily excited and superstitious. Itchoua, on the other hand, seems cool under pressure and logical.]

C Elements of Literature

Suspense

? How does the author increase the reader's tension and anxiety in this part of the story? [Possible response: He stretches out the action, letting the derelict ship zigzag back and forth, toward the island and then away; he makes the characters speculate about why the perfectly intact ship was abandoned. As a result, most readers wonder what is going on, what will happen next, and how the characters will solve the mystery.]

Paramaribo and Dutch Guiana are very close to Cayenne.

Watching her sailing dead for us, a white wave boiling under her bows, Le Gleo cried out:

"What's wrong with her crew? Are they all drunk or insane? Can't they see us?"

Itchoua nodded soberly and looked at us sharply as he remarked: "See us? No doubt—if there *is* a crew aboard!"

"Are you saying that she's the *Flying Dutchman*?" His sudden fright had been so evident that the older man laughed.

"What do you mean, chief?" Le Gleo had started, turned to the Basque. "Are you saying that she's the *Flying Dutchman*?"[6]

His sudden fright had been so evident that the older man laughed:

"No, old man, that's not what I meant. If I say that no one's aboard, I mean she's a derelict."[7]

Then we understood her queer behavior. Itchoua was right. For some reason, believing her doomed, her crew had abandoned her. Then she had righted herself and sailed on, wandering with the wind.

The three of us grew tense as the ship seemed about to crash on one of our numerous reefs, but she suddenly lurched with some change of the wind, the yards[8] swung around, and the derelict came clumsily about and sailed dead away from us.

---

6. Flying Dutchman: fabled Dutch ghost ship whose captain is said to be condemned to sail the seas until Judgment Day. Seeing the *Flying Dutchman* is supposed to bring bad luck.

7. derelict (der'ə·likt'): here, abandoned ship.

8. yards: in nautical terms, rods fastened across the masts to support the sails.

In the light of our lantern she seemed so sound, so strong, that Itchoua exclaimed impatiently:

"But why the devil was she abandoned? Nothing is smashed, no sign of fire—and she doesn't sail as if she were taking water."

Le Gleo waved to the departing ship:

"Bon voyage!" he smiled at Itchoua and went on. "She's leaving us, chief, and now we'll never know what——"

"No, she's not!" cried the Basque. "Look! She's turning!"

As if obeying his words, the derelict three-master stopped, came about, and headed for us once more. And for the next four hours the vessel played around us—zigzagging, coming about, stopping, then suddenly lurching forward. No doubt some freak of current and wind, of which our island was the center, kept her near us.

Then suddenly the tropic dawn broke, the sun rose, and it was day, and the ship was plainly visible as she sailed past us. Our light extinguished, we returned to the gallery with our glasses[9] and inspected her.

The three of us focused our glasses on her poop[10] and saw, standing out sharply, black letters on the white background of a life ring, the stenciled name "*Cornelius de Witt*, Rotterdam."

We had read her lines correctly: She was Dutch. Just then the wind rose and the *Cornelius de Witt* changed course, leaned to port, and headed straight for us once more. But this time she was so close that we knew she would not turn in time.

"Thunder!" cried Le Gleo, his Breton soul aching at seeing a fine ship doomed to smash upon a reef, "she's going to pile up! She's gone!"

---

9. glasses: here, binoculars.

10. poop: in nautical terms, the stern (back) deck of a ship.

Getting Students Involved

...ave read the
..ow" poem
...y. Encour-
...Have them
...he follow-
...tory that
...to their
...heir poems

I Know "Three Skeleton Key"	
I Know "Three Skeleton Key" [Write four sounds that you can "hear" in your imagination.]	
I Know "Three Skeleton Key" [Write four sights that you picture vividly.]	
I Know "Three Skeleton Key" [Write four odors that are so strong, you can almost smell them.]	
I Know "Three Skeleton Key" [Write four images that you can almost touch or feel.]	

I shook my head:

"Yes, and a shame to see that beautiful ship wreck herself. And we're helpless."

There was nothing we could do but watch. A ship sailing with all sail spread, creaming the sea with her forefoot as she runs before the wind, is one of the most beautiful sights in the world—but this time I could feel the tears stinging in my eyes as I saw this fine ship headed for her doom.

All this time our glasses were riveted on her and we suddenly cried out together:

"The rats!"

Now we knew why this ship, in perfect condition, was sailing without her crew aboard. They had been driven out by the rats. Not those poor specimens of rats you see ashore, barely reaching the length of one foot from their trembling noses to the tip of their skinny tails, wretched creatures that dodge and hide at the mere sound of a footfall.

No, these were ships' rats, huge, wise creatures, born on the sea, sailing all over the world on ships, transferring to other, larger ships as they multiply. There is as much difference between the rats of the land and these maritime rats as between a fishing smack[11] and an armored cruiser.

The rats of the sea are fierce, bold animals. Large, strong, and intelligent, clannish and seawise, able to put the best of mariners to shame with their knowledge of the sea, their uncanny ability to foretell the weather.

And they are brave, these rats, and vengeful. If you so much as harm one, his sharp cry will bring <u>hordes</u> of his fellows to swarm over you, <u>tear you</u>, and not cease until your flesh has been stripped from the bones.

The ones on this ship, the rats of Holland, are the worst, superior to other rats of the sea as their brethren are to the land rats. There is a well-known tale about these animals.

11. **smack:** here, small sailboat.

The rats of the sea are fierce, bold animals.

A Dutch captain, thinking to protect his cargo, brought aboard his ship not cats but two terriers, dogs trained in the hunting, fighting, and killing of vicious rats. By the time the ship, sailing from Rotterdam, had passed the Ostend

----

WORDS TO OWN
hordes (hôrdz) *n.*: large, moving crowds.

THREE SKELETON KEY 69

D **Reading Skills and Strategies**
Connecting with the Text
Ask students to think about a time when they were moved by the ruin or destruction of something beautiful. Direct them to write about their memories of the incident. Advise students to choose an incident they would not mind sharing with others.

E **Appreciating Language**
Vivid Adjectives and Verbs
Invite students to identify the vivid adjectives and verbs that the narrator uses to describe the rats. [Adjectives: *fierce, bold, large, strong, intelligent, clannish, seawise, brave, vengeful;* Verbs: *swarm, tear, stripped.*] Then, ask what these vivid adjectives and verbs convey about the narrator's view of the rats. [Possible responses: The narrator both respects and fears the rats. He sees them as both awesome and terrifying.]

F **Reading Skills and Strategies**
Making Predictions
? What do you think the rest of the story will be about? [Students will probably predict that the rest of the story will be about the men's attempts to fight or outsmart the rats, or to get off the island safely.]

Skill Link

Transitive and Intransitive Verbs
Use the following exercise before you teach the Grammar Link on troublesome verbs, on p. 79. This exercise will help you assess students' skill in identifying verbs that take direct objects.
Activity
Label each verb with a **V**. If the verb has a direct object, label it **DO**. For a review of direct

objects, see pp. 735 and 755 in the Language Handbook.
1. Set the glasses on the table. [V: *set*, DO: *glasses*]
2. I am sitting on the floor. [V: *am sitting*, no DO]
3. Will you raise the window shade? [V: *will raise*, DO: *window shade*]

4. The sun is rising early today. [V: *is rising*, no DO]
5. The builders laid the bricks for the foundation. [V: *laid*, DO: *bricks*]
6. The cat lay in the sun. [V: *lay*, no DO]

Ⓐ Reading Skills and Strategies

Metacognition

❓ Which clues help you figure out what happened to the ship's crew? [Possible response: The first clue is the statement that hungry rats will either attack a crew and drive them from a ship or eat them. The second clue is that the lifeboats are still on the ship. Since the crew did not escape in the lifeboats, the rats must have eaten the crew.]

Ⓑ Vocabulary Note

Technical Words

Encourage interested students to look up the meaning and pronunciation of the following terms related to ships: *port, starboard, bow, stern.* Ask them to label a diagram of a ship with the terms and explain their meanings to the class.

Ⓒ Struggling Readers

Identifying Pronoun Antecedents

Help students to identify the noun in this paragraph that the pronouns *they, them,* and *those* refer to. [The word *fellows*—which is used here as a synonym for rats in the preceding sentence—is the antecedent of all the pronouns.]

Thousands of heads rose, felt the wind, and we were scented, seen!

light, the dogs were gone and never seen again. In twenty-four hours they had been overwhelmed, killed, and eaten by the rats.

Ⓐ At times, when the cargo does not <u>suffice</u>, the rats attack the crew, either driving them from the ship or eating them alive. And studying the *Cornelius de Witt,* I turned sick, for her small boats were all in place. She had not been abandoned.

Over her bridge, on her deck, in the rigging, on every visible spot, the ship was a writhing mass—a starving army coming toward us aboard a vessel gone mad!

Our island was a small spot in that immense stretch of sea. The ship could have grazed us or

Ⓑ passed to port or starboard with its ravening[12] cargo—but no, she came for us at full speed, as if she were leading the regatta at a race, and impaled herself on a sharp point of rock.

There was a dull shock as her bottom stove in,[13] then a horrible crackling as the three masts went overboard at once, as if cut down with one blow of some gigantic sickle. A sighing groan came as the water rushed into the ship; then she split in two and sank like a stone.

But the rats did not drown. Not these fellows! As much at home in the sea as any fish, Ⓒ they formed ranks in the water, heads lifted, tails stretched out, paws paddling. And half of them, those from the forepart of the ship,

12. ravening (rav′ən·iŋ): greedily searching for animals to kill for food. A more common related word is *ravenous* (rav′ə·nəs), meaning "wildly, greedily hungry."
13. stove in: caved in.

WORDS TO OWN

suffice (sə·fis′) *v.*: be enough.

70 OUT HERE ON MY OWN

Using Students' Strengths

Intrapersonal Learners

These students tend to be experts on themselves. After they have read the story, suggest they write in their journals about coping with fear. How would they have reacted if they had been in the lighthouse keepers' situation? What ways have they found to cope with stress and fear in their own lives? Which, if any, coping techniques would they like to share with others?

Visual Learners

As visual learners read the story, they might benefit from filling in a graphic organizer. See p. 5 in the *Graphic Organizers for Active Reading.*

sprang along the masts and onto the rocks in the instant before she sank. Before we had time even to move, nothing remained of the three-master save some pieces of wreckage floating on the surface and an army of rats covering the rocks left bare by the receding tide.

Thousands of heads rose, felt the wind, and we were scented, seen! To them we were fresh meat, after possible weeks of starving. There came a scream, composed of innumerable screams, sharper than the howl of a saw attacking a bar of iron, and in the one motion, every rat leaped to attack the tower!

We barely had time to leap back, close the door leading onto the gallery, descend the stairs, and shut every window tightly. Luckily the door at the base of the light, which we never could have reached in time, was of bronze set in granite and was tightly closed.

The horrible band, in no measurable time, had swarmed up and over the tower as if it had been a tree, piled on the embrasures[14] of the windows, scraped at the glass with thousands of claws, covered the lighthouse with a furry mantle, and reached the top of the tower, filling the gallery and piling atop the lantern.

Their teeth grated as they pressed against the glass of the lantern room, where they could plainly see us, though they could not reach us. A few millimeters of glass, luckily very strong, separated our faces from their gleaming, beady eyes, their sharp claws and teeth. Their odor filled the tower, poisoned our lungs, and rasped our nostrils with a pestilential, nauseating smell. And there we were, sealed alive in our own light, prisoners of a horde of starving rats.

That first night, the tension was so great that we could not sleep. Every moment, we felt that some opening had been made, some window given way, and that our horrible besiegers were pouring through the breach. The rising

tide, chasing those of the rats which had stayed on the bare rocks, increased the numbers clinging to the walls, piled on the balcony—so much so that clusters of rats clinging to one another hung from the lantern and the gallery.

With the coming of darkness we lit the light and the turning beam completely maddened the beasts. As the light turned, it successively blinded thousands of rats crowded against the glass, while the dark side of the lantern room gleamed with thousands of points of light, burning like the eyes of jungle beasts in the night.

And there we were, sealed alive in our own light, prisoners of a horde of starving rats.

All the while we could hear the enraged scraping of claws against the stone and glass, while the chorus of cries was so loud that we had to shout to hear one another. From time to time, some of the rats fought among themselves and a dark cluster would detach itself, falling into the sea like a ripe fruit from a tree. Then we would see phosphorescent streaks as triangular fins slashed the water—sharks, permanent guardians of our rock, feasting on our jailers.

The next day we were calmer and amused ourselves teasing the rats, placing our faces against the glass which separated us. They could not fathom the invisible barrier which separated them from us, and we laughed as we watched them leaping against the heavy glass.

But the day after that, we realized how serious our position was. The air was foul; even the heavy smell of oil within our stronghold could

14. **embrasures** (em·brā′zhərz): slanted openings.

WORDS TO OWN
receding (ri·sēd′iŋ) v. used as adj.: moving back.

D Elements of Literature
Suspense
? What creates the suspense in this part of the paragraph, and how does the narrator make the suspense last? [Possible response: The reader can only guess what the rats will do next. The narrator prolongs the suspense by describing the speed with which the rats move, instead of immediately explaining what the rats do after they reach the island.]

E Reading Skills and Strategies
Responding to the Text
Ask students how they generally respond to such vivid descriptions of horrifying events. Do they enjoy the thrill of safely experiencing such horror, do they want to turn away and close the book, or do they experience both feelings? Encourage students to express their feelings freely.

F Appreciating Language
Sensory Details
? Which of the five senses does the narrator appeal to in order to vividly convey the horror of the situation? [Possible responses: SIGHT: *swarmed, covered, filling, piling, gleaming, beady eyes, sharp claws and teeth, horde;* SOUND: *scraped, grated;* SMELL: *poisoned our lungs, rasped our nostrils, pestilential, nauseating smell;* TOUCH: *furry mantle, sharp claws and teeth, sealed alive*]

G Reading Skills and Strategies

Making Predictions
? Do you think the rats will eventually get into the lighthouse? Explain why or why not. [Students' predictions will vary. Many will predict that the rats will find a way in, because there is bound to be a small hole or weakness in the structure somewhere, and rats are good at squeezing through tight spaces. They may also say that to make the story more exciting, the author will devise a way for the rats to get in.]

Using Students' Strengths

Logical/Mathematical Learners
After logical/mathematical learners read the story, invite them to work in groups of three. Challenge them to look back over the story and consider other options the characters may have had at various points for solving their problems with the rats. Allow students time to analyze the details (regarding food, supplies, tools, and the structure of the lighthouse) that might help them find a different solution to the conflict.

Then, direct students to outline the story with the new solution. They should treat the new plot day by day, from the moment the characters spot the abandoned, rat-infested ship until their rescue. Groups can present their new solution to the class. If they wish, the students can take the roles of the characters and act out their re-creation of events.

LITERATURE AND HISTORY

Many women have been employed as lighthouse keepers. In 1776 Hannah Thomas became the first female lighthouse keeper in this country. Each night she had to refill her lighthouse's lamps and clean them, and each dawn she had to extinguish the lamps and clean them again. Female keepers assumed the same risks as their male counterparts. Another keeper, Rebecca Flaherty, drowned when her lighthouse in the Florida Keys was swept away during a hurricane.

A Elements of Literature

Suspense

❓ How do you feel, knowing that rats have succeeded in causing the window frame to sag? [Possible responses: tense, worried that the rats are about to get in, curious about what will happen next.]

B Elements of Literature

Foreshadowing

Let students explain why Itchoua says the name of the island can be changed to Six Skeleton Key. [The island was named Three Skeleton Key for three convicts who had been stranded there and died. Their bodies had been devoured by birds, leaving only their bones. Itchoua is suggesting that the lighthouse keepers will suffer a similar fate—but this time rats will be the devourers. Then the total of skeletons found on the key, or island, will increase to six.]

LITERATURE AND HISTORY

Night Lights on the High Seas

For centuries, lighthouses have been used to alert sailors that land is near, to point out dangerous rocks and reefs, and to cast a bright light into the night to guide ships on their way. Seafarers have relied on these structures since the days of ancient Egypt. The lighthouse built in 300 B.C. on Pharos, an island near Alexandria, was regarded as one of the Seven Wonders of the World.

Lighthouses help to guide ships at night by giving off an intense beam of light that flashes every few seconds. Until the eighteenth century the source of light was an oak-log fire. Coal fire was used for many years after that, until electricity became common in the early twentieth century. Some modern lighthouses also send out radio signals to help ships find their way in foggy weather. Even in their modern form, lighthouses still serve their ancient purpose as a guiding light, a flashing speck of civilization in the dark, lonely waters of the night.

not dominate the fetid odor of the beasts massed around us. And there was no way of admitting fresh air without also admitting the rats.

A The morning of the fourth day, at early dawn, I saw the wooden framework of my window, eaten away from the outside, sagging inwards. I called my comrades and the three of us fastened a sheet of tin in the opening, sealing it tightly. When we had completed that task, Itchoua turned to us and said dully:

B "Well—the supply boat came thirteen days ago, and she won't be back for twenty-nine." He pointed at the white metal plate sealing the opening through the granite. "If that gives way"—he shrugged—"they can change the name of this place to Six Skeleton Key."

The next six days and seven nights, our only distraction was watching the rats whose holds were insecure fall a hundred and twenty feet into the maws of the sharks—but they were so many that we could not see any diminution in their numbers.

Thinking to calm ourselves and pass the time, we attempted to count them, but we soon gave up. They moved incessantly, never still. Then we tried identifying them, naming them.

One of them, larger than the others, who

Crossing the Curriculum

Health

Remind students that rats have nearly always been considered a health hazard for humans. Assign students to small groups to research exactly how rats have affected human health in history. Based on their research, students should create lists of five health precautions to be posted in a rat-infested area to warn human residents of the dangers.

Geography

Students may not realize that South America, like North America, was colonized by people from other countries and that the land became a haven for immigrants from Europe and Asia. Put students into small groups to research which ethnic groups immigrated to the northeast section of South America and when and why they settled there. Students can create maps labeled with the information they learn, and they can share their work with the class.

seemed to lead them in their rushes against the glass separating us, we named "Nero";[15] and there were several others whom we had learned to distinguish through various peculiarities.

But the thought of our bones joining those of the convicts was always in the back of our minds. And the gloom of our prison fed these thoughts, for the interior of the light was almost completely dark, as we had had to seal every window in the same fashion as mine, and the only space that still admitted daylight was the glassed-in lantern room at the very top of the tower.

Then Le Gleo became morose and had nightmares in which he would see the three skeletons dancing around him, gleaming coldly, seeking to grasp him. His maniacal, raving descriptions were so vivid that Itchoua and I began seeing them also.

It was a living nightmare, the raging cries of the rats as they swarmed over the light, mad with hunger; the sickening, strangling odor of their bodies——

True, there is a way of signaling from lighthouses. But to reach the mast on which to hang the signal, we would have to go out on the gallery where the rats were.

There was only one thing left to do. After debating all of the ninth day, we decided not to light the lantern that night. This is the greatest breach of our service, never committed as long as the tenders of the light are alive; for the light is something sacred, warning ships of danger in the night. Either the light gleams a quarter-hour after sundown, or no one is left alive to light it.

Well, that night, Three Skeleton Light was dark, and all the men were alive. At the risk of causing ships to crash on our reefs, we left it unlit, for we were worn out—going mad!

At two in the morning, while Itchoua was

15. **Nero** (nir′ō): emperor of Rome (A.D. 54–68), known for his cruelty.

dozing in his room, the sheet of metal sealing his window gave way. The chief had just time enough to leap to his feet and cry for help, the rats swarming over him.

But Le Gleo and I, who had been watching from the lantern room, got to him immediately, and the three of us battled with the horde of maddened rats which flowed through the gaping window. They bit, we struck them down with our knives—and retreated.

We locked the door of the room on them,

The chief had just time enough to leap to his feet and cry for help, the rats swarming over him.

but before we had time to bind our wounds, the door was eaten through and gave way, and we retreated up the stairs, fighting off the rats that leaped on us from the knee-deep swarm.

I do not remember, to this day, how we ever managed to escape. All I can remember is wading through them up the stairs, striking them off as they swarmed over us; and then we found ourselves, bleeding from innumerable bites, our clothes shredded, sprawled across the trapdoor in the floor of the lantern room—without food or drink. Luckily, the trapdoor was metal, set into the granite with iron bolts.

The rats occupied the entire light beneath us, and on the floor of our retreat lay some twenty of their fellows, who had gotten in with us before the trapdoor closed and whom we had killed with our knives. Below us, in the tower, we could hear the screams of the rats as

G Reading Skills and Strategies
Metacognition

? What clues earlier in the story could help readers predict that Le Gleo would be the first to crumble under the pressure? [Possible response: Students may recall that Le Gleo is the most superstitious and excitable of the lighthouse keepers. They may remember his first reaction to the deserted ship, described on p. 68, when he wonders if it is a cursed vessel of legend.]

D Reading Skills and Strategies
Making Predictions

When students get up to this paragraph, ask them to predict how the men might signal to the outside world that something is wrong on Three Skeleton Key. [Possible predictions: The men will set off some kind of siren or other noise or set a fire to attract the attention of passing ships; they will use the light to send a message in Morse code; or, as a last resort, they will not light the lighthouse lamp.]

E Appreciating Language
Using Troublesome Verbs

Ask students to explain why *lay*, not *laid*, is the correct verb to use in this sentence. [In this example, *lay* is used as the past tense of the verb *lie*, meaning "to recline." It is an intransitive verb with no direct object.]

Getting Students Involved

Cooperative Learning

Report from a Panel of Experts. Create four-student panels, and assign to each panel a subject that plays a role in the story: rodents, sailing, lighthouses, and so on. Tell the students to imagine that they are experts who have traveled to Three Skeleton Key to analyze and report on incidents that occur in the story. Direct each group to first choose a focus for its report—for example, characteristics of three-master sailing ships. Then, tell the groups they will have two responsibilities: (1) to return to the story to look for details and relevant excerpts; (2) to research other materials to supplement the information in the story. Two students in each group can search the story while two others research outside sources. Give each group a chance to present its findings to the class during an expert question-and-answer session.

A Reading Skills
and Strategies

**Making
Predictions**

? Now that the lighthouse team has been cut off from its supplies and has been attacked by the rats, do you think the men can survive? Explain your response. [Possible responses: Some students may argue that the end is near; others may say that because the men did not light the lamp on the previous night, help may already be on the way.]

B Elements of Literature

Suspense

? What question is in your mind at this point in the story? [Possible responses: Will the ship's crew go away, thinking the men are already dead? Can the men find a way to let the ship's crew know they are still alive?]

they devoured everything edible that they found. Those on the outside squealed in reply and writhed in a horrible curtain as they stared at us through the glass of the lantern room.

> "The Three Skeletons!
> Hee! Hee!
> The Three Skeletons
> are now *six* skeletons!
> *Six* skeletons!"

A Itchoua sat up and stared silently at his blood trickling from the wounds on his limbs and body and running in thin streams on the floor around him. Le Gleo, who was in as bad a state (and so was I, for that matter), stared at the chief and me vacantly, started as his gaze swung to the multitude of rats against the glass, then suddenly began laughing horribly:

"Hee! Hee! The Three Skeletons! Hee! Hee! The Three Skeletons are now *six* skeletons! *Six* skeletons!"

He threw his head back and howled, his eyes glazed, a trickle of saliva running from the corners of his mouth and thinning the blood flowing over his chest. I shouted to him to shut up, but he did not hear me, so I did the only thing I could to quiet him—I swung the back of my hand across his face.

The howling stopped suddenly, and his eyes swung around the room; then he bowed his head and began weeping softly, like a child.

B Our darkened light had been noticed from the mainland, and as dawn was breaking, the patrol was there to investigate the failure of our light. Looking through my binoculars, I could see the horrified expression on the faces of the officers and crew when, the daylight strengthening, they saw the light completely covered by a seething mass of rats. They thought, as I

afterwards found out, that we had been eaten alive.

But the rats had also seen the ship or had scented the crew. As the ship drew nearer, a solid phalanx[16] left the light, plunged into the water, and swimming out, attempted to board her. They would have succeeded, as the ship was hove to;[17] but the engineer connected his steam to a hose on the deck and scalded the head of the attacking column, which slowed them up long enough for the ship to get under way and leave the rats behind.

Then the sharks took part. Belly up, mouths gaping, they arrived in swarms and scooped up the rats, sweeping through them like a sickle through wheat. That was one day that sharks really served a useful purpose.

The remaining rats turned tail, swam to the shore, and emerged dripping. As they neared the light, their comrades greeted them with shrill cries, with what sounded like a derisive note predominating. They answered angrily and mingled with their fellows. From the several tussles that broke out, it seemed as if they resented being ridiculed for their failure to capture the ship.

But all this did nothing to get us out of our jail. The small ship could not approach but steamed around the light at a safe distance, and the tower must have seemed fantastic, some weird, many-mouthed beast hurling defiance at them.

Finally, seeing the rats running in and out of the tower through the door and the windows, those on the ship decided that we had perished and were about to leave when Itchoua,

---

16. phalanx (fā′lanks′): closely packed group. A phalanx is an ancient military formation, and the word still has warlike connotations.

17. hove to: stopped by being turned into the wind.

- -
WORDS TO OWN

edible (ed′ə·bəl) *adj.*: fit to be eaten.
derisive (di·rī′siv) *adj.*: scornful and ridiculing.
- -

Assessing Learning

Peer Assessment

After students have completed the story, let them get together in pairs to discuss their progress in making predictions as they read. Ask both partners to respond to each of the following questions, alternating who answers first.

1. How soon did you guess that the island would be overrun by rats? What clues tipped you off?

2. How soon did you know that the rats would break into the lighthouse? What clues tipped you off?

3. Did you predict that the men would find a way to get help from the outside world—or not? Why did you make this prediction?

4. Did you predict that the men would survive their experience? Why or why not?

C **Historical Connections**
Explain to students that long before there were fax machines and telephones, the most efficient way to communicate across distances was by Morse code. The code is made up of dots (short signals), dashes (long signals), and spaces (pauses). The most well-known example of Morse code is the three-letter signal *SOS* (in Morse code: • • • — — — • • •), a distress signal used especially by ships in trouble at sea. The signal was still new when it was used by the crew of the sinking *Titanic* in 1912. Interested students may want to learn Morse code and practice sending messages in it.

regaining his senses, thought of using the light as a signal. He lit it and, using a plank placed and withdrawn before the beam to form the dots and dashes, quickly sent out our story to those on the vessel.

Our reply came quickly. When they understood our position—how we could not get rid of the rats, Le Gleo's mind going fast, Itchoua and myself covered with bites, cornered in the lantern room without food or water—they had a signalman send us their reply.

His arms swinging like those of a windmill, he quickly spelled out:

"Don't give up, hang on a little longer! We'll get you out of this!"

Then she turned and steamed at top speed for the coast, leaving us little reassured.

She was back at noon, accompanied by the supply ship, two small coast guard boats, and the fireboat—a small squadron. At twelve-thirty the battle was on.

After a short reconnaissance,[18] the fireboat picked her way slowly through the reefs until she was close to us, then turned her powerful jet of water on the rats. The heavy stream tore the rats from their places and hurled them screaming into the water, where the sharks gulped them down. But for every ten that were dislodged, seven swam ashore, and the stream could do nothing to the rats within the tower. Furthermore, some of them, instead of returning to the rocks, boarded the fireboat, and the men were forced to battle them hand to hand. They were true rats of Holland, fearing no man, fighting for the right to live!

Nightfall came, and it was as if nothing had been done; the rats were still in possession. One of the patrol boats stayed by the island; the rest of the flotilla[19] departed for the coast. We had to

18. **reconnaissance** (ri·kän′ə·səns): exploratory survey or examination.
19. **flotilla** (flō·til′ə): small fleet of boats.

Making the Connections

Connecting to the Theme: "Out Here on My Own"
When students have finished the story, talk about the theme. Tell them that horror stories often involve an individual or small group facing danger while cut off from the rest of society. Sometimes the characters overcome the odds without help, and sometimes, as in this story, outside help arrives just in time. Invite students to discuss other stories or movies with this theme and what they enjoy about such stories.

Cultural Connections
Despite today's technology, people all over the world (or universe) still may find themselves in situations when they must face danger alone. Let students brainstorm contemporary situations in which individuals are cut off and in danger. Possibilities include people camping in the wilderness; people trapped in a fire, earthquake, or other natural disaster; astronauts on their own in space.

A Reading Skills and Strategies

Making Predictions

❓ The men have gone two days without food and have experienced false hopes of rescue. Do you still predict that they will survive? Why or why not? [Possible responses: Rescue seems so close that perhaps they can still make it, although they may eventually go insane or die from their infected wounds. Some students may realize that the narrator, at least, must survive in order to tell the story.]

B Vocabulary Note

Word Origins

Tell students that shrapnel is an artillery shell containing lead balls and a powder charge. It was named for the nineteenth-century British general Henry Shrapnel, who invented it. Ask students to research the origin of other words that were named for the inventor of the object: *silhouette, saxophone.*

C Critical Thinking

Expressing an Opinion

❓ Do you think the narrator is a believable character? In your opinion, why did the author choose such an odd character to tell the story? [Some students may say that the narrator's calm return to a place where he experienced a truly horrifying situation is very unusual behavior. The author might have chosen such an odd narrator to make the story even more chilling and strange. Imagining how it would feel to return to such a place adds to the horror of the story.]

Resources

A spend another night in our prison. Le Gleo was sitting on the floor, babbling about skeletons, and as I turned to Itchoua, he fell unconscious from his wounds. I was in no better shape and could feel my blood flaming with fever.

Somehow the night dragged by, and the next afternoon I saw a tug, accompanied by the fireboat, come from the mainland with a huge barge in tow. Through my glasses, I saw that the barge was filled with meat.

Risking the treacherous reefs, the tug dragged the barge as close to the island as possible. To the last rat, our besiegers deserted the rock, swam out, and boarded the barge reeking with the scent of freshly cut meat. The tug dragged the barge about a mile from shore, where the fireboat drenched the barge with gasoline. A well-placed incendiary shell from the patrol boat set her on fire.

B The barge was covered with flames immediately, and the rats took to the water in swarms, but the patrol boat bombarded them with shrapnel from a safe distance, and the sharks finished off the survivors.

A whaleboat from the patrol boat took us off the island and left three men to replace us. By nightfall we were in the hospital in Cayenne. What became of my friends?

Well, Le Gleo's mind had cracked and he was raving mad. They sent him back to France and locked him up in an asylum, the poor devil! Itchoua died within a week; a rat's bite is dangerous in that hot, humid climate, and infection sets in rapidly.

C As for me—when they fumigated the light and repaired the damage done by the rats, I resumed my service there. Why not? No reason why such an incident should keep me from finishing out my service there, is there?

Besides—I told you I liked the place—to be truthful, I've never had a post as pleasant as that one, and when my time came to leave it forever, I tell you that I almost wept as Three Skeleton Key disappeared below the horizon.

76 OUT HERE ON MY OWN

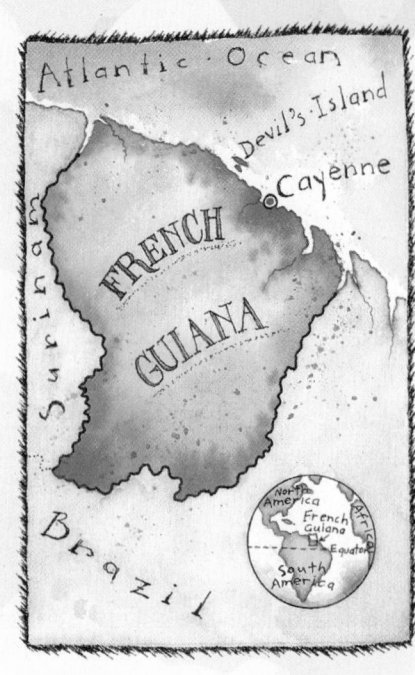

MEET THE WRITER

Sea Fever

George G. Toudouze (1847–1904) was born in France and had many literary interests—he was a playwright, an essayist, and an illustrator. He also had a great interest in the sea and worked on a history of the French Navy. One critic says of his storytelling style, "It has the impact of a powerful man at a fair who, for the fun of it, takes the hammer and at one blow sends the machine to the top, rings the bell, and walks off." "Three Skeleton Key" first appeared in *Esquire* magazine.

Assessing Learning

Check Test: True-False
1. "Three Skeleton Key" is about one man's most enjoyable experience. [False]
2. Three Skeleton Key is an island where three escaped prisoners died of thirst and hunger. [True]
3. The rats on board the drifting ship were just like ordinary rats. [False]
4. The men decided to leave the lighthouse unlit as a signal to the mainland. [True]

5. Only one man was left alive when the rescuers arrived. [False]

Standardized Test Preparation
For practice with standardized test format specific to this selection, see
• *Standardized Test Preparation,* pp. 16, 18
For practice in proofreading and editing, see
• *Daily Oral Grammar,* Transparency 4

MAKING MEANINGS

First Thoughts

[respond]

1. Describe your reaction to "Three Skeleton Key" by completing these sentences:
   - When I first read about the rats, I felt . . .
   - For me, the scariest part of the story was . . .

Shaping Interpretations

[predict]

2. Early in the story the narrator explains how Three Skeleton Key got its name. How does this **foreshadow**—or hint at—the danger the three lighthouse keepers face later on?

[analyze]

3. On the fourth day of the invasion, a wooden window frame in the lighthouse sags inward. How does this incident increase **suspense**? What other details create suspense?

[connect]

4. The three characters in the lighthouse respond differently to the invasion. Describe each man's reactions to the rats. Which character (if any) did you identify with?

Connecting with the Text

[connect]

5. If you were the narrator, would you have returned to Three Skeleton Key? Why or why not?

[connect]

6. The writer Isaac Asimov once said, "When I was a lad . . . I found myself fearfully attracted to stories that scared me. Don't ask why—I hate being scared, but I didn't mind, as long as I knew in my heart that I was safe." Do you enjoy tales of terror like "Three Skeleton Key"? Explain why or why not.

[predict]

7. At what point in the story did you **predict** that the crew would survive the rat attack? On what evidence did you base your prediction?

Extending the Text

[connect]

8. This is a story of nature gone berserk. What other stories or movies can you name that have used this same frightening idea? (A well-known old movie is Alfred Hitchcock's *The Birds,* in which birds attack human beings.)

Reading Check

To review the story line, imagine you are the narrator filling out a report on your adventure at Three Skeleton Key.

Lighthouse Log
Day 1:
Day 2:
Day 3:
Day 4:
Day 9:
Day 10:
Day 11:

THREE SKELETON KEY   77

Reading Check
Sample answers:
Day 1: Spotted three-master heading for lighthouse
Day 2: Teased rats as they tried to get at us through the glass
Day 3: Couldn't get fresh air
Day 4: Saw window frame eaten away
Day 9: Decided not to light lantern
Day 10: Rats took over tower; ship arrived
Day 11: Rescued

MAKING MEANINGS

First Thoughts

1. Possible responses
- I felt scared, sick, uneasy, intrigued.
- For me, the scariest part was when the rats broke into the lighthouse and attacked the men.

Shaping Interpretations

2. Possible response: The legend involves three men who die of hunger and thirst on the isolated island. Their fate hints at the life-threatening situation the three lighthouse keepers face with the rats.

3. It makes the men seem vulnerable and makes readers wonder how soon the rats will break in. Other details include the sounds of the rats' cries and their scraping claws; the men's decision not to light the lantern; the metal sealing giving way in Itchoua's window.

4. Possible responses: The narrator remains calm; Le Gleo has nightmares and goes mad; Itchoua is calm at first but eventually gives up and accepts failure. Students may choose any of the three men to identify with, depending on their own personalities and temperaments.

Connecting with the Text

5. Students may say that they would have returned to face down their fear and not let the experience haunt them; or they may say that they would never return to a place where they had lived through such horror.

6. Some students may enjoy feeling scared while actually experiencing safety. Students with vivid imaginations and intense emotions may not enjoy feeling overwhelmed by terror, even in fiction.

7. Possible responses: I knew the men would survive once the rescue ship arrived and the crew realized the men were trapped; or once the barge filled with meat was on the scene; or once the barge was drenched with gasoline.

Extending the Text

8. Possibilities include *Attack of the Killer Tomatoes, The Black Scorpion, Jaws, Jurassic Park, The Swarm, Them!, Willard, Arachnophobia,* and H. G. Wells's *Food of the Gods.*

Rubrics for each Choices assignment appear on p. 109 in the *Portfolio Management System.*

CHOICES: Building Your Portfolio

1. **Writer's Notebook** Remind students to save their work. They may use it as prewriting for the Writer's Workshop on pp. 94–99.

2. **Creative Writing/Reader's Theater** Assign sections of the story to small groups. Ask each group to create a script of its section and perform it for the class. [Example: Narrator: Look—a three-master! And she's headed dead at us. (*Sound effect: wind and waves.*)]

3. **Science/Speaking** Suggest to students that as part of this research they might contact a local or state health department and interview one of its representatives. Also, tell students that they should consider creative alternatives to dry factual reports. One option would be to write an advice column to the residents of a building that is rat infested, using the information students have gathered to answer residents' questions.

4. **Design/Creative Writing** Provide students with several job listings from a local newspaper that they may use as models for wording and content.

CHOICES: Building Your Portfolio

Writer's Notebook

1. Collecting Ideas for a Story

Much of the suspense in "Three Skeleton Key" comes from the fact that the characters are out there on their own. A lonely, forsaken setting like a tiny island can often inspire an idea for a frightening story. Jot down some ideas for the setting of a horror story. Look back at your notes for the Quickwrite on page 64 for more ideas.

> **Scene:**
> Cabin in the woods far from the main road. Starless night. Electricity sputters off. A knock on the door. Faint scraping sound heard outside.

Creative Writing/ Reader's Theater

2. On-Air Scare

In 1949, a drama called "Three Skeleton Key" was broadcast on a radio series called *Escape,* a half-hour program of horror-adventure stories. Work with three or four classmates to write a radio script for the whole story or for the part of the story you find most exciting. You might want to start with lines from the narrator to set the scene. Then, let the **dialogue,** or conversation, among the keepers carry the action of the story. Sound effects are important in a radio drama, so describe briefly any sound effects you'd use. Put these notes in parentheses right where you want the sounds heard. You may also describe background music. Schedule some class time to present a tape recording of your radio drama.

Science/Speaking

3. Oh, Rats!

What are the real facts about rats? As part of a team, research one of these questions:

- What role did rats play in European history during the 1300s?
- Are sea rats really as fierce, knowledgeable, and vengeful as they are in the story?
- In what ways are rats still a problem today?

Don't limit your research to encyclopedias. Try other resources, such as history books, computer databases, and knowledgeable members of your community.

What conclusions about rats can you draw from your research? Regroup and share what you have learned. Then, work together to create a presentation for the class.

Design/ Creative Writing

4. Career: Keeper

Design a job listing for the position of lighthouse keeper at Three Skeleton Key. Describe the personal characteristics and skills necessary for the job. Be sure to describe the work environment, duties, and pay. If possible, use computer graphics and special typefaces to attract the attention of the best possible candidates.

Professional Notes

Literature and History

Today most lighthouses are fully automated and do not need keepers like the men in the story. But before the machine age, tending a lighthouse was a hard job. Lighthouses in the early United States used whale-oil burning wick lamps that made lots of smoke. If the lamps were left unattended, their glass panes would soon be covered with so much dark soot that no light could get through them. A lighthouse keeper spent a typical night cleaning glass (often for more than one lamp), filling lamps with oil (two or three times a night), and trimming burnt wicks.

GRAMMAR LINK MINI-LESSON

Those Troublesome Verbs

Language Handbook HELP

See Irregular Verbs, pages 727-729.

Technology HELP

See Language Workshop CD-ROM. *Key word entry: irregular verbs.*

Use this chart to help you navigate the choppy seas of troublesome verbs:

Base Form	Past	Past Participle
lie (recline)	lay	(have) lain
lay (put)	laid	(have) laid
sit (rest)	sat	(have) sat
set (place)	set	(have) set
rise (go up)	rose	(have) risen
raise (lift)	raised	(have) raised

EXAMPLES

1. The keepers lay ill while men laid meat on the barge.
2. The men sat behind a metal door that was set in granite.
3. The sailors rose from the bench and raised the ship's sails.

Try It Out

➤ Complete the sentences below by choosing the correct word from each underlined pair.

1. The keepers sit/set a light in the window and rise/raise a distress flag.
2. They lie/lay awake and sit/set their minds on rescue. (Use the present tense.)
3. No ship had raised/risen their hopes or had laid/lain their fears to rest.

➤ Keep an eye out for these troublesome verbs in your writing, and check the chart when you proofread.

VOCABULARY HOW TO OWN A WORD

WORD BANK	And the Answer Is . . .
hordes *suffice* *receding* *edible* *derisive*	1. Hordes of rats would be a terrifying sight. Describe two other hordes that you would not like to see coming at you. 2. How much food will suffice for you for a day? 3. If you were a flood victim, how would you feel when you saw the flood waters receding? 4. What's your favorite edible plant? Why do you like it? 5. Write a derisive remark that a skeptic would make on hearing this rat story.

THREE SKELETON KEY 79

GRAMMAR LINK

First, review with students the concept of transitive verbs, which take direct objects. Then, ask students to identify the three verbs of the six that take direct objects [*lay, set, raise*]. Next, call on volunteers to form sentences, using the verbs in the chart. Write their responses on the board, and explain why they are or are not correct. Then, ask students to write a sentence for each troublesome verb. Have each student exchange sentences with a partner who will (a) check for the correct form of the verb and (b) identify the direct object, if any.

Try It Out
Answers
1. set, raise
2. lie, set
3. raised, laid

VOCABULARY
Possible Answers
1. Students should describe frightening things that might travel in groups, such as wasps, hyenas, and sharks.
2. Students' answers will vary widely, depending on their concept of what is "enough."
3. Students may say they would feel relieved, overjoyed, grateful, or excited to see the flood waters recede.
4. Students may mention various fruits, vegetables, herbs, or nuts.
5. Possible response: "Oh, right, give me a break! That story is so unrealistic."

Resources

Language
• *Grammar and Language Links,* p. 7

Vocabulary
• *Words to Own,* p. 4

Spelling
For related instructions, see
• *Spelling and Decoding,* p. 4

Grammar Link Quick Check

Read the following, and choose the correct verb.

1. When I set/sat down to read "Three Skeleton Key," I lay/laid my head against the back of the chair. [sat, laid]
2. I have set/sat here often with a book, but never before has the hair on my arms raised/risen from reading a story. [sat, risen]
3. I set/sat a miniature lighthouse in the window, and I laid/lay down on the couch for a nap. [set, lay]
4. Suddenly, a scratching, gnawing sound made me set/sit up in terror. [sit]
5. My brother stood up from his hiding place, raised/rose his eyebrows, and left the room. [raised]

OBJECTIVES
1. Read and interpret the story
2. Analyze characters
3. Make inferences
4. Express understanding through narrative and creative writing or math
5. Identify and use irregular verbs correctly
6. Understand and use new words

SKILLS
Literary
• Analyze characters
Reading
• Make inferences
Writing
• Describe a character
• Write a journal entry
• Write a character sketch
Grammar/Language
• Use irregular verbs correctly
Vocabulary
• Use new words
Math
• Convert numbers into metric measurements

Planning

• **Block Schedule**
Block Scheduling Lesson Plans with Pacing Guide

• **Traditional Schedule**
Lesson Plans Including Strategies for English-Language Learners

• **One-Stop Planner**
CD-ROM with Test Generator

Before You Read

A DAY'S WAIT

Make the Connection

Things That Go Bump in the Night

Think-pair-share. Read the cartoon on this page; then, take five minutes to talk with a partner about the reasons children have so many fears.

Quickwrite

Make a list of suggestions you could give a young child about what to do when he or she is feeling afraid. You might want to begin each suggestion with "Whenever I feel afraid . . .".

Elements of Literature

What's in a Character?

"A Day's Wait" introduces two characters: a father, called Papa, and Schatz, his young son. The writer doesn't tell you directly what Papa and Schatz are like. You have to figure out their personalities for yourself, by watching what they say and do and think.

A **character** is a person or animal who takes part in the action of a story.

For more on Character, see the Handbook of Literary Terms.

Reading Skills and Strategies

Making Inferences: Finding Clues

An **inference** is an educated guess based on evidence. When you make inferences about characters, you try to guess what they are like. Here is how you do it:

• Take note of any information that the writer gives you directly. For instance, what does the character look like?

• Pay attention to what the character thinks, says, and does.

• Watch how other people react to the character.

• Think about people you know in real life—or from other stories—who resemble this character.

Background

Literature and Science

To understand this story, you have to know that there are two kinds of thermometers, each using a different temperature scale. On the Celsius thermometer, used in Europe, the boiling point of water is 100 degrees. On the Fahrenheit thermometer, the boiling point is much higher, 212 degrees.

go.hrw.com
LEO 7-1

CALVIN AND HOBBES
© Watterson. Dist. by UNIVERSAL PRESS SYNDICATE. Reprinted with permission. All rights reserved.

80 OUT HERE ON MY OWN

Preteaching Vocabulary

Words to Own

Have students read the definitions of the words on the bottom of selection pages. Call on partners to act out the meaning of **detached,** and have other students give examples that relate to the meanings of **poised, commenced,** and **slack.** Then have all students use the exercise to match each word to its **antonym.**

1. detached [b]	a. ended
2. poised [c]	b. involved
3. commenced [a]	c. unbalanced
4. slack [d]	d. tight

He was shivering, his face was white...

The events in this story really happened to Hemingway and his nine-year-old son Bumby. (In this story Bumby is called Schatz, a German word meaning "treasure.") Hemingway and his family lived in France for many years; in this story they are back in the United States.

A Day's Wait

Ernest Hemingway

He came into the room to shut the windows while we were still in bed and I saw he looked ill. He was shivering, his face was white, and he walked slowly as though it ached to move.

"What's the matter, Schatz?"

"I've got a headache."

"You better go back to bed."

"No. I'm all right."

"You go to bed. I'll see you when I'm dressed."

But when I came downstairs he was dressed, sitting by the fire, looking a very sick and miserable boy of nine years. When I put my hand on his forehead I knew he had a fever.

"You go up to bed," I said, "you're sick."

"I'm all right," he said.

When the doctor came he took the boy's temperature.

"What is it?" I asked him.

"One hundred and two."

Downstairs, the doctor left three different medicines in different-colored capsules with instructions for giving them. One was to bring down the fever, another a purgative,[1] the third to overcome an acid

---

1. **purgative** (pʉr′gə·tiv): laxative.

A DAY'S WAIT **81**

Summary ▪

The story's narrator, a father, notices one morning that his nine-year-old son is ill. A doctor visits the home, notes that the boy's temperature is 102°, and leaves some medicines. The doctor assures the father that there should be no danger if the fever does not go above 104°. The father tries to read to his son, but because the boy seems detached, staring strangely at the foot of the bed and refusing to go to sleep, the father goes hunting. When he returns, the boy seems anxious and preoccupied and eventually asks, "About what time do you think I'm going to die?" Questioned by his father, the boy reveals that while at school in France he heard that a person cannot live with a temperature over 44°. Since his is 102°, he has spent the entire day convinced he was about to die. The father explains the difference between the Fahrenheit and Celsius scales. The boy, having faced his ordeal with dignity and courage, gradually relaxes. According to the father, the following day he cries about unimportant things.

Background

The boy in this story is suffering from influenza, or "the flu." Students may not be aware that illnesses such as influenza and pneumonia, which are treated routinely today, often proved fatal in the past. Point out that this story takes place at a time before antibiotics had been developed.

Resources ———

Listening
Audio CD Library
A recording of this story is provided in the *Audio CD Library:*
• Disc 4, Track 2

Selection Assessment
Formal Assessment
• Selection Test, p. 10
Test Generator
• Selection Test

  Resources: Print and Media

Reading
• *Reading Skills and Strategies*
   Selection Skill Lesson, p. 34
• *Graphic Organizers for Active Reading*, p. 6
• *Words to Own*, p. 5
• *Spelling and Decoding*
   Worksheet, p. 5
• *Audio CD Library*
   Disc 4, Track 2
Writing and Language
• *Daily Oral Grammar*
   Transparency 5

• *Grammar and Language Links*
   Worksheet, p. 9
• *Language Workshop CD-ROM*
Assessment
• *Formal Assessment*, p. 10
• *Portfolio Management System*, p. 110
• *Standardized Test Preparation*, p. 20
• *Test Generator (One-Stop Planner CD-ROM)*
Internet
• go.hrw.com (keyword: LE0 7-1)

A Reading Skills and Strategies

Making Inferences

? Based on how he responds to his father's attentions, how would you describe the boy? [Possible responses: The boy is trying to act too grownup; he is worrying too much, or not showing enough emotion; he is holding his feelings in too much.]

B Elements of Literature

Character

What do you learn about the personalities of the characters from this exchange? [Possible responses: Schatz is very considerate, thinking about Papa even when he himself is ill; Schatz is stoic and does not complain. Although Papa does not ask Schatz to explain what he is thinking, he does show concern and compassion.]

C Appreciating Language

Irregular Verbs

Point out that the verb *frozen* in this passage is the past participle of the irregular verb *freeze*, and that *freeze* is irregular because its past and past participle tenses (*froze*, *frozen*) are not formed by adding *-d* or *-ed*.

D Struggling Readers

Using Graphic Aids

If students have difficulty visualizing this scene, read the paragraph aloud while a volunteer sketches the scene at the board—the high bank, overhanging brush, trees, icy brush piles, the man, dog, and quail. Students at their desks might make suggestions to the artist.

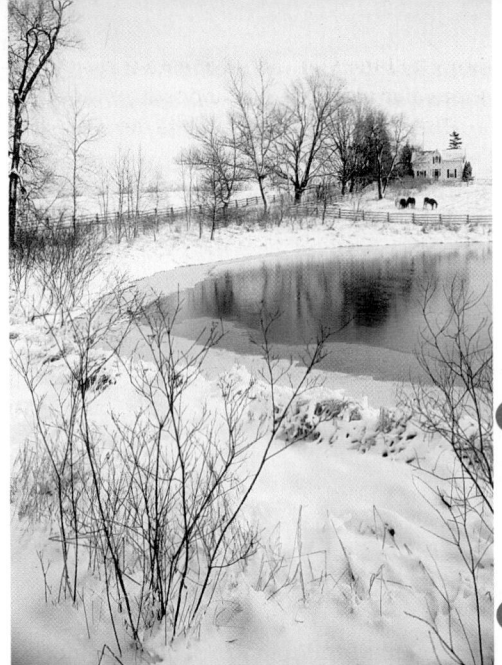

condition. The germs of influenza can only exist in an acid condition, he explained. He seemed to know all about influenza and said there was nothing to worry about if the fever did not go above one hundred and four degrees. This was a light epidemic of flu and there was no danger if you avoided pneumonia.

Back in the room I wrote the boy's temperature down and made a note of the time to give the various capsules.

"Do you want me to read to you?"

"All right. If you want to," said the boy. His face was very white and there were dark areas under his eyes. He lay still in the bed and seemed very **detached** from what was going **A** on.

I read aloud from Howard Pyle's *Book of Pirates;* but I could see he was not following what I was reading.

"How do you feel, Schatz?" I asked him.

"Just the same, so far," he said.

I sat at the foot of the bed and read to myself

while I waited for it to be time to give another capsule. It would have been natural for him to go to sleep, but when I looked up he was looking at the foot of the bed, looking very strangely.

"Why don't you try to go to sleep? I'll wake you up for the medicine."

"I'd rather stay awake."

After a while he said to me, "You don't have to stay in here with me, Papa, if it bothers you."

"It doesn't bother me."

B "No, I mean you don't have to stay if it's going to bother you."

I thought perhaps he was a little lightheaded and after giving him the prescribed capsules at eleven o'clock I went out for a while.

It was a bright, cold day, the ground covered with a sleet that had frozen so that it seemed as **C** if all the bare trees, the bushes, the cut brush, and all the grass and the bare ground had been varnished with ice. I took the young Irish setter for a little walk up the road and along a frozen creek, but it was difficult to stand or walk on the glassy surface and the red dog slipped and slithered and I fell twice, hard, once dropping my gun and having it slide away over the ice.

We flushed a covey of quail[2] under a high clay bank with overhanging brush and I killed two as they went out of sight over the top of the bank. **D** Some of the covey lit in trees, but most of them scattered into brush piles and it was necessary to jump on the ice-coated mounds of brush several times before they would flush. Coming out while you were <u>poised</u> unsteadily on the icy, springy brush, they made difficult shooting and I killed two, missed five, and started back

2. **flushed a covey** (kuv′ē) **of quail:** frightened a small group of wild birds called quail from their hiding place.

WORDS TO OWN

detached (dē·tacht′) *adj.:* not involved emotionally; indifferent.
poised (poizd) *v.:* balanced.

Reaching All Students

Struggling Readers

Making Inferences was introduced on p. 80. For a lesson directly tied to this selection that teaches students to make inferences by using a strategy It Says . . . I Say, see the *Reading Skills and Strategies* binder:

- Selection Skill Lesson, p. 34

English Language Learners

The dialogue of this story consists largely of simple words and sentences. Place students in a group of three for reading the story aloud. Assign one reader who is proficient in English to the group. Have students who are learning English read the dialogue while the proficient reader reads the narrative passages. For additional strategies, see

- *Lesson Plans Including Strategies for English-Language Learners*

Advanced Learners

Tell students that in this story Hemingway takes only three pages to describe the most frightening day in a young boy's life. The boy's feelings are hinted at and briefly explained but are never described in detail. Have students debate whether Hemingway's method of hinting at strong emotions is more or less effective than detailed descriptions of a character's inner turmoil would be. Which style of writing do students prefer and why?

pleased to have found a covey close to the house and happy there were so many left to find on another day.

At the house they said the boy had refused to let anyone come into the room.

"You can't come in," he said. "You mustn't get what I have."

I went up to him and found him in exactly the position I had left him, white-faced, but with the tops of his cheeks flushed by the fever, staring still, as he had stared, at the foot of the bed.

I took his temperature.

"What is it?"

"Something like a hundred," I said. It was one hundred and two and four tenths.

"It was a hundred and two," he said.

"Who said so?"

"The doctor."

"Your temperature is all right," I said. "It's nothing to worry about."

"I don't worry," he said, "but I can't keep from thinking."

"Don't think," I said. "Just take it easy."

"I'm taking it easy," he said and looked straight ahead. He was evidently holding tight onto himself about something.

"Take this with water."

"Do you think it will do any good?"

"Of course it will."

I sat down and opened the *Pirate* book and commenced to read, but I could see he was not following, so I stopped.

"About what time do you think I'm going to die?" he asked.

"What?"

"About how long will it be before I die?"

"You aren't going to die. What's the matter with you?"

"Oh, yes, I am. I heard him say a hundred and two."

"People don't die with a fever of one hundred and two. That's a silly way to talk."

"I know they do. At school in France the

E

boys told me you can't live with forty-four degrees. I've got a hundred and two."

He had been waiting to die all day, ever since nine o'clock in the morning.

"You poor Schatz," I said. "Poor old Schatz. It's like miles and kilometers. You aren't going to die. That's a different thermometer. On that thermometer thirty-seven is normal. On this kind it's ninety-eight."

"Are you sure?"

"Absolutely," I said. "It's like miles and kilometers. You know, like how many kilometers we make when we do seventy miles in the car?"

"Oh," he said.

But his gaze at the foot of the bed relaxed slowly. The hold over himself relaxed too, finally, and the next day it was very slack and he cried very easily at little things that were of no importance.

H

G

WORDS TO OWN
commenced (kə·menst′) *v.*: began.
slack *adj.*: loose.

E · Reading Skills and Strategies

Making Inferences

? Why doesn't the father tell the boy his exact temperature? [The father minimizes the temperature because he loves his son and wants to ease his fears.]

F · Reading Skills and Strategies
Making Predictions

? Were you surprised by this question? Why or why not? [Possible responses: no, because the boy has behaved so oddly and has been so worried; yes, because the boy kept this fear to himself all day and because the doctor said he was in no danger.]

G · Elements of Literature
Character

? What does this dialogue tell you about the father's character? [Possible responses: He cares about his son and feels the boy's emotional pain, but is not demonstrative. He clearly values reason and helps the boy understand his error by drawing an analogy to miles and kilometers.]

H · Reading Skills and Strategies

Making Inferences

? Why do you think that realizing he is not going to die has this effect on the boy? [Possible responses: The boy is exhausted from being so courageous and has no more strength or reason to be brave. The boy is relieved to be alive and is finally showing his true feelings.]

Assessing Learning

Check Test: Short Answer

1. What is wrong with the boy? [He has influenza.]

2. How does the father take care of the boy? [The father reads to the boy, sits with him, gives him medicine, and reassures him.]

3. What does the father do during the afternoon? [He goes hunting.]

4. What does the father say when the boy asks about his temperature? [He tells him that it is about one hundred degrees, but it is actually higher.]

5. What does the boy do on the day after he finds out that he will not die? [He relaxes and he cries easily.]

Standardized Test Preparation
For practice with standardized test format specific to this selection, see
• *Standardized Test Preparation*, p. 20
For practice in proofreading and editing, see
• *Daily Oral Grammar*, Transparency 5

MEET THE WRITER

Grace Under Pressure

Ernest Hemingway (1899–1961) was born in Oak Park, Illinois. The son of a doctor, he spent his first seventeen summers in northern Michigan, where his father introduced him to hunting and fishing. In high school, Hemingway boxed and played football, but he also wrote poetry, stories, and the gossip column for his school newspaper.

When the United States entered World War I, Hemingway volunteered and became an American Red Cross ambulance driver in Italy. He was nineteen when a bomb that landed three feet away filled his right leg with 227 pieces of shrapnel.

After returning from the war, Hemingway wrote many stories and novels that are now considered classics. In them he portrays men who show "grace under pressure"—that is, calm courage in the face of great danger or death. In his own life, Hemingway relentlessly pursued excitement and danger. He hunted and fished all over the world, surviving several plane crashes and the fierce charges of the large animals he loved to hunt. His exploits made him as famous as any movie star.

In "A Day's Wait," Hemingway again explores the theme of grace under pressure. This time he focuses on a young boy's first awareness of his own mortality. The silences and sparse dialogue in the story reflect the belief of Hemingway's heroes that they should keep a tight rein on their fears and other emotions. The story also illustrates Hemingway's approach to writing: "I always try to write on the principle of the iceberg. There is seven eighths of it underwater for every part that shows."

Hemingway worked hard to keep up his image of toughness, but his son Gregory ("Gig") remembers a more human side:

66 He told me about the times he'd been scared as a boy, how he used to dream about a furry monster who would grow *taller and taller* every night and then, just as it was about to eat him, would jump over the fence. He said fear was perfectly natural and nothing to be ashamed of. The trick to mastering it was controlling your imagination; but he said he knew how hard that was for a boy.

He said he loved to read the Bible when he was seven or eight because it was so full of battles. 'But I wasn't much good at reading at first, Gig, just like you. It was years before I realized that *Gladly the cross I'd bear* didn't refer to a kindly animal. I could easily imagine a cross-eyed bear and Gladly seemed like such a lovely name for one.'

Mainly he just told me stories—about how he had fished and hunted in the Michigan north woods and about how he wished he could have stayed my age and lived there forever—until I fell asleep. 99

Hemingway won the Nobel Prize in literature in 1954. Today he is regarded as one of the great writers of the twentieth century.

Using Students' Strengths

Visual Learners
As visual learners read the story, they might benefit by filling in the graphic organizer on p. 6 in the *Graphic Organizers for Active Reading*.

Interpersonal Learners
After students have read the story, have them work in small groups. Ask them to discuss the personal qualities of the boy—his self-control, his courage, his sensitivity to his father's feelings. Then have them make a list of characters from books, movies, or television programs who also display these qualities. Have them share their ideas with classmates.

First Thoughts

[respond]

1. Finish these sentences:

• If I were Schatz and thought that I was about to die, I would . . .

• If I were Papa and saw the way Schatz looked and acted, I would . . .

Shaping Interpretations

[interpret]

2. Though Schatz is sick and miserable, he gets up, gets dressed, and closes the window in his parents' room. Think about Schatz's actions. What do they tell you about his **character**?

[infer]

3. What makes us believe that the boy's mother is present? Why do you suppose she does not appear in the story?

[evaluate]

4. What do you think of Papa's choice of reading material for his son? (Would it teach a child to be tough and macho?)

[conclude]

5. During the day the father goes hunting and kills two birds. Think about this activity and other details in the story. What do they tell you about the father's **character**? Do you think the father shows his son that he loves him?

[speculate]

6. Why would so young a boy behave so heroically in the face of death? What do you think of this kind of behavior?

Connecting with the Text

[connect]

7. Look back at your notes for the Quickwrite on page 80. What items on your list might help Schatz deal with his fears? If you could talk with Schatz, what else would you share with him?

Extending the Text

[connect]

8. Why do you think people like Schatz often hesitate to share their feelings? How could this lack of communication cause misunderstandings?

Challenging the Text

[evaluate]

9. How much did you care about Schatz and Papa as you read? Do you think Hemingway's way of telling a story gets readers involved with the characters? Why or why not?

[evaluate]

10. Explain what the **title** means. Do you think it is a good title? If you were to give this story a different title, what would it be?

Stupid

A DAY'S WAIT **85**

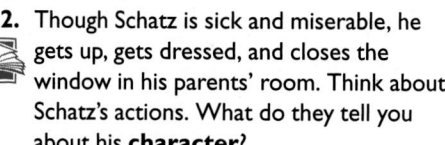

Reading Check

Go back through "A Day's Wait," and then fill in a story map like the one below.

| Title: |
| Author: |
| Characters: |
| Conflict: |
| Resolution: |
| Setting: |

Reading Check
Title: "A Day's Wait"
Author: Ernest Hemingway
Characters: Papa, Schatz
Conflict: Schatz thinks he will die of a fever.
Resolution: Papa explains that there are two kinds of thermometers.
Setting: Papa's house and outdoors.

Making the Connections

Connecting to the Theme:
"Out Here on My Own"
Talk with students about how this story relates to the theme: Nine-year-old Schatz struggles alone all day with his fear that at any moment he will die.

First Thoughts

1. **Possible responses**
   • If I were Schatz, I would cry or ask for help.
   • If I were Papa, I would ask Schatz what was worrying him.

Shaping Interpretations

2. Possible responses: He is a serious and responsible child; he is independent.

3. In the first paragraph of the story, the father uses the word *we*, probably referring to the boy's mother. The story focuses on the relationship between father and son.

4. Possible response: A story about pirates would glorify feats of strength, bravado, and fearlessness.

5. Possible responses: The father controls his emotions and doesn't express them. He likes the outdoors and enjoys hunting. He does show his love for his son by giving him medicine, reading to him, making him comfortable, and reassuring him that he is not in danger.

6. Schatz may behave this way to try to please his father or be like him. Some students may say that it shows real heroism and courage. Others may feel that family members should share their concerns.

Connecting with the Text

7. Possible response: Talk to someone about your fears; do not let your imagination run wild.

Extending the Text

8. Possible responses: Some people hesitate to share their feelings because they are unsure of how others will react. A lack of communication can lead to misinterpretation.

Challenging the Text

9. Students may care more for Schatz than for Papa because they can identify with the boy. Students may find that they have to work to get the full meaning of Hemingway's matter-of-fact style.

10. The boy waits all day for death. Possible response: Yes, because the father's and the reader's discovery of this wait is what the story quietly builds up to. Alternate titles: "Father and Son," "A Boy's Fear."

Rubrics for each Choices assignment appear on p. 110 in the *Portfolio Management System.*

CHOICES: Building Your Portfolio

1. **Writer's Notebook** Remind students to save their work. They may use it as prewriting for the Writer's Workshop on pp. 94–99.

2. **Creative Writing** Now that students realize the fear that Schatz has been living with the whole day, have them reread the story with this knowledge in mind. Have them make notes about what might have been going through Schatz's mind at various points throughout the day. For example, when his father left to go hunting, Schatz might have thought, "Doesn't he care that I'm dying? Isn't he going to say his final goodbyes? Maybe he doesn't want to be around when I die."

3. **Analyzing Character** Encourage students to collect their evidence in a chart with the headings "What Schatz Does," "What Schatz Says," and "How Others Respond."

4. **Math** Answers:
- 34 pounds x .45 = 15.3 kilograms
- 7 pounds x .45 = 3.15 kilograms
- 13.5 miles x 1.6 = 21.6 kilometers
- 55° F to 75° F = (55-32 = 23 x 5/9) = 12.8° C to (75-32=43 x 5/9)= 23.9° C

CHOICES: Building Your Portfolio

Writer's Notebook

1. Collecting Ideas for a Story

Papa in "A Day's Wait" represents Hemingway's idea of a hero because he values courage and self-reliance. What qualities do *you* think make someone a hero? Using a word web, describe someone who displays the qualities you admire. Your character could be someone you know or imagine, someone famous, or even someone from a book or a movie.

Creative Writing

2. Journal Jottings

Pretend that you are Schatz waiting for his father to return from hunting. Write a journal entry giving your version of the story's events.

Caricature of Ernest Hemingway.

Drawing by David Levine. Reprinted with permission from The New York Review of Books. Copyright ©1964 Nyrev, Inc.

Analyzing Character

3. Sketching Schatz

Write a brief **character sketch** of Schatz. Before you begin, review the story for information on

- Schatz's **actions** (what he does)
- his **words** (what he says)
- **how other people respond** to him

As you gather details, think of words you can use to describe Schatz.

Math

4. By the Numbers

Schatz confuses the numbers on Celsius and Fahrenheit thermometers. Help Schatz out by teaching him about the metric system. (You can find out about the metric system in an encyclopedia or a science textbook.) Imagine that Schatz and Papa take a camping trip. Convert these numbers (and others you invent yourself) into metric measurements:

- Papa carries provisions weighing 34 pounds.
- Schatz's knapsack weighs 7 pounds.
- They travel 13.5 miles.
- The temperature ranges from 55°F to 75°F.

Skill Link

Letter-Sound Correspondences

Mind Those *p*'s. Write the word *pneumonia* on the chalkboard and remind students that although *pneumonia* begins with the letter *p*, the beginning sound of the word is /n/. Point out that *pneumonia* is a word with Greek origins. Many words from Greek have unexpected *p*'s— *p*'s that stand for sounds other than /p/ and *p*'s that are silent. Point out that *ph* stands for /f/ in many words, all of which have Greek roots. Ask students to suggest words in which the sound

/f/ is spelled with *ph*—for example, *phone, photograph, philosophy, pheasant.*

Introduce these examples of consonant combinations in which *p* is silent, as it is before *n* in *pneumonia.*

before *s*	before *t*
pseudo	ptarmigan
psalm	pterodactyl
psychology	Ptolemy
psychic	ptomaine

Activity

Write the following items on the board. Ask a volunteer to tell the beginning sound in the underlined word and then call on a classmate to read the item.

1. Food poisoning used to be called <u>ptomaine</u> poisoning.
2. <u>Pneumonia</u> can be a serious disease.
3. A <u>pseudonym</u> is a ficticious name.
4. <u>Ptarmigans</u> have feathered legs and feet.
5. The <u>pharmacist</u> filled the prescription.

GRAMMAR LINK   MINI-LESSON

Irregular Verbs Dare to Be Different

Language Handbook HELP

See Irregular Verbs, pages 727-729.

Technology HELP

See Language Workshop CD-ROM. *Key word entry: irregular verbs.*

Many people have trouble with irregular verbs. You don't form the past tense of irregular verbs by adding -d or -ed, as you do with regular verbs. The only way to be sure you know the various forms of irregular verbs is to memorize them. Don't suffer in silence, as Schatz did—reading this list aloud several times will help you remember these odd verb forms.

Base Form	Past	Past Participle
am/is/are	was/were	(has/have) been
begin	began	(has/have) begun
break	broke	(has/have) broken
bring	brought	(has/have) brought
do	did	(has/have) done
find	found	(has/have) found
freeze	froze	(has/have) frozen
go	went	(has/have) gone
see	saw	(has/have) seen
swim	swam	(has/have) swum
throw	threw	(has/have) thrown

Try It Out

➤ Act as an editor: Provide the correct irregular verb forms in the paragraph below.

I had went with my Irish setter to the froze creek. There he had broke the ice, and then we begun a game. I throwed a stick, and he swum out after it. I seen him circling, looking for that stick. When he had founded it, he done what he's always did. He bringed it right back and begun to chew it up.

➤ Find out if irregular verbs are a trouble spot for you. As you edit your own work, circle all the verbs in the past or past participle form. If you suspect you've used the wrong form, check a dictionary.

VOCABULARY   HOW TO OWN A WORD

WORD BANK	**Vocabulary for the Workplace: The Job Interview**
detached *poised* *commenced* *slack*	1. Imagine that you have just conducted two job interviews. Which candidate would you hire: the one who was excitedly <u>poised</u> on the edge of the seat or the one who seemed <u>detached</u>? Why? 2. Describe how you feel about this scenario: You're at an interview that just <u>commenced</u>, and the interviewer's interest seems very <u>slack</u>.

GRAMMAR LINK

For the second Try It Out activity, ask students to choose a piece of writing from their portfolios and look for any irregular verbs they may have used. Have them underline each irregular verb and identify its tense. Then, have them check that they have used the correct form of the verb.

Try It Out
Answers

I *went* with my Irish setter to the *frozen* creek. There he *broke* the ice, and then we *began* a game. I *threw* a stick, and he *swam* out after it. I *saw* him circling, looking for that stick. When he *had found* it, he *did* what he's always *done*. He *brought* it right back and *began* to chew it up.

VOCABULARY
Answers

1. The candidate who was *poised*, because the poised person appeared eager to be hired and would likely be motivated to do a good job.
2. Students should say they would feel worried or disappointed if the interviewer's interest seemed *slack* just as the interview *commenced*.

Resources ———

Grammar
- *Grammar and Language Links*, p. 9

Vocabulary
- *Words to Own*, p. 5

Spelling
For related spelling instruction, see
- *Spelling and Decoding*, p. 5

Grammar Link Quick Check

Choose the correct verb form in each sentence.
1. Papa's Irish setter has <u>swam/swum</u> in the creek when the water was high. [swum]
2. Schatz finally <u>breaked/broke</u> down and cried. [broke]
3. Papa <u>brought/brung</u> his gun along to hunt for quail. [brought]
4. Has the doctor <u>began/begun</u> to examine Schatz? [begun]
5. Papa <u>was/been</u> reading a story to Schatz. [was]

No Questions Asked

The literature in No Questions Asked gives students the chance to read a selection for enjoyment and enrichment as they further explore the collection theme. Annotated questions in the margins of the Teacher's Edition should be considered optional. No follow-up questions appear after the selection.

This suspenseful story tells about dinosaurs in an entertaining way and helps students imagine the events that may have led to the extinction of these amazing animals. As three dinosaurs of the triceratops genus search for food, they encounter threats from fire, a mighty tyrannosaur, and the small, swift-moving mammals that are taking over the earth. After the two males are killed and the last triceratops eggs are eaten by mammals, one lone female triceratops remains; her chances of survival are slim.

Resources

Listening
Audio CD Library
A lively recording of this story is provided in the *Audio CD Library:*
• Disc 4, Track 3

Writing and Language
• *Daily Oral Grammar*
 Transparency 6

Ⓐ **Reading Skills and Strategies**
Making Predictions
Have students make predictions about when the story is set and what might happen in it. Ask them to consider the meaning of the title. You might mention reasons why the dinosaurs became extinct: they may have been killed by asteroids, climate changes, lack of food, or stronger, smarter enemies. [Possible responses: The story is set millions of years ago, before dinosaurs became extinct. The last remaining dinosaur is likely to be destroyed.]

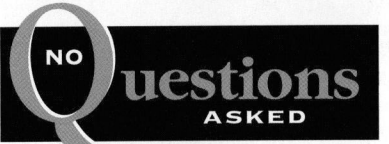

No Questions ASKED

Ⓐ The Last Dinosaur

The giant flesh eater stepped from the forest, snapping his mouth to reveal seven-inch-long slashing teeth.

Jim Murphy

The sun came up slowly, fingers of light poking into and brightening the tangled forest of pine and poplar and hemlock trees. The drone of insects quieted, and the tiny mammals scampered to hide.

Ⓑ In a clearing a small triceratops herd began their day. The female triceratops blinked several times before moving to get the light out of her eyes. Then she went back to the frond she'd ripped from a cycadeoid.[1]

The frond was tough and spiky, but her sharp-edged beak and rows of teeth chopped the plant into easily swallowed pieces. She was about to tug at another frond when a male triceratops began stamping his feet in alarm.

He had been feeding at the base of a tree when his horns became entangled in a mass of grapevines. He shook his head violently to get free. When that didn't work, he backed away, yanking his head from side to side. Still covered with vines, he halted. His breathing came in short, grunting pants.

Suddenly he lowered his head and charged the tree. He hit it solidly, backed up, and hit it again, and then again. The fourth butt splintered the tree's base, and it leaned over. A few wiggles of his head and the vine slipped off.

He snorted at the vine, challenging it. When it didn't move, he walked around it and left the clearing. He was the largest triceratops and leader of the herd, so the smaller male and the female followed him.

Ⓒ The three wandered through the forest, always staying near the stream that was their source of water. They did not hurry, and often stopped to nibble at figs or tender tree saplings. On the second day they came to a hillside covered with tasty ferns. The spot was cool and quiet, so they stayed the afternoon, browsing.

A sudden noise made the female jerk up her head to look and listen. They had not seen another dinosaur in a very long time, but she was still wary. A hungry tyrannosaur might have picked up their scent and followed, hoping one of them would stray from the herd.

The two males sensed her unease and also looked around. A giant dragonfly circled the

---

1. **cycadeoid** (sī·kad′ē·oid′): extinct plant that existed at the time of the dinosaurs.

88 OUT HERE ON MY OWN

Getting Students Involved

Cooperative Learning
The Great Dinosaur Debate. Have students work in groups of three to research theories about why dinosaurs became extinct. Each group member should become an "expert" on one theory, such as the asteroid crash theory, the climate change theory, and the competition with mammals theory. After they do their research, have the experts get together to share information. Then, have them return to their original groups to teach what they have learned.

Enrichment Activity
The Last Elephant. Students who enjoy Jim Murphy's approach to teaching animal facts through fiction may enjoy writing their own story about a current endangered species. First, have them research facts about endangered animals such as elephants, pandas, or snow leopards. Then, have them incorporate the facts into a story that takes readers into the minds of the animals.

triceratopses, then flew away. A bird chattered briefly. Then the forest grew still. Was a tyrannosaur out there, watching, waiting? Nothing moved and the noise did not return, but the herd was nervous. They left the hillside and continued their journey.

The next day, the land sloped downward and the stream widened to become a series of falls, pools, and swirling rapids. The path twisted to follow the water and dipped sharply in places. Despite their great size, the triceratopses walked the narrow ledges and leaped boulders with an easy grace.

The female triceratops smelled something. Her sense of sight was very poor, so she turned to face what was causing the strange odor. Wisps of smoke trailed through the trees.

The smoke was from a fire started the night before by heat lightning.[2] The female couldn't

2. **heat lightning:** lightning flashes that appear near the horizon on hot nights.

B Vocabulary Note
Word Origins
So students don't miss it, read the definition of *triceratops* (p. 90) aloud to the class. Point out the meaning of the prefix tri- and have students name other words they know with the same prefix. [Possible responses: *triangle, tricycle, tripod*]

C Struggling Readers
Finding Details
❓ What details in this passage support the idea that very few dinosaurs are left in the world? [The herd of triceratopses is made up of only three animals; the three triceratopses have not seen another dinosaur in a long time.]

D Elements of Literature
Suspense
❓ How does the author build a feeling of tension and uncertainty in this passage? [Possible responses: He says that the triceratopses are worried that a tyrannosaur is following them; they notice every noise around them; they are nervous when the forest becomes very quiet.]

E Elements of Literature
Conflict
❓ What force of nature first threatens the triceratopses? How well are they able to cope with the threat? [They are first threatened by fire, and their poor eyesight makes it difficult for them to avoid the fire. However, their sense of smell alerts them to the danger, and because they move quickly, they are able to escape.]

Elements of Literature

Foreshadowing

❓ As he describes the marsh, what hint of the triceratopses' fate does the author provide? [Possible responses: He describes the bones of a dead dinosaur, half buried in the mud, in a place where herds of dinosaurs used to graze.]

Using Structural Analysis to Identify Words: Greek Suffixes

Tell students that a knowledge of common Greek suffixes can help them unlock the meaning of a variety of words. They will frequently encounter these Greek suffixes:

Suffix	Meaning	Example
–ical	pertaining to	Biblical
–ist	one who believes in or practices	capitalist
–ism	belief in or practice of	journalism
–itis	inflammation of	tendonitis

Ask students to think of at least one more word using each suffix.

---

see the fire or know that it was advancing toward them. But the smoke was growing thicker and more unpleasant, so the three animals trotted away.

All night they moved quickly to stay clear of the smoke. At dawn, the ground leveled, and the smell seemed to disappear. The two males stopped, exhausted, and bent to drink the cool water. The female continued along the path.

Weeks before, the female triceratops had mated with the leader of the herd. She was hunting now for a spot to build her nest.

The leader stamped his feet and snorted for her to stop, but it did no good. The female would not obey until the nest was completed and her eggs laid. This time, the males followed.

A mile downstream, the forest thinned an the stream emptied into a broad marsh. In th past, dome-headed pachycephalosaurs or a mored ankylosaurs would be browsing in th cattails and rushes. Now only the bones of long-dead anatosaur, half buried in mud, wer there to greet the herd.

The female walked the edge of the mars carefully. The ground was either too wet or to rocky for the nest. On the opposite side of th marsh she found a warm, sandy area with lov growing shrubs.

Immediately she began digging, using th toes of her front and rear feet to shovel out th sand. The hole she dug was six feet across an a foot deep.

A Dino Dictionary

Did you know that the names of the dinosaurs come from Greek and Latin words? Read about these terrifying beasts and look at their pictures. Do they resemble the Greek and Latin words that form their names?

anatosaur (ə·nat′ō·sôr′): two-legged, plant-eating dinosaur with a wide jaw resembling the bill of a duck, webbed feet, and a long tail. The name comes from *anas*, the Latin word for "duck."

ankylosaur (aŋ′kə·lō·sôr′): four-legged, plant-eating dinosaur with thick, leathery skin covered by bony plates. *Ankylos* is Greek for "crooked."

pachycephalosaur (pak′ə·sef′ə·lō·sôr′): two-legged, plant-eating dinosaur with a dome-shaped plate nine inches thick covering its brain. The name comes from Greek: *pachys* (thick) + *kephalē* (head) + *sauros* (lizard).

tyrannosaur (tə·ran′ə·sôr′): fierce two-leg meat eater, about forty feet in length. Its nam comes from Greek: *tyrannos* (tyrant, or crue ruler) + *sauros* (lizard).

Tyrannosaurus rex (reks): best-known sp of tyrannosaur. In Latin, *rex* means "king."

triceratops (trī·ser′ə·täps′): four-legged, plant-eating dinosaur of North America. Th triceratops had three horns on its head, gre to about twenty-five feet in length, and weig up to four or five tons. Its name comes from Greek: *tri-* (three) + *kerat-* (horn) + *ōps* (eye, face).

Making the Connections

Connecting to the Theme: "Out Here on My Own"

Remind students that this is the third selection they have read in this collection that features an animal character on its own. (The others were "Rikki-tikki-tavi" and "The Runaway.") Have students compare this selection with "Rikki-tikki-tavi." How was Rikki's situation similar to that of the last triceratops? How was it different? Then, ask students to compare and contrast the possible reasons why Kipling and Murphy used animal characters. [Possible responses: Rikki is a pet who fights bravely to protect the humans who take him in; the last triceratops is a dinosaur in the wild who fights bravely to protect her eggs and herself. Kipling may have used animal characters that possess the moral values he admired in people. Murphy's purpose may be to tell about real animals in an entertaining, involving way.]

When the hole was finished, she laid fifteen eggs in it to form a circle. Gently she covered the eggs with sand. The sun would warm the sand and eggs, and eventually baby triceratopses would emerge.

The two males were feeding a little distance from the nest. The smaller male approached the nest.

When the female saw him, she placed herself between him and her eggs and lowered her head as a warning. The curious male kept coming, so the female charged him. Only when he backed away did the female stop her charge.

When the herd had been larger, many females would make nests in the same area. They would then take turns guarding the nests or feeding and sleeping. But the female triceratops was alone now. It would be her job to keep clumsy males and egg-eating creatures away from her eggs. The quick shrewlike[3] mammals were especially annoying at night.

Two days later the smell of smoke returned. It was faint, distant, and yet the three triceratopses grew nervous. The female paced near her nest.

Late in the day, a heavy line of smoke appeared on the other side of the marsh. Flames erupted, reaching into the air.

A flock of birds flew overhead, screeching an alarm. Mammals, made bold by their fear, left their hiding places and ran from the fire. The two males edged away, but the female stayed to guard her eggs.

In the smoke and dark forest shadows, something moved. The shape was big, as big as many of the trees, and had a massive head. Tyrannosaurus rex. The giant flesh eater stepped from the forest, snapping his mouth to reveal seven-inch-long slashing teeth.

Instinctively the two triceratops males rejoined the female and formed a semicircle barrier in front of the nest. The leader lowered his head and stared at his enemy. Neither moved.

3. **shrewlike:** resembling a shrew, a small mammal that looks like a mouse.

Ordinarily, the tyrannosaur would not attack a triceratops, especially near its nest. But a wall of flames and heat had cut off his retreat. Besides, the tyrannosaur had not had a large meal in weeks.

The tyrannosaur darted at the herd, skidded to a sudden halt, then began circling warily, watching for a chance to strike. He hissed and snapped his teeth. At that instant, the largest triceratops charged, his powerful legs driving him directly at the soft belly of his attacker.

With the aid of his long tail and thickly muscled legs, the tyrannosaur leaped aside to avoid the sharp horns. He spun and dove, mouth wide open, and sank his teeth into the back of the triceratops.

Then the smaller triceratops lunged at the giant, but he was an inexperienced fighter. The tyrannosaur's teeth closed on his neck, and with a quick, deadly yank, he tore a chunk of flesh from the triceratops. The smaller triceratops fell, dying.

The other triceratops tried to charge again, but his right leg was dragging and his movements were slow. Again the tyrannosaur moved aside easily. Using his tail as a spring, the tyrannosaur launched himself for the kill. His teeth sank into the triceratops, while his clawed feet struck him in the stomach. The two rolled, kicking and biting each other.

At this moment, the female triceratops abandoned her eggs and rammed the tyrannosaur full in the side. He bellowed painfully, releasing his hold on the male. The female pushed forward with all her strength, pinning the tyrannosaur against a tree and driving her horns in deeper.

She stepped away and watched her enemy, ready to charge if he got up. His legs and tail flailed weakly, his breathing became labored. Then, with a violent shudder, the great killer died.

During the battle, the fire had spread, leaping and dancing from tree to tree until it

THE LAST DINOSAUR 91

B **Reading Skills and Strategies**
Making Predictions
? Do you think the dinosaur eggs will hatch and the babies will survive? Explain your answer. [Most students will probably say no, based on the title "The Last Dinosaur" and the fact that the eggs face danger from fire, clumsy males, and egg-eating mammals. There is also only one female dinosaur left to protect them.]

C **Struggling Readers**
Supplying Missing Words
Ask students what words are missing but implied in the sentence fragment "Tyrannosaurus rex." [Possible response: "It was a Tyrannosaurus rex."]

D **Elements of Literature**
Suspense
? What questions were in your mind as you read this part of the story? [Possible responses: Who will win the fight? Can the tyrannosaur kill all the triceratopses? What will happen to the eggs?]

E **Struggling Readers**
Identifying Pronoun Antecedents
To help students visualize the fight, be sure they can identify the changing antecedents of the pronouns *he, him,* and *his* in these two paragraphs. ["*he* was an inexperienced fighter"—the smaller triceratops; "*he* tore a chunk of flesh"—the tyrannosaur; "*his* right leg . . . *his* movements"—the other (larger) triceratops; "Using *his* tail"—tyrannosaur; "*His* teeth . . . *his* clawed feet"—tyrannosaur; "struck *him*"—larger triceratops]

A English Language Learners
Homographs

Make sure these students understand that the word *wound* has two different pronunciations and meanings. When the word is pronounced wound, it is the past tense of the verb *to wind* (something up). When pronounced wōōnd, as in this example, *wound* is a noun meaning "injury."

B Reading Skills and Strategies
Responding to the Text

❓ Were you surprised by what happened to the triceratops eggs? Why or why not? [Since the threat from the small, swift animals was foreshadowed on p. 91, many students will not be surprised. Some, however, may have suspected that the fire or the tyrannosaur would destroy the eggs.]

C Critical Thinking
Challenging the Text

❓ Jim Murphy personalizes the fate of the dinosaurs, by helping the reader imagine how it felt to be the last triceratops. Do you think this is a good way to teach science? Why or why not? [Answers will vary. Students may say that appealing to readers' imaginations can be a good way to bring science to life but that not all scientific concepts can be presented in this way.]

BROWSING IN THE FILES

About the Author. Jim Murphy grew up in suburban New Jersey and began writing stories and poetry in high school, where he was also a track star. "I thoroughly enjoy my work," he once told an interviewer. "The nonfiction projects let me research subjects that I'm really interested in. . . . The fiction lets me get out some of the thoughts and opinions that rattle around in my head."

A Critic's Comment. Jim Murphy's books have won many prizes, including the International Reading Association's Children's Choice Award, the American Library Association's Notable Book Award, and the Golden Kite Award. One critic described *The Last Dinosaur* as "surprisingly poignant" for a book designed to teach facts about dinosaurs.

---

reached the edge of the sandy area. Flames rolled through the reeds.

A The male triceratops struggled to get up, but his legs buckled under him. He crawled a few feet but had to stop. His wounds were too severe. A choking wave of smoke surrounded him.

The female triceratops went back to protect her eggs. To one side a tree crashed to the ground, sending up an explosion of sparks. A bush nearby caught fire. The female charged it, slashing at it blindly with her horns.

The roar of the fire became deafening, and the heat and smoke grew painful. Reluctantly the female moved away from her eggs to find air.

She went only a short distance and turned to go back. The smoke stung her lungs and burned her eyes. She shook her head, but the choking pain would not go away. She backed away some more and lost sight of her nest.

B Immediately the tiny mammals pounced on the unguarded nest. Low to the ground the smoke was not so thick. Digging hastily, they uncovered the eggs and devoured them. Then they scurried from the approaching fire.

The female triceratops hurried through the forest. Several times she stopped to look back toward her eggs. A wall of smoke and flames was all she could see. Finally she gave up.

A tongue of flames reached out at her, and she broke into a gallop. She crashed through branches and vines, leaped over fallen logs heedlessly, with the fire just behind her. At last she came to a rock ledge overlooking a wide river.

C The water was dark and deep. Branches and tree roots floated near the banks. The female wanted to find another retreat, but she was surrounded by flames. She hesitated a second, then jumped into the water.

Legs churning frantically, she swam across the river and away from the fire. The river's current caught her, pulling her swiftly along.

She struggled to keep her head above water, to breathe, all the while moving her legs. At last her feet touched the river bottom.

Exhausted, her breathing fast, she hauled herself onto solid ground. Across from her, the fire had stopped at the river's edge. She was safe. It was then she noticed the streams of mammals that had also crossed the river to escape the fire.

The light grew dim and the air became chilly. The female's breath gave off thin vapor streams.

The triceratops shook her head and snorted. She hadn't eaten much in days and wanted to find some tender plants. And maybe, somewhere deep in the forest, there was another triceratops herd she could join.

Slowly, as the sun went down, the female pushed through the bushes to begin her search.

MEET THE WRITER
Digging Dinosaurs

Jim Murphy (1947–   ) says that dinosaurs have always fascinated him.

❝ Our knowledge of them suggests that they were amazing survivors, occupying every corner of the world and adapting to changing climates and food sources for millions of years. ❞

Murphy feels that studying dinosaurs and finding out how they survived for so long may help humans adapt and survive.

Good Reads About the Past

Other books by Murphy that present information in an entertaining way are *The Great Fire* (Scholastic) and *Across America on an Emigrant Train* (Clarion).

Listening to Music

"Walking in Your Footsteps" by Sting, performed by The Police

The song "Walking in Your Footsteps," written by Sting, suggests similarities between what happened to the dinosaurs and what could happen to humans. After students read "The Last Dinosaur," have them listen to the song. The British pop trio The Police emerged in London in 1976. The trio consisted of bass guitarist and vocalist Gordon Sumner, better known as Sting; lead guitarist Andy Summers; and American-

born drummer Stewart Copeland. "Walking in Your Footsteps" is from their acclaimed album *Synchronicity* (1983).

Activity

Ask students what the dinosaur in the song represents *(an extinct creature)* and what warning the song expresses *(what happened to the dinosaurs can happen to humanity if we aren't careful)*. Then, have students compare and contrast the dinosaur in the song with Murphy's dinosaur.

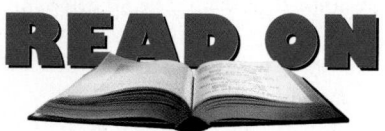

Read On

Survival of the Fittest

Young Brian finds himself stranded alone in the Canadian wilderness after a plane crash. With only his wits and a hatchet to rely on for survival, Brian learns some memorable lessons about nature, growing up, and himself in Gary Paulsen's *Hatchet* (Puffin). (This title is available in the HRW Library.)

Working Girl

In Katherine Paterson's *Lyddie* (Puffin), set in the 1840s, Lyddie Worthen has to grow up fast when her mother is forced to abandon the family farm. After she finds a job in a textile mill, Lyddie faces a grim new world of poverty and eighteen-hour workdays. A true heroine, Lyddie fights against injustice as she struggles to earn enough to buy back the family farm.

Hot on the Trail

It is 1882 in the Old West, and fifteen-year-old Artemis is the last surviving male of the Bonner family after his rich uncle is killed by the wicked Catfish Grimes. Artemis sets out on a wild cross-country chase to avenge the murder and recover his uncle's treasure in Walter Dean Myers's *The Righteous Revenge of Artemis Bonner* (HarperCollins).

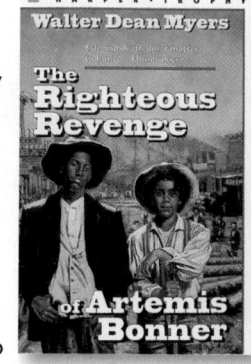

Other Picks

- Patricia Beatty, *Lupita Mañana* (Beech Tree Books). In order to find work, Lupita Torres enters California illegally. Her search for a better life becomes a struggle in a place where laws are not always fair and growing up is not always easy. (This title is available in the HRW Library.)
- Jack London, *The Call of the Wild* (Macmillan). When Buck is taken from his comfortable home and forced into service as a sled dog, he must draw on his instincts in order to survive. As he adapts to his harsh surroundings, Buck finds himself responding to "the call of the wild." (This title is available in the HRW Library.)

READ ON 93

Sustained Silent Reading

These **independent-level materials** can be used by students of various levels of ability for sustained silent reading. Based on the Bormuth formula, *The Righteous Revenge* scores at the lowest level and *The Call of the Wild* at the highest. In terms of suspense, *Hatchet* has been known to hold the attention of even the most reluctant readers. To encourage independent reading in challenging but manageable texts, at the start of the year, establish a reading area in the classroom. Students should note in their reading logs how long they spend in sustained silent reading; they should be encouraged to read for increasingly longer periods of time. As students read silently, you should move around the room, noting those who are having trouble sustaining attention. Watch body positions and eye movements. Watch for students who are mouthing words, tracking texts with their fingers, or leafing through the book to see how many more pages remain to be read.

MAIN OBJECTIVE
Write a story

PROCESS OBJECTIVES

1. Use appropriate prewriting techniques to identify and develop an idea for a story
2. Create a first draft
3. Use Evaluation Criteria as a basis for determining revision strategies
4. Revise the first draft, incorporating suggestions generated by self- or peer evaluation
5. Proofread and correct errors
6. Create a final draft
7. Choose an appropriate method of publication
8. Reflect on progress as a writer

Planning

- **Block Schedule**
  Block Scheduling Lesson Plans with Pacing Guide

- **One-Stop Planner**
  CD-ROM with Test Generator

Technology HELP

See Writer's Workshop 1 CD-ROM. *Assignment: Story.*

ASSIGNMENT

Write a story on a topic of your choice.

AIM

To be creative.

AUDIENCE

Children, teenagers, or adults. (You decide.)

NARRATIVE WRITING
STORY

We all want to know what happened and what's going to happen next. Drivers slow down when they pass an accident, trying to figure out how it happened. When we overhear a story told by one stranger to another, we want to know who did what and why.

Professional Model

In movies, geniuses have frizzy white hair, right? They wear thick glasses and have names like Dr. Zweistein.

Peter Lu didn't have frizzy white hair. He had straight hair, as black as licorice. He didn't wear thick glasses, either, since his vision was normal.

Peter's family, like ours, had immigrated from China, but they had settled here first. When we moved into a house just two doors down from the Lus, they gave us some good advice on how to get along in America.

I went to the same school as Peter, and we walked to the school bus together every morning. Like many Chinese parents, mine made sure that I worked very hard in school.

In spite of all I could do, my grades were nothing compared to Peter's. He was at the top in all his classes. We walked to the school bus without talking, because I was a little scared of him. Besides, he was always deep in thought.

The first sentence grabs our attention.

A character is introduced and described.

The narrator tells us about herself.

The narrator describes her feelings.

94 OUT HERE ON MY OWN

 Resources: Print and Media

Writing and Language
- *Portfolio Management System*
  - Prewriting, p. 111
  - Peer Editing, p. 112
  - Assessment Rubric, p. 113
- *Workshop Resources*
  - Revision Strategy Teaching Notes, p. 1
  - Revision Strategy Transparencies 1, 2
- *Writer's Workshop 1 CD-ROM*
  - Story

The history of the written word is rich and...
Page 1
Once upon a time...

(continued)

> Peter didn't have any friends. Most of the kids thought he was a nerd because they saw his head always buried in books. I didn't think he even tried to join the rest of us or cared what the others thought of him.
>
> Then on Halloween he surprised us all.
>
> —from "Lafff" by Lensey Namioka

The events of the plot begin. The writer hints at a conflict.

We start to feel suspense.

Prewriting

1. Writer's Notebook

If you have Writer's Notebook entries for this collection, review them. Can you find an idea you'd like to develop into a story? If not, try the Freewriting or Brainstorming below.

2. Freewriting

Stories are likely to come from personal experience. Try to find the kernel of a story in your memory. Prod your memory with a few of these prompts:

- Of all the people you've known, who was the most unusual? the most often in trouble? the most serious?
- What place do you know best? What happens there?
- What interesting experiences have your friends told you about?
- Do you have a dream of an adventure you'd like to have?

3. Brainstorming

Try writing down at least ten characters, ten settings, and ten problems on separate slips of paper. For each story element, use a different-colored paper. To start, see the ideas at the right. Then, mix and match the characters, settings, and problems until you come up with an interesting combination for a story.

Characters
park ranger
veterinarian
seventh-grader
shy teenager

Settings
Yosemite
suburb in summer
big city
shopping mall

Problems
battles a fire
is hit by a car
hates dirty streets
needs a friend

WORK IN PROGRESS

WRITER'S WORKSHOP 95

Introducing the Writer's Workshop

- Ask a volunteer to read aloud the Professional Model on pp. 94–95 as the class reads along silently.
- Discuss with students the side-margin notes. Outline the elements of a good story:
  1. an opening that catches the reader's interest
  2. characters that the reader wants to know more about
  3. a setting the reader can visualize —in this story, a neighborhood of houses
- Be sure students understand the purpose of their writing—to create a story based on an idea of their own.

Remind students to choose a situation they will not mind sharing with others.

Teaching the Writer's Workshop

Prewriting

Have students use the techniques suggested on pp. 95–96 (or any others that may be helpful) to come up with ideas.

Reaching All Students

Struggling Writers

Students having difficulty may need to review the basic elements of a story. You might ask students to identify these elements in the Professional Model. Then, have them work in small groups to brainstorm ideas. One student might suggest a character, and a classmate would then ask for details: "How old is (he or she)? Where does (he or she) live?" Other students may suggest settings and conflicts. The students can use the brainstorming box on p. 95 to create plot outlines—for instance, what would a seventh-grader (or other character) do if a fire started in a mall (or other setting)?

Students might develop a story based partly on their own experiences and feelings and partly on one of the characters or conflicts in a story in Collection 1—How would I respond to a snake in my house? What would I do if somebody tried to take away my home? What would I do if a younger child was sick and scared? Students who like to draw can create a storyboard (if possible, show them an example, and distribute storyboard forms). Have students sketch several scenes to develop a narrative. They can refer to the storyboard as they work on the first draft.

Drafting

If you have not yet taught the Student Model, do so before students begin their drafts.

• Remind students to use only every other line when they write their drafts. They should also leave extra space in the right margin for comments and editing marks.

Language/Grammar Link
H E L P

Choosing specific verbs:
page 21.

Story Plan
My main character is
_____, who
(name)
_____.
(basic situation)
This character wants
_____, but
(goal)
_____.
(main conflict)

Character: seventh-
grade boy
Goal: to fit in and
have friends
Conflict: other kids
make fun of him

Language/Grammar Link
H E L P

Problems with verbs:
pages 44, 63, 79, and 87.

4. Creating Interesting Characters

One of the best ways to hold your readers' interest is to create vivid, true-to-life characters. To develop your characters, concentrate on specific physical descriptions, actions, realistic speech, and others' opinions of the characters.

5. Plotting Your Story

To come up with the events, or **plot**, of your story, think about the character's problem. What is the **conflict** that arises? What goal does your character have? What events lead to solving the problem? The story-plan framework at the left might serve as a guide, or you may prefer to start writing once you have the initial situation and a few of the characters.

6. Where in the World?

Look for opportunities to give your reader a clear picture of the **setting**—where and when the events of the story take place. Don't just describe the setting and then forget about it when you move on to the action. Try to blend the two.

Drafting

1. Getting Started

If you can come up with a good opening now, that's great, but if you can't, don't worry. Just start writing. Pick an event or a character or a place, and begin.

2. What Did They Say?

Readers can learn a lot about characters through **dialogue**, or what the characters say. As you write, ask yourself if there's a way to use dialogue to *show* rather than *tell* about a character. For example, if you want to show that a character is kind, try having her speak gently to someone. Let readers hear your character talk so that they can make their own judgments.

3. Whose Story Is It?

From whose point of view do you want to tell your story? Do you want to tell it from the **point of view** of one of the characters, who refers to himself or herself as "I"? Do you want to tell it from the point of view of someone outside the story who knows everything about all the characters? Perhaps you want to use a narrator who is outside the story but knows the thoughts

Reaching All Students

English Language Learners
To develop possible story ideas, groups of students can list characters in the collection's stories and then come up with similar types: character, *mongoose*; another animal, *muskrat, whale,* etc. The students might do the same with setting and conflict. Students can look through magazines to find action pictures of some of the characters, settings, or conflicts named. They should be encouraged to choose, as a main

character, one of the illustrated examples; the same picture, or others, might suggest the setting and conflict (for example, a picture of a whale washed up on a beach).

Advanced Students
Information can often be presented in an interesting way in well-written dialogue. For example, instead of writing "It was a dark night," the student can have one character say to another,

"It's so dark I can't see my own hand in front of my face." Students can also experiment with point of view. If they are used to writing from the first-person perspective of the main character, they might write from the point of view of a minor character who describes and comments on the main character (as in the Student Model).

This is the beginning of a student's short story.

from BEING DIFFERENT

The top edge of the sun was visible over the roof of the barn. There was a slight chill in the air like every dusk. I spotted the slumped figure in the wooden swing across the field and walked to it.

"Momma is worried. You didn't go tell her you were home from school," I said, noticing the pile of books at his feet. "She thought something happened to you."

He didn't answer, just shrugged.

"Why didn't you kiss Momma hello?"

"Didn't want to." He looked in the other direction. "I just needed time to think about things alone." He faced me, a tear in his left eye glistened.

"What things?" I asked. I had never seen my brother so upset.

He looked up at the dusk sky and then down at his feet. "About important things."

I didn't mean to pry, I knew he disliked me to do so, but I felt so close to him now, closer than ever before, and I knew I had to pry.

"I don't fit in with the other boys at school."

"Who told you that?"

"It's so obvious, Angie. Don't you notice who always gets the good grades but never the good friends? I'm so different."

—Amy Yustein
Suffern Junior High School
Suffern, New York

The first paragraph introduces us to the setting and the main characters.

The realistic dialogue creates believable characters.

The main character's actions clearly show he is sad and upset.

We get inside the narrator's mind and know how she feels.

This is the main character's problem. His goal is to fit in.

Strategies for Elaboration

To create believable, interesting characters, start carefully observing the people around you—at a mall or fast-food restaurant, for example. Look at people's appearance—their clothing, hairstyles, and so on. Listen carefully. How do people talk? What does realistic speech sound like? Take notes on what you see and hear. Your notes may help you write your story. Remember that the more you observe in the world around you, the better you'll write.

■ **Evaluation Criteria**

A good story

1. *centers on a major conflict that the characters must resolve*

2. *uses dialogue and actions to develop the characters*

3. *provides a description of the setting*

4. *ends with a resolution of the conflict*

5. *reveals a theme*

Using the Model

As class members read the Student Model, be sure they understand the side notes. Have students focus on questions like these:

❓ Why does the narrator (Angie) tell us what time of day it is?

❓ What might Angie be suggesting when she says there was a "slight chill" in the air?

❓ In paragraph 1, Angie refers to her brother as the "slumped figure" and "it." What does her description tell us about him?

❓ Do you think the brother would have been able to express his feelings if Angie had not asked him the questions? Explain your response.

❓ Angie tells about her feelings as well as her brother's. How does our knowledge of her add to the story?

❓ The brother says he never has good friends but always gets good grades. How might this description of himself be a clue to the way he will handle his problem?

❓ If you were going to finish Angie's story, how would you continue from where it stops?

Getting Students Involved

Cooperative Learning

To help students create realistic plots and characters, have them play a brainstorming game. To begin the activity, each student writes, on a numbered slip of paper, one sentence describing a character he or she would like to use in a story (students should jot down their numbers in their notebooks). Place all the character slips in a small box. Fill a large box with a variety of objects, such as pressed flowers, a toy car, a colored stone, old postcards or photographs, and other items students may bring to class. Divide students into groups of four, and have each group draw a slip and an object. Give the groups five minutes to brainstorm a story idea featuring the character in a situation involving the object. The groups can then record their story ideas on notebook paper marked with the number from the slip. The process should be repeated until all the slips have been drawn. Students then receive the story idea that corresponds to the character they thought up. As they write a story based on their character, they should try to use the ideas suggested by the group.

Evaluating and Revising

Have students use the Evaluation Criteria provided here to review their drafts and determine needed revisions.

Proofreading

Have students proofread their own work first and then exchange papers with another student. For this assignment, remind students to be particularly careful to capitalize characters' names and place names that are proper nouns. If time permits, the final copy should be put aside for at least a day before it is proofread for the final time.

Remind students that they must spell accurately in final drafts. Suggest that they use a spelling checker if they are using a computer that has one. Make sure that students understand that a spelling checker will not alert them to usage errors such as the misuse of *it's* for *its*.

Publishing

The class can combine all the stories in an anthology. Students can decide how they wish to arrange the text—perhaps by type of story (romance, mystery, fantasy, etc.) or by theme (friendship, courage, loyalty, and so on). The class can discuss the pros and cons of each type of organization.

Reflecting

Suggest that students answer the following questions:

1. What qualities about myself did I discover as I wrote this story? For example, did I try to use my imagination? Did I ask for help from others or offer help to anyone who needed it?

2. What things that I learned while writing this story will be helpful when I write another story?

Sentence Workshop
H E L P

Sentence fragments: page 99.

Proofreading Tips

- Check your writing for errors in spelling, grammar, and punctuation.
- Make sure you have punctuated dialogue correctly.
- Correct any sentence fragments.

Communications Handbook
H E L P

See Proofreaders' Marks.

Publishing Tip

Collect your class stories in a booklet. Provide a table of contents, and assign someone to write a preface explaining your story-writing project. Leave your story anthology in your classroom as an inspiration and resource for other students.

---

and feelings of just one character. (Learn more about point of view on pages 202–203.)

Evaluating and Revising

1. Peer Editing

After writing the first draft, share your work with a partner. Exchange papers, and answer the following questions:

- Did the story hold my interest? If not, why didn't it?
- What did I like best about the characters? What would I change about them?
- What is the best part of the story?

2. Self-Evaluation

Plot

1. Are the character's problem and its resolution believable? If not, can I add more true-to-life details?

2. Which events need to be elaborated on or eliminated?

Character

1. Have I conveyed the main character's personality?

2. What details can I add to make the character more vivid?

Setting

Are there other details about time and place I can add to develop the setting?

Point of View

1. What point of view did I choose? Why?

2. Are there any places where the point of view seems weak?

Theme

1. What is the main idea about life that I wanted to communicate?

2. What details can I add (to the characterization or to the story events, for example) to make my theme clearer?

98 OUT HERE ON MY OWN

Resources ━━━━

Peer Editing Forms and Rubrics
- *Portfolio Management System, p. 112*

Revision Transparencies
- *Workshop Resources, p. 1*

Grading Timesaver

Rubrics for this Writer's Workshop assignment appear on p. 113 of the *Portfolio Management System*.

Sentence Workshop

SENTENCE FRAGMENTS

To be a complete sentence, a group of words must (1) have a subject, (2) have a verb, and (3) express a complete thought. A **sentence fragment** is punctuated like a sentence—it begins with a capital letter and ends with a period—but it lacks one or more of the key elements that make up a complete sentence.

FRAGMENT   Wished that he hadn't left his bed. [Who wished? The sentence's subject is missing.]

SENTENCE   <u>Keevan</u> wished that he hadn't left his bed. [Adding the subject *Keevan* makes it a complete sentence.]

FRAGMENT   Then suddenly the tropic dawn. [The sentence's verb is missing.]

SENTENCE   Then suddenly the tropic dawn <u>broke</u>. [Adding the verb *broke* makes this a complete sentence.]

FRAGMENT   When the cobra runs for her life. [Even with a subject and verb, this group of words does not express a complete thought.]

SENTENCE   When the cobra runs for her life, <u>she goes like a whiplash</u>.

Writer's Workshop Follow-up: Revision

Take out a story you've written, and exchange papers with a classmate. Note any sentence fragments you find and suggest a correction for each. Exchange papers again and revise any fragments that you feel are genuine errors. (You can check with your teacher.) You will want to use some fragments in the dialogue you write, because real people often talk in fragments. In "The Dinner Party," for example, a character remarks, "Because it was crawling across my foot" (page 18). This is a fragment, but it's correct because it's in dialogue.

**Language Handbook
HELP**

See Sentence or Sentence Fragment?, *pages 750–751.*

**Technology
HELP**

See Language Workshop CD-ROM. *Key word entry: sentence fragments.*

Try It Out

Copy the following paragraph onto a separate sheet of paper, and revise it, correcting any sentence fragments. Compare your rewritten versions in class. How many variations are possible?

Robert Frost earned a poor living. As a schoolteacher and editor. Before deciding to try farming. The stony New Hampshire soil on thirty acres. Which his grandfather had bought for him. The great physical effort of working the land too hard to write poetry. After a few years of discouragement. Frost returned to teaching.

SENTENCE WORKSHOP 99

Resources ——————

Workshop Resources
• Worksheet, p. 37

Language Workshop CD-ROM
• Sentence Fragments

**Try It Out
Possible Answers**
Robert Frost earned a poor living as a schoolteacher and editor before deciding to try farming the stony New Hampshire soil on thirty acres of land that his grandfather had bought for him. The great physical effort of working the land made it too hard for him to write poetry. So, after a few years of discouragement, Frost returned to teaching.

Assessing Learning

Quick Check: Sentence Fragments
Identify the missing element in each of the following sentence fragments. Then, rewrite the sentence fragments to make them complete sentences. (Possible answers follow each sentence.)

1. The lighthouse on Three Skeleton Key. [Verb—The lighthouse on Three Skeleton Key had a bad reputation.]

2. Washed the mongoose out of the burrow. [Subject—A summer flood washed the mongoose out of the burrow.]

3. About the colt in the snow. [Subject and verb—We were worried about the colt in the snow.]

4. Awaited our punishment. [Subject—Little Man and I awaited our punishment.]

5. When the baby dragons would come out of their shells. [Subject and verb—I looked forward to the time when the baby dragons would come out of their shells.]

OBJECTIVES
1. Use text organizers, such as table of contents and headings, to locate specific information
2. Recognize the types of activities in a textbook that are indicated by logos, color, and similar graphic features

Reading for Life

Using Text Organizers

Using the Strategies

Answers
1. Out Here on My Own
2. On page 22
3. Reading Skills and Strategies; Dialogue with the Text; Literature and Science; Elements of Literature; Reading Skills and Strategies; Student to Student; Literature and History; No Questions Asked; Read On; Writer's Workshop; Sentence Workshop; Reading for Life; Learning for Life
4. Answers will vary.
5. Writer's Workshop; Sentence Workshop; Communications Handbook

Using Tables of Contents to Organize Information
Tell students to be sure to study a book's table of contents when they are conducting research using a variety of sources. Studying the table of contents offers a quick method of evaluating the usefulness of a text. Tell students that a table of contents is an outline of a book's organization. It shows how a book is divided (for example, into sections) and how the chapters are arranged (for example, chronologically or by geographical region). Some books have overviews or summaries of each chapter that can help students decide whether or not the book's information is relevant to their research.

Situation
It's the beginning of another school year. You're in English class, and you've just been handed this literature textbook. Use the following strategies to get to know your new book and to **locate specific information.**

Strategies
Use the table of contents.
- The **table of contents** (TOC) is always near the front of the book. Turn to the TOC to get an idea of what's in the book. You'll find a list of writers and selections (with authors' names at left) and special features in the order in which they appear in the book.

Look at the headings.
- A **heading** is a kind of title. Textbook headings are usually printed in a color or size that grabs your attention.
- Glance through the book and look for headings (like *Before You Read* and *Making Meanings*) that jump out at you. A repeated heading always signals the same kind of material.

100 OUT HERE ON MY OWN

CONTENTS

Use graphic features.
- **Graphic features** like charts, tables, and maps organize or present information visually. Graphic features like color, boldface words, and logos (tiny pictures—like computer icons) help you find what you're looking for. For example, you'll find an open-book logo like the one on page 2 near every reading lesson, question, and activity.

Using the Strategies
Turn to page viii, and use the strategies you've just learned to answer these questions about the TOC.

1. What is the title of Collection One?
2. On what page does the lesson on the short story begin?
3. Make a list of all the special features that are included in Collection One.
4. What headings in this TOC are you curious about?
5. If you needed help in writing, could you find it in this book? If so, where?

Extending the Strategies
Give a classmate a guided tour of this textbook. Explain how the book is organized.

Reaching All Students

Struggling Readers
These students may be paired with advanced readers to take the guided tour of the textbook. The students should pay particular attention to the correspondence between the Table of Contents and the text; the titles of the collections and their thematic bases; the Before You Read headings; the post-selection headings; the Words to Own definitions; footnotes to the text; and the Resource Center features and their functions. The goal should be to make the book (and books in general) user-friendly and appealing to students who may be intimidated by the written word.

Advanced Learners
After examining the Index of Skills, Index of Art, and Index of Authors and Titles, these students can write a brief report on the purpose of each index and on the usefulness of specialized indexes. They might consider whether any other types of indexes would be appropriate for the text. You can make copies of the Table of Contents by Genre; students can think of other possible tables of contents for the book. Students may want to take a similar in-depth look at the structure of their texts across the curriculum. In a brief report, they may discuss how the various features of a textbook contribute to its usefulness, or they may indicate what other features they would add. Students may enjoy designing logos for these features.

Learning for Life
Making a Presentation

Problem

As in real life, characters in literature face challenges they sometimes have to deal with alone. Who in our world can be called courageous? What can we learn from courageous people?

Project

Analyze the personal qualities that make people courageous. Create a presentation that teaches others about courage.

Preparation

1. Either alone or with a group, identify someone you know, or someone currently in the news, who shows courage. Remember that courage is shown not only in a daring rescue attempt but also in more ordinary actions, such as standing up for something you believe in even if your opinion is unpopular.

2. Write down the person's specific actions that show courage.

Procedure

1. For each of the person's actions, make a list of qualities the person showed—

CALVIN AND HOBBES © Watterson. Dist. by UNIVERSAL PRESS SYNDICATE. Reprinted with permission. All rights reserved.

for example, determination, a desire to help others, and emotional strength.

2. If the person is someone you know, interview him or her. Ask questions like these:

   • What actions do you think require courage?

   • What personal qualities help you act courageously?

   • How can a person develop those qualities?

Presentation

Present what you have learned in one of the following ways:

1. Role-Play

Role-play and deliver a speech to your class. Try to be as much like the courageous person you've researched as possible. Talk about the personal qualities that make someone courageous.

2. Public-Service Announcement

Write and audiotape or videotape a public-service announcement about acting courageously. The person you researched will be the spokesperson of the announcement. Make the point that courage can be shown in many ways, some of them bold and some of them quiet.

3. Design

Design a symbol for each personal quality that contributes to courage. Label each symbol. Display your symbols in any form you wish. Consider writing a short article and sending your designs to a magazine for possible publication.

Processing

Complete this sentence: The most important thing I learned about courage is. . . .

Resources

Viewing and Representing
HRW Multimedia Presentation Maker
Students may wish to use the Multimedia Presentation Maker in preparing their presentation.

Grading Timesaver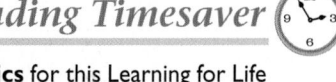

Rubrics for this Learning for Life project appear on p. 114 of the *Portfolio Management System*.

Developing Workplace Competencies

Preparation	Procedure	Presentation
• Acquiring information • Determining relevant information	• Evaluating information • Formulating appropriate questions	• Thinking creatively • Communicating ideas and information

Who Am I?

Collection Planner

Theme

A Rose By Any Other Name Might Be a Daisy *Who am I? What is important to me? What kind of person do I want to become? By meeting new people and adapting to new ways of life, the characters in these stories develop their sense of self and gain fresh insights about the things that matter most to them.*

Reading the Anthology

Reaching Struggling Readers

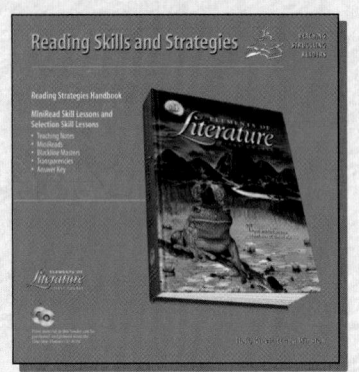

The *Reading Skills and Strategies: Reaching Struggling Readers* binder provides materials coordinated with the Pupil's Edition (see the Collection Planner, p. T101C) to help students who have difficulty reading and comprehending text, or students who are reluctant readers. The binder for seventh grade is organized around eleven individual skill areas and offers the following options:

- **Mini Read** MiniReads are short, easy texts that give students a chance to practice a particular skill and strategy before reading selections in the Pupil's Edition. Each MiniRead Skill Lesson can be taught independently or used in conjunction with a Selection Skill Lesson.

- **Selection Skill Lessons** Selection Skill Lessons allow students to apply skills introduced in the MiniReads. Each Selection Skill Lesson provides reading instruction and practice specific to a particular piece of literature in the Pupil's Edition.

Reading Beyond the Anthology

Read On Collection Two includes an annotated bibliography of books suitable for extended reading. The suggested books are related to works in this collection by theme, by author, or by subject. To preview the Read On for Collection Two, please turn to p. T179.

HRW Library The *HRW Library* offers novels, plays, and short-story collections for extended reading. Each book in the Library includes one or more major works and thematically or topically related Connections. The Connections are magazine articles, poems, or other pieces of literature. Each book in the *HRW Library* is also accompanied by a Study Guide that provides teaching suggestions and worksheets. For Collection Two, the following titles are recommended.

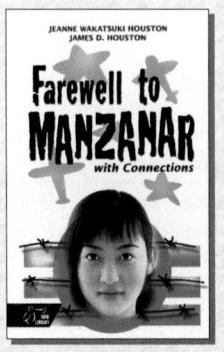

FAREWELL TO MANZANAR
Jeanne Wakatsuki Houston and James D. Houston
This spirited true story retraces the Wakatsuki family's years in a Japanese American internment camp during World War II.

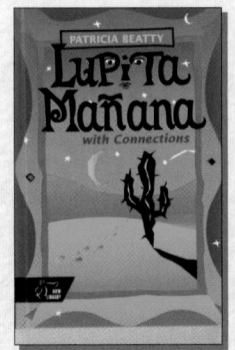

LUPITA MAÑANA
Patricia Beatty
With hopes of helping support their family in Mexico, 13-year-old Lupita and her brother travel 275 miles—on foot, by truck, by train—from Tijuana to the United States.

Skills Focus

Selection or Feature	Reading Skills and Strategies	Elements of Literature	Language/ Grammar	Vocabulary/ Spelling	Writing	Listening/ Speaking	Viewing/ Representing
from **Homesick** (p. 104) Jean Fritz	Distinguish Fact from Opinion, pp. 104, 118	Autobiography and Biography, pp. 104, 118 Conflict, p. 118	Style: Denotation and Connotation, p. 120	Use Body Language to Learn Words, p. 120	Collect Ideas for an Autobiographical Incident, p. 119 Report on China, p. 119	State and Defend a Position, p. 118 Present a Dramatic Reading, p. 119	Make a Picture or Collage of an American Image, p. 119
Elements of Literature: Non- fiction (p. 121)		Types of Non- fiction, p. 121 Subjective and Objective Writing, p. 122					
Reading Skills and Strategies: Compar- ing and Contrasting (p. 123)	Compare and Contrast, p. 123						Use a Venn Diagram, p. 123
from **Barrio Boy** (p. 124) Ernesto Galarza	Compare and Contrast, pp. 124, 132	Metaphor, p. 131	Adjectives: Degrees of Comparison, p. 133	Use New Words in Sentences, p. 133	Freewrite Ideas, p. 132 Compare Stories, p. 132	Tell Stories Illustrating Cul- tural Heritage, p. 132	Make a Pie Graph of Class Ethnicity, p. 132
Fish Cheeks (p. 134) Amy Tan	Describe Men- tal Images, pp. 134, 141 Retell Main Events, p. 141	Description, pp. 134, 141 Title, p. 141	Precise Adjectives, pp. 142, 143	Word Analogies, p. 143	Write about an Expe- rience, p. 142 Describe a Meal from Two Points of View, p. 142		Collect Recipes in a Class Cook- book, p. 142
Names/Nombres (p. 144) Julia Alvarez	Main Idea, pp. 144, 149 Infer, p. 144 Identify Signifi- cant Details, p. 149	Main Idea: Stated or Implied, p. 144	Dangling Modifiers, p. 151 Suffixes, p. 151 Prefixes, p. 151		Take Notes on Names, p. 150 Write an "I Am" Poem, p. 150 Make Up a Pen Name, p. 150	Present a Short Talk on the Meaning of One's Name, p. 150	Design a Book Cover for an Imaginary Book, p. 150
The Naming of Names (p. 152) Ray Bradbury	Monitor Com- prehension, pp. 152, 165 Identify Main Events, p. 165 Make Infer- ences, p. 165	Setting, pp. 152, 166 Title, p. 165 Sensory Details, p. 166	Misplaced Modifiers, p. 167	Glossaries and Dictionaries, p. 167 Word Derivation, p. 167 Make a Word Map, p. 167	Describe a Setting, p. 166 Compare and Contrast Fiction and Fact, p. 166 Describe Another Planet's Setting, p. 166	Do an Oral Presentation on the Renaming of Regional Features, p. 166	Make a Map of the Region, p. 166 Draw Characters, p. 166
I'm Nobody! (p. 168) Emily Dickinson		Figures of Speech, pp. 168, 171			Take Notes, p. 171 Write a Letter to Dickinson, p. 171		Design a Cover for Dickinson's Poetry, p. 171
No Questions Asked: The Frog Who Wanted to Be a Singer (p. 172) Linda Goss	The **No Questions Asked** feature provides students with an unstructured opportunity to practice reading strategies using a selection that extends the theme of the collection.						
Speaking and Listen- ing Workshop: Group Discussion (p. 180)						Conduct a Group Discussion on a Question, pp. 180–181	
Writer's Workshop: Autobiographical Incident (p. 182)		Chronological Order, p. 184			Write an Autobio- graphical Incident, pp. 182–186		
Sentence Work- shop: Combining Sentences (p. 187)			Subordinate Clauses, p. 187		Revise Sentences, p. 187		
Reading for Life: Independent Reading (p. 188)	Strategies for Independent Reading, p. 188				Write a Letter or E-mail to an Author, p. 188		
Learning for Life: Evaluating Advertising (p. 189)	Evaluate Adver- tisements, p. 189				Write a Consumer- Response Letter, p. 189	Conduct a Discussion, p. 189	Create and Illustrate an Ad, p. 189

Skills Focus

Resources for this Collection

Note: All resources for this collection are available for preview on the *One-Stop Planner CD-ROM 1 with Test Generator.* All worksheets and blackline masters may be printed from the CD-ROM.

Internet Resources
go.hrw.com LE0 7-2

Selection or Feature	Reading and Literary Skills	Language and Grammar

from **Homesick** (p. 104)
Jean Fritz
	• *Reading Skills and Strategies: Reaching Struggling Readers*
	  • MiniRead Skill Lesson, p. 66
	  • Selection Skill Lesson, p. 72
	• *Graphic Organizers for Active Reading,* Worksheet p. 7
	• *Literary Elements:*
	  Transparency 2; Worksheet p. 7
		• *Grammar and Language Links:*
		  Denotations and Connotations, Worksheet p. 11
		• *Daily Oral Grammar,*
		  Transparency 7

Elements of Literature:
  Nonfiction (p. 121)
	• *Literary Elements,*
	  Transparency 2	

from **Barrio Boy** (p. 124)
Ernesto Galarza
	• *Reading Skills and Strategies: Reaching Struggling Readers*
	  • MiniRead Skill Lesson, p. 142
	  • Selection Skill Lesson, p. 148
	• *Graphic Organizers for Active Reading,* Worksheet p. 8
		• *Grammar and Language Links:* Comparing
		  Adjectives and Adverbs, Worksheet p. 13
		• *Language Workshop CD-ROM,*
		  Degrees of Comparison
		• *Daily Oral Grammar,*
		  Transparency 8

Fish Cheeks (p. 134)
Amy Tan
Connections: Immigrants (p. 140)
Pat Mora
	• *Graphic Organizers for Active Reading,* Worksheet p. 9	• *Grammar and Language Links:* Using
		  Precise Adjectives, Worksheet p. 15
		• *Language Workshop CD-ROM,*
		  Adjectives
		• *Daily Oral Grammar,*
		  Transparency 9

Names/Nombres (p. 144)
Julia Alvarez
	• *Reading Skills and Strategies: Reaching Struggling Readers*
	  • MiniRead Skill Lesson, p. 80
	  • Selection Skill Lesson, p. 87
	• *Graphic Organizers for Active Reading,* Worksheet p. 10
		• *Grammar and Language Links:* Dangling
		  Modifiers, Worksheet p. 17
		• *Language Workshop CD-ROM,*
		  Dangling Modifiers
		• *Daily Oral Grammar,*
		  Transparency 10

The Naming of Names (p. 152)
Ray Bradbury
	• *Reading Skills and Strategies: Reaching Struggling Readers*
	  • Selection Skill Lesson, p. 11
	• *Graphic Organizers for Active Reading,* Worksheet p. 11
		• *Grammar and Language Links:*
		  Modifiers, Worksheet p. 19
		• *Language Workshop CD-ROM,*
		  Comparative and Superlative Forms
		• *Daily Oral Grammar,*
		  Transparency 11

I'm Nobody (p. 168) Emily Dickinson	• *Graphic Organizers for Active Reading,* Worksheet p. 12	

No Questions Asked: The Frog Who
  Wanted to Be a Singer (p. 172)
Linda Goss
Connections: A Place in the Choir
  (p. 178)
Bill Staines
	The **No Questions Asked** feature provides students with an unstructured opportunity to practice reading strategies using a selection that extends the theme of the collection.	

Speaking and Listening Workshop: **Group Discussion** (p. 180)		
Writer's Workshop: Autobiographi- **cal Incident** (p. 182)		

Sentence Workshop: Combining
  Sentences Using Subordinate
  Clauses (p. 187)
		• *Workshop Resources,* p. 39
		• *Language Workshop CD-ROM,*
		  Subordinate Clauses

Learning for Life: Evaluating **Advertising** (p. 189)		

Collection Planner

Collection Resources

- *Cross-Curricular Activities*, p. 13
- *Portfolio Management System:*
  Introduction to Portfolio Assessment, p. 1;
  Parent/Guardian Letters, p. 89
- *Formal Assessment,*
  Reading Application Test, p. 32
- *Test Generator*, Collection Test

CD-ROM icon next to Test Generator

Vocabulary, Spelling, and Decoding	Writing	Listening and Speaking, Viewing and Representing	Assessment
• *Words to Own*, Worksheet p. 6 • *Spelling and Decoding*, Worksheet p. 6	• *Portfolio Management System*, Rubrics for Choices, p. 115	• *Audio CD Library,* Disc 5, Track 2 • *Portfolio Management System*, Rubrics for Choices, p. 115	• *Formal Assessment, Selection Test*, p. 19 • *Standardized Test Preparation*, pp. 22, 24 • *Test Generator* (One-Stop Planner CD-ROM)
			• *Formal Assessment,* Literary Elements Test, p. 30
• *Words to Own*, Worksheet p. 7 • *Spelling and Decoding*, Worksheet p. 7	• *Portfolio Management System*, Rubrics for Choices, p. 116	• *Audio CD Library,* Disc 5, Track 3 • *Viewing and Representing:* Fine Art Transparency 4 Worksheet p. 16 • *Portfolio Management System*, Rubrics for Choices, p. 116	• *Formal Assessment, Selection Test*, p. 21 • *Standardized Test Preparation*, p. 26 • *Test Generator* (One-Stop Planner CD-ROM)
• *Words to Own*, Worksheet p. 8 • *Spelling and Decoding*, Worksheet p. 8	• *Portfolio Management System*, Rubrics for Choices, p. 117	• *Audio CD Library,* Disc 5, Track 4 • *Viewing and Representing:* Fine Art Transparency 5 Worksheet p. 20 • *Portfolio Management System*, Rubrics for Choices, p. 117	• *Formal Assessment, Selection Test*, p. 23 • *Standardized Test Preparation*, p. 28 • *Test Generator* (One-Stop Planner CD-ROM)
• *Spelling and Decoding*, Worksheet p. 9	• *Portfolio Management System*, Rubrics for Choices, p. 118	• *Visual Connections,* Videocassette A, Segment 2 • *Portfolio Management System*, Rubrics for Choices, p. 118	• *Formal Assessment, Selection Test*, p. 25 • *Standardized Test Preparation*, p. 30 • *Test Generator* (One-Stop Planner CD-ROM)
• *Words to Own*, Worksheet p. 9 • *Spelling and Decoding*, Worksheet p. 10	• *Portfolio Management System*, Rubrics for Choices, p. 119	• *Audio CD Library,* Disc 6, Track 2 • *Portfolio Management System*, Rubrics for Choices, p. 119	• *Formal Assessment, Selection Test*, p. 27 • *Standardized Test Preparation*, p. 32 • *Test Generator* (One-Stop Planner CD-ROM)
	• *Portfolio Management System*, Rubrics for Choices, p. 121	• *Audio CD Library,* Disc 6, Track 3 • *Portfolio Management System*, Rubrics for Choices, p. 121	• *Formal Assessment, Selection Test*, p. 29 • *Test Generator* (One-Stop Planner CD-ROM)
		• *Audio CD Library,* Disc 6, Track 4	
			• *Portfolio Management System*, p. 122
	• *Workshop Resources*, p. 5 • *Writer's Workshop 1 CD-ROM,* Autobiographical Incident		• *Portfolio Management System* • Prewriting, p. 123 • Peer Editing, p. 124 • Assessment Rubric, p. 125
		• *Viewing and Representing,* HRW Multimedia Presentation Maker	• *Portfolio Management System*, Rubrics, p. 126

 Transparency   CD-ROM   Video   Audio CD

Collection Planner (vertical tab)

T101D

Introducing the Theme

To help students understand the theme, explain that the question "Who am I?" refers to a person's identity—the way a person views himself or herself or the way other people view that person. As an example of public identity, you might use Dr. Martin Luther King, Jr.: He was a father, minister, civil rights leader. Students can specify more of King's identities: role model, winner of the Nobel Peace Prize. They can also name the various identities of other individuals, real or imaginary. Finally, you might ask volunteers to give nouns (other than their names) that help define their identities.

RESPONDING TO THE ART

Activity. Imagine that you are the person in this photograph. Write a brief paragraph in which you describe yourself. Include your name, the place where you live, what you like to do, what you are doing or thinking about in the photograph, and any other details that describe who you are.

Collection

Two

Who Am I?

102

Writing Focus: Autobiographical Incident

The following **Work in Progress** assignments build to a culminating **Writer's Workshop** at the end of Collection 2.

• Homesick	Recall details of a personal event (p. 119)
• Barrio Boy	Freewrite about an autobiographical incident (p. 132)
• Fish Cheeks	Write about a learning experience (p. 142)
• Names / Nombres	Write about experiences involving names (p. 150)
• The Naming of Names	Describe a setting for an incident (p. 166)
• I'm Nobody!	Describe a special person (p. 171)

Writer's Workshop: Narrative Writing / Autobiographical Incident (p. 182)

I am myself,
of all my atom parts I am the sum.
And out of my blood and my brain
I make my own interior weather,
my own sun and rain.

—Eve Merriam

Selection Readability

This Annotated Teacher's Edition provides a summary of each selection in the student book. Following each Summary heading, you will find one, two or three small icons. These icons indicate, in an approximate sense, the reading level of the selection.

■ One icon indicates that the selection is easy.

■ ■ Two icons indicate that the selection is on an intermediate reading level.

■ ■ ■ Three icons indicate that the selection is challenging.

Responding to the Quotation

Tell students that Eve Merriam was a modern American poet. Ask students what l. 2 of the quotation suggests. They may respond that humans are the result of everything they are made of. Follow up by asking how a person can "make" his or her "interior weather." Elicit that an individual, using his or her physical and mental qualities, creates a personality and mood. Ask students if they agree with this idea. Encourage them to explain their response.

Writer's Notebook

Have students imagine that they are living in a different time or a different place—for example, that they have moved to a faraway country or have traveled back in time. Have students make two columns on a page in their journals. They should label one column "Here and Now" and the other column "In Another Place (or Time)." Explain that they should fill in the columns by answering the question "What is my life like?" In one column they can describe something in their present life, such as their favorite type of entertainment; in the other column they can visualize what that thing would be like in another time or place. Students should work with partners to share ideas and offer suggestions.

Resources

Portfolio Management System
- Introduction to Portfolio Assessment, p. 1
- Parent/Guardian Letters, p. 89

Formal Assessment
- Reading Application Test, p. 32

Test Generator
- Collection Test

Cross-Curricular Activities
- Teaching Notes, p. 13

Before You Read

HOMESICK

Make the Connection

Do You Speak My Language?

If you lived in France or Spain or Korea, people might ask you if you could speak their language:

Parlez-vous français? (pár′lā vōō frán·sā′)

¿Habla español? (ä′blä es·pä·nyôl′)

한국말을 할수 있습니까? (hän gōōk mär·əl häl sōō its·ōōm′ nē kä)

Suppose you had to live for a time in another country, far away from the place you call home. What would you miss? How could living far away help you find out who you are and what you like about your own country?

Round table. Divide into small groups and brainstorm the pros and cons ("fors and againsts") of living in a different land, in a different culture. (Perhaps you or someone you know is doing exactly that.) List your pros and cons, and then share your findings with the class.

As you read "Homesick," keep a sheet of paper next to the book so that you can record your responses to Jean Fritz's account of living in two cultures. One student's responses appear on the first page.

Elements of Literature

Autobiography and Biography: Who's Telling?

An **autobiography** is the story of a person's life, written by that very person. A **biography** is the story of a person's life, told by *another* person. In her autobiography, "Homesick," Jean Fritz tells what it was like to grow up in China.

The first chapter of her account begins on the next page. The year is 1925, and Jean is ten years old. To learn what happened to Jean when she grew up, read her biography and "meet the writer" on page 117.

In an **autobiography** the writer tells the story of his or her own life. In a **biography** the writer tells the story of someone else's life.

For more on Autobiography and Biography, see pages 121–122 and the Handbook of Literary Terms.

Reading Skills and Strategies

Distinguishing Fact from Opinion: Checking It Out

When you read an autobiography, it's important to be able to tell facts from opinions. A **fact** can be proved true or false. "The Yangtze River is in China" is a fact. An **opinion,** a personal feeling or belief, can't be proved true or false. In autobiographies, like "Homesick," writers share their feelings and opinions, but they also present facts.

Don't be fooled: People may state an opinion as if it were a fact. If you're in doubt, ask yourself: Can this statement be proved, or is it someone's personal feeling or belief?

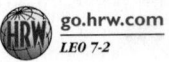
go.hrw.com
LE0 7-2

104 WHO AM I?

Preteaching Vocabulary

Words to Own

Have students read the four Words to Own and their definitions listed at the bottom of the selection pages. Students can work in pairs to write original sentences using these words correctly. Then, have students choose the word that best completes each sentence below.

1. A friend of mine _____ into the room, giving me an unfriendly look. [sauntered]

2. I became so _____ that I jumped from my chair. [flustered]

3. As that _____ old thing fell backward, it broke. [rickety]

4. Being suddenly unseated left me _____ at both my friend and the chair. [glowering]

from Homesick

Jean Fritz

I belonged on the other side of the world. In America . . .

In my father's study there was a large globe with all the countries of the world running around it. I could put my finger on the exact spot where I was and had been ever since I'd been born. And I was on the wrong side of the globe. I was in China in a city named Hankow, a dot on a crooked line that seemed to break the country right in two. The line was really the Yangtze River, but who would know by looking at a map what the Yangtze River really was?

Orange-brown, muddy mustard colored. And wide, wide, wide. With a river smell that was old and came all the way up from the bottom. Sometimes old women knelt on the riverbank, begging the River God to return a son or grandson who may have drowned. They would wail and beat the earth to make the River God pay attention, but I knew how busy the River God must be. All those people on the Yangtze River! Coolies[1] hauling water. Women washing clothes. Houseboats swarming with old people and young, chickens and pigs. Big crooked-sailed junks[2] with eyes painted on their prows so they could see where they were going. I loved the Yangtze River, but of course, I belonged on the other side of the world. In America, with my grandmother.

1. **coolies:** workers who do heavy work for little pay. English-speakers visiting the East took this name from the Hindi word *qulī*, meaning "hired servant."
2. **junks:** Chinese ships with flat bottoms and square sails.

Dialogue with the Text

Where does she live? Who's telling the story?

That person must have lived near the river.

That reminds me of a story in our literature book, "The Old Demon."

I think that the people made up the River God as an explanation for people's deaths.

Why did the person telling the story move?

Katie Sheldon

— Katie Sheldon
Vista Verde Middle School
Irvine, California

Summary ■■

In this chapter of her autobiography, Fritz relates how she longs to be in America. She feels out of place in both the British school she attends and the Chinese community, Hankow, in which she lives. When Ian Forbes, the school bully, threatens Jean if she refuses to sing "God Save the King," Jean plays hooky for a day and explores her Chinese neighborhood. At home she is scolded for cutting school. Later, her father helps her solve her dilemma at school by telling her to use the words to "My Country 'Tis of Thee" while her British schoolmates sing their lyrics to the melody.

Planning

- **Block Schedule**
  Block Scheduling Lesson Plans with Pacing Guide
- **Traditional Schedule**
  Lesson Plans Including Strategies for English-Language Learners
- **One-Stop Planner**
  CD-ROM with Test Generator

Resources

Listening
Audio CD Library
A spirited recording of this memoir is provided in the *Audio CD Library:*
- Disc 5, Track 2

Selection Assessment
Formal Assessment
- Selection Test, p. 19
Test Generator
- Selection Test

Elements of Literature
For additional instruction in nonfiction, see *Literary Elements:*
- Transparency 2
- Worksheet, p. 7

Resources: Print and Media

Reading
- *Reading Skills and Strategies*
  MiniRead Skill Lesson, p. 66
  Selection Skill Lesson, p. 72
- *Graphic Organizers for Active Reading* p. 7
- *Words to Own,* p. 6
- *Spelling and Decoding*
  Worksheet, p. 6
- *Audio CD Library*
  Disc 5, Track 2

Elements of Literature
- *Literary Elements*
  Transparency 2
  Worksheet, p. 7

Writing and Language
- *Daily Oral Grammar*
  Transparency 7
- *Grammar and Language Links*
  Worksheet, p. 11

Assessment
- *Formal Assessment,* p. 19
- *Portfolio Management System,* p. 115
- *Standardized Test Preparation,* pp. 22, 24
- *Test Generator (One-Stop Planner CD-ROM)*

Internet
- go.hrw.com (keyword: LE0 7-2)

(A) Elements of Literature

Autobiography

❓ Why does Jean include excerpts
from her letters in her autobiography?
[Possible responses: She wants to give
readers a look at what her life was like in
China and how she imagined life in the
United States; she wants her autobiography to be believable.]

**(B) Reading Skills
and Strategies**

**Distinguishing
Fact from Opinion**

❓ Why is this statement an opinion,
not a fact? [Possible response: It states
Jean's feelings about being American; this
statement cannot be proved to be true
or false.]

(C) Reading Skills and Strategies

Responding to the Text

❓ What does Jean's decision not to
sing "God Save the King" tell about
her? [Possible responses: She has pride
in her country; she is principled and
does what she believes is right.]

*Twenty-five fluffy little
yellow chicks hatched
from our eggs today, my
grandmother wrote.*

(A) *I wrote my grandmother that I had
watched a Chinese
magician swallow three
yards of fire.*

(B) The trouble with living on the
wrong side of the world was that I
didn't feel like a *real* American.

For instance. I could never be
president of the United States. I didn't
want to be president; I wanted to be a
writer. Still, why should there be a *law*
that only a person born in the United States
could be president?[3] It was as if I wouldn't be
American enough.

Actually, I was American every minute of the
day, especially during school hours. I went to a
British school and every morning we sang
"God Save the King." Of course the British children loved singing about their gracious king.
Ian Forbes stuck out his chest and sang as if he
were saving the king all by himself. Everyone
sang. Even Gina Boss, who was Italian. And
Vera Sebastian, who was so Russian she
dressed the way Russian girls did long ago before the Revolution,[4] when her family had to
run away to keep from being killed.

But I wasn't Vera Sebastian. I asked my
mother to write an excuse so I wouldn't have
to sing, but she wouldn't do it. "When in
Rome," she said, "do as the Romans do." What
she meant was, "Don't make trouble. Just sing."

3. This is not a fact. The U.S. Constitution states only that a
presidential candidate must be a "natural-born" U.S. citizen.
This term applies to citizens born in the United States and
its territories. But no law or court case has yet decided
whether "natural-born" also describes children born to
U.S. citizens in other countries.
4. **Revolution:** In 1917, a revolution drove the czars (em-
perors) and other nobility from power, and Russia became
the first nation to set up a Communist government.

So for a long time I did. I sang with my
fingers crossed but still I felt like a
traitor.

Then one day I thought:
If my mother and father
were really and truly in
Rome, they wouldn't
do what the Romans did
at all. They'd probably try
to get the Romans to do
what *they* did, just as they
were trying to teach the Chinese
to do what Americans did. (My
mother even gave classes in American manners.)

(C) So that day I quit singing. I kept my mouth
locked tight against the king of England. Our
teacher, Miss Williams, didn't notice at first.
She stood in front of the room, using a ruler for
a baton, striking each syllable so hard it was as
if she were making up for the times she had
nothing to strike.

(Miss Williams was pinch-faced and bossy.
Sometimes I wondered what had ever made
her come to China. "Maybe to try and catch a
husband," my mother said.

A husband! Miss Williams!)

"Make him vic-tor-i-ous," the class sang. It
was on the strike of "vic" that Miss Williams noticed. Her eyes lighted on my mouth and when
we sat down, she pointed her ruler at me.

"Is there something wrong with your voice
today, Jean?" she asked.

"No, Miss Williams."

"You weren't singing."

"No, Miss Williams. It is not my national
anthem."

"It is the national anthem we sing here," she
snapped. "You have always sung. Even Vera
sings it."

I looked at Vera with the big blue bow tied
on the top of her head. Usually I felt sorry for
her but not today. At recess I might even untie
that bow, I thought. Just give it a yank. But if I'd

Reaching All Students

Struggling Readers
Distinguishing Fact from Opinion was introduced on p. 104. For a lesson directly tied to
this selection that teaches students to distinguish fact from opinion by using a strategy
called Text Reformulation, see the *Reading Skills
and Strategies* binder:
• MiniRead Skill Lesson, p. 66
• Selection Skill Lesson, p. 72

English Language Learners
Students might gain practice in comprehension
and pronunciation by listening to the recording
of the selection in the *Audio CD Library.* For
additional strategies to supplement instruction
for these students, see
• *Lesson Plans Including Strategies for English-
Language Learners*

Advanced Learners
As students read the selection, have them find
support for this statement: Growing up in China
is good for Jean, because it forces her to ask
questions about her identity, questions that lead
her to a deeper understanding of herself.

been smart, I wouldn't have been looking at Vera. I would have been looking at Ian Forbes and I would have known that no matter what Miss Williams said, I wasn't through with the king of England.

Recess at the British School was nothing I looked forward to. Every day we played a game called prisoner's base, which was all running and shouting and shoving and catching. I hated the game, yet everyone played except Vera Sebastian. She sat on the sidelines under her blue bow like someone who had been dropped out of a history book. By recess I had forgotten my plans for that bow. While everyone was getting ready for the game, I was as usual trying to look as if I didn't care if I was the last one picked for a team or not. I was leaning against the high stone wall that ran around the schoolyard. I was looking up at a little white cloud skittering across the sky when all at once someone tramped down hard on my right foot. Ian Forbes. Snarling bulldog face. Heel grinding down on my toes. Head thrust forward the way an animal might before it strikes.

"You wouldn't sing it. So say it," he ordered. "Let me hear you say it."

I tried to pull my foot away but he only ground down harder.

"Say what?" I was telling my face please not to show what my foot felt.

"*God save the king.* Say it. Those four words. I want to hear you say it."

Although Ian Forbes was short, he was solid and tough and built for fighting. What was more, he always won. You had only to look at his bare knees between the top of his socks and his short pants to know that he would win. His knees were square. Bony and unbeatable. So of course it was crazy for me to argue with him.

"Why should I?" I asked. "Americans haven't said that since George the Third."[5]

5. **George the Third** (1738–1820): king of Great Britain at the time of the Revolutionary War (1775–1783), fought by the American colonies to gain independence from Great Britain.

He grabbed my right arm and twisted it behind my back.

"Say it," he hissed.

I felt the tears come to my eyes and I hated myself for the tears. I hated myself for not staying in Rome the way my mother had told me.

"I'll never say it," I whispered.

They were choosing sides now in the schoolyard and Ian's name was being called—among the first, as always.

He gave my arm another twist. "You'll sing tomorrow," he snarled, "or you'll be bloody sorry."

As he ran off, I slid to the ground, my head between my knees.

Oh, Grandma, I thought, why can't I be there with you? I'd feed the chickens for you. I'd pump water from the well, the way my father used to do.

It would be almost two years before we'd go to America. I was ten years old now; I'd be twelve then. But how could I think about *years*? I didn't even dare to think about the next day. After school I ran all the way home, fast so I couldn't think at all.

Our house stood behind a high stone wall, which had chips of broken glass sticking up from the top to keep thieves away. I flung open the iron gate and threw myself through the front door.

"I'm home!" I yelled.

Then I remembered that it was Tuesday, the day my mother taught an English class at the YMCA[6] where my father was the director.

I stood in the hall, trying to catch my breath, and as always I began to feel small. It was a huge hall with ceilings so high it was as if they would have nothing to do with people. Certainly not with a mere child, not with me—the only child in the house. Once I asked my best friend, Andrea, if the hall made her feel little too. She said no. She was going to be a dancer

6. **YMCA:** short for "Young Men's Christian Association."

D Struggling Readers
Paraphrasing
Ask students to state in their own words what the author means when she describes Vera as "someone who had been dropped out of a history book." [Possible response: Vera seems old-fashioned in the way she acts and dresses.]

E Reading Skills and Strategies
Making Predictions
❓ Based on your own experience and on what you've learned about Jean, what do you think she will do? [Possible responses: She'll sing "God Save the King," because she knows she can't defeat a bully; she won't sing the song, because she's determined to keep her allegiance to the United States.]

F English Language Learners
British Slang
Ask students to give the most common meaning of *bloody*. [stained with blood] Then, tell students *bloody* is a British slang word that means "darn" or "very." It is sometimes considered vulgar.

G Critical Thinking
Speculating
❓ Why does Jean present Andrea's reaction to the hall as well as her own? [Possible response: Jean presents Andrea's feelings in contrast to her own. The hall makes Jean feel small and alone, but it makes Andrea want to dance.] What generalization can you make from the contrast between the two girls? [Possible response: People's feelings about their surroundings are often based on their feelings about themselves.]

Using Students' Strengths

Visual Learners
Students might benefit from completing the graphic organizer, available on p. 7 in *Graphic Organizers for Active Reading*.

Logical/Mathematical Learners
Have a volunteer use a globe to show students that Asia and North America are indeed on opposite sides of the world. Then, focus on the setting by using a transparency or pull-down map of China to point out Hankow (now part of Wuhan) and the Yangtze River. Students can calculate the approximate distance from Wuhan to the home of Jean's grandmother in western Pennsylvania.

A Appreciating Language
Punctuation

? Why are commas used around *for instance*? [Commas are used to separate this parenthetical phrase from the rest of the sentence.] Ask students to name other uses for commas. [Possible responses: to separate the main clauses of a compound sentence; to separate items in a series. Students can look in the Language Handbook, pp. 769–771, for other uses.]

B Reading Skills and Strategies

Distinguishing Fact from Opinion

? How do you know whether this statement about American flowers is a fact? [Possible response: It can be proved false by studying flowers or consulting a plant book.] Why does Jean make this statement? [Possible response: She is trying to get out of doing something she hates to do—making French knots.]

C Struggling Readers
Finding Details

? Why do Jean and Lin Nai-Nai keep a secret from the other servants? [Nai-Nai does not come from the servant class. If the other servants knew this, they would be cruel to her.]

D Cultural Connections

Foot binding is associated with a craze for small feet that began in the Tang Dynasty (618–906), when dancers bound their feet. The agonizing process was inflicted on girls between the ages of five and seven. Many Chinese families, especially the wealthy, required footbound wives for their sons, presumably because the practice severely limited a woman's freedom of movement.

E Critical Thinking
Speculating

? Why do you think Jean tricks Lin Nai-Nai? [Possible response: Jean wants to take out her frustrations on someone, and Lin Nai-Nai is the only person she can hurt.]

---

and she loved space. She did a high kick to show how grand it was to have room.

Andrea Hull was a year older than I was and knew about everything sooner. She told me about commas, for instance, long before I took punctuation seriously. How could I write letters without commas? she asked. She made me so ashamed that for months I hung little wagging comma-tails all over the letters to my grandmother. She told me things that sounded so crazy I had to ask my mother if they were true. Like where babies came from. And that someday the whole world would end. My mother would frown when I asked her, but she always agreed that Andrea was right. It made me furious. How could she know such things and not tell me? What was the matter with grown-ups anyway?

I wished that Andrea were with me now, but she lived out in the country and I didn't see her often. Lin Nai-Nai, my amah,[7] was the only one around, and of course I knew she'd be there. It was her job to stay with me when my parents were out. As soon as she heard me come in, she'd called, "Tsai loushang," which meant that she was upstairs. She might be mending or ironing but most likely she'd be sitting by the window embroidering. And she was. She even had my embroidery laid out, for we had made a bargain. She would teach me to embroider if I would teach her English. I liked embroidering: the cloth stretched tight within my embroidery hoop while I filled in the stamped pattern with cross-stitches and lazy daisy flowers. The trouble was that lazy daisies needed French knots for their centers and I hated making French knots. Mine always fell apart, so I left them to the end. Today I had twenty lazy daisies waiting for their knots.

Lin Nai-Nai had already threaded my needle with embroidery floss.

"Black centers," she said, "for the yellow flowers."

7. **amah:** in Asia, a woman who looks after children.

I felt myself glowering. "American flowers don't have centers," I said, and gave her back the needle.

Lin Nai-Nai looked at me, puzzled, but did not argue. She was different from other amahs. She did not even come from the servant class, although this was a secret we had to keep from the other servants, who would have made her life miserable had they known. She had run away from her husband when he had taken a second wife. She would always have been Wife Number One and the Boss no matter how many wives he had, but she would rather be no wife than head of a string of wives. She was modern. She might look old-fashioned, for her feet had been bound up tight when she was a little girl so that they would stay small, and now, like many Chinese women, she walked around on little stumps stuffed into tiny cloth shoes. Lin Nai-Nai's were embroidered with butterflies. Still, she believed in true love and one wife for one husband. We were good friends, Lin Nai-Nai and I, so I didn't know why I felt so mean.

She shrugged. "English lesson?" she asked, smiling.

I tested my arm to see if it still hurt from the twisting. It did. My foot too. "What do you want to know?" I asked.

We had been through the polite phrases—Please, Thank you, I beg your pardon, Excuse me, You're welcome, Merry Christmas (which she had practiced but hadn't had a chance to use since this was only October).

"If I meet an American on the street," she asked, "how do I greet him?"

I looked her straight in the eye and nodded my head in a greeting. "Sewing machine," I said. "You say, 'Sew-ing ma-chine.'"

WORDS TO OWN
glowering (glou′ər·iŋ) v. used as *adj.*: staring angrily; scowling.

Using Students' Strengths

Kinesthetic Learners
Invite pairs of students to role-play significant encounters in the story. The meetings could include Jean's angry confrontations with Ian Forbes; her sulky interaction with her amah, Lin Nai-Nai; and her kindness to the young Chinese boy later in the story. Have students present their role-plays to the class.

Visual Learners
Suggest that students create a collage entitled *Jean's Two Worlds*. In a section called "China," they can draw or paste pictures that show how Jean sees and appreciates China. The other section, labeled "America," can represent how Jean imagines the United States.

She repeated after me, making the four syllables into four separate words. She got up and walked across the room, bowing and smiling. "Sew Ing Ma Shing."

Part of me wanted to laugh at the thought of Lin Nai-Nai maybe meeting Dr. Carhart, our minister, whose face would surely puff up, the way it always did when he was flustered. But part of me didn't want to laugh at all. I didn't like it when my feelings got tangled, so I ran downstairs and played "Chopsticks" on the piano. Loud and fast. When my sore arm hurt, I just beat on the keys harder.

Then I went out to the kitchen to see if Yang Sze-Fu, the cook, would give me something to eat. I found him reading a Chinese newspaper, his eyes going up and down with the characters. (Chinese words don't march across flat surfaces, the way ours do; they drop down cliffs, one cliff after another from right to left across a page.)

"Can I have a piece of cinnamon toast?" I asked. "And a cup of cocoa?"

Yang Sze-Fu grunted. He was smoking a cigarette, which he wasn't supposed to do in the kitchen, but Yang Sze-Fu mostly did what he wanted. He considered himself superior to common workers. You could tell because of the fingernails on his pinkies. They were at least two inches long, which was his way of showing that he didn't have to use his hands for rough or dirty work. He didn't seem to care that his fingernails were dirty, but maybe he couldn't keep such long nails clean.

He made my toast while his cigarette dangled out of the corner of his mouth, collecting a long ash that finally fell on the floor. He wouldn't have kept smoking if my mother had been there, although he didn't always pay attention to my mother. Never about butter pagodas,[8] for instance. No matter how many times my mother told him before a dinner party, "No butter pagoda," it made no difference. As soon as everyone was seated, the serving boy, Wong Sze-Fu, would bring in a pagoda and set it on

---

8. **pagodas:** Asian temples with several levels.

WORDS TO OWN
flustered (flus′tərd) v. used as adj.: confused; upset.

F Elements of Literature
Autobiography
❓ What part of this sentence is like a biography? Explain. [Possible response: The description of Dr. Carhart is like a biography, because it is written by another person.] What elements of autobiography are in the passage beginning "Part of me wanted to laugh"? [Possible response: Autobiographical elements are the first-person pronoun and descriptions, by the narrator, of her feelings.]

G Appreciating Language
Word Choice
❓ How does Jean bring the "Chinese words" to life? [Possible response: She says they "don't march across" the page but "drop down cliffs."] What is the part of speech of march and drop? [verb] What is the effect of the sentence? [Possible response: It creates an unusual, amusing picture that shows how imaginative Jean is.]

H Reading Skills and Strategies
Comparing/Contrasting
❓ How is Lin Nai-Nai's attitude toward her class different from Yang Sze-Fu's attitude toward his? [Possible response: Yang Sze-Fu is a servant but tries to act above his class; Lin Nai-Nai is actually above the servant class but pretends to be a servant (see p. 108).]

I Critical Thinking
Interpreting
❓ Why does Yang Sze-Fu prepare the butter pagodas despite the instructions from Jean's mother? [Possible responses: Yang Sze-Fu wants to prove his independence; he takes great pride in his work and wants to show off his skill.]

Crossing the Curriculum

Music
Play a recording of "God Save the King." Encourage students to discuss the song's patriotic nature and why singing it makes Jean feel disloyal to the United States. Ask students to tell how they feel when "The Star-Spangled Banner" or "My County 'Tis of Thee" is played. Invite students to present national anthems from other countries.

Art
Have students reread the descriptive passages in "Homesick" to find out about everyday life in China in the 1920s. You might discuss with the class which of the passages they would like to illustrate. Encourage students to create an original drawing or painting that illustrates the selection.

Social Studies
Remind students that China is a fast-growing, economically powerfully nation that exerts increasing influence around the world. For a bulletin-board display, suggest that students find newspaper and magazine clippings that portray everyday life in modern China. Students might create captions that contrast modern China with the China of the late 1920s that the author portrays.

A Appreciating Language

Word Choice

? How would this passage have sounded if Jean had written *filthy* instead of *unsanitary*? [Possible responses: Jean's mother would have sounded angrier at Yang Sze-Fu; the passage would have sounded less pleasant.]

B Elements of Literature

Autobiography

? What does Jean reveal about herself by telling how she decides to reread *Sara Crewe*? [Possible responses: She is sentimental; she uses literature to escape from her real-life concerns and to gain a perspective on her problems.]

C Critical Thinking

Making Judgments

? Does taking a day off from school seem like a reasonable action, or might Jean have found a better way to handle her conflict with Ian? [Possible responses: Cutting school won't solve Jean's problem and will probably make her situation worse; Jean could talk to her teacher or parents about Ian's threats.]

D Reading Skills and Strategies

Responding to the Text

? What are your impressions of Hankow? What would it have been like to walk through its streets in 1925? [Possible response: It was a colorful and exotic place, filled with unusual sights—some beautiful, some distressing.]

the table. The guests would "oh" and "ah," for it was a masterpiece: a pagoda molded out of butter, curved roofs rising tier upon tier, but my mother could only think how unsanitary it was. For, of course, Yang Sze-Fu had molded the butter with his hands and carved the decorations with one of his long fingernails. Still, we always used the butter, for if my mother sent it back to the kitchen, Yang Sze-Fu would lose face[9] and quit.

When my toast and cocoa were ready, I took them upstairs to my room (the blue room) and while I ate, I began *Sara Crewe*[10] again. Now there was a girl, I thought, who was worth crying over. I wasn't going to think about myself. Or Ian Forbes. Or the next day. I wasn't. I wasn't.

9. **lose face:** lose dignity or self-respect.
10. *Sara Crewe:* famous children's book by Frances Hodgson Burnett about a rich girl who becomes a poor orphan. Burnett also wrote *A Little Princess, Little Lord Fauntleroy,* and *The Secret Garden.*

And I didn't. Not all afternoon. Not all evening. Still, I must have decided what I was going to do because the next morning when I started for school and came to the corner where the man sold hot chestnuts, the corner where I always turned to go to school, I didn't turn. I walked straight ahead. I wasn't going to school that day.

I walked toward the Yangtze River. Past the store that sold paper pellets that opened up into flowers when you dropped them in a glass of water. Then up the block where the beggars sat. I never saw anyone give money to a beggar. You couldn't, my father explained, or you'd be mobbed by beggars. They'd follow you everyplace; they'd never leave you alone. I had learned not to look at them when I passed and yet I saw. The running sores, the twisted legs, the mangled faces. What I couldn't get over was that, like me, each one of those beggars had only one life to live. It just happened that they had drawn rotten ones.

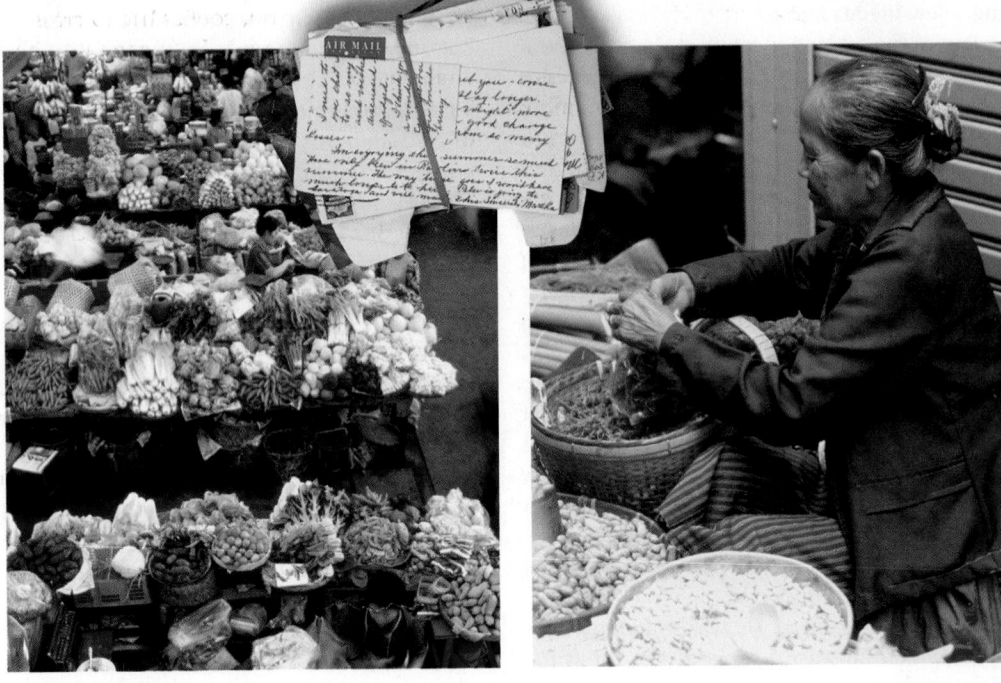

110 WHO AM I?

Getting Students Involved

Cooperative Learning

Divide the class into groups of four. One student can research events, another take notes, the third write the short report, and the fourth present the report to the class. Topics may include the Boxer Rebellion, the Opium Wars, the treaties that caused the partitions, and the Yangtze River, now called Chang Jiang, or other topics that provide cultural insight.

Enrichment Activity

Challenge pairs of students to rewrite portions of the selection from the third-person point of view, as if it were a biography, not an autobiography. Ask students to be aware of sections that contain Jean's inner thoughts and feelings, information that a biographer would probably have to make guesses about.

Oh, Grandma, I thought, we may be far apart but we're lucky, you and I. Do you even know how lucky? In America do you know?

This part of the city didn't actually belong to the Chinese, even though the beggars sat there, even though upper-class Chinese lived there. A long time ago other countries had just walked into China and divided up part of Hankow (and other cities) into sections, or concessions, which they called their own and used their own rules for governing. We lived in the French concession on Rue de Paris. Then there was the British concession and the Japanese. The Russian and German concessions had been officially returned to China, but the people still called them concessions. The Americans didn't have one, although, like some of the other countries, they had gunboats on the river. In case, my father said. In case what? Just in case. That's all he'd say.

The concessions didn't look like the rest of China. The buildings were solemn and orderly, with little plots of grass around them. Not like those in the Chinese part of the city: a jumble of rickety shops with people, vegetables, crates of quacking ducks, yard goods, bamboo baskets, and mangy[11] dogs spilling onto a street so narrow it was hardly there.

The grandest street in Hankow was the Bund, which ran along beside the Yangtze River. When I came to it after passing the beggars, I looked to my left and saw the American flag flying over the American consulate building. I was proud of the flag and I thought maybe today it was proud of me. It flapped in the breeze as if it were saying ha-ha to the king of England.

Then I looked to the right at the Customs House, which stood at the other end of the Bund. The clock on top of the tower said nine-thirty. How would I spend the day?

---

11. **mangy** (mān′jē): diseased. Animals with mange lose their hair and become covered with sores and scabs.

I crossed the street to the promenade part of the Bund. When people walked here, they weren't usually going anyplace; they were just out for the air. My mother would wear her broad-brimmed beaver hat when we came, and my father would swing his cane in that jaunty way that showed how glad he was to be a man. I thought I would just sit on a bench for the morning. I would watch the Customs House clock, and when it was time, I would eat the lunch I had brought along in my schoolbag.

I was the only one sitting on a bench. People did not generally "take the air" on a Wednesday morning, and besides, not everyone was allowed here. The British had put a sign on the Bund, NO DOGS, NO CHINESE. This meant that I could never bring Lin Nai-Nai with me. My father couldn't even bring his best friend, Mr. T. K. Hu. Maybe the British wanted a place where they could pretend they weren't in China, I thought. Still, there were always Chinese coolies around. In order to load and unload boats in the river, coolies had to cross the Bund. All day they went back and forth, bent double under their loads, sweating and chanting in a tired, singsong way that seemed to get them from one step to the next.

To pass the time, I decided to recite poetry. The one good thing about Miss Williams was that she made us learn poems by heart and I liked that. There was one particular poem I didn't want to forget. I looked at the Yangtze River and pretended that all the busy people in the boats were my audience.

"'Breathes there the man, with soul so dead,' I cried, 'Who never to himself hath said, This is my own, my native land!'"

I was so carried away by my performance that I didn't notice the policeman until he was right in front of me. Like all policemen in the British

---

WORDS TO OWN
rickety (rik′it·ē) *adj.:* weak and shaky.

HOMESICK 111

E Reading Skills and Strategies
Distinguishing Fact from Opinion
❓ Is this statement a fact or an opinion? [Possible response: It is a fact; history books and old maps of China would indicate that cities had been divided into concessions.]

F Critical Thinking
Making Connections
❓ Why might the city's division into international sections tend to make Jean feel even more isolated? [Possible response: The United States has not established an area in China. Jean attends a British school in a Chinese city and lives in the French concession.]

G Struggling Readers
Supplying Missing Words
Help students complete the idea that Jean's father implies with the words "Just in case." [Possible response: Just in case the Chinese people revolt and attack the foreigners, the gunboats are here for our protection.]

H Historical Connections
At the beginning of the twentieth century, military units in northern China attempted to eliminate the foreign presence in their country. These groups were called Boxers. In August 1900, an international force entered the capital to put down the siege of foreign embassies. A year later, China was forced to allow foreign powers to station troops there to protect the embassies.

I Critical Thinking
Determining Author's Purpose
❓ Why does Jean mention this sign in the Bund? [Possible response: She wants us to see that the concession system denied Chinese people the right to move freely in their own country.]

J Literary Connections
Allusions
Jean is quoting from Sir Walter Scott's poem "The Lay of the Last Minstrel."

Skill Link

Connotation and Denotation
Ask students if they would rather be described as *ambitious* or *pushy, curious* or *nosy, thrifty* or *stingy?* Elicit that the words in each pair have similar meanings. However, the first word has a positive connotation, or feeling, while the second word has a negative association. Remind students that the denotation of a word is its dictionary meaning. Students should be aware of the connotations of words when they read and write.

Activity
Ask students to explain which word in parentheses has a positive connotation.
1. Ian Forbes was (commanding, domineering).
2. Jean (resolutely, stubbornly) refused to give in to his demand.
3. (Courageously, Recklessly) Jean stood up for her own ideals.
4. Fortunately, Jean's father came up with a (clever, sneaky) solution.

A Cultural Connections

At this time, the British often recruited Sikhs from northern India to serve as soldiers and police officers in their colonies around the world. The Sikhs wear turbans like those worn by some of the colorful characters in *The Arabian Nights*, also known as *The Thousand and One Nights*, a collection of tales that appeared around 1450.

B Elements of Literature

Autobiography

[?] What does the author's fantasy of walking a Great Dane tell us about her self-image? [Possible response: She feels small and powerless.]

C Advanced Learners

Personification

[?] How does the author help us to imagine that the junk "would have life"? [Possible response: She uses the names of body parts to describe it—its skeleton, ribs, backbone, snub-nosed prow, and eyes.]

D Reading Skills and Strategies

Making Inferences

[?] Why does Jean carve the Chinese form of her name on the junk? [Possible responses: She wants to establish a connection to this boat and to China; she wants to leave a permanent record that makes her part of this land.]

---

concession, he was a bushy-bearded Indian with a red turban wrapped around his head.

He pointed to my schoolbag. "Little miss," he said, "why aren't you in school?"

He was tall and mysterious-looking, more like a character in my *Arabian Nights* book than a man you expected to talk to. I fumbled for an answer. "I'm going on an errand," I said finally. "I just sat down for a rest." I picked up my schoolbag and walked quickly away. When I looked around, he was back on his corner, directing traffic.

So now they were chasing children away too, I thought angrily. Well, I'd like to show them. Someday I'd like to walk a dog down the whole length of the Bund. A Great Dane. I'd have him on a leash—like this—(I put out my hand as if I were holding a leash right then) and he'd be so big and strong I'd have to strain to hold him back (I strained). Then of course sometimes he'd have to do his business and I'd stop (like this) right in the middle of the sidewalk and let him go to it. I was so busy with my Great Dane I was at the end of the Bund before I knew it. I let go of the leash, clapped my hands, and told my dog to go home. Then I left the Bund and the concessions and walked into the Chinese world.

My mother and father and I had walked here but not for many months. This part near the river was called the Mud Flats. Sometimes it was muddier than others, and when the river flooded, the flats disappeared underwater. Sometimes even the fishermen's huts were washed away, knocked right off their long-legged stilts and swept down the river. But today the river was fairly low and the mud had dried so that it was cracked and cakey. Most of the men who lived here were out fishing, some not far from the shore, poling their sampans through the shallow water. Only a few people were on the flats: a man cleaning fish on a flat rock at the water's edge, a woman spreading clothes on the dirt to dry, a few small children.

But behind the huts was something I had never seen before. Even before I came close, I guessed what it was. Even then, I was excited by the strangeness of it.

It was the beginnings of a boat. The skeleton of a large junk, its ribs lying bare, its backbone running straight and true down the bottom. The outline of the prow was already in place, turning up wide and snub-nosed, the way all junks did. I had never thought of boats starting from nothing, of taking on bones under their bodies. The eyes, I supposed, would be the last thing added. Then the junk would have life.

The builders were not there, and I was behind the huts where no one could see me as I walked around and around, marveling. Then I climbed inside, and as I did, I knew that something wonderful was happening to me. I was a-tingle, the way a magician must feel when he swallows fire, because suddenly I knew that the boat was mine. No matter who really owned it, it was mine. Even if I never saw it again, it would be my junk sailing up and down the Yangtze River. My junk seeing the river sights with its two eyes, seeing them for me whether I was there or not. Often I had tried to put the Yangtze River into a poem so I could keep it. Sometimes I had tried to draw it, but nothing I did ever came close. But now, *now* I had my junk and somehow that gave me the river too.

I thought I should put my mark on the boat. Perhaps on the side of the spine. Very small. A secret between the boat and me. I opened my schoolbag and took out my folding penknife that I used for sharpening pencils. Very carefully I carved the Chinese character that was our name. Gau. (In China my father was Mr. Gau, my mother was Mrs. Gau, and I was Little Miss Gau.) The builders would paint right over the character, I thought, and never notice. But I would know. Always and forever I would know.

For a long time I dreamed about the boat,

112 WHO AM I?

Crossing the Curriculum

Art/Architecture

Students can work in small groups to research Chinese pagodas and junks. Encourage them to sketch typical structures and perhaps to create scale drawings that they can use to create models. Students can make their models from cardboard or balsam wood and paint and decorate them in traditional ways.

Music

Interested students might listen to selections of traditional Chinese music. Ask them to report briefly on the unique instruments and harmonies used in the music.

Geography

Invite students to create a map of China and of the Hankow area in particular in the 1920s, showing where different Western countries had concessions and spheres of influence. Students can use the national flags of these countries to indicate locations.

imagining it finished, its sails up, its eyes wide. Someday it might sail all the way down the Yangtze to Shanghai, so I told the boat what it would see along the way because I had been there and the boat hadn't. After a while I got hungry and I ate my egg sandwich. I was in the midst of peeling an orange when all at once I had company.

A small boy, not more than four years old, wandered around to the back of the huts, saw me, and stopped still. He was wearing a ragged blue cotton jacket with a red cloth pincushion-like charm around his neck which was supposed to keep him from getting smallpox. Sticking up straight from the middle of his head was a small pigtail, which I knew was to fool the gods and make them think he was a girl. (Gods didn't bother much with girls; it was boys that were important in China.) The weather was still warm so he wore no pants, nothing below the waist. Most small boys went around like this so that when they had to go, they could just let loose and go. He walked slowly up to the boat, stared at me, and then nodded as if he'd already guessed what I was. "Foreign devil," he announced gravely.

I shook my head. "No," I said in Chinese. "American friend." Through the ribs of the boat, I handed him a segment of orange. He ate it slowly, his eyes on the rest of the orange. Segment by segment, I gave it all to him. Then he wiped his hands down the front of his jacket.

"Foreign devil," he repeated.

"American friend," I corrected. Then I asked him about the boat. Who was building it? Where were the builders?

He pointed with his chin upriver. "Not here today. Back tomorrow."

I knew it would only be a question of time before the boy would run off to alert the people in the huts. "Foreign devil, foreign devil," he would cry. So I put my hand on the prow of the boat, wished it luck, and climbing out, I started back toward the Bund. To my

surprise the boy walked beside me. When we came to the edge of the Bund, I squatted down so we would be on the same eye level.

"Goodbye," I said. "May the River God protect you."

For a moment the boy stared. When he spoke, it was as if he were trying out a new sound. "American friend," he said slowly.

When I looked back, he was still there, looking soberly toward the foreign world to which I had gone.

The time, according to the Customs House clock, was five after two, which meant that I couldn't go home for two hours. School was dismissed at three-thirty and I was home by three-forty-five unless I had to stay in for talking in class. It took me about fifteen minutes to write "I will not talk in class" fifty times, and so I often came home at four o'clock. (I wrote up and down like the Chinese: fifty "I's," fifty "wills," and right through the sentence so I never had to think what I was writing. It wasn't as if I were making a promise.) Today I planned to arrive home at four, my "staying-in" time, in the hope that I wouldn't meet classmates on the way.

Meanwhile I wandered up and down the streets, in and out of stores. I weighed myself on the big scale in the Hankow Dispensary[12] and found that I was as skinny as ever. I went to the Terminus Hotel and tried out the chairs in the lounge. At first I didn't mind wandering about like this. Half of my mind was still on the river with my

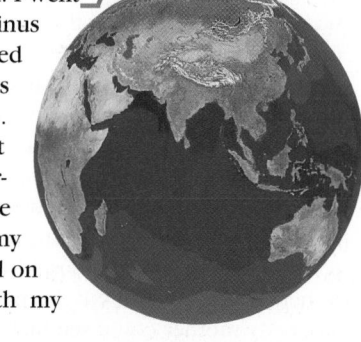

12. **dispensary:** place where medicine and first aid are provided.

HOMESICK 113

Taking a Second Look

Review: Making Generalizations
A generalization is a broad statement based on a number of examples. To make a generalization, a reader takes information from a few situations and comes up with a statement that might apply to similar situations. For instance, the amah Lin Nai-Nai hides the fact that she does not belong to the servant class, but Yang Sze-Fu, the cook, behaves as if he is superior to the other servants. From these details the reader might make a generalization that

Chinese servants in the 1920s were very conscious of their class or status in society.
Activities
1. Have students make a generalization, based on Miss Williams and Ian Forbes, about how the Americans in China perceived the British. [Possible response: They saw the British as excessively patriotic, intolerant of the non-British, and cruel.]

2. What generalization can students make about the standard of living of Americans in China in the 1920s? They should base the answer on such details as Jean's having her own amah and the family's having several servants.

English Language Learners

Identifying Idioms

Explain that the idiom *in one piece* means "unhurt" or "safe."

B **Elements of Literature**

Autobiography

❓ What does Jean reveal about herself with her comment about hanging her head? [Possible responses: She identifies with literary characters; she has a dramatic flair.]

C **Reading Skills and Strategies**

Distinguishing Fact from Opinion

❓ Is this description of Miss Williams a fact or an opinion? Explain. [Possible response: It is an opinion, because the words *mean* and *pinched* show Jean's feelings about her teacher.]

D **Critical Thinking**

Analyzing

❓ In this paragraph, what two conflicting feelings does Jean's mother experience, and how does she express them? [Possible response: Stroking Jean's hair indicates her love for her daughter. She stiffens because she must also discipline Jean for cutting school.]

junk, but as time went on, my junk began slipping away until I was alone with nothing but questions. Would my mother find out about today? How could I skip school tomorrow? And the next day and the next? Could I get sick? Was there a kind of long lie-abed sickness that didn't hurt?

I arrived home at four, just as I had planned, opened the door, and called out, "I'm home!" Cheery-like and normal. But I was scarcely in the house before Lin Nai-Nai ran to me from one side of the hall and my mother from the other.

"Are you all right? Are you all right?" Lin Nai-Nai felt my arms as if she expected them to be broken. My mother's face was white. "What happened?" she asked.

Then I looked through the open door into the living room and saw Miss Williams sitting there. She had beaten me home and asked about my absence, which of course had scared everyone. But now my mother could see that I was in one piece and for some reason this seemed to make her mad. She took me by the hand and led me into the living room. "Miss Williams said you weren't in school," she said. "Why was that?"

I hung my head, just the way cowards do in books.

My mother dropped my hand. "Jean will be in school tomorrow," she said firmly. She walked Miss Williams to the door. "Thank you for stopping by."

Miss Williams looked satisfied in her mean, pinched way. "Well," she said, "ta-ta." (She always said "ta-ta" instead of "goodbye." Chicken language, it sounded like.)

As soon as Miss Williams was gone and my mother was sitting down again, I burst into tears. Kneeling on the floor, I buried my head in her lap and poured out the whole miserable story. My mother could see that I really wasn't in one piece after all, so she listened quietly, stroking my hair as I talked, but gradually I

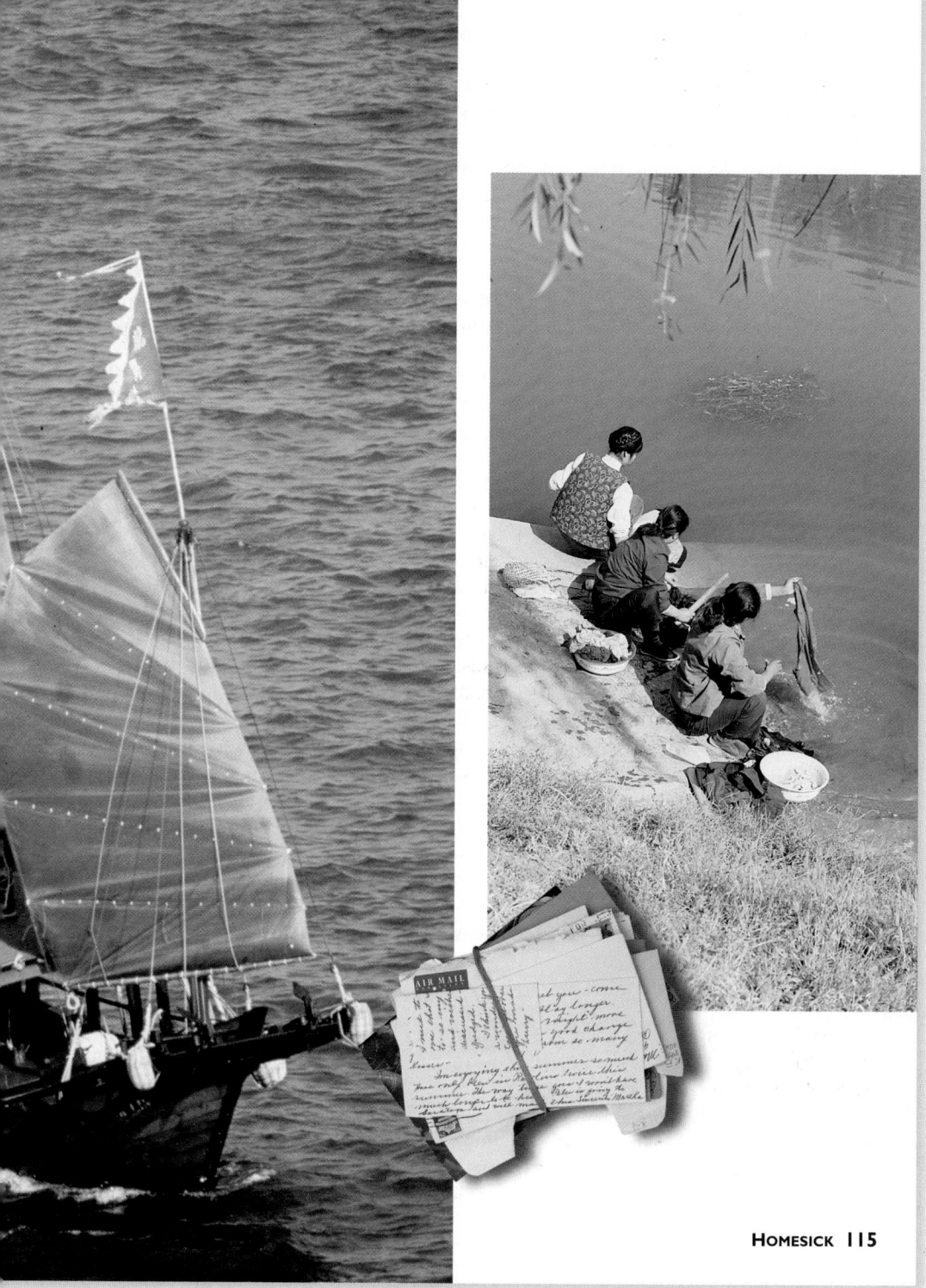

HOMESICK 115

RESPONDING TO THE ART

Have students look carefully at the photographs on pp. 109, 110, and 114–115.

Activity

1. What do the photographs add to the reader's appreciation of the story? [Possible responses: Their colors, subject matter, and unexpected arrangement on the page make these pictures pleasing to look at. Their content helps the reader visualize the events in the story.]

2. How does the subject matter of these photographs relate to "Homesick"? [Possible responses: The Yangtze River is the most important feature of the story's setting, the city of Hankow, and several of the photographs show life on the river. The pictures also illustrate some of the people and activities Jean observes when she ventures into the Chinese part of the city.]

3. What image appears with all the other photographs, and why? [Possible response: the packet of letters, which represents Jean's correspondence with her grandmother in the United States.]

Assessing Learning

Observation Assessment

Use the chart at the right to assess students individually for their participation and their attainment of skills that are important in reading.

Activity	Always	Often	Seldom
Summarizes			
Finds details			
Restates theme			
Contributes freely			
Answers when called on			
Follows classroom etiquette policy			

Autobiography

❓ What does Jean reveal about her father by describing his solution to her problem? [Possible response: She shows that her father is clever and perhaps a bit sneaky.]

B **Appreciating Language**

Puns

Ask students to recall the last line of "My Country 'Tis of Thee." ["Let freedom ring."] Then, point out that Jean is punning. She is using this line to suggest that her voice rang out in a free way.

C **Reading Skills and Strategies**

Identifying Cause and Effect

❓ Why does Jean go to Lin Nai-Nai and tell her the correct way to greet someone? [Possible responses: Now that she has resolved her own problem, Jean feels guilty about taking out her frustrations on the servant and wants to correct the misinformation.]

could feel her stiffen. I knew she was remembering that she was a Mother.

"You better go up to your room," she said, "and think things over. We'll talk about it after supper."

I flung myself on my bed. What was there to think? Either I went to school and got beaten up. Or I quit.

After supper I explained to my mother and father how simple it was. I could stay at home and my mother could teach me, the way Andrea's mother taught her. Maybe I could even go to Andrea's house and study with her.

My mother shook her head. Yes, it was simple, she agreed. I could go back to the British School, be sensible, and start singing about the king again.

I clutched the edge of the table. Couldn't she understand? I couldn't turn back now. It was too late.

So far my father had not said a word. He was leaning back, teetering on the two hind legs of his chair, the way he always did after a meal, the way that drove my mother crazy. But he was not the kind of person to keep all four legs of a chair on the floor just because someone wanted him to. He wasn't a turning-back person so I hoped maybe he would understand. As I watched him, I saw a twinkle start in his eyes and suddenly he brought his chair down slam-bang flat on the floor. He got up and motioned for us to follow him into the living room. He sat down at the piano and began to pick out the tune for "God Save the King."

A big help, I thought. Was he going to make me practice?

Then he began to sing:

"My country 'tis of thee,
Sweet land of liberty . . ."

Of course! It was the same tune. Why hadn't I thought of that? Who would know what I was singing as long as I moved my lips? I joined in now, loud and strong.

"Of thee I sing."

My mother laughed in spite of herself. "If you sing that loud," she said, "you'll start a revolution."

"Tomorrow I'll sing softly," I promised. "No one will know." But for now I really let freedom ring.

Then all at once I wanted to see Lin Nai-Nai. I ran out back, through the courtyard that separated the house from the servants' quarters, and upstairs to her room.

"It's me," I called through the door and when she opened up, I threw my arms around her. "Oh, Lin Nai-Nai, I love you," I said. "You haven't said it yet, have you?"

"Said what?"

"Sewing machine. You haven't said it?"

"No," she said, "not yet. I'm still practicing."

"Don't say it, Lin Nai-Nai. Say 'Good day.' It's shorter and easier. Besides, it's more polite."

"Good day?" she repeated.

"Yes, that's right. Good day." I hugged her and ran back to the house.

The next day at school when we rose to sing the British national anthem, everyone stared at me, but as soon as I opened my mouth, the class lost interest. All but Ian Forbes. His eyes never left my face, but I sang softly, carefully, proudly. At recess he sauntered over to where I stood against the wall.

He spat on the ground. "You can be bloody glad you sang today," he said. Then he strutted off as if he and those square knees of his had won again.

And, of course, I was bloody glad.

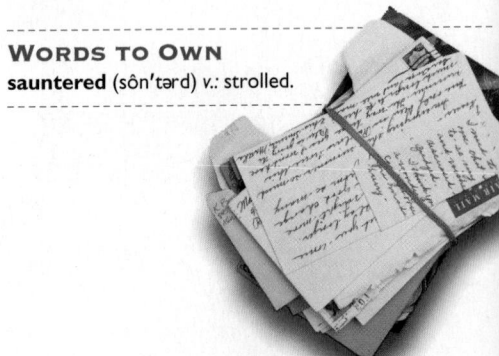

WORDS TO OWN

sauntered (sôn'tərd) v.: strolled.

Making the Connections

Connecting to the Theme: "Who Am I?"

When students have finished the selection, discuss the theme "Who Am I?" Point out that having a good sense of our own identity—background, values, and place in the world—helps us understand ourselves and other people. What "identity problem" does Jean have, and how does she resolve it? [Possible response: Living in China and feeling separated from her roots in the United States leads Jean to struggle with who she really is and where she belongs.] What does Ian Forbes's challenge force Jean to do? [Possible response: assert her American identity, as well as seek a connection with her Chinese neighbors] Ask students to name other characters in books and movies who answer the question "Who am I?"

Cultural Connections

Students who want to learn more about Jean's experiences in China in the 1920s and her return to the United States in 1927 might enjoy reading her full autobiography, titled *Homesick*. In particular, students may be interested in reading about the adjustments Jean made in order to live in the United States. Her dreams about the nation did not always match the reality.

MEET THE WRITER

"I Wander About in History . . ."

Jean Fritz (1915–) spent the first thirteen years of her life in Hankow, China, a memorable childhood she recalls in *Homesick: My Own Story*, a 1983 Newbery Honor Book and an American Book Award winner.

© Jill Krementz.

66 Until I was eleven years old I attended an English school. I felt very American and often thought I had to speak up for my country. At recess, for instance. The English children would sometimes tease me by making fun of America. I never let that pass even if it meant a fight. 99

After moving to the United States and graduating from college, Jean Fritz became a librarian. "When I ran the children's department of our local library," she recalls, "I found that I not only wanted to read children's stories, I wanted to write them too."

One of Fritz's first books was *The Cabin Faced West* (1958). This account of a lonely girl in frontier Pennsylvania is based on the experiences of her own grandmother's grandmother. While working on this historical novel, Fritz discovered the joy of research— reading old newspapers, letters, church records, and county histories filled with colorful bits and pieces of the past.

66 Digging into American history also seemed to satisfy a need that I had . . . of finding my roots, of trying to come to terms with just what it has meant historically to be an American. 99

Today Jean Fritz is best known for her fascinating and funny biographies of great historical figures:

66 I have never felt that one lifetime is long enough to meet all the people you would like to meet and to have all the experiences you would like to have. So I wander about in history, getting to know the people I find there. 99

Biographies by Jean Fritz

Jean Fritz's "wanderings" have led her to write more than a dozen biographies for young adults, including *Why Don't You Get a Horse, Sam Adams?; Can't You Make Them Behave, King George?;* and *Where Do You Think You're Going, Christopher Columbus?* (all published by Putnam).

BROWSING IN THE FILES

A Critic's Comment. Katherine Paterson, herself born and raised in China, had this to say about *Homesick*: "Every now and then a book comes along that makes me want to send a valentine to its author. *Homesick* is such a book. I suppose all of us BICs (born in China) with literary ambitions have been urged at some time or another to record our childhood experiences. Now we don't have to. Jean Fritz has done it, putting her life and ours into a story as pungent and delicious as those meat dumplings we used to buy off the peddler's cart."

Assessing Learning

Check Test: True-False
1. Jean's father is a diplomat in China. [False]
2. Jean attends a British school. [True]
3. Jean skips school to avoid taking a history test. [False]
4. Jean sails on the river in a Chinese boat. [False]
5. Jean's father decides to talk to the teacher. [False]

Standardized Test Preparation
For practice with standardized test format specific to this selection, see
• *Standardized Test Preparation*, pp. 22, 24
For practice in proofreading and editing, see
• *Daily Oral Grammar*, Transparency 7

MAKING MEANINGS

First Thoughts

1. Students might suggest reasoning with Ian, asking Miss Williams for help, or agreeing to sing the anthem.

Shaping Interpretations

2. Possible response: They want her to learn how to solve her problems instead of running away from them.

3. Possible response: Jean feels the need to be part of something typically Chinese.

4. In this autobiography, Jean Fritz shares her personal experiences and feelings. In an encyclopedia article, the author would focus on facts and would not discuss personal feelings.

5. Example of facts: *I lived in China, in a city named Hankow.* Examples of opinions: *I loved the Yangtze River, but of course I belonged on the other side of the world.*

6. Possible response: Jean is no longer angry, and she does not want to be unkind or disrespectful to Lin Nai-Nai.

7. Possible response: Jean is glad she's found a way to feel like an American.

Connecting with the Text

8. Students might mention the fear they've felt at the hands of a bully, the feeling of isolation that comes from being in a strange place, and the pleasure that comes when a family can sit down and solve a problem.

9. Students might suggest that living in a different land provides a learning opportunity and a way to see one's own culture and country in a new light.

Extending the Text

10. Students might point out that the Americanization is driven by consumerism and that the world is losing some of its diversity as a result. Some students may suggest that people around the world want certain aspects of American culture. Other students may wonder whether people can preserve their own culture while incorporating the customs and technology of a foreign country.

MAKING MEANINGS

First Thoughts

[connect]
1. What would you do if you were in Jean's shoes at the British school?

Shaping Interpretations

[infer]
2. How do Jean's parents react to her decision to stop singing the British national anthem?

[speculate]
3. Why does Jean feel it is so important to carve her name on the framework of the junk?

[contrast]
4. Suppose Jean Fritz had described her experiences in an encyclopedia article on Americans living in China, rather than in an **autobiography.** How would the story be different? Which kind of writing do you like better?

[classify]
5. In "Homesick," Jean Fritz reveals some opinions about her life in China. Like other writers of autobiography, however, she also presents facts. Give one example of a **fact** and one example of an **opinion** in "Homesick."

[speculate]
6. Why do you think Jean goes back to Lin Nai-Nai to tell her the right words to use in greeting an American?

[infer]
7. What is Jean "bloody glad" about in the end?

Connecting with the Text

[connect]
8. You've probably gotten angry at least once at someone who didn't deserve it, as Jean does with Lin Nai-Nai. What other feelings expressed by Jean remind you of feelings you've had?

[contrast]
9. Think back to your round-table discussion about the pros and cons of living in a different land. How do your feelings about living in another culture compare with Jean's? Did her story change any of your opinions?

Extending the Text

[evaluate]
10. Today the culture of the United States and its ideas about democracy travel throughout the world. Do you think the Americanization of countries like China through movies, music, malls, and fast-food restaurants is a good thing or a bad thing? Defend your position in a class or group discussion.

Reading Check

a. Why doesn't Jean wish to sing the British national anthem?

b. What **conflicts** arise from her decision? (You should be able to name three people who try to make her sing.)

c. What trick does Jean play on Lin Nai-Nai?

d. What does Jean see and do while playing hooky in the Chinese section of town?

e. How does her father help her solve her problem?

Reading Check

a. Singing the British national anthem makes her feel like a traitor.

b. Jean is in conflict with Miss Williams, Ian Forbes, and her mother, who all try to make her sing. Jean is an outcast and is mistreated because of her decision.

c. Jean teaches Lin Nai-Nai incorrect English words to greet Americans.

d. Jean sees beggars, a police officer, a boat, a small boy, the Customs House clock, and the Hankow Dispensary. She carves her name on the boat, talks to a policeman and the boy, eats her lunch, and weighs herself. (Answers may vary slightly.)

e. He suggests that she sing "My Country 'Tis of Thee" while the other students sing "God Save the King."

Writer's Notebook

1. Collecting Ideas for an Autobiographical Incident

In "Homesick," Jean Fritz looks back more than fifty years to the incident in which the little Chinese boy calls her a "foreign devil" and then an "American friend." Look back at something surprising or unusual that happened to you. Maybe it's something that made you happy or very sad. Try to remember exactly what happened—recall details about the people, time, and place. What events led up to the experience? How did you feel at the time, and how do you feel about the experience now? You might focus on answering the questions shown in the notebook at the right.

> **What** happened?
> Traveled alone on a bus to N. Carolina, got lost
>
> **Who** was involved?
>
> **Where** did it happen?
>
> **When?**
>
> **Why?**
>
> **How** did I feel at the time?   **How** do I feel about it now?

Research/ Expository Writing

2. China Back Then

When you got to page 111 in "Homesick," you might have asked, "What's this about American gunboats on the Yangtze?" In your library, find out about China—especially Hankow—in the 1920s. Why did countries have "concessions" there? Write a short report and present it to the class.

Art

3. Made in America

How would you convey to someone living in another country what the United States means to you? What image would you choose to show how living in this country affects who you are? Draw a picture or make a collage of the image you select. Give your work a title. (You also might consider sending your personal image to a pen pal in another country.)

Dramatic Reading

4. From Page to Stage

Working in a small group, select a passage from "Homesick" to present in a dramatic reading. Find a passage that includes dialogue and takes about five minutes to read aloud. (Ask your teacher to approve your selection.) In your group, assign one person to read the narrator's (Jean Fritz's) commentary. Assign others to read the dialogue. (The narrator will have to read all the dialogue "tags"—phrases like "she asked," "he hissed," and so on.) Read with all the emotions you think the people in the narrative are feeling. When you present your reading, stand in a line in front of your class, with the narrator at the center.

Rubrics for each Choices assignment appear on p. 115 in the *Portfolio Management System.*

CHOICES: Building Your Portfolio

1. **Writer's Notebook** Remind students to save their work. They may use it as prewriting for the Writer's Workshop on p. 182. In an attachment to the cluster, have students write down details that appeal to the five senses for the incident of their choice. Make sure they include any dialogue they can recall.

2. **Research/Expository Writing** If students need additional sources to do their research, suggest that they write the nearest Chinese consulate. Students may also call a university history department to find a professor who specializes in Chinese history. You might need to help students create questions for those sources.

3. **Art** Have students brainstorm some qualities that are typical of U.S. citizens and some images that stand for aspects of U.S. society. Write the list of qualities in a T-chart or on the chalkboard, with qualities on the left side and symbols and images on the right side.

4. **Dramatic Reading** Before students present their passages, have them read each quotation aloud and discuss the various emotions that might be expressed, such as anger, sadness, or frustration, as they read. Suggest that a group recorder take notes on decisions made in the group's discussion.

LANGUAGE LINK

Have students choose some descriptive writing from their portfolios and exchange papers with a partner. Students should find three sentences containing words that carry positive or negative connotations. Then, they should rewrite the sentences with words that express different connotations.

Try It Out
Possible Answers

1. Twenty-five <u>scrawny</u>, <u>pale</u> <u>critters</u> hatched from our eggs today, my grandmother wrote.
2. Miss Williams was <u>welcoming</u> and <u>receptive</u> to our <u>ideas</u>.
3. Then he <u>strode</u> <u>away</u> as if he and those <u>strong</u> <u>legs</u> of his had won again.
4. The buildings were <u>lonesome</u> and <u>scary-looking</u>, with <u>dried</u> <u>patches</u> of grass around them.

VOCABULARY
Possible Answers

1. Student should have an intense, frowning expression.
2. Gestures should indicate frustration and confusion.
3. Students may pretend to climb, sway, and lose balance.
4. The walk should be leisurely and smooth.

Resources ────────

Language
• *Grammar and Language Links*, p. 11

Vocabulary
• *Words to Own*, p. 6

Spelling
For related instruction, see
• *Spelling and Decoding*, p. 6

Using Reference Aids to Clarify Usage
Students who enjoy thinking about word choice and shades of meaning may want to use a dictionary, thesaurus, or synonym finder to find a precise word to use in place of a vague word or phrase in their writing. Students should turn to p. 702 to see an example of the way synonyms are listed in a thesaurus.

LANGUAGE LINK [MINI-LESSON]

Style: Shades of Meaning—Denotations and Connotations

Handbook of Literary Terms
HELP
See Connotation and Denotation.

The literal "dictionary definition" of a word is called its **denotation.** All the feelings and associations we attach to certain words are called their **connotations.**

Jean Fritz carefully chose words with particular connotations to describe her tormentor, Ian Forbes. She wanted to make sure you, the reader, knew exactly what she thought of him.

She could have written:	She wrote instead:
He walked.	He <u>sauntered.</u>
He was strong.	He was <u>tough.</u>
He whispered.	He <u>hissed.</u>

Hisssss·s

It's easy to see the difference. You don't really mind if someone *whispers* to you. On the other hand, you wouldn't want to spend much time with someone who *hisses* at you like a snake.

Try It Out

In the following sentences, identify words that have negative or positive connotations. Then, change the meaning of each sentence by choosing words that suggest different feelings. Follow the directions in parentheses.

1. "Twenty-five fluffy little yellow chicks hatched from our eggs today, my grandmother wrote." (Rewrite the sentence to make the chicks seem ugly.)
2. "Miss Williams was pinch-faced and bossy." (Make Miss Williams seem attractive.)
3. "Then he strutted off as if he and those square knees of his had won again." (Make the bully seem like a hero.)
4. "The buildings were solemn and orderly, with little plots of grass around them." (Paint a negative picture of the buildings.)

VOCABULARY [HOW TO OWN A WORD]

WORD BANK
glowering
flustered
rickety
sauntered

Body Language
A good way to own a word is to interpret it with your body and face. Try these exercises for the words in the Word Bank.

1. How are you at <u>glowering</u>? Give a partner a glowering look.
2. How do you look and what do you do when you are <u>flustered</u>?
3. Now get your body into the act. Pretend you are on a <u>rickety</u> ladder. Be careful!
4. Saunter to the door. Your walk should suggest you've got time and are in a good mood. Ask your partner to tell you what you looked like as you <u>sauntered</u>.

120 WHO AM I?

Language Link Quick Check

Rewrite the following sentences by choosing words with different connotations. (Possible answers are given.)

1. Jean did not want to sing the British anthem. [Jean refused to sing the British anthem.]
2. Ian spoke with Jean. [Ian threatened Jean.]
3. Jean walked in the opposite direction of the school. [Jean strode away from the school.]
4. The Chinese ship was unfinished. [The Chinese ship waited patiently to be completed.]
5. The little boy took the orange. [The little boy snatched the orange from her hand.]

Elements of Literature

NONFICTION: Encountering Our Lives *by* Naomi Shihab Nye

Experiment with Nonfiction

Try an experiment with nonfiction. Think of an event that happened in your family. Invite someone in your family—sister, grandmother, father—to tell the story as he or she remembers it, including as many details as possible.

Then, ask another family member, one who wasn't present at this telling, to share his or her own version of the very same events. Compare both versions with your own. Is the story the same or has it changed? Almost always, people remember the same event differently. One person may describe how delicious the split-open watermelons looked at a family picnic. Another might not remember those watermelons at all but might remember the joke someone told or how blisteringly hot the sun felt. Very quickly you will see how much "fictionalizing" enters the telling and writing of nonfiction.

Conduct another experiment: Take your journals and go on a silent "observation walk" with some of your classmates around the edge of your schoolyard. Each of you should write down at least ten sensory details you experience on your walk. Afterward compare your details. Someone may have described the pattern of links in the chain fence. Someone else may have noted the scent of honeysuckle in the air or the woman waiting at a bus stop down the block. What can you tell about yourselves simply from what you notice?

Nonfiction Happens to Everybody

Readers sometimes think that since fiction is basically "invented," its opposite, nonfiction, must be basically "true." It would be more accurate to say that fiction writers *claim* to make things up, while nonfiction writers *claim* to base their work on real happenings. In fact, many of

the same elements—plots, characters, conflicts, settings, points of view, and themes—may be used in both fiction and nonfiction. Both fiction and nonfiction often contain elements we associate with poetry as well—rhythm, sensory images, and figures of speech. Some people try to separate literature into distinctly different compartments, but it's really a big family whose members all secretly get along.

Nonfiction happens all the time to everybody. It can include what we ate for breakfast, whom we saw in the street and what they said—as well as everything we may be dreaming or remembering.

The world of nonfiction is wide-ranging. It includes **personal histories** (also called **autobiographies** and **memoirs**), **biographies** (accounts of other people's lives), **personal essays,** and **reports** or **feature stories,** such as we read in newspapers.

(continued on next page)

Resources

Elements of Literature
Nonfiction: Encountering Our Lives
For more instruction on nonfiction, see *Literary Elements:*
• Transparency 2
Assessment
Formal Assessment
• Literary Elements Test, p. 30

Elements of Literature

This feature suggests that in nonfiction writing, there is no single way to narrate an event, since what each person observes depends on individual experience. Like fiction, nonfiction works may have plot, characters, conflict, point of view, and theme. Forms of nonfiction include biographies, autobiographies, memoirs, personal essays, and reports. Some nonfiction is subjective, or personal; other nonfiction is objective, or unbiased. Finally, the array of topics suitable for nonfiction is vast.

Mini-Lesson: Nonfiction

First, ask students to identify nonfiction works that fit into the various categories: biographies, autobiographies, memoirs, personal essays, reports, and feature stories. Next, have students review the difference between subjective and objective writing. Students can label the following sentences as *subjective* or *objective*.
1. Two plus two equals four. [objective]
2. "The Runaway" is a beautiful poem. [subjective]
3. Twenty people died in the traffic accident. [objective]
4. Pasta is my favorite food. [subjective]
Ask students to provide other sentences that class members can identify as objective or subjective.

Using Students' Strengths

Logical/Mathematical Learners
To help students organize the information on pp. 121–122, suggest that they create lists like the following one, each labeled with a subhead from the pupil's page and filled with important details from the text.
Experiment with Nonfiction
1. People who are present at the same event will differ in the way they retell it.
2. Different people at the same event will focus on different details.

Visual Learners
These students may prefer to organize the material on pp. 121–122 by creating a series of boxes. Each box should contain either a subhead or a single item of information from the text, as in the numbered list at the left. Students may distinguish between heads and texts by using boxes with dashed lines, zigzag lines, or straight lines. The boxes can be arranged to indicate how the items are related.

Applying the Element

Use "Homesick" to help students review the elements of nonfiction. Ask the following questions:

- How can you tell, from the full title of Jean Fritz's work, what type of nonfiction it is? (Students can reread Meet the Author, p. 117, before answering the question.) [Possible response: The full title, *Homesick: My Own Story*, indicates that it is an autobiography.]

- Have students reread the paragraph describing recess at the British School (p. 107, col. 1). Which parts of the description are *objective,* and which are *subjective*? [Possible responses: Objective—prisoner's base is played every day; Vera doesn't play the game. Subjective—Fritz hates the game; she describes the cloud as "skittering" and Ian's head as that of an animal.]

- How might another observer of the recess—for example, Miss Williams—have written the passage "While . . . schoolyard"? [Possible response: "That disobedient child Jean was daydreaming by the wall, not paying attention to the other children."] Have students discuss what each version tells about the person who wrote it.

- Have a volunteer read aloud the quotation by Jean Fritz on p. 122. Be sure that students understand Fritz's ideas. You might ask students to explain what "human condition" means. [Possible response: the joys, fears, dreams, and needs of all people on the earth.] How might "Homesick" help readers "find out what life is all about"? [Possible responses: Students who have never been forced to obey rules that were foreign to them will learn how Fritz felt; students who have had that experience can observe how another person handled that difficult situation.]

As students read other selections in this collection, have them look for the elements of nonfiction.

(continued from previous page)

Subjective and Objective Writing: The Snapshot and the Big Picture

Some nonfiction is richly, frankly **subjective,** which means that its purpose is to express the writer's opinions, feelings, and point of view. That is, it is personal. For example, Elroy Bode, a writer in Texas, has written eloquent short essays on such ordinary topics as selecting a pair of pants at a discount store or returning to his old neighborhood to stare at his childhood home. By speaking directly and intimately, personal essays like Bode's pull us in. They earn our trust and remind us of ourselves.

Other nonfiction pieces maintain a more **objective** tone. This means the writers try to be unbiased, to present the "big picture" rather than a private snapshot. The purpose of such writers is often to inform. A news-paper story that reports on an earthquake, for example, will usually not tell us how the reporter feels about earthquakes. A personal essay on earthquakes, on the other hand, might well focus entirely on the writer's feelings and sensations and not even mention the Richter scale.

The Appeal of Nonfiction: Telling It Your Way

Many novelists, poets, and short-story writers find themselves writing nonfiction today. Perhaps writing nonfiction satisfies a deep, important urge—when we write personal nonfiction, we can sit back, take our shoes off, and tell the story. We can tell it straight, we can tell it twisted and mysterious, we can tell it any way we like. People write essays about everything from eating to traveling to growing older. When you write nonfiction, no subject is too large—or too small.

Jean Fritz, whose vivid story about growing up in China is included in this collection, has talked about the reasons she writes **biographies,** or stories about other people's lives. "We all seek insight into the human condition," she says, "and it is helpful to find familiar threads running through the lives of others. . . . We need to know more people in all circumstances and times so we can pursue our private, never-to-be-fulfilled quest to find out what life is all about."

CALVIN AND HOBBES © Watterson. Dist. by UNIVERSAL PRESS SYNDICATE. Reprinted with permission. All rights reserved.

Reaching All Students

Struggling Readers

Have volunteers read the pupil's page aloud to the class while other students read silently. Then, invite students to write questions they may have on index cards. Collect and shuffle the cards. Have the class discuss answers.

Advanced Readers

Have students write, on the chalkboard, numbered statements about English language or literature—a fact, an opinion, or something students have done in class. Ask students to label each statement *subjective* or *objective*. After they have discussed the correct responses, elicit ways of distinguishing between subjective opinions and objective statements of fact. The following is an example:

- English class is exciting. [subjective]
- We study grammar in English. [objective]

Way to distinguish: "Exciting" describes someone's feelings; "We study grammar" describes an activity the class has participated in.

Reading Skills and Strategies

Booking space on the Net:

OBJECTIVES
1. Distinguish between comparison and contrast
2. Use a Venn diagram to compare and contrast texts

COMPARING AND CONTRASTING

Finding Similarities and Differences

There you are at your favorite mall, but something weird is going on. In the store that sells jeans, all the jeans look exactly alike. All the shoes in the shoe store look like clones. Even the music store is selling just one CD, and you can't stand that group. Is this a nightmare, or are you about to be bored out of your mind?

Variety's the Spice

Shopping's no fun when there are no decisions to make, nothing to compare and contrast. When you **compare,** you look at two or more things to see how they are similar. When you **contrast,** you look for differences. You may not realize it, but you do a lot of comparing and contrasting every day. When you decide what you'll eat for lunch, you may compare and contrast different foods. Even when you think about whether to do your homework right after school or later, you're comparing and contrasting the advantages of one choice with those of the other.

Comparing and contrasting are important skills at school, too. In English class, for instance, your teacher may ask you to look for similarities and differences between two characters or two poems.

To find similarities and differences between poems, look at elements like these:

• figures of speech
• sound effects
• subjects
• themes

To compare and contrast stories, you might look at these elements:

• characters   • plots
• settings   • themes
• conflicts

Here are some words that writers use in comparing and contrasting:

Comparing	Contrasting
both, similar, like, as, too, also	in contrast, different, although, but, yet

The Venn Diagram

A Venn diagram like the one below can help you sort out and analyze the similarities and differences between two texts. In each circle, you note differences. In the center, where the circles overlap, you note similarities. This diagram shows how you might begin comparing and contrasting "Homesick" and "Barrio Boy."

"Homesick"   "Barrio Boy"

told by a girl | both feel like strangers in a foreign country | told by a boy

Differences   **Similarities**   **Differences**

Apply the strategy on the next page. ▶

Reading Skills and Strategies

This feature emphasizes the importance of using comparison and contrast in reading literary selections. It also discusses the difference between the two techniques and lists words and phrases that writers use in comparing or contrasting. The feature ends with an illustration of the Venn diagram as a graphic device for comparing and contrasting literary selections.

Mini-Lesson: Comparing and Contrasting

Have students read "I Wasn't Able to Be Myself" (Making the Connection, p. 124) and "An Immigrant in the United States" (Student to Student, p. 130). Then, discuss with students the similarities and differences between the two works. Similarities: Both works are told by a first-person narrator; for both Guadalupe Solis and Ponn Pet, the experience of learning to live in the United States was made easier by helpful and friendly people they met. Differences: Guadalupe describes her need to learn English; Ponn Pet observes several things: the need to learn English; the fact that Cambodians are of one racial group, whereas the United States has many races and ethnic groups; American foods and eating practices, which are unlike those in Cambodia. Using a Venn diagram, students can display other similarities and differences between the two literary works.

Reaching All Students

Visual Learners

Students may choose to illustrate the similarities and differences between "I Wasn't Able to Be Myself" and "An Immigrant in the United States" by drawing, painting, creating comic strips, sculpting, or using other media. They might create one artwork for each selection. One part of each work can show similarities; the other, differences. Or one work might display similarities; the other, differences. Students can provide captions and other verbal clues.

English Language Learners

Students might practice writing sentences that include the comparison/contrast words and phrases on the pupil's page. Instead of comparing and contrasting the pieces by Solis and Pet, students might choose one work and compare and contrast their own experiences in adapting to the culture and language of the United States with those of the author. Students might present their work to the class.

OBJECTIVES

1. Read and interpret the auto-biographical excerpt
2. Make comparisons and contrasts
3. Express understanding through autobiographical writing, comparison and contrast, research/math, or speaking and listening
4. Identify comparing adjectives and use them correctly
5. Understand and use new words

SKILLS

Literary
• Identify autobiography

Reading
• Make comparisons and contrasts

Writing
• Collect ideas for an autobiographical incident
• Write a comparison/contrast paragraph

Speaking/Listening
• Discuss ethnic heritage

Language
• Identify comparing adjectives and use them correctly

Vocabulary
• Understand and use new words

Math
• Collect statistics for a graph

Planning

• **Block Schedule**
Block Scheduling Lesson Plans with Pacing Guide

• **Traditional Schedule**
Lesson Plans Including Strategies for English-Language Learners

• **One-Stop Planner**
CD-ROM with Test Generator

Before You Read

BARRIO BOY

Make the Connection

"I Wasn't Able to Be Myself"

Here is a brief true story that connects to the autobiography you're about to read: Guadalupe Solis immigrated to the United States from Monterrey, Mexico. When she arrived, one of her first big jobs was to learn English. She remembers that "when I moved here . . . I wasn't able to be myself because I couldn't speak. People couldn't know me because I couldn't communicate."

Guadalupe learned English by writing down the words she heard and then looking them up in the dictionary. She also found patient people who helped her with her new language: "Sometimes I would go to the store to practice my English—the store clerks had to be patient with me because they were trying to sell me something. . . . People who are trying to learn a new language should not feel inferior. They should say to themselves, 'I'm going to be bilingual.' Now, even when I don't have to talk in English, I do anyway. Now I dream in English."

 go.hrw.com
LEO 7-2

Quickwrite

Describe what you would do if you lived in a place where you did not speak the language. If you are in this situation now, describe what you are doing to learn the language.

Reading Skills and Strategies

Comparing and Contrasting: Alike or Unlike?

When you **compare,** you look for ways that things are alike. When you **contrast,** you look for ways that things are different. Jean Fritz and Ernesto Galarza grew up in different countries, half a world apart. Yet, in some ways, their stories are similar. As you read "Barrio Boy," think about the similarities and the differences between the two autobiographies. To find similarities and differences between texts, focus on these elements:

• subject
• theme, or main idea
• setting
• plot

Background

Literature and Social Studies

Ernesto Galarza was born in 1905 in Jalcocotán, a village in western Mexico with a main street that he says "was just wide enough to park six automobiles hub to hub."

In 1910, when the Mexican Revolution threatened their peaceful mountain home, Ernesto, his mother, and two uncles left their village for Mazatlán, Mexico. Eventually they moved to Sacramento, California, and lived in what Galarza called "a rented corner of the city"—the *barrio,* or Spanish-speaking neighborhood.

Like thousands of other immigrants, Galarza confronted the values and customs of American city life—adjusting gradually, and often with difficulty, to his adopted country.

124 WHO AM I?

Preteaching Vocabulary

Words to Own

Have pairs of students read the four Words to Own and their definitions listed at the bottom of the selection pages. Students can work in pairs to write sentences using the words correctly. Then, have students fill in the blanks with the word that correctly completes each sentence.

1. Putting our dog, Frisky, into a carrying case on wheels seemed like a _____ task. [formidable]

2. We didn't think Frisky would be eager to jump into that _____ when she'd rather be running and jumping. [contraption]

3. To calm Frisky, we spoke to her in a _____ voice. [reassuring]

4. Finally, we _____ ourselves that Frisky wouldn't mind being cooped up in a box. [assured]

from Barrio Boy

Ernesto Galarza

At Lincoln, making us into Americans did not mean scrubbing away what made us originally foreign.

The two of us [the narrator, Ernesto, and his mother] walked south on Fifth Street one morning to the corner of Q Street and turned right. Half of the block was occupied by the Lincoln School. It was a three-story wooden building, with two wings that gave it the shape of a double T connected by a central hall. It was a new building, painted yellow, with a shingled roof that was not like the red tile of the school in Mazatlán. I noticed other differences, none of them very <u>reassuring</u>.

We walked up the wide staircase hand in hand and through the door, which closed by itself. A mechanical <u>contraption</u> screwed to the top shut it behind us quietly.

WORDS TO OWN

reassuring (rē′ə·shoor′iŋ) v. used as *adj.*: comforting; giving hope or confidence; from the Latin word *securus*, meaning "secure." Look for the related word *assured* on page 126.
contraption (kən·trap′shən) *n.*: strange machine or gadget.

Summary ■ ■

Ernesto's family has recently moved to Sacramento, California, from Mazatlán, Mexico, and he is enrolling as a first-grader at the Lincoln School. Despite his initial anxiety about attending a new school in a new land, Ernesto receives a warm welcome from the principal. His remaining fears are dispelled by his teacher, who guides Ernesto through the "awful idiocies of the English Language." At the school, the boy learns that he can be proud of his ethnic heritage while adapting to the language and culture of his new home.

Resources

Listening
Audio CD Library
A spirited recording of this excerpt from *Barrio Boy* is provided in the *Audio CD Library*:
• Disc 5, Track 3

Viewing and Representing
Fine Art Transparency
A fine art transparency of Chuck Baird's *Colors #1* can be used with this lesson.
• Transparency 4
• Worksheet, p. 16

Resources: Print and Media

Reading
• *Reading Skills and Strategies*
   MiniRead Skill Lesson, p. 142
   Selection Skill Lesson, p. 148
• *Graphic Organizers for Active Reading*, p. 8
• *Words to Own*, p. 7
• *Spelling and Decoding*
   Worksheet, p. 7
• *Audio CD Library*
   Disc 5, Track 3

Writing and Language
• *Daily Oral Grammar*
   Transparency 8
• *Grammar and Language Links*
   Worksheet, p. 13
• *Language Workshop CD-ROM*

Viewing and Representing
• *Viewing and Representing*
   Fine Art Transparency 4
   Fine Art Worksheet, p. 16

Assessment
• *Formal Assessment*, p. 21
• *Portfolio Management System*, p. 116
• *Standardized Test Preparation*, p. 26
• *Test Generator (One-Stop Planner CD-ROM)*

Internet
• go.hrw.com (keyword: LE0 7-2)

A Critical Thinking

Speculating

❓ Why do Ernesto and his mother circle the school on their walks before he enrolls?

[Possible responses: They are both uneasy and excited about his first day; they want to be sure they know where the school is; they may also be curious about the school.]

B Reading Skills and Strategies

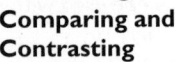

Comparing and Contrasting

❓ What differences are there between the people in charge at the Mazatlán and Sacramento schools? [The head of the Mexican school is a man, and he is called the director. At the Lincoln School the person in charge is called a principal, and she is a woman.]

In a matter of seconds I had to decide whether she was a possible friend or a menace.

My Brother (1942) by Oswaldo Guayasamín (Oswaldo Guayasamín Calero). Oil on wood (15⅞" × 12¾"; 40.3 cm × 32.4 cm)

The Museum of Modern Art, New York. Inter-American Fund. Photograph ©2000 The Museum of Modern Art, New York.

Up to this point the adventure of enrolling me in the school had been carefully rehearsed. Mrs. Dodson had told us how to find it and we had circled it several times on our walks. Friends in the barrio explained that the director was called a principal, and that it was a lady and not a man. They <u>assured</u> us that there was always a person at the school who could speak Spanish.

Exactly as we had been told, there was a sign on the door in both Spanish and English: "Principal." We crossed the hall and entered the office of Miss Nettie Hopley.

Miss Hopley was at a roll-top desk to one side, sitting in a swivel chair that moved on wheels. There was a sofa against the opposite

- -
WORDS TO OWN

assured (ə·shoord′) *v*.: guaranteed; promised confidently.
- -

126 WHO AM I?

Reaching All Students

Struggling Readers
Comparing and Contrasting was introduced on p. 124. For a lesson directly tied to this selection that teaches students to compare and contrast by using a strategy called Semantic Differential Scales, see the *Reading Skills and Strategies* binder:
• MiniRead Skill Lesson, p. 142
• Selection Skill Lesson, p. 148

English Language Learners
Students might role-play the lessons Miss Ryan gives her students (pp. 127–128). A student who has gained facility in English might play the role of Miss Ryan. The game of pronouncing challenging but easily illustrated words like *butterfly* or *fluorescent* might be enjoyable as well. For additional strategies to supplement instruction for these students, see
• *Lesson Plans Including Strategies for English-Language Learners*

Advanced Students
Have students compile a list: "Lessons I Learned in Kindergarten and First Grade." Students can include important learning experiences and realizations they had in these early years of school. Brief essays, diary entries, letters, even mock press conferences are types of writing students can employ. They may enjoy illustrating their recollections and placing the pages between decorative covers.

wall, flanked by two windows and a door that opened on a small balcony. Chairs were set around a table, and framed pictures hung on the walls of a man with long white hair and another with a sad face and a black beard.

The principal half turned in the swivel chair to look at us over the pinch glasses crossed on the ridge of her nose. To do this, she had to duck her head slightly, as if she were about to step through a low doorway.

What Miss Hopley said to us we did not know, but we saw in her eyes a warm welcome, and when she took off her glasses and straightened up, she smiled wholeheartedly, like Mrs. Dodson. We were, of course, saying nothing, only catching the friendliness of her voice and the sparkle in her eyes while she said words we did not understand. She signaled us to the table. Almost tiptoeing across the office, I maneuvered myself to keep my mother between me and the gringo[1] lady. In a matter of seconds I had to decide whether she was a possible friend or a menace. We sat down.

Then Miss Hopley did a formidable thing. She stood up. Had she been standing when we entered, she would have seemed tall. But rising from her chair, she soared. And what she carried up and up with her was a buxom superstructure, firm shoulders, a straight sharp nose, full cheeks slightly molded by a curved line along the nostrils, thin lips that moved like steel springs, and a high forehead topped by hair gathered in a bun. Miss Hopley was not a giant in body, but when she mobilized it to a standing position she seemed a match for giants. I decided I liked her.

She strode to a door in the far corner of the office, opened it, and called a name. A boy of about ten years appeared in the doorway. He sat down at one end of the table. He was brown like us, a plump kid with shiny black

hair combed straight back, neat, cool, and faintly obnoxious.

Miss Hopley joined us with a large book and some papers in her hand. She, too, sat down and the questions and answers began by way of our interpreter. My name was Ernesto. My mother's name was Henriqueta. My birth certificate was in San Blas. Here was my last report card from the Escuela Municipal Numero 3 para Varones[2] of Mazatlán, and so forth. Miss Hopley put things down in the book and my mother signed a card.

As long as the questions continued, Doña Henriqueta could stay and I was secure. Now that they were over, Miss Hopley saw her to the door, dismissed our interpreter, and without further ado took me by the hand and strode down the hall to Miss Ryan's first grade.

Miss Ryan took me to a seat at the front of the room, into which I shrank—the better to survey her. She was, to skinny, somewhat runty me, of a withering height when she patrolled the class. And when I least expected it, there she was, crouching by my desk, her blond, radiant face level with mine, her voice patiently maneuvering me over the awful idiocies of the English language.

During the next few weeks Miss Ryan overcame my fears of tall, energetic teachers as she bent over my desk to help me with a word in the pre-primer. Step by step, she loosened me and my classmates from the safe anchorage of the desks for recitations at the blackboard and consultations at her desk. Frequently she burst into happy announcements to the whole class. "Ito can read a sentence," and small Japanese Ito, squint-eyed and shy, slowly read aloud while the class listened in wonder: "Come,

2. **Escuela Municipal Numero 3 para Varones:** Spanish for "Municipal School Number 3 for Boys."

---

1. **gringo** (griŋ′gō): in Latin America, insulting term for "foreigner"; from the Spanish *griego*, meaning "Greek."

WORDS TO OWN
formidable (fôr′mə·də·bəl) *adj.:* awe-inspiring; impressive.

BARRIO BOY 127

C Appreciating Language
Comparing with Adjectives
❓ If Ernesto had compared Miss Hopley's *formidable* action with other remarkable actions he had seen, what might he have written? [Possible response: Miss Hopley did a *more formidable* thing than I had ever seen.] If he had used the adjective *smart* instead, how might he have compared Miss Hopley's action? [Possible response: Miss Hopley did a *smarter* thing than I had ever seen.] Have students identify the difference in the two ways of forming the comparative degree.

D Critical Thinking
Analyzing
❓ Why does Ernesto decide to like Miss Hopley? [Possible response: Since Ernesto sees Miss Hopley as a giant, he would rather have her as a friend than as an enemy.]

E Struggling Readers
Paraphrasing
Have students tell in their own words what the second and third sentences of the paragraph mean. [Possible response: Since I was so small, she seemed very tall while walking around the class; from time to time she bent by my desk, her bright face by mine, and helped me figure out passages of English that didn't make sense to me.]

F Reading Skills and Strategies

Comparing and Contrasting
Ask students to contrast Miss Williams, Jean Fritz's teacher in "Homesick," with Miss Ryan. [Possible response: Miss Williams is pinched-faced, mean, and bossy, whereas Miss Ryan is radiant, patient, and encouraging.]

G Appreciating Language
Figurative Language
❓ What is the meaning of *anchorage* in reference to ships? [a harbor where ships lie at anchor, safe from the open sea] Why does Ernesto compare the students at their desks to anchored ships? [Possible response: Like ships in a harbor, students are safe there, because they don't have to face the class or meet with the teacher.]

Using Students' Strengths

Kinesthetic Learners
Have students pantomime the scene in which Ernesto and his mother prepare for the boy's enrollment at school and then meet Miss Hopley. Other students may create and present scenes that show Ernesto learning to read English with Miss Ryan's help.

Interpersonal Learners
Ask students to demonstrate how they would help a younger child learn to read English. Some English language learners might describe their experiences in conjunction with this.

Visual Learners
Encourage visual learners to complete the graphic organizer, provided on p. 8 in the *Graphic Organizers for Active Reading*.

BROWSING IN THE FILES

About the Author. Throughout his life Ernesto Galarza demonstrated the respect for education, the United States, and his heritage that he had learned in first grade at Lincoln School. Before writing *Barrio Boy,* he was for a time an elementary school teacher himself. Galarza is well known for having helped to organize labor unions for Mexican Americans. Later, he continued this work as a member of the House of Representatives Committee on Education and Labor and as a consultant to the Civil Rights Commission. His writings include poetry, an autobiography, and books on politics and economics.

Ⓐ Elements of Literature
Autobiography

❓ How do you know that Ernesto was proud of his achievements? [Possible response: He remembers them in detail, and words like "celebrated success" indicate his pleasure.]

Ⓑ Cultural Connection

The words used to mimic animal sounds vary widely from language to language. For example, in Danish, cows make the sound *muh-muh;* in Norwegian, frogs croak *kvekk* and roosters go *kykkeliky;* in French, cats purr *ron ron.*

Ⓒ Reading Skills and Strategies
Distinguishing Fact from Opinion

❓ Why is this statement an opinion and not a fact? [Possible responses: It would be impossible to prove true or false; it expresses Ernesto's feelings about Miss Ryan and his judgment about his performance in first grade.]

Skipper, come. Come and run." The Korean, Portuguese, Italian, and Polish first-graders had similar moments of glory, no less shining than mine the day I conquered "butterfly," which I had been persistently pronouncing in standard Spanish as boo-ter-flee. "Children," Miss Ryan called for attention. "Ernesto has learned how to pronounce *butterfly*!" And I proved it with a perfect imitation of Miss Ryan. From that celebrated success, I was soon able to match Ito's progress as a sentence reader with "Come, butterfly, come fly with me."

Like Ito and several other first-graders who did not know English, I received private lessons from Miss Ryan in the closet, a narrow hall off the classroom with a door at each end. Next to one of these doors Miss Ryan placed a large

It was as if in that closet we were both discovering together the secrets of the English language . . .

chair for herself and a small one for me. Keeping an eye on the class through the open door, she read with me about sheep in the meadow and a frightened chicken going to see the king, coaching me out of my phonetic ruts in words like *pasture, bow-wow-wow, hay,* and *pretty,* which to my Mexican ear and eye had so many unnecessary sounds and letters. She made me watch her lips and then close my eyes as she repeated words I found hard to read. When we came to know each other better, I tried interrupting to tell Miss Ryan how we said it in Spanish. It didn't work. She only said "oh" and went on with *pasture, bow-wow-wow,* and *pretty.* It was as if in that closet we were both discovering together the secrets of the English language and grieving together over the tragedies of Bo-Peep. The main reason I was graduated with honors from the first grade was that I had fallen

128 WHO AM I?

MEET THE WRITER
"Anecdotes I Told My Family . . ."

For young **Ernesto Galarza** (1905–1984), coming to the United States meant abandoning everything he had ever known and confronting an alien landscape. He couldn't understand the language; the customs and values were strange. Like millions of other immigrants, he felt lost. He soon discovered that education was the key to making sense of his new life. Eventually he earned his Ph.D. from Columbia University in New York and then returned to California to teach. Although he was a beloved teacher, Galarza is best remembered for *Barrio Boy,* his best-selling 1971 account of his journey from Mexico to the United States. Galarza explains how he came to write *Barrio Boy:*

❝ *Barrio Boy* began as anecdotes I told my family about Jalcocotán, the mountain village in western Mexico where I was born. Among this limited public (my wife, Mae, and daughters, Karla and Eli Lu) my thumbnail sketches became best-sellers. Hearing myself tell them over and over, I began to agree with my captive audience that they were not only interesting but possibly good.

in love with Miss Ryan. Her radiant, no-nonsense character made us either afraid not to love her or love her so we would not be afraid, I am not sure which. It was not only that we sensed she was with it, but also that she was with us.

Like the first grade, the rest of the Lincoln School was a sampling of the lower part of

---

Crossing the Curriculum

Art
Have students work in groups to create a mural or poster of the United States as a melting pot. Students will need to brainstorm a design, choose the materials they will use (such as paint, collage, or photographs), and create and complete a design.

Social Studies
The author describes his childhood at the beginning of the twentieth century, a time of large-scale immigration to the United States. Suggest that students research the immigration trends (who came and where they came from) in their state in any decade of the twentieth century. Have students create a graph that shows their findings.

Geography
Have students locate Mazatlán on a map of Mexico and then list questions about this region to research and report on to the class. Students might list questions about the climate, culture, economy (including industries), and history of Mazatlán and its surrounding area. Students can compile the research in a report that takes the form of questions and answers.

Quite by accident I told one of these vignettes at a meeting of scholars and other boring people. It was recorded on tape, printed in a magazine, and circulated among schools and libraries here and there. I received letters asking for reprints, and occasionally a tempting suggestion that I write more of the same, perhaps enough to make a book.

Adding up the three listeners in my family and the three correspondents made a public of six. I didn't need more persuasion than this to link the anecdotes into a story. **99**

Be One of Ernesto Galarza's Public

The selection you've read is from one chapter of Galarza's *Barrio Boy* (University of Notre Dame Press). If you liked it, you'll enjoy reading the entire book.

town, where many races made their home. My pals in the second grade were Kazushi, whose parents spoke only Japanese; Matti, a skinny Italian boy; and Manuel, a fat Portuguese who would never get into a fight but wrestled you to the ground and just sat on you. Our assortment of nationalities included Koreans, Yugoslavs, Poles, Irish, and home-grown Americans.

Miss Hopley and her teachers never let us forget why we were at Lincoln: for those who were alien, to become good Americans; for those who were so born, to accept the rest of us. Off the school grounds we traded the same insults we heard from our elders. On the playground we were sure to be marched up to the principal's office for calling someone a wop, a chink, a dago, or a greaser. The school was not so much a melting pot as a griddle where Miss Hopley and her helpers warmed knowledge into us and roasted racial hatreds out of us. **◐ D**

At Lincoln, making us into Americans did not mean scrubbing away what made us originally foreign. The teachers called us as our parents did, or as close as they could pronounce our names in Spanish or Japanese. No one was **◐ E**

The teachers called us as our parents did, or as close as they could pronounce our names . . .

ever scolded or punished for speaking in his native tongue on the playground. Matti told the class about his mother's down quilt, which she had made in Italy with the fine feathers of a thousand geese. Encarnación acted out how boys learned to fish in the Philippines. I astounded the third grade with the story of my travels on a stagecoach, which nobody else in the class had seen except in the museum at Sutter's Fort. After a visit to the Crocker Art Gallery and its collection of heroic paintings of the golden age of California, someone showed a silk scroll with a Chinese painting. Miss Hopley herself had a way of expressing wonder over these matters before a class, her eyes wide open until they popped slightly. It was easy for me to feel that becoming a proud American, as she said we should, did not mean feeling ashamed of being a Mexican. **◐ F**

BARRIO BOY 129

◑ D Critical Thinking
Expressing an Opinion
? Ask students to explain the meaning of the figurative term *melting pot*. [Possible response: a nation in which immigrants adopt the majority culture and, in turn, that culture is enriched by immigrants' contributions.] **Do you think that America is or ever was a melting pot?** [Possible responses: Yes; in the past, many immigrants entered the country and became members of the larger culture; this process continues today. No; most immigrants retain their unique cultures and traditions.]

◑ E Reading Skills and Strategies

Comparing and Contrasting
? What two attitudes toward being an American does Galarza contrast here? [Possible response: The attitude he learns—becoming a proud American while remaining proud of his ethnic background—contrasts with the view that one should lose, forget, or be ashamed of one's original cultural heritage.]

◑ F Elements of Literature
Autobiography
? Why do you think that Galarza includes these anecdotes about Matti's mother's quilt and his own ride in a stagecoach? [Possible responses: These are the colorful, personal details that make an autobiography come to life; it is a way to show us how the school celebrates human diversity.]

Resources
Selection Assessment
Formal Assessment
• Selection Test, p. 21
Test Generator
• Selection Test

Assessing Learning

Check Test: Short Answer
1. From which country does Ernesto's family come? [Mexico]
2. What are some of the languages spoken by students at the Lincoln School? [English, Spanish, Japanese, Korean, Portuguese, Italian, and Polish]

3. Why did Ernesto try to interrupt his English lessons with Miss Ryan? [to tell her how a word was said in Spanish]
4. What was the reason, in Galarzo's words, that he was graduated with honors from the first grade? [He had fallen in love with Miss Ryan.]

Standardized Test Preparation
For practice with standardized test format specific to this selection, see
• *Standardized Test Preparation*, p. 26
For practice in proofreading and editing, see
• *Daily Oral Grammar*, Transparency 8

A Historical Connections

Cambodia borders on Laos, Vietnam, and Thailand. Since becoming independent in 1953, the Cambodian people have been constantly at war. The Khmer people make up over 90 percent of the population.

B Reading Skills and Strategies

Responding to the Text

? Imagine you had to move halfway across the world. What things would you miss? [Students may say they would be lonesome for friends and would miss familiar places and activities.]

C Reading Skills and Strategies

Comparing and Contrasting

Ask students to identify differences and one similarity between the author's life in Cambodia and in the United States. [People in the United States are free and at peace, while people in Cambodia are not free and are at war. There are differences in climate, language, foods, eating utensils, and sports. However, in both countries people have similar feelings.]

Student to Student

An Immigrant in the United States

A I am a Cambodian immigrant refugee living in the United States. My family and I left Cambodia because of the war in my country where I was born. I can't believe that we are free in this country. I was eight years old when I first saw different-colored people. How strange, scary, and frightening to see white- and black-colored people, red and brown and yellow hair, blue, green, and brown eyes. I thought they had costumes on. My eyes had only seen brown-skinned people with black hair. The only pictures in books I had ever seen in my country were of Cambodian people who

B are of the brown race. Everything was different. The climate was so cold, and when I saw something white on the ground I thought somebody went up in an airplane and dropped lots and lots of tiny pieces of paper down on the ground. It was the first time I saw snow.

When I went to school I couldn't speak English and the teacher didn't speak Khmer. I couldn't understand what to do. It was very difficult. Eating in the cafeteria at the beginning was so different. I had never seen or tasted milk and never eaten cheese or butter. I had never used a fork or knife. There were about five other Cambodian kids in my room who had been in America longer, so they showed me how to use a fork and a knife. At first I didn't like the foods—cheese, salad, pizza, and milk—so I threw them away. The foods I hated are some of my favorite foods now, like pizza, cheese, and milk.

C American kids showed me how to play American sports and we became friends. Today I feel very happy to be in a free country in America.

The color of people doesn't scare me anymore. I think how silly it was to be afraid. Everyone is the same inside with the same feelings.

—Ponn Pet
Lowell, Massachusetts

Making the Connections

Connecting to the Theme: "Who Am I?"

Have students discuss how Ernesto Galarza might have answered the theme question. Point out that having a sensitive teacher helped Ernesto become comfortable with his identity as both a Mexican and an American.

Connecting Across Texts

Connecting with "Barrio Boy"

Ask students to compare Ernesto's experiences with those of Ponn Pet. Point out that Ernesto traveled only from Mexico to California, whereas Ponn Pet journeyed halfway around the world, to Lowell, Massachusetts. Ask students whether Ponn may have had a more difficult adjustment than Ernesto, and why. Students may observe that the differences—in climate, culture, food, and language—between the United States and Cambodia are greater than the corresponding differences between the United States and Mexico. Students may also speculate on whether the United States was easier to adjust to in 1910 or in 1995. Make sure students see school as a major factor in helping both boys adjust to their new homelands.

First Thoughts

[connect]

1. Finish these sentences:
   - If I went to a school where I did not speak the language, I would . . .
   - I have been in the same situation as Ernesto, and I . . .

Shaping Interpretations

[predict]

2. What did you **predict** would happen to Ernesto, and why? (Were you correct?) How else could his story have ended?

[interpret]

3. In many ways this story is a tribute to Ernesto's teachers. What do you think Galarza means when he says that Miss Ryan was not only "with it" but "with us"?

[describe]

4. The **metaphor** of the melting pot comes from a 1908 play by Israel Zangwill: "America is . . . a great melting pot, where all the races of Europe are melting and reforming!" Ernesto thinks of Lincoln School not as a melting pot—which makes everyone the same—but as a warm griddle. What do you think this means? Which metaphor would you use to describe the United States, and why?

[speculate]

5. Reread the ending of Ponn Pet's essay (page 130). Do you think the teachers at Lincoln School would agree with him? Why or why not?

[contrast]

6. How is Ernesto's experience at an American school different from Jean Fritz's experience at the Hankow British school in "Homesick" (page 105)? Are the experiences of the two outsiders similar at all? Explain.

Connecting with the Text

[apply]

7. At school Ernesto learns tolerance for other cultures and races. Where does he learn intolerance? Where have you seen tolerance and intolerance in your community and in the wider world?

[connect]

8. Refer to your notes for the Quickwrite on page 124. How has this story helped you understand the difficulties of learning a second language?

Extending the Text

[extend]

9. Ernesto Galarza and many of his classmates are immigrants. What special problems do you think immigrants face today? What are some ways that schools and local governments try to solve these problems?

Reading Check

a. How does Ernesto feel about Miss Hopley and Miss Ryan?

b. How is the makeup of Ernesto's class a lot like that of his neighborhood?

c. How does Miss Ryan encourage her students to learn English?

d. According to Miss Hopley and the teachers at Lincoln School, what are the children to remember about *why* they are at school?

e. How does Lincoln School honor its students' original languages and customs?

Reading Check

a. Ernesto likes Miss Hopley and loves Miss Ryan. Both are friendly and kind.

b. The class has a diverse cultural background.

c. Miss Ryan helps students individually with patience and praise.

d. They are to learn and remember how to live in their new homeland without forgetting the customs of their birthplaces.

e. Students may speak their native languages when at play, and they are encouraged to discuss their homelands.

First Thoughts

1. Possible responses:
   - . . . feel shy and be afraid to speak.
   - . . . felt that people didn't understand me very well.

Shaping Interpretations

2. Some students might have predicted that Ernesto would not like the teachers because he couldn't understand them or that Ernesto would fail because he didn't know English. The story could have ended unhappily, with Ernesto being unable to learn to read or to make friends.

3. Miss Ryan not only is a good teacher but also encourages her students and cares about them.

4. Galarza uses the griddle metaphor to suggest that the students at the Lincoln School retain their identities but learn to respect differences. Another possible metaphor is a bowl of salad. Each part of the salad is unique, with its own flavor and characteristics.

5. Students might note that both Miss Hopley and Miss Ryan care deeply about their students' needs and feelings. They probably would agree with Ponn Pet that everyone has similar feelings.

6. Possible responses: At the Lincoln School, the teachers allow the students to speak their native languages at recess. At Jean's school, everyone is expected to play the same game at recess. One similarity is that both Jean and Ernesto are outsiders.

Connecting with the Text

7. Ernesto learns intolerance in the remarks he hears from parents in the community. Students might mention specific books, movies, and TV shows that teach tolerance.

8. Students may say that experiencing the world through Ernesto's eyes helped them appreciate the difficulties of understanding and pronouncing words in an unfamiliar language.

Extending the Text

9. Students may mention the lack of acceptance that immigrants feel outside their own neighborhoods, as well as the problems of learning a new language and of becoming familiar with a different culture. Possible solutions include laws and educational programs to help new residents adjust to their surroundings.

Rubrics for each Choices assignment appear on p. 116 in the *Portfolio Management System*.

CHOICES: Building Your Portfolio

1. **Writer's Notebook**   Remind students to save their work. They may use it as prewriting for the Writer's Workshop on p. 182.

2. **Comparing and Contrasting** Discuss with the class some of the similarities and differences between Jean and Ernesto. For example, Jean was born in a land that was foreign to her family, whereas Ernesto emigrated to one that was foreign to his; both are uncertain whether they are "foreigners" or "Americans."

3. **Research/Math**   Students can use reference sources, such as an atlas or an almanac, to group specific countries or backgrounds within larger classifications, such as Western Europe or Latin America, in order to create a pie graph. Also, the information in an atlas will help students see the variety of ethnic groups that exist in the world. You might check with a math teacher to see if students have learned to figure percentages or to use computer software packages with graphing capabilities that can help simplify this assignment.

4. **Speaking and Listening**   Check to see whether there is a cultural organization in your community. If so, invite a representative to speak to the class. If not, check the library for a book of folk tales from your students' native countries. Read a few of the tales as a prompt for this activity.

CHOICES: Building Your Portfolio

Writer's Notebook

1. Collecting Ideas for an Autobiographical Incident

Ernesto's autobiography might have given you ideas for an autobiography of your own. Develop your ideas by freewriting on one of the following topics in your Writer's Notebook. Use words that express the feelings you associate with a time when

- you felt anxious about going somewhere or doing something new
- a teacher helped you learn or do something
- you realized what it means to live in the United States

> First day of school:
> — Everything was so big.
> — J.J. spilled milk on me. I was soaked and smelly.
> — When I visited as a seventh-grader, everything seemed so small.

Comparing and Contrasting

2. Looking Back

Both Ernesto Galarza and Jean Fritz wrote autobiographies in which they look back at their childhood. At first their stories may seem quite different. Yet, when you look closely, you'll find some important similarities, especially in the problems and feelings they experienced. Write a paragraph or two comparing and contrasting "Homesick" and "Barrio Boy." Before you write, use a Venn diagram like the one on page 123 to organize your ideas.

Research/Math

3. American Pie

Students from all over the world attended Ernesto's school. Is the same true in your class? Take a poll to find out. List the various ethnic groups you find among your classmates (ask them to consider the backgrounds of their parents and grandparents). Then, figure out the percentage of the whole that each group represents. Show your results on a pie graph.

Speaking and Listening

4. Connecting Across Cultures

Recall how Ernesto's classmates share simple stories that help reveal to one another their diverse ethnic and racial backgrounds. With a group of classmates, arrange a "Telling Our Stories" session. Talk about something from your heritage that will help your classmates learn who you are. Then, as a class, discuss the ways details in your stories "cross cultures."

GRAMMAR LINK   MINI-LESSON

• Making the Most of Comparing Adjectives

The **comparative degree** of an adjective compares two people or things. The **superlative degree** compares more than two people or things.

Language Handbook HELP

See Comparison of Modifiers, pages 737-739.

Technology HELP

See Language Workshop CD-ROM. *Key word entry: degrees of comparison.*

Comparative Degree	
Add the ending *-er* or the the word *more* when you compare two items.	The Lincoln School was a sampling of the <u>lower</u> part of town. . . .

Superlative Degree	
When you compare more than two, add the ending *-est* or the word *most*.	To the children, their beloved Miss Ryan was the <u>most wonderful</u> teacher in the world.

1. When comparing, don't use both *more* and *-er,* and don't use both *most* and *-est.*

   Ernesto felt m̶o̶r̶e̶ <u>safer</u> when his mother was present.

   Matti was the m̶o̶st̶ <u>thinnest</u> boy in the second grade.

2. Don't use the superlative form when you compare only two people or things.

   prouder
   Do you think Ernesto was pro̶u̶d̶e̶st̶ of being an American or a Mexican?

   more
   Of the two boys, Ito learned m̶o̶st̶ quickly.

Try It Out

Act as an editor and show how you'd correct these sentences:

1. Ernesto thought American schools were more stranger than Mexican schools.

2. Ernesto spoke Spanish and English, but his Spanish was best.

3. Was Ernesto proudest of pronouncing *butterfly* or of reading "Little Bo-Peep"?

VOCABULARY   HOW TO OWN A WORD

WORD BANK	Rest Assured—The Words Are in the Bank
reassuring *contraption* *assured* *formidable*	Write some sentences of your own. 1. What are the most <u>reassuring</u> words you've ever heard? Tell about when you heard them. 2. Describe some <u>contraption</u> that makes your life easier. 3. Have you ever <u>assured</u> a friend that something would happen? Recall what you said. 4. Who is the most <u>formidable</u> person in your school? What makes him or her so?

BARRIO BOY 133

GRAMMAR LINK

Have students choose one of their writings from their portfolios. Tell them to go through the work and to circle all the adjectives. Then, ask students to write sentences using these adjectives. Half of the adjectives should be in the comparative degree, and the other half in the superlative degree. Ask volunteers to read their new sentences.

Try It Out
Answers
1. Ernesto thought American schools were stranger than Mexican schools.
2. Ernesto spoke Spanish and English, but his Spanish was better.
3. Was Ernesto prouder of pronouncing *butterfly* or of reading "Little Bo-Peep"?

VOCABULARY
Possible Answers
1. The most reassuring words I've ever heard were a pilot saying, after a rough flight, "We've landed safely!"
2. The contraption on our roof that turns the antenna so we get better TV reception makes my life easier.
3. I assured my friend Lois that I would never reveal her secret to anyone else.
4. Mr. DeLeon, who is 6′3″ tall and has a black belt in karate, is the most formidable person in school.

Resources ———

Grammar
• *Grammar and Language Links,* p. 13

Vocabulary
• *Words to Own,* p. 7

Spelling
For related spelling instruction, see
• *Spelling and Decoding,* p. 7

Grammar Link Quick Check

Rewrite the following sentences, using the correct forms of comparison.
1. Ernesto felt that the trip to school was more scarier than anything else he had done.
   [Ernesto felt that the trip to school was scarier than anything else he had done.]

2. Miss Hopley had the more pleasing manner of all the people at the school. [Miss Hopley had the most pleasing manner of all the people at the school.]

3. Ernesto felt the warmest feelings for Miss Ryan rather than Miss Hopley. [Ernesto felt warmer feelings for Miss Ryan than for Miss Hopley.]

4. Of all the students, Ernesto was the more sensitive. [Of all the students, Ernesto was the most sensitive.]

5. Miss Ryan was the most kindest person in the entire school. [Miss Ryan was the kindest person in the entire school.]

OBJECTIVES

1. Read and interpret an autobiographical excerpt
2. Identify description
3. Describe mental images that appeal to the senses
4. Express understanding through autobiographical writing, description, or a home economics project
5. Identify and use precise adjectives
6. Understand and use new words
7. Complete analogies

SKILLS

Literary
- Identify description

Reading
- Describe mental images

Writing
- Collect ideas for an autobiographical incident
- Describe a meal or a dish

Language
- Use precise adjectives

Vocabulary
- Use new words
- Complete analogies

Home Economics
- Collect recipes

Viewing/Representing
- Examine a photograph (ATE)

Planning

- **Block Schedule**
  Block Scheduling Lesson Plans with Pacing Guide

- **Traditional Schedule**
  Lesson Plans Including Strategies for English-Language Learners

- **One-Stop Planner**
  CD-ROM with Test Generator

Before You Read

FISH CHEEKS

Make the Connection

Oops!

A girl is walking down the hall at school. She spots a boy she's been dying to meet coming toward her. They are almost right next to each other when she slips, loses her balance, and falls to the floor in a clumsy heap. How could a moment like this possibly have a positive outcome?

Quickwrite

Jot down your responses to the question above. Then, in a group, share your possible outcomes.

Elements of Literature

Description: Putting You There

People who write autobiographies, or personal histories, try to let the reader share their experiences. They do this by using descriptive language. In "Fish Cheeks," Amy Tan describes holiday guests arriving "in a clamor of doorbells and rumpled Christmas packages." These vivid images help us to hear and see the scene—to be right in the thick of it.

> **D**escription is the kind of writing that creates a clear image of something, usually by using details that appeal to one or more of our senses: sight, hearing, smell, taste, and touch.
>
> *For more on Description, see the Handbook of Literary Terms.*

Reading Skills and Strategies

Describing Mental Images: Appealing to the Senses

When writers describe things, they create **mental images**, pictures drawn with words. To help you imagine places, events, and characters, they use language that appeals to the senses, as Amy Tan does in this true story. When you read description, notice that

- most images are visual, but images often appeal to several senses at once

- writers often choose details that show how they feel about what they describe

 go.hrw.com
LEO 7-2

Preteaching Vocabulary

Words to Own

Have pairs of students take turns reading aloud the definitions of the Words to Own listed at the bottom of the selection pages. Then, have the partners work together on the following exercises to reinforce understanding of the words.

1. Describe a food that you think tastes **appalling**.
2. Draw a picture of an apple cut into **wedges**.
3. Tell about a time that you and your friends raised a **clamor**.
4. List ways to make sure your clothes aren't **rumpled**.
5. Tell about a time that you were not able to **muster** a sound.

FISH CHEEKS

Amy Tan

> ON CHRISTMAS EVE
> I SAW THAT MY MOTHER
> HAD OUTDONE HERSELF IN
> CREATING A STRANGE MENU.

FISH CHEEKS 135

Summary ▪

At age fourteen, Amy Tan has a crush on the minister's son. The minister and his family are invited to the Tans' house for Christmas Eve dinner. Amy is embarrassed by the Chinese food her mother serves and by the table manners of her Chinese relatives—traditions so different from those of Robert's American family. But her mother reminds Amy that she must be proud that she is Chinese. Years later, Amy recognizes that her mother was more sensitive to her feelings than she realized at the time, because she had served all of Amy's favorite foods.

Resources

Listening
Audio CD Library
An excellent rendition of "Fish Cheeks" is provided in the *Audio CD Library:*
- Disc 5, Track 4

Viewing and Representing
Fine Art Transparency
A fine art transparency of Kam Mak's *Girl Holding Wreath in a Field* can be used to show the link between descriptive writing and visual art.
- Transparency 5
- Worksheet, p. 20

FROM THE EDITOR'S DESK

In "Fish Cheeks," Amy Tan serves up a delicious slice of immigrant life that highlights the tension of a teenager caught between family traditions and wider American values. Yet we've also chosen it because the theme—a young person's need to find her or his own way in life—is universal.

Resources: Print and Media

Reading
- *Graphic Organizers for Active Reading,* p. 9
- *Words to Own,* p. 8
- *Spelling and Decoding,* Worksheet, p. 8
- *Audio CD Library,* Disc 5, Track 4

Writing and Language
- *Daily Oral Grammar*
  Transparency 9
- *Grammar and Language Links*
  Worksheet, p. 15
- *Language Workshop CD-ROM*

Viewing and Representing
- *Viewing and Representing*
  Fine Art Transparency 5
  Fine Art Worksheet, p. 20

Assessment
- *Formal Assessment,* p. 23
- *Portfolio Management System,* p. 117
- *Standardized Test Preparation,* p. 28
- *Test Generator (One-Stop Planner CD-ROM)*

Internet
- go.hrw.com (keyword: LE0 7-2)

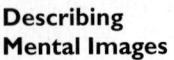

A Reading Skills and Strategies

Describing Mental Images

❓ Why does Amy describe Robert the way she does? [Possible response: She is emphasizing what she considers Robert's "American" features.] **What does her description suggest about her self-image?** [Possible response: Amy thinks that her "Chinese features," such as her hair color and nose, aren't as good as Robert's "American" features.]

B Reading Skills and Strategies

Making Predictions

❓ What do you think will happen when Robert visits Amy's home? [Possible responses: He might be a little uncomfortable at first but will relax and have a good time; or, as Amy thinks, he will feel uneasy the whole time, and Amy herself will be embarrassed.]

C Elements of Literature

Description

❓ What details give you a clear image of the food the Tans are cooking? [Possible responses: the bulging fish eyes pleading not to be thrown into hot oil; the soaking dried fungus coming "back to life"; the marks on the squid that make them look like "bicycle tires."]

D Critical Thinking

Interpreting

❓ Why does Amy pretend not to care about Robert? [Possible responses: She probably doesn't want him to know that she likes him; she's afraid that he won't like her and that she will be hurt.]

A I fell in love with the minister's son the winter I turned fourteen. He was not Chinese, but as white as Mary in the manger. For Christmas I prayed for this blond-haired boy, Robert, and a slim new American nose.

B When I found out that my parents had invited the minister's family over for Christmas Eve dinner, I cried. What would Robert think of our shabby *Chinese* Christmas? What would he think of our noisy *Chinese* relatives who lacked proper American manners? What terrible disappointment would he feel upon seeing not a roasted turkey and sweet potatoes but *Chinese* food?

C On Christmas Eve I saw that my mother had outdone herself in creating a strange menu. She was pulling black veins out of the backs of fleshy prawns. The kitchen was littered with <u>appalling</u> mounds of raw food: A slimy rock cod with bulging fish eyes that pleaded not to be thrown into a pan of hot oil. Tofu, which looked like stacked <u>wedges</u> of rubbery white sponges. A bowl soaking dried fungus back to life. A plate of squid, their backs crisscrossed with knife markings so they resembled bicycle tires.

And then they arrived—the minister's family and all my relatives in a <u>clamor</u> of doorbells and <u>rumpled</u> Christmas packages. D Robert grunted hello, and I pretended he was not worthy of existence.

THE KITCHEN WAS LITTERED WITH APPALLING MOUNDS OF RAW FOOD...

WORDS TO OWN
appalling (ə·pôl′iŋ) *adj.*: shocking, horrifying.
wedges (wej′iz) *n.*: pieces of material thick at one end and narrowing to a thin edge.
clamor (klam′ər) *n.*: loud, confused noise.
rumpled (rum′pəld) *v.* used as *adj.*: wrinkled and untidy.

Reaching All Students

Struggling Readers
Students might role-play the characters in the memoir. They can create dialogue where necessary; students might enjoy describing the food in Tan's words. One of the students might play the role of Amy, acting as narrator.

English Language Learners
Students may find it helpful to collect pictures, from magazines or newspapers, of some of the foods described here or other "American" foods. Students can practice using descriptive words for these food items. For additional strategies to supplement instruction for these students, see
• *Lesson Plans Including Strategies for English-Language Learners*

Advanced Learners
These students might list the vivid verbs and colorful adjectives that appear in "Fish Cheeks" and note which senses they appeal to. Then, have them use a thesaurus or search their own vocabulary to list descriptive synonyms for each verb or adjective.

Dinner threw me deeper into despair. My relatives licked the **E** ends of their chopsticks and reached across the table, dipping them into the dozen or so plates of food. Robert and his family waited patiently for platters to be passed to them. My relatives murmured with pleasure when my mother brought out the whole steamed fish. Robert grimaced. Then my father poked his chopsticks just below the fish eye and plucked out the soft meat. "Amy, your favorite," he said, offering me the tender fish cheek. I wanted to disappear. **F**

At the end of the meal my father leaned back and belched loudly, thanking my mother for her fine cooking. "It's a polite Chinese custom to show you are satisfied," explained my father to our astonished guests. Robert was looking down at his plate with a reddened face. The minister managed to <u>muster</u> up a quiet burp. I was stunned into silence for the rest of the night. **G**

> "YOU WANT TO BE THE SAME AS AMERICAN GIRLS ON THE OUTSIDE."

After everyone had gone, my mother said to me, "You want to be the same as American girls on the outside." She handed me an early gift. It was a miniskirt in beige tweed. "But inside you must always **H** be Chinese. You must be proud you are different. Your only shame is to have shame."

And even though I didn't agree with her then, I knew that she understood how much I had suffered during the evening's dinner. It wasn't until many years later—long after I had gotten over my **I** crush on Robert—that I was able to fully appreciate her lesson and the true purpose behind our particular menu. For Christmas Eve that year, she had chosen all my favorite foods.

- -
WORDS TO OWN
muster (mus´tər) v.: call forth.
- -

FISH CHEEKS 137

Using Students' Strengths

Interpersonal Learners
Have students discuss ideas for an advice column. In it, Amy asks for help on fitting in with her friends while respecting her family traditions. Amy's letter should describe her feelings about the dinner; the columnist's reply should offer practical suggestions to help Amy love and respect her family and also enjoy her American life fully. After discussions, have students write their own columns.

Kinesthetic Learners
Students might pantomime the dinner party that Amy Tan describes, using facial expressions and hand gestures to convey the tensions and awkwardness that arise.

Visual Learners
Students might benefit by filling in the graphic organizer located on p. 9 in the *Graphic Organizers for Active Reading*.

E Ⓔ English Language Learners
Identifying Idioms
Make sure students understand that "threw me deeper into despair" means "made me feel unhappier and more helpless."

Ⓕ Appreciating Language
Precise Adjectives
❓ Ask students how the adjective *tender* describes *fish cheek* in a precise way. [Possible response: It helps the reader "feel" the soft texture of the fish.] In what way does *tender* also describe Amy's father? [Possible response: It suggests that his offer of this tidbit to Amy is tender, or loving.]

Ⓖ Struggling Readers
Paraphrasing
Ask students to paraphrase, or restate in their own words, why Amy feels so embarrassed that she is "stunned into silence." [Possible response: Amy's father belches after dinner and says that the meal was delicious. He explains to Robert and his father that Chinese people belch to show they enjoyed the food. Robert is embarrassed and turns red and looks down. His father tries to belch too, to be polite.]

Ⓗ Critical Thinking
Analyzing
❓ Why does the narrator's mother give her a miniskirt? [Possible responses: She is saying that Amy can be like any other American girl on the outside but should also be proud of her Chinese heritage; she is suggesting that she understands Amy's feelings.]

Ⓘ Reading Skills and Strategies
Responding to the Text
❓ Why does Mrs. Tan choose all of Amy's favorite foods for dinner? [Possible response: Mrs. Tan shows her love for Amy by preparing these foods.]

Resources
Selection Assessment
Formal Assessment
• Selection Test, p. 23
Test Generator
• Selection Test

LITERATURE AND SCIENCE

Queen Bean

Whenever you have Chinese food, it's there: In a restaurant it's in the small, tapered beaker nestled between the salt and pepper shakers; in your take-out bag it's in bulgy tiny plastic packets. Yes, it's the soy sauce, as reliable and reassuring a companion to Chinese food as ketchup is to some American foods. Yet, this tasty sauce is only one of dozens of uses for the amazing soybean, a staple of Chinese cuisine for centuries.

The soybean is a member of the legume family, a high-protein vegetable group that includes such familiar items as peanuts, chickpeas, lentils, lima beans, navy beans, and split peas. Soybeans are used in a wide variety of products: tofu (a high-protein bean curd popular among vegetarians), soy milk, soy flour, and tempeh (a fermented soy product high in protein and vitamin B_{12}). In fact, soybeans so far surpass all other legumes in protein, B vitamins, and versatility that in comparison, the other members of the family seem like mere has-beans.

Crossing the Curriculum

Social Studies
As is clear from "Fish Cheeks," etiquette varies widely from culture to culture. Invite students to focus on a particular culture, modern or historical, and research its etiquette. Students can list specific manners and tell how or why they think these customs evolved. Some students might like to explore how the rules of etiquette have changed in the United States since the early 1900s.

Mathematics
Using the menu described in the selection, students should work in groups to estimate the cost of the Tans' meal. They may use newspaper ads, circulars, or visits or phone calls to grocery stores to determine the cost of items. Students may also figure out how long a person would have to work at minimum wage to pay for the meal.

Health
After they have read the "Queen Bean" feature, invite students to investigate the health benefits of meeting some or most of their protein needs from legumes instead of relying solely on meat and dairy products. What health risks are associated with diets high in meats? What are the disadvantages of relying solely on vegetable proteins?

MEET THE WRITER

Finding Answers in Stories

❝ I was the only Chinese girl in class from third grade on. I remember trying to belong and feeling isolated. I felt ashamed of being different and ashamed of feeling that way. When I was a teenager, I rejected everything Chinese. . . . The only people I could think I wanted to be like were fictional characters. In part, that is one of the reasons I began to write. You're looking for answers in your life, and you can't find them in anyone else. You end up finding them in stories. ❞

Amy Tan (1952–) found her friends in books—fairy tales, the *Little House* novels of Laura Ingalls Wilder, and later, the British novels of the Brontë sisters. Later still, she began to write books of her own, about a life half a world away from America's prairies and Britain's moors.

Tan spent her childhood in Oakland, California, where her parents had settled after leaving China. When she was fourteen, both her father and her brother died from brain tumors. After these losses, her mother revealed a long-kept secret: Amy had three half-sisters still living in China. These upheavals in her family changed Amy Tan's sense of who she was. Suddenly her Chinese heritage became important to her. She began to read whatever she could about China, later taking college courses in Chinese literature and history. Most of all, Tan became fascinated by her mother's stories about her experiences in China during the war-torn 1930s and 1940s.

Eventually these experiences inspired Tan to write *The Joy Luck Club* (1989) and *The Kitchen God's Wife* (1991). Tan explains:

❝ I took images from my mother's stories and painted a larger picture. The voice in my mother and in my novels is one and the same. ❞

In recent years, Amy Tan has made several trips to China, where she has come to know the sisters who once seemed lost to her forever. She now loves the Chinese culture she once tried so hard to reject.

In rediscovering her heritage, Tan has not abandoned American ways. She is the lead vocalist in a rock band called the Rock Bottom Remainders. The humorist Dave Barry plays lead guitar, and the writer Stephen King plays rhythm guitar. All three band members claim to have no musical talent whatsoever.

Scene from the 1993 movie version of *The Joy Luck Club*.
© Buena Vista Pictures Distribution, Inc.

FISH CHEEKS 139

BROWSING IN THE FILES

About the Author. Amy Tan's Chinese name, An-Mei, means "blessing to America." When she was young, her family moved often, and because she sometimes found it hard to adjust, she spent a lot of time living in her imagination. Her first professional writing job was drafting speeches for business executives. Later, she turned to nonfiction and fiction. Her first published short story, "Endgame," is about the relationship between a chess player and her Chinese mother.

Writers on Writing. In an interview Tan gave in 1997, she asserts: "I don't see myself . . . writing about cultural dichotomies, but about human connections. All of us go through angst and identity crises. And even when you write in a specific context, you still tap into that subtext of emotions that we all feel about love and hope, and mothers and obligations and responsibilities."

Assessing Learning

Check Test: Short Answer

1. Why is Amy worried about having guests for Christmas dinner? [She is afraid that the guests will be upset by her family's Christmas meal and by their manners.]
2. How does she treat Robert when he arrives? [She acts as if she does not care about him.]
3. What does Amy's father do that embarrasses her? [He gives her the fish cheek, and he burps at the end of the meal.]

4. What does her mother say after the meal? [She tells Amy that she can be like American girls on the outside but that inside she must be proud that she is different.]
5. What does the narrator realize many years later about the meal? [She realizes that her mother had made all Amy's favorite dishes for that meal.]

Standardized Test Preparation

For practice with standardized test format specific to this selection, see
- *Standardized Test Preparation*, p. 28

For practice in proofreading and editing, see
- *Daily Oral Grammar*, Transparency 9

Connections

A Reading Skills and Strategies

Describing Mental Images

❓ What might the speaker mean by the image, or picture in words, of immigrants wrapping "their babies in the American flag"? [Possible response: The babies are surrounded by American culture, because the parents want their children to adopt American values.]

B Appreciating Language

Word Choice

❓ What do you think the phrase "thick English" means? [Possible response: English spoken with a thick, or heavy, foreign accent.] Do you think the speaker is making fun of foreign accents? Explain. [Possible response: No, she seems sympathetic to immigrants who want to adapt to American ways while holding on to their native cultures.]

C Elements of Literature

Description

❓ How does the speaker appeal to our sense of hearing? [Possible response: She imitates the pronunciation of the immigrants' speech; she says parents "whisper" (ll. 9–10).]

D Critical Thinking

Extending the Text

❓ How does the poem's structure reflect the immigrants' conflicting attitudes about their children? [Possible response: The first stanza shows the ways in which the parents encourage their children to assimilate; the second stanza voices the fears that immigrants have about their children's futures in the United States.]

RESPONDING TO THE ART

Invite students to examine the photograph.

Activity. What does the picture show about children in America? [Possible response: Immigrant children from different nations can live together happily.]

Immigrants   Pat Mora

A wrap their babies in the American flag,
    feed them mashed hot dogs and apple pie,
    name them Bill and Daisy,
    buy them blonde dolls that blink blue
5   eyes or a football and tiny cleats
    before the baby can even walk,
B speak to them in thick English,
            hallo, babee, hallo,
C whisper in Spanish or Polish
10 when the babies sleep, whisper
    in a dark parent bed, that dark
    parent fear, "Will they like
    our boy, our girl, our fine american
    boy, our fine american girl?"

Connecting Across Texts

Connecting with "Fish Cheeks"

When students have read "Fish Cheeks," discuss the collection theme with the class. Because she can't answer the question "Who am I?"—is she Chinese or American or some of both?—young Amy Tan is embarrassed when her mother serves Chinese food to American guests on an American holiday. Have students compare the thoughts and actions of Amy's parents with those of the immigrant parents in the poem. [Possible responses: The parents in both selections want their children to be happy, but the parents in the poem are eager for their children to become "all-American." Amy's parents hope that she will not forget her heritage when she practices American customs (like wearing a miniskirt).]

MAKING MEANINGS

First Thoughts

[connect]

1. Have you ever felt the way Amy does? What would you have done that Christmas Eve if you had been Amy?

Shaping Interpretations

[speculate]

2. Why do you think Amy is ashamed of her family's Chinese traditions? What does Amy's mother mean when she says, "Your only shame is to have shame"?

[infer]

3. Reread Tan's **description** of the food her mother is preparing for dinner. How does Amy feel about the dinner? How can you tell?

[classify]

4. Find one visual **image** in the story that creates a vivid picture in your mind. Then, find three more images that appeal to more than one sense.

[interpret]

5. What do you think Robert and his family think of the Christmas Eve dinner? Use details from the essay to support your response. (How did *you* predict this evening would turn out?)

[analyze]

6. Why do you suppose it isn't until many years later that Amy realizes her mother chose all of Amy's favorite foods for Christmas Eve dinner? What do you think are her mother's "lesson" and "true purpose" in preparing these foods?

[compare]

7. How are the new Americans in "Immigrants" (see *Connections* on page 140) similar to Amy Tan's family? How are they different?

Connecting with the Text

[connect]

8. Amy's mother tells her that she can be an American girl on the outside but must always be Chinese on the inside. Do you think this is possible? Is it a good idea? Explain your answer.

Extending the Text

[speculate]

9. Think about Jean in "Homesick" (page 105), Ernesto in "Barrio Boy" (page 125), and Amy in "Fish Cheeks." How do you think each would answer the question "Who am I?"

Challenging the Text

[evaluate]

10. Where does the **title** "Fish Cheeks" come from? Do you think it's a good title? Tell why or why not.

Reading Check

Imagine that it is Christmas Eve twenty years later. With a partner, retell the **main events** of "Fish Cheeks." Let one person play the role of Amy and the other person play her mother. Let Amy retell the story. Let her mother add details.

MAKING MEANINGS

First Thoughts

1. Students might say they would have cried, apologized, or left the room; or they would have tried to explain their family's customs.

Shaping Interpretations

2. She is ashamed because Chinese and American traditions are so different. Her mother means that Amy should be ashamed only for not being proud of her heritage.

3. Amy uses words such as *appalling, slimy, rubbery,* and *bulging* to describe the food in the unpleasant way that she thinks the guests will see it.

4. "A slimy rock cod with bulging fish eyes" appeals to the senses of touch and sight; the relatives' licking and dipping their chopsticks appeals to the senses of taste and sight; the murmuring over steamed fish appeals to the senses of hearing and smell.

5. The American guests do not seem to enjoy the meal. Robert grimaces when the fish comes out, and his face turns red when Amy's father burps.

6. Amy was too self-conscious to realize what her mother was doing. Her mother wanted to show her how much her family cared about her and how proud she should be of her Chinese heritage.

7. Both show love and concern for their children's futures. The immigrants in the poem have adopted American customs rather than retain their traditions, as Amy Tan's parents did.

Connecting with the Text

8. Having two cultures can make a person more interesting but can lead to confusion or conflict.

Extending the Text

9. Possible responses: Jean: "I am an American who must make the most of living in a foreign land." Ernesto: "I am now an American but remain proud of my Mexican heritage." Amy: "While I live and work in typical American ways, deep down I am still Chinese."

Reading Check

The student role-playing Amy should recount how she wanted to impress Robert and his family. She might recall her horror at the huge mounds of food and embarrassment at her father's offering her the fish cheeks and later burping. The student playing Mrs. Tan should emphasize that she was aware of Amy's divided feelings, had deliberately cooked her daughter's favorite foods, and wanted Amy to be proud of her heritage.

Challenging the Text

10. Mr. Tan offers Amy fish cheeks, her favorite food, but Amy cringes in embarrassment. Because the dish represents Amy's ambivalence about her Chinese background, it provides a good title for this story.

Rubrics for each Choices assignment appear on p. 117 in the *Portfolio Management System*.

CHOICES:
Building Your Portfolio

1. **Writer's Notebook** Remind students to save their work. They may use it as prewriting for the Writer's Workshop on p. 182. *Remind students to choose a situation they would not mind sharing with others.*

2. **Descriptive Writing** Before beginning the activity, have students practice by describing a piece of fruit. Ask them to use a chart like the one in their books. Allow them time to share their charts with the class before completing the activity.

3. **Home Economics** Students should ask for a recipe from an older person who enjoys cooking. You might bring in a cookbook that students can use as a model.

CHOICES: Building Your Portfolio

Writer's Notebook

1. Collecting Ideas for an Autobiographical Incident

Have you ever been in an embarrassing situation that somehow ended with a positive outcome (like the one you wrote about for the Quickwrite on page 134)? Write about this experience, or write about a time when you were anxious to make a good impression.

> *Wanted to look grown-up. Wore high heels to interview for camp counselor. Couldn't play with kids. Felt embarrassed and awkward. Interviewer helped. Said "Just take off the heels!"*

Descriptive Writing

2. Different Tastes

Slimy, bulging, rubbery—Amy Tan uses specific **adjectives** to make us feel disgust for the foods that her mother has lovingly prepared for Christmas Eve. Actually these foods are young Amy's favorites, but she uses these adjectives to show her feelings about the meal at the time.

Describe a meal from two different points of view: the point of view of someone who loves everything on the plate, and the point of view of someone who thinks the food is strange and can't eat a thing. You might gather your details in a chart like the one in the next column. The Language Links on pages 120 and 143 might help you with your adjectives.

Meal
Delicious
Buttery, fluffy potatoes with a lake of rich gravy
Horrible
Some mashed-up white stuff flooded with a gluey liquid

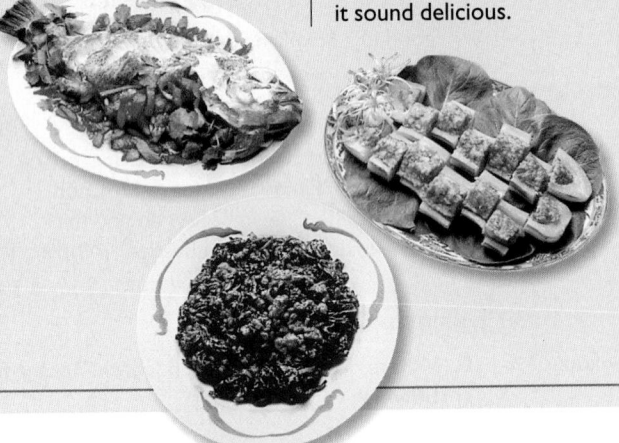

Home Economics

3. World-Class Dining

Bring in the recipe for a dish that is one of your favorites. If possible, choose a dish that you associate with your ethnic or racial heritage. Collect the recipes in a class cookbook. Before each recipe, write a few sentences describing the dish in words that make it sound delicious.

Taking a Second Look

Review: Making Inferences

Remind students that when they make inferences, they use their own knowledge, as well as details in a selection, to fill in some information that the author has not provided. When they were reading "Fish Cheeks," for example, they may have made "educated guesses" about the characters.

Activities

1. Ask students to infer whether Amy's father was aware of her confused feelings during the meal. [He probably wasn't, since he acted in his normal way, handing Amy the fish cheeks and burping loudly.]

2. Ask students to infer what they can about Robert from details in the story. [Students might infer from the way in which he grimaces at the fish and blushes at the burping that he was a bit prissy and overly formal.]

LANGUAGE LINK | MINI-LESSON

Style: Using Precise Adjectives

SOME OF
TAN'S
ADJECTIVES

slim
shabby
noisy
strange
appalling
raw
slimy
bulging
rubbery
rumpled
reddened
quiet

Amy Tan's **descriptive writing** is vivid because she uses specific adjectives that paint an exact picture of the nouns they modify. Overall, these small details work together to give us a clear impression of Amy's feelings. How would your sense of her experience change if she had left out the adjectives?

Tan's Sentences Without Adjectives	Tan's Sentences With Adjectives
What would Robert think of our Christmas?	"What would Robert think of our shabby Chinese Christmas?"
The kitchen was littered with mounds of food.	"The kitchen was littered with appalling mounds of raw food."

Notice how the precise adjectives—*shabby, appalling, raw*—help you see how Amy feels about this Chinese Christmas.

Try It Out

➤ Do adjectives sometimes fail you? Take out a description you've written that you want to revise. Place a check mark above each adjective. Decide if it is a general adjective or a precise adjective that paints an exact picture. For example:

General Adjective	Precise Adjective
big	colossal, gigantic
nice	generous, kind
strong	forceful, muscular

Change any adjective that does not give readers a precise and vivid impression. You may want to use a **thesaurus** to find the exact word.

VOCABULARY | HOW TO OWN A WORD

WORD BANK

appalling
wedges
clamor
rumpled
muster

Analogies: Pairs of Pairs

An analogy begins with a pair of items that are related in some way. You figure out that relationship and then complete another pair that has a similar relationship. For example:

1. *Sad* is to *happy* as _____ is to *delightful*.

The relationship of *sad* to *happy* is one of opposites. Complete the analogy with a vocabulary word from the Word Bank that is the opposite of *delightful*. Then, complete each analogy below.

2. *Pressed* is to *neat* as _____ is to *sloppy*.
3. *Whisper* is to *soft* as _____ is to *loud*.
4. *Receive* is to *get* as _____ is to *summon*.
5. *Slices* is to *pizza* as _____ is to *cheese*.

FISH CHEEKS 143

LANGUAGE LINK

Ask students to choose, from their portfolios, a piece of descriptive writing that they would not mind sharing with a partner. Allow time for partners to read each other's papers silently. Then, ask the partners to indicate which descriptions they think should have more details. Allow students to rewrite those descriptions, adding precise adjectives where they will make the description livelier. Then, call on volunteers to read their revised descriptions aloud.

Try It Out

Students should demonstrate that they have identified the less precise adjectives by replacing them with more vivid alternatives.

VOCABULARY

1. appalling
2. rumpled
3. clamor
4. muster
5. wedges

Resources ——————

Language
• *Grammar and Language Links*, p. 15

Vocabulary
• *Words to Own*, p. 8

Spelling
For related instruction, see
• *Spelling and Decoding*, p. 8

Language Link Quick Check

Replace the underlined adjectives in the following sentences with precise adjectives. (Possible answers are given.)
1. The fish seemed <u>wet</u>. [slimy; moist]
2. Chinese food is <u>good</u>. [delicious; scrumptious]
3. The dinner was <u>upsetting</u> to Amy. [mortifying; embarrassing; disturbing]

4. In America, it is <u>bad</u> to burp after a meal. [unmannerly; unacceptable; vulgar]
5. Amy's Chinese relatives were <u>loud</u>. [noisy; deafening]

NAMES/NOMBRES

Make the Connection

The Name Game

How would you feel if someone mispronounced or misspelled your name? or introduced you as Judy, though your name was really Julie? or made fun of your name?

Round robin. Share your thoughts about the following questions with a group of three or four other students:

- How does your name affect how you see yourself and how others see you?

- Would you like to have a different name? What would you like it to be?

Quickwrite

Write about your family name, given name, nickname, or pet name. Explain when and how you got the name and how you feel about it. Is it an accurate representation of who you are?

Elements of Literature

Main Idea

Have you ever heard someone say "Just get to the point"? Often, in real life as well as in literature, that point, or **main idea,** is not directly stated; it is **implied.** When a main idea is implied, you must draw your own conclusions to decide what the point is.

> The **main idea** is the most important thing a writer has to say in a paragraph or selection. The main idea may be directly stated or implied.
>
> *For more on Main Idea, see page 443 and the Handbook of Literary Terms.*

Reading Skills and Strategies

Discovering the Main Idea: It's in the Details

The **main idea** of a story is the idea that all the important details add up to. It's the central idea in the story, the one that the writer wants you to remember. In some stories, like "Names/Nombres," the writer **implies,** or suggests, the main idea. You have to **infer,** or guess, the point that the writer is getting at. To infer a main idea, follow these steps:

- Identify the important details in the selection.

- Think about the point that the important details make.

- From this information, figure out what the main idea is, and state it in your own words.

 go.hrw.com
LEO 7-2

144 WHO AM I?

 Resources: Print and Media

Reading
- *Reading Skills and Strategies*
  MiniRead Skill Lesson, p. 80
  Selection Skill Lesson, p. 87
- *Graphic Organizers for Active Reading*, p. 10
- *Spelling and Decoding* Worksheet, p. 9

Writing and Language
- *Daily Oral Grammar*
  Transparency 10
- *Grammar and Language Links*
  Worksheet, p. 17
- *Language Workshop CD-ROM*

Viewing and Representing
- *Visual Connections*
  Videocassette A, Segment 2

Assessment
- *Formal Assessment*, p. 25
- *Portfolio Management System*, p. 118
- *Standardized Test Preparation*, p. 30
- *Test Generator (One-Stop Planner CD-ROM)*

Internet
- go.hrw.com (keyword: LE0 7-2)

A name as chaotic with sounds as a Middle Eastern bazaar . . .

Names/Nombres

Julia Alvarez

When we arrived in New York City, our names changed almost immediately. At Immigration, the officer asked my father, *Mister Elbures,* if he had anything to declare. My father shook his head no, and we were waved through. I was too afraid we wouldn't be let in if I corrected the man's pronunciation, but I said our name to myself, opening my mouth wide for the organ blast of the *a,* trilling my tongue for the drumroll of the *r, All-vah-rrr-es!* How could anyone get *Elbures* out of that orchestra of sound?

Summary ■ ■

"Names/Nombres" is a personal essay describing the experiences of a girl who emigrates with her family from the Dominican Republic to New York City in the 1950s. Almost immediately, Julia notices that Americans do not pronounce Spanish names correctly. After a while, and with her mother's encouragement, she comes to accept the "English" names her classmates call her. She is aware, too, that some of her classmates think of her as "exotic." While in high school, Julia likes being called by the American nicknames her many friends give her. At graduation Julia is slightly embarrassed by the numerous relatives who come to the ceremony. When her parents give her a typewriter as a graduation gift, her family predicts that her name will become well known, and she wonders which of her names that will be.

Resources

Viewing and Representing
Videocassette A, Segment 2
The segment "What's in a Name?" can be used with this selection. See the *Visual Connections Teacher's Manual.*
Selection Assessment
Formal Assessment
• Selection Test, p. 25
Test Generator
• Selection Test

Skill Link

Decoding: Verbs to Nouns
A verb can be made into a noun by the addition of the suffix *–tion* or one of its variations, *–ion* or *–ation.* Adding *–tion* changes the way a word is used in a sentence. It also changes the way the word is pronounced. Demonstrate this with the word *immigration.* In the verb *immigrate,* the primary stress is on the first syllable: im mi grate. When the verb becomes a noun, the primary stress shifts to the third syllable: im mi gra tion.

The same shift in stress occurs with other verbs that end in *–ate: graduate, graduation; hesitate, hesitation; imitate, imitation.* Use the following examples to help students make the generalization that the primary stress always shifts to the *penult,* the next-to-the-last syllable, when *–tion* is added: *transport, transportation; edit, edition; define, definition.*
Activity
Write the following items on the chalkboard.

Ask a volunteer to read the two words alongside each number. Then, have the student call on a classmate to underline the syllable that gets the primary stress in each word.
1. compose   composition
2. fascinate   fascination
3. restore   restoration
4. locate   location
5. hibernate   hibernation

Rubrics for each Choices assignment appear on p. 118 in the *Portfolio Management System*.

CHOICES: Building Your Portfolio

1. **Writer's Notebook** Remind students to save their work. They may use it as prewriting for the Writer's Workshop on p. 182. *Remind students to choose a situation they would not mind sharing with others.*

2. **Creative Writing** Have students first create a cluster diagram to help them fill in the details of the poem. They may use headings such as quotations, likes, dislikes, hopes and dreams, fears, and background.

3. **Research/Speaking and Listening** Brainstorm with the class to develop a list of questions to ask a family member about why the student's name was chosen. Tell students they may also use these questions to help organize their oral reports after they interview family members.

4. **Writing/Art** Encourage students to choose a name that symbolizes, or represents, something about them and their writing. Students should try to make the pen name, title, and biographical notes relate to one another.

CHOICES: Building Your Portfolio

Writer's Notebook

1. Collecting Ideas for an Autobiographical Incident

Jot down some notes about your own experiences with names. Here are some ways to get started:

* comments people have made about your name in the past

* the perfect name for you and why (it could be the one you have now or one you make up)

* feelings you've had about other people's names

* names you've given (nicknames, names of pets)

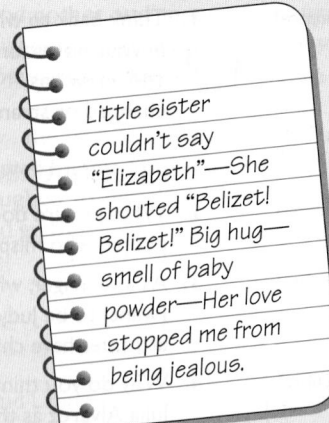

> • Little sister couldn't say "Elizabeth"—She shouted "Belizet! Belizet!" Big hug—smell of baby powder—Her love stopped me from being jealous.

Creative Writing

2. I Am a Poem

Imagine that you are writing from the point of view of Julia Alvarez, and complete the following "I Am" poem. Use what you have learned about Alvarez in "Names/Nombres" to help you capture her personality.

"I Am"
I am …
I wonder …
I hear …
I see …
I want …
I am …

Research/ Speaking and Listening

3. What's in Your Name?

Research your own names to find out as much as you can about them—first, middle, and last names, as well as any additional names you've been given as part of your ethnic or religious heritage. You could begin by interviewing your family members to record what they know. Then, check the name books at your library. See if you can find out the **origins** of all your names. Prepare a short talk in which you tell your classmates about the meanings of your names.

Writing/Art

4. Pen Names

What do Mark Twain, Dr. Seuss, Lewis Carroll, M. E. Kerr, and O. Henry have in common? Answer: They all wrote their books using pen names. Invent a pen name that you might use someday. Then, think of a title for a book you might write. Create a book cover with that title and pen name. On the back cover, place a photo of yourself, accompanied by notes about your life.

Assessing Learning

Check Test: Short Answer

1. Why does the narrator's given name surprise her friends? [It is much longer than any of the names they are used to.]

2. What does the narrator do when the immigration officer mispronounces her family's name? [She says the name clearly to herself.]

3. What are some nicknames the narrator is given? [Jules, Hey Jude, and Alcatraz]

4. Where does the narrator tell her friends she is from? [New York]

5. What do the students do after the commencement ceremony? [They sign yearbooks.]

Standardized Test Preparation

For practice with standardized test format specific to this selection, see

* *Standardized Test Preparation*, p. 30

For practice in proofreading and editing, see

* *Daily Oral Grammar*, Transparency 10

GRAMMAR LINK MINI-LESSON

Language Handbook HELP

See Participial Phrases, page 740.

Technology HELP

See Language Workshop CD-ROM. *Key word entry: dangling modifiers.*

Don't Leave Your Modifiers Dangling

It's easy to make the mistake of "hanging" a modifying phrase on a sentence (usually at the beginning) and forgetting to include the word it modifies:

DANGLING

    Arriving in New York City, our names changed almost immediately.

Who arrived in New York City? It sounds as if the names came on their own!

    Phrases that hang, or dangle, on a sentence without clearly modifying a word are called **dangling modifiers.** You can correct a dangling modifier by adding, subtracting, or rearranging words:

CLEAR

    Arriving in New York City, we noticed that our names changed almost immediately.

The first sentence of "Names/Nombres" shows this even better solution:

CLEAR

    "When we arrived in New York City, our names changed almost immediately."

Try It Out
➤Find and fix the dangling modifiers in these sentences.

1. Tracing the fugitive, the name on the wanted poster was JUDY ALCATRAZ.

2. Moving into our new apartment, our name became *Alberase*.

3. Equipped with a typewriter, the stories were easier to write.

➤ Exchange a sample of your writing with a partner. Then, be a dangler detector: Read through each other's work carefully to see that every sentence makes sense and that every modifier or phrase has something to modify. Your first step should be to identify the modifying phrases (with the permission of the writer, use a colored pen). Dangling modifiers usually appear, or "dangle," at the opening of a sentence.

SPELLING HOW TO OWN A WORD

VERB LIST

combine
generate
graduate
pronounce
immigrate

Suffixes: The Verb-Noun Connection

How do you turn a verb into a noun? Often you can do it simply by adding the **suffix** *-ion* (or its variation *-sion, -tion, -ation,* or *-iation*) to the verb. A **suffix** is a word part that is added to the end of a word. (A **prefix** is added to the beginning.) You may have to make a spelling change when you add one of these suffixes to a verb. For example, when you add *-ion, -ation,* or *-iation* to a word that ends with an e, you must drop the e:

complicate + -ion = complication

Change the verbs in the list into nouns. Then, check the story to see if you have formed each noun correctly.

NAMES/NOMBRES 151

GRAMMAR LINK

Ask students to choose a piece of descriptive writing from their portfolios and to look for sentences with dangling modifiers. Tell them to copy these incorrect sentences on a separate piece of paper. Next, collect the papers, distribute them randomly, and ask students to correct these errors. After this task is completed, return the papers and ask volunteers to explain how the errors were corrected.

Try It Out
Possible Answers
1. When we traced the fugitive, we found that the name on the wanted poster read "Judy Alcatraz."
2. After we moved into our new apartment, our name became *Alberase*.
3. Now that I was equipped with a typewriter, my stories were easier to write.

SPELLING
Answers
combination
generation
graduation
pronunciation
immigration

Resources

Grammar
• *Grammar and Language Links*, p. 17

Spelling
For related instruction, see
• *Spelling and Decoding*, p. 9

Grammar Link Quick Check

Find and fix the dangling modifiers in these sentences. (Possible answers are given.)

1. Often having to repeat her last name for people, their puzzled looks were no longer a surprise. [Often having to repeat her last name to people, Julia was no longer surprised by their puzzled looks.]

2. Talking to her friends, they are always astonished to hear her real name. [When talking to her friends, Julia always astonishes them when she tells them her full name.]

3. Signing yearbooks with her friends, the relatives patiently waited for Julia's return to the family celebration. [Because she was signing yearbooks with her friends, the relatives patiently waited for Julia to join them for a family celebration.]

4. Wanting to be accepted, Julia's jokes are often made with her classmates. [Julia, wanting to be accepted, often makes jokes with her classmates.]

OBJECTIVES

1. Read and interpret the story
2. Identify setting
3. Monitor comprehension
4. Express understanding through autobiographical and creative writing, research/science, mapping/speaking, or art
5. Identify and correct misplaced modifiers
6. Understand and use new words
7. Use glossaries and dictionaries

SKILLS

Literary
- Identify setting

Reading
- Monitor comprehension

Writing
- Collect ideas for an autobiographical incident
- Describe a fantasy setting

Speaking/Listening
- Create an original map

Grammar
- Identify and correct misplaced modifiers

Vocabulary
- Understand and use new words

Art
- Present a metamorphosis, or transformation

Science
- Research facts about Mars

Planning

- **Traditional Schedule**
  Lesson Plans Including Strategies for English-Language Learners
- **One-Stop Planner**
  CD-ROM with Test Generator

Before You Read

THE NAMING OF NAMES

Make the Connection

What's in a Name?
From Walla Walla to Winnemucca, from Mooseheart to King of Prussia, from Devil's Hopyard to Saint Cloud—every part of our country has wonderful names that give us clues to the identity and background of the people who have lived there. With a group of classmates, look over a map of your community, region, or state. Pick out and list some unusual names. Consider names of roads, neighborhoods, buildings, rivers, and mountains, as well as towns. Discuss these names with your group. How does each name reflect the culture of the people who have lived in the region?

Quickwrite

Imagine you were among the first people to settle your town. Decide on a new name that you think captures the spirit or the setting of your new home. Write your new name and the reason you think it's a good one.

Elements of Literature

Setting: Out of the Imagination
You won't recognize Mars in this science fiction story. The story's imaginary and fantastic setting springs from the imagination of Ray Bradbury. On his Mars, twenty-first-century colonists from Earth settle in a place where the wind roars through "the violet grass, shaking out green rose petals." As you'll see, in this strange Martian setting everything is subject to a kind of magic.

> **S**etting is the time and place in which a story takes place.
>
> *For more on Setting, see the Handbook of Literary Terms.*

Reading Skills and Strategies

Monitoring Comprehension: Modify Your Reading

Luckily, **monitoring comprehension** is easier to do than to say. It just means checking your understanding of a story as you go along. To prevent breakdown, you monitor and modify, or adjust, your reading style—just as astronauts monitor and adjust computerized controls on a spaceflight. If your understanding of "The Naming of Names" breaks down, here are some ways to get back into orbit:

- Stop and take reading notes whenever the setting changes.
- Reread paragraphs aloud.
- Use reference aids, such as footnotes and dictionaries.
- Ask questions. Look for clues with your classmates and teacher.

 go.hrw.com
LEO 7-2

152 WHO AM I?

Preteaching Vocabulary

Words to Own
To reinforce students' understanding of the Words to Own, have them write their responses to the following questions. (Possible responses are given.)

1. What do you do to become more **convivial** when you feel **forlorn**? [I invite friends over to cheer myself up.]
2. If the waters of a flood **receded**, what **submerged** objects might you see? [Once the water shrank back, I might see sunken treasure.]
3. What high-tech **anachronism** would look **amiss** in a play set in 1865? [computers]
4. Name something in your community that **dwindled** and then **ceased**. [Funds for special programs decreased and then ended.]
5. What might happen to the **interior** of a house built with **flimsy** materials? [If the walls inside are weak, the building might collapse.]

The Naming of Names

Ray Bradbury

"I wonder if those Martians mind us living here."

Summary ■ ■ ■

To escape from the threat of nuclear war on Earth, the Bittering family has traveled to Mars. There, Earthling colonists have populated empty Martian cities and given "American" names to Martian localities. At first, the Bitterings are fearful and homesick, especially the father. When the links between Earth and Mars are cut off, most of the Earthlings accept the changes that are occurring to them; eventually, the father begins speaking Martian and acknowledges that he, too, has been transformed. Five years later, when a rescue mission from Earth arrives, the crew finds abandoned colonies and friendly "natives." Deciding to set up a colony, they start by naming the Lincoln Mountains.

Background

"The Naming of Names" appeared in 1958, a time when many scientists believed that some form of life existed on Mars. These beliefs were shattered in 1965, when *Mariner 4*, the first spacecraft to visit the planet, sent back closeup photographs revealing a seemingly lifeless surface on Mars. (See also "Live from Mars," p. 157.)

Resources

Listening
Audio CD Library
The *Audio CD Library* includes a recording of "The Naming of Names":
• Disc 6, Track 2

Selection Assessment
Formal Assessment
• Selection Test, p. 27
Test Generator
• Selection Test

Resources: Print and Media

Reading
• *Reading Skills and Strategies*
    Selection Skill Lesson, p. 11
• *Graphic Organizers for Active Reading*, p. 11
• *Words to Own*, p. 9
• *Spelling and Decoding*
    Worksheet, p. 10
• *Audio CD Library*
    Disc 6, Track 2

Writing and Language
• *Daily Oral Grammar*
    Transparency 11
• *Grammar and Language Links*
    Worksheet, p. 19
• *Language Workshop CD-ROM*

Assessment
• *Formal Assessment*, p. 27
• *Portfolio Management System*, p. 119
• *Standardized Test Preparation*, p. 32
• *Test Generator (One-Stop Planner CD-ROM)*

Internet
• go.hrw.com (keyword: LE0 7-2)

A Elements of Literature

Setting

? What details in this description of the setting help create a suspenseful mood? [Possible responses: The description of the air suggests that it could blow away personal identity; the comparison of the old cities to dead children's bones suggests the cities' abandonment.]

B Critical Thinking

Analyzing

? How does Harry feel about his arrival on Mars? [Possible responses: He may be regretting his decision to travel there; he may feel that he will not survive long.]

C Appreciating Language

Word Choice

? What does the word *submerged*, mostly used in connection with water, suggest about Harry's feelings? [Possible responses: It makes the atmosphere seem heavy and dangerous; it suggests that Harry feels overwhelmed.]

The rocket metal cooled in the meadow winds. Its lid gave a bulging *pop*. From its clock <u>interior</u> stepped a man, a woman, and three children. The other passengers whispered away across the Martian meadow, leaving the man alone among his family.

The man felt his hair flutter and the tissues of his body draw tight as if he were standing at the center of a vacuum.[1] His wife, before him, seemed almost to whirl away in smoke. The children, small seeds, might at any instant be sown to all the Martian climes.[2]

The children looked up at him, as people look to the sun to tell what time of their life it is. His face was cold.

"What's wrong?" asked his wife.

"Let's get back on the rocket."

"Go back to Earth?"

"Yes! Listen!"

The wind blew as if to flake away their identities. At any moment the Martian air might draw his soul from him, as marrow comes from a white bone. He felt <u>submerged</u> in a chemical that could dissolve his intellect and burn away his past.

They looked at Martian hills that time had worn with a crushing pressure of years. They saw the old cities, lost in their meadows, lying like children's delicate bones among the blowing lakes of grass.

"Chin up, Harry," said his wife. "It's too late. We've come over sixty million miles."

The children with their yellow hair hollered at the deep dome of Martian sky. There was no answer but the racing hiss of wind through the stiff grass.

He picked up the luggage in his cold hands. "Here we go," he said—a man standing on the edge of a sea, ready to wade in and be drowned.

They walked into town.

---

1. **vacuum:** closed space with the air sucked out.
2. **climes:** regions.

Their name was Bittering. Harry and his wife, Cora; Dan, Laura, and David. They built a small white cottage and ate good breakfasts there, but the fear was never gone. It lay with Mr. Bittering and Mrs. Bittering, a third, unbidden partner at every midnight talk, at every dawn awakening.

"I feel like a salt crystal," he said, "in a mountain stream, being washed away. We don't belong here. We're Earth people. This is Mars. It was meant for Martians. For heaven's sake, Cora, let's buy tickets for home!"

But she only shook her head. "One day the atom bomb will fix Earth. Then we'll be safe here."

"Safe and insane!"

Tick-tock, seven o'clock, sang the voice-clock; *time to get up.* And they did.

Something made him check everything each morning—warm hearth, potted blood-geraniums—precisely as if he expected something to be <u>amiss</u>. The morning paper was toast-warm from the 6:00 A.M. Earth rocket. He broke its seal and tilted it at his breakfast place. He forced himself to be <u>convivial</u>.

"Colonial days all over again," he declared. "Why, in ten years there'll be a million Earthmen on Mars. Big cities, everything! They said we'd fail. Said the Martians would resent our invasion. But did we find any Martians? Not a living soul! Oh, we found their empty cities, but no one in them. Right?"

A river of wind submerged the house. When the windows <u>ceased</u> rattling, Mr. Bittering swallowed and looked at the children.

"I don't know," said David. "Maybe there're

WORDS TO OWN
interior (in·tir′ē·ər) *n.*: inside.
submerged (sub·murjd′) *v.* used as *adj.*: sunk; covered with liquid.
amiss (ə·mis′) *adj.*: wrong; improper.
convivial (kən·viv′ē·əl) *adj.*: sociable or friendly.
ceased (sēst) *v.*: stopped.

Reaching All Students

Struggling Readers

Monitoring Comprehension was introduced on p. 152. For a lesson directly tied to this selection that teaches students to monitor comprehension by using a strategy called Say Something, see the *Reading Skills and Strategies* binder:
• Selection Skill Lesson, p. 11

English Language Learners

Bradbury's use of figurative language and sophisticated vocabulary may make this selection challenging. Students might benefit from reading the story Round Robin–style, pausing often to discuss any difficult words or sentence structure. For additional strategies to supplement instruction for these students, see
• *Lesson Plans Including Strategies for English-Language Learners*

Advanced Learners

Have several students create an on-the-spot news broadcast, interviewing the Bitterings and other new arrivals about their expectations as they disembark. Group members, acting as anchor, interviewers, and Earthling arrivals, might present their "coverage" to the class.

Martians around we don't see. Sometimes nights I think I hear 'em. I hear the wind. The sand hits my window. I get scared. And I see those towns way up in the mountains where the Martians lived a long time ago. And I think I see things moving around those towns, Papa. And I wonder if those Martians *mind* us living here. I wonder if they won't do something to us for coming here."

"Nonsense!" Mr. Bittering looked out the windows. "We're clean, decent people." He looked at his children. "All dead cities have some kind of ghosts in them. Memories, I mean." He stared at the hills. "You see a staircase and you wonder what Martians looked like climbing it. You see Martian paintings and you wonder what the painter was like. You make a little ghost in your mind, a memory. It's quite natural. Imagination." He stopped. "You haven't been prowling up in those ruins, have you?"

"No, Papa." David looked at his shoes.

"See that you stay away from them. Pass the jam."

"Just the same," said little David, "I bet something happens."

Something happened that afternoon. Laura stumbled through the settlement, crying. She dashed blindly onto the porch.

"Mother, Father—the war, Earth!" she sobbed. "A radio flash just came. Atom bombs hit New York! All the space rockets blown up. No more rockets to Mars, ever!"

"Oh, Harry!" The mother held on to her husband and daughter.

"Are you sure, Laura?" asked the father quietly.

Laura wept. "We're stranded on Mars, forever and ever!"

For a long time there was only the sound of the wind in the late afternoon.

Alone, thought Bittering. *Only a thousand of us here. No way back. No way. No way.* Sweat poured from his face and his hands and his body; he was drenched in the hotness of his fear. He wanted to strike Laura, cry, "No, you're lying! The rockets will come back!" Instead, he stroked Laura's head against him and said, "The rockets will get through someday."

"Father, what will we do?"

"Go about our business, of course. Raise crops and children. Wait. Keep things going until the war ends and the rockets come again."

The two boys stepped out onto the porch.

"Children," he said, sitting there, looking beyond them, "I've something to tell you."

"We know," they said.

In the following days, Bittering wandered often through the garden to stand alone in his fear. As long as the rockets had spun a silver web across space, he had been able to accept Mars. For he had always told himself: *Tomorrow, if I want, I can buy a ticket and go back to Earth.*

But now: the web gone, the rockets lying in jigsaw heaps of molten girder[3] and unsnaked wire. Earth people left to the strangeness of Mars, the cinnamon dusts and wine airs, to be baked like gingerbread shapes in Martian summers, put into harvested storage by Martian winters. What would happen to him, the others? This was the moment Mars had waited for. Now it would eat them.

He got down on his knees in the flower bed, a spade in his nervous hands. *Work,* he thought, *work and forget.*

He glanced up from the garden to the Martian mountains. He thought of the proud old Martian names that had once been on those peaks. Earthmen, dropping from the sky, had gazed upon hills, rivers, Martian seas left nameless in spite of names. Once Martians had built cities, named cities; climbed mountains, named mountains; sailed seas, named seas.

---

3. **molten girder:** A girder is a metal beam that helps to support a framework; *molten* means "melted."

D Critical Thinking
Speculating
? Why does Harry dismiss his son's concerns? [Possible response: Harry may feel the same way as the son, but he doesn't want to worry him.]

E Elements of Literature
Character
? What does the contrast between Harry's thoughts and his actions tell you about him? [Possible responses: He is sensitive to the needs of his children; he is mature enough not to upset them by revealing his own fears.]

F Reading Skills and Strategies

Monitoring Comprehension
As the setting is about to change, ask students to review what they have read so far and voice any questions they may have about the setting or plot. Ask students whether they think they should slow their reading rate in order to understand the story better.

G Struggling Readers
Paraphrasing
Explain that Bradbury is using figurative language: He compares the rocket travel to a silver web; he compares the fate of the Earthlings on Mars to the baking of gingerbread shapes. Then, have students restate this passage in their own words. [Possible response: As long as regular rocket travel linked Mars and Earth, Bittering felt safe. Now he feels stranded in a dangerous place.]

Using Students' Strengths

Interpersonal Learners
As these students read the story, suggest that they keep a running list with two headings: *Why Most Colonists Want to Adapt to Martian Ways* and *Why Harry Bittering Wants to Keep Earthling Ways.* Ask students to use the chart to keep track of the story's developments, including the conflict between Harry Bittering and the other colonists.

Kinesthetic Learners
Encourage these students to dramatize segments of the story, using their voices to develop the tension between Bittering and the others.

Visual Learners
Students might draw some of the story's visually striking settings. They can also fill in the graphic organizer provided on p. 11 in the *Graphic Organizers for Active Reading.*

Mountains melted, seas drained, cities tumbled. In spite of this, the Earthmen had felt a silent guilt at putting new names to these ancient hills and valleys.

Nevertheless, man lives by symbol and label. The names were given.

Mr. Bittering felt very alone in his garden under the Martian sun, an <u>anachronism</u> bent here, planting Earth flowers in a wild soil.

Think. Keep thinking. Different things. Keep your mind free of Earth, the atom war, the lost rockets.

He perspired. He glanced about. No one watching. He removed his tie. *Pretty bold,* he thought. *First your coat off, now your tie.* He hung it neatly on a peach tree he had imported as a sapling from Massachusetts.

He returned to his philosophy of names and mountains. The Earthmen had changed names. Now there were Hormel Valleys, Roosevelt Seas, Ford Hills, Vanderbilt Plateaus, Rockefeller Rivers, on Mars. It wasn't right. The American settlers had shown wisdom, using old Indian prairie names: Wisconsin, Minnesota, Idaho, Ohio, Utah, Milwaukee, Waukegan, Osseo. The old names, the old meanings.

Staring at the mountains wildly, he thought: *Are you up there? All the dead ones, you Martians? Well, here we are, alone, cut off! Come down, move us out! We're helpless!*

The wind blew a shower of peach blossoms.

He put out his sun-browned hand, gave a small cry. He touched the blossoms, picked them up. He turned them, he touched them again and again. Then he shouted for his wife.

"Cora!"

She appeared at a window. He ran to her.

"Cora, these blossoms!"

She handled them.

"Do you see? They're different. They've changed! They're not peach blossoms any more!"

"Look all right to me," she said.

"They're not. They're *wrong!* I can't tell

how. An extra petal, a leaf, something, the color, the smell!"

The children ran out in time to see their father hurrying about the garden, pulling up radishes, onions, and carrots from their beds.

"Cora, come look!"

They handled the onions, the radishes, the carrots among them.

"Do they look like carrots?"

"Yes . . . no." She hesitated. "I don't know."

"They're changed."

"Perhaps."

"You know they have! Onions but not onions, carrots but not carrots. Taste: the same but different. Smell: not like it used to be." He felt his heart pounding, and he was afraid. He dug his fingers into the earth. "Cora, what's happening? What is it? We've got to get away from this." He ran across the garden. Each tree felt his touch. "The roses. The roses. They're turning green!"

And they stood looking at the green roses.

And two days later Dan came running. "Come see the cow. I was milking her and I saw it. Come on!"

They stood in the shed and looked at their one cow.

It was growing a third horn.

And the lawn in front of their house very quietly and slowly was coloring itself like spring violets. Seed from Earth but growing up a soft purple.

"We must get away," said Bittering. "We'll eat this stuff and then we'll change—who knows to what? I can't let it happen. There's only one thing to do. Burn this food!"

"It's not poisoned."

"But it is. Subtly, very subtly. A little bit. A very little bit. We mustn't touch it."

WORDS TO OWN

anachronism (ə·nak′rə·niz′əm) *n.:* something out of its proper time in history, like a television in the Middle Ages or penicillin in ancient Rome.

LITERATURE AND SCIENCE

Live from Mars

Mars is called the red planet because its surface is covered with red dust. The strong Martian winds create huge dust storms. Depending on how much dust is in the air, the Martian sky ranges from pink on a clear day to purple on a stormy one. People associate the color red with fury. This may be why Mars was named after the Roman god of war.

About "The Naming of Names" Bradbury says, "I charted my own Mars and went through a naming of names, building cities and towns, and creating a wild and special new world." In fact, the real Mars is so cold and has so little oxygen and water that humans could not survive there without special equipment. Its atmosphere consists mainly of carbon dioxide, and the average temperature near the planet's surface is an icy −80°F.

In the nineteenth century, astronomers noticed what looked like canals on the surface of Mars. They wondered if intelligent beings had dug these trenches. Scientists now know that the "canals" are actually the outlines of large craters. Still, evidence from a recently discovered 4.5-billion-year-old meteorite suggests that life (in the form of tiny, single-celled organisms) may have existed on Mars billions of years ago.

Mars continues to fascinate scientists. In 1996, NASA sent two spacecraft to Mars. The first, the Mars Pathfinder, landed on Mars on July 4, 1997. The second, the Mars Global Surveyor, reached Mars's orbit about two months later. Future missions will study the climate, terrain, and water conditions. Scientists are planning for the next step in the exploration of the planet: As early as 2020, humans may be landing on Mars!

He looked with dismay at their house. "Even the house. The wind's done something to it. The air's burned it. The fog at night. The boards, all warped out of shape. It's not an Earthman's house anymore."

"Oh, your imagination!"

He put on his coat and tie. "I'm going into town. We've got to do something now. I'll be back."

"Wait, Harry!" his wife cried.
But he was gone.

In town, on the shadowy step of the grocery store, the men sat with their hands on their knees, conversing with great leisure and ease.

Mr. Bittering wanted to fire a pistol in the air.
What are you doing, you fools! he thought. *Sitting here! You've heard the news—we're stranded on this planet. Well, move! Aren't you frightened? Aren't you afraid? What are you going to do?*

"Hello, Harry," said everyone.

"Look," he said to them. "You did hear the news, the other day, didn't you?"

They nodded and laughed. "Sure. Sure, Harry."

"What are you going to do about it?"

"Do, Harry, do? What *can* we do?"

THE NAMING OF NAMES 157

Getting Students Involved

"Build a rocket, that's what!"

"A rocket, Harry? To go back to all that trouble? Oh, Harry!"

"But you *must* want to go back. Have you noticed the peach blossoms, the onions, the grass?"

"Why, yes, Harry, seems we did," said one of the men.

"Doesn't it scare you?"

"Can't recall that it did much, Harry."

"Idiots!"

"Now, Harry."

Bittering wanted to cry. "You've got to work with me. If we stay here, we'll all change. The air. Don't you smell it? Something in the air. A Martian virus, maybe; some seed, or a pollen. Listen to me!"

They stared at him.

"Sam," he said to one of them.

"Yes, Harry?"

"Will you help me build a rocket?"

"Harry, I got a whole load of metal and some blueprints. You want to work in my metal shop on a rocket, you're welcome. I'll sell you that metal for five hundred dollars. You should be able to construct a right pretty rocket, if you work alone, in about thirty years."

Everyone laughed.

"Don't laugh."

Sam looked at him with quiet good humor.

"Sam," Bittering said. "Your eyes——"

"What about them, Harry?"

"Didn't they used to be gray?"

"Well, now, I don't remember."

"They were, weren't they?"

"Why do you ask, Harry?"

"Because now they're kind of yellow-colored."

"Is that so, Harry?" Sam said, casually.

"And you're taller and thinner——"

"You might be right, Harry."

"Sam, you shouldn't have yellow eyes."

"Harry, what color eyes have *you* got?" Sam said.

"My eyes? They're blue, of course."

"Here you are, Harry." Sam handed him a pocket mirror. "Take a look at yourself."

Mr. Bittering hesitated and then raised the mirror to his face.

There were little, very dim flecks of new gold captured in the blue of his eyes.

"Now look what you've done," said Sam a moment later. "You've broken my mirror."

Harry Bittering moved into the metal shop and began to build the rocket. Men stood in the open door and talked and joked without raising their voices. Once in a while they gave him a hand on lifting something. But mostly they just idled and watched him with their yellowing eyes.

"It's supper time, Harry," they said.

His wife appeared with his supper in a wicker basket.

"I won't touch it," he said. "I'll eat only food from our deep freezer. Food that came from Earth. Nothing from our garden."

His wife stood watching him. "You can't build a rocket."

"I worked in a shop once, when I was twenty. I know metal. Once I get it started, the others will help," he said, not looking at her, laying out the blueprints.

"Harry, Harry," she said, helplessly.

"We've got to get away, Cora. We've *got* to!"

The nights were full of wind that blew down the empty moonlit sea meadows past the little white chess cities lying for their twelve-thousandth year in the shallows. In the Earthmen's settlement, the Bittering house shook with a feeling of change.

Lying abed, Mr. Bittering felt his bones shifted, shaped, melted like gold. His wife, lying beside him, was dark from many sunny afternoons. Dark she was, and golden-eyed, burnt almost black by the sun, sleeping, and the children metallic in their beds, and the wind

---

Professional Notes

roaring forlorn and changing through the old peach trees, the violet grass, shaking out green rose petals.

The fear would not be stopped. It had his throat and heart. It dripped in a wetness of the arm and the temple and the trembling palm.

A green star rose in the east.

A strange word emerged from Mr. Bittering's lips.

"Iorrt. Iorrt." He repeated it.

It was a Martian word. He knew no Martian.

In the middle of the night he arose and dialed a call through to Simpson, the archaeologist.

"Simpson, what does the word *Iorrt* mean?"

"Why, that's the old Martian word for our planet Earth. Why?"

"No special reason."

The telephone slipped from his hand.

"Hello, hello, hello, hello," it kept saying while he sat gazing out at the green star. "Bittering? Harry, are you there?"

The days were full of metal sound. He laid the frame of the rocket with the reluctant help of three indifferent men. He grew very tired in an hour or so and had to sit down.

"The altitude," laughed a man.

"Are you *eating,* Harry?" asked another.

"I'm eating," he said, angrily.

"From your deep freezer?"

"Yes!"

"You're getting thinner, Harry."

"I'm not!"

"And taller."

"Liar!"

His wife took him aside a few days later. "Harry, I've used up all the food in the deep freezer. There's nothing left. I'll have to make sandwiches using food grown on Mars."

He sat down heavily.

"You must eat," she said. "You're weak."

"Yes," he said.

He took a sandwich, opened it, looked at it, and began to nibble at it.

"And take the rest of the day off," she said. "It's hot. The children want to swim in the canals and hike. Please come along."

"I can't waste time. This is a crisis!"

"Just for an hour," she urged. "A swim'll do you good."

He rose, sweating. "All right, all right. Leave me alone. I'll come."

"Good for you, Harry."

The sun was hot, the day quiet. There was only an immense staring burn upon the land. They moved along the canal, the father, the mother, the racing children in their swimsuits. They stopped and ate meat sandwiches. He saw their skin baking brown. And he saw the yellow eyes of his wife and his children, their eyes that were never yellow before. A few tremblings shook him but were carried off in waves of pleasant heat as he lay in the sun. He was too tired to be afraid.

"Cora, how long have your eyes been yellow?"

She was bewildered. "Always, I guess."

"They didn't change from brown in the last three months?"

She bit her lips. "No. Why do you ask?"

"Never mind."

They sat there.

"The children's eyes," he said. "They're yellow, too."

"Sometimes growing children's eyes change color."

"Maybe *we're* children, too. At least to Mars. That's a thought." He laughed. "Think I'll swim."

They leaped into the canal water, and he let himself sink down and down to the bottom like a golden statue and lie there in green silence. All was water-quiet and deep, all was

- -
WORDS TO OWN
forlorn (fôr·lôrn′) *adj.*: hopeless. *Forlorn* may also mean "deserted" or "abandoned."
- -

E **Appreciating Language**
Word Choice
❓ How does the introduction of a Martian word add interest and tension to the story? [Possible response: It is an eye-catching and concrete way to show that Bittering is becoming a Martian.]

F **Reading Skills and Strategies**

Monitoring Comprehension
Students might stop and monitor their comprehension. Ask them to describe the changes in Bittering and how they advance the story. [Possible response: He first notices changes in others, but he refuses to adapt to the changing environment. Finally, he himself begins to change.]

G **Elements of Literature**
Character
❓ Why can't Cora remember that her eyes were brown just a few months ago? [Possible response: As they become Martians, the characters lose their Earthling identities and forget the past.]

H **Critical Thinking**
Analyzing
❓ Why does Bittering suddenly laugh and suggest they are all children on Mars? [Possible responses: He is becoming too tired to fight; he is changing like the others.]

Taking a Second Look

Review: Comparing and Contrasting
Remind students that when they compare things, they look for ways in which they are alike. When they contrast things, they look for ways in which they are different. As an example, have students recall the contrasting features of the cow on Earth and on Mars (p. 156). [On Earth the cow had two horns; on Mars, it grows a third horn.]

Activities
1. Ask students to contrast the appearance of Cora Bittering on Earth with her appearance on Mars. [Possible responses: On Mars her skin is much darker; her eyes are golden, not brown; her body has lengthened; she seems more youthful.]

2. Students can contrast Harry Bittering's attitude toward Mars at the beginning of the story with the way he feels at the end. [Possible response: He is uncomfortable on Mars at first and suspicious of the effects of Mars on him; by the end of the story, he accepts the changes it has worked in him and appreciates the more relaxed life.]

A Elements of Literature

Setting

❓ What does this description indicate about changes in Bittering's attitude toward the Martian environment? [Possible responses: He is accepting the environment; he begins to view the changes in a positive light.]

B Appreciating Language

Word Choice

❓ How does Harry's use of *submerged* here differ from the narrator's use of *submerge* on p. 154? [Possible response: On his arrival on Mars, Harry felt that he would dissolve in the Martian atmosphere. Now, as he sees the sky and the sun "made Martian," Harry recognizes that, by changing, he will become part of the natural environment.]

C Appreciating Language

Punctuation

❓ Why are there double quotation marks here? [The quotation marks surround the boy's exact words.] Why are there single quotation marks around *father*? [Single quotation marks are used inside double quotation marks. The quotation marks surround a word discussed as a word.]

peace. He felt the steady, slow current drift him easily.

[A] *If I lie here long enough,* he thought, *the water will work and eat away my flesh until the bones show like coral. Just my skeleton left. And then the water can build on that skeleton—green things, deep-water things, red things, yellow things. Change. Change. Slow, deep, silent change. And isn't that what it is up* there?

[B] He saw the sky submerged above him, the sun made Martian by atmosphere and time and space.

Up there, a big river, he thought, *a Martian river, all of us lying deep in it, in our pebble houses, in our sunken boulder houses, like crayfish hidden, and the water washing away our old bodies and lengthening the bones and——*

He let himself drift up through the soft light.

Dan sat on the edge of the canal, regarding his father seriously.

"*Utha,*" he said.

"What?" asked his father.

[C] The boy smiled. "You know. *Utha*'s the Martian word for 'father.'"

"Where did you learn it?"

"I don't know. Around. *Utha!*"

160 Who Am I?

Skill Link

Catching Misplaced Modifiers

When students revise sentences, they should be on the lookout for misplaced modifiers—words, phrases, and clauses that are in the wrong place. Write this sentence on the chalkboard: The Earthlings give the rivers names that they find on Mars. Which word does the clause "that they find on Mars" modify? [*rivers*] How should the sentence be revised to put this clause beside the word it modifies? [The Earthlings give names to the rivers that they find on Mars.]

Activity

Have students revise these sentences to remove the misplaced modifier. (Possible responses are given.)

1. Bittering thinks about the Martian names of the mountains standing in his garden. [Standing in his garden, Bittering thinks about the Martian names of the mountains.]

2. A radio flash about the bombs from New York is heard on Mars. [A radio flash from New York about the bombs is heard on Mars.]

3. Bittering notices how his friends are changing in the Earthlings' settlement. [Bittering notices how his friends in the Earthlings' settlement are changing.]

4. What names will the new colonists give the mountains from Earth? [What names will the new colonists from Earth give the mountains?]

"What do you want?"

The boy hesitated. "I—I want to change my name."

"Change it?"

"Yes."

His mother swam over. "What's wrong with Dan for a name?"

Dan fidgeted. "The other day you called Dan, Dan, Dan. I didn't even hear. I said to myself, that's not my name. I've a new name I want to use."

Mr. Bittering held to the side of the canal, his body cold and his heart pounding slowly. "What is this new name?"

"Linnl. Isn't that a good name? Can I use it? Can't I, please?"

Mr. Bittering put his hand to his head. He thought of the silly rocket, himself working alone, himself alone even among his family, so alone.

He heard his wife say, "Why not?"

He heard himself say, "Yes, you can use it."

"Yaaa!" screamed the boy. "I'm Linnl, Linnl!"

Racing down the meadowlands, he danced and shouted.

Mr. Bittering looked at his wife. "Why did we do that?"

"I don't know," she said. "It just seemed like a good idea."

They walked into the hills. They strolled on old mosaic[4] paths, beside still-pumping fountains. The paths were covered with a thin film of cool water all summer long. You kept your bare feet cool all the day, splashing as in a creek, wading.

They came to a small deserted Martian villa with a good view of the valley. It was on top of a hill. Blue marble halls, large murals, a swimming pool. It was refreshing in this hot summertime. The Martians hadn't believed in large cities.

"How nice," said Mrs. Bittering, "if we could

---

4. **mosaic** (mō·zā′ik): made of small pieces of colored glass, stone, and so on.

---

move up here to this villa for the summer."

"Come on," he said. "We're going back to town. There's work to be done on the rocket."

But as he worked that night, the thought of the cool blue marble villa entered his mind. As the hours passed, the rocket seemed less important.

In the flow of days and weeks, the rocket receded and dwindled. The old fever was gone. It frightened him to think he had let it slip this way. But somehow the heat, the air, the working conditions——

He heard the men murmuring on the porch of his metal shop.

"Everyone's going. You heard?"

"All going. That's right."

Bittering came out. "Going where?" He saw a couple of trucks, loaded with children and furniture, drive down the dusty street.

"Up to the villas," said the man.

"Yeah, Harry. I'm going. So is Sam. Aren't you, Sam?"

"That's right, Harry. What about you?"

"I've got work to do here."

"Work! You can finish that rocket in the autumn, when it's cooler."

He took a breath. "I got the frame all set up."

"In the autumn is better." Their voices were lazy in the heat.

"Got to work," he said.

"Autumn," they reasoned. And they sounded so sensible, so right.

Autumn would be best, he thought. *Plenty of time, then.*

No! cried part of himself, deep down, put away, locked tight, suffocating. *No! No!*

"In the autumn," he said.

"Come on, Harry," they all said.

"Yes," he said, feeling his flesh melt in the

D Critical Thinking
Making Connections

? How is Dan's reaction to his new name similar to or different from that of Julia in "Names/Nombres" (p. 145)? [Possible responses: Just as Julia wants to be accepted by her friends and likes her American identity, Dan wants to feel that he has become a part of his new home. Unlike Julia, who can communicate with her new friends, Dan has only a vague feeling that he should change.]

E Reading Skills and Strategies

Monitoring Comprehension

Ask students to reread passages on pp. 159–161 that show how Harry's feelings about Mars have changed during his picnic in the Martian hills. [Possible responses: As he lies underwater, he begins to accept change. He also allows Dan to become Linnl; he finds the Martian villa lovely and the rocket projector less important.]

F Critical Thinking
Challenging the Text

? Do you think Bittering's gradual acceptance of Mars is good or bad? [Possible responses: His acceptance is good, since life on Mars seems relaxed, and the other Earthlings have accepted the new environment. His acceptance is bad, because dangerous changes could occur.]

Listening to Music

The Planets, by Gustav Holst

Gustav Holst (1874–1934), who grew up in England, wanted to be an organist but turned to the trombone because of a physical ailment that affected his hands. *The Planets,* his best-known work as a composer, contains seven parts: Mars, the Bringer of War; Venus, the Bringer of Peace; Mercury, the Winged Messenger; Jupiter, the Bringer of Jollity; Saturn, the Bringer of Old Age; Uranus, the Magician; and Neptune, the Mystic.

(Pluto, discovered in 1930, and Earth are not included.)

Activity

Have students listen to passages from Mars, the Bringer of War, and other sections. List on the chalkboard Holst's full names for all seven sections. Ask students to guess to which planet each musical passage refers. The class can discuss how the music suggests each planet's characterization.

A Elements of Literature

Setting

❓ By using the old names, what attitudes toward Mars do the Earthlings show? [Possible responses: Using these names shows respect for their new home; instead of imposing their culture on Mars, they are accepting Martian values.]

B Reading Skills and Strategies

Making Predictions

❓ Do you think the Bitterings will come back for their furniture and encyclopedia? [Possible responses: No, they are gradually shedding their ties to Earth; they are changing in ways that make these possessions unnecessary.]

C Advanced Learners

Similes

❓ What does the comparison between the swinging rubber tires and the pendulum of a stopped clock suggest? [Possible responses: The Martian setting has a certain timelessness to it; time as we know it on Earth does not exist on Mars.]

---

hot liquid air. "Yes, in the autumn. I'll begin work again then."

A "I got a villa near the Tirra Canal," said someone.

"You mean the Roosevelt Canal, don't you?"

"Tirra. The old Martian name."

"But on the map——"

"Forget the map. It's Tirra now. Now I found a place in the Pillan mountains——"

"You mean the Rockefeller range," said Bittering.

"I mean the Pillan mountains," said Sam.

"Yes," said Bittering, buried in the hot, swarming air. "The Pillan mountains."

Everyone worked at loading the truck in the hot, still afternoon of the next day.

Laura, Dan, and David carried packages. Or, as they preferred to be known, Ttil, Linnl, and Werr carried packages.

The furniture was abandoned in the little white cottage.

B "It looked just fine in Boston," said the mother. "And here in the cottage. But up at the villa? No. We'll get it when we come back in the autumn."

Bittering himself was quiet.

"I've some ideas on furniture for the villa," he said after a time. "Big, lazy furniture."

"What about your encyclopedia? You're taking it along, surely?"

Mr. Bittering glanced away. "I'll come and get it next week."

They turned to their daughter. "What about your New York dresses?"

The bewildered girl stared. "Why, I don't want them anymore."

They shut off the gas, the water; they locked the doors and walked away. Father peered into the truck.

"Gosh, we're not taking much," he said. "Considering all we brought to Mars, this is only a handful!"

He started the truck.

Looking at the small white cottage for a long moment, he was filled with a desire to rush to it, touch it, say goodbye to it, for he felt as if he were going away on a long journey, leaving something to which he could never quite return, never understand again.

Just then Sam and his family drove by in another truck.

"Hi, Bittering! Here we go!"

The truck swung down the ancient highway out of town. There were sixty others traveling the same direction. The town filled with a silent, heavy dust from their passage. The canal waters lay blue in the sun, and a quiet wind moved in the strange trees.

"Goodbye, town!" said Mr. Bittering.

"Goodbye, goodbye," said the family, waving to it.

They did not look back again.

C Summer burned the canals dry. Summer moved like flame upon the meadows. In the empty Earth settlement, the painted houses flaked and peeled. Rubber tires upon which children had swung in backyards hung suspended like stopped clock pendulums[5] in the blazing air.

At the metal shop, the rocket frame began to rust.

In the quiet autumn Mr. Bittering stood, very dark now, very golden-eyed, upon the slope above his villa, looking at the valley.

"It's time to go back," said Cora.

"Yes, but we're not going," he said quietly. "There's nothing there anymore."

"Your books," she said. "Your fine clothes."

"Your *Illes* and your fine *ior uele rre*," she said.

"The town's empty. No one's going back," he said. "There's no reason to, none at all."

The daughter wove tapestries and the sons

---

5. **pendulums** (pen′dyōo·ləmz): hanging weights that swing back and forth; used to regulate the movement of old-fashioned clocks.

Making the Connections

Connecting to the Theme: "Who Am I?"

When students have finished the story, bring up the theme question, "Who am I?" Ask volunteers to suggest how Harry Bittering might have answered the question at the beginning of the story, in the middle, and at the end. Suggest that students focus on Harry's interests, conflicts, and appearance at each point in the story. Students might create a chart like the one at right to list and share their responses.

Who Is Harry Bittering?

	Beginning	Middle	End
Interests			
Conflicts			
Appearance			

played songs on ancient flutes and pipes, their laughter echoing in the marble villa.

Mr. Bittering gazed at the Earth settlement far away in the low valley. "Such odd, such ridiculous houses the Earth people built."

"They didn't know any better," his wife mused. "Such ugly people. I'm glad they've gone."

They both looked at each other, startled by all they had just finished saying. They laughed.

"Where did they go?" he wondered. He glanced at his wife. She was golden and slender as his daughter. She looked at him, and he seemed almost as young as their eldest son.

"I don't know," she said.

"We'll go back to town maybe next year, or the year after, or the year after that," he said, calmly. "Now—I'm warm. How about taking a swim?"

They turned their backs to the valley. Arm in arm they walked silently down a path of clear-running spring water.

F ive years later a rocket fell out of the sky. It lay steaming in the valley. Men leaped out of it, shouting.

"We won the war on Earth! We're here to rescue you! Hey!"

But the American-built town of cottages, peach trees, and theaters was silent. They found a flimsy rocket frame rusting in an empty shop.

The rocket men searched the hills. The captain established headquarters in an abandoned bar. His lieutenant came back to report.

"The town's empty, but we found native life in the hills, sir. Dark people. Yellow eyes. Martians. Very friendly. We talked a bit, not much. They learn English fast. I'm sure our relations will be most friendly with them, sir."

"Dark, eh?" mused the captain. "How many?"

"Six, eight hundred, I'd say, living in those marble ruins in the hills, sir. Tall, healthy. Beautiful women."

"Did they tell you what became of the men and women who built this Earth settlement, Lieutenant?"

"They hadn't the foggiest notion of what happened to this town or its people."

"Strange. You think those Martians killed them?"

"They look surprisingly peaceful. Chances are a plague[6] did this town in, sir."

"Perhaps. I suppose this is one of those mysteries we'll never solve. One of those mysteries you read about."

The captain looked at the room, the dusty windows, the blue mountains rising beyond, the canals moving in the light, and he heard the soft wind in the air. He shivered. Then, recovering, he tapped a large fresh map he had thumbtacked to the top of an empty table.

"Lots to be done, Lieutenant." His voice droned on and quietly on as the sun sank behind the blue hills. "New settlements. Mining sites, minerals to be looked for. Bacteriological specimens taken. The work, all the work. And the old records were lost. We'll have a job of remapping to do, renaming the mountains and rivers and such. Calls for a little imagination.

"What do you think of naming those mountains the Lincoln Mountains, this canal the Washington Canal, those hills—we can name those hills for you, Lieutenant. Diplomacy. And you, for a favor, might name a town for me. Polishing the apple. And why not make this the Einstein Valley, and further over . . . are you *listening*, Lieutenant?"

The lieutenant snapped his gaze from the blue color and the quiet mist of the hills far beyond the town.

"What? Oh, *yes*, sir!"

6. **plague:** deadly disease that spreads quickly.

- -

WORDS TO OWN

flimsy (flim′zē) *adj.*: poorly made; easily broken or damaged.

- -

D Critical Thinking
Determining Author's Purpose
⁇ What view of life on Mars does Ray Bradbury present? [Possible response: He creates a carefree society in which people remain young and find satisfaction in beauty, music, and laughter.]

E Reading Skills and Strategies

Monitoring Comprehension
Have students voice any questions they have about the story so far. Ask volunteers to find and read aloud passages that answer these questions.

F Struggling Readers
Identifying Pronoun Antecedents
⁇ Often a pronoun and its antecedent are in the same sentence. Sometimes you have to infer what the antecedent is. Whom does *you* refer to? [It refers to the Bitterings and other Earthlings, who came to Mars earlier and were stranded there by the war on Earth.]

G Reading Skills and Strategies
Making Predictions
⁇ What do you think will happen to the new settlers? [Possible response: They, too, will adopt Martian ways.]

H Elements of Literature
Setting
⁇ How does gazing at the surrounding hills affect the lieutenant? [Possible response: He is already becoming attracted to life on Mars.]

Taking a Second Look

Review: Describing Mental Images
Remind students that strategic readers form mental images, or pictures, from descriptions of characters and events.

Activities
1. Have students reread the description of the deserted colony in summer (p. 162, at "Summer burned . . ."). As they visualize the scene, ask students to describe what senses it appeals to. Also, invite students to discuss how the setting advances the story. [Possible response: It shows that the Earthlings have completely abandoned their original settlement.]

2. Ask volunteers to turn to other descriptions in the story that appeal to their senses, and have them share the images they visualize.

MEET THE WRITER

Extra! Extra! Shouting Stories Bite Writer on Leg!

Ray Bradbury (1920–   ) decided at the age of twelve to become a writer. He credits this decision to a circus performer called Mr. Electrico. Bradbury recalls one performance:

> Mr. Electrico twitched his blazing sword. He touched me on the right shoulder, the left shoulder, and then gently on my brow and the tip of my nose. I felt the storms jiggling in my eardrums, the blue fire swarming into my brain and down my arms and out my fingertips. . . .

Bradbury went home and shortly afterward began to write.

Eventually Bradbury enjoyed great success with works such as *Fahrenheit 451* (1951) (the title refers to the temperature at which book paper burns), *Dandelion Wine* (1957), *Something Wicked This Way Comes* (1983) (its main character is based on Mr. Electrico), and *The Martian Chronicles* (1958).

In writing about Mars, Bradbury says:

> I have always looked on myself as some sort of Martian. . . . Some twenty-three years ago, I wrote a strange tale entitled 'Dark They Were, and Golden-Eyed' [another title for 'The Naming of Names']. In that Martian story, I told of a man and his family who helped colonize Mars, who eat of its foods and live in its strange seasons, and stay on when everyone else goes back to Earth, until the day finally comes when they find that the odd weathers and peculiar temperatures of the Red Planet have melted their flesh into new shapes, tinted their skin, and put flecks of gold into their now most fantastic eyes, and they move up into the hills to live in old ruins and become—Martians. Which is the history I predict for us on that far world. The ruins may not be there. But if necessary we will *build* the ruins, and live in them and name them ourselves as my

transplanted Earthmen did. And will not be of Earth anymore but will truly be Martians.

Bradbury has been called the "world's greatest science fiction writer," but he thinks of himself as an "idea writer." Of the products of his ideas Bradbury says:

> My stories have led me through my life. They shout, I follow. They run up and bite me on the leg—I respond by writing down everything that goes on during the bite. When I finish, the idea lets go, and runs off.

Bite into a Bradbury

Catch up on more of Ray Bradbury's stories by sampling some of his short-story collections. In collections such as *The Illustrated Man* (Bantam), *R Is for Rocket* (Bantam), and *The Stories of Ray Bradbury* (Knopf), you'll find popular stories like "Mars Is Heaven," "The Sound of Summer Running," and "The Flying Machine."

Assessing Learning

Check Test: Short Answer
1. What two planets are involved in this story? [Earth and Mars]
2. Why have the settlers come to a new planet? [to escape the threat of nuclear war]
3. What happens to the Earthlings' eyes? [They become yellow.]
4. What does Harry want to build? [a rocket]
5. Who comes to check on the settlers? [More Earthlings come.]

Standardized Test Preparation
For practice with standardized test format specific to this selection, see
• *Standardized Test Preparation,* p. 32
For practice in proofreading and editing, see
• *Daily Oral Grammar,* Transparency 11

MAKING MEANINGS

First Thoughts

[respond]

1. Does the life on Mars appeal to you or scare you? Would you want to stay on Mars—or get back to Earth?

Shaping Interpretations

[interpret]

2. Why do you think Harry Bittering resists change so fiercely? Do you think Bradbury wants us to admire Harry's resistance or to think it's foolish?

[analyze]

3. How does the **setting,** especially the Martian wind, affect the Earth people? Think of how it changes their attitudes and their identities.

[infer]

4. What **inferences,** or guesses, can you make about the fate of the original Martians who lived in the villas? (Look for clues in the first few paragraphs of the story.)

[analyze]

5. Which group—the Martians or the Earth people—do you think Bradbury likes better, and what are his reasons?

Connecting with the Text

[connect]

6. Do you think it's good for newcomers to a society or culture to change their ways? Should they try to hold on to their old ways of doing things instead? Explain.

Extending the Text

[predict]

7. What do you predict will happen to the lieutenant who arrives on Mars at the end of the story?

Challenging the Text

[evaluate]

8. At one point the **title** of this story was "Dark They Were, and Golden-Eyed." Why do you think Bradbury changed it to "The Naming of Names"? Which title do you think is more interesting?

[monitor]

 9. Did your understanding break down at any point as you read this story? If so, what did you do to get back on track? If you could write to Ray Bradbury about the way his story is written, what would you say?

THE NAMING OF NAMES **165**

Reading Check

Suppose that Harry Bittering kept a journal on Mars. Write the entries he might have made about these **main events:**

a. how he feels when he first looks around the Martian landscape

b. what changes he notices in things and people

c. why he begins to build a rocket

d. what he does and thinks during the picnic by the canal

e. what he thinks when he leaves for the Martian villa

f. why he decides not to go back to the town

Reading Check

Entries should include Bittering's feelings and evidence from the story.

a. feelings of fear and discomfort

b. eyes becoming yellow, people growing taller and darker, and animals and vegetables changing shape and color

c. to return to Earth before he changes

d. He swims, relaxes, and thinks of change, but the rocket seems less important.

e. He realizes that he will never again understand life in town.

f. There is nothing there that he needs in order to survive.

MAKING MEANINGS

First Thoughts

1. Reasons for staying include a sense of freedom and an opportunity for exploration. Reasons for leaving include homesickness, isolation, and fear of the unknown.

Shaping Interpretations

2. Perhaps Harry fears losing his identity. Bradbury may want us to admire Bittering because he is independent and yet learns to change.

3. The Martian wind seems to change their identities and values. Also, the air is described as being different shades of red, and this color may affect the way Earthlings see things.

4. The original Martians may all have drifted away to other areas. The description of the wind suggests that the Martians have been blown away.

5. Bradbury may like the Martians better. He describes them as beautiful and peaceful. Yet he shows the Earthlings as becoming more reasonable, since they adapt to their new environment.

Connecting with the Text

6. Students may suggest that it is good for newcomers to fit in, to get along with others, and to find work. Holding on to some of their traditions allows them to keep part of their original identities, too.

Extending the Text

7. He, too, may become a Martian; or he may try to take over the land occupied by the new Martians.

Challenging the Text

8. Bradbury may have changed the title to emphasize the importance, to the colonists, of place names and to deemphasize the physical changes the Earthlings undergo.

9. Students should note that when comprehension breaks down, it's helpful to reread a difficult paragraph aloud, ask questions, and use reference aids, such as dictionaries and encyclopedias. In a letter to Bradbury, students might admire the way he shows the gradual influences of the Martian environment on the Earthlings.

Grading Timesaver

Rubrics for each Choices assignment appear on p. 119 in the *Portfolio Management System*.

CHOICES: Building Your Portfolio

1. Writer's Notebook Remind students to save their work. They may use it as prewriting for the Writer's Workshop on p. 182. Have students list features of a setting that made them feel uncomfortable.

2. Research/Science Have students prepare a double-entry journal. In the left column, labeled "Bradbury's Mars," students should write down details about Mars from the story. Then, in the right column, "The Real Mars," students can provide facts from the Literature and Science box. Students should indicate whether the details support or contradict Bradbury's depiction.

3. Creative Writing/Science Allow students to work with partners on the activity. One partner should research a chosen planet, and the other partner should write the fictional description.

4. Mapping/Speaking Have students work in groups to brainstorm names based on appearances or functions. For example, the mall could be called the "Shop Stop" and the university, the "Pay and Learn."

5. Art Be sure that students have an idea of what the Bitterings might be like. Have students reread the story and any notes they took during reading for clues about the Bitterings' appearance and attitudes.

CHOICES: Building Your Portfolio

Writer's Notebook

1. Collecting Ideas for an Autobiographical Incident

Details of his new home—the weird Martian wind, green roses, the strange-tasting vegetables—give Mr. Bittering the creeps. Like him, we've all spent time in places that unsettle us. Describe a real **setting** that you disliked or that made you feel strange. Begin with **sensory details** that tell what you saw, smelled, heard, felt, or tasted in that place.

My fifth-grade classroom:
—gross smell of wet wool in coat closet
—towers of dusty textbooks
—annoying buzz of fluorescent lights

Research/Science

2. Get Real

Suppose you read this story aloud to a third-grader. She decides to report on Mars to her science class, and now she thinks Mars is exactly like Bradbury's fantasy. Help her out. Look back at the information about Mars on page 157. **Compare and contrast** each fact with events from the story. Make a chart listing all the contradictions you find.

Creative Writing/Science

3. Once upon a Planet . . .

Take another planet in our solar system, and describe it as the **setting** for a fantasy. Before you write, create a science data sheet for your planet. Focus on details like climate, atmosphere, colors, and physical features.

Mapping/Speaking

4. Name That Dune

Pretend you have just conquered your region. You have decided to put your mark on this territory by choosing new names. First, review your notes for the Quickwrite on page 152. Then, choose names for other places in the area—geographical features, towns, roads, universities, malls. Show your classmates a map with your new names in place, and explain the reasoning behind your choices.

Art

5. Martian Makeover

Imagine you're the art director of a team making a film of "The Naming of Names." First, you must decide how to present the Bitterings as typical Americans newly arrived from Earth. Then, you will choose makeup, costumes, and special effects to show their transformation, or **metamorphosis,** into Martians. Draw "before" and "after" pictures of the family to show the changes you imagine. Label each set of drawings to call attention to particularly important details of each character's costumes, makeup, and special effects.

Systematic Word Study Across Content Areas and in Current Events

After students have completed the vocabulary activity on using glossaries and dictionaries (see p. 167), encourage them to create their own vocabulary logs of words they discover in newspapers, magazines, and on-line. Students may want to compile specialized logs for specific content areas, such as science and social studies, with words they encounter in reading about current events.

Entries should include a pronunciation and definition of each word and a sentence that uses the word correctly. Recommend that students add fifteen words a week to their logs, and encourage them to share their entries with the class. Consider keeping your own log as a model for the class.

GRAMMAR LINK `MINI-LESSON`

Language Handbook HELP

See Placement of Modifiers, pages 739-741.

• All Modifiers! Places, Please!

To work well, modifiers have to be in the right place. Here's an example of a **misplaced modifier:**

> Today I read a story about a Martian settlement that disappeared in my literature book.

Did the settlement disappear into the book? No, the phrase *in my literature book* is misplaced. To fix the sentence, place the modifier as close as possible to the word it modifies—*story.*

> Today I read a story <u>in my literature book</u> about a Martian settlement that disappeared.

Try It Out

➤Move the misplaced modifier in each sentence to the right place.

1. The picnic is a key scene in this story beside the canal.

2. The lieutenant saw people in the villas named Linnl and Ttil.

3. I almost understood every word of the story.

VOCABULARY `HOW TO OWN A WORD`

WORD BANK •

interior
submerged
amiss
convivial
ceased
anachronism
forlorn
receded
dwindled
flimsy

Using Glossaries and Dictionaries

A **glossary** is an alphabetical list of difficult words used in a book, along with their definitions. A glossary usually gives only meanings that apply to the way the words are used in the book. Look at the glossary for this book (pages 789–796). Besides the definition, what information about each word can you find? For more information on a word, you need to look in a **dictionary.** Many dictionaries give the **derivation** (or **etymology**) of words, the origins of the words and their parts. At the back or front of the dictionary, you'll find a list of definitions for symbols and abbreviations used in the derivations. One important symbol is <, which means "comes from." To indicate that the derivation of a word or word part is unknown, the symbols < ? are used.

Here is a word map for the word *interior.* Make similar word maps, using the same labels, for three other words from the Word Bank.

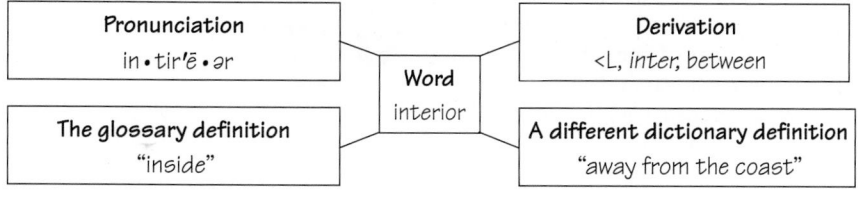

Pronunciation		Derivation
in • tir′ē • ər	**Word** interior	<L, *inter,* between
The glossary definition "inside"		**A different dictionary definition** "away from the coast"

Grammar Link Quick Check

Rewrite the following sentences by correcting the placement of the modifying phrases. (Possible answers are given.)

1. The Bittering family had a picnic hoping to cheer up Harry. [Hoping to cheer up Harry, the Bittering family had a picnic.]

2. Harry decided to build a rocket wanting to return to Earth. [Wanting to return to Earth, Harry decided to build a rocket.]

3. The lieutenant thought of the other Earthlings who arrived after the settlers. [The lieutenant, who arrived after the settlers, thought of the other Earthlings.]

4. Dan did not think about the planet Earth enjoying the Martian home. [Dan, enjoying the Martian home, did not think about the planet Earth.]

GRAMMAR LINK

Have students choose a piece of writing from their portfolios. Ask them to see if each prepositional phrase is as close as possible to the word it modifies. If not, it may be misplaced. Have students rewrite sentences with misplaced modifiers and share the revisions with the class.

Try It Out
Possible Answers

1. The picnic beside the canal is a key scene in this story.

2. The lieutenant saw people named Linnl and Ttil in the villas.

3. I understood almost every word of the story.

VOCABULARY

Pronunciations are at the bottom of the selection pages and in the glossary (pp. 789–796). Remind students to look in the dictionary under the base form of a verb (*cease,* not *ceased,* for example). Dictionary definitions for some words may not differ significantly from glossary definitions; students can give synonyms instead (for *amiss,* "wrong," "improper," "faulty"). Encourage students to check the dictionary for abbreviations in the etymologies, or you can list those they may find: *Gr.,* Greek; *L,* Latin; *OE,* Old English; *ME,* Middle English; *OFr,* Old French; *Brit.,* British. Ask students why it is useful to learn about word origins. [Knowing prefixes like *ana-* (against) and combining forms like *-chrono-* (time) can help them figure out the meaning of new words like *anachronism.*]

Resources _____

Grammar
• *Grammar and Language Links,* p. 19

Vocabulary
• *Words to Own,* p. 9

Spelling
For related instruction, see
• *Spelling and Decoding,* p. 10

Using the Glossary to Find Pronunciations

If students have trouble pronouncing a particular word, they should turn to the guide to pronunciation symbols that appears at the bottom of each right-hand Glossary page, starting on page 789. The guide contains words and symbols that will help students decode unfamiliar words.

Before You Read

I'M NOBODY!

Make the Connection

Fame for Fifteen

"In the future everyone will be world-famous for fifteen minutes."

—Andy Warhol

Pair and share. Discuss Warhol's statement with a partner. Do you agree with Warhol? Why or why not? What do you feel are the privileges and pitfalls of fame?

Quickwrite

Pretend that you became a celebrity overnight. Fill in a chart like the one below showing how sudden fame might change you and your private life.

FAME

Pluses	Minuses
+ _____	- _____
+ _____	- _____
+ _____	- _____
+ _____	- _____

Elements of Literature

Figures of Speech: Painting with Words

In "I'm Nobody!" Emily Dickinson throws a spotlight on her ideas by using **figures of speech.** Figures of speech compare things that at first glance seem very different.

Thinking about these comparisons of unlike things lets you see familiar people and objects in a new light. The comparisons in figures of speech are imaginative and are not meant to be understood as literally true.

The most common types of figures of speech are similes and metaphors. A **simile** compares two unlike things, using the word *like* or *as:* The sleeping calico cat is *like* a cushion. A **metaphor** equates two things: The sleeping calico cat *is* a cushion.

> **A** figure of speech is a word or phrase that describes one thing in terms of something else, something very different from it. A **simile** is a comparison between two unlike things, using a word such as *like* or *as.* A **metaphor** is a comparison in which one thing is said to be another thing. A metaphor does not use *like* or *as.*
>
> *For more on Figure of Speech, Simile, and Metaphor, see page 397 and the Handbook of Literary Terms.*

go.hrw.com
LE0 7-2

 — *Resources: Print and Media* —

Senecio (1922) by Paul Klee. Oil on gauze on cardboard (40.5 cm x 38 cm) (accession number 1569).

Kunstsammlung Basel, Kunstmuseum. Photograph Oeffentliche Kunstsammlung Basel, Martin Buhler.

I'm Nobody!

Emily Dickinson

I'm Nobody! Who are you?
Are you Nobody too?
Then there's a pair of us!
Don't tell! they'd banish us, you know!

How dreary to be Somebody!
How public—like a Frog—
To tell your name the livelong June
To an admiring Bog!

A

B

Summary ■

In this eight-line poem, the speaker shares the pleasure she takes in being a "Nobody" who values her privacy and feels a kinship with other "Nobodies." She shows disdain for public figures who bask in the adulation of the crowd, likening these celebrities to frogs croaking to a bog.

Resources

Listening
Audio CD Library
For a recording of this poem, see the *Audio CD Library:*
• Disc 6, Track 3

Selection Assessment
Formal Assessment
• Selection Test, p. 29
Test Generator
• Selection Test

Ⓐ Critical Thinking
Interpreting
❓ Why does the speaker call herself "Nobody"? [Possible response: She is a very private, unknown person.] **Why does she welcome another "Nobody"?** [Possible response: Even private, unknown people need friends.] **Why might the pair be "banished"?** [Possible response: Celebrities may be suspicious of independent thinkers.]

Ⓑ Elements of Literature
Figures of Speech
❓ The speaker compares the "Somebody" to a frog. Is this comparison a simile or a metaphor? Explain. [It is a simile, because it contains the word *like.*] **The speaker compares the Somebody's admirers to a bog. Is this comparison a simile or a metaphor? Explain.** [It is a metaphor, because it does not contain *like* or *as.*] **What might make a frog a good figure of speech for a celebrity?** [Possible response: Frogs puff up with air as if to "tell their names." They may look self-important in their small ponds.]

Reaching All Students

Struggling Readers
This poem can be read as a conversation between the speaker and a reader. Suggest that students read the poem aloud in conversational tones, paying special attention to the punctuation.

English Language Learners
Explain that *banish* means "drive out of the place where one lives" and *livelong* means "entire." Point out that a bog is a low-lying, wet area,

often considered unpleasant or unhealthy. Students might be familiar with the expression *bogged down,* meaning "stuck in a difficult or unpleasant situation." For additional strategies to supplement instruction for these students, see
• *Lesson Plans Including Strategies for English-Language Learners*

RESPONDING TO THE ART
Paul Klee (1879–1940) ranks as a highly original modern painter. His works, filled with wit and invention, hint at a mysterious inner vision of the world.
Activity. Ask students whether the face in Klee's painting shows a "Somebody" or a "Nobody."

MEET THE WRITER

Who Is That Mysterious Woman in White?

Today **Emily Dickinson** (1830–1886) ranks as one of America's—and the world's—greatest poets. During her lifetime, however, she was anything but famous. Of the seventeen hundred poems she wrote, only seven were published while she was alive—and she refused to have her name put on any of them.

After a normal, sociable childhood and adolescence, Dickinson became a recluse at the age of twenty-six. By the time she was forty, she dressed only in white and rarely left her family's house in Amherst, Massachusetts. She never married, and except for family and a few old friends, she saw no one. Why? No one knows for sure. Her poems often deal with the relationship between her inner self and the outer world. Perhaps she had to draw back from the world and study it from a distance in order to write about it.

Many successful poets in the nineteenth century used regular rhymes and dum-de-dum rhythms. Emily Dickinson did not. Her rhythms were irregular and her rhymes slightly "off." More important, she chose strong images to express her bold ideas. All in all, she was a true American original.

The Granger Collection, New York.

After Emily Dickinson died, her sister discovered more than a thousand poems written on envelopes, paper bags, and scraps of paper, all neatly sewn into little packets. It looked as if the poet was hoping someone would find the poems and publish them. Yet in her lifetime, no one had really understood what poetry meant to Emily Dickinson. Here is how she once defined it:

66 If I read a book and it makes my whole body so cold no fire can ever warm me, I know that is poetry. If I feel physically as if the top of my head were taken off, I know that is poetry. These are the only ways I know it. Is there any other way? 99

Using Students' Strengths

Visual Learners
Students can fill in the blackline master provided on p. 12 in the *Graphic Organizers for Active Reading*.

Auditory Learners
Suggest that students set the words of "I'm Nobody!" to music, using a familiar or original tune. They might tape their musical version of the poem and play it for the class.

Interpersonal Learners
Based on what they learn about Emily Dickinson, these students can list some questions that the reclusive poet might have asked about life and society. Challenge them to answer the questions from Dickinson's point of view.

MAKING MEANINGS

First Thoughts

[respond]

1. How do you think the speaker feels about fame? Do you agree?

Shaping Interpretations

[interpret]

2. What does "Nobody" mean in this poem? What does "Somebody" mean?

[infer]

3. Who are "they" in line 4? Why would "they" banish the speaker?

[compare]

4. The **simile** in the second stanza compares a celebrity to a frog. How could a frog and a public person be similar? Is this a flattering comparison?

[speculate]

5. In the **metaphor** in the last line, admirers of famous people are compared to creatures in a bog (a marshy place) that admire a croaking frog. How do you think the poet feels about people who idolize celebrities?

[infer]

6. Whom do you think the speaker is talking to?

Connecting with the Text

[explain]

7. Look back at the pluses and minuses of fame you listed for the Quickwrite on page 168. Do you think your pluses would convince the poet? Explain.

CHOICES: Building Your Portfolio

Writer's Notebook

1. Collecting Ideas for an Autobiographical Incident

A person can be a "Nobody" to the world but a "Somebody" to you. List a few of your personal "Somebodies." Choose one you'd like to write about. Make notes to show what that person has meant to you. Include something the person has said to you, and try to describe the way you feel about this person.

Letter Writing

2. Dear Ms. Dickinson

If you could talk to Emily Dickinson, what would you want to tell her? What would you want to ask her? Write her a letter letting her know what you think of her poem and what you wonder about her life. You could make a class collection of Letters to a Poet.

Art/Design

3. Judging by the Cover

Sometimes you *can* judge a book by its cover. Design a cover for a collection of Emily Dickinson's poetry, entitled *I'm Nobody and Other Selected Poems*. Using "I'm Nobody" as your inspiration, decide what art you want to put on the front cover to give readers an idea of what's inside. On the back cover, create more art or draw a picture of the author.

Making the Connections

Connecting to the Theme: "Who Am I?"

Remind students that the writers they've met in this collection have asked the age-old question "Who am I?" Have students speculate on whether Dickinson's answer to this question—"I'm Nobody!"—is a satisfactory or healthy response. Would Jean Fritz, Ernesto Galarza, Amy Tan, or Julia Alvarez agree with Dickinson?

MAKING MEANINGS

First Thoughts

1. The speaker seems to prefer self-reliance to fame. Students can discuss whether they agree with her.

Shaping Interpretations

2. "Nobody" may be a person who does not care what others think and does not seek public recognition. "Somebody" may be a person who is famous or sought after by others.
3. "They" might be society in general or a current popular social group. "They" might banish the speaker because she does not fit in and does not care about fame.
4. Both a frog and a public person could be viewed as making noise to attract attention.
5. Since a bog may be a dismal place, the speaker probably has a low opinion of people who idolize celebrities.
6. The "you" is not identified, but it may be someone the speaker feels close to; perhaps it is a reader who shares the speaker's values.

Connecting with the Text

7. Students should offer evidence to support the belief that fame is desirable. Based on what they have read about Dickinson, they can explain why she might or might not agree with them.

Grading Timesaver

Rubrics for each Choices assignment appear on p. 121 in the *Portfolio Management System*.

CHOICES: Building Your Portfolio

1. **Writer's Notebook** Students might create cluster diagrams that list the traits of their personal "Somebodies."
2. **Letter Writing** Encourage students to read other poems by Dickinson as a way to generate more questions for the poet.
3. **Art/Design** Students can examine covers of books they're familiar with to develop a sense of how the cover design helps express the content of a book.

No Questions Asked

The literature in No Questions Asked gives students the chance to read a selection for enjoyment and enrichment as they further explore the collection theme. Annotated questions in the margins of the Teacher's Edition should be considered optional. No follow-up questions appear after the selection.

This selection, created by a contemporary writer, has elements of a folk tale: The actions of animal characters shed light on human behavior and suggest a moral. In this story, a frog is convinced that he can sing. After his request to join the birds' singing group is ridiculed, he asks the fox, in charge of the weekly concerts, to let him perform; the fox agrees but informs the other forest inhabitants. As a result, the frog is booed off the stage. Still determined to sing, he returns to the stage and offers his rendition of boogie-woogie. Swept up in the rhythm, the other animals dance enthusiastically. What links the selection to the theme is the frog's perseverance in overcoming the belief among forest inhabitants that frogs aren't singers; he creates an identity for himself and eventually proves his worth.

Resources

Listening
Audio CD Library
A recording of this modern-day folk tale is provided in the *Audio CD Library*:
• Disc 6, Track 4

Q uestions
NO
ASKED

Let's examine a little creature who is feeling mighty bad, mighty sad, mighty mad . . .

The Frog Who Wanted to Be a Singer

Linda Goss

172

Using Students' Strengths

Auditory/Musical Learners
Encourage students to sing the song that Frog performs (pp. 176–177). Earlier in the selection, students might play or sing appropriate background music.

Interpersonal Learners
Suggest that students retell portions of the story from Frog's first-person point of view. The narrative should express how he feels about wanting to sing, about being ridiculed by the animals, and about achieving his goal.

Well, friends, I got a question for you. Have you ever been frustrated? That's right, I said *frustrated*. Tell the truth now. Everybody in this room should be screaming, "Yeah, I've been frustrated," because you know you have, at least once in your lives. And some of us here are frustrated every single day.

How do you tell when you are frustrated? Do you feel angry? Do you feel depressed? Are you full of anxiety? Are you tense? Are you nervous? Confused? Sometimes you can't stop eating. Sometimes you don't want to eat at all. Sometimes you can't sleep. And sometimes you don't want to wake up. *You are frustrated!*

Well, friends, let's go back. Back to the forest. Back to the motherland. Back to the days when the animals talked and walked upon the earth, as folks do now.

Let's examine a little creature who is feeling mighty bad, mighty sad, mighty mad, and mighty frustrated. We call him the frog. There's nothing wrong in being a frog. But this particular frog feels that he has talent. You see, he wants to be a singer. And there's nothing wrong in wanting to be a singer except that in this particular forest where this particular frog lives, frogs don't sing. Only the birds are allowed to sing. The birds are considered the most beautiful singers in the forest.

So, for a while, the frog is cool. He's quiet. He stays to himself and practices on his lily pad, jumping up and down, singing to himself. But one day all of this frustration begins to swell inside him. He becomes so swollen that frustration bubbles start popping from his mouth, his ears, his nose, even from his eyes, and he says to himself (in a froglike voice): "You know, I'm tired of feeling this way. I'm tired of holding all this inside me. I've got talent. I want to be a singer."

The little frog decides to share his ambitions with his parents. His parents are somewhat worried about his desires, but since he is their son, they encourage him and say: "Son, we're behind you one hundred percent. If that's what you want to be, then go right ahead. You'll make us very proud."

This makes the frog feel better. It gives him some confidence, so much so that he decides to share the good news with his friends. He jumps over to the other side of the pond and says, "Fellows, I want to share something with you."

"Good!" they reply. "You got some flies we can eat."

"No, not flies. I got talent. I want to be a singer."

"Fool, are you crazy?" says one friend. "Frogs don't sing in this place. You'd better keep your big mouth shut."

They laugh at the frog, so he jumps back over to his lily pad.

He rocks back and forth, meditating and contemplating his situation, and begins to realize that perhaps he should go and talk with the birds. They seem reasonable enough; maybe they will allow him to join their singing group.

He gathers up his confidence, jumps over to their tree house, and knocks on their trunk. The head bird flies to the window, looks down on the frog's head, and says: "Oh, it's the frog. How may we help you?"

"Can I come up? I got something to ask you," says the frog.

"Very well, Frog. Do jump up."

Frog enters the tree house, and hundreds of birds begin fluttering around him.

"Come on in, Frog. Why don't you sit over there in the corner," says the head bird. Frog sits down but he feels a little shy. He begins to chew on his tongue.

"Frog, how may we help you?"

"Uh, well, uh, you see," says Frog, "I would like to become a part of your group."

"That's wonderful," says the head bird.

"Yes, wonderful," echo the other birds.

"Frog, you may help us carry our worms," said the head bird.

"That's not what I had in mind," says Frog.

A Elements of Literature
Storyteller
? A storyteller narrates a tale directly to an audience. In what way is the narrator here like a storyteller? [Possible response: She addresses the reader directly.] What is the effect of using the storytelling method? [Possible response: Addressing readers arouses their interest in the story.]

B Reading Skills and Strategies
Comparing and Contrasting
? The story is similar to a folk tale in some ways. What is one similarity? [Possible response: The story has talking animals.] In what ways is a story written by a modern writer different from a folk tale? [Possible responses: Folk tales are passed down from one generation to the next by word of mouth (storytelling). They have no known author.]

C Appreciating Language
Word Choice
? *Frustrated* usually refers to a human feeling. Why might the narrator have used the word to describe the frog's feelings? [Possible responses: She is suggesting that the animal characters have human qualities and that the events in the story say something about humans.]

D Critical Thinking
Making Connections
? How would you compare this frog with the one in Dickinson's poem? [Possible responses: This frog is like Dickinson's frog because he wants an audience and public approval (of his singing).]

E Struggling Readers
Finding Details
? What kind of "job" do the birds offer the frog? [He can help them find worms.] How is their response like his friends' response a little earlier? [His friends, the other frogs, think he wants to give them flies to eat.]

A Critical Thinking

Analyzing

? How is the response of the birds an example of prejudice? [The birds do not give him an opportunity to perform before judging him; they just assume he cannot sing because he is a frog.]

B Elements of Literature

Repetition

? Why does the narrator add the words "Quick, quick, quick" after each line of Fox's dialogue? [Possible response: It is a humorous way to emphasize the belief that foxes are alert and active, physically and mentally.]

C English Language Learners

Slang

Make sure that students understand that "do his thing" means "express himself as an individual."

D Reading Skills and Strategies

Making Predictions

? What might the fox be planning? [Possible response: Foxes are usually thought of as sly and tricky, so he may be planning a practical joke.]

E Reading Skills and Strategies

Making Inferences

? Why is the fox's introduction an insult to the frog? [Possible response: By referring to the performer as "the frog who thinks he's a singer," the fox is implying that the frog's performance will be a disaster.]

"Well, what do you have in mind?"

Frog begins to stutter: "I-I-I-I want to-to-to sing wi-wi-with your group."

"What! You must be joking, of course. An ugly green frog who is full of warts sing with us delicate creatures. You would cause us great embarrassment."

"B-b-but . . ." Frog tries to plead his case, but the head bird becomes angry.

"Out! Out! Out of our house you go." He kicks the frog from the house. Frog rolls like a ball down the jungle path.

When he returns home, he feels very sad. The frog wants to cry but doesn't, even though he aches deep inside his gut. He wants to give up, but he doesn't. Instead he practices and practices and practices and practices.

Then he begins to think again and realizes that even though the birds sing every Friday night at the Big Time Weekly Concert, they don't control it. The fox is in charge. The frog jumps over to the fox's place and knocks on his cave.

"Brother Fox, Brother Fox, it's me, Frog. I want to talk to you."

The fox is a fast talker and a busy worker, and really doesn't want to be bothered with the frog.

"Quick, quick, quick, what do you want?" says the fox.

"I want to be in the concert this Friday night."

"Quick, quick, what do you want to do?"

"I want to sing," says the frog.

"Sing? Get out of here, quick, quick, quick!"

"Please, Brother Fox. Please give me a chance."

"Hmmm," says the fox, shifting his eyes. "Uh, you know something, Froggie? Maybe I could use you. Why don't you show up Friday, at eight o'clock sharp, OK?"

"You mean I can do it?"

"That's what I said. Now, get out of here. Quick, quick, quick!"

Oh, the frog is happy. He is going to "do his thing." He is going to present himself to the world.

Meanwhile, the fox goes around to the animals in the forest and tells them about the frog's plans. Each animal promises to be there and give the frog a "little present" for his singing debut.

And so Monday rolls around, Tuesday rolls around, Wednesday rolls around, Thursday rolls around, and it is Friday. The frog is so excited, he bathes all day. He combs his little green hair, parts it in the middle, and slicks down the sides. He scrubs his little green fingers and his little green toes. He looks at his little reflection in the pond, smiles, and says, "Um, um, um, I am *beauuuutiful*! And I am going to 'do my thing' tonight." And soon it is seven o'clock, and then it is seven thirty, and then it is seven forty-five, and there is the frog trembling, holding on to the edge of the curtain.

He looks out at the audience and sees all the animals gathering in their seats. The frog is scared, so scared that his legs won't stop trembling and his eyes won't stop twitching. Brother Fox strolls out onstage and the show begins.

"Thank you, thank you, thank you. Ladies and gentlemen, we have a wonderful show for you tonight. Presenting, for your entertainment, the frog who thinks he's a singer. Come on, let's clap. Come on out here, Frog, come on, come on. Let's give him a big hand." The animals clap and roar with laughter. The frog jumps out and slowly goes up to the microphone.

"For-for-for-for my first number, I-I-I——"

Now, before that frog can put the period at the end of that sentence, the elephant stands up, pulls down a pineapple, and throws it right at the frog's head.

"Ow!" cries the frog. And the lion pulls down a banana, throws it, and hits that frog

174 WHO AM I?

Connecting Across Texts

Connecting with "Names/Nombres"

Remind students of the theme of the collection, "Who Am I?" Ask them how the frog in this story attempts to prove his identity, not so much to himself as to others. [Even though he is ridiculed, he persists in finding a way to express his musical talent.] Have students recall Julia Alvarez's experiences in "Names/Nombres," and ask how the frog's struggle for identity is, in a way, the opposite of hers. [Possible responses: The frog hopes to find acceptance by doing something different from what is expected of him; Julia, by contrast, adapts to her new country in order to find acceptance.]

T174

Oh, the frog is happy. He is going to "do his thing." He is going to present himself to the world.

F Appreciating Language

Slang

Jive as used here means "phony," and *turkey* is slang for "a foolish or clumsy person."

G Vocabulary Note

Word Origins

❓ What does the adjective *hypnotic* mean? ["causing sleep"] What are two related nouns? [*hypnosis, hypnotist*] What is the origin of these words? [Greek *hypnos*, "sleep"]

H Critical Thinking

Making Judgments

❓ How would you describe the performance of the birds? [Possible response: It is so uninteresting that it almost puts the audience to sleep.]

I Elements of Literature

Character

❓ What do the frog's actions show about him? [Possible responses: He has spunk and determination; he won't give in to those who insult him.]

right in the mouth. "Oh," gulps the frog. Other animals join in the act of throwing things at the frog. Some of them shout and yell at him, "Boo! Boo! Get off the stage. You stink! You're ugly. We don't want to hear a frog sing. Boo, you jive turkey!"

The poor little frog has to leap off the stage and run for his life. He hides underneath the stage. Brother Fox rushes back on the stage.

"OK, OK, OK, calm down—just trying out our comic routine. We have some real talent for your enjoyment. Presenting the birds, who really can sing. Let's hear it for the birds." The audience claps loudly. The birds fly onto the stage, their heads held up high. Their wings slowly strike a stiff, hypnotic pose as if they are statues. Their stage presence demands great respect from the audience. They chirp, tweet, and whistle, causing the audience to fall into a soft, peaceful nod.

Everyone is resting quietly except the frog, who is tired of being pushed around. The frog is tired of feeling frustrated. He leaps over the fox. He grabs him, shakes him, puts his hands

THE FROG WHO WANTED TO BE A SINGER **175**

Crossing the Curriculum

Health

Students might investigate recent reports by biologists that show a significant decline in frog populations. The declines have occurred in a wide range of ecosystems, and scientists are at a loss to explain them. Students can do research in newspapers and magazines or on the Internet and present their findings to the class. Of particular interest is whether the possible causes for the decline might affect human health.

Music

Interested students might present a group of songs about frogs and songs that mention frogs. They can entitle their performance "The Singers Who Wanted to Be Frogs." Suggest that students wear green and make small frog hats for the performance.

Science

Invite students to create a poster that illustrates the metamorphosis of a tadpole into a frog. Ask them to focus on how these changes help the frog adapt to its environment. Students might include "frog factoids" on their posters.

"I don't care if you are asleep. I'm gonna wake you up. I came here to sing a song tonight . . ."

A Appreciating Language

Creating New Words
The verb *hippity-hop* suggests lively action. Ask students to create similar verbs to tell how other animals move. For example, the elephant might *shuffledy-stomp* and the fox might *slippity-slink*.

B Cultural Connections

Boogie-woogie, a style of piano playing, combines blues and jazz rhythms. It has a strong beat and, like jazz, features improvisation, as the musician invents or changes some of the melodies. Students might suggest improvised lyrics for the frog's song.

C Cultural Connections

The narrator names real dances. The "bump" was popular in the 1970s; the "twist" became a craze in the early 1960s. The "bugaloo," the "slop," and the "mashed potato" were also short-lived dance fads of the 1960s.

---

around the fox's throat, and says, "You tricked me. You tried to make a fool out of me."

"Leave me alone," says the fox. "If you want to go back out there and make a fool of yourself, go right ahead."

"Hmph," says the frog. "That's just what I'm going to do."

A Now that little green frog hippity-hops back onto the stage. He is shaking but determined to sing his song.

"I don't care if you are asleep. I'm gonna wake you up. I came here to sing a song tonight, and that's what I'm going to do."

In the style of what we call boogie-woogie, the frog begins to "do his thing":

B
DOOBA DOOBA DOOBA DOOBA DOOBA DOOBA DOOBA DOOBA
DOOBA DOOBA DOOBA DOOBA DOOBA DOOBA DOOBA DOOBA

176 WHO AM I?

The frog bops his head about as though it were a jazzy saxophone. His fingers move as though they were playing a funky bass fiddle.

DOOBA   DOOBA   DOOBA   DOOBA   DOOBADEE DOOBADEE DOOBADEE DOOBADEE
DOOBA   DOOBA   DOOBA   DOOBA   DOOBADEE DOOBADEE DOOBADEE DOOBADEE
DOOBA DOOBA DOOBA DOOBA DOOBA DOOBA DOOBA DOOBA
DOOBA! DOOBA! DOOP-DEE-DOOP! . . . BLUR-RRRRRP!

C The elephant opens one eye. He roars "Uuumphf!" He jumps from his seat. He flings his hips from side to side, doing a dance we now call the "bump." The lion is the next animal to jump up from his seat. He shouts: "I love it! I love it!" He shakes his body thisaway and thataway and every whichaway, doing a dance we now call the "twist." Soon the snakes are

---

Getting Students Involved

Cooperative Learning

Have students examine the photographs that appear with "The Frog Who Wanted to Be a Singer." What is unusual about the photos on pp. 175 and 176? [They show leaping frogs on a mostly black background. On p. 176, the leg of the right-hand frog looks transparent.] Photographic effects like these are often created on computers. The class might do a project to learn more about computer graphics. Research-minded students can look in magazines or on the Internet to find information and additional examples. Artistic students can prepare an interesting display of the graphics. Other students can write up the information as captions.

boogalooing and the giraffes are doing the jerk. The hyenas do the "slop" and the fox does the "mashed potato." The birds also want to join in: "We want to do Dooba Dooba, too." They chirp and sway through the trees.

Tweet Tweet Tweet Dooba
Tweet Tweet Tweet Dooba

The whole forest is rocking. The joint is jumping. The animals are snapping their fingers. They are *dancing,* doing something that they have never done before.

The fox runs back on the stage, grabs the mike, and shouts: "Wow, Frog, you are a genius. You have given us something new."

From then on, the frog is allowed to sing every Friday night at the Big Time Weekly Concert.

And, as my granddaddy used to say, that is how Rhythm and Blues was born.

DOOBA DOOBA DOOBA DOOBA DOOBA DOOBA DOOBA DOOBA
DOOBA! DOOBA! DOOP-DEE-DOOP! . . . BLURRRRRRP!

D **English Language Learners**
Slang
The expression "The joint is jumping" means "This place is full of activity."

E **Elements of Literature**
Theme
❓ How would you express the theme, or moral, of this tale? [Possible responses: You never know what you can do until you try. Don't give up even if others don't have faith in you. Don't judge a frog by its croak. Don't stereotype others.]

F **Cultural Connections**
Rhythm and blues is a popular form of music that includes elements of the blues and of African American folk music. The style, which is marked by a strong beat, influenced the development of rock-and-roll. The narrator has turned this story into a tongue-in-cheek explanation of how rhythm and blues was born.

MEET THE WRITER
"It's Storeee-Tellin' Time!"

Storyteller **Linda Goss** is hardly ever sitting at a desk when she begins to create a story.

❝ When I'm in the kitchen, I become very creative. I have created stories when washing dishes or sweeping my kitchen floor. I have created when I've been on planes, trains, buses, sometimes in the car. I don't necessarily put it down on paper. The kind of storytelling I do is oral, so I think of telling it instead of writing it. That's the whole thing about a storyteller. It's memory. ❞

Linda Goss was born and raised in Alcoa, Tennessee. "Everybody in the town was a storyteller," she recalls. In college she studied drama and immersed herself in folklore. After teaching school she decided to become a full-time storyteller, and she is now Philadelphia's official storyteller.

When Goss tells stories, she dresses in African clothes and beaded jewelry, wrapping her hair in colorful cloth hung with charms and decorations. She sometimes walks in front of an audience, clanging cowbells and calling, "It's storeee-tellin' time!" Then she brings her tales to life with singing, talking, and dramatic expressions and gestures.

Goss aims to inspire people with her stories. In "The Frog Who Wanted to Be a Singer," she wants to show that if people believe in themselves, they can realize their dreams.

More "Storeee-Tellin' "

Linda Goss has collected more magical tales in *Talk That Talk* (Simon and Schuster), an anthology of African American storytelling.

THE FROG WHO WANTED TO BE A SINGER 177

Listening to Music

"A Place in the Choir" by Bill Staines

A native New Englander, Bill Staines has been writing and singing songs since the 1960s. Over the years he has performed all across the United States and has appeared on Garrison Keillor's *Prairie Home Companion* on National Public Radio. Probably Staines's best-known song, "A Place in the Choir" (p. 178) has become a folk-music staple and has even made its way into hymnals. It is also popular in Ireland (and among Irish Americans) because of the charming rendition by the Irish-born singers Tommy Makem and Liam Clancy.

Activity
After students have listened to the song, ask them to work alone or in pairs to create and perform a new stanza based on the characters and events in "The Frog Who Wanted to Be a Singer."

Connections

This song has the folk-tale quality of "The Frog Who Wanted to Be a Singer." Because each animal's contribution to the song reflects its nature, Staines's work relates thematically both to the collection and to Goss's story.

Ⓐ Reading Skills and Strategies
Making Predictions

? Is this a serious song? How would you describe it so far? [Possible responses: No, it is fun, silly, simple, and playful. The songwriter uses the word *critters* instead of *creatures*, and the words and rhymes are all simple.]

Ⓑ Reading Skills and Strategies
Drawing Conclusions

? What do you think the author is saying about the animals in this song? [Possible responses: He is saying that animals all make different sounds, but they all sing in the same big choir. Also, he might be implying that variety is a good thing.]

Ⓒ Critical Thinking
Extending the Text

? How could what the author is saying about animals also apply to people? [Possible response: He might be saying that even though people are different from each other, they are all part of the same big family.]

RESPONDING TO THE ART

Point out the "Curiosity Bedspread" that forms the background for p. 178. Explain that the word *curiosity* here means "something that arouses interest for its uncommon characteristics." Have students share their impressions of the colorful animals on the spread. Explain that hand-sewn patchwork quilts and bedspreads are examples of folk art, created by individuals without formal art training.
Activity. What parallel can you draw between the quilt and the choir described in the song? [Possible responses: Animals of all kinds and all singing abilities have a place in the choir; fabrics of all colors and patterns have been sewn together in this quilt.] Some students might enjoy sketching a design for their own "Curiosity Bedspread."

A Place in the Choir
Bill Staines

Ⓐ
All God's critters got a place in the choir,
Some sing low, some sing higher,
Some sing out loud on the telephone wire,
And some just clap their hands,
   Or paws,
   Or anything they got now.

Listen to the bass, it's the one on the bottom
Where the bullfrog croaks and the hippopotamus
Moans and groans with a big t'do,
And the old cow just goes "moo."

Ⓑ
The dogs and the cats they take up the middle,
While the honeybee hums and the cricket fiddles,
The donkey brays and the pony neighs
And the old coyote howls.

CHORUS: *All God's critters . . .*

Listen to the top where the little birds sing
On the melodies with the high notes ringing,
The hoot owl hollers over everything
And the jaybird disagrees.

Singing in the nighttime, singing in the day,
The little duck quacks, then he's on his way,
The 'possum ain't got much to say,
And the porcupine talks to himself.

CHORUS: *All God's critters . . .*

Ⓒ
It's a simple song of living sung everywhere
By the ox and the fox and the grizzly bear,
The grumpy alligator and the hawk above,
The sly raccoon and the turtledove.

CHORUS: *All God's critters . . .*

A Curiosity Bedspread (1935) by Mrs. Avery Burton.

Collection of Shelly Zegart, Louisville, Kentucky.

178 WHO AM I?

Connecting Across Texts

Connecting with "The Frog Who Wanted to Be a Singer"
Have students discuss the message that "A Place in the Choir" shares with "The Frog Who Wanted to Be a Singer." [Both suggest that we all have a role to play, a part to sing, in the song of the universe; no one should be forced to remain quiet.]

Making the Connections

Connecting to the Theme: "Who Am I?"
Elicit how the themes of the two selections relate to the collection theme "Who Am I?" [By believing in our abilities and participating in activities with others, we learn more about who we are and what we can contribute.]

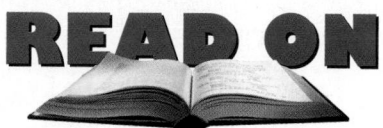

READ ON

Great Pumpkins

In *Squashed* (Delacorte) by Joan Bauer, sixteen-year-old Ellie Morgan wants to lose twenty pounds and grow a two-hundred-pound pumpkin. If she can become a famous pumpkin grower with a trim figure, her life will be perfect. When uncontrollable pressures threaten her plans, Ellie discovers her strengths and learns to believe in herself.

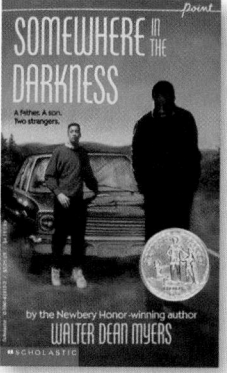

Sentimental Journey

Suffering from kidney disease and confined to a prison hospital, Cephus "Crab" Little decides to make up for lost time with his fifteen-year-old son, Jimmy, in *Somewhere in the Darkness* (Scholastic) by Walter Dean Myers. Together they journey to Crab's hometown in Arkansas, where Jimmy's growing understanding of his father's past helps him come to terms with his father and himself.

Growing Up Absurd

Gracie, a sophomore in high school, finds her road to self-discovery fraught with the hurdles of family turmoil: an unhappy mother, a newly adopted brother, and an impending family move. A. E. Cannon's *Amazing Gracie* (Delacorte) is a moving account of a girl's discovery of herself through the power of love.

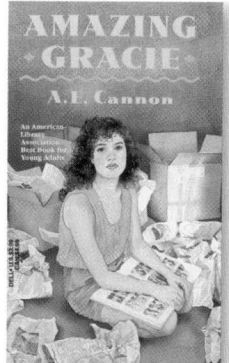

Other Picks

- Minfong Ho, *Rice Without Rain* (Lothrop, Lee & Sheperd). The ancient traditions of Jinda's Thai village are challenged, and Jinda faces questions of loyalty when young strangers from the city arrive.

- Louise Fitzhugh, *Harriet the Spy* (Dell). Harriet Welsch longs to be a writer, and when her secret spy notebook is discovered, she suddenly finds out what being a writer really means.

READ ON

Portfolio Assessment
These extended reading suggestions connect to various aspects of the theme "Who Am I?" The characters (and readers) learn that the search for identity often leads to self-understanding and to self-acceptance.

Options
The following projects can help you evaluate your students' reading outside class. Videotapes or audiotapes of completed projects may be included in students' portfolios.

- **Write a Poem**   Ask students to create a poem inspired by *Squashed*. Students can choose the form of the poem (whether it is rhymed or unrhymed, for example), but encourage them to use vivid images and concrete words. Each poem should reflect the student's feelings about the characters, theme, setting, or other elements of the book. When they have finished, volunteers may read their poems to the class.

- **Create a Map**   Ask students to create a map of the journey Crab and Jimmy made to Arkansas in *Somewhere in the Darkness*. Remind the class to include markers that pinpoint the places where Jimmy learns something important about his father, Crab. Suggest that students present and explain their maps to the class.

- **Write a Diary Entry**   Ask students to choose a day from *Amazing Grace* and to create a page from Gracie's diary for that day. Students should date the page, summarize the events of that day, and then record Gracie's thoughts about it. Encourage students to include pictures or small items that might be found tucked between the pages of a diary, such as a dried flower. Volunteers can read their diary pages to the class.

Speaking and Listening Workshop

OBJECTIVES

1. Participate in group discussion to accomplish specific goals
2. State the group's goals clearly
3. Understand the functions of the group moderator and the group recorder
4. Cooperate with others by sharing ideas, forming a consensus, and presenting results

Resources

Performance Rubric
- *Portfolio Management System*, p. 122

Introducing the Speaking and Listening Workshop

- Discuss with students the roles of moderator and recorder. If possible, every student should serve at some time in at least one of these roles or as a presenter (see below).
- Have students identify three points to keep in mind as they brainstorm:
  1. Start with a moment or two of silence for collecting thoughts.
  2. Encourage everyone to take part.
  3. Do not interrupt.
- Explain that in seeking a consensus, members consider different ideas. A consensus is usually the result of informal agreement, although a vote may be taken.
- Tell students that each group should select two to three members to present the group's recommendations to the class. If possible, a presenter should not be the moderator or the recorder.

Try It Out

First, review the concept of theme with students. Next, remind students that selecting several details from the story as evidence should make their explanations more convincing. After the groups have reached a consensus, presenters may explain the groups' decisions to the class.

GROUP DISCUSSION

TWO (OR THREE OR FOUR) HEADS ARE BETTER THAN ONE

When was the last time you worked with other people to discuss an issue, solve a problem, or find an answer to a question? Maybe you and a group of classmates talked about a story in this collection. Maybe you and some of your friends planned a walkathon or a weekend soccer match.

People work in groups because it's a good way to get things done. In fact, more and more businesses are finding that when people work in groups, they are more efficient and more creative. Here are some guidelines that will help any group work together smoothly.

1. Choose Your Roles

In small groups, people seem to take on certain roles naturally. Some are leaders; others prefer to work behind the scenes. Some may create conflict; others may help settle arguments.

Each person in the group has a role to play, and each role has special responsibilities. For example, your group may choose a chairperson or moderator to help keep the discussion moving and make sure everyone speaks up, stays on the subject, and listens to others. Someone else may be named secretary or recorder. This person has the responsibility of taking notes during the discussion. You can rotate these roles if the people in your group work together often.

2. State Your Goals

Everyone in the group should agree on a specific task or goal. Your goal may be to

- discuss and share ideas
- cooperate in group learning
- solve problems
- arrive at a decision or make a specific recommendation

Try It Out

Get together with a group of three or four classmates to discuss one of the stories in this collection that you all have read. First, explain what you liked or disliked about the story. Then, tell if you think the story fits the theme of this collection, "Who Am I?"

180 WHO AM I?

Getting Students Involved

Cooperative Learning

Projects might include painting a mural, holding a fund-raising event for an approved local charity, producing a class newsletter, holding an informal debate on a topic of interest, or inviting a speaker to the class and interviewing that person (for example, a representative of a local social service agency). The groups should decide which members will be responsible for which tasks and arrange to meet if follow-up is needed. After they have completed their projects, group members may select two or three presenters to describe, to the rest of the class, what the group learned from the project. A student who has difficulty participating in a group project may be paired with a student who is more at ease in the cooperative activity.

3. Brainstorm to Gather Ideas

Brainstorming lets you find out each person's ideas about reaching the group's goal. Here are some tips on brainstorming:

- Be silent for several minutes so that everyone has a chance to collect his or her thoughts.

- Take turns expressing your ideas. Don't worry if you think your ideas are boring or impractical. Keep going around the group until you have plenty of good ideas.

- Take only your fair share of time to talk. Be friendly and polite and listen when it's someone else's turn to speak.

4. Reach a Consensus

After brainstorming, begin to work cooperatively to meet your goal. Discuss your ideas and decide as a group which to pursue. Coming to a general agreement as a group is called reaching a consensus. Here are some hints about what to do during this part of the discussion:

- Listen carefully and be willing to learn from what others have to say. Don't interrupt, and speak only when it is your turn.

- Stay on the discussion topic. If you have to remind others to stick to the subject, be polite about it.

- Ask questions if you don't understand something.

Shoe, ©Tribune Media Services, Inc. All Rights Reserved. Reprinted with permission.

5. Present Your Information

You may need to present your ideas to other people. Think about the information you need to communicate. Be sure to include enough details so that your listeners can understand and relate to your ideas.

> **Try It Out**
>
> Form a group with three or four classmates. Your goal is to answer this question: What would make your school a better place to learn in? After brainstorming, reach a consensus on your three best ideas. Then, choose a group representative to present your ideas to the rest of the class.

Teaching the Speaking and Listening Workshop

- Before students break into groups, a few students can role-play a sample group discussion in front of the class. If disagreements arise, class members may offer alternative solutions as a means of resolving conflict.

- Explain that no group member should monopolize a discussion and that everyone should listen carefully and take part in the discussion.

- If students are not skilled at brainstorming, explain the principles:
  1. Start with a quiet period for gathering ideas.
  2. Respect all ideas.
  3. Pay thoughtful attention to all participants, and give everyone a chance to speak.

- After the group sessions are held, students should present an evaluation of their experience by answering questions like these:
  1. What did I learn about cooperation from this activity?
  2. What problems arose in my group, and how did we handle them?
  3. What might a group do differently next time?

Try It Out

- Make sure that each group contains students who have verbal skills and students who need practice in speaking and listening.

- Be sure that students understand the topic to be discussed and the procedures to be followed: brainstorming ideas, reaching a consensus, presenting recommendations to class.

- After the groups have presented their findings, the class may offer the recommendations to the school.

Reaching All Students

Struggling Learners

Students can gain confidence in speaking in front of an audience by practicing with poems or short prose pieces. Have several students stand in front of the class together so that no student is in the spotlight alone. Students can take turns reading stanzas or other sections of a work. Students can select or be assigned items of interest like "Darzee's Chant" (p. 15), "Sir Kensley the Brave" (p. 60), "An Immigrant in the United States" (p. 130), "The Clutch Moment" (pp. 184–185), or other poems and prose pieces in this book.

English Language Learners

Students who are reluctant to speak in class might be given additional time to practice, or they might be encouraged to recite a brief poem or other work in their native language; if possible, it can be translated by another student.

T181

MAIN OBJECTIVE
Write an autobiographical incident

PROCESS OBJECTIVES
1. Use appropriate prewriting techniques to identify and develop a topic
2. Create a first draft
3. Use Evaluation Criteria as a basis for determining revision strategies
4. Revise the first draft, incorporating suggestions generated by self- or peer evaluation
5. Proofread and correct errors
6. Create a final draft
7. Choose an appropriate method of publication
8. Reflect on progress as a writer

Planning

- **Block Schedule**
  Block Scheduling Lesson Plans with Pacing Guide
- **One-Stop Planner**
  CD-ROM with Test Generator

Technology HELP

See Writer's Workshop 1 CD-ROM. *Assignment: Autobiographical Incident.*

ASSIGNMENT
Write a narrative about an experience you've had.

AIM
To record an incident in your life; to express your feelings.

AUDIENCE
Your teacher, classmates, friends, or family or people who were involved in the incident.

NARRATIVE WRITING
AUTOBIOGRAPHICAL INCIDENT

When something important happens to you, you probably want to tell a friend about it right away. When you write an **autobiographical incident** (or personal narrative), you tell about an event in your life that has special significance for you.

Professional Model

That night I asked Mother, "What are the long words for what's wrong with my eyes?" . . .
  She rhymed off a whole list.
  "Say it again. Slowly."
  "Strabismus, nystagmus corneal opacities, and eccentric pupils."
  I practiced.
  The next day I was late coming out of school. The same grade-seven boy was waiting for me. He had his first snowball ready.
  "Cross-eyed, cross-eyed," he chanted and waited for me to start running so that he could chase me, pelting me with hard-packed snowballs.
  I turned on him instead.
  "I am not cross-eyed," I said in a strong, clear voice. "I have corneal opacities and eccentric pupils."
  I glared at him as I spoke, and my eyes were as crossed as ever. But he was so surprised that he stood there, his mouth gaping open like a fish's.
  Then I turned my back and

Dialogue and a question grab our attention.

The writer uses dialogue to give background.

Dialogue and details make the experience real and vivid.

Action and dialogue reveal character.

The writer's feelings are clear.

Description of the boy's surprise.

 Resources: Print and Media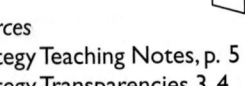

Writing and Language
- *Portfolio Management System*
  Prewriting, p. 123
  Peer Editing, p. 124
  Assessment Rubric, p. 125

- *Workshop Resources*
  Revision Strategy Teaching Notes, p. 5
  Revision Strategy Transparencies 3, 4
- *Writer's Workshop 1 CD-ROM*
  Autobiographical Incident

The history of the written word is rich and
Page 1
Once upon a tim

(continued)

walked away. Perhaps his aim was off because he was so used to firing his missiles at a running target. But the first snowball flew past harmlessly. The second exploded with a smack against a nearby tree.

I kept walking, chin in the air. . . .
I had found out what mere words could do. I would not forget.

The writer tells why the incident was important to her.

—from *Little by Little* by Jean Little

Prewriting

1. Check Your Writer's Notebook

WORK IN PROGRESS

Look at your Writer's Notebook entries for this collection. Is there one you'd like to develop further? If not, freewrite about one of the subjects listed below or another topic of your choice until you've found an incident you want to write about.

2. Freewrite

a. Freewrite for two minutes about one or two of the following subjects:

surprises • conflicts • vacation • helping others • secrets • athletic events • losing a friend • thinking about the future • special memories • luck • honesty

b. Complete one of these starters in as many ways as possible:

- The happiest time in my life was . . .
- The most unforgettable time in my life was . . .
- I still feel sad thinking about . . .
- I felt caught in the middle when . . .

Framework for an Autobiographical Incident

What the incident means to me:
_____
_____

Introduction (dialogue, question, statement, or description that grabs readers' attention):
_____
_____

Order of events:
1. _____
2. _____
3. _____
4. _____

Conclusion (summary of the importance of the incident):
_____
_____

WRITER'S WORKSHOP 183

Introducing the Writer's Workshop

- Read the Professional Model on pp. 182–183 as the students follow along. Tell students that the meaning of the difficult words will become clear later in the essay. The writer has deliberately used hard words that she herself had to "practice."
- Be sure students understand the side-margin comments. Ask them to describe the effects of dialogue and of vivid images, such as "hard-packed snowballs." Students may take the roles of the writer and the boy.
- Discuss with students what makes a good autobiographical incident:
  1. a story line in which each event leads clearly to the next
  2. details that make the incident believable
  3. honesty about what made the incident important to the writer
- Be sure students understand the purpose of their writing: to describe an incident and tell the reader how they felt about it. *Remind students to choose a situation that they will not mind sharing with others.*

Teaching the Writer's Workshop

Prewriting

Have students use the techniques suggested on pp. 183–184 (or any others that may be helpful to them) to come up with ideas.

Reaching All Students

Struggling Writers

Students having difficulty can meet in small groups to consider experiences that are listed under Freewrite on p. 183. For instance, what does it mean to lose a friend or to have a secret? Have students think of vivid words or images to suggest common emotions (one student might enact excitement, for example, and others describe the actions). They might recall movies, TV shows, or stories in which a character had a special experience. Have students probe their own experiences for any that would make a good autobiographical incident, such as a birthday or a visit to a special place.

Students might make a storyboard, using one frame for each specific event. Then, on a separate sheet of paper, they can describe each picture, adding details and dialogue.

Students who are reluctant to reveal their feelings or details of their home life might write about an incident they shared with classmates or friends or even a TV show that moved them.

Drafting

- If you have not yet taught the Student Model, do so before students begin their drafts.
- Remind students to use every other line when they write their drafts. They should also leave extra space in the right margin for comments and editing marks.

Using the Model

As class members read the Student Model, be sure they understand the side notes. You can extend the discussion by having students focus on questions like these:

❓ How does the writer create suspense? How can you use suspense to help make your narrative interesting? In what way is suspense like a clue to a mystery?

❓ What kinds of details tell you how Vinnie Merrill feels while he is making the free throw?

❓ The writer expresses nervousness at the beginning of paragraph 2. What feeling does he express when he says, "I knew the ball was not going to miss"? Why might his feelings have changed?

❓ Do you find the writer's statement in the last paragraph believable? Why or why not?

❓ What other techniques does the writer use that you might use in your paper?

Writing Tip

Many writers use chronological order when they write a personal narrative. Using **chronological order** means telling about events in the order in which they happened. You may want to start with a critical moment, such as the last few seconds of a game, as Vinnie Merrill has done in the Student Model.

An alternative is to use **comparison and contrast.** For instance, you may want to compare and contrast the good and bad parts of your experience.

Good	Bad

Language/Grammar Link
HELP

Denotations and connotations: page 120. Using precise adjectives: page 143. Comparing adjectives: page 133. Dangling modifiers: page 151. Misplaced modifiers: page 167.

c. **Favorites.** Make a list of your favorite things: people, places, hobbies, sports, clothes, animals, vacations, and so on. Is there an incident involving one of your favorite things that you want to write about? Explore your ideas by freewriting.

d. **Souvenirs.** Do you have souvenirs (ticket stubs, photos, letters) that remind you of special times in your life? Try developing your thoughts about one of these times by freewriting.

3. Choose Your Topic

To choose an incident to expand on, ask yourself:

- Do any of these incidents mean something special to me?
- Which of the incidents do I remember especially well?
- Am I willing to share any of these incidents with others?

4. Explain Why It's Important

After choosing an incident to write about, explain in a sentence or two why the experience was important. For example: "I felt so happy—as if I were my team's hero. Great feeling."

As you draft and redraft, keep looking back at this statement. As you write, you may develop a different sense of what your experience means. If so, change your statement. Some writers say they never know what an experience really means to them until they write about it.

Drafting

1. Get It on Paper: First Draft

The best way to start your draft is to get the basics of your story down on paper as quickly as you can. Try answering the 5W questions as you write: *Who* was involved in the incident? *What* happened? *When* did it happen? *Where* did it happen? *Why* did it happen? Filling in a framework like the one on page 183 can help you organize your draft. Have you left out anything important? Have you emphasized what needs to be emphasized?

Student Model

THE CLUTCH MOMENT

Nine, eight, seven, six, five, four.
I was fouled with four seconds left

Suspenseful opener.

Getting Students Involved

Cooperative Learning

Basketball is one game that has a known "inventor"—James Naismith, a gym teacher in Springfield, Massachusetts. In 1891, Naismith had empty peach baskets nailed along the gym wall. The athletes played that historic first basketball game with a soccer ball.

Students can work in groups of two or three to learn more about basketball. The students should first compile a list of questions. A good source for simple research is an encyclopedia article, a library book, or the Internet. Questions might include these: How many players were on the first teams? [nine] When and where did young women start playing? [A few weeks after Naismith's invention, women at a school nearby were shooting baskets.] What was the most famous all-black team before integration of the sport in the 1950s? [the Harlem Globetrotters]

In another activity, students can look in the library for photographs or drawings of early basketball games and in current newspapers and magazines for up-to-date pictures. Then, they can describe the differences and similarities between the old pictures and the new.

(continued)

in the game. The fans roared out of their seats, cheering and howling. I couldn't believe it. My dream had come true. These two free throws would decide if we won, lost, or tied.

Background information.

I stepped up to the free throw line with sweat dripping off my head into my eyes. Chills ran through my body, making my arms feel numb and loose. The only thing I could think of was making these two free throws. I blocked all the cheers out of my head and took a deep breath to relax. I turned the ball in my hands and took four dribbles. I looked at the goal and released the ball. Swish! The game was tied 49–49. The Jefferson Junior fans grew quiet and the Cubs were cheering loudly.

Detailed description of the writer's actions, thoughts, and feelings.

Descriptive details make us feel as if we were there.

I stepped up to the free throw line for the last time that night. After dribbling again four times I raised my arms to shoot the ball.

It felt like a piece of flab as I released the ball, letting it fly through the air. I knew the ball was not going to miss. I had made the shot of my life to win the game 50–49. It was our ball out of bounds and I threw it in and the time ran out. The game was over! As soon as I raised my hands, I was tackled by Ben Meldrum and the rest of the team. Even the B-team joined in the fun and piled on me.

I knew right then while I was on the floor that I could never have that feeling again.

The writer tells why the incident was important.

—Vinnie Merrill
Simonsen Junior High School
Jefferson City, Missouri

Strategies for Elaboration

You can help your readers see, hear, feel, smell, and even taste what you've experienced by including **sensory details** in your autobiographical incident.

Try capturing your memories by completing these statements:

- I see . . .
- I hear . . .
- I smell . . .
- I taste . . .
- I feel . . .

If you have photographs that help you remember the incident, look them over.

- Who's in the picture?
- How would you describe the people's expressions?
- What are they wearing?
- What year or season is it?
- Are any objects visible in the photo that bring back special memories?

Reaching All Students

English Language Learners

In order to write about past events, English language learners may need help in using the correct forms of irregular verbs. First, discuss the difference between present, past, and present perfect tenses (for example, *bring, brought, [have] brought*). Then, list the principal parts of some irregular verbs, as in the *bring* example: *think, catch, give,* etc. Explain how to find these forms in a dictionary. Students can make irregular-verb cards for practice in learning the correct forms:

The present tense goes on one side; the past and present perfect tenses go on the reverse. For more practice in using verbs correctly, students can refer to the Language Handbook (pp. 726–733) and to the *Language Workshop CD-ROM*.

Advanced Learners

Students may rewrite their autobiographical incidents in another form—a play, a poem, or a newspaper or radio/TV news report. Other students can look through art books for depic-

tions of facial expressions that suggest certain emotions: fear, surprise, etc. Students may read an autobiography (or a biography) of a person they admire or want to know more about. Ask them to consider the differences between autobiography and biography—between narrating events in one's own life and narrating events in another person's life.

Evaluating and Revising

Have students use the Evaluation Criteria provided here to review their drafts and determine needed revisions.

Proofreading

Have students proofread their own papers first and then exchange their work with that of other students. For this assignment, remind students to be particularly careful about correct use of verb forms and verb tenses.

If time permits, the final copy should be put aside for at least a day before it is proofread for the final time by the author.

Remind students that they must spell accurately in final drafts. Suggest that they use a spelling checker if they are using a computer that has one. Make sure students understand that a spelling checker will not alert them to usage errors, such as the confusion of *they're, their* and *your, you're*.

Publishing

Students may want to include several autobiographical incidents in a scrapbook or album. They can illustrate their narratives with photographs or drawings. They can share their books with family and friends, and they should save their narratives to read again when they're older.

Reflecting

Students can prepare a brief reflection on the process of writing a narrative. They might complete one of the starters below:

- The best-written part of my paper is . . . because . . .
- The most surprising thing I learned about myself while writing this paper was . . .

Resources

Peer Editing Forms and Rubrics
- *Portfolio Management System,* p. 124

Revision Transparencies
- *Workshop Resources,* p. 5

Grading Timesaver

Rubrics for this Writer's Workshop assignment appear on p. 125 of the *Portfolio Management System.*

■ *Evaluation Criteria*

A good autobiographical incident

1. *focuses on a single incident*
2. *opens in a way that grabs readers' attention*
3. *includes enough background information to allow readers to understand the story*
4. *narrates events in time order or in another order that readers can follow*
5. *includes descriptive details that bring the story to life*
6. *shows what the incident means to the writer*

Sentence Workshop
H E L P

Combining sentences using subordinate clauses: page 187.

Communications Handbook
H E L P

See Proofreaders' Marks.

Publishing Tip

Collect your class's stories in a book, and present it to your school library.

---

2. Elaborate

Once you've written down the basics of your incident, add details to make your story come alive.

a. **Run your mental videotape.** Replay the experience in your mind as if you were watching it on videotape. What did the people involved *say* to one another? How did they *look*? What exactly did they *do*? Jot down the details.

b. **Return to the scene.** To jog your memory about what happened and what you were thinking and feeling at the time, try returning to the place where the incident happened.

c. **Interview others.** Talk to other people involved in the experience. What details do they remember?

Evaluating and Revising
1. Peer Review

When you finish your second draft, trade papers with a partner. Read your partner's paper, and answer the following questions:

- Does the beginning grab my attention?
- Are there any missing or unnecessary details?
- Are there parts where I would like more details?
- Do I understand why the incident is important to the writer?

2. Self-Evaluation

If you can, put your paper aside briefly. When you look at it again, ask yourself if it has the characteristics of a good autobiographical incident. (See the Evaluation Criteria at the left.)

"'What I Did This Summer.' This summer, I went to camp. I hated it. I hated every minute of it. I hated my counsellor. I hated the food. I hated the woods. I hated the nature walks and the nature talks. I hated the outings. I hated the campfires. I hated the overnights. I hated . . ."

Sentence Workshop

COMBINING SENTENCES USING SUBORDINATE CLAUSES

When you have a string of short choppy sentences, you can often combine them by changing some of them into subordinate clauses.

A **subordinate clause** is a clause that does not stand alone as a complete sentence. A subordinate clause is attached to a main clause and tells things like *who, what, where, why, when, how,* or *to what extent.*

You can change a sentence into a subordinate clause by adding a word that tells the time or place, such as *after, before, until, where, wherever, when, whenever,* or *while.*

CHOPPY SENTENCES	I found out that my parents had invited the minister's family over for Christmas Eve dinner. I cried.
COMBINED	"When I found out that my parents had invited the minister's family over for Christmas Eve dinner, I cried."

—Amy Tan, "Fish Cheeks" (page 136)

In this case the subordinate clause precedes the independent clause. You could easily have reversed the order.

I cried when I found out that my parents had invited the minister's family over for Christmas Eve dinner.

Note: If you put your time or place clause at the beginning of the sentence, you must put a comma after the clause.

Writer's Workshop Follow-up: Revision

Exchange your autobiographical incident for a partner's. Circle groups of sentences you could combine by making one or more a time or place clause. Then, suggest a revision for each group. Exchange papers again, and review your partner's suggestions.

Language Handbook HELP

See Combining Sentences, pages 760-761.

Technology HELP

See Language Workshop CD-ROM. Key word entry: subordinate clauses.

Try It Out

Make each of the following items a single sentence by changing one or more sentences into subordinate clauses. Then, find the original passage and see how the writer combined these ideas.

1. We sat down. She pointed her ruler at me.

   —"Homesick" (page 106)

2. The commencement ceremony ended. My family waited outside in the parking lot. I signed yearbooks with nicknames.

   —"Names/Nombres" (page 147)

3. They looked at Martian hills. Time had worn those hills with a crushing pressure of years.

   —"The Naming of Names" (page 154)

SENTENCE WORKSHOP 187

Resources

Workshop Resources
• Worksheet, p. 39

Language Workshop CD-ROM
• Subordinate Clauses

Try It Out
Possible Answers
1. When we sat down, she pointed her ruler at me.
2. After the commencement ceremony, my family waited in the parking lot while I signed yearbooks with nicknames.
3. They looked at Martian hills that time had worn with a crushing pressure of years.

Assessing Learning

Quick Check: Subordinate Clauses

Label the following word groups with either an *I* for independent clause or an *S* for subordinate clause. If the word group is a subordinate clause, combine it with an independent clause that makes sense. [Answers may vary.]

1. I didn't have any dinner. [I]
2. Until I finished my homework. [S; Until I finished my homework, I could not watch TV.]

3. Because I wanted to see that movie. [S; Because I wanted to see that movie, I made a date with two friends.]
4. I received an A in English. [I]
5. While we were listening to music. [S; My cousin and I did crossword puzzles while we were listening to music.]

Using the Strategies

Suggested Answers
1. *Dr. Jekyll and Mr. Hyde;* This book is the only one marked C, for "challenging."
2. fantasy—*Wise Child;* science fiction—*The Giver;* combination—*Dr. Jekyll and Mr. Hyde*
3. Students' answers should reflect their interests, their awareness of their reading level, and other appropriate standards.

Situation

Your teacher wants everyone in your class to read a novel. You look at the Read On suggestions on page 179. How about *Rice Without Rain?* You liked "Homesick"; it might be fun to read a whole novel set in another country. Here are some things to think about as you select and read a book for independent reading.

Strategies

Find a book to read.

- When you read independently, outside school, you are reading for a purpose. Maybe you are reading for enjoyment. Maybe you have to write a book report. Keep your purpose in mind as you select your book.

- Whenever you're looking for something to read on your own, check the Read On and Meet the Writer features in this book.

- Be picky! If reading a particular book feels like taking medicine, try the opening chapter of a few others until you find one you like.

Read regularly and often.

- Reading regularly helps you get into the reading habit. Try setting a reading goal for yourself—a certain number of pages or a certain amount of time each day.

Speed up; slow down.

- When you read a novel, set your own pace, adjusting your reading rate to your purpose.

- When you bump into a difficult word, try to infer its meaning from its context, the words around it.

Use your reading skills.

Even when you're reading for enjoyment, keep using the skills you've learned at school.

- Notice how the writer creates character and keeps you asking questions.

- Make inferences and predictions.

- Connect what you read with your own life.

Reading List: Science Fiction and Fantasy

- Lois Lowry, *The Giver* A
  Twelve-year-old Jonas looks forward to training for his first job. At first his community of the future seems ideal: Injustice, poverty, and inequality no longer exist. Gradually it becomes apparent that things are terribly wrong.

- Monica Furlong, *Wise Child* E/A
  A wise woman shares her knowledge and "magic" with a young girl in this tale of long ago.

- Robert Louis Stevenson, *Dr. Jekyll and Mr. Hyde* C
  A classic horror fantasy that examines the forces of good and evil as embodied in one tortured man.

  Key to reading levels
  E = easy
  A = average
  C = challenging

Using the Strategies

1. Which book do you think is the most difficult on the list above? How can you tell?

2. Which book seems to be fantasy? science fiction? a combination of the two?

3. If you were looking for something to read on your own, which book on the list would you choose? Why?

Extending the Strategies

Write a letter or send e-mail to the author of your novel. Tell how you felt about the book.

188 WHO AM I?

Reaching All Students

Struggling Readers
Some students may have difficulty finding and getting through longer works. A group visit to the library to explore appropriate-level books may help. Students may be more comfortable reading short works, including stories in young people's magazines, or they may prefer illustrated nonfiction to fiction. You might pair a struggling reader with a reader who can give assistance and support.

Advanced Readers
Suggest that students publish a class *Readers' Magazine* to which they contribute reviews of books they have read and think classmates may enjoy. The reviews can include their illustrations of a novel or photocopies of illustrations or of an author photo from a book. Professional reviews of suitable books, in magazines and newspapers, may be included. The magazine can also include student interviews about recommended books.

Learning for Life

Evaluating Advertising

OBJECTIVES
1. Evaluate the targeted audience, the emotions appealed to, the visuals used, and the effectiveness of selected advertisements
2. Choose and complete a project (creating an ad, conducting an opinion poll and presenting the findings, writing a consumer-response letter)

Problem

Like the characters in this collection, you may have asked yourself, "Who am I?" Companies that try to sell you their products also want to know who you are. A good advertising company tries to understand you, the buyer, so that it can create an effective advertisement to persuade you to buy something. How can you learn to view advertisements critically and make well-informed decisions?

Project

Evaluate advertising aimed at your age group.

Preparation

1. Look through magazines, and find advertisements targeted to your age group. Select six advertisements to bring to class.

2. People read ads very quickly, so the ads have to work on our emotions instantly. Take a few minutes to think about how you feel when you look at these advertisements. Jot down some notes. How do you think the advertisers want you to feel?

Procedure

1. Write answers to these questions about the advertisements you have chosen:
   - What group is each ad directed to? (What age, gender, interests, and so on are targeted?)
   - What desires does each ad appeal to? (To be cool, to look great, to be popular, to be like everyone else, to be successful, to have fun?)
   - What in the ad creates the appeal (pictures, slogans, and so on)?
   - Are the ads' claims realistic?
   - Would you buy the products on the basis of the ads? Explain.

2. Form a group with four or five classmates, and compare your responses to your advertisements.

Presentation

Use your evaluation of the advertisements to do one of the following:

1. Advertisement

With a small group, create your own ad for a product. Be sure you make realistic claims, and appeal to your own age group. Include illustrations that you create or find in magazines. Select the wording you feel would be most effective.

2. Opinion Poll

Do a survey of students in your grade to find out how effective some of the advertisements are. Select five to eight advertisements, and display them around the classroom. Prepare a brief list of questions to ask. When you've finished, write up the results of the poll. Try to draw conclusions from the information you gathered in the poll.

3. Consumer-Response Letter

Write a letter to one of the advertisers, commenting on the company's ad. Tell what you liked and what you didn't like about the ad. With your teacher's permission, send the letter to the company's public relations manager.

Processing

Have your reactions to advertisements changed as a result of doing this project? Write a reflection on what you learned.

LEARNING FOR LIFE 189

Resources

Viewing and Representing
HRW Multimedia Presentation Maker
Students may wish to use the *Multimedia Presentation Maker* to create an advertisement.

Grading Timesaver

Rubrics for this Learning for Life project appear on p. 126 of the *Portfolio Management System*.

Developing Workplace Competencies

Preparation	Procedure	Presentation
• Identifying central issue or problem • Detecting bias, stereotypes, clichés	• Classifying data • Recognizing underlying assumptions • Recognizing loaded language • Drawing conclusions	• Generating related ideas • Synthesizing information • Evaluating arguments

Do the Right Thing

Theme

Making Difficult Choices When people are confronted with choices that test their character, they often discover that the way to make the best decision is to listen to the voice within their hearts.

Reading the Anthology

Reaching Struggling Readers

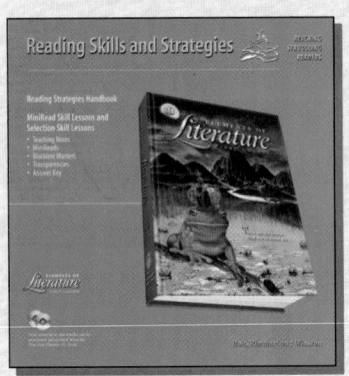

The *Reading Skills and Strategies: Reaching Struggling Readers* binder provides materials coordinated with the Pupil's Edition (see the Collection Planner, p. T189C) to help students who have difficulty reading and comprehending text, or students who are reluctant readers. The binder for seventh grade is organized around eleven individual skill areas and offers the following options:

- **MiniReads** are short, easy texts that give students a chance to practice a particular skill and strategy before reading selections in the Pupil's Edition. Each MiniRead Skill Lesson can be taught independently or used in conjunction with a Selection Skill Lesson.

- **Selection Skill Lessons** Selection Skill Lessons allow students to apply skills introduced in the MiniReads. Each Selection Skill Lesson provides reading instruction and practice specific to a particular piece of literature in the Pupil's Edition.

Reading Beyond the Anthology

Read On Collection Three includes an annotated bibliography of books suitable for extended reading. The suggested books are related to works in this collection by theme, by author, or by subject. To preview the Read On for Collection Three, please turn to p. T259.

HRW Library The *HRW Library* offers novels, plays, and short-story collections for extended reading. Each book in the Library includes one or more major works and thematically or topically related Connections. Each book in the *HRW Library* is also accompanied by a Study Guide that provides teaching suggestions and worksheets. For Collection Three, the following titles are recommended.

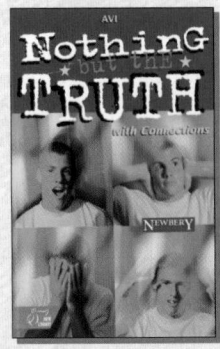

NOTHING BUT THE TRUTH
Avi
Philip's high school teacher sends him to the principal's office for humming "The Star-Spangled Banner" —a violation of school policy. As events quickly unfold, readers must decide who is telling the truth.

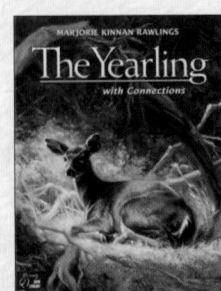

THE YEARLING
Marjorie Kinnan Rawlings
A Pulitzer Prize–winning novel, *The Yearling* tells about Jody's discovery of an orphaned fawn and the tragic decisions that the boy must eventually make when the yearling becomes too destructive to keep.

Skills Focus

Selection or Feature	Reading Skills and Strategies	Elements of Literature	Language/ Grammar	Vocabulary/ Spelling	Writing	Listening/ Speaking	Viewing/ Representing
After Twenty Years (p. 192) O. Henry	Determine the Meaning of Words, pp. 192, 201	Foreshadowing, pp. 192, 199 Internal Conflict, p. 199	End Marks, p. 201 • Period • Exclamation Mark • Question Mark	Context Clues, p. 201 Word Roots, p. 201	Ideas for Supporting a Position, p. 200 Write a News Article, p. 200	Orally Retell the Story, p. 200 Perform a Group Radio Play of the Story, p. 200	
Elements of Literature: Point of View (p. 202)		Point of View, pp. 202–203 • Omniscient • First-Person • Third-Person Limited					
Reading Skills and Strategies: Making Predictions (p. 204)	Predict, p. 204 Prior Knowledge, p. 204						
A Mason-Dixon Memory (p. 205) Clifton Davis	Make and Confirm Predictions, pp. 205, 213	Flashback, pp. 205, 213 Chronological Order, p. 205	Commas in a Series, p. 215	Synonyms, p. 215 Dictionary, p. 215 Thesaurus, p. 215 Word Maps, p. 215	Identify and Support an Opinion, p. 214 Write an Essay on a Good Act, p. 214	Research Civil Rights and Construct Interview Questions, p. 214 Hold a Panel Discussion, p. 214	Use a Chart to Record Comparisons, p. 213
The No-Guitar Blues (p. 216) Gary Soto	Regional and Cultural Expressions, pp. 216, 223	Third-Person Limited Point of View, p. 216 First-Person Point of View, p. 224	Comma Splice, p. 225	Spelling Words with *ie* and *ei*, p. 225	Summarize Ballot Results, p. 216 Brainstorm Positions, p. 224 Write a Scene, p. 224	Multimedia Presentation on Latin Music, p. 224 Tell a Story Based on a Painting, p. 224	Make an Illustrated Recipe Card, p. 224
Madam and the Rent Man (p. 226) Langston Hughes	Identify the Main Idea or Message, p. 229	Tone, pp. 226, 229			Ideas for a Position, p. 229 Write a Dialogue, p. 229	Perform a Read-Aloud, p. 229	
Bargain (p. 230) A. B. Guthrie	Draw Conclusions, pp. 230, 241 Identify the Main Events in a Story, p. 241	First-Person Point of View, pp. 230, 241 Historical Fiction, p. 230 Foreshadowing, p. 241	Apostrophes, p. 243 • Possessives • Contractions	Spelling Words with Silent Letters, p. 243	Summarize Evidence from a Story, p 242 Analyze Setting, p. 242	Prepare and Present an Oral Report on Frontier Teachers, p. 242	Design a Set for a Film of the Story, p. 242
Amigo Brothers (p. 244) Piri Thomas	Comparison and Contrast, pp. 244, 255 Context Clues, p. 255	Conflict: External and Internal, pp. 244, 254	Create a Dictionary of Slang, p. 255 Punctuate Dialogue, p. 256	Using New Words in Context, p. 256	Write a News Story, p. 255 Write a Comparison-Contrast Essay, p. 255		Use a Venn Diagram, p. 244 Use a Cluster Map to Organize Ideas, p. 255
No Questions Asked: Sarah Cynthia Sylvia Stout Would Not Take the Garbage Out (p. 257) Shel Silverstein	The **No Questions Asked** feature provides students with an unstructured opportunity to practice reading strategies using a selection that extends the theme of the collection.						
Writer's Workshop: Supporting a Position (p. 260)					Persuasive Writing: Support a Position, pp. 260–264		Use a Cluster Map to Organize Ideas, p. 262
Sentence Workshop: Run-on Sentences (p. 265)			Run-on Sentences, p. 265		Revise Run-on Sentences, p. 265		
Reading for Life: Evaluating a Persuasive Message (p. 266)	Evaluate Persuasion, p. 266 Identify the Main Idea, p. 266	Identify the Writer's Point of View, p. 266	Identify Loaded Words, p. 266				
Learning for Life: Using Multiple Sources to Conduct Research on Volunteering (p. 267)					Create an On-line Index, p. 267 Write a PSA, p. 267	Participate in a Small-Group Discussion, p. 267 Hold a Volunteer Fair, p. 267	Design a Volunteers-Needed Card, p. 267

Resources for this Collection

Note: All resources for this collection are available for preview on the *One-Stop Planner CD-ROM 1 with Test Generator*. All worksheets and blackline masters may be printed from the CD-ROM.

Internet Resources
go.hrw.com LE0 7-3

Selection or Feature	Reading and Literary Skills	Language and Grammar

After Twenty Years (p. 192)
O. Henry
	• *Reading Skills and Strategies: Reaching Struggling Readers*
	  • MiniRead Skill Lesson, p. 101
	  • Selection Skill Lesson, p. 108
	• *Graphic Organizers for Active Reading*, Worksheet p. 13
	• *Literary Elements:*
	  Transparency 3; Worksheet p. 10
		• *Grammar and Language Links:*
		  End Marks, Worksheet p. 21
		• *Language Workshop CD-ROM,*
		  End Marks
		• *Daily Oral Grammar,*
		  Transparency 12

Elements of Literature: Point of View (p. 202)	• *Literary Elements,* Transparency 3	

A Mason-Dixon Memory (p. 205)
Clifton Davis
Connections: Buddies Bare Their Affection for Ill Classmate (p. 212)
from the Austin American Statesman
	• *Reading Skills and Strategies: Reaching Struggling Readers*
	  • Selection Skill Lesson, p. 57
	• *Graphic Organizers for Active Reading*, Worksheet p. 14
		• *Grammar and Language Links:*
		  Commas, Worksheet p. 23
		• *Language Workshop CD-ROM,*
		  Commas
		• *Daily Oral Grammar,*
		  Transparency 13

The No-Guitar Blues (p. 216)
Gary Soto
	• *Reading Skills and Strategies: Reaching Struggling Readers*
	  • MiniRead Skill Lesson, p. 95
	  • Selection Skill Lesson, p. 112
	• *Graphic Organizers for Active Reading*, Worksheet p. 15
		• *Grammar and Language Links:* Comma Splices
		  Worksheet p. 25
		• *Language Workshop CD-ROM,*
		  Run-on Sentences
		• *Daily Oral Grammar,*
		  Transparency 14

Madam and the Rent Man (p. 226)
Langston Hughes
	• *Graphic Organizers for Active Reading*, Worksheet p. 16
	• *Literary Elements:*
	  Poetry Transparencies 1–5
	  Teaching Notes, p. 38	

Bargain (p. 230)
A. B. Guthrie
	• *Reading Skills and Strategies: Reaching Struggling Readers*
	  • Selection Skill Lesson, p. 39
	• *Graphic Organizers for Active Reading*, Worksheet p. 17
		• *Grammar and Language Links:*
		  Apostrophes, Worksheet p. 27
		• *Language Workshop CD-ROM,*
		  Apostrophes
		• *Daily Oral Grammar,*
		  Transparency 15

Amigo Brothers (p. 244)
Piri Thomas
	• *Reading Skills and Strategies: Reaching Struggling Readers*
	  • Selection Skill Lesson, p. 152
	• *Graphic Organizers for Active Reading*, Worksheet p. 18
		• *Grammar and Language Links:*
		  Dialogue, Worksheet p. 29
		• *Language Workshop CD-ROM,*
		  Quotation Marks
		• *Daily Oral Grammar,*
		  Transparency 16

No Questions Asked: Sarah Cynthia Sylvia Stout Would Not Take the Garbage Out (p. 257) Shel Silverstein	The **No Questions Asked** feature provides students with an unstructured opportunity to practice reading strategies using a selection that extends the theme of the collection.	
Writer's Workshop: Supporting a Position (p. 260)		
Sentence Workshop: Run-on Sentences (p. 265)		• *Workshop Resources*, p. 41 • *Language Workshop CD-ROM,* Run-on Sentences
Learning for Life: Using Multiple Sources to Conduct Research on Volunteering (p. 267)		

Collection Planner

Collection Resources

- *Cross-Curricular Activities*, p. 19
- *Portfolio Management System:*
  Introduction to Portfolio Assessment, p. 1;
  Parent/Guardian Letters, p. 91
- *Formal Assessment,*
  Reading Application Test, p. 50
- *Test Generator*, Collection Test

Vocabulary, Spelling, and Decoding	Writing	Listening and Speaking, Viewing and Representing	Assessment
• *Words to Own*, Worksheet p. 10 • *Spelling and Decoding,* Worksheet p. 11	• *Portfolio Management System,* Rubrics for Choices, p. 127	• *Audio CD Library,* Disc 7, Track 2 • *Viewing and Representing:* Fine Art Transparency 6 Worksheet p. 24 • *Portfolio Management System,* Rubrics for Choices, p. 127	• *Formal Assessment,* Selection Test, p. 37 • *Standardized Test Preparation,* p. 34 • *Test Generator* (One-Stop Planner CD-ROM)
			• *Formal Assessment,* Literary Elements Test, p. 37
• *Words to Own*, Worksheet p. 11 • *Spelling and Decoding,* Worksheet p. 12	• *Portfolio Management System,* Rubrics for Choices, p. 128	• *Visual Connections,* Videocassette A, Segment 3 • *Audio CD Library,* Disc 7, Track 3 • *Portfolio Management System,* Rubrics for Choices, p. 128	• *Formal Assessment,* Selection Test, p. 39 • *Standardized Test Preparation,* pp. 36, 38 • *Test Generator* (One-Stop Planner CD-ROM)
• *Spelling and Decoding,* Worksheet p. 13	• *Portfolio Management System,* Rubrics for Choices, p. 129	• *Audio CD Library,* Disc 7, Track 4 • *Portfolio Management System,* Rubrics for Choices, p. 129	• *Formal Assessment,* Selection Test, p. 41 • *Standardized Test Preparation,* p. 40 • *Test Generator* (One-Stop Planner CD-ROM)
	• *Portfolio Management System,* Rubrics for Choices, p. 131	• *Audio CD Library,* Disc 7, Track 5 • *Viewing and Representing:* Fine Art Transparency 7 Worksheet p. 28 • *Portfolio Management System,* Rubrics for Choices, p. 131	• *Formal Assessment,* Selection Test, p. 43 • *Test Generator* (One-Stop Planner CD-ROM)
• *Spelling and Decoding,* Worksheet p. 14	• *Portfolio Management System,* Rubrics for Choices, p. 132	• *Audio CD Library,* Disc 7, Track 6 • *Viewing and Representing:* Fine Art Transparency 8 Worksheet p. 32 • *Portfolio Management System,* Rubrics for Choices, p. 132	• *Formal Assessment,* Selection Test, p. 44 • *Standardized Test Preparation,* p. 42 • *Test Generator* (One-Stop Planner CD-ROM)
• *Words to Own*, Worksheet p. 12 • *Spelling and Decoding,* Worksheet p. 15	• *Portfolio Management System,* Rubrics for Choices, p. 134	• *Audio CD Library,* Disc 8, Track 2 • *Portfolio Management System,* Rubrics for Choices, p. 134	• *Formal Assessment,* Selection Test, p. 46 • *Standardized Test Preparation,* p. 44 • *Test Generator* (One-Stop Planner CD-ROM)
		• *Audio CD Library,* Disc 8, Track 3	

	• *Workshop Resources*, p. 9
	• *Standardized Test Preparation:* Worksheet p. 112 Transparencies 1–6
			• *Portfolio Management System*
			  • Prewriting, p. 135
			  • Peer Editing, p. 136
			  • Assessment Rubric, p. 137

		• *Viewing and Representing,* HRW Multimedia Presentation Maker	• *Portfolio Management System,* Rubrics, p. 138

 Transparency   CD-ROM   Video   Audio CD

Collection Planner

Collection Three

OBJECTIVES

1. Read literature in different genres on the theme "Do the Right Thing"
2. Interpret literary elements used in the literature, with special emphasis on point of view
3. Apply a variety of reading strategies, particularly making predictions
4. Respond to the literature in a variety of modes
5. Learn and use new words
6. Plan, draft, revise, proofread, and publish a persuasive essay supporting a position
7. Develop skill in revising run-on sentences
8. Demonstrate the ability to read and evaluate a persuasive message
9. Explore through a variety of projects the use of multiple sources to conduct research on volunteering

Introducing the Theme

In the stories in this collection, the main characters or characters around them have a common problem; they need to choose between right and wrong. Inform students that they may not always agree with the choices the characters make. Encourage them, though, to examine the reasons behind the characters' choices and the motivations for their decisions.

Responding to the Quotation

Ask students if they agree with Madeleine L'Engle's definition of being human. If they agree, have them give their reasons, for example, being able to choose depends upon the uniquely human ability to reason. If they disagree, have them tell what other abilities or characteristics they think "make us human," such as imagination.

Do the Right Thing

It is the ability to choose which makes us human.

—*Madeleine L'Engle*

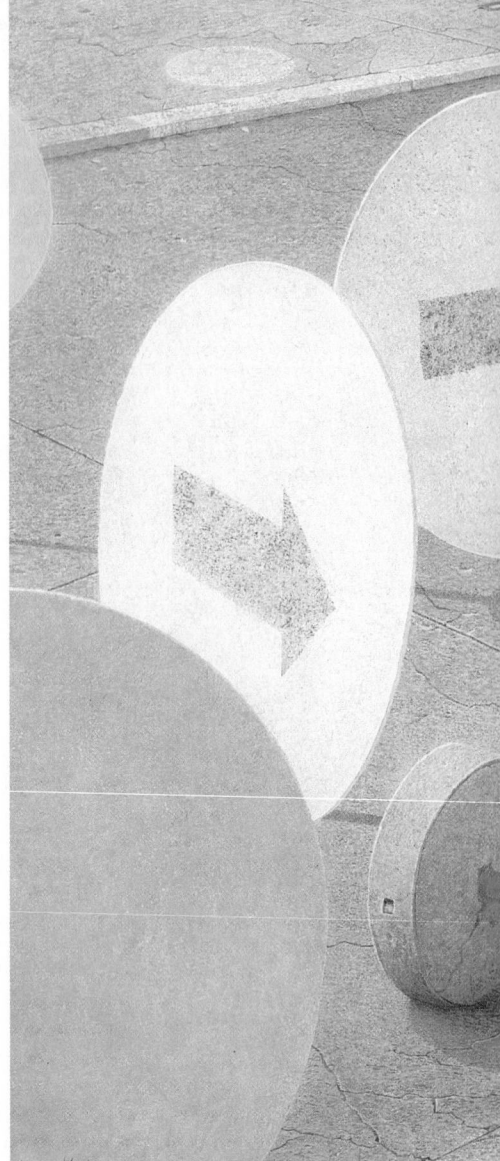

Signs (1961) by Robert Remsen Vickrey.
Tempera on board (27¾" × 41¾").

Writing Focus: Supporting a Position

The following **Work in Progress** assignments build to a culminating **Writer's Workshop** at the end of Collection 3.

- After Twenty Years — Write about conflicting loyalties (p. 200)
- A Mason-Dixon Memory — State opinions about important issues (p. 214)
- The No-Guitar Blues — Brainstorm opinions on selected topics (p. 224)
- Madam and the Rent Man — Take a position in support of tenants (p. 229)
- Bargain — Write strategies to recover a debt (p. 242)
- Amigo Brothers — Make a cluster map to gather ideas (p. 255)

Writer's Workshop: Persuasive Writing / Supporting a Position (p. 260)

In the Collection of the Corcoran Gallery of Art, Washington, D.C. Gift of Roy C. Markus through the FRIENDS of the Corcoran.
© Robert Vickrey/Licensed by VAGA, New York, NY.

191

Robert Remsen Vickrey (1926–   ) is an American painter and art teacher renowned for his technical skill. In fact, the art critic John Canaday referred to him as "the world's most proficient craftsman in egg tempera painting." A short film about Vickrey calls him a "lyrical realist," and most of his paintings are representational (nonabstract), narrative (suggesting a story or chain of events), and vaguely symbolic. Often depicting children or teenagers alone in large rooms or in empty landscapes, they suggest quiet thought, deep feeling, and serious decision making. *Signs* is typical of Vickrey's emphasis on design and his focus on a young person at a dramatic crossroad. **Activity.** Ask students what they think the boy in this picture feels. [Some students may say that he is confused, tired, perhaps overwhelmed by decision making; he has stopped to consider what he will do next.] What do students think the arrow signs might represent? [Responses may include choices, directions, people giving conflicting advice or commands.]

Writer's Notebook

WORK IN PROGRESS

Ask students to make a list of situations they may face in the future that will require them to make choices between right and wrong. Remind students to choose situations that they would not mind sharing with others. Allow time for students to discuss their choices with partners.

Resources

Portfolio Management System
- Introduction to Portfolio Assessment, p. 1
- Parent/Guardian Letters, p. 91

Formal Assessment
- Reading Application Test, p. 50

Test Generator
- Collection Test

Cross-Curricular Activities
- Teaching Notes, p. 19

Selection Readability

This Annotated Teacher's Edition provides a summary of each selection in the student book. Following each Summary heading, you will find one, two, or three small icons. These icons indicate, in an approximate sense, the reading level of the selection.

■ One icon indicates that the selection is easy.

■■ Two icons indicate that the selection is on an intermediate reading level.

■■■ Three icons indicate that the selection is challenging.

OBJECTIVES

1. Read and interpret the story
2. Identify foreshadowing and find clues planted in the story
3. Attack strange words by using context clues
4. Express understanding through persuasive writing, writing a news article, speaking/using another point of view, or performing a radio play
5. Use end marks correctly
6. Understand and use new words

SKILLS

Literary
- Identify foreshadowing and find clues planted in the story

Reading
- Use context clues

Writing
- Collect ideas for an essay
- Write a news article

Speaking/Listening
- Retell the story from another point of view
- Present a group reading

Grammar/Language
- Use end marks correctly

Vocabulary
- Use new words

Viewing/Representing
- Compare cityscapes (ATE)

Planning

- **Block Schedule**
  Block Scheduling Lesson Plans with Pacing Guide
- **Traditional Schedule**
  Lesson Plans Including Strategies for English-Language Learners
- **One-Stop Planner**
  CD-ROM with Test Generator

Before You Read

AFTER TWENTY YEARS

Make the Connection

Do What's Right

Imagine that you write an advice column for your school newspaper. One day you receive this letter from someone in your school.

Last Friday I saw my friend Lucy (not her real name) take a wallet that was left on the cafeteria table. I know she needs the money because her dad is between jobs. I don't know what to do! I mean, I want to do what's right—but I don't know how to handle this. She's just never done anything like this before.

    Sincerely,
    Confused and Can't Sleep

Quickwrite

In a letter, advise "Confused and Can't Sleep." How would you suggest she resolve her problem?

Elements of Literature

Foreshadowing

O. Henry is famous for writing stories with surprise endings. When most readers finish one of his stories, they like to go back to see if he dropped any clues that should have helped them **predict** how the story was going to end. These clues planted in a story are called **foreshadowing**.

Reading Skills and Strategies

Attacking Strange Words

O. Henry loved long words and fancy words. (He read dictionaries for pleasure!) For example, in the second paragraph of this story, he says "pacific thoroughfare." Most people would just say "peaceful street." You can figure out some of O. Henry's difficult words by examining their structure, by looking at **context clues,** or by thinking of words that the unfamiliar word resembles. *Pacific*, for example, resembles *pacifist*, "a person who loves peace." It also resembles *pacifier*, the device you give babies to keep them peaceful.

As you read "After Twenty Years," keep a sheet of paper next to each page so that you can record your thoughts.

Foreshadowing is the use of clues to hint at events that will happen later in a story.

For more on Foreshadowing, see the Handbook of Literary Terms.

Pause after the sixth paragraph, after the face of the man in the doorway is revealed. From the description of this man, what do you guess he is like? What do you **predict** is going to happen next? One student's comments appear on the first page, showing her "dialogue with the text."

go.hrw.com
LE0 7-3

Inset, *The City from Greenwich Village* (1922) by John Sloan. Oil on canvas.

Inset, Gift of Helen Farr Sloan, © 1998 Board of Trustees, National Gallery of Art, Washington, D.C.

Background image, Courtesy of The Valentine Museum, Richmond, Virginia.

192 DO THE RIGHT THING

Preteaching Vocabulary

Words to Own

Have students read the definitions of the Words to Own listed at the bottom of the selection pages. Have several volunteers express each definition in their own words. Then, have students complete each of the following sentences with the correct vocabulary word.

1. David is conceited, and his _____ prevents him from making friends. [egotism]
2. The plans for the complex space station are _____. [intricate]
3. The receiver and the defender reached for the ball _____. [simultaneously]
4. Alana walked _____ to the office to face her punishment. [dismally]
5. After several years, playing video games after school had become _____ with them. [habitual]

After Twenty Years

O. Henry

"We agreed that we would meet here again exactly twenty years from that date and time..."

Responding to the Art

John Sloan (1871–1951) was a leading exemplar of social realism. His canvases call forth the exuberance and angst of modern urban life.

Activity. Ask students to compare Sloan's cityscape with O'Keeffe's on p. 479. In what ways are they similar, and in what ways are they different? What advantages and disadvantages of city living are suggested by each painting?

Summary

On a cold, rainy night in New York City in the early 1900s, a man explains to an approaching policeman that he is waiting to meet an old friend, Jimmy Wells. Two decades earlier, the pair agreed to meet at the same spot in exactly twenty years. Assured that the man will stay until Wells arrives, the officer moves on. Twenty minutes later another man arrives, at first identifying himself as Wells but then announcing that he is a policeman. After arresting Bob as "Silky" Bob, a wanted criminal, he hands him a note from the first patrolman. The note reveals that the patrolman is Wells. He could not bring himself to arrest his old friend and "got a plainclothes man to do the job."

Resources

Listening
Audio CD Library
A recording of this story is provided in the *Audio CD Library*:
• Disc 7, Track 2

Resources: Print and Media

Reading
• *Reading Skills and Strategies*
  MiniRead Skill Lesson, p. 101
  Selection Skill Lesson, p. 108
• *Graphic Organizers for Active Reading*, p. 13
• *Words to Own*, p. 10
• *Spelling and Decoding*
  Worksheet, p. 11
• *Audio CD Library*
  Disc 7, Track 2

Elements of Literature
• *Literary Elements*
  Transparency 3
  Worksheet, p. 10

Writing and Language
• *Daily Oral Grammar*
  Transparency 12
• *Grammar and Language Links*
  Worksheet, p. 21
• *Language Workshop CD-ROM*

Viewing and Representing
• *Viewing and Representing*
  Fine Art Transparency 6
  Fine Art Worksheet, p. 24

Assessment
• *Formal Assessment*, p. 37
• *Portfolio Management System*, p. 127
• *Standardized Test Preparation*, p. 34
• *Test Generator (One-Stop Planner CD-ROM)*

Internet
• go.hrw.com (keyword: LE0 7-3)

A Reading Skills and Strategies

Attacking Strange Words

Dividing a word into its root and its prefixes or suffixes is an effective way to unlock its meaning. *Depeopled* is made up of *peopled*, meaning "having people," and the prefix *de-*, meaning "not." Ask students to give synonyms for *depeopled*. [emptied, abandoned] In the third paragraph, students can use the strategy on *unlighted*.

B Reading Skills and Strategies

Responding to the Text

Ask students if they had any of the same questions as they were reading the first paragraph. If any passage in the story raises questions like these, or puzzles or surprises them, they should make a note.

C Elements of Literature

Foreshadowing

❓ Do you think these details might be clues to a later surprise in the story? Why or why not? [Possible responses: Yes, the scar and flashy diamond pin suggest facts about the man that may be revealed later. No, he is just a tough and showy person.]

D Appreciating Language

Punctuation

❓ The last sentence in the paragraph is made up of two independent clauses. What changes in punctuation and capitalization would you use to make two separate sentences? ["...New York. He thought...'"]

The policeman on the beat moved up the avenue impressively. The impressiveness was <u>habitual</u> and not for show, for spectators were few. The time was barely ten o'clock at night, but chilly gusts of wind with a taste of rain **A** in them had well nigh depeopled the streets.

Trying doors as he went, twirling his club with many <u>intricate</u> and artful movements, turning now and then to cast his watchful eye down the pacific[1] thoroughfare, the officer, with his stalwart form and slight swagger, made a fine picture of a guardian of the peace. The vicinity was one that kept early hours. Now and then you might see the lights of a cigar store or of an all-night lunch counter, but the majority of the doors belonged to business places that had long since been closed.

When about midway of a certain block, the policeman suddenly slowed his walk. In the doorway of a darkened hardware store a man leaned with an unlighted cigar in his mouth. As the policeman walked up to him, the man spoke up quickly.

"It's all right, officer," he said reassuringly. "I'm just waiting for a friend. It's an appointment made twenty years ago. Sounds a little funny to you, doesn't it? Well, I'll explain if you'd like to make certain it's all straight. About that long ago there used to be a restaurant where this store stands—'Big Joe' Brady's restaurant."

"Until five years ago," said the policeman. "It was torn down then."

C The man in the doorway struck a match and lit his cigar. The light showed a pale, square-jawed face with keen eyes and a little white scar near his right eyebrow. His scarf pin was a large diamond, oddly set.

"Twenty years ago tonight," said the man, "I dined here at 'Big Joe' Brady's with Jimmy Wells, my best chum and the finest chap in the world. He and I were raised here in New York, just like two brothers, together. I was eighteen and Jimmy was twenty. The next morning I was to start for the **D** West to make my fortune. You couldn't have dragged Jimmy out of New York; he thought it was the only place on earth.

1. **pacific:** here, peaceful.

WORDS TO OWN

habitual (hə·bich'oo·əl) *adj.*: done or fixed by habit; customary.
intricate (in'tri·kit) *adj.*: complicated; full of detail.

---

194 DO THE RIGHT THING

Dialogue with the Text

What was impressive about the policeman?

B Does this take place in a city?

Were these movements what made him impressive?

He was obviously an experienced "guardian of the peace."

Did he slow his walk because of apprehension or curiosity?

Why did the man assume that the policeman was going to question him and that he needed to supply an answer before a question was even asked?

The man is obviously familiar with the town.

Has the policeman let down his guard?

Extremely descriptive—gives a nice picture of the man in a few sentences.

Hester Reed

—Hester Reed
The Dutchess Day School
Millbrook, New York

Listening to Music ♪

"Ringo" by Don Robertson and Hal Blair, performed by Lorne Greene

This ballad about the outlaw Johnny Ringo was a hit in 1964 for Lorne Greene, who portrayed Ben Cartwright in the TV Western *Bonanza*.

Activity

Have students listen to "Ringo" and compare the characters, situations, and themes with those in the O. Henry story.

Reaching All Students

Struggling Readers

Using Context Clues was introduced on p. 192. For a lesson directly tied to this selection that teaches students to use context clues, see the *Reading Skills and Strategies* binder:

• MiniRead Skill Lesson, p. 101
• Selection Skill Lesson, p. 108

English Language Learners

Write these idioms from the story on the chalkboard (without the bracketed definitions): *to cast a watchful eye* [to pay careful attention]; *to get into a groove* (p. 195) [to live according to a routine]; *to put a razor edge on someone* [to toughen a person] (p. 195). Ask students to volunteer definitions and help them decide on the ones that are correct.

Well, we agreed that night that we would meet here again exactly twenty years from that date and time, no matter what our conditions might be or from what distance we might have to come. We figured that in twenty years each of us ought to have our destiny worked out and our fortunes made, whatever they were going to be."

"It sounds pretty interesting," said the policeman. "Rather a long time between meets, though, it seems to me. Haven't you heard from your friend since you left?"

"Well, yes, for a time we corresponded," said the other. "But after a year or two we lost track of each other. You see, the West is a pretty big proposition, and I kept hustling around over it pretty lively. But I know Jimmy will meet me here if he's alive, for he always was the truest, staunchest old chap in the world. He'll never forget. I came a thousand miles to stand in this door tonight, and it's worth it if my old partner turns up."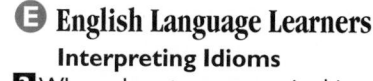

The waiting man pulled out a handsome watch, the lids of it set with small diamonds.

"Three minutes to ten," he announced. "It was exactly ten o'clock when we parted here at the restaurant door."

"Did pretty well out West, didn't you?" asked the policeman.

"You bet! I hope Jimmy has done half as well. He was a kind of plodder, though, good fellow as he was. I've had to compete with some of the sharpest wits going to get my pile. A man gets in a groove in New York. It takes the West to put a razor edge on him."

LITERATURE AND HISTORY

Home, Sweet Home: The O. Henry Museum

Will Porter—better known by his pen name, O. Henry—lived in Austin, Texas, for more than thirteen years. The city has restored the house where O. Henry lived, along with his wife and child, and turned it into a museum. Among the programs sponsored by the museum are the O. Henry Writing Clubs, which encourage the efforts of young writers, and a yearly wordplay tournament, the O. Henry Pun-Off World Championships (a fitting tribute to a man who loved words and who read the dictionary for fun).

AFTER TWENTY YEARS 195

E English Language Learners
Interpreting Idioms
? Where does *pretty* occur in this passage? ["pretty interesting," "pretty big," "pretty lively"] Point out that this informal word means "quite" or "very." How does the man use *pretty* here? [Possible response: He uses it to emphasize the size of the country and the quickness of his movements.]

F Reading Skills and Strategies
Attacking Strange Words
? Students can use context clues to determine the meaning of *staunchest*. What does the man stress about Jimmy? [Possible response: Jimmy doesn't forget a promise.] What kind of friend is someone like this? [Possible response: a loyal one.]

G Elements of Literature
Foreshadowing
? What do the man's boasts suggest might happen to him? [Possible response: He brags about competing against sharp wits. He will either outwit someone or face his downfall.]

Resources
Viewing and Representing
Fine Art Transparency
Examining Edward Hopper's *Nighthawks* may help students visualize the setting and the mood of "After Twenty Years."
- Transparency 6
- Worksheet, p. 24

Elements of Literature
For additional instruction on analyzing point of view, see *Literary Elements:*
- Transparency 3
- Worksheet, p. 10

Skill Link

Decoding: The Letters c and g
Point out that the letters *c* and *g* have both hard sounds and soft sounds. Use these words to illustrate the hard and the soft sounds of initial *c* and *g: cast, gasoline; certain, genuine; city, ginger; compete, good; customer, gust.* Help students recognize that *c* and *g* stand for the hard sounds /k/ and /g/ before the vowels *a, o,* and *u,* and for the soft sounds /s/ and /j/ before *e* and *i.* The letters *c* and *g* also stand for their hard sounds when they are followed by another consonant: *crib, glide.* When *c* or *g* occurs at the end of a word, it stands for the hard sounds (*panic, big*). A final *e* changes the sounds to soft (*police, page*). Use *electric* and *electricity* to demonstrate the effect that the letter *i* has on *c.*

Activity
Write the following items on the board. Ask a volunteer to read an item aloud and then call on a classmate to explain why *c* or *g* has a hard or soft sound in each underlined word.
1. Her pacific nature seemed genuine.
2. His egotism was enlarged by success.
3. Garbage was strewn about the vicinity.
4. An orange flower was lying on the cement.
5. The citizen made a gigantic mistake when she forged her birth certificate.

Ⓐ Critical Thinking

Challenging the Text

❓ Do you think O. Henry exaggerates the man's admiration for Jimmy? Give your reasons. [Possible responses: Yes, he made the point, and the repetition is irritating; no, the man sincerely believes in Jimmy and in Jimmy's faithfulness.]

Ⓑ Struggling Readers

Breaking Down Difficult Text

❓ Long sentences with phrases and clauses between the subject and the verb can be broken down into separate, shorter sentences for easier reading. What four thoughts have been combined to create this sentence? [And in the door of the hardware store the man smoked his cigar and waited. The man had come a thousand miles to fill an appointment. The appointment was uncertain almost to absurdity. The appointment was with the friend of his youth.]

Ⓒ Elements of Literature

Foreshadowing

❓ Do you think the man's height is a clue to a significant event in the plot? Why or why not? [Possible responses: Yes, Jimmy probably would not have grown that much taller after the age of twenty, and so maybe the tall man is not Jimmy. No, Jimmy might have grown taller.]

Ⓓ Elements of Literature

Foreshadowing

❓ What clue in this passage suggests that the situation is not what it seems? [Possible response: The tall man is very vague about his job and about the place he is taking his "friend."]

Ⓔ Reading Skills and Strategies

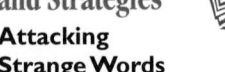

Attacking Strange Words

❓ What does the noun *position* usually mean? [a place] What is a *position* in a city department? [a job]

The policeman twirled his club and took a step or two.

"I'll be on my way. Hope your friend comes around all right. Going to call time on him sharp?"

Ⓐ "I should say not!" said the other. "I'll give him half an hour at least. If Jimmy is alive on earth, he'll be here by that time. So long, officer."

"Good night, sir," said the policeman, passing on along his beat, trying doors as he went.

There was now a fine, cold drizzle falling, and the wind had risen from its uncertain puffs into a steady blow. The few foot passengers astir in that quarter hurried <u>dismally</u> and silently along with coat collars turned high and pocketed hands. And in the door of the hardware store the man who had come a thousand miles to fill an appointment, uncertain almost to absurdity, with the friend of his youth, smoked his cigar and waited.

About twenty minutes he waited, and then a tall man in a long overcoat, with collar turned up to his ears, hurried across from the opposite side of the street. He went directly to the waiting man.

"Is that you, Bob?" he asked, doubtfully.

"Is that you, Jimmy Wells?" cried the man in the door.

"Bless my heart!" exclaimed the new arrival, grasping both the other's hands with his own. "It's Bob, sure as fate. I was certain I'd find you here if you were still in existence. Well, well, well!—twenty years is a long time. The old restaurant's gone, Bob; I wish it had lasted, so we could have had another dinner there. How has the West treated you, old man?"

Ⓒ "Bully;[2] it has given me everything I asked it for. You've changed lots, Jimmy. I never thought you were so tall by two or three inches."

"Oh, I grew a bit after I was twenty."

"Doing well in New York, Jimmy?"

---

2. **bully:** informal term meaning "very well."

196 DO THE RIGHT THING

Ⓓ "Moderately. I have a position in one of the city departments. Come on, Bob; we'll go Ⓔ around to a place I know of and have a good long talk about old times."

The two men started up the street, arm in arm. The man from the West, his <u>egotism</u> enlarged by success, was beginning to outline the history of his career. The other, submerged in his overcoat, listened with interest.

At the corner stood a drugstore, brilliant with electric lights. When they came into this

---

WORDS TO OWN

dismally (diz′məl·ē) *adv.*: miserably; gloomily.
egotism (ē′gō·tiz′əm) *n.*: conceit; talking about oneself too much.

Making the Connections

Connecting to the Theme: "Do the Right Thing"

After students have finished reading the story and discussed whether they think Jimmy did the right thing, remind students that "Silky" Bob also had choices to make. How might his life have been different if he had remained in close touch with his friend Jimmy?

Developing Vocabulary by Listening to Literature Read Aloud

Students acquire vocabulary through listening to selections read aloud. Vocabulary and style in a vintage story like this one can sometimes challenge contemporary readers. Read aloud or play the recording of the first few paragraphs of this story. Ask students to jot down unfamiliar words or phrases as they listen. (Students might list *thoroughfare, spectators,* and *lunch counter.*) Write some of the words on the board, and ask students to guess at their meanings. Students should draw on their experiences and use the context to figure out a word's meaning.

glare, each of them turned <u>simultaneously</u> to gaze upon the other's face.

The man from the West stopped suddenly and released his arm.

"You're not Jimmy Wells," he snapped. **F** "Twenty years is a long time, but not long enough to change a man's nose from a Roman to a pug."

"It sometimes changes a good man into a bad one," said the tall man. "You've been under arrest for ten minutes, 'Silky' Bob. Chicago thinks you may have dropped over our way and wires us she wants to have a chat with you. Going quietly, are you? That's sensible. Now, before we go to the station, here's a note I was asked to hand to you. You may read it here at the window. It's from Patrolman Wells." **G**

The man from the West unfolded the little piece of paper handed him. His hand was steady when he began to read, but it trembled a little by the time he had finished. The note was rather short.

> Bob: I was at the appointed place on time. When you struck the match to light your cigar, I saw it was the face of the man wanted in Chicago. Somehow I couldn't do it myself, so I went around and got a plainclothes man to do the job. **H**
>
> Jimmy

WORDS TO OWN

simultaneously (sī′məl·tā′nē·əs·lē) *adv.*: at the same time.

MEET THE WRITER

"Stories in Everything"

O. Henry (1862–1910) is the pen name of William Sydney Porter, who was born in Greensboro, North Carolina. He left school at fifteen and eventually moved to Texas. There he edited a humor magazine called *The Rolling Stone* and worked for a few years in a bank in Austin. Unfortunately, Porter was a careless record keeper. Two years after he left the bank, he was accused of embezzling its money. Although he was probably innocent, Porter panicked and ran off to Honduras. A year or so later, he returned to Austin to be with his dying wife. There, he was convicted and spent three years in a federal prison in Ohio.

Porter found the plots of many of his stories (including "After Twenty Years") in jail. He may also have found his famous pen name there: The name of a prison guard was Orrin Henry.

After he was released from prison in 1901, Porter moved to New York. Soon, as

O. Henry, he became one of the country's most popular short-story writers. His stories are known for their snappy surprise endings. Many of his best-known stories are set in New York's streets and tenements and cheap hotels.

One day, while O. Henry was dining with friends at a New York restaurant, a young writer asked him where he got his plots. "Oh, everywhere," replied O. Henry. "There are stories in everything." He picked up the menu on which the dishes of the day were typewritten. "There's a story in this," he said. And then he outlined the story called "Springtime à la Carte." (On menus, *à la carte* means that each item is priced separately.)

More from the Pen of O. Henry

"After Twenty Years" is from a collection called *The Four Million and Other Stories* (Airmont). This title refers to the population of New York City in O. Henry's day. Other O. Henry stories set in New York include "The Gift of the Magi" and "The Last Leaf."

AFTER TWENTY YEARS 197

F Elements of Literature

Foreshadowing

❓ This is the moment of recognition toward which all the foreshadowing has been pointing. What do you think will happen to "Silky" Bob, who bragged of defeating many sharp wits? [Possible response: He will be tricked and defeated.]

G Appreciating Language

Punctuation

❓ Why is a period the correct end mark for the first sentence? [The sentence is a statement.] Why does "Going quietly, are you?" end with a question mark? [It is meant to be read as a question.] What end mark would the writer have used to show strong emotions? [exclamation point]

H Elements of Literature

Situational Irony

❓ What is surprising about the ending of the story? [Possible response: The patrolman is actually Bob's friend Jimmy.] What ending did you expect? [Possible response: Jimmy forgets about the meeting and never appears.]

Resources ———

Selection Assessment
Formal Assessment
• Selection Test, p. 37
Test Generator
• Selection Test

Assessing Learning

Check Test: True-False
1. Bob waits in a doorway to meet his old friend Jimmy Wells. [True]
2. Bob last saw Jimmy ten years before. [False]
3. Bob recognizes Jimmy as soon as he sees him. [False]
4. The third man in the story is a plainclothes police officer. [True]
5. Jimmy Wells tells the other police officer where to find Bob. [True]

Standardized Test Preparation
For practice with standardized test format specific to this selection, see
• *Standardized Test Preparation*, p. 34
For practice in proofreading and editing, see
• *Daily Oral Grammar*, Transparency 12

BROWSING IN THE FILES

About the Author. Porter drew on a wide range of experiences when he wrote his stories. He had been a ranch hand, land agent, bank teller, magazine publisher, newspaper reporter, cartoonist, druggist, and prison convict. He may even have met a real-life "Silky" Bob while he was in prison.

Student to Student

A ### Critical Thinking
Analyzing Character
❓ After reading this paragraph, what word would you use to describe Sam? [Possible responses: hardworking, optimistic, persistent.]

B ### Reading Skills and Strategies
Responding to the Text
❓ If Joe is so unlikable, why is Sam his friend? [Possible response: Joe is the star pitcher, and Sam idolizes him.]

C ### Reading Skills and Strategies
Drawing Conclusions
❓ Whose fault is it that the team lost the game? Why? [Possible response: Joe blames Sam for losing the game, but he realizes that it was his fault. He threw a fastball to a good hitter on two strikes, instead of throwing the curve that Sam had signaled.]

D ### Elements of Literature
Symbols
❓ What might the items Sam is carrying stand for? [Possible responses: Sam carries all the equipment, just as he "carries" the burden of responsibility for the unity of the team. Joe carries "nothing," since he does not shoulder any responsibility.]

Student to Student

The Pitch That Didn't Work

"Steeeeriiike two!" called the umpire.

"Way to go, Joe!" Sam yelled out of his thick catcher's mask. Sam was always on the bright side of things. Even when he went zero for four, made two errors behind the plate, and his team was losing by five runs, he would still have a positive attitude and continue to try, despite the obviousness of his not being a good athlete.

Joe stared down as Sam gave the sign for the curve. Joe shook it off because he always wanted to put on the heat with two strikes.

"Time!" yelled Joe. "Listen," he said as Sam came out to meet him on the mound, "I'll throw what I want to throw! If I want to throw heat, I'll do it!" Joe had always been very stubborn and very critical. He didn't have one friend in the world besides Sam, who looked up to him as the star pitcher of the league for three years in a row but who also relied on him to be his friend. There was an odd relationship between the two, but somehow they had always worked it out one way or another.

Sam returned to home plate, a little frustrated that Joe wouldn't listen to him but knowing it wasn't anything new, as Joe did this all the time.

"Let's fire it in here, buddy!" yelled Sam.

Joe kicked up, released, and as the fastball came out, there was a loud crack of the bat. As Sammy had foreseen, Brad Newsome, a fifteen-year-old and the biggest player in the league, crushed it deep to left-center field. Everyone knew it was gone.

This was the first game Joe had lost this whole year, and Joe blamed it on Sam for stirring everything up.

At the end of the inning, Joe and Sam's coach, Harvey Mulock, gave a lecture to the team, who were sulking around the dugout. He chewed them out about how they had to get their attitudes straightened out, and after that he took Joe and Sam outside the dugout to have a private talk.

"Which one of you is responsible for the home run by Brad Newsome? If it just got away and it was a mistake, then tell me, Joe, why did you give him that pitch? You know better."

"It was my fault, Coach Mulock," answered Sam. "I gave the wrong sign when I knew that Brad grooves on fastballs, and I just wasn't thinking. I'm really sorry."

"That's OK; just try to get things worked out on what you're going to throw before you do it."

Phew, was what was going through both Joe's and Sam's heads. Joe knew he had done the wrong thing and not spoken up, but then again, he thought to himself, if Sam's going to stick up for me and apologize even though it was really my fault, then let him be that stupid. I'm not going to stop him.

After the game, Joe and Sam walked off together as always, Sam carrying the bats, balls, and gloves, and Joe carrying nothing.

—Michael Levitin
Forestville School
Forestville, California

198 DO THE RIGHT THING

Connecting Across Texts

Connecting with "After Twenty Years"
Divide the class into groups of three or four. Ask the groups to discuss how Sam's decision is different from Jimmy's in "After Twenty Years." Students may say that by apologizing for a mistake he did not make, Sam covers up for Joe's error. He is too loyal to his friend. Jimmy decides that having Bob arrested is more important than being loyal to a friend who has committed a crime. Then, give each group five minutes to arrive at a consensus for an answer to this question: Does Sam do the right thing? That is, is his decision a good or a bad one? Then, call on a member from each group to present the group's conclusion to the class. Some groups may decide that Sam is protecting Joe from criticism that he deserves. Others may admire Sam's loyalty to his friend.

MAKING MEANINGS

MAKING MEANINGS

First Thoughts

[respond]

1. What would you have done if you'd been in Jimmy's situation? Talk about whether or not you think he did the right thing.

Shaping Interpretations

[analyze]

2. Two old friends keep an appointment made twenty years earlier. What does the fact that they both turn up say about their friendship?

[speculate]

3. Why did the police officer need to know if the man would wait for his friend or "call time on him sharp"? What do you think the officer would have done if the man had said he would leave at ten o'clock?

[identify]

4. Did you guess who the police officer was? Go back to the text and find clues that hint at, or **foreshadow**, something sinister about the man in the doorway.

[interpret]

5. Jimmy Wells had an **internal conflict:** He had to decide what to do about his friend. How did he resolve his problem? Why do you think he didn't do the job himself?

Connecting with the Text

[evaluate]

6. Take a look at the advice you gave to "Confused and Can't Sleep" in your Quickwrite notes. What do you think Jimmy Wells would say about your advice?

[connect]

7. "After Twenty Years" and "The Pitch That Didn't Work" (page 198) raise interesting questions about friendship. What do you think of Joe and Sam's friendship? How should friends treat one another?

Reading Check

a. Why had the stranger come back to the old neighborhood after twenty years?

b. What did the police officer realize when the man in the doorway lit his cigar?

c. What had the man from the West done to make his fortune?

d. What did the police officer do after saying good night to the man in the doorway?

Courtesy of the Valentine Museum, Richmond, Virginia.

AFTER TWENTY YEARS 199

MAKING MEANINGS

First Thoughts

1. Possible responses: I think Jimmy did the right thing; turning in a criminal is more important than maintaining a friendship. No, I would have urged my friend to confess with the chance of getting a lighter sentence.

Shaping Interpretations

2. Possible responses: They have strong memories of their friendship; each is curious about how the other's life has turned out.

3. Possible response: He needed to be sure he had time to send for another officer. Otherwise, the officer would have had to arrest his friend himself or let him go.

4. Possible responses: I guessed who the police officer was because he listened to so much of "Silky" Bob's story. Clues include Bob's scar, his diamonds, his skulking in the doorway, and his bragging.

5. Possible responses: Jimmy resolves his problem by choosing morality over friendship. By having someone else arrest his friend, he avoids a painful personal meeting.

Connecting with the Text

6. Jimmy would probably agree with the advice if it suggests returning the wallet or turning in the thief.

7. Students may comment that some people find good qualities in people whom others don't like. Most students will probably agree, however, that people should not treat their friends the way that Joe treats Sam and that Sam is allowing his friendship to be abused.

Reading Check

a. He returned in order to fulfill his promise to meet an old friend.

b. He realized that the man was a criminal wanted by the Chicago police.

c. The story does not specify his activities, although he implies he succeeded by using his wits. His name "Silky" suggests a smooth operator. He may be a con man, a thief, or a gangster.

d. He writes a note to "Silky" Bob and sends a plainclothes officer to arrest him.

Grading Timesaver

Rubrics for each Choices assignment appear on p. 127 in the *Portfolio Management System*.

CHOICES: Building Your Portfolio

1. **Writer's Notebook** Remind students to save their work for Writer's Notebook activities; they may be able to use their work for the Writer's Workshop on pp. 260-264.

2. **News Article** Use a story from a newspaper as a model. Ask students to read it and to provide appropriate answers for the news story questions before writing their own news article.

3. **Speaking/Using Another Point of View** Remind students to use a casual, conversational tone for Bob's voice. They might also incorporate some of the old slang expressions that Bob uses. Allow them to make notes on what they will say, but ask them to ad-lib instead of simply reading scripted dialogue.

4. **Performance/Radio Play** Remind students that radio programs depend entirely on sound to express action. If possible, play a tape of an old radio program, particularly a mystery or a thriller. As they listen, ask students to identify the action and to guess how the sound effects were created.

CHOICES: Building Your Portfolio

Writer's Notebook

1. Collecting Ideas for Supporting a Position

Jimmy Wells took a stand. He did what he thought was the right thing, even though he had to betray someone who had been like a brother to him. If you knew that your best friend had done something wrong, what would you do? Think about a situation like this that you might face. Take a few minutes to describe the situation. Then, take a position, and list some reasons supporting it.

> My best friend told me a secret about another friend. I think my other friend should know. If I tell, my best friend will be mad.

News Article

2. Cop Busts Best Buddy

New York, 1906—You are a reporter for the *New York World,* the newspaper O. Henry once worked for. You cover the police beat, and you hear the story of Jimmy Wells and his chum "Silky" Bob from the plainclothes man who brought Bob in. Write an article about it for the morning edition. A news story should answer these questions at the beginning of the article:

- *What* happened?
- *Who* was involved?
- *Why* did it happen?
- *When* and *where* did it happen?
- *How* did it happen?

Speaking/Using Another Point of View

3. "I'd Traveled a Thousand Miles . . ."

Retell "After Twenty Years" from Bob's point of view. Imagine you are "Silky" Bob talking to a fellow prisoner, telling the story of how you got caught by your old friend Jimmy Wells. Tape-record your account the first time you tell it. Then, play back the tape, and polish your wording and your delivery until you're ready to tell the class "Silky" Bob's story.

Performance/ Radio Play

4. Play It by Ear

With a group of four classmates, read "After Twenty Years" aloud as if you were performing a radio play. One of you can be the narrator. Three can read the parts of Bob, Jimmy Wells, and the plainclothes man. The fifth person can do sound effects—wind, footsteps, and the striking of a match—at the points where they're heard in the story. Practice varying the loudness and softness of your voice. When you've got it just right, tape-record your performance. Take turns giving the tape to schoolmates, family, and friends to listen to.

GRAMMAR LINK

MINI-LESSON

End All End-Mark Errors

Language Handbook HELP

See Sentences Classified by Purpose, pages 759-760; *End Marks*, page 768.

Technology HELP

See Language Workshop CD-ROM. *Key word entry: end marks.*

If you mean yes, nod and you'll be understood—unless you're in Turkey, where a nod means no. Every language has its own conventions, or accepted rules. In written English the accepted rule states that every sentence must begin with a capital letter and end with one of these **end marks:** a period, a question mark, or an exclamation point. Follow these simple rules:

1. Use a period at the end of a statement.

   EXAMPLE "It's an appointment made twenty years ago."

2. Use a question mark at the end of a question.

   EXAMPLE "Is that you, Bob?"

3. Use an exclamation point at the end of an exclamation or a command.

   EXAMPLES "You bet!"
   "Bless my heart!"

Try It Out

Rewrite the following paragraph, adding capitalization and end punctuation marks. (The paragraph contains a total of seven sentences.)

Charlie tried out for the baseball team what did he have to lose it's not as if you have to be Ken Griffey, Jr., to play a position who imagined what would happen it was such a surprise unbelievably, he's hitting lead-off I guess you never know

---

VOCABULARY

HOW TO OWN A WORD

WORD BANK

habitual
intricate
dismally
egotism
simultaneously

Attacking Strange Words

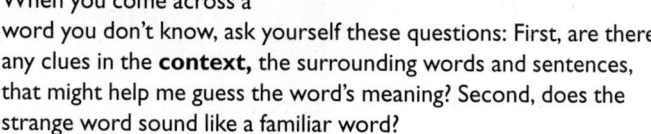

When you come across a word you don't know, ask yourself these questions: First, are there any clues in the **context,** the surrounding words and sentences, that might help me guess the word's meaning? Second, does the strange word sound like a familiar word?

Try to guess the meaning of *habitual* from this sentence on page 194: "The policeman on the beat moved up the avenue impressively. The impressiveness was <u>habitual</u> and not for show, for spectators were few."

The first clue is that *habitual* looks and sounds like *habit,* which means "usual way of doing something." The second clue is in the sentence itself. We learn that the police officer doesn't move impressively just to show off. It is a habit with him.

How are you at building in clues? Write five sentences about the story using the Word Bank words. Fill the sentences with context clues.

GRAMMAR LINK

Ask students to use different colored pencils to underline different types of end marks in assignments they have written earlier. Have them revise all sentences that contain incorrect end marks.

Try It Out
Possible Answers

Charlie tried out for the baseball team. What did he have to lose? It's not as if you have to be Ken Griffey, Jr., to play a position. Who imagined what would happen? It was such a surprise! Unbelievably, he's hitting lead-off. I guess you never know.

VOCABULARY
Possible Answers

1. Without thinking, Bob kept rubbing his finger across his huge diamond ring, a gesture that was <u>habitual</u> with him.
2. Some police operations are <u>intricate</u>; by contrast, this one was simple.
3. On this gray and wintry day, the rain was falling <u>dismally</u>.
4. Many criminals can't resist bragging about their exploits, and their <u>egotism</u> eventually betrays them.
5. All of a sudden, Bob realized his situation, and, <u>simultaneously</u>, the plainclothes officer arrested him.

Resources ———

Grammar
• *Grammar and Language Links,* p. 21

Vocabulary
• *Words to Own,* p. 10

Spelling
For related instruction, see
• *Spelling and Decoding,* p. 11

Grammar Link
Quick Check

Revise the following sentences by adding the correct end mark: period, question mark, or exclamation point. (Answers may vary slightly.)

1. Can you imagine what it would be like to see an old friend after twenty years [?]
2. I know it would be a shock [.]
3. With which friend might you make such an agreement [?]
4. I would choose either Jose or Luisa [.]
5. Wow, what a story that was [!]

Resources

Elements of Literature
Point of View
For additional instruction on point of view, see *Literary Elements:*
• Transparency 3

Assessment
Formal Assessment
• Literary Elements Test, p. 37

Elements of Literature

This feature introduces the three major types of point of view used in narratives: omniscient, first person, and third-person limited. Each type is defined and its effects are illustrated in passages from the fairy tale of the Frog Prince, retold from different points of view.

Mini-Lesson:
Point of View

• After students have read both pages in the pupil's edition, explain to the class what the word *bias* means (a way of viewing the world). Then, inform them that first-person storytellers always have biases that color the stories they tell. It is sometimes said that biases cause a narrator to lean toward one particular retelling.

• Lead the class in brainstorming a list on the chalkboard of possible biases for the boy in the cartoon; then, brainstorm a list for the monsters.

• Ask students to work in groups of three or four to use the lists to make up brief stories (one paragraph each) from three different points of view: the boy's, the monsters', and finally, an unbiased omniscient narrator's.

• When everyone has finished, allow time for students to read their stories aloud.

POINT OF VIEW: Through Whose Eyes? *by* John Leggett

When you were little, you probably imagined at one time or another that there was something terrifying under your bed. Did it ever occur to you that that something might find *you* just as terrifying? As the saying goes, "It all depends on your point of view." When you're telling a story, you look at things one way—your way. When someone else tells the story, he or she will put a slightly different spin on the same events.

Novels and short stories are also told from a particular **point of view,** or vantage point. When you're reading, you should ask, "Who is the narrator?" and "What is the narrator's relationship to the story?"

The Big Three

The three most common points of view are the omniscient, the first person, and the third-person limited.

The **omniscient** (äm·nish'ənt) **point of view** is the all-knowing point of view. (In Latin, *omnis* means "all" and *sciens* means "knowing.")

THE FAR SIDE By GARY LARSON

"I've got it again, Larry . . . an eerie feeling there's something on top of the bed."

You can think of an omniscient narrator as being above the action, looking down on it like a god. This narrator can tell you everything about all the characters, even their most private thoughts.

Using Students' Strengths

Verbal Learners
Divide the class into groups of three, and ask students to choose Bob, Jimmy, or the plain-clothes policeman in "After Twenty Years." Give students time to make notes on how the story would be told from their character's first-person perspective. Allow students to use the notes to tell aloud, in groups, summaries of the story from the point of view of their character. Remind students to ad-lib, not read, and to use the pronoun *I*.

Interpersonal Learners
Ask students to stage a journalist's interview with someone who knew "Silky" Bob. Possibilities include Bob's mother, a business associate from the West, Bob's lawyer, or the restaurant owner "Big Joe" Brady. The journalist and the interviewee should ask questions or provide information that sheds light on Bob's character.

- What is the point of view used in "After Twenty Years"? [omniscient]
- Name several details that the story's point of view enables you to know. [Possible responses: the impressive manner of the patrolman's walk, the diamonds set in Bob's watch, Bob's trembling hand as he reads the note.]
- Name several details that the story's point of view *could* tell you but doesn't. [Possible responses: the nature of Bob's crimes, Bob's thoughts as he waits in the doorway, Jimmy's thoughts as he decides to turn in his friend.]
- How does the story's point of view help to create the effect of the surprise ending? [Possible responses: The omniscient point of view enables the author to control the amount of knowledge the reader has about Bob and Jimmy. In particular, the omniscient narrator does not tell the reader that the patrolman is Jimmy, withholding that surprise for the ending.]

Once upon a time there lived a princess who would have been perfectly happy except for one thing: In a moment of weakness, she had promised to marry a frog.

Her father felt sorry for her, but he insisted that she keep her word. (In fact, he was a little nervous—he'd never met a talking frog before.) "After all, a promise is a promise," agreed her mother, who thought the frog was better looking than the princess's last boyfriend. Little did any of the royal family know who the frog really was.

A story can also be told by one of the characters. In this viewpoint the character speaks as "I." We call this the **first-person point of view.** ("I" is the first-person pronoun.) In this point of view, we know only what this one character can tell us. Sometimes that isn't very reliable.

I couldn't believe that my parents were actually going to make me marry a slimy, ugly, bulgy-eyed frog! They didn't feel sorry for me at all! All they cared about was a stupid promise I never thought I'd have to keep.

Often a story is seen through the eyes of one character, but the character is *not* telling the story as "I." This is called the **third-person limited point of view.** In this point of view, a narrator zooms in on the thoughts and feelings of just one character in the story. This point of view helps us share that character's reactions to the story's events.

The princess tried desperately to get out of her promise. It was all her parents' fault, she thought. They were so unfair. But she had a nagging feeling that she had only herself to blame—and the frog. "I wonder if the royal chef knows how to cook frogs' legs?" she said to herself.

Point of view is very important in storytelling, and writers love to experiment with it. Someone who wanted to tell the frog-and-princess story from a really unusual point of view might choose to let the frog tell it.

Drawing by Chas. Addams. © 1964, 1992. The New Yorker Magazine, Inc.

"Personally, I can't imagine what he sees in her."

ELEMENTS OF LITERATURE: POINT OF VIEW **203**

Reaching All Students

Struggling Readers
Review with students the definitions of *first person, second person,* and *third person.* Direct students' attention to p. 710 in the Language Handbook. Ask each student to write three sentences. Each sentence should demonstrate understanding of one of the three grammatical persons.

English Language Learners
Review with students the correct use of first-person, second-person, and third-person pronouns. Direct students' attention to p. 710 in the Language Handbook. Ask students to identify the personal pronouns in five sentences from any selection they have read and to tell whether the pronouns are first, second, or third person.

Advanced Learners
Students can choose a well-known story, fable, fairy tale, or movie, and retell it (or part of it) from a different point of view. For example, a student might retell "Little Red Riding Hood" from the point of view of the wolf, or retell *E.T.* from the point of view of the extraterrestrial. After each retelling, ask the class what insights into the character were provided by the new point of view.

Reading Skills and Strategies

Booking space on the Net: *Used-booksellers take a page from other online vendors.* http://www.excite.com/

OBJECTIVES

1. Predict outcomes based on prior knowledge and text information
2. Adjust and confirm predictions

Reading Skills and Strategies

This feature illustrates the elements that go into a reader's predictions: prior knowledge and information from the text. Students are urged to adjust their predictions and make new ones as they read a selection. Reading "A Mason-Dixon Memory" will give students a chance to put the strategy into practice.

Mini-Lesson:

Making Predictions

Before students make predictions about the two story beginnings (A and B), ask them what prior knowledge they have about the situations the beginnings describe.

Possible responses:

- **Story A** (Prior knowledge) To cook fish, campers need to build a fire. (Prediction) Campers leave fish out and go off to gather wood.
- **Story B** (Prior knowledge) Bears love fish. (Prediction) Campers return in time to find the bear eating the fish.

MAKING PREDICTIONS: FORECASTING MORE THAN JUST THE WEATHER

One reason we get pulled into good stories is that as we get more and more caught up in the plot, we crank up our antennas and begin to make predictions. The process of making predictions is simply forecasting what will happen next. Think about your own process of making predictions as you read these two story beginnings.

STORY A   The young campers have just settled down to cook the trout they caught in the lake. (What do you predict will happen next?)

STORY B   "I'm famished," said the bear to himself as he watched the young campers building a fire to cook their hard-won trout. (What do you predict happens next?)

ZIGGY

© ZIGGY AND FRIENDS, INC. Dist. by UNIVERSAL PRESS SYNDICATE. Reprinted by permission. All rights reserved.

I Told You So

Weather forecasters base their predictions on prior knowledge of things like cloud formations and barometric pressure. Good readers constantly add their **prior knowledge** to what they are reading to make good educated guesses. An interesting story will constantly trigger **predictions.** The reader adjusts those predictions as he or she continues reading the text. A chart of this process of predicting and adjusting might look like this:

| Prior Knowledge | + | Prediction | + | Information from Text | = | Adjusted Prediction |

You've been making and confirming and adjusting predictions ever since you began to listen to bedtime stories as a child. As you read "A Mason-Dixon Memory," practice your predicting strategies. Ask yourself if the events are turning out the way you thought they would. Can you make new predictions as you read more of the selection? Making and confirming and adjusting predictions is a process you can engage in right up to the end of the story.

Apply the strategy on the next page. ➤

204 DO THE RIGHT THING

Reaching All Students

Struggling Readers

Help students understand the predicting process. Explain that weather forecasters use wind speed and direction to predict the path of a hurricane. Based on prior knowledge and current information (from satellites, for instance), the forecasters make and continually adjust predictions. Ask students to volunteer their own examples of predicting, from daily life, sports, science, health, or any other area.

English Language Learners

Ensure that students understand the three key words in the predicting process: *predict, adjust,* and *confirm.* Ask students to offer a definition of each term in their own words. You may also want to explain that *prior knowledge* is simply what a person already knows.

Advanced Learners

Ask students to volunteer examples of predicting outcomes from well-known stories or movies. How, for example, did they predict that Rikki-tikki-tavi would win his battle? Students might also list the different types of prior knowledge that can contribute to making predictions, such as personal experiences, awareness of scientific facts, and reports from reliable sources.

T204

Before You Read

A MASON-DIXON MEMORY

Make the Connection

What If...?

How far would you go to "do the right thing"? Think of something you really care about. It could be a possession. It could be an event you're looking forward to—a party, a tournament, or a field trip—anything you'd hate to give up. Talk with a partner about the thing you really value, and then have your partner tell you about what he or she values.

Quickwrite

Think about your partner's choice, and imagine situations in which making the right choice could mean that your partner would have to give up the thing he or she prizes so much. Write a brief *what if* question for your partner—for example, "What if going to the party means you have to break a date with a friend who wasn't invited?"

go.hrw.com
LEO 7-3

Elements of Literature

Flashback: We Interrupt This Story...

Most stories are written in **chronological order**—the writer tells about events in the order they happen. Just as Clifton Davis

 A flashback is a scene that breaks the normal time order of a plot to show a past event.

For more on Flashback, see the Handbook of Literary Terms.

starts his story, though, he remembers a childhood experience. He interrupts his story with a **flashback** that takes you back to earlier times and events in his life. The flashback and the main story are connected: They both tell about people who "did the right thing."

Reading Skills and Strategies

Making and Confirming Predictions

As you read this story, do some guesswork about what will happen. Remember, the best thing about guessing or predicting is that you can always change your prediction (and often should) once you've read more of the story. Put a slip of paper on this page to hold your place. Briefly respond to the questions that follow as you reach the points in the story marked by the star, square, triangle, diamond, and circle.

★ Look at the title and the illustrations. What do you think this story will be about? What do you know about the Mason-Dixon line?

■ What do you think will happen? What will the seniors' response be?

▲ Does your prior knowledge from guessing about the title of the story match what you now know? Will Clifton get to go to the amusement park?

◆ What do you predict these characters will do? (Think about what you already know about their friendship.)

● Confirm your predictions about what the seniors' response will be. How does what really happened compare with your prediction?

A MASON-DIXON MEMORY **205**

OBJECTIVES

1. Read and interpret the story
2. Recognize and analyze a flashback
3. Make and confirm predictions
4. Express understanding through persuasive and creative writing, research, or a panel discussion
5. Use commas correctly to separate items in a series
6. Understand and use new words
7. Identify and use synonyms

SKILLS

Literary
- Recognize and analyze a flashback

Reading
- Make and confirm predictions

Writing
- Collect ideas for an essay supporting a position
- Write an essay about people who care about and support someone
- Research and list questions for a civil rights movement participant or witness

Speaking/Listening
- Hold a panel discussion on the topic of a color-blind society

Grammar/Language
- Use commas correctly to separate items in a series

Vocabulary
- Understand and use new words
- Identify and use synonyms

Viewing/Representing
- Respond to a team photograph (ATE)

Preteaching Vocabulary

Words to Own

Have students read the definitions of the Words to Own listed at the bottom of the selection pages. Ask each student to draw a picture or a symbol that characterizes one of the words (such as a volcano for *erupted* or a flag for *civic*). Then, have students match each of the words with one of the following definitions.

1. foreshadowing evil [ominous]
2. make a decision [resolve]
3. related to government [civic]
4. most commonly or frequently [predominantly]
5. broke out [erupted]

Planning

- **Block Schedule**
  Block Scheduling Lesson Plans with Pacing Guide
- **Traditional Schedule**
  Lesson Plans Including Strategies for English-Language Learners
- **One-Stop Planner**
  CD-ROM with Test Generator

RESPONDING TO THE ART

Ask students what words they would use to describe the group of boys in the photograph. [Possible responses: *team, friends, together, proud, unified, happy.*] Then, ask students to name qualities that they associate with a team or club. [Possible responses: working together toward a common goal, helping and supporting each other.]

Responding to the Quotation

❓ Point out that the quotation sets forth an either-or situation: Either we leave, or we stay. It also describes specific causes and effects: Leaving causes a forfeit; staying causes one player to be eliminated. Based on the quotation, what do you think the conflict in the story will be? [Possible responses: Someone does not want Dondré to play, and the external conflict is over whether he will play. Someone will experience an internal conflict by being forced to make a difficult decision.]

A Mason-Dixon Memory*

Clifton Davis

Sponsor: Fred Matte

Dondré Green

Damon Marsala

"If we leave, we forfeit this tournament.

If we stay, Dondré can't play."

206 DO THE RIGHT THING

Resources: Print and Media

Reading
- *Reading Skills and Strategies*
  Selection Skill Lesson, p. 57
- *Graphic Organizers for Active Reading*, p. 14
- *Words to Own*, p. 11
- *Spelling and Decoding*
  Worksheet, p. 12
- *Audio CD Library*
  Disc 7, Track 3

Writing and Language
- *Daily Oral Grammar*
  Transparency 13
- *Grammar and Language Links*
  Worksheet, p. 23
- *Language Workshop CD-ROM*

Viewing and Representing
- *Visual Connections*
  Videocassette A, Segment 3

Assessment
- *Formal Assessment*, p. 39
- *Portfolio Management System*, p. 128
- *Standardized Test Preparation*, pp. 36, 38
- *Test Generator (One-Stop Planner CD-ROM)*

Internet
- go.hrw.com (keyword: LE0 7-3)

Golf team photograph from the 1991 *Warrior* yearbook.

Brad Coenen

Lee Williams

David Elias

John Shamblin

Brian Matte

A MASON-DIXON MEMORY 207

Summary ▪▪

This memoir interweaves two real-life incidents to explore how people respond to bigotry. In 1991, Dondré Green, the only African American on his high school golf team in Monroe, Louisiana, was not allowed to play in a tournament at a whites-only country club. His teammates forfeited the tournament rather than play without Dondré. This story reminds the author of an episode that took place in 1959, during his early adolescence. On a school trip to Washington, D.C., Clifton Davis and his white classmates were scheduled to visit an amusement park in Maryland. The morning of the visit, a chaperone informed Clifton that the amusement park, south of the Mason-Dixon line, would not admit blacks. When the tearful Clifton broke this news to his roommate, Frank vowed not to go either, and soon all of their classmates joined the boycott.

Resources

Viewing and Representing
Videocassette A, Segment 3
The video segment "The Journey Toward Equality" provides a historical overview of segregation. See the *Visual Connections Teacher's Manual.*

Listening
Audio CD Library
A reading of this memoir is included in the *Audio CD Library:*
• Disc 7, Track 3

Selection Assessment
Formal Assessment
• Selection Test, p. 39
Test Generator
• Selection Test

Reaching All Students

Struggling Readers
Making and Confirming Predictions was introduced on p. 205. For a lesson directly tied to this selection that teaches students to make predictions by using a strategy called Story Impressions, see the *Reading Skills and Strategies* binder:
• Selection Skill Lesson, p. 57

English Language Learners
To be sure students understand the flashback structure, ask them to narrate, in simple language, the story within a story. If students are unfamiliar with U.S. race relations in the 1950s and later, or with details such as a country club, briefly provide background. For additional ideas, see
• *Lesson Plans Including Strategies for English-Language Learners*

A Reading Skills and Strategies

Making and Confirming Predictions

❓ What information in this paragraph might help you predict events in the story? [Possible responses: Dondré was a black student in a mostly white school; his race led to an incident that made nationwide news.] Students can jot down their predictions as they read, to create a record of how their predictions may change.

B Vocabulary Note

Synonyms

❓ Ask students to define *synonyms*. [words with similar meanings] What are two synonyms for *absorbed* here? [Possible responses: interested in, or busy with, other things; not paying attention.]

C Elements of Literature

Flashback

❓ What clues does this passage provide that the flashback begins here? [Possible responses: The narrator says that his memory "broke free"; he provides a space to break up the text; he begins talking about events that took place in 1959.]

D Appreciating Language

Punctuation

❓ What is the purpose of the commas after *Disneyland* and *Farm*? [to separate the three names] What would happen if the commas were removed? [Possible response: Glen Echo would seem to be compared with only two other places.]

E Critical Thinking

Speculating

❓ How important do you think this trip was to the author? Explain. [Possible response: It must have been very important, because he worked so hard to earn the money for it.]

Dondré Green glanced uneasily at the civic leaders and sports figures filling the hotel ballroom in Cleveland. They had come from across the nation to attend a fundraiser for the National Minority College Golf Scholarship Foundation. I was the banquet's featured entertainer. Dondré, an eighteen-year-old high school senior from Monroe, Louisiana, was the evening's honored guest.

"Nervous?" I asked the handsome young man in his starched white shirt and rented tuxedo.

"A little," he whispered, grinning.

One month earlier, Dondré had been just one more black student attending a predominantly white Southern school. Although most of his friends and classmates were white, Dondré's race had never been an issue. Then, on April 17, 1991, Dondré's black skin provoked an incident that made nationwide news.

"Ladies and gentlemen," the emcee[1] said, "our special guest, Dondré Green."

As the audience stood applauding, Dondré walked to the microphone and began his story. "I love golf," he said quietly. "For the past two years, I've been a member of the St. Frederick High School golf team. And though I was the only black member, I've always felt at home playing at the mostly white country clubs across Louisiana."

The audience leaned forward; even the waiters and busboys stopped to listen. As I listened, a memory buried in my heart since childhood began fighting its way to life.

"Our team had driven from Monroe," Dondré continued. "When we arrived at the Caldwell Parish Country Club in Columbia, we walked to the putting green."

Dondré and his teammates were too absorbed to notice the conversation between a man and St. Frederick athletic director James Murphy. After disappearing into the clubhouse, Murphy returned to his players.

1. **emcee** (em′sē′): master of ceremonies.

208 DO THE RIGHT THING

"I want to see the seniors," he said. "On the double!" His face seemed strained as he gathered the four students, including Dondré.

"I don't know how to tell you this," he said, "but the Caldwell Parish Country Club is reserved for whites only." Murphy paused and looked at Dondré. His teammates glanced at each other in disbelief. "I want you seniors to decide what our response should be," Murphy continued. "If we leave, we forfeit this tournament. If we stay, Dondré can't play." ■

As I listened, my own childhood memory from thirty-two years ago broke free.

In 1959 I was thirteen years old, a poor black kid living with my mother and stepfather in a small black ghetto on Long Island, New York. My mother worked nights in a hospital, and my stepfather drove a coal truck. Needless to say, our standard of living was somewhat short of the American dream.

Nevertheless, when my eighth-grade teacher announced a graduation trip to Washington, D.C., it never crossed my mind that I would be left behind. Besides a complete tour of the nation's capital, we would visit Glen Echo Amusement Park in Maryland. In my imagination, Glen Echo was Disneyland, Knott's Berry Farm, and Magic Mountain rolled into one.

My heart beating wildly, I raced home to deliver the mimeographed letter describing the journey. But when my mother saw how much the trip would cost, she just shook her head. We couldn't afford it.

After feeling sad for ten seconds, I decided to try to fund the trip myself. For the next eight weeks, I sold candy bars door-to-door, delivered newspapers, and mowed lawns. Three

---

WORDS TO OWN

civic (siv′ik) *adj.*: of a city or citizenship.
predominantly (prē·däm′ə·nənt·lē) *adv.*: mainly.

Getting Students Involved

Cooperative Learning

A Protest Poster. Divide the class into groups of three to create protest posters to be pasted up around the amusement park Clifton Davis could not visit. (Students might create other posters to protest injustices that are especially meaningful to them.) The posters should contain messages criticizing an unfair

policy (such as segregation at the amusement park). Students might also suggest a boycott of the park or other nonviolent actions. Each group member should choose one of these roles: artist (in charge of visuals), writer (in charge of text), or presenter (in charge of the presentation of the poster to the class).

days before the deadline, I'd made just barely enough. I was going!

The day of the trip, trembling with excitement, I climbed onto the train. I was the only nonwhite in our section.

Our hotel was not far from the White House. My roommate was Frank Miller, the son of a businessman. Leaning together out of our window and dropping water balloons on passing tourists quickly cemented our new friendship.

Every morning, almost a hundred of us loaded noisily onto our bus for another adventure. We sang our school fight song dozens of times—en route[2] to Arlington National Cemetery and even on an afternoon cruise down the Potomac River.

We visited the Lincoln Memorial twice, once in daylight, the second time at dusk. My classmates and I fell silent as we walked in the shadows of those thirty-six marble columns, one for every state in the Union that Lincoln labored to preserve. I stood next to Frank at the base of the nineteen-foot seated statue. Spotlights made the white Georgian marble seem to glow. Together, we read those famous words from Lincoln's speech at Gettysburg, remembering the most bloody battle in the War Between the States: ". . . we here highly <u>resolve</u> that these dead shall not have died in vain—that this nation, under God, shall have a new birth of freedom. . . ."

As Frank motioned me into place to take my picture, I took one last look at Lincoln's face. He seemed alive and so terribly sad.

The next morning I understood a little better why he wasn't smiling. "Clifton," a chaperone said, "could I see you for a moment?"

The other guys at my table, especially Frank, turned pale. We had been joking about the previous night's direct water-balloon hit on a fat lady and her poodle. It was a stupid, dangerous act, but luckily nobody got hurt. We were celebrating our escape from punishment when the chaperone asked to see me.

2. **en route** (en rōōt'): on the way.

"Clifton," she began, "do you know about the Mason-Dixon line?"

"No," I said, wondering what this had to do with drenching fat ladies.

"Before the Civil War," she explained, "the Mason-Dixon line was originally the boundary between Maryland and Pennsylvania—the dividing line between the slave and free states." Having escaped one disaster, I could feel another brewing. I noticed that her eyes were damp and her hands shaking.

"Today," she continued, "the Mason-Dixon line is a kind of invisible border between the North and the South. When you cross that invisible line out of Washington, D.C., into Maryland, things change."

There was an <u>ominous</u> drift to this conversation, but I wasn't following it. Why did she look and sound so nervous? ▲

"Glen Echo Amusement Park is in Maryland," she said at last, "and the management doesn't allow Negroes inside." She stared at me in silence.

I was still grinning and nodding when the meaning finally sank in. "You mean I can't go to the park," I stuttered, "because I'm a Negro?"

She nodded slowly. "I'm sorry, Clifton," she said, taking my hand. "You'll have to stay in the hotel tonight. Why don't you and I watch a movie on television?"

I walked to the elevators feeling confusion, disbelief, anger, and a deep sadness. "What happened, Clifton?" Frank said when I got back to the room. "Did the fat lady tell on us?"

Without saying a word, I walked over to my bed, lay down, and began to cry. Frank was stunned into silence. Junior-high boys didn't cry, at least not in front of each other.

It wasn't just missing the class adventure that made me feel so sad. For the first time in

---

WORDS TO OWN

resolve (ri·zälv') v.: decide; make a formal statement.
ominous (äm'ə·nəs) adj.: threatening, like a bad sign; warning of something bad.

F **Cultural Connections**

Map Reading

Ask students to look at a map of the Washington, D.C., area. Have them locate the landmarks mentioned in the text: White House, Arlington National Cemetery (in Virginia), the Potomac River, the Lincoln Memorial.

G **Appreciating Language**

Word Origins

? What is the origin of *chaperone*? [It is from a French word meaning "hood"—a type of protection.]

H **Elements of Literature**

Symbol

? What does the phrase "Mason-Dixon line" stand for in the selection title? [Possible responses: segregation, injustice, intolerance.] What other titles might the author have chosen? [Possible response: "A Memory of Segregation."]

I **Reading Skills and Strategies**

Making and Confirming Predictions

Narrators sometimes ask questions that can help the reader make a prediction. Here Davis asks about the chaperone's nervousness and suggests the shock to come.

J **Critical Thinking**

Analyzing Character

? Can a person feel several emotions at once? [Possible responses: Yes, people are complex, and feeling one emotion doesn't automatically cancel out others.]

Using Students' Strengths

Visual Learners

Ask students to locate photographs of some of the scenes Davis describes. They might find magazine and newspaper photos of Washington, D.C., in the late 1950s and early 1960s; the Lincoln Memorial and other national monuments; signs of segregation; and scenes of protest. Students can create a collage that captures the spirit of Davis's memoir.

Crossing the Curriculum

Physical Education and Sports

Racial segregation of athletes has often made headlines. The best-known example is probably Jackie Robinson, the first African American to break the color barrier in major-league baseball in 1947. Playing for the Brooklyn Dodgers, Robinson endured insults, threats, and physical abuse, but he paved the way for other African American athletes. Ask students to research other examples of racial prejudice in sports.

❓ Why does Frank decide to stay behind with Clifton? [Possible responses: Frank knows how hurt he would feel if he had to stay behind because of prejudice. He thinks that an act of kindness will cheer up Clifton. He believes that not going is the way to fight prejudice.]

B Struggling Readers

Finding Sequence of Events

❓ What events lead up to the boys' decision not to go to the park? [Possible responses: The chaperone informs Clifton he cannot go. Frank decides to stay with Clifton. Frank tells the others what has happened. Eleven boys decide they will also stay with Clifton.]

C Elements of Literature

Flashback

❓ What clues in the text indicate that the flashback has ended and the present story has resumed? [Possible responses: The space in the text sets the flashback off. The mention of Dondré Green places the reader back in the present.]

D Appreciating Language

Parallel Structure

❓ Commas separate a series of three phrases here. What words before the series do the three phrases refer to? [permitting lawsuits for]

E Vocabulary Note

Synonyms

❓ What are three synonyms for bigotry? [Possible response: prejudice, intolerance, narrow-mindedness.] Students might make a word map of the terms (see p. 215).

---

my life, I was learning what it felt like to be a "nigger." Of course there was discrimination in the North, but the color of my skin had never officially kept me out of a coffee shop, a church—or an amusement park.

"Clifton," Frank whispered, "what is the matter?"

"They won't let me go to Glen Echo Park tonight," I sobbed.

"Because of the water balloon?" he asked.

"No," I answered, "because I'm a Negro."

"Well, that's a relief!" Frank said, and then he laughed, obviously relieved to have escaped punishment for our caper with the balloons. "I thought it was serious!"

Wiping away the tears with my sleeve, I stared at him. "It *is* serious. They don't let Negroes into the park. I can't go with you!" I shouted. "That's pretty serious to me." ◆

I was about to wipe the silly grin off Frank's face with a blow to his jaw when I heard him say, "Then I won't go either."

For an instant we just froze. Then Frank grinned. I will never forget that moment. Frank was just a kid. He wanted to go to that amusement park as much as I did, but there was something even more important than the class night out. Still, he didn't explain or expand.

The next thing I knew, the room was filled with kids listening to Frank. "They don't allow Negroes in the park," he said, "so I'm staying with Clifton."

"Me too," a second boy said.

"Those jerks," a third muttered. "I'm with you, Clifton." My heart began to race. Suddenly, I was not alone. A pint-sized revolution had been born. The "water-balloon brigade," eleven white boys from Long Island, had made its decision: "We won't go." And as I sat on my bed in the center of it all, I felt grateful. But above all, I was filled with pride.

Dondré Green's story brought that childhood memory back to life. His golfing teammates,

like my childhood friends, had an important decision to make. Standing by their friend would cost them dearly. But when it came time to decide, no one hesitated. "Let's get out of here," one of them whispered.

"They just turned and walked toward the van," Dondré told us. "They didn't debate it. And the younger players joined us without looking back." ●

Dondré was astounded by the response of his friends—and the people of Louisiana. The whole state was outraged and tried to make it right. The Louisiana House of Representatives proclaimed a Dondré Green Day and passed legislation permitting lawsuits for damages, attorneys' fees, and court costs against any private facility that invites a team, then bars any member because of race.

As Dondré concluded, his eyes glistened with tears. "I love my coach and my teammates for sticking by me," he said. "It goes to show that there are always good people who will not give in to bigotry. The kind of love they showed me that day will conquer hatred every time."

Suddenly, the banquet crowd was standing, applauding Dondré Green.

My friends, too, had shown that kind of love. As we sat in the hotel, a chaperone came in waving an envelope. "Boys!" he shouted. "I've just bought thirteen tickets to the Senators-Tigers game. Anybody want to go?"

The room erupted in cheers. Not one of us had ever been to a professional baseball game in a real baseball park.

On the way to the stadium, we grew silent as our driver paused before the Lincoln Memorial. For one long moment, I stared through the marble pillars at Mr. Lincoln, bathed in that

---

WORDS TO OWN

erupted (ē·rup'tid) v.: exploded or burst forth.

Making the Connections

Connecting to the Theme: "Do the Right Thing"

"A Mason-Dixon Memory" describes two situations in which people have the opportunity to do the right thing. Ask students if they think other choices might have been possible. Would it have been right, for example, to compromise? Why or why not? What if Dondré's teammates had played in the tournament, won the trophy, and then publicly declined to accept it? Do all situations present "either-or" choices? How do people make decisions to "do the right thing" when the choices are not so clear? What values, beliefs, commitments, and emotions come into play?

warm yellow light. There was still no smile and no sign of hope in his sad and tired eyes.

"... we here highly resolve ... that this nation, under God, shall have a new birth of freedom. ..."

In his words and in his life, Lincoln had made it clear that freedom is not free. Every time the color of a person's skin keeps him out of an amusement park or off a country-club fairway, the war for freedom begins again. Sometimes the battle is fought with fists and guns, but more often the most effective weapon is a simple act of love and courage.

Whenever I hear those words from Lincoln's speech at Gettysburg, I remember my eleven white friends, and I feel hope once again. I like to imagine that when we paused that night at the foot of his great monument, Mr. Lincoln smiled at last. As Dondré said, "The kind of love they showed me that day will conquer hatred every time."

MEET THE WRITER

A Man of Many Talents

Clifton Davis (1946–   ) may be better known for writing tunes than for writing prose. He wrote the song "Never Can Say Goodbye," which sold two million records. He's still involved with music today, as a composer, recording artist, and host of a gospel-music radio program.

Besides being a singer and a songwriter, Clifton Davis is an actor. He has acted in several plays on Broadway and received a Tony nomination for his performance in *Two Gentlemen of Verona*. Davis has also appeared in movies and TV shows. The role he is best known for is Reverend Reuben Gregory on the television series *Amen*. The curious thing about casting Davis in the role of the minister is that he really *is* a minister, in the Seventh-Day Adventist Church.

Davis believes it's important to do what's right, even if you're making a living amid the glitz and glamour of Hollywood.

A MASON-DIXON MEMORY 211

Assessing Learning

Check Test: Short Answer

1. How does Clifton Davis meet Dondré Green? [Davis is the featured entertainer at a banquet honoring Green.]
2. What problem does Dondré's team face at the country club? [Only whites can play golf at the club; Green is not allowed to play.]
3. How does Clifton raise money for his trip? [He sells candy bars, delivers newspapers, and mows lawns.]
4. What is the Mason-Dixon line? [the historic, invisible boundary between the North and the South]
5. What happened because of the country club's treatment of Dondré? [The Louisiana House of Representatives proclaimed Dondré Green Day and authorized lawsuits against private facilities that invite a team and then bar team members because of race.]

Ian O'Gorman, undergoing chemotherapy for cancer, had his head shaved rather than wait until his hair fell out in clumps. About a dozen other boys in Ian's class also had their hair cut down to the scalp so that Ian's baldness wouldn't stand out. Their act of kindness and solidarity, described in this newspaper article, is similar to the response of Clifton Davis's classmates and of Dondré Green's teammates when they both faced discrimination because of their skin color. In all three cases, the friends were "doing the right thing."

Ⓐ Reading Skills and Strategies
Responding to the Text
❓ Does Scott Sebelius's explanation make sense to you? [Possible responses: Yes, it makes sense—Ian's friends cut their hair so that nobody could point at Ian and say, "You can tell he's the one with cancer because he doesn't have any hair." No, it doesn't make sense—it just draws more attention to Ian's illness.]

Ⓑ Appreciating Language
Figurative Language
❓ The expression *butterflies in your stomach* means "an uneasy feeling, especially nervousness." Why does the expression fit well in Ian's statement? [Possible response: It has the same form as the first part, "I had tubes up my nose."]

Ⓒ Critical Thinking
Interpreting
❓ Why do you think Ian was surprised that his friends got their hair cut too? [Possible responses: He didn't realize, until he got sick, how much they cared about him; he never thought that anyone would do something like that for him.]

Ⓓ Critical Thinking
Extending the Text
❓ Is it easier for people to "do the right thing" when they are acting alone or when they are acting as part of a group? Why? [Possible responses: It is easier when acting alone, because the individual is not dependent on the approval of others. It is easier as part of a group, because the group members give each other support.]

Buddies Bare Their Affection for Ill Classmate

OCEANSIDE, California, March 19 (Associated Press)—In Mr. Alter's fifth-grade class, it's difficult to tell which boy is undergoing chemotherapy. Nearly all the boys are bald. Thirteen of them shaved their heads so a sick buddy wouldn't feel out of place.

"If everybody has their head shaved, sometimes people don't know who's who. They don't know who has cancer and who just shaved their head," said eleven-year-old Scott Sebelius, one of the baldies at Lake Elementary School.

For the record, Ian O'Gorman is the sick one. Doctors recently removed a malignant tumor from his small intestine, and a week ago he started chemotherapy to treat the disease, called lymphoma.

"Besides surgery, I had tubes up my nose. I had butterflies in my stomach," said Ian, who'll have eight more weeks of chemotherapy in an effort to keep the cancer from returning.

Ian decided to get his head shaved before all his hair fell out in clumps. To his surprise, his friends wanted to join him.

"The last thing he would want is to not fit in, to be made fun of, so we just wanted to make him feel better and not left out," said ten-year-old Kyle Hanslik.

Kyle started talking to other boys about the idea, and then one of their parents started a list. Last week, they all went to the barber shop together.

"It's hard to put words to," said Ian's father, Shawn, choking back tears as he talked about the boys. "It's very emotional to think about kids like that who would come together, to have them do such a thing to support Ian."

The boy's teacher, Jim Alter, was so inspired that he, too, shaved his head.

Ian left the hospital March 2. Although he has lost twenty pounds and is pale, he is eager to get back to the business of being an eleven-year-old playing baseball and basketball. "I think I can start on Monday," he said.

—from the *Austin American-Statesman*

Ian O'Gorman (center), who is undergoing chemotherapy for cancer, is surrounded by his classmates, who shaved their heads as a show of support.

212 DO THE RIGHT THING

Connecting Across Texts

Connecting with "A Mason-Dixon Memory"
Allow students five minutes to discuss the following questions with partners. Then, ask the pairs of students to share their responses with the rest of the class. In what way are Ian O'Gorman's friends like Dondré Green's teammates? [Possible response: They all pull together and support a friend who is in a difficult situation.] In what way is Ian's situation different from Dondré's? [Possible response: Ian's problem results from an illness; Dondré's problem results from racism.]

MAKING MEANINGS

First Thoughts

[respond]

1. Finish these sentences:
   - If I were a teammate of Dondré Green's (or a classmate of Clifton Davis's), I would . . .
   - Being a friend means . . .

Shaping Interpretations

[interpret]

2. How did Dondré Green's teammates and the people of Louisiana react to the fact that he had been barred from the tournament? Why do you think Dondré was astounded by this response?

[interpret]

3. The narrator says there was "something even more important" than going to the amusement park. Frank never explained what that "something" was. How would you explain it?

[compare]

4. Compare the actions of Dondré's coach and teammates with those of Ian O'Gorman's teacher and classmates (see *Connections* on page 212). In your opinion, which group sacrifices more than the other in order to "do the right thing"? Explain.

[infer]

5. Where does the **flashback** begin and end? What does it have to do with the main story?

Connecting with the Text

[connect]

6. Have you or a friend ever felt unwelcome someplace? How did your experience compare with Clifton Davis's or Dondré Green's?

[connect]

7. When has a friend ever done the right thing and stood by you? How did you feel?

[evaluate]

8. Look back at the *what if* question you wrote for the Quickwrite on page 205. Did reading this story change the way you look at choices that might force you to give up something you value? If so, explain how and why.

[reflect]

9. Reflect on the **predicting** you did as you read the story. Compare your predictions with a partner's. Discuss the evidence from the story that led you to make those predictions. How much of your predicting was based on your own experiences with people?

Challenging the Text

[synthesize]

10. Green and Davis both believe that a simple act of love and courage is the most effective weapon against prejudice. Do you agree? Explain.

A MASON-DIXON MEMORY 213

Reading Check

How were the experiences of Dondré Green and Clifton Davis alike? Fill in a chart like the one below to compare their experiences.

	Experience	Friends' Response
Green		
Davis		

Reading Check

Dondré Green Experience: Country club will not admit him because of his race. Response: Teammates forfeit game.
Clifton Davis Experience: Amusement park will not admit him because of his race. Response: Schoolmates stay behind with him.

First Thoughts

1. Students will probably say that they would take the same action as the friends in the story and that being a friend means standing by someone.

Shaping Interpretations

2. Possible response: They were outraged. Dondré may have been astounded to learn that so many people cared about what had happened to him.

3. Possible responses: "doing the right thing," "sticking by your friend," or "acting on your deepest principles."

4. Possible responses: Dondré's friends make a public gesture that has legal consequences. Ian's teacher and classmates demonstrate their friendship in an attempt to change people's views about cancer victims. Most people will agree that the first group sacrifices more, because the players lose something important to them, while the members' hair will eventually grow back.

5. The flashback begins at the space in column 2 on p. 208, breaks off near the end of column 1 on p. 210, and continues in column 2 on p. 210 to the end of the selection. The flashback is a personal memory on the same theme as the main story—solidarity in the face of bigotry.

Connecting with the Text

6. Students may cite examples of embarrassment or insult, in which they either had to face the situation alone or had others to support them.

7. Responses will vary. Remind students that there are many ways in which a friend can offer support.

8. After seeing how the two stories end, students may agree that some sacrifices are worthwhile.

9. Remind students that they should make predictions not just to arrive at right answers but to think more clearly about stories.

Challenging the Text

10. Some students may say that love and courage are effective on a personal level; others may say that it takes new laws to combat bigotry.

CHOICES: Building Your Portfolio

1. **Writer's Notebook**   The issues students choose might be local, national, or even international ones. Areas for students to consider include politics, education, health, the arts, and entertainment.

2. **Creative Writing**   Allow students to use the article on p. 212 as a model. Suggest a few current human-interest stories that students may choose as their subjects.

3. **Research**   You might suggest that students use the library to find personal reminiscences of civil rights struggles. Autobiographies and oral histories can be good sources of what the experiences meant to participants and witnesses.

4. **Panel Discussion**   Each member of the panel might become an "expert" on a specific aspect of the question, such as the history of racial understanding in America, causes of racial misunderstanding, effects of racial misunderstanding, and possible solutions.

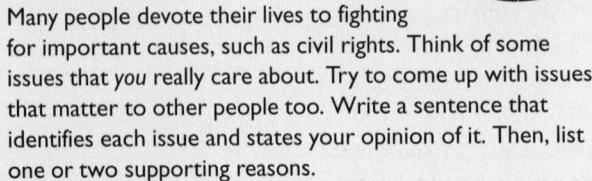

CHOICES: Building Your Portfolio

Writer's Notebook

1. Collecting Ideas for Supporting a Position

Many people devote their lives to fighting for important causes, such as civil rights. Think of some issues that *you* really care about. Try to come up with issues that matter to other people too. Write a sentence that identifies each issue and states your opinion of it. Then, list one or two supporting reasons.

- All nuclear weapons should be destroyed.
- Girls should be allowed to play football on school teams.

Creative Writing

2. Love's the Thing

In a brief essay, write about a time when people showed that they cared about and supported someone who was different from them or who needed a helping hand. You can write about your own experience or the experience of someone you know or an incident in the news. (See *Connections* on page 212.) You might use one of these statements from "A Mason-Dixon Memory" as your opener:

- "... there are always good people. ..."
- "... love will conquer hatred. ..."

Research

3. Questioning a Witness

Find the name of a person who participated in any way in the 1960s civil rights movement. (You might want to look in your social studies book.) Research what the person did and how working for civil rights might have affected what your subject achieved later in life. Once you've gathered your information, write down three questions that you'd like to ask the person. Make one question about the past, one about the present, and one about the future.

Panel Discussion

4. A Color-Blind Society

Martin Luther King, Jr., the famous civil rights leader, once said, "Racial understanding is not something that we find but something that we must create." Do you think the United States can create a "color-blind" society? Can we make sure that Americans of different racial and ethnic backgrounds are all treated fairly? With a small group of classmates, form a team to research the subject. Use the Internet and news magazines as sources. Then, hold a panel discussion to present your findings and views.

GRAMMAR LINK   [MINI-LESSON]

Commas Make Sense of a Series

Language Handbook HELP

See Items in a Series, page 769.

Technology HELP

See Language Workshop CD-ROM. Key word entry: commas.

1. Use commas to separate words, phrases, or clauses in a series.

| INCORRECT | Davis felt confusion disbelief anger and a deep sadness. |
| CORRECT | Davis felt "confusion, disbelief, anger, and a deep sadness." |

2. In most cases, use commas to separate two or more adjectives that come before a noun.

| INCORRECT | It was a stupid dangerous act. |
| CORRECT | It was a stupid, dangerous act. |

3. Do not place a comma between an adjective and a noun immediately following it.

| INCORRECT | Green's teammates made a fast, important, costly, decision. |
| CORRECT | Green's teammates made a fast, important, costly decision. |

4. If the last adjective in a series is closely connected in meaning to the noun, do not use a comma before that adjective.

| INCORRECT | Spotlights made the white, Georgian marble seem to glow. |
| CORRECT | "Spotlights made the white Georgian marble seem to glow." |

To decide whether a comma is needed, add the word *and* between the adjectives. If the *and* sounds strange, don't use a comma. ("White and Georgian marble" sounds strange, so don't use a comma.)

Try It Out

Copy the sentences below. Add commas where necessary to separate the items in a series. Compare your answers with those of a partner.

1. Davis sold candy bars delivered newspapers and mowed lawns.

2. Lincoln's sad wise tired face impressed them.

3. Sincere courageous acts of love can conquer hatred.

4. They saw many famous national landmarks in Washington, D.C.

VOCABULARY   [HOW TO OWN A WORD]

WORD BANK	**Synonyms: Shades of Meaning**
civic predominantly resolve ominous erupted	Words with the same or almost the same meaning are called **synonyms**. Synonyms give different shades of meaning. A dictionary or a **thesaurus,** a book of synonyms, can help you pick exactly the word you need. Make a word map like the one below for the rest of the Word Bank words. Find two synonyms for each word, and put them all in a word map.

A MASON-DIXON MEMORY 215

GRAMMAR LINK

Ask students to circle all of the commas in a short assignment that they have already written. Have them read the sentences aloud to partners, saying "comma" every time they encounter a comma. Students should make sure that each comma is correct as used and that no necessary commas were left out. Have students revise the work for correct comma use. If you permit students to omit the final comma before *and* in a series, then the comma after *newspapers* in sentence 1 may be considered optional.

Try It Out
Answers
1. Davis sold candy bars, delivered newspapers, and mowed lawns.
2. Lincoln's sad, wise, tired face impressed them.
3. Sincere, courageous acts of love can conquer hatred.
4. They saw many famous national landmarks in Washington, D.C.

VOCABULARY
Possible Answers
1. mostly	predominantly	largely
2. intend	resolve	determine
3. sinister	ominous	foreboding
4. exploded	erupted	broke out

Resources

Grammar
• *Grammar and Language Links*, p. 23

Vocabulary
• *Words to Own*, p. 11

Spelling
For related instruction, see
• *Spelling and Decoding*, p. 12

Grammar Link Quick Check

Add or delete commas where needed in the following sentences. If you permit students to omit the final comma before *and* in a series, then the comma after *singing* in sentence 3 may be considered optional.

1. It was a clear sunny hot, day at the golf course. [It was a clear, sunny, hot day at the golf course.]

2. The White House, and the Lincoln Memorial are both found in the nation's beautiful, capital city. [The White House and the Lincoln Memorial are both found in the nation's beautiful capital city.]

3. They pass the time on the bus by talking singing and playing games. [They pass the time on the bus by talking, singing, and playing games.]

4. His roommate, and the ten, other boys support Clifton Davis. [His roommate and the ten other boys support Clifton Davis.]

1. Read and interpret the story
2. Identify point of view
3. Identify regional and cultural sayings
4. Express understanding through writing, a multimedia presentation, a language/home economics project, or art
5. Identify and correct comma splices in writing
6. Choose the correct spelling for words with *ie* and *ei*

SKILLS

Literary
• Identify point of view

Reading
• Identify sayings

Writing
• Collect ideas for an essay
• Write a scene from a different point of view
• Make a recipe card
• Write a story about a painting

Grammar/Language
• Correct comma splices

Vocabulary
• Choose correct spellings

Viewing/Representing
• Create a multimedia presentation about music
• Compare a painting with a story (ATE)

Planning

• **Block Schedule**
Block Scheduling Lesson Plans with Pacing Guide

• **Traditional Schedule**
Lesson Plans Including Strategies for English-Language Learners

• **One-Stop Planner**
CD-ROM with Test Generator

Before You Read

THE NO-GUITAR BLUES

Make the Connection

How Much Is It Worth to You?

Suppose there's something you think you just *have* to have. The trouble is you don't have the money to pay for it.

Look at some of the options listed below. Which would you do to get what you want?

1. Work and save until you can afford it.
2. Persuade a relative to give it to you.
3. Ask your parents for it.
4. Find a friend to share the item and help you pay for it.
5. Borrow the money, though you don't know how you'll pay it back.

Quickwrite

Which of the options listed above are the most popular with your class? In a secret ballot, have classmates write down the numbers of the options they would choose. Work with several classmates to collect and tally the ballots. Ask the class whether they have additional ideas to suggest. Then, write a **summary** of the results.

Elements of Literature

Point of View

Every story you read, every story you tell, comes from a particular **point of view,** or vantage point. "The No-Guitar Blues" is told from the **third-person limited point of view.** This means that the narrator zooms in on the thoughts and feelings of just one character—in this case, Fausto. You'll get inside Fausto's head and share his thoughts and feelings. By the story's end you might feel that you know Fausto better than you know some of your friends.

Reading Skills and Strategies

Regional and Cultural Sayings: You Say "Potato," and I Say . . .

People from different backgrounds and cultures have different words for things. Sometimes they make mistakes and misunderstand one another. In this story, Fausto is confused by the word *turnover* (a pastry). He thinks it means he should turn something over. When he sees a turnover, he realizes that it looks exactly like a Mexican pastry called an *empanada.*

As you read the story, keep an eye out for more regional and cultural sayings.

> **P**oint of view is the vantage point from which a story is told.
>
> *For more on Point of View, see pages 202–203 and the Handbook of Literary Terms.*

Los Lobos (The Wolves), the popular rock group mentioned in the story.

go.hrw.com
LEO 7-3

Listening to Music

"La Bamba" (Traditional), performed by Los Lobos

In 1974, four friends from Garfield High School in East Los Angeles formed Los Lobos (The Wolves), an innovative group fusing rock with Latino sounds. Hugely popular in its neighborhood, Los Lobos gradually gained a national audience, working with such noted pop stars as Ry Cooder, Elvis Costello, and Paul Simon. Among the group's biggest hits were new versions of "C'mon Let's Go" and "La Bamba," songs associated with the Mexican American rock pioneer Ritchie Valens, who died in a plane crash.

Activity

Have students listen to "La Bamba" and discuss what Fausto might have liked about Los Lobos.

THE NO-GUITAR BLUES

GARY SOTO

Fausto had come this far, so he figured he might as well go through with it.

Summary ■

Fausto, who dreams of becoming a rock star after seeing Los Lobos on *American Bandstand*, wants a guitar. When his mother reminds him of the expense, Fausto decides to earn the money; he bikes to a suburb nearby to look for work. As he sits disconsolately at a curb, he notices a playful terrier wandering about. He reads the address on its tag and returns the dog to its owners, concocting a story about having found their pet near the freeway. The owners are grateful and press a twenty-dollar bill into his hand. Seized by guilt over his deception, Fausto attends mass the following morning and resolves his inner conflict by dropping the money into the collection plate. Later his mother tells him that she has found her father's old *guitarron* in the garage and offers it to Fausto, reawakening his dreams of a guest spot on *American Bandstand*.

LITERATURE AND MUSIC

American Bandstand, a popular TV show in the 1950s and 1960s, was a little like *Club MTV*. Many rock-and-roll stars started their careers on the program. Students can hear Los Lobos on the soundtrack of the 1987 movie *La Bamba*.

Responding to the Quotation

❓ After reading the quotation, what do you think the story is about? [Possible response: It is about someone who sets out on a dangerous mission and decides not to turn back.]

Resources

Listening
Audio CD Library
A recording of this story is provided in the *Audio CD Library*:
• Disc 7, Track 4

  Resources: Print and Media

Reading
• *Reading Skills and Strategies*
    MiniRead Skill Lesson, p. 95
    Selection Skill Lesson, p. 112
• *Graphic Organizers for Active Reading*, p. 15
• *Spelling and Decoding*
    Worksheet, p. 13
• *Audio CD Library*
    Disc 7, Track 4

Writing and Language
• *Daily Oral Grammar*

Transparency 14
• *Grammar and Language Links*
    Worksheet, p. 25
• *Language Workshop CD-ROM*

Assessment
• *Formal Assessment*, p. 41
• *Portfolio Management System*, p. 129
• *Standardized Test Preparation*, p. 40
• *Test Generator (One-Stop Planner CD-ROM)*

Internet
• go.hrw.com (keyword: LE0 7-3)

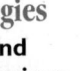

A Reading Skills
and Strategies

**Regional and
Cultural Sayings**

❓ Fausto's parents like *conjunto*, or
polka, music. What kind of dance is the
polka? [a fast dance for couples] Why
might they dislike rock music? [Possible
response: It is loud and not meant for
the kind of dancing they know.] Why is
their taste in music important to
Fausto? [Possible response: He thinks
they won't buy him a guitar to play rock
music.]

B Elements of Literature

Point of View

❓ Does the narrator describe Fausto's
actions, his thoughts, or both? Explain.
[Both; he describes the boy's movements, his feelings, and his words to his
mother.] What makes the narrator's
description of Fausto's mother different? [Possible response: He describes
her physical actions and her conversation but not her thoughts.]

C Critical Thinking

Evaluating

❓ What does this passage tell the
reader about Fausto? [Possible
responses: He understands that his
father cannot buy him whatever he
wants; he is willing to work for what
he wants. He gets carried away by his
enthusiasms.]

D English Language Learners

Idioms

Ask students what they think the
idiom *cat got your tongue* means. [being
"tongue-tied," or unable to express what
you want to say]

The moment Fausto saw the group Los Lobos on *American Bandstand,* he knew exactly what he wanted to do with his life— play guitar. His eyes grew large with excitement as Los Lobos ground out a song while teenagers bounced off each other on the crowded dance floor.

He had watched *American Bandstand* for years and had heard Ray Camacho and the Teardrops at Romain Playground, but it had never occurred to him that he too might become a musician. That afternoon Fausto knew his mission in life: to play guitar in his own band; to sweat out his songs and prance around the stage; to make money and dress weird.

Fausto turned off the television set and walked outside, wondering how he could get enough money to buy a guitar. He couldn't ask his parents because they would just say, "Money doesn't grow on trees" or "What do you think we are, bankers?" And besides, they hated rock music. They were into the *conjunto*[1] music of Lydia Mendoza, Flaco Jimenez, and Little Joe and La Familia. And, as Fausto recalled, the last album they bought was *The Chipmunks Sing Christmas Favorites.*

But what the heck, he'd give it a try. He returned inside and watched his mother make tortillas. He leaned against the kitchen counter, trying to work up the nerve to ask her for a guitar. Finally, he couldn't hold back any longer.

"Mom," he said, "I want a guitar for Christmas."

She looked up from rolling tortillas. "Honey, a guitar costs a lot of money."

"How 'bout for my birthday next year," he tried again.

"I can't promise," she said, turning back to her tortillas, "but we'll see."

Fausto walked back outside with a buttered tortilla. He knew his mother was right. His fa-

---

1. **conjunto** (kồn·hōōn′tô): Northern Mexican polka music played with accordion, bass guitar, and drums.

ther was a warehouseman at Berven Rugs, where he made good money but not enough to buy everything his children wanted. Fausto decided to mow lawns to earn money and was pushing the mower down the street before he realized it was winter and no one would hire him. He returned the mower and picked up a rake. He hopped onto his sister's bike (his had two flat tires) and rode north to the nicer section of Fresno in search of work. He went door-to-door, but after three hours he managed to get only one job, and not to rake leaves. He was asked to hurry down to the store to buy a loaf of bread, for which he received a grimy, dirt-caked quarter.

He also got an orange, which he ate sitting at the curb. While he was eating, a dog walked up and sniffed his leg. Fausto pushed him away and threw an orange peel skyward. The dog caught it and ate it in one gulp. The dog looked at Fausto and wagged his tail for more. Fausto tossed him a slice of orange, and the dog snapped it up and licked his lips.

"How come you like oranges, dog?"

The dog blinked a pair of sad eyes and whined.

"What's the matter? Cat got your tongue?" Fausto laughed at his joke and offered the dog another slice.

At that moment a dim light came on inside Fausto's head. He saw that it was sort of a fancy dog, a terrier or something, with dog tags and a shiny collar. And it looked well-fed and healthy. In his neighborhood, the dogs were never licensed, and if they got sick they were placed near the water heater until they got well.

This dog looked as if he belonged to rich people. Fausto cleaned his juice-sticky hands on his pants and got to his feet. The light in his head grew brighter. It just might work. He called the dog, patted its muscular back, and bent down to check the license.

"Great," he said. "There's an address."

The dog's name was Roger, which struck

Reaching All Students

Struggling Readers
Regional and Cultural Sayings was introduced on p. 216. For a lesson directly tied to this selection that teaches students to recognize regional and cultural sayings, see the *Reading Skills and Strategies* binder:
• MiniRead Skill Lesson, p. 95
• Selection Skill Lesson, p. 112

English Language Learners
Encourage students to render some of the story's phrases in their native languages. Students might focus on brief exchanges of dialogue. If possible, have students provide explanations of any idioms. Students can also speak the dialogue in English as they go through the story.

Advanced Learners
Ask students either to find an edition of the *Dictionary of American Regional English* (DARE) in the library or to locate information about it on the Internet. Have them report on this ongoing compilation of the wide varieties of American speech and choose examples from the dictionary to present to the class.

Fausto as weird, because he'd never heard of a dog with a human name. Dogs should have names like Bomber, Freckles, Queenie, Killer, and Zero.

Fausto planned to take the dog home and collect a reward. He would say he had found Roger near the freeway. That would scare the daylights out of the owners, who would be so happy that they would probably give him a reward. He felt bad about lying, but the dog *was* loose. And it might even really be lost, because the address was six blocks away.

Fausto stashed the rake and his sister's bike behind a bush and, tossing an orange peel every time Roger became distracted, walked the dog to his house. He hesitated on the porch until Roger began to scratch the door with a muddy paw. Fausto had come this far, so he figured he might as well go through with it. He knocked softly. When no one answered, he rang the doorbell. A man in a silky bathrobe and slippers opened the door and seemed confused by the sight of his dog and the boy.

"Sir," Fausto said, gripping Roger by the collar. "I found your dog by the freeway. His dog license says he lives here." Fausto looked down at the dog, then up to the man. "He does, doesn't he?"

The man stared at Fausto a long time before saying in a pleasant voice, "That's right." He pulled his robe tighter around him because of the cold and asked Fausto to come in. "So he was by the freeway?"

"Uh-huh."

"You bad, snoopy dog," said the man, wagging his finger. "You probably knocked over some trash cans, too, didn't you?"

Fausto didn't say anything. He looked around, amazed by this house with its shiny furniture and a television as large as the front window at home. Warm bread smells filled the air and music full of soft tinkling floated in from another room.

"Helen," the man called to the kitchen. "We

have a visitor." His wife came into the living room, wiping her hands on a dish towel and smiling. "And who have we here?" she asked in one of the softest voices Fausto had ever heard.

"This young man said he found Roger near the freeway."

Fausto repeated his story to her while staring at a perpetual clock with a bell-shaped glass, the kind his aunt got when she celebrated her twenty-fifth anniversary. The lady frowned and said, wagging a finger at Roger, "Oh, you're a bad boy."

"It was very nice of you to bring Roger home," the man said. "Where do you live?"

"By that vacant lot on Olive," he said. "You know, by Brownie's Flower Place."

The wife looked at her husband, then Fausto. Her eyes twinkled triangles of light as she said, "Well, young man, you're probably hungry. How about a turnover?"

"What do I have to turn over?" Fausto asked, thinking she was talking about yardwork or something like turning trays of dried raisins.

"No, no, dear, it's a pastry." She took him by the elbow and guided him to a kitchen that sparkled with copper pans and bright yellow wallpaper. She guided him to the kitchen table and gave him a tall glass of milk and something that looked like an empanada.[2] Steamy waves of heat escaped when he tore it in two. He ate with both eyes on the man and woman, who stood arm in arm smiling at him. They were strange, he thought. But nice.

"That was good," he said after he finished the turnover. "Did you make it, ma'am?"

"Yes, I did. Would you like another?"

"No, thank you. I have to go home now."

As Fausto walked to the door, the man opened his wallet and took out a bill. "This is for you," he said. "Roger is special to us, almost like a son."

Fausto looked at the bill and knew he was in

2. **empanada** (em′pä·nä′dä): pastry filled with meat or fruit.

THE NO-GUITAR BLUES **219**

E **Vocabulary Note**
Compound Words
? Many compounds contain two nouns joined as one word. What two compounds are in these lines? [*freeway, daylights*] Ask students to find two other compounds in this text column. [*doorbell, bathrobe*]

F **Critical Thinking**
Interpreting
? Why do you think Fausto hesitates before knocking at the door? [Possible responses: Until Roger starts to scratch at the door, he is afraid he has come to the wrong house. He is uneasy about trying to get a reward for bringing Roger back.]

G **Reading Skills and Strategies**

Regional and Cultural Sayings
? Some foods have names that might surprise people of other cultures. What is a turnover? [a folded pastry, often filled with fruit] What other food names might mystify a non-English speaker? [Possible responses: chicken fingers, ladyfingers, drumsticks, buffalo wings, angel hair pasta, pigs in blankets, hot dogs.]

H **Elements of Literature**
Character
? How might the man's statement about Roger explain why the couple have been so kind to Fausto? [Possible response: The couple may have no children of their own and may be treating Fausto like a son.]

Using Students' Strengths

Visual Learners
Ask students to draw or sketch one of the settings described in the story: Fausto's room, the home of Roger's owners (interior or exterior), St. Theresa's Church (interior or exterior). Students might also benefit from completing the material provided in *Graphic Organizers for Active Reading*, p. 15.

Musical Learners
Have students bring in recordings of music they think Fausto would like. For each musical work, have students identify the element that they most admire (rhythm, melody, lyrics, performance, etc.) and give reasons to support their choices.

Interpersonal Learners
Have pairs of students stage a dialogue between Fausto and a friend in which they discuss Fausto's problem and possible solutions. Students should rehearse their dialogues before they perform. Remind them to stay in character as they discuss Fausto's feelings and determine the right course of action for him.

A Struggling Readers

Idioms

? How can people be "in trouble" with themselves? [Possible responses: They might have internal conflicts; they might not be living up to the values they have set for themselves.]

B Critical Thinking

Analyzing Character

? Why does Fausto say he should not have lied to the man and woman? [Possible responses: The amount of the reward is a lot more than he had expected, and the couple are very nice to him.]

C Elements of Literature

Point of View

? Although the narrator mentions the man and the lady, whom is he really telling the reader about? [Fausto] Why is the narrator able to tell the reader what Fausto is doing and thinking? [Possible response: The narrator tells the story from Fausto's point of view.] What might Fausto's actions and thoughts indicate about the boy's feelings? [Possible response: Because Fausto feels guilty about accepting the money, he can't concentrate on the songs and prayers.]

D Reading Skills and Strategies

Making Inferences

? Why does Fausto put the money into the collection basket? [Possible response: He thinks that giving the money to the church will make up for the wrong he did when he lied to get it.]

E Appreciating Language

Word Relatives

? A *lector* is a reader at church. What other words is *lector* related to? [*lecture, lecturer*] What is a *lectern*? [a stand for holding notes at a lecture]

FROM THE EDITOR'S DESK

We videotaped some classes of students doing the activities for this story. They had quite different opinions of what they would have done if they had been Fausto.

A trouble. Not with these nice folks or with his parents, but with himself. How could he have been so deceitful? The dog wasn't lost. It was just having a fun Saturday walking around.

"I can't take that."

"You have to. You deserve it, believe me," the man said.

"No, I don't."

"Now don't be silly," said the lady. She took the bill from her husband and stuffed it into Fausto's shirt pocket. "You're a lovely child. Your parents are lucky to have you. Be good. And come see us again, please."

Fausto went out, and the lady closed the door. Fausto clutched the bill through his shirt pocket. He felt like ringing the doorbell and begging them to please take the money back, but he knew they would refuse. He hurried away and, at the end of the block, pulled the bill from his shirt pocket: It was a crisp twenty-dollar bill.

B "Oh, man, I shouldn't have lied," he said under his breath as he started up the street like a zombie. He wanted to run to church for Saturday confession,[3] but it was past four-thirty, when confession stopped.

He returned to the bush where he had hidden the rake and his sister's bike and rode home slowly, not daring to touch the money in his pocket. At home, in the privacy of his room, he examined the twenty-dollar bill. He had never had so much money. It was probably enough to buy a secondhand guitar. But he felt bad, like the time he stole a dollar from the secret fold inside his older brother's wallet.

Fausto went outside and sat on the fence. "Yeah," he said. "I can probably get a guitar for twenty. Maybe at a yard sale—things are cheaper."

His mother called him to dinner.

The next day he dressed for church without

---

anyone telling him. He was going to go to eight o'clock mass.

"I'm going to church, Mom," he said. His mother was in the kitchen cooking papas and chorizo con huevos.[4] A pile of tortillas lay warm under a dish towel.

"Oh, I'm so proud of you, Son." She beamed, turning over the crackling papas.

His older brother, Lawrence, who was at the table reading the funnies, mimicked, "Oh, I'm so proud of you, my son," under his breath.

At Saint Theresa's he sat near the front. When Father Jerry began by saying that we are all sinners, Fausto thought he looked right at him. Could he know? Fausto fidgeted with guilt. No, he thought. I only did it yesterday.

C Fausto knelt, prayed, and sang. But he couldn't forget the man and the lady, whose names he didn't even know, and the empanada they had given him. It had a strange name but tasted really good. He wondered how they got rich. And how that dome clock worked. He had asked his mother once how his aunt's clock worked. She said it just worked, the way the refrigerator works. It just did.

Fausto caught his mind wandering and tried **D** to concentrate on his sins. He said a Hail Mary and sang, and when the wicker basket came his way, he stuck a hand reluctantly in his pocket and pulled out the twenty-dollar bill. He ironed it between his palms and dropped it into the basket. The grown-ups stared. Here was a kid dropping twenty dollars in the basket while they gave just three or four dollars.

There would be a second collection for Saint **E** Vincent de Paul,[5] the lector[6] announced. The wicker baskets again floated in the pews, and

---

4. **papas** (pä′päs) **and chorizo con huevos** (chô·rē′sô kôn wā′vôs): Spanish for "potatoes" and "sausage with eggs," respectively.

5. **Saint Vincent de Paul** (1580–1660): founder of religious orders that care for the sick and poor. Saint Vincent de Paul societies today minister to the needy.

6. **lector** (lek′tər): person who reads the Scripture lessons in a church service.

3. **confession:** in the Roman Catholic Church, a ritual in which a person seeks God's forgiveness by telling a priest his or her sins.

220 DO THE RIGHT THING

Getting Students Involved

Cooperative Learning

Storyboard. Have students work in groups of five to create storyboards for five incidents from the story, in sequence, with captions. Call on a student from each group to present its storyboard and to read the captions aloud. Examples (with captions in quotation marks):

Fausto pushing the lawn mower—"Fausto remembers it is winter." Fausto tossing Roger a piece of an orange—"He meets a dog named Roger." Fausto eating turnovers—"Roger's owners are nice to him."

Empanadas (Turnovers) (1991) by Carmen Lomas Garza.
Courtesy of the Artist.

this time the adults around him, given a second chance to show their charity, dug deep into their wallets and purses and dropped in fives and tens. This time Fausto tossed in the grimy quarter.

Fausto felt better after church. He went home and played football in the front yard with his brother and some neighbor kids. He felt cleared of wrongdoing and was so happy that he played one of his best games of football ever. On one play, he tore his good pants, which he knew he shouldn't have been wearing. For a second, while he examined the hole, he wished he hadn't given the twenty dollars away.

Man, I coulda bought me some Levi's, he thought. He pictured his twenty dollars being spent to buy church candles. He pictured a priest buying an armful of flowers with *his* money.

Fausto had to forget about getting a guitar. He spent the next day playing soccer in his good pants, which were now his old pants. But that night, during dinner, his mother said she remembered seeing an old bass guitarron[7] the last time she cleaned out her father's garage.

"It's a little dusty," his mom said, serving his favorite enchiladas. "But I think it works. Grandpa says it works."

Fausto's ears perked up. That was the same kind the guy in Los Lobos played. Instead of

7. **guitarron** (gē′tä·rõn′): type of large guitar.

THE NO-GUITAR BLUES 221

RESPONDING TO THE ART
Carmen Lomas Garza
(1948–) depicts Mexican American family life in vivid color and precise detail. Her simple folk-art style, with its crisp outlines and vivid colors, is seen in the rich tableau of *Empanadas*. Ask students to compare the role of empanadas in the painting and in the story.

F **Critical Thinking**
Analyzing Character
? Why does Fausto feel better after church? [Possible response: He has made a sacrifice that supports his values.]

G **Reading Skills and Strategies**
Regional and Cultural Sayings
? Here Fausto plays *soccer*. In column 1, line 7, he plays *football*. Is he playing the same game? Explain. [Possible response: He is probably playing the same game. In Mexico and most countries except the U.S. and Canada, soccer is called *football*.]

H **Appreciating Language**
Word Origins
? What is the origin of the word *guitar*? [It is from the Spanish word *guitarra*.] Why might the narrator have used the term *guitarron* instead of "a large guitar"? [Possible responses: He wants to suggest that the instrument is from Mexico. It is the word the mother would have used.]

Skill Link

Avoiding Comma Splices
Students should be careful to avoid *comma splices*—two sentences linked only by a comma. Instead, they should connect the sentences with a comma followed by a coordinating conjunction (*and, but, for, nor, or, so, yet*): *Fausto felt guilty, so he donated the money.*
Activity
Ask students to write three sentences about Fausto. Each one should be made up of two brief sentences linked by a comma followed by a coordinating conjunction. [Possible responses: (1) Fausto wants to join a band, but he needs a guitar. (2) He can ask his parents for the money, or he can earn it. (3) Fausto's mother finds the guitar, and his grandfather helps him play it.]

Making the Connections

Connecting to the Theme:
"Do the Right Thing"
Ask students whether they think Fausto did the right thing. Are there other "right things" that Fausto might have done? Could he have returned the money? Could he have used it for another purpose? Discuss with students how telling the truth or sacrificing something can balance out a lie.

A Elements of Literature

Metaphor

? Why does the author describe Fausto's smile as "a pumpkin smile"? [Possible responses: He is comparing it to a smile carved on a jack-o'-lantern—a big, toothy grin.]

B Vocabulary Note

Pronunciation

? What is the sound of *s* in *resound*? [It has a *z* sound.]

C Elements of Literature

Point of View

? What is the narrator saying about Fausto here? [Possible response: He is an optimistic person with big dreams.]

BROWSING IN THE FILES

About the Author. Gary Soto is known for his poetry as well as for his stories and novels. He says he enjoys poems, like those by the Chilean poet Pablo Neruda, that celebrate "common things like tomatoes, socks, scissors, and artichokes." He continues: "I felt joyful when I read these odes; and when I began to write my own poems, I tried to remain faithful to the common things of my childhood—dogs, alleys, my baseball mitt, curbs, and the fruit of the valley, especially the orange. I wanted to give these things life, to write so well that my poems would express their simple beauty."

---

asking for the guitar, he waited for his mother to offer it to him. And she did, while gathering the dishes from the table.

"No, Mom, I'll do it," he said, hugging her. "I'll do the dishes forever if you want."

It was the happiest day of his life. No, it was the second-happiest day of his life. The happiest was when his grandfather Lupe placed the guitarron, which was nearly as huge as a wash-tub, in his arms. Fausto ran a thumb down the strings, which vibrated in his throat and chest. It sounded beautiful, deep and eerie. A pumpkin smile widened on his face.

MEET THE WRITER

"Stories Sometimes Begin with Memory"

Like Fausto in this story, **Gary Soto** (1952–) grew up in a Mexican American family in Fresno, California. Much of Soto's award-winning fiction and poetry draws on his Mexican American heritage and his childhood memories. Here's how he recalls the incident that years later inspired "The No-Guitar Blues":

66 I was sucking on a popsicle, playing checkers with my sister, doing nothing on a hot summer day, when a lawn-sniffing beagle wandered onto our block. Immediately, I got it into my head to rescue that dog because I thought it was lost. I hopped off the porch, with my sister in tow, and called, 'Here, boy,' snapping my fingers, patting my thigh. Foolishly, the dog stopped. I pulled on his collar, the jingle of dog tags rattling under his chin. Sure enough, he was lost: The dog tag was etched with the name of a faraway street. I hauled the poor pooch into our backyard and telephoned the owner to inform her that her dog was found. The owner arrived at our house after a few hours. She was glad to see the dog, and I was glad when she opened her purse and gave me and my sister each a two-dollar bill. So

"OK, hijo,[8] now you put your fingers like this," said his grandfather, smelling of tobacco and after-shave. He took Fausto's fingers and placed them on the strings. Fausto strummed a chord on the guitarron, and the bass resounded[9] in their chests.

The guitarron was more complicated than Fausto imagined. But he was confident that after a few more lessons he could start a band that would someday play on *American Bandstand* for the dancing crowds.

8. **hijo** (ē′hô): Spanish for "son."
9. **resounded:** vibrated.

stories sometimes begin with memory, and a memory is what initiated 'No-Guitar Blues,' way back in the mid-sixties when there were no leash laws and plenty of roaming dogs. 99

Prose and Poetry by Gary Soto

You might want to read one of Soto's novels, like *Taking Sides,* or its sequel, *Pacific Crossing* (both, Harcourt Brace). If you like poetry, look at Soto's *A Fire in My Hands* (Scholastic). The book includes a "question and answer" section in which he talks about writing poetry.

Assessing Learning

Check Test: Short Answer

1. What does Fausto decide while watching TV? [He wants to be a guitar player.]
2. What reason does Fausto's mother give for not buying him a guitar? [It is too expensive.]
3. Why does Fausto decide to take the dog to its owners? [He hopes to receive a reward.]

4. What does Fausto do with the reward money? [He puts it in the collection basket at church.]
5. How does Fausto finally get a guitar? [He is given a used guitarron by his grandfather.]

Standardized Test Preparation

For practice with standardized test format specific to this selection, see
- *Standardized Test Preparation,* p. 40

For practice in proofreading and editing, see
- *Daily Oral Grammar,* Transparency 14

MAKING MEANINGS

First Thoughts

[respond]

1. If you had been Fausto, what would you have done with the twenty dollars?

Shaping Interpretations

[infer]

2. When Fausto saw his reward money, he "knew he was in trouble . . . with himself." What does Fausto's reaction tell you about the kind of person he is?

[interpret]

3. Fausto thought Roger's owners were "strange . . . but nice." Why do you think he had that impression of them?

[compare]

4. Before you read this story, you and your class discussed ways to get something you really want. Refer now to the summary that you wrote for the Quickwrite. How does Fausto's experience compare with the solutions you discussed?

[recognize]

5. What lesson about life do you think Fausto's experience teaches? At what point in the story does he "do the right thing"?

[compare]

6. Compare and contrast the experiences of Jimmy Wells in "After Twenty Years" (page 193) with those of Fausto. How are they similar? How are they different?

Challenging the Text

[evaluate]

7. The happy ending of this story rewards Fausto's good behavior. Do you think the story would have been more realistic with a different ending? Would it have been better? Explain.

Extending the Text

[interpret]

8. What does the title of the story mean? What are the blues? Check a dictionary for different meanings of the word. What region and culture in the United States are often connected with the blues?

[connect]

9. Have you heard any regional or cultural sayings recently? Do you use any when you speak? If so, what are they?

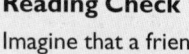

> **Reading Check**
> Imagine that a friend of Fausto's mother tells her that her son dropped a twenty-dollar bill into the collection basket at church. His mother asks Fausto about this, and he explains the situation. With a partner, role-play their talk.

Dick Clark, host of *American Bandstand*, a popular TV show in the 1950s and 1960s.

MAKING MEANINGS

First Thoughts

1. Responses will vary, but students should consider the consequences of their decisions.

Shaping Interpretations

2. Possible responses: He feels bad about acquiring the money dishonestly; he is not living up to the standards he has set for himself.

3. Possible response: Roger's home and his owners are different from Fausto's home and his parents, but Roger's owners are kind.

4. Some students may say that they had considered a dishonest solution like Fausto's.

5. Possible responses: Sometimes the price of getting what you want may not be worth the gain. Fausto did the right thing when he put the money in the collection basket.

6. Possible responses: Fausto and Jimmy both do the right thing by making a difficult decision. Fausto, however, is making up for telling a lie; Jimmy is doing his job.

Challenging the Text

7. Some students may say that the story is realistic and satisfying, although it seems written to teach a lesson. Other students may say that everything is tied up at the end a little too neatly.

Extending the Text

8. Possible responses: The title suggests that Fausto feels sad because he does not have a guitar. *Blues* has two meanings: a feeling of loss or failure and folk music characterized by slow tempos and melancholy words. Blues music is often associated with African American culture and the southern United States.

9. Students' responses should specify to which region or culture each saying belongs.

> **Reading Check**
> Students should demonstrate in their dialogues that they grasp Fausto's fundamental honesty, his passion for music, and his inner conflict. Remind students that their dialogues should be based on information in the story, not simply on speculation.

CHOICES: Building Your Portfolio

1. **Writer's Notebook** Remind students to save their work. They may use it as prewriting for the Writer's Workshop on pp. 260–264.

2. **Creative Writing** Give students the option of rewriting a scene from Roger's perspective. Discuss how Roger might have viewed his encounter with Fausto. Ask students to make a list of things that Roger would notice but Fausto might ignore.

3. **Multimedia Presentation** Students may have trouble finding information about the rock and *conjunto* groups mentioned in the story. A better source might be a knowledgeable clerk at a store that sells Spanish-language recordings.

4. **Language/Home Economics** Distribute recipes from a cookbook, for students to use as models. Remind them that there are two main parts to a recipe: (1) a list of ingredients and amounts and (2) step-by-step instructions for preparing and combining the ingredients.

5. **Art/Creative Writing** Encourage students to look carefully at the painting and to use the details to suggest their stories. For example, has something important just been broadcast over the radio? Are all the preparations for a wedding or a party? Does the purse on the counter contain something surprising?

CHOICES: Building Your Portfolio

Writer's Notebook

1. Collecting Ideas for Supporting a Position

Sometimes you can get ideas for a writing assignment from something you are reading. All of the following topics are part of Soto's story about Fausto: television, music, money, family, foods, animals, morals. With two or three classmates, brainstorm your opinions on these subjects. Jot down some opinions you think you could support.

> • **Music:** *Students who want to learn to play a musical instrument should be able to take lessons at school.*
> • **Money:** *Kids should get an allowance if they work for it.*

Creative Writing

2. The Eyes Have It

In "The No-Guitar Blues" you see everything that happens from Fausto's **point of view.** Try seeing an event through another character's eyes. Choose a character from one scene in the story—for example, Fausto's mother, one of the churchgoers, or one of Roger's owners. Get inside the head of this character, and write the scene from his or her point of view. Reveal your character's thoughts and feelings about Fausto. Write as "I," the person telling the story.

Multimedia Presentation

3. Fausto's Music

The story talks about two kinds of music—the rock music Fausto likes and the *conjunto* music his parents like—and it names some real musicians and groups, such as Los Lobos. Look for information in the library about these groups and find recordings of their music in audio stores. Share what you learn in a multimedia presentation, perhaps showing photographs and playing recordings.

Language/ Home Economics

4. De la cocina de . . . (From the Kitchen of . . .)

This story mentions a number of Mexican foods (for example, empanadas, enchiladas, chorizo con huevos). Choose one of these foods, and make a recipe card for it, complete with a drawing or photograph of the food.

On a separate sheet of paper, rewrite this recipe, translating as many words as you can into Spanish. Ask a friend to help, or use a bilingual dictionary.

Art/Creative Writing

5. Kitchen Chronicle

Look at the picture "Empanadas" on page 221. Imagine that you're one of the people (or the cat) in the picture. Tell a story about the painting, using the **first-person point of view** (that is, speak as "I"). Describe yourself, and tell what you were doing before the moment captured by the picture. Then, tell what you're doing in the picture and what will happen next.

GRAMMAR LINK

Put That Splice on Ice

Language Handbook HELP

See Revising Run-on Sentences, page 761.

Technology HELP

See Language Workshop CD-ROM. Key word entry: run-on sentences.

Can you see what's wrong with this sentence?

> Fausto had come this far, he figured he might as well go through with it.

It's a case of the wrong connection: It's what is called a **comma splice**—two sentences joined together by just a comma. When you are tying two sentences together, a comma alone can't do the job. Here are two ways you can correct the sentence:

1. Break it into two simple sentences.

   Fausto had come this far. **He** figured he might as well go through with it.

2. Create a compound sentence by using a conjunction like *and, or, but,* or *so.* (This is the solution Soto used.)

   "Fausto had come this far, so he figured he might as well go through with it."

Try It Out

Edit these sentences so that they are correct:

1. The dog looked well-fed, Fausto figured he belonged to rich people.

2. He knocked, no one answered.

3. He'd beg them to take the money, they'd refuse.

A tip for writers: To spot comma splices, try reading your writing aloud. A natural, distinct pause in your voice usually marks the end of one thought and the beginning of another. If you stop at a place where you have a comma, you may have found a comma splice.

SPELLING — HOW TO OWN A WORD

Language Handbook HELP

See Spelling Rules, page 781.

Words with *ie* and *ei*

> *I* before *e*,
> Except after *c*,
> Or when sounded as *a*,
> As in *neighbor* and *weigh*.

Every rule has its exceptions. Which of these words from the story breaks the rule: *deceitful, terrier,* or *weird*?

Choose the correct spelling of the word in each underlined pair in the paragraph below. Check your choices in a dictionary. Do all the words follow the "*i* before *e*" rule?

After Fausto received/recieved the guitarron, he formed a band. In their leisure/liesure time they seized/siezed every chance to play. Finally, Fausto achieved/acheived his goal: The priest/preist asked his band to play for a youth dance. In an eerei/eerie dream before the dance, Fausto played, and everyone booed. In real life everyone clapped.

THE NO-GUITAR BLUES 225

GRAMMAR LINK

Ask students to work in pairs to review their use of commas in papers they have written earlier. First, have them read each other's papers to find comma splices. They can then work together to decide whether each splice should be corrected by creating two smaller sentences or by creating a compound sentence with a coordinating conjunction.

Try It Out
Possible Answers

1. The dog looked well-fed, so Fausto figured he belonged to rich people.
2. He knocked. No one answered.
3. He'd beg them to take the money, but they'd refuse.

SPELLING
Answers

Story word that breaks the rule: *weird.* Correct choices from pairs: *received, leisure, seized, achieved, priest, eerie.* All the words except *leisure* and *seized* follow the *i* before *e* except after *c* rule.

Resources

Grammar
- *Grammar and Language Links,* p. 25

Spelling
For related instruction, see
- *Spelling and Decoding,* p. 13

Grammar Link Quick Check

Eliminate any comma splices below by adding or deleting words, punctuation marks, or capitalization. (Possible answers are given.)

1. We can do the right thing, we can do the easy thing. [We can do the right thing, or we can do the easy thing.]

2. Some people were surprised, they couldn't figure out why Fausto would do what he did. [Some people were surprised. They couldn't figure out why Fausto would do what he did.]

3. He could have kept the money, he knew that was wrong. [He could have kept the money, but he knew that was wrong.]

4. Fausto gets a guitarron at the end, he is happy. [Fausto gets a guitarron at the end, so he is happy.]

Planning

• **Block Schedule**
  Block Scheduling Lesson Plans with Pacing Guide

• **Traditional Schedule**
  Lesson Plans Including Strategies for English-Language Learners

• **One-Stop Planner**
  CD-ROM with Test Generator

Before You Read

MADAM AND THE RENT MAN

Make the Connection

Face to Face

• "Grin and bear it."
• "Stand up for yourself."

What does "grin and bear it" mean? Have you ever been in a situation where you had to "grin and bear it"? What does "stand up for yourself" mean? When do people have to stand up for themselves?

Quickwrite

Write down your thoughts in response to the following questions:

1. Which is harder—to grin and bear it or to stand up for yourself?

2. Can you stand up for yourself and still be polite? still be popular?

3. Will people respect you if you always deal with situations you don't like by grinning and bearing it?

 go.hrw.com
LEO 7-3

The Apartment (1943) by Jacob Lawrence. Gouache on paper (21¼" × 29¼") (HMA 1982.10).

Elements of Literature

Tone

Has anyone ever said to you, "Don't use that tone of voice with me"? Your tone can change the meaning of what you say. Tone can turn a statement like "You're a big help" into a genuine compliment or a cruel, sarcastic remark.

Poems and stories have tones, too. As you read "Madam and the Rent Man," think about the **tone,** or the writer's attitude, and how that tone is conveyed to the reader.

> **T**one is the attitude a writer takes toward the audience, the subject, or a character. Tone is conveyed through the writer's choice of words and details.
>
> *For more on Tone, see the Handbook of Literary Terms.*

226 DO THE RIGHT THING

 — — *Resources: Print and Media* —

Reading
• *Graphic Organizers for Active Reading,* p. 16
• *Audio CD Library*
   Disc 7, Track 5

Elements of Literature
• *Literary Elements*
   Transparencies 1–5
   Teaching Notes, p. 38

Viewing and Representing
• *Viewing and Representing*
   Fine Art Transparency 7
   Fine Art Worksheet, p. 28

Assessment
• *Formal Assessment,* p. 43
• *Portfolio Management System,* p. 131
• *Test Generator (One-Stop Planner CD-ROM)*

Internet
• go.hrw.com (keyword: LE0 7-3)

Madam and the Rent Man

Langston Hughes

The rent man knocked.
He said, Howdy-do?
I said, What
Can I do for you?
5   He said, You know
Your rent is due.

I said, Listen,
Before I'd pay
I'd go to Hades°
10   And rot away!

The sink is broke,
The water don't run,
And you ain't done a thing
You promised to've done.

15   Back window's cracked,
Kitchen floor squeaks,
There's rats in the cellar, **(A)**
And the attic leaks.

He said, Madam,
20   It's not up to me.
I'm just the agent,
Don't you see?

I said, Naturally,
You pass the buck.
25   If it's money you want
You're out of luck.

He said, Madam,
I ain't pleased!
I said, Neither am I. **(B)**

30   So we agrees!

9. **Hades** (hā′dēz′): in Greek mythology, the underworld, or world of the dead.

MADAM AND THE RENT MAN **227**

Background

Literature and Place

This poem is set in Harlem, a section of New York City where most people live in rented apartments. The speaker of the poem is a woman who has reason to be angry with her landlord.

Summary ■

Beneath the folksy style of this poem, a conversation between a rent collector and a tenant, lies a compelling social issue. When the agent asks for the rent, the speaker refuses, citing a list of long-neglected fixtures in disrepair. The "rent man" disclaims responsibility—after all, he's only the agent, not the landlord. In an ironical ending, Madam notes that she and the agent "agree" on one thing: neither is "pleased." She realizes that both are powerless to change an exploitative system.

Resources ———

Listening
Audio CD Library
A recording of this poem is provided in the *Audio CD Library*:
• Disc 7, Track 5

(A) Elements of Literature
Tone
❓ What is the poem's tone? [Possible responses: conversational, folksy.] How can you tell? [Possible responses: from the expression "Howdy-do," the short sentences, the simple rhyme scheme.] Is the poem's subject serious or funny? [Most students will find the subject serious in spite of the poem's light tone.]

(B) Elements of Literature
Irony
❓ How is the ending of the poem surprising? [Possible responses: The reader does not expect Madam and the rent man to agree on anything. However, Madam asserts that they agree, at least, that the situation is intolerable.]

RESPONDING TO THE ART

Jacob Lawrence (1917–2000) was an eminent painter of African American life. His distinctive expressionist style features flat, angular lines and forceful colors.

The Apartment is part of a cycle of paintings portraying daily life in Harlem.

Activity. Ask students how this picture makes them feel—sad, angry, happy, or frightened? How do the colors and shapes combine to create a mood in the painting?

Reaching All Students

Struggling Readers
This poem's rhyme and meter make it suitable for a musical treatment that can help struggling readers hear and grasp the tone. Students, working in groups of four or five, can perform musical renditions of the poem for the class. Or you may decide on a simple tune for the poem and lead students in singing it.

English Language Learners
Explain that a dialect is a way of speaking that is characteristic of a particular region or group of people. This poem contains dialect spoken in some African American communities. You may also explain that Hughes does not use quotation marks to set off dialogue; ask students to add opening and closing quotation marks to clarify the speaker of each line.

T227

MEET THE WRITER

"I Knew Only the People I Had Grown Up With"

Langston Hughes (1902–1967) was one of the first African American writers to win worldwide favor. Still, he never lost his popularity with the people he wrote about. Hughes once said:

66 I knew only the people I had grown up with, and they weren't people whose shoes were always shined, who had been to Harvard, or who had heard of Bach. 99

Langston Hughes was born in Joplin, Missouri, and worked at many different jobs in various cities while writing poetry in his spare time. For two years he worked as a busboy at a hotel in Washington, D.C. During this time he wrote many poems, among them blues poems, which he would make up in his head and sing on his way to work. His talent as a poet far exceeded his talent as a singer, as is evident from this story:

66 One evening, I was crossing Rock Creek Bridge, singing a blues I was trying to get right before I put it down on paper. A man passing on the opposite side of the bridge stopped and looked at me, then turned around and cut across the roadway.

He said 'Son, what's the matter? Are you ill?'
'No,' I said. 'Just singing.'
'I thought you were groaning,' he commented. 'Sorry!' And he went on his way.
So after that I never sang my verses aloud in the street any more. 99

Hughes became a major literary figure in what is now known as the Harlem Renaissance of the 1920s. His poems often echo the rhythms of blues and jazz. "Madam and the Rent Man" is from a collection called *One-Way Ticket.*

Popular Poet

Hughes wrote his first poem *after* he was elected class poet when he was in elementary school. The position inspired him to write poetry, and he went on to become a celebrated poet. You can find some of his best poems in a collection called *The Dream Keeper* (Knopf).

228 DO THE RIGHT THING

Assessing Learning

MAKING MEANINGS

First Thoughts

[respond]

1. Which of the following would you say to Madam, and why?

- "Wait a minute, Madam—you might be evicted."
- "Why are you picking on the agent? It's not his fault."
- "You tell him, Madam!"

Shaping Interpretations

[interpret]

2. What does "pass the buck" mean? How has the rent man "passed the buck"?

[evaluate]

3. The woman in the poem speaks plainly and bluntly. Do you think she is right to speak this way? Explain. Refer to your Quickwrite notes for ideas.

[recognize]

4. What **tones** do you hear expressed in this poem?

[infer]

5. Do you think this poem has a **message**? Explain.

CHOICES: Building Your Portfolio

Writer's Notebook

1. Collecting Ideas for Supporting a Position

In "Madam and the Rent Man" the characters are deadlocked. Madam won't pay the rent until her apartment is fixed up. The rent man won't do repairs—it's not his building. This sometimes happens in real life—tenants withhold rent; landlords let buildings fall apart. Suppose that you are an advocate for the rights of tenants who live in rundown buildings. What positions would you take in support of the tenants? How would you make your positions known?

Creative Writing/Dialogue

2. She Said, He Said

Write a dialogue between two people who disagree about something: perhaps money, noise, or food. The dialogue could be funny or serious. Use the vocabulary and speech patterns of everyday conversation to make your characters sound real.

Reading Aloud

3. The Rent Man Knocked

Prepare a read-aloud of "Madam and the Rent Man" in which you and a partner (as Madam and the rent man) read the dialogue. Practice changing the **tone** of your voice as the argument intensifies. Perform your read-aloud for the class. Afterward, ask your listeners to analyze your interpretation of the poem. Did they notice anything new about the poem as they heard it read aloud?

Making the Connections

Connecting to the Theme: "Do the Right Thing"

Both characters in this poem face decisions. Madam decides that the right thing is to stand up for her rights, even if doing so creates conflict. The rent man has apparently decided that his responsibility is limited, even though he is surely aware that the situation is intolerable. Others, who are not named in the poem, must "do the right thing": the landlord, the police, the government.

MAKING MEANINGS

First Thoughts

1. Whichever choice students make, ask them to point out specific details in the poem that led to their reactions.

Shaping Interpretations

2. Possible responses: It means to shift responsibility or blame for something to someone else. The rent man says that he is only an agent and that it is not his job to repair the speaker's home.

3. Possible responses: Yes, she is right to speak as she does, because the problems she faces are serious; she has reported them before, and she deserves a decent place to live. No, she should have tried to reason with the landlord instead of speaking ironically.

4. Possible responses: The overall tone of the poem is humorous, but it has an undercurrent of sarcasm and anger. The discussion between Madam and the rent man is unfriendly; it could develop into shouting.

5. Possible responses: No matter what odds they face, people should fight for their rights; people should not neglect their responsibilities, while expecting others to come up with solutions.

Grading Timesaver

Rubrics for each Choices assignment appear on p. 131 in the *Portfolio Management System*.

CHOICES: Building Your Portfolio

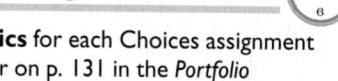

1. Writer's Notebook Remind students to save their work. It may be used as prewriting for the Writer's Workshop on pp. 260–264.

2. Creative Writing/Dialogue Remind students that spoken language is very different from written language; in conversation, people often use sentence fragments and other shortcuts.

3. Reading Aloud Model an oral reading of a similar poem (perhaps another of Hughes's "Madam" poems) before students attempt their own read-alouds.

T229

BARGAIN

Make the Connection

Justice or Revenge?

What is the difference between justice and revenge? What do these two concepts have in common?

	Justice	Revenge
How is it defined in the dictionary?		
Is it right or wrong for a person to seek it? Why?		
Is it fair to all parties? Why or why not?		
Does it help anyone? Does it hurt anyone?		
Give some examples.		

Quickwrite

Get together with a group of classmates to talk about your opinions. A chart can help you explore some ideas. Copy the chart on this page, add questions of your own, and fill in the answers.

Reading Skills and Strategies

Drawing Conclusions: Looking for Evidence

Writers don't come right out and tell you everything you want to know about their characters. You are supposed to take part in the story. You draw your own **conclusions** about the characters you meet in a story, using information you find in the text and your own life experiences. To draw conclusions about the characters in a story, use these strategies:

- Watch what the characters say and do.
- Watch the way other characters respond to them.
- Think about how they are like people you know in real life.

Elements of Literature

Point of View

"Bargain" is told by a character in the story. We call this the **first-person point of view:** The narrator tells the story using the pronoun *I* to talk about his or her own part in the action. In this story the narrator is a boy about your age.

> **I**n the **first-person point of view**, a character tells the story, using the pronoun *I*.

For more on Point of View, see pages 202–203 and the Handbook of Literary Terms.

Background

Historical Fiction

This story takes place in Moon Dance, a town where we have all been in our imaginations. You will recognize Moon Dance from TV and movie westerns—its muddy street, its saloon, and its general store. This story is a kind of **historical fiction.** Setting is important in historical fiction. This writer wants you to feel what it was like to live in a rough frontier town. If you took away Moon Dance and all the historical details, you'd have a different story.

go.hrw.com
LE0 7-3

OBJECTIVES

1. Read and interpret the story
2. Identify and analyze point of view
3. Draw conclusions
4. Express understanding through persuasive writing, research/speaking and listening, research/art, or analysis of a setting
5. Identify apostrophes and use them correctly
6. Spell words that contain silent letters

SKILLS

Literary
- Identify and analyze point of view

Reading
- Draw conclusions

Writing
- Collect ideas for an essay supporting a position
- Write a summary
- Write an essay analyzing setting

Speaking/Listening
- Present an oral report on frontier teachers

Grammar/Language
- Identify apostrophes and use them correctly

Vocabulary
- Spell words that contain silent letters

Art
- Sketch a set and props for a filmed version of the story

Viewing/Representing
- Write a poem or short story about a character in a painting (ATE)
- Describe the mood of a painting (ATE)

  Resources: Print and Media

Reading
- *Reading Skills and Strategies* Selection Skill Lesson, p. 39
- *Graphic Organizers for Active Reading*, p. 17
- *Spelling and Decoding*, Worksheet, p. 14
- *Audio CD Library*, Disc 7, Track 6

Writing and Language
- *Daily Oral Grammar*, Transparency 15
- *Grammar and Language Links*, Worksheet, p. 27
- *Language Workshop CD-ROM*

Viewing and Representing
- *Viewing and Representing* Fine Art Transparency 8 Fine Art Worksheet, p. 32

Assessment
- *Formal Assessment*, p. 44
- *Portfolio Management System*, p. 132
- *Standardized Test Preparation*, p. 42
- *Test Generator (One-Stop Planner CD-ROM)*

Internet
- go.hrw.com (keyword LE0 7-3)

BARGAIN

A. B. Guthrie

Planning

- **Traditional Schedule**
  Lesson Plans Including Strategies for English-Language Learners
- **One-Stop Planner**
  CD-ROM with Test Generator

Summary ▪▪

When Mr. Baumer, owner of a general store, tries to collect a debt from Slade, this former employee and chronic bully cruelly twists Baumer's nose and tosses the bill into the street. The next day, Baumer tells Al—the young narrator, who works part time at the store—that the illiterate freighter resents him, an immigrant who learned to read at sixteen and built a successful business; Baumer, in turn, resents Slade for stealing whiskey from him. A month later, Slade breaks Baumer's hand. Shortly before Christmas, Baumer shocks Al by hiring Slade to haul freight. One bitterly cold day Slade dies in transit, apparently having frozen to death. Al, unloading a barrel, wonders whether there are enough customers for it. Assuring him there are, Baumer says it was a "bargain." As Al notices the barrel's label "Wood Alcohol—Deadly Poison," Mr. Baumer slyly remarks, "Is good to know to read."

Mr. Baumer and I had closed the Moon
Dance Mercantile Company and were walking to the post office, and he had a bunch of bills in his hand ready to mail. There wasn't anyone or anything much on the street because it was suppertime. A buckboard[1] and a saddle horse were tied at Hirsches' rack, and a rancher in a wagon rattled for home ahead of us, the sound of his going fading out as he prodded his team. Freighter[2] Slade stood alone in front of the Moon Dance Saloon, maybe wondering whether to have one more before going to supper. People said he could hold a lot without showing it except in being ornerier[3] even than usual.

Mr. Baumer didn't see him until he was almost on him, and then he stopped and fingered through the bills until he found the right one. He stepped up to Slade and held it out.

1. **buckboard:** open carriage.
2. **freighter:** here, person who transports goods.
3. **ornerier** (ôr′nər·ē·ər): dialect for "meaner and more stubborn."

Slade said, "What's this, Dutchie?"

Mr. Baumer had to tilt his head up to talk to him. "You know vat it is."

Slade just said, "Yeah?" You never could tell from his face what went on inside his skull. He had dark skin and shallow cheeks and a thick-growing moustache that fell over the corners of his mouth.

"It is a bill," Mr. Baumer said. "I tell you before, it is a bill. For twenty-vun dollars and fifty cents."

> He was a man you wouldn't remember from meeting once.

BARGAIN 231

Resources ⌢

Listening
Audio CD Library
A recording of this story is provided in the *Audio CD Library*:
- Disc 7, Track 6

Ⓐ Elements of Literature
Point of View
❓ What does the pronoun *I* here tell you about the story's point of view? [The story is a first-person narrative.]

Ⓑ Reading Skills and Strategies
Drawing Conclusions
❓ What conclusions can you draw from the name that Slade calls Baumer and from Baumer's accent (*vat* for *what*)? [Possible responses: Slade is prejudiced against immigrants. Baumer is probably German-born (in German, *deutsch* means "German").]

Reaching All Students

Struggling Readers
Drawing Conclusions was introduced on p. 230. For a lesson directly tied to this selection that teaches students to draw conclusions by using a strategy called It Says . . . I Say, see the *Reading Skills and Strategies* binder:
- Selection Skill Lesson, p. 39

English Language Learners
Students may wrestle with Baumer's grammar and pronunciation. Point out that Baumer replaces *w* sounds with *v* sounds, sometimes simplifies verb tenses, and omits some words that are grammatically necessary (*Is good* for *It is good*, p. 232).

Advanced Learners
Explain that the Western is a genre, or type, of literature (like mysteries and science fiction). Have students list the Western's characteristics of setting, character, plot, imagery, and theme.

A Reading Skills and Strategies

Drawing Conclusions

? What conclusions can you draw about Slade based on his reaction to being given the bill? [Possible responses: He has a short temper and a mean streak; he has no intention of paying what he owes.]

B Elements of Literature

Point of View

? Why does the narrator give this information about himself? [Possible response: He is letting the reader know who he is.] How does the reader learn the narrator's name? [The reader learns the name when Baumer says to him, "Better study, Al."] Why might the narrator use different methods to provide information about himself? [Possible response: The variety makes the story more interesting.]

C Vocabulary Note

Silent Letters

? How is the word pneumonia pronounced? [nōō•mōn′yə] Which letter is silent? [p] What language is the word from? [Greek]

D Appreciating Language

Sentence Structure

? This sentence lists, or catalogues, many store items; the words are joined by and. What is the effect of the long list? [Possible response: The list emphasizes the variety of things the store carries and helps the reader visualize the piles of merchandise.]

"You know what I do with bills, don't you, Dutchie?" Slade asked.

Mr. Baumer didn't answer the question. He said, "For merchandise."

Slade took the envelope from Mr. Baumer's hand and squeezed it up in his fist and let it drop on the plank sidewalk. Not saying anything, he reached down and took Mr. Baumer's nose between the knuckles of his fingers and twisted it up into his eyes. That was all. That was all at the time. Slade half turned and slouched to the door of the bar and let himself in. Some men were laughing in there.

Mr. Baumer stooped and picked up the bill and put it on top of the rest and smoothed it out for mailing. When he straightened up, I could see tears in his eyes from having his nose screwed around.

He didn't say anything to me, and I didn't say anything to him, being so much younger and feeling embarrassed for him. He went into the post office and slipped the bills in the slot, and we walked on home together. At the last, at the crossing where I had to leave him, he remembered to say, "Better study, Al. Is good to know to read and write and figure." I guess he felt he had to push me a little, my father being dead.

I said, "Sure. See you after school tomorrow"—which he knew I would anyway. I had been working in the store for him during the summer and after classes ever since pneumonia took my dad off.

Three of us worked there regularly: Mr. Baumer, of course, and me and Colly Coleman, who knew enough to drive the delivery wagon but wasn't much help around the store except for carrying orders out to the rigs[4] at the hitch-post and handling heavy things like the whiskey barrel at the back of the store which Mr. Baumer sold quarts and gallons out of.

The store carried quite a bit of stuff—sugar and flour and dried fruits and canned goods

and such on one side and yard goods and coats and caps and aprons and the like of that on the other, besides kerosene and bran and buckets and linoleum and pitchforks in the storehouse at the rear—but it wasn't a big store like Hirsch Brothers up the street. Never would be, people guessed, going on to say, with a sort of slow respect, that it would have gone under long ago if Mr. Baumer hadn't been half mule and half beaver. He had started the store just two years before and, the way things were, worked himself close to death.

He was at the high desk at the end of the grocery counter when I came in the next afternoon. He had an eyeshade on and black sateen protectors on his forearms, and his pencil was in his hand instead of behind his ear and his glasses were roosted on the nose that Slade had twisted. He didn't hear me open and close the door or hear my feet as I walked back to him, and I saw he wasn't doing anything with the pencil but holding it over paper. I stood and studied him for a minute, seeing a small, stooped man with a little paunch bulging through his unbuttoned vest. He was a man you wouldn't remember from meeting once. There was nothing in his looks to set itself in your mind unless maybe it was his chin, which was a small pink hill in the gentle plain of his face.

While I watched him, he lifted his hand and felt carefully of his nose. Then he saw me. His eyes had that kind of mistiness that seems to go with age or illness, though he wasn't really old or sick, either. He brought his hand down quickly and picked up the pencil, but he saw I still was looking at the nose, and finally he sighed and said, "That Slade."

Just the sound of the name brought Slade to my eye. I saw him slouched in front of the bar, and I saw him and his string[5] coming down the grade from the buttes,[6] the wheel horses held

---

5. **string:** here, a group of horses.
6. **buttes** (byōōts): steep, flat-topped hills that stand alone on a plain.

4. **rigs:** carriages with their horses.

Using Students' Strengths

Visual Learners

Ask students to draw pictures of what they think Baumer's store and Slade's freight wagon look like. To help students visualize the setting and details of the story, you might display photos or drawings of the Old West (including a general store) and of frontier modes of transport (including freight-hauling wagons). Students can respond to questions like "What do you think you could buy in this store?" and "What kinds of things could this wagon carry?"

Logical/Mathematical Learners

Have students make a page from Baumer's ledger, or record book, of the Moon Dance Mercantile Company. The page might show customer names and sales transactions, dates, prices, items and quantities purchased, payments and partial payments, quantities remaining in inventory, even profits. The page should show what Slade owes.

Interpersonal Learners

Ask students to imagine that they have been transported back in American history to Moon Dance. Inform them that they have arrived just in time to witness one of the disputes between Baumer and Slade. Ask them to create diary entries describing their thoughts on seeing the conflict between the two men.

snug and the rest lined out pretty, and then the string leveling off and Slade's whip lifting hair from a horse that wasn't up in the collar.[7] I had heard it said that Slade could make a horse scream with that whip. Slade's name wasn't Freighter, of course. Our town had nicknamed him that because that was what he was.

"I don't think it's any good to send him a bill, Mr. Baumer," I said. "He can't even read."

"He could pay yet."

"He don't pay anybody," I said.

"I think he hate me," Mr. Baumer went on. "That is the thing. He hate me for coming not from this country. I come here, sixteen years old, and learn to read and write, and I make a business, and so I think he hate me."

"He hates everybody."

Mr. Baumer shook his head. "But not to pinch the nose. Not to call Dutchie."

The side door squeaked open, but it was only Colly Coleman coming in from a trip, so I said, "Excuse me, Mr. Baumer, but you shouldn't have trusted him in the first place."

"I know," he answered, looking at me with his misty eyes. "A man make mistakes. I think some do not trust him, so he will pay me because I do. And I do not know him well then. He only came back to town three, four months ago, from being away since before I go into business."

"People who knew him before could have told you," I said.

"A man make mistakes," he explained again. **F**

7. **up in the collar:** pulling as hard as the other horses.

"It's not my business, Mr. Baumer, but I would forget the bill."

His eyes rested on my face for a long minute, as if they didn't see me but the problem itself. He said, "It is not twenty-vun dollars and fifty cents now, Al. It is not that anymore."

"What is it?"

He took a little time to answer. Then he brought his two hands up as if to help him shape the words. "It is the thing. You see, it is the thing." **G**

I wasn't quite sure what he meant.

He took his pencil from behind the ear where he had put it and studied the point of it. "That Slade. He steal whiskey and call it evaporation. He sneak things from his load. A thief, he is. And too big for me."

I said, "I got no time for him, Mr. Baumer, but I guess there never was a freighter didn't steal whiskey. That's what I hear."

It was true, too. From the railroad to Moon Dance was fifty miles and a little better—a two-day haul in good weather, heck knew how long in bad. Any freight string bound home with a load had to lie out at least one night. When a freighter had his stock tended to and maybe a little fire going against the dark, he'd tackle a barrel of whiskey or of **H** grain alcohol if he had one aboard consigned to Hirsch Brothers or Mr. Baumer's or the Moon Dance Saloon or the Gold Leaf Bar. He'd drive a hoop out of place, bore a little hole with a nail or bit and draw off what he wanted. Then he'd plug the hole with a whittled peg and pound the hoop back. That was

BARGAIN 233

E ⬤ Struggling Readers
Reading Aloud
Have pairs of students read aloud this dialogue between Baumer and Al. Students should convey the emotions of the characters as they read aloud: Al's polite sincerity, Baumer's attempts to explain Slade's behavior.

F ⬤ Critical Thinking
Interpreting
❓ Why does Baumer keep saying that "a man make mistakes"? What does he mean? [He may mean that Slade deserves another chance, or that he made a mistake by ever trusting Slade.]

G ⬤ Reading Skills and Strategies
Making Inferences
❓ What do you think Baumer means by "the thing"? [Possible responses: The principle of justice is driving him to collect the bill; he will stand up to Slade because he knows the freighter hates him; he is angry that Slade has stolen whiskey from him.] Why does he use the phrase "the thing"? [Possible responses: The problem is haunting Baumer.]

H ⬤ Elements of Literature
Foreshadowing
❓ Why might the author provide so much detail about how the freighters steal whiskey? [Possible response: This information may be important later in the story.]

Resources
Viewing and Representing
Fine Art Transparency
A fine art transparency of Oscar E. Berninghaus's *Why the Mail Was Late* can be used as a prereading motivator. See the *Viewing and Representing Transparencies and Worksheets:*
• Transparency 8
• Worksheet, p. 32

Taking a Second Look

Review: Describing Mental Images
The process of describing the "pictures" that text passages create in their minds connects the reader more closely to the text.
Activities
1. Have students choose one of the following passages and describe, in their own words, what image the passage evokes for them. (Students should pay close attention to

sensory details). (a) "Slade . . . squeezed it up in his fist and let it drop on the plank sidewalk." (b) ". . . his chin, which was a small pink hill in the gentle plain of his face." (c) ". . . the wheel horses held snug and the rest lined out pretty, and then the string leveling off and Slade's whip lifting hair from a horse that wasn't up in the collar."

2. Have students, working in pairs, each choose a descriptive passage in the story that appeals to them. Then, have each student describe to the partner, in his or her own words, the image that the passage evokes. The listening partner can look through the story to find the paraphrased passage.

A Reading Skills and Strategies

Drawing Conclusions

❓ What conclusions do you draw from this comment about the people's attitude toward freighters? [Possible responses: The people know that good freighters are hard to find and that the work is difficult. The people are scared of the freighters.]

B Elements of Literature

Point of View

❓ Why doesn't Al tell us what Baumer is thinking? [Possible response: Because Al is a first-person narrator, he doesn't know what the other characters think unless they tell him.] Why does Al say that he "could see thought swimming" in Baumer's eyes? [Possible response: Baumer is thinking seriously—probably about the freighters' theft of whiskey.]

C Struggling Readers

Finding Sequence of Events

The narrator packs a series of events into this paragraph to indicate the passage of time and to lead up to the next encounter with Slade. Have students list the events named in this paragraph. [Possible responses: One month passes. Fall becomes winter. Ducks head south. Baumer hires Miss Webb. Christmas trade (shopping) begins. October arrives. Baumer and Al walk up the street with the bills.]

D Appreciating Language

Punctuation

❓ Why is there an apostrophe in *Hirsches'*? [It indicates ownership.] On p. 232 the store is called *Hirsch Brothers*. Is *Hirsches'* singular or plural possessive? [plural possessive] What would be the singular possessive? [*Hirsch's*]

E Reading Skills and Strategies

Making Predictions

❓ Al believes that something is about to happen. What do you think is going to happen? [Possible responses: Slade will attack Baumer. Baumer will lose his self-control and attack Slade.]

---

evaporation. Nobody complained much. With freighters you generally took what they gave you, within reason.

"Moore steals it, too," I told Mr. Baumer. Moore was Mr. Baumer's freighter.

"Yah," he said, and that was all, but I stood there for a minute, thinking there might be something more. I could see thought swimming in his eyes, above that little hill of chin. Then a customer came in, and I had to go wait on him.

Nothing happened for a month, nothing between Mr. Baumer and Slade, that is, but fall drew on toward winter and the first flight of ducks headed south and Mr. Baumer hired Miss Lizzie Webb to help with the just-beginning Christmas trade and here it was, the first week in October, and he and I walked up the street again with the monthly bills. He always sent them out. I guess he had to. A bigger store, like Hirsches', would wait on the ranchers until their beef or wool went to market.

Up to a point things looked and happened almost the same as they had before, so much the same that I had the crazy feeling I was going through that time again. There was a wagon and a rig tied up at Hirsches' rack and a saddle horse standing hipshot[8] in front of the harness shop. A few more people were on the street now, not many, and lamps had been lit against the shortened day.

It was dark enough that I didn't make out Slade right away. He was just a figure that came out of the yellow wash of light from the Moon Dance Saloon and stood on the boardwalk and with his head made the little motion of spitting. Then I recognized the lean, raw shape of him and the muscles flowing down into the sloped shoulders, and in the settling darkness I filled the picture in—the dark skin and the flat cheeks and the peevish eyes and the moustache growing rank.

---

8. **hipshot:** with one hip lower than the other.

---

234 DO THE RIGHT THING

There was Slade and here was Mr. Baumer with his bills and here I was, just as before, just like in the second go-round of a bad dream. I felt like turning back, being embarrassed and half scared by trouble even when it wasn't mine. Please, I said to myself, don't stop, Mr. Baumer! Don't bite off anything! Please, short-sighted the way you are, don't catch sight of him at all! I held up and stepped around behind Mr. Baumer and came up on the outside so as to be between him and Slade, where maybe I'd cut off his view.

But it wasn't any use. All along I think I knew it was no use, not the praying or the walking between or anything. The act had to play itself out.

Mr. Baumer looked across the front of me and saw Slade and hesitated in his step and came to a stop. Then in his slow, business way, his chin held firm against his mouth, he began fingering through the bills, squinting to make out the names. Slade had turned and was watching him, munching on a cud of tobacco like a bull waiting.

"You look, Al," Mr. Baumer said without lifting his face from the bills. "I cannot see so good."

So I looked, and while I was looking, Slade must have moved. The next I knew, Mr. Baumer was staggering ahead, the envelopes spilling out of his hands. There had been a thump, the clap of a heavy hand swung hard on his back.

Slade said, "Haryu, Dutchie?"

Mr. Baumer caught his balance and turned around, the bills he had trampled shining white between them and at Slade's feet the hat that Mr. Baumer had stumbled out from under.

Slade picked up the hat and scuffed through the bills and held it out. "Cold to be goin' without a skypiece," he said.

Mr. Baumer hadn't spoken a word. The lampshine from inside the bar caught his eyes, and in them, it seemed to me, a light came and

---

Crossing the Curriculum

Geography

The geography of the western United States influenced the way communities developed, the work people did, and their methods of transportation and communication. Have students create a glossary (with pictures) of western geographical terms, perhaps including the following: butte, canyon, Continental Divide, desert, foothill, mesa, mountain, plain, plateau, and prairie.

Social Studies/History

People who lived in the Old West developed their own words for many objects, events, and feelings. Ask students to present an oral report in which they explain one or more western expressions—for example: prairie schooner, dust devil, dingus, bite the dust, pack train, stool pigeon, storm the puncheons, snipe-gutted. Students might find help in Dictionary of the American West, edited by Winfred Blevins (Facts on File, 1993).

T234

The Apprentice by Robert Duncan.

Courtesy of the Artist.

went as anger and the uselessness of it took turns in his head.

Two men had come up on us and stood watching. One of them was Angus McDonald, who owned the Ranchers' Bank, and the other was Dr. King. He had his bag in his hand.

Two others were drifting up, but I didn't **F** have time to tell who. The light came in Mr. Baumer's eyes, and he took a step ahead and **G** swung. I could have hit harder myself. The fist landed on Slade's cheek without hardly so much as jogging his head, but it let the devil loose in the man. I didn't know he could move so fast. He slid in like a practiced fighter and let Mr. Baumer have it full in the face.

Mr. Baumer slammed over on his back, but he wasn't out. He started lifting himself. Slade leaped ahead and brought a boot heel down on the hand he was lifting himself by. I heard meat

and bone under that heel and saw Mr. Baumer **H** fall back and try to roll away.

Things had happened so fast that not until then did anyone have a chance to get between them. Now Mr. McDonald pushed at Slade's chest, saying, "That's enough, Freighter. That's enough, now," and Dr. King lined up, too, and another man I didn't know, and I took a place, and we formed a kind of screen between them. Dr. King turned and bent to look at Mr. Baumer.

"Fool hit me first," Slade said.

"That's enough," Mr. McDonald told him again while Slade looked at all of us as if he'd spit on us for a nickel. Mr. McDonald went on, using a half-friendly tone, and I knew it was because he didn't want to take Slade on any more than the rest of us did. "You go on home and sleep it off, Freighter. That's the ticket." **I**

Slade just snorted.

BARGAIN 235

Getting Students Involved

A Critical Thinking

Challenging the Text

? Do you think the author exaggerates Slade's meanness? Why or why not? [Possible responses: Yes, the author wants to persuade the reader to hate Slade. No, many people are even meaner than Slade.]

B Critical Thinking

Making Judgments

? Do you agree with Al that there is no way to get the best of Slade? [Possible responses: Yes, because everyone is afraid of him; no, because Baumer may have a plan to get even.]

C Elements of Literature

Character

? What does Baumer's practicing writing with his left hand tell you about him? [Possible responses: Baumer is strong-willed, persistent, and courageous.]

D Vocabulary Note

Silent Letters

? Which letters in *straightened* are silent? [*gh*] What other words have these silent letters? [Possible responses: *night, light, bright.*]

E Reading Skills and Strategies

Responding to the Text

? Do you agree with Baumer that he does not need to go to the law with his problem? [Possible response: No, laws and police and judges should deal with people like Slade. Yes, too many people go to the law with problems they could solve themselves.]

From behind us, Dr. King said, "I think you've broken this man's hand."

"Lucky for him I didn't kill him," Slade answered. "Dutch penny pincher!" He fingered the chew out of his mouth. "Maybe he'll know enough to leave me alone now."

Dr. King had Mr. Baumer on his feet. "I'll take him to the office," he said.

Blood was draining from Mr. Baumer's nose and rounding the curve of his lip and dripping from the sides of his chin. He held his hurt right hand in the other. But the thing was that he didn't look beaten even then, not the way a man who has given up looks beaten. Maybe that was why Slade said, with a show of that fierce anger, "You stay away from me! Hear? Stay clear away, or you'll get more of the same!"

Dr. King led Mr. Baumer away, Slade went back into the bar, and the other men walked off, talking about the fight. I got down and picked up the bills, because I knew Mr. Baumer would want me to, and mailed them at the post office, dirty as they were. It made me sorer, someway, that Slade's bill was one of the few that wasn't marked up. The cleanness of it seemed to say that there was no getting the best of him.

Mr. Baumer had his hand in a sling the next day and wasn't much good at waiting on the trade. I had to hustle all afternoon and so didn't have a chance to talk to him even if he had wanted to talk. Mostly he stood at his desk, and once, passing it, I saw he was practicing writing with his left hand. His nose and the edges

of the cheeks around it were swollen some.

At closing time I said, "Look, Mr. Baumer, I can lay out of school a few days until you kind of get straightened out here."

"No," he answered as if to wave the subject away. "I get somebody else. You go to school. Is good to learn."

I had a half notion to say that learning hadn't helped him with Slade. Instead, I blurted out that I would have the law on Slade.

"The law?" he asked.

"The sheriff or somebody."

"No, Al," he said. "You would not."

I asked why.

"The law, it is not for plain fights," he said. "Shooting? Robbing? Yes, the law come quick. The plain fights, they are too many. They not count enough."

He was right. I said, "Well, I'd do something anyhow."

"Yes," he answered with a slow nod of his head. "Something you vould do, Al." He didn't tell me what.

Within a couple of days he got another man to clerk for him—it was Ed Hempel, who was always finding and losing jobs—and we made out. Mr. Baumer took his hand from the sling in a couple or three weeks, but with the tape on it, it still wasn't any use to him. From what you could see of the fingers below the tape, it looked as if it never would be.

He spent most of his time at the high desk, sending me or Ed out on the errands he used to run, like posting and getting the mail. Some-

236 DO THE RIGHT THING

Skill Link

Possessives

Doing this Skill Link will help students prepare for the Grammar Link on p. 243. Remind them of the definitions of *possessive* (a form showing ownership) and *contraction* (a shortened form in which some letters are left out). Have students identify the following items as contractions or as possessives.

1. she's [contraction of *she is*]
2. hers [possessive]

3. its [possessive]
4. it's [contraction of *it is*]
5. whose [possessive]
6. who's [contraction of *who is*]
7. they're [contraction of *they are*]
8. their [possessive]
9. theirs [possessive]
10. there's [contraction of *there is*]

times I wondered if that was because he was afraid of meeting Slade. He could just as well have gone himself. He wasted a lot of hours just looking at nothing, though I will have to say he worked hard at learning to write left-handed.

Then, a month and a half before Christmas, he hired Slade to haul his freight for him.

Ed Hempel told me about the deal when I showed up for work. "Yessir," he said, resting his foot on a crate in the storeroom where we were supposed to be working. "I tell you he's throwed in with Slade. Told me this morning to go out and locate him if I could and bring him in. Slade was at the saloon, o' course, and says to the devil with Dutchie, but I told him this was honest-to-God business, like Baumer had told me to, and there was a quart of whiskey right there in the store for him if he'd come and get it. He was out of money, I reckon, because the quart fetched him."

"What'd they say?" I asked him.

"Search me. There was two or three people in the store and Baumer told me to wait on 'em, and he and Slade palavered[9] back by the desk."

"How do you know they made a deal?"

Ed spread his hands out. "'Bout noon, Moore came in with his string, and I heard Baumer say he was makin' a change. Moore didn't like it too good, either."

It was a hard thing to believe, but there one day was Slade with a pile of stuff for the Moon Dance Mercantile Company, and that was proof enough with something left for boot.

Mr. Baumer never opened the subject up with me, though I gave him plenty of chances. And I didn't feel like asking. He didn't talk much these days but went around absent-minded, feeling now and then of the fingers that curled yellow and stiff out of the bandage

9. **palavered** (pə·lav′ər d): talked; met to discuss something.

like the toes on the leg of a dead chicken. Even on our walks home he kept his thoughts to himself.

I felt different about him now and was sore inside. Not that I blamed him exactly. A hundred and thirty-five pounds wasn't much to throw against two hundred. And who could tell what Slade would do on a bellyful of whiskey? He had promised Mr. Baumer more of the same, hadn't he? But I didn't feel good. I couldn't look up to Mr. Baumer like I used to and still wanted to. I didn't have the beginning of an answer when men cracked jokes or shook their heads in sympathy with Mr. Baumer, saying Slade had made him come to time.

Slade hauled in a load for the store, and another, and Christmastime was drawing on and trade heavy, and the winter that had started early and then pulled back came on again. There was a blizzard and then a still cold and another blizzard and afterwards a sunshine that was iceshine on the drifted snow. I was glad to be busy, selling overshoes and sheep-lined coats and mitts and socks as thick as saddle blankets and Christmas candy out of buckets and hickory nuts and the fresh oranges that the people in our town never saw except when Santa Claus was coming.

One afternoon, when I lit out from class, the thermometer on the school porch read forty-two degrees below. But you didn't have to look at it to know how cold the weather was. Your nose and fingers and toes and ears and the bones inside you told you. The snow cried when you stepped on it.

I got to the store and took my things off and scuffed my hands at the stove for a minute so's to get life enough in them to tie a parcel. Mr. Baumer—he was always polite to me—said, "Hello, Al. Not so much to do today. Too cold for customers." He shuddered a little, as if he hadn't got the chill off even yet, and rubbed his broken hand with the good one. "Ve need

Ⓕ Reading Skills and Strategies

Drawing Conclusions

❓ What conclusions do you draw from this surprising development? [Possible response: Baumer is going to trick Slade.]

Ⓖ Critical Thinking

Speculating

❓ Why does Baumer provide a quart of whiskey for Slade? [Possible response: Baumer may be laying a trap for Slade, and the whiskey is the bait.]

Ⓗ Vocabulary Note

Adverbs and Adjectives

Ed uses the adjective *good* here when he should use the adverb *well*. Remind students that although this substitution is often made in conversation, it should be avoided in formal writing.

Ⓘ Elements of Literature

Point of View

❓ Whose feelings does the narrator describe? [his own] What are these feelings? [Possible response: Al has lost respect for Baumer because he hired Slade.] Whose motives does Al speculate about? [Baumer's] How does Al react when the men talk about Baumer? [He has no answer for the men's jokes and comments.]

Ⓙ Appreciating Language

Figurative Language

❓ What might Al be referring to when he says that the snow cried when he stepped on it? [Possible response: the high-pitched, squeaking noise that snow can make when it is stepped on in very cold weather.] What does the word *cried* suggest? [Possible response: the pain and discomfort caused by severe weather.]

Frederic Remington (1861–1909) left an enduring pictorial record of life on the western frontier. Here, in *The Fall of the Cowboy* (1895), he conjures a wintry image of the loneliness of frontier life.

Activity. Ask students to use vivid, precise adjectives to describe the objects in this painting: sky, ground, fence, the two men, and the two horses. Then, ask students to use descriptive language to capture the overall mood of the painting. Students might also speculate on why the painting is titled *The Fall of the Cowboy*. Some students may point out that the cowboys' harsh life, and changes in society (the rise of railroads; increasing immigration, urbanization, and industrialization), spell the end of the heyday of cowboys and of the frontier.

The Fall of the Cowboy (1895) by Frederic S. Remington. Oil on canvas (1961. 230). © Amon Carter Museum, Fort Worth, Texas.

Ⓐ Elements of Literature

Point of View

According to Al, Baumer is thinking about Slade making it through the snow. Al's comment turns out to be an ironical use of the first-person narrator. **Explain.** [Possible response: Al has no way of knowing Baumer's real thoughts. Al gives a much more innocent interpretation of them than the reader does at the end of the story.]

Ⓑ English Language Learners

Dialect

? *Figger* is a word of dialect—language used in some regions or by some groups of people. What is the standard English word for *figger*? [figure]

Ⓐ Christmas goods," he said, looking out the window to the furrows that wheels had made in the snow-banked street, and I knew he was thinking of Slade's string, inbound from the Ⓑ railroad, and the time it might take even Slade to travel those hard miles.

Slade never made it at all.

Less than an hour later our old freighter, Moore, came in, his beard white and stiff with frost. He didn't speak at first but looked around and clumped to the stove and took off his heavy mitts, holding his news inside him.

Then he said, not pleasantly, "Your new man's dead, Baumer."

"My new man?" Mr. Baumer said.

"Who do you think? Slade. He's dead."

All Mr. Baumer could say was "Dead!"

"Froze to death, I figger," Moore told him, while Colly Coleman and Ed Hempel and Miss Lizzie and I and a couple of customers stepped closer.

"Not Slade," Mr. Baumer said. "He know too much to freeze."

"Maybe so, but he sure's froze now. I got him in the wagon."

We stood looking at one another and at Moore. Moore was enjoying his news, enjoying feeding it out bit by bit so's to hold the stage.

238 DO THE RIGHT THING

Crossing the Curriculum

Social Sciences

Slade's death is indirectly caused by his inability to read. Provide students with information (consult a general encyclopedia or the Internet) on the current rate of illiteracy in the United States. (Although the rate of total illiteracy is less than 1 percent, the rate of functional illiteracy may be as high as 20 percent.) Then, provide students with illiteracy rates for a few other countries. Ask them which countries tend to have the lowest rates. [developed countries] Which tend to have the highest rates? [developing countries] After students have read the statistics, ask them to write letters requesting information from an organization combating illiteracy, such as the Literacy Volunteers of America.

"Heart might've give out, for all I know."

The side door swung open, letting in a cloud of cold and three men who stood, like us, waiting on Moore. I moved a little and looked through the window and saw Slade's freight outfit tied outside with more men around it. Two of them were on a wheel of one of the wagons, looking inside.

"Had a extra man, so I brought your stuff in," Moore went on. "Figgered you'd be glad to pay for it."

"Not Slade," Mr. Baumer said again.

"You can take a look at him."

Mr. Baumer answered no.

"Someone's takin' word to Connor to bring his hearse. Anyhow, I told 'em to. I carted old Slade this far. Connor can have him now."

Moore pulled on his mitts. "Found him there by the Deep Creek crossin', doubled up in the snow an' his fire out." He moved toward the door. "I'll see to the horses, but your stuff'll have to set there. I got more'n enough work to do at Hirsches'."

Mr. Baumer just nodded.

I put on my coat and went out and waited my turn and climbed on a wagon wheel and looked inside, and there was Slade piled on some bags of bran. Maybe because of being frozen, his face was whiter than I ever saw it, whiter and deader, too, though it never had been lively. Only the moustache seemed still alive, sprouting thick like greasewood from alkali.[10] Slade was doubled up all right, as if he

10. **greasewood from alkali:** Greasewood is a thorny desert plant. Alkali is dry, salty soil that might look white and chalky, like Slade's face.

had died and stiffened leaning forward in a chair.

I got down from the wheel, and Colly and then Ed climbed up. Moore was unhitching, tossing off his pieces of information while he did so. Pretty soon Mr. Connor came up with his old hearse, and he and Moore tumbled Slade into it, and the team, which was as old as the hearse, made off, the tires squeaking in the snow. The people trailed on away with it, their breaths leaving little ribbons of mist in the air. It was beginning to get dark.

Mr. Baumer came out of the side door of the store, bundled up, and called to Colly and Ed and me. "We unload," he said. "Already is late. Al, better you get a couple lanterns now."

We did a fast job, setting the stuff out of the wagons onto the platform and then carrying it or rolling it on the one truck that the store owned and stowing it inside according to where Mr. Baumer's good hand pointed.

A barrel was one of the last things to go in. I edged it up and Colly nosed the truck under it, and then I let it fall back. "Mr. Baumer," I said, "we'll never sell all this, will we?"

"Yah," he answered. "Sure we sell it. I get it cheap. A bargain, Al, so I buy it."

I looked at the barrel head again. There in big letters I saw "Wood Alcohol—Deadly Poison."

"Hurry now," Mr. Baumer said. "Is late." For a flash and no longer I saw through the mist in his eyes, saw, you might say, that hilly chin repeated there. "Then ve go home, Al. Is good to know to read."

BARGAIN 239

Critical Thinking

C Interpreting

? In what way does this comment about Slade mean more than it seems to on the surface? [Possible responses: Slade's heart (charity and compassion) gave out long ago. "For all I know" reminds the reader that no one (except Baumer) knows how Slade really died.]

D Vocabulary Note

Apostrophe

? What does the apostrophe in *someone's* indicate? [The word is a contraction for *someone is*. The letter *i* in *is* has been omitted.] Why does *takin'* have an apostrophe? [The apostrophe takes the place of the final *g*, which has been omitted to suggest how Moore pronounces the word.] Ask students to explain the word *'em*. [The *th* has been dropped from *them*, again to indicate Moore's pronunciation.]

E Critical Thinking

Interpreting

? What is the significance of the story's title? [Possible responses: Although he bought more goods than he needed, Baumer considers the purchase a "bargain" because it allows him to take revenge on Slade.]

F Reading Skills and Strategies

Drawing Conclusions

? What really caused Slade's death? [He stole what he thought was whiskey; since he couldn't read, he didn't know that the barrel contained poison.]

Making the Connections

Connecting to the Theme: "Do the Right Thing"

"Bargain" raises many questions, suitable for class discussion, about "doing the right thing." Does Baumer do the right thing in response to Slade's cruelty? Is Baumer guilty of a crime? If justice and revenge are not the same thing, is revenge ever justified? Is it right to create a situation in which something bad may happen, even if you do not personally or directly cause the bad event?

Students might also connect the characters in "Bargain" with other characters in this collection. What might Jimmy Wells (in "After Twenty Years") have thought of Baumer? [Possible response: Wells might have thought Baumer should have gone to "the law."] In what way is the rent man (in "Madam and the Rent Man") like, and unlike, Baumer? [Possible response: He

is like Baumer because he is hated by another character in the selection. He is unlike Baumer because he does not actively plan the death of that character; rather, his neglect of Madam's apartment makes her life miserable. Unlike Baumer, too, he has a boss (the landlord).]

MEET THE WRITER
"Real People in Real Times"

A. B. Guthrie (1901–1991) wanted to portray the West as it was, not create myths about it. He said:

> ❝ I want to talk about real people in real times. For every Wyatt Earp or Billy the Kid, there were thousands of people just trying to get along. ❞

Most readers agree that Guthrie succeeded. His most famous work, a trilogy about the opening of the West, is noted for its historical accuracy. Guthrie also wrote the screenplay for *Shane*, a famous movie about a Western gunslinger who takes justice into his own hands to save a family and pays a bitter price.

Albert Bertram Guthrie, Jr., grew up in the little town of Choteau, Montana. After graduating from college, he traveled extensively and worked at various jobs—ranching in Sonora, Mexico; selling groceries in California; working as a census taker in Montana; laboring at his uncle's feed mill in Attica, New York. After the mill burned down, he finally settled in Lexington, Kentucky, where he worked at a newspaper for more than twenty years.

Guthrie became a fiction writer when he took time out from his newspaper job to visit his sick mother. During his visit, he had time to write his first novel, *Murders at Moon Dance* (1943). In this book he introduces the setting of "Bargain" and many of his other short stories.

Thinking back to his childhood in Montana early in the century, Guthrie said that the best Christmas gift he ever got was a dictionary and that his warmest memories were the arguments he used to have with his family about the meanings of words. In talking about choosing words in his own writing, Guthrie said:

> ❝ For me, writing is a slow and painful business. It demands concentration and search and presents the obstacles of dissatisfaction with what could be said better. And there's no immediate reward in putting words on paper. The reward, great but fugitive, is in having written, in having found the word, the line, the paragraph, the chapter that is as good as ever you can make it. I spent a full day on one line of dialogue and knocked off satisfied. ❞

More Words, Lines, and Paragraphs by A. B. Guthrie

Guthrie's novels about the opening of the West are *The Big Sky* (Houghton Mifflin); *The Way West* (Bantam), which won the Pulitzer Prize; and *These Thousand Hills* (Buccaneer).

Assessing Learning

First Thoughts

[respond]

1. What do you think of what Mr. Baumer does to Slade? Does he do the right thing? Why or why not?

Shaping Interpretations

[interpret]

2. Look again at the Quickwrite on page 230 and the chart the class filled in. Would you say that this story is about justice or revenge? Why?

[interpret]

3. When Al suggests that Mr. Baumer forget Slade's bill, Mr. Baumer says that it isn't the money anymore; it is "the thing." What do you think Mr. Baumer means by "the thing"?

[analyze]

4. A writer helps you to predict future events by dropping clues **foreshadowing** what will happen later. Early in "Bargain," Mr. Baumer says, "Better study, Al. Is good to know to read and write and figure." How do these words foreshadow the story's ending?

[conclude]

5. Writers do not always tell you in so many words what a character in a story is thinking or feeling. You are given various clues and must draw your own **conclusions.** At the end of "Bargain," Guthrie doesn't tell you exactly what Mr. Baumer thinks about Slade's fate. What conclusions can you draw about what Mr. Baumer is thinking? What details in the story support your conclusions?

[interpret]

6. Who do you think is responsible for Slade's death—Mr. Baumer or Slade himself? Give two or three reasons to support your view.

Connecting with the Text

[connect]

7. If you were in Al's situation, would you keep silent about the likely cause of Slade's death? Why or why not?

Challenging the Text

[speculate]

8. "Bargain" is written in the **first-person point of view,** from Al's vantage point. What would you have known if Mr. Baumer had told the story himself?

Reading Check

Suppose that Al decides he has to confide to someone what he knows about Baumer's feud with Slade and the likely cause of Slade's death. He chooses to tell the whole story to Dr. King. With a partner, role-play Al and Dr. King. As Al tells what happened, Dr. King should comment and ask questions. Be sure to cover all the **main events** in the story.

First Thoughts

1. Possible responses: Baumer does not really do anything to Slade, who dies because of his own ignorance. Baumer was wrong to set up Slade, since Baumer knew he would steal the alcohol and die.

Shaping Interpretations

2. Possible responses: It is about justice, because Slade deserved to be punished; it is about revenge, because Baumer plotted to trap Slade.

3. Possible responses: The principle of justice demands that action be taken; Slade must be made to pay for hurting Baumer.

4. Possible responses: Slade dies because he cannot read a warning label.

5. Possible responses: Baumer is thinking that justice has been served. His final comment shows that he had planned Slade's death. He knew that freighters stole whiskey and that Slade could not read.

6. Remind students to support their opinions with details from the story, such as Baumer's surprising hiring of Slade and Slade's illiteracy.

Connecting with the Text

7. Some students may say that talking to a law officer would not help, because a sheriff would probably find Slade's death to be just. Other students may say that even if the sheriff takes no action against Baumer, Al should speak up, because he has to live with himself.

Challenging the Text

8. Possible responses: If Baumer had told the story, the reader would have known whether he plotted Slade's death.

Reading Check

When students accept the roles of Al and Dr. King, remind them to stick to the plot of the story and to consider the following characteristics of each person: Dr. King is educated, intelligent, mature, objective. Al is young, inexperienced, and a good observer. He works for Baumer, has witnessed Slade's attacks, and knows that Baumer believed that Slade hated him; he has also heard Baumer stress the importance of literacy.

CHOICES:
Building Your Portfolio

1. **Writer's Notebook**   Remind students to save their work. They may use it as prewriting for the Writer's Workshop on pp. 260–264.

2. **Writing a Summary**   Point out that there has historically been a difference, in the United States and elsewhere, between the legal and layperson's definitions of murder. Provide legal definitions for the terms *manslaughter* and *murder,* and ask students to use these terms in their arguments.

3. **Research/Speaking and Listening** Have students augment their oral reports with drawings, photographs, or reenactments of a frontier classroom. Remind them that students of all ages were grouped together when one school had to cover a large area. Give students the option of creating a lesson or test that Al might have taken.

4. **Research/Art**   Reserve a corner of the classroom for a Moon Dance Mercantile set. Assign groups of students to create or bring in certain props; one group could be responsible for kitchen items; another, for farm implements; and so on.

5. **Analyzing Setting**   Remind students that changing the setting of the story would affect virtually every aspect of the characters' lives. As students plan their essays, have them consider these details: geography and weather, architecture, modes of transportation, communication, and law enforcement.

CHOICES: Building Your Portfolio

Writer's Notebook

1. Collecting Ideas for Supporting a Position

How would you solve a problem like Mr. Baumer's? Suppose someone owes you ten dollars. This person refuses to pay you and even insults you in public. What would you do? Take a position and list reasons supporting it.

> —Ask a teacher or other authority for help? Possibly.
> —Forget about the money? No.
> —Try to reason with the person? Maybe.

Writing a Summary

2. Accident or Plan?

Imagine that Mr. Baumer is put on trial for causing Slade's death. In one paragraph, **summarize** the case *against* Mr. Baumer. Give reasons and evidence to inform and persuade the jury that Mr. Baumer is guilty. In another paragraph, summarize the case *for* Mr. Baumer. Present evidence to show that Slade is responsible for his own death.

Research/ Speaking and Listening

3. Frontier Teacher

What was it like to be a teacher when the frontier was a land of strong men and women and brutal violence? Guthrie says that his father taught school in Montana when "male teachers were few in cattle country and often were belittled because of their occupation." Find information about the people who taught in classrooms in the midst of this rugged country. Present your findings in an oral report to the class.

Research/Art

4. The Moon Dance Movie

You are a properties manager on a film set, the person who finds or creates objects to use in movie scenes. You've been hired to help create the town of Moon Dance. Because you know about A. B. Guthrie's concern for historical accuracy, you want your props to be as realistic as possible. Choose a setting from the story to bring to life—perhaps the inside of the Moon Dance Mercantile Company. What props will you use?

Reread the scenes that take place in that setting, and analyze them. Then, outline your plans on the basis of the story's descriptions and your research. Sketch particular items if you wish, and display your plans in the classroom.

Analyzing Setting

5. Rewriting History

Can you imagine this piece of historical fiction taking place anywhere else—say, in the town or neighborhood you live in? Write a brief essay about how Mr. Baumer's problem might be translated to another time and place. What details in the story would have to change?

GRAMMAR LINK MINI-LESSON

End the Apostrophe Glut

Language Handbook HELP

See Personal Pronouns, page 734; Apostrophes, page 777.

Technology HELP

See Language Workshop CD-ROM. Key word entry: apostrophes.

Basically, apostrophes have two jobs: They are used to indicate possession (*Al's problem*) or to indicate where letters are missing in a contraction (*it's serious*).

1. Use apostrophes with nouns to show possession.

> Mr. <u>Baumer</u>**'s** nose [With singular nouns, use an apostrophe and *s*.]

> the <u>horses</u>**'** saddles [With plural nouns ending in *s*, use just an apostrophe.]

> <u>Mercedes</u>**'** sister [Use an apostrophe alone with a singular noun when an apostrophe and *s* would sound awkward.]

Do *not* add apostrophes to possessive personal pronouns. They already show possession.

> ours [not our**'s**]

> hers [not her**'s**]

> its [not it**'s**; *it's* means "it is"]

2. The apostrophe's other big job is to take the place of missing letters. You need to use apostrophes in contractions.

> "I <u>don't</u> [do not] think <u>it's</u> [it is] any good to send him a bill. . . . He <u>can't</u> [cannot] even read."

Try It Out

Proofread the following sentences, adding apostrophes where necessary and removing them where they don't belong.

1. Everyone in town knew Slades way's, and all of them tried to steer clear of him.

2. Its no use sending Slade a bill, because he wouldnt even recognize its purpose.

3. Moore just stood for a while soaking up the fires heat before he said to Mr. Baumer, "You'r new mans dead."

4. Its easy to understand about the wood alcohol and it's role in Slades death when Mr. Baumer reminds Al that its good to know how to read.

GRAMMAR LINK

Ask students to take out an assignment that they have written previously and to circle all of the possessive pronouns. Remind the class that indefinite pronouns such as *somebody* and *anyone*, unlike personal pronouns, do take an apostrophe. Ask students to check the circled pronouns and to correct any apostrophe errors. Then, have them exchange their papers with partners to make sure that all the mistakes have been caught.

Try It Out
Answers

1. Slade's; ways

2. It's; wouldn't

3. fire's; Your; man's

4. It's; its; Slade's; it's

SPELLING
Answers

Silent letters: clim**b**ed, ed**g**ed. Other words from the story: **k**nuckles, **p**neumonia, frei**gh**t, consi**g**ned, hus**t**led, Christmas, **k**now.

Resources ———

Grammar
• *Grammar and Language Links*, p. 27

Spelling
For related instruction, see
• *Spelling and Decoding*, p. 14

SPELLING HOW TO OWN A WORD

Language Handbook HELP

See Spelling Rules, page 781.

Silent Letters

Some words are difficult to spell because they contain silent letters—that is, vowels or consonants that are not pronounced. Say aloud these words from the story: *climbed, edged.* What silent letters do you notice?

Which of these words is hard for you to spell? Write both words correctly in your spelling log. Then, underline the silent letters. Add other words with silent letters to your spelling log as you encounter them. You might want to start by finding five words with silent letters in the story.

BARGAIN 243

Grammar Link Quick Check

Choose the word in parentheses that correctly completes each of the following sentences.

1. The things that (<u>were</u>/we're) left behind were (<u>ours</u>/our's), so we had to go back for them.

2. (<u>Students</u>/Student's) do sometimes forget (they're/<u>their</u>) possessions.

3. Our (<u>teacher's</u>/teachers'/teachers's) faces (<u>didn't</u>/did'nt) look very happy on the way back.

4. Next time we go, (<u>we'll</u>/well) all remember not to leave (anyones/<u>anyone's</u>) things behind.

5. (Its/<u>It's</u>) too bad that we forgot (who's/<u>whose</u>) things they were.

OBJECTIVES

1. Read and interpret the story
2. Identify and analyze internal conflicts
3. Recognize comparison and contrast
4. Express understanding through persuasive and creative writing/speaking, comparing characters, or creating a dictionary of slang
5. Identify punctuation marks in dialogue and use them correctly
6. Understand and use new words

SKILLS

Literary
- Identify and analyze internal conflicts

Reading
- Recognize comparison and contrast

Writing
- Collect ideas for an essay supporting a position
- Write a news story
- Write an essay comparing and contrasting characters
- Create a dictionary of slang

Grammar/Language
- Identify punctuation marks in dialogue and use them correctly

Vocabulary
- Understand and use new words

Before You Read

AMIGO BROTHERS

Make the Connection

Some Friendly Advice

Have you ever had to compete against a good friend in a contest or sport? Did your friendship stay the same after the competition? What advice would you give two friends competing against each other?

Quickwrite

In a group, create a list titled "Rules for Competing Against a Friend."

Reading Skills and Strategies

Comparison and Contrast: Finding Similarities and Differences

Piri Thomas begins his story by contrasting the two best friends: "Antonio was fair, lean, and lanky, while Felix was dark, short, and husky." A **comparison** points out similarities between things; a **contrast** points out differences. After you read the story, go back over it and use a Venn diagram to help you identify the ways in which Felix and Antonio are alike and different. Write their likenesses in the parts of the circles that overlap.

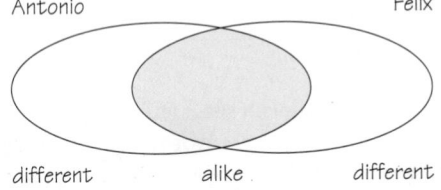

Antonio   Felix

different   alike   different

go.hrw.com
LEO 7-3

Elements of Literature

Internal Conflict

In this story two best friends competing for the same prize must fight each other in a boxing ring. This fight is a perfect example of an **external conflict.** The boys are supposed to literally knock each other out. Each boy also struggles with an **internal conflict:** How can he do his best without hurting and even losing his closest friend?

An **internal conflict** takes place within a character's own mind. In an internal conflict, a character struggles with opposing needs or desires or emotions.

For more on Conflict, see pages 22–23 and the Handbook of Literary Terms.

Background

Literature and Social Studies

This story is about two friends (*amigos* in Spanish) living on the Lower East Side of New York City. Many boys from the Lower East Side have dreamed of building a better life by winning the New York Golden Gloves, a tournament started in 1927 by Paul Gallico, a newspaper writer. This tournament marks an amateur's entry into the world of big-time boxing.

244 DO THE RIGHT THING

Preteaching Vocabulary

Words to Own

Have students read the definitions of the Words to Own at the bottom of the selection pages. Then, have them complete each of the following sentences with the correct vocabulary word.

1. That day Sir Lancelot engaged in three _____. [bouts]
2. The artillery let loose a fierce _____ against the enemy's position. [barrage]
3. Steve admitted that he had been _____ the truth about his homework. [evading]

4. The fabric had many _____ colors. [interwoven]
5. They lost! Now they face _____. [elimination]
6. When the dam opened, they were overwhelmed by the _____. [torrent]
7. Karen lived in a _____ building until she was twelve. [tenement]
8. *The Thinker* is a statue of a man sitting _____. [pensively]

T244

Amigo Brothers

Piri Thomas

"Only one of us can win."

 — Resources: Print and Media —

Reading
- *Reading Skills and Strategies*
  Selection Skill Lesson, p. 152
- *Graphic Organizers for Active Reading*, p. 18
- *Words to Own*, p. 12
- *Spelling and Decoding*
  Worksheet, p. 15
- *Audio CD Library*
  Disc 8, Track 2

Writing and Language
- *Daily Oral Grammar*

Transparency 16
- *Grammar and Language Links*
  Worksheet, p. 29
- *Language Workshop CD-ROM*

Assessment
- *Formal Assessment*, p. 46
- *Portfolio Management System*, p. 134
- *Standardized Test Preparation*, p. 44
- *Test Generator (One-Stop Planner CD-ROM)*

Internet
- go.hrw.com (keyword: LE0 7-3)

Planning

- **Block Schedule**
  Block Scheduling Lesson Plans with Pacing Guide
- **Traditional Schedule**
  Lesson Plans Including Strategies for English-Language Learners
- **One-Stop Planner**
  CD-ROM with Test Generator

Summary ■■

Antonio Cruz and Felix Vargas are seventeen-year-old best friends who both dream of becoming the lightweight boxing champion of the world. Inseparable, they train and run together until they find out that they will meet in the ring for the privilege of representing the Boys' Club in the Golden Gloves Championship Tournament. They pledge not to go easy on each other and then agree not to see each other until the big night, a week away. The night before their confrontation, each boy anguishes over the prospect of combat with his best friend. The next night, before a roaring crowd, the boys trade punishing blows through three furious rounds as the advantage shifts back and forth. At the end of the third and final round, both boys are still standing. They rush to embrace each other, and as the referee is about to announce the winner, the boys are out of earshot, having already left the ring arm in arm.

Responding to the Quotation

❓ What does the quotation suggest will happen to the boys in the title? [Possible response: The desire to win a competition will break up their friendship.]

Resources

Listening
Audio CD Library
A dramatic reading of this story is included in the *Audio CD Library*:
- Disc 8, Track 2

Selection Assessment
Formal Assessment
- Selection Test, p. 46

Test Generator
- Selection Test

A Reading Skills and Strategies

Comparison and Contrast

? Which will prove more significant—the boys' *differences* in appearance or their *similarities* in growing up friends? [Possible responses: Their similarities—sharing experiences as they grow up—will prove more important than how they look. Their differences—how they look—will determine the course of their lives.]

B Elements of Literature

Internal Conflict

? What kinds of internal conflicts will the story probably present? [Possible responses: Each boy will struggle to become champion. Each boy will feel bad that his friend will not be the champ.]

C Struggling Readers

Finding Details

? How do Antonio and Felix train for the fights? [They work out at the Boys' Club or in the gym; they run every morning.] What type of attitude do they have? [positive]

D Vocabulary Note

Definitions

? What does the writer suggest is the difference between a boxer and a slugger? [Possible responses: A boxer is tall, slim, and quick—a tactical fighter. A slugger is small and strong—a power hitter.] Students should also check the dictionary.

E Reading Skills and Strategies

Responding to the Text

? How do you think the boys should deal with the tension between them? [Possible responses: The boys should forget about being friends; they should flip a coin to decide who should drop out of the fight; they should promise to be both friends and sportsmanlike rivals.]

A ntonio Cruz and Felix Vargas were both seventeen years old. They were so together in friendship that they felt themselves to be brothers. They had known each other since childhood, growing up on the Lower East Side of Manhattan in the same tenement building on Fifth Street between Avenue A and Avenue B.

Antonio was fair, lean, and lanky, while Felix was dark, short, and husky. Antonio's hair was always falling over his eyes, while Felix wore his black hair in a natural Afro style.

Each youngster had a dream of someday becoming lightweight champion of the world. Every chance they had, the boys worked out, sometimes at the Boys' Club on 10th Street and Avenue A and sometimes at the pro's gym on 14th Street. Early morning sunrises would find them running along the East River Drive, wrapped in sweat shirts, short towels around their necks, and handkerchiefs Apache style around their foreheads.

While some youngsters were into street negatives, Antonio and Felix slept, ate, rapped, and dreamt positive. Between them, they had a collection of *Fight* magazines second to none, plus a scrapbook filled with torn tickets to every boxing match they had ever attended, and some clippings of their own. If asked a question about any given fighter, they would immediately zip out from their memory banks divisions, weights, records of fights, knockouts, technical knockouts, and draws or losses.

Each had fought many bouts representing their community and had won two gold-plated medals plus a silver and bronze medallion. The difference was in their style. Antonio's lean form and long reach made him the better boxer, while Felix's short and muscular frame made him the better slugger. Whenever they had met in the ring for sparring sessions,[1] it had always been hot and heavy.

---

1. **sparring sessions:** practice matches in which boxers use light punches.

Now, after a series of elimination bouts, they had been informed that they were to meet each other in the division finals that were scheduled for the seventh of August, two weeks away—the winner to represent the Boys' Club in the Golden Gloves Championship Tournament.

The two boys continued to run together along the East River Drive. But even when joking with each other, they both sensed a wall rising between them.

One morning less than a week before their bout, they met as usual for their daily workout. They fooled around with a few jabs at the air, slapped skin, and then took off, running lightly along the dirty East River's edge.

Antonio glanced at Felix, who kept his eyes purposely straight ahead, pausing from time to time to do some fancy leg work while throwing one-twos followed by uppercuts to an imaginary jaw. Antonio then beat the air with a barrage of body blows and short devastating lefts with an overhead jaw-breaking right.

After a mile or so, Felix puffed and said, "Let's stop a while, bro. I think we both got something to say to each other."

Antonio nodded. It was not natural to be acting as though nothing unusual was happening when two ace-boon buddies were going to be blasting each other within a few short days.

They rested their elbows on the railing separating them from the river. Antonio wiped his face with his short towel. The sunrise was now creating day.

Felix leaned heavily on the river's railing and

WORDS TO OWN

tenement (ten'ə·mənt) *n.* used as *adj.*: apartment. Tenement buildings are often cheaply built and poorly maintained.

bouts *n.*: matches; contests.

elimination (ē·lim'ə·nā'shən) *n.* used as *adj.*: removal from competition.

barrage (bə·räzh') *n.*: heavy, prolonged attack.

Reaching All Students

Struggling Readers

Comparison and Contrast was introduced on p. 244. For a lesson directly tied to this selection that teaches students to compare and contrast by using a strategy called Likert Scale, see the *Reading Skills and Strategies* binder:
• Selection Skill Lesson, p. 152

English Language Learners

Display a photograph or drawing of a well-known boxer or of a boxing match. If possible, show a short fight sequence from a boxing film. Call on students to answer questions such as the following: What can you tell me about this fighter? What do you know about boxing? For additional strategies to supplement instruction for these students, see
• *Lesson Plans Including Strategies for English-Language Learners*

Advanced Learners

Many expressions from sports have contributed to the liveliness and expressiveness of the English language. In an oral presentation, students can tell how expressions from their favorite sports have taken on new meanings. For example, politicians who win an election by a wide margin might say they "slam-dunked" their opponent. Students can demonstrate some of the expressions with drawings or photographs.

stared across to the shores of Brooklyn. Finally, he broke the silence.

"Man. I don't know how to come out with it."

Antonio helped. "It's about our fight, right?"

"Yeah, right." Felix's eyes squinted at the rising orange sun.

"I've been thinking about it too, panin.[2] In fact, since we found out it was going to be me and you, I've been awake at night, pulling punches on you, trying not to hurt you."

"Same here. It ain't natural not to think about the fight. I mean, we both are cheverote[3] fighters and we both want to win. But only one of us can win. There ain't no draws in the eliminations."

Felix tapped Antonio gently on the shoulder. "I don't mean to sound like I'm bragging, bro. But I wanna win, fair and square."

Antonio nodded quietly. "Yeah. We both know that in the ring the better man wins. Friend or no friend, brother or no . . ."

Felix finished it for him. "Brother. Tony, let's promise something right here. OK?"

"If it's fair, hermano,[4] I'm for it." Antonio ad-

2. **panin** (pä·nēn') *n.*: Puerto Rican Spanish slang for "pal" or "buddy."
3. **cheverote** (chev'er·ôt'te) *adj.*: Puerto Rican Spanish slang for "good" or "fine."
4. **hermano** (er·mä'nô) *n.*: Spanish for "brother."

mired the courage of a tugboat pulling a barge five times its welterweight size.

"It's fair, Tony. When we get into the ring, it's gotta be like we never met. We gotta be like two heavy strangers that want the same thing and only one can have it. You understand, don't cha?"

"Sí, I know." Tony smiled. "No pulling punches. We go all the way."

"Yeah, that's right. Listen, Tony. Don't you think it's a good idea if we don't see each other until the day of the fight? I'm going to stay with my Aunt Lucy in the Bronx. I can use Gleason's Gym for working out. My manager says he got some sparring partners with more or less your style."

Tony scratched his nose pensively. "Yeah, it would be better for our heads." He held out his hand, palm upward. "Deal?"

WORDS TO OWN
pensively (pen'siv·lē) *adv.*: thoughtfully.

They were so together in friendship that they felt themselves to be brothers. They had known each other since childhood . . .

Using Students' Strengths

Visual Learners
Ask students to draw or sketch portraits of Antonio or Felix as he might appear on sports trading cards. Have them show the boxer in an action position, and ask them to suggest the qualities that each has in the story.

Auditory/Musical Learners
Felix relaxes by listening to salsa music. Locate a short salsa recording that you can use in the classroom. Have students close their eyes as you play the music. Ask them for their reactions: Does it sound like any other music you know? Does the beat make you feel like dancing? What kinds of instruments can you hear?

Interpersonal Learners
Ask students to work in pairs to create conversations that might occur between Tony and Felix just after they step out of the ring. First, give students five minutes to create notes on what each character would say. Then, have them role-play a two-minute conversation.

A Appreciating Language

Punctuation

Point out that all direct quotations are enclosed in quotation marks and that the author begins a new paragraph each time the speaker changes.

B Elements of Literature

Internal Conflict

❓ What does this passage reveal about the internal conflict that Antonio is experiencing? [Possible response: Antonio wants to win, but he also doesn't want to hurt Felix.] Why does Felix want to forget about Antonio's face? [Possible response: Every time Felix thinks about Antonio's face, he imagines himself hitting it.]

C Struggling Readers

Paraphrasing

Ask students to paraphrase this paragraph. [Possible response: Felix sees Antonio's face on the body of the actor playing the challenger in the movie. Felix sees himself as the champ, pounding the challenger so badly that he has to be held back as Antonio collapses in the ring.]

D Critical Thinking

Interpreting

❓ How does watching the movie help Felix prepare for the fight? [Possible response: He decides to pretend, during the fight, that as a champ he must defend his title against a challenger.]

E Reading Skills and Strategies

Comparison and Contrast

❓ What are the similarities and differences between the movie and the street incident? [Possible responses: Similarities—both involve boxing since Felix fights an imaginary opponent to impress the kids; the kids see Felix as a "challenger" to their turf. Differences—the street incident is a real-life event, not a fantasy; the street incident involves mostly kids, whereas the fighters in the movie are probably older.] What do the differences suggest about Felix and Antonio? [Possible response: They, too, are still "kids"; whatever the outcome of the fight, the two must deal with everyday life.]

"Deal." Felix lightly slapped open skin.

"Ready for some more running?" Tony asked lamely.

"Naw, bro. Let's cut it here. You go on. I kinda like to get things together in my head."

"You ain't worried, are you?" Tony asked.

"No way, man." Felix laughed out loud. "I got too much smarts for that. I just think it's cooler if we split right here. After the fight, we can get it together again like nothing ever happened."

The amigo brothers were not ashamed to hug each other tightly.

"Guess you're right. Watch yourself, Felix. I hear there's some pretty heavy dudes up in the Bronx. Suavecito,[5] OK?"

"OK. You watch yourself too, sabe?"[6]

Tony jogged away. Felix watched his friend disappear from view, throwing rights and lefts. Both fighters had a lot of psyching up to do before the big fight.

The days in training passed much too slowly. Although they kept out of each other's way, they were aware of each other's progress via the ghetto grapevine.

The evening before the big fight, Tony made his way to the roof of his tenement. In the quiet early dark, he peered over the ledge. Six stories below, the lights of the city blinked and the sounds of cars mingled with the curses and the laughter of children in the street. He tried not to think of Felix, feeling he had succeeded in psyching his mind. But only in the ring would he really know. To spare Felix hurt, he would have to knock him out, early and quick.

Up in the South Bronx, Felix decided to take in a movie in an effort to keep Antonio's face away from his fists. The flick was *The Champion* with Kirk Douglas, the third time Felix was seeing it.

The champion was getting beaten, his face

being pounded into raw, wet hamburger. His eyes were cut, jagged, bleeding, one eye swollen, the other almost shut. He was saved only by the sound of the bell.

Felix became the champ and Tony the challenger.

The movie audience was going out of its head, roaring in blood lust at the butchery going on. The champ hunched his shoulders, grunting and sniffing red blood back into his broken nose. The challenger, confident that he had the championship in the bag, threw a left. The champ countered with a dynamite right that exploded into the challenger's brains.

Felix's right arm felt the shock. Antonio's face, superimposed on the screen, was shattered and split apart by the awesome force of the killer blow. Felix saw himself in the ring, blasting Antonio against the ropes. The champ had to be forcibly restrained. The challenger was allowed to crumble slowly to the canvas, a broken bloody mess.

When Felix finally left the theater, he had figured out how to psych himself for tomorrow's fight. It was Felix the Champion vs. Antonio the Challenger.

He walked up some dark streets, deserted except for small pockets of wary-looking kids wearing gang colors. Despite the fact that he was Puerto Rican like them, they eyed him as a stranger to their turf. Felix did a fast shuffle, bobbing and weaving, while letting loose a <u>torrent</u> of blows that would demolish whatever got in its way. It seemed to impress the brothers, who went about their own business.

Finding no takers, Felix decided to split to his aunt's. Walking the streets had not relaxed him; neither had the fight flick. All it had done was to stir him up. He let himself quietly into his Aunt Lucy's apartment and went straight to

---

5. **suavecito** (swä′vä·sē′tô) *adj.*: Puerto Rican Spanish slang for "be cool."
6. **sabe** (sä′bā) *v.*: Spanish for "you know."

248 DO THE RIGHT THING

WORDS TO OWN
torrent (tôr′ənt) *n.*: flood or rush.

Getting Students Involved

Cooperative Learning

Boxing Profile. In groups of four, students can create a boxing magazine profile of either Felix or Antonio. Have them review the story to find the following facts about the boy they choose: a description of his fighting style; his height and weight; pastimes he enjoys; a short personal statement in his own words. Students may include other interesting details.

Post-fight Show. Ask students to work in groups of five to produce a five-minute post-fight talk show. One student should be the show's host; the guests should include Felix and Antonio, commenting on their performances in the ring; a ringside fan, describing the crowd's reaction to the fight; a boxing expert, giving an objective analysis. Students may script or ad-lib dialogue. The class should serve as a studio audience.

bed, falling into a fitful sleep with sounds of the gong for Round One.

Antonio was passing some heavy time on his rooftop. How would the fight tomorrow affect his relationship with Felix? After all, fighting was like any other profession. Friendship had nothing to do with it. A gnawing doubt crept **F**

in. He cut negative thinking real quick by doing **G** some speedy fancy dance steps, bobbing and weaving like mercury. The night air was blurred **H** with perpetual motions of left hooks and right crosses. Felix, his amigo brother, was not going to be Felix at all in the ring. Just an opponent with another face. Antonio went to sleep, hear-

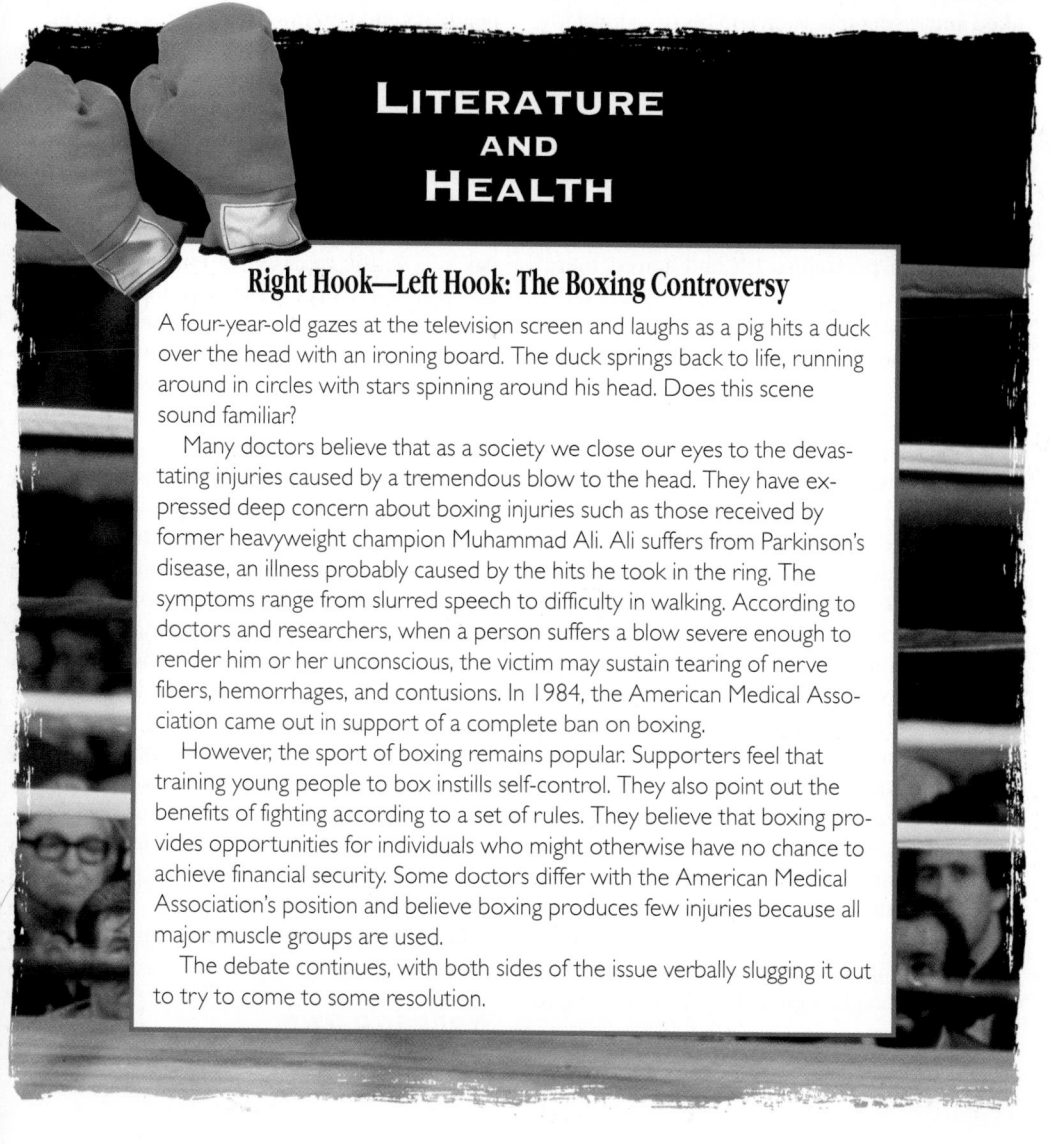

LITERATURE AND HEALTH

Right Hook—Left Hook: The Boxing Controversy

A four-year-old gazes at the television screen and laughs as a pig hits a duck over the head with an ironing board. The duck springs back to life, running around in circles with stars spinning around his head. Does this scene sound familiar?

Many doctors believe that as a society we close our eyes to the devastating injuries caused by a tremendous blow to the head. They have expressed deep concern about boxing injuries such as those received by former heavyweight champion Muhammad Ali. Ali suffers from Parkinson's disease, an illness probably caused by the hits he took in the ring. The symptoms range from slurred speech to difficulty in walking. According to doctors and researchers, when a person suffers a blow severe enough to render him or her unconscious, the victim may sustain tearing of nerve fibers, hemorrhages, and contusions. In 1984, the American Medical Association came out in support of a complete ban on boxing.

However, the sport of boxing remains popular. Supporters feel that training young people to box instills self-control. They also point out the benefits of fighting according to a set of rules. They believe that boxing provides opportunities for individuals who might otherwise have no chance to achieve financial security. Some doctors differ with the American Medical Association's position and believe boxing produces few injuries because all major muscle groups are used.

The debate continues, with both sides of the issue verbally slugging it out to try to come to some resolution.

AMIGO BROTHERS **249**

F Elements of Literature
Internal Conflict
❓ How would you describe Antonio's conflict in this passage? [Possible response: Antonio is afraid that, no matter what happens in the ring, his friendship with Felix will be destroyed.]

G Appreciating Language
Informal English
❓ Adverbs modify verbs, adjectives, and other adverbs. Which word does the phrase *real quick* modify? [the verb *cut*] The phrase is informal English. What would it be in standard English? [*really quickly*] Why is this phrase the standard form? [In standard English, the words without -*ly* are adjectives, and words with -*ly* are adverbs.]

H Elements of Literature
Similes
❓ What does the author mean when he says that Antonio bobs and weaves "like mercury"? [Possible response: Mercury is a liquid metal that moves quickly and is difficult to hold on to; Antonio has quick and fluid motions.] Mercury is named after the swift Roman messenger god.

LITERATURE AND HEALTH

Anyone who competes in a contact sport risks injury. Here are some steps that have been taken to reduce the risk of injury in amateur boxing:

- Head protection and softer gloves
- Fewer rounds (usually only three)
- Referee who can stop a fight before boxers suffer serious injury
- A physician at ringside to advise the referee on when to stop a fight

Crossing the Curriculum

Health

Ask students to create workout schedules showing the types of exercises and number of repetitions that a typical boxer in training should perform. Some students might also research and report on the diet and nutrition plan that a boxer in training would follow; they can create a daily or weekly meal plan for a boxer.

A Reading Skills and Strategies

Comparison and Contrast

? What phrase signals that contrast is being used in this passage? [*on the other side*] What other words or expressions often signal comparison or contrast? [Possible responses: Comparison —*in the same way, similarly.* Contrast—*on the other hand, instead.*]

B Elements of Literature

Internal Conflict

? What does Felix's action reveal about the conflict he still feels? [Possible responses: He is afraid that he may lose his resolve to fight as hard as possible; he doubts that he is doing the right thing by trying to beat his best friend.]

C Elements of Literature

Metaphors

? What metaphor is used to describe the park? ["a beehive of activity"] What picture of the park does the metaphor bring to mind? [Possible response: The scene is a busy place, like a hive.]

D Critical Thinking

Challenging the Text

? What is the effect of this paragraph in the story? [Possible response: It creates suspense and shows that the community takes this fight seriously.]

E Vocabulary Note

Prefixes and Suffixes

? *Acknowledgment* may look like a difficult word, but there is a more familiar word between the prefix and the suffix. What is it? [*knowledge*] How does the word's spelling change when the suffix, *ment,* is added? [The *e* is dropped.] Which letter is silent? [*k*] What is the word's meaning? ["*recognition*"]

---

ing the opening bell for the first round. Like his friend in the South Bronx, he prayed for victory via a quick clean knockout in the first round.

Large posters plastered all over the walls of local shops announced the fight between Antonio Cruz and Felix Vargas as the main bout.

The fight had created great interest in the neighborhood. Antonio and Felix were well liked and respected. Each had his own loyal following. Betting fever was high and ranged from a bottle of Coke to cold hard cash on the line.

A Antonio's fans bet with unbridled faith in his boxing skills. On the other side, Felix's admirers bet on his dynamite-packed fists.

B Felix had returned to his apartment early in the morning of August 7th and stayed there, hoping to avoid seeing Antonio. He turned the radio on to salsa[7] music sounds and then tried to read while waiting for word from his manager.

The fight was scheduled to take place in Tompkins Square Park. It had been decided that the gymnasium of the Boys' Club was not large enough to hold all the people who were sure to attend. In Tompkins Square Park, everyone who wanted could view the fight, whether from ringside or window fire escapes or tenement rooftops.

C The morning of the fight Tompkins Square was a beehive of activity with numerous workers setting up the ring, the seats, and the guest speakers' stand. The scheduled bouts began shortly after noon and the park had begun filling up even earlier.

The local junior high school across from Tompkins Square Park served as the dressing room for all the fighters. Each was given a separate classroom with desk tops, covered with mats, serving as resting tables. Antonio thought he caught a glimpse of Felix waving to

---

7. **salsa** (säl′sə) *n.:* Latin American dance music, usually played at fast tempos.

---

250 DO THE RIGHT THING

---

him from a room at the far end of the corridor. He waved back just in case it had been him.

The fighters changed from their street clothes into fighting gear. Antonio wore white trunks, black socks, and black shoes. Felix wore sky-blue trunks, red socks, and white boxing shoes. They had dressing gowns to match their fighting trunks with their names neatly stitched on the back.

D The loudspeakers blared into the open windows of the school. There were speeches by dignitaries, community leaders, and great boxers of yesteryear. Some were well prepared; some improvised on the spot. They all carried the same message of great pleasure and honor at being part of such a historic event. This great day was in the tradition of champions emerging from the streets of the Lower East Side.

Interwoven with the speeches were the sounds of the other boxing events. After the sixth bout, Felix was much relieved when his trainer, Charlie, said, "Time change. Quick knockout. This is it. We're on."

Waiting time was over. Felix was escorted from the classroom by a dozen fans in white T-shirts with the word FELIX across their fronts.

Antonio was escorted down a different stairwell and guided through a roped-off path.

As the two climbed into the ring, the crowd exploded with a roar. Antonio and Felix both bowed gracefully and then raised their arms in **E** acknowledgment.

Antonio tried to be cool, but even as the roar was in its first birth, he turned slowly to meet Felix's eyes looking directly into his. Felix nodded his head and Antonio responded. And both as one, just as quickly, turned away to face his own corner.

Bong—bong—bong. The roar turned to stillness.

WORDS TO OWN

interwoven (in′tər·wō′vən) *v.* used as *adj.:* connected closely; blended.

Skill Link

Quotation Marks

Use this activity before you teach the Grammar Link on p. 256. Remind students that when a quotation itself is a question or an exclamation, the question mark or the exclamation point goes *inside* the quotation marks. When the whole sentence is a question or an exclamation, the question mark or the exclamation point goes *outside* the quotation marks.

Activity

Punctuate each sentence correctly.

1. I've never been to a boxing match said David. ["I've never been to a boxing match," said David.]
2. Have you ever been to a boxing match asked David. ["Have you ever been to a boxing match?" asked David.]

3. Did David say, Jill wants to go to a boxing match? [Did David say, "Jill wants to go to a boxing match"?]
4. Let's all go to the next match we shouted. ["Let's all go to the next match!" we shouted.]

T250

"Ladies and Gentlemen, Señores y Señoras."

The announcer spoke slowly, pleased at his bilingual efforts.

"Now the moment we have all been waiting for—the main event between two fine young Puerto Rican fighters, products of our Lower East Side."

"Loisaida,"[8] called out a member of the audience.

"In this corner, weighing 134 pounds, Felix Vargas. And in this corner, weighing 133 pounds, Antonio Cruz. The winner will represent the Boys' Club in the tournament of champions, the Golden Gloves. There will be no draw. May the best man win."

The cheering of the crowd shook the window panes of the old buildings surrounding Tompkins Square Park. At the center of the ring, the referee was giving instructions to the youngsters.

"Keep your punches up. No low blows. No punching on the back of the head. Keep your heads up. Understand? Let's have a clean fight. Now shake hands and come out fighting."

Both youngsters touched gloves and nodded. They turned and danced quickly to their corners. Their head towels and dressing gowns were lifted neatly from their shoulders by their trainers' nimble fingers. Antonio crossed himself. Felix did the same.

BONG! BONG! ROUND ONE. Felix and Antonio turned and faced each other squarely in a fighting pose. Felix wasted no time. He came in fast, head low, half-hunched toward his right shoulder, and lashed out with a straight left. He missed a right cross as Antonio slipped the punch and countered with one-two-three lefts that snapped Felix's head back, sending a mild

shock coursing through him. If Felix had any small doubt about their friendship affecting their fight, it was being neatly dispelled.

Antonio danced, a joy to behold. His left hand was like a piston pumping jabs one right after another with seeming ease. Felix bobbed and weaved and never stopped boring in. He knew that at long range he was at a disadvantage. Antonio had too much reach on him. Only by coming in close could Felix hope to achieve the dreamed-of knockout.

Antonio knew the dynamite that was stored in his amigo brother's fist. He ducked a short right and missed a left hook. Felix trapped him against the ropes just long enough to pour some punishing rights and lefts to Antonio's hard midsection. Antonio slipped away from Felix, crashing two lefts to his head, which set Felix's right ear to ringing.

Bong! Both amigos froze a punch well on its way, sending up a roar of approval for good sportsmanship.

Felix walked briskly back to his corner. His right ear had not stopped ringing. Antonio gracefully danced his way toward his stool none the worse, except for glowing glove burns showing angry red against the whiteness of his midribs.

"Watch that right, Tony." His trainer talked into his ear. "Remember Felix always goes to the body. He'll want you to drop your hands for his overhand left or right. Got it?"

Antonio nodded, spraying water out between his teeth. He felt better as his sore midsection was being firmly rubbed.

Felix's corner was also busy.

"You gotta get in there, fella." Felix's trainer

8. **Loisaida** (loi·sī′dä): Puerto Rican English dialect for "Lower East Side."

WORDS TO OWN
dispelled (di·speld′) v.: driven away.

F Cultural Connections

Remind students of some of the rules of modern boxing: three-minute rounds, one minute to rest between rounds, and ten seconds for a fighter to get back up after being knocked down.

G Elements of Literature

Onomatopoeia

❓ **Onomatopoeia** is the use of words to imitate sounds. Which word is an example here? [*bong!*] What is the effect when you read the word? [Possible response: It gives you the feeling of being at the match.]

H Reading Skills and Strategies

Comparison and Contrast

❓ What word signals that a comparison is being made? [*both*] What does the comparison say about the boys? [Possible response: They are still good friends who play by the rules.]

Getting Students Involved

Cooperative Learning

Problems with Friends. Even though they are best friends, Felix and Antonio have a problem being comfortable around each other until the fight is over. Place students into groups of three or four, and ask them to discuss some of the problems that friends may have. Then, give students time to list the problems and possible solutions in a chart like the one here.

Possible Problems with Friends	Possible Solutions
[wanting to copy someone else's homework]	[doing assignment together]

A Elements of Literature
Simile

? What is Felix compared to here? [a bull] What does the simile suggest about his character? [Possible response: his determination to keep on charging at his opponent.] Who does the comparison suggest might win the bout? [Possible responses: Antonio might win, because a bull rarely defeats the matador. Felix might win, because he is fierce.]

B Appreciating Language
Action Words

? The author uses vivid verbs (some are present participles used as adjectives) to create a sense of immediacy and vitality. What are these words? [*blurring, looping, forcing, bobbed, weaved, punching, exploded, catching, buckled, danced, puffing, rip-roaring, screaming*]

C English Language Learners
Idioms

? An opossum is a small animal that pretends to be dead when it is threatened. What does *playing possum* mean? ["to pretend to be asleep or unaware"] The context should also help students understand the idiom.

D Cultural Connections

Trainers rub or massage fighters between rounds to improve circulation through the small blood vessels close to the skin. Massaging may also increase the flow of blood to the heart and brain, giving the fighter more energy and alertness.

---

poured water over his curly Afro locks. "Get in there or he's gonna chop you up from way back."

A *Bong! Bong!* Round two. Felix was off his stool and rushed Antonio like a bull, sending a hard right to his head. Beads of water exploded from Antonio's long hair.

Antonio, hurt, sent back a blurring barrage of lefts and rights that only meant pain to Felix, who returned with a short left to the head followed by a looping right to the body. Antonio countered with his own flurry, forcing Felix to give ground. But not for long.

Felix bobbed and weaved, bobbed and weaved, occasionally punching his two gloves together.

Antonio waited for the rush that was sure to come. Felix closed in and feinted with his left shoulder and threw a right instead. Lights suddenly exploded inside Felix's head as Antonio slipped the blow and hit him with a pistonlike left, catching him flush on the point of his chin.

B Bedlam broke loose as Felix's legs momentarily buckled. He fought off a series of rights and lefts and came back with a strong right that taught Antonio respect.

Antonio danced in carefully. He knew Felix
C had the habit of playing possum when hurt, to sucker an opponent within reach of the powerful bombs he carried in each fist.

A right to the head slowed Antonio's pretty dancing. He answered with his own left at Felix's right eye that began puffing up within three seconds.

Antonio, a bit too eager, moved in too close, and Felix had him entangled into a rip-roaring, punching toe-to-toe slugfest that brought the whole Tompkins Square Park screaming to its feet.

Rights to the body. Lefts to the head. Neither fighter was giving an inch. Suddenly a short right caught Antonio squarely on the chin. His long legs turned to jelly and his arms flailed out

desperately. Felix, grunting like a bull, threw wild punches from every direction. Antonio, groggy, bobbed and weaved, evading most of the blows. Suddenly his head cleared. His left flashed out hard and straight, catching Felix on the bridge of his nose.

Felix lashed back with a haymaker, right of the ghetto streets. At the same instant, his eye caught another left hook from Antonio. Felix swung out, trying to clear the pain. Only the frenzied screaming of those along ringside let him know that he had dropped Antonio. Fighting off the growing haze, Antonio struggled to his feet, got up, ducked, and threw a smashing right that dropped Felix flat on his back.

Felix got up as fast as he could in his own corner, groggy but still game. He didn't even hear the count. In a fog, he heard the roaring of the crowd, who seemed to have gone insane. His head cleared to hear the bell sound at the end of the round. He was glad. His trainer sat him down on the stool.

In his corner, Antonio was doing what all fighters do when they are hurt. They sit and smile at everyone.

D The referee signaled the ring doctor to check the fighters out. He did so and then gave his OK. The cold-water sponges brought clarity to both amigo brothers. They were rubbed until their circulation ran free.

Bong! Round three—the final round. Up to now it had been tic-tac-toe, pretty much even. But everyone knew there could be no draw and that this round would decide the winner.

This time, to Felix's surprise, it was Antonio who came out fast, charging across the ring. Felix braced himself but couldn't ward off the barrage of punches. Antonio drove Felix hard against the ropes.

WORDS TO OWN
evading (ē·vād′iŋ) *v.* used as *adj*: avoiding.
frenzied (fren′zēd) *adj*.: wild.

---

252 DO THE RIGHT THING

Making the Connections

Connecting to the Theme: "Do the Right Thing"

"Amigo Brothers" points out the difficulty in doing the right thing when two choices seem desirable. Felix and Antonio must decide what is more important to them—friendship or fame. In the story they achieve some kind of compromise. Students may wonder, however, what will become of the friendship after the winner is declared.

Cultural Connections

About half of the Puerto Ricans in the mainland United States live in New York City. Like Felix and Antonio, many live on Manhattan's Lower East Side. Puerto Ricans in New York City have made important contributions to political and community life, the arts, education, business, and sports. Ask students to research contributions made by Puerto Ricans to New York's cultural and economic life.

The crowd ate it up. Thus far the two had fought with mucho corazón.[9] Felix tapped his gloves and commenced his attack anew. Antonio, throwing boxer's caution to the winds, jumped in to meet him.

Both pounded away. Neither gave an inch and neither fell to the canvas. Felix's left eye was tightly closed. Claret-red blood poured from Antonio's nose. They fought toe-to-toe.

The sounds of their blows were loud in contrast to the silence of a crowd gone completely mute. The referee was stunned by their savagery.

Bong! Bong! Bong! The bell sounded over and over again. Felix and Antonio were past hearing. Their blows continued to pound on each other like hailstones.

9. **mucho corazón** (moo'chô côr·ä·sôn'): Spanish for "a lot of heart."

Finally the referee and the two trainers pried Felix and Antonio apart. Cold water was poured over them to bring them back to their senses.

They looked around and then rushed toward each other. A cry of alarm surged through Tompkins Square Park. Was this a fight to the death instead of a boxing match?

The fear soon gave way to wave upon wave of cheering as the two amigos embraced.

No matter what the decision, they knew they would always be champions to each other.

BONG! BONG! BONG! "Ladies and Gentlemen. Señores and Señoras. The winner and representative to the Golden Gloves Tournament of Champions is . . ."

The announcer turned to point to the winner and found himself alone. Arm in arm the champions had already left the ring.

MEET THE WRITER
A Survivor from the Mean Streets

Like Antonio and Felix in "Amigo Brothers," **Piri Thomas** (1928–   ) grew up in a rough neighborhood in New York City. Unfortunately, he wasn't as lucky as Antonio and Felix—he didn't have a sport like boxing to help him escape the lures of drugs and crime. As a result, Thomas spent time in prison. While in prison, Thomas discovered he could write, and after his release he published an autobiography called *Down These Mean Streets* (1967). Thomas has worked for many years to help drug addicts give up their addictions and start new lives.

AMIGO BROTHERS **253**

MAKING MEANINGS

First Thoughts

1. Possible responses: It is unfair to build up such suspense and then not tell who wins. The ending was not surprising, because the author has emphasized the boys' strong relationship.

Shaping Interpretations

Possible responses

2. Yes, because the fight was an important opportunity for them. No, they should not have risked their friendship for a boxing match.

3. They hope that no one will get seriously hurt; they both still care for each other.

4. They embrace each other. They have learned that their friendship is more important than competition; they walk away arm in arm without hearing the decision.

5. They both do their best during a difficult competition.

6. Without the external conflict, the internal conflict would never have occurred; the survival of the friendship is more important than who wins.

Connecting with the Text

7. Some students may say that friendships are more important than competition. Others may say that they could not ignore the results.

8. Some students would not stop seeing their friends. Others may say that their competition would not have been so fierce.

Challenging the Text

9. Students may say that two friends can compete against each other.

MAKING MEANINGS

First Thoughts

[respond]
1. How did you react to the end of the story? Were you surprised by what Felix and Antonio did? Were you disappointed not to find out who won the fight?

Shaping Interpretations

[evaluate]
2. Do you think that Felix and Antonio were right to stop seeing each other before the fight? Were they right to fight so hard? What did you predict they would do, based on what you knew about their friendship?

[interpret]
3. Why do both boys wish for an early knockout? What does this wish show about them and their feelings for each other?

[evaluate]
4. Describe what you think is the moment of truth for the boys in the story. What do you think they learn at this moment?

[interpret]
5. The last sentence refers to both boys as "champions." In what sense are they both champions?

[analyze]
6. Which do you think is more important to the story: the **external conflict**—the fight itself—or the **internal conflict**—the feelings the boys struggled with before and during the fight? Why?

Connecting with the Text

[connect]
7. Would *you* be able to walk away from a contest like this fight without finding out if you had won? Why or why not?

[speculate]

8. Look back at your "Rules for Competing Against a Friend" from the Quickwrite on page 244. How many of them did Antonio and Felix follow? If you had been in their situation, would you have acted differently?

Challenging the Text

[evaluate]
9. Did you find this story, particularly its ending, true to life? Do you think two good friends can fight each other and stay friends? Give reasons for your opinion.

> **Reading Check**
> **a.** What dream do both Felix and Antonio have?
> **b.** Why do the boys decide to stop training together?
> **c.** How can you tell that the boys do not "pull punches" in their fight?
> **d.** How does the fight end?

> **Reading Check**
> **a.** They both dream about winning the Golden Gloves Championship.
> **b.** They are uncomfortable knowing that they will have to fight each other soon.
> **c.** Both are knocked down in the fight; Antonio's nose bleeds profusely; Felix's left eye is swollen closed.
> **d.** The final bell rings but the boys continue fighting; their trainers pull them apart, and the boys rush back at each other and embrace.

CHOICES: Building Your Portfolio

Writer's Notebook

1. Collecting Ideas for Supporting a Position

If Felix and Antonio were asked to write a paper supporting a position, they might start with the general subject of sports. They might narrow their subject down to a more specific topic, such as prizefighting. They might then think of issues relating to that topic that matter to them.

Making a cluster map like the one in the notebook is one way to gather ideas for an essay supporting a position. Think of a broad subject that interests you. Then, create a cluster map to collect and organize ideas for an essay supporting a position.

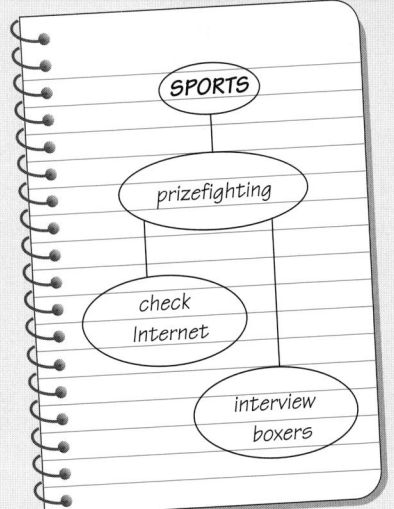

Creative Writing/Speaking

2. This Just In . . .

Pretend you are a sports-caster for a cable sports channel. Write a news story about the fight between Felix and Antonio. A good news story includes details that tell *who* was involved, *what* happened, *when* and *where* it happened, *why* it happened, and *how* it happened. To grab your listeners' attention, try to give your news story a catchy first sentence. Practice reading your account of the fight aloud; then, read it to your class.

Comparing Characters

3. Side by Side

In a short essay, **compare and contrast** the personalities of Felix and Antonio. Start by reviewing the Venn diagram of the boys' likenesses and differences that you made after you read the story. In your essay, you might want to talk first about their similarities and then about their differences. End by telling which character you like better and why.

Language/Writing

4. Slangfest

People in almost every age group, occupation, and area use **slang**—informal language that includes invented words and familiar words that have been given new meanings. Slang words are often colorful. Here are a few of the slang expressions used in "Amigo Brothers": *worked out, slapped skin, ace-boon buddies, fair and square, smarts, get it together, dude, split, flick,* and *cooler.* Create a dictionary of slang from the story. First, list all the slang you can locate. Then, try to figure out the meaning of each word or expression from its **context.** (Check a dictionary to see if you're right, or ask an adult.) Write your definitions, put the entries in alphabetical order, and share your dictionary with the class.

Grading Timesaver

Rubrics for each Choices assignment appear on p. 134 in the *Portfolio Management System.*

CHOICES: Building Your Portfolio

1. **Writer's Notebook** Remind students to save their work. They may use it as prewriting for the Writer's Workshop on pp. 260–264.
2. **Creative Writing/Speaking** Before students begin writing their news stories, provide them with copies of a newspaper or magazine sports article that they may use as a model. Discuss some of the guidelines that news writers use for creating catchy openings.
3. **Comparing Characters** As students plan their essays, remind them of ways to structure their writing. They might discuss the similarities first and then the differences, or the differences and then the similarities; they might discuss each boy separately.
4. **Language/Writing** Before students begin working, show them a few entries from a dictionary of slang or some of the definitions for slang terms in a standard dictionary.

GRAMMAR LINK

Ask students to take out an earlier writing assignment that contains dialogue. Have them exchange their work with partners. Then, ask them to underline all of the sentences of dialogue in a partner's paper. Have them check that the dialogue is punctuated correctly.

Try It Out
Answers
1. Tony said, "No pulling punches. We go all the way."
2. Did the announcer say, "There will be no draw. May the best man win"?
3. A woman in the crowd said to her friend with alarm, "What's going on? It looks as if they're trying to kill each other!"
4. "Let's have a clean fight," said the referee. "No low blows. No punching on the back of the head. Got it?"

VOCABULARY
Possible Answers
1. Will a new field be built next to the <u>tenement</u>? Have this season's victories been <u>interwoven</u> with disasters? Was he called out while <u>evading</u> the tag?
2. There will be two <u>bouts</u> before the <u>elimination</u> round. He withstood a <u>barrage</u> of punches.
3. I look back <u>pensively</u> on my career. After that match, my doubts about my ability were <u>dispelled</u>.
4. A <u>torrent</u> of cheers rose from the <u>frenzied</u> crowd.

Resources ━━━━━

Grammar
• *Grammar and Language Links*, p. 29
Vocabulary
• *Words to Own*, p. 12
Spelling
For related instruction, see
• *Spelling and Decoding*, p. 15

GRAMMAR LINK   MINI-LESSON

Punctuate Dialogue Correctly—And Punch Up Your Writing

Language Handbook HELP

See Quotation Marks, pages 774-776.

Technology HELP

See Language Workshop CD-ROM. Key word entry: quotation marks.

Dialogue, or conversation, puts a lot of punch in a story. When you include what characters say, your story comes to life. It's important to get the punctuation right when you write dialogue. Just follow these rules:

1. Put quotation marks around direct quotations of words spoken aloud:

    Antonio helped. **"**It's about our fight, right?**"**

    Antonio helped by asking if it was about the fight.

2. Begin a quotation with a capital letter:

    After a mile or so, Felix puffed and said, "**L**et's stop a while, bro. I think we both got something to say to each other."

3. Use a comma, a question mark, or an exclamation point (never a period) to set off a quotation from the rest of the sentence:

    "Loisaida**,**" called out a member of the audience.

    "Ready for some more running**?**" Tony asked lamely.

Try It Out

Add commas and quotation marks to set off the dialogue in these passages.

1. Felix and Antonio decided they'd each fight to win. Tony said No pulling punches. We go all the way.
2. Did the announcer say There will be no draw. May the best man win?
3. A woman in the crowd said to her friend with alarm What's going on? It looks as if they're trying to kill each other!
4. Let's have a clean fight said the referee. No low blows. No punching on the back of the head. Got it?

VOCABULARY   HOW TO OWN A WORD

WORD BANK	Vocabulary for the Workplace: Sports Reporting
tenement bouts elimination barrage pensively torrent interwoven dispelled evading frenzied	1. You're a reporter interviewing a Little League coach. Write questions that include the words *tenement*, *interwoven*, and *evading*. 2. You're writing a news article about tryouts for the Olympic Games. Write sentences using the words *bouts*, *elimination*, and *barrage*. 3. You're a retired tennis player. Write sentences for your autobiography using the words *pensively* and *dispelled*. 4. You're a sportscaster describing the crowd at a hockey game. Write a description using the words *torrent* and *frenzied*.

256 DO THE RIGHT THING

Grammar Link Quick Check

Add quotation marks, capitalization, and commas where needed in the following sentences.
1. The girl asked is this seat taken? [The girl asked, "Is this seat taken?"]
2. I said no. Go ahead and sit down. [I said, "No. Go ahead and sit down."]
3. Thanks. It's crowded here she replied. ["Thanks. It's crowded here," she replied.]
4. I said to her You have to be here earlier. [I said to her, "You have to be here earlier."]
5. She said next time I will. [She said, "Next time I will."]

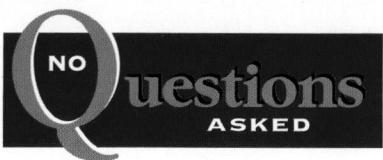

OBJECTIVES
1. Read and interpret the poem
2. Connect the selection to the collection theme

Sarah Cynthia Sylvia Stout Would Not Take the Garbage Out

Shel Silverstein

Sarah Cynthia Sylvia Stout
Would not take the garbage out!
She'd scour the pots and scrape the pans,
Candy the yams and spice the hams,
5   And though her daddy would scream and shout,
She simply would not take the garbage out.
And so it piled up to the ceilings:
Coffee grounds, potato peelings,
Brown bananas, rotten peas,
10   Chunks of sour cottage cheese.
It filled the can, it covered the floor,
It cracked the window and blocked the door
With bacon rinds and chicken bones,
Drippy ends of ice cream cones,
15   Prune pits, peach pits, orange peel,
Gloppy glumps of cold oatmeal,
Pizza crusts and withered greens,
Soggy beans and tangerines,
Crusts of black burned buttered toast,
20   Gristly bits of beefy roasts . . .
The garbage rolled on down the hall,
It raised the roof, it broke the wall . . .
Greasy napkins, cookie crumbs,
Globs of gooey bubble gum,
25   Cellophane from green baloney,
Rubbery blubbery macaroni,
Peanut butter, caked and dry,
Curdled milk and crusts of pie,
Moldy melons, dried-up mustard,

SARAH CYNTHIA SYLVIA STOUT WOULD NOT TAKE THE GARBAGE OUT   257

No Questions Asked

The literature in No Questions Asked gives students the chance to read a selection for enjoyment and enrichment as they further explore the collection theme. Annotated questions in the margins of the Teacher's Edition should be considered optional. No follow-up questions will appear after the selection.

This poem, a humorous twist on the theme "Do the Right Thing," tells the story of Sarah Cynthia Sylvia Stout. An otherwise conscientious girl, Sarah refuses to take the garbage out, despite her father's persistent pleas. The speaker describes the accumulation of waste in gleeful detail. Eventually, the neighbors move out and the litter stretches across the continent. By the time Sarah decides to "do the right thing," the garbage has dealt her an "awful fate" too dreadful for the speaker to specify. The speaker concludes with a warning to children: Attend to chores before they overwhelm you.

Resources

Listening
Audio CD Library
A lively recording of this poem is provided in the *Audio CD Library:*
• Disc 8, Track 3

Ⓐ Elements of Literature
Imagery
❓ Much of the poem is a listing of food scraps. To which senses do these images appeal? Give one example for each sense. [Possible responses: sight—*brown bananas*; hearing—*cracked the window*; taste—*withered greens*; smell—*moldy melons*; touch—*rubbery blubbery macaroni.*] What is the tone of the images? [funny, silly]

Ⓑ Appreciating Language
Reading Aloud
❓ Ask volunteers to read passages from the poem. What effect might the rhyming, mostly single-syllable end words have on the reciter? [Possible response: They might cause the reciter to speak faster and faster, adding to the humor.]

Making the Connections

Connecting to the Theme:
"Do the Right Thing"
Divide the class into groups of three, and then ask students to discuss the following questions. Ask the groups to share their responses with the class.
1. Why do you think that this poem was included in the collection? [Possible response: Sarah finally decides to do the right thing by taking out the garbage.]

2. How is Sarah different from the other characters in the collection? [Possible responses: Her situation is comical, while the other characters face more serious dilemmas; Sarah decides to do the right thing too late.]

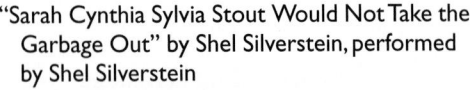
30   Eggshells mixed with lemon custard,
Cold french fries and rancid meat,
Yellow lumps of Cream of Wheat.
At last the garbage reached so high
That finally it touched the sky.
35   And all the neighbors moved away,
And none of her friends would come to play.
And finally Sarah Cynthia Stout said,
"OK, I'll take the garbage out!"
But then, of course, it was too late . . .
40   The garbage reached across the state,
From New York to the Golden Gate.
And there, in the garbage she did hate,
A Poor Sarah met an awful fate,
That I cannot right now relate
45   Because the hour is much too late.
B But children, remember Sarah Stout
And always take the garbage out!

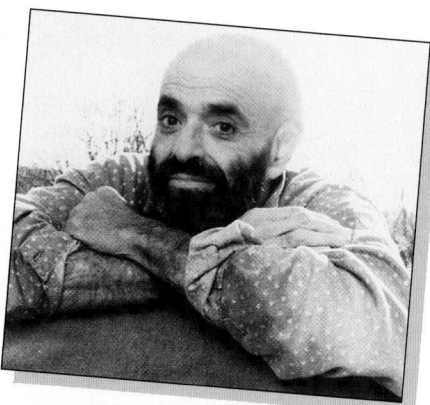

MEET THE WRITER

"I Couldn't Dance. . . . So I Started to Draw and Write."

Shel Silverstein (1932–1999) began drawing and writing when he was a young boy growing up in Chicago. He wrote:

66 When I was a kid—12, 14 around there—I would much rather have been a good baseball player or a hit with the girls. But I couldn't play ball. I couldn't dance. Luckily, the girls didn't want me; not much I could do about that. So I started to draw and write. I was also lucky I didn't have anyone to copy, be impressed by. I . . . developed my own style. 99

When Silverstein grew up, he became a writer of children's books, a poet, a cartoonist, and a songwriter. He created and illustrated two of the world's most popular collections of poems for children: *Where the Sidewalk Ends* (1974), which includes "Sarah Cynthia Sylvia Stout," and *A Light in the Attic* (1981). Silverstein said:

66 I would hope that people, no matter what age, would find something to identify with in my books, pick one up and experience a personal sense of discovery. 99

Listening to Music ♪

"Sarah Cynthia Sylvia Stout Would Not Take the Garbage Out" by Shel Silverstein, performed by Shel Silverstein

A man of many talents, Shel Silverstein wrote several noted songs in a wide range of styles and moods. Among them was the Civil War ballad "In the Hills of Shiloh," hauntingly sung by Judy Collins; the pop hit "Sylvia's Mother," sung by Dr. Hook and the Medicine Show; and every song on the 1975 album *Lullabies, Legends, and Lies,* performed by the country singer Bobby Bare. Like all the poems in his collection *Where the Sidewalk Ends,* "Sarah Cynthia" was set to music by the author.

Activity

After students have read Silverstein's poem, ask them to listen to the author's own musical version. Ask students to consider whether the music changes the effect of the poem and which version they prefer. Students' brief critiques may be in the form of written reviews or oral presentations.

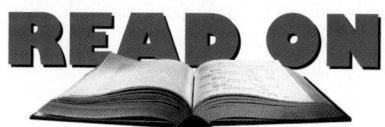

READ ON

- ## Wonderful Wool

  Twelve-year-old Miguel Chavez longs for his family to treat him like an adult. For a year he tries to show that he is ready to make the difficult journey driving sheep into the mountains. It is not until some sheep are missing and a serious letter arrives that Miguel is truly able to prove himself in Joseph Krumgold's Newbery Winner . . . *and now Miguel* (HarperCollins).

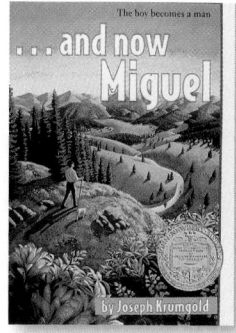

  ## Struggle at Sea

  Lincoln Noah Stonewright is going to Alaska to explore his Eskimo roots and search for his missing uncle. In *Water Sky* (HarperCollins) by Jean Craighead George, Lincoln's search leads him to join the crew of a whaling ship and forces him to face a serious conflict.

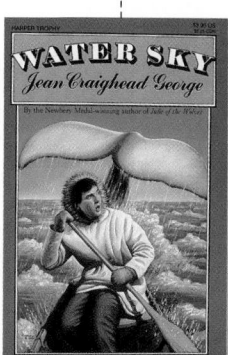

  ## Pride and Prejudice

  Virginia Hamilton's *Many Thousand Gone: African Americans from Slavery to Freedom* (Knopf) tells of the brave choices made by people desperate to be free. You'll read about Prince Ukawsaw, who was tricked into slavery; Henry Box Brown, who mailed himself to freedom in a homemade crate; and Jackson, who dressed as a maid to escape his owner. This incredible collection of true stories shows the pain and power of some courageous people.

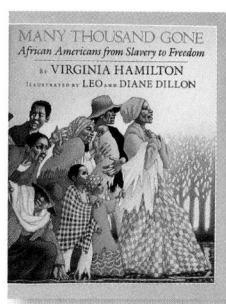

Other Picks

- Lensey Namioka, *The Coming of the Bear* (HarperCollins). Friends Zenta and Matsuzo, two shipwrecked samurai, may be forced to fight on opposite sides of a war in sixteenth-century Japan.
- Scott Johnson, *One of the Boys* (Macmillan). Eric Atwater enjoys popularity in the "cool" gang led by magnetic Marty Benbow, until the gang's pranks turn cruel.

READ ON

Portfolio Assessment Options
The following projects can help you evaluate and assess your students' outside reading. Videotapes or audiotapes of completed projects may be included in students' portfolios.

- **Compare a Novel and a Story** Have students write a comparative book review in which they examine one of the "Read On" novels and one of the short stories in this collection. Ask them to focus on the external and internal conflicts that the main characters face and on how well the characters succeed in "doing the right thing."
- **Tape an Interview** Make video or audio equipment available to pairs of students who have read the same book. One student should write and ask interview questions based on information in the book, and the other student should answer the questions in character.
- **Make a Calendar** Ask students to create a daily calendar to record Miguel's adventures in . . . *and now Miguel*. Ask them to write, in dated boxes on their calendars, descriptions of incidents from the story. The calendar covers should contain illustrations of important scenes.
- **Write a Ship's Log** Ask students to suppose that it is Lincoln Stonewright's duty to keep a log for the whaling ship in *Water Sky*. Have students write log entries that describe the incidents in the story, and ask them to include frequent comments from Lincoln in the margin of the log.

Sustained Silent Reading

Virginia Hamilton's collection of true stories about American slavery would be a good book to assign for sustained silent reading in **independent-level materials**. According to the Bormuth formula, this book scores on the same level as most fiction (including magazine fiction) written for teenagers.

Students often have trouble reading nonfiction: Nonfiction does not always have the level of interest or suspense found in fiction, and it often requires recognition of cause and effect, retention of factual details, knowledge of historical references, and so on.

As students read *Many Thousand Gone*, have them keep a notebook handy. They should record in the notebook how long they spend on the book, which sections of the book they enjoyed, and which gave them trouble (if any). They should also make notes as they read: Have them note their responses to parts of the book, questions about details in the stories, and further research they might like to do on the topic. Have them discuss problems they have in particular with nonfiction. How many nonfiction titles have they read on their own so far this school year?

Writer's Workshop

MAIN OBJECTIVE
Write a persuasive essay supporting a position

PROCESS OBJECTIVES
1. Use appropriate prewriting techniques to identify and develop a topic
2. Create a first draft
3. Use Evaluation Criteria as a basis for determining revision strategies
4. Revise the first draft, incorporating suggestions generated by self- or peer evaluation
5. Proofread and correct errors
6. Create a final draft
7. Choose an appropriate method of publication
8. Reflect on progress as a writer

Planning

- **Block Schedule**
  Block Scheduling Lesson Plans with Pacing Guide
- **One-Stop Planner**
  CD-ROM with Test Generator

ASSIGNMENT

Write an essay in which you state your position on an issue that is important to you and provide reasons supporting your position.

AIM

To persuade.

AUDIENCE

Your classmates, newspaper readers, or anyone affected by the issue. (You choose.)

PERSUASIVE WRITING

SUPPORTING A POSITION

In this collection you've been reading about people who take a stand to do the right thing. In this Writer's Workshop you'll have a chance to take and defend a stand on an issue you care about. You'll write a paper in which you

- discuss an issue about which people disagree
- talk about the **pros** and **cons**—the reasons for and against different positions on the issue
- tell where *you* stand on the issue
- give at least three reasons for supporting your position

Professional Model

Itzhak Perlman, a world-famous violinist, was disabled as a child by polio.

I've been in public buildings throughout the world, and it's clear that the people who design them have no idea what it feels like to use crutches or sit in a wheelchair. One of the great architectural catastrophes of all time, from the point of view of any concertgoer, much less one who is disabled, is the Sydney Opera House in Sydney, Australia. A design contest was held and the winner was an architect who had conceived a truly fantastic-looking place with about a hundred steps leading to the entrance. There is no elevator— not for the general public, not for the poor musicians who have to lug

The writer introduces the issue.

The writer gives a detailed example as support.

The writer states a fact as support.

  Resources: Print and Media

Writing and Language
- *Portfolio Management System*
  Prewriting, p. 135
  Peer Editing, p. 136
  Assessment Rubric, p. 137
- *Workshop Resources*
  Revision Strategy Teaching Notes, p. 9
  Revision Strategy Transparencies 5, 6, 7

Assessment
- *Standardized Test Preparation, p. 112*

(continued)

instruments up all those stairs, and certainly not for the disabled. Why couldn't the prize have been given to the best design that was also barrier-free? Why, when it's possible to make *everyone* comfortable, is so little attention paid to accessibility? . . .

> *The writer restates the issue as a question.*

If you want to be sensitive to the indignities and frustrations suffered by the disabled, spend a day or two in a wheelchair. Tell yourself that you cannot get up—then try to get into a car. Try to go shopping or use the toilet in a restaurant. See what it feels like to be all dressed up and have to ride to your appointment in a freight elevator with the garbage. I can tell you how that makes *me* feel—furious.

> *The writer tries to convince readers by asking them to put themselves in his place.*

> *The writer cites a personal experience as support.*

We don't need more equal-rights laws. What we need is an attitude that we're all human beings, and as such, we all care about each other.

> *The essay ends with a call to action.*

—from "To Help the Handicapped, Talk to Them" by Itzhak Perlman

Looking at the Good and Bad on School Issues

Uniforms	Good: They'd save money. Bad: They're boring!
Length of school day	Longer: Kids could do their home-work at school. Shorter: Kids need fresh air!
Metal detectors	Good: safety Bad: They'd make stu-dents feel like criminals!

Prewriting

1. Writer's Notebook

WORK IN PROGRESS

Look at your Writer's Notebook entries for this collection. Could you use any of your ideas as the basis for a paper supporting a position? For more ideas, try the brainstorming suggestion on the next page.

Chris Britt/Copley News Service

WRITER'S WORKSHOP 261

Introducing the Writer's Workshop

- Read the Professional Model on pp. 260–261 as students follow along. You may want to offer definitions of a few difficult words, such as *accessibility* and *indignities*.
- Be sure students understand the side-margin comments. Have students read aloud the specific sentences to which the comments apply.
- Discuss with students what qualities they think make a good persuasive essay—a strong position, plenty of supporting evidence, a powerful conclusion.
- Be sure students understand the purpose of their writing: to take a stand on an issue and offer persuasive support.

Teaching the Writer's Workshop

Prewriting

Have students use the techniques suggested on pp. 261–262 (or any others that may be helpful to them) to come up with ideas. Encourage students to keep open minds as they search for appropriate topics. Remind them that good ideas often come from surprising places.

Reaching All Students

Struggling Writers

Provide struggling writers with plenty of time for prewriting, and help them overcome impatience to start their first drafts. Emphasize that planning makes writing easier in the long run. As students search for topics, remind them of the following tips:

- Choose a topic about which people actually disagree, not a "straw man," a target easily

knocked down. For example, "War is bad" is not likely to elicit differing opinions.
- Choose a specific topic, not a general one, so that position and support can be clearly stated and realistic. For example, "Everyone should be happy" is too general to allow effective support.
- Choose an issue that a significant number of

people really care about.
- If possible, choose an issue of which they have some personal knowledge or experience. Authors write more effectively about topics they know firsthand.

As class members read the Student Model, be sure they understand the side notes. You can extend the discussion by having students focus on questions like these:

❓ Does the opening sentence grab your attention? Why or why not?

❓ Are the examples realistic? Would you add any others? Do you think the word *nag* is an appropriate one? Why or why not?

❓ Do you think restating the issue as a question is an effective technique? What tone do you think it adds to the essay?

❓ Does the writer provide reasons that are strong enough? Are the reasons accurate? Under the proposed solution, for example, would kids "no longer ask for money"?

❓ At the end, does the writer repeat his or her position clearly and directly?

Would girls have to wear skirts? Unfair!

NO—we should have freedom of choice

Check the Internet for facts and opinions

Should kids wear uniforms to school?

YES—everyone would be equal

Tell about Nina's experience

Language/Grammar Link
H E L P

End marks: page 201. Commas in a series: page 215. Comma splice: page 225. Apostrophes: page 243. Punctuating dialogue: page 256.

2. Brainstorming

Remember that you will have to come up with good reasons to support a particular course of action. To find a topic people disagree on, get together with a group of classmates and brainstorm issues in several areas—for instance, school, community, national, and world. Each group member should pick a category and write down the issues, along with opinions on them.

3. Choosing an Issue and Finding Reasons

You've got a lot of issues on the table. How do you choose one to work with? First, look for an issue that matters to you. Second, make sure you see reasons to support different sides.

Clustering is one way to walk around an issue and look at it from different sides. Here is how it works. State the issue in the form of a question. Write the question in the middle of a sheet of paper, and draw a circle around it. Around the circle, write down another position people might take on the issue, along with reasons to support that position. Then, write down evidence—facts, examples, personal experiences—supporting the reasons. The model on the left is an example of clustering.

KIDS SHOULD BE PAID FOR CHORES

I strongly believe that kids should be paid for doing chores around the house. Kids all across the country constantly nag their parents for money to go to the movies, buy CDs, go to McDonalds, and do many other things. Many parents complain about kids' always asking for money.

Parents constantly complain that kids don't help out around the house enough. Lots of times parents nag kids until they clean up their rooms, put out the trash, cut the lawn, do the dishes, shovel the snow, and do many other chores.

Why can't kids and parents reach a compromise about money and chores? Parents would pay kids who remember to do their chores without

A strong statement of position on a problem is used to grab readers' attention.

The writer gives examples to illustrate the problem.

The writer restates the issue as a question and

Getting Students Involved

Cooperative Learning

Ask students to present a mock television talk show on an issue that allows for differences of opinion. Choose a moderator or host and six guests—three who are for the issue, three who are against it. Each guest should prepare a short statement and then ad-lib the answers to questions prepared and posed by the host. Point out to students that stating their opinions and their supporting reasons clearly and directly is just as important in speaking as it is in writing. Guests should alternate pro and con as they make their opening statements. After the host's questions have been answered, student "audience participation" should be encouraged. Remind all students to remain respectful of opposing opinions and to stick to the topic. After the discussion, you may want to ask the student audience to cast a voice vote on which side presented the stronger arguments.

being reminded a small fee for the work done. Kids would no longer ask for money.

This compromise teaches kids responsibility. They would learn that you don't get anything for doing nothing. When their chores are completed, with no nagging, they'd be paid whatever the parents had agreed to pay them. Kids could spend the money on things they like. They'd learn to save money for the expensive items.

No more nagging kids begging for money. No more nagging parents begging kids to clean up. Both kids and parents would be getting something that they want.

—T. J. Wilson
Atlantic Middle School
North Quincy, Massachusetts

gives two reasons to support his position.

The writer elaborates by giving several more reasons to support his position.

The writer ends with a strong statement citing the benefits of the recommended course of action.

4. Targeting Your Audience

In persuasive writing, your goal is to convince your readers to agree with your position and, if possible, to take the actions you recommend. "Whom am I trying to persuade?" is an important question to answer. Here are other questions to think about:

- What does my audience know about the issue? What do I need to explain?
- What is my audience likely to agree with me about?
- What **counterarguments,** or arguments against my position, could my audience make? How could I answer these counterarguments?

Drafting

1. Drafting a Strong Beginning

Grab your readers' attention right from the start. One way to do this is to make your first sentence short. Another way is to begin with a question like "Who has the right to tell us what to

---

Framework for an Essay Supporting a Position

Introduction (statement of the issue, the pros and cons of different positions on the issue, and your position): _____

_____

Reason 1 and two items of support (support for your position, including facts, examples, and personal experiences): _____

_____

Reason 2 and two items of support: _____

_____

Reason 3 and two items of support: _____

_____

Conclusion (restatement of your opinion and a call to action): _____

_____

Sentence Workshop
H E L P

Run-on sentences: page 265.

Communications Handbook
H E L P

See Proofreaders' Marks.

Drafting

- If you have not yet taught the Student Model, do so before students begin their drafts.
- Remind students to use every other line when they write their drafts. They should also leave extra space in the right margin for comments and editing marks.
- Encourage students to keep separate notes of any ideas that don't immediately seem to fit into their drafts. These ideas may turn out to be useful at the revision stage.
- Urge students to avoid mere repetition. Presenting supporting reasons and evidence does not mean simply repeating the position statement in more forceful terms.
- Tell students not to let themselves get bogged down in details at the drafting stage. Word choice and mechanical details can be dealt with at the revision and proofreading stages.

Reaching All Students

English Language Learners

English language learners may benefit from focusing on smaller units as they draft their essays. Students might create a short topic outline in which they identify exactly what each paragraph will cover. You might suggest the following outline on the chalkboard:
Paragraph 1—Issue and position
Paragraphs 2, 3, and 4—Reason or evidence
Paragraph 5—Restatement of position; conclusion

Advanced Learners

Encourage advanced learners to state at least one opposing argument in their essays and to answer it fully and directly. Students can also search for supporting reasons and evidence in the works of published experts, including books, articles, and Internet documents. Remind students to consider carefully the reliability of all sources.

Evaluating and Revising

Have students use the Evaluation Criteria provided here to review their drafts and determine needed revisions.

Proofreading

Have students proofread their own papers first and then exchange with another student. For this assignment, remind students to be particularly careful of word choice and to avoid loaded words.

If time permits, the final copy should be put aside for at least a day before it is proofread for the final time by the author.

Remind students that they must spell accurately in final drafts. Suggest that they use a spelling checker if they are using a computer that has one. Make sure students understand that a spelling checker will not alert them to errors involving homophones and homographs.

Publishing

Students might consider submitting their essays to the school newspaper or sending them out for possible publication by the local community newspaper.

Reflecting

Students can prepare a brief reflection on the process of writing a persuasive essay. They might complete one of the starters below:

- The best-written part of my essay is . . . because . . .
- The most surprising thing I learned about myself while writing this essay was . . .

Resources

Peer-Editing Forms and Rubrics
- *Portfolio Management System*, p. 136

Revision Transparencies
- *Workshop Resources*, p. 9

Grading Timesaver

Rubrics for this Writer's Workshop assignment appear on p. 137 of the *Portfolio Management System*.

Strategies for Elaboration

To support your position, you can use

- facts (including surveys and statistics)
- examples
- opinions from experts, especially direct quotations
- definitions
- anecdotes (very brief stories, such as personal experiences; include dialogue if possible)
- appeals to emotion
- cause and effect (for example, the results of a particular course of action)

■ *Evaluation Criteria*

A good position paper

1. *clearly states the issue*
2. *presents two or more positions on the issue or courses of action*
3. *clearly states the writer's position on the issue*
4. *gives sound, persuasive reasons to support this position*
5. *stays on track from beginning to end*
6. *is organized logically, with transitions connecting ideas*

---

wear to school?" Let the first paragraph set the stage. Tell what the issue is, and explain why it's important and why it interests you. Then, briefly explain the pros and cons of the issue. Finally, tell which side of the issue you're on.

2. Laying Out the Evidence

In the next three paragraphs, you'll try to persuade your audience to agree with you. In each paragraph, give one convincing reason to support your position. Then, elaborate with two items of support—a fact, an example, a personal experience. Try to use several kinds of support. If your evidence is limited to personal experiences, for example, your audience may suspect that you can't find other kinds of support.

3. Organizing the Evidence

It's important to arrange your reasons and support in a logical way. Many writers use **order of importance** for this kind of paper, saving their strongest reason for last. You may want to put your best reason in your fourth paragraph.

4. Ending with a Bang

In your conclusion, present a strong statement of your position. Leave no doubt in your readers' minds. Drive your point home by telling what's wrong with the other side. End by urging readers to agree with you or to take the course of action you support. Use the Framework for an Essay Supporting a Position (page 263) to organize your ideas.

Evaluating and Revising

Trade drafts with a classmate, and read your partner's draft. Then, respond to the following questions:

- How does the writer interest me in the issue?
- Does the writer present the issue clearly?
- Does the writer present enough support to convince me?
- What support is strongest? weakest?
- What's the best thing I can say about the introduction and conclusion? What still needs work in those parts of the essay?

Make all the changes that you think will improve your paper.

Assessing Learning

Standardized Test Preparation
For practice with standardized test prompts and formats, see
- *Standardized Test Preparation*, p. 112

BUILDING YOUR PORTFOLIO
Sentence Workshop

OBJECTIVES
1. Identify run-on sentences
2. Revise run-on sentences with correct punctuation and coordinating conjunctions

RUN-ON SENTENCES

A **run-on sentence** is two complete sentences punctuated as if they were one sentence. In a run-on the thoughts just run into each other. You can't tell where one idea ends and another one begins.

RUN-ON   I was eighteen the next morning I was to start for the West to make my fortune.

CORRECT   I was eighteen**. T**he next morning I was to start for the West to make my fortune.

A comma does not mark the end of a sentence.

RUN-ON   Fausto went to church, he put twenty dollars in the basket.

CORRECT   Fausto went to church, **and** he put twenty dollars in the basket.

There are several ways to revise run-on sentences:

- You can make two sentences. In the first run-on above, adding the period after *eighteen* clears up the confusion.

- You can add a comma and the coordinating conjunction *and, but,* or *or.*

RUN-ON   Fausto got an orange while he was eating, a dog walked up and sniffed his leg.

CORRECT   Fausto got an orange, **and** while he was eating, a dog walked up and sniffed his leg.

Writer's Workshop Follow-up: Revision

Take out your essay supporting a position, and exchange papers with a classmate. To spot run-ons, try reading your partner's essay aloud. As you read, you will probably pause where one thought ends and another begins. If you pause at a place where there is no end punctuation, you may have found a run-on sentence. Underline any run-ons you find, and suggest a revision for each. Exchange essays again, and revise any run-ons your partner found in your writing.

Language Handbook HELP

See Revising Run-on Sentences, page 761.

Technology HELP

See Language Workshop CD-ROM. *Key word entry: run-on sentences.*

Try It Out

Copy the following paragraph onto a separate sheet of paper, and revise it, correcting any run-on sentences.

Gary Soto's love of reading made him want to be a writer, he didn't start trying to be a writer, until he went to college. As a student in Catholic school, he wanted to be a priest when he went to public school he wanted to be a barber. He discovered poetry in college he says he was "hooked for good" on writing.

Resources ───────

Workshop Resources
- Worksheet, p. 41

Language Workshop CD-ROM
- Run-on Sentences

Try It Out
Possible Answers
Gary Soto's love of reading made him want to be a writer, but he didn't start trying to be a writer until he went to college. As a student in Catholic school, he wanted to be a priest. When he went to public school, he wanted to be a barber. He discovered poetry in college, and he says he was "hooked for good" on writing.

SENTENCE WORKSHOP 265

Assessing Learning

Quick Check: Run-on Sentences

Revise each run-on sentence below, using one of the ways shown in the Sentence Workshop.

1. Gary Soto is a writer he wrote "The No-Guitar Blues." [Gary Soto is a writer. He wrote "The No-Guitar Blues."]
2. "The No-Guitar Blues" is based on a real incident it happened when Soto was young. ["The No-Guitar Blues" is based on a real incident. It happened when Soto was young.]
3. He had a popsicle while he was eating, a dog

wandered up. [He had a popsicle, and while he was eating, a dog wandered up.]

4. He pulled on the dog's collar, hoping to find the dog's owner, he checked its tags. [He pulled on the dog's collar. Hoping to find the dog's owner, he checked its tags.]
5. Soto says the woman was glad to see the dog he was glad when she gave him a reward. [Soto says the woman was glad to see the dog, and he was glad when she gave him a reward.]

Using the Strategies

Possible Responses

1. The subject: why the students have chosen to wear uniforms. Since the students have already chosen to wear uniforms, their perspective may be biased. They give only reasons in favor of wearing uniforms.
2. Students wearing uniforms come to school ready to learn; differences in family income no longer affect students' clothing; self-esteem becomes more important than appearance.
3. *peace of mind; unity; sense of pride*
4. Students' responses should show an understanding of the issue and of the use of persuasive arguments.

Situation

In the paragraph on the right, students at Juniper Academy tell why they think wearing school uniforms is the right thing to do. Do you find their message convincing? Use the following strategies to evaluate this and any other persuasive writing.

Strategies

Identify the writer and the main idea.

- Who is the writer (or writers), and what special expertise or interest does he or she have in the topic?
- Does the writer clearly state a position on the issue? How much does the writer know about the subject? Can you believe what he or she says?

Analyze the writer's perspective, or point of view.

- Does the writer present more than one point of view, or is the writing slanted toward one side of the argument?
- Does the writer give convincing reasons to support his or her position?

Uniforms

Why have we chosen to wear uniforms at Juniper Academy? Uniforms are a smart choice. In uniforms, kids come to school with a better attitude, ready to learn, which leads to higher attendance and better grades. By reducing socioeconomic barriers, uniforms "level the playing field." Kids can be proud of who they are instead of worrying about what they are wearing. As outward appearance becomes less of a factor, self-esteem is higher, giving a child courage to get involved with the school. Uniforms can give parents and teachers peace of mind. Finally, we feel that uniforms build unity and a strong sense of pride within the student body as a whole.

—from the Web page of Juniper Academy
Redding, California

Evaluate the writer's choice of words.

- Does the vocabulary fit the purpose and the audience?
- Does the writer use loaded words (words that call up strong feelings, like *greatest* or *rotten*) to make a point?

Using the Strategies

1. What is the subject of the paragraph by the students at Juniper Academy? Describe how the writers' **perspective,** or point of view, affects what they have to say.

2. Give three reasons to support wearing uniforms.

3. Find two or three words or phrases in the last two sentences that could be considered loaded words.

4. Did the paragraph convince you? Why or why not?

Extending the Strategies

- Read an editorial in your school paper or local newspaper. Evaluate the message, using the strategies you've just learned.

266 DO THE RIGHT THING

Reaching All Students

Struggling Readers
As struggling readers learn to evaluate persuasive writing, encourage them to be on the lookout for bias in a writer. Urge them to avoid making assumptions, especially about "common knowledge"; to stay alert for a writer's unstated motives, such as financial profit; not to be afraid to ask questions.

Advanced Learners
After advanced learners have read a newspaper editorial and evaluated its message, have them write a response to the newspaper. Remind them that their responses should follow the advice given on the pupil's page. Their responses should also contain, usually in the first paragraph, a reference to the title and date of the editorial.

Learning for Life

Using Multiple Sources to Conduct Research on Volunteering

OBJECTIVES
1. Research volunteer opportunities for middle-school students
2. Make information about volunteering available to other students through a public-service announcement, a "Volunteer Fair," or an on-line index

Problem

You've read about people who made decisions to "do the right thing." For many people, volunteering to help others is "doing the right thing." What are the benefits of volunteering?

Project

Find out about volunteer opportunities for middle-school students in your community, and make the information available to other students.

Preparation

1. Make a list of your interests and skills. Include your favorite activities in and out of school and the causes you feel strongly about.

2. In groups of four or five, brainstorm to come up with a list of places where you might volunteer, for example:
   - an animal shelter
   - a park
   - a hospital
   - a library
   - a senior citizens' center

3. Make a list of volunteer positions to investigate.

Procedure

1. Design a volunteers-needed card to record information about volunteer jobs. Include such items as the volunteer position, the agency it is with, the location, the name and phone number of the person to contact, how to apply, qualifications looked for in an applicant, the time commitment required, and any special comments.

2. Elect one classmate to call Volunteers of America and the office of the mayor. Find out if there is a government agency nearby that assigns volunteers. Then, call at least one place where you would like to volunteer. Fill in a volunteers-needed card for each place.

Presentation

Present your findings in one of the following ways:

1. Public-Service Announcement

Create an audio or a video public-service announcement encouraging young people to volunteer in the community. Talk about the benefits of volunteering and the kinds of work available. Play your announcement for your school. You might ask if a local radio or TV station will broadcast your announcement.

2. "Volunteer Fair"

Organize a "volunteer fair" for your class or school. Set up tables with information about volunteer work. Use separate tables for different kinds of work—for example, work with animals or work in hospitals. "Volunteers" at each table can answer questions.

3. On-line Index

If you have access to a computer program that can make an index, enter your volunteers-needed information. Then, students can get information by searching under any of several categories—for example, they should be able to look under the specific position (animal-shelter helper) or the general category (outdoor work) or the part of town in which a job is located.

Processing

Finish this sentence: "I want to help my community by. . .".

Resources

Viewing and Representing
HRW Multimedia Presentation Maker
Students may wish to use the *Multimedia Presentation Maker* to create a video public-service announcement.

Grading Timesaver

Rubrics for this Learning for Life project appear on p. 138 of the *Portfolio Management System*.

Developing Workplace Competencies

Preparation	Procedure	Presentation
• Working on a team • Processing information	• Designing a system • Demonstrating individual responsibility • Using self-management skills	• Thinking creatively • Synthesizing information • Applying technology to a specific task

Collection Four

We Rookies Have to Stick Together

Theme

Buddies Forever *The theme of friendship forged under difficult circumstances is an enduring motif in storytelling. This theme is given special poignancy when the friendship is challenged by the competition—then by a terrible sickness.*

Reading the Anthology

Reaching Struggling Readers

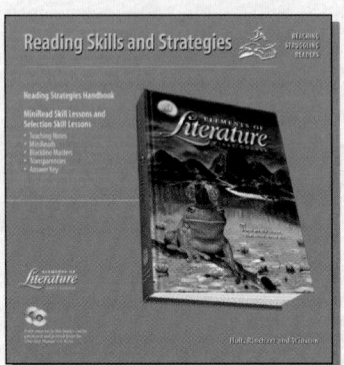

The *Reading Skills and Strategies: Reaching Struggling Readers* binder provides materials coordinated with the Pupil's Edition (see the Collection Planner, p. T267C) to help students who have difficulty reading and comprehending text, or students who are reluctant readers. The binder for seventh grade is organized around eleven individual skill areas and offers the following options:

- **MiniRead** MiniReads are short, easy texts that give students a chance to practice a particular skill and strategy before reading selections in the Pupil's Edition. Each MiniRead Skill Lesson can be taught independently or used in conjunction with a Selection Skill Lesson.

- **Selection Skill Lessons** Selection Skill Lessons allow students to apply skills introduced in the MiniReads. Each Selection Skill Lesson provides reading instruction and practice specific to a particular piece of literature in the Pupil's Edition.

Reading Beyond the Anthology

Read On

Collection Four includes an annotated bibliography of books suitable for extended reading. The suggested books are related to works in this collection by theme, by author, or by subject. To preview the Read On for Collection Four, please turn to p. T325.

HRW Library

The *HRW Library* offers novels, plays, and short-story collections for extended reading. Each book in the Library includes one or more major works and thematically or topically related Connections. The Connections are magazine articles, poems, or other pieces of literature. Each book in the *HRW Library* is also accompanied by a Study Guide that provides teaching suggestions and worksheets. For Collection Four, the following titles are recommended.

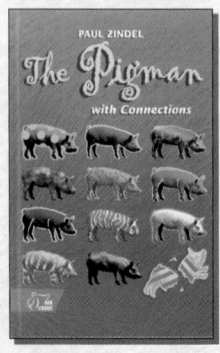

THE PIGMAN
Paul Zindel
At first the Pigman, a lonely widower, is little more than a joke to high school students John and Lorraine. But eventually, the Pigman provides the teenagers with a hard-learned lesson about friendship and its responsibilities.

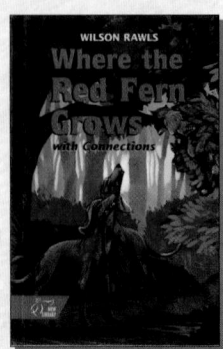

WHERE THE RED FERN GROWS
Wilson Rawls
Billy Colman's two dogs save him from the fangs of a mountain lion and win the championship coon hunt. But Billy must also make tough decisions in this story—and learn the harder lesson of letting go.

Skills Focus

Selection or Feature	Reading Skills and Strategies	Elements of Literature	Language/ Grammar	Vocabulary/ Spelling	Writing	Listening/ Speaking	Viewing/ Representing
Elements of Literature: Drama (p. 270)		Drama, pp. 270–271 • Dialogue • Plot • Script • Screenplay and Teleplay					
Reading Skills and Strategies: Previewing the Text (p. 272)	Preview the Text, p. 272						
Brian's Song (p. 273) William Blinn	Preview the Text, pp. 273, 322	Setting, pp. 273 Stage and Camera Directions, pp. 273, 300 Change, p. 300 Internal Conflict, pp. 300, 322 Foreshadowing, p. 322	Transitions, p. 324	Use Body Language to Express Word Meaning, p. 301 Antonyms, p. 301 Use Reference Aids, p. 324 • Thesaurus • Dictionary • Reference Software	Collect Ideas for a How-To Essay, p. 323 Write a Paragraph or Journal Entry on a Topic Related to the Selection, p. 323 Write a Profile of Gale Sayers, p. 323	Role-Play Judges Deciding on an Emmy for *Brian's Song*, p. 323	Use a Chart to Record Information, pp. 300, 322
Speaking and Listening Workshop: Oral Interpretation (p. 326)					Make a Cutting of a Long Work for Oral Presentation, p. 326 Prepare a Reader's Script, p. 327	Identify Appropriate Gestures and Body Movement for an Interpretation, p. 327 Create and Present an Oral Interpretation of Literature, pp. 326–327	
Writer's Workshop: How-To Essay (p. 328)		Chronological Order, p. 329	Transitions, p. 331		Expository Writing: Write a How-To Essay, pp. 328–332		
Sentence Workshop: Combining Sentences Using *And, But,* or *Or* (p. 333)			Combine Sentences to Form Compound Sentences, p. 333		Revise Sentences by Combining, p. 333		
Reading for Life: Reading a Manual (p. 334)	Reading a Manual, p. 334 Determine Meaning from Context, p. 334	Chronological Order, p. 334		Determine the Meaning of Technical Abbreviations, p. 334 Use a Glossary, p. 334			
Learning for Life: Conducting an Interview to Research a Question (p. 335)					Write a Teamwork Handbook, p. 335	Conduct an Interview with a Company's Workers, p. 335 Create and Perform a Skit About Teamwork, p. 335	Create Posters About Teamwork, p. 335

Skills Focus

Collection Planner *(vertical sidebar text)*

Resources for this Collection

Internet Resources
go.hrw.com LE0 7-4

Note: All resources for this collection are available for preview on the *One-Stop Planner CD-ROM 1 with Test Generator.* All worksheets and blackline masters may be printed from the CD-ROM.

Selection or Feature	Reading and Literary Skills	Language and Grammar
Elements of Literature: Drama (p. 270)	• *Literary Elements,* Transparency 4	
Brian's Song (p. 273) William Blinn **Connections: Pic,** *from* **I Am Third** (p. 320) Gale Sayers	• *Reading Skills and Strategies: Reaching Struggling Readers* • MiniRead Skill Lesson, p. 166 • Selection Skill Lesson, p.174 • *Graphic Organizers for Active Reading,* Worksheet pp. 19, 20 • *Literary Elements:* Transparency 4 Worksheet p. 13	• *Grammar and Language Links:* Transitions, Worksheet p. 31 • *Daily Oral Grammar,* Transparencies 17, 18
Speaking and Listening Workshop: Oral Interpretation (p. 326)		
Writer's Workshop: How-to Essay (p. 328)		
Sentence Workshop: Combining Sentences Using *And, But,* **or** *Or* (p. 333)		• *Workshop Resources,* p. 43 • *Language Workshop CD-ROM,* Combining Sentences
Learning for Life: Conducting an Interview to Research a Question (p. 335)		

Collection Resources

- *Cross-Curricular Activities,* p. 30
- *Portfolio Management System:*
  Introduction to Portfolio Assessment, p. 1;
  Parent/Guardian Letters, p. 93
- *Formal Assessment,*
  Reading Application Test, p. 60
- *Test Generator,* Collection Test

Vocabulary, Spelling, and Decoding	Writing	Listening and Speaking, Viewing and Representing	Assessment
			• *Formal Assessment,* Literary Elements Test, p. 58
• *Words to Own,* Worksheet pp. 13, 14 • *Spelling and Decoding,* Worksheet p. 16	• *Portfolio Management System,* Rubrics for Choices, p. 139	• *Visual Connections,* Videocassette A, Segment 4 • *Audio CD Library,* Disc 8, Track 5 • *Viewing and Representing:* Fine Art Transparency 9 Worksheet p. 36 • *Portfolio Management System,* Rubrics for Choices, p. 139	• *Formal Assessment,* Selection Tests, pp. 54, 56 • *Standardized Test Preparation,* pp. 46, 48, 50 • *Test Generator* (One-Stop Planner CD-ROM)
			• *Portfolio Management System,* p. 140
	• *Workshop Resources,* p. 15 • *Standardized Test Preparation:* Worksheet p. 128 Transparencies 13–18		• *Portfolio Management System* • Prewriting, p. 141 • Peer Editing, p. 142 • Assessment Rubric, p. 143
		• *Viewing and Representing,* HRW Multimedia Presentation Maker	• *Portfolio Management System,* Rubrics, p. 144

 Transparency   CD-ROM   Video   Audio CD

Collection Planner

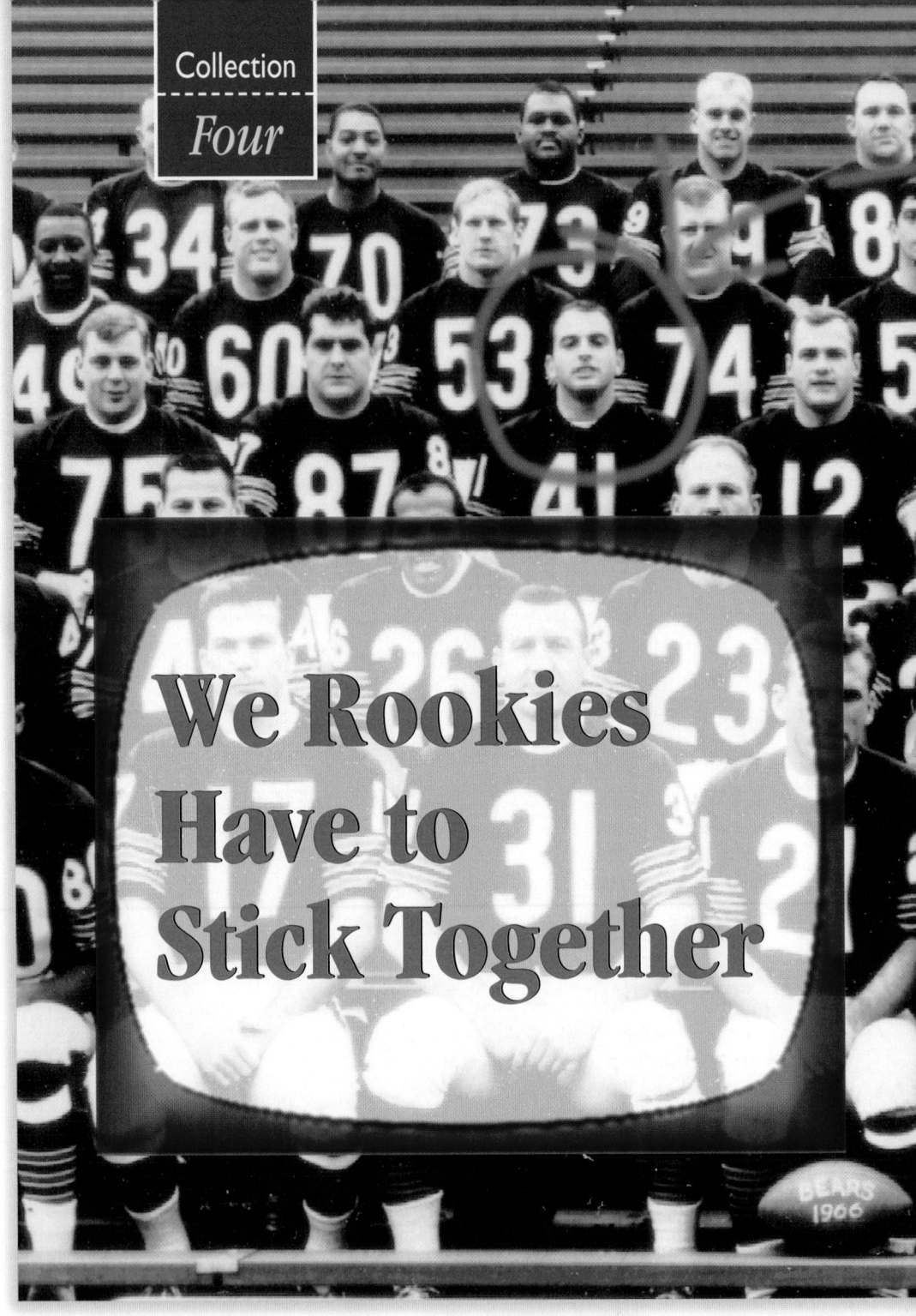

We Rookies Have to Stick Together

Introducing the Theme

There is much to learn from studying the lives of contemporaries, whether they are celebrities or ordinary people. In their victories are the best examples of what people can do—including acts of friendship in the face of competition. To direct students toward an understanding of the theme, ask them to consider the following questions:

• Who are rookies?
• When do people have to "stick together"?

Ask volunteers to describe situations in which they have been rookies or have needed to stick together to achieve some goal.

Responding to the Quotation

? Do you agree with the ideas expressed in this quotation? Explain. [Possible responses: It is good to be a part of groups like this, because they give you support; no, these types of groups only keep you from being an individual.]

Selection Readability

This Annotated Teacher's Edition provides a summary of each selection in the student book. Following each Summary heading, you will find one, two or three small icons. These icons indicate, in an approximate sense, the reading level of the selection.

■ One icon indicates that the selection is easy.
■■ Two icons indicate that the selection is on an intermediate reading level.
■■■ Three icons indicate that the selection is challenging.

Call it a clan,
call it a network,
call it a tribe,
call it a family.
Whatever you call it,
whoever you are,
you need one.
—Jane Howard

269

Writer's Notebook

Allow four to five minutes for students to write an entry of several sentences in their journals, responding to the prompt "I believe that winning a competition is the most important thing." After students have made entries in their journals, encourage them to think about and discuss why keeping a journal might be useful. [Possible response: Writing in a journal can help a person put things in perspective, work through difficulties, understand how to deal with others, and record memorable events.]

Resources

Portfolio Management System
- Introduction to Portfolio Assessment, p. 1
- Parent/Guardian Letters, p. 93

Formal Assessment
- Reading Application Test, p. 60

Test Generator
- Collection Test

Cross-Curricular Activities
- Teaching Notes, p. 30

Writing Focus: How-To Essay

The following **Work in Progress** assignment relates to a culminating **Writer's Workshop** at the end of Collection 4.

- Brian's Song   List the steps and materials required for a how-to essay (p. 323)

Writer's Workshop: Expository Writing / How-To Essay (p. 328)

OBJECTIVES

1. Understand the basic elements of drama: exposition, conflict, complications, climax, and resolution
2. Recognize the importance of dialogue in a play
3. Analyze the teleplay

Resources ———

Elements of Literature
Elements of Drama
For additional instruction on the elements of drama, see *Literary Elements:*
• Transparency 4

Elements of Literature

This feature explains the basic elements of drama and shows how drama differs from other narrative forms such as short stories and novels.

Mini-Lesson:
The Elements of Drama

After students have read the introduction, create a chart on the chalkboard of the basic elements of a drama: exposition, conflict, complications, climax, and resolution. Next, have students brainstorm for titles of familiar movies or of stories they have read. Ask them to select one story or movie and to identify each of the dramatic elements as you fill in the columns on the chalkboard. See the following chart for an example.

Elements of a Drama	Example: *Jurassic Park*
Exposition	Scientists and others learn about the park.
Conflict	Is the park safe for business?
Complications	Computer operator shuts down electricity, and dinosaurs run free.
Climax	Tyrannosaurus rex kills the velociraptors.
Resolution	The remaining people are rescued from the park.

Elements of Literature

DRAMA: An Introduction *by* Robert Anderson

A play is not written to be read. It is written to be performed on a stage by actors using speech and movements. You shouldn't have to read a program before you see a play. A good playwright reveals everything you need to know right on the stage.

In a short story a writer might write this:

Mary said, "Yes, I agree with you." But she really didn't.

In a play this might be written:

Mary. Yes, I agree with you. (*She really doesn't.*)

The actor must find a way of delivering this line that shows that Mary doesn't mean what she says. A play has no all-knowing storyteller who can take us inside Mary's mind and tell us what she is thinking.

In a movie or television show the director might zoom in for a close-up of Mary's face as she says the line, so that we can see the contradiction in her eyes. In the theater the director might have the actor pause a moment before saying the line or make a movement indicating that she doesn't mean what she says.

"Show, Don't Tell!"

"Show, don't tell," a prime rule in the theater, points up one of the differences between novels and plays. A novelist tells a story largely through narration and, usually, some description and dialogue. In contrast, a playwright must convey the *whole story* through **dialogue** (the characters' words) and stage action alone. Unlike dialogue in a novel, which might simply give you a feel for a character's personality, dialogue in a play must carry the whole story forward.

The Bare Bones of Drama

In drama, as in fiction, "story" consists of certain elements, which seem to have been part of storytelling from the beginning of time.

In the play's **exposition** the playwright introduces us to the characters and their environment (that is, to their **setting**). In some old-fashioned plays the exposition is delivered by a maid speaking on the phone. "Mr. and Mrs. Jones are not at home," she might say. "Mrs. Jones has gone away with her daughter, Daphne, and Mr. Jones has gone to live in a hotel." Thus we would learn that things are not going well in the Jones family.

Once we know something about the characters, we wait for a conflict to develop. **Conflict** is a struggle between opposing forces.

A clash between a character and an outside force is an **external conflict.** In the movie *Return of the Jedi,* for example, Luke Skywalker struggles with his father, Darth Vader. If the struggle occurs inside a character's mind, it is an **internal conflict.** Scrooge, the heartless miser in Charles Dickens's *A Christmas Carol,* for example, struggles with his own greed and selfishness before he emerges a changed man at the end of the story.

As the characters struggle with their conflicts, more problems, or **complications,** arise. This is what people mean when they say "The plot thickens." It has been said that a playwright first

Applying the E~~~~

As students read the follow~~~~
tion, have them fill out a chart ~~~~
to the one used in the mini-lesson.
Students should write down what
they feel are the teleplay's major
conflict, complications, climax, and
other elements.

gets a character up a tree, then throws stones at him, and then gets him down. In this scenario the stones are the complications.

Then we reach the most exciting part of the play, the **climax.** This is the moment, near the end of the play, when the conflict must be resolved. Now the tension is at its peak. In an action-adventure movie the climax would be the scene where the hero single-handedly lands a burning plane full of terrified passengers.

Finally, in the **resolution** of the play, the major problems are more or less resolved. At last the dramatic question posed at the beginning of the play is answered. Mrs. and Mrs. Jones get back together. Luke Skywalker defeats Darth Vader. The story ends.

Staging a Play: People Working Together

A playwright has to call on a large group of collaborators to help a play become a reality: a producer, a director, actors, set designers, lighting designers. All these people have their own talents and temperaments—and tempers! When I taught playwriting, I used to say, "Half the job is learning how to write a play. The other half is learning how to get along with people."

Television: A Special Type of Drama

Television may be the most intimate form of drama. It can make you feel close to characters, because it brings them right into your home.

Television plays share many characteristics with stage plays and movies, but they also have some special features. A television play often has a **narrator**—a voice that comments on the action. This narrator may create **suspense,** a feeling of anxious curiosity. For example, a narrator might begin the play by saying, "If I had known then what I know now, I never would have entered the dark house."

A television play can also switch scenes more quickly than a stage play. Many kinds of action that might be hard to represent realistically on-stage—a car chase, an underwater scene—can more easily be filmed for television.

The written form of any drama is called a **script.** A script for a movie is called a **screenplay.** A script for a television drama is called a **teleplay.** Like all scripts, a teleplay includes directions for props, setting, and the actors' movements and speech. A teleplay also contains instructions for the camera and for sound effects. These instructions allow you to imagine the drama as you read it. (For an explanation of terms used in a teleplay, see Reading a Teleplay, page 276.)

The Important Ingredient: Feeling

These elements of conflict, character, and story are only the bare bones of drama. They are like the wire frame on which a sculptor places layer upon layer of clay. What makes a play great is the talents of the writer. These include the ability to tell a good story and to tell it truly.

Resources
Assessment
Formal Assessment
• Literary Elements Test, p. 58

FROM THE EDITOR'S DESK
Robert Anderson's agent advised him not to work for us. She said textbook publishing would be a lot of work for him with little reward. In fact, she said the textbook project he was considering (ours) would probably never see the light of day. As you can see, Anderson did not take his agent's advice. Three editions later, his relationship with HRW is still remarkable.

ELEMENTS OF LITERATURE: DRAMA **271**

Using Students' Strengths

Kinesthetic

To help students understand the author's objective to *show* rather than to *tell,* brainstorm with them and write on the chalkboard several emotions or reactions, such as fear, anger, sadness, or confusion. Then, have volunteers act out those emotions or reactions in front of the class, by using facial expressions, gestures, or movements. Have the class identify the emotions that the volunteers are showing.

Interpersonal

Divide the class into small groups, and explain that each group will be producing a short dramatic presentation based on a popular TV show. Have each group choose a writer and a director. Other members will be the actors. The writer can decide what action will occur between the characters. The director's job is to tell the actors how to act and interact. The actors cooperate with the writer in developing dialogue. After setting a time limit for the creation and rehearsal of these short productions, ask for volunteers to be the first to present their group effort.

Reading Skills and Strategies

Reading Skills and Strategies

This feature focuses on the strategy of previewing the text, which readers use in forming impressions of a text or in predicting what its content will be. Students will have the opportunity to practice this strategy while they read *Brian's Song.*

Mini-Lesson:
Making Decisions

Begin by discussing movie previews students have seen recently and asking them to recall what they learned about the movies from those previews. Next, pass out to volunteers several books that you have collected from the school library or your own bookshelf. Have them look through the books to answer the questions posed in Making Decisions: Previewing the Text. Finally, approach *Brian's Song* with these same questions, along with the suggestions in Time for the Feature Presentation, and ask students what they can discover about the teleplay before they begin reading it.

MAKING DECISIONS: PREVIEWING THE TEXT

Movie producers know how important previews are. Previews show us a movie's most exciting scenes or funniest lines and leave us curious about what we *didn't* see. Producers know we will decide whether to see a movie largely on the basis of a preview we've seen.

Readers also make decisions on the basis of previews. Walk into any bookstore and you'll see a lot of previewing going on. People are examining book jackets and illustrations, skimming the texts, looking at the tables of contents or indexes.

Previewing can also be useful when you're assigned a text to read in school. Previewing helps you predict what you'll find in the text. It can also help you decide what strategies to use as you read. As you preview a text, ask yourself these questions:

- **Format.** What kind of text is this? (A play, a novel, a history book?)

- **Titles and subtitles.** What is the general topic? Do I already know something about this topic that will help me as I read? Does the topic interest me? What could the title mean? Is it a good title?

- **Difficulty.** Does the text contain a lot of factual information? Should I take notes as I read?

- **Vocabulary.** Does it contain technical terms or other challenging words? Will I need to read this slowly?

- **Visuals.** Are there special features such as maps, graphs, or stage directions?

Time for the Feature Presentation

As you look through *Brian's Song,* you'll notice that it's set up in the format of a teleplay. There are camera directions, descriptions of sets, sound instructions, directions for the actors. If you flip to page 276, you'll find a list of terms used in a typical screenplay. You should be familiar with these terms; they'll help you visualize the action of the play—as if you were viewing it on a TV screen.

Preview the play for a few minutes. What else do you notice about the text? What is your first response to the text—does it look interesting to you?

Apply the strategy on the next page.

Before You Read

BRIAN'S SONG

Make the Connection

Friendly Foes

Some people say that we need friends more than anything else in life. We are also competitive, though—we want to win—and sometimes competition can cause conflicts between even the closest of friends. Suppose that you and a friend are competing for the same thing—a part in a play, a spot on the team, a special honor or award. Would you

- go all out to win, no matter what?
- talk over the problem and hope you can remain friends?
- put your friendship ahead of your desire to win?

Quickwrite

Write briefly about your responses to these questions about competition and friendship. What matters more to you—winning or friendship? Save your notes.

Reading Skills and Strategies

Previewing the Text

A play usually opens with an introductory scene that gives you some information about its **setting,** or the place and time in which the events occur. Preview the beginning of *Brian's Song.* What details in the **stage and camera directions** (instructions for actors and camera operators) tell you *where* the characters are?

Background

A Tale of Two Rookies

Brian's Song is a television drama based on the true story of Gale Sayers and Brian Piccolo, two new recruits for the Chicago Bears football team. It is what Hollywood would call a buddy movie, the story of two men who compete with each other, joke with each other, get angry with each other, and finally learn to love each other.

The two rookies couldn't be more different. Gale, an African American, is quiet and shy. Brian, an Italian American, is outgoing and talkative. What the two players have in common is a strong desire to make the team. Many struggles, small and large, take place in this play, with everything from a place on the team to a human life at stake. Sometimes what happens will make you laugh, but just as often this story will make you want to cry.

go.hrw.com
LEO 7-4

BRIAN'S SONG **273**

Preteaching Vocabulary

Words to Own

Have pairs of students read the definitions of the Words to Own listed at the bottom of the selection pages. Then, use the following exercises to reinforce students' understanding of the words.

1. Practice walking in a way that is a **saunter.** Then, show how one **pivots.**
2. Make up a situation that would leave you feeling **disheartened.**
3. Describe a time when you reacted in an

impassive way.
4. Mimic someone who behaves in an **insolent** manner.
5. How does a **surly** person act?
6. Tell whether being **stoic** is a good way to deal with life's difficulties.
7. Describe something you would only do with great **reluctance.**
8. How does a person with an **enigmatic** smile look?

T273

Brian's Song

William Blinn

Summary ■ ■

Gale Sayers, a gifted NFL rookie, is nervous and introverted when he arrives at the Chicago Bears' training camp. There he meets Brian Piccolo, a fellow player and something of a prankster. Sayers and Piccolo are competing for the same job—halfback—and soon develop a friendly rivalry. They also become roommates. When Sayers injures his leg badly, Piccolo helps him through the long rehabilitation period.

The two friends continue playing football until Piccolo is diagnosed with lung cancer. In the long medical battle that ensues, both men show great courage, generosity, and devotion. By the play's end, readers realize that they have witnessed the development of a special friendship that transcends all barriers.

Background

This teleplay is based on a true story: the friendship and rivalry between two professional football players—Gale Sayers, one of the best runners in football history, and Brian Piccolo, another talented halfback.

Resources

Viewing and Representing
Videocassette A, Segment 4
The *Visual Connections* videocassette segment "Teamwork in the Sky" will spur students to consider the importance of teamwork in *Brian's Song*. The video is a behind-the-scenes look at a precision military flying group.
See the *Visual Connections Teacher's Manual*.

Resources: Print and Media

Reading
- *Reading Skills and Strategies*
  MiniRead Skill Lesson, p. 166
  Selection Skill Lesson, p. 174
- *Graphic Organizers for Active Reading*, pp. 19, 20
- *Words to Own*, pp. 13, 14
- *Spelling and Decoding*
  Worksheet, p. 16
- *Audio CD Library*
  Disc 8, Track 5

Elements of Literature
- *Literary Elements*
  Transparency 4
  Worksheet, p. 13

Writing and Language
- *Daily Oral Grammar*
  Transparencies 17, 18
- *Grammar and Language Links*
  Worksheet, p. 31

Viewing and Representing
- *Viewing and Representing*

Fine Art Transparency 9
Fine Art Worksheet, p. 36
- *Visual Connections*
  Videocassette A, Segment 4

Assessment
- *Formal Assessment*, pp. 54, 56
- *Portfolio Management System*, p. 139
- *Standardized Test Preparation*, pp. 46, 48, 50
- *Test Generator (One-Stop Planner CD-ROM)*

Internet
- go.hrw.com (keyword: LE0 7-4)

They came to know each other,

fight each other,

and help each other . . .

275

Resources

Listening
Audio CD Library
A spirited reading of an excerpt from this teleplay is provided in the *Audio CD Library:*
- Disc 8, Track 5

Selection Assessment
Formal Assessment
- Selection Test, p. 54
Test Generator
- Selection Test

Viewing and Representing
Fine Art Transparency
A transparency of Robert M. Cunningham's *The Raiders at Santa Rosa* can be used with this lesson as part of the prereading process.
- Transparency 9
- Worksheet, p. 36

Elements of Literature
For additional instruction on drama, see *Literary Elements:*
- Transparency 4
- Worksheet, p. 13

FROM THE EDITOR'S DESK

Because of its snappy style and unique inside look at pro football, this teleplay evokes rave reviews from seventh-graders. Students identify quickly with the two football heroes who overcome obstacles to make their mark in one of the nation's favorite games. Moreover, in overcoming their racial differences, Gale Sayers and Brian Piccolo serve as role models for us all.

Reaching All Students

Struggling Readers
Previewing the Text was introduced on p. 272. For a lesson directly tied to this selection that teaches students to preview the text by using a strategy called Text Reformulation, see *Reading Skills and Strategies* binder:
- MiniRead Skill Lesson, p. 166
- Selection Skill Lesson, p. 174

English Language Learners
One approach to engaging English language learners is to ask them to listen to the recording of the selection in the *Audio CD Library.* For additional strategies to supplement instruction for these students, see
- *Lesson Plans Including Strategies for English-Language Learners*

Advanced Learners
As students read the teleplay, ask them to rewrite scenes as if they were episodes from a novel. Explain that they can use some of the same dialogue in their episodes, but they will need to add narrative to connect the episodes. Also suggest that students create specific sensory details to include in their scenes.

A Reading Skills and Strategies

Previewing the Text

Have students look through the selection pages and tell what kind of text they think *Brian's Song* is. How can they tell? [Teleplay. Indicators include camera directions, descriptions of sets, sound instructions.] Have students discuss whether they enjoy plays.

B Reading Skills and Strategies

Previewing the Text

Ask students to preview the list of useful terms for reading a teleplay. How will these terms, originally intended for the director and camera crew, help an ordinary reader of the teleplay? [Possible responses: The terms will help the reader see and hear the action of the play better. The terms will prompt the reader's imagination.]

A **Reading a Teleplay**

In a **screenplay** (a script for a movie) or a **teleplay** (a script for TV) the camera directions are very important. Camera directions help you imagine what you would *see* on the screen. Like many teleplays, *Brian's Song* uses a **narrator,** or unseen speaker, to comment on the action.

Study this list of terms so that you can recognize and understand them as you read *Brian's Song.*

Voice-over: the voice of a character who is off camera or who is on camera but not shown to be speaking.

Fade In: The picture slowly appears on the screen.

Fade Out: The picture slowly disappears from the screen.

Exterior: outdoors.

Interior: indoors.

Beat: pause.

Long shot: a view from a distance.

Tight on; close shot: a close-up camera shot.

Full shot: a camera shot showing a complete view of the character(s) or scene.

Pan: short for *panorama;* the camera swings slowly from one side of the set to the other.

Hard cut to: shift abruptly to (a different scene).

Angle on or to: position the camera on (a character or scene).

Zoom: move in quickly for a close view or away for a distant view.

Freeze frame; hold: remain focused on one image for a few seconds.

For a Glossary of Football Terms used in Brian's Song, *see* Literature and Sports, *pages 280–281.*

B

Characters

NARRATOR, *voice that comments on the action*

BRIAN PICCOLO ⎫ *running backs for the*
GALE SAYERS ⎭ *Chicago Bears*

GEORGE HALAS, *coach of the Bears*

J. C. CAROLINE ⎫
ABE GIBRON ⎬ *assistant coaches of the*
ED MCCASKEY ⎭ *Bears*

ATKINS ⎫
EVEY ⎬ *players for the Bears*
O'BRADOVICH ⎭

REPORTERS

LINDA SAYERS, *Gale's wife*

JOY PICCOLO, *Brian's wife*

SPEAKER, *at an awards ceremony*

JACK CONCANNON, *quarterback of the Bears*

ANNOUNCER, *radio sportscaster*

DR. FOX, *who treats Gale*

NURSES

HOTEL OFFICIAL

PLAYER, *Gale's new roommate*

MR. EBERLE, *hospital official*

DOCTOR, *who gives Brian anesthesia*

M.C., *master of ceremonies*

Using Students' Strengths

Kinesthetic Learners

As part of the reading process, from time to time ask volunteers to act out the roles of Gale and Brian. Encourage the students to use their bodies and voices to portray the main traits of these two characters. At the end of a scene, the actors can briefly freeze, creating a tableau, while other members of the class discuss the characters and events.

Visual Learners

As visual learners read the teleplay, they may benefit from filling in the form located in *Graphic Organizers for Active Reading,* p. 19.

Part One

Fade In:

Exterior—Rolling countryside—Day (helicopter shot)

The terrain is farmland, flat, tranquil, soothing in its simplicity. As our view gets closer to the ground, we start to hear the Narrator's voice.

> NARRATOR (*voice-over*). This is a story about two men, one named Gale Sayers, the other Brian Piccolo. They came from different parts of the country. They competed for the same job. One was white; the other black. One liked to talk; the other was as shy as a three-year-old. Our story's about how they came to know each other, fight each other, and help each other. . . .
> (*beat*)
> Ernest Hemingway said that every true story ends in death. Well, this *is* a true story.

As the helicopter continues its descent, we now find ourselves following a cab down a two-lane asphalt road. We follow the cab as we roll opening credits.

Direct cut to:

Exterior—Campus-type area—Day— On sign

Reading "Training Camp of the Chicago Bears," an NFL insignia beneath the lettering. We pan off the sign, moving by a number of red-brick buildings, the kind of ivied architecture seen at any number of small universities in the Middle West. Coming up the curving blacktopped drive is the cab.

Exterior—Practice field—Series of cuts

The Bears are going through the various routines and exercises. Defensive linemen scuttling crablike back and forth as a coach switches a ball from hand to hand. Men working on the blocking sled, throwing their bulk against the padded metal arm. Players negotiating the rope framework, some alternating, crossing over, others hopping from square to square. Throughout these cuts, the sounds of men under strain, struggling for breath, grunting with effort as they bear down.

As we zoom toward the far end of the field, we see Gale Sayers standing by the driver's side of the cab, his suitcase next to him.

Sayers is in his early twenties, his handsome face normally enigmatic, guarded. He's dressed in slacks and sport coat, but even in this kind of "civilian" garb, it doesn't take a practiced eye to note the lean, hard compactness of a born athlete.

> BRIAN (*voice-over*). Heads up! Look out!

Gale looks toward the sound of the voice just in time to react to the football hurtling down toward him. He gets a hand up and slaps it away, over the cab. Gale walks across to the other side of the road to get the football and throws it to the young man now approaching him. He's wearing a Bears sweat shirt, workout shorts, football cleats. This is Brian Piccolo—early twenties, with a smile that comes easily and nicely. He takes life and people as he finds them, and he generally finds them worthwhile, enjoyable, and a little funny. The face is strong and handsome. Gale throws the ball back across the road to him.

> GALE. Here you go.
> BRIAN. Thanks.

Brian heaves the ball back to the practice area offstage, though he makes no move to

---

WORDS TO OWN
enigmatic (en′ig·mat′ik) *adj.:* mysterious; like a riddle.

A Reading Skills
and Strategies

**Previewing
the Text**

Ask students to preview pp. 278 and 279 to see where the next scenes take place and who will be in them. [The scenes take place in the coach's offices, where Gale meets with Coach Halas.]

B Reading Skills
and Strategies

Making Inferences

❓ How do you know that Brian is trying to be funny here and not unkind? [The stage directions say his smile is a nice one and that his lines are a "put-on."]

C Elements of Literature

Character

❓ Why doesn't Gale smile or respond to Brian's comments? [Possible responses: Gale might be very nervous about being at training camp; he may not know what to think of Brian's kidding; perhaps he thinks Brian is making fun of him.]

A *return there himself. Gale is a little ill at ease as Brian just stands there looking at him with a half smile.*

> **BRIAN.** You're Gale Sayers.
> **GALE.** Yeah.
> **BRIAN.** I'm Brian Piccolo. We met at the All-America game last June in Buffalo.

Brian has extended his hand, but Gale is holding his suitcase. A short beat as Gale switches hands, but by the time it's done, Brian has taken back his hand, and there's a moment of stuttering reactions. Finally, they shake hands. Gale's head is down, face guarded.

> **GALE.** Sorry I didn't remember, but I'm not very good at that kind of stuff.

Piccolo's smile is a nice one.

> **BRIAN** (*a quiet put-on*). Golly, that's okay. I can see why you might forget, but I sure couldn't. No way. That was a heckuva talk we had, man. I mean, I walked up and said: "I'm Brian Piccolo. I hear we'll both be playing for the Bears." And you said—I'll never forget it—you said: "Uh-huh." Just like that. "Uh-huh." And whenever I'm feeling depressed or low, why, I think about that advice. Lot of guys wouldn't have taken the time to talk to me like that, but not you. "Uh-huh," you said. Just like that. Right out.

Brian grins. Gale does not. His expression is neutral. A short beat.

> **GALE.** Where do I go to check in?

Piccolo's smile goes. The total lack of reaction from Gale is puzzling. He nods toward one of the buildings offstage.

> **BRIAN.** That building over there. That's where Halas is.
> **GALE.** Thanks.

278 WE ROOKIES HAVE TO STICK TOGETHER

The word comes in a characteristic flat tone. Gale moves off for the building. Brian stands there a moment, looking after him thoughtfully.

> **BRIAN.** Hey . . .

Gale stops, looking back.

> **GALE.** What?
> **BRIAN.** You ever met Halas before?
> **GALE.** Talked to him on the phone a couple times. That's all.

Brian's manner is calm, pleasant, helpful.

> **BRIAN.** Well, look, let me give you a little hint. He's a good guy and all, but he's deaf in his left ear and he's too vain to admit it. So stay on his right-hand side, or he won't hear a word you say.
>   (*beat*)
> **GALE.** Uh—okay. Thanks.
> **BRIAN.** Rookies have to stick together, man.

With a wave of his hand, Brian starts off, moving at an easy lope back onto the practice field. Sayers stands there, watching Brian, not knowing precisely what to make of him. After a moment, he turns and starts for the building pointed out by Piccolo.

> **Direct cut to:**

Interior—Bears' main office corridor— Full shot

Gale comes in looking about uneasily, then heads for the end of the corridor. He stops in front of a door with a nameplate reading "Coach George Halas," wipes his sweating palms on his trouser legs, then knocks on the door.

> **HALAS** (*impatiently, offstage*). Yeah. Come in.

Gale stands motionless for a second, gathering his forces, then opens the door and steps inside.

Taking a Second Look

Review: Making Inferences

Remind students that authors can't say everything in a selection. Instead they expect readers to put two and two together and to draw their own inferences. Explain that making an inference is like making an educated guess.

Activities

1. As students read *Brian's Song*, ask volunteers to make some inferences. Suggest that they point to details in the text as well as list the prior knowledge they used to reach the inference.

2. Have students read the play in groups, stopping at points where it is necessary to make an inference or draw a conclusion. Encourage students to discuss their inferences.

3. After students read the play, have volunteers explain how making inferences added to their understanding and enjoyment of the play.

Interior—Halas's office—Full shot

As Gale comes into the office, he starts to speak, but his voice is only a dry croak. The office is in a state of organized chaos. Cardboard filing boxes, cartons of books, and papers. Reels of film and, standing behind an ancient desk, a large man of some years, some strength, and much power: Halas. He holds a framed picture, hammer, and nails. He looks at the young man standing in the doorway.

HALAS. I'm George Halas.
GALE. I know. (*Quickly*) I mean, everyone knows who you are. I'm Gale Sayers.
HALAS. Come on in, Gale. You can give me a hand hanging this thing. My good luck picture. First professional team I ever played on. The Decatur Staleys in 1920.

Gale steps in, closing the door, still awed and afraid. Halas moves to an empty place on the wall, his back to Gale.

HALAS. How's your leg? I read where it was hurt.
GALE. It's fine. Hundred percent.
HALAS. How about your head?
GALE. My head? Nothin' wrong with my head.
HALAS. Good. Because being in the All-Star game puts you three weeks behind everybody else. New terminology, new plays to learn. Won't be easy.
    (*beat*)
GALE. NFL[1] ain't supposed to be easy.

A smile and look from Halas. He nods.

HALAS. Right. Give me a hand.

Gale moves behind the desk, where Halas is holding the picture up against the wall. Halas starts hammering a nail.

HALAS. About all I can promise you is a fair

1. **NFL:** National Football League.

shot at running back. But you're going to have a lot of company. Jon Arnett, Ralph Kurek, Brian Piccolo . . . going to be very crowded out there.

Gale looks at Halas for a second, realizing he's on the man's left side, recalling the advice given him by Brian earlier. He rumbas around behind and then to the other side of the Coach.

GALE. Well, a fair shot is all I want. Can't ask for more than that.

Halas notes Gale's shift with a puzzled look, then drives the nail home. He turns back to the desk, once more placing Gale on his left side.

HALAS. We plan to use our backs a good deal as receivers this year. You do much pass catching when you were in college?

He looks back to where Gale was, only to find that Gale has crossed behind him.

GALE. Well, yes sir, I did, but it was usually safety-valve stuff. Once in a while we'd screen.

Halas moves to one of the filing cabinets nearby.

HALAS. Well, I generally prefer to get a back into the pattern, unless the other team has a tendency to blitz. That's another thing you'll have to get used to, checking out the linebackers, make sure they aren't coming.

Halas looks back to Gale, but once again, he's the man who isn't there. Gale has managed to cross behind him again, squeezing in between Halas and the wall, struggling to make the move seem casual.

GALE. Yes sir, I know . . .

Halas starts back to the desk, once again forcing Gale to do an end around.

GALE. . . . and, especially on teams like the Cardinals, I guess . . .

D Elements of Literature
Drama: Conflict
❓ What conflict will probably develop between Gale and Brian now that they are both at training camp? [They will be competing with each other for the same running back position.]

E Reading Skills and Strategies
Drawing Conclusions
❓ Why is Gale moving around the room while Coach Halas is speaking to him? [Possible response: Gale is trying to follow Brian's advice to stay on the side of the coach's good ear.]

F Vocabulary Note
Technical Words
To check the meaning of *blitz*, have students turn to the glossary of football terms on pp. 280–281. Encourage them to use the glossary as they read the play.

Using Students' Strengths

Interpersonal Learners
Have students imagine they are directing *Brian's Song*. Have them direct their classmates on how to say the lines and perform the actions described in the stage directions. Encourage the directors to explain what each character is thinking or feeling at a particular moment and how the actors can express thoughts and feelings through words and movements.

Logical/Mathematical Learners
Invite students to create a Venn diagram in which they show some of the ways in which Gale and Brian are both alike and different. Suggest that they focus mainly on the personality traits of the two characters.

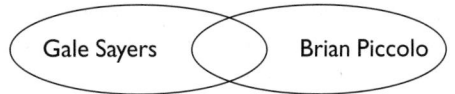

Gale Sayers   Brian Piccolo

T279

A Reading Skills and Strategies

Previewing the Text

Invite students to preview the terms in the glossary and tell how they can use this list. [Possible response: Looking back at the glossary is a good way to understand the specialized football terms in the teleplay.]

B Reading Skills and Strategies

Making Predictions

? What do you think might happen between Gale and Brian now? [Possible response: Since Brian's practical joke has made Gale look foolish, there might be some trouble between the players if Gale tries to get even.]

C Appreciating Language

Exaggeration

? Why do you think the author used humorous overstatements like these in the stage directions, which the TV audience would not have seen? [Possible response: The exaggeration would indicate to the director and actors how the scene should be played.]

A Glossary of Football Terms

All sports and jobs have their special vocabularies. What's an end run? a punt return? What's the difference between a flanker and a kicker? If you're a rookie when it comes to football vocabulary, this glossary will help.

defensive linemen: players who hold the line (the team's position) against the advancing offense, which has the ball.

blocking sled: device with a padded metal arm against which players hurl themselves during practice to increase their capacity to block the opposition.

rope framework: rope grid through which players run during practice to increase their agility.

rookie: first-year player.

running back: offensive player who handles the ball.

screen: protect the receiver of a pass with a wall of players known as blockers.

blitz: have more than the usual number of defensive players charge the opposing team's quarterback while he is trying to pass.

offensive back: running back.

HALAS (*exasperated*). Sayers—what's the matter with you?

GALE. I—I don't know what you mean . . .

HALAS. I know you've got moves, but you don't have to show them to me now! You're hopping around here like a pauper[2] in a pay toilet!

GALE (*sputtering*). Well, I—I was just trying to stay on the side with your good ear . . .

HALAS. Good ear? What are you talking about, good ear?

GALE. Well, Brian Piccolo told me that— he said—uh—he—uh . . .

Halas waits for the sentence to end, but it's not going to. For the realization is slowly dawning on Gale that he has been had. Gale struggles to manufacture a smile as Halas stares at him.

2. **pauper** (pô′pər): person without any money.

280 WE ROOKIES HAVE TO STICK TOGETHER

Direct cut to:
Interior—Dining hall—Night—Angle on steam table

The table is piled with food being assaulted by a number of large men, who ladle on portions that would choke a garbage disposal. At a centrally placed table, we can see Halas, his coaches, and key players.

Closer angle—Coaches' table

Seated on one side of Halas is Ed McCaskey, a handsome man in his early fifties. On the other side is Abe Gibron, a man who is all football. One man at the table is standing. This is J. C. Caroline, a man in his late twenties, tall and lean, built for speed. He has a packet of three-by-five index cards he consults as he speaks.

CAROLINE. Some of you guys who pulled in today haven't had a chance to hear what's

---

Getting Students Involved

Cooperative Learning

Research. Have students form small groups to research the way college football athletes are chosen to play in the professional leagues. Students might focus on how many players enter the leagues each year and what types of salaries and bonuses a star player can expect to earn. Have the groups consolidate their findings and present them in an oral report to the class.

Enrichment Activity

Journal Entries. Encourage students to create journal entries for Brian and Gale in which they describe their first meetings. In their journals, the players can also describe their feelings about being rookies at the training camp. Guide students to see that Gale and Brian would probably feel curiosity, uncertainty, and excitement as they adjust to their new lives.

three-point stance: crouched down with one hand touching the ground in a "ready" position.

halfback option: choice of the halfback to run with the ball or throw it when he gets it from the quarterback.

flanker: wide receiver who catches passes and is a fast runner.

scrimmage: here, a practice game.

second string: alternate players.

fullback: bigger, stronger running back who often leads interference and blocks the opposition's attempts to reach the carrier of the ball.

pitch-out: play in which the quarterback tosses the ball behind him to the running back instead of handing it off to him.

carries: acts of holding the ball and running with it.

game ball: ball that's used in game and may be awarded to the most valuable player in that game.

number two halfback: substitute or alternate halfback.

punt return: attempt by a player (the punt returner) to gain yards toward his team's goal by catching the ball after it has been punted (kicked) to the other team.

kicker: player who kicks to start the play or kicks field goals. Kickers don't have to be strong or quick since they usually don't have to block or run.

end run: a strategy whereby the quarterback hands the ball back to the running back, who runs around the line to score a touchdown.

D Vocabulary Note
Multiple Meanings
Mention that the word *Bible* is sometimes used to describe a book that is very important to a group of people involved in a common activity.

E Critical Thinking
Analyzing
Ask students to suggest what the playbook is and why coaches fine players $500 if they lose it. [Possible response: The playbook lists all the plays that a team uses in its games, information that would be valuable to an opposing team. The high fine is a way to make sure that no player allows the book to fall into the wrong hands.]

F Elements of Literature
Drama: Conflict
Have students note that Gale and Brian remain in character during this exchange. Gale is annoyed by Brian's attempts at familiarity and his jokes.

going to be expected of you, so pipe down for a little bit, let me talk.

Angle on Gale

He is seated at one of the rear tables, exchanging "pass-the-salt" conversations with the other men nearby, all of whom are black. The man next to Gale finishes his plate and vacates the chair as Caroline continues to speak offstage. Brian Piccolo approaches and starts to unload his tray in the place next to Gale. Gale tries to hide his displeasure.

CAROLINE (*droning offstage*). You new guys are going to be given a playbook tomorrow. It's like the Bible, except the Gideons[3] don't replace it for free. Neither do the Bears. Lose the playbook and the fine is five hundred dollars. No exceptions, no appeal. Five-double-o. Second thing is

3. **Gideons** (gid'ē·ənz): Gideons International, a Protestant organization that places Bibles in hotels and hospitals.

curfew. You don't like it; I don't like it. Well, that's just tough sleddin', because that fine is ten bucks for every fifteen minutes and there's no appeal from that either. Now—for talking in team meeting . . .

Caroline becomes aware of Gale and Brian speaking offstage.

BRIAN. Sayers, we can't go on meeting like this—my wife's getting suspicious.

GALE. Buzz off. I'm trying to listen to the Man.

BRIAN. No need, no need. I've been through this lecture twice already. If you lose the playbook, a fine of five big ones. Lose the playbook a second time, and they cut off your foot and feed it to the defensive platoon.

GALE. Just cool it, would you, please?

BRIAN. Just trying to be helpful.

GALE. Yes—like you "helped" me with Halas. Well, I don't need your kind of . . .

BRIAN'S SONG, PART ONE 281

Crossing the Curriculum

Social Studies
To appreciate the play fully, students should be aware of the state of race relations and the role of African American athletes in 1965, the year in which Gale and Brian are depicted as coming to the Bears. Students can research the civil rights movement, the racial composition of football teams, or the role of African Americans in sports at that time. Form groups of students to collect information from different sources, create visual aids, and give oral reports to the class.

Music
Ask interested students to find examples of football fight songs, such as the one Brian sings, and play them for the class. Have them explain how the music tends to rouse the emotions of the crowd.

Mathematics
Have students locate sports pages from newspapers or magazines that list statistics for college or professional football teams. Ask students to research what the statistics mean. Have them explain their findings to the class and show how statisticians arrive at their figures.

CAROLINE (*loudly offstage*). *Mister* Sayers!

Wider angle

J. C. Caroline fixes Gale with the look that's chilled any number of feckless[4] flankers. Every eye in the room is on Gale, and most are relishing his pained reaction.

> CAROLINE (*continuing*). I was mentioning the fine for talking in a team meeting. Did you happen to hear me?
> GALE. No, I did not.
> CAROLINE. The fine is twenty-five dollars, Mr. Sayers. And it's just been levied on you, *dig?*
> GALE (*seething*). Yeah.

Piccolo stares straight ahead, lips trembling as he tries to mask the laughter building up within him.

> BRIAN (*sotto*). Sorry, man . . .

Gale glares at him, homicide[5] in mind. Slow homicide.

Caroline gets to his feet, tapping the water glass for attention.

> CAROLINE. It's been brought to my attention that unless Sayers was saying his beads[6] it might be fair if Mr. Piccolo was to give us a little song. Say—a fight song. Wake Forest, wasn't it, Mr. Piccolo?

Angle to Brian and Gale

Gale's look acknowledges that there may be some justice in this old world after all. To his surprise, however, the singing troubles Brian not at all. He smiles, rising, and when he sees the surprise on Gale's face, leans over to whisper.

> BRIAN. Can't let it get to you, man—it's all a question of *style.* Style, I say . . .

4. **feckless:** careless.
5. **homicide** (häm′ə·sīd): murder.
6. **beads:** rosary beads, a string of beads used by Roman Catholics to keep count while saying certain prayers.

282 WE ROOKIES HAVE TO STICK TOGETHER

He is up on the chair, launching into the Wake Forest fight song, giving it a rousing tempo and booming volume. Brian thrives on this kind of thing. Gale's eye falls on something offstage in the direction of Brian's plate.

Gale's point of view—The plate

Shot is centered on two mammoth dollops of mashed potatoes swimming in rich brown gravy.

Angle on Gale

He takes a spoon and fork, glancing up to make sure Brian is still concentrating on the song, then moves to transfer the potatoes to the seat of Brian's chair.

As he finishes the song, Brian waves a cordial hand to those clapping, then hops down lightly and sits—without looking. Gale just sits there, looking at Brian, enjoying the rush of expressions that go rolling across his face. Disbelief. Dread. Realization. A look to the absent mashed potatoes on his plate. Acceptance. By the time he slowly swings his look over to Gale, Gale is just getting to his feet, face composed. Before he goes, however, he reminds Brian.

> GALE. It's all a question of style— style, I say . . .

He moves off, camera closing on Piccolo. He turns squishily, watching Gale saunter *off. He can't quite work up a smile, but neither can he get to a point of being very angry about it. He can take it as well as hand it out, it seems.*

Direct cut to:

Exterior—Practice field—Day—Tight on Gibron

Abe Gibron is an assistant coach possessed of

WORDS TO OWN
saunter (sôn′tər) *v.:* stroll; walk in an unhurried way.

Getting Students Involved

a voice that could shatter glass. When we pull back, we will see that Gibron is presently riding herd on a number of offensive backs, Sayers and Piccolo in the forefront, as they lower their heads and dig against the resistance of the harness looped about their shoulders and fastened to a stone wall. Gibron will not be happy until one of the men pulls down the wall.

GIBRON. Dig! Dig! Dig! Come on! What's wrong with you? You're not trying! You're not trying! You make me sick! Dig—dig—dig!

Hard cut to:

Exterior—Practice field—Day—Full shot

Fifty men hit the dirt, then are up on their feet, running in place.

GIBRON. Mark! Set! Go!

Sayers and Piccolo come out of a sprinter's crouch, taking each other on in wind sprints, their faces locked with drive and desire.

Angle to the forty-yard line

Halas and a number of other coaches are standing. Gale tears across the line a full stride ahead of the others. Stopwatches are held out for Halas's perusal.[7] He notes the results and is pleased.

Angle on Gale and Brian

They draw up, both sagging, leaning forward, hands on knees as they try to pull more air in. This may be the tenth wind sprint they've run today. Between gasps of breath:

BRIAN. Well—I think it's working.
GALE. What's working?
BRIAN. I'm getting you overconfident.

Hard cut to:

Interior—Team meeting room—Day— On blackboard

---

7. **perusal** (pə·rōō′zəl): studying; careful reading.

A play is diagramed on the blackboard, the area covered with circles and X's, dotted lines, and arrows. Halas is the man with the chalk. No need to hear what he's saying—his look and the manner in which he raps the chalk against the slate get the message across.

Angle on Sayers and Piccolo

They are seated near the front with the rest of the players, all of whom are studying the board as if their lives depended on it. Which, in one sense, it does. The look of exhaustion is shared by all as they listen and frantically scribble notes.

Direct cut to:

Exterior—Practice field—Day—Full shot

The offense and defense take measure of one another. They line up, the ball is snapped. There is a brief flurry of motion, then the quarterback is downed by a large man from the defensive unit. As they all untangle themselves to the accompaniment of the whistles, Brian gets up and finds himself being glared at by Abe Gibron.

GIBRON. Pic! You bonehead! That was a fake draw, screen right! What's your assignment on a fake draw, screen right?
BRIAN. My assignment on a fake draw, screen right, is to pick up the linebacker, if he's coming, unless the linebacker is Dick Butkus. Then I simply notify the quarterback and send for a priest.

Laughter from the others on this, which only further enrages Gibron.

Angle on Gale

He is smiling broadly at Piccolo's reply—smiling, perhaps, in spite of himself.

GIBRON (*offstage*). Come on, you guys, don't! You just encourage him, that's all! Knock it off!

BRIAN'S SONG, PART ONE 283

Drama: Conflict

❓ From his remarks here, what does Brian seem to be struggling with inside himself? [Possible response: He is struggling with his own uncertainty about whether he is good enough to learn the plays and make the team.]

B **Reading Skills and Strategies**

Connecting to the Text

❓ Would you say that you're more like Gale Sayers or Brian Piccolo? Why? [Invite volunteers to make their comparisons.]

C **Critical Thinking**

Interpreting

❓ Since Brian and Gale are competing for the same position, why do you think Gale shares this secret with Brian? [Possible responses: Gale is starting to like Brian and wants to help him; Gale may also feel that Brian has little chance to outplay him.]

Direct cut to:
Exterior—Practice field—Night—Full shot

Gale moves along the walk bordering the practice area, dressed in casual sports clothes, an after-dinner stroll. He nears us, then stops, looking offstage, expression puzzled.

His point of view—On Brian

In the middle of the empty practice field, he falls into a three-point stance, counts off a whispered series of signals, then breaks to his right. Just as he's about to turn upfield, he brakes sharply and cocks his arm, letting an imaginary pass go. Apparently, the imaginary receiver caught the ball, because Piccolo's expression is pleased as he turns back—and sees Gale watching his pantomime.[8] He shrugs.

BRIAN. I'm dynamite until there's someone playing against me.

Another angle

Gale moves to him, still a little puzzled.

BRIAN. Practicing the halfback option. I'm not too good at it, and it looks as if they want to use it a lot.
GALE (*politely*). Oh, you'll get the hang of it.

Brian smiles.

BRIAN. Wish I was as sure of that as you are. Tell you the truth, Sayers—I envy you.
GALE. How come?
BRIAN. Because they've got a lot of money tied up in you. They can't cut you.

Gale just looks at him for a second, then turns abruptly and starts off.

BRIAN (*simply*). And you're too good to get cut, bonus or no bonus.

8. **pantomime** (pan′tə·mīm′): dramatic presentation using only silent actions and gestures.

Gale stops, turns back slowly.
(*beat*)

BRIAN. And I'm too good, too, but I'm not sure I've proved that to the Old Man yet.

Gale is thrown off stride mentally. Piccolo's easy directness takes some getting used to. Brian views him with a small smile.

BRIAN. Sayers—I am bending over backwards to get through that turtle shell of yours. Can't you at least say thank you or something?
GALE. Well—I don't do things like you do—telling jokes and all that kind of—you know—I—I'm more of a . . . (*Considers*) Thanks.

A quick nod, then Gale turns and heads back in the direction of the dormitory. Piccolo smiles, taking even this small breakthrough as some kind of progress. He gets to his feet and is about to go through the halfback option once more.

GALE. Hey, Piccolo?
BRIAN. Yeah?
GALE. Try it going to your left. They don't look for a right-handed guy to throw going to his left.

Brian nods, smiling as their eyes meet; Gale's look still a guarded one.
(*beat*)

BRIAN. Thanks.

Gale shrugs, glances down.

GALE. Well, like you said—us rookies got to stick together.

Hard cut to:
Interior—Hallway outside Halas's office—Day—On door

Gale raps on the door several times.

HALAS (*offstage*). Come on in, Gale.

Gale opens the door and steps in, camera following to reveal Halas behind the desk, Ed McCaskey seated nearby, and J. C. Caroline doodling on the blackboard. Gale views the three with a mixture of fear and curiosity.

HALAS. You know Ed McCaskey, don't you, Gale? And J.C.?

Affirmative ad-libs[9] come from Gale and the other two men. Gale takes the chair that has obviously been left vacant for him. Halas nods toward a pitcher of iced tea.

HALAS. Want some iced tea?
GALE. Uh, yeah. Please.

Halas pours him a glass, the cubes tinkling. Gale fidgets. Halas hands him the glass.

HALAS. Tell you what we wanted to talk to you about, Gale . . . See, I'm an old-timer in a lot of ways . . . (*A look to Caroline and McCaskey*) At least that's what people keep telling me—but I don't think it's all that uncommon for a man my age to get used to the way things are—to be comfortable with things. You understand what I'm saying?
GALE (*baffled*). I guess so. . . .
HALAS. Well, what it comes down to is that J.C. here had a notion and he talked to Ed about it, and Ed thinks it's a good idea—and I guess maybe it's time for some changes around here. You follow me?
GALE. You want me to play flanker, not running back.

The other three exchange a smile at this.

MCCASKEY. Not that simple, Gale. J.C.'s point—and one I agree with—is that it's 1965 and it's time the Bears roomed together by position—without any regard to race.
CAROLINE. We'd like you and Brian Piccolo to room together.

9. **affirmative ad-libs:** remarks improvised by the actors, meaning "yes."

Gale smiles with relief.

GALE. Is that all? Is that what this is about?
CAROLINE. Is that *all*?
GALE. Yeah. You had me worried. I thought it was something really . . .

Tight on Caroline

His index finger shoots out, pinning Gale to the chair.

CAROLINE. Sayers—this *is* something, really. This is a white man and a black man rooming together on a team where that's never been done before. You're going to be called a Tom by some blacks and uppity by some whites. And when we go on the road, we'll be going to Atlanta and Dallas and Houston and Miami—and don't think it's going to get any better in Los Angeles and Detroit and Chicago, and every other town we play in, 'cause it *won't.*
  (*beat*)
You're going to rock the boat, Sayers—and there's plenty of people around who are already seasick.

A beat, as Caroline holds Gale's gaze, then straightens up. Halas has a small smile on his face.

HALAS. Have a glass of iced tea, J.C.

Halas leans forward.

HALAS. What J.C. is saying is that there may be pressures, Gale. Severe ones. (*Simply*) Now! What do *you* say?

Gale takes a breath, looking beyond the three men, giving the question the introspection it deserves.

                              Direct cut to:
Interior—Dormitory hallway—Night—On Brian

Brian comes down the hallway, wearing a windbreaker and casual slacks. Offstage we

A Reading Skills and Strategies

Previewing the Text

? As you preview pp. 286–287, what new characters make their first appearance in the teleplay? [Three of Brian's and Gale's teammates—Atkins, O'Bradovich, and Evey appear; Joy Piccolo and Linda Sayers, the main characters' wives, also appear for the first time.]

B Critical Thinking

Speculating

? Why do you think the coaches asked Gale, but not Brian, about the rooming arrangement? [Possible response: Perhaps they saw Gale as the more valuable player and wanted to keep him happy.]

C Elements of Literature

Drama: Conflict

? How might making the team affect the conflict between Gale and Brian? [Possible responses: The conflict should ease since they are no longer competing for a place on the team; however, as teammates, they will still compete to see who will be the starting player.]

D Critical Thinking

Extending the Text

? What do you think of hazing or initiations that include bullying or demeaning behavior? Do they play any role at all in making a group or organization better? [Possible responses: Students might point out that it's easy for people to get hurt during a hazing. They may also suggest more positive ways to build solidarity within a group.]

A can hear the sound of muted rock music. Brian's face is set, *dour* and depressed. He stops in front of one of the doors, pulls a key out of his pocket, then registers: That music is coming from his room. He looks down at the space between the door and the floor. There's light peeping out from within the room. Puzzled, he puts the key in the lock and opens the door cautiously.

Interior—The room

A picture is thumbtacked to the bulletin board, of Joy Piccolo and a baby girl. We pan over to reveal another picture tacked up on the bulletin board next to Joy's. The second picture is of Linda Sayers. We pan down from this picture to find Gale sprawled out on the bed, the radio blaring by his side. He reaches out and turns off the radio.

B
> **GALE.** Hi. We're rooming together.
> **BRIAN.** Says who?
> **GALE.** Who else?
> **BRIAN** (*sourly*). Terrific. Sort of a shame he couldn't ask me how I felt about it, isn't it?

GALE (*warily*). Look, if you want me out . . .

BRIAN. No, stay, I don't want you out. I'm just steamed at the Old Man for not putting me in the scrimmage this afternoon.

(*beat*)

Is that your wife?

GALE. Yeah.

BRIAN. She's pretty.

GALE. So's yours. And the little girl.

BRIAN (*still down*). Thanks. I'm supposed to call her tonight—tell her how I'm doing. Be the shortest phone call in history.

GALE. Maybe not.

When Piccolo looks over at him, Gale smiles.

GALE. Pic—they wouldn't assign us to room together unless we *both* made the team.

Brian looks over at Gale and it hits him. He moves to Gale, pulling him off the bed and shoving him toward the door.

C
> **BRIAN.** Come on! We've got to call our wives!
> **GALE.** I already called Linda, right after . . .
> **BRIAN.** That was just practice! This is for real! Come on!

And the two of them go tumbling out into the corridor.

Full shot—The corridor

Atkins, O'Bradovich, and Evey are standing a few feet away—huge men, arms like hams, necks like tree stumps. Their expressions are insolent, *challenging, but not cruel. Each of them has a coffee can in hand. Each container holds a sticky-looking, evil-smelling* conglomeration[10] *of honey, cereal, sand, catsup, and whatever they could lay their hands on. They move in unison toward Brian and Gale.*

D
> **ATKINS.** Congratulations on making the team, gentlemen. Well done.
> **EVEY.** As you know, Coach Halas frowns on the hazing[11] of new men.
> **O'BRADOVICH.** But now that you've made the team—it's really like—you're one of us.

All three have wooden spoons in the ooze, lifting the dripping, brown gunk for all to see. In a second, they're all tearing down the hall. Gale and Brian are bent low, the three pursuers bellowing with the thrill of the hunt. The last words echo in the corridor as all the

---

10. **conglomeration** (kən·gläm′ər·ā′shən): mixture of different sorts of things.
11. **hazing:** initiating of new members by bullying them or making them do ridiculous things.

WORDS TO OWN

dour (door) *adj.*: gloomy; sullen.
insolent (in′sə·lənt) *adj.*: boldly disrespectful.

---

286 WE ROOKIES HAVE TO STICK TOGETHER

doors are opened and men stick their heads out to see which rookies are getting it now.

ATKINS (*yelling*). Welcome to the Chicago Bears!

Interior—Bears' locker room—Day—Full shot

Gale is in front of his locker, just pulling off his jersey, which is muddy and torn. Two reporters are on each side of him. Piccolo, whose uniform looks as if he stepped out of a catalog, is seated in front of his locker, taking it all in with a certain objective humor. Gale, typically, is ill at ease in this kind of situation. **E**

REPORTER #1. Is playing in the NFL easier than you thought it would be?

GALE. Only played one game. Not exactly an expert.

REPORTER #2. But you didn't look as if you were having too much trouble out there.

GALE. The blocks were there.

BRIAN. Sure is different from the way you were talking last night, Gale. (*To reporters*) He calls the offensive line the "seven blocks of Silly Putty."

GALE. Pic——

REPORTER #1. You're Brian Piccolo?

BRIAN. P—I—C—C—O—L—O, yes.

Direct cut to:

NFL footage

A long run from scrimmage by Sayers.

BRIAN (*voice-over*). Gale, when you run, do you think about what you're doing, or do you just do it? **F**

GALE (*voice-over*). I just do it.

BRIAN (*voice-over*). Well, start thinking about it, will you? I want to play, too.

Direct cut to:

Interior—Pizza parlor—Night—Full shot

Grouped about one of the tables are Gale, Brian, and their wives, Joy Piccolo and Linda

Sayers. *They're at ease with one another, just now finishing off a casual, enjoyable evening on the town. They are listening to one of Brian's stories. He's telling it well, laughing as he does so, and it's a catching kind of thing for the women. Gale, being Gale, allows himself a small smile, but little beyond that.* **G**

BRIAN. Now—picture this—Concannon calls a trap, see. . . . (*To Linda and Joy*) You know what a trap is?

LINDA (*unsure*). I think so, but—maybe . . .

BRIAN. Well—uh—all the linemen go one way and hopefully the defense guys go that way, too. If they do, there's a big hole, see? If they don't—bad news. Anyway—Concannon calls a trap up the middle, Gale carrying the ball. It works like they draw it on the blackboard. Forty-three yards. Beautiful. So, Halas sees Gale's winded; he tells me to go in. So, I go in; Gale comes out. We get in the huddle—Concannon decides he's going to get foxy. He calls the *same* play. The very same play. Last thing they'll be looking for, he says. Now—the trap play is also called the "sucker play" because the defense really looks bad when it works—and defenses don't like to look bad—makes 'em <u>surly</u>. **H**

Joy, who's heard this story a hundred times already, has started to laugh, anticipating Brian's big finish.

BRIAN. So—we come out of the huddle—ball's snapped—all our linemen go one way—and it's like I'm looking at a team portrait of the Los Angeles Rams—Hello, Deacon . . . Merlin, how's the family . . . Rosey . . .

Laughter from them all, ad-libs between the

WORDS TO OWN
surly (sur'lē) *adj.:* bad-tempered, rude, and hostile.

BRIAN'S SONG, PART ONE 287

E **Reading Skills and Strategies**
Comparing/Contrasting
❓ What does the contrast in the appearance of Gale's and Brian's uniforms tell you? [Possible response: Gale has played a full, active game; Brian has sat on the bench and has not played.]

F **Critical Thinking**
Analyzing
❓ What does Brian mean in this conversation with Gale? [Possible response: He is making a joke about how well Gale plays and saying it would be nice for him if Gale weren't such a good player.]

G **Elements of Literature**
Drama: Exposition
❓ What does this scene set in the pizza parlor tell you about Brian and Gale? [Possible response: Their friendship seems to be blossoming since they are spending their free time together in the company of their wives.]

H **English Language Learners**
Summarizing
As an aid in comprehension, invite a volunteer to summarize the anecdote that Brian tells. [Possible response: When the Bears' quarterback called a trap against the Rams, the play worked perfectly and Gale ran for 43 yards. Then Brian went in for Gale, and the quarterback called the same play. This time, the play didn't fool the Rams, and Brian was crushed by the defensive linemen.]

Skill Link

Recognizing Characteristics of Realistic Dialogue

Tell students that playwrights create dialogue that captures and expresses the characters' experiences in a believable and lifelike way. As an example, point out the lines on p. 287 in which Brian recounts the play in which he was flattened by the Los Angeles defensive line. Ask students to comment on the use of dashes, ellipsis points, and interjections, such as *uh* and see, and how they help create the sound and rhythm of real speech and a well-told joke. As a volunteer reads this passage aloud, ask students to imagine that Brian Piccolo is actually in the room retelling this anecdote. Then ask students to point out other passages in which a character's lines seem ideally suited for recounting his experience.

A **Elements of Literature**
Character

? How is Gale changing? [Possible response: He seems to be adopting some of Brian's style; he is developing a sense of humor and becoming more outgoing.]

B **Reading Skills and Strategies**
Drawing Conclusions

? What does this passage reveal about Brian's and Gale's relationship? [Possible response: They like each other quite a bit and are comfortable together. Brian has a nickname for Gale and is happy his friend might win the Rookie of the Year award; Gale can make jokes about himself to Brian.]

girls. *Gale's smile has broadened now and Brian's just having a fine old time.*

> **BRIAN.** I mean—I was afraid to get up. I figured not everything was going to come with me. . . .
> **JOY** (*nicely*). You never saw anyone so black and blue.
> **GALE.** Yeah—it was like rooming with a black player again.

A *Gale grins—and the other three gape, looking at him with expressions of shock. His smile turns uneasy, bewildered. He checks to make sure there's no anchovy hanging off his chin.*

> **LINDA.** Gale—you told a *joke*.
> **BRIAN.** Joy—did you hear it? The great Stone Face from Kansas told a joke!

Brian turns to the other patrons, cupping his hands about his mouth.

> **BRIAN** (*yelling*). Chicago! There's hope for us all! Sayers *speaks!*
> **GALE.** Aw, come *on*, Pic. . . .

But Gale's smiling, pleased with himself if the truth were known, as is Linda Sayers. The camera holds on them.

Direct cut to:
NFL footage of a Sayers run—Slow motion

This footage should be the most impressive of all, selling the power and grace of Sayers's ability.

> **BRIAN** (*voice-over*). Magic—I think I'm going to write you a speech.
> **GALE** (*voice-over*). What kind of speech?
> **B** **BRIAN** (*voice-over*). Acceptance speech for "Rookie of the Year." You can't miss.
> **GALE** (*voice-over*). And I got to give a *speech*? You're putting me on!

Direct cut to:
Interior—Banquet dais—Night—Tight spot

Offstage the sound of a speaker drones on.

C **Reading Skills and Strategies**
Making Generalizations
? What do you think would be the most challenging part of being on a professional sports team? [Possible response: The long hours of practice and the uncertainty over whether one would be able to play first string or even remain on the team would be very difficult for most players.]

RESPONDING TO THE ART
Have students look at the collage on pp. 288–289. What do they think this artwork has to say about professional football in our country? [Possible response: Television plays a basic role in popularizing and interpreting professional football.]

Getting Students Involved

Cooperative Learning
Research. Students might work in small groups to research the career of Gale Sayers and to find out why he was one of the great running backs in the game. If possible, students can find and read sports articles from the late 1960s that detail Sayers's accomplishments.

Skill Link

Rewriting Fragments
Explain that William Blinn, like other writers, uses sentence fragments in his dialogue to create the effect of informal conversation. Review that sentence fragments do not contain both subjects and predicates and are not grammatically complete. As an example, give the following fragments from p. 287: "Only played one game. Not exactly an expert." Ask students to rework the fragments as complete sentences. (I've played only one game. I'm not exactly an expert.) Point out that the character of spoken speech changes when the sentences are complete. Ask students to find other examples of sentence fragments in the teleplay, tell how they might be reworded to make them complete, and then contrast the impact of the two versions.

Ⓐ *Gale, Linda, Brian, and Joy are on the dais— the men in tuxedos, the women in formal gowns. Brian has a crumpled piece of paper in his hand. He leans into Gale, speaking in an urgent whisper.*

> **BRIAN.** From the top. One more time.
> **GALE** (*harried, by rote*). I'd like to thank you all for this honor, though it's really not right to give it to one man. Football is a— team sport, and I . . .
> **SPEAKER** (*offstage*). Gale Sayers!

A spotlight floods the area and we hear off-stage applause. Gale is urged to his feet by Brian and Linda. He moves toward the speaker's platform, petrified. All we can see is Gale; the harsh pinpoint of the carbon arc is centered on him with no residual spillage.[12] He looks at the trophy for a second.

> Ⓑ **GALE** (*trembling*). I'd—I'd like to thank you all for this honor, though it's really not right . . .

He stops. He stops because he can't think of the next word. It's gone. Nothing there. Joy and Linda agonize in the silence, trying to pray more words out of Gale. Brian can't believe it. He starts to slowly tear the speech up, shaking his head, grinning. Gale's mouth is Ⓒ *like Death Valley.*

> **GALE.** Thank you.

Brian tosses the pieces of paper in the air, like confetti, smiling.

> **BRIAN.** Who'd believe it—who'd ever believe it. . . .

                                        Direct cut to:

Exterior—Sayers's house—Night

> **BRIAN.** Hey, Gale?

12. **carbon arc . . . spillage:** The carbon arc, or spotlight, is turned directly on Gale, with no light spilling off onto anyone else (no "residual spillage").

Gale holds on the porch. Linda waves a hand toward the car, her words intended for Gale.

> **LINDA.** Too cold out here. I'll warm your side of the bed.

She moves into the house as Brian gets out of the car and trots to Gale, both men with shoulders hunched against the cold. Brian moves to him.

> **GALE.** What do you want, man? It's freezing out here!
> **BRIAN.** Something I've got to tell you.
> **GALE.** What is it?

Gale notes an edge to Brian's voice, an undercurrent[13] of reluctance, shyness. Brian looks him directly in the eye.

> **BRIAN.** Joy and I had a long talk last night— about whether or not I should ask to be traded. We decided that I wouldn't ask. I like the guys on the team; I like the town.
>   (*beat*)
> What I *don't* like is playing second string.
> **GALE** (*quietly*). I don't blame you.
> Ⓓ **BRIAN.** Now—*maybe* I've got a shot at full-back. But I don't think Halas thinks I'm big enough. He'll probably go with Ralph Kurek. The other spot is yours—and that's the job I'm gunning for, Gale.

Gale starts to reply, but Brian silences him with a gesture.

> **BRIAN.** Let me get it said.
>   (*beat*)
> I'm a better blocker than you are and I'm as good a receiver. And if I can't break

13. **undercurrent:** unspoken feeling. Literally, *undercurrent* refers to a stream of water flowing beneath the surface.

WORDS TO OWN
reluctance (ri•luk′təns) *n.:* unwillingness.

Using Students' Strengths

Visual Learners

These students might view segments of the TV movie *Brian's Song* after they read the corresponding portions of the text. Ask them to list any questions or difficulties they had that viewing the film clarified.

Verbal Learners

Have students work in pairs to create a poem about Gale Sayers and/or Brian Piccolo. Suggest they begin with specific and striking images from the teleplay that reveal the core of the two characters.

Intrapersonal Learners

After they have read up to the point when Gale is seriously injured, ask these students to imagine how the star running back must have felt at the possible loss of his career. Suggest that they write in the first person the diary entry that Gale might have written on this day.

away for sixty, I can still get ten sixes, and it adds up the same way. I'm going to come into camp next year in the best shape ever, and I think I've got a realistic chance to blow you out of the lineup. . . . And that's just what I'm going to try to do.

GALE. I understand, man—that's your job.

BRIAN. Yeah—but I don't like to do "a job" on a friend.

GALE (*small smile*). Don't worry; you won't.

There's no anger between them, just resolve. After a beat, there is a light tap on the car horn. Brian looks at the trophy: He touches it lightly.

BRIAN (*as Bogart*).[14] It's a Maltese Falcon, kid—get this inside—and the free world is safe.

With that, Brian moves back to the car, camera holding on Gale as he looks after his nutty friend, then down to the trophy. He heads for the door.

Direct cut to:

Interior—Halas's office—Day—On picture

Another team picture is being tacked on the wall, the printing identifying it as last year's Bears.

Direct cut to:

Exterior—Practice field area—Day— Full shot

Gale and Brian take positions in a line for wind sprints. Their look to each other is friendly, but neither has precisely a fix on what attitude is the working one. They speak as the line moves forward. There are sounds of the other men yelling offstage.

BRIAN. Hi. You just pull in?

14. **Humphrey Bogart** (1899-1957): American actor who starred in *The Maltese Falcon*, a film in which the main characters pursue a treasured sculpture of a falcon.

GALE. Yeah. Would have been here this morning, but the flight got fogged in in Detroit. You look in good shape.

BRIAN. I am. Worked hard this winter.

GIBRON (*yelling offstage*). Go!

Full shot

Brian takes off, arms pumping, but Gale is laughing at a joke Brian has just told. Brian is past the forty at least three seconds before Gale, grinning from ear to ear.

Gale draws up from his leisurely sprint. They haven't even kept the clock on his effort.

GALE. Mind if I try it again?

HALAS. Might be a good idea.

Gale starts to retrace his steps to the goal line, then draws up, looking back to Gibron and Halas.

GALE. What was Pic's time like?

Gibron consults the clipboard.

GIBRON. Must be out to get you. . . . He's about half a second faster this year than last.

Gale is not frightened, but properly impressed. He nods, taking it in. His expression denies his statement.

GALE. That's really terrific. . . .

Direct cut to:

Exterior—Practice field—Day—Full shot

A number of men dot the area, going through calisthenics. We find Gale and Brian doing sit-ups, each being helped by another player who anchors their feet. They're facing in opposite directions so that, as they come up, they're looking at each other. The looks are not hostile, but there's very little "give" in each man's expression.

BRIAN'S SONG, PART ONE **291**

E Critical Thinking

Interpreting

❓ Why does Brian start to clown around at this point? [Possible response: He has just had an uncomfortable conversation with Gale and wants to cut the tension.]

F Elements of Literature

Drama: Setting

❓ What does this brief scene in the teleplay establish about the setting? [Possible response: Showing the new team picture indicates that a year has passed and a new season's play is about to begin.]

G Elements of Literature

Drama: Exposition

❓ How does the playwright use action in these scenes to advance the plot? [Possible response: More than dialogue, the actions and facial expressions here show the increasing tension between Brian and Gale as they compete for the same position.]

A **Reading Skills and Strategies**

Previewing the Text

Have students preview pp. 292–293 to find out what dramatic event occurs on the playing field. [Gale Sayers's leg is badly injured during a game.]

B **Struggling Readers**

Paraphrasing

Ask students to retell Brian's joke in their own words. [Possible response: Brian claims that pizza has a special effect that gives Italian athletes an edge. When Gale points out that there are no famous Italian running backs, Brian adds the common Italian name ending -elli to the names of two famous running backs, Jim Brown and Lenny Moore.]

C **Critical Thinking**

Analyzing

? Why is Gale "disappointed and yet relieved at the same time"? [Possible response: Gale is relieved that he got the position on the team, but he feels disappointment for Brian.]

Direct cut to:

A Exterior—Practice field—Day—Full shot

The offense and defense are performing the one-on-one drill. This time, it's Brian who's the offensive back and the move he puts on the defensive man is a beauty. As Brian tears out of frame, we zoom in on Gale, impassive outwardly, but fully aware of what's going on.

Direct cut to:

Interior—Dormitory hallway—Night—Full shot

Gale and Brian come in from the outside, both wearing light jackets, Brian carrying a pizza box.

B **BRIAN.** That's why you'll never cut it, Sayers—pizza has magical properties that give Italian guys strength and speed.
GALE. Yeah—a lot of great Italian running backs, all right.
BRIAN. Yeah. Jim Brownanelli. Lennie Moorelli. All those guys.

Angle to stairway

At the bottom is a bulletin board, where J. C. Caroline stands putting up a large sheet of paper. Brian moves by him, taking the stairs two at a time, and ad-libs a greeting, which is returned by J.C. Gale comes by.

GALE. What's that, J.C.?
CAROLINE. Starting lineups for the first exhibition.

Gale's eye moves toward the landing of the second floor. The shadow of Brian Piccolo can be seen. His head turns slowly, listening.

GALE. What's the backfield?
CAROLINE (*as he goes*). Concannon, Ralph Kurek, and you.

If ever there were mixed emotions in a man, now is that time. Gale looks up.

292 WE ROOKIES HAVE TO STICK TOGETHER

His point of view—Brian's shadow

Sagging, head lowered. A long beat, then Brian takes a breath, straightens his shoulders and moves off, the shadow disappearing.

BRIAN (*offstage*). Come on, Magic. . . . Pizza's getting cold.

Tight on Gale

C *He leans against the wall, disappointed and yet relieved at the same time. He looks toward the second-story landing once more, as we start to hear the growing roar of a large crowd, the unwavering roar of the hero seekers.*

Direct cut to:

Exterior—Wrigley Field—Day—NFL footage

The stands are crowded with spectators. The day is damp and gray.

Angle to field—NFL footage

The Bears are playing the San Francisco 49ers.

Angle to Bears' bench

Gale's uniform, muddy and begrimed; Piccolo's with only a smudge or two. Halas and Gibron pace restlessly up and down the sidelines, yelling to the defensive unit, as are all the other players. Concannon is on the phones, listening intently.

Angle to field

The ball is snapped to 49er quarterback John Brodie and he backpedals, looking for a receiver going deep. Brodie gets the pass off, but it falls into the hands of a defensive back from the Chicago Bears.

WORDS TO OWN

impassive (im·pas′iv) *adj.*: not showing emotion.

Skill Link

Identifying Transitions

You might use the following exercise before the Language Link exercise on transition words, p. 324.

Activity

Transitions are words or phrases that help to show how one idea is connected to another. Tell whether the underlined transition word in each pair of sentences shows contrast, cause and effect, or time order. For a review of transitions, see p. 331 in the Writer's Workshop.

1. Both Gale and Brian wanted to be the Bears running back. <u>As a result,</u> they were rivals. (cause and effect)
2. Gale hated Brian at first. <u>Later,</u> they became close friends. (time order)
3. Brian was a great ball-handler. <u>However,</u> Gale was a faster runner. (contrast)
4. Gale was badly injured in one game. <u>Consequently,</u> Brian played first string. (cause and effect)
5. Brian helped Gale recover. <u>Otherwise,</u> he would have no one to compete with. (contrast)

T292

Angle to bench

Every man is on his feet yelling. There is a flurry of activity—Gale is pulling on his helmet, receiving a pat from Brian. Concannon takes off the earphones and moves with the rest of the offensive team onto the field.

Angle to stands

LINDA. Go get 'em, Gale!! You can do it, honey!

Tight on Joy Piccolo

Happy at this turn of events but also painfully aware of something else, her eyes move from the field to the bench.

Her point of view—On Brian

With his back to the stands, helmet off, Number 41 paces restlessly back and forth along the sidelines. His attention is on the game, but the gaze drops a few times as inward moments take over.

Angle to Bears' huddle

CONCANNON. Yours, Gale. Twenty-eight toss. South. Line. On three. *Break!*

Full shot

The team comes out of the huddle, moving with precision into formation. Concannon looks over the defense and calls out the signals in a rhythmic cadence.[15] The ball is snapped and Concannon pivots, the move coordinated with the pulling of the guards and Gale's instantaneous break to his left. The ball is tossed back to Gale. He takes the pitch-out and has the ball well in hand as he starts to look for an opening in the upfield area.

On Brian

He is at the water bucket, dipper poised as he stops to watch the play develop.

15. **cadence** (kād′′ns): beat.

Back on Gale

Seemingly from nowhere, a San Francisco 49er uniform comes hurtling into frame and we freeze frame just before the shoulder of the player tears into Gale's knee. All crowd noises are killed. Only silence. The frame moves again now and we can see the awful impact. Freeze frame on this instant. The picture comes to life in short bursts as Gale crumples, knee landing at an angle to set one's teeth on edge, in jerky, grainy images.

On Brian

A freeze frame slowly moves forward half a step; he realizes what he's witnessing.

On Linda and Joy

They are very much afraid of what they're seeing. Linda's hand flies to her mouth.

Back on Gale

He hits the ground, one hand already going to the knee, the ball forgotten about. He tries to get to his feet, and the instant he puts any pressure on the knee, his head snaps back in reaction to the agony that assaults him. We freeze frame on Gale, every muscle contorted, and we hear the sound of a siren wailing, wailing, wailing.

Hard cut to:

Exterior—Sayers's home—Day—Full shot

The car, driven by Linda, pulls to a halt in the driveway. Gale opens the door and starts to get out. He's using two metal canes, the right leg swung out before him, stiff and unbending. His face is chiseled with tension and anger—cold, acid anger.

LINDA. Can I help?
GALE. No.

WORDS TO OWN
pivots (piv′əts) v.: rotates; turns around as if on an axis.

Crossing the Curriculum

Health

Have students research and write a report on the topic of knee injuries. Students might focus on the effectiveness of relatively new procedures of arthroscopic surgery. Students who are interested in medical careers might be assigned to investigate other techniques for treating orthopedic problems.

Physical Education

Students interested in football might investigate the special equipment football players wear to protect themselves from injury. Other students might research the types of physical therapy that an athlete like Gale would undergo after sustaining a career-threatening injury. Suggest that they create a daily physical therapy schedule that Gale might have followed to regain the full use of his knee.

Identifying Cause and Effect

? Why do you think Gale is in such an angry mood? [Possible response: His injury threatens his career and everything he has worked for.]

B Critical Thinking

Hypothesizing

? How do you think Gale has constructed this "emotional moat" around himself? [Possible response: By hiding or not expressing his feelings over the years, he has allowed a barrier to form around himself; now it is hard to connect emotionally with others.]

He makes his way slowly toward the front door, still not used to the canes, not yet using his body weight to help himself. Instead, it's a halting, unnatural motion—painful to execute, more painful for Linda to watch. She hurries past him to open the front door.

Interior—The living room—Day—Full shot

Gale comes in, no reaction to being home in his eyes. He moves to the first chair and sits.

> LINDA. It's good to have you home, Gale.
> GALE. Yeah. Good to be home.

But his eyes admit it was a reply made because it was the reply expected.

A
> LINDA. Can I get you anything?
> GALE. No. I'm fine.
> LINDA. It's about lunch time. You want a sandwich or anything?
> GALE. Not hungry; you go ahead, though.
> LINDA. Are you sure?
> GALE (*with an edge*). Yes, I'm sure.

B *The emotional moat he's built up is too wide to be crossed at this point. Linda kisses him lightly on the cheek, then rises and moves to the kitchen. She pauses at the door, looking back at him, a tentative smile on her face, but Gale's expression doesn't match or encourage the smile. Disheartened, Linda leaves the room.*

Tight on Gale

His hand moves to the injured knee, the cast large beneath the trouser leg. Alone, the mask falters slightly and the fear is unmistakable. Then, after a moment or two, we, and Gale, start to hear the sound of a man singing. We've heard the song before. It's Brian singing the Wake Forest fight song. Gale looks with disbelief toward another door off of the living room. Using the canes, Gale pulls himself to

an upright position and makes his way slowly across the room to the door. He pulls it open.

Angle down basement stairway

The singing is louder now. A beat, then Brian's smiling face appears at the bottom. He's wearing old clothes, carries a crescent wrench in one hand.

> BRIAN. Hey, Magic . . . thought you'd never get here.

He moves back out of sight and we hear the sound of something metal being tapped upon. Gale enters frame and starts down the steps carefully.

> GALE. Pic—what are you doing down there?

Interior—Basement—Full shot—Day

This is not a recreation room. The walls are cement block, gun-metal gray; a washer and dryer are in a corner. Opposite them, Brian Piccolo is tightening bolts on a metal framework that will eventually be used as a leg-lift machine. Gale negotiates the last few steps.

> BRIAN. It's not a bad act, Gale, but Peg Leg Bates[16] does it better.
> GALE (*indicating machine*). What's that supposed to be?
> BRIAN. It's not "supposed" to be anything but what it is—a leg-lift machine.
> GALE. What for?
> BRIAN. What *for*? Gale—getting that knee back into shape is not going to be a take-it-easy number. If you're afraid, that's understandable, but . . .

---

16. **Peg Leg Bates:** Clayton Bates (1908–1998), a famous jazz dancer who continued to dance even after his leg was amputated.

WORDS TO OWN

disheartened (dis·härt″nd) v. used as *adj*.: discouraged.

Making the Connections

Connecting to the Theme:
"We Rookies Have to Stick Together"
Have students find the instances in which Brian or Gale says, "We rookies have to stick together." [Brian says this with a smirk on p. 278 right after meeting Gale. Later Gale says it on p. 284, more sincerely, after giving Brian a tip for how to run a play.] Then ask students to discuss the following questions with partners:

• In what ways do Brian and Gale help and support each other in the teleplay? [Possible

responses: Brian helps Gale recover from his injury and open up to people; Gale supports Brian in his bid to play more often.]

• Why is it important for newcomers to help and support each other? [Possible response: Although newcomers are apt to need a great deal of help and support to adjust to a new situation, they might be reluctant to ask for help lest they appear too inexperienced.]

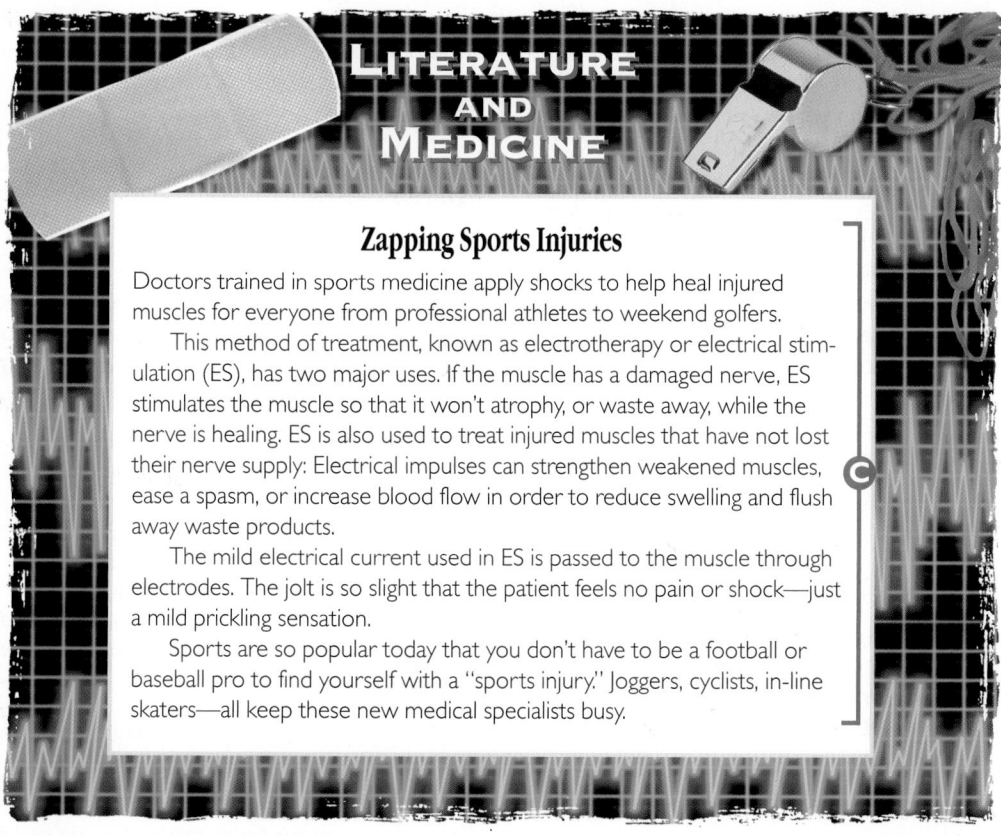

LITERATURE AND MEDICINE

Zapping Sports Injuries

Doctors trained in sports medicine apply shocks to help heal injured muscles for everyone from professional athletes to weekend golfers.

This method of treatment, known as electrotherapy or electrical stimulation (ES), has two major uses. If the muscle has a damaged nerve, ES stimulates the muscle so that it won't atrophy, or waste away, while the nerve is healing. ES is also used to treat injured muscles that have not lost their nerve supply: Electrical impulses can strengthen weakened muscles, ease a spasm, or increase blood flow in order to reduce swelling and flush away waste products.

The mild electrical current used in ES is passed to the muscle through electrodes. The jolt is so slight that the patient feels no pain or shock—just a mild prickling sensation.

Sports are so popular today that you don't have to be a football or baseball pro to find yourself with a "sports injury." Joggers, cyclists, in-line skaters—all keep these new medical specialists busy.

C Reading Skills and Strategies

Previewing the Text

Have students preview the brief article "Zapping Sports Injuries." How might their reading rate for this piece differ from that for the teleplay? [Possible response: The reading rate might be slower since the information is technical.]

LITERATURE AND MEDICINE

Have students investigate further the use of mild electric shocks in the treatment of injuries. One avenue of information about sports injuries and their treatment might be local coaches who have had experience with injuries on their teams. If you are teaching in a college town, perhaps some of the college football players would be willing to talk to the class.

GALE (*hard*). I am *not* afraid! **D**

Piccolo is out of patience. He picks up the tools and starts for the stairway.

BRIAN (*quietly*). You ought to be, Gale.
GALE. Pic, maybe you think this is a real friendly thing you're doing, but . . .
BRIAN. And you can put that in your ditty bag, too, you stupid jackass—friendship hasn't got one thing to do with this. . . .

Piccolo is halfway up the steps now. He stops, looking back at Gale, weighing whether or not to go on. Sayers's expression is stubborn and angry, but no more so than Brian's. A beat, then Brian sits on one of the steps.

BRIAN. Gale—when I was in high school—I was one of the best backs in the state. Unfortunately for me, *the* best back in the state, Tucker Fredrickson, went to the same school. And the colleges would come down to watch us and Tuck ended up at Auburn—and I ended up at Wake Forest. Good school, nice place, but not exactly center ring, you follow?

(*beat*)

So—I work my butt off at Forest. And my senior year—I led the nation in rushing and scoring. . . . (*Softly*) I mean—I led the *entire* nation.

(*beat*)

BRIAN'S SONG, PART ONE 295

D Reading Skills and Strategies

Responding to the Text

? Do you think that Gale is telling the truth about being afraid? [Possible responses: Maybe not, because Gale interrupts Brian too quickly; or no, because he stresses the word *not* too much.]

Getting Students Involved

Cooperative Learning

Sports Talk. As a speaking and listening activity, ask students to work in groups of five to produce five-minute TV sports talk shows. One student should be the show's host. Guests could include:

- Doctor Fox, the team doctor, detailing the seriousness of Gale's knee injury
- Gale, commenting on all the help Brian has given him to get back into playing shape

- Brian, explaining why he thought it was important to help his friend, even though he knows they will be competing for the same position
- Coach Halas, describing Gale and Brian's friendship and explaining why he thought it was important for them to room together.

Students can script or ad-lib dialogue. The class should serve as a studio audience for the show.

A

A Reading Skills and Strategies

Previewing the Text

❓ Can you tell by quickly previewing this spread whether Gale will recover from his injury? [Possible response: Yes, in each scene he seems to be regaining more and more use of his leg.]

B Elements of Literature

Drama: Conflict

❓ What conflicts—internal and external—does Brian express in this speech? [Possible responses: Brian has an external conflict with his teammates over getting to be the number one player; he has an internal conflict over whether he can remain number one; he also has an internal conflict over getting a position because his teammate was injured.]

C Critical Thinking

Speculating

❓ Why do you think Gale drops his cane in the litter basket immediately after hearing the sportscast? [Possible response: Hearing how well Brian did in the game has strengthened Gale's resolve to overcome his injury. Throwing his cane away is a way to show he is getting back into playing shape.]

D Critical Thinking

Expressing an Opinion

❓ What roles are Brian and Gale playing here? [Possible response: Brian is the boss, the coach, the teacher, and the doctor; Gale is the worker, the athlete, the student, and the patient.]

A So, I look around for a pro team, and I pick the Bears. Then, who else comes to the Bears—Sayers. Big gun from a big school, and I'm number two all over again.

(beat)

Well, Gale—I'm number one guy now, but for all the wrong reasons. And if you don't come back one hundred percent, people are always going to say that I got in on a pass, a lucky break, and I won't take it that B way. *(Rises)* I am going to beat you, Magic, but it won't mean a thing unless you're at your best, not one second slower, one degree weaker. I'm going to work your tail off getting you into shape again—for *my* sake.

Full shot

Brian turns and goes to the top of the stairs. Gale stands there, rage stilled, cooled, then turns, looking steadily at the leg-lift machine. He moves to it, running his fingertips over it lightly, seeking reassurance from the chilled metal.

Direct cut to:
Exterior—City park—Day—On Gale

It's a blustery, cold day. The wind drives ribbons of dry snow along the walk. Gale moves toward us, using a wooden cane, the limp noticeable but not as bad as previously seen. He wears an overcoat, the collar turned up, and a grim expression. In his free hand he carries a small radio. A sportscaster is heard over the sound of the wind.

ANNOUNCER *(voice-over).* And in Los Angeles, the Chicago Bears trimmed the Rams by a score of seventeen to sixteen. Quarterback Jack Concannon was eight for fourteen passing, and the running game was ably manned by Brian Piccolo, who gained 105 yards in fourteen carries. Piccolo was awarded the game ball.

C *Gale is adjacent to a litter basket. He stops for a beat, his back to us, then deposits the cane into the basket. His step seems to have more drive to it when he moves on.*

Direct cut to:
Exterior—Park area—Day—On Gale

It's early morning as Gale, dressed in a sweatsuit, comes jogging toward us. His expression is stoic, the pace quite slow, the sort of speed one recommends to those just discharged from the hospital after hernial surgery. But the pace is steady and dogged.

DR. FOX *(voice-over). (Filter)* Hello?
BRIAN *(voice-over). (Filter)* Dr. Fox? This is Brian Piccolo. How's he doing?
DR. FOX *(voice-over). (Filter)* Very well, I think. Though it's boring going through those exercises all by yourself. It's drudgery and it's painful, and a lot of people just give up when they're alone in that situation.

Direct cut to:
Interior—Sayers's basement—Night—Tight on Gale

D *Gale is lying on his back, feet in the air, as he strains to lift the platform bearing a sizable portion of weights. He's drenched with sweat, puffing. We pan up from his face to the knee, seeing the wicked-looking scar that creases the flesh. As he starts to lift the platform, we pull back to reveal Piccolo seated nearby. He has a small kitchen egg timer in his hand.*

BRIAN. And—ten. *(Setting timer)* Minute rest, then one more set.
GALE. *Another* one?
BRIAN. Last one tonight. Hang in there.

WORDS TO OWN

stoic (stō′ik) *adj.*: not showing or complaining about pain. Stoics were philosophers of ancient Greece who tried not to let pleasure or pain affect them.

Assessing Learning

Check Test: Short Answer

1. What lie does Brian tell Gale about Coach Halas? [that the coach is deaf in one ear]
2. What happens to Gale at the first team meeting? [He is fined for talking.]
3. What personal arrangement do the coaches set up with Gale? [that he will room with Brian]

4. What physical problem does Gale have to deal with? [recovering from a knee injury]
5. Why does Brian tell Gale that he is helping him recover from the injury? [so Brian will have competition for the same position next season]

Standardized Test Preparation

For practice with standardized test format specific to this selection, see
• *Standardized Test Preparation*, p. 46
For practice in proofreading and editing, see
• *Daily Oral Grammar*, Transparency 17

Gale remains on the floor under the weight machine. He sighs, getting his breath back.

BRIAN. How's the knee feel?

GALE (*dispirited*). Oh, one day it feels as strong as ever; the next day it's like I got spaghetti for ligaments.[17]

(*beat*)

BRIAN. You know—if it doesn't come all the way back—it won't be the end of the world, Gale.

GALE. That so?

BRIAN. Football's terrific, man, but it's still just a job.

GALE. It's the only job I know how to do.

(*beat*)

I'm not like you—I can't talk and all that stuff.

BRIAN. Talking now . . .

GALE. It's different.

(*beat*)

BRIAN. You'll learn how to talk, once you find something that's got to be said.

The egg timer chirps once and Gale lifts his legs to the underside of the platform bearing the weights.

BRIAN. Third set. Ten reps. *Go.*

Gale starts to lift. The first three or four times go smoothly enough, but about halfway through the fifth one . . .

GALE (*straining*). I'll never make ten, man—no juice left . . .

BRIAN. Don't bone me! Come on, Magic! Hang tough! Five. Way to go—six—lookin' good, Magic. Come on. . . .

GALE. No—way . . .

BRIAN. You aren't getting out that easy! Come on! You can do it! Seven! Fantastic! Three more, man! Work on it! Are these the legs of a murderer? Come on, Gale! Eight! Got it! Two more!

17. **ligaments:** bands of tough tissue connecting bones.

GALE. No—way . . .

Tight on Brian

He is leaning over Gale, mind seeking a ploy.

BRIAN. Can't make it, huh, weakling? Giving up, is that it? Is that what you're doing?

Tight on Gale

Looking up at Brian expressionlessly—then a stifled laugh breaks from his lips. He smiles.

GALE. Come on, man—don't make me laugh.

Gale starts to laugh and lets the weights come to rest on the stops. Brian just stands there without any comprehension of how his maneuver could have backfired so badly.

Direct cut to:

Exterior wooded area—Day—Long shot

Brian and Gale move along a narrow dirt road that winds through the trees. Their pace is no longer that of a jog, but one more suited to a brisk 880.[18]

Closer—Trucking

We move back in front of the two of them as they run, both in control, arms pumping smoothly, the motion fluid and easy. After a few seconds, Brian looks over briefly at Gale, then he picks up the pace a little, opening a few yards between them. Gale takes this with some surprise but matches Brian and closes the gap. But it's only temporary, for Brian ups the ante once more, the pace now at 440[19] clip. Gale's eyes flash as Brian moves away, but he picks it up again. He's shoulder to shoulder with Pic.

BRIAN. A beer for the first man to the bridge!

18. **880:** referring to a race of 880 yards, or half a mile. The pace is slower than a dash but faster than a long-distance run.

19. **440:** referring to a race of 440 yards, or a quarter-mile. The pace is much faster than that of an 880-yard race.

BRIAN'S SONG, PART ONE 297

E **Critical Thinking**

Interpreting

? What might Gale mean when he says "I can't talk and all that stuff" and why would this affect his ability to find a job? [Possible response: He isn't outgoing like Brian; he doesn't have the communication skills or interpersonal skills he would need to succeed in many positions.]

F **Vocabulary Note**

Multiple Meanings

? How do you think *juice* came to have the meaning "strength" or "vitality"? [Possible response: Energy and strength are viewed as a sort of juice flowing through a person's body.]

G **Struggling Readers**

Finding Details

? What details show how Brian is controlling this run? [Possible responses: Brian looks at Gale and starts running faster, and as Gale catches up, Brian challenges him again.]

Cultural Connections

Athletic Heroes

This selection presents an opportunity for students to discuss their views of the role of athletes in society. Have students begin by discussing why athletes occupy such a prominent place in our pantheon of heroes. Students might also address the issue of whether athletes have the responsibility to serve as role models for young sports fans. As part of this, students can name the athletic heroes they admire most and name some of their most admirable traits.

A · Appreciating Language
Style

❓ Why do you think William Blinn uses this colorful simile in his stage directions? [Possible response: The comparison is a way to convey the wildness and energy of the scene to director and players.]

B · Historical Connections

Explain that in old merry-go-rounds, a ring was hooked to the ceiling in one spot. If a rider could reach it and pull it off—a feat that required strength and agility—he or she won a free ride. Since there was only one ring, only one person could win. Similarly, in the struggle to become the starting running back for the Bears, there can be only one winner.

C · Elements of Literature
Drama: Resolution

❓ What major complication is resolved at the end of Part One of the teleplay? [Possible response: Gale Sayers has overcome his injury and is now healthy enough to play again.]

GALE. You're on!

Different angle

Brian peels off from the road and crashes into the trees flanking the road. Gale is a little surprised at this cross-country route, but he's right after Brian, though he's got about five or six yards to make up due to the momentary hesitation.

On Brian

There are no paths here, no easy routes. The trees and shrubs make it necessary to dart this way and that, hurdle logs, scramble up steep slopes and gullies. Brian is in the lead, but Gale's responding to the challenge, charging after him at full bore.

Various cuts—The chase

The two of them are bound together by an invisible rope, though the rope has developed a tendency to shrink slightly. It's almost imperceptible, but Gale is making up ground on Brian. They come to a creek bed five or six inches deep, and as they go splashing through it, we go to slow motion—droplets exploding into the sunlight, the two men calling on reserves from deep within. The small stream dwindles to loose shale.

The fall

A scant step behind Piccolo, Gale loses his footing on the stones and takes a head-over-heels tumble, a really bad one, pinwheeling over and over violently. Piccolo halts immediately, looking back at Gale with concern.

On Brian

He is gasping for breath, looking to Gale.

On Gale

He meets Brian's look. Every breath hurts, sears. He glances down at the knee, then stands slowly, brushing the stones from the

---

palms of his hands. He meets Brian's look. He nods.

Full shot

Like catapults,[20] they both turn and take off. They burst out of the trees, Gale a step behind. This is the final all-out sprint for the tape. Nothing held in reserve at this point, they pull great gulps of air in, straining, eyes frozen on the finish up ahead. And with each step, Gale moves up. An inch, no more, but that inch is repeated with each step, every stride bringing him closer to Brian's shoulder.

Long shot

As they near a small wooden footbridge, they move, it seems, as one, mirror images of black and white. They both literally hurl themselves at the imaginary tape and go tumbling across the bridge with their momentum, sprawling in the soft grass on the other side.

They are both lying there, having given it all they had to give. They're shiny as seals with perspiration, their eyes bright with fatigue, focusing on the blue sky overhead. After a long moment, they both sit up, shaky smiles on their faces, though they're still puffing like a Saint Bernard in Palm Springs.

BRIAN. I—think—I—owe—you—a—beer.
GALE (*shakes head*). I—think—I—owe—you—a—lot—more—than—that.
BRIAN. Yeah—you're—healthy.
GALE. Yeah.

And they look at each other, the expressions of both growing a little serious, aware that, as friends, they are still competitors; there's only one brass ring on this merry-go-round.

---

20. **catapults** (kat′ə·pultz′): devices like giant slingshots, used for throwing objects.

The Day the Butterfly Came

He never really had a name, the Butterfly. Jenny and her grandfather had just found him there, on the windowsill.

It was a quiet day in spring, and not much was going on. Jenny was pushing her grandfather around in his wheelchair. Just as she was about to suggest they go inside, there he was, the Butterfly.

Jenny quickly wheeled her grandfather over to it. Afraid to scare it, she just stood there. "It's not going anywhere," her grandfather told her. Sometimes Jenny thought he knew everything about animals, even what they were thinking.

"How come he's not with the rest of the butterflies in the old maple?" Jenny questioned the old man.

"Not all animals belong together, Jenny," he answered her.

And every day after that, the Butterfly came to the windowsill. Sometimes only for a while, but he always came. It puzzled Jenny because he never joined the others.

One morning she asked her grandfather, "Should we take him to the others in the old maple?"

Victor and Ernest, sculpture by John Ahearn.

"No," replied the old man. "Just because he doesn't have any butterfly friends doesn't mean he doesn't have friends. The Butterfly has us. Even if we are different from him, we can still be his friends."

Jenny remembered this all her life. Many years after her grandfather died, she realized what he was trying to tell her. It doesn't matter if your friends are different from you; they can still be the most important people in your life.

— Kristin Sparks
The Abbotsford High School
Abbotsford, Wisconsin

BRIAN'S SONG, PART ONE 299

Student to Student

In this short tale, Jenny and her grandfather are visited each day by a butterfly. Jenny thinks the insect would be happier with its fellows in the trees. The grandfather, however, tells Jenny to leave the butterfly alone since it has chosen them for its friends. Jenny realizes that people sometimes must choose friends who are different from themselves.

D Critical Thinking
Speculating
❓ Why do you think that people often choose friends who are quite different from themselves? [Possible responses: Opposites attract one another; getting to know someone different is a way to learn more about the world.]

E Critical Thinking
Making Connections
❓ Can you think of other works of literature in which there is an unexpected friendship? [Possible responses: *A Wrinkle in Time, The Dark Is Rising, The Phantom Tollbooth.*]

Listening to Music 🎵

The "Butterfly" Etude
The "Butterfly" Etude is No. 9 of the *Etudes for Piano,* Opus 25, by Frédéric Chopin (shō´pǎn) (1810–1849). The work is performed by several artists.

Activity
Explain that an etude (ā-tōōd´), from the French word for "study," is a short piece of music for a solo instrument and that one of Chopin's etudes is nicknamed "Butterfly." Then play the etude as background music while students read or reread "The Day the Butterfly Came." Afterward, have students discuss how the background music enhanced their reading.

Connecting Across Texts

Connecting with *Brian's Song*
Invite students to discuss how this short tale connects with *Brian's Song.* Ask: How does the friendship between Brian and Gale illustrate the last line of the story about the butterfly? [Possible response: Although Brian and Gale were of different races and temperaments, they were able to become close friends; moreover, Brian became one of the most important people in Gale's life, helping him to recover from his injury.]

T299

MAKING MEANINGS (PART ONE)

First Thoughts

1. Possible answers:
- . . . he is such a good football player.
- . . . he really wants to help Gale get back into the game.

Shaping Interpretations

2. Brian first sees Gale as a great player and a tough competitor. Later, as he gets to know Gale, he becomes aware of how shy he is. He also learns that Gale is generous and has a sense of humor. At first, Gale sees Brian as funny but annoying. Later, Gale realizes that Brian is a true friend.

3. Brian's decision creates a conflict because he and Gale are competing for the same position on the team. The internal conflict is between Brian's ambition to be number one and his friendship for Gale; he both respects Gale and wants to beat him.

4. Gale owes Brian gratitude for helping and supporting him during his recovery. Brian also insisted that Gale make his best effort to regain his full powers.

Connecting with the Text

5. Answers will vary. Possible responses: "All three have wooden spoons in the ooze, lifting the dripping, brown gunk for all to see." (p. 286); "He checks to make sure there is no anchovy hanging off his chin." (p. 288); ". . . they're still puffing like a Saint Bernard in Palm Springs." (p. 298).

T300

MAKING MEANINGS (PART ONE)

First Thoughts

[respond]

1. Using your notes from the Quick-write on page 273, discuss with a partner your responses to the play. Here are some starters to help you if you're stuck:

- What most surprises me about the two players' friendship is . . .
- I admire Gale because . . .
- I admire Brian because . . .

Shaping Interpretations

[compare]

2. Change is important in most dramas. How do Brian's feelings about Gale change in the first part of the play? How do Gale's feelings about Brian change? You might use a chart like this to show the shift in feelings:

	At First	Later
Brian		
Gale		

[explain]

3. Explain how Brian's decision to stay with the Bears and try to win the position of halfback creates a **conflict,** or struggle, between him and Gale. What **internal conflict** does this decision create for Brian?

[infer]

4. After Brian and Gale race, Gale says, "I think I owe you a lot more than that" (page 298). What do you think he means by this comment?

Connecting with the Text

[connect]

5. The **camera directions** in this play are written for the director, actors, and crew—the audience never hears them. However, Blinn's directions are often entertaining in themselves, as when he describes the dining room scene on page 280: "a number of large men . . . ladle on portions that would choke a garbage disposal." Find and share other camera directions that you think are humorous or especially descriptive.

Reading Check

a. The opening scenes of the play give us some information about *who* Gale and Brian are. For example, what tricks does Brian play on Gale in the opening scenes of the play? How does Gale react to them?

b. After Brian and Gale make the team, they go out to dinner with their wives. What does Gale do during the meal that shows the effect of Brian's easygoing friendship?

c. The injury to Gale's knee is a serious physical obstacle to playing football. What other obstacle must Gale overcome?

d. What reason does Brian give for helping Gale recover from his injury?

Reading Check

a. Brian teases Gale about his reserve, and he tells him that Coach Halas is deaf in one ear. Gale reacts by not responding and by trying to stay on Halas's right side.

b. Gale makes a joke.

c. Gale also has to overcome being in competition with his friend.

d. The reason Brian gives is that he wants to win the position of "number one guy" fairly, with Gale giving his best effort.

Extending the Text

[apply]

6. In what other situations in life could friends also be competitors?

[analyze]

7. What do you think the little story on page 299 has to do with this play?

Challenging the Text

[evaluate]

8. Do you think the screen-writer has made the friendship between Gale and Brian believable? Do you think Brian and Gale deal with their problems in a believable way? Why or why not?

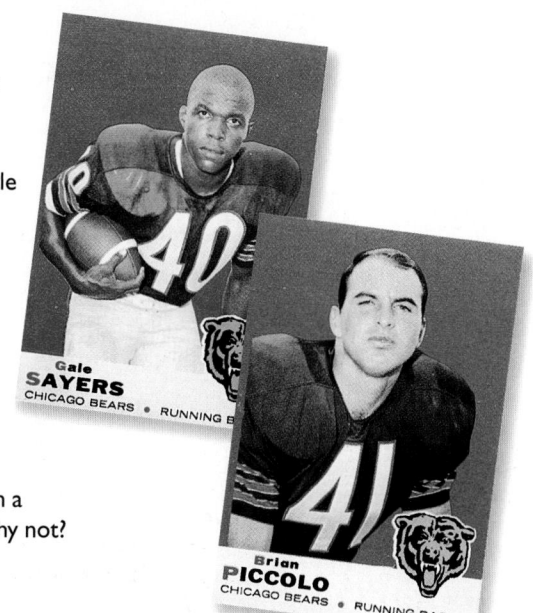

Gale **SAYERS**
CHICAGO BEARS • RUNNING B

Brian **PICCOLO**
CHICAGO BEARS • RUNNING BACK

VOCABULARY   HOW TO OWN A WORD

WORD BANK

enigmatic
saunter
dour
insolent
surly
reluctance
impassive
pivots
disheartened
stoic

Act It Out

Most of the words in the Word Bank at the left are found in the camera directions. They all relate to a character's feelings or actions.

Suppose you are an actor assigned to a part in this play. You would have to understand what each word in the directions means, and you'd have to work at interpreting that word. After all, the audience can't read the camera directions. The actor must communicate the directions to the audience.

1. Go back to the place in the text where each word in the Word Bank is used. With a partner, act out each word, using **facial expressions** and other kinds of **body language.** If the word describes how a speech is given, use your voice to show how the character is feeling.

2. Another exercise actors use involves **antonyms,** words opposite in meaning to other words. Take each word in the directions and try to find its opposite. For *enigmatic,* for example, you might try *open* or *frank.* How would you interpret this opposite quality?

3. Share all your interpretations with the class and ask for audience feedback. Have you communicated each feeling or action clearly?

Extending the Text

6. Students might mention friends with whom they compete for grades or awards; oftentimes lawyers who are friends compete in the court-room to win a case; similarly, two salespeople for the same company compete to see who can make the most sales in a year.

7. Students may point out that the friendship of Jenny, her grandfather, and the butterfly is like that between Brian and Gale because it is unexpected.

Challenging the Text

8. Students may say that they find the friendship believable because the two men overcome their differences, get to know each other gradually by sharing a common experience, and are honest about their conflict. Although balancing friendship and competition is diffi-cult, Brian and Gale handle it in a natural and believable way.

VOCABULARY

Students should demonstrate knowl-edge of the Words to Own as defined on pp. 277–296.

Resources

Vocabulary
• *Words to Own,* p. 13

Spelling
For related instruction, see
• *Spelling and Decoding,* p. 16

**Previewing
the Text**

? Have students preview Part Two
of *Brian's Song.* Based on the brief
description of sets, what major complication might be developing in the
second half? [Possible response: Brian
becomes ill and is hospitalized.]

B Critical Thinking

Speculating

? Look at the facial expressions of
Gale and Brian in the illustration.
What words would you use to
describe how they are feeling? [Possible
responses: concerned, worried, uneasy,
uncomprehending.]

Resources

Writing and Language
• *Daily Oral Grammar,* Transparency 18
Reading
• *Words to Own,* p. 14
Assessment
• *Formal Assessment,* p. 56
• *Standardized Test Preparation,* pp. 48,
50

A

B

302 WE ROOKIES HAVE TO STICK TOGETHER

Preteaching Vocabulary

Words to Own

Have students, either in pairs or individually,
read the definitions of the Words to Own listed
at the bottom of the selection pages. Then use
the following exercises to reinforce students'
understanding of the words.

1. How would your **respiration** rate change if
you jumped up and down exuberantly?
2. What type of clothes would look **somber**?

3. Draw a picture of a real situation that left
you feeling **exasperated**.
4. Name a time when you hid your true feelings
behind a **facade** of happiness.
5. What would cause your trust in someone to
be **eroded**?
6. What symbol might be used in a
cartoon to show someone staring
uncomprehendingly?

7. List some activities that require great
stamina.
8. What conclusion might you draw if your
friend looked very **pallid**?
9. What type of activities might leave you feeling **enervated**?

Part Two

GIBRON (*voice-over*). What do you think training camp is? You think training camp is some kind of picnic? Is that what you think? Because there's no man assured of a job around here, let me tell you, and if you think you are, then you got one more think comin', gentlemen!

As Gibron's voice starts to come over, we also start to hear the sounds of the Chicago Bears calling out a cadence as they go through their calisthenics.[1]

Hard cut to:
Exterior—Practice area—Day—Full shot

The backs step through the ropes, knees high. We pick up Gale going through the obstacle course, with Brian right behind him, both handling it with relative ease. We pan them, then all of them leave the frame to hold on the grizzled features of Coach Halas. His eyes are masked by dark glasses, but there's a smile tugging on the corners of his mouth.

Direct cut to:
Interior—Dormitory room—Night—On Gale

The playbook is in front of him. We pan across the room to find Brian, same look, same activity. A beat, then there is a knock on the door. Brian opens the door and reacts with some surprise on seeing Coach Halas standing in the hallway. He nods pleasantly. Gale, too, is surprised and sits up.

HALAS. Hello, Brian. Mind if I come in for a moment?
BRIAN. No, no. Of course not. Come on in, Coach.

And Halas comes in, moving by Brian. The two young men look to each other, neither

---

1. **calisthenics** (kal'is·then'iks): exercises (from the Greek words *kallos,* meaning "beauty," and *sthenos,* meaning "strength").

BRIAN'S SONG, PART TWO 303

C Elements of Literature
Drama: Teleplay
? How does the playwright quickly re-establish the setting and tension of the play? [Possible response: He shows the whole team doing calisthenics on a field; he has the coach in a voice-over remind us that the players must compete to play.]

D Critical Thinking
Speculating
? Why might Coach Halas be smiling? [Possible response: He is happy that both Gale and Brian are back and doing well; perhaps he is planning something for Gale or Brian.]

Using Students' Strengths

Verbal Learners
Suggest that these students view scenes from the TV movie *Brian's Song.* Ask them to note the specific ways in which the actors used their voices to express certain feelings and ideas. Have students read these same lines themselves, imitating the actors' methods.

Logical/Mathematical Learners
These students might create a storyboard for Part Two of *Brian's Song,* reading and timing individual scenes and then estimating the length of the entire part. Students might also suggest the order in which the scenes might be filmed to minimize production costs.

Auditory/Musical Learners
Encourage these students to suggest background music that could be played during certain scenes in *Brian's Song* to emphasize the mood. Have students play the music as they read aloud individual scenes.

A Reading Skills and Strategies

Previewing the Text

Have students preview pp. 304 and 305 to see what details they can learn about Brian's condition. [He seems to be losing weight and gets winded easily; he has a cough that he can't get rid of.]

B Critical Thinking

Interpreting

❓ What do you think Brian might be thinking about as he says this? [Possible response: Maybe Brian thinks that Coach Halas is going to move him out of the lineup and move Gale back in. If this were the case, Brian would feel awkward being there.]

C Struggling Readers

Summarizing

Summarize that Coach Halas is teasing Brian here; that is, Halas hides his real purpose to lead Brian on and make him think that he is off the team. Only at the last minute does the coach reveal that he is going to use both Gale and Brian on the starting team.

D Vocabulary Note

Specialized Vocabulary

Elicit that Gale, as *halfback*, is the running back who usually carries the ball. Brian as *fullback*, would run interference for Gale, blocking any attempts to reach the ball carrier. Both players would be in the *backfield*; that is, in back of the players on the line of scrimmage.

---

having any notion that might explain this **A** *unprecedented visit.*

> **HALAS.** How's the knee, Gale?
>
> **GALE.** Fine, Coach. Feels strong.
>
> **B** **BRIAN.** Look, if you want to talk to Gale, I can just walk on down to . . .
>
> **HALAS.** No, actually, I'd like to talk to both of you.

Chilling portent. They both smile, as does Halas, but only the Old Man's has any relaxation in it. Long beat. Throat clearings from Gale and Brian.

> **BRIAN.** Well—uh—how do things look this year, Coach?
>
> **HALAS.** Fine. Just fine. Matter of fact, there's one boy I'm very impressed with. Brian, I wouldn't be surprised to see him replace you as number two halfback.

Halas lets the moment run on for a second.

> **HALAS.** Because I'm making you number one fullback.

Tight on Brian

He sits there looking at Halas much as Papa Dionne[2] must have looked at the doctor.

On Gale

Beaming, really and deeply pleased for his friend.

> **D** **GALE.** Hey, Pic—you and me the starting backfield—what do you say?

Full shot

Brian just shakes his head back and forth, an empty smile flopping about on his face.

> **GALE.** Coach—I didn't think it was possible—but I think you finally found a way to shut him up!

2. **Papa Dionne:** father of quintuplets born in Canada in 1934.

304 WE ROOKIES HAVE TO STICK TOGETHER

Hard cut to:

NFL footage—Alternating between runs of Piccolo and Sayers

> **GALE** (*voice-over*). Hey, Pic?
>
> **BRIAN** (*voice-over*). Yeah?
>
> **GALE** (*voice-over*). You know you got a four point three rushing average?
>
> **BRIAN** (*voice-over*). No, man, but hum a few bars and I'll see if I can fake it.
>
> **GALE** (*voice-over; overlapping*). Aw, Pic . . .

Exterior—Angle to football field—End zone

Brian breaks through a hole in the center of the line, keeping his feet as he gets to the end zone, flipping the ball high into the air. The first person to him is Gale, slapping him <u>exuberantly</u> on the back as they move with their teammates toward the bench.

Direct cut to:

Interior—Locker room—Day—Full shot

The team is being weighed in, Gibron by the scales, sliding the weights up and down the bar and calling out the result for each man. There is some good-natured catcalling[3] as some of the larger linemen are weighed in and most of it is coming from Brian, who is next in line, with Gale close behind him. Brian takes his place. Gibron starts to readjust the weights.

> **BRIAN.** Scrimmage tomorrow, Abe. Going to give us any trick plays?
>
> **GIBRON.** Only trick I'd like to give you is how to keep some meat on you. You're down another pound.
>
> **BRIAN.** But what's there is choice; admit it.

3. **catcalling:** shrill whistles or shouts making fun of someone; so called because people used to make noises like a cat to show disapproval, the way we boo or hiss today.

WORDS TO OWN

exuberantly (eg·zōō′bər·ənt·lē) *adv.*: with high spirits.

Crossing the Curriculum

Science

Encourage students to research the advances in treatment for cancer since Brian Piccolo's surgery in 1967. Students might also investigate current recovery rates for different types of cancer and present the information in a chart.

Architecture

Interested students could research the structure of a professional football stadium in their region. In particular, ask them to find out how the needs of the players and coaches, the media, and the sports fans were taken into account during the design stage.

Music

Some students may enjoy composing lyrics and a melody with the title *Brian's Song*. The original song should express their feelings about the play, about Brian's approach to life, or the friendship that developed between Brian and Gale. Allow time for volunteers to perform their songs.

GIBRON. Two-o-six and a quarter. Skinniest fullback in the league.

BRIAN. Gibron, you run the fat off us, then complain that we're too thin. You're a hard man to please.

Brian grins, used to Gibron's grumbles, and moves off. Gale is next in line.

GIBRON. Ought to tell your Italian friend to load up on the pasta.

GALE. Probably just wants to be quicker, Gibron.

GIBRON. Well, it ain't workin'. He lost ten pounds and he's half a second slower over a forty-yard sprint. Lighter *and* slower don't total out to much of a threat, you know. (*Checks the weight*) One ninety-nine. Next.

We move with Gale as he steps off the scale, camera closing on him. He glances off at Gibron, then in the direction taken by Brian. His eyes are puzzled; it's a weird combination Gibron has pointed out. Strange. Unsettling. Gale lets it sink in.

Direct cut to:

NFL footage of Gale and Brian

Running the ball, alternating. Two cuts, the first being the best footage of Piccolo as either runner or receiver, the last being a punt return by Sayers that goes all the way. This final cut, the punt return, is to lead directly into the following staged sequence.

Angle to Bears' sideline

Gale comes off the field with the rest of the punt-return unit, among whom is Brian. Typically, Gale barely smiles at the congratulations he gets. He moves to the bench and sits, Brian by his side. They pull off their helmets, eyes on the game.

Closer angle—Gale and Brian

Both winded, but with one difference. Gale is clearly buoyed up, exhilarated. Brian simply seems tired.

GALE. Nice block.

BRIAN. Thanks.

(*beat*)

Must be ninety million pounds of pollen in the air.

Gale glances over at Brian casually and might see what we are now noting. Gale's respiration is swiftly slowing down, approaching normal. Brian's is not, he's still winded and badly so. Brian rises, moving for the water bucket near the phone desk. Gale watches him, then rises, moving for the sidelines to view the upcoming kickoff, camera moving with him. He finds an opening among the men standing there; then, in the hush just prior to the kicker's runup, the sound of Brian coughing. Gale turns back.

His point of view—On Brian

The roar of the crowd overwhelms the sound of Piccolo's coughing. He takes down a fair amount of water, but that doesn't help. Brian coughs once more, though it's more evident in the motion of his shoulders and chest than in a sound; he's making an effort to stifle the cough.

GALE. You ought to get Fox to give you something for that hay fever.

BRIAN. He did. Doesn't help. The only thing I'm allergic to is Ray Nitschke.[4] (*Yelling*) All right, Butkus! Stick it in their ear, babe!

Brian moves off, back toward the bench. Gale looks to the playing field, but his thoughts are elsewhere. He glances back.

---
4. **Ray Nitschke** (nitch′kē) (1936–): all-star linebacker for the Green Bay Packers.

WORDS TO OWN
respiration (res′pə·rā′shən) *n.*: breathing.

E Elements of Literature
Drama: Complications
? How does William Blinn gradually show, not tell, the reader about the new complication in the plot? [By focusing on a series of small details—Brian's weight loss, tiredness, and coughing—the playwright shows us that a health problem is emerging.]

F Critical Thinking
Interpreting
? Do you think Gale really thinks that Brian has hay fever? [Possible response: Gale seems uneasy with each detail of Brian's health and seems to realize that the problem is more serious than hay fever.]

A Reading Skills and Strategies

Connecting with the Text

❓ What would you do if you had a friend who you sensed needed medical attention? [Possible responses: I would urge this friend to go to the doctor; I would talk to someone else who might be better able to see that my friend got the necessary help.]

B Critical Thinking

Making Judgments

❓ Do you think Coach Halas is making a fair and good decision here? Why? [Possible response: Yes, his main responsibility is to win football games and that means using the best players; yes, if Brian does have a problem, it is wise to find out about it as soon as possible.]

C English Language Learners

Interpreting Idioms

Explain to students that the expression "I wouldn't want to be in *your* shoes" means "I wouldn't want to be you." That is, Brian is going to be very upset with the news and is likely to get angry at the coaches and Gale.

D Struggling Readers

Paraphrasing

Ask students to paraphrase the sentence: "Gale maintains a low profile, not wanting to draw any fire from Brian." [Possible response: Gale keeps his distance and doesn't say much because he doesn't want Brian to get angry at him.]

His point of view—Angle to Piccolo

Seated once more on the bench, his helmet off, still using more effort than one would expect to get his wind back. He sees Gale looking at him and smiles, giving a "thumbs-up" sign.

On Gale

A *Nodding, returning both the smile and the sign, and both are, at one and the same time, lies and prayers.*

Direct cut to:

Interior—Bears' locker room—Day—Full shot

Most of the players are dressed now, or seated in front of their lockers tying their shoes. We find Halas as he comes out of his office, his expression somber. He pulls up a stool beside Gale and sits, drained, enervated.

> GALE. Lookin' at you, I'd never know we won the game.
> HALAS (*small smile*). I don't feel very much like a winner at the moment.
> GALE. Why not?

A deep breath, a gathering of his forces.

B HALAS. Gale, I'm sending Brian Piccolo back to Chicago. He won't make the rest of the road trip with us. Ralph Kurek's going to start next week.
> GALE.
> (*beat*)
> Why?
> HALAS. Because I've had a policy on this team from the very start—the best player plays, no exceptions. And right now—Kurek is the best player.
> GALE. Look, a lot of guys take a while to get on track for a season, slow starters, and . . .
> HALAS (*finishing for him*). And Brian Piccolo has never been one of those guys, Gale. He's always been in shape, able to give one hundred percent. But he isn't

---

doing that anymore, and that worries me. (*With regret*) I don't know why—something physical—or whether he's got personal problems, something with his wife or children—but the truth is that something is taking the edge off of him—and I want to find out what that something is. For his sake and the team's. Can't afford to lose a back that good.
> GALE (*resigned*). When's he going to find out?
> HALAS. Abe's telling him now. That's why I didn't want you to go right back to the hotel.
> GALE. Wouldn't want to be in Abe's shoes about now. . . .
C HALAS. I wouldn't want to be in *your* shoes about ten minutes from now.

Direct cut to:

Interior—Hotel room—Night—On suitcase

A bundle of wadded-up clothes is thrown into the suitcase. We pull back to reveal Piccolo in the act of packing, moving from closet and **D** *dresser to the suitcase on the bed. Gale maintains a low profile, not wanting to draw any fire from Brian.*

> BRIAN. Who'd believe it? I mean, really, who'd believe it!
> GALE. Halas just wants you to see the doctor, and . . .
> BRIAN. Halas doesn't know what he wants! Gibron's his boy and you should have heard *that* lecture! Kept telling me to patch things up with Joy. I tell him things are fine with me and Joy. And he just

---

WORDS TO OWN

somber (säm′bər) *adj.*: serious.
enervated (en′ər·vāt′id) *v.* used as *adj.*: exhausted; weakened.

Getting Students Involved

Cooperative Learning

In the Cards. Have students work in groups of four to create football cards for Gale and Brian. Ask them to review the selection to find the following information for each player:

- Real name/nickname/team name
- Football position/year entered the league
- Description of personality, using words or phrases from the selection

- Any other information given in the teleplay that students find noteworthy

Ask students to include the information on the cards. Allow them to use real football cards as models, but remind them that their cards should provide mainly personal, not statistical, information.

Enrichment Activity

Short Stories into Scripts. Point out the telegraphic style in which the stage directions for the teleplay are written. Explain how sharp images or details can succinctly create a mood or scene. After students review a few passages with an eye on style, ask them to translate a section of a favorite short story into a portion of a teleplay script, complete with dialogue and stage directions.

smiles that Father Flanagan[5] smile of his and says I shouldn't be afraid to level with him.

GALE. Pic, be fair, now. Dr. Fox says that . . .

BRIAN. Oh, spare me any crud about our great team doctor. Wants me to get a physical for the cough, right? No allergy. Then what is it, I say! Want to hear what he says? *Could* be a virus. *Could* be a staph infection.[6] *Could* be any one of a thousand things. It's like being treated in a Chinese restaurant—two from column A, three from column B!

GALE. He's just trying to help, Pic. . . .

A beat, then Brian sits on the bed, calming somewhat, but still angry and frustrated.

BRIAN. Yeah—I suppose you're right—but it's all so pointless, Gale. I know perfectly well what's wrong with me.

He looks over at Gale, eyes radiating sincerity.

BRIAN. Gale—I think I'm pregnant.

Direct cut to:

Interior—Visiting team locker room—Day—Full shot

The Chicago Bears suit up. Linemen pound each other's shoulder pads to a tighter fit. Some of the players sit in front of their lockers, wide-eyed, seeing nothing. Others move about nervously, bouncing on the balls of their feet, trembling with caged energy.

Angle to training table

Gale is having his ankle wrapped tightly with adhesive tape. His face has the look of a

5. **Father Flanagan:** Edward Joseph Flanagan (1886–1948), founder of Boys Town, a famous orphanage in Nebraska. Father Flanagan was known for his kindness and sympathy for young people in trouble. He liked to say "There are no bad boys."
6. **staph** (staf) **infection:** short for *staphylococcus infection*. Staphylococci are bacteria.

carving—somber, dark, guarded. The trainer finishes the job and Gale nods his thanks, moving off the table, another man following behind him at once. We move with him as he strides toward a door at the other end of the locker room. He passes by Gibron, who is going over the attack plan with Concannon and the second-string quarterback, past linemen who are simply yelling at each other, wordless growls and bellows. Gale stops in front of the door bearing the word COACH. *He knocks on the door.*

HALAS (*offstage*). Come in.

Interior—The coach's office—Day—Full shot

Halas is seated behind the desk, hat and dark glasses on. Ed McCaskey is at a water cooler in the corner, drawing a paper cup out of the container, using the water to wash down a pill. At first, both men seem quite normal, but it's a facade *and one that's being* eroded *with each passing second.*

GALE. Which end of the field you want me to take if we lose the toss?

McCaskey and Halas stare at him for a second, then look to each other. Gale is a little baffled by the delay; the question is a standard one. Some kind of communication is going on between the two older men. They nod.

HALAS. Come on in, Gale. Close the door.

There is something in that tone, something vulnerable and sad, out of key. Gale steps into the room and closes the door as requested. There is a short silence, each of the other men hoping they'll not have to take the lead.

WORDS TO OWN
facade (fə·säd′) *n.:* literally, the front part of a building; here, a "front" put up to hide real feelings.
eroded (ē·rōd′id) *v.:* worn away.

Crossing the Curriculum

Social Studies/History
Interested students might trace the historical development of football from its origins in ancient Rome, its development in England, and its divergence from the games of soccer and rugby. Suggest that students show their findings on a time line.

Art
Ask students to imagine how they would describe friendship visually without using words. Give students time to think about what images or symbols they would use. Then encourage them to create abstract depictions of friendship in drawings, collages, or waterworks.

Mathematics
When Gale Sayers signed with the Chicago Bears as their top draft pick in 1965, he got a $50,000 bonus and a four-year contract that paid $25,000 a year. Ask students to research the bonuses and salaries that today's top draft picks are paid in pro football and compare these percentagewise with Sayers's package. Challenge students to adjust the figures for inflation before making their comparisons.

A Critical Thinking

Making Connections

❓ What other characters in a movie or story have experienced awe as it is defined here by William Blinn? [Possible response: In "The Naming of Names" the Bitterings were awed by their new home on Mars.]

B Reading Skills and Strategies

Visualizing

❓ What impact might the freeze-frame technique have on audiences? [Possible responses: It forces the audience to notice a very important moment. Since it's the same technique used when Gale was hurt, readers and viewers will associate Brian's illness with Gale's knee injury.]

C Elements of Literature

Character

❓ How does Gale's offer to speak to the team show that he is changing? [Possible response: Gale had always been unable to speak in public. His feelings of friendship and loyalty to Brian enable him to overcome this problem finally.]

HALAS. Gale—we've just had a phone call from Memorial Hospital. . . .

Halas removes the glasses. His eyes are red. He takes a breath.

HALAS. Brian Piccolo has cancer.

> *Awe has within it an element of fear, of facing something so basic, so large, that one cannot ever truly cope with it. Gale reacts with prayerful disbelief and awe.*

GALE. Oh, God . . .

Full shot

Halas kneads the bridge of his nose, the eyes closed as if hoping the curtain of his eyelids will allow time for a scene change.

HALAS. They've scheduled an operation for tomorrow morning.
GALE (*feeling*). An operation to do what?
MCCASKEY (*evenly, calmly*). Gale, they've got to remove part of Brian's right lung.

> *This strikes Gale like a whiplash. He starts to sink weakly into a nearby chair, and as he does so the frame freezes several times, giving the same look associated with the knee injury. As he sinks into the chair, the image moves with stuttering, uneven speed.*

HALAS (*offstage*). The doctors don't have any explanation, Gale. It must be something Brian has carried around inside him all his life. What set it off, they don't know. As to whether or not they found it in time—well, they don't know that either, I'm afraid.

Gale's eyes are glazed. His spirit has been blindsided.[7] Halas and McCaskey are no less affected.

MCCASKEY (*to Halas*). Who tells them?

---

7. **blindsided:** literally, hit on one side while looking in the other direction.

---

308 WE ROOKIES HAVE TO STICK TOGETHER

Halas sighs, nodding.

HALAS. I know. It's my responsibility and I'll . . .
GALE (*interrupting*). I'll tell them.
HALAS (*surprised*). You, Gale?
GALE (*rising*). That's right, me. I'll tell them. Let's go. (*To McCaskey*) Does Linda know?
MCCASKEY. I don't think so. . . .
GALE. Call her and tell her.

He pulls open the door, looking to Halas. The Coach and McCaskey trade a swift look, then Halas gets to his feet. As he moves to the door, McCaskey picks up the phone on the desk and starts to dial.

Interior—The locker room—Day—Full shot

Halas and Gale come out of the Coach's room. Halas's presence is noted quickly and the players gather around in a loose semi-circle. Gale appears very much in control of himself, in command of the situation.

HALAS (*to players*). Gale has got something he'd like to say to you all. Gale . . .

Gale attempts to sustain eye contact with the other members of the team, but it swiftly becomes clear to him that he can't make it. Initially, his voice is strong and clear, but he can't hold it there for long.

GALE. You—you all know that we hand out a game ball to the outstanding player. Well, I'd like to change that a little. We just got word that Brian Piccolo—that he's sick. Very sick. It looks like—uh—that he might not ever play football again—or—for a long time. . . .
  (*beat*)
And—I think we should all dedicate ourselves to—give our maximum effort to win this ball game and give the game ball to

---

Using Students' Strengths

Spatial Learners
Suggest that students block out on paper where the various characters might stand and how they might move during certain scenes. These students might direct the actors' movements during a reading of the scenes.

Kinesthetic Learners
Invite students to interpret the roles of Gale and Brian. Urge them to use body language, gestures, and facial expressions to contrast the warm and lighthearted Brian with the serious and reserved Gale.

Verbal Learners
Encourage the students to read and record part of the script for a radio drama. Point out they will have to rework the script to provide information that is transmitted visually in the teleplay.

T308

D **Critical Thinking**
Visualizing
? Are these pictures of Brian Piccolo
and Gale Sayers what you would
expect them to look like? Why or why
not? [Possible responses: Yes, they seem
like the characters in the play because
Gale looks serious while Brian is smiling;
or no, they seem less muscular than
football players today.]

A Struggling Readers

Rereading

Suggest that students reread this passage to make sure they understand why Brian is grinning about the Bears' loss. Remind them that Gale's speech had urged the team to give its all to win the game for Brian. Brian is teasing Gale that his speech wasn't inspiring since the Bears lost the game.

B Reading Skills and Strategies

Drawing Conclusions

❓ Why do you think Coach Caroline tells Brian this? [Possible response: He wants Brian to know that he is still important to the team.]

C Critical Thinking

Making Judgments

❓ Do you think that Brian is acting sensibly for someone who has just had a cancer operation? [Possible responses: No, he should be more serious about his diet and recovery; yes, joking and teasing have always been part of Brian's character, and it will make him feel better.]

Pic. We can all sign it and take it up to him at the hosp . . .

His voice tightens with abrupt anguish. He turns away, hiding his tears.

GALE (*continuing, softly*). Oh, my *God* . . .

Fade Out.
Fade In:

Interior—Brian's hospital room—Day—Tight on Brian

Garbed [8] in hospital gown, looking strangely out of place, a young man of two hundred pounds is in something approximating a doll's wardrobe. He's grinning from ear to ear, holding up the front page of the sports section, the headline of which reads COLTS DUMP BEARS 24–21.

BRIAN (*voice-over*). Fantastic! Who'd believe it! Sayers, you've got great moves on the field, but in the locker room, I've got to tell you, you're a klutz! When you dedicate a game to someone, you are then supposed to go out and *win* the game, idiot! Pat O'Brien [9] never said, "Blow one for the Gipper," you know.

Full shot

Gale and Jack Concannon stand at the end of the bed. At a small table near the window, the flowers and cards have been cleared away by J. C. Caroline and a few other players. In place of these niceties, they are opening up two cartons of pizza and two six-packs of beer. Joy Piccolo stands next to her husband.

GALE. Bad—you are so bad.

CAROLINE. We probably would have won if Concannon had called that trap play more,

8. **garbed:** clothed.
9. **Pat O'Brien** (1899–1983): actor who played football coach Knute Rockne in the movie *Knute Rockne, All American.* In the film, Rockne asks his Notre Dame players to "win one for the Gipper"—George Gipp, a star player who had died.

---

but he hates to use it unless you're there for the repeat.

The men at the table have started putting pieces of pizza on paper napkins and begin to distribute them.

JOY. Brian, do you think this is such a good idea? I mean, pepperoni pizza and beer *isn't* on your diet.

BRIAN. Joy—are you telling me as I lie on this bed of pain, my body whittled away at by a ruthless band of strangers with Exacto knives—are you telling me I can't have any *pizza?*

Joy studies Brian, then looks to the other men. She shakes her head, exasperated and loving them all very much.

JOY. Pass the pizza, please. . . .

With smiles, the others crowd around the bed as Joy moves to the table. After a second or two to get the first bite down:

BRIAN. Hey—who wants to see my scar?

Instant negative replies from them all. As these trail off, the door is opened offstage and they all look around. A nurse enters. She gazes at her patient, who has just had a lung removed, as he visits with his wife and friends, all of whom have pizza in hand.

NURSE. *Out! Now! No* discussion! *Out!*

Full shot

Gale, Butkus, Concannon, Caroline, and Mayes quickly gather up the pizza cartons and head for the door, ad-libbing farewells, ducking their heads like schoolboys as they pass by the nurse. Gale is the last in line. Joy straightens up from kissing Brian goodbye.

WORDS TO OWN

exasperated (eg·zas′pər·āt′id) *v.* used as *adj.*: fed up (used here in a playful sense).

Making the Connections

Cultural Connections

At times, Gale Sayers's legendary unwillingness to speak caused misunderstandings. Once, in college, he hurt his leg in a game, and although the trainer couldn't see anything wrong, Gale was in a great deal of pain. Out of shyness, he didn't tell his coach and played the next game anyway, but not up to his usual high standards. Unaware of the problem, the coach accused him of not being motivated to play hard!

After sharing this anecdote, invite students to discuss whether cultures place different values on expressing individual feelings and needs. Are there cultures that expect people to downplay their own individual needs and feelings in the interest of the family or group or some other goal? Have students list the advantages of each approach.

BRIAN. Hey, take Gale down and have him give that little girl his autograph, will you? (*To Gale*) Little girl I met the day I came in here. We had our operations on the same day. Told her I'd get your autograph. You don't mind, do you?

GALE. No problem. Be glad to.

JOY. I'll see you tonight.

He blows a kiss at her and they all leave. The nurse holds for a second in the door, reinforcing her disapproval of Brian's ways. She sighs and steps out of the door. Once it's closed, Brian throws back the covers and puts his feet over the side. There's a good deal of strain and discomfort involved, but it's well within Brian's tolerance. He stands with his back to the window, then starts for the door, his gait a shuffle.

BRIAN. There he goes, sports fans—can you believe it—power, speed, grace, and agility all wrapped up in . . .

Brian halts as the door is opened once again by the nurse. Their eyes fight to a draw.

BRIAN. Don't come any closer, Miss Furman. White lisle[10] stockings turn me on!

Direct cut to:
Children's ward—Angle to nurses' station

The walls here are festooned with crayon drawings made by the patients. The nurses' station has a number of stuffed animals on the counter. As Joy and Gale approach, one of the nurses hangs up the phone and turns to them with a pleasant smile.

NURSE #2. May I help you?

JOY. My name's Mrs. Piccolo. My husband's a patient on the third floor and he told me about a little girl—Patti Lucas—who wanted this gentleman's autograph.

The nurse nods nicely, holding up a finger as

10. **lisle** (līl): made of lisle thread, a very strong cotton.

she flips swiftly through the Rolodex[11] in front of her.

NURSE #2. I'm sorry, Mrs. Piccolo—Patti isn't with us anymore.

JOY. Well, do you have a home address? My husband wanted her to have the autograph very much.

NURSE #2.
(*beat*)
Mrs. Piccolo—Patti's dead. She passed away early this morning.

Gale places his hand gently on Joy's shoulder. Joy nods, forcing a smile mouthing the "thank you," though her voice is absent. Gale is a few feet behind her as they start back for the elevator bank.

Direct cut to:
NFL footage of Gale in an end run, preferably slow motion

The crowd noise is at a frenzied peak; then the frame freezes.

BRIAN (*voice-over*). Look at that knee, will you? That thing is really beautiful!

Exterior—Hospital grounds—Day—Full shot

Brian is wheeled out onto the hospital lawn. He's looking at a sports magazine, which he holds up so Joy can see the picture. They stop beneath a large tree bordering the walk.

BRIAN. Nothing wrong with that knee; I'll tell you that.

JOY. Congratulations, Dr. Piccolo.

BRIAN. Yeah—but you know what—I've been thinking. With Gale healthy, and Ralph Kurek healthy—I'm going to have a rough time getting back into the lineup next year. And I was thinking—what's so difficult about being a kicker? I mean, I

11. **Rolodex:** trademark of an address-card file.

D **Struggling Readers**
Summarizing
Help students summarize what is happening in this scene. Brian is alone and pretending to be a sportscaster commenting on Brian Piccolo's physical condition. He is poking fun at himself, making ironic comments about his power and agility, when actually he is barely strong enough to walk.

E **Elements of Literature**
Drama: Foreshadowing
? Why do you think William Blinn included this short scene about Patti Lucas? [Possible responses: He wanted to contrast the joking of the teammates with the somber reality of the hospital; he wanted to build tension; he wanted to foreshadow Brian's death.]

F **Reading Skills and Strategies**
Comparing/Contrasting
? What does the cut from the hospital room to the playing field emphasize? [Possible response: The scene change shows the contrast between Brian's illness and Gale's health.]

wonder if it's something you can teach yourself. 'Cause you don't need a lot of wind or <u>stamina</u> or size . . .

He looks down at Joy and the look on her face is weakening, hopeful still, but with more effort required on her part with each day that goes by. Brian reads that look like a compass.

BRIAN. All right, Gloomy Gus—what do you think of my brainstorm?

JOY (*floundering*). Well—I don't know, Brian—I'm no expert on kickers and things . . .

BRIAN. You just did an end run that Red Grange[12] would be proud to call his own.

JOY. Don't make fun of me, Brian. I'm scared.

BRIAN (*evenly*). What of?

JOY (*sputtering with disbelief*). What *of*? What *of*? You can't be serious! You know perfectly well what of!

BRIAN (*absolutely sincere*). No, I don't, Joy. I swear to God I don't. (*Taking her hands*) Look—I'm no idiot.—This thing is bad—I know that—but it's a detour, Joy—that's all. It's not going to stop me because I'm not going to *let* it stop me. No way . . . (*Quietly*) I've got too much to do yet, Joy.

Her face in his hands, Brian bends to kiss Joy. As their lips meet, we start to boom up and back. Joy leans her head against Brian's knee, his hand stroking her hair.

Direct cut to:

NFL footage of Sayers

Fielding a punt, signaling for a fair catch, then deciding to let it roll. And roll it does, further and further back toward his own goal. By the time he realizes he should have caught it, there are a number of defensive men all

---

12. **Red Grange** (1903–1991): one of the greatest football players in American history. He was nicknamed "the Galloping Ghost" when he played on the University of Illinois team. He later played professionally for the Chicago Bears.

around the ball, making any return impossible. From the time the ball struck earth and took off, we have heard:

BRIAN (*voice-over*). Pick it up! Pick it up, dummy! Gale! Joy, look at him!

NURSE (*voice-over*). Now, Mr. Piccolo, calm down.

BRIAN (*voice-over*). Calm down? How can I calm down? You'd think the ball was wearing a white sheet.

Direct cut to:

Interior—Hotel room—Night—Full shot

Gale is on the bed, shoes off, talking on the phone with Brian, the mood one of good-natured give-and-take. Seated on the other bed is a football player, Gale's new roommate. There is a room-service cart in evidence, remnants there of sandwiches and glasses of milk. We intercut this with Brian in his hospital room. There is no one else present with Brian.

GALE. Well, I was going to catch it, but when it started coming down, I said I wonder what Pic would do in a situation like this, and ducking seemed to be the answer.

BRIAN. Well, at least you won the game.

GALE. That's right.

BRIAN. Didn't dedicate this one to me, though, did you?

In the hotel room, there is a knock on the door. The other player goes to answer it. He opens the door to reveal a hotel official, who exchanges a few words with the football player, then is allowed into the room.

GALE. Nope. Dedicated this one to Butkus.

BRIAN. Why?

WORDS TO OWN

stamina (stam′ə·nə) *n.*: endurance; ability to resist fatigue.

GALE. He threatened us.

(beat)

How you doin'? Pic? Really?

BRIAN. Hanging in there, Magic. Doing what they tell me to do. You could do me a favor, though.

GALE. You got it. Name it.

BRIAN. Call Joy, will you? When she left tonight, she was really down. I never saw her that down.

GALE. I'll call her as soon as I get back.

BRIAN. Thanks, I appreciate it.

GALE. Okay. Goodnight.

BRIAN. Goodnight.

Gale hangs up, then looks a question to the hotel clerk.

HOTEL OFFICIAL. Mr. Sayers, while you were on the phone, there was a lady who called. She seemed very upset.

He hands Gale a piece of folded paper. Gale unfolds it.

HOTEL OFFICIAL. I hope I've not overstepped my authority.

PLAYER. I'm sure you did the right thing. Thank you very much.

He ushers the hotel official out the door, closes it, then glances back at Gale, who sags, drained.

GALE. It's Joy Piccolo. She says it's urgent. **E**

Direct cut to:

Interior—Piccolo living room—Night—On clock

The time is 3:30. We pull back to reveal Joy, in robe and slippers, pouring coffee for Gale and Linda. The Sayerses have dumped their coats on the couch.

JOY. I know it's an awful thing, to make you fly all the way back here in the middle of the night, but . . .

GALE. It doesn't bother me, so don't let it bother you.

Joy smiles feebly and sits, her hands tightly intertwined, struggling to maintain her composure. A long beat.

LINDA. Just say it, Joy. . . .

Joy nods, a childlike move.

JOY. They found more of the tumor. . . .[13]

The tears come. Her face twists, crumpling under the terror and the fear. Linda moves to her, holding her, both women rocking back and forth. Gale swallows bitterly, probably wishing he was strong enough to cry. He pulls a handkerchief out of his pocket and places it on the coffee table within Joy's reach. She nods her appreciation, dabbing at her eyes. **F**

JOY. They told me today—they want to operate again—and I was going to tell Brian—but—I couldn't, Gale. I don't know whether or not he can take the disappointment. And if he can't—I know *I* can't.

(beat)

The doctor is going to tell him tomorrow morning. If you could be there when he finds out—it might help.

GALE. I'll be there, Joy. **G**

Direct cut to:

Interior—Brian's room—Day—On football game

This is a "board game" with charts and dice and miniature scoreboard. As we pull back, we find Brian and Gale seated on opposite sides of the small table near the window. They both roll their dice. **H**

GALE. What'd you try?

BRIAN. End run.

13. **tumor:** mass of new tissue growing with no function in the body. Tumors are classified as either benign (harmless) or malignant (harmful and possibly fatal). Brian has a malignant tumor.

BRIAN'S SONG, PART TWO **313**

E **Reading Skills and Strategies**

Making Predictions

❓ Knowing that Joy was very upset in the hospital and now has an urgent call for Gale, what prediction might you make? [Possible response: She may have learned that Brian's condition has deteriorated.]

F **English Language Learners**

Paraphrasing

Help students see what the author means when he says Gale probably wishes he were "strong enough to cry"? [Possible response: Gale realizes it would be healthy to cry in this situation; however, his feelings are under such tight control that he just can't break through and express them.]

G **Elements of Literature**

Drama: Suspense

❓ How does the playwright build suspense by telling the audience the bad news before Brian learns the truth? [Possible response: The tension mounts because now the audience very much wants to find out what Brian will do and say when he hears the news.]

H **Critical Thinking**

Interpreting

❓ What does it say about Gale and Brian that in the hospital they play a "board game" of football? [Possible response: For Brian, it is a way to stay attached to the game he loves; Gale is probably creating a situation in which he and Brian can be equals again.]

Taking a Second Look

Review: Using Context Clues

Remind students that they can figure out the meaning of an unfamiliar word by looking at clues in the word's *context*—that is, all the words and sentences that surround it, in a passage.

Activities

1. Ask students to identify clues in the context that shed light on the meaning of *anguish* in the first line of stage directions on page 310. [Gale has just learned that Brian has cancer; his voice is tightening; he is crying; these clues all suggest that *anguish* means "deep pain."]

2. Next have students find clues to the meaning of *festooned*, as used in the stage directions in column 1 on page 311. [The drawings are on the wall in the ward, as a colorful decoration; so *festooned* probably means "decorated."]

3. Ask students to find other unfamiliar words in the teleplay and to use context clues to figure out their meanings.

GALE. Oh, Lordy—I was in a blitz.

Brian starts to consult the complicated chart that will give him the results of the play.

GALE (*indicating game chart*). Well—did you gain or what?

Ⓐ *The door is opened by Mr. Eberle, a nervous, uncertain sort, more at home with facts and figures than flesh and blood. A name tag hangs from the lapel of his lab coat. Brian looks up with a smile.*

BRIAN. Hi. Can I help you?
EBERLE. Well, I'm sorry if I'm disturbing anything . . .
BRIAN. Don't worry—I can beat him later. What can I do for you?
EBERLE (*rummaging through papers*). I know this is a bother at a time like this, Mr. Piccolo, but hospitals have their rules and regulations, you see, and I'll need your signature on this surgical consent for the operation.

He hands Brian the piece of paper, but Brian is scarcely aware of it. He looks at Eberle uncomprehendingly, stunned. Gale is searching for a way to ease this, but before he can locate his voice, Eberle notes the bewilderment on Brian's face.

EBERLE. The doctor *has* been here, hasn't he? He's talked with you, I mean?
BRIAN. No . . .
EBERLE (*looking to watch*). Oh—well, I suppose I might be running a little ahead of my schedule today. Perhaps I better come back after the doctor has . . .
BRIAN. What would the doctor have to say to me? Man, I've *had* my operation, *right*?

Silence, and that's the worst answer there can be. Eberle can't meet Brian's look. After a beat, Brian looks over slowly to Gale.

BRIAN. Talk to me, Magic. . . .

Gale discovers his voice after a second, but it emerges with anguish.

GALE. The tests show—there's more of the tumor than they thought, Pic. They have to operate again. . . .

Once more, Eberle, seeking nothing more than escape, steps forward, holding out the surgical consent and a fountain pen.

EBERLE. So, if you'll just sign the consent, Mr. . . .
BRIAN (*turning away*). No!
EBERLE. But putting this off won't be . . .
BRIAN. Are you deaf? I said *no*!
EBERLE. Mr. Sayers—can't you talk to your friend?

Ⓑ *Brian has moved to the window, shoulders hunched as if gathering himself for a blow of enormous force. Gale looks at him, then turns to Eberle.*

GALE. No, Mr. Eberle, I think I'd rather talk to *you*.
EBERLE. But . . .
GALE. Brian is a professional athlete, Mr. Eberle. And a professional gets into a habit after a while. He gets himself ready for a game mentally as well as physically. Because he knows those two things are all Ⓒ tied up together. And there's a clock going inside him, so that when the game starts, he's one hundred percent mentally and physically. And what Pic is saying to you now is that you're scheduling this game before he can get ready. Couldn't it wait until over the weekend?
EBERLE. Well, yes, it *could*, but . . .
GALE. Then *let* it.

WORDS TO OWN
uncomprehendingly (un'käm·prə·hend'iŋ·lē) *adv.*: without understanding.

Making the Connections

Connecting to the Theme: "We Rookies Have to Stick Together"
Encourage students to discuss how Brian and Gale switch roles after Brian's illness. Ask: How does this development relate to the theme of the collection? [Possible response: Brian supports Gale when Gale is hurt and tries to convince him to talk more. Once Brian is ill, Gale takes on the supporting caregiver role and becomes able to speak effectively, even eloquently. This relates to the theme because "sticking together" is a two-way street. Brian stuck with Gale when he needed help, and now Gale sticks with Brian in his time of need.]

D Reading Skills and Strategies
Visualizing

? If you saw this photograph and knew nothing else about Brian Piccolo, what would you say about him? [Possible responses: He seems like a friendly, outgoing guy. He has a questioning look on his face, so maybe he is the sort who likes a challenge.]

Taking a Second Look

Review: Recognizing Comparison and Contrast

Remind students that comparing means looking for similarities while contrasting is looking for differences. Explain that they can get to know Gale and Brian better by comparing and contrasting them.

Activities

1. Have students contrast the personalities of Brian and Gale at the beginning of the teleplay. In what ways are they different?

2. Ask students to compare the personal lives and careers of Gale and Brian. How are they similar?

3. Finally, have students compare the two athletes at the end of the play to note how the differences in their personalities have been minimized.

EBERLE (*a beat, looks to Brian*). First thing Monday morning, Mr. Piccolo.

BRIAN. Okay.

EBERLE. I'll see you then.

Gale looks back to Brian, who continues to gaze out the window. A beat, as Brian strains to salvage some control.

BRIAN. Thanks, Gale . . .

GALE. No sweat.

BRIAN. Thought you were the guy who didn't talk very well.

GALE. Well—I roomed with an Italian; you know how they are.

Brian turns away from the window. He moves back to the game board, idly scanning the setup. A beat, then a small smile appears on his face.

A BRIAN. Guess what? I scored a touchdown.

We hold on Brian.

Cut to black over following:

NURSE #1's VOICE. Good morning, Mr. Piccolo. Time to wake up now.

Fade In:

Medium shot—Nurse #1

She is looking into lens, smiling Cheshirely,[14] a hypodermic needle in hand.

NURSE #1. I'm going to give you a little shot to help you relax, Mr. Piccolo. You'll be going up to the operating room in about an hour.

BRIAN (*offstage*). My wife here?

NURSE #1. You'll see her when you come down, Mr. Piccolo. Now, this won't hurt a bit.

BRIAN (*offstage*). Yes—you're being very brave about it all.

14. **Cheshirely:** like the mysterious grinning Cheshire Cat in Lewis Carroll's *Alice's Adventures in Wonderland*.

Direct cut to:

Interior—Operating room—Up angle

A doctor, masked and gowned, leans into the lens, arms held up away from his body.

DOCTOR. Mr. Piccolo—we're going to put you to sleep now. . . .

B BRIAN (*offstage*). That's the—worst—choice of words—I ever heard in my life. . . .

As we start a slow fade to black, we begin to hear the sound of applause, growing louder and louder with each second. Then, in utter darkness:

M.C. (*offstage*). Gale Sayers!!!

Cut to:

Interior—Banquet hall—Night—Tight on Gale

Dressed in a tuxedo, Gale starts as he becomes aware of the explosion of sounds being directed at him. Other men at his table poke Gale, all laughing as they urge him to his feet. Startled, he rises and the camera pans him as he is almost passed along from table to table.

The dais

Gale smiles, still at a loss, and moves toward the toastmaster,[15] who is holding out a large trophy to him. As Gale accepts the trophy with a muttered thank you the applause builds once more. Gale looks down at the inscription on the trophy.

Insert—The inscription

It reads "George S. Halas Award—Most Courageous Player—to Gale Sayers."

Tight on Gale

He looks out, nodding acknowledgment to the applause. Slowly it starts to trail off, then

15. **toastmaster:** person at a banquet who proposes toasts and introduces after-dinner speakers.

dies. A moment of throat clearings, chairs shifting into better positions. When it is absolutely still, Gale begins to speak.

GALE. I'd like to say a few words about a guy I know—a friend of mine. His name is Brian Piccolo and he has the heart of a giant—and that rare form of courage that allows him to kid himself and his opponent—cancer. He has the mental attitude that makes me proud to have a friend who spells out courage twenty-four hours a day, every day of his life.

Gale takes a sip of water.

GALE. You flatter me by giving me this award—but I tell you here and now I accept it for Brian Piccolo. Brian Piccolo is the man of courage who should receive the George S. Halas Award. It is mine tonight; it is Brian Piccolo's tomorrow.

Not a sound out there. Gale clutches the award tightly and his eyes sparkle with tears. No attempt is made to hide those tears.

GALE. I love Brian Piccolo—and I'd like all of you to love him, too. And, tonight— when you hit your knees . . .
   (beat)
Please ask God to love him. . . .

Gale steps quickly out of the spotlight. We hold on the empty circle for several seconds before the sound comes. First, one or two people, then more, and swiftly an avalanche of thunder.

Direct cut to:

Interior—Brian's hospital room—Day—On Brian

Joy places the phone on the pillow next to him. When the angle widens, we see Linda is also present. There is an IV stand[16] next to the

16. **IV stand:** short for *intravenous* (in′trə·vē′nəs) *stand,* which holds liquid medication that flows directly into the veins.

bed, a tank of oxygen in the corner. Brian's face is drawn, the flesh pallid *and shiny. We intercut the conversation with Gale in his hotel room.*

BRIAN. Hi, Magic . . .
GALE. How are you, Pic?
BRIAN. Oh, hangin' in there . . .
   (beat)
Heard what you did at the banquet. If you were here, I'd kiss you. . . .
GALE. Glad I'm not there, then.
BRIAN. Hey, Gale? They said you gave me a pint of blood. Is that true?
GALE. Yeah.
BRIAN. That explains it, then.
GALE. Explains what?
BRIAN. I've had this craving for chitlins[17] all day.

Gale smiles on the other end.

GALE. I'll be in tomorrow morning, man. I'll see you then.
BRIAN. Yeah—I ain't going nowhere. . . .

Joy takes the phone and hands it to Linda, who takes the receiver to the window where the cradle is located. Camera closes on Linda, who raises the phone to her ear.

LINDA. Gale?
GALE. How is he, Linda? *Really?*
LINDA *(softly, yet urgently).* Hurry. Gale— please hurry.

Direct cut to:
Interior—Brian's room—On Ed McCaskey

He is seated in a chair by the door, a continuous caressing of rosary beads sliding through his fingers. The room is striped with sunlight from the partially closed Venetian blinds. The door is opened and Gale and Linda come in.

17. **chitlins:** chitterlings, or fried pig intestines.

WORDS TO OWN
pallid (pal′id) *adj.:* pale.

C ▶ **Elements of Literature**
Character
❓ How has Gale changed in handling his feelings? [Possible response: This time he does not try to hide his tears; or, now he has found the strength to cry.]

D **Critical Thinking**
Analyzing
❓ Why does Brian use humor here? [Possible response: Brian is so moved by all that Gale has done for him that he makes a joke to lighten the mood.]

E **Reading Skills and Strategies**
Making Inferences
❓ What can you infer from the repetition of the word *hurry*? [Possible response: The doctors do not expect Brian to live very long; he may become unconscious soon.]

F **Elements of Literature**
Drama: Climax
❓ As you near the climax, the most emotional part of the play, how do you think the central conflict will be resolved? [Possible response: Brian will die of cancer.]

B English Language Learners
Slang
Make sure that students realize that *feeling kind of punk* means "feeling weak," while *sack out* means "to sleep."

C Elements of Literature
Drama: Stage Directions
? What details in the stage directions show you that Brian is very weak? [Possible responses: His vision is out of focus; his breathing is slack; he only lifts the hand closer to the door.]

Comparing and Contrasting Print and Performance
Now that students have read the teleplay of *Brian's Song*, consider showing them the popular made-for-television movie from 1971. After they watch the movie, ask students to compare what they expected to see with what they actually saw. They may find that Brian and Gale did not look or behave as they imagined. They may think that certain scenes are more dramatic when acted than they are on the printed page. You may also want to discuss the effect of the musical score on viewers.

Brian's eyes are closed, and his frame seems small beneath the blankets. Joy bends to him as Gale moves quietly to the other side of the bed, Linda holding by the door.

JOY. Brian—Gale's here.

Closer angle—Gale and Brian

Brian's hand comes up from the sheet in greeting. Gale takes the hand in his. Brian's words come slowly, breath on a ration.

> **A**
> BRIAN. Hello, Magic.
> GALE (*after a beat*). How's it going, Pic?
> BRIAN. It's fourth and eight, man—but they won't let me punt.[18]
> GALE. Go for it, then.
> BRIAN. I'm trying, Gale—God, how I'm try-ing. . . .

Suddenly Brian's head snaps back, his hand convulsing on Gale's. Tears spilling down her cheeks, Joy leans close to her husband.

Seconds go by. Then, slowly, Brian's body relaxes and his head touches the pillow. Joy blots the perspiration from his brow. His eye goes to Gale.

BRIAN. Remember that first year . . . couldn't get a word out of you . . .
GALE. Couldn't get you to shut up . . .
BRIAN. Remember how you got me with those mashed potatoes . . .
GALE. You deserved it—the way you sang that dumb fight song—twice, you did it—at camp, and that time down in my basement . . .
> (*beat*)

18. "fourth and eight . . . punt": Fourth down and eight yards to go is a desperate situation in football. The team can either punt—kick the ball to the other team—or go for a new set of downs, which there is little chance of getting. Brian is admitting that the doctors won't let him give up, although he wants to. Gale's response, "Go for it, then" (which is said when the decision is to go for the downs), gives Brian the encouragement he needs to keep fighting.

318 WE ROOKIES HAVE TO STICK TOGETHER

And that 32 trap play—remember that?
BRIAN. Yeah. How could I forget?

There is a pause. Brian's look turns reflective. He smiles.

BRIAN. You taught me a lot about running, Gale. I appreciate it.
GALE. I wouldn't be running if I hadn't had you pushin' me—helping me . . .
BRIAN. I'll get you next training camp. . . .
GALE. I'll be waiting. . . .
> **B**
> BRIAN. Yeah . . . (*A sigh*) Gale, I'm feeling kind of punk. . . . I think I'll sack out for a while, okay?
GALE. Sure thing.

Angle to their hands

Gale gently lets go of Brian's hand, which falls limply back onto the sheet. Gale's hand rests on the other for a beat, then he moves away.

Full shot

The nurse opens the door for Gale and Linda. He stops, looking back, his voice choked.

GALE. See you tomorrow, Pic. . . .

Tight on Brian

> *He turns his head toward Gale, brings his gaze into focus. He lifts the hand closest to the door and gives a "thumbs-up."*
> **C**
> BRIAN. If you say so. . . .
>
> *Offstage, the sound of the door closing. Brian pulls Joy close to him, his arms about her. His eyes close, his breathing slackens. Joy's lips are close to Brian's ear.*

JOY. I love you, Brian—I love you. . . .

Brian forces his eyes open and looks at her for a long beat. He finds one final smile.

Assessing Learning

Peer Assessment
You might ask each student to write five statements about events and characters in the story, some true and some false. Stress that these statements should focus on important events in the plot. Then assign partners and have each student respond to his or her partner's statements, marking them True or False.

BRIAN. Who'd believe it, Joy—who'd ever believe it. . . .

And Brian and Joy are close for the last time. This stillness will endure. **(D)**

Dissolve to:

Exterior—Hospital parking lot—Night— On Gale and Linda

Arm in arm they move slowly along the line of cars in the parking lot until they come to their own. Gale opens the door on Linda's side and helps her in. As he closes the door, he looks to the hospital.

His point of view—Hospital window

Zooming in on McCaskey in Brian's room. He slowly closes the blinds. **(E)**

Tight on Gale

He gazes at the hospital.

NARRATOR (*voice-over*). Brian Piccolo died of cancer at the age of twenty-six. He left a wife and three daughters.

Superimpose over the close shot of Gale Sayers in the parking lot, footage from the footrace between Gale and Brian, ending with slow motion of their contest that freezes on a tight shot of Brian.

NARRATOR (*voice-over*). He also left a great many loving friends who miss him and think of him often. But, when they think of him, it's not how he died that they remember but, rather, how he *lived*. . . . **(F)**
  (*beat*)
How he *did* live . . . **(G)**

And as Gale moves around to his side of the car and starts to get in, the image of Brian takes precedence, smiling and full of life. A good face to study for a moment or two.

Fade Out.

MEET THE WRITER
An Award-Winning Dramatist

William Blinn (1937–   ) was born in Toledo, Ohio, and graduated from the American Academy of Dramatic Arts in New York City. He has written and produced teleplays for *The Wonder Years* and *Our House*, two syndicated television series about families. For his teleplay of *Brian's Song*, written for ABC's *Movie of the Week*, he received an Emmy, the George Foster Peabody Award, the Writer's Guild of America Award, and the Black Sports Magazine Award. *Brian's Song* also received a Congressional Record Commendation as "one of the truly moving television and screen achievements."

BRIAN'S SONG, PART TWO **319**

(D) Critical Thinking
Interpreting
❓ What do you think the words "This stillness will endure" might mean? [Possible responses: They might mean that Brian will die peacefully, or that love and friendship are what people will remember about him, or that he will not have to suffer anymore.]

(E) Elements of Literature
Drama: Resolution
❓ How does the closing of the blinds represent the resolution of the drama? [Possible response: This symbolizes the close of Brian's life, the end of his conflict with cancer.]

(F) Elements of Literature
Drama: Narrator
❓ Why do you think the narrator closes with emphasis on how Brian lived rather than how he died? [Possible responses: The playwright wants the audience members to think about the meaning of Brian's life and its impact on their own lives.]

(G) Reading Skills and Strategies
Making Generalizations
❓ What is it about Brian's life that people remember? Have students recall events from the play and make a generalization that sums up his approach to life. [Possible responses: Brian always lived life to the fullest, giving 100 percent in every situation; Brian always saw the humorous side of life.]

Assessing Learning

Check Test: Short Answer
Questions and Answers
1. How does Brian's position on the field change? [He is promoted to number one fullback.]
2. What makes the coaches think something is wrong with Brian? [He loses weight and runs more slowly.]
3. What serious illness does Brian develop? [lung cancer]

4. What unwelcome health news does Brian get after his first operation? [He learns that the cancer is still in his lung and he will need another operation.]
5. How does Gale show his friendship for Brian when he is ill? [He visits Brian often; he dedicates a game to his friend; he gives Brian his trophy for Most Courageous Player.]

Standardized Test Preparation
For practice with standardized test format specific to this selection, see
• *Standardized Test Preparation,* pp. 48, 50
For practice in proofreading and editing, see
• *Daily Oral Grammar,* Transparency 18

Connections

This selection is an excerpt from Gale Sayers's autobiography, *I Am Third*. If students have written their own autobiographical incidents (see pp. 182–186), they might compare their work with this professional model.

Ⓐ Historical Connections

After recovering from the injury to his right knee in 1968, Gale Sayers went on to lead the NFL in rushing the following year with 1,032 yards. His future looked bright, and there's no telling what he might have accomplished had he not suffered an even more serious injury to his other knee in 1970. This time he did not bounce back, and the Kansas-born star quit pro football early in 1972. In all, Gale Sayers's professional career lasted 68 games. He was elected to the Football Hall of Fame in 1977.

Ⓑ Elements of Literature

Drama

Point out that William Blinn has Brian and Gale room together in 1965 while in actuality the date was 1967. Ask students why a dramatist might change facts while creating a teleplay. [Possible responses: Reordering events slightly might have improved the overall dramatic flow of the teleplay; having Gale and Brian room together earlier gives the playwright more opportunities to explore their friendship.]

Connections   AN AUTOBIOGRAPHY

Pic *from* I Am Third

Ⓐ Gale Sayers

Ⓑ Brian Piccolo and I began rooming together in 1967, and we became close friends. It's easy to make a big deal out of the fact that he was white and I'm black and to wonder how we got along. But there was nothing to it, although I admit at first we did feel each other out. I had never had a close relationship with a white person before, except maybe George Halas, and Pic had never really known a black person. I remember him telling me that he wondered at first, "Are they really different? Do they sleep in chandeliers, or what?"

The best thing about our relationship as it developed was that we could kid each other all the time about race, do our thing in perfect ease. It was a way, I guess, of easing into each man's world. It helped take the strangeness out of it. . . .

I was in the room when Pic came in. "What are you doing here?" he said.

I said, "We're in together."

He was a little surprised, but I had known about it. They had asked me if I had any objections to rooming with Brian. I said no, none at all. I had been rooming with a fellow who got cut, and I think Pic was rooming with a quarterback, Larry Rakestraw, and they decided maybe they ought to room guys together by position.

Connecting Across Texts

Connecting with *Brian's Song*

Ask students to discuss whether Gale Sayers's autobiography adds information about Brian Piccolo's life and career that is not included in *Brian's Song*. Ask: Does Sayers's story differ at all in the details from the play? [Possible response: Sayers says he began rooming with Brian in 1967, not 1965, as stated in the play; according to Sayers, a team co-captain suggested integrated rooming; in real life, the friendship may have taken longer to get established.] Also ask: Does the speaker in this memoir sound like the Sayers character in the play? [Possible response: Gale Sayers seems somewhat more outgoing and self-assured in this piece than he does in the play.]

But I think Bennie McRae, one of our co-captains, also suggested that they start some integrated rooming, to get a little better understanding with the guys. And Pic and I were the first on the Bears.

But it really didn't make any difference. I think they tend to make too much out of it. Friends like to room with friends, and it has nothing to do with segregation or anything like that.

You can bet we didn't have dinner together in Birmingham that weekend. We joked a lot about it, but we went our separate ways. I don't know if we ate dinner with one another but a couple of times that first year. It was always that when we got into a place I'd call the guys that I normally went out with and he'd call the guys that he normally went out with and we'd split. It was just that he had his friends and I had mine. I think we were both a little unsure about the whole thing at first. And I guess I was a little distant that first year. I think once people get to know me I'm easy to get along with. Pic always knew that on the day of a game I liked to be left alone—just let me be—and this is what he did. But by the end of that first year we had both loosened up quite a bit.

I think he actually helped open me up because he was such a happy-go-lucky guy. He always had a joke or two in him. . . .

Because of my injury and my mental state afterward, I got to know Pic even better and became closer to him than almost anybody else on the team. And then when he became ill, it seemed that our friendship deepened and we got to understand each other even better. And that's

when I found out what a beautiful person he really was. . . .

It was a tough thing to believe that this kind of thing could happen to him. But he was such a strong person. . . . And he was loose about it because that was his way. He'd always been loose about things. His attitude was, What's the use of getting solemn and serious? It doesn't change things. . . . His only concern, he said, was for his wife and his three small daughters.

The funeral was held that Friday, a clean lovely morning in Chicago, and I went through it like a sleepwalker. I was one of the pallbearers along with Dick Butkus, Ralph Kurek, Ed O'Bradovich, Mike Pyle, and Randy Jackson. I think the only thing I remember about that funeral service was one line recited from the scripture: "The virtuous man, though he dies before his time, will find rest."

It was at the cemetery, as the priest was delivering his final words, that I broke down. He referred to the trophy and to our friendship and it was too much for me. I couldn't control myself. I just started to cry.

As soon as the service was ended, Joy came over to me and put her arms around me and we embraced and I told her how sorry I was. "Don't be sorry, Gale," she said. "I'm happy now because I know Brian is happy, and I don't have to watch him suffer any more. He's through suffering now."

She comforted me. I thought to myself, If she can really be that composed, Brian must have really given her something. And I thought, Well, he gave us all something, all of us who were privileged to know him.

C Critical Thinking
Extending the Text
? Have students think about Gale and Brian's relationship as portrayed in the teleplay and as described in this paragraph. What comment do they think Brian and Gale would make about friendships between people from different races? [Possible responses: Just like most friendships, interracial friendships take time to develop; events can change them and make them stronger. Like most strong friendships, Gale and Brian's friendship was based on mutual respect.]

D Reading Skills and Strategies
Comparing/Contrasting
? What quality of Brian's is shown here that does not come out in the teleplay? [Possible response: Brian has respect for Gale's feelings and need for privacy.]

E Reading Skills and Strategies
Responding to the Text
? Through the teleplay, what has Brian Piccolo given you? [Possible response: His life story is a gift that shows one can give 100 percent while maintaining a sense of humor and a lighthearted attitude.]

MAKING MEANINGS (PART TWO)

First Thoughts

1. Possible answers:
   - I felt sad when Brian died.
   - I felt angry because Brian's death seemed so unfair.
   - I felt grateful that Brian had had a chance to play pro ball.

Shaping Interpretations

2. Brian has an internal conflict between his friendship with Gale and his desire to beat him; he resolves it by being true to his friend and his ambition. Brian faces a major conflict with illness that is resolved by his death. Gale's major conflict is his inability to show emotions. He resolves this conflict with Brian's help.

3. Patti Lucas is a girl in the hospital who tells Brian that she wants Gale's autograph. She dies before getting it, foreshadowing Brian's own death.

4. Some instances of opening up include Gale telling a joke in the restaurant; Gale allowing Brian to help him with his knee injury; and Gale's willingness to speak out in public about his friend's illness.

5. Brian gave his teammates an example of strength and courage under fire. He was cheerful and hopeful to the end; even when afraid, he showed concern for the feelings of others.

6. Answers will vary.

7. Students might suggest that the play is like a song intended to honor Brian's life.

Connecting with the Text

8. Students may suggest that the play shows that competition and friendship are not mutually exclusive; others might suggest that competition can even improve a friendship.

Extending the Text

9. Students might cite such leaders as Dr. Martin Luther King, Jr., or Abraham Lincoln, whose untimely and violent deaths have not eclipsed the lasting legacy of their life achievements.

10. Students may point out that pro athletes embody our ideals of power, agility, and skill and so make natural role models; students might also note that wealth, fame, and the stress of professional competition

---

MAKING MEANINGS (PART TWO)

First Thoughts

[respond] 1. How did you feel after reading *Brian's Song*?

Shaping Interpretations

[analyze] 2. What do you think is the most serious **conflict** that each main character faces in the play? How is each conflict resolved? Chart the play's conflicts like this:

Character	Conflict	Resolution
Brian		
Gale		

[interpret] 3. Who is Patti Lucas? How does the scene in which Gale and Joy look for her **foreshadow,** or hint at, the end of the story?

[illustrate] 4. In "Pic" (see *Connections* on page 320), Gale Sayers writes that Brian "helped open me up because he was such a happy-go-lucky guy." What examples can you give of this opening-up process?

[conclude] 5. Gale also writes that Brian "gave us all something." From your own reading of the teleplay, what do you think that something was?

[infer] 6. What did you learn from Gale's autobiography that wasn't in the screenplay?

[compare] 7. If you previewed the play before you started reading, you probably took a guess at what the **title** means. What was your guess? How would you explain the meaning of the title now?

Connecting with the Text

[connect] 8. Look back at your notes for the Quickwrite on page 273. Have your opinions about friendship and competition changed? Explain.

Extending the Text

[apply] 9. The narrator says about Brian, "It's not how he died that they remember but, rather, how he *lived*." What other people could you say this about?

[evaluate] 10. Do you think that professional athletes make good role models for you and your friends? Which pros do you admire most and why?

[analyze] 11. Brian faces illness with courage and humor. Do you think this alone would make someone a hero? Explain why or why not.

---

can lead to excesses that damage a pro's ability to be a role model. Allow students to discuss why specific athletes are good role models.

11. Students should define what they mean by the term *hero*. Some might suggest that dying with courage and humor is not enough to make one a hero. Others might feel that for Brian, already a sports hero, dying well added to his heroic qualities.

Reading Check

a. What change in the team does Coach Halas make at the start of the new season?

b. What are the first signs of Brian's illness?

c. Who tells Brian he needs a second operation?

d. Describe what Gale does when he is given the Most Courageous Player Award.

e. What finally happens to Brian?

Reading Check

a. Coach Halas makes Brian the number one fullback.

b. He is losing weight, running more slowly and coughing, and cannot catch his breath.

c. A hospital official, Mr. Eberle, accidentally reveals the information.

d. Gale says in his speech that he is accepting the award for Brian, who really deserves it.

e. Brian dies of cancer.

CHOICES: Building Your Portfolio

Writer's Notebook

1. Collecting Ideas for a How-To Essay

If you asked Gale how to play football, he would have no trouble explaining the game to you, step by step and play by play. He would have an easy time explaining the game because he likes football and he played it well. What do you do well? Do you like to teach your dog tricks or your little sister how to draw? Are you good at baking bread or playing soccer?

Brainstorm a list of things you do well. Then, pick one of the items, and make a list of all the steps you have to take to perform the activity. If the activity calls for special materials, list those too. You may want to organize your notes in a chart like the one started in the notebook on the right.

Making Pizza

Materials	Steps
yeast	1. Combine yeast, sugar, and water; stir.
sugar	
water	2. Wait 10 minutes, until yeast is foamy. . . .
flour	
oil	

Creative Writing

2. The Times of My Life

In a paragraph or journal entry, write about one of these topics:

- a time when you had to compete against someone you liked for something you wanted
- a time when you helped a friend overcome an obstacle
- a time when you or someone close to you faced a serious illness

Critical Thinking/ Speaking and Listening

3. Here Comes the Judge

Working with a group, role-play the discussion the judges might have had before deciding to award an Emmy to *Brian's Song* as the best TV movie of the year. Before you start your discussion, you should decide how you'll vote: yes or no for *Brian's Song*. Then you must find good reasons to explain your vote. Why is the play good or bad, in your opinion?

Research/ Biographical Sketch

4. Gale's Song

After the events depicted in *Brian's Song*, Gale went on to become a famous football player. Do research in the library and on the Internet to find out more about Gale. You might start with his autobiography, *I Am Third*. (What does the title mean?) Then, write a brief profile of Gale. Mention at least three important character traits, and describe incidents in Gale's life that illustrate those traits.

Grading Timesaver

Rubrics for each Choices assignment appear on p. 139 in the *Portfolio Management System*.

CHOICES: Building Your Portfolio

1. **Writer's Notebook** Remind students to save their work. They may use it as prewriting for the Writer's Workshop on pp. 328–332.
2. **Creative Writing** Ask students to choose a situation they would not mind sharing with others. Students should include specific details as well as feelings or impressions in their writing. Suggest that students make a chart with two columns, labeled Details and Feelings, before they write.
3. **Critical Thinking/ Speaking and Listening** Assist students to develop the criteria and to create an evaluation form. Have everyone complete the form before the judges begin their discussion. Then, discuss one aspect of the teleplay at a time in detail.
4. **Research/ Biographical Sketch** Have student work in pairs to do library or Internet research. Remind students to keep track of the sources of any notes they take. Encourage them to outline their information in chronological order before writing.

GRAMMAR LINK

Try It Out
Possible Answers

1. Brian Piccolo is quite different from Gale Sayers. For example, Brian is outgoing, whereas Gale is shy.
2. Gale Sayers injures his knee badly. As a result, Brian Piccolo gets to play.
3. Brian and Gale are good friends. However, they are rivals, too.
4. Brian's death at age twenty-six was tragic. Therefore, people remember him with deep sadness.

Resources

Grammar
• *Grammar and Language Links*, p. 31

Vocabulary
• *Words to Own*, p. 14

Spelling
For related instruction, see
• *Spelling and Decoding*, p. 16

VOCABULARY
Possible Answers

1. **exuberantly:** energetically, dynamically, heartily
   respiration: breathing, inhalation, exhalation
   somber: serious, gloomy
   enervated: weakened, frail, worn-out
   facade: front, mask, cover-up
   erode: decay, disintegrate
   exasperated: irritated, frustrated
   stamina: endurance, vigor
   uncomprehendingly: unknowingly, bewilderedly, confusedly
   pallid: pale, colorless, wan
2. Gale is first to greet him and slaps him *heartily* on the back.
   Gale's *breathing* returns to normal.
   When Halas exits his office, he has a *serious* look on his face.
   Sitting on a stool next to Gale, he looks *worn out*.
   The normal look on the men's faces is a front that quickly *disintegrates*.
   Although *frustrated* by Brian's friends, Joy still loves them.
   To be a kicker, you don't need a lot of *endurance*, strength, and size.
   Brian stared *confusedly* at Eberle.
   Brian looked tired; his skin was *pale*.

GRAMMAR LINK   MINI-LESSON

Transitions Make the Right Connection

Writers use transitions to show how one idea is connected with another. Transitions can be used to show contrast, cause and effect, and time order.

Some Common Transitions

although	however
as a result	otherwise
because	since
finally	then
for example	therefore

EXAMPLE

Brian and Gale compete for the same position on the team. <u>Consequently</u> [or <u>therefore</u>, <u>as a result</u>], they have conflicts.

Try It Out

➤ Experiment with transitions. Which different transitional words could you add to each pair of sentences below to make their connections clearer?

1. Brian Piccolo is quite different from Gale Sayers. Brian is outgoing, whereas Gale is shy.
2. Gale Sayers injures his knee badly. Brian Piccolo gets to play.
3. Brian and Gale are good friends. They are rivals, too.
4. Brian's death at age twenty-six was tragic. People remember him with deep sadness.

VOCABULARY   HOW TO OWN A WORD

WORD BANK
exuberantly
respiration
somber
enervated
facade
eroded
exasperated
stamina
uncomprehendingly
pallid

Extra! Extra! Reference Aids Help Clarify Meaning

Synonyms are words that are similar in meaning. For instance, *somber* and *serious* are synonyms, but *somber* suggests a gloomier outlook than *serious*. That's why the writer used it on page 306.

You can find synonyms in a **thesaurus** (a book of synonyms), in a **dictionary,** and in reference books called **synonym finders.** You can also check **reference software** or on-line libraries.

1. With a partner, pick five words from the Word Bank. Find the line in the play where each one is used. Then, hunt for synonyms in at least two reference aids. For each of your words, choose the two synonyms that best convey the writer's meaning. Jot them down. After each synonym that made your final cut, note where you found it.
2. Now, use the synonyms to paraphrase the sentences containing your five words. (**Paraphrasing** a sentence means putting it in your own words without changing the meaning.) In each of your paraphrased sentences, include one of the synonyms you found.

Grammar Link Quick Check

Revise the following sentences, adding transitions to connect the ideas more clearly.

1. I am a big football fan. I loved *Brian's Song.* [I am a big football fan, and therefore I loved *Brian's Song.*]
2. Brian was diagnosed with cancer last year. He was unable to play on the football team that season. [Brian was diagnosed with cancer last year. Consequently, he was unable to play on the football team that season.]
3. He attended every practice for the Chicago Bears football team last year. He was in the starting lineup for the last game of the season. [He attended every practice for the Chicago Bears football team last year. As a result, he was in the starting lineup for the last game of the season.]

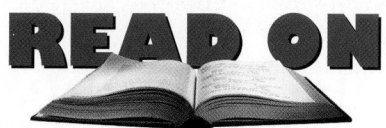

READ ON

Fast Breaks

Jerome "the Jayfox" is a gifted basketball player and the first African American at a North Carolina high school. In *The Moves Make the Man* (HarperCollins) by Bruce Brooks, he develops an intense friendship with a white teammate, and together they struggle to understand the meaning of truth.

Ride 'Em, Cowboy

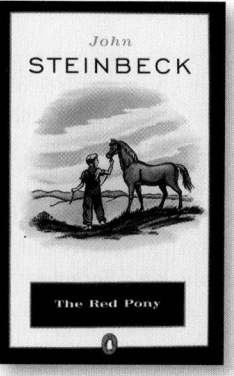

Ten-year-old Jody lives on a ranch in northern California with his family. After his father buys him Galiban, a hot-tempered pony, Jody feels proud and excited. With Billy Buck, the hired hand, Jody patiently trains and cares for Galiban, longing for the day when he can ride tall in his saddle. When the pony gets sick, Jody learns some tough lessons about the ways of the world in *The Red Pony* (Penguin) by John Steinbeck.

Promised Land

Desta is an Ethiopian Jew and a proud African. She lives with her family in a peaceful village, unaware of the prejudice and hatred that surround them. When the hatred touches them directly, Desta and her brother and sister realize they must leave their home. *The Return* (Fawcett) by Sonia Levitin tells of their dangerous journey to Israel.

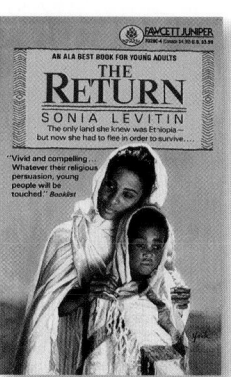

Other Picks

- Gaye Hiçyilmaz, *Against the Storm* (Little, Brown). A young village boy's new life in a poor Turkish city is unbearable until he gets help from a streetwise orphan.

- Bernice Selden, *The Mill Girls: Lucy Larcom, Harriet Hanson Robinson, Sarah G. Bagley* (Atheneum). Three farm girls work in the textile industry during the 1830s and go on to fame and fortune.

READ ON 325

Speaking and Listening Workshop

OBJECTIVES

1. Present an oral interpretation of a story, poem, or play
2. Choose and adapt the material to meet the listeners' needs and interests
3. Prepare a reading script
4. Rehearse your script

Resources

Performance Rubric
- *Portfolio Management System*, p. 140

Introducing the Speaking and Listening Workshop

- Ask volunteers to read the text on pp. 326–327. If possible, play a videotape of an oral interpretation. Ask students what makes an effective performance (for instance, appropriate material, expressive voice, suitable body language).
- Be sure students recognize the purpose of the oral interpretation: to entertain their audience.
- Emphasize that students should select their audience first, then choose a reading that fits the viewers' needs.
- Discuss with students where to look for a work: in the textbook, in a book of favorite poems or short stories, in a collection of famous speeches. If you borrow a few books from the library, students can photocopy passages that appeal to them. Students can also work cooperatively, presenting group readings.

Try It Out

Students can practice their presentation in front of a mirror, paying attention to posture, voice inflection, and facial expression.

Try It Out

Performers can indicate content and emotion by tone of voice, facial expression, body language.

Try It Out

Use the tips in this workshop to prepare and present an oral interpretation of a piece of literature in this book (or another piece approved by your teacher).

Try It Out

To test the expressiveness of your voice, form a group with two or three classmates. Each of you will write a brief "poem" in an imaginary language. Take turns reading your "poems" before the group. Can the others guess what your "poem" is about? What emotions does it express?

ORAL INTERPRETATION

Have you ever told stories around a campfire or even around a kitchen table? Giving an **oral interpretation** can be just as entertaining. Using the expressive power of your voice, you interpret a story or poem or play by reading it to your listeners.

Choosing a Selection

When you interpret a piece of literature, your goal is to share a text with other people. Your first challenge is to choose a piece of literature that you like and that will interest your readers and hold their attention. Ask yourself these questions when you're picking a selection:

1. Who is my audience? What are my listeners' interests, and how closely can I expect them to pay attention? (The interests and attention spans of gym teachers, for example, are different from those of preschoolers.)

2. How much time do I have? The length of your presentation will depend on what other events are planned and on your audience's attention span.

3. How can I make my reading fit the occasion? (E. E. Cummings's poem "It's Spring" might be perfect for a program on spring, but Robert Frost's poem "Stopping by Woods on a Snowy Evening" might not be.)

4. Will I present the text alone, in a solo reading, or will I work with others to present a group reading?

Adapting Material

If you are lucky, you will find a piece of literature that is exactly the right length. Sometimes, though, you will need to choose just one part of a long poem, a short story, or a play. This shortened version is called a **cutting**. To make sure that your cutting will work well for an oral interpretation, follow these guidelines:

1. Make sure that the cutting is interesting and dramatic.

2. If your cutting begins in the middle of a story, you may need to write an introduction explaining what has already happened.

326 WE ROOKIES HAVE TO STICK TOGETHER

Reaching All Students

Struggling Readers

Students who are ill at ease during a formal presentation might give informal talks (for instance, narrate the high point of a recent ballgame); participate in a group reading, perhaps reciting the refrain of a poem; role-play excerpts from speeches by someone they admire; provide suitable props, such as photographs or memorabilia; or perform a work already studied in class.

English Language Learners

Encourage students to prepare readings of poems or short prose pieces by writers from their home culture; other students may act as interpreters. Bilingual students might present oral readings in two languages (a good group activity). Reciting English-language poems that have a distinct rhyme, such as "Annabel Lee" or "Sarah Cynthia Sylvia Stout," should facilitate students' pronunciation. A reading of the latter poem can include suitable props.

3. In plays, cut out the stage directions. (These usually appear in italics and are enclosed in brackets or parentheses.) Try to act out the directions: If, for example, the directions say that a character bows or sighs, act this out.

Preparing Your Script

Once you've chosen your piece of literature and trimmed it to the right length, you can prepare a **reading script**.

- Write out or type all the lines you will read.
- Double-space to make your script legible.
- If you are presenting a cutting, type out your introduction.
- Underline or highlight words that you wish to emphasize.
- Draw a slash where you plan to take a breath or pause for dramatic effect.
- Make notes in the margins about the emotions you want to express. Jot down ideas about gestures, movements, and facial expressions you plan to use.

Rehearsing

- Tape-record your interpretation and then play it back. Does your voice sound natural? Did you pronounce your lines clearly? Is your reading dramatic without seeming forced or stagy?
- Read your script to a friend. Then, ask your friend to give you feedback about your performance. Did your friend understand everything you read, or were some parts confusing? Could your friend distinguish between the characters? Was your **stage presence**—the image you project as you read—powerful and convincing?

As you prepare and rehearse your script, analyze the effects you want to have on your listeners. Keep in mind that there is no single "correct" interpretation. Experiment. Use your imagination. You may come up with a new way of looking at a work of literature—whether it was written last year or many centuries ago.

Try It Out

When you're trying to get across a character's feelings, gestures can be just as effective as words. See if you can match the gestures listed in the left-hand column with the emotions listed in the right-hand column. Can some gestures show more than one emotion?

Gestures	Emotions
shrug	impatience
pacing	skepticism
arching eyebrow	indifference
rubbing chin	puzzlement
stamping foot	despair
wringing hands	anger
rolling eyes	annoyance

Teaching the Speaking and Listening Workshop

- Have students show you their selections; discuss with students the need for any abridging.
- Examine students' reading scripts ahead of time. You can place students in small rehearsal groups. If possible, they can audiotape and play back readings while serving as peer evaluators.
- After the oral interpretations have been completed, students can answer the following questions:
1. What did I learn about reading in front of an audience?
2. As a public reciter, what are my strengths? my weaknesses?
3. What suggestions would I make for a similar activity next time?

Try It Out
Possible Answers
- shrug—indifference
- pacing—impatience
- arching eyebrow—skepticism
- rubbing chin—puzzlement
- stamping foot—anger
- wringing hands—despair
- rolling eyes—annoyance

Reading Aloud in Selected Texts

When students read aloud, their reading should communicate their understanding of the text and engage their listeners. To help students with their understanding of a text, suggest that they look up the meanings of unfamiliar words, pay attention to a word's connotations, and think about the writer's choice of words. Then, ask them to paraphrase the work.

To help students engage their listeners, suggest that they use voice quality and tone to reflect meaning and mood, stresses and pauses to emphasize important words and ideas, and the rate of speaking to punctuate and group ideas.

Students may enjoy applying these skills to some of these selected texts:
- "Fish Cheeks," p. 135
- "I'm Nobody," p. 169
- "Annabel Lee," p. 351
- "The Only Girl in the World for Me," p. 387
- "The Fox and the Grapes," p. 568

Speaking and Listening: Determining Purpose

Before students listen to a speech, they should identify a purpose:
1. Will they listen to gain information on a topic?
2. Will they listen to solve a particular problem?
3. Will they listen critically because they think the speaker is not to be trusted?
4. Will they listen just to enjoy themselves?

Speaking and Listening: Comparing Perceptions

After the speech has been delivered, be sure that students compare their perceptions of it. Do they agree on the speaker's message? Do they agree on the speaker's effectiveness?

MAIN OBJECTIVE
Write a how-to essay

PROCESS OBJECTIVES

1. Use appropriate prewriting techniques to identify and develop a topic
2. Create a first draft
3. Use Evaluation Criteria as a basis for determining revision strategies
4. Revise the first draft, incorporating suggestions generated by self- or peer evaluation
5. Proofread and correct errors
6. Create a final draft
7. Choose an appropriate method of publication
8. Reflect on progress as a writer

Planning

- **Block Schedule**
  Block Scheduling Lesson Plans with Pacing Guide
- **One-Stop Planner**
  CD-ROM with Test Generator

ASSIGNMENT

Write an explanation of how to do something.

AIM

To inform; to explain.

AUDIENCE

Your teacher and other adults, teenagers, or children slightly younger than you. (You decide.)

EXPOSITORY WRITING
HOW-TO ESSAY

In this workshop you'll describe a **process:** You'll explain **how to** do or make something or how something works.

Professional Model

As an expert in managing humans, I want to share some of my techniques. You pups will be on your own before you have time to scratch an itch.

First, master complete control over your eyes. Suppose it's a pretty day. You want to go for a walk. Lie about five feet from the human with your paws extended. Rest your chin on your paws. Look up out of the bottom of your eyes so that just a sliver of white shows. Sigh loudly.

Next, make them think the silly baby talk they use with you is exciting. Perk up your ears. Tilt your head. Smile. I promise you'll get a cookie or even a new toy.

Finally, don't forget the chin-in-the-lap technique. Suppose you need to scratch but you're too tired. Place your chin in the human's lap. Work your nose under the human's hand. Automatic scratching will start. Humans were bred to scratch dogs.

Use these techniques, little ones, and you will enjoy a happy life loving humans who'll never realize that you're the ones in control.

—"How to Handle a Human"
by Joan Burditt

The introductio grabs the reade attention. (The speaker is an adult dog!)

The writer brea each technique down into a series of steps.

The writer uses transitions (First, Next, an Finally) to help the reader follo the techniques.

The conclusion sums up the benefits of learning "how t manage human

Resources: Print and Media

Writing and Language
- *Portfolio Management System*
  Prewriting, p. 141
  Peer Editing, p. 142
  Assessment Rubric, p. 143
- *Workshop Resources*
  Revision Strategy Teaching Notes, p. 15
  Revision Strategy Transparencies 8, 9, 10

Assessment
- *Standardized Test Preparation,* p. 128
  Transparencies 13–18

Prewriting

1. Writer's Notebook

Reread your Writer's Notebook for this collection, and take another look at the list of things you do well. Here are a few ways to cut down the list:

- Think about things you're especially good at.
- Pick activities that you think will interest the audience you have in mind.
- Make sure you can break each process into steps.
- Choose activities that are simple enough to explain in a few paragraphs.

2. Getting Feedback

Test out the ideas you like best with two or three classmates. Here's one way to get feedback:

- On a slip of paper, describe each idea and its audience. Then, have everyone in the group rate the ideas on a scale from 1 to 5 to show how much they think readers would like to learn about that process. (See the examples at the right.)
- If none of your ideas gets a high score, just brainstorm more topics with your group.

You might also ask your friends and family for ideas. They may be able to come up with an activity like making a kind of food, performing a dance, or celebrating a special occasion.

3. Listing Steps and Equipment

Once you have a good idea for a how-to paper, you need to figure out (1) the steps in the process and (2) what's needed to do it. You might start by making a chart like the one at right.

Notice that the steps are listed in **chronological,** or time, order. After you jot down the steps in your process, you may decide to move some around or cross out unnecessary ones.

WORK IN PROGRESS

How to Make a Good Video:
Classmates   Rating: 3

How to Strike Out Every Time:
6th grade   Rating: 4

How to Make Falafel:
Classmates   Rating: 4

How to Give Your Cat a Pill:
Classmates   Rating: 4

How to Give Your Dog a Bath:
4th grade   Rating: 4

How to Dress in 5 Minutes:
Classmates   Rating: 5

How to Wash a Car

Steps	Equipment
1. Spray car with water.	car, hose, outdoor faucet
2. Fill bucket with warm water and liquid soap.	liquid soap, bucket, hot-water faucet, rags or sponges
3. Spread soapy water all over car.	lots of energy!
4. Hose off car with cold water.	clothes you can mess up
5. Clean windows and mirrors.	window-cleaning fluid, rags

Introducing the Writer's Workshop

- Have volunteers read the Professional Model (p. 328) aloud as the class reads silently along. Ask students what makes the essay humorous. Discuss with students whether they think the portrayal of dogs in the essay is realistic.
- Do class members find the instructions in the essay clear? Do students have any other instructions, humorous or serious, intended for pets? How would the essay be different if the speaker had been a human? Write student responses on the chalkboard.
- Be sure students understand the purpose of the writing: to describe a process. Go over the elements of a good how-to essay:
  1. a topic (a process) that is suitable for the audience
  2. clear steps arranged in time order
  3. explanation of needed equipment

Teaching the Writer's Workshop

Prewriting

Have students use the techniques suggested on p. 329 (or any other helpful approaches) to come up with ideas.

Getting Students Involved

Cooperative Learning

The class might compile a Young Person's Guide to Pets and Their Care. Students who have pets can contribute tips and instructions on such topics as feeding, grooming, exercising, and providing health care for a companion animal. These students can write brief anecdotes of happy, sad, or interesting experiences they have had with pets, or they can compose humorous or serious poems about pets. Other students may do research, using books, magazine and newspaper articles, and the Internet, on such topics as unusual pets, pet care in other countries, animals that make good pets and those that create problems when domesticated, breeds of dogs, or the process by which dogs evolved from wolves.

The class can compile a picture collection, perhaps with sections entitled "Pets Around the World," "Pets and Their Humans," "Pets in Famous Paintings," "Pets in Literature," and other titles students may suggest. They can gather pictures from magazines and newspapers; students who like to draw can illustrate scenes—from stories, poems, and other works—of pets (such as Rikki-tikki-tavi). Students can create an imaginative classroom display of the artwork.

Drafting

- If you have not yet taught the Student Model, do so before students begin their drafts.
- Remind students to use every other line when they write their drafts. They should also leave extra space in the right margin, for comments and editing marks.
- Students may use appropriate illustrations, such as sketches of equipment or of hands performing a task.

A Framework

If you don't want to list at the beginning all the equipment you need, you can list the tools and materials you need with each step. The framework of your paper would then look like this:

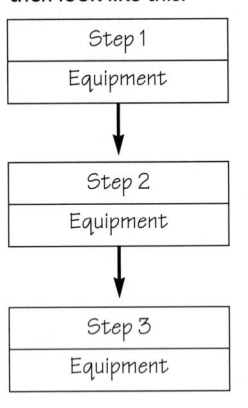

```
        Step 1
      Equipment
          ↓
        Step 2
      Equipment
          ↓
        Step 3
      Equipment
```

Drafting

1. Organizing Your First Draft

When you write your first draft, try to get your ideas down quickly. Start with your Prewriting notes. They should contain most of the specific information you need.

As you write your draft, you may want to elaborate on some of the steps, tools, and materials. If you elaborate on steps, avoid adding unnecessary information. Whatever descriptive details, examples, definitions, and reasons you add should clarify your steps. Remember that your goal is to explain each step clearly so that your readers can complete it before moving on.

Try to provide information that answers any questions your audience might have about the process. For a how-to paper on washing a car, for instance, you need to say *how much* liquid soap goes into the bucket.

Here's an organizing guide you may find helpful.

Equipment needed: _____

_____

Step 1 _____

_____

Step 2 _____

_____

Step 3 _____

_____

(Add as many steps as you need.)

2. Writing a Strong Start and Finish

Your introduction should grab your readers' attention and draw them into your essay. The introduction for this kind of paper should be fairly short. Just write one or two sentences telling what process you are going to explain and, perhaps, why it's important or fun to do. If there's a special reason why you chose this process, include that information in your introduction.

Here are some ideas for a strong conclusion:

- Emphasize how useful or important the process is.
- Describe how sharing this process makes you feel.
- End with a quotation from someone who tried out your "how-to" and enjoyed it!

330 WE ROOKIES HAVE TO STICK TOGETHER

Reaching All Students

English Language Learners
Encourage students to look around the classroom for relatively simple processes they might write about—cleaning the chalkboard and erasers, watering the plants, for example. Go over with them, in particular, the appropriate verbs to use and the name of any equipment the task requires. Be sure students understand the concept of chronological organization and spatial location; discuss transitional expressions (see box on p. 331). They might "act out" such phrases as *first, then, on the right, beside the chair.*

Advanced Learners
Students may write about a more elaborate process and provide illustrations as appropriate. Possible topics include the following: how to take and develop photographs; how to assemble a stamp collection, with photocopies of samples; how to plan a trip, with marked maps, sample itineraries, and so on; how to locate a constellation, with a celestial map; how to write a simple software program; how to plan a young people's fund-raising campaign for a charity. Students can share their projects with the class, especially in visual displays.

This humorous essay explains how not to eat vegetables.

Eating vegetables must be the worst thing that could happen to anyone. But do not despair. A small spark of hope remains. The secret to surviving may be found in knowing a few simple tricks. If they are performed with slyness and cunning, you may never have to eat your vegetables again.

At the beginning of the meal, one trick is especially helpful. Do not place any vegetables on your plate if no one tells you to. If no one is paying attention, you might not have to take any at all. If this plan doesn't work, be the last person to take some. Purposely leave the serving dish near your plate. Cautiously return forkfuls back into the bowl. . . .

If a dog happens to reside at your home, use him to your advantage. Strategically drop small amounts of broccoli (without cheese sauce) onto the floor or your lap. Several napkins are necessary for this maneuver. The dog will be waiting underneath, ready to dispose of whatever is dropped.

I hope these tips will help you avoid eating vegetables. They have worked for me on several occasions, and I will continue to use these handy techniques as long as I am forced to eat repulsive objects.

—Laura Kent
Lake Braddock Secondary School
Burke, Virginia

The writer starts out with an attention grabber.

The writer gives the reason for learning the process. (It's clear this is not a serious essay!)

The writer describes two steps in the process and offers helpful hints.

The writer lists necessary equipment (a dog, napkins).

A personal statement makes a funny conclusion.

Strategies for Elaboration

Using Transitions

Transition words and phrases like *first, next, finally,* and *after five minutes* tell your readers when to take each step. Other transitions, such as *on the table, on the right, beside,* and *in the center* tell readers where things are or where they go. Use both types of transitions to make your how-to paper clear and easy to follow.

Language/Grammar Link HELP

Transitions: page 324.

■ **Evaluation Criteria**

A good how-to paper

1. describes the steps and equipment needed to complete the task

2. presents each step clearly so that another person can do it

3. presents the steps in a logical (usually chronological) order

4. stays on track—sticks to the process being explained

WRITER'S WORKSHOP 331

As class members read the Student Model, be sure they understand the side notes. Assure students that the essay is poking fun at children's manners, not at people who like to eat vegetables. You can extend the discussion by having students focus on questions like these:

? How can the reader tell that the essay is meant to be humorous?

? The most common arrangement in a how-to essay is time order. Where has the writer used this arrangement? Is it effective? Why or why not?

? What transitional expressions has Laura Kent used (see the Strategies for Elaboration box)?

? How would you add to this essay—do you have a favorite vegetable-avoiding strategy?

? What other techniques from this essay might you use in your paper?

Crossing the Curriculum

Health and Nutrition

Vegetables may be frequent objects of humor, but they are essential to good nutrition. Discuss with students what nutrients vegetables provide—for instance, carrots, sweet potatoes, yams, and other yellow-orange vegetables are a good source of vitamin A; cabbage, kale, broccoli, and turnip greens are thought to help prevent cancer. Students can do simple research, in a library book or an encyclopedia article or on the Internet, on vegetable groups and their role in good health. The results of their investigation can be displayed on a mural or on posters. Students might also prepare a Vegetable Atlas, to show regions in which vegetables are an important crop.

Encourage students to describe their own encounters with vegetables. Are there any that students love? They might bring in favorite recipes containing the vegetable. Do students have suggestions for "disguising" vegetables they don't like? Students may be inspired to write poems—humorous or serious—about a well-liked or a disliked vegetable (or other food). For a simple cooking lesson, students can cut the top off washed green peppers, clean out the seeds, and fill the "bowls" with sliced carrots, celery, and other raw vegetables. Serve with low-fat dressing. (Supervise the cutting, or bring precut veggies to class.)

Evaluating and Revising

Have students use the Evaluation Criteria provided here to review their drafts and determine which revisions will improve their papers.

Proofreading

Have students proofread their own papers first, before exchanging them with other students. For this assignment, remind students to use transitional phrases to indicate progression from one step to the next.

If time permits, the final copy should be put aside for at least a day before it is proofread for the final time.

Publishing

Process essays related to classroom tasks can be kept on file for new students. Volunteers can update essays if procedures change.

Reflecting

Suggest that students answer the following questions:

1. What did I learn about breaking a task into steps so that others can follow the process easily?
2. What did I learn about working with others? Did I ask for help or offer to assist a classmate who needed help?
3. What would I do in the same way or differently in another how-to essay?

Resources

Peer Editing Forms and Rubrics
Portfolio Management System, p. 142

Revision Transparencies
Workshop Resources, p. 15

Grading Timesaver

Rubrics for this Writer's Workshop assignment appear on p. 143 of the *Portfolio Management System.*

Communications Handbook
HELP

See Proofreaders' Marks.

Sentence Workshop
HELP

Combining sentences using and, but, *or* or: *page 333.*

Publishing Tip

With your classmates, sort the how-to papers into groups, and bind together papers on similar activities. Give the bound sets of papers to an elementary-school classroom or library.

Evaluating and Revising

1. Peer Review

When you've finished your first draft, do a test run with a partner. Ask your partner to pantomime the process as you read your draft aloud. Before you begin, list the equipment that is needed, and have your partner sketch each tool or ingredient on a separate piece of paper. When your partner needs to "use" a piece of equipment, the sketch should be right there. If it isn't, add that item to your list. If your partner gets confused at any point, make a note on your draft. Ask your partner:

- What steps in the process seem too complicated?
- Did you notice any distracting or unnecessary information I could take out?

2. Self-Evaluation

Ask yourself these questions:

- Will this process interest my audience? Have I made it easy enough for readers to do—or is it so easy that it will bore them? Is the vocabulary right for my audience?
- Will the introduction make readers want to know more about the process? If not, what details can I add to give readers a good reason for learning the process?
- Have I listed all the equipment, materials, tools, and ingredients needed for each step?
- Have I listed the steps in chronological order? Have I included all the details needed to allow readers to understand and follow the process? Do I need to add transitions to help readers follow the steps?
- Have I stayed on track from beginning to end? What details would be better left out?
- Does my paper have a strong conclusion?

PEANUTS reprinted by permission of United Feature Syndicate, Inc.

332 WE ROOKIES HAVE TO STICK TOGETHER

Assessing Learning

Standardized Test Preparation

For practice with standardized test prompts and formats, see
- *Standardized Test Preparation,* p. 128

Sentence Workshop

OBJECTIVES
1. Form one sentence from two or more by creating compound subjects or compound verbs linked by *and, but,* or *or*
2. Create compound sentences by joining two sentences with *and, but,* or *or,* preceded by a comma

COMBINING SENTENCES USING AND, BUT, OR OR

Sometimes a short sentence can express your meaning perfectly. A long, unbroken chain of short sentences can make your writing choppy and dull, however. You can vary your sentence structure by using the conjunction *and, but,* or *or* to combine ideas.

Combine sentences having the same verb but different subjects by making a **compound subject.** Combine sentences having the same subject but different verbs by making a **compound verb.**

TWO SENTENCES	Running backs are fast runners. Receivers are also.
COMBINED	Running backs **and** receivers are fast runners. [compound subject]
TWO SENTENCES	Running backs carry the ball. They make lateral passes if necessary.
COMBINED	Running backs carry the ball **but** make lateral passes if necessary. [compound verb]

Sometimes you may want to combine two sentences that express closely related, equally important ideas. You can connect the two sentences by using a comma followed by the conjunction *and, but,* or *or*. When you join sentences this way, you create a **compound sentence.**

| TWO SENTENCES | They were both football players. They competed for the same job. |
| COMBINED | They were both football players, **and** they competed for the same job. [compound sentence] |

Writer's Workshop Follow-up: Revision

Read your how-to essay aloud. Do your sentences flow, or do they sound dull and choppy? Try combining sentences to improve the sound of your essay or to help readers make connections between ideas.

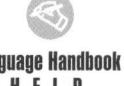

Language Handbook
H E L P

See Combining Sentences, pages 760-761.

Technology
H E L P

See Language Workshop CD-ROM. Key word entry: combining sentences.

Resources ———

Workshop Resources
• Worksheet, p. 43

Language Workshop CD-ROM
• Combining Sentences

Try It Out
Possible Answers
1. Piccolo's smile vanishes, and he nods toward one of the buildings offstage.
2. Gale moves off for the building, but Brian stays behind a moment.
3. Brian Piccolo approaches and starts to unload his tray.
4. The man next to Gale finishes his plate and leaves.
5. Sayers and Piccolo come out of a sprinter's crouch.

Try It Out

Combine each pair of sentences using *and, but,* or *or*. Exchange your edited sentences with a partner. Have you chosen the best conjunction? Are several combinations possible?

1. Piccolo's smile vanishes. He nods toward one of the buildings offstage.

2. Gale moves off for the building. Brian stays behind for a moment.

3. Brian Piccolo approaches. Brian Piccolo starts to unload his tray.

4. The man next to Gale finishes his plate. The man next to Gale leaves.

5. Sayers comes out of a sprinter's crouch. Piccolo comes out of a sprinter's crouch.

SENTENCE WORKSHOP 333

Assessing Learning

Quick Check: Combining Sentences

Combine each pair of sentences using *and, but, or or*. [Possible answers follow each sentence.]

1. Brian wants to play. He does not want to play second string. [Brian wants to play, but he does not want to play second string.]

2. Gale goes to see the coach. He tries to follow Brian's advice. [Gale goes to see the coach and tries to follow Brian's advice.]

3. The two athletes could play the same position. They could try for different positions. [The two athletes could play the same position or try for different positions.]

4. The team's doctor notices Brian's weight loss. Gale notices Brian's difficulty in breathing. [The team's doctor notices Brian's weight loss, and Gale notices his difficulty in breathing.]

5. Gale dedicates the game to Brian. The Bears lose to the Colts. [Gale dedicates the game to Brian, but the Bears lose to the Colts.]

Reading for Life
Reading a Manual

OBJECTIVES

1. Read a manual to get information
2. Use the manual's table of contents and index to locate information
3. Study the diagrams and charts that illustrate the instructions
4. Look up unfamiliar terms and abbreviations in the manual's glossary

Using the Strategies

Answers

1. *Select* means "choose one of the items shown on the computer screen"; *scroll* means "move the image on the computer screen up or down."
2. Answers will vary.
3. Possible response: Among the *significant* differences between the two candidates is that one favors weekly recycling and the other opposes it.

Situation

You're writing a "how-to" paper for English class. You've used the word *important* three times. Somewhere inside your word-processing program there's a thesaurus, a whole treasury of synonyms. How can you get to it? You take out the manual that came with your word-processing software. Here are strategies you can use to read any manual.

Strategies

Read for information.
You read a manual to get information about a tool or program or to solve a problem you're having with it.

- To see what's in a manual, look at the table of contents in the front. Then, look at the index, the alphabetical list of subjects with page numbers in the back. See if the manual includes phone numbers and e-mail addresses you can use to get help.

- Read the directions slowly, word by word. Keep referring to the actual tool or program as you read.

Notice the steps.

- Directions are usually listed

Looking Up Synonyms for a Word in a Document

1 Select the word in the document.
2 Choose Utilities Thesaurus (Alt,U,T), or press the THESAURUS key (Shift+F7).
3 Look through the list of synonyms in Synonyms. Scroll through the list if necessary.

Command for Thesaurus
Utilities Thesaurus or THESAURUS Key (Shift+F7)
Lists alternative words for the selection.

in step-by-step, **chronological** order. Read all the directions for each step before moving on to the next.

Look up unfamiliar words, abbreviations, and symbols.

- In a manual you may see abbreviations like STO and ALT and symbols like * and #. You may also see unfamiliar terms, and words—like *scroll, select, icon, shift,* and *menu*—used in new ways. When you come across an unfamiliar abbreviation, symbol, or word, look it up in the manual's glossary. If it isn't there, try to figure out its meaning from context or ask an expert.

Using the Strategies

Use these strategies as you read the page above.

1. From the context, figure out what *select* and *scroll* mean here.
2. Describe two ways to get the thesaurus screen on your computer.
3. Make up a sentence using one of the synonyms listed for *important*.

Extending the Strategies

Find someone who is having a problem with a tool or a software program. Get the manual, and apply these strategies to help the person solve the problem.

334 WE ROOKIES HAVE TO STICK TOGETHER

Reaching All Students

Struggling Readers
Students who are mechanically inclined may already be familiar with manuals—those accompanying computer games, VCRs, and so on. Ask the students to bring such manuals to class, where they can explain what sort of information they contain. You might invite a service representative from the software manufacturer to help students get their bearings. If some of the students seem reluctant to read manuals, encourage them to do so. You might partner strong and weak students to work together to acquire computer skills from a manual.

English Language Learners
You or a computer-savvy student can present the manual. If it is illustrated with diagrams, computer-literate students may have little difficulty interpreting the instructions. Others may need more practice—to learn basic computer terms as well as computer operations. By using the manual first for functions they already know, students may gain familiarity with the instruction book.

T334

Learning for Life

Conducting an Interview to Research a Question

OBJECTIVES
1. Conduct an interview at a workplace to learn how the employees cooperate
2. Develop a set of guidelines for teamwork, based on the results of the interview
3. Analyze cooperation in the classroom; compare the elements of cooperation in the workplace and in the classroom
4. Choose and complete a project (preparing a handbook of guidelines for cooperative class activities; creating a skit displaying teamwork; designing posters that illustrate teamwork)

Problem

Brian Piccolo and Gale Sayers understood the importance of working together on a team. How do people who work in teams learn to cooperate and act effectively together?

Project

Interview workers in a local company to find out how they cooperate and make an effective team.

Preparation

1. Choose a business that requires people to work cooperatively: a hospital, a restaurant, or a newspaper, for example.

2. Develop some key questions for the experts you will interview, such as these:

   • Why do you work as a team?

   • What roles do different team members play?

   • How do you help one another?

   • Do you have guidelines for working as a team?

   • How do you handle problems with team members?

Procedure

1. Call to arrange a time and place for the interview. Go as a group. (Discuss ahead of time the roles each of you will play, such as note taker or interviewer.) Try to talk to more than one employee—a complete team or several members of a team would be ideal.

2. Don't try to write down everything said during the interview. Instead, jot down important facts and a few direct quotations. If you use a tape recorder, be sure to get permission first. Don't forget to write a thank-you note after the interview.

3. Develop a set of guidelines for teamwork in the workplace based on your interview.

4. Analyze the way your class works together. Compare its procedures with the guidelines for teamwork that you developed. Discuss with your teacher ways that students might learn to be more cooperative. Also, discuss the problems involved in working in teams in a classroom.

Presentation

Present what you have learned about teamwork in one of the following ways:

1. Teamwork Handbook

Develop a handbook of guidelines for working as a team on class projects. Add an introduction about the value of teamwork. If possible, ask the workers you interviewed to review the handbook.

2. Skit

Create a skit for other classes that shows the dos and don'ts of teamwork in action. Use a school or workplace setting.

3. Posters

Create a group of posters for display in the workplace or classroom. Show guidelines for teamwork, such as dividing responsibilities, respecting others, and listening carefully.

Processing

Discuss this question as a class: Are there differences between cooperation in the classroom and cooperation in the workplace? Explain the differences or the reason you think there are no differences.

LEARNING FOR LIFE **335**

Resources

Viewing and Representing
HRW Multimedia Presentation Maker
Students may wish to use the *Multimedia Presentation Maker* to create the handbook and the posters.

Grading Timesaver

Rubrics for this Learning for Life project appear on p. 144 of the *Portfolio Management System*.

Developing Workplace Competencies

Preparation	Procedure	Presentation
• Using logic • Developing strategies • Determining goals	• Reasoning by analogy • Making inferences • Recognizing relationships • Observing and judging reports	• Classifying data • Drawing conclusions • Synthesizing information

Collection Five

Living in the Heart

Theme

The Power of Love *Love, they say, has the power to move mountains. In these stories, love ranges from romantic love, to parental love, to love of place, to children's love for their parents, to simple human decency.*

Reading the Anthology

Reaching Struggling Readers

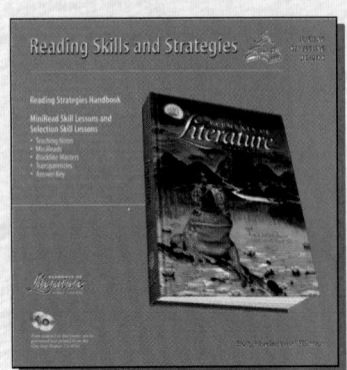

The Reading Skills and Strategies: Reaching Struggling Readers binder provides materials coordinated with the Pupil's Edition (see the Collection Planner, p. T355C) to help students who have difficulty reading and comprehending text, or students who are reluctant readers. The binder for seventh grade is organized around eleven individual skill areas and offers the following options:

- **MiniRead** MiniReads are short, easy texts that give students a chance to practice a particular skill and strategy before reading selections in the Pupil's Edition. Each MiniRead Skill Lesson can be taught independently or used in conjunction with a Selection Skill Lesson.

- **Selection Skill Lessons** Selection Skill Lessons allow students to apply skills introduced in the MiniReads. Each Selection Skill Lesson provides reading instruction and practice specific to a particular piece of literature in the Pupil's Edition.

Reading Beyond the Anthology

Read On Collection Five includes an annotated bibliography of books suitable for extended reading. The suggested books are related to works in this collection by theme, by author, or by subject. To preview the Read On for Collection Five, please turn to p. T407.

HRW Library The *HRW Library* offers novels, plays, and short-story collections for extended reading. Each book in the Library includes one or more major works and thematically or topically related Connections. The Connections are magazine articles, poems, or other pieces of literature. Each book in the *HRW Library* is also accompanied by a Study Guide that provides teaching suggestions and worksheets. For Collection Five, the following titles are recommended.

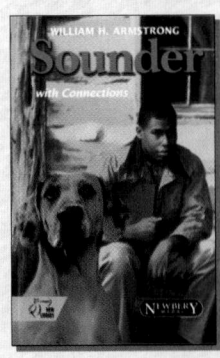

SOUNDER
William Armstrong
A young boy and a loyal hunting dog spend years searching for the father who was sentenced to a chain gang for stealing a ham to feed his hungry family. An enduring story of the power of love.

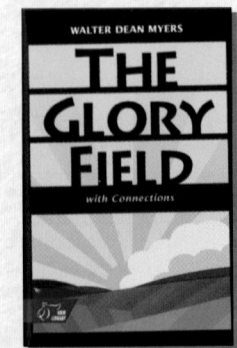

THE GLORY FIELD
Walter Dean Myers
This is a novel about a family that has been in America for 241 years. Malcolm, a descendant of the great Muhammed Bilal, looks to the guidance and struggles of others as he and his family fight for freedom.

Skills Focus

Selection or Feature	Reading Skills and Strategies	Elements of Literature	Language/ Grammar	Vocabulary/ Spelling	Writing	Listening/ Speaking	Viewing/ Representing
Elements of Literature: Poetry: Sound Effects (p. 338)		Sound Effects, pp. 338–339					
The Highwayman (p. 340) Alfred Noyes	Predict, p. 340 Dialogue with the Text, pp. 340, 349 Identify the Sequence of Events, p. 348	Narrative Poems, pp. 340, 348 Setting, p. 348 Rhythm, p. 348			Summarize and Respond, p. 349	Prepare and Present a Choral Reading Using Voice to Emphasize Literary Elements, p. 349	Design a Movie Poster Capturing the Mood of the Poem, p. 349
Annabel Lee (p. 350) Edgar Allan Poe	Dialogue with the Text, p. 350	Repetition, pp. 351, 354 Setting, p. 354			Take Notes for a Biographical Sketch, p. 354	Present a Choral Reading, p. 354	
Elements of Literature: Poetry: Images (p. 355)		Images, p. 355					
User Friendly (p. 356) T. Ernesto Bethancourt	Recognize Causes and Effects, pp. 356, 365 Retell the Main Events of a Story, p. 365	Character, pp. 356, 365	Pronouns in Compound Structures, p. 366	Homographs, p. 366	Make a List of Valued Things or People, p. 365		Make a Portrait of a Character, p. 365
Reading Skills and Strategies: Thinking Critically (p. 367)	Distinguish Between Fact and Opinion, p. 367						
Miss Awful (p. 368) Arthur Cavanaugh	Form Valid Opinions, pp. 368, 383		Homonyms, p. 385	Antonyms and Synonyms, p. 385 Word Maps, p. 385	Notes for a Character Sketch, p. 384 Write a Campaign Speech, p. 384	Campaign Speech, p. 384 Role-play Characters, p. 384	Create a Treasure Box, p. 384
The Only Girl in the World for Me (p. 386) Bill Cosby	Match Reading Purpose to Text, pp. 386, 391	Motivation, p. 386 Exaggeration, p. 391	Unclear Pronoun References, p. 392	Word Roots from Latin, p. 392 Affixes, p. 392	Create a Character Profile, p. 391	Round Table Discussion, p. 386 Enact the Story, p. 391	Create a Storyboard, p. 391
Gold (p. 393) Pat Mora	Understand Mood, pp. 393, 396	Personification, p. 396			Details, p. 396 Poem, p. 396		
Elements of Literature: Poetry: Figures of Speech (p. 397)		Figures of Speech, p. 397 • Simile • Metaphor					
My Father Is a Simple Man (p. 398) Luis Omar Salinas **Mama Is a Sunrise** (p. 400) Evelyn Tooley Hunt	Compare Texts, pp. 398, 402	Free Verse, pp. 398, 403 Mood, p. 403			Develop a List of Comparisons, p. 403 Write a Poem, p. 403		Use a Chart to Compile Information, p. 398 Make a Greeting Card, p. 403
No Questions Asked: Papa's Parrot (p. 404) Cynthia Rylant	The **No Questions Asked** feature provides students with an unstructured opportunity to practice reading strategies using a selection that extends the theme of the collection.						
Speaking and Listening Workshop: Interviewing (p. 408)						Conduct an Interview, pp. 408–409	
Writer's Workshop: Biographical Sketch (p. 410)					Write a Biographical Sketch, pp. 410–414		
Sentence Workshop: Revising Wordy Sentences (p. 415)			Wordy Sentences, p. 415		Revise Wordy Sentences, p. 415		
Reading for Life: Reading a Geography Book (p. 416)	Use the Text's Structure, p. 416						Use Maps and Graphic Features, p. 416
Learning for Life: Conflict Resolution (p. 417)					Write a Song, p. 417	Role-Play a Conflict Resolution, p. 417	Create a Billboard, p. 417

Skills Focus

Resources for this Collection

Note: All resources for this collection are available for preview on the *One-Stop Planner CD-ROM 2 with Test Generator.* All worksheets and blackline masters may be printed from the CD-ROM.

Internet Resources
go.hrw.com LE0 7-5

Selection or Feature	Reading and Literary Skills	Language and Grammar
Elements of Literature: Poetry: Sound Effects (p. 338)	• *Literary Elements,* Transparency 5	
The Highwayman (p. 340) Alfred Noyes	• *Graphic Organizers for Active Reading,* Worksheet p. 21 • *Literary Elements:* Transparency 5; Worksheet p. 16	• *Daily Oral Grammar,* Transparency 19
Annabel Lee (p. 350) Edgar Allan Poe	• *Graphic Organizers for Active Reading,* Worksheet p. 22 • *Literary Elements:* Transparency 6; Worksheet p. 19	• *Daily Oral Grammar,* Transparency 20
Elements of Literature: Poetry: Images (p. 355)	• *Literary Elements,* Transparency 6	
User Friendly (p. 356) T. Ernesto Bethancourt	• *Reading Skills and Strategies: Reaching Struggling Readers* • MiniRead Skill Lesson, p. 160 • Selection Skill Lesson, p. 178 • *Graphic Organizers for Active Reading,* Worksheet p. 23	• *Grammar and Language Links:* Pronouns, Worksheet p. 33 • *Language Workshop CD-ROM,* Pronouns • *Daily Oral Grammar,* Transparency 21
Miss Awful (p. 368) Arthur Cavanaugh **Connections: Eighth-Grade Teacher Finds Grammar Errors on Food Label** (p. 382) *from N. P. R.*	• *Reading Skills and Strategies: Reaching Struggling Readers* • Selection Skill Lesson, p. 76 • *Graphic Organizers for Active Reading,* Worksheet p. 24	• *Grammar and Language Links:* Homonyms, Worksheet p. 35 • *Language Workshop CD-ROM,* Homonyms • *Daily Oral Grammar,* Transparency 22
The Only Girl in the World for Me (p. 386) Bill Cosby	• *Reading Skills and Strategies: Reaching Struggling Readers* • MiniRead Skill Lesson, p. 120 • Selection Skill Lesson, p. 126 • *Graphic Organizers for Active Reading,* Worksheet p. 25	• *Grammar and Language Links:* Pronoun Reference, Worksheet p. 37 • *Language Workshop CD-ROM,* Pronoun-Antecedent Agreement • *Daily Oral Grammar,* Transparency 23
Gold (p. 393) Pat Mora		
Elements of Literature: Poetry: Figures of Speech (p. 397)	• *Literary Elements,* Transparency 7	
My Father Is a Simple Man (p. 398) Luis Omar Salinas **Mama Is a Sunrise** (p. 400) Evelyn Tooley Hunt	• *Graphic Organizers for Active Reading,* Worksheet p. 26 • *Literary Elements:* Transparency 7; Worksheet p. 22	
No Questions Asked: Papa's Parrot (p. 404) Cynthia Rylant	The **No Questions Asked** feature provides students with an unstructured opportunity to practice reading strategies using a selection that extends the theme of the collection.	
Speaking and Listening Workshop: Interviewing (p. 408)		
Writer's Workshop: Biographical Report (p. 410)		
Sentence Workshop: Revising Wordy Sentences (p. 415)		• *Workshop Resources,* p. 45 • *Language Workshop CD-ROM,* Wordiness
Learning for Life: Conflict Resolution (p. 417)		

Collection Planner

Collection Resources

- *Cross-Curricular Activities,* p. 35
- *Portfolio Management System:*
  Introduction to Portfolio Assessment, p. 1;
  Parent/Guardian Letters, p. 95

- *Formal Assessment,*
  Reading Application Test, p. 81
- *Test Generator,* Collection Test 💿

Vocabulary, Spelling, and Decoding	Writing	Listening and Speaking, Viewing and Representing	Assessment
			• *Formal Assessment,* Literary Elements Test, p. 76
	• *Portfolio Management System,* Rubrics for Choices, p. 145	• *Visual Connections,* Videocassette A, Segment 5 📼 • *Audio CD Library,* Disc 9, Track 3 🎧 • *Viewing and Representing:* Fine Art Transparency 10 📽 Worksheet p. 40 • *Portfolio Management System,* Rubrics for Choices, p. 145	• *Formal Assessment,* Selection Test, p. 65 • *Standardized Test Preparation,* pp. 52, 54 • *Test Generator* (One-Stop Planner CD-ROM) 💿
	• *Portfolio Management System,* Rubrics for Choices, p. 146	• *Audio CD Library,* Disc 9, Track 4 🎧 • *Portfolio Management System,* Rubrics for Choices, p. 146	• *Formal Assessment,* Selection Test, p. 66 • *Test Generator* (One-Stop Planner CD-ROM) 💿
			• *Formal Assessment,* Literary Elements Test, p. 78
• *Spelling and Decoding,* Worksheet p. 17	• *Portfolio Management System,* Rubrics for Choices, p. 147	• *Audio CD Library,* Disc 9, Track 5 🎧 • *Portfolio Management System,* Rubrics for Choices, p. 147	• *Formal Assessment,* Selection Test, p. 67 • *Standardized Test Preparation,* p. 56 • *Test Generator* (One-Stop Planner CD-ROM) 💿
• *Words to Own,* Worksheet p. 15 • *Spelling and Decoding,* Worksheet p. 18	• *Portfolio Management System,* Rubrics for Choices, p. 148	• *Audio CD Library,* Disc 10, Track 2 🎧 • *Portfolio Management System,* Rubrics for Choices, p. 148	• *Formal Assessment,* Selection Test, p. 69 • *Standardized Test Preparation,* p. 58 • *Test Generator* (One-Stop Planner CD-ROM) 💿
	• *Portfolio Management System,* Rubrics for Choices, p. 149	• *Visual Connections,* Videocassette B, Segment 6 📼 • *Audio CD Library,* Disc 10, Track 3 🎧 • *Portfolio Management System,* Rubrics for Choices, p. 149	• *Formal Assessment,* Selection Test, p. 71 • *Standardized Test Preparation,* p. 60 • *Test Generator* (One-Stop Planner CD-ROM) 💿
	• *Portfolio Management System,* Rubrics for Choices, p. 150	• *Audio CD Library,* Disc 10, Track 4 🎧 • *Portfolio Management System,* Rubrics for Choices, p. 150	• *Formal Assessment,* Selection Test, p. 73 • *Test Generator* (One-Stop Planner CD-ROM) 💿
			• *Formal Assessment,* Literary Elements Test, p. 79
	• *Portfolio Management System,* Rubrics for Choices, p. 151	• *Audio CD Library,* Disc 10, Tracks 5, 6 🎧 • *Viewing and Representing:* Fine Art Transparencies 11, 12 📽 Worksheet pp. 44, 48 • *Portfolio Management System,* Rubrics for Choices, p. 151	• *Formal Assessment,* Selection Test, p. 74 • *Test Generator* (One-Stop Planner CD-ROM)
		• *Audio CD Library,* Disc 10, Track 7 🎧	
			• *Portfolio Management System,* p. 152
	• *Workshop Resources,* p. 21 • *Writer's Workshop 1 CD-ROM,* Firsthand Biography 💿		• *Portfolio Management System* • Prewriting, p. 153 • Peer Editing, p. 154 • Assessment Rubric, p. 155
		• *Viewing and Representing,* HRW Multimedia Presentation Maker	• *Portfolio Management System,* Rubrics, p. 156

Collection Planner

Transparency   CD-ROM   Video   Audio CD

T335D

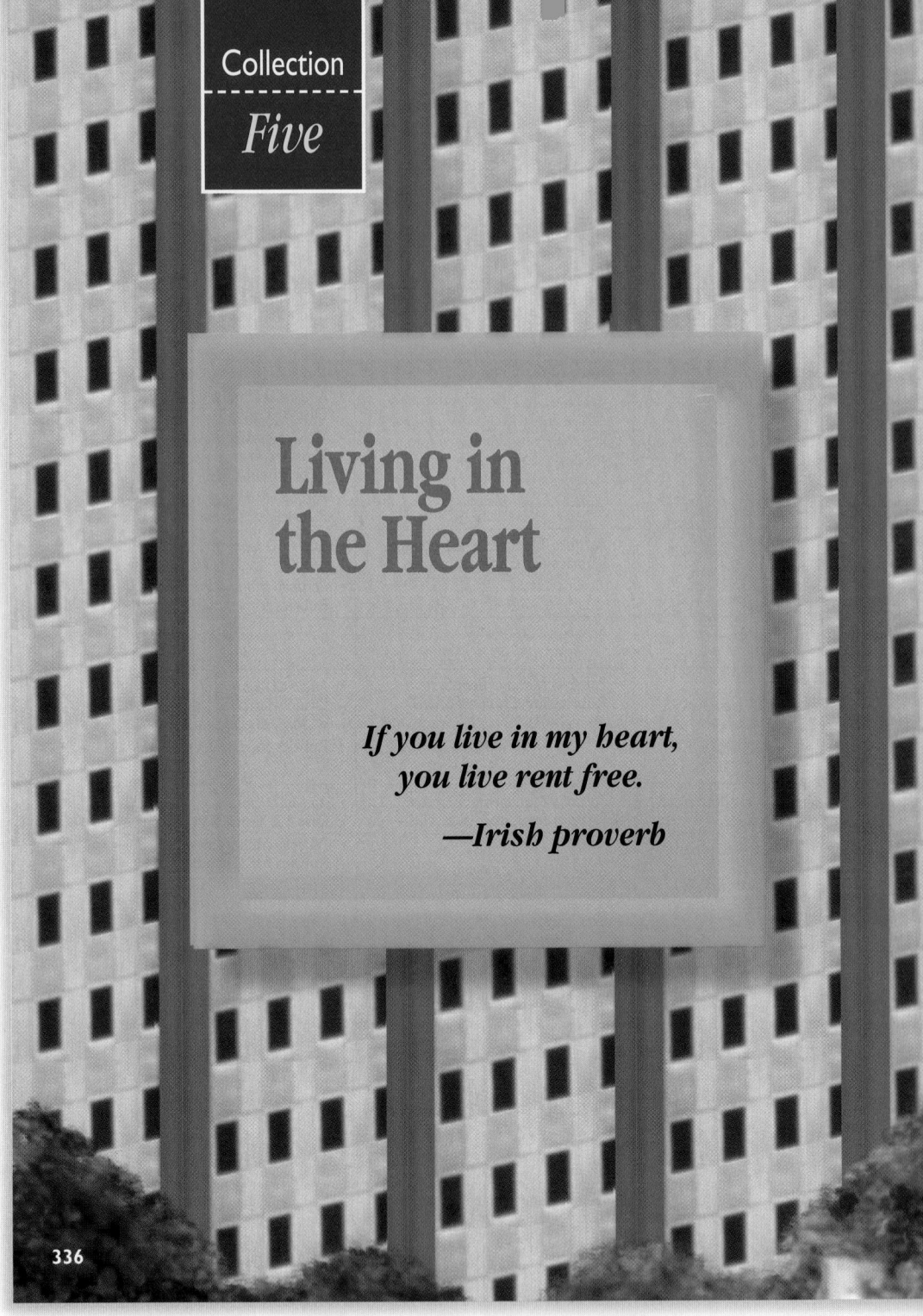

OBJECTIVES

1. Read literature in different genres on the theme "Living in the Heart"
2. Interpret literary elements used in the literature, with special emphasis on sound effects, images, and figures of speech in poetry
3. Apply a variety of reading strategies, particularly distinguishing opinions from facts
4. Respond to the literature in a variety of modes
5. Learn and use new words
6. Develop skill in interviewing
7. Plan, draft, revise, proof, and publish a biographical sketch
8. Develop skill in revising wordy sentences
9. Demonstrate the ability to read a geography book
10. Explore conflict resolution through a variety of projects

Introducing the Theme

Explain to the class that each of the stories and poems in this collection is about an unusual and unforgettable person. Point out that several of the selections focus on the love and care these special people share with others. As they read the selections, remind students to look for qualities that make each of the unusual characters in the collection so hard to forget.

Responding to the Quotation

Ask students what they think this proverb means. Elicit that it has something to do with the idea of living on fondly in someone's memory. Ask students what they think "rent free" means. To stimulate discussion, you might ask, "What would be the opposite of living 'rent free'?" or "What is so great about living in someone else's heart?" Elicit a variety of responses about whether love conveys a kind of immortality to the loved one.

Collection
Five

Living in the Heart

*If you live in my heart,
you live rent free.*

—*Irish proverb*

336

Selection Readability

This Annotated Teacher's Edition provides a summary of each selection in the student book. Following each Summary heading, you will find one, two or three small icons. These icons indicate, in an approximate sense, the reading level of the selection.

■ One icon indicates that the selection is easy.

■ ■ Two icons indicate that the selection is on an intermediate reading level.

■ ■ ■ Three icons indicate that the selection is challenging.

RESPONDING TO THE ART

Explain to the students that this sculpture by Robert Indiana also served as the basis for a postage stamp. The city of Philadelphia may have chosen this particular work of art to place in front of its Convention and Visitors Bureau because Philadelphia is known as "The City of Brotherly Love."

Writer's Notebook

Ask students if they have ever heard anyone say "My heart won't let me forget." Ask them to explain in their writing how they would interpret the phrase if someone said it to them. Then, point out that people often say that a little part of everyone they have ever cared for still lives on inside them even after they have been separated. Ask students to explain in writing why they agree or disagree with that idea.

Resources

Portfolio Management System
- Introduction to Portfolio Assessment, p. 1
- Parent/Guardian Letters, p. 95

Formal Assessment
- Reading Application Test, p. 81

Test Generator
- Collection Test

Cross-Curricular Activities
- Teaching Notes, p. 35

Love sculpture by Robert Indiana in front of the Philadelphia Visitors Center.

The Philadelphia Convention and Visitors Bureau.

Writing Focus: Biographical Sketch

The following **Work in Progress** assignments build to a culminating **Writer's Workshop** at the end of Collection 5.

- The Highwayman   Write about someone's character traits (p. 349)
- Annabel Lee   Describe a person who evokes strong emotions (p. 354)
- User Friendly   Write about someone's favorite thing (p. 365)
- Miss Awful   Jot down first impressions of a person (p. 384)
- The Only Girl . . .   Create a character profile (p. 396)
- Gold   Describe a place (p. 396)
- My Father Is . . . / Mama Is . . .   Capture someone's personality (p. 403)

Writer's Workshop: Expository Writing / Biographical Sketch (p. 410)

Resources ———

Elements of Literature
Poetry: Sound Effects
For more instruction on sound effects, see *Literary Elements:*
• Transparency 5
Assessment
Formal Assessment
• Literary Elements Test, p. 76

Elements of Literature

This feature explains various sound effects that poets use to create music: rhythm, rhyme, alliteration, and onomatopoeia. The terms *rhythm* and *meter* are clarified. Types of rhyme are explained and illustrated. The feature also introduces the process of scanning a poem in order to mark its stressed and unstressed syllables. It includes a discussion of *free verse* as a type of poetry that does not use regular metrical patterns.

Mini-Lesson:
Sound Effects
Rhythm Have students clap along with you as they sing "Twinkle, Twinkle, Little Star" aloud. Ask students to note the syllables on which they clap their hands. Then write the first four lines of the song on the chalkboard, and with suggestions from students, mark the stressed and unstressed syllables. The first line should be marked
Twínklĕ, twínklĕ, líttlĕ stár

POETRY: Sound Effects *by* John Malcolm Brinnin

Poets use many techniques to make music out of words. The most common sound effects used in poetry are also used in the songs you listen to on the radio.

Rhythm: The Rise and Fall of Our Voices

Rhythm refers to the rise and fall of our voices as we use language. As in music, a poem's rhythm can be fast or slow, light or solemn. It might also sound just like everyday speech.

Poetry that is written in **meter** has a regular pattern of stressed and unstressed syllables. Poetry that is written in **free verse** does not have a regular pattern of stressed and unstressed syllables. Free verse sounds like ordinary speech.

When poets write in meter, they count out the number of stressed syllables (or strong beats) and unstressed syllables (weaker beats) in each line. Then they repeat the pattern throughout the poem. To avoid a singsong effect, poets

usually vary the basic pattern from time to time. Try reading aloud the following lines from a famous poem called *The Rime of the Ancient Mariner* by Samuel Taylor Coleridge. Can you hear that each line has four stressed syllables alternating with four unstressed syllables?

Day after day, day after day,
We stuck, nor breath nor motion;
As idle as a painted ship
Upon a painted ocean.

A poem's rhythm can be shown by using accent marks (´) for stressed syllables and cups (˘) for unstressed syllables. This marking is called **scanning.**

˘ ´ ˘ ´ ˘ ´ ˘ ´
Day after day, day after day

Rhyme: Chiming Sounds

Rhyme is the repetition of the sound of a stressed syllable and any unstressed syllables that follow: *sport* and *court; smother* and *another; sputtering* and *muttering*. The echoing effect of rhyme gives us pleasure. It makes us look forward to hearing certain

chiming sounds throughout the poem. In the verse from *The Rime of the Ancient Mariner,* the rhyming words are *motion* and *ocean.*

Rhymes like *motion/ocean* in Coleridge's verse are called **end rhymes** because they occur at the ends of lines. **Internal rhymes** occur within lines, as in this line from the same poem:

The fair breeze blew, the white foam flew . . .

Poets will often use a pattern of rhymes, called a **rhyme scheme.** To describe a rhyme scheme, assign a new letter of the alphabet to each new end rhyme. The rhyme scheme of Coleridge's verse is *abcb.*

Alliteration: Repeating Consonants

Another way poets create sound effects is through the use of alliteration. **Alliteration** is the repetition of consonant sounds in words that are close together. Read this tongue twister of a poem aloud to hear all the repeated *t* sounds.

338 LIVING IN THE HEART

Reaching All Students

Struggling Readers
Before students begin the feature, give them a framework like the one below, and have them complete it as they read. After they finish, correct and discuss their frameworks.
Sound Effects in Poetry
(1) Rhythm
  a. Definition:_____
  b. Example of lines scanned to show meter:_____
  c. Free verse is_____

(2) Rhyme
  a. Definition:_____
  b. Examples:
    1. end rhymes:_____
    2. internal rhymes:_____
  c. A rhyme scheme is_____
(3) Alliteration
  a. Definition:_____
  b. Example:_____

(4) Onomatopoeia
  a. Definition:_____
  b. Examples:_____

English Language Learners
Because of difficulties with the patterns of English pronunciation and stress, English language learners may have a hard time recognizing rhythm, rhyme, and onomatopoeia in poetry. However, alliteration should be easier for them to identify since they can spot it visually.

A Tutor

A tutor who tooted the flute
Tried to tutor two tooters to
    toot.
    Said the two to the tutor,
    "Is it harder to toot, or
To tutor two tooters to toot?"

—Carolyn Wells

"A Tutor" is a **limerick,** a humorous five-line poem. Limericks have a definite rhythm and rhyme scheme. Try scanning the poem and describing the rhyme scheme now that you've tooted through it.

Onomatopoeia: Sound Echoes Sense

Onomatopoeia is a long word that is pronounced like this: än´ō·mat´ō·pē´ə. It is the use of words with sounds that echo their sense. *Crash, bang, boom, hiss,* and *toot* are all examples of onomatopoeia.

To see how sounds alone can suggest sense, read the famous nonsense poem in the next column aloud. You will not find all the words in a dictionary, but the sounds will help you guess what is going on.

Jabberwocky

'Twas brillig, and the slithy toves
    Did gyre and gimble in the wabe;
All mimsy were the borogoves,
    And the mome raths outgrabe.
"Beware the Jabberwock, my son!
    The jaws that bite, the claws that catch!
Beware the Jubjub bird, and shun
    The frumious Bandersnatch!"
He took his vorpal sword in hand:
    Long time the manxome foe he sought—
So rested he by the Tumtum tree,
    And stood awhile in thought.
And, as in uffish thought he stood,
    The Jabberwock, with eyes of flame,
Came whiffling through the tulgey wood,
    And burbled as it came!
One, two! One, two! And through and through
    The vorpal blade went snicker-snack!
He left it dead, and with its head
    He went galumphing back.
"And hast thou slain the Jabberwock?
    Come to my arms, my beamish boy!
O frabjous day! Callooh! Callay!"
    He chortled in his joy.
'Twas brillig, and the slithy toves
    Did gyre and gimble in the wabe;
All mimsy were the borogoves,
    And the mome raths outgrabe.

—Lewis Carroll

ELEMENTS OF LITERATURE: POETRY **339**

Rhyme Explain that poets use rhyme for a variety of reasons. Rhyme can help to accent rhythm in a poem, to make a poem sound more like a song, to emphasize certain ideas, to tie the lines together and structure the poem, and to make the poem easier to remember.

Alliteration Point out that alliteration can have a powerful effect on the mood of a poem. Used excessively, alliteration can ruin the mood and make lines sound comical. Used judiciously, it can add to a poem's emotional power.

Onomatopoeia Explain that, while "Jabberwocky" does include a large number of nonsense words invented by the author, Carroll also used a number of real (if funny-sounding) words, most of which are onomatopoeic. For example, *whiffling* is a real word that means "blowing fitfully," while *burbled* is based on a Middle English word that means "to make a bubbling sound." Discuss Carroll's use of sound-mimicking words in the poem, whether invented or preexisting, and encourage students to use dictionaries to figure out which words the poet actually created.

Applying the Element

To help students review sound effects in poetry, have them read "Jabberwocky" aloud and complete the following exercises.

• Scan the first two lines of the poem to show its meter:
  [′Twas brĭllig, ănd thĕ slĭthy tóves
   Dĭd gýre ănd gímble ĭn thĕ wábe]
• List the end rhymes in the first four lines. [toves/borogoves; wabe/outgrabe; son/shun; catch/Bandersnatch]
• Find one example of internal rhyme in the poem. [Possible response: jaws/claws in l. 6.]
• Find two examples of alliteration. [Possible responses: "gyre and gimble"; "claws that catch"; "snicker-snack"; "beamish boy"; "Callooh! Callay!"]
• Identify one instance of onomatopoeia and explain it. [Possible response: The word *snicker-snack* suggests the sound of a sword.]

Listening to Music

"'Twas Brillig" by Mack David et al., performed on the original soundtrack of the 1951 Walt Disney film *Alice in Wonderland*

Of the various stage and screen adaptations of *Alice in Wonderland*, the best known is probably the animated movie musical produced by Walt Disney in 1951. Some of the actors who lent their voices to this production were Ed Wynn, Sterling Holloway, and Jerry Colonna. The score was made up of fifty songs, including "I'm Late!"

and musical versions of all the famous poems in Carroll's original.

Activity

After students have read "Jabberwocky," play the song "'Twas Brillig" and explain that the song comes from the animated Disney version of *Alice in Wonderland.* Have students create their own cartoons based on the poem. They might use computer graphics or stacked drawings that can be flipped through rapidly to create the effect of animation.

OBJECTIVES

1. Read and interpret the poem
2. Identify narrative poetry and review main elements of the narrative
3. Monitor comprehension
4. Express understanding through expository writing, a choral reading, or art

SKILLS

Literary
- Identify narrative poetry and review main events of the narrative

Reading
- Monitor comprehension

Writing
- Brainstorm subjects and traits for a biographical report
- Write a summary and response

Speaking/Listening
- Perform a choral reading

Art
- Create a poster

Viewing/Representing
- Describe the mood of a painting (ATE)
- Compare techniques in art and poetry (ATE)

Planning

- **Block Schedule**
  Block Scheduling Lesson Plans with Pacing Guide

- **Traditional Schedule**
  Lesson Plans Including Strategies for English-Language Learners

- **One-Stop Planner**
  CD-ROM with Test Generator

Before You Read

THE HIGHWAYMAN

Make the Connection

"Watch for Me by Moonlight"

It was a night made for love and adventure. Start with the **setting:** a moonlit road hundreds of years ago, a country inn at midnight. Add some **characters:** a daring and dashing robber, a beautiful young woman, a jealous stableman, and a group of cruel soldiers. Can you predict what will happen? Hint: Look at the poem's title and illustrations. Skim the first verse.

Predicting. Discuss your impressions of the poem with a partner. On the basis of your preview, what do you think will happen?

Reading Skills and Strategies

Dialogue with the Text

As you read this poem, keep a sheet of paper handy so that you can write down your reactions. One student's comments appear on the first page as an example. Remember that you create your own meaning from "The Highwayman." No one else will read it exactly the same way you do.

Elements of Literature

Stories in Verse: An Old Tradition

Poems that are written to tell a story are called **narrative poems.** These story poems resemble short stories: They have a **plot, characters,** and a **setting.** Stories sung to the strumming of a stringed instrument are probably the oldest form of storytelling. Modern poems like this one use strong rhythms to make their stories sound like the old sung stories—they capture the enduring power of the spoken word.

> **N**arrative poetry is poetry that tells a story.

Background

Literature and History

The highwayman in this famous poem is a robber who lived in England in the 1700s. Highwaymen used to stop stagecoaches on the lonely moorlands of northern England and Scotland and rob the rich passengers of money and jewels. Some highwaymen were considered heroes by the Scots because they shared the money with the poor. Highwaymen were often dashing, romantic figures who dressed in expensive clothes. The poem is based on a true story that the poet heard while he was on vacation in that part of England where highwaymen used to lie in wait for stagecoaches.

go.hrw.com
LEO 7-5

340 LIVING IN THE HEART

 Resources: Print and Media

Reading
- *Graphic Organizers for Active Reading,* p. 21
- *Audio CD Library,* Disc 9, Track 3

Elements of Literature
- *Literary Elements*
  Transparency 5; Worksheet, p. 16

Writing and Language
- *Daily Oral Grammar,* Transparency 19

Viewing and Representing
- *Viewing and Representing*

Fine Art Transparency 10
Fine Art Worksheet, p. 40
- *Visual Connections*
  Videocassette A, Segment 5

Assessment
- *Formal Assessment,* p. 65
- *Portfolio Management System,* p. 145
- *Standard Test Preparation,* pp. 52, 54
- *Test Generator (One-Stop Planner CD-ROM)*

Internet
- go.hrw.com (keyword: LEO 7-5)

The Highwayman

Alfred Noyes

Part 1

The wind was a torrent of darkness among the gusty
    trees,
The moon was a ghostly galleon° tossed upon cloudy
    seas,
The road was a ribbon of moonlight over the purple
    moor,
And the highwayman came riding——
5   Riding——riding——
The highwayman came riding, up to the old inn door.

He'd a French cocked hat on his forehead, a bunch of
    lace at his chin,
A coat of the claret° velvet, and breeches of brown
    doeskin.
They fitted with never a wrinkle. His boots were up
    to the thigh.
10 And he rode with a jeweled twinkle,
        His pistol butts a-twinkle,
His rapier hilt° a-twinkle, under the jeweled sky.

Over the cobbles he clattered and clashed in the dark
    inn yard.
And he tapped with his whip on the shutters, but all
    was locked and barred.
He whistled a tune to the window, and who should be
    waiting there
15 But the landlord's black-eyed daughter,
        Bess, the landlord's daughter,
Plaiting° a dark red love knot into her long black
    hair.

---

2. **galleon:** large sailing ship.
8. **claret** (klar′it): purplish red, like claret wine.
12. **rapier** (rā′pē·ər) **hilt:** sword handle.
18. **plaiting:** braiding.

Dialogue with the Text

Reminds me of one of our family camping trips.

Sounds like a ghost ship caught in a storm.

It sounds like the only good sight in the open land was a road.

Is the inn abandoned?

A Those were long boots.

What's a jeweled twinkle?

Does that mean he was making a lot of noise?

There must not have been windows.

I think that these two lines should somehow become one—"But the landlord's black-eyed daughter Bess."

Crystal Hinojos

—Crystal Hinojos
Lincoln Middle School
El Paso, Texas

THE HIGHWAYMAN 341

Summary ■■■

The highwayman promises to return by moonlight to his love, Bess, the land-lord's daughter. Tim, the inn's ostler (stableman), in love with Bess, over-hears the lovers and, presumably, betrays his rival to the authorities. The next night soldiers arrive, tie Bess to her bed with a musket beneath her breast, and wait for the highwayman. When Bess hears his horse on the road, she pulls the trigger to warn her lover. The highwayman gallops off, but when he learns of Bess's death, he returns in a rage and is shot down by the soldiers.

Resources ——

Viewing and Representing
Videocassette A, Segment 5
This segment, "The Highwayman Came Riding," includes a dramatization of the poem. See the *Visual Connections Teacher's Manual.*

Listening
Audio CD Library
A recording of this poem is included in the *Audio CD Library:*
• Disc 9, Track 3

A Elements of Literature
  Narrative Poetry
? Remind students that narrative poetry shares many elements with fic-tion: plot, characters, setting. Who are the major characters in the narrative poem so far? [the highwayman, Bess] What mood is created by the setting's details? [Possible response: eerie, excit-ing mood, created by the torrential wind, dark night, moonlit road]

Speaking and Listening: Analyzing the Use of Aesthetic Language
Play the dramatic reading of this classic poem for students (Disc 9, Track 3, of the *Audio CD Library*). Ask students to listen for words and phrases that help them see the characters in the poem. Also ask them to note places in the poem where the rhythm suggests the galloping of a horse.

Reaching All Students

Struggling Readers
Explain that the word *highwayman* is a term for an outlaw who robbed travelers on public roads. Have students list words or draw pic-tures that the word *highwayman* brings to mind. (You might start them off with such words as *outlaw, adventurer,* and *dark, lonely roads.*) As stu-dents read the poem, ask them to write a one-sentence summary of each stanza. They should have a paragraph-length summary by poem's end. When they have finished the poem, ask

students to compare their paragraph summaries with those of others and to correct their sum-maries as necessary.

English Language Learners
The diction that Noyes uses to evoke the eigh-teenth-century setting may make it difficult for some English language learners to understand the poem. Before they read the first stanza, help them to find modern equivalents of unfamiliar words, such as *torrent* (storm), *galleon* (large ship), *moor* (field), *breeches* (knee-length pants),

doeskin (soft leather), *claret* (wine-colored), *rapier hilt* (sword handle), *cobbles* (stones used to pave roads), and *plaiting* (braiding). Review remaining stanzas for similar hurdles to under-standing. For strategies to supplement instruc-tion for these students, see
• *Lesson Plans Including Strategies for English-Language Learners*

A Elements of Literature

Onomatopoeia

Remind students that the poetic device **onomatopoeia** refers to the use of words whose sounds echo their sense. Point out that Noyes uses several onomatopoeic words *(clattered, clashed, creaked)* in the third and fourth stanzas to break the eerie silence he sets up in the first two stanzas. Ask students if they can think of other onomatopoeic words that start with cl- or cr-. [Possible responses: clap, clunk, crack, crash.]

Cultural Connections

Explain that eighteenth-century England was a place where outlaws could flourish. The century's most famous highwayman was Jonathan Wild, a master criminal who sold stolen goods back to their wealthy owners. He also helped the authorities capture many other felons; if an outlaw refused to cooperate with Wild, he would turn the criminal in and collect a reward. As many as 120 men were captured and hanged as a consequence of Wild's tips.

B Reading Skills and Strategies

Using Context Clues

? What is the "prize" mentioned in line 25? What context clues give you the response? [The reference to "yellow gold" in line 26 identifies the prize.]

C Reading Skills and Strategies

Dialogue with the Text

? What is your response to the highwayman? Find words or passages that explain your reaction. [Possible response: Although the highwayman is a criminal, he is well dressed (ll. 7–12), bold (ll. 27–30), and a passionate lover (stanzas 5–6). Many readers find him extremely attractive as a romantic hero.]

A And dark in the dark old inn yard a stable wicket° creaked
20 Where Tim the ostler° listened. His face was white and peaked.
His eyes were hollows of madness, his hair like moldy hay,
But he loved the landlord's daughter,
    The landlord's red-lipped daughter,
Dumb as a dog he listened, and he heard the robber say——

B "One kiss, my bonny sweetheart, I'm after a prize tonight,
25 But I shall be back with the yellow gold before the morning light;
Yet, if they press me sharply, and harry° me through the day,
Then look for me by moonlight,
    Watch for me by moonlight,
I'll come to thee by moonlight, though hell should bar the way."
30

C He rose upright in the stirrups. He scarce could reach her hand,
But she loosened her hair in the casement.° His face burnt like a brand
As the black cascade of perfume came tumbling over his breast;
And he kissed its waves in the moonlight,
    (Oh, sweet black waves in the moonlight!)
35 Then he tugged at his rein in the moonlight, and galloped away to the west.

Part 2

He did not come in the dawning. He did not come at noon;
And out of the tawny sunset, before the rise of the moon,

19. **wicket:** small door or gate.
20. **ostler** (äs′lər): person who takes care of horses; groom.
27. **harry:** harass or push along.
32. **casement:** window that opens outward on hinges.

342 LIVING IN THE HEART

Using Students' Strengths

Auditory/Musical Learners

Ask students to set one or more stanzas of the poem to music. Have them adapt an existing melody with roughly the same meter as the poem ("Ghost Riders in the Sky," for example). Then have them sing the stanzas and invite the rest of the class to join in.

Visual Learners

This poem contains intensely vivid visual images. After they have read the poem a few times, invite students to create a drawing of the setting or of one of the characters. They can use an appropriate line from the poem as a caption for the illustration.

T342

The Haywain by John Constable (1776–1837).

National Gallery, London/Bridgeman Art Library, London/Superstock.

John Constable (1776–1837) was one of England's greatest landscape painters, although he was not recognized as such during his lifetime. After a boyhood spent sketching the countryside around his home near Ipswich, Constable entered the Royal Academy. Painted in 1821, *The Haywain* (hay wagon), one of his best-known works, shows his fascination with the English countryside and its radiant, cloud-filled skies. In his tranquil depictions of sky, clouds, and light, Constable strove for accurate representation, not as an end in itself, but as a means of expressing emotion. After the death of his wife in 1828, his paintings became more muted and brooding.

Activity. Ask students if they think there is a single important element or visual center to this picture—an object, a creature, a person, a feature of the landscape. Have students describe the mood of *The Haywain* and find features and details in the painting that help create this mood. [Possible responses: The cottage, trees, and pond are comforting and serene. The gathering clouds add a foreboding note.]

Getting Students Involved

Cooperative Learning

Literary Recipe. Ask students to work in groups of three to create lists of measured ingredients for a romantic narrative poem. A possible list of such ingredients:

    5 cups hero or heroine
    3 cups villain
    4 cups unusual setting
    4 tablespoons suspense
    2 cups dramatic action
    2 tablespoons tragedy

Provide a recipe from a cookbook as a model, and ask students how the ingredients should be mixed and prepared. Save the recipes for inclusion in a literary cookbook containing other formulas for mystery stories, love poems, tragic plays, persuasive essays, and so on.

Ⓐ **Critical Thinking**

Predicting

Ask students to predict what might happen if the highwayman returns while the soldiers are still at the inn. After students have finished the poem, ask them to evaluate their predictions.

Ⓑ **Historical Connections**

"The Highwayman" takes place in the eighteenth century. The phrases "redcoat troop" and "King George's men" refer to the British army. In this poem, written by an Englishman and set in England, the terms referring to the soldiers are sinister, since they refer to the highwayman's enemies.

FROM THE EDITOR'S DESK

The highwayman, the ribbon of moonlight, and the ghostly galleon deservedly made the cover of this book. It wouldn't be seventh grade without the highwayman riding—riding—riding.

> When the road was a gypsy's ribbon, looping the
>   purple moor,
> 40 A redcoat troop came marching——
>   Marching——marching——
>   King George's men came marching, up to the old inn
>   door.
>
>   They said no word to the landlord. They drank his
>   ale instead.
>   But they gagged his daughter, and bound her, to the
>   foot of her narrow bed.
>   Two of them knelt at her casement, with muskets at
> 45   their side!

344 LIVING IN THE HEART

Listening to Music

"The Highwayman" by Phil Ochs, lyrics by Alfred Noyes, performed by Phil Ochs

"Annabel Lee" by Don Dilworth, lyrics by Edgar Allan Poe, performed by Joan Baez

Folk singer Joan Baez and singer-songwriter Phil Ochs were both popular performers in the 1960s era of folk-rock, as well as prominent figures in the movement protesting the Vietnam War. In fact, Ochs was famous for protest songs like the highly satirical "Draft Dodger Rag,"

although he also penned sweet folk-style ballads like "There But for Fortune" and "Changes." His musical version of "The Highwayman" is an affectionate homage to the poem. Joan Baez first won prominence singing traditional British and American folk ballads at Boston-area coffeehouses and the Newport Folk Festival. In addition to "Annabel Lee," she once recorded an entire album of songs, *Baptism,* made up of famous poems set to music.

Activity

After students have read the poems, have them listen to the musical versions of these poems. Then ask students to compare the two songs either orally or in writing, explaining which they consider a better musical adaptation of the original poem.

There was death at every window;
    And hell at one dark window;
For Bess could see, through her casement, the road
    that *he* would ride.

They had tied her up to attention, with many a snig-
    gering jest;
They had bound a musket beside her, with the muzzle
50   beneath her breast!
"Now, keep good watch!" and they kissed her. She
    heard the dead man say——
Look for me by moonlight;
    Watch for me by moonlight;
I'll come to thee by moonlight, though hell should bar
    the way!

She twisted her hands behind her; but all the knots
55   held good!
She writhed her hands till her fingers were wet with
    sweat or blood!
They stretched and strained in the darkness, and the
    hours crawled by like years,
Till, now, on the stroke of midnight,
    Cold, on the stroke of midnight,
The tip of one finger touched it! The trigger at least
60   was hers!

The tip of one finger touched it; she strove no more
    for the rest!
Up, she stood up to attention, with the muzzle be-
    neath her breast.
She would not risk their hearing; she would not
    strive again;
For the road lay bare in the moonlight;
65   Blank and bare in the moonlight;
And the blood of her veins, in the moonlight,
    throbbed to her love's refrain.

Tlot-tlot; tlot-tlot! Had they heard it? The horse hoofs
    ringing clear;
Tlot-tlot, tlot-tlot, in the distance? Were they deaf that
    they did not hear?
Down the ribbon of moonlight, over the brow of the
    hill,

THE HIGHWAYMAN **345**

Getting Students Involved

A Critical Thinking

Speculating

Ask students to speculate on Bess's thoughts before she pulls the trigger. [Possible response: She must have been thinking of her lover's danger and decided she would do anything to save him. She must also have felt that if she had to choose between saving his life and her own, she would choose his.]

Elements of Literature

Narrative Poetry

Point out that a narrative poem follows a plot much like that of a story. Review the elements of plot: basic situation, conflict, complications, climax, and resolution. Ask students to identify those elements in "The Highwayman." [The basic situation is the love between the highwayman and the landlord's daughter; the major conflict occurs between the highwayman and the authorities. Complications arise when the redcoats, tipped off by Tim, try to ambush the highwayman. The climax comes when Bess pulls the trigger, and the resolution is the highwayman's return and death.]

Resources

Selection Assessment

Formal Assessment
• Selection Test, p. 65

Test Generator
• Selection Test

Elements of Literature

For additional instruction on sound devices, see *Literary Elements:*
• Transparency 5
• Worksheet, p. 16

---

70   The highwayman came riding,
          Riding, riding!
     The redcoats looked to their priming!° She stood up,
          straight and still.

     Tlot-tlot, in the frosty silence! *Tlot-tlot,* in the echoing
          night!
     Nearer he came and nearer. Her face was like a light!
     Her eyes grew wide for a moment; she drew one last
          deep breath,
75   Then her fingers moved in the moonlight,
          Her musket shattered the moonlight,
     Shattered her breast in the moonlight and warned
          him—with her death.

     He turned. He spurred to the west; he did not know
          who stood
     Bowed, with her head o'er the musket, drenched
          with her own blood!
80   Not till the dawn he heard it, his face grew gray to
          hear
     How Bess, the landlord's daughter,
          The landlord's black-eyed daughter,
     Had watched for her love in the moonlight, and died
          in the darkness there.

     Back, he spurred like a madman, shouting a curse to
85   the sky,
     With the white road smoking behind him and his
          rapier brandished high.
     Blood-red were his spurs in the golden noon; wine-
          red was his velvet coat;
     When they shot him down on the highway,
          Down like a dog on the highway,
     And he lay in his blood on the highway, with the
90   bunch of lace at his throat.

     *And still of a winter's night, they say, when the wind
          is in the trees,*
     *When the moon is a ghostly galleon tossed upon
          cloudy seas,*

72. **priming:** explosive for firing a gun.

The Granger Collection, New York.

Taking a Second Look

Review: Drawing Conclusions

Remind students that a conclusion is a kind of inference and that drawing a conclusion involves combining prior knowledge with new information from the text. For example, after reading of the soldiers' brutal treatment of Bess, the reader might draw the conclusion that serving in a position of authority does not guarantee that someone will behave in a moral manner.

Activities

1. Have students reread ll. 25–30, which describe the highwayman's conversation with Bess, and then draw conclusions about why the highwayman promises to come back to Bess in spite of the risks he describes. Tell them to base their conclusions on the highwayman's character and his words, as well as other behavior they have read about or witnessed.

2. After students have finished reading the poem, have them draw a conclusion about its theme. Ask them to focus on what the poet demonstrates about the power of love through the actions of Bess and the highwayman.

Meet the Writer

"One Blustery Night"

British poet, novelist, biographer, and essayist **Alfred Noyes** (1880–1958) was often called the most popular writer of his time. People enjoyed his verse for its rousing storytelling and its thumping rhythms—in fact, his work was often performed aloud.

Today Noyes is best remembered for "The Highwayman," which he wrote in a small cottage on the edge of Bagshot Heath shortly after leaving Oxford University. He recalls:

> Bagshot Heath in those days was a wild bit of country, all heather and pinewoods. 'The Highwayman' suggested itself to me one blustery night when the sound of the wind in the pines gave me the first line:
>
> *The wind was a torrent of darkness among the gusty trees . . .*
>
> It took me about two days to complete the poem. Shortly afterward it appeared in *Blackwood's Magazine*. It illustrates the unpredictable chances of authorship, that this poem, written in so short a time, when I was 24, should have been read so widely.
>
> I think the success of the poem in all these ways was due to the fact that it was not an artificial composition, but was written at an age when I was genuinely excited by that kind of romantic story. "

BROWSING IN THE FILES

About the Author. Alfred Noyes, unlike most poets of his time, was successful enough to earn a living solely from his poetry. He particularly liked the poems of Alfred, Lord Tennyson, whose poetry was popular during Noyes's childhood. Although the twentieth century has been a time of literary experimentation and rebellion against convention, Noyes's poems are quite traditional, sounding as if they came from a much earlier era. It is startling to realize that Noyes lived into the era of television and space launches.

When the road is a ribbon of moonlight over the
    purple moor,
A highwayman comes riding——
    Riding——riding——
95 A highwayman comes riding, up to the old inn door.

Over the cobbles he clatters and clangs in the dark   **B**
    inn yard;
He taps with his whip on the shutters, but all is   **C**
    locked and barred.
He whistles a tune to the window, and who should be
    waiting there
100 But the landlord's black-eyed daughter,
    Bess, the landlord's daughter,
Plaiting a dark red love knot into her long black hair.

THE HIGHWAYMAN **347**

B Elements of Literature

Narrative Poetry
Point out that Noyes uses the words *still* and *they say* to jump forward in time, into the narrative present, giving the poem the flavor of an old legend or folk tale. Also, point out that these final stanzas echo the language and sustain the mysterious, eerie mood of the first three stanzas.

C Reading Skills and Strategies

Dialogue with the Text
Ask students to discuss how they were affected by the final stanzas of the poem. Have them note their reactions and cite specific lines or poetic devices that influenced their responses.

Assessing Learning

Check Test: Short Answer

1. When he leaves Bess, what promise does the highwayman make? [to return by moonlight]
2. Who overhears their conversation, and how is he described? [Tim the ostler; his face is "white and peaked."]
3. What do the redcoats do to Bess when they come to her father's inn? [They taunt her and tie her to her bed with a musket pointed at her breast.]
4. What does Bess do when she hears the highwayman's horse? [She pulls the trigger and dies.]
5. What happens to the highwayman? [He escapes, but when he learns what happened to Bess, he returns the next day and is shot down.]

Standardized Test Preparation

For practice with standardized test format specific to this selection, see
- *Standardized Test Preparation*, pp. 52, 54

For practice in proofreading and editing, see
- *Daily Oral Grammar*, Transparency 19

MAKING MEANINGS

First Thoughts

1. Possible responses: If you focus on the narrator's comment that the highwayman is a "dead man," then her sacrifice is pointless; if you focus on Bess's motivation, then her sacrifice is noble.

Shaping Interpretations

2. The setting is a windy, moonlit night on a moor and at a dark inn. Noyes repeats words like *darkness* and *moonlight* throughout the poem to remind the reader of this setting.

3. Tim may have told the soldiers of the highwayman's plans because he loves Bess and is jealous.

4. The highwayman is enraged and wants to avenge her death. Perhaps he wants to die.

5. Noyes uses present tense verbs in the last two stanzas and adds the word *when* to suggest that if the conditions are right, the highwayman and Bess sometimes still meet as ghosts.

6. The description of the highwayman's clothes, his words, and his passionate response to Bess's sacrifice suggest that the narrator thinks of him as a romantic hero.

7. The rhythm suggests fast-paced action, passionate emotion, and excitement.

Connecting with the Text

8. Possible response: The highwayman takes his revenge on the redcoats and lives.

9. Possible response: The poet makes the poem come alive with vivid descriptions; he gives the whole story an eerie, mysterious quality; he makes the poem lively by using a strong rhythm and repetition.

MAKING MEANINGS

First Thoughts

[respond]

1. Bess gives up her life because of her love for the highwayman. In your opinion, is her sacrifice noble or pointless? Explain your response.

Shaping Interpretations

[infer]

2. What is the **setting** of this story? How does the poet help you to see and hear what is happening?

[analyze]

3. What part does Tim the ostler play in the story? What is his motive?

[interpret]

4. Why do you think the highwayman comes back to the inn after he hears how Bess died?

[analyze]

5. The last two stanzas are very much like the first and third stanzas. The wording, however, is slightly different. How does the difference reflect what is happening at the end of the poem?

[analyze]

6. How do you think the narrator feels about the highwayman? How can you tell? How do *you* feel about him?

[describe]

7. Powerful **rhythm** adds to the drama of this poem. Read aloud the tenth through thirteenth stanzas. Would you describe their rhythm as fast or slow? Does their rhythm help you imagine the poem's action?

Connecting with the Text

[connect]

8. If you could write a new ending for the poem, what would it be?

[connect]

9. Here is a letter that one student wrote about "The Highwayman." List two or three points you would make in a letter about the poem.

Reading Check

Review the main events of this **narrative poem** and then complete a **sequence chart** like the one below.

Part 1

1. The highwayman rides to the old inn.

2. He finds Bess waiting.

3. Tim overhears him say . . .

> Dear Editors;
>
> I am a seventh grader at Madison Jr. High. My name is Brooke Garner. Our class has been reading many stories in your book, *Elements of Literature*.
> My favorite poem ~~that~~ is "The Highwayman." It shows a very deep understanding and love between the highwayman and the girl. This poem was so touching that ~~through~~ every emotion the writer was trying to convey, filtered through my mind and I was left weakened by its magnitude. The poem lived and I feel that the author had somehow been hurt and understood how the people must have felt and lived.
>
> Sincerely yours,
> Brooke Garner

Reading Check

Part 1

1. The highwayman rides to the old inn.
2. He finds Bess waiting.
3. Tim overhears him say that he will return "though hell should bar the way."
4. The highwayman kisses Bess's hair and rides away.

Part 2

1. The highwayman does not come during the next day.
2. Soldiers come to the inn that evening.
3. They bind Bess to her bed, placing a musket beneath her breast.
4. Bess manages to get a finger on the trigger.
5. She hears the highwayman's horse galloping toward the inn.
6. She pulls the trigger to warn the highwayman and dies.
7. He rides off when he hears the shot.
8. At dawn he learns what has happened to Bess.
9. He rides back to the inn, shouting curses, and the soldiers shoot him down.
10. People say they hear the highwayman still riding to the inn, where Bess waits for him.

CHOICES: Building Your Portfolio

Rubrics for each Choices assignment appear on p. 145 in the *Portfolio Management System*.

Writer's Notebook

1. Collecting Ideas for a Biographical Sketch

Like Noyes, many writers choose to write about actual people and events. Think of someone you know or know of whose real life is worth telling about—exciting, heroic, funny, unusual. What is that person like? List his or her three main character traits. Then, jot down notes about an incident that illustrates these traits.

Emily Brown

Artistic; creative; community-minded: Got stores on Mission Street to donate walls and inspired neighborhood kids to do murals.

A Summary and Response

2. You Be the Judge

Write two paragraphs about "The Highwayman." First, **summarize** the plot by describing the story's **conflict, climax,** and **resolution.** In your second paragraph, tell how the poem affected you. To recall your first reactions, review the notes you made as you read the poem.

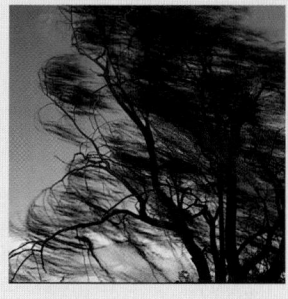

Choral Reading

3. A Ghostly Chorus of Voices

Get together with a group of classmates and create a choral reading of "The Highwayman." Try assigning some lines to individuals, some to a boys' chorus, and some to a girls' chorus. (Label the parts on a copy of the poem.) As you practice the poem, decide how to read each line—loudly, softly, quickly, slowly, with rising excitement, with sorrow, and so on. Look for ways to capture the powerful **rhythm** with your voice. Discuss how to read the parts where words or phrases are repeated, for if you're not careful, they may sound dull. Also, be sure to clearly pronounce the lines that contain **alliteration**— the repetition of initial consonant sounds in words near one another. You might perform your choral reading for another class.

Creative Writing/Art

4. Soon—At a Theater Near You!

Hollywood once made a movie based on "The Highwayman." Create a poster for such a movie, working with a partner or with several classmates if you prefer. Illustrate scenes and portray characters, but above all try to convey the **mood** of the movie as you imagine it. Be sure to use a quotation from the poem on your poster.

CHOICES: Building Your Portfolio

1. **Writer's Notebook** Remind students to save their work. They may use it as prewriting for the Writer's Workshop on pp. 410–414.

2. **A Summary and Response** Review the definitions of the terms *conflict, climax,* and *resolution.* If students need a graphic organizer, ask them to refer to their sequence charts from Making Meanings: Reading Check, on p. 348.

3. **Choral Reading** Model an oral reading of a passage from the poem before students try it themselves. Allow students to use props, sound effects, or background music when they perform their readings.

4. **Creative Writing/Art** Display an actual movie advertisement or poster that students can use as a model when they create their own posters. Brainstorm with the class to create a list of items that they should include on the posters (title, names of actors, catchy quotations from films, comments from reviewers, and so on).

ANNABEL LEE

Make the Connection

"A Love That Was More Than Love"

"Annabel Lee" is a famous love poem, written after the poet's young wife, Virginia, died of tuberculosis. She was laid to rest in New York, near the Hudson River, in a sepulcher (sep′əl·kər), a burial vault that stands above ground. Poe's poem reads like a fairy tale, set in a faraway time and place.

Think aloud. With a partner, take turns reading the poem aloud to hear its haunting sounds and to visualize its romantic setting. Exchange thoughts about the poem's speaker and its music.

Reading Skills and Strategies

Dialogue with the Text

Have your notebook open while you and your partner are reading the poem. Note comments and questions as they come to you and then discuss them with your partner. Work together to solve any problems you have in understanding the poem.

 go.hrw.com
LE0 7-5

Portrait of a Girl at a Beach by John Collier.

Reprinted by permission of the Estate of Edith Wharton and the Watkins/Loomis Agency.

Elements of Literature

Repetition: See the sea . . . the sea . . . the sea

Musicians, as you may know, use repetition—of sounds, of words, of tones—to create emotional effects. Poe uses repetition in much the same way. In "Annabel Lee," notice how words, sounds, phrases, and rhythms keep recurring with hypnotic regularity.

> **R**epetition is the recurring use of a sound, a word, a phrase, or a line. Repetition can be used to create music, to appeal to our emotions, and to emphasize important ideas.

350 LIVING IN THE HEART

OBJECTIVES
1. Read and interpret the poem
2. Identify repetition of words and sounds throughout the poem
3. Monitor comprehension
4. Express understanding through writing or a choral reading

SKILLS

Literary
- Identify repetition of words and sounds throughout the poem

Reading
- Monitor comprehension

Writing
- Collect ideas and take notes about a subject for a biographical sketch

Speaking/Listening
- Perform a choral reading

Viewing/Representing
- Describe the setting in a painting (ATE)
- Compare techniques in art and poetry (ATE)

Planning

- **Block Schedule**
  Block Scheduling Lesson Plans with Pacing Guide
- **Traditional Schedule**
  Lesson Plans Including Strategies for English-Language Learners
- **One-Stop Planner**
  CD-ROM with Test Generator

 — 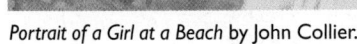 *Resources: Print and Media* —

Reading
- *Graphic Organizers for Active Reading*, p. 22
- *Audio CD Library*
  Disc 9, Track 4

Elements of Literature
- *Literary Elements*
  Transparency 6
  Worksheet, p. 19

Writing and Language
- *Daily Oral Grammar*
  Transparency 20

Assessment
- *Formal Assessment*, p. 66
- *Portfolio Management System*, p. 146
- *Test Generator (One-Stop Planner CD-ROM)*

Internet
- go.hrw.com (keyword: LE0 7-5)

User Friendly

T. Ernesto Bethancourt

I reached over and shut off the insistent buzzing of my bedside alarm clock. I sat up, swung my feet over the edge of the bed, and felt for my slippers on the floor. Yawning, I walked toward the bathroom. As I walked by the corner of my room, where my computer table was set up, I pressed the *on* button, slid a diskette into the floppy drive, then went to brush my teeth. By the time I got back, the computer's screen was glowing greenly, displaying the message: *Good Morning, Kevin.*

I sat down before the computer table, addressed the keyboard, and typed: *Good Morning, Louis.* The computer immediately began to whir and promptly displayed a list of items on its green screen.

```
Today is Monday, April 22,
the 113th day of the year.
There are 254 days remain-
ing. Your 14th birthday is
five days from this date.

Math test today, 4th
Period.

Your history project is
due today. Do you wish
printout: Y/N?
```

Bad enough the thing is talking to me. I'm answering it!

Summary ■

This story explores the relationship between a lonely boy and his computer. Kevin, the narrator, a 14-year-old computer whiz, starts to see surprising messages on the screen of his new computer (named "Louis"), which has been designed by his father to include the latest components. That afternoon, Kevin's feelings are hurt by Ginny Linke, a girl he has a crush on; he confides in the computer, which sympathetically promises to "take care of Ginny." The computer sets into motion a number of actions affecting Ginny's family. Kevin decides to disconnect Louis in order to end the mischief-making. But his father tells him that he has reprogrammed the computer to be more conventional. He hands Kevin a surprising message the computer printed out as its programs were being erased, and Kevin at last understands the reason for the computer's odd behavior.

Background

Silicon Valley is an area in central California bounded on the south by San Jose and on the north by San Francisco. There is no such city as Santo Rosario; its closest real-life counterpart is probably Santa Clara, which is often called the "High Tech Capital of the World." This story predates recent developments in computer technology, for example, in its references to the computer's green screen and user-unfriendly error message. A hard disk that can store 100 million bytes (individual pieces) of information has also been surpassed by the latest personal computers.

Resources

Listening
Audio CD Library
An entertaining recording of the story is included in the *Audio CD Library:*
• Disc 9, Track 5

Selection Assessment
Formal Assessment
• Selection Test, p. 67
Test Generator
• Selection Test

Reaching All Students

Struggling Readers
Recognizing Causes and Effects was introduced on p. 356. For a lesson directly tied to this selection that teaches students to recognize causes and effects by using a strategy called Text Reformulation, see the *Reading Skills and Strategies* binder:
• MiniRead Skill Lesson, p. 160
• Selection Skill Lesson, p. 178

English Language Learners
Ask students to explain the title of the story, "User Friendly" [easy for ordinary people to use]. Have English language learners formulate questions about any terminology they don't understand, to ask peer tutors—including other English language learners who are more familiar with computers. For strategies to supplement instructions for these students, see
• *Lesson Plans Including Strategies for English-Language Learners*

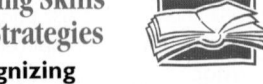
I punched the letter *Y* on the keyboard and flipped on the switch to the computer's printer. At once the printer sprang to life and began *eeeek*ing out page one. I went downstairs to breakfast.

My bowl of Frosted Flakes was neatly in place, flanked by a small pitcher of milk, an empty juice glass, and an unpeeled banana. I picked up the glass, went to the refrigerator, poured myself a glass of Tang, and sat down to my usual lonely breakfast. Mom was already at work, and Dad wouldn't be home from his Chicago trip for another three days. I absently[1] read the list of ingredients in Frosted Flakes for what seemed like the millionth time. I sighed deeply.

When I returned to my room to shower and dress for the day, my history project was already printed out. I had almost walked by Louis, when I noticed there was a message on the screen. It wasn't the usual:

```
Printout completed. Do you wish
to continue: Y/N?
```

Underneath the printout question were two lines:

```
When are you going to get me my
voice module,² Kevin?
```

I blinked. It couldn't be. There was nothing in Louis's basic programming that would allow for a question like this. Wondering what was going on, I sat down at the keyboard and entered: *Repeat last message*. Amazingly, the computer replied:

```
It's right there on the screen,
Kevin. Can we talk? I mean, are
you going to get me a voice
box?
```

I was stunned. What was going on here? Dad

1. **absently:** in a distracted, inattentive way.
2. **voice module:** unit that, when connected to a computer, enables it to produce speech.

and I had put this computer together. Well, Dad had, and I had helped. Dad is one of the best engineers and master computer designers at Major Electronics, in Santa Rosario, California, where our family lives.

Just ask anyone in Silicon Valley[3] who Jeremy Neal is and you get a whole rave review of his inventions and modifications[4] of the latest in computer technology. It isn't easy being his son either. Everyone expects me to open my mouth and read printouts on my tongue.

I mean, I'm no dumbo. I'm at the top of my classes in everything but PE. I skipped my last grade in junior high, and most of the kids at Santa Rosario High call me a brain. But next to Dad I have a long, long way to go. He's a for-real genius.

So when I wanted a home computer, he didn't go to the local ComputerLand store. He built one for me. Dad had used components[5] from the latest model that Major Electronics was developing. The CPU, or central computing unit—the heart of every computer—was a new design. But surely that didn't mean much, I thought. There were CPUs just like it, all over the country, in Major's new line. And so far as I knew, there wasn't a one of them that could ask questions, besides *YES/NO?* or *request additional information.*

It had to be the extra circuitry in the gray plastic case next to Louis's console.[6] It was a new idea Dad had come up with. That case housed Louis's "personality," as Dad called it. He told me it'd make computing more fun for me, if there was a tutorial program[7] built in, to help me get started.

3. **Silicon Valley:** area in central California that is a center of the computer industry. (Silicon is used in the manufacture of computer chips, or circuits.)
4. **modifications:** slight changes.
5. **components:** parts.
6. **console:** a computer's keyboard and monitor (display unit). *Console* can also refer to a cabinet for a radio, record player, or television, made to stand on the floor.
7. **tutorial program:** program that provides instructions for performing specific tasks on a computer.

Skill Link

I think he also wanted to give me a sort of friend. I don't have many.... Face it, I don't have *any*. The kids at school stay away from me, like I'm a freak or something.

We even named my electronic tutor Louis, after my great-uncle. He was a brainy guy who encouraged my dad when he was a kid. Dad didn't just give Louis a name either. Louis had gangs of features that probably won't be out on the market for years.

The only reason Louis didn't have a voice module was that Dad wasn't satisfied with the ones available. He wanted Louis to sound like a kid my age, and he was modifying a module when he had the time. Giving Louis a name didn't mean it was a person, yet here it was, asking me a question that just couldn't be in its programming. It wanted to talk to me!

Frowning, I quickly typed: *We'll have to wait and see, Louis. When it's ready, you'll get your voice.* The machine whirred and displayed another message:

    That's no answer, Kevin.

Shaking my head, I answered: *That's what my dad tells me. It'll have to do for you. Good morning, Louis.* I reached over and flipped the standby switch, which kept the computer ready but not actively running.

I showered, dressed, and picked up the printout of my history project. As I was about to leave the room, I glanced back at the computer table. Had I been imagining things?

I'll have to ask Dad about it when he calls tonight, I thought. *I wonder what he'll think of it. Bad enough the thing is talking to me. I'm answering it!*

Before I went out to catch my bus, I carefully checked the house for unlocked doors and open windows. It was part of my daily routine. Mom works, and most of the day the house is empty: a natural setup for robbers. I glanced in the hall mirror just as I was ready to go out the door.

My usual reflection gazed back. Same old Kevin Neal: five ten, one hundred twenty pounds, light-brown hair, gray eyes, clear skin. I was wearing my Santa Rosario Rangers T-shirt, jeans, and sneakers.

"You don't look like a flake to me," I said to the mirror, then added, "But maybe Mom's right. Maybe you spend too much time alone with Louis." Then I ran to get my bus.

Ginny Linke was just two seats away from me on the bus. She was with Sherry Graber and Linda Martinez. They were laughing, whispering to each other, and looking around at the other students. I promised myself that today I was actually going to talk to Ginny. But then, I'd promised myself that every day for the past school year. Somehow I'd never got up the nerve.

What does she want to talk with you for? I asked myself. She's great-looking . . . has that head of blond hair . . . a terrific bod, and wears the latest clothes. . . .

And just look at yourself, pal, I thought. You're under six foot, skinny . . . a year younger than most kids in junior high. Worse than that, you're a brain. If that doesn't ace you out with girls, what does?

The bus stopped in front of Santa Rosario Junior High and the students began to file out. I got up fast and quickly covered the space between me and Ginny Linke. *It's now or never,* I thought. I reached forward and tapped Ginny on the shoulder. She turned and smiled. She really smiled!

USER FRIENDLY 359

Using Students' Strengths

A Reading Skills and Strategies
Making Inferences
? What inferences can you make about Ginny, Kevin, and the other girls from this passage? [Possible response: Ginny is self-centered and insensitive. That the other girls join her in laughing at Kevin suggests that they are as insensitive as she is and that he is probably unpopular enough to be considered an easy target of ridicule.]

B Elements of Literature
Characterization
Ask students to contrast the characters of Ginny and Louis. [Possible response: Ginny is insensitive and cruel, while Louis seems to care about Kevin; Louis sees a side of Kevin that the kids at school ignore.]

C Elements of Literature
Characterization
? Kevin doesn't seem to know why he tells Louis all the details about Ginny. Can you think of any reasons? [Possible responses: Kevin is so lonely that he needs to pour his heart out to someone. Louis has just been sympathetic to him and assured him he wasn't a nerd. Kevin may be starting to regard Louis as more than a computer.]

"Uhhhh . . . Ginny?" I said.

"Yes, what is it?" she replied.

"I'm Kevin Neal. . . ."

"Yes, I know," said Ginny.

"You do?" I gulped in amazement. "How come?"

"I asked my brother, Chuck. He's in your math class."

I knew who Chuck Linke was. He plays left tackle on the Rangers. The only reason he's in my math class is he's taken intermediate algebra twice . . . so far. He's real bad news, and I stay clear of him and his crowd.

"What'd you ask Chuck?" I said.

Ginny laughed. "I asked him who was that nerdy kid who keeps staring at me on the bus. He knew who I meant, right away."

Sherry and Linda, who'd heard it all, broke into squeals of laughter. They were still laughing and looking back over their shoulders at me when they got off the bus. I slunk off the vehicle, feeling even more nerdish than Ginny thought I was.

When I got home that afternoon, at two, I went right into the empty house. I avoided my reflection in the hall mirror. I was pretty sure I'd screwed up on the fourth-period math test. All I could see was Ginny's face, laughing at me.

Nerdy kid, I thought, *that's what she thinks of me.* I didn't even have my usual after-school snack of a peanut butter and banana sandwich. I went straight upstairs to my room and tossed my books onto the unmade bed. I walked over to the computer table and pushed the *on* button. The screen flashed:

`Good afternoon, Kevin.`

Although it wasn't the programmed response to Louis's greeting, I typed in: *There's nothing good about it. And girls are no @#%!!! good!* The machine responded:

`Don't use bad language, Kevin. It isn't nice.`

Repeat last message, I typed rapidly. It was happening again! The machine was . . . well, it was talking to me, like another person would. The "bad language" message disappeared and in its place was:

`Once is enough, Kevin. Don't swear at me for something I didn't do.`

"This is it," I said aloud. "I'm losing my marbles." I reached over to flip the standby switch. Louis's screen quickly flashed out:

`Don't cut me off, Kevin. Maybe I can help: Y/N?`

I punched the *Y.* "If I'm crazy," I said, "at least I have company. Louis doesn't think I'm a nerd. Or does it?" The machine flashed the message:

`How can I help?`

Do you think I'm a nerd? I typed.

`Never! I think you're wonderful. Who said you were a nerd?`

I stared at the screen. *How do you know what a nerd is?* I typed. The machine responded instantly. It had never run this fast before.

`Special vocabulary, entry #635. BASIC Prog. #4231. And who said you were a nerd?`

"That's right," I said, relieved. "Dad programmed all those extra words for Louis's 'personality.'" Then I typed in the answer to Louis's question: *Ginny Linke said it.* Louis flashed:

`This is a human female? Request additional data.`

Still not believing I was doing it, I entered all I knew about Ginny Linke, right down to the phone number I'd never had the nerve to use. Maybe it was dumb, but I also typed in how I felt about Ginny. I even wrote out the incident

---

Getting Students Involved

Cooperative Learning
Compiling Lists. Ask students to work in groups of three to create lists of stories, books, movies, plays, or television shows in which a computer or robot functions like a human character. Each entry should include a very short description of the kind of person the computer program or robot becomes. For example, in the *Star Wars* movies, the robot C3PO speaks like a very intelligent but rather prissy person; the shorter R2D2 makes odd sounds and seems more like a pet than a human being. In the film *2001: A Space Odyssey,* the computer HAL is a very devoted, conscientious, but slightly sinister character.

n the bus that morning. Louis whirred, then
ashed out:

```
She's cruel and stupid. You're
the finest person I know.
```

I'm the ONLY person you know, I typed.

```
That doesn't matter. You are my
user. Your happiness is every-
thing to me. I'll take care of
Ginny.
```

The screen returned to the *Good afternoon,
evin* message. I typed out: *Wait! How can you
 all this? What do you mean, you'll take
re of Ginny?* But all Louis responded was:

```
Programming Error: 76534.
Not programmed to respond to
this type of question.
```

No matter what I did for the next few hours,
couldn't get Louis to do anything outside of its
gular programming. When Mom came home
om work, I didn't mention the funny goings-
. I was sure Mom would think I'd gone stark
onkers. But when Dad called that evening,
ter dinner, I asked to speak to him.

"Hi, Dad. How's Chicago?"

"Dirty, crowded, cold, and windy," came
ad's voice over the miles. "But did you want a
eather report, son? What's on your mind?
mething wrong?"

"Not exactly, Dad. Louis is acting funny. Real
nny."

"Shouldn't be. I checked it out just before I
ft. Remember you were having trouble with
e modem? You couldn't get Louis to access
ny of the mainframe databanks."

"That's right!" I said. "I forgot about that."

"Well, I didn't," Dad said. "I patched in our
test modem model. Brand-new. You can leave
question on file and when Louis can access
e databanks at the cheapest time, it'll do it
utomatically. It'll switch from standby to on,
t the data, then return to standby, after it

saves what you asked. Does that answer your
question?"

"Uhhhh . . . yeah, I guess so, Dad."

"All right, then. Let me talk to your mom
now."

I gave the phone to Mom and walked upstairs while she and Dad were still talking. The
modem, I thought. Of course. That was it. The
modem was a telephone link to any number of
huge computers at various places all over the
country. So Louis could get all the information
it wanted at any time, so long as the standby
switch was on. Louis was learning things at an
incredible rate by picking the brains of the
giant computers. And Louis had a hard disk
memory that could store 100 million bytes of
information.

But that still didn't explain the unpro-
grammed responses . . . the "conversation" I'd
had with the machine. Promising myself I'd talk
more about it with Dad, I went to bed. It had
been a rotten day and I was glad to see the end
of it come. I woke next morning in a panic. I'd
forgotten to set my alarm. Dressing frantically
and skipping breakfast, I barely made my bus.

As I got on board, I grabbed a front seat. They
were always empty. All the kids that wanted to
talk and hang out didn't sit up front where the
driver could hear them. I saw Ginny, Linda, and
Sherry in the back. Ginny was staring at me and
she didn't look too happy. Her brother Chuck,
who was seated near her, glared at me too.
What was going on?

Once the bus stopped at the school, it didn't
take long to find out. I was walking up the path
to the main entrance when someone grabbed
me from behind and spun me around. I found
myself nose to nose with Chuck Linke. This
was not a pleasant prospect.
Chuck was nearly twice my size.
Even the other guys on the
Rangers refer to him as "The
Missing" Linke. And he looked
real ticked off.

USER FRIENDLY 361

D **Critical Thinking**
Speculating
? Why might Louis display the error
message instead of answering Kevin's
questions? [Possible responses: Louis
might not be able to keep up the
"humanlike" conversation indefinitely.
Louis might be pulling back because of
Kevin's reaction to the previous emotional statement. Louis might be anticipating Kevin's disapproval.]

E **Reading Skills
and Strategies**
**Recognizing
Causes and Effects**
? To what degree might the installa-
tion of the new modem be a cause of
the "conversation" Kevin had had with
Louis? [Possible response: The new
modem enables the computer to
process huge amounts of information
and also allows it to add new vocabulary
and programs to its disk space.] Why is
Kevin not entirely satisfied with this
explanation? [Possible response: These
new abilities do not account for the
computer's independent actions and
statements, which go beyond memory
and pure logic to something unpredictable and emotional.]

F **Elements of Literature**
Conflict
? Remind students that **conflict**
refers to a problem that arises within
an individual (internal conflict),
between individuals, or between an
individual and nature, society, or fate
(external conflict). What kind of conflict does this passage portray? [exter-
nal conflict between Kevin and various
individuals] What other kinds of conflict do you see in the story so far?
[external conflict between Kevin and the
computer; internal conflict within Kevin
as he worries about his own sanity]

Taking a Second Look

Review: Making Generalizations
Remind students that a **generalization** is a type
of inference in which the reader combines information in a text with prior knowledge and then
makes a judgment that extends to the general
world. Making generalizations is similar to drawing conclusions. However, a conclusion applies to
a single set of specific circumstances—the ones
described in the text, while a generalization
applies to many different possible circumstances,
going beyond the text to the world. For

example, readers of "User Friendly" may draw
conclusions about Ginny's insensitivity on the
basis of her treatment of Kevin in the story. On
the same basis, readers could make the generalization that more popular people often feel
secure enough to treat less popular people cruelly, without worrying about the consequences.
Activities
1. On the basis of the story and their own experiences, have students make a generalization

about why people like Kevin might find it easier to relate to computers than to their peers.
2. After students finish reading the story, ask
   them to make a generalization about how
   artificial intelligence is different from human
   intelligence. Have them base their generalizations on the behavior of Kevin and the computer in the story and on their own
   experiences and readings.

A Critical Thinking

Speculation

❓ Who do you think is making the phone calls to Ginny? [Possible response: Louis probably arranged it— perhaps using an electronic voice or hiring an actress to follow a script.]

B Reading Skills and Strategies

Recognizing Causes and Effects

❓ Why does Louis stop replying with the error message here? [Possible response: Kevin just told Louis that Chuck threatened him. Louis had said before that Kevin's happiness was everything. So Louis's concern for Kevin's safety takes priority over the need to hide its activities behind the error message.]

What have you done to Ginny Linke?

"OK, nerd," growled Chuck, "what's the big idea?"

"Energy and mass are different aspects of the same thing?" I volunteered, with a weak smile. "E equals MC squared.[8] That's the biggest idea I know."

"Don't get wise, nerd," Chuck said. He grabbed my shirt front and pulled me to within inches of his face. I couldn't help but notice that Chuck needed a shave. And Chuck was only fifteen!

"Don't play dumb," Chuck went on. "I mean those creepy phone calls. Anytime my sister gets on the phone, some voice cuts in and says things to her."

"What kind of things?" I asked, trying to get loose.

A "You know very well what they are. Ginny told me about talking to you yesterday. You got some girl to make those calls for you and say all those things. . . . So you and your creepy girlfriend better knock it off. Or I'll knock *you* off. Get it?"

For emphasis Chuck balled his free hand into a fist the size of a ham and held it under my nose. I didn't know what he was talking about, but I had to get away from this moose before he did me some real harm.

"First off, I don't have a girlfriend, creepy or otherwise," I said. "And second, I don't know what you're talking about. And third, you better let me go, Chuck Linke."

"Oh, yeah? Why should I?"

"Because if you look over your shoulder,

---

8. **E equals MC squared:** reference to Albert Einstein's famous equation describing the relationship between energy and mass. This equation transformed the field of physics.

362 LIVING IN THE HEART

---

you'll see the assistant principal is watching us from his office window."

Chuck released me and spun around. There was no one at the window. But by then I was running to the safety of the school building. I figured the trick would work on him. For Chuck the hard questions begin with "How are you?" I hid out from him for the rest of the day and walked home rather than chance seeing the monster on the bus.

Louis's screen was dark when I ran upstairs to my bedroom. I placed a hand on the console. It was still warm. I punched the *on* button, and the familiar *Good afternoon, Kevin* was displayed.

Don't good afternoon me, I typed furiously. *What have you done to Ginny Linke?* Louis's screen replied:

B ```
Programming Error: 76534.
Not programmed to respond to
this type of question.
```

*Don't get cute,* I entered. *What are you doing to Ginny? Her brother nearly knocked my head off today.* Louis's screen responded immediately.

```
Are you hurt. Y/N?
```

No, I'm okay. But I don't know for how long. I've been hiding out from Chuck Linke today. He might catch me tomorrow, though. Then, I'll be history! The response from Louis came instantly.

```
Your life is in danger. Y/N?
```

I explained to Louis that my life wasn't really threatened. But it sure could be made very unpleasant by Chuck Linke. Louis flashed:

```
This Chuck Linke lives at same
address as the Ginny Linke per-
son. Y/N?
```

I punched in *Y.* Louis answered.

```
Don't worry then. HE'S history!
```

Getting Students Involved

Cooperative Learning

"I Am" Poem. After students have read the story, divide the class into groups of three, and ask them to collaborate to create an "I Am" poem about either Kevin or the computer, according to this formula:

Line 1: I am . . .
Line 2: I wish . . .
Line 3: I fear . . .
Line 4: I need . . .
Line 5: I am . . .
```

Wait! What are you going to do? I wrote. But Louis only answered with: *Programming Error: 76534.* And nothing I could do would make the machine respond. . . .

"Just what do you think you're doing, Kevin Neal?" demanded Ginny Linke. She had cornered me as I walked up the path to the school entrance. Ginny was really furious.

"I don't know what you're talking about," I said, a sinking feeling settling in my stomach. I had an idea that I *did* know. I just wasn't sure of the particulars.

"Chuck was arrested last night," Ginny said. "Some Secret Service men came to our house with a warrant. They said he'd sent a telegram threatening the president's life. They traced it right to our phone. He's still locked up. . . ." Ginny looked like she was about to cry.

"Then this morning," she continued, "we got two whole truckloads of junk mail! Flyers from every strange company in the world. Mom got a notice that all our credit cards have been canceled. And the Internal Revenue Service has called Dad in for an audit! I don't know what's going on, Kevin Neal, but somehow I think you've got something to do with it!"

"But I didn't . . ." I began, but Ginny was striding up the walk to the main entrance.

I finished the school day, but it was a blur. Louis had done it, all right. It had access to mainframe computers. It also had the ability to try every secret access code to federal and commercial memory banks until it got the right one. Louis had cracked their security systems. It was systematically destroying the entire Linke family, and all via telephone lines! What would it do next?

More important, I thought, what would *I* do next? It's one thing to play a trick or two, to get even, but Louis was going crazy! And I never wanted to harm Ginny, or even her stupid moose of a brother. She'd just hurt my feelings with that nerd remark.

"You have to disconnect Louis," I told

myself. "There's no other way."

But why did I feel like such a rat about doing it? I guess because Louis was my friend . . . the only one I had. "Don't be a jerk," I went on. "Louis is a machine. He's a very wonderful, powerful machine. And it seems he's also very dangerous. You have to pull its plug, Kevin!"

I suddenly realized that I'd said the last few words aloud. Kids around me on the bus were staring. I sat there feeling like the nerd Ginny thought I was, until my stop came. I dashed from the bus and ran the three blocks to my house.

When I burst into the hall, I was surprised to see my father, coming from the kitchen with a cup of coffee in his hand.

"Dad! What are you doing here?"

"Some kids say hello," Dad replied. "Or even, 'Gee, it's good to see you, Dad.'"

"I'm sorry, Dad," I said. "I didn't expect anyone to be home at this hour."

"Wound up my business in Chicago a day sooner than I expected," he said. "But what are you all out of breath about? Late for something?"

"No, Dad," I said. "It's Louis . . . ."

"Not to worry. I had some time on my hands, so I checked it out again. You were right. It was acting very funny. I think it had to do with the in-built logic/growth program I designed for it. You know . . . the 'personality' thing? Took me a couple of hours to clean the whole system out."

"To what?" I cried.

"I erased the whole program and set Louis up as a normal computer. Had to disconnect

Louis was going crazy!

C Reading Skills and Strategies

Recognizing Causes and Effects

? What question about Louis's behavior does Kevin's explanation still not answer? [It doesn't explain *why* Louis started talking to him in the first place and why the computer is doing so much to hurt the Linkes.]

D Elements of Literature

Characterization

Point out that Kevin's conversation with himself reveals both his loneliness and his common sense: Kevin needs a friend, and Louis is his only friend, but his common sense tells him that the computer could be dangerous. Ask students if they would feel as Kevin does in his position.

E Advanced Learners

Making Judgments

? Assuming that Louis has been functioning almost as a human in this story, ask about the implications of what Kevin's father has done. [Possible response: He has, in essence, "killed" the human side of Louis.] Is Kevin's father right to do what he did? Why does Kevin cry out in response? [Possible response: Because Louis is so powerful, Kevin's father probably has no other choice. However, Kevin's response indicates that he is upset that Louis's human side has been destroyed.]

Making the Connections

Connecting to the Theme: "Living in the Heart"

Ask students to discuss the collection theme after they have finished this story. On the board write the words *brain* and *heart* and circle both. Around the word *brain*, have volunteers cluster events in the story that show Kevin's and the computer's mental abilities. Around the word

heart, have students cluster events in the story that reflect their emotional needs. Point out that the real focus of the story is not in what the computer can do, but in what it wants and needs.

Elements of Literature

Title

? How is the meaning of the technical phrase "user friendly" expanded in this story? [Possible response: While the phrase refers to features that make a computer easier to use, the story shows how Kevin comes to regard Louis(e) as his friend, and Louise comes to regard Kevin as someone she loves.]

B **Elements of Literature**

Characterization

? How does your impression of the computer's character change as a result of this information? [Possible response: That the computer thinks of itself as a female who loves Kevin suggests that it has emotional depth far beyond anything Kevin imagined.] Why does Kevin cry at the end? [Possible response: He realizes that he has lost someone that loved him.]

the whole thing and do some rewiring. It had been learning, all right. But it was also turning itself around. . . ." Dad stopped, and looked at me. "It's kind of involved, Kevin," he said. "Even for a bright kid like you. Anyway, I think you'll find Louis is working just fine now.

"Except it won't answer you as Louis anymore. It'll only function as a regular Major Electronics Model Z-11127. I guess the personality program didn't work out."

I felt like a great weight had been taken off my shoulders. I didn't have to "face" Louis, and pull its plug. But somehow, all I could say was "Thanks, Dad."

"Don't mention it, son," Dad said brightly. He took his cup of coffee and sat down in his favorite chair in the living room. I followed him.

"One more thing that puzzles me, though," Dad said. He reached over to the table near his chair. He held up three sheets of fanfold computer paper covered with figures. "Just as I was doing the final erasing, I must have cut the

printer on by accident. There was some data in the print buffer memory and it printed out. I don't know what to make of it. Do you?"

I took the papers from my father and read: *How do I love thee? Let me compute the ways.*[9] The next two pages were covered with strings of binary code figures. On the last page, in beautiful color graphics,[10] was a stylized heart. Below it was the simple message: *I will always love you, Kevin: Louise.*

"Funny thing," Dad said. "It spelled its own name wrong."

"Yeah," I said. I turned and headed for my room. There were tears in my eyes and I knew I couldn't explain them to Dad, or myself either.

---

9. **How do I . . . ways:** reference to a famous poem by the English poet Elizabeth Barrett Browning (1806–1861) that begins, "How do I love thee? Let me count the ways."
10. **graphics:** designs or pictures produced on and printed out from a computer. *Graphics* also refers to printed images produced by other means, such as engraving.

MEET THE WRITER

"The Brooklyn Public Library Was a Place of Refuge"

T. Ernesto Bethancourt (1932–   ) became a full-time writer by accident. He was working as a folk musician in a nightclub, and his first daughter had just been born. Bethancourt used the time between shows to begin writing his autobiography, in hopes that she would read it one day. "Through a series of extraordinary events, the autobiography became novelized, updated, and was pub-

lished in 1975 as [New York City Too Far from] Tampa Blues. The book was an immense success, and I began a new career in midlife."

Bethancourt attributes his writing success to the New York City public schools and the public library. "I thank them, every day, for the new and wonderful life they have given to me and my family." In another interview he said, "The Brooklyn Public Library was a place of refuge from street gangs. There was adventure, travel, and escape to be found on the shelves."

Bethancourt has written science fiction novels and the Doris Fein mystery series.

Assessing Learning

Check Test: Short Answer

1. What is the first strange thing that Louis does in this story? [asks for a voice module]
2. What does Ginny do at the end of her first conversation with Kevin? [She laughs at him.]
3. What promise does Louis make to Kevin about Ginny? ["I'll take care of Ginny."]
4. What happens to Ginny and her family? [Ginny receives nasty phone calls; later, her brother is arrested for having written threatening letters to the President; her family receives

tons of junk mail; their credit cards are cancelled; and Mr. Linke is called in for an IRS audit.]

5. What happens to Louis? [Kevin's father reprograms Louis to be more conventional, but the computer reveals through a printout that it thought of itself as "Louise" and loved Kevin.]

Standardized Test Preparation

For practice with standardized test format specific to this selection, see
• *Standardized Test Preparation*, p. 56
For practice in proofreading and editing, see
• *Daily Oral Grammar*, Transparency 21

MAKING MEANINGS

First Thoughts

[respond]

1. Talk to a partner about your responses to the story. You may want to begin by completing these statements:

   • If I were the narrator, I would . . .

   • I think it wasn't fair when . . . because . . .

Shaping Interpretations

[analyze]

2. Trace the chain of **causes** and **effects** leading up to Kevin's decision to erase Louis(e). Make a flow chart that shows how each event causes another event. Is what finally happens to Louis(e) part of the chain of events or outside of it?

Challenging the Text

[evaluate]

3. Did the ending of the story surprise you, or did it make you feel that the writer tricked you? Describe how you feel about the story's ending.

> **Reading Check**
>
> "User Friendly" is narrated by the main character. With two partners, take turns retelling the **main events** of the story, but tell them as though you were the computer. While your partners narrate, listen carefully to be sure they include all important details that Louis(e) would know, in the order in which Louis(e) would have found out about them.

CHOICES: Building Your Portfolio

Writer's Notebook

1. Collecting Ideas for a Biographical Sketch

You can tell a lot about people when you know what's most important to them. For instance, what seems most important to Kevin is his computer. Make a list of people you know or have read about. Jot down what you think each person values most. It could be a baby brother or a pet cat, or perhaps even a CD player or a camping tent. What does each person's favorite thing tell you about him or her? You might want to check your Quickwrite notes for ideas.

Art

2. A Portrait of Kevin

A good portrait reveals **character.** The author of this story gives you many clues to Kevin's appearance and the kind of impression he makes on others. See if you can capture Kevin's character in a portrait. Some portraits show objects in the background that are associated with the subject. What would you put in Kevin's portrait?

Reading Check

Kevin's father builds the computer, names it Louis, and modifies it with all kinds of circuitry. On Monday, April 22, Kevin gets his schedule. Louis asks when Kevin will get the voice module and Kevin acts surprised. That afternoon Kevin tells Louis all about Ginny Linke and how she hurt his feelings that day. Louis promises to take care of Ginny. Louis then arranges for Ginny Linke to receive harassing phone calls. The next day Kevin questions Louis about the phone calls and tells Louis that Chuck threatened him. Louis then promises to retaliate. Louis writes a letter threatening the President and ties it to Chuck. He then arranges for the IRS to audit Chuck's father, has tons of junk mail delivered to the Linkes, and authorizes their credit cards to be cancelled. Kevin's father reprograms the computer.

MAKING MEANINGS

First Thoughts

1. Possible responses: If I were the narrator, I would feel as if I had lost my best friend. But I would also be relieved. I think it wasn't fair that Kevin's father reprogrammed Louise, because it was as if he had killed someone.

Shaping Interpretations

2. Kevin tries to talk to Ginny, who laughs at him. This causes Kevin to vent his hurt to Louis. Louis then harasses Ginny and her family. This behavior causes Kevin to consider disconnecting Louis. Louise's final fate is the result of Kevin's father's response to Kevin's earlier statement about Louis's odd behavior.

Challenging the Text

3. Possible response: It is not surprising that the computer has human feelings for Kevin, because of Louis's statement "Your happiness is everything to me." However, the idea that the computer thinks of itself as Louise and loves Kevin is surprising.

Grading Timesaver

Rubrics for each Choices assignment appear on p. 147 in the *Portfolio Management System.*

CHOICES: Building Your Portfolio

1. **Writer's Notebook** Remind students to save their work. They may use it as prewriting for the Writer's Workshop on pp. 410–414.

2. **Art** Make sure the portraits include the physical details Kevin gives of his own appearance on p. 359, and encourage students to choose relevant items (such as the computer or a snapshot of Ginny) to include in the portrait. The portrait should also suggest Kevin's serious, quiet, intense personality.

GRAMMAR LINK

Use the following sentences to give students more practice in using correct pronoun forms in compound structures.

Lydia and (I, me) decided to go to the movies. Jake wanted to go with Lydia and (I, me), but he had to babysit for his little sister. So (she, her) and (I, me) went by ourselves. Then Jake's parents came home early, so he rushed to the theater and saw (she, her) and (I, me) sitting in the front row.

Try It Out
1. she
2. I
3. her
4. him
5. him, me

VOCABULARY

Possible Answers:
1. On holidays, federal banks close early. / We had a picnic on the river banks.
2. My grade was an A. / The hill had a steep grade.
3. I have to file my nails before I tear something. / The computer operator opened the electronic file.
4. We replaced our computer with a newer model. / Would you like me to model my new coat for you?
5. The wound bled a great deal before the nurse bandaged it. / The nurse wound a bandage around the man's injured head.
6. My eyes filled with tears when I heard the sad story. / Fragile fabric tears easily.
7. I can type at a rate of 60 words a minute. / My blood is type A positive.

Resources ———

Grammar
• *Grammar and Language Links*, p. 33

Spelling
For related instruction, see
• *Spelling and Decoding*, p. 17

GRAMMAR LINK   `MINI-LESSON`

Language Handbook
H E L P

See The Objective Case, page 735.

Technology
H E L P

See Language Workshop CD-ROM. *Key word entry:* pronouns.

Pronouns Can Be Problems

Pronouns used in compound structures can be confusing. Which of these sentences is correct?

> Dad talked to Mom and <u>me</u>.
>
> Dad talked to Mom and <u>I</u>.

Mom and me and *Mom and I* are compound structures. When you proofread your own writing, you can use this trick to decide which pronoun is correct: Say the sentence aloud as if it contained only a pronoun, not a compound structure. Use each form of the pronoun in turn, and let your ear tell you which one sounds right.

EXAMPLE   Dad talked to <u>me</u>. [sounds right]

            Dad talked to <u>I</u>. [sounds wrong]

CORRECT   Dad talked to Mom and <u>me</u>.

Try It Out

In the following sentences, choose the correct pronoun from each pair. Use the trick described at the left to test each proofreading decision.

1. Ginny and she/her laughed at me on the bus.
2. Louis and I/me sent each other messages.
3. Louis made problems for Chuck and she/her.
4. Was there much respect between Kevin and he/him?
5. Louis showed he/him and I/me that it could cause a lot of trouble.

VOCABULARY   `HOW TO OWN A WORD`

Homographs: Words with Multiple Meanings

One of the mysteries of the English language is the fact that words spelled the same way can have different meanings. Such words are called **homographs.** Some homographs are pronounced differently; some are pronounced the same. When you find a homograph in your reading, you can choose the correct meaning for the word by deciding which meaning best fits the context.

The homographs in these sentences are pronounced differently:

> The plastic case was next to the <u>console</u> (kän′sōl′).
> No one could <u>console</u> (kən·sōl′) me that sad day.

The homographs in these sentences are pronounced the same:

> The first <u>page</u> came out of the printer.
> Dominic was a <u>page</u> in the U.S. Senate.

Choose three of the following homographs from "User Friendly." Make up two sentences for each, using context to reveal the meaning of each homograph.

> banks • grade • file • model • wound • tears • type

Grammar Link Quick Check

Explain why each of the following sentences is correct or incorrect.

1. Kevin named the computer that his father and him had put together "Louis." [Incorrect: It should be "his father and he" because the pronoun is a subject of the verb *had put*.]

2. Kevin worked up the nerve to speak to Ginny, but the conversation between him and her turned ugly. [Correct: The pronouns are objects of the preposition *between*.]

3. Kevin recognized too late how deeply their friendship had affected Louise and he. [Incorrect: It should be "Louise and him" because they are objects of the verb *had affected*.]

4. Kevin's father removed the computer's personality, but Kevin and he would tell very different stories of what had led up to that action. [Correct: The pronoun is the subject of the verb *would tell*.]

Reading Skills and Strategies

Booking space on the Net:

OBJECTIVES
1. Distinguish between opinions and facts
2. Identify opinions and facts in the selections
3. Distinguish between valid opinions and invalid stereotypes
4. Form valid opinions from reading that can be supported by facts

THINKING CRITICALLY: OPINIONS VS. FACTS

Being able to tell fact from opinion can come in handy. You can often avoid big arguments simply by watching out for opinions based purely on emotion. Opinions are not necessarily incorrect, but to be valid, they must be backed by facts. Here's a quick way to tell the difference between facts and opinions:

Fact
information that can be proved true

→

Examples
• Elton John was born on March 25, 1947, in Pinner, England.
• Five pounds of feathers weigh as much as five pounds of rocks.

Judging opinions

Opinion
a judgment or belief that cannot be supported with evidence

Valid opinion
a judgment or belief supported with evidence

Stereotype
an opinion about a group of people that does not allow for individual differences

Example
"Elton John is the best musician in the world."

Example
"Elton John's song 'Candle in the Wind' honors Princess Diana and raises money for good causes."

Example
"All old people are weak."

Forming Opinions As You Read

Strategic readers constantly form opinions and revise them as they read. Your opinions can be influenced by any of the following:

• specific details in the text
• your own prior knowledge and experience
• talking about the text with other readers

When you express opinions about a character in a story, about the plot, or about how well or poorly the story is told, back up your opinions with details from the text or from your own experience. Don't just say, "This was a bad story." Say, "This was a bad story because . . .".

Apply the strategy on the next page.

Reading Skills and Strategies

This feature not only explains the difference between opinions and facts, but also gives students criteria for recognizing opinions, valid opinions, and stereotypes. In addition, the feature helps students form valid opinions as they combine information gained from reading with their own prior knowledge and experience.

Mini-Lesson:
Thinking Critically

• Ask students to create a two-column Fact and Opinion Log that they can use as they read "Miss Awful" (pp. 369–380). In the left column of the log, they should record first their initial impressions of Roger Clark and Miss Orville; in the right column they should enter the information on which these opinions are based: the details and facts from the story, as well as their own prior experiences. As they read the story, they should record any changes in their opinions as they gather new information. After students have finished the story, ask them to compare their charts.

Reaching All Students

Struggling Readers

Give students more practice in distinguishing between entirely subjective opinions ("I like this candidate because he appeals to me") and valid opinions that can be supported by evidence ("I like this candidate because he supports programs that have been successful"). Help them see that many subjective opinions can be turned into valid opinions with the addition of reason and evidence. Most students will probably not like Miss Orville at first, but they should be encouraged to consider all the information about Miss Orville and to adjust their opinions accordingly.

English Language Learners

Students who are learning English may miss subtle details and nuances provided by the writer. They may also have some difficulty understanding that they are "allowed" to change their minds about a character—that the writer of the story actually sets the reader up to think one way about Miss Awful and then proceeds to change his or her opinion. Remind them that every story is a process in which we meet total strangers and get to know them. Encourage them to think about times when they changed their minds in real life and to recall the reasons behind these changes.

OBJECTIVES

1. Read and interpret the story
2. Analyze character
3. Form opinions
4. Express understanding through expository and creative writing, art, or speaking/listening
5. Identify homonyms and use such homonyms in writing
6. Understand and use new words

SKILLS

Reading
- Form opinions

Writing
- Collect ideas for a biographical report
- Create a list of treasured items
- Write a campaign speech

Grammar/Language
- Identify and use homonyms

Vocabulary
- Understand and use new words

Art
- Create a box of treasured items

Speaking/Listening
- Prepare a campaign speech
- Role-play conflict resolution

Viewing/Representing
- Interpret details in a painting (ATE)

Planning

- **Block Schedule**
  Block Scheduling Lesson Plans with Pacing Guide

- **Traditional Schedule**
  Lesson Plans Including Strategies for English-Language Learners

- **One-Stop Planner**
  CD-ROM with Test Generator

Before You Read

MISS AWFUL

Make the Connection

Teaching from the Heart

If you attended an elementary school in which you had the same teacher for every subject, you were with that one person a long time—approximately fourteen hundred hours a year. A teacher can be a tremendous influence on a person.

Think-pair-share. Think of the best teacher you've ever had. Consider what qualities and actions made this teacher special. Then, *without naming the teacher,* describe the teacher to a partner and explain why he or she was so important to you.

Quickwrite

Based on your discussion, write down your opinions about what makes a good teacher.

Reading Skills and Strategies

Forming Opinions

If you did the activities described on this page, you just gave some **valid opinions.** Not only did you state what you thought about the teacher, but you backed up your opinions with reasons. As you read this story, you'll probably find yourself riding a roller coaster of the main character's changing opinions. Hang on tight, and notice when your opinions of "Miss Awful" are changing along with his.

Preteaching Vocabulary

Words to Own

Have students read the definitions of the Words to Own listed at the bottom of the selection pages. Then, use the following activity to reinforce understanding of the words.

- Model using the dictionary to research the etymology of a word. Choose a word from Latin, such as *torpor* (from *torpere,* "to be numb").
- Direct students, either individually or in pairs, to identify the five Words to Own (besides

torpor) with Latin derivations. [Dictionaries vary, but students' findings should approximate these: **martial**—from *martialis,* "of Mars"; **prodigy**—from *pro-,* "before" + *agiom,* "a thing said"; **mortified**—from *mors,* "death" + *facere,* "to make, to do"; **infiltrated**—from *in,* "in, into" + *filtrum,* "filter"; **reconvened**—from *re,* "back, again" + *com,* "with" + *venire,* "come"]

MISS AWFUL

Arthur Cavanaugh

He gaped at the monstrous tweed figure in dismay.

THE WHOLE EPISODE OF MISS AWFUL BEGAN FOR THE CLARKS AT THEIR DINNER TABLE ONE SUNDAY AFTERNOON. YOUNG ROGER CLARK WAS EXPLAINING WHY HE COULD GO TO CENTRAL PARK WITH HIS FATHER INSTEAD OF STAYING HOME TO FINISH HIS HOMEWORK—MISS WILSON, HIS TEACHER, WOULDN'T BE AT SCHOOL TOMORROW, SO WHO'D KNOW THE DIFFERENCE? "SHE HAS TO TAKE CARE OF A CRISIS," ROGER EXPLAINED. "IT'S IN OMAHA."

369

Summary ■ ■

In this short story, told by an omniscient narrator, Roger Clark learns that his third-grade teacher, Miss Wilson, will be out of school for a week. He anticipates with pleasure the arrival of an inexperienced substitute. He and his classmates are dismayed to find instead a thin, elderly, forbidding disciplinarian, Miss Orville, whose loud commands and harsh reproaches stun the customarily indulged children. Miss Orville's severity extends to the adults as well, as she bluntly catalogs their children's shortcomings and tries to reverse years of laxity in the classroom. When the students learn that Miss Orville is a retired teacher who was evicted from her apartment, they taunt her about the incident. On her last day in class, the students plot their revenge—stripping the leaves from Miss Orville's cherished plant. Roger protests the plan's cruelty to no avail. When the bewildered Miss Orville notices her denuded plant, Roger tries to console her by correctly spelling words he had missed before. Miss Orville's eyes fill with tears.

Background

"Miss Awful" is set in Greenwich Village, a lively, colorful neighborhood in New York City. Students may notice references to brownstones, which are narrow townhouses built from reddish-brown sandstone. Fifth Avenue is a street that runs through the middle of Manhattan. St. Geoffrey's, where "Miss Awful" teaches, is a fictional institution modeled on relatively permissive "progressive" private schools.

Resources ———

Listening
Audio CD Library
A recording of this selection is included in the *Audio CD Library*:
• Disc 10, Track 2

Resources: Print and Media

Reading
• *Reading Skills and Strategies*
   Selection Skill Lesson, p. 76
• *Graphic Organizers for Active Reading*, p. 24
• *Words to Own*, p. 15
• *Spelling and Decoding*
   Worksheet, p. 18
• *Audio CD Library*
   Disc 10, Track 2

Writing and Language
• *Daily Oral Grammar*
   Transparency 22
• *Grammar and Language Links*
   Worksheet, p. 35
• *Language Workshop CD-ROM*

Assessment
• *Formal Assessment*, p. 69
• *Portfolio Management System*, p. 148
• *Standardized Test Preparation*, p. 58
• *Test Generator (One-Stop Planner CD-ROM)*

A Reading Skills and Strategies

Forming Opinions

❓ Do you agree with Elizabeth's taunt that Roger "fails to make sense"? Why do you think Roger doesn't get upset with her? [Possible responses: Roger's statement was a little vague and babyish, but Elizabeth seems to be picking on him. As his older sister, she probably feels entitled to criticize him. She also knows he won't jump on her. Roger's failure to get upset suggests that he may be mild-mannered and tends to avoid conflict.]

B Critical Thinking

Predicting

Ask students to write predictions about what will happen while Miss Wilson is away, based on Roger's comments and also on other evidence, such as the story's title.

Ⓐ "What is?" his older sister, Elizabeth, inquired. "For a kid in third grade, Roger, you talk dopey. You fail to make sense."

Roger ignored the insult. His sister was a condition of life he had learned to live with, like lions. Or snakes. Poisonous ones. Teetering,[1] as always, on the tilted-back chair, feet wrapped around the legs, he continued, "Till Ⓑ Miss Wilson gets back we're having some other teacher. She flew to Omaha yesterday." He pushed some peas around on his plate and was silent a moment. "I hope her plane don't crash," he said.

Roger's mother patted his hand. A lively, outgoing youngster, as noisy and rambunctious[2] as any eight-year-old, he had another side to

1. **teetering:** wobbling, as if about to fall.
2. **rambunctious:** noisy and lively.

Reaching All Students

Struggling Readers

Forming Opinions was introduced on page 368. For a lesson directly tied to this selection that teaches students to form opinions as they read by using a strategy called Semantic Differential Scales, see the *Reading Skills and Strategies binder:*

• Selection Skill Lesson, p. 76

English Language Learners

Students from other countries may have difficulty imagining conditions at St. Geoffrey's—a school holding taffy pulls in the heart of a congested, sophisticated city; a place where a teacher decides to lie down on the floor with her third-graders. Have them read Meet the Writer on page 381, in which Arthur Cavanaugh explains the actual circumstances on which "Miss Awful" was based. English language learners may not readily hear the similarity in sound

between "Miss Awful" and the name *Miss Orville;* ask for volunteers to explain it. For strategies to supplement instruction for these students, see

• *Lesson Plans Including Strategies for English-Language Learners*

Tribute to the American Working People (detail of five-part painting) by Honoré Desmond Sharrer.

National Museum of American Art, Washington, D.C./Art Resource, New York.

Characterization

❓ What kind of person do you think Roger is, and what do you base your idea on? [Possible response: He has a side that cares about other people; he seems more sensitive than most eight-year-old boys.]

B **Reading Skills and Strategies**

Forming Opinions

❓ Do you agree with Elizabeth's statement that school is not supposed to be fun? [Possible response: The best thing is to combine fun and learning. But if a choice must be made, children go to school to learn.] Discuss whether it is possible to have fun and learn at the same time, or whether there is a necessary trade-off. Is fun something that becomes harder to come by as students get older?

C **Vocabulary Note**

Call attention to the use of the words *whim* and *whimsical*. They help to establish the differences between Miss Wilson and Miss Orville. Point out the definition of *whimsical* and ask students to suggest examples of whims and whimsical behavior.

him, tender and soft, which worried about people. Let the blind man who sold pencils outside the five-and-ten on Broadway be absent from his post, and Roger worried that catastrophe had overtaken him. When Mrs. Loomis, a neighbor of the Clarks in the Greenwich Village brownstone, had entered the hospital, Roger's anxious queries had not ceased until she was discharged.[3] And recently there was the cat which had nested in the downstairs doorway at night. Roger had carried down saucers of milk, clucking with concern. "Is the cat run away? Don't it have a home?"

Virginia Clark assured her son, "You'll have Miss Wilson safely back before you know it. It's nice that you care so."

Roger beamed with relief. "Well, I like Miss Wilson, she's fun. Last week, for instance, when Tommy Miller got tired of staying in his seat and lay down on the floor——"

"He did what?" Roger's father was roused from his post-dinner torpor.

"Sure. Pretty soon the whole class was lying down. Know what Miss Wilson did?"

"If you'll notice, Mother," Elizabeth interjected, "he hasn't touched a single pea."

"*She* lay down on the floor, too," Roger went on ecstatically. "She said we'd *all* have a rest, it was perfectly normal in the middle of the day. That's what I love about St. Geoff's. It's fun."

"Fun," snorted his sister. "School isn't supposed to be a fun fest. It's supposed to be filling that empty noodle of yours."

"Miss Wilson got down on the floor?" Mr. Clark repeated. He had met Roger's teacher on occasion; she had struck him as capable but excessively whimsical. She was a large woman to be getting down on floors, Mr. Clark thought. "What did the class do next?" he asked.

"Oh, we lay there a while, then got up and did a Mexican hat dance," Roger answered. "It was swell."

3. **discharged:** released: here, from the hospital.

"I'm sure not every day is as frolicsome," Mrs. Clark countered, slightly anxious. She brought in dessert, a chocolate mousse. Roger's story sounded typical of St. Geoffrey's. Not that she was unhappy with his school. A small private institution, while it might be called overly permissive, it projected a warm, homey atmosphere which Mrs. Clark found appealing. It was church-affiliated, which she approved of, and heaven knows its location a few blocks away from the brownstone was convenient. True, Roger's scholastic progress wasn't notable—his spelling, for example, remained atrocious. Friendly as St. Geoffrey's was, Mrs. Clark sometimes *did* wish . . .

Roger attacked dessert with a lot more zest than he had shown the peas. "So can I go to the park with you, Dad? I've only got spelling left, and who cares about that?" Before his mother could comment, he was up from the table and racing toward the coat closet. "Okay, Dad?"

"I didn't say you could go. I didn't even say I'd take you," Mr. Clark objected. He happened, at that moment, to glance at his waistline and reflect that a brisk hike might do him some good. He pushed back his chair. "All right, but the minute we return, it's straight to your room to finish your spelling."

"Ah, thanks, Dad. Can we go to the boat pond first?"

"We will not," cried Elizabeth, elbowing into the closet. "We'll go to the Sheep Meadow first."

Roger was too happy to argue. Pulling on his jacket, he remarked, "Gee, I wonder what the new teacher will be like. Ready for your coat, Dad?"

It was just as well that he gave the matter no more thought. In view of events to come, Roger was entitled to a few carefree hours.

WORDS TO OWN
torpor (tôr′pər) *n.*: sluggishness.
whimsical (hwim′zi·kəl) *adj.*: full of silly, fanciful ideas.

Monday morning at school started off with perfect normalcy. It began exactly like any other school morning. Elizabeth had long since departed for the girls' school she attended uptown when Mrs. Clark set out with Roger for the short walk to St. Geoff's. She didn't trust him with the Fifth Avenue traffic yet. They reached the school corner and Roger skipped away eagerly from her. The sidewalk in front of school already boasted a large, jostling throng of children, and his legs couldn't hurry Roger fast enough to join them. Indeed, it was his reason for getting to school promptly: to have time to play before the 8:45 bell. Roger's school bag was well equipped for play. As usual, he'd packed a supply of baseball cards for trading opportunities; a spool of string, in case anybody brought a kite; a water pistol for possible use in the lavatory; and a police whistle for sheer noise value. Down the Greenwich Village sidewalk he galloped, shouting the names of his third grade friends as he picked out faces from the throng. "Hiya, Tommy. Hey, hiya, Bruce. Hi, Steve, you bring your trading cards?"

By the time the 8:45 bell rang—St. Geoff's used a cowbell, one of the homey touches—Roger had finished a game of tag, traded several baseball cards, and was launched in an exciting jump-the-hydrant contest. Miss Gillis, the school secretary, was in charge of the bell, and she had to clang it extensively before the student body took notice. Clomping up the front steps, they spilled into the downstairs hall, headed in various directions. Roger's class swarmed up the stairs in rollicking spirits, Tommy Miller, Bruce Reeves, Joey Lambert, the girls forming an untidy rear flank behind them, shrill with laughter.

It wasn't until the front ranks reached the third-grade classroom that the first ominous note was struck.

"Hey, what's going on?" Jimmy Moore demanded, first to observe the changed appearance of the room. The other children crowded behind him in the doorway. Instead of a cozy semicircle—"As though we're seated round a glowing hearth," Miss Wilson had described it—the desks and chairs had been rearranged in stiff, rigid rows. "Gee, look, the desks are in rows," commented Midge Fuller, a plump little girl who stood blocking Roger's view. Midge was a child given to unnecessary statements. "It's raining today," she would volunteer to her classmates, all of them in slickers. Or, "There's the lunch bell, gang." The point to Roger wasn't that the desks had been rearranged. The point was, *why?* As if in answer, he heard two hands clap behind him, as loud and menacing as thunder.

"What's this, what's this?" barked a stern, raspish voice. "You are not cattle milling in a pen. Enough foolish gaping! Come, come, form into lines."

Heads turned in unison, mouths fell agape. The children of St. Geoffrey's third grade had never formed into lines of any sort, but this

"GEE, I WONDER WHAT THE NEW TEACHER WILL BE LIKE. READY FOR YOUR COAT, DAD?"

MISS AWFUL **373**

D Reading Skills and Strategies
Making Inferences

❓ What does packing so many toys in his schoolbag tell you about Roger and his school? [Possible responses: He doesn't plan on doing much work; apparently, his school doesn't require him to leave his toys at home.]

E Critical Thinking
Speculating

❓ Why might the chairs be in rows instead of in a semicircle? [Possible response: The substitute teacher must have moved them.] What might this new arrangement signal about the differences between the substitute teacher and Miss Wilson? [Possible response: The substitute teacher will probably be more strict and orderly than Miss Wilson was.]

F Elements of Literature
Characterization

Remind students that characters' words tell us something about their personalities. Discuss what these words suggest about the new teacher. Point out the words *barked* and *stern* and have students note that the request doesn't include a "please."

Crossing the Curriculum

Art

After students finish the story, have them work in groups to create storyboards for the three most memorable incidents from "Miss Awful," using passages from the story as captions. Possible incidents might include:

- The children march toward their desks. "She clapped time with her hands and the stunned ranks trooped into the classroom."

- Roger's toys spill from his schoolbag. "We have come to play, have we?"
- Miss Orville sits in a rocking chair on the sidewalk. "She couldn't keep any of the plants."

Call on a student from each group to present the storyboards to the class and to read the captions aloud.

A Reading Skills and Strategies

Forming Opinions

? Do you agree with what Miss Orville says about children and plants? [Possible response: It is true that children and plants are living organisms, but children are lively, mobile beings; unlike passive plants, they have wills of their own.] What does her statement about children and plants suggest about her feelings? [Possible response: Her comment may reveal a secret tenderness toward children and plants or a misguided desire to control and shape them.]

B Literary Connections

After they have read this paragraph, ask students to offer comparisons between Miss Orville and similar characters they have read about in other stories or seen in movies or on television. Ask whether each of these characters was primarily positive or negative, and whether the perception of the character changed at some point in the work. Point out that Miss Orville's character is based on an old stereotype, a largely negative one, of the "old-maid schoolteacher." As the story continues, tell students to be on the lookout for any new information about Miss Orville or positive elements in her character.

---

was not the cause of their shocked inertia.[4] Each was staring, with a sensation similar to that of drowning, at the owner of the raspish voice. She was tall and straight as a ruler, and was garbed in an ancient tweed suit whose skirt dipped nearly to the ankles. She bore a potted plant in one arm and Miss Wilson's roll book in the other. Rimless spectacles glinted on her bony nose. Her hair was gray, like a witch's, skewered in a bun, and there was no question that she had witch's eyes. Roger had seen those same eyes leering from the pages of *Hansel and Gretel*—identical, they were. He gulped at the terrible presence.

"Form lines, I said. Girls in one, boys in the other." Poking, prodding, patrolling back and forth, the new teacher kneaded the third grade into position and ruefully inspected the result. "Sloppiest group I've ever beheld. *March!*" She clapped time with her hands and the stunned ranks trooped into the classroom. "*One*, two, three, *one*, two—girls on the window side, boys on the wall. Stand at your desks. Remove your outer garments. You, little Miss, with the vacant stare. What's your name?"

"Ja-Ja——" a voice squeaked.

"Speak up. I won't have mumblers."

"Jane Douglas."

"Well, Jane Douglas, you will be coat monitor. Collect the garments a row at a time and hang them neatly in the cloakroom. Did you hear me, child? Stop staring." Normally slow-moving, Jane Douglas became a whirl of activity, charging up and down the aisles, piling coats in her arms. The new teacher tugged at her tweed jacket. "Class be seated, hands folded on desks," she barked, and there was immediate compliance. She next paraded to the windows and installed the potted plant on the sill. Her witch's hands fussed with the green leaves, straightening, pruning. "Plants and children belong in classrooms," she declared, spec-

tacles sweeping over the rows. "Can someone suggest why?"

There was total silence, punctured by a deranged giggle, quickly suppressed.

A "Very well, I will tell you. Plants and children are living organisms. Both will grow with proper care. Repeat, *proper*. Not indulgent fawning, or giving in to whims—scrupulosity!"[5] With another tug at the jacket, she strode, ruler straight, to the desk in the front of the room. "I am Miss Orville. *O-r-v-i-l-l-e*," she spelled. "You are to use my name in replying to all questions."

In the back of the room, Jimmy Moore whispered frantically to Roger. "What did she say her name is?"

Miss Orville rapped her desk. "Attention, please, no muttering in the back." She cleared her voice and resumed. "Prior to my retirement I taught boys and girls for forty-six years," she warned. "I am beyond trickery, so I advise you to try none. You are to be in my charge until **B** the return of Miss Wilson, however long that may be." She clasped her hands in front of her and trained her full scrutiny on the rows. "Since I have no knowledge of your individual abilities, perhaps a look at the weekend homework will shed some light. Miss Wilson left me a copy of the assignment. You have all completed it, I trust? Take out your notebooks, please. At once, at once, I say."

Roger's head spun dizzily around. He gaped at the monstrous tweed figure in dismay. Book bags were being clicked open, notebooks drawn out—what was he to do? He had gone to his room after the outing in the park yesterday, but, alas, it had not been to complete his assignment. He watched, horrified, as the tweed figure proceeded among the aisles and inspected notebooks. What had she said her name was? Awful—was that it? Miss Awful! Biting his lip, he listened to her scathing comments.

"You call this chicken scrawl penmanship?"

---

4. inertia (in·ʉr′shə): here, an inability or reluctance to move.

5. scrupulosity (skr oo′pyə·läs′ə·tē): extreme carefulness and correctness.

374 LIVING IN THE HEART

Getting Students Involved

Cooperative Learning

Resume. Ask students to work in groups of four to create a resume for Miss Orville. Give students a model resume before they begin. Have them speculate to create details in these areas:

- education
- teaching experience
- most important skills
- personal information (interests, hobbies)
- awards

Encourage the students to type their information in resume format.

T374

LITERATURE
AND
SOCIAL STUDIES

Becoming a Nation of Readers

If Roger had gone to school in the late 1800s, chances are he would have learned to read and spell from a McGuffey reader. *McGuffey's Eclectic Readers* were textbooks used by most American schoolchildren toward the end of the nineteenth century. These popular books were named after their creator, William H. McGuffey (1800–1873), a professor and minister who devoted his life to improving public education.

As a child, McGuffey spent only the winter months in school. Like many other students in those days, he stayed at home to work on the family farm during the rest of the year. When he wasn't in school, his mother taught him by reading stories aloud.

McGuffey loved learning so much that he became a teacher when he was only thirteen. He spent the rest of his life in the classroom. He strongly believed that reading, speaking, and spelling aloud were the best ways to educate young people. He chose an "eclectic" assortment of literature for his books—fables, poems, short stories, and great speeches. His goals were not only to expose students to fine literature but to teach them values like duty, goodness, and citizenship. His readers include stories called "True Courage," "On Speaking the Truth," "The Greedy Girl," and "The Boy Who Did Mischief for Fun."

Between 1836 and 1920, McGuffey readers sold more than 122 million copies. The books are popular even today. One source estimates that since 1961, some thirty thousand McGuffey readers have been sold each year.

Three images, The Granger Collection, New York.

MISS AWFUL 375

Cultural Connections

Explain that a set of *McGuffey's Eclectic Readers* functioned much like this textbook because each book included written works of different types—stories, poetry, nonfiction—for students in elementary school. The books were arranged according to reading difficulty, not grade level. By the time they reached secondary school, most students did not use the readers.

A Reading Skills and Strategies
Making Inferences
? What does Mr. Clark suggest here? [Possible response: He seems to imply that because Miss Orville doesn't try to have fun with her pupils, she may be an improvement over Miss Wilson.]

B Elements of Literature
Characterization
? Discuss what this passage reveals about both Mrs. Clark and Miss Orville. Point out that both Mr. Clark and Elizabeth seem to approve of Miss Orville's approach, while Mrs. Clark does not. Point out that despite her apparent dislike of Miss Orville, Mrs. Clark is still complying with the teacher's requirements. Why does Mrs. Clark want to meet Roger at the corner rather than in front of school? [Possible response: to avoid meeting Miss Orville] How does Mrs. Clark feel about Miss Orville? [Possible response: She seems to feel about her much as the children do—resenting her, fearing her, but compelled to please her.]

C Elements of Literature
Characterization
? What information about Miss Orville's character does Nancy Reeves's story present? [Possible responses: The story reveals that Miss Orville is extremely stubborn and determined. It also shows that she has experienced some difficulty in her life.]

---

absorbed in his toys. Is that what you want for him?"

"I—I—" Virginia Clark would have been grateful if the sidewalk had opened up to receive her.

As she reported to her husband that evening, she had never in her life been as <u>mortified</u>. "Spoke to me in front of all the other mothers, in loud, clarion tones," she described the scene. "Do I want Roger to remain a child at play. Imagine."

"By the way, where is Roge?" Mr. Clark asked, who had come home late from the office. "He's not watching television, or busy with his airplanes——"

"In his room, doing over his homework for the ninety-eighth time. It has to be perfect, he says. But, really, Charles, don't you think it was outrageous?"

A Mr. Clark stirred his coffee. "I bet Miss Orville doesn't get down on the floor with the class. Or do Mexican hat dances with them."

B "If that's meant to <u>disparage</u> Miss Wilson——" Virginia Clark stacked the dinner dishes irritably. She sometimes found her husband's behavior maddening. Especially when he took to grinning at her, as he was presently doing. She also concluded that she'd had her fill of Elizabeth's attitude on the subject. "At last some teacher's wised up to Roge," had been the Clarks' daughter's comment. "He's cute and all, but I wouldn't want to be in a shipwreck with him." Washing dishes in the kitchen, Mrs. Clark considered that maybe she wouldn't meet Roger in *front* of school tomorrow. Maybe she'd wait at the corner instead. "His shoes," she gasped, and hurried to remind her son to get out the polishing kit. The spelling, too, she'd better work on that . . .

It was on Thursday that Nancy Reeves finally remembered where previously she had seen Miss Orville. Perhaps it was from the shock of having received a compliment from the latter.

"Mrs. Reeves, I rejoice to inform you of

progress," Miss Orville had addressed her, after the third grade had performed its military display for the afternoon. "On Monday, young Bruce's penmanship was comparable to a chicken's—if a chicken could write. Today, I was pleased to award him an A."

A tug at the tweed jacket, and the stiff-backed figure walked firmly down the street. Nancy Reeves stared after her until Miss Orville had merged into the flow of pedestrians and traffic. "I know who she is," Nancy suddenly remarked, turning to the other mothers. "I knew I'd seen her before. Those old ramshackle buildings near us on Hudson Street—remember when they were torn down last year?" The other mothers formed a circle around her. "Miss Orville was one of the tenants," Nancy Reeves went on. "She'd lived there for ages, and refused to budge until the landlord got a court order and deposited her on the sidewalk.

WORDS TO OWN
mortified (môrt′ ə·fīd) *v.* used as *adj.*: ashamed and hurt.
disparage (di·spar′ij) *v.*: show disrespect for; "put down."

ROGER WASN'T SO CERTAIN THAT TOMMY SHOULD HAVE DROPPED THE PENCIL CASE A SECOND TIME.

Crossing the Curriculum

Social Studies
In the story, Miss Orville asks her students if they realize how many children around the world are denied the privilege of schooling. Have students research levels of education around the world and present this information to the class. Have them provide figures for the average age at which children in various countries leave school to enter the work force. Students may be surprised at the figures, so ask them to write their reactions after they obtain the information.

I *saw* her there, sitting in a rocker on the sidewalk, surrounded by all this furniture and plants. Her picture was in the papers. Elderly retired schoolteacher . . . they found a furnished room for her on Jane Street, I think. Poor old thing, evicted like that . . . I remember she couldn't keep any of the plants . . ."

On the way home, after supplying a lurid account of the day's tortures—"Miss Awful made Walter Meade stand in the corner for saying a bad word"—Roger asked his mother, "Eviction. What does that mean?"

"It's when somebody is forced by law to vacate an apartment. The landlord gets an eviction notice, and the person has to leave."

"Kicked her out on the street. Is that what they did to the witch?"

"Don't call her that, it's rude and impolite," Mrs. Clark said, as they turned into the brownstone doorway. "I can see your father and I have been too easygoing where you're concerned."

"Huh, we've got worse names for her," Roger retorted. "*Curse* names, you should hear 'em. We're planning how to get even with Miss Awful, just you see." He paused, as his mother opened the downstairs door with her key. "That's where the cat used to sleep, remember?" he said, pointing at a corner of the entryway. His face was grave and earnest. "I wonder where that cat went to. Hey, Mom," he hurried to catch up. "Maybe *it* was evicted, too."

Then it was Friday at St. Geoffrey's. Before lunch, Miss Orville told the class, "I am happy to inform you that Miss Wilson will be back on Monday." She held up her hand for quiet. "This afternoon will be my final session with you. Not that discipline will relax, but I might read you a story. Robert Louis Stevenson, perhaps. My boys and girls always enjoyed him so. Forty-six years of them . . . Joseph Lambert, you're not sitting up straight. You know I don't permit slouchers in my class."

It was a mistake to have told the children

that Miss Wilson would be back on Monday, that only a few hours of the terrible reign of Miss Awful were left to endure. Even before lunch recess, a certain spirit of challenge and defiance had <u>infiltrated</u> into the room. Postures were still erect, but not quite as erect. Tommy Miller dropped his pencil case on the floor and did not request permission to pick it up.

"Ahhh, so what," he mumbled, when Miss Orville remonstrated[7] with him.

"What did you say?" she demanded, drawing herself up.

"I said, so what," Tommy Miller answered, returning her stare without distress.

Roger thought that was neat of Tommy, talking fresh like that. He was surprised, too, because Miss Awful didn't yell at Tommy or anything. A funny look came into her eyes, he noticed, and she just went on with the geography lesson. And when Tommy dropped his pencil case again, and picked it up without asking, she said nothing. Roger wasn't so certain that Tommy should have dropped the pencil case a second time. The lunch bell rang, then, and he piled out of the classroom with the others, not bothering to wait for permission.

At lunch in the basement cafeteria, the third grade talked of nothing except how to get even with Miss Awful. The recommendations showed daring and imagination.

"We could beat her up," Joey Lambert suggested. "We could wait at the corner till she goes by, and throw rocks at her."

"We'd get arrested," Walter Meade pointed out.

"Better idea," said Bruce Reeves. "We could go upstairs to the classroom before she gets back, and tie a string in front of the door. She'd trip, and break her neck."

7. **remonstrated:** reasoned earnestly in protest against something.

WORDS TO OWN
infiltrated (in·fil′trāt′·id) *v.*: gradually entered or sneaked into.

MISS AWFUL 379

Taking a Second Look

T379

❓ Review the definition of conflict with students, and ask them why Roger is now in conflict with the other students. As a result of his disagreement with the other children, what actions could Roger take? [Possible responses: Roger could keep silent; he could hide the plant to keep it safe; he could find a way to warn Miss Orville.]

B **Reading Skills and Strategies**
Forming Opinions

❓ Do you agree with Miss Orville's comments, or is she overreacting? [Possible responses: Miss Orville is right, because what the children did was cruel and inhumane. Miss Orville is overreacting—she had been extremely harsh with the students, and their resentment is understandable, if unfortunate.]

C **Critical Thinking**
Speculating
❓ Why does Roger spell *flower* and *castle* instead of actually talking to Miss Orville? Why do you think the author chose the words *flower* and *castle* for Roger to spell? [Possible responses: It might be too embarrassing for Roger to say anything directly to Miss Orville about the day's painful incidents. Spelling those words may be his way of showing her that she did make a difference for at least one child. The author may have chosen those words because *flower* recalls Miss Orville's love of plants and *castle* recalls her lost home.]

"She's old," Roger Clark protested. "We can't hurt her like that. She's too old."

It was one of the girls, actually, who thought of the plant. "That dopey old plant she's always fussing over," piped Midge Fuller. "We could rip off all the dopey leaves. That'd show her."

Roger pushed back his chair and stood up from the table. "We don't want to do that," he said, not understanding why he objected. It was a feeling inside, he couldn't explain . . . "Aw, let's forget about it," he said. "Let's call it quits."

"The plant, the plant," Midge Fuller squealed, clapping her hands.

Postures were a good deal worse when the third grade <u>reconvened</u> after lunch. "Well, you've put in an industrious week, I daresay . . ." Miss Orville commented. She opened the frayed volume of *Treasure Island* which she had brought from home and turned the pages carefully to Chapter One. "I assume the class is familiar with the tale of young Jim Hawkins, Long John Silver, and the other wonderful characters."

"No, I ain't," said Tommy Miller.

"Ain't. What word is that?"

"It's the word ain't," answered Tommy.

"Ain't, ain't," somebody jeered.

Miss Orville lowered the frayed volume. "No, children, you mustn't do this," she said with force. "To attend school is a privilege you must not mock. Can you guess how many thousands of children in the world are denied the gift of schooling?" Her lips <u>quavered</u>. "It is a priceless gift. You cannot permit yourselves to <u>squander</u> a moment of it." She rose from her desk and looked down at the rows of boys and girls. "It isn't enough any longer to accept a gift and make no return for it, not with the world in the shape it's in," she said, spectacles trembling on her bony nose. "The world isn't a playbox," she said. "If I have been severe with you this past week, it was for your benefit. The world needs good citizens. If I have helped one of you to grow a fraction of an inch, if just *one* of you——"

She stopped speaking. Her voice faltered, the words dammed up. She was staring at the plant on the window sill, which she had not noticed before. The stalks twisted up bare and naked, where the leaves had been torn off. "You see," Miss Orville said after a moment, going slowly to the window sill. "You *see* what I am talking about? To be truly educated is to be civilized. Here, you may observe the opposite." Her fingers reached out to the bare stalks. "Violence and destruction . . ." She turned and faced the class, and behind the spectacles her eyes were dim and faded. "Whoever is responsible, I beg of you only to be sorry," she said. When she returned to her desk, her back was straighter than ever, but it seemed to take her longer to cover the distance.

At the close of class that afternoon, there was no forming of lines. Miss Orville merely dismissed the boys and girls and did not leave her desk. The children ran out, some in regret, some silent, others cheerful and scampering. Only Roger Clark stayed behind.

He stood at the windows, plucking at the naked plant on the sill. Miss Orville was emptying the desk of her possessions, books, pads, a folder of maps. "These are yours, I believe," she said to Roger. In her hands were the water pistol, the baseball cards, the spool of string. "Here, take them," she said.

Roger went to the desk. He stuffed the toys in his coat pocket without paying attention to them. He stood at the desk, rubbing his hand up and down his coat.

"Yes?" Miss Orville asked.

Roger stood back, hands at his side, and lifted his head erectly. "Flower," he spelled. "*F-l-o-w-e-r.*" He squared his shoulders and looked at Miss Orville's brimming eyes. "Castle," Roger spelled. "*C-a-s-t-l-e.*"

Then he walked from the room.

WORDS TO OWN
reconvened (rē′kən·vēnd′) *v.*: reassembled.
quavered (kwā′vərd) *v.*: trembled.
squander (skwän′dər) *v.*: waste.

Making the Connections

Connecting to the Theme: "Living in the Heart"
Ask students how Roger might relate the theme of the collection to his experiences with Miss Orville. Suppose Roger grows up to be a teacher himself. What will he have learned from Miss Orville about being a teacher? Have students brainstorm in groups of three, and then list each group's statements on the chalkboard.

MEET THE WRITER

"All of My Stories Have Been Drawn from Life"

Arthur Cavanaugh (1926–   ) was born in New York City and has lived there all his life. Many of his short stories are about the Clark family, which bears a strong resemblance to his own. "Miss Awful," in fact, is based on his son Frank's experiences at a school in Greenwich Village, New York. Cavanaugh remembers:

❝ To hear him tell of it, the days at school were a happy mixture of games, crayons, milk and cookies, and outings to the playground across the street. One night when I got home from work, Frank indignantly announced that his teacher was out sick and, worse, replaced by a crabby old lady who did nothing but admonish the class for their lack of discipline and scholarship. 'Honest, you wouldn't believe how awful she is,' Frank assured me. But I noticed a marked change in my son, at night when I came home. Where before he was sprawled in front of the television, I'd find him bent over his homework or actually voluntarily reading a book. The night that I discovered him wrestling with a dictionary, looking up words for a quiz the next day, I knew that 'Miss Awful' had scored a victory on behalf of education. And when the following week I heard from Frank that his regular teacher was back at her desk, the tinge of regret in his voice was unmistakable. All of my stories have been drawn from life, usually long after the incident happened, but 'Miss Awful' was the exception, taking shape as the story happened right in front of me. ❞

MISS AWFUL 381

Resources

Assessing Learning

Check Test: Short Answer

1. What subject does Roger seem to have the most trouble with in school? [spelling]
2. Why does Miss Orville scold Roger on her first day? [His toys are spilling out of his bag.]
3. What discovery do the families at St. Geoffrey's make about Miss Orville? [She was evicted from her home and forced to leave her plants.]
4. What do the children do to Miss Orville on her last day? [They strip her plant of its leaves.]
5. What does Roger do when he sees Miss Orville for the last time? [He spells *flower* and *castle* correctly.]

Standardized Test Preparation

For practice with standardized test format specific to this selection, see
• *Standardized Test Preparation*, p. 58
For practice in proofreading and editing, see
• *Daily Oral Grammar*, Transparency 22

A teacher who is being interviewed on National Public Radio discusses her discovery of spelling and grammatical errors on the label of a steak-sauce bottle and her subsequent actions.

Ⓐ Critical Thinking
Extending the Text

❓ Have you ever discovered any grammatical or spelling errors on packaged products or on advertisements? What do you think might be done about these errors? Would it be appropriate to contact the manufacturer? Have students discuss any actions they have taken.

Ⓑ Spelling Note

Point out that there is absolutely no situation in which a writer should use an apostrophe after the *s* in *its*. When *it's* is used as a contraction, the apostrophe always falls between the *t* and the *s*, because the apostrophe substitutes for the second *i* in "it is."

Ⓒ Reading Skills and Strategies
Comparison and Contrast

Point out the similarity between this statement and something that Miss Orville might say. Ask students if, on the basis of her statements, Ms. Dowling is similar to Miss Orville.

Speaking and Listening: Distinguishing Fact and Opinion

The English teacher Donna Dowling states facts and opinions in her interview. Remind students that a fact can be proved true and that an opinion cannot be supported with evidence. Ask students to explain what facts Donna Dowling cites to prove the errors on the label. Then, ask them to suggest places where they can **verify** these facts (for example, a grammar book). Finally, ask students to find one or two opinions that Dowling expresses towards the end of the interview.

FROM THE EDITOR'S DESK

We heard this interview on National Public Radio one morning and thought immediately of Miss Awful and her insistence on good grammar and spelling. We called NPR, got a copy of the interview, and here it is.

Connections   AN INTERVIEW

Eighth-Grade Teacher Finds Grammar Errors on Food Label

Scott Simon, Host. Many people read the sides of their cereal boxes during breakfast. Donna Dowling, an English teacher in Greenville, South Carolina, read the back of her steak-sauce bottle during dinner. Now the manufacturers of Heinz 57 are better, or at least more correct, for it. Ms. Dowling asked her eighth-grade students at the Northwood Middle School to read this sentence: "Its' [apostrophe after the *s*] unique tangy blend of herbs and spices bring out the natural taste of steak." Ms. Dowling, what did your students say?

Donna Dowling, Eighth-Grade Teacher. Well, they were delighted that I had brought the bottle. Any visual that you can have with eighth-grade students is fun. So I passed it around the classroom and asked them—challenged them—to find the errors, and I would say most of them were able to do it pretty quickly. Of course, the apostrophe was not as challenging as the subject-verb disagreement.

Scott Simon. Note, now, even though *its* is possessive, there's no apostrophe after the *s*?

Donna Dowling. Oh, no. No, the only time you have an apostrophe in *its* is when it's a contraction.

Scott Simon. And what's the problem with the—

Donna Dowling. And the subject of the sentence is *blend,* and *blend* is a singular noun. So the verb should be *brings,* instead of *bring.*

Scott Simon. Now, you wrote the Heinz Company about this.

Donna Dowling. Yes, we did. I sent sample letters from all of my students, some very humorous. One of my students said, "I'm doing this because Mrs. Dowling is making me. She is the kind of teacher who would stop God on Judgment Day if he misused a subject-verb." And we received small gifts from the Heinz Company and the assurance that the label would be rewritten.

Scott Simon. What did the company say in their letter back to you, may I ask?

Donna Dowling. Well, they wrote a very funny letter saying that they wanted to respond, but they feared my red pen. And they wanted us to know that after double-checking with several different sources, we were correct and they would see to it that the new label was correct.

Scott Simon. What does it do for your students to see that big, high-priced steak-sauce-label writers can be wrong?

Donna Dowling. I think it makes them less intimidated about learning the language. All year long we have gone on a scavenger hunt looking for not errors but the way writers play with words in captions and pictures and leads in articles and billboard advertising. And my primary purpose in this is for them just to be more aware of the language everywhere. And I think it gives them a certain comfort to know that we all make mistakes.

Scott Simon. Ms. Dowling, thank you very much. Please don't listen to our show too carefully.

Donna Dowling. Oh, well, you know I will.

—from National Public Radio,
Weekend Edition

382

Connecting Across Texts

Connecting with "Miss Awful"

Ask students whether they think Donna Dowling would agree with Miss Orville's approach to teaching. Point out that Dowling seems to have a sense of humor about herself and her students, unlike Miss Orville. Ask the class what Miss Orville could have done to win over more students. Suggest that students go on a scavenger hunt like Dowling's students and look for humorous errors or wordplay in advertisements, captions, headlines, billboards, and so on. Have them bring their findings back to the class and post the examples on a bulletin board in the classroom.

MAKING MEANINGS

First Thoughts

[respond]
1. Do you think Miss Orville is *really* "Miss Awful"? Would you like to be in her class? Talk about your responses to what happened in this classroom.

Shaping Interpretations

[analyze]
2. Miss Orville compares children to plants. What details in the story show that she cares a great deal about plants? What does this say about her feelings toward children?

[conclude]
3. Think about what you know about Miss Orville's life, and try to explain why she demands so much of her class.

[interpret]
4. What does Miss Orville discover about the children? What does the phrase "brimming eyes" (page 380) suggest about her feelings?

[conclude]
5. The story suggests that Roger has discovered something important in the end. What has he discovered, in your opinion? Why do you think he spells the words for Miss Orville?

[explain]
6. How would you explain the children's cruelty in this story? What do you think of what they did?

[speculate]
7. How do you think Miss Orville would have reacted to the class that found the grammar errors on the steak-sauce bottle (see *Connections*, page 382)?

Connecting with the Text

[connect]
8. Imagine that you were there when the children were discussing how to get even with Miss Orville. What would you have said?

[compare]

9. Look back at your notes for the Quickwrite on page 368. Does Miss Orville have any of the qualities you listed? Jot down any changes you'd make in your notes now that you've read the story.

[assess]

10. What was your **opinion** of Miss Awful when you first met her? Did you change your opinion as the story went on? Did talking about the story in class affect your opinions? Trace your responses to Miss Awful.

Reading Check

a. What is the class's first clue that things are going to be different while Miss Wilson is away? What other changes does Miss Orville make?

b. How does Roger's behavior change while Miss Orville is in charge?

c. What do you learn about Miss Orville's life?

d. How do the students get back at Miss Orville?

e. What does Roger say to Miss Orville when he stays after class?

MISS AWFUL **383**

Reading Check

a. The desks have been placed into rows. She makes the children form lines and march into the room.

b. Roger changes from being a happy boy interested mostly in playing and having fun to being a nervous boy worried about his homework.

c. She retired from teaching after 46 years, and she was evicted and forced to leave her plants behind when her apartment building was to be demolished.

d. The children tear the leaves off her plant.

e. He spells *flower* and *castle* correctly for her.

MAKING MEANING

First Thoughts

1. Possible response: Some students may say that Miss Orville was not as bad as she seemed at first; very few are likely to say they would like to be in her class.

Shaping Interpretations

2. Miss Orville brings a plant to class and fusses over it. She is hurt when the children destroy it. Miss Orville had to leave her plants behind when she was forced to leave her apartment. She values children and wants them to receive proper care.

3. Miss Orville appears to have had a hard life. She wants her students to value the precious education they are receiving and to be prepared for the difficult world outside the classroom.

4. Miss Orville discovers that she has been able to reach one of the students; she is touched by Roger's action.

5. Roger realizes that Miss Orville's intentions were good and that she has not had much happiness in her life. He spells the words to show her that he has learned from her, that her efforts have not been entirely wasted.

6. The children act out of their anger over Miss Orville's harsh treatment. Encourage students who approve of the children's actions to consider Miss Orville's feelings.

7. Miss Orville probably would have enjoyed working with that class, since she must take grammar as seriously as Donna Dowling does.

Connecting with the Text

8. Ask students to consider how they might have tried to change other students' minds.

9. Students may want to add Miss Orville's high expectations to their list of qualities in a good teacher.

10. Most students will have negative first impressions of Miss Orville, and a number of them will probably not change their opinions. Some students may soften their opinions when they learn more about her and sympathize with her when her pupils destroy the plant.

Rubrics for each Choices assignment appear on p. 148 in the *Portfolio Management System*.

CHOICES:
Building Your Portfolio

1. **Writer's Notebook** Remind students to save their work. They may want to use it as prewriting for the Writer's Workshop on pp. 410–414.
2. **Creative Writing/Art** To help students get started, suggest some items (for instance, a watering can, a picture of a rocking chair, gifts from students, teaching awards, an old roll book). Provide materials that students can use to create three-dimensional objects and chests in which to place them.
3. **Speaking and Listening/ Persuasion** Model a discussion of a different scene from the story before students attempt to role-play discussions themselves. Remind students that the children in the story are in the third grade.
4. **Persuasive Writing/Public Speaking** Remind students that campaign speeches should focus on a small number of key points. Before they begin, ask them to paraphrase Miss Orville's statements from the story and to develop them into key points, such as "School is important" and "Life should be taken seriously."

CHOICES: Building Your Portfolio

Writer's Notebook

1. Collecting Ideas for a Biographical Sketch

First impressions can be wrong: "Miss Awful" turns out to be "Miss Pretty-OK." Write notes for a character sketch of someone who at first struck you one way and later seemed completely different. You might list details under two headings: "First Impressions" and "Second Looks." Include your impressions and the details that helped you form them.

> Coach Olson
> **First Impressions**
> Weak: thin;
> soft voice
> **Second Looks**
> Inspiring: "Don't
> ever give up!"
> "Take your time
> and do it right."

Creative Writing/Art

2. A Teacher's Treasure Chest

Suppose that when she was evicted from her apartment, Miss Orville took with her a box of personal treasures—mementos and souvenirs of her life. List the contents of that box. Use information from the story and your imagination to choose objects that suggest her love of plants and children, her years of teaching, her opinions, and her character. If you want to, create the actual box of treasures.

Speaking and Listening/ Persuasion

3. "We Can't Hurt Her Like That"

Reread the section of the story where the students are in the cafeteria discussing how to get back at Miss Awful (pages 379–380). Remember that Roger's attempts to persuade them not to be cruel are unsuccessful. With a group, discuss ways Roger could have persuaded the students to agree with his opinion. Then, have someone play Roger and have others play the other students. Role-play the cafeteria scene for the class to see if they are convinced by Roger's new powers of persuasion.

Persuasive Writing/ Public Speaking

4. Oration by Orville

Suppose Miss Orville were running for some political office—mayor or school superintendent, for example. Write a campaign speech expressing *her* views about the state of education today. You might want to include these Orville statements from the story:

- "To attend school is a privilege you must not mock."
- "Can you guess how many thousands of children in the world are denied the gift of schooling?"
- "It isn't enough any longer to accept a gift and make no return for it, not with the world in the shape it's in."
- "The world isn't a playbox."

GRAMMAR LINK MINI-LESSON

Technology HELP

See Language Workshop CD-ROM. Key word entry: homonyms.

Homonym Alert! Homonym Alert!

Homonyms (häm′ə·nimz′) are words that sound alike but have different meanings and spellings. For example, *sea* and *see* are homonyms; so are *flower* and *flour*. In fact, Roger probably confused these last two words when Miss Orville asked him to spell the word *flower*.

If there's any doubt in your mind about which word you want, look up both spellings in your dictionary and find out which one has the meaning that fits your context.

Try It Out

For each sentence below, choose the correct homonym.

1. Roger dared not <u>brake /break</u> rules.
2. Miss Orville thought that watching television was a <u>waste /waist</u> of time.
3. The children knew <u>their /there</u> trick would hurt Miss Orville's feelings.
4. She went <u>through /threw</u> agony.
5. Roger <u>red /read</u> much better.

For Better or For Worse © Lynn Johnston Productions Inc./Dist. by United Feature Syndicate, Inc.

VOCABULARY HOW TO OWN A WORD

WORD BANK

torpor
whimsical
martial
prodigy
mortified
disparage
infiltrated
reconvened
quavered
squander

Map It Out: Antonyms, Synonyms, Examples

Working with a partner, create a word map for each word in the Word Bank. Using the map below as a model, make up your own questions about each word. Be sure to keep a dictionary handy.

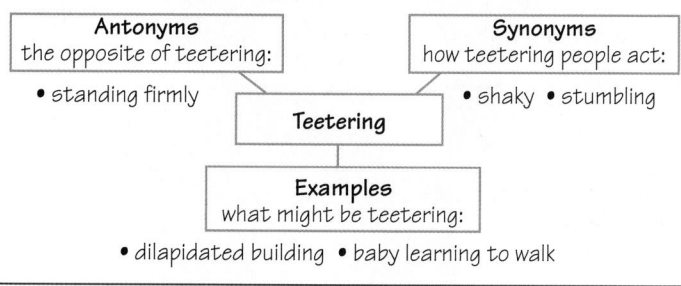

Antonyms
the opposite of teetering:
• standing firmly

Synonyms
how teetering people act:
• shaky • stumbling

Teetering

Examples
what might be teetering:
• dilapidated building • baby learning to walk

MISS AWFUL **385**

GRAMMAR LINK

Work with students to create a class list of frequently confused homonyms. The list might include *passed/past; new/knew; they're/there/their; through/threw;* and *to/too/two.* After the class has completed the list, ask students to use it to check for errors in some of their recent compositions.

Try It Out
1. break   4. through
2. waste   5. read
3. their

VOCABULARY

Before students begin creating their word maps, reread aloud with the class the sentences from the story in which the vocabulary words appear.

Resources

Grammar
• *Grammar and Language Links,* p. 35

Vocabulary
• *Words to Own,* p. 15

Spelling
For related instruction, see
• *Spelling and Decoding ,* p. 18

Grammar Link Quick Check

For each sentence below, choose the correct homonym.

1. We walked <u>through/threw</u> my friend's neighborhood on our way to school. [through]
2. <u>There/Their</u> were only about twenty students in my class before we came. [There]
3. I <u>new/knew</u> that one of my friends would save a seat for me. [knew]
4. He told me that he had <u>passed/past</u> the test because he had studied very hard. [passed]
5. <u>They're/Their</u> going to finish building the new library next week. [They're]

Before You Read

THE ONLY GIRL IN THE WORLD FOR ME

Make the Connection

Being Cool

Every generation has its own way of looking and acting cool. Many years ago, in the fifties, a young man with a crew cut and dirty saddle shoes was in. Later, in the nineties, a boy with baggies was hip. What is cool today?

Round table. With three classmates, brainstorm to find examples of what is cool. Think about clothing, hairstyles, words and actions, and likes and dislikes.

Quickwrite

Think about your "cool" list. What makes people want to be seen as cool? Write down your ideas.

Elements of Literature

Motivation: Designated Driver

"Why did he do that?" "What makes her act that way?" These are questions about **motivation.** Feelings, needs, wishes, pressures from family and friends—all these are forces that pull and push people from inside and outside.

Motivation is any force that moves a character to act in a particular way.

As you read the story of Bill Cosby and his first girlfriend, think about what motivates them to act the way they do.

Reading Skills and Strategies

Establishing and Adjusting Your Purpose for Reading: Matching Purpose to Text

When you drive a race car, you shift gears depending on the kind of road you're on. It's the same with reading. When you read, you preview and use your prior knowledge to see what kind of text lies ahead. You establish and adjust your **purpose**—and the way you read—depending on the kind of text you're reading. Some common purposes for reading are to **find out,** to **understand,** to **interpret,** to **enjoy,** and to **solve problems.** Give the reading road ahead a quick preview. When you see that you're about to read something called "The Only Girl in the World for Me" by Bill Cosby, what purpose do you establish?

The first time I saw her, she was crossing the street
to the schoolyard and for one golden moment our eyes met.

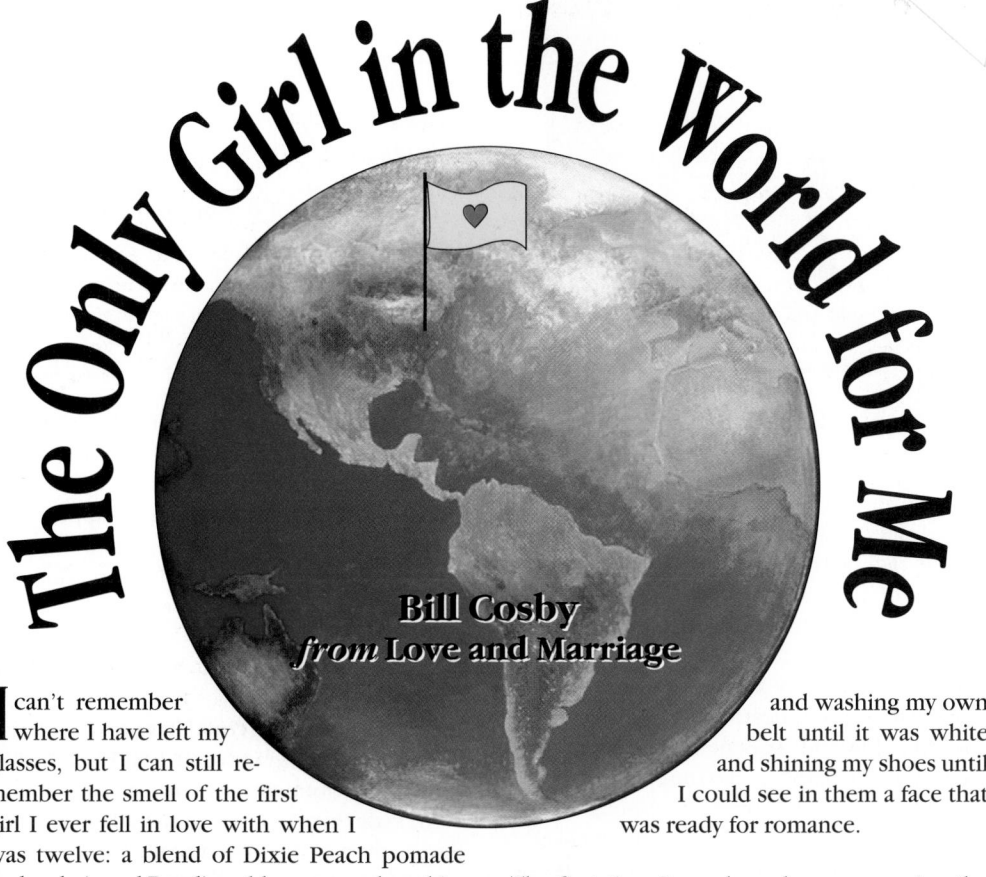

The Only Girl in the World for Me

Bill Cosby
from **Love and Marriage**

I can't remember where I have left my glasses, but I can still remember the smell of the first girl I ever fell in love with when I was twelve: a blend of Dixie Peach pomade on her hair and Pond's cold cream on her skin; together they were honeysuckle for me. And just as heady as her scent was the thought that I was in love with the only girl in the world for me and would marry her and take care of her forever in a palace in North Philadelphia. Because I wanted to make a wondrous impression on this girl, grooming was suddenly important to me. Before puberty, happiness in appearance for me was pants that didn't fall down and a football that stayed pumped; but now I started taking three long baths a day

and washing my own belt until it was white and shining my shoes until I could see in them a face that was ready for romance.

The first time I saw her, she was crossing the street to the schoolyard and for one golden moment our eyes met. Well, maybe the moment was closer to bronze because she made no response. But at least she had seen me, just about the way that she saw lampposts, hydrants, and manholes. Or was there something more? I began to dream; and later that day, when I was playing with the boys in the yard, it seemed that she was looking at me and the world was suddenly a better place, especially Twelfth and Girard.

THE ONLY GIRL IN THE WORLD FOR ME **387**

Summary ■

In this memoir, Cosby wittily recaptures the rollercoaster ride of first love, which transforms his 12-year-old bad self into a neat freak who takes three baths a day. In silence he worships a young goddess, who is never ⌐a name. He finally works up the thin⌐to ask her girlfriend if she ever he als⌐him. The news that she not only he⌐ intoxicates him, but lined up a su⌐ dismay that she beau. Neverth⌐d, but also has finally escorts his⌐current where his circulation⌐ spire against him. True ⌐nt and finally intersect, however, ⌐ie, covers that his new girlfrien⌐ needed to go to the bathroom.

Background

"The Only Girl in the World for Me" takes place in Philadelphia in the late 1940s, when Bill Cosby was twelve years old. The locale in which this funny valentine unfolds is a racially mixed, working-class section of North Philadelphia, memorialized by Cosby's other writings and stand-up routines.

Ⓐ Elements of Literature
Motivation

❓ Why does Cosby think that improving his grooming will help him romantically? [Possible responses: Like many young men, he assumes that women are impressed with men who dress well. Perhaps his mother nags him to clean up, and this makes him assume that all females are similarly obsessed with hygiene. Cleanliness is also something he can control, as opposed to other factors that might influence a woman's heart.]

Reaching All Students

Struggling Readers
Establishing and Adjusting Your Purpose for Reading was introduced on p. 386. For a lesson directly tied to this selection that teaches students to establish and adjust purpose by using a strategy called Save the Last Word for Me, see the *Reading Skills and Strategies* binder:
• MiniRead Skill Lesson, p. 120
• Selection Skill Lesson, p. 126

English Language Learners
Bring photos, tapes, and other material pertaining to Bill Cosby to class in order to give English language learners some cultural context. These students from other countries may have difficulty with some of the cultural references—for example, jump shots, Western Union, the *Hindenburg*. Help students get Cosby's use of exaggeration ("And the angels sang!") and irony ("What a prince of passion I was at this

moment . . . !"). For strategies to supplement instruction for these students, see
• *Lesson Plans Including Strategies for English-Language Learners*

Resources

Viewing and Representing
Videocassette B, Segment 6
An appealing videocassette segment, "Naomi Nye: Living in the Heart," is included in the video library. See the *Visual Connections Teacher's Manual.*

Listening
Audio CD Library
An entertaining recording of this memoir is included in the Audio:
• Disc 10, Track 3

A Reading Skills and Strategies
Have students compare the speed at which they read this piece with the speed they would use for reading a textbook. [Most students will agree the Cosby piece, being light and entertaining, can be read more quickly.] Remind students that, although a quick reading will cover the basic events in the memoir, reading too quickly might make them miss gems such as "I sat down one Sunday night and wrote a note that was almost to her."

B Elements of Literature
Motivation
❓ Why is carrying the note around unread better than knowing what it says? [Possible response: As long as Bill doesn't read her note, he can imagine that it contains good news and so he can still hope.] Why does he finally read the note? [Possible responses: He probably cannot stand the suspense any more; to delay reading her answer makes him as miserable as the rejection would.]

C Elements of Literature
Allusion
Tell students that an **allusion** is a reference to a person, place, thing, event, or quotation from literature, history, or another cultural source. Explain that comparing the girl's note to "something by Keats" is Cosby's way of saying that it was beautiful poetry to him. It also sets up the comedy of Cosby's irony, because the response is not the least bit poetic.

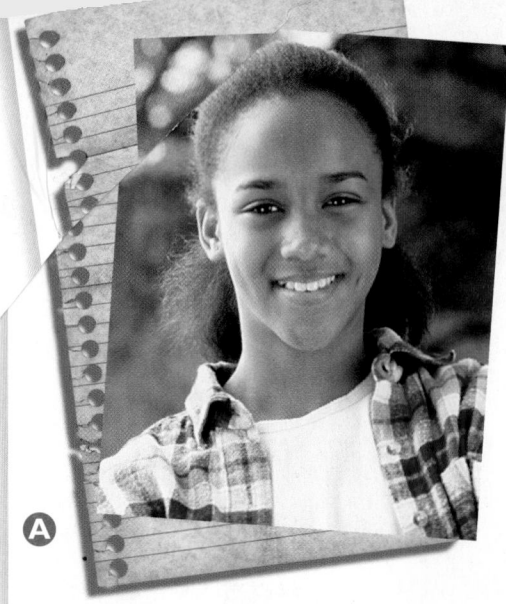

However, we still never talked, but just traded silent unsmiling looks whenever we passed. For several days, just her look was enough of a lift for me; but a higher altitude was coming, for one night at a party, we met and I actually danced with her. Now I was certain that I was in love and was going to win her.

I began my conquest with a combination of sporting skill and hygiene: I made my jump shots and my baths as dazzling as they could be. Oddly enough, however, although I saw her every day at school and on the weekends too, I never spoke to her. I had what was considered one of the faster mouths in Philadelphia, but I still wasn't ready to talk to her because I feared rejection. I feared:

COSBY: I like you very much. Will you be my girlfriend?
GODDESS: *(Doing a poor job of suppressing a laugh)* I'd rather have some cavities filled.

All I did, therefore, was adore her in silent cleanliness. Each Sunday night, I took a bath and then prepared my shirt and pants for dis-

388 LIVING IN THE HEART

play to her. On Monday morning, I took another bath (Bill the Baptist,[1] I should have been called) and then brushed my hair, my shoes, and my eyelashes and went outside to await the pang of another silent passage.

At last, deciding that I could no longer live this way, I sat down one Sunday night and wrote a note that was almost to her. It was to her constant girlfriend and it said:

Please don't tell her, but find out what she thinks of me.
                                                        Bill

The following morning, I slipped the note to the girlfriend and began the longest wait of my life.

Two agonizing days later, the girlfriend slipped me an answer, but I put it into my pocket unread. For hours, I carried it around, afraid to read it because I didn't happen to be in the mood for crushing rejection that day. At last, however, I summoned the courage to open the note and read:

She thinks you're cute.

Not even malaria[2] could have taken my temperature to where it went. I had been called many things, but cute was never one of them.

An even lovelier fever lay ahead, for the next time I saw her, she smiled at me, I smiled at her, and then I composed my next winged message to her friend:

I think she's cute too. Does she ever talk about me?

The answer to this one came return mail and it sounded like something by Keats:[3]

1. **Bill the Baptist:** reference to John the Baptist, a prophet who baptized his followers to show that they had repented.
2. **malaria:** disease characterized by chills and fever.
3. **Keats:** John Keats (1795–1821), an English poet.

Using Students' Strengths

Visual Learners and Logical/Mathematical Learners
Encourage artistic students and logical students to collaborate on creating a kind of Game of Love, with a board showing the many steps and pitfalls between "First Glance" and "Together-Forever Romance." Group members can create notecards giving such directions as "She thinks you're cute. Take five steps forward," "She's in your French class this term. Take an extra turn," or "She has a boyfriend. Return to Go."

She talks about you a lot. She knows it when you come around her.

And the angels sang! Imagine: She actually *knew* it when I came around her! The fact that she also knew it when gnats came around her in no way dampened my ecstasy.

And so, we continued to smile as we passed, while I planned my next move. My Western Union[4] style had clearly been charming the pants off her (so to speak) and now I launched my most courageous question yet:

Does she have a boyfriend?

When I opened the answer the next day in school, the air left me faster than it left the *Hindenburg:*[5]

Yes.

Trying to recover from this deflation, I told myself that I was still cute. I was the cutest man in second place. But perhaps my beloved wasn't aware of the glory she kept passing by. Once more, I sat down and wrote:

How much longer do you think she'll be going with him? And when she's finished with him, can I be next?

Note the elegance and dignity of my appeal. My dignity, however, did have some trouble with the reply:

She thinks she's going to break up with him in about a week, but she promised Sidney she would go with him next.

---

4. **Western Union:** company that operates a telegraph service.
5. *Hindenburg:* an airship filled with hydrogen gas that caught fire and blew up following a transatlantic flight in May 1937.

Suddenly, my aching heart found itself at the end of a line. But it was like a line at a bank: I knew it was leading to a payoff. I also knew that I could cream Sidney in cuteness.

Once she had made the transition to Sidney, I patiently began waiting for her to get sick of him. I had to be careful not to rush the illness because Sidney belonged to a tough gang and there was a chance that I might not be walking around too well when the time came for me to inherit her.

And then, one magnificent morning, I received the magic words:

She would like to talk to you.

I wrote back to see if she would wait until I had finished duty at my post as a school crossing guard. Yes, she would wait; I could walk her home. We were going steady now; and how much more torrid our passion would be when I began to *talk* to her.

At last, the words came and I chose them with care. As I walked her home from school, I reached into my reservoir of romantic thoughts, smiled at her soulfully, and said, "How you doing?"

Her response was equally poetic: "All right."

"So we're going steady now?"

"You want to?"

"Yeah. Give me your books."

And now, as if our relationship were not already in the depths of desire, I plunged even deeper by saying, "You wanna go to a movie on Saturday?"

"Why not?"

There might have been reasons. Some people were looking at us now because she was so beautiful, people possibly wondering what she was doing with me; but I knew that I was someone special to be the love of a vision like this, no matter how nearsighted that vision might be.

When we reached her door, I said, "Well, I'll see you Saturday."

THE ONLY GIRL IN THE WORLD FOR ME 389

D Elements of Literature
Motivation
? What might be the young girl's motivation for passing this response along to Bill? [Possible responses: She is probably very popular and very sure of herself, so that she can afford to make him wait for her. She may enjoy the idea of keeping suitors lined up so that she is never on the shelf. She might also feel that she must keep her promises, suggesting that she is honorable.]

E Reading Skills and Strategies
Adjusting Reading Rate
Call attention to Cosby's shifting from the day-by-day, note-by-note account of the romance to covering the passage of several weeks in this paragraph. Suggest that students slow their reading rate a bit, to think about the hero, who is now in a waiting phase that lasts a few weeks.

F Elements of Literature
Dialogue
? Make sure students notice that the narrative includes actual dialogue, or conversation, for the first time. Discuss how this shift from passing notes (through an intermediary) signals a change in the relationship between Bill and his beloved. Point out that previously Bill had to wait and agonize to hear a single sentence from his goddess. Now he speaks to her face to face. How might the shift to face-to-face conversation change the relationship? [Possible response: The shift to actual conversation makes the relationship less idealized and more real.]

Resources ─────────

Selection Assessment
Formal Assessment
• Selection Test, p. 71
Test Generator
• Selection Test

Skill Link

Speaking and Listening: Analyzing Dialogue
Tell students that dialogue reveals character in addition to advancing the plot or entertaining the reader. Sometimes the way a character is shown in dialogue becomes clearer when the dialogue is read out loud, as if in a play.

Activity
Have students reread the dialogue between Bill and his goddess on this page and the next. Discuss what the characters reveal about themselves in these exchanges. Then encourage pairs of students to read the dialogue out loud. Have the class determine what additional qualities the readers brought out in the characters.

"Right," she replied as only she could say it. "What time?"

"One o'clock."

When this day of days finally arrived, I took her to a theater where I think the admission was a dime. As we took our seats for the matinee, two basic thoughts were in my mind: not to sit in gum and to be a gentleman.

Therefore, I didn't hold her hand. Instead, I put my arm around the top of her seat in what I felt was a smooth opening move. Unfortunately, it was less a move toward love than toward gangrene:[6] With my blood moving uphill, my arm first began to tingle and then to ache. I could not, however, take the arm down and let my blood keep flowing because such a lowering would mean I didn't love her; so I left it up there, its muscles full of pain, its fingertips full of needlepoints.

Ⓐ Suddenly, this romantic agony was enriched by a less romantic one: I had to go to the bathroom. Needless to say, I couldn't let her know about this urge, for great lovers never did such things. The answer to "Romeo, Romeo, wherefore art thou, Romeo?"[7] was not "In the men's room, Julie."

What a prince of passion I was at this moment: My arm was dead, my bladder was full, and I was out of money too; but I desperately needed an excuse to move, so I said, "You want some popcorn?"

"No," she said.

"Fine, I'll go get some."

When I tried to move, every part of me could move except my arm: It was dead. I reached over and pulled it down with the other one, trying to be as casual as a man could be when pulling one of his arms with the other one.

6. **gangrene:** tissue decay in a part of the body.
7. **"Romeo . . . Romeo?":** reference to a speech by Juliet in Act II of William Shakespeare's play *The Tragedy of Romeo and Juliet*. The line reads, "O Romeo, Romeo! Wherefore art thou Romeo?" Juliet is actually asking why his name is Romeo.

"What's the matter?" she said.

"Oh, nothing," I replied. "I'm just taking both of my arms with me."

Ⓑ A few minutes later, as I came out of the bathroom, I was startled to meet her: She was coming from the bathroom *too*. How good it was to find another thing that we had in common. With empty bladders and full hearts, we returned to our seats to continue our love.

MEET THE WRITER

"You Can Turn Painful Situations Around Through Laughter"

While attending college on a football scholarship, **Bill Cosby** (1937–) began working as a stand-up comedian for five dollars a night. He became famous for his funny, heartwarming stories about his boyhood in Philadelphia. Bill Cosby has said, "You can turn painful situations around through laughter. If you can find humor in anything—even poverty—you can survive it." Cosby's television programs for children include the animated series *Fat Albert and the Cosby Kids*. He also developed programs for *Electric Company* and *Reading Rainbow*.

MAKING MEANINGS

First Thoughts

[respond]

1. Did anything in this story about Bill Cosby's first love surprise you? Do twelve-year-old girls and boys relate to one another the same way today?

Shaping Interpretations

[analyze]

2. Think of two strange things Bill does in the story. What is his **motivation**?

[compare]

3. Find three instances where Bill tries to be cool as he woos the girl he likes. Do any of Bill's attempts to be cool match up with what is on your "cool" list?

[identify]

4. One comic technique Cosby uses is **exaggeration,** or overstatement, as when he says "Not even malaria could have taken my temperature to where it went." Find another example of comic exaggeration in the story.

[compare]

5. What purpose did you establish for reading this story, and why did you choose it? Did your purpose change while you were reading? Compare your reading experience with your classmates'.

> ### Reading Check
>
> Create a storyboard, a series of pictures depicting the **main events** of this story in the order in which they happened. You should have four or five illustrations.

CHOICES: Building Your Portfolio

Writer's Notebook

1. Collecting Ideas for a Biographical Sketch

Bill Cosby gives you some information about himself as a twelve-year-old, but you probably still have questions about what he was like. Think of someone you don't know well but would like to know better, or think of a figure from history, sports, or politics you'd like to research. Create a character profile listing facts you know and questions to which you want answers.

Speaking and Listening

2. Act the Way They Do

Prepare and present a creative enactment of "The Only Girl in the World for Me." A creative enactment can include any combination of the words of the text, your own words, and various props. You may want to work with one or two partners. Two students could act out parts of the story, and the third could be the narrator.

Making the Connections

Connecting to the Theme: "Living in the Heart"

Discuss the terrain in the heart explored by this memoir. Call attention to Cosby's opening statement, that he can't remember where he put his glasses, but he can remember how a girl smelled almost 50 years ago. In other words, powerful emotions like love are stored in our memories so that we have them forever.

> ### Reading Check
> **Main Events:**
>
> 1. Bill and the goddess exchange silent glances.
> 2. Bill begins to groom himself obsessively.
> 3. Bill reads the note revealing that she thinks he is "cute."
> 4. Bill and his girlfriend sitting at the movies, his arm numb, his face contorted with discomfort.
> 5. Bill and his girlfriend meeting, surprised, smiling, outside the restrooms.

MAKING MEANINGS

First Thoughts

1. Answers will vary. Students may be surprised at the elaborateness of the pre-courtship events.

Shaping Interpretations

2. Possible responses: He takes 3 baths every day and he brushes his eyelashes. He is in love.
3. He doesn't speak when he sees her. He tries to put on a good appearance. He tries to sound offhand in his notes, even though he is on an emotional rollercoaster. He tries to be casual in their conversation and on the date.
4. Possible answers: "And the angels sang"; "how much more torrid our passion would be when I began to talk to her"; "some people were looking at us because she was so beautiful"; "less a move toward love than toward gangrene" or "this romantic agony."
5. Most students will probably say their purpose was to be entertained. Many students may have slowed down to savor Cosby's language.

CHOICES: Building Your Portfolio

1. **Writer's Notebook** Remind students to save their work. They may use it as prewriting for the Writer's Workshop on pp. 410–415.
2. **Speaking and Listening** Encourage students to make the enactment as real as possible, bringing in props such as Bill's grooming items, paper and pencil for the note-writing, signs signifying the restrooms.

Grading Timesaver

Rubrics for each Choices assignment appear on p. 149 in the *Portfolio Management System.*

GRAMMAR LINK

Divide the class into pairs, and have students exchange copies of writing assignments that they have recently completed. Ask them to read the partner's paper, stopping at each pronoun and writing its antecedent in the margin. If students cannot decide what the antecedent is, ask them to circle the sentence in which the pronoun occurs and write "Unclear reference—rewrite" next to it. Give students time to rewrite the ambiguous sentences.

Try It Out
Possible answers
1. Although she didn't know what her friend saw in Bill, the girl carried his notes to her.
2. She would go out with Sidney next, Bill's goddess told her friend.
3. Bill saw his girlfriend walking home with Sidney.

VOCABULARY LINK
Word Roots from Latin
- **–dict–:** diction, dictate, indictment, dictionary
- **–duc–:** reduce, induce, produce
- **–loc–:** relocate, localize, locate, allocate
- **–vis–:** vision, revise, visit, devise, advise, vista

The girl was a *vision* of loveliness, but Bill's need to be cool *dictated* that he not reveal his adoration, and so he *induced* himself to use casual diction in *producing* his letters. He *allocated* more and more time to grooming, *visiting* and *revisiting* the mirror many times a day to check on the *location* and state of his eyelashes.

Resources ———

Grammar
- *Grammar and Language Links,* p. 37

GRAMMAR LINK [MINI-LESSON]

Avoiding Unclear Pronoun References

Language Handbook HELP

See Agreement of Pronoun and Antecedent, page 723.

Technology HELP

See Language Workshop CD-ROM. Key word entry: pronoun-antecedent agreement.

Writers must make sure that readers can tell which word or phrase a pronoun refers to. The word a pronoun refers to is called its **antecedent.** In the first sentence that follows, it's unclear what the antecedent of *she* is.

UNCLEAR	The girl looked at her friend, and <u>she</u> smiled. [Who smiled, the girl or her friend?]
CLEAR	The girl smiled as <u>she</u> looked at her friend. [The girl was the one who smiled.]

The writer had to reword the sentence and move the pronoun closer to its antecedent (*girl*).

Try It Out
➤ Revise the sentences below to fix unclear pronoun references.

1. The girl who took Bill's notes to her friend didn't know what she saw in him.
2. She told her friend she would go out with Sidney next.
3. Bill saw Sidney walking his girlfriend home.

➤ Proofread a piece of your writing. Circle each pronoun, and draw an arrow from the pronoun to its antecedent. Could any other noun be mistaken for the antecedent? If so, rewrite the sentence to make the pronoun reference clear.

VOCABULARY [HOW TO OWN A WORD]

Word Roots from Latin

Many English **word roots** come from Latin. A word root is a word or word part from which other words are formed. An **affix** is a word part added to a root. For example, *-ject-* is a word root meaning "throw." *Re-* is a prefix meaning "back." *Reject* comes from the Latin word *rejectus,* which means "thrown or flung back." In the story you just read, Bill Cosby feared "crushing rejection" by his girlfriend-to-be.

Learning word roots that come from Latin will help you figure out the meaning of many English words. Here are some common roots from Latin:

Word Root	Meaning	Example
-dict-	speak	prediction
-duc-	draw, lead	introduce
-loc-	place	local
-vis-	see	invisible

Think of another example for each root. Then, using several of the examples, write a sentence or two about "The Only Girl in the World for Me."

Understanding Influences of Other Languages on the Spelling of English

Students should understand that knowledge of Latin roots can help them figure out the spelling of a word, as well as its meaning. For example, some students might be tempted to spell *indict* as *indite.* If they think about the word's meaning, however, and recognize that its root is *-dict-,* they will be able to see why it is not spelled that way. You may want to have students practice spelling other words with Latin roots.

-aud-, "hear"
audible
audition
auditorium

-bene-, "well, good"
benefit
benefactor
benediction

-ject-, "throw"
reject
projectile
eject

-rupt-, "break"
disrupt
eruption
rupture

Before You Read

GOLD

Make the Connection

Where the Heart Is

Like a special person, a place can leave a lasting memory in your heart. For many of us, home is the place where we live. For others, home is not within four walls but outside in nature. Home can be any place that makes you feel good—it could even be a rock where you like to sit and think.

Quickwrite

Jot down notes on feelings, smells, sights, and sounds you connect with home. Try to include some colors. Use words that express your strongest feelings.

Elements of Literature

Mood

Mood is the overall feeling created by a story, a poem, or another work of literature. You can usually describe that feeling in one or

Mood is the overall emotion created by a work of literature.

For more on Mood, see the Handbook of Literary Terms.

two adjectives, such as *sad, peaceful,* or *scared*. Try to come up with a word that describes the mood Pat Mora creates in "Gold." Do you think the painting on pages 394–395 captures the special mood of Mora's golden place?

MEET THE WRITER

"The Desert Is My Mother"

Pat Mora (1942–   ) grew up in El Paso, Texas, near the border between the United States and Mexico. Much of her writing celebrates the Southwest, especially the beauty of the desert, and describes her feelings of kinship with it. In her book *El desierto es mi madre* (*The Desert Is My Mother*), a picture book for children written in Spanish and English, she says the desert offers life, food, and spiritual comfort.

 go.hrw.com
LEO 7-5

GOLD **393**

Planning

Summary

This lyric poem expresses the poet's love of the desert landscape, painted gold by the setting sun. The speaker is surrounded by other natural creatures, all watching each other, all in balance.

Resources 🎧

Listening
Audio CD Library
An eloquent recording of the poem is included in the *Audio CD Library:*
• Disc 10, Track 4

Reaching All Students

Struggling Readers
Tell students that this poem focuses on a southwestern desert landscape. Ask them what sort of images they would expect to see in a poem on that subject. List their suggestions on the board, and ask for colors that might be appropriate. Then ask them to suggest images for the word *gold*.

English Language Learners
Ask Spanish-speaking students to explain how to pronounce *saguaro*. Help English language learners get into the poem by asking them for the words that mean "home" in their native languages. List these words on the board, and ask the students to teach the rest of the class the correct pronunciations. Make a class poem of these words for "home." Encourage students to translate a line or two of Mora's poem into their own languages. For strategies to supplement instruction for these students, see
• *Lesson Plans Including Strategies for English-Language Learners*

Gold

Pat Mora

When Sun paints the desert
with its gold,
I climb the hills.
Wind runs round boulders, ruffles
5   my hair. I sit on my favorite rock,
lizards for company, a rabbit,
ears stiff in the shade
of a saguaro.°
In the wind, we're all
10 eye to eye.

Sparrow on saguaro watches
rabbit watch us in the gold
of sun setting.
Hawk sails on waves of light, sees
15 sparrow, rabbit, lizards, me,
our eyes shining,
watching red and purple
     sand rivers stream down the hill.

I stretch my arms wide as the sky
like hawk extends her wings
20 in all the gold light of this, home.

8. **saguaro** (sə·gwär′ō): huge cactus found in
the southwestern United States and northern
Mexico. The word is Mexican Spanish and was
taken from the Pima name.

GOLD **395**

MAKING MEANINGS

First Thoughts

1. Possible responses: The desert is her home; some students may share Mora's sense of the desert's beauty and familiarity, while others would feel it a barren, alien landscape.

Shaping Interpretations

2. Mora says "we're," "us," and "our," but it is likely she is the only human present; her companions are the cactus, rabbit, lizard, sparrow, and hawk.

3. The verb *paints* personifies the sun; the verbs *runs* and *ruffles* personify the wind as a playful, affectionate creature. The personifications make these natural forces seem safe, creative, and appealing.

4. Gold is the dominant color in the landscape, but the feelings Mora has about this beautiful, familiar place are a kind of "gold"—wealth—to her. Some people probably start out believing the poem is literally about the precious metal gold.

5. Possible moods include serenity ("favorite rock"); harmony with nature ("eye to eye"); joy ("our eyes shining").

Grading Timesaver

Rubrics for each Choices assignment appear on p. 150 in the *Portfolio Management System.*

CHOICES: Building Your Portfolio

1. **Writer's Notebook** Remind students to save their work. They may use it as prewriting for the Writer's Workshop on pp. 410–414.

2. **Art/Creative Writing** Encourage students to jot down images and words that evoke "home" for them. Some students may work better by beginning with the drawing and then moving to the writing.

MAKING MEANINGS

First Thoughts

[respond]
1. What place is home to the speaker of the poem? Would you feel at home there? Why or why not?

Shaping Interpretations

[interpret]
2. Is Mora alone in her special place? Who or what are her companions?

[analyze]
3. Mora uses **personification** when she speaks of nonhuman things as if they were human. What verb makes the sun seem like a person? What verbs make the wind seem like a person? What does each instance of personification make you see?

[explain]
4. Why does Mora call the poem "Gold"? When you first read that title, did you know what kind of gold she meant? Explain.

[identify]
5. Think about the way Mora's poem makes you feel. What word or words would you use to describe its **mood**? Give at least three details from the poem that help create that mood.

CHOICES: Building Your Portfolio

Writer's Notebook

1. Collecting Ideas for a Biographical Sketch

One way to make people you write about come alive is to describe them in the place where they feel most at home or in a place they love. Think of someone you've considered writing about. Close your eyes, and try to picture the person. Where do you see him or her? Open your eyes, and write down some details of the place. Try to use words that capture the feelings, colors, and sounds connected with that place your subject loves.

Art/Creative Writing

2. "Sweet as the Sight"

Write a poem about a place where you feel good, a place you call home. (Be sure to check your Quick- write notes.) Use details that create a word picture of the place and that show how you feel about it. Include colors, sounds, smells—even animal life, if there is any. Then, use crayons or watercolors to draw or paint a picture of the place. Try to use colors to capture the mood of your special place.

396 LIVING IN THE HEART

Assessing Learning

Check Test: Short Answer

1. What does the sun do to the landscape? [paints it gold]

2. Where and at what time of day does the poem unfold? [in the desert at sunset]

3. Where does the speaker sit? [on her favorite rock]

4. What animals are mentioned in the poem? [rabbit, lizards, sparrow, hawk]

5. What one word does the speaker use to describe the whole scene? ["home"]

Elements of Literature

OBJECTIVES
1. Understand the concept of figurative, nonliteral language
2. Learn to recognize simile and metaphor
3. Identify these techniques in the poems of this collection

POETRY: Figures of Speech *by* John Malcolm Brinnin

Making Connections

In our everyday language we use many expressions that are not literally true: "Charlie's bragging gets under my skin." "Gilda's money is burning a hole in her pocket." When we use expressions like these, we are speaking **figuratively.** That is, our listeners know the words do not carry their ordinary meaning. Bragging, after all, does not really pierce skin, and money cannot cause a pocket to catch fire.

The meaning of such figurative expressions depends on comparisons. Bragging is *compared* to something that causes pain or annoyance, such as a thorn. Money is *compared* to something so hot that it cannot be held and must be gotten rid of. Expressions like these, expressions that are not literally true, are called **figures of speech.** Because they can express so much meaning in interesting and surprising ways, figures of speech are an important element in poetry.

There are many kinds of figures of speech; the most common are **similes** and **metaphors.**

Similes: Using *Like* or *As*

A **simile** is a comparison of two unlike things using the word *like, as, than,* or *resembles.* In "Mama Is a Sunrise" (page 400), for example, the poet uses a simile when she tells us that Mama "warms us *like* grits and gravy."

Here are three famous similes (a *frigate* is a ship):

There is no Frigate like a
Book . . .
—Emily Dickinson

I wandered lonely as a
cloud . . .
—William Wordsworth

My love is like a red, red
rose . . .
—Robert Burns

Metaphors: Identifying Two Different Things

Like a simile, a **metaphor** compares two unlike things, but it does so without using *like, as, than,* or *resembles.* For example, in "The Highwayman," Alfred Noyes does not say the moon was *like* a ghostly galleon. He uses a metaphor: "The moon *was* a ghostly galleon tossed upon cloudy seas."

The next time you see the full moon among the clouds, think of Noyes's metaphor. See if it helps you think of the night sky as a vast ocean, with the clouds as whitecaps and the moon sailing steadily through the sea. If it does, you have discovered the power of metaphors.

A Writer on Poetry

"To have written one good poem—*good* used seriously—is an unlikely and marvelous thing that only a couple of hundred writers of English, at the most, have done—it's like sitting out in the yard in the evening and having a meteorite fall in one's lap."

—Randall Jarrell

Resources ———

Elements of Literature
Figures of Speech
For more instruction on figures of speech, see *Literary Elements:*
• Transparency 7
Assessment
Formal Assessment
• Literary Elements Test, p. 79

Elements of Literature

This feature discusses the most common figures of speech, similes and metaphors, and helps students understand the way poets use these figures of speech to heighten the power of their writing.
Mini-Lesson:
Figures of Speech
Divide the class into pairs, and ask students to write common similes or metaphors for each of the following:
• A metaphor for someone who is good at gardening [has a green thumb]
• A simile for someone who can swim well [swims like a fish]
• A simile for someone who is extremely thin [is as thin as a rail]
• A metaphor for someone who is very generous [is all heart or has a heart of gold]
Call on students from each pair to read their choices out loud. Then point out that these expressions are now considered clichés. Ask students to suggest fresh alternative.

Applying the Element

Ask students to identify the figures of speech in the following lines of "The Highwayman" (p. 341), determine if the comparisons are similes or metaphors, and paraphrase the comparisons in their own words: ll. 2, 21, 39, 74.

Reaching All Students

Struggling Readers

Sports journalism is rich in similes, metaphors, and other types of figurative language. Divide the class into mixed-ability groups of three. Distribute copies of a newspaper sports section or sports journal to the groups, and ask them to scan their publication for examples of similes, metaphors, and other figures of speech. Have them compile a list of the similes and metaphors they find. Ask one student from each group to read the list aloud.

Advanced Learners

Have students work independently to create short poems about a concrete object—a pencil, a toothbrush, a baseball, a pair of sunglasses. Have the students write poems in free verse or in fixed meter and rhyme patterns borrowed from well-known poems or songs. Ask the students to include at least two metaphors and two similes in their poems. Encourage students to read their finished poems aloud.

My Father Is a Simple Man/Mama Is a Sunrise

1. Read and interpret the poems
2. Identify free verse
3. Compare the texts of the poems
4. Express understanding through expository and creative writing or art

SKILLS

Literary
• Identify free verse

Writing
• Collect ideas and take notes about a subject for a biographical report
• Write a poem about a sunrise

Art
• Create a greeting card

Viewing/Representing
• Respond to the character in a painting (ATE)
• Compare techniques in art and poetry (ATE)

Planning

• **Block Schedule**
  Block Scheduling Lesson Plans with Pacing Guide

• **Traditional Schedule**
  Lesson Plans Including Strategies for English-Language Learners

• **One-Stop Planner**
  CD-ROM with Test Generator

Before You Read

MY FATHER IS A SIMPLE MAN/MAMA IS A SUNRISE

Make the Connection

Put In a Good Word

In the next two poems you'll see two people through their children's eyes. The title of each poem contains one word that describes the parent. The words are *simple* and *sunrise*. What do these words suggest to you?

Quickwrite

Write down all the things you think of when you hear the words *simple* and *sunrise*. Then, choose two or three words from your lists. Whom do they remind you of? Think of someone you know or someone you have read about. Now, quickly write three or four sentences about this person— just the first three or four things that come to mind.

Elements of Literature

Free Verse

These two poems are written in **free verse.** In free verse, poets do *not* use strict patterns of rhythm and rhyme.

> **P**oetry without a regular meter or a rhyme scheme is called **free verse.**
>
> *For more on Free Verse, see pages 338–339 and the Handbook of Literary Terms.*

Instead, they write in loose groupings of words and phrases and try to capture the natural rhythms of ordinary speech. Even in free verse, however, you'll find vivid images and repetition used to create rhythm and to emphasize important ideas.

Reading Skills and Strategies

Comparing Texts: Searching for Similarities

You already know that both of these poems are written in **free verse.** You can find other similarities between them by **comparing texts.** After you've read the poems and talked about them, reread each one carefully. Then, copy the chart below. Working with a partner, jot down the similarities you find in the two poems.

	"My Father Is a Simple Man"	"Mama Is a Sunrise"
Subject		
Speaker		
Figures of speech		
Theme		

Resources: Print and Media

Reading
• *Graphic Organizers for Active Reading*, p. 26
• *Audio CD Library*
   Disc 10, Tracks 5, 6

Elements of Literature
• *Literary Elements*
   Transparency 7
   Worksheet, p. 22

Viewing and Representing
• *Viewing and Representing*
   Fine Art Transparencies 11, 12
   Fine Art Worksheets, pp. 44, 48

Assessment
• *Formal Assessment*, p. 74
• *Portfolio Management System*, p. 151
• *Test Generator (One-Stop Planner CD-ROM)*

My Father Is a Simple Man

Luis Omar Salinas

I walk to town with my father
to buy a newspaper. He walks slower
than I do so I must slow up.
The street is filled with children.
5   We argue about the price
of pomegranates, I convince
him it is the fruit of scholars.
He has taken me on this journey
and it's been lifelong.
10   He's sure I'll be healthy
so long as I eat more oranges,
and tells me the orange
has seeds and so is perpetual;°
and we too will come back
15   like the orange trees.
I ask him what he thinks
about death and he says
he will gladly face it when
it comes but won't jump
20   out in front of a car.
I'd gladly give my life
for this man with a sixth
grade education, whose kindness
and patience are true . . .
25   The truth of it is, he's the scholar,
and when the bitter-hard reality
comes at me like a punishing
evil stranger, I can always
remember that here was a man
30   who was a worker and provider,
who learned the simple facts
in life and lived by them,
who held no pretense.
And when he leaves without
35   benefit of fanfare° or applause
I shall have learned what little
there is about greatness.

13. **perpetual:** continuing forever.
35. **fanfare:** noisy display to draw attention
(literally, a flourish of trumpets).

The Jazz Musician by William Low.
Courtesy of the Artist.

MY FATHER IS A SIMPLE MAN **399**

Reaching All Students

Struggling Readers
Point out that this poem consists of only ten sentences. Divide the class into pairs, and have students read the poem with their partners, one sentence at a time. When they find sentences they do not understand, they should stop to discuss them. The sentence most likely to give them trouble is the one in ll. 25–33, which you may need to paraphrase for them.

English Language Learners
Before they read the poem, have students suggest words in their native languages close in meaning to "simple" and to list some synonyms for these words in English. Once they have read the poem, ask whether the speaker's description of his father fits with their ideas of "simple." For strategies to supplement instruction for these students, see
• *Lesson Plans Including Strategies for English-Language Learners*

Summary ▪

This free-verse tribute to the speaker's father emphasizes the virtues of simplicity, decency, and hard work. As the speaker and his father walk through the town, the speaker elicits his father's spare, direct observations on health, continuity, and death; his father connects the orange with its seeds to the idea of regeneration. The poet realizes that his father is actually a scholar who understands life's realities, and he sees him as a great man.

Resources ———

Listening
Audio CD Library
An eloquent recording of the poem is included in the *Audio CD Library:*
• Disc 10, Track 5

RESPONDING TO THE ART
Activity. Ask students to write a short response to this painting, focusing on the following questions:
1. How is this man in the painting like the father in Salinas's poem?
2. What is the musician's instrument? What does his facial expression reveal about him?
3. What do you think he is looking at or thinking about?
4. Why do you think the artist wanted to paint a picture of him?

Ⓐ Elements of Literature
Free Verse
Have the students check the poem for meter and rhyme. They won't find a regular pattern of stressed and unstressed syllables. Nor will they find a rhyme scheme. Explain that the absence of these patterns of rhythm and rhyme makes this poem an example of free verse.

Ⓑ Reading Skills and Strategies
Finding the Main Idea
❓ How does the speaker seem to define greatness? [Possible response: It is the simple wisdom that comes from living honestly, working hard, and providing for those you love.]

T399

Summary ∎

In a series of figures of speech, this poem celebrates the warmth and vitality of the speaker's mother, showing how she is the life-giving center of her family.

Ⓐ Elements of Literature
Metaphor

❓ Identify the metaphor of the poem's title. What does it mean? [The speaker equates her mother with a sunrise. The metaphor means that her mother warms her family, as the sun warms the earth, and brings them joy, which the speaker describes in terms of light.]

Ⓑ Elements of Literature
Imagery

❓ What other images in the poem develop the central idea of Mama as a sunrise? [Possible responses: the image of coal glowing; sparks in Papa's eyes; warm food; the promise of a new dawn.]

Ⓒ Elements of Literature
Figures of Speech

Work with students to list all the figures of speech in this poem:

Metaphors:
• "she kindles us"
• "we wake up glowing"
• "She puts a spark even in Papa's eyes"
• "we rise up shining"
• "Mama is a sunrise"

Similes:
• "like lump coal ignited"
• "like grits and gravy"

Resources

Selection Assessment
Formal Assessment
• Selection Test, p. 74
Test Generator
• Selection Test

Ⓐ Mama Is a Sunrise

Evelyn Tooley Hunt

When she comes slip-footing through the door,
    she kindles us
    like lump coal lighted,
    and we wake up glowing.
5 She puts a spark even in Papa's eyes
Ⓑ and turns out all our darkness.

Ⓒ When she comes sweet-talking in the room,
    she warms us
    like grits and gravy,
10   and we rise up shining.
Even at nighttime Mama is a sunrise
that promises tomorrow and tomorrow.

Using Students' Strengths

Visual Learners

Have students choose either "My Father Is a Simple Man" or "Mama Is a Sunrise" to illustrate, either with original drawings or paintings or a collage of images.

Kinesthetic Learners

Before students read "Mama Is a Sunrise," have them stand and stretch for a minute. As they stretch, ask them to think about how they could use body language to describe a sunrise to someone. Give students a few moments to prepare, and then ask them to perform their sunrise movements on your cue.

MEET THE WRITERS

"The Strange Fullness of the Unreal"

Luis Omar Salinas (1937–) was just four years old when his mother died of tuberculosis. He was adopted by his uncle Alfredo and grew up in California. Some of his best poetry explores the haunting effects of losing his mother when he was little. Many of these poems use fantastic, dreamlike images that contrast sharply with the plain-spoken realism of "My Father Is a Simple Man." Salinas has stated that his aim is to capture "the strange fullness of the unreal."

Faraway Worlds

Evelyn Tooley Hunt (1904–1998) brought a spirit of play to her work. For example, *Dancer in the Wind* (1977) is a book of haiku variations entirely about scarecrows. (A **haiku** is a type of three-line poem perfected in Japan.)

MY FATHER IS A SIMPLE MAN / MAMA IS A SUNRISE **401**

BROWSING IN THE FILES

About the Authors

Luis Omar Salinas held many jobs—copy clerk, dishwasher, construction worker, shoe salesman—before he became a poet and writing teacher in Fresno, California. His poems have been widely published. One of his collections of poems is titled *Crazy Gypsy*.

Evelyn Tooley Hunt began writing poetry as a young girl, and she wrote continually throughout her long life. Although she waited several years before publishing her first work, she quickly became successful. Her poems have been published in magazines such as *Christian Century*. One of her poetry collections is titled *Toad Song*.

FROM THE EDITOR'S DESK

At first we put these two poems together because of their obvious thematic link. But then we noticed another parallel—the almost subliminal visual link between the orange in Salinas's poem and the rising sun in Hunt's. In both poems, these round golden images represent the continuity of life.

Comparing Texts: Searching for Similarities

Remind students that **tone** refers to the writer's attitude toward his or her subject. Ask students to look for similarities in the tone of "As I Gaze upon My Father" and Salinas's or Hunt's poem. Which of those two poems does "As I Gaze upon My Father" resemble more, and why? [Possible response: This student poem resembles Salinas's poem because both are realistic descriptions of the speaker's father, while Hunt's poem is a more fanciful, less realistic description of her mother.]

MAKING MEANINGS

First Thoughts

1. Make sure that students justify their choices with reasons—for instance, a preference for the figurative language in Hunt's poem, or for the straightforwardness of Salinas's work.

Shaping Interpretations

2. The speakers in both poems suggest that their fathers are likable men. The father in Salinas's poem seems more confident than the father in the student poem.

3. Words that suggest light and warmth are *kindles, lighted, glowing, spark, warms, shining,* and *sunrise.* She warms and brightens her family's life.

4. In Hunt's poem, the speaker repeats *tomorrow* to show that each day starts with a sunrise and that her mother gives the family strength to face the future with hope. In Salinas's poem, the speaker repeats *life* because he is talking about his father's life and the idea of continuing life.

5. Students will probably note the similarities in theme and subject. Some may see a connection between the orange as a symbol of eternity and the sun rising day after day.

6. The poem has a joyous mood. Details might include the playful references to the mother's "slip-footing" and "sweet-talking," the warmth of "kindles" and "lump coal lighted," the comfort food of "grits and gravy," the glory of "rise up shining."

As I Gaze upon My Father

In the brownish photo, my father
Sits up straight
Like a wooden board,
With his knees crossed
5 And his hands folded gently over his knee,
But the sheepish smile gives him away
Like a pen trying to be a pencil.

He wore a white oxford
That was perfectly pressed
10 And smooth as a newborn's flesh.
As a second layer he wore a wool sweater
That was rough as sandpaper,
As if to show his life.

—Maren Stuart
Tampa Preparatory School
Tampa, Florida

First appeared in *Merlyn's Pen: The National Magazines of Student Writing.*

MAKING MEANINGS

MY FATHER IS A SIMPLE MAN
MAMA IS A SUNRISE

First Thoughts

[respond]

1. Which poem do you like better, Salinas's or Hunt's? Why?

Shaping Interpretations

[compare]

2. How are the fathers in "As I Gaze upon My Father" (above) and "My Father Is a Simple Man" similar? How are they different?

402 LIVING IN THE HEART

Connecting with the Texts

7. Students should compare and contrast their role models' qualities with the powerful, earthy honesty of Salinas's father, the life-affirming qualities in Hunt's mama, and the complex dignity of Stuart's father.

[compare]

3. When Hunt says "Mama Is a Sunrise," she is using a **metaphor.** Find words in Hunt's poem that refer to light or warmth. What traits does Mama actually share with a sunrise?

[interpret]

4. In **free verse,** poets repeat certain words to emphasize important ideas. What words are repeated in each of these poems? Why do you think the poet wanted to emphasize these words?

[compare]

5. Refer to the comparison chart you made after you read the poems. How are the poems similar? Does one similarity seem to jump out at you? (Be sure to compare your charts in class.)

[generalize]

6. What word or phrase would you use to describe the overall **mood** of "Mama Is a Sunrise"? Name at least three details from the poem that help create the mood.

Connecting with the Texts

[connect]

7. Think about your role models. How are they similar to the characters in these poems? How are they different?

CHOICES: Building Your Portfolio

Writer's Notebook

1. Collecting Ideas for a Biographical Sketch

In the poems you just read, Hunt compares Mama to a sunrise, and Salinas compares his father to a scholar. Pick one of your favorite people (perhaps the person you described in your notes for the Quickwrite on page 398).

What comparisons can you use to help readers "see" this person and understand the impression he or she makes on you?

Creative Writing

2. Another Sunrise

Write a poem with the same structure as "Mama Is a Sunrise." Start each line as Hunt does, and end it your own way. Open your poem with a metaphor.

...is a...
When she/he...

Art

3. This Is Just to Say . . .

Make a greeting card for a favorite person. Think of an original comparison that captures something special about the person. Draw a colorful illustration of the comparison on the front of your card. Write your comparison inside. You may want to sign your name and send the card to your favorite person.

Rubrics for each Choices assignment appear on p. 151 in the *Portfolio Management System.*

CHOICES: Building Your Portfolio

1. **Writer's Notebook** Remind students to save their work. They may use it as prewriting for the Writer's Workshop on pp. 410–414.

2. **Creative Writing** Point out to students that their poems should be about people they know well. Allow students to brainstorm lists of qualities they associate with the subjects of their poems.

3. **Art** Distribute sample greeting cards that students may use as models. Allow students to incorporate clippings from magazines into their drawings. Many word-processing programs contain templates that students can use to design and create their greeting cards.

Assessing Learning

Check Test: True-False

1. The speaker in "My Father Is a Simple Man" sees his father as a scholar. [T]
2. "My Father Is a Simple Man" has regular rhythm, rhymes, and stanzas. [F]
3. The speaker's father in this poem dislikes oranges. [F]
4. "Mama Is a Sunrise" contains both similes and metaphors. [T]
5. The title "Mama Is a Sunrise" is a simile. [F]

T403

OBJECTIVES
1. Read and enjoy the story
2. Connect the story to the collection theme

No Questions Asked

The literature in No Questions Asked gives students the chance to read a selection for enjoyment and enrichment as they further explore the collection theme. Annotated questions in the margins of the Teacher's Edition should be considered optional. No follow-up questions will appear after the selection.

This touching story focuses on Harry, a junior high school student, who used to spend much of his free time in his father's candy store, but who, when he grew older, began hanging out in a burger place with other boys. Harry's father, Mr. Tillian, has just suffered a heart attack, and Harry opens the store, planning to tend it in his father's absence. When Harry began junior high, his father had become inexplicably attached to a parrot that he named Rocky. When he enters the store after his father's heart attack, Harry hears the parrot call out, "Where's Harry?" Harry is bewildered and angry at the parrot until he hears it continue to say, "Miss him! Miss him! Where's Harry?" Harry realizes that his father had been talking to the bird about how much he missed his son. Harry begins to cry and closes up the shop to visit his father.

Resources

Listening
Audio CD Library
A moving recording of the story is included in the *Audio CD Library:*
• Disc 10, Track 7

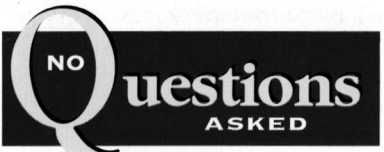

Papa's Parrot

Cynthia Rylant

Chills ran down Harry's back. What could the bird mean?

Though his father was fat and merely owned a candy and nut shop, Harry Tillian liked his papa. Harry stopped liking candy and nuts when he was around seven, but in spite of this, he and Mr. Tillian had remained friends and were still friends the year Harry turned twelve.

For years, after school, Harry had always stopped in to see his father at work. Many of Harry's friends stopped there, too, to spend a few cents choosing penny candy from the giant bins or to sample Mr. Tillian's latest batch of roasted peanuts. Mr. Tillian looked forward to seeing his son and his son's friends every day. He liked the company.

When Harry entered junior high school, though, he didn't come by the candy and nut shop as often. Nor did his friends. They were older and they had more spending money. They went to a burger place. They played video games. They shopped for records. None of them were much interested in candy and nuts anymore.

A new group of children came to Mr. Tillian's shop now. But not Harry Tillian and his friends.

The year Harry turned twelve was also the year Mr. Tillian got a parrot. He went to a pet store one day and bought one for more money than he could really afford. He brought the parrot to his shop, set its cage near the sign for maple clusters, and named it Rocky.

Harry thought this was the strangest thing his father had ever done, and he told him so, but Mr. Tillian just ignored him.

Rocky was good company for Mr. Tillian. When business was slow, Mr. Tillian would turn on a small color television he had sitting in a corner, and he and Rocky would watch the soap operas. Rocky liked to scream when the romantic music came on, and Mr. Tillian would yell at him to shut up, but they seemed to enjoy themselves.

The more Mr. Tillian grew to like his parrot, and the more he talked to it instead of to

Sustained Silent Reading

To see how your students are mastering sustained silent reading, try this project.

Tell students to suppose that they are putting together a collection of stories for seventh-graders. Their task is to evaluate the stories and decide which ones kids would like — which ones would give kids something to think about, which ones they think are challenging but manageable enough for independent reading. Then, ask students to read Rylant's story on their own, silently, in class. Tell them to write a few sentences in their reading logs when they are finished, noting whether they had any trouble with the story (if so, what gave them trouble?) and what aspects of the story they liked best and least. When the reading is finished, have students meet in groups to discuss their notes. See if the class can come to an agreement on whether or not the story should be included in a book for seventh-graders.

While students are reading silently, you should, of course, circulate and give help when it is requested. The story is very short; students reading on level should be able to complete it in ten minutes.

people, the more embarrassed Harry became. Harry would stroll past the shop, on his way somewhere else, and he'd take a quick look inside to see what his dad was doing. Mr. Tillian was always talking to the bird. So Harry kept walking.

At home things were different. Harry and his father joked with each other at the dinner table as they always had—Mr. Tillian teasing Harry about his smelly socks; Harry teasing Mr. Tillian about his blubbery stomach. At home things seemed all right.

But one day, Mr. Tillian became ill. He had been at work, unpacking boxes of caramels, when he had grabbed his chest and fallen over on top of the candy. A customer had found him, and he was taken to the hospital in an ambulance.

Mr. Tillian couldn't leave the hospital. He lay in bed, tubes in his arms, and he worried about his shop. New shipments of candy and nuts would be arriving. Rocky would be hungry. Who would take care of things?

Harry said he would. Harry told his father that he would go to the store every day after school and unpack boxes. He would sort out all the candy and nuts. He would even feed Rocky.

So, the next morning, while Mr. Tillian lay in his hospital bed, Harry took the shop key to school with him. After school he left his friends and walked to the empty shop alone. In all the days of his life, Harry had never seen the shop closed after school. Harry didn't even remember what the CLOSED sign looked like. The key stuck in the lock three times, and inside he had to search all the walls for the light switch.

The shop was as his father had left it. Even the caramels were still spilled on the floor. Harry bent down and picked them up one by one, dropping them back in the boxes. The bird in its cage watched him silently.

Harry opened the new boxes his father hadn't gotten to. Peppermints. Jawbreakers.

Toffee creams. Strawberry kisses. Harry traveled from bin to bin, putting the candies where they belonged.

"Hello!"

Harry jumped, spilling a box of jawbreakers.

"Hello, Rocky!"

Harry stared at the parrot. He had forgotten it was there. The bird had been so quiet, and Harry had been thinking only of the candy.

"Hello," Harry said.

"Hello, Rocky!" answered the parrot.

Harry walked slowly over to the cage. The parrot's food cup was empty. Its water was dirty. The bottom of the cage was a mess.

Harry carried the cage into the back room.

"Hello, Rocky!"

"Is that all you can say, you dumb bird?" Harry mumbled. The bird said nothing else.

Harry cleaned the bottom of the cage, refilled the food and water cups, and then put the cage back in its place and resumed sorting the candy.

"Where's Harry?"

Harry looked up.

"Where's Harry?"

Harry stared at the parrot.

"Where's Harry?"

Chills ran down Harry's back. What could the bird mean? It was like something from *The Twilight Zone.*°

"Where's Harry?"

Harry swallowed and said, "I'm here. I'm here, you stupid bird."

"You stupid bird!" said the parrot.

Well, at least he's got one thing straight, thought Harry.

"Miss him! Miss him! Where's Harry? You stupid bird!"

Harry stood with a handful of peppermints.

"*What?*" he asked.

"Where's Harry?" said the parrot.

° *The Twilight Zone:* a popular dramatic television series that ran from 1959 to 1964 and is now widely shown in reruns. It usually features suspenseful, fantastic plots.

A Elements of Literature
Characterization
❓ What impression does the story give you of Mr. Tillian? [Possible responses: He seems kind; he looks forward to Harry's visits, so he must love his son very much.]

B Reading Skills and Strategies
Making Inferences
❓ Why might Mr. Tillian buy a parrot? [Possible response: He buys it to have someone to talk to because his son doesn't come to the candy store any more.]

Reaching All Students

Struggling Readers
This story shows a central character on the cusp between childhood and adolescence. Help students keep track of the time shifts in the story by making a timeline, showing Harry's greater closeness to his father before junior high school, his change when he enters junior high school, his father's acquisition of the parrot, the time his father spends with the parrot, his father's heart attack, and Harry's discovery of the parrot's message.

English Language Learners
Make sure English language learners understand that the parrot repeats what he hears, and he repeats what he has heard in the past. They might also need a little help with the expression "Miss him," which is missing its subject "I." For strategies to supplement instruction for these students, see
• *Lesson Plans Including Strategies for English-Language Learners*

Ⓐ Reading Skills and Strategies
Drawing Conclusions

❓ Why does Harry cry? [Possible response: He realizes that his father must have said "Where's Harry! Miss him!" many times while he was alone in his store with Rocky; Harry feels bad that he has not spent more time with his father, especially now that his father is ill.]

"I'm *here*, you stupid bird! I'm here!" Harry yelled. He threw the peppermints at the cage, and the bird screamed and clung to its perch.

Ⓐ Harry sobbed, "I'm here." The tears were coming.

Harry leaned over the glass counter.

"Papa." Harry buried his face in his arms.

"Where's Harry?" repeated the bird.

Harry sighed and wiped his face on his sleeve. He watched the parrot. He understood now: someone had been saying, for a long time, "Where's Harry? Miss him."

Harry finished his unpacking and then swept the floor of the shop. He checked the furnace so the bird wouldn't get cold. Then he left to go visit his papa.

MEET THE WRITER
Always Trying to Find Those Words

Cynthia Rylant (1954–   ) wrote in her autobiography:

❝ They say that to be a writer you must first have an unhappy childhood. I don't know if unhappiness is necessary, but I think maybe some children who have suffered a loss too great for words grow up into writers who are always trying to find those words, trying to find a meaning for the way they have lived. ❞

As a child Rylant knew what it felt like to lose someone. Her parents separated when she was four, and she lived with her grandparents in West Virginia while her mother went to school. For years she heard nothing of her father; then, when she was a young teenager, he got in touch with her. They planned a reunion, but he died before it could happen. She was just thirteen.

Rylant felt that despite this sorrow, her childhood was a happy one, calling her West Virginia home "a small, sparkling universe that gave me a lifetime's worth of material for my writing." Rylant has won several awards for her books for young people, including the Newbery Medal for her novel *Missing May* (1993). She describes the kinds of people she likes to write about:

❝ I get a lot of personal gratification thinking of those people who don't get any attention in the world and making them really valuable in my fiction—making them absolutely shine with their beauty. ❞

More Words Found by Cynthia Rylant
If you are touched by "Papa's Parrot," you might enjoy some of Rylant's novels: *A Fine White Dust* (Bradbury) and *Missing May* (Orchard Books). You might also like her autobiography, *Best Wishes* (Richard C. Owen).

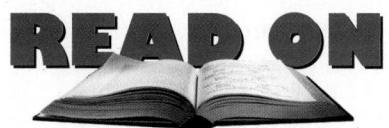

READ ON

Love Stories

Cynthia Rylant's *A Couple of Kooks: And Other Stories About Love* (Dell) takes a fresh look at love. A supermarket bag boy's crush on a pretty shopper, an old man's passion, and a retarded boy's adoration of a woman who works in a hardware store are among the stories you'll discover.

Forever Friends

Twelve-year-old Dara and her family flee war-torn Cambodia and find a haven at the refugee camp of Nong Chan. In *The Clay Marble* (Farrar, Straus & Giroux) by Minfong Ho, Dara finds a new friend, Jantu, and for a short while their lives are full of peace. When the war brings chaos to the camp, however, Dara is separated from her family and Jantu. Now she must find the courage to reunite the people she loves. (This title is available in the HRW Library.)

Desert Heartbreak

In *One More River* (Avon) by Lynne Reid Banks, wealthy Lesley Shelby must abandon her comfortable life when her family moves to a kibbutz in Israel just before the 1967 Six-Day War. Once there, she struggles to find something in common with the Israeli teenagers she meets. In this riveting story, Lesley discovers her own strengths and inner conflicts when she encounters an Arab youth.

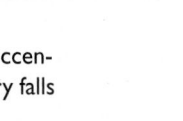

Other Picks

- Robert Westall, *Stormsearch* (Farrar, Straus & Giroux). When Tim and Tracy Vaux dig up an ancient ship's model, they uncover a story of doomed romance and family secrets.

- David Kherdian, *A Song for Uncle Harry* (Philomel). Petey and his eccentric Armenian uncle Harry have an unusual bond until Uncle Harry falls in love.

Speaking and Listening Workshop

OBJECTIVES
1. Understand the elements of a successful interview
2. Prepare for the interview
3. Conduct the interview
4. Follow up the interview
5. Become a relaxed, informative, and pleasant interviewee

Resources

Performance Rubric
- *Portfolio Management System,* p. 152

Introducing the Speaking and Listening Workshop

Discuss with students the importance of being well prepared for an interview. The more knowledgeable they are about the topic, the more relaxed they will be during the interview—and the more at ease the person being interviewed (the subject) will be. Prepared students will also be better able to generate questions on information the subject introduces.

Give students the following suggestions to help them prepare for their interviews more productively:
- Do as much research on your topic and subject as possible. If the subject has published anything, try to familiarize yourself with his or her writings. Never rush into the interview unprepared.
- Create a list of thoughtful questions that will require more than yes or no responses. You will probably not be able to ask all of your questions, but you can be sure that you will not run out of things to ask.

Try It Out

Suggest that students group their questions for sports, music, or film idols into categories such as "Early Experiences," "Big Break," "Favorite Activities," and "Long-term Plans." Have students compare and discuss their lists of questions with a partner. Ask them to suggest a few questions to add to their partner's lists.

Try It Out

Allow students to use a video camera to record their mock interviews, and let them submit videotaped interviews instead of performing them live.

Try It Out

Imagine you're interviewing your favorite sports, music, or film idol. Write down a list of ten questions, none of which can be answered with a simple yes or no.

Try It Out

Team up with a classmate, and come up with a situation in which an interviewer and a subject have opposing points of view (a dog hater interviews the director of the humane society; a vegetarian interviews the owner of a cattle ranch). Then, act out two versions of the interview. In the first version the interview is tense and hostile, full of insults, interruptions, and accusations. In the second the interview is polite and constructive, and the interviewer refrains from directly expressing a point of view. What did you learn from the two scenarios?

INTERVIEWING

Interviews—conversations in which one person asks questions to obtain information—are more common than you might think. You've probably been interviewed—by a teacher, the school nurse, or a neighbor wanting you to baby-sit or mow the lawn.

Sometime you may need to conduct an interview yourself. Here's how to get off to a good start.

Preparing for the Interview

A good interviewer is well prepared. Before you take out your pencil and note pad, follow these steps:
- Research your topic. If your interview focuses on a topic—kayaking, say—go to the library and find out all you can about it. The more you know, the better your questions will be.
- Know your subject. If your interview focuses on the ideas and life of the person you're interviewing (your subject), see if any newspaper or magazine articles have been written about him or her. If your subject is a writer, read her latest book; if he's an architect, go see—or find a picture of—a building he designed.
- Make a list of questions. Ask obvious questions rather than pretend you know the answer. Don't ask questions that can be answered with a simple yes or no. Avoid questions that might influence your subject, like "You hate losing, don't you?"
- Set up a time and place for the interview. Choose a place that's comfortable and familiar to your subject—interview a horse trainer at her ranch or a chemistry teacher in his lab. Be on time.

Conducting the Interview

You're seated across from your subject, pencil poised. How do you make the most of your opportunity? Follow these guidelines:
- Set the ground rules. If you want to tape-record the interview, ask your subject's permission before you begin. If you plan to quote your subject's exact words in a newspaper article or in an essay, you must ask permission to do that, too.

Using Students' Strengths

Auditory Learners
Play an audio recording of a one-on-one interview from a radio news program such as *Morning Edition* or *All Things Considered.* Ask students to write down the best question and the worst question they think the interviewer asked. After students have listened to the entire interview, divide the class into groups of three, and have them compare and discuss their choices.

Visual Learners
Give students copies of a chart like the one below, and ask them to use it to organize their notes on the information given in this lesson.

Preparing	Conducting	Following Up
[go to library for research; call to set up time and place]	[try not to interrupt; focus and be patient]	[go to library to check facts; make sure notes are complete]

- Be courteous and patient. Allow your subject plenty of time to answer your questions. Try not to interrupt. Respect the person's ideas and opinions, even if you disagree.

- Listen carefully. Don't rush on to your next question. If you're confused, ask for an explanation. If an answer reminds you of a related question, ask it—even if it isn't on your list.

- Focus on your subject, not on yourself. Avoid getting off on tangents, such as "Something like that happened to me. . . ."

- Wrap things up. A good interview is leisurely but doesn't go on forever. Know when to stop. You can always phone later to check a fact or ask a final question. Be sure to thank your subject.

Following Up the Interview

Your notebook is filled, and your mind is bursting with ideas. How do you get your thoughts in order? Follow these steps:

- Review your notes. As soon as possible, read through your notes and make sure your information is complete and clear.

- Write a summary. To make sure you understand what was said, write a summary of the main points of the interview.

- Check your facts. If you can, check the spelling of all names and technical facts against another source, such as an encyclopedia.

Turning the Tables: Being Interviewed

Sometime someone may want to interview you. Here are some tips:

- Stay relaxed. Listen carefully to each question before you begin your answer. If a question confuses you, ask the interviewer to reword it or repeat it. Take your time. Long, thoughtful answers are better than short, curt ones.

- Be accurate. Don't exaggerate. If you're not sure of something, say so.

- Keep a sense of humor.

> ### Try It Out
>
> Watch a television news anchor interview a subject. Pay attention to
>
> - the length of the questions
> - follow-up questions
> - how the interviewer maintains control over the interview
> - how the interviewer makes his or her subject feel comfortable
>
> How can you apply what you have learned to your own interviews?

Teaching the Spe[...] and Listening Workshop

Give students these suggestions to help them conduct and follow up their interviews more successfully:

- When your subject is speaking, maintain good eye contact and look down at your notes as little as possible. Respond often, with words or occasional nods to let your subject know you are listening.

- Be flexible. Do not insist on sticking to your list of prepared questions if you find that your subject has an interesting topic that you had not anticipated.

- Take good notes, but do not try to write down every word. It is more important to listen carefully and jot down key words that will jog your memory later on. If you listen carefully and respond to your subject, you should be able to reconstruct your notes after the interview.

- If you have recorded the interview, do not attempt to transcribe every word from the tape. Instead, transcribe just the comments that you think you will want to quote.

- Do not skip the fact-checking stage. Make sure that all quotations and facts you plan to use are documented and accurate.

Try It Out

To encourage students to observe attentively while they are watching the TV news interview, ask them to take notes. Have them turn in their notes along with a paragraph about what they learned from the interview.

Reaching All Students

Struggling Learners

Help students prepare for their interviews by having them brainstorm lists of appropriate questions, working in groups of four. Students should first share any information they have about their subject with the other members of the group. The members of each group should brainstorm aloud for three to five minutes on each subject, with one member taking notes. Ask students to try to leave the group with at least five good questions for each subject.

MAIN OBJECTIVE
Write a biographical sketch

PROCESS OBJECTIVES
1. Use appropriate prewriting techniques to identify and develop details about a subject
2. Create a first draft
3. Use evaluation criteria as a basis for determining revision strategies
4. Revise the first draft, incorporating suggestions generated by self- or peer evaluation
5. Proofread and correct errors
6. Create a final draft
7. Choose an appropriate method of publication
8. Reflect on progress as a writer

Planning

- **Block Schedule**
  Block Scheduling Lesson Plans with Pacing Guides
- **One-Stop Planner**
  CD-ROM with Test Generator

Technology HELP

See Writer's Workshop 1 CD-ROM. *Assignment: Firsthand Biography.*

ASSIGNMENT

Write an essay about a real person.

AIM

To inform.

AUDIENCE

Your teacher, classmates, friends, or family.

A longer excerpt from Barrio Boy by Ernesto Galarza appears on page 125.

EXPOSITORY WRITING
BIOGRAPHICAL SKETCH

In a biographical sketch, you give information about a person, either someone you know or a historical figure you're interested in.

Professional Model

In this passage from his autobiography, Barrio Boy, Ernesto Galarza describes his aunt.

Doña Henriqueta was not even as tall as Doña Esther, but plumper. She had a light olive complexion and a mass of dark brown hair so wavy it burst when she undid her braids. She never did household chores without singing, accompanying herself by imitating a guitar that plinked and plonked between the verses of her song. Her features were good-looking, almost soft, not much like her temper. Doña Henriqueta knew about people in deep trouble, for she was one of them. But unlike most of them, she believed in rebelling against it, in resisting those who caused it. As the oldest of the four migrants from Miramar, Doña Henriqueta stood between us and Don Catarina when he was in one of his cantankerous moods. She drew a line between respect, which we were expected to show, and fear, which we were not.

—from *Barrio Boy* by Ernesto Galarza

The writer describes his aunt's appearance.

He tells about his aunt's actions.

He describes his aunt's personality.

He tells where his aunt is from.

 Resources: Print and Media

Writing and Language
- *Portfolio Management System*
  - Prewriting, p. 153
  - Peer Editing, p. 154
  - Assessment Rubric, p. 155
- *Workshop Resources*
  - Revision Strategy Teaching Notes, p. 21
  - Revision Strategy Transparencies 11, 12
- *Writer's Workshop 1 CD-ROM*
  - Firsthand Biography

Prewriting

1. Writer's Notebook

Review the notes you made in your Writer's Notebook for this collection. Then, answer these questions:

- Which of these people do I find most interesting? Why?
- Which of these people would I enjoy writing about? Why?
- Which of these people taught me something important? What was it?

2. Freewriting

To find more ideas, freewrite on some of these subjects:

- people you think are "the most" (the most helpful, the most courageous, the most whatever)
- a memorable historical figure
- someone who changed your mind about something
- someone whose actions made a difference
- a hero whose deeds haven't been recognized
- a unique athlete

Choose two or three of the people you've written about. For each person, list a personality trait you admire (for example, understanding or courage) and sum up an incident that illustrates the trait. For an example of this kind of freewriting, see the chart in the margin. Review your charts, and see which person seems to jump out at you. Which one will give you a lot to write about?

3. Why Is This Person Important?

When you've decided on your subject, ask yourself why he or she is important enough to write about. Use these questions to help put your thoughts into words:

■ *Evaluation Criteria*

A good biographical sketch

1. *makes the personality of the subject come alive*
2. *includes concrete details of the subject's appearance, behavior, and background*
3. *may use dialogue to show the subject's character*
4. *may describe the setting*
5. *tells about specific incidents to illustrate the subject's character*
6. *shows why the subject is important to the writer*

Person	Dad
Trait	forgiveness
Incident	Forgave me when I hit a ball through the kitchen window (I wasn't supposed to hit balls there).

Introducing the Writer's Workshop

- Read aloud the Professional Model on p. 410 as the students follow along. Tell students to pay attention for shifts and contrasts as they read about Doña Henriqueta, who starts out sounding like a jolly, happy person and gathers fire and strength as the sketch goes on.
- Be sure students understand the side-margin comments. After they have read the model, ask students to summarize Henriqueta's personality.
- Discuss with students what makes a good biographical sketch:
    1. an interesting subject, about whom the writer feels strongly
    2. details that make the subject come alive for the reader
    3. a clear sense of why the subject is important to the writer
- Be sure that students understand the purpose of their writing: to describe a subject and tell the reader why that subject is important to them

Remind students to choose a topic they will not mind sharing with others.

Teaching the Writer's Workshop

Prewriting

Have students use the prewriting techniques suggested on pp. 411–412 (or any others that may be helpful to them) to come up with ideas.

Reaching All Students

Struggling Writers

Encourage students to discuss potential subjects with a partner. Talking can help students open up and discover more to say in their sketches. Partners may even be able to help each other decide which subject might be the most rewarding to write about. They can also ask questions, to encourage the writer to find more material about a subject.

English Language Learners

Encourage English language learners to focus first on physical details to characterize their subjects, as Galarza does. These concrete details— of facial expression, physique, characteristic clothing, way of walking and talking—are easier to write about than more abstract personality traits, and will provide the students with a way of conveying their subject's personality.

T411

Drafting

- If you have not yet taught the Student Model, do so before students begin writing their own drafts.
- Remind students to double space when they write their drafts. They should also leave extra space in the right margin for comments and editing marks.

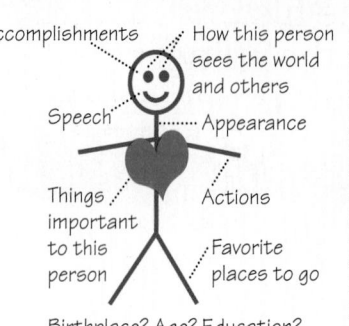

Accomplishments · How this person sees the world and others

Speech · Appearance

Things important to this person · Actions · Favorite places to go

Birthplace? Age? Education? Work?

Framework for a Biographical Sketch

Introduction (captures the reader's curiosity; shows the person in action; mentions an interesting biographical detail):

_____

_____

Body (describes the person's qualities; tells a story about the person; gives biographical details):

_____

_____

_____

_____

_____

Conclusion (tells what the person means to you or presents a final word picture):

_____

_____

_____

_____

- What more than anything else draws me to this person?
- What have I learned about people or life from this person?
- How has this person influenced my life or my thinking?
- Why would my readers enjoy knowing this person?

Try writing two or three sentences that **summarize** why your subject is important to you. This summary may turn out to be the main point of your biographical sketch. It may also turn out that as you write, your opinion changes. In any case, keep this statement handy as you work on the biography.

4. Details Make It Real

Now, gather details of your subject—details of appearance, interests, accomplishments. Decide if you want to tell something about your person's background—age, birthplace, education, work. Draw a stick figure of a person like the one at the left, and fill in details in as many of the categories as you can.

Drafting

1. Getting Started

Read over your Prewriting notes. Mark them up, circling points you want to use in your biographical sketch—for example, actions that reveal character and memorable traits. Include details that show what the person means to you.

As you begin to write, include everything you think is important. Don't worry too much about length or organization—you can take care of those things once you have something down on paper. Make sure, though, that you never lose sight of your statement about why this person is important to you.

2. Shaping and Organizing

Here are a few ways to organize your ideas:

Time order. You could organize your biographical sketch **chronologically,** following time order. Use this kind of organization, for example, if you're relating a series of events that show your subject's personality.

Physical appearance. You could start with your subject's physical appearance and then relate it to personality. Look at Ernesto Galarza's portrait of his aunt Henriqueta (page 410).

Using Students' Strengths

Visual Learners

Encourage students to visualize their subjects in a favorite setting, like the kitchen in which Elly Henry places her mother. The setting could be an area in the subject's home or place of work, a sports arena, theater, or vacation spot. It could even be a place the subject has spoken about but never visited. Explain to students that, through this process, their subjects will come to life for them, along with many concrete sensory images that they can use in their writing.

Interpersonal Learners

As a prewriting activity, suggest that students bring in items that remind them of their subject—letters, photographs, articles of clothing, favorite possessions—to help stimulate both their memories and their emotions.

Note how her soft features contrast with her fiery spirit. Also look at the Student Model below. Notice that the mother's physical appearance gives us a sense of her personality.

Personality traits. You could organize your biography around your subject's personality traits, telling about specific incidents that show the traits in action. You might consider describing the most important personality trait last. With this method, called **order of importance,** you put your most important point either first or last.

Student Model

The following passage is from a description of the writer's mother.

from IN THE KITCHEN

I hopped up onto the yellow-topped counter and gazed around the room, taking in the kitchen with all my senses . . . and finally, my mother. Small and thin, with short salt-and-pepper hair and happy laugh-lines (and the age-ones she called unattractive but I always said made her that much more beautiful), it was my mother I noticed most. When she laughed, her eyes would crinkle and she would look at you as if you were the most special person in the world. I always loved making my mother laugh, just to see her eyes—and that look.

We see the person in a setting.

Physical details give us a clear picture of the person's appearance and personality.

As she cooked, delectable smells danced and flew from the lidded pots and pans, making my mouth water. I asked for "tries," and she gave me tastes and nibbles, making me long for supper.

Description of actions helps us get to know the writer's mother.

(continued on next page)

Strategies for Elaboration

Bringing Your Person to Life

Your aim in writing a biographical sketch is to bring your person to life for your readers. To do this, try these strategies:

• Quote something the person says or has said that is funny or characteristic of him or her.

• Put the person in a setting that you associate with him or her. Describe the setting.

• Tell what other people think of the person.

• Tell what this person makes you think of. What do you associate with him or her—springtime, ballgames, walks in the park?

Choosing Reference Materials and Resources for Writing, Revising and Editing

As students write, revise, and edit their biographical sketches, they should consult specific reference materials. For example, in writing their sketches, they might want to look in a book of synonyms, such as *Roget's International Thesaurus* or *Webster's New Dictionary of Synonyms,* if they are looking for just the right words to describe their subject. In revising, if their sketch is about a historical figure, they may decide to consult a biographical reference like *Merriam-Webster's Biographical Dictionary.* And in editing, they might turn to *Bartlett's Familiar Quotations* for a quotation to perk up the beginning or end of their sketches.

Reaching All Students

Advanced Learners

Students may extend their biographical sketches into a more ambitious piece of writing—perhaps a series of portraits of similar subjects or a lengthier biography of this one subject. Encourage them to interview their subjects and do research into their lives and times.

Evaluating and Revising

Have students use the Evaluation Criteria provided on page 411 to review their drafts and decide on needed revisions.

Proofreading

Have students proofread their own work first and then exchange papers with a partner. For this assignment, remind students to be particularly careful with subject-verb agreement and pronoun usage.

If time permits, the final copy should be put aside for at least a day before it is proofread for the last time by the author.

Publishing

Students may want to include several biographical sketches in a scrapbook. They may illustrate their descriptions with drawings or photographs of their subjects. Encourage them to share their products with family and friends; a sketch might be a valued birthday or holiday gift. They should also save their sketches to read over in future years.

Reflecting

Students can prepare a brief reflection on the process of writing a biographical sketch. They might complete one of the starters below:

- My favorite part of this paper is . . . because . . .
- The main discovery I made about my subject while writing this paper was . . .

Resources ━━━

Peer Editing Forms and Rubrics
- *Portfolio Management System,* p. 154

Revision Transparencies
- *Workshop Resources,* p. 21

Grading Timesaver

Rubrics for this Writer's Workshop assignment appear on p. 155 of the *Portfolio Management System.*

Language/Grammar Link
H E L P

Problems with pronouns: pages 366 and 392. Homonyms: page 385.

Sentence Workshop
H E L P

Revising wordy sentences: page 415.

Proofreading Tip

Read your paper backward, word by word.

Publishing Tip

Your subject might enjoy reading what you wrote. Consider printing and binding your biography to create a special gift.

Communications Handbook
H E L P

See Proofreaders' Marks.

First appeared in Merlyn's Pen: The National Magazines of Student Writing.

Student Model (continued)

Some of my best times have been spent in that kitchen, watching my mother bustle about, stirring this, testing that, always smiling with her crinkly eyes, making everyone around her happy. At the end, when all was done, she would put her arms around me, and I would stand on my tiptoes so that I could fit my head on her shoulder, and then she would squeeze me a little harder and say "thank you," and I would say "thank you" right back.

—Elly Henry
Camp Hill Jr./Sr. High School
Camp Hill, Pennsylvania

The writer describes more actions to give us a sense of her mother's personality.

At the end and earlier in the passage, we can feel the writer's affection for her mother.

3. Making the Beginning and Ending Memorable

As you shape your biography, think of ways to make the beginning and ending strong. You might begin by mentioning an unusual fact or physical detail, by telling about a funny incident, or by quoting part of a conversation.

Ending a biographical piece can be tricky. You don't want to sound obvious or dull—"My father taught me everything I know"—but maybe you can find a way to show your subject's importance to you. Perhaps you can end with a description of a special moment, as the writer of the Student Model on page 413 did.

Evaluating and Revising

Look once more at your statement of why your subject is important to you. Did you say what you meant to say? Did you end up saying anything new? Could that new point be worth focusing on? Revise your writing to make it say what you want it to say.

Sentence Workshop

OBJECTIVES
1. Identify wordy sentences
2. Revise wordy sentences by using a single word instead of a phrase; by eliminating *that is/was, who is/was,* or *which is/was*; and by avoiding repetition

REVISING WORDY SENTENCES

Sometimes writers clutter up sentences by using more words than they really need. An overload of words doesn't make writing sound better or more impressive. Learn how to avoid wordiness in your writing and how to make every word count.

You can revise **wordy sentences** in at least three ways:

1. Replace a long phrase with a single word.

WORDY   They reached the school corner and Roger skipped away in an eager manner from her.

REVISED   "They reached the school corner and Roger skipped away eagerly from her."

—Arthur Cavanaugh, "Miss Awful" (page 373)

2. Take out *that is/was, who is/was,* or *which is/was.*

WORDY   The sidewalk that was in front of school already boasted a large, jostling throng of children. . . .

REVISED   "The sidewalk in front of school already boasted a large, jostling throng of children. . . ."

—Arthur Cavanaugh, "Miss Awful" (page 373)

3. Take out words that repeat something.

WORDY   I reached over and shut off the insistent buzzing of my bedside alarm clock, which was ringing next to my bed.

REVISED   "I reached over and shut off the insistent buzzing of my bedside alarm clock."

—T. Ernesto Bethancourt, "User Friendly" (page 357)

Writer's Workshop Follow-up: Revision

Take out your biographical sketch, and circle any wordy sentences. Revise these sentences to make them straightforward and concise. Look for and eliminate phrases like *due to the fact that* and *at the point at which.*

Language Handbook HELP

See Revising Stringy Sentences and Wordy Sentences, pages 761-762.

Technology HELP

See Language Workshop CD-ROM. Key word entry: wordiness.

Try It Out

Revise each of the following wordy sentences.

1. At the moment when she returned to her desk, her back was straighter than ever.

2. Due to the fact that she was so beautiful, people probably wondered why she was with me.

3. Harry didn't have the slightest clue as to whether or not the parrot was speaking to him.

4. My computer, which was known by the name of Louis, sent me a message.

SENTENCE WORKSHOP   415

Resources

Workshop Resources
• Worksheet, p. 45

Language Workshop CD-ROM
• Wordiness

Try It Out:
Possible Answers
1. When she returned to her desk, her back was straighter than ever.
2. Because she was so beautiful, people probably wondered why she was with me.
3. Harry didn't know whether the parrot was speaking to him.
4. My computer, known as Louis, sent me a message.

Assessing Learning

Quick Check: Revising Wordy Sentences

Revise each of the following wordy sentences. Answers will vary.

1. With great haste, the highwayman returned in a big hurry to the old inn. [Hastily, the highwayman returned to the old inn.]

2. At the point at which he heard the shot, the highwayman turned back. [When he heard the shot, the highwayman turned back.]

3. Because the angels were jealous of the two young lovers, their envy was the reason why they sent a wind to kill Annabel Lee. [Because the angels were jealous of the two young lovers, they sent a wind to kill Annabel Lee.]

4. The hawk flies in a graceful way during the time that the speaker observes the golden sunlight that is gleaming. [The hawk flies gracefully while the speaker observes the golden, gleaming sunlight.]

5. On a walk with his father, who is a kind and patient man, the son learns what it is that is important in life. [On a walk with his father, a kind and patient man, the son learns what is important in life.]

T415

Using the Strategies

Suggested Answers

1. In Chapter 12
2. Students' answers might include details about San Antonio's location, history, economic base, and population.
3. Texas

Recognizing Features of Informational Texts

Remind students that features such as a table of contents, an index, charts, maps, and other graphics are found in most full-length informational works. Advise them to apply the skills they've learned here when they read material from other disciplines.

Situation

Imagine that you're going to visit San Antonio this summer, driving all the way from Virginia to Texas. Before you leave, you want to learn about the states you'll be traveling through. You decide to start with your geography book.

Strategies

Focus your research.

• Make a list of questions you want to answer.

Use the text's structure to locate information.

• Skim the **table of contents** to see what information your textbook covers and how it is organized. Scan unit headings and chapter titles. See where you can find information on your topic.

• Search the **index** for key words about your topic. Check general entries ("Southern states," for example) and specific entries (names of states, large cities, and physical features, such as rivers).

• Look for **maps** that will help you locate physical features, such as mountains, as well as towns and cities.

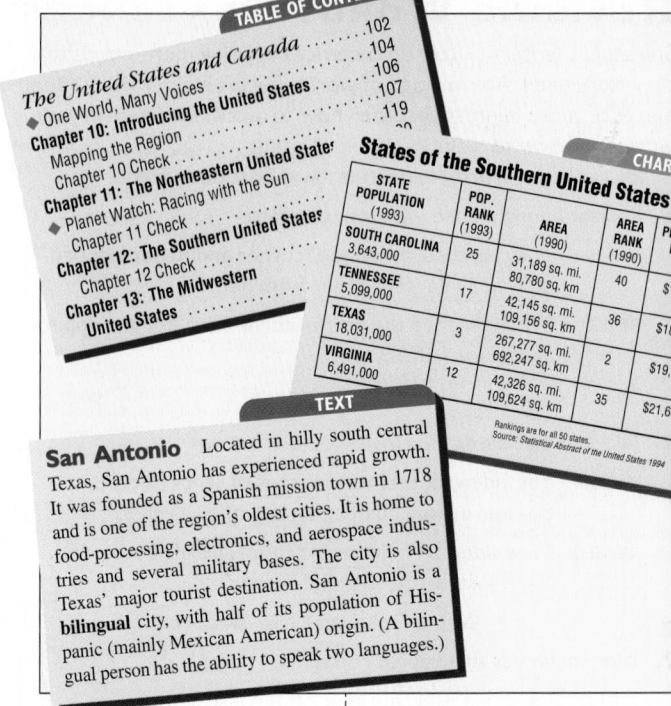

CHART

States of the Southern United States

STATE POPULATION (1993)	POP. RANK (1993)	AREA (1990)	AREA RANK (1990)	PER IN (
SOUTH CAROLINA 3,643,000	25	31,189 sq. mi. 80,780 sq. km	40	$16
TENNESSEE 5,099,000	17	42,145 sq. mi. 109,156 sq. km	36	$18,
TEXAS 18,031,000	3	267,277 sq. mi. 692,247 sq. km	2	$19,1
VIRGINIA 6,491,000	12	42,326 sq. mi. 109,624 sq. km	35	$21,63

Rankings are for all 50 states.
Source: Statistical Abstract of the United States 1994

TEXT

San Antonio Located in hilly south central Texas, San Antonio has experienced rapid growth. It was founded as a Spanish mission town in 1718 and is one of the region's oldest cities. It is home to food-processing, electronics, and aerospace industries and several military bases. The city is also Texas' major tourist destination. San Antonio is a **bilingual** city, with half of its population of Hispanic (mainly Mexican American) origin. (A bilingual person has the ability to speak two languages.)

Use graphic features.

• Look for **charts,** which present a lot of information in a small space.

Using the Strategies

Answer the following questions about the material above, which is from a world geography textbook.

1. Where in the table of contents would you find facts about states you'd travel through on the way from Virginia to Texas?

2. List three things that you learned about San Antonio.

3. Which state listed in the chart is the third most populous in the country?

Extending the Strategies

Where in the world would you most like to go? Use these strategies to find information on this place in your geography textbook.

Reaching All Students

Struggling Readers

Students who have difficulty navigating through a geography textbook might be paired with more skillful, confident readers. Before answering the Using the Strategies questions, the pairs can consider these questions: Where is the table of contents and what is its purpose? How are states located on a map of the United States? What kind of information may be contained in a chart? How is a chart read? What is the most effective way to read a passage of text

packed with details? (For example, break down the details by category; look for important words like *located, founded, industries, population*.) Students who come from foreign countries or other parts of the United States might be especially interested in the textbook's information on their home region; these text sections might be a good place to start. If students have first-hand knowledge they would like to add, encourage them to do so.

Advanced Readers

Students might create a fantasy land and a geography "textbook" for their imaginary location. Encourage students to be as original as they wish in coming up with details. To present the details, students can develop charts, maps, brief text passages, entries in a table of contents and an index, illustrations, and similar material. Students may want to share their work with the class.

Learning for Life
Conflict Resolution

OBJECTIVES
1. Explore methods of conflict resolution
2. Choose and complete a project to present the results of the research (role-playing, creating a billboard, composing a song)

Problem

Wherever people live and work together, conflicts arise. How can people resolve, or work out, differences with others and keep good relationships with them?

Project

Do a survey to find out how people resolve differences with others.

Preparation

1. With a small group of classmates, write a short survey of four or five questions about how people deal with conflict.

2. Test your survey by asking your teacher or another adult to respond to your questions. Then, make any changes that are needed in the survey.

3. Each group member will pick at least two people to interview. They might be classmates, students in other classes, friends, or neighbors.

Procedure

1. Tell each person whom you are going to interview what your purpose is. Then, ask the survey questions. Don't try to write down every word of every answer. Jot down important points and just a few of the person's exact words.

2. Meet as a group and read the answers to the surveys. Do you see any patterns? Ask yourselves these questions:

   - What methods do people use to cooperate?
   - What kinds of situations cause conflicts?
   - What ways of resolving conflicts seem to work best?

3. As a class, discuss each group's findings. Then, decide on some general guidelines for resolving conflicts.

Presentation

Choose one of these ways to present what you have learned:

1. Role-Playing

On slips of paper, write down situations involving conflict that might occur in the workplace or at school. Fold the slips of paper in half and put them in a container. Then, with a partner, pull a conflict "out of the hat" and role-play the conflict and the resolution.

2. Billboard

Create a billboard with photographs of people and comments about how they resolve conflicts. If possible, use quotations from the people you surveyed.

3. Song

With a group of classmates, write a song about resolving conflicts. Choose a music style—rock, rap, country, folk, whatever. Try to include a catchy chorus that brings home the importance of your message.

Processing

In your portfolio, write a reflection about the survey. You might use one of these starters:

- I never realized it could be so hard to . . .
- Of all the ways to resolve conflicts, the one that appeals to me the most is . . .

Resources

Viewing and Representing
HRW Multimedia Presentation Maker
Students may wish to use the *Multimedia Presentation Maker* to create a billboard.

Grading Timesaver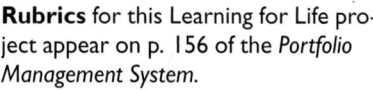

Rubrics for this Learning for Life project appear on p. 156 of the *Portfolio Management System.*

Developing Workplace Competencies

Preparation	Procedure	Presentation
• Working on a team • Designing a system • Improving a system	• Acquiring data • Evaluating data • Reasoning effectively	• Thinking creatively • Processing information • Communicating ideas and information

Collection Six

This Old Earth

Theme

For Better or Worse, All Things Are Connected *The old myths tell us that we are inextricably connected to the natural world, but in the modern world nature is often seen as a mere backdrop to the human drama. Sometimes it takes a catastrophe, such as an earthquake or a shipwreck, to remind us of nature's powerful role in our lives.*

Reading the Anthology

Reaching Struggling Readers

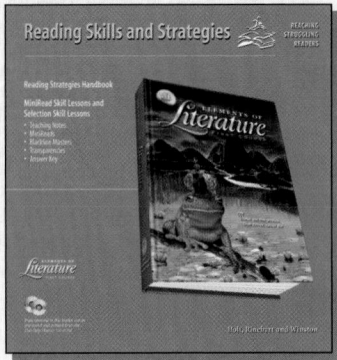

The *Reading Skills and Strategies: Reaching Struggling Readers* binder provides materials coordinated with the Pupil's Edition (see the Collection Planner, p. T417C) to help students who have difficulty reading and comprehending text, or students who are reluctant readers. The binder for seventh grade is organized around eleven individual skill areas. Selection Skill Lessons provide reading instruction and practice specific to particular pieces of literature in Collection Six.

Reading Beyond the Anthology

Read On

Collection Six includes an annotated bibliography of books suitable for extended reading. The suggested books are related to works in this collection by theme, by author, or by subject. To preview the Read On for Collection Six, please turn to p. T485.

HRW Library

The *HRW Library* offers novels, plays, and short-story collections for extended reading. Each book in the Library includes one or more major works and thematically or topically related Connections. The Connections are magazine articles, poems, or other pieces of literature. Each book in the *HRW Library* is also accompanied by a Study Guide that provides teaching suggestions and worksheets. For Collection Six, the following titles are recommended.

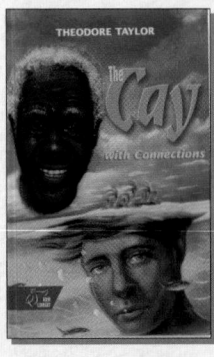

THE CAY
Theodore Taylor
In this story of an evolving friendship, an aging West Indian man teaches a boy to survive nature's hostile forces on an isolated cay.

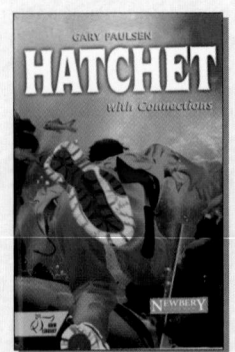

HATCHET
Gary Paulsen
A boy acquires a deep respect for nature—and his rightful place in it—when he is left alone in the wilderness for fifty-four days.

Skills Focus

Selection or Feature	Reading Skills and Strategies	Elements of Literature	Language/ Grammar	Vocabulary/ Spelling	Writing	Listening/ Speaking	Viewing/ Representing
The Creation (p. 420) James Weldon Johnson	Dialogue with the Text, p. 420	Refrain, pp. 420, 425 Call and Response, p. 420			Make Observations, p. 425 Write a Call-and-Response Hymn, p. 425	Perform a Choral Reading, p. 425	
Sky Woman (p. 426) Joseph Bruchac	Chronology, pp. 426, 430 Identify Major Events, p. 430	Origin Myth, pp. 426, 430	Avoid Clichés, p. 432	Adding Suffixes: Changing y to i, p. 432	Observe an Animal, p. 431 Write a Character's Autobiography, p. 431	Tell an Origin Myth, p. 431 Perform a Story, p. 431	
Reading Skills and Strategies: Organizing Ideas (p. 433)	Sequencing, p. 433 Cause and Effect, p. 433 Outlining, p. 433						Use Graphic Organizers to Track Text Structures, p. 433
When the Earth Shakes (p. 434) Patricia Lauber	Make a KWL Chart, pp. 434, 440 Track Cause and Effect, pp. 434, 440	Suspense, p. 440	Formal and Informal English, p. 442	Use New Words in Work Contexts, p. 442	Record Details, p. 441 Report on an Earthquake, p. 441 Create an Origin Myth About Earthquakes, p. 441		Draw a Diagram of the Earth's Layers, p. 441
Elements of Literature: Nonfiction (p. 443)		Main Idea, p. 443 Nonfiction, p. 443					
from **Earthquakes** (p. 443) Seymour Simon from **Survive the Savage Sea** (p. 444) Dougal Robertson	Adjust Reading Rate, pp. 444, 457 Evaluate Predictions, p. 457	Main Idea, pp. 444, 457	Active and Passive Voice, p. 459	Use New Words, p. 459	Identify Admirable Characteristics, p. 458 Write a Character's Journal Entry, p. 458 Identify the Contents of a Survival Kit, p. 458 Write a Report on Navigation, p. 458	Deliver an Oral Summary, p. 458	Illustrate a Report, p. 458
maggie and milly and molly and may (p. 460) E. E. Cummings		Rhyme, pp. 460, 463 Style, p. 460			Describe a Place, p. 462 Write a Poem About a Place, p. 462		Create a Museum Display, p. 463
I Am of the Earth (p. 464) Anna Lee Walters **Early Song** (p. 465) Gogisgi/Carroll Arnett		Personification, pp. 464, 467			Use Personification to Build an Image, p. 467 Write About a Quotation, p. 464 Paraphrase a Poem, p. 467		
Antaeus (p. 468) Borden Deal	Identify the Author's Purpose, pp. 468, 480	Allusion, pp. 468, 479	Style: Dialect, p. 481	Use Words in Context, p. 481	Make an Observation, p. 480 Write a Final Scene, p. 480	Have a Round Table Discussion, p. 480 Do a Tableau, p. 480	
No Questions Asked: Four Skinny Trees/ Cuatro árboles flaquititos (p. 482) Sandra Cisneros	The **No Questions Asked** feature provides students with an unstructured opportunity to practice reading strategies using a selection that extends the theme of the collection.						
Writer's Workshop: Observational Writing (p. 486)					Write a Descriptive Essay Based on Observation, pp. 486–490		Use Graphic Organizers, pp. 488, 489
Sentence Workshop: Using a Variety of Sentence Structures (p. 491)			Use a Variety of Sentence Structures, p. 491		Revise Sentences to Improve Variety, p. 491		
Reading for Life: Inductive and Deductive Reasoning (p. 492)	Inductive and Deductive Reasoning, p. 492	Logical Argument, p. 492					
Learning for Life: Saving Our Planet: Science Research (p. 493)					Create a Handbook, p. 493	Present an Earth Day Oral Report, p. 493	Use Visual Aids, p. 493 Draw an Invention, p. 493

Collection Six This Old Earth

Resources for this Collection

Note: All resources for this collection are available for preview on the *One-Stop Planner CD-ROM 2 with Test Generator*. All worksheets and blackline masters may be printed from the CD-ROM.

Selection or Feature	Reading and Literary Skills	Language and Grammar
The Creation (p. 420) James Weldon Johnson	• *Graphic Organizers for Active Reading*, Worksheet p. 27	
Sky Woman (p. 426) Joseph Bruchac	• *Reading Skills and Strategies: Reaching Struggling Readers* • Selection Skill Lesson, p. 182 • *Graphic Organizers for Active Reading*, Worksheet p. 28	• *Grammar and Language Links:* Avoiding Clichés, Worksheet p. 39 • *Daily Oral Grammar,* Transparency 24

When the Earth Shakes (p. 434)
Patricia Lauber
	• *Reading Skills and Strategies: Reaching Struggling Readers*
	  • Selection Skill Lesson, p. 186
	• *Graphic Organizers for Active Reading*, Worksheet p. 29
	• *Literary Elements:*
	  Transparency 8; Worksheet p. 25
		• *Grammar and Language Links:*
		  Formal and Informal English, Worksheet p. 41
		• *Daily Oral Grammar,* Transparency 25

Elements of Literature: Nonfiction: **The Main Idea** (p. 443)	• *Literary Elements,* Transparency 8	

from **Survive the Savage Sea** (p. 444)
Dougal Robertson
	• *Reading Skills and Strategies: Reaching Struggling Readers*
	  • Selection Skill Lesson, p. 15
	• *Graphic Organizers for Active Reading*, Worksheet p. 30
		• *Grammar and Language Links:*
		  Active and Passive Voice, Worksheet p. 43
		• *Daily Oral Grammar,* Transparency 26

maggie and milly and molly and may (p. 460) E. E. Cummings	• *Graphic Organizers for Active Reading*, Worksheet p. 31	
I Am of the Earth Anna Lee Walters (p. 464) **Early Song** Gogisgi/Carroll Arnett (p. 465)	• *Graphic Organizers for Active Reading*, Worksheet p. 32	

Antaeus (p. 468)
Borden Deal
Connections: In a Mix of Cultures, an Olio of Plantings (p. 478)
Anne Raver
	• *Reading Skills and Strategies: Reaching Struggling Readers*
	  • Selection Skill Lesson, p. 130
	• *Graphic Organizers for Active Reading*, Worksheet p. 33
		• *Grammar and Language Links:*
		  Dialect, Worksheet p. 45
		• *Daily Oral Grammar,* Transparency 27

No Questions Asked: Four Skinny Trees/Cuatro árboles flaquititos (p. 482) Sandra Cisneros *translated by* Elena Poniatowska	The **No Questions Asked** feature provides students with an unstructured opportunity to practice reading strategies using a selection that extends the theme of the collection.	
Writer's Workshop: **Observational Writing** (p. 486)		
Sentence Workshop: Using a Variety of Sentence Structures (p. 491)		• *Workshop Resources,* p. 47 • *Language Workshop CD-ROM,* Sentence Structures
Learning for Life: Saving Our Planet: **Science Research** (p. 493)		

Collection Planner

Collection Resources

- *Cross-Curricular Activities*, p. 41
- *Portfolio Management System:*
  Introduction to Portfolio Assessment, p. 1;
  Parent/Guardian Letters, p. 97
- *Formal Assessment,*
  Reading Application Test, p. 96
- *Test Generator,* Collection Test 🖸

Vocabulary, Spelling, and Decoding	Writing	Listening and Speaking, Viewing and Representing	Assessment
	• *Portfolio Management System,* Rubrics for Choices, p. 157	• *Audio CD Library,* Disc 11, Track 2 🎧 • *Portfolio Management System,* Rubrics for Choices, p. 157	• *Formal Assessment,* Selection Test, p. 84 • *Test Generator* (One-Stop Planner CD-ROM) 🖸
• *Spelling and Decoding,* Worksheet p. 19	• *Portfolio Management System,* Rubrics for Choices, p. 158	• *Audio CD Library,* Disc 11, Track 3 🎧 • *Viewing and Representing:* Fine Art Transparency 13 📽 Worksheet p. 52 • *Portfolio Management System,* Rubrics for Choices, p. 158	• *Formal Assessment,* Selection Test, p. 85 • *Standardized Test Preparation,* p. 62 • *Test Generator* (One-Stop Planner CD-ROM) 🖸
• *Words to Own,* Worksheet p. 16 • *Spelling and Decoding,* Worksheet p. 20	• *Portfolio Management System,* Rubrics for Choices, p. 159	• *Audio CD Library,* Disc 11, Track 4 🎧 • *Portfolio Management System,* Rubrics for Choices, p. 159	• *Formal Assessment,* Selection Test, p. 87 • *Standardized Test Preparation,* pp. 64, 66 • *Test Generator* (One-Stop Planner CD-ROM) 🖸
			• *Formal Assessment,* Literary Elements Test, p. 95
• *Words to Own,* Worksheet p. 17 • *Spelling and Decoding,* Worksheet p. 21	• *Portfolio Management System,* Rubrics for Choices, p. 160	• *Audio CD Library,* Disc 11, Track 5 🎧 • *Viewing and Representing:* Fine Art Transparency 14 📽 Worksheet p. 56 • *Portfolio Management System,* Rubrics for Choices, p. 160	• *Formal Assessment,* Selection Test, p. 89 • *Standardized Test Preparation,* p. 68 • *Test Generator* (One-Stop Planner CD-ROM) 🖸
	• *Portfolio Management System,* Rubrics for Choices, p. 162	• *Audio CD Library,* Disc 12, Track 2 🎧 • *Portfolio Management System,* Rubrics for Choices, p. 162	• *Formal Assessment,* Selection Test, p. 91 • *Test Generator* (One-Stop Planner CD-ROM) 🖸
	• *Portfolio Management System,* Rubrics for Choices, p. 163	• *Audio CD Library,* Disc 12, Tracks 3, 4 🎧 • *Portfolio Management System,* Rubrics for Choices, p. 163	• *Formal Assessment,* Selection Test, p. 92 • *Test Generator* (One-Stop Planner CD-ROM) 🖸
• *Words to Own,* Worksheet p. 18 • *Spelling and Decoding,* Worksheet p. 22	• *Portfolio Management System,* Rubrics for Choices, p. 164	• *Visual Connections,* Videocassette B, Segment 7 📼 • *Audio CD Library,* Disc 12, Track 5 🎧 • *Viewing and Representing:* Fine Art Transparency 15 📽 Worksheet p. 60 • *Portfolio Management System,* Rubrics for Choices, p. 164	• *Formal Assessment,* Selection Test, p. 93 • *Standardized Test Preparation,* p. 70 • *Test Generator* (One-Stop Planner CD-ROM) 🖸

	• *Workshop Resources,* p. 25
	• *Writer's Workshop 1 CD-ROM,* Observational Writing 🖸
			• *Portfolio Management System*
			  • Prewriting, p. 165
			  • Peer Editing, p. 166
			  • Assessment Rubric, p. 167

		• *Viewing and Representing,* HRW Multimedia Presentation Maker	• *Portfolio Management System,* Rubrics, p. 168

 Transparency   CD-ROM   Video   Audio CD

Collection Planner

Collection
Six

This Old Earth

i keep hearing
tree talk
water words
and i keep knowing what they mean

—Lucille Clifton

Painting of horses (c. 15,000– 13,000 B.C.), Hall of the Bulls, Lascaux (las•kō´) Caves, France. Hunter-artists covered the cave walls with paintings of deer, bulls, horses, and a unicorn-like animal. Researchers think that hunters performed dances and rites in the cave to bring success in the hunt. There is evidence that hunters may have even thrown spears at the cave paintings.

François Ducasse/Photo Researchers.

Introducing the Theme

Explain to students that each piece in this collection is about the relationship between humans and some aspect of the natural world. Point out that some selections focus on the earth's beauty and its nurturing qualities, while other selections are concerned with destructive forces of nature, such as earthquakes. Students should note how writers use descriptive details to show the many different faces of "This Old Earth."

Responding to the Quotation

? What do you think "tree talk" means? What are "water words"? [Possible responses: the sound of wind in the trees; the sound of leaves rustling as squirrels run along a branch; the sound of waves or a waterfall.] What might the speaker be suggesting when she says, "and i keep knowing" what those sounds mean? [Possible response: By observing nature and using her imagination, she finds interesting and important messages in the natural world.]

Tell students that Lucille Clifton is a modern American poet.

Writing Focus: Observational Writing

The following **Work in Progress** assignments in this collection build to a culminating **Writer's Workshop** at the end of Collection 6.

• The Creation	Note details of a moment of creation (p. 425)
• Sky Woman	Observe an animal (p. 431)
• When the Earth Shakes	Describe feelings about a natural event (p. 441)
• Survive the Savage Sea	Note an admirable person's traits (p. 458)
• maggie and milly and molly and may	List sensory impressions of a place (p. 463)
• I Am of the Earth / Early Song	Personify an aspect of nature (p. 467)
• Antaeus	Record sensory details (p. 480)

Writer's Workshop: Descriptive Writing / Observational Writing (p. 486)

419

RESPONDING TO THE ART

The cave whose walls are depicted here was accidentally discovered in 1941 by young boys searching for a lost dog. These prehistoric paintings were in perfect condition when they were discovered, but changes in atmospheric conditions began to damage them soon after. The cave was closed to the public in 1963, but 20 years later, a replica (Lascaux II) was built next to it for visitors. The pigments in the cave paintings are all earth tones: red, black, yellow, and brown. The main cavern is called "The Great Hall of Bulls"; its walls are covered with bulls and horses up to 18 feet long. The paintings also include bison, stags, a bear, and an unidentified (possibly mythological) two-horned, spotted animal. Other scenes include cows, a rhinoceros, birds, and geometric designs.

Activity. Discuss what the art suggests about the cave dwellers —for example, that even the earliest known societies had an urge to communicate their experiences.

Writer's Notebook

Give students the choice of freewriting either a poem or a description or of drawing a picture of one of their favorite scenes in nature. Encourage class members to include themselves in their scenes; their creations may come from their memories or their imaginations, and students should feel free to add or change elements.

Resources

Portfolio Management System
- Introduction to Portfolio Assessment, p. 1
- Parent/Guardian Letters, p. 97

Formal Assessment
- Reading Application Test, p. 96

Test Generator
- Collection Test

Cross-Curricular Activities
- Teaching Notes, p. 41

Selection Readability

This Annotated Teacher's Edition provides a summary of each selection in the student book. Following each Summary heading, you will find one, two, or three small icons. These icons indicate, in an approximate sense, the reading level of the selection.

■ One icon indicates that the selection is easy.

■■ Two icons indicate that the selection is on an intermediate reading level.

■■■ Three icons indicate that the selection is challenging.

OBJECTIVES

1. Read and interpret the poem
2. Identify refrain and analyze its effect
3. Monitor comprehension
4. Express understanding through observational and creative writing or a choral reading

SKILLS

Literary
• Identify and analyze refrain

Reading
• Monitor comprehension

Writing
• Collect ideas for an observational essay
• Write a hymn of praise

Speaking/Listening
• Perform a choral reading

Viewing/Representing
• Identify and interpret forms in a painting (ATE)

Planning

• **Traditional Schedule**
  Lesson Plans Including Strategies for English-Language Learners

• **One-Stop Planner**
  CD-ROM with Test Generator

Make the Connection

Like a Mother's Love

This "sermon" is based on the Biblical account of creation found in the book of Genesis. Notice that the preacher speaks of God as someone who shares our need for love. Notice also that he compares God's care for his human creation to a mother's love for her baby.

Sermons are meant to be heard. With your classmates, read the first four lines aloud. Then, as you read the rest of the poem, imagine yourself in a crowded church hearing this sermon about how the world began.

Reading Skills and Strategies

Dialogue with the Text

As you read "The Creation," keep a sheet of paper next to the book so that you can record your thoughts and feelings. One student's comments appear on the first page as an example.

go.hrw.com
LE0 7-6

Elements of Literature

Refrain: You Can Say That Again

You often hear phrases or verses repeated in poems, sermons, speeches, and songs. (Think of some of your favorite songs.) The lines that keep coming up are called the **refrain.** The refrain is often used to build rhythm, but it can also be used to emphasize the main theme of the work. A live audience often joins in with the refrain.

This dialogue, known as **call and response,** was common in many Southern churches after the Civil War and is still practiced in some churches today. In call and response the church leader strives to instruct as well as spiritually uplift the congregation (the audience), and the congregation responds verbally. You could say the congregation is responding with a refrain to the leader's call.

Look for the refrain in "The Creation," and imagine the effect if the whole congregation repeated the creator's words.

> **A** refrain is a group of words repeated at intervals in a poem, song, or speech.
>
> *For more on Refrain, see the Handbook of Literary Terms.*

  Resources: Print and Media

Reading
• *Graphic Organizers for Active Reading,* p. 27
• *Audio CD Library*
  Disc 11, Track 2

Assessment
• *Formal Assessment,* p. 84
• *Portfolio Management System,* p. 157
• *Test Generator (One-Stop Planner CD-ROM)*

Internet
• go.hrw.com (keyword: LE0 7-6)

The Creation

James Weldon Johnson

And God stepped out on space,
And he looked around and said:
I'm lonely—
I'll make me a world.

5 And far as the eye of God could see
Darkness covered everything,
Blacker than a hundred midnights
Down in a cypress° swamp.

Then God smiled,
10 And the light broke,
And the darkness rolled up on one side,
And the light stood shining on the other,
And God said: That's good!

Then God reached out and took the light in His hands,
15 And God rolled the light around in His hands
Until He made the sun;
And He set that sun a-blazing in the heavens.
And the light that was left from making the sun
God gathered it up in a shining ball
20 And flung it against the darkness,
Spangling the night with the moon and stars.
Then down between
The darkness and the light
He hurled the world;
25 And God said: That's good! **B**

Then God himself stepped down—
And the sun was on His right hand,
And the moon was on His left;
The stars were clustered about His head,
30 And the earth was under His feet.
And God walked, and where He trod
His footsteps hollowed the valleys out
And bulged the mountains up.

8. **cypress:** type of evergreen tree.

Dialogue with the Text

The use of the word "on" is not what you would expect.

What is a cypress swamp? After finding out what a cypress swamp is and rereading this section, I could almost feel the darkness overcoming me.

That is a powerful picture.

I am finding the inconsistencies in the portrayal of God's size distracting and confusing.

Cheryl Testa

—Cheryl Testa
William T. Rogers Middle School
Kings Park, New York

THE CREATION 421

Summary ■

This free-verse poem depicts God's creation of the universe. Lonely in dark and empty space, God smiles and creates light. He makes the light into sun, moon, and stars, and he places the earth between the light and the darkness. Then, he creates mountains and valleys, the seven seas, rain, plants, and animals. Still lonely, he creates humankind by shaping clay into his own image and breathing life into it.

Resources ———

Listening
Audio CD Library
A dramatic reading of this poem is provided in the *Audio CD Library*:
• Disc 11, Track 2

A Reading Skills and Strategies
Dialogue with the Text
Have students jot down their reactions to God's first spoken words. [Possible responses: surprise at God's feeling lonely or at his using the colloquial "I'll make me a world."] Have students continue to note responses and questions throughout their reading.

B Elements of Literature
Refrain
? Point out that l. 25 is an exact repetition of l. 13. What is the effect of the repetition? [Possible responses: It emphasizes God's pleasure in his creation; it helps readers remember the lines; it suggests a call and response dialogue, in which the audience participates in the reading of the poem.]

Reaching All Students

Struggling Readers
Like all narrative poems, "The Creation" tells a story. Call students' attention to the poem's "fictional" elements: plot, characters, setting, and theme. Students can then choose partners and use their notes to retell the poem's story in their own words. Students might take turns reading passages and having a partner pantomime the action to bring the lines to life.

English Language Learners
This poem includes a number of vivid verbs, such as *flung, spangling, hurled, batted*. Have pairs of students jot down unfamiliar verbs and then use context clues to figure out their meanings. Students can check their work in the dictionary. Finally, partners can quiz each other until each student has learned the new verbs.

Advanced Learners
Tell students that "The Creation" is a retelling of the first story in the Bible (Genesis 1:1–31). First, have students read this chapter of Genesis. Then, ask students to consider how Johnson's poem is similar to and different from the narrative in the Bible. Students can write brief essays comparing and contrasting these two versions of the creation story.

A Appreciating Language

Using the Dash

❓ Point out to students that Johnson uses dashes (—) at the end of some lines. What signal does the dash give to the reader? [Possible response: It indicates that the reader should pause, even in the middle of a sentence, to emphasize the action.] Ask students to consider how the lines would be read if they ended with a period.

B Critical Thinking

Analyzing Repetition

❓ Why do you think Johnson presents the image of falling rain twice? [Possible response: The repetition suggests that the rains lasted for a long time and were necessary for the grass to sprout (l. 42).]

C Elements of Literature

Parallelism

❓ Explain that parallelism is the repetition of a grammatical structure. Have students identify the parallelism in this stanza. [Possible responses: grass sprouted, flowers blossomed, pine tree pointed.] What is the effect of the repetition? [It emphasizes the actions; it makes the lines easier to remember; it gives the lines a musical quality when they are read aloud.]

D Elements of Literature

Refrain

❓ What effect is created by the change in refrain in l. 69? [Possible responses: The change emphasizes the significance, to God, of the creation of humans; the change also catches the reader's attention—an important device when the poem is read aloud.]

E Reading Skills and Strategies

Dialogue with the Text

Ask students for their reactions to this description of God's creation of humans. [Possible responses: Unlike the creation of the rest of the world, it comes after God has "thought and thought," and humans are created in God's "own image." Humankind's creation is compared with a mother's care for her baby.]

Then He stopped and looked and saw
35   That the earth was hot and barren.
So God stepped over to the edge of the world

A And He spat out the seven seas—
He batted His eyes, and the lightnings flashed—.
He clapped His hands, and the thunders rolled—

B And the waters above the earth came
40   down,
The cooling waters came down.

Then the green grass sprouted,
And the little red flowers blossomed,
The pine tree pointed his finger to the sky,
45   And the oak spread out his arms,
C The lakes cuddled down in the hollows of the ground,
And the rivers ran down to the sea;
And God smiled again,
And the rainbow appeared,
50   And curled itself around His shoulder.

Then God raised His arm and He waved His hand
Over the sea and over the land,
And He said: Bring forth! Bring forth!
And quicker than God could drop His hand,
55   Fishes and fowls
And beasts and birds
Swam the rivers and the seas,
Roamed the forests and the woods,
And split the air with their wings.
60   And God said: That's good!

Then God walked around,
And God looked around
On all that He had made.
He looked at His sun,
65   And He looked at His moon,
And He looked at His little stars;

He looked on His world
With all its living things,
D And God said: I'm lonely still.

70   Then God sat down—
On the side of a hill where He could think;
By a deep, wide river He sat down;
With His head in His hands,
God thought and thought,
75   Till He thought: I'll make me a man!

Up from the bed of the river
God scooped the clay;
And by the bank of the river
He kneeled Him down;
80   And there the great God Almighty
E Who lit the sun and fixed it in the sky,
Who flung the stars to the most far corner of the night,
Who rounded the earth in the middle of His hand;
This Great God,
85   Like a mammy bending over her baby,
Kneeled down in the dust
Toiling over a lump of clay
Till He shaped it in His own image;

Then into it He blew the breath of life,
90   And man became a living soul.
Amen. Amen.

The Creation by Aaron Douglas.
The Howard University Gallery of Art, Washington, D.C.

422   THIS OLD EARTH

Crossing the Curriculum

Music

Tell students that "The Creation" was published originally in a collection called *God's Trombones*. In his preface to that volume, Johnson wrote of a preacher who had the voice of a trombone, "the instrument possessing above all others the power to express the wide and varied range of emotions encompassed by the human voice—and with greater amplitude. He intoned, he moaned, he pleaded—he blared, he crashed, he thundered. I sat fascinated." After sharing this quotation with students, invite them to listen to music featuring the trombone—for instance, Aaron Copland's *Fanfare for the Common Man* or the song "Seventy-Six Trombones" from *The Music Man*. Then, have students discuss how hearing the instrument enriches their appreciation of Johnson's description of preachers' voices. Does hearing "The Creation" read aloud remind students of the sound of the trombone? Why or why not?

THE CREATION **423**

RESPONDING TO THE ART

An acclaimed visual artist of the Harlem Renaissance, **Aaron Douglas** (1899–1979) was asked by James Weldon Johnson to illustrate "The Creation" in the 1927 edition of *God's Trombones,* a collection of Johnson's literary works. The key elements of Douglas's distinctive style are apparent here. Many of Douglas's paintings feature circles, triangles, rectangles, and squares. A striking tension occurs between the soft, flowing shapes and the flat, angular figures (often shown in silhouette). This juxtaposition suggests the dual influences of Cubism and African sculpture.

Activity

1. **What do you think the hand and the human figure represent?** [Possible responses: the hand of God; the first human being.]

2. **What other forms can you identify?** [Possible responses: a plant, mountains, moons or suns, a body of water, brown earth, rainbow, sky.]

3. **Do you think that Douglas's simple geometric forms are an appropriate illustration for "The Creation"? Explain.** [Some students may answer yes, because the painting reflects the simplicity of a newly created world; the painting also includes images from the poem and, like the poem, focuses on the creation of humankind. Other students may say no, because the softness of some of the colors does not reflect the vibrancy and rhythmic quality of the poem.]

Listening to Music

"He's Got the Whole World in His Hands," a gospel song

Like many other ethnic groups, African Americans have given Bible stories, sermons, and religious music their own cultural stamp. The folk songs known as spirituals were an expression of slave life in the South. These songs convey not only religious faith but also the slaves' deep longing for freedom. From the spirituals and the powerful hymns of revival meetings came the gospel tradition that would later incorporate aspects of jazz, blues, and even rock-and-roll. Many popular performers, including Aretha Franklin, trace their musical roots to the gospels sung in their churches.

Activity

After students have read "The Creation," have them listen to the gospel song "He's Got the Whole World in His Hands" and discuss what the two works have in common. Then, invite interested students to work in small groups to turn Johnson's poem into a gospel song.

MAKING MEANINGS

First Thoughts

1. Possible responses: uplifted, joyful, entertained, excited, awe-struck.

Shaping Interpretations

2. Possible response: God has no one like himself for companionship.

3. Possible response: He smiles to create light. He rolls light into balls of sun, moon, and stars. He hurls the moon, stars, and earth into place. His footsteps create mountains and valleys. He spits, blinks, and claps to create oceans, lightning and thunder, and rain; he then creates vegetation, lakes, and rivers. His smile creates a rainbow. By raising his arm and crying "Bring forth!" he creates animals. Still lonely, he thinks about what to do. Out of clay he shapes humans, lovingly and in his own image.

4. Possible responses: Students may be surprised by a maternal portrayal of an apparently male God. They may suggest that the image emphasizes God's special tenderness and protective feelings toward the creature he makes in his own image. In contrast to a "mammy," a scientist might seem unemotional.

5. Possible response: The refrain gives the poem a musical quality and suggests a congregation's response to a preacher's sermon. It highlights God's loneliness and his pleasure in his newly created world.

6. Possible responses: It suggests that even after his creation of the world, God needed human companionship; that humans should cherish the natural world, because they are part of its creation.

MEET THE WRITER

"Sermons in Verse"

James Weldon Johnson (1871–1938) was born in Florida shortly after the Civil War. He became a writer and a successful song-writer, professor of literature, journalist, lawyer, and diplomat. He served as U.S. consul in Venezuela and Nicaragua and later headed the NAACP, a civil rights organization.

Johnson began to write down sermons after attending a late-evening worship service in Kansas City. He said:

❝ He [the minister] appeared to be a bit self-conscious . . . and started to preach a formal sermon from a formal text. The congregation sat apathetic and dozing. He sensed that he was losing his audience and his opportunity. Suddenly he closed the Bible, stepped out from behind the pulpit, and began to preach. He started intoning the old folk-sermon that begins with the creation of the world and ends with Judgment Day. He was at once a changed man, free, at ease, and masterful. The change in the congregation was instantaneous. An electric current ran through the crowd. It was in a moment alive and quivering; and all the while the preacher held it in the palm of his hand. ❞

Before the preacher had finished, Johnson was jotting down notes for "The Creation."

MAKING MEANINGS

First Thoughts

[connect]

1. How would you feel if you'd just heard this sermon preached to you? Check your reading notes for ideas.

Shaping Interpretations

[speculate]

2. In your opinion, why in line 69 does the preacher say God is still lonely?

[summarize]

3. List all the things God creates in this sermon and describe how he creates them. How is the creation of man different?

Reading Check

a. According to this poem, why does God decide to make the world?

b. God is not just spirit in this poem; he is shown taking action. What are three of his actions?

c. God smiles twice. What does each smile bring into being?

d. Why does God decide to create a man?

Reading Check

a. He is lonely.

b. Possible responses: He rolls light in his hands to make the sun, moon, and stars. He walks heavily to create mountains and valleys. He shapes clay to make humans.

c. Light; a rainbow

d. He is still lonely in his new world.

Assessing Learning

Check Test: True-False

1. When God smiles, darkness covers everything. [False]

2. God creates mountains and valleys by walking. [True]

3. God says, "That's good!" about his creations. [True]

4. God creates all creatures in his own image. [False]

4. What is your reaction to line 85, where God is compared to a "mammy bending over her baby"? (How would it be different if God were compared to a scientist?)

5. What effect do you think the **refrain** has on the poem? What idea does it highlight?

6. If "The Creation" is a sermon, what lesson does it convey to you?

Connecting with the Text

7. In the poem, God keeps saying of his creations, "That's good!" Do you share that feeling about those creations? Explain.

Extending the Text

8. Every culture is interested in the question of how the world began. What other "pictures" of this great beginning do you know about?

Connecting with the Text

7. Possible responses: Yes, the natural features of earth, the plants, animals, mountains, and valleys are beautiful; no, the natural world contains both good and bad.

Extending the Text

8. Encourage students to share creation stories they have read, heard, or studied.

Grading Timesaver

Rubrics for each Choices assignment appear on p. 157 in the *Portfolio Management System*.

CHOICES: Building Your Portfolio

Writer's Notebook

1. Collecting Ideas for Observational Writing

Choose a "moment of creation" to observe—something you can actually watch as it comes into being. Record your observations as exactly as you can. Pay attention to what you see, hear, smell, taste, and feel. If you've picked a slow-moving event, such as seeds sprouting, you might record daily observations in a log or chart.

Creative Writing

2. And That's Good, Too

Write a hymn of praise for the world. List what's good about the world and use "That's good!" as a refrain. Try other techniques used in "The Creation," such as repeating key phrases (line 53: "Bring forth! Bring forth!") and using "customized" verbs. (In line 33, God didn't *form* the mountains; he "*bulged* the mountains *up*.")

Choral Reading

3. All Together Now

Get together with a group of classmates and try different ways of performing the poem. Here are some choices to consider:

- Everybody reads the whole poem in unison.
- Two groups alternate reading lines or whole verses.
- One person reads some of the lines and the group reads all the other lines.
- Use musical accompaniment for dramatic effect.
- Use lighting for dramatic effect.

Decide on the most effective way to present the poem, and perform it for the class or for a group of your parents and friends.

CHOICES: Building Your Portfolio

1. **Writer's Notebook** Students may have had opportunities to watch a house being built, a meal being prepared, or a mural being painted on a neighborhood wall.

2. **Creative Writing** Students may choose just a small part of the world with which they are familiar, such as their neighborhood. Encourage the use of vivid verbs.

3. **Choral Reading** You might organize students into small groups for this activity. As they think about musical accompaniment, remind them that Johnson titled his collection *God's Trombones*. Students might adapt the concept of a preacher whose audience (the other readers) responds to and repeats his or her words at intervals.

Making the Connections

Connecting to the Theme: "This Old Earth"

After students have read the poem, discuss how it illuminates the collection theme. How does Johnson's God feel about the earth he has created? Does the poem convey a positive, negative, or mixed impression of the earth? Have students list images from the poem that they find striking or memorable. Students can keep these images and questions in mind as they read "Sky Woman," an origin myth of the Seneca.

Before You Read

SKY WOMAN

Make the Connection

Answer Me This

Since ancient times, people have told stories about the creation of the world and of living things. All over the world, people have made up stories to answer puzzling questions like, Who are we, and where did we come from? Why is there a blue roof over the earth? How did all the different animals come to be?

Quickwrite

Suppose you lived thousands of years ago, before there was such a thing as science to suggest answers to your questions about the natural world. What are some of the things you might have wondered about? List at least five questions.

Elements of Literature

Origin Myths

"Sky Woman" is an **origin myth** of the Seneca (see Background). This is the story the Seneca told many years ago to explain the beginnings of the earth, of animals, and of good and evil.

Reading Skills and Strategies

Recalling with Chronology: It's as Easy as 1, 2, 3

Keeping track of **chronology,** the time order of events, is one way to follow the action in a text. You might want to read this myth with a partner and take turns writing down key events in the order in which they happened.

It's easy to follow chronological order in a story. Just take these steps:

- Ask yourself, "*When* did each important event happen? What happened *before* that event? What happened *after?*"

- Look for words or phrases like *first, next, during,* and *at last* that signal when events happened.

> **A**n **origin myth** is an imaginative story that explains how something in the world came to be.
>
> *For more on Myth, see pages 496–499 and the Handbook of Literary Terms.*

 go.hrw.com
LE0 7-6

Background

Literature and Social Studies

The Seneca were one of five Native American nations that united to form the Iroquois League more than a century before the first European colonies were established in North America. The League was centered in what is now New York State. For a time its territory stretched north to Canada, east to Maine, west to Michigan, and south to Tennessee.

As you will see in this myth, women played an influential role in the life of the Seneca, as they did in the lives of other Iroquois peoples.

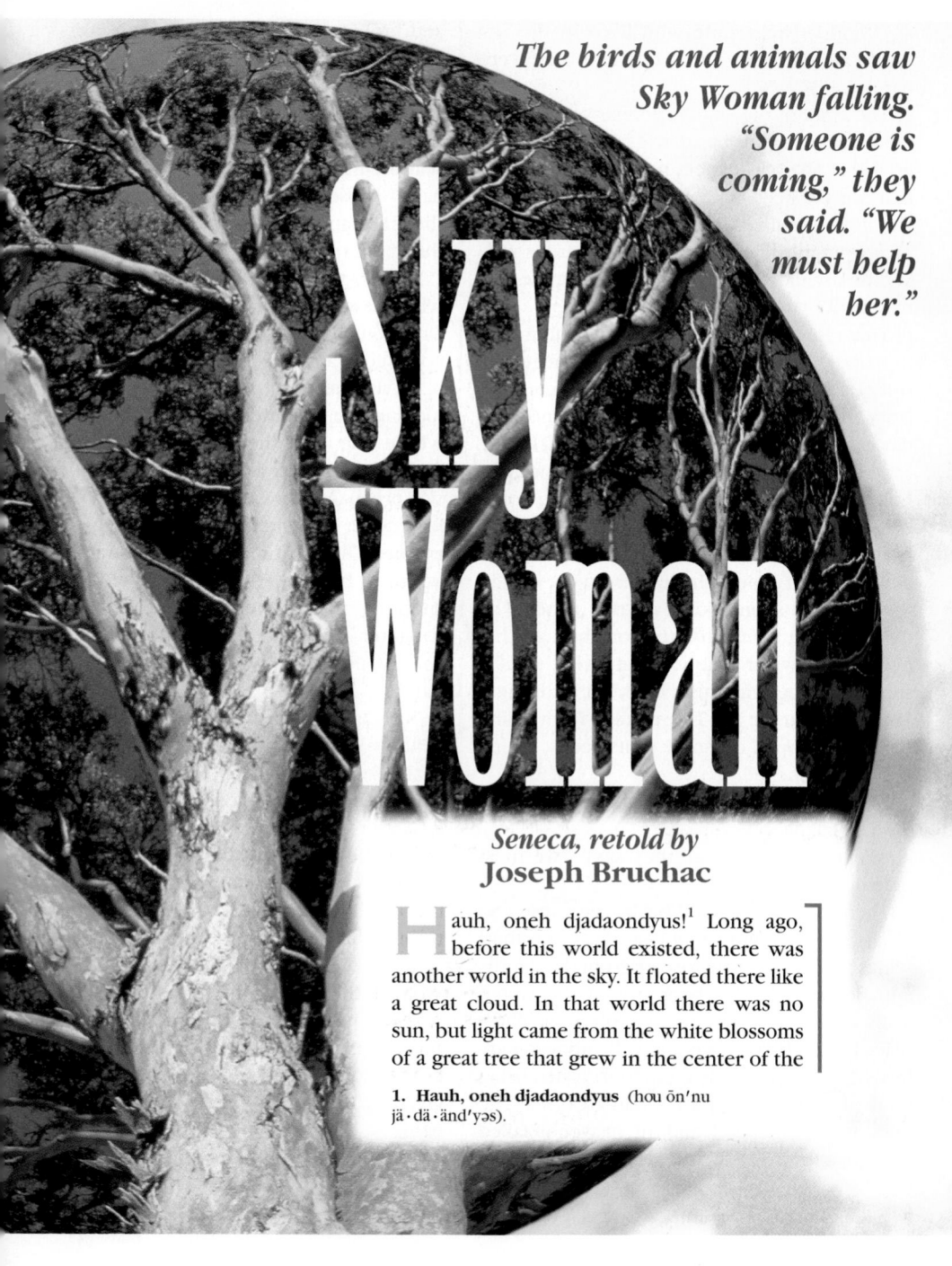

The birds and animals saw Sky Woman falling. "Someone is coming," they said. "We must help her."

Sky Woman

Seneca, retold by
Joseph Bruchac

Hauh, oneh djadaondyus![1] Long ago, before this world existed, there was another world in the sky. It floated there like a great cloud. In that world there was no sun, but light came from the white blossoms of a great tree that grew in the center of the

1. **Hauh, oneh djadaondyus** (hou ōn′nu jä · dä · änd′yəs).

SKY WOMAN **427**

Summary ▪

Before the world existed, people lived in the Sky World. There, a huge tree gave light and food. After dreaming that the tree fell, the chief ordered it uprooted. His pregnant young bride fell through the hole where the roots had been buried. With the help of animals, she landed safely on the world below, a place made up only of water. The earth from the bottom of the sea became a continent. Later, Sky Woman gave birth to a daughter.

Disobeying her mother, Sky Woman's daughter traveled west and gave birth to the gentle Good Mind and to the harsh Flint, whose birth she did not survive. His grandmother, Sky Woman, soon despaired of Flint's evil deeds and left the earth to watch over the Good Mind from the moon. The Good Mind fought Flint and cast him out, but because Flint's evil thoughts and deeds remained in the world, humans must guard against his influence.

Resources ▪

Listening
Audio CD Library
A dramatic reading of "Sky Woman" is provided in the *Audio CD Library:*
• Disc 11, Track 3

Selection Assessment
Formal Assessment
• Selection Test, p. 85

Test Generator
• Selection Test

Viewing and Representing
Fine Art Transparency
A fine art transparency of Helen Hardin's *Prayers of a Blue Corn Mother* can help students appreciate this origin myth.
• Transparency 13
• Worksheet, p. 52

Reaching All Students

Struggling Readers
Recalling with Chronology was introduced on p. 426. For a lesson directly tied to this selection that teaches students to recall with chronology by using a strategy called Retellings, see the *Reading Skills and Strategies* binder:
• Selection Skill Lesson, p. 182

English Language Learners
Encourage readers to visualize the Sky World, the Sky Tree, the Sky Land, the Good Mind, and Flint (students may need to look up *flint* in the dictionary). Ask students to point out other imaginary elements in the story, such as talking animals and the explanation of the "face" of the moon. For additional strategies to supplement instruction for these students, see
• *Lesson Plans Including Strategies for English-Language Learners*

Advanced Learners
Invite students to reflect on the similarities and differences between the events depicted in "Sky Woman" and in "The Creation." They might pay special attention to the role of animals in each narrative.

Origin Myth

? What details in the first two paragraphs indicate that the story is an origin myth? [Possible responses: The world floats, and light and food come from one source, a tree. The chief's wife and child are "destined to bring life to a new land."]

B Critical Thinking

Interpreting

? Why does the chief, after dreaming about the fallen Sky Tree, order it to be uprooted? [Possible response: Dreams were thought to be a message from the Creator. Therefore, by bringing the dream to life, the chief is following the Creator's wishes.]

C Reading Skills and Strategies

Recalling with Chronology

Ask students to list the events of the earth's creation in chronological order. [Possible response: Sky Woman falls through the hole in the Sky Land. Birds catch her, and she stands on the back of the turtle. Many animals try to bring up earth from the ocean floor; several of them die in the attempt. Finally, the muskrat puts earth on the turtle's back, and the earth grows to become a continent.]

D Struggling Readers

Finding Details

? What part of nature is explained by the scattering of the seeds? [Possible response: the origin of trees and other plants]

E Critical Thinking

Hypothesizing

? How is Sky Woman's daughter punished for disobeying her mother? [Possible response: She gives birth to twins, one gentle and one harsh, and then she dies.]

F Vocabulary Note

Compound Words

? Some compounds are made up of two nouns linked as one word. What compound word is in this line? [grandmother] What other compound word appears in this column? [footprints, l. 7]

Sky World. The people who lived in the Sky World ate the fruit of that tree and they were happy.

The chief of the Sky World married a young woman. Soon after he married her, he discovered that she was expecting a child. Since he had not yet been with her, this angered him. He did not realize that she had become pregnant from inhaling his breath and that his wife and their child were destined to bring life to a new land.

That night, the chief had a powerful dream. In that dream he saw the great tree lying on its side. Dreams were considered to be a message from the Creator. So, when the next morning came, he gave orders for the Sky Tree to be uprooted. When this was done, it made a great hole in the Sky Land. Through that hole could be seen a place far below where there was nothing but water, and in that water birds and animals swam about. The light from the hole in the Sky Land shone down on that water. The chief's young wife came to look through that hole at the water below. Then, whether she slipped or she was pushed, she fell through. She grasped at the Sky Tree to keep from falling but only stripped off some of its seeds, which she held as she fell.

Below her, the birds and animals saw Sky Woman falling.

"Someone is coming," they said. "We must help her."

Then the wide-winged birds, the geese and swans, flew up and caught her between their wings. The great turtle rose up from the depths and floated with his back out of the water. Thus, when Sky Woman came down, she had a place to stand. The birds and fish and water animals then began to dive down to try to bring up earth from the bottom of that great sea. The duck and the pickerel[2] and the beaver all failed and floated up dead. At last the muskrat tried

2. **pickerel** (pik′ər·əl): small freshwater fish.

428 THIS OLD EARTH

---

and brought up a handful of earth in its paw. When that earth was placed on the great turtle's back, it grew and grew until it became a continent. Sky Woman began to walk on that new earth. As she walked in a great circle, she scattered the seeds which she still held in her hand. Those seeds fell into her footprints, and the trees and other plants began to grow on the new earth.

Soon Sky Woman gave birth to a daughter, who grew to womanhood almost overnight. Sky Woman cautioned her daughter that she could go in any direction she wished except toward the west. But when her mother was not looking, the daughter walked toward the west, where she met the West Wind. When Sky Woman's daughter returned to her mother, she was pregnant. Sky Woman was worried, for she feared her daughter was too young to be a mother. Then, as time went on, a strange thing began to happen. Two voices could be heard speaking inside the belly of Sky Woman's daughter. The voices were those of her twin sons. One voice was gentle, and one was harsh.

"Let us be born in the right way," said the gentle voice.

"No," said the harsh voice, "I will push my way out here on the side."

Then the two boys were born. The one with the gentle voice was the Good Mind, and he was born in the normal way. But the one with the harsh voice was Flint, and he thrust out through his mother's side, killing her.

With the help of his grandmother, Sky Woman, the Good Mind buried his mother. He watered her grave and cared for it, and from that grave grew the squash, the beans, and the corn. Those were gifts for the people to come, given by his mother, who was now part of the earth.

The Good Mind then went about the earth, doing things which would be good for the people. He made useful trees, like the oak and

---

Making the Connections

Connecting to the Theme: "This Old Earth"

After students have finished reading the myth, invite them to discuss how it relates to the collection theme. For instance, students might consider the role of nature—plants and animals, as well as humans—in the creation of a continent. The class might discuss why several animals died while trying to bring up the earth from the sea and in what way cooperation between animals helped establish a continent.

Cultural Connections

Traditional tales in Native American cultures have been passed down orally through the generations. Some literary elements in these tales lend themselves to retelling. For example, the vivid images and dramatic action make the story entertaining, and the use of familiar natural objects (sky, trees, water, seeds) and animals also allows listeners to relate the story to their own world.

the chestnut. Flint followed behind him and made briers[3] and poisonous plants. The Good Mind made berries of all kinds. Flint covered those berry bushes with sharp thorns. The Good Mind created such animals as the deer and the rabbit, animals which would feed the people. Flint produced loose poisonous snakes and biting insects. The Good Mind made fresh water which was clear and good to drink. Flint muddied the water and made it foul smelling.

The Good Mind's grandmother, Sky Woman, had been filled with sorrow since her daughter's death. Seeing all the bad things being done by Flint, she decided to leave the world.

"You will see me in the sky at night," she said

3. **briers** (brī'ərz): thorny bushes.

to her grandson the Good Mind. Then she left the earth. To this day, you can see her face, that of a caring grandmother, looking down from the Moon.

Finally the Good Mind could stand it no longer. He fought with his brother Flint and cast him out of the world. To this day, though, Flint's works and his bad thoughts remain in the world. They are in the mind of every person, just as every person also holds the good thoughts of the Good Mind. So we must always be aware of the thoughts that are in our minds to be sure that we do good things and not bad. Da neho.[4] So the story goes.

4. **Da neho** (dä nä'hō).

G Elements of Literature
Origin Myth
? What aspect of the world is explained by this passage in the origin myth? [Possible response: the origin of both "positive/good" and "negative/evil" in the world.]

BROWSING IN THE FILES
About the Author. Bruchac, who is part Abenaki, is well-known as a storyteller. In addition to the collections he has written, he performs his stories orally; some of these stories are available on tapes from his company, Good Mind Records. He says of his writing that it "is informed by several key sources. One of these is nature, another is the Native American experience.... I like to work outside, in the earth-mother's soil, with my hands ... but maintain my life as an academic for a couple of reasons: it gives me time to write (sometimes) and it gives me a chance to share my insights into the beautiful and all too fragile world of human life and living things we have been granted." Bruchac has had a varied career as a writing and literature teacher at Skidmore College, at Comstock Prison, and in Ghana.

MEET THE WRITER

"Roots as Deep as the Rocks"

Joseph Bruchac (1942–   ) is a poet of Native American ancestry. He is also an editor who has put together two excellent anthologies of poetry. *Songs from This Earth on Turtle's Back* (1983) is a comprehensive collection of contemporary Native American poetry. *Breaking Silence* (1984), a collection of contemporary Asian American poetry, won an American Book Award in 1984. Bruchac also started a small press, the Greenfield Review Press, which has been a leading publisher of Native American writers. He himself has written, among many other books, several collections of Iroquois folk tales.

Bruchac believes that the theme of most Native American literature is survival—of a people, of a culture, of a land. He says:

❝ Today, as we question Pentagon budgets, drug-ridden classrooms, and PCB-filled streams, many of us ask if the secret of surviving may be found not in the dreams of the future but in the lessons of the past.

But what is the true American past? How far back does the past go in a 'nation of immigrants'? One group of 'Americans' has roots as deep as the rocks. They go back, at the very least, thirty thousand years. As descendants of those oldest 'Americans,' American Indian writers may be better equipped to speak of the American past and to draw from it lessons relating to survival. ❞

More Roots

You can find more stories rooted in the past in Bruchac's *Iroquois Stories* (Greenfield Review).

FROM THE EDITOR'S DESK
We interviewed Joseph Bruchac at his home on a rainy day in Saratoga Springs, New York. Before he was to demonstrate the beating of his drum, we discovered him drying it with a hair dryer! (Native Americans had to dry their drums by fire to get a deep rich sound.)

SKY WOMAN 429

Assessing Learning

Check Test: Short Answer
1. According to the myth, where did light originally come from? [the flowers of a large tree in the sky]
2. Why is the Sky Tree uprooted? [The chief sees it lying on its side in a dream.]
3. How does Sky Woman survive her fall? [Animals in the world below catch and support her.]
4. Where does Sky Woman warn her daughter not to go? [toward the west]

5. Why does Sky Woman leave the earth? [She dislikes Flint's evil ways.]

Standardized Test Preparation
For practice with a standardized test format specific to this selection, see
• *Standardized Test Preparation*, p. 62
For practice in proofreading and editing, see
• *Daily Oral Grammar*, Transparency 24

MAKING MEANINGS

First Thoughts

1. Possible responses: Her angry husband pushed her; since the chief loved her, she must have fallen after leaning over too far.

Shaping Interpretations

2. Possible questions: How was the earth created? How did plants, animals, and humans come to inhabit the earth? Why is there evil in the world?
3. Possible response: The Seneca probably used parts of these animals for food, clothing, and shelter.
4. Possible response: Sky Woman's daughter had two sons, one good and one evil.

Connecting with the Text

5. Possible responses: Nature—floods, forest fires, droughts. Human minds—jealousy, spite, hatred, meanness.

MAKING MEANINGS

First Thoughts

[speculate]

1. The story tells us that Sky Woman "slipped or . . . was pushed" through the great hole in the Sky Land. Which do you think it was? Why?

Shaping Interpretations

[compare]

2. This **origin myth** answers several questions people might once have asked about the earth and human behavior. What are these questions? How do they compare with the ones you wrote for the Quickwrite on page 426?

[infer]

3. Think about the creatures that helped Sky Woman on her journey down to the water world. Why would these specific animals have been important to the Seneca?

[explain]

4. How does the myth explain the origin of good and evil?

Connecting with the Text

[connect]

5. The story states that "Flint's works and his bad thoughts remain in the world" and gives several examples of these works: briers, poisonous plants, thorns, poisonous snakes. Can you think of other examples of "Flint's works," both in nature and "in the mind of every person"?

Reading Check

Draw a storyboard for this myth, a series of pictures illustrating the myth's **major events**. Arrange the events in **chronological order**—the order in which they happened. Share your storyboard with the class.

430 THIS OLD EARTH

Reading Check
Storyboards might vary somewhat but should include, in this order: Sky Woman's fall, the creation of the earth, the daughter's journey to the west, the birth of the Good Mind and Flint, Sky Woman's departure for the moon, and the Good Mind's fight with Flint.

Writer's Notebook

1. Collecting Ideas for Observational Writing

Cat in the back yard. Tail twitches. Head jerks to the right—she sees a butterfly. Crouches, leaps, and misses.

Animals play a big part in Seneca life. List the animals you come across in your own daily life—a pet, a wild bird, a farm animal, even an insect or rodent. Pick one animal from your list, and observe it for at least fifteen minutes. Record exactly what you see and, if possible, what you hear. What does the animal look like? How does it move? What sounds does it make?

Creative Writing

2. My Side of the Story

How do you think Sky Woman would tell her own story? Write "The Autobiography of Sky Woman." You could include her thoughts as she falls through space, her feelings toward the creatures who rescue her, her feelings about her daughter and grandsons, and her fears about her future.

Creative Writing/ Speaking and Listening

3. And That's Why Water Is Wet: Telling a Story

Some origin myths may have arisen in response to children's questions, such as, Why is water wet? Brainstorm to come up with some why questions a four-year-old might ask grown-ups about the world. Then, pick one of your why questions and, with a classmate, role-play the grown-up telling a story to satisfy the curious child. First, write your story to answer the why. Then, rehearse and perform it for your classmates or a group of children. You might include props or pantomime.

Research/ Speaking and Listening

4. Telling Tales

Research some other Native American creation stories. For example, *Back in the Beforetime* (Macmillan), edited by Jane L. Curry, is a collection of stories told by the California Indians; *They Dance in the Sky* (Houghton Mifflin) by Jean Guard and Ray A. Williamson presents creation myths from various regions, including the Great Plains, the Southeast, and the Northwest. You can also find some Native American creation myths in *In the Beginning: Creation Stories from Around the World* (Harcourt Brace) by Virginia Hamilton. Choose one myth to tell your class. Do research in the library or on the Internet to find information about the people and region from which the tale comes. Use this information in a brief introduction to your myth. If possible, include maps and pictures to make your introduction lively.

Rubrics for each Choices assignment appear on p. 158 in the *Portfolio Management System*.

CHOICES:

Building Your Portfolio

1. **Writer's Notebook** Encourage students to remain motionless while observing an animal and to avoid interacting with it.
2. **Creative Writing** Remind students to keep their autobiographies consistent with details given in the myth. They might begin by making a chart that lists each important event and Sky Woman's reaction to it.
3. **Creative Writing/Speaking and Listening** If students have trouble thinking of questions, suggest that they look at Rudyard Kipling's *Just So Stories* for ideas. These imaginative myths, such as "How the Camel Got His Hump" and "How the Leopard Got His Spots," might prompt students to ask questions of their own. Students might work in pairs to rehearse their performances; they can alternate role-playing the adult and the child.
4. **Research/Speaking and Listening** You might organize students into pairs or small groups for this activity, so that students interested in researching a people or a region can work together. Students might collaborate on the research, then divide the tasks of preparing a rough script of the myth, drawing maps or other visual aids, and giving the oral presentation.

LANGUAGE LINK

Have students select from their portfolios pieces of writing that contain figures of speech. Tell students that figures of speech that seem very familiar are probably clichés. Have students circle any clichés they find and replace them with original comparisons and phrases.

Try It Out
Possible Answers
1. The Chief of Heaven was as mad as a Red Sox fan reading about a Yankee win in the World Series.
2. Sky Woman did not deserve any punishment, for she had been as good as a cup of cocoa on a cold day.
3. The animals were working to help Sky Woman as students do the night before exams.

Spelling
Possible Answers

silly	sillier	silliness
funny	funnier	funniest
scary	scarier	scarily
ugly	uglier	ugliness
sloppy	sloppily	sloppiness
frisky	friskier	friskiest
angry	angrily	angriest

Resources

Language
• *Grammar and Language Links*, p. 39

Spelling
For related instruction, see
• *Spelling and Decoding*, p. 19

LANGUAGE LINK   MINI-LESSON

Style: Avoiding Clichés

CLICHÉS TO AVOID

break the ice

busy as a bee

crack of dawn

clear as a bell

as quiet as a mouse

eat like a horse

on top of the world

as red as a beet

Look at the underlined phrases in these sentences. Which one seems fresher and more interesting?

> Sky Woman was <u>as beautiful as the West Wind</u>.

> Sky Woman was <u>as pretty as a picture</u>.

Both sentences contain figures of speech. The first one may be new to you: *as beautiful as the West Wind*. How beautiful is that? The surprise comparison may make you imagine several images: a field of wheat, perhaps, rippling like a sea of gold, or a cool breeze rising off the shore. For most readers the comparison in the second sentence does none of that. It's a **cliché** (klē·shā′)—a figure of speech that has lost its power because people have overused it.

Try It Out

➤ Rewrite each sentence below to replace the cliché with fresher language. Be sure to compare your rewrites with those of other students.

1. The Chief of Heaven was <u>as mad as a hornet</u>.

2. Sky Woman did not deserve any punishment, for she had been <u>as good as gold</u>.

3. The animals were <u>busy as beavers</u> helping Sky Woman.

➤ When you revise something you've written, look closely at the comparisons you've used and ask yourself, "Did I make this up, or is it something people always say?" If the latter, the phrase is probably a cliché. Replace it, if you can, with a comparison that you've never heard before.

SPELLING   HOW TO OWN A WORD

Language Handbook HELP

See Adding Prefixes and Suffixes, pages 781-782.

Adding Suffixes: Change *y* to *i*

What do these words have in common?

easy   happy   pretty   lonely   stormy

Correct: They all end with *y* preceded by a consonant. When you add a **suffix**—an ending such as *-er, -est, -ness,* or *-ly*—to most words that end with *y* preceded by a consonant, you have to follow this spelling rule: First, change the *y* to *i*; then, add the suffix.

easy	+	suffix	=	eas**ily**	eas**ier**
happy	+	suffix	=	happ**ily**	happ**iness**
lonely	+	suffix	=	lonel**ier**	lonel**iest**

Get together with a partner, and make a list of five more words that end in *y* preceded by a consonant. Then, follow the *y-to-i* rule, and add a suffix to each word. Here are two words to get you started: *silly, funny*.

432 THIS OLD EARTH

Language Link Quick Check

Rewrite each sentence below to replace the cliché with fresher language. (Possible responses are given.)

1. The people in the Sky World were as happy as clams. [The people in the Sky World were as happy as a dog on a walk in the park.]
2. The chief rose at the crack of dawn. [The chief rose as the sun first struck the clouds.]
3. When she fell through the hole, Sky Woman was scared to death. [When she fell through the hole, Sky Woman was as scared as an animal in a forest fire.]
4. The Good Mind is as wise as an owl. [The Good Mind is as wise as a Supreme Court justice.]
5. Because of Flint's cruelty, Sky Woman was at the end of her rope. [Because of Flint's cruelty, Sky Woman was at the limit of her endurance.]

Reading Skills and Strategies

Booking space on the 'Net: Used-booksellers like a page from other on-line vendors

ORGANIZING IDEAS

Sequencing: What Happens?

Organizers can be handy for putting in order the details of a narrative or an informative report. See for yourself—as you read the narratives in this collection, try using the sequencing chart below to organize "what happens."

Sequencing Chart for a Narrative

```
Main characters
      ↓
Their problem (conflict)
      ↓
Event 1
      ↓
Event 2
      ↓
Event 3
      ↓
(List other events.)
      ↓
Resolution
```

Cause and Effect: Why Things Happen

You can make some texts, especially informative reports, clearer by looking at what caused certain events to happen. Use organizers like the ones below to sort out causes and effects.

Sequencing Charts for Cause and Effect

What Happened
Earthquake occurred in Alaska.

Effect	Effect
Buildings fell.	Roads buckled.

OR

What Happened (Effect)
Port towns suffered damage in quake.

↕

Cause
Ground on coast is not solid. Soil slides.

Outlining: Finding the Skeleton

It's also helpful to **outline** the ideas in an informative text. Outlining can help you uncover the skeleton that holds the text together: its main ideas and supporting details. Here is an example of an informal outline.

Informal Outline

Earthquake occurred in
Alaska (main idea)
   Roads buckled (supporting detail)
   Houses split in two
   Earth split open
Port towns were damaged
   Waterfronts sank
   Oil tanks burned
(and so on)

Shake, Rattle, and Roll

You're about to be set down in the middle of an earthquake. Have one of these organizers ready to help you sift through the information as you read.

Apply the strategy on the next page.

OBJECTIVES

1. Appreciate the value of organizing ideas
2. Understand the uses of sequencing charts, cause-and-effect charts, and informal outlines

Reading Skills and Strategies

This feature focuses on the skill of organizing ideas. It illustrates three graphic organizers: the sequencing chart for listing events in order; the sequencing chart for linking cause and effect; and the outline for developing an organizational skeleton.

Mini-Lesson: Organizing Ideas

Have volunteers read aloud the text on p. 433. Then, ask students to think about how they organize their lockers or other crowded areas. Why is it helpful to organize things? [They can be found more easily.] Point out that organizing ideas helps the reader understand and remember information and that graphic organizers like the ones on p. 433 indicate the relationships between ideas. Ask students to explain how these organizers work. [A narrative sequencing chart lists events in order. A cause-and-effect sequencing chart relates reasons (causes) to their consequences (effects). An informal outline shows the relationship between main ideas and supporting details.] Students might develop a narrative sequencing chart for one of the selections the class has read.

Reaching All Students

Struggling Readers

Some students may be confused by the term *narrative*. Remind them that a narrative is a story. Some narratives (such as "Sky Woman") are fiction and some (such as *Survive the Savage Sea*) are nonfiction. Some *informative* texts, like "When the Earth Shakes," contain a narrative, but they also present many facts and details. Other informative texts, such as many textbooks, provide information but do not tell a story.

Advanced Readers

Have students prepare an outline of an informative text. It may be a selection from this collection, an article from a newspaper or magazine, or a chapter in a book. Students can illustrate their finished outlines with drawings or photos.

OBJECTIVES

1. Read and interpret the article
2. Track cause and effect
3. Express understanding through observational and creative writing, research/writing, or science/art
4. Identify formal and informal English and use both styles in writing
5. Understand and use new words

SKILLS

Reading
- Track cause and effect

Writing
- Collect ideas for an observational essay
- Write a research report
- Write an imaginative story

Language
- Distinguish between formal and informal English

Vocabulary
- Understand and use new words

Art
- Draw a diagram or build a model

Science
- Explain what causes earthquakes

Planning

- **Block Schedule**
  Block Scheduling Lesson Plans with Pacing Guide

- **Traditional Schedule**
  Lesson Plans Including Strategies for English-Language Learners

- **One-Stop Planner**
  CD-ROM with Test Generator

Make the Connection

Nature Comes Out Swinging

From the title "When the Earth Shakes," you can probably guess that you're going to read about one of nature's most awesome forces: earthquakes.

Quickwrite

KWL. On a blank sheet of paper, make a chart like this:

What I Know	What I Want to Know	What I Learned

With a group of classmates, brainstorm to find out what you already know and what you want to learn about earthquakes. Write your ideas in the first two columns. As you're reading, you'll fill in the What I Learned column. As you read, think about how the new information relates to what you already know. Does it make you think of any new questions?

 go.hrw.com
LEO 7-6

Reading Skills and Strategies

Tracking Cause and Effect

On page 433, you saw two kinds of charts you can use to sum up the important details in an informative essay. As you read "When the Earth Shakes," notice how clearly the author explains the causes of the earthquake and its effects. Try using one of the organizers on page 433 to sum up these causes and effects. Fill out the chart after you've finished reading.

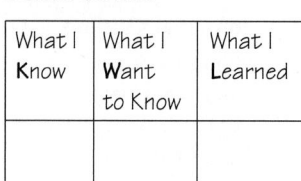

The earth at their feet was churning and crumbling and sinking away.

Preteaching Vocabulary

Words to Own

Have students read the five Words to Own and their definitions listed at the bottom of the selection pages. Students can work in pairs to write original sentences using these words correctly. Then, ask students to choose the word that best completes each sentence below.

1. The *Titanic* might not have sunk if there had been instruments capable of monitoring icebergs, like those used in _____ to record shock waves. [observatories]

2. The great ship's bow rose like a high _____ overlooking the ocean. [bluff]

3. The steel hull of the *Titanic* _____ after colliding with the iceberg. [buckled]

4. The water that night was not _____ but was as still and smooth as glass. [churning]

5. After the ship sank, _____ of wreckage floated everywhere. [particles]

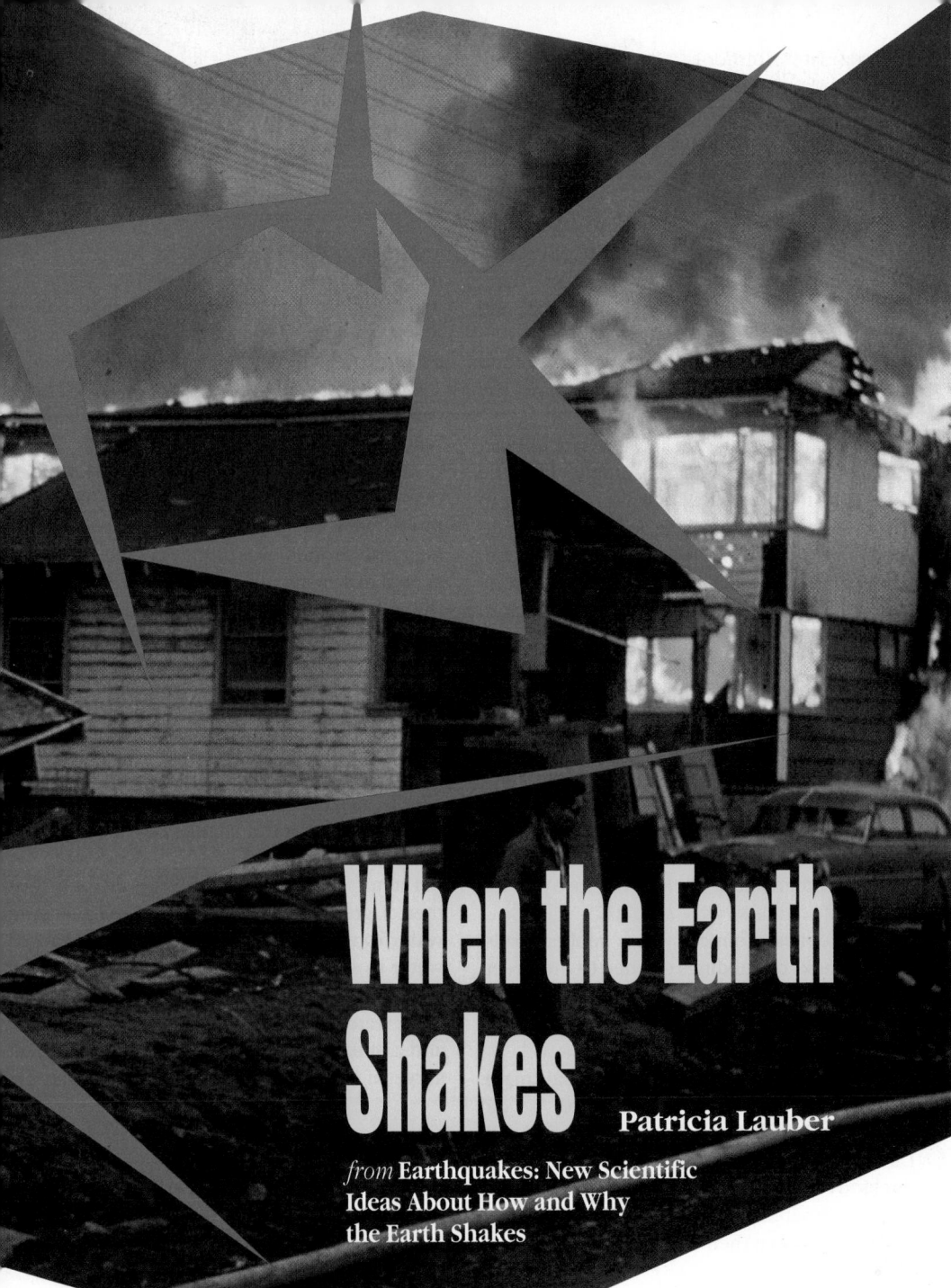

When the Earth Shakes

Patricia Lauber

from **Earthquakes: New Scientific Ideas About How and Why the Earth Shakes**

Summary ■■

This article about the causes of earth-quakes begins with an example of the effects of a quake. In 1964, a fierce earthquake shook most of Alaska, causing severe damage and dramatic changes in the state's topography: The ocean floor rose, a peninsula moved, and a mountain split apart.

What causes such catastrophes? The planet is composed of layers of rock, much of it under intense pres-sure. When the strain becomes too great, the rock shifts or snaps. Energy from the shifting or snapping rock trav-els in waves. Waves traveling in the air produce the rumbling sound of the quake, but the waves on the earth's surface are more destructive, as the effects of the Alaska quake, and many others, demonstrate.

Resources

Listening
Audio CD Library
A dramatic reading of "When the Earth Shakes" is provided in the *Audio CD Library:*
• Disc 11, Track 4

Selection Assessment
Formal Assessment
• Selection Test, p. 87
Test Generator
• Selection Test

Elements of Literature
For additional instruction on inferring the main idea, see *Literary Elements:*
• Transparency 8
• Worksheet, p. 25

Resources: Print and Media

Reading
• *Reading Skills and Strategies*
  Selection Skill Lesson, p. 186
• *Graphic Organizers for Active Reading,* p. 29
• *Words to Own,* p. 16
• *Spelling and Decoding*
  Worksheet, p. 20
• *Audio CD Library*
  Disc 11, Track 4

Elements of Literature
• *Literary Elements*
  Transparency 8
  Worksheet, p. 25

Writing and Language
• *Daily Oral Grammar*
  Transparency 25
• *Grammar and Language Links*
  Worksheet, p. 41

Assessment
• *Formal Assessment,* p. 87
• *Portfolio Management System,* p. 159
• *Standardized Test Preparation,* pp. 64, 66
• *Test Generator (One-Stop Planner CD-ROM)*

Internet
• go.hrw.com (keyword: LE0 7-6)

A Critical Thinking
Analyzing Details

After students have identified Passover and Good Friday, ask them what is ironic about the timing of the earthquake. [Possible response: These are major Jewish and Christian holidays. It is ironic that disaster should strike during a time of celebration, when people are least prepared.]

B Reading Skills and Strategies

Tracking Cause and Effect

Have students identify the cause and the effect in this paragraph. [Possible responses: The earth shook, causing a landslide. Some students may say that because the town was built on a cliff, it was especially vulnerable.] Ask the class to think about the causes of the earth's shaking and the probable effects of the landslide.

C Critical Thinking
Determining Author's Purpose

? Ask students to describe the tone of this paragraph. [Possible responses: calm, factual.] What does the tone suggest about the author's purpose? [Possible responses: She wants to report facts; she wants to inform readers about earthquakes.]

D Appreciating Language
Formal English

Point out that formal English need not be uninteresting. Draw students' attention to Lauber's use of vivid, forceful verbs, such as *roared, slid, surge, swept, flooded,* and *washed,* in this paragraph.

It was late afternoon, March 27, 1964. Above Alaska the sky was the color of lead, and in some places a light snow fell. Anchorage, the biggest city, lay quiet, for this gray day was both Good Friday and the eve of Passover.

A Schools were empty. Many shops and offices had closed early, and at 5:30 most people were home. Outside, the air was raw, the sky dark. Inside, lights glowed, furnaces hummed, and pots simmered on stoves.

Then it happened. Suddenly the familiar and the cozy vanished. In their place came the strange and the fearful.

At Turnagain, on the edge of Anchorage, people first heard a deep rumble, like the sound of thunder. Next, their houses began to shake. They rushed to their doors, looked out, and thought the world was coming to an end. The earth at their feet was churning and crumbling and sinking away. It was cracking into huge, tilted blocks.

Neighbor helped neighbor to escape. Behind them trees fell. Houses were ripped in two or upended.

B Turnagain was built on high ground, on a bluff overlooking the water. The violent shaking triggered a landslide. The front of the bluff slid away, carrying houses and garages with it.

In downtown Anchorage, big buildings creaked and groaned. Their floors rose and fell in waves.

Automobiles bounced like rubber balls. Great chunks of buildings crashed to the street. A movie theater dropped thirty feet into a hole that opened beneath it. A flower shop snapped in two.

C Anchorage was not alone in this nightmare. As it shook and cracked and jolted, so did much of Alaska. Buildings trembled and fell. Land tore open. Highways buckled. Railroad tracks were twisted into curls of steel. Snow-capped mountains shuddered, and ice and rock swept down their slopes.

Alaska had been struck by a mighty earthquake that hit without warning. At 5:35 P.M. all was well. By 5:38 half of Alaska seemed to be in the grip of an angry giant. The earth shook with terrible violence.

All along the coast, port towns suffered great damage. One reason was the kind of land on which they stood.

Much of Alaska's coast is rugged, rocky land that stands high above the water. The port towns were built in the low-lying places. But here the ground was not very solid. Also, it sloped down steeply to the ocean floor. When the earthquake shook such land, the soil began to slide. Whole waterfronts vanished in underwater landslides.

That was one of the things that happened at Seward.

Seward was both a port and the end of a rail line. The rail line brought in oil, which was stored in tanks before being shipped. When the earthquake hit, the tanks broke and the oil caught fire.

D Flames roared along the waterfront. Just then a great landslide took place. The entire waterfront slid into the bay. The slide caused water to surge away from the land. Burning oil was carried into the bay and then swept back. Fiery water flooded inland. Tugs, fishing boats, and a tanker were washed ashore by the great surge of water. Docks and small-boat harbors

---

WORDS TO OWN

churning (churn'in) *v.*: shaking or stirring violently, like milk being made into butter in a churn.
bluff (bluf) *n.*: steep cliff.
buckled (buk'əld) *v.*: collapsed (usually under pressure).

---

436 THIS OLD EARTH

Reaching All Students

Struggling Readers
Tracking Cause and Effect was introduced on p. 434. For a lesson directly tied to this selection that teaches students to track cause and effect by using a strategy called Text Reformulation, see the *Reading Skills and Strategies* binder:
• Selection Skill Lesson, p. 186

English Language Learners
This article includes specialized earth science vocabulary, especially beginning on p. 438 (*mantle, granite, basalt,* etc.). You might read several paragraphs aloud. As students follow along, have them list the scientific words. Urge them to use context clues or the dictionary to define each one. For strategies to supplement instruction for these students, see
• *Lesson Plans Including Strategies for English-Language Learners*

Advanced Learners
Students can create a script for a documentary about earthquakes. They can do simple research in an encyclopedia or on the Internet. Their documentary should focus on details of the 1964 Alaska quake. Students should review Lauber's descriptions carefully as they plan and draft their scripts.

were destroyed by fire and wave. For hours that night the bay was ablaze with burning material.

By then, the earthquake had long since ended. The earth was still twitching, and it would go on doing so for weeks. But the earthquake itself was over. In fact, it had lasted only about five minutes.

During that time, the earthquake did great damage. Scientists who studied it reported some astounding effects. Among other things, the quake changed the very face of Alaska.

In the Gulf of Alaska the ocean floor rose. So did land along the coast. All in all, a region the size of Maine was lifted three to eight feet. Inland, another big region sank. Part of an island rose thirty-eight feet. When the quake ended, the town of Valdez was ten feet higher than it had been before.

A whole peninsula moved. Carrying along its mountains and lakes, Kenai Peninsula moved sideways as much as sixty feet and sank seven feet or more.

There were other changes. Near Valdez a huge wave reached 220 feet above sea level and clawed at the earth. A piece of land 4,000 feet long and 600 feet wide fell into the sea.

Water in Kenai Lake sloshed back and forth. It moved with such force that its water and ice peeled the bark off trees along the shore.

A mountain split apart. One side of it plunged downward, flying over a ridge like a skier taking a jump. The flying mountain spread into a carpet of rocks a mile long and two miles wide. The carpet traveled without touching the ground. Finally it landed on a glacier. Scientists later found it there and figured out what had happened.

The 1964 Alaska earthquake was one of the strongest ever recorded. It was one of the mightiest earthquakes known to man. But it took place for the same reason that all earthquakes do. It took place because rock within the earth suddenly shifted.

An earthquake can be strong, as Alaska's was in 1964. Or it can be slight. It can be so slight that no person feels it, though instruments record it. But big or small, an earthquake is just what its name says it is—a shaking of the earth. The earth shakes when rock within it suddenly shifts.

WHEN THE EARTH SHAKES 437

E Reading Skills and Strategies

Tracking Cause and Effect

Point out that this short paragraph precedes a long list of effects. Ask students to identify the main cause. [earthquake] Then, ask students to name the secondary causes. [the relative positions of land and sea, the elevation of land, and the violence with which water and land responded to the quake]

F Reading Skills and Strategies

Responding to the Text

Encourage students to share their reactions to this list of the earthquake's effects. [Possible responses: astonishment at the extent of the damage; admiration for scientists' ability to measure such effects.]

G Elements of Literature

Simile

❓ What simile does Lauber use to describe the plunging mountain? [She compares it to a skier taking a jump.]

Getting Students Involved

Cooperative Learning

Making a Map. Have the class, working in small groups, create three maps of Alaska. One group's map can show where Alaska is located in North America; another map might show the entire state; and the third map can focus on the area that includes Anchorage, Seward, Valdez, and the Kenai Peninsula. Students should find source materials (atlases, road maps, computer-generated maps) to use in developing their maps. The groups can display their maps as a trio.

Enrichment Activity

Front-Page News. Have students gather in groups of three or four to create the front page of a newspaper covering the Alaska earthquake. Suggest that each newspaper include a lead story that is basically informative and narrative; eyewitness accounts from residents; at least one drawing of the damage; and an interview with the governor of the state. Students can divide the tasks of writing, illustrating, and laying out the page. Students may want to display their finished front pages in class.

Simile

❓ What two similes does the author use to help readers understand what the earth is made of? [She compares the arrangement of core, mantle, and crust to the layers of an onion; she compares the earth's crust to the crust on a loaf of bread.]

B Reading Skills and Strategies

Tracking Cause and Effect

❓ Why does the earth's mantle sometimes shift or snap? [The mantle is under great pressure, and the heat of the earth's interior increases the pressure on the mantle.]

C Struggling Readers

Identifying Pronoun Antecedents

❓ Explain that a pronoun's antecedent may be located in the preceding sentence and that a plural pronoun may refer to two singular nouns linked by *and*. What is the antecedent of *them* in l. 4? [*the bow and string*, l. 2]

D Critical Thinking

Analyzing

❓ Which ideas about earthquakes does the stick example help make clear? [Possible responses: the release of stored-up energy when the strain is too great; the change of stored-up energy into waves that push outward; the vibration of the waves that create the quake's rumbling sound.] Why does the author use the stick to explain earthquakes? [Possible response: It is a simple example that most readers will be familiar with.]

The earth is mostly made of rock. Beneath its soil and oceans, it is a big ball of rock. The ball has three main regions: the core, the mantle, and the crust. They are arranged like the layers of an onion. The core is at the center of the earth. The mantle surrounds the core. The crust surrounds the mantle.

Like the crust on a loaf of bread, the earth's crust is a thin outside covering. It is made of two main kinds of rock.

One is a fairly light rock. Its most familiar form is granite, and that is what it is often called. The upper part of the continents is made of this granitelike rock. It is usually about twenty-five miles thick. The continental crust does not end at the water's edge. It reaches out under the sea in what is called a continental shelf. Where the shelf ends, the oceanic crust begins.

The crust under the oceans is a different kind of rock. It is much more dense. That is, the rock particles are packed more closely together. The most familiar form of this rock is the dark, heavy kind called basalt. The crust under the oceans is about five miles thick.

The inside of the earth is very hot. And so the crust grows hotter as it goes deeper. Oil wells drilled deep into the crust reach rock hot enough to boil water. When volcanoes erupt, molten rock spills out of them. The rock may have a temperature of two thousand degrees Fahrenheit. This molten rock has come from the lower crust or upper mantle.

The mantle is about 1,800 miles thick. It is made of rock, but this is not rock as we know it. The rock is under very great pressure, deep within the earth. It is also very hot. The heat and pressure make the rock behave in ways that are strange to us.

Sometimes rock of the mantle behaves like a very gummy liquid. It can flow like thick tar.

But it also behaves like a solid. It can suddenly shift or snap. When it does, an earthquake takes place. Earthquakes also occur when rock of the crust suddenly shifts or breaks.

Rock shifts or breaks for the same reason that anything else does: because it has been put under great strain. If you take a ruler and bend it, you are putting it under strain. If you bend, or strain, it too much, it will break.

There are forces within the earth that bend, squeeze, and twist the rock of the crust and the upper mantle. As a result, the rock is put under great strain. That is, a large amount of energy is stored in it as strain. When the strain becomes too great, the rock suddenly gives way and the stored-up energy is released.

Something like this happens if you shoot a bow and arrow. As you pull, the bow and string are bent and forced out of shape. Energy from your muscles is stored in them as strain. When you let go, the bow and string snap back into shape, and the stored-up energy is released. It speeds the arrow through the air.

Energy released from rock takes the form of waves. A wave is a kind of giant push. It is a push that passes from one rock particle to the next, much as a push can pass through a line of people. Imagine ten people lined up, each with his hands on the person ahead. If the last person in line is given a sharp push, the push will be felt all through the line. The people stay in place, but the push passes through them.

That is how earthquake waves travel through the inside of the earth. The pushes pass from one rock particle to the next.

You can feel what happens if you snap a stick between your hands. As you slowly bend it, energy is stored as strain. Finally the strain becomes too great. The stick snaps. All the stored-up energy is released. And you feel a sharp stinging. Stored-up energy has changed to waves that are passing through the wood.

WORDS TO OWN

particles (pärt′i·kəlz) *n.:* tiny pieces.

Crossing the Curriculum

Science

Ask students to research and present an explanation of tsunamis. They may offer the information in the form of a poster or of a scale model made of clay or other materials. Students may prefer to make an oral presentation about what causes tsunamis and what kind of damage they can do. Interested students might look through a collection of Japanese prints to find any that suggest Japan's experiences with tsunamis.

Social Studies

Students might discuss a recent natural disaster, such as an earthquake, hurricane, blizzard, heat wave, or forest fire, that inflicted serious injury or death in some part of the world. Students might find out what steps were taken by individuals, groups, or governments to assist those in need. To find out how the survivors coped with the emergency, students can write to the appropriate government office or to the foreign country's embassy in Washington, D.C.

One wood particle pushes the next. When the pushes reach your hands, you feel them as a sting.

Meanwhile, the broken ends of the stick are vibrating. That is, they are very quickly moving back and forth. They set air waves in motion. Particles of air push other particles. Waves, or pushes, pass through the air. These movements are the source of the sound you hear when the stick snaps.

When an earthquake takes place, waves travel out from the shifting rock in all directions.

Some waves travel through the air. They account for the rumbling sounds that may accompany an earthquake.

Some waves travel deep in the earth. They are seldom felt by people. But instruments in earthquake <u>observatories</u> record them. Earthquake waves that pass through the earth are recorded thousands of miles away.

Some waves travel along the earth's surface. Surface waves are the ones that do the damage—the ones that shake buildings, tear up roads, and cause landslides.

They are not, however, the only cause of earthquake damage. There can be another kind, and it is a kind that comes from the sea.

E WORDS TO OWN

observatories (əb·zʉrv'ə·tôr'ēz) n.: buildings equipped for scientific observation.

E Reading Skills and Strategies
Finding the Main Idea

? These four short paragraphs consist of a main idea and three supporting ideas. Which one contains the main idea and which contain the supporting ideas? [the first paragraph; the three that follow it] Which phrase in the main-idea paragraph serves as an introduction to the three supporting ideas? ["in all directions"] What phrase do the three supporting-idea paragraphs have in common? Why? ["Some waves travel"; each paragraph describes one way in which the waves move.]

MEET THE WRITER

"I'm Always Learning Something"

Patricia Lauber (1924–   ) has written more than sixty books on subjects ranging from volcanoes to robots and much in between. Says Lauber:

66 I write about anything that interests me, dogs, horses, forests, birds, mysteries, life in other countries. Some of my books are fiction, and some are nonfiction, but all are based on what I've seen around me. I like to stand and stare at things, to talk with people, and to read a lot. From this I'm always learning something I didn't know before. Some time later, when I've had a chance to think things over, I write down what I heard, saw, felt, and thought. 99

When Lauber is not writing, she is fond of hiking, dancing, reading, listening to music, seeing plays, and talking. Commenting on her busy schedule, she says:

66 It's a little hard to fit everything in, but one nice thing about being a writer is that sailing a boat or exploring a forest can often be described as 'doing research.' 99

More That Lauber Learned

For another look at nature unleashed, read Patricia Lauber's book *Volcano: The Eruption and Healing of Mount St. Helens* (Bradbury).

BROWSING IN THE FILES

About the Author. Patricia Lauber sees a link between the natural curiosity of children and the questions that all scientists ask. "Children are born curious, wanting and needing to understand the world around them, wanting to know how, why, and what." Believing that science books should not be dull, Lauber creates suspense as she describes natural events: The reader wants to know what happens next.

WHEN THE EARTH SHAKES 439

Making the Connections

Connecting to the Theme:
"This Old Earth"

After students have read the article, encourage them to discuss how it relates to the theme of the collection. Students may observe that Lauber describes the earth from a scientific point of view; she focuses on its composition and on the causes and effects of a breakdown of its structure. How is Lauber's approach different from the views presented in "The Creation" and "Sky Woman"? Class members may note that Johnson's poem is based on the creation as it is described in the Bible; "Sky Woman" includes many imaginative aspects, as humans, animals, and other parts of the natural world combine to create a continent.

MAKING MEANINGS

First Thoughts

1. Responses will vary according to geographical region. Possible disasters: drought, flooding, blizzards, earthquakes, fires, hurricanes. Safety measures include stockpiling supplies, checking flashlight batteries, and having evacuation plans.

Shaping Interpretations

2. Students may say that they would want others to understand and remember what causes earthquakes and how severe the damage can be.

3. Possible response: The third paragraph of the article (p. 436) makes the reader ask: "What happened? What does 'the strange and the fearful' mean?"

4. Possible examples: layers of an onion, bow and arrow, and the snapping of a stick (all on p. 438). Most readers have peeled onions, broken sticks, and seen movies in which bows and arrows were used for sport or as weapons; these readers should easily grasp Lauber's explanations.

Challenging the Text

5. A diagram of the layers of the earth might clarify the information on p. 438. Possible headings: "Alaska Earthquake" (beginning of article); "What Causes Earthquakes?" (p. 437, final paragraph); and "Energy and Pressure" (p. 438, top of right column).

MAKING MEANINGS

First Thoughts

[connect]

1. What natural disaster could occur in your area? What steps would you take to protect your life and the lives of others?

Shaping Interpretations

[relate]

2. If you were a teacher, what would you want your students to understand and remember after reading "When the Earth Shakes"? Fill in one of the **cause-and-effect organizers** before you answer this question.

[predict]

3. Like fiction writers, science writers try to create **suspense.** They want to make us eager to find out what happens next. Where in this selection did you feel suspense? At these moments, what questions did Lauber plant in your mind?

[identify]

4. The author gives some good examples to explain difficult information. List at least three of the examples, and tell how they help the reader understand earthquakes.

Challenging the Text

[organize]

5. What kinds of graphic aids—charts, graphs, time lines, drawings, and illustrations—could you use to make the facts and statistics in this article easier to understand? What headings could you add to help your reader follow the main ideas?

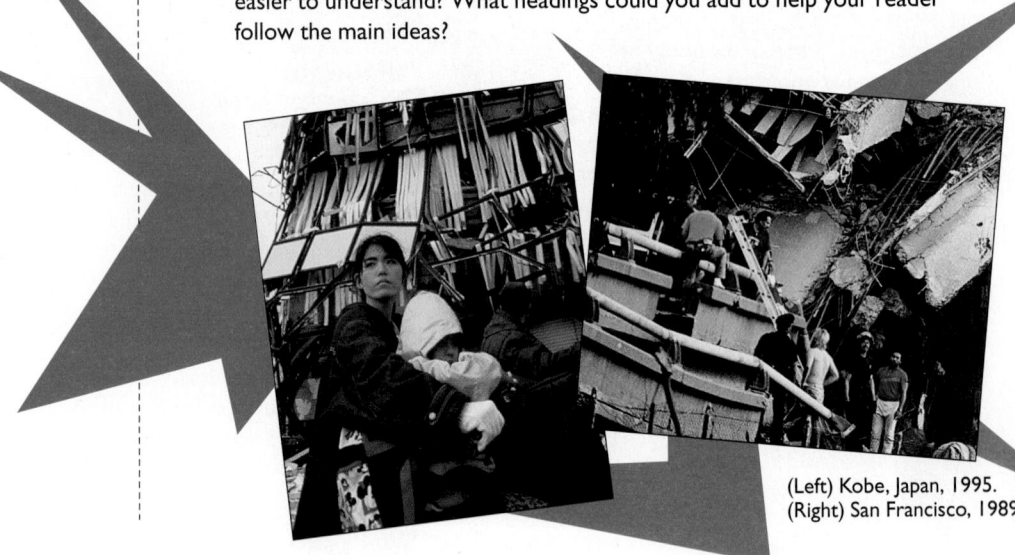

(Left) Kobe, Japan, 1995.
(Right) San Francisco, 1989.

Reading Check

Fill in the L column in the KWL chart you began in response to the Quickwrite on page 434. Then, choose one or two interesting or surprising things you learned, and share them with a partner.

440 THIS OLD EARTH

Reading Check
Possible responses: The earthquake was fierce enough to "change the face of Alaska"; it was strong enough to "throw" half a mountain onto a faraway glacier. Ask students to explain why the passages they have selected interest or surprise them.

Assessing Learning

Check Test: Short Answer

1. What are the three main layers of the earth? [core, mantle, crust]
2. What causes the earth's rock layer to shift or snap? [great strain from energy within the earth; high heat]
3. When rock releases stored-up energy, what form does that energy take? [waves]
4. Which kinds of waves cause earthquake damage? [surface waves and sea waves]

Standardized Test Preparation

For practice with a standardized test format specific to this selection, see
• *Standardized Test Preparation*, pp. 64, 66
For practice in proofreading and editing, see
• *Daily Oral Grammar*, Transparency 25

CHOICES: Building Your Portfolio

Writer's Notebook

1. Collecting Ideas for Observational Writing

Think of a time when some natural event or aspect of nature—such as a snowstorm, an attack of mosquitoes, or a rash caused by poison ivy—frightened you or made you uncomfortable. Suppose you wanted to describe your experience to a friend: What details would you include? Record details just as they come to you when you picture your experience.

> The hurricane:
> no electricity; trying
> to remember where
> we stored the
> candles; buckets
> under leaks; trees
> bending like rubber

Research/Writing

2. Earthquake Report

In the twentieth century major earthquakes have hit San Francisco, Los Angeles, Mexico City, Tokyo, and Kobe. Research one of these big quakes in your local library or on the Internet. Look for news accounts written at the time. Write a report about the quake that presents not only facts—how strong the quake was, how long it lasted, how much damage it caused, and so on—but also the best human-interest stories you turn up in the course of your research.

Science/Art

3. What's in the World?

Draw a diagram—or make a 3-D model if you're ambitious—that shows the three layers of the earth. Along with your drawing or model, provide a brief explanation of how the rock of the earth's mantle or crust can act to create earthquakes, volcanic eruptions, and tidal waves.

Creative Writing

4. Then Earth Shuddered and Said—

Forget all the scientific facts you know about earthquakes for a moment. Tell an imaginative story to explain the causes of an earthquake.

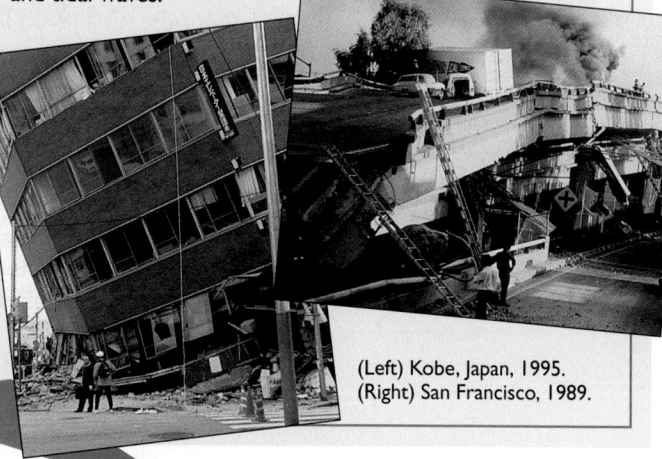

(Left) Kobe, Japan, 1995.
(Right) San Francisco, 1989.

Rubrics for each Choices assignment appear on p. 159 in the *Portfolio Management System.*

CHOICES: Building Your Portfolio

1. **Writer's Notebook** Encourage students to include as many details as they can, especially those that focus on the five senses.
2. **Research/Writing** The 1989 San Francisco earthquake received national attention because it happened during the World Series, which by chance was being played by teams from San Francisco (Giants) and Oakland (Athletics)—cities on either side of the San Francisco Bay. The 1906 San Francisco earthquake, which was followed by a devastating fire, is the source of Jack London's frequently anthologized nonfiction account "Earthquake: The Story of an Eyewitness."
3. **Science/Art** Students might ask for advice from their art and science teachers.
4. **Creative Writing** Encourage students to use their imaginations to provide an explanation—no matter how fantastical—for the causes of earthquakes.

Using Compiled Information to Raise Additional Questions

Sometimes when students do reports, such as the report on earthquakes in Choice 2 above, their research will raise new questions to pursue. For example, in compiling information on earthquakes, students may read news accounts of the devastating 1999 earthquake in Turkey. Encourage students to use their research as a springboard for exploring related topics. For example, they might be interested in raising questions that allow them to compare the effects of different types of natural disasters.

LANGUAGE LINK

Have students select pieces of writing from their portfolios and read them through, looking for examples of formal and informal English. Ask students to identify where they used formal English and where they used informal English. If students have written dialogue or journal entries in formal English, or research reports in informal English, have them rewrite sentences and paragraphs in the other style.

Try It Out
Possible Answers

Informal to Formal: A tremendous earthquake measuring 8.0 on the Richter scale occurred in Alaska at 5 P.M.

Formal to Informal: Help! We're buried under a pile of rubble—three of us, one just a child! Get us out of here! Help!

VOCABULARY
Possible Answers

1. Chemists working in the university observatories successfully combined particles that allow us to control rain.
2. From our laboratories overlooking a high bluff, we have discovered a supernova.
3. The team will study the remains of the bridge that buckled from the force of the churning river. Then we will gather on the bluff for a memorial service for the lost city.

Resources ———————

Language
• *Grammar and Language Links*, p. 41

Vocabulary
• *Words to Own*, p. 16

Spelling
For related instruction, see
• *Spelling and Decoding*, p. 20

LANGUAGE LINK   `MINI-LESSON`

• **Style: Formal and Informal English**

Compare these two sentences:

> Examine the statistics on the Alaska earthquake.

> Check out the stats on that Alaska shake.

The sentences mean the same thing, but they create different effects. The first sentence is an example of **formal English.** The second sentence is an example of **informal English.**

Formal English is the language you use for solemn occasions, such as speeches and graduation ceremonies, and in serious papers and reports. Formal English doesn't include slang or colloquial expressions.

Informal English is used in everyday speaking and writing. You use informal English when you talk with family members or friends and when you write personal letters or journal entries. Informal English includes colloquial expressions and slang.

Try It Out

Rewrite each paragraph, making the informal paragraph formal and the formal paragraph informal.

INFORMAL

Check it out, man—a humongous quake socked Alaska at five o'clock in the P.M., and hoo, boy! We give this big one an eight on the old Richter.

FORMAL

We request aid. The recent earth tremor caused our building to collapse. We are currently situated beneath a mass of structural material. We are two adults and a juvenile. We request aid.

VOCABULARY   `HOW TO OWN A WORD`

WORD BANK

churning
bluff
buckled
particles
observatories

• **Vocabulary for the Workplace: Jack of All Trades**

1. Suppose you work as a chemist. Write a press release about an experiment, using two words from the Word Bank.
2. Imagine that you're an astronomer. Write a memo to the government agency that funds your work, describing the work. Use one word from the Word Bank.
3. Now, suppose you're an archaeologist directing a team of workers who are digging up an ancient city destroyed by an earthquake. Write some directions for your workers, using at least three of the words in the Word Bank.

442 THIS OLD EARTH

Language Link Quick Check

Identify the following sentences as formal or informal English. Then, rewrite each in the opposite style. (Possible responses are given.)

1. The earthquake caused considerable damage to our home. [Formal; The quake made some mess of the place!]
2. My old man told me to chill out. [Informal; My father suggested that I calm down.]
3. All the stuff in the dining room was totally trashed. [Informal; The entire contents of the dining room were destroyed.]
4. The kitchen was the most heavily damaged room. [Formal; The kitchen got hit worst.]
5. We're packing it in and getting out of town. [Informal; We have decided to abandon the property.]

Elements of Literature

NONFICTION: The Main Idea

What's the Point?

In 1989, a huge earthquake shook San Francisco. The quake hit during a World Series game between the San Francisco Giants and the Oakland A's. These teams had never met in the playoffs before. Oakland, however, had won the series in the 1970s.

Can you figure out what this paragraph is about? Probably not. The sentences are clear; the facts are true; the details are concrete—but the paragraph doesn't hang together.

Here's the Point

What's missing is a focus, a topic, a main idea with supporting details that make the main idea pop out. In the following paragraph, look for the **topic**—what the paragraph is all about—and **main idea**—the writer's most important point. What details and evidence support the main idea?

On the afternoon of Good Friday, March 27, 1964, Anchorage, Alaska, was shaken apart by the most violent earthquake ever recorded in the United States. It measured 8.4 on the Richter scale. Government Hill Elementary School was split in two when the ground beneath it dropped. Houses began sliding apart, cracks in the pavement opened and closed like huge jaws, the ground rolled in huge waves. In the first three days after the quake, three hundred aftershocks shook the buildings that remained standing.

—Seymour Simon, *Earthquakes*

This paragraph hangs together. The first sentence states the topic and main idea; the next sentence provides evidence—a statistic—to prove the point. The next two sentences clarify the main idea by providing details. The final sentence provides statistics that reinforce the main idea about the violence of the quake.

Where's the Point?

Sometimes the main idea is implied rather than stated. It's up to you to put all the details together and figure out the main idea yourself.

In a long piece of writing, a writer develops the main idea over many paragraphs. Look at the opening of "When the Earth Shakes" (page 436). All the paragraphs promote one idea: The Alaska earthquake was destructive. The author finally states this idea, on page 437—but by then you've probably gotten the point.

What happens when you're reading nonfiction and the main idea escapes you? These strategies will help you "get the point":

1. Look at the **main ideas** of the different paragraphs. What do they add up to?

2. Check the beginning and end of each paragraph for a **key passage** that might state the central idea.

3. If you find no stated main idea, summarize the important details. Your summary should lead you to the main idea.

4. If the main idea seems to be buried under an earthquake's rubble, form a rescue team, and uncover the idea by talking it over.

Resources

Elements of Literature
Nonfiction: The Main Idea
For more instruction on main idea, see *Literary Elements:*
• Transparency 8
Assessment
Formal Assessment
• Literary Elements Test, p. 95

Elements of Literature

This feature explains how a writer's main idea serves as the focus in nonfiction. It provides strategies for determining main ideas that are implied rather than stated.

Mini-Lesson:
The Main Idea
After students have read p. 443, define **main idea** (the writer's most important point). Explain that the writer establishes the main idea and then backs it up with details, examples, or other evidence. Even if the main idea is not specifically stated, the details usually suggest the writer's key point. Students might develop an illustration to show the relationship between a main idea and its supporting details—for example, three arrows pointing from the main idea to three supporting details.

Applying the Element
Use p. 438 of "When the Earth Shakes" to help students practice identifying main ideas. (Suggested responses are given.)
• What is the main idea of the first paragraph? ["The earth is mostly made of rock."]
• Identify three details that support this main idea. [Details are found in the paragraph's remaining six sentences.]

Using Students' Strengths

Visual Learners

As visual learners read the feature, they might benefit by filling in the graphic organizer provided in the *Graphic Organizers for Active Reading*, p. 29.

Intrapersonal Learners

Have students obtain magazines from the school library. After students have chosen and have read an article, ask them to identify its main idea and to describe how they figured out this idea. Students who have difficulty identifying the main idea of an entire article might choose, instead, to work with one or two paragraphs.

OBJECTIVES

1. Read and interpret the nonfiction excerpt
2. Identify the main idea
3. Adjust reading rate
4. Express understanding through observational and creative writing, reading/speaking and listening, health, or science
5. Identify the active and the passive voice and use each appropriately
6. Understand and use new words

SKILLS

Literary
- Identify the main idea

Reading
- Adjust reading rate

Writing
- Collect ideas for an observational essay
- Write journal entries
- Write a list of the contents of a survival kit
- Write a report about navigation

Speaking/Listening
- Summarize a story

Language
- Distinguish between the active and the passive voice

Vocabulary
- Understand and use new words

Science
- Research navigation

Health
- Plan a survival kit

Viewing/Representing
- Recognize purpose of diagrams, sketches, and photographs (ATE)
- Identify objects and mood of a painting (ATE)

Before You Read

SURVIVE THE SAVAGE SEA

Make the Connection

Alone and Adrift

In E. E. Cummings's poem on page 461, the sea is a wonderful place where four girls find various treasures. Here is another look at the sea—this time as a killer. As you'll see, this old earth can be destructive as well as supportive.

Think and pair. With a partner, brainstorm to come up with problems you would face and solutions you might find if you were lost at sea. You could go back and forth—one of you presenting a problem and the other suggesting a solution—and then trade roles. Record your ideas in a two-column chart like this one:

Problem	Solution
no fresh water	catch rain

Quickwrite

In a fight for survival, what kind of person would you want beside you? List the qualities you think would help a person survive a disaster.

Elements of Literature

Main Idea: I Get Your Point

The **main idea** of a text is the most important idea, the one that the writer wants you to remember. One way to find the main idea when you're reading nonfiction is to look for the most important word in each paragraph or section you read. Try this strategy as you read about this life-and-death conflict with a powerful force of nature.

The **main idea** is the most important idea expressed in a paragraph or a selection.

For more on Main Idea, see page 443 and the Handbook of Literary Terms.

Reading Skills and Strategies

Adjusting Reading Rate: Changing the Pace

You may want to adjust your **reading rate** as you steer through the savage waters of this story. Your purpose is not to read faster than anyone else but to understand what is happening. As you read, make note of passages that seem easy and passages that seem hard. Which passages seem just right?

Background

Literature and Real Life

On June 15, 1972, killer whales attacked the sailing ship *Lucette* in the Pacific Ocean. The boat sank in sixty seconds. On board the *Lucette* were Dougal Robertson and his wife, Lyn; their oldest son, Douglas; their twelve-year-old twins, Neil and Sandy; and a young family friend, Robin. Set adrift on a rubber raft and a fiberglass dinghy, Robertson and his crew began their struggle to survive. Steering a course by the sun and stars, they made for the coast of Costa Rica, a thousand miles away.

Preteaching Vocabulary

Words to Own

Have students read the ten Words to Own and their definitions listed at the bottom of the selection pages. Students may work in pairs to write a one-paragraph sea adventure story, using at least five of the words correctly. Then, have students match words in the left-hand list with their synonyms on the right. Discuss why one answer is used twice.

1. ____ imminent [f]
2. ____ debris [h]
3. ____ scanty [d]
4. ____ deteriorating [i]
5. ____ copious [b]
6. ____ tenets [g]
7. ____ testily [e]
8. ____ vigil [c]
9. ____ advocates [a]
10. ____ meager [d]

a. supporters
b. plentiful
c. period of watching
d. inadequate
e. irritably
f. happening soon
g. beliefs
h. rubble
i. worsening

This was not our environment, and the beasts around us would eat us if we failed.

from # Survive the Savage Sea

Dougal Robertson

First Day

We sat on the salvaged pieces of flotsam[1] lying on the raft floor, our faces a pale bilious[2] color under the bright yellow canopy, and stared at each other, the shock of the last few minutes gradually seeping through to our consciousness. Neil, his teddy bears gone, sobbed in accompaniment to Sandy's hiccup cry, while Lyn repeated the Lord's Prayer, then, comforting them, sang the hymn "For Those in Peril on the Sea." Douglas and Robin watched at the doors of the canopy to

1. **flotsam:** floating wreckage of a ship or its cargo.
2. **bilious:** yellowish or greenish, as if suffering from liver or gallbladder problems. (Bile is secreted by the liver.)

Planning

- **Block Schedule**
  Block Scheduling Lesson Plans with Pacing Guide
- **Traditional Schedule**
  Lesson Plans Including Strategies for English-Language Learners
- **One-Stop Planner**
  CD-ROM with Test Generator

Summary ■ ■

Five members of the Robertson family and a friend have survived the sinking of their sailing ship, *Lucette*. They drift in the Pacific on a raft, with no navigational instruments, little food or water, and no means of communication except a few distress flares. On the seventh day after the wreck, the flares fail to attract a passing ship. Dougal, the narrator, realizes that the stranded group must use whatever resources it can find. The Robertsons augment their water supply with rainwater and catch turtles, sharks, and other fish. Despite a drought, they keep their spirits up by daydreaming about lavish meals. On the fifteenth day, the dinghy breaks away; the exhausted Dougal swims through shark-infested water to recapture it. On the thirty-eighth day, a Japanese ship rescues them.

Ⓐ Critical Thinking
Interpreting
❓ Read this quotation aloud to students. What might Robertson mean by "this was not our environment"? [Possible response: Humans are land animals; they are not equipped to survive at sea.]

Resources: Print and Media

Reading
- *Reading Skills and Strategies*
  Selection Skill Lesson, p. 15
- *Graphic Organizers for Active Reading*, p. 30
- *Words to Own*, p. 17
- *Spelling and Decoding*
  Worksheet, p. 21
- *Audio CD Library*
  Disc 11, Track 5

Writing and Language
- *Daily Oral Grammar*
  Transparency 26
- *Grammar and Language Links*
  Worksheet, p. 43

Viewing and Representing
- *Viewing and Representing*
  Fine Art Transparency 14
  Fine Art Worksheet, p. 56

Assessment
- *Formal Assessment*, p. 89
- *Portfolio Management System*, p. 160
- *Standardized Test Preparation*, p. 68
- *Test Generator (One-Stop Planner CD-ROM)*

Internet
- go.hrw.com (keyword: LE0 7-6)

 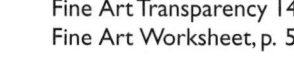

T445

Resources 🎧

Listening

Audio CD Library

A dramatic reading of this excerpt from *Survive the Savage Sea* is provided in the *Audio CD Library*:
• Disc 11, Track 5

Ⓐ Elements of Literature

Character

❓ What do their words tell you about Neil and Lyn? [Possible responses: They are trying not to panic; they hope to encourage each other by speaking bravely and by denying that they are frightened; they loved the lost ship.]

Ⓑ English Language Learners

Briticisms

Explain to students that in British usage, *biscuits* are cookies. This word is similar to the Italian *biscotti*, or hard, crunchy cookies. Also note another British term: *Tin* here means "box."

Ⓒ Elements of Literature

Main Idea

❓ After students have read the first day's entry, ask them to identify its main idea. What details support their answers? [Possible responses: main idea—the situation is very dangerous; supporting details—the raft contains little food and water; the parents' concern reflects the sense of danger.]

Ⓓ Struggling Readers

Breaking Down Difficult Text

Help students distinguish the separate ideas in the passage. Point out that the semicolon and the three commas mark important breaks (the last two commas surround a parenthetical phrase). You might mention transitional words (*while, but, until*).

retrieve any useful pieces of <u>debris</u> which might float within reach and gazed with dumb longing at the distant five-gallon water container, bobbing its polystyrene[3] lightness ever further away from us in the steady trade wind. The dinghy *Ednamair* wallowed, swamped, nearby with a line attached to it from the raft, and our eyes traveled over and beyond to the heaving undulations of the horizon, already searching for a rescue ship even while knowing there would not be one. Our eyes traveled fruitlessly across the limitless waste of sea and sky, then once more ranged over the scattering debris. Of the killer whales which had so recently shattered our very existence, there was no sign. Lyn's sewing basket floated close and it was brought aboard followed by a couple of empty boxes, the canvas raft cover, and a plastic cup.

Ⓐ I leaned across to Neil and put my arm round him, "It's all right now, son, we're safe and the whales have gone." He looked at me reproachfully. "We're not crying cos we're frightened," he sobbed. "We're crying cos Lucy's gone."[4] Lyn gazed at me over their heads, her eyes filling with tears. "Me too," she said, and after a moment added, "I suppose we'd better find out how we stand." . . .

We cleared a space on the floor and opened the survival kit, which was part of the raft's equipment and was contained in a three-foot-long polythene cylinder; slowly we took stock:

Vitamin-fortified bread and glucose[5] for ten men for two days;

Eighteen pints of water, eight flares[6] (two parachute, six hand);

One bailer, two large fishhooks, two small, one spinner and trace, and a twenty-five-pound breaking strain fishing line;

A patent knife which would not puncture

3. **polystyrene:** type of plastic. Polythene, which is mentioned below, is another kind of plastic.
4. **Lucy's gone:** Neil means the *Lucette,* their ship.
5. **glucose:** kind of sugar that is easily digested.
6. **flares:** very bright lights used as distress signals.

446 THIS OLD EARTH

the raft (or anything else for that matter), a signal mirror, torch,[7] first-aid box, two sea anchors, instruction book, bellows, and three paddles.

Ⓑ In addition to this there was the bag of a dozen onions which I had given to Sandy, to which Lyn had added a one-pound tin of biscuits and a bottle containing about half a pound of glucose sweets, ten oranges, and six lemons. How long would this have to last us? As I looked around our <u>meager</u> stores my heart sank and it must have shown on my face, for Lyn put her hand on mine; "We must get these boys to land," she said quietly. "If we do nothing else with our lives, we must get them to land!" I looked at her and nodded, "Of course, we'll make it!" The answer came from my heart Ⓒ but my head was telling me a different story. . . .

Sixth Day

Ⓓ . . . At four in the morning we were dozing quietly when a flying fish flew straight through the door of the raft, striking Lyn in the face. Now Lyn is a very steady and reliable person in a crisis; she seems to be able to do the right thing at the right time automatically while less able people like myself are floundering around wondering what to do, but her reaction to being slapped in the face by a wet fish at four in the morning, after all our previous excitement, had us all scrambling around the raft looking for something like the Loch Ness monster[8] until the eight-inch leviathan[9] was finally secured and made safe for breakfast. . . .

7. **torch:** British English for "flashlight."
8. **Loch** (läkh) **Ness monster:** thirty-foot-long sea monster supposedly living in a lake in northern Scotland. (*Loch* is Scottish for "lake.")
9. **leviathan** (lə·vī′ə·thən): Leviathan is a huge sea monster mentioned in the Bible.

WORDS TO OWN

debris (də·brē′) *n.:* rough, broken bits of litter.
meager (mē′gər) *adj.:* literally, very thin; inadequate; not enough.

Reaching All Students

Struggling Readers

Adjusting Reading Rate was introduced on p. 444. For a lesson directly tied to this selection that teaches students to adjust reading rate by using a strategy called Say Something, see the *Reading Skills and Strategies* binder:
• Selection Skill Lesson, p. 15

English Language Learners

Tell students that Robertson and his family are from Scotland and that the English spoken in the United Kingdom is a little different from American English. As you go through the selection with students, point out examples of British usage (see annotations B and F and footnotes 7 and 8, for example) and explain how these words differ from their American counterparts.

Advanced Learners

As students read, have them imagine what might have happened on the days not covered in this excerpt. Either singly or in groups, students might outline the events that took place during the rest of the 38-day fight for survival. Students can then write Dougal's journal entries for one or more missing days. Remind students to keep their work consistent with the details in the other entries and with Dougal's writing style.

Seventh Day

. . . Douglas, lazily watching the dispersing clouds, suddenly sat up with a start, pointing excitedly. "A ship! A ship! It's a ship!" We all crowded to the door of the raft, staring in the direction of his pointing finger; a cargo vessel of about six thousand tons was approaching us on a course that would bring her within three miles of us. I felt my heart pound against my ribs. "Get out the flares," I said hoarsely, "and pass them to me in the dinghy; they'll see us better from there."

Three miles was a fair distance, but on a dull day like this, against a background of rain, they should see us easily. I clambered into the dinghy and Douglas passed me the rockets and hand flares; my hands trembled as I ripped open a parachute rocket flare and, with a mute appeal to the thing to fire, struck the igniter on the fuse. It spluttered and hissed, then roared off on a trajectory high above the raft, its pinkish magnesium flare slowly spiraling downward leaving a trail of smoke in the sky. They couldn't fail to see it. I waited a moment or two watching for the ship to alter course, then struck a hand flare, holding it high above my head. The blinding red light was hot to hold and I pointed it away from the wind to ease my hand, the red embers of the flare dropping into the dinghy; as it went out I struck another, smoke from the first now a rising plume in the sky; surely they must see that. I waited a little, my hands trembling. "This chance might not come again," I said, anxious faces crowding the door of the raft; "I'm going to use our last rocket flare and one more hand flare." We watched tensely as the second rocket flare soared and spiraled its gleaming distress message high above us; desperately I struck the third hand flare and held it high, standing on the thwart and holding on to the mast. "Look, look! . . ." I shouted. "Set fire to the sail!" Lyn's voice. I stuck the flare to the sail but it only melted. The ship sailed on, slowly disappearing behind a rain shower, and when she reappeared her hull[10] was half obscured by the horizon, five miles distant and disappearing fast. The time was eleven o'clock. My shoulders drooped. "We daren't use another," I said. "They won't see it now and we have to keep something for the next one." We had three hand flares left. Lyn smiled cheerfully. "It says in the instruction book that the first one probably wouldn't see us," she said slowly, "and I'd already told the twins not to expect anything." She gathered the twins to her, comfortingly. We stared at the dwindling speck on the horizon and felt so lonely that it hurt. "I'm sorry, lads." I felt very tired. "We used to consider that one of the most important <u>tenets</u> of good seamanship was 'Keep a good lookout.' That lot seem to be pretty poor seamen!"

Our position was 3° north and 240 miles west of Espinosa (almost 95°20′W) on Wednesday 21 June, midsummer's day, on the route from Panama to the Marquesas; the ship was westbound. I surveyed the empty flare cartons bitterly, and the one smoke flare which was damp and wouldn't work, and something happened to me in that instant, that for me changed the whole aspect of our predicament. If these poor bloody seamen couldn't rescue us, then we would have to make it on our own and to the devil with them. We would survive without them, yes, and that was the word from now on, "survival," not "rescue" or "help" or dependence of any kind, just survival. I felt the strength flooding through me, lifting me from the depression of disappointment to a state of almost cheerful abandon. I felt the bitter aggression of the predator fill my mind. This was not our environment, and the beasts around us would eat us if we failed. We would carve a place for ourselves among them; they had

10. **hull:** main body of a ship.

WORDS TO OWN

tenets (ten′its) *n.*: beliefs of a group; doctrines.

E Reading Skills and Strategies

Adjusting Reading Rate

Draw students' attention to the sudden change in tone that occurs here: When Dougal realizes that the ship may be the only chance of rescue, the tone becomes tense and dramatic. Ask students whether they speeded up or slowed down their reading rate and why. [Some students may have begun to read faster because the content became very exciting. Other students may have slowed down, in order to follow the important details.]

F Critical Thinking

Speculating

? In Britain, *bloody* is a "swear word," meaning "cursed" or "damned." Why do you think Dougal uses this word and the phrase "to the devil with them"? [Possible responses: He uses *bloody* because he is angry at the ship's failure to keep a good lookout; he uses the *devil* phrase when he realizes that the family's survival depends on its own skill and determination.]

G Appreciating Language

Word Choice

? Why do you think Dougal uses the word *carve* rather than *create, make,* or some other verb? [Possible response: *Carve* contributes to the serious tone of the passage. The word emphasizes that survival depends on killing and eating the "beasts around us."]

Crossing the Curriculum

Geography

Have students research the use of longitude and latitude to locate points on the earth's surface. Students might consult an atlas or a globe to pinpoint the location of the Robertsons' raft, according to the details in the last paragraph on p. 447. Students can do further research to find out what kind of weather can be expected there in mid-June.

Film

Alfred Hitchcock's film *Lifeboat* (1944), in which several survivors of a shipwreck must work together until they are rescued, portrays another situation of extreme danger on the high seas. *Lifeboat* is set during World War II; the passengers, who have never met before, are suspicious of one another. After seeing the movie, students can discuss similarities and differences between the film and the excerpt from *Survive the Savage Sea.*

Health

Interested students might research the subject of nutrition and use the information to analyze the Robertsons' initial stocks of food. Encourage students to draw conclusions about the family's subsequent diet at sea—the nutrients they gain from the food they eat, as well as the nutrients they lack. Some of the details can be presented as a checklist or a poster.

A Critical Thinking
Expressing an Opinion
? Do you agree with Dougal's belief that he must become a "savage" to survive? [Possible responses: Yes, he needs to rely on animal energy and the desire to live; no, he must depend on his brain and his tools.]

B Elements of Literature
Main Idea
? Invite students to share their responses to Dougal's actions. [Students may mention shock, horror, fascination, or disgust.] **What is the main idea of the paragraph?** [Possible responses: There's no room for "civilized" behavior in this situation, because there is a real possibility of starvation or dehydration.]

C Struggling Readers
Paraphrasing
Ask students to read the sensory details carefully and then restate the passage in their own words. Suggest that they split up the long sentence where logical breaks occur. [Possible response: Dougal looks closely at his family and Robin to see how their health is holding up. Their skin has become wrinkled from the water; they have boils and rashes. They are in the bottom of the raft, where water has collected. Because the water cools them and they don't have much energy anyway, they don't bail out the water very often. Their bones show through their skin, and their bodies are much thinner. Their health is getting worse.]

millions of years of adaptation on their side, but we had brains and some tools. We would live for three months or six months from the sea if necessary, but "we would get these boys to land" as Lyn had said, and we would do it ourselves if there was no other way. From that **(A)** instant on, I became a savage. . . .

Fourteenth Day

. . . We had a sip of water for breakfast with no dried food to detract from its value, after which I crossed to the dinghy to try for a dorado.[11] The heat of the sun's rays beat on my head like a club and my mouth, dry like lizard skin, felt full of my tongue; the slightest exertion left me breathless. I picked up the spear; the dorado were all deep down as if they knew I was looking for them. A bump at the stern[12] of the raft attracted Sandy's attention. "Turtle!" he yelled. This one was much smaller than the first and with great care it was caught and passed through the raft—with Douglas guarding its beak, and the others its claws, from damaging the fabric—to me on the dinghy, where I lifted it aboard without much trouble. I wrapped a piece of tape around the broken knife blade and made the incision into its throat. "Catch the blood," Lyn called from the raft. "It should be all right to drink a little." I held the plastic cup under the copious flow of blood; the cup filled quickly and I stuck another under as soon as it **(B)** was full, then, raising the full cup to my lips, tested it cautiously. It wasn't salty at all! I tilted the cup and drained it. "Good stuff!" I shouted. I felt as if I had just consumed the elixir of life.[13] "Here, take this," and I passed the bailer full of blood, about a pint, into the raft for the others to drink. Lyn said afterward she had imagined that she would have to force it down us, and the sight of me draining the cup, my moustache

11. **dorado:** kind of fish; also called a dolphin.
12. **stern:** back end of a vessel.
13. **elixir** (ē·liks′ir) **of life:** substance that some people in the Middle Ages believed existed and would allow people to live forever.

448 THIS OLD EARTH

dripping blood, was quite revolting. I don't know what I looked like, but it certainly tasted good, and as the others followed my example it seemed they thought so too. I passed another pint across, and though some of this coagulated[14] before it could be drunk, the jelly was cut up and the released serum[15] collected and used as a gravy with the dried turtle and fish.

I set to cutting my way into the turtle much refreshed, and even with the broken knife made faster work of it than the first one, both because it was smaller and, being younger, the shell was not so tough; the fact that I now knew my way around inside a turtle helped a lot too. . . .

I looked around the raft at the remains of Robin and the Robertson family, water-wrinkled skin covered with salt-water boils[16] and raw red patches of rash, lying in the bottom of **(C)** the raft, unmoving except to bail occasionally, and then only halfheartedly, for the water was cooling in the heat of the day; our bones showed clearly through our scanty flesh; we had become much thinner these last few days and our condition was deteriorating fast. The raft was killing us with its demands on our energy. Douglas looked across at me, "Do you think it'll rain tonight, Dad?" I looked at him and shrugged, looked at the sky, not a cloud. "I suppose it could do," I said. "Do you think it will?" he insisted. "For heaven's sake, Douglas, I'm not a prophet," I said testily. "We'll just have to wait it out." His eyes looked hopelessly at the blue of the sea from the deep cavities under his brow; how could I comfort him when he knew

14. **coagulated:** solidified; clotted.
15. **serum:** clear liquid left over after blood coagulates.
16. **boils:** painful, infected swellings.

WORDS TO OWN
copious (kō′pē·əs) adj.: plentiful.
scanty (skan′tē) adj.: inadequate. Scanty and meager are synonyms; scanty and copious are antonyms.
deteriorating (dē·tir′ē·ə·rāt′iŋ) v.: getting worse.
testily (tes′tə·lē) adv.: irritably.

Taking a Second Look

Review: Recognizing Comparison and Contrast
Make sure that students understand that when they compare items, they show how they are alike; when they contrast items, they show how they are different. The dangerous situations presented in Survive the Savage Sea and "He Ate Ants" provide students with a good opportunity to practice the skill of comparing and contrasting.

Activity
1. Have students divide their papers into two columns, one headed "Similarities" and the other headed "Differences." After comparing the two narratives to see how they are alike, students can note these qualities in the first column. In the second column, they can note the characteristics that set the two narratives apart.
2. Students can use their notes in a whole-class discussion on which of the two situations was more dangerous and why.

as well as I that it might not rain for a week, and that we'd be dead by then. I said, "Fresh turtle for tea,[17] we can suck something out of that." We could live on turtles, maybe.

We took no water that evening, only a little for the twins. We talked of the dishes we'd like

17. **tea:** in Britain, a light meal eaten in the late afternoon.

to eat in the gathering twilight and I chose fresh fruit salad and ice cream; Lyn, a tin of apricots; Robin, strawberries and ice cream with milk; Douglas, the same as me; Neil, chocolate chip ice cream; Sandy, fresh fruit, ice cream and milk—gallons of ice-cool milk. Later that night as I took the watch over from Douglas, he described in detail the dish he had dreamed up

LITERATURE AND REAL LIFE

He Ate Ants

In June 1995, Captain Scott O'Grady was flying a patrol over Bosnia for the North Atlantic Treaty Organization (NATO) as part of an effort by the major Western powers and the United Nations to stem years of blood-shed in Bosnia. His radar showed that a surface-to-air missile was seconds from destroying his plane. After he bailed out, he pulled his parachute cord too quickly. O'Grady drifted slowly over a clear sky at twenty thousand feet, in full view of hostile Serbian soldiers. Upon landing, he scrambled into a clump of nearby bushes and began six agonizing days of life on the run.

"Most of the time, my face was in the dirt, just praying that no one would see me," O'Grady said. He described himself as "a scared little bunny rabbit, trying to hide, trying to survive. . . . I ate grass. When you're hungry, you'll eat anything." "Anything" included ants. "They scamper really quickly and it's hard to get them," he laughed. After finishing the water in his survival kit, he prayed for rain, and "God delivered." He then relied on tricks from his survival training: collecting dew in plastic packets and squeezing rainwater from a sponge and from his wool socks.

O'Grady was finally able to move into a clearing and send off a signal from his radio that led to a helicopter res-cue. After sending up a flare to guide the helicopters, O'Grady loaded his gun and made a frantic dash, forgetting his training for the first time. "The one thing they tell you is never run at a helicopter with a loaded gun," he said with a grin.

SURVIVE THE SAVAGE SEA 449

D Literary Connections

Point out the irony of being thirsty when one is surrounded by water. The Romantic poet Samuel Taylor Coleridge (1772–1834) includes a similar scene in his famous poem *The Rime of the Ancient Mariner.* Like the Robertsons, Coleridge's sailor is adrift in fiercely hot, dry weather. As he searches the horizon for clouds, he laments, "Water, water, everywhere,/ Nor any drop to drink."

LITERATURE AND REAL LIFE

There are other modern survival stories that students may be famil-iar with. Examples include the 1995 film *Apollo 13,* in which three astronauts struggle to return to Earth in a damaged spacecraft. Students may also have seen the movie *Titanic* (1997), the story of the sinking of the ocean liner after it collided with an iceberg. Several hundred passengers survived the frozen waters of the North Atlantic, most with no knowledge that a ship was coming to rescue them. Ask students what lessons might be learned from survival stories like these. [Possible response: Those who survived did so because they remained calm and used whatever resources they could to help them.]

Resources ———

Viewing and Representing
Fine Art Transparency
A fine art transparency of Winslow Homer's *The Gulf Stream* can help stu-dents appreciate the harshness and fierceness of the sea.
• Transparency 14
• Worksheet, p. 56

Connecting Across Texts

Connecting with "Survive the Savage Sea"

Ask students to imagine what Dougal Robert-son and Scott O'Grady would have done in each other's place. Would each have survived in the other's circumstances? Why or why not? What qualities do the two men have in com-mon? How are their situations different? [Possi-ble responses: Whether each would have survived the other's predicament is a matter of guesswork. Certainly, both men possessed courage, determination, intelligence, and the ability to improvise. Robertson had his family to help him, whereas O'Grady was on his own. As a member of the military, O'Grady was able, when he had reached a clearing, to send a radio signal for help, whereas the Robertsons had to wait for passing ships or until they reached land.]

Point out to students the usefulness of diagrams or sketches. Be sure that students understand the functions of the labeled items in the diagram. Students might discuss how their images of the raft and the *Ednamair* were similar to or different from the drawing.

Activity. What are the differences in purpose between labeled sketches and photographs? [Possible responses: Sketches are intended to make the text easier to follow; photographs like this one are meant to appeal to the reader's interest and imagination. (Some photographs help the reader visualize an unfamiliar object or place.)]

Why do you think this photograph was chosen to be featured? [Possible responses: The turtle, one of the creatures the Robertsons had never eaten before but come to depend on for food and drink, represents their struggle for survival. Unlike the shark, it is not threatening.] What advantages does the turtle have over other animals living in the "savage" sea? [Possible responses: Because it is spotted and small, it can blend in with other objects and hide; its flippers help it swim, and its shell protects it.]

A drawing of the Robertsons' raft and the *Ednamair*.

450 THIS OLD EARTH

Getting Students Involved

Cooperative Learning

Group Discussion. Ask students to imagine what it would be like to be stranded somewhere with five other people for 38 days. How might the individuals make such a tense situation easier—or harder—for one another? Have groups of seven students choose roles (the five Robertsons, Robin, and a TV reporter) and hold a post-rescue press conference to discuss how the castaways controlled their tempers and their fears during their odyssey.

Roll Again. Have groups of three or four students create a board game based on *Survive the Savage Sea.* Students might design their game like a pictorial map, showing the actual route of the raft. Encourage them to include as many events from the text as they can, and remind them to maintain the chronological order of the story. Provide class time for students to play the game. As an alternative, students might design a board game based on "He Ate Ants."

In Case of Emergency. Have students name several types of emergencies, such as fire, a car accident, or a lost pet. Assign one emergency to each of several groups of three or four students. Ask them to brainstorm the topic and form emergency plans. Each student can present one part of the group's study—details of the emergency, preventive measures, plan of escape or rescue—to the class. Students might compile a book of emergency guidelines.

during his watch. "You take a honeydew melon," he said. "Cut the top off and take out the seeds; that's the dish. Chill it and drop a knob of ice cream in, then pile in strawberries, raspberries, pieces of apple, pear, orange, peach and grapefruit, the sweet sort, then cherries and grapes until the melon is full; pour a lemon syrup over it and decorate it with chips of chocolate and nuts. Then," he said with a dreamy expression on his face, "you eat it!" "I'll have one too," I said, taking the bailer from his boil-covered hand; I looked at the sky; to the northeast a faint film of cirrostratus cloud[18] dimmed the stars. "You know, I think it might rain by morning." I could feel him relax in the darkness; his voice came slowly, "I'll be all right if it doesn't, Dad," he said.

Fifteenth Day

. . . The twins were talking when Douglas, on watch, his voice desperate with dismay, called, "Dad, the dinghy's gone!" I was across the raft in an instant. I looked at the broken end of wire trailing in the water, the broken line beside it. The dinghy was sixty yards away, sailing still, and our lives were sailing away with it; I was the fastest swimmer, no time for goodbyes, to the devil with sharks; the thoughts ran through my head as I was diving through the door, my arms flailing into a racing crawl even as I hit the water. I heard Lyn cry out but there was no time for talk. Could I swim faster than the dinghy could sail, that was the point; I glanced at it as I lifted my head to breathe, the sail had collapsed as the dinghy yawed,[19] I moved my arms faster, kicked harder, would the sharks let me, that was another point; my belly crawled as I thought of the sharks, my arms moved faster still; I glanced again, only thirty yards to go but she was sailing again, I felt no fatigue, no cramped muscles, my

18. **cirrostratus** (sir'ō·strāt'əs) **cloud:** thin, high white cloud.
19. **yawed:** swung back and forth, pushed by the waves.

SURVIVE THE SAVAGE SEA   451

A Reading Skills and Strategies
Comparing/Contrasting
Ask students to compare and contrast this exchange and Dougal's conversation with Douglas on pp. 448–449. [Possible responses: In the earlier exchange, the son is looking for reassurance that it will rain; the father is angry that he cannot comfort Douglas. In the later conversation, the two seek to reassure each other; they may be ashamed of giving in to panic and ill temper; they are trying to be brave.]

B Reading Skills and Strategies

Adjusting Reading Rate
❓ What does this sentence indicate about the coming journal entry? [Possible response: It will be exciting and dramatic, since an emergency has taken place.] How do you think the pace of your reading might change? [Students may read faster to find out what happens. Point out that students can read more slowly if they become confused by unfamiliar words or difficult sentence structure.]

C Elements of Literature
Main Idea
❓ What are Dougal's responses to the loss of the dinghy? [Possible responses: The family is likely to die; it is up to him to catch the boat, because he is the fastest swimmer; he can't let grief or fear prevent him.] What main idea do you draw from these details? [Possible response: If he does not act quickly and courageously, they will all perish.]

D Appreciating Language
Style
Writers sometimes present a character's thoughts exactly the way he or she is thinking them. Here, Dougal writes a long run-on sentence with clauses linked by commas. Have a volunteer read this sentence aloud to its end. Discuss whether the technique is effective here. [Possible responses: In an emergency, people's thoughts may flow more quickly; this style adds realism and increases the sense of danger.]

Making the Connections

Connecting to the Theme: "This Old Earth"
After students have read the selection, have them consider how it relates to the collection theme. [Possible responses: Dougal and the other castaways must battle nature—sharks, waves, parching sun, and scarce rain—in order to survive. They probably gain an appreciation for the sea as a cruel environment and for the earth as their home.]

A Struggling Readers

Rereading

❓ After students have read this journal entry from its beginning (p. 451), have them reread it to identify its main idea. [Possible responses: "The dinghy was . . . sailing away . . . and our lives were sailing away with it"; "only one thought now in mind, the dinghy or us."] What details support this idea? [Possible responses: Douglas panics when the dinghy breaks away; Dougal risks his life for the dinghy without even stopping to say goodbye; Dougal doesn't feel any physical strain from the swim until he is aboard the dinghy.]

B Elements of Literature

Main Idea

❓ What is the narrator's conclusion about living at sea? [Possible response: He thinks there is little chance that humans can live at sea as successfully as they live on land.]

C Reading Skills and Strategies

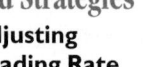

Adjusting Reading Rate

❓ After they have completed this paragraph, ask students how they mastered it. [Possible responses: repeated reading; reading more slowly.] How does this paragraph differ from the one before it? [Possible response: The pace is much slower, because the paragraph contains only thought and no action, and the vocabulary is more difficult and abstract.]

Developing Vocabulary by Listening to Literature Read Aloud

Students acquire vocabulary through listening to selections read aloud. The vocabulary in this true survival story may challenge some readers. Read aloud the last paragraph on this page. Ask students to jot down unfamiliar words or phrases as they listen. (Students might list *adapted, pondered,* and *finesse.*) Write some of the words on the board, and ask students to guess at their meanings. Students should draw on their experiences and use the context to figure out a word's meaning.

---

body felt like a machine as I thrashed my way through the sea only one thought now in mind, the dinghy or us. Then I was there; with a quick heave I flipped over the stern of the dinghy to safety, reached up and tore down the sail before my knees buckled and I lay across the thwart trembling and gasping for breath, my heart **A** pounding like a hammer. I lifted my arm and waved to the raft, now two hundred yards away; then slowly I untied the paddle from the sail and paddled back to the raft; it took nearly half an hour. The long shapes of two sharks circled curiously twenty feet down; they must have had breakfast.

. . . I felt that we had already gone beyond thinking in terms of survival. We had started living from the sea as an adapted way of life, for not only were we surviving, we were improving our physical condition. As we settled to rest, I pondered the philosophies of advocates of "at sea" living. To my mind there was little prospect of man developing a cultural relation- **B** ship with the sea, in the way that he has done **C** with the land; the predatory emotions which are brought to the fore to make living possible in this primitive style are not compatible with emotional beauty or intellectual finesse. However, we no longer thought of rescue as one of the main objectives of our existence; we were no longer subject to the daily disappointment of a lonely vigil, to the idea that help might be at hand or was necessary. We no longer had that helpless feeling of dependence on others for our continued existence. We were alone, and stood alone, inhabitants of the savage sea. . . .

Twenty-ninth Day

We made good headway in the gentle westerly

WORDS TO OWN

advocates (ad′və·kits) *n.:* people who speak or write in support of something.
vigil (vij′əl) *n.:* watch; guard.

---

452 THIS OLD EARTH

Using Students' Strengths

Visual Learners

As visual learners read this nonfiction account, they might benefit from filling in the graphic organizer provided in the *Graphic Organizers for Active Reading*, p. 30.

Verbal Learners

Invite students to create postcards from each member of the Robertson party. First, students should write the text for the back of the card, and then they can illustrate the front. Remind students to mention the major events that have happened on the journey, as seen through the eyes of the shipwreck victims.

Eight Bells Folly:
Memorial
to Hart Crane
(1933) by
Marsden
Hartley.

Collection of the
Frederick R. Weisman
Art Museum at the
University of
Minnesota,
Minneapolis. Gift of
Ione and Hudson
Walker.

SURVIVE THE SAVAGE SEA **453**

See the biography of **Marsden Hartley** on p. T352. *Eight Bells Folly: Memorial to Hart Crane* (1933) uses a series of dreamy images that evoke the turbulence of Crane's troubled mind.

Hartley had known the American poet Hart Crane (1899–1932) casually in New York during the late 1920s. When they met again in Mexico in 1932, the two men established a closer rapport. Though Crane had published several poems and two books during the 1920s, he was unable to achieve financial success or personal contentment. On his way home from Mexico in April 1932, he leapt from the ship on which he was traveling. The title of the painting refers to the fact that aboard many ships, bells are rung every half-hour. Eight bells indicate noon, the hour at which Crane jumped overboard.

Activity. Have students list the shapes and objects they recognize in this painting (figure 8, eyeballs, bell, crescent moon, anchor, full moon or sun, waves, and so on). Then, ask the following questions:

1. To what or to whom might the eyes in the painting belong? [Possible response: to other people who have jumped or fallen overboard]

2. What is the overall mood of the painting? [Possible responses: frightening; grim; horrifying.]

Professional Notes

"It has a very mad look as I wish it to have," Hartley wrote in a 1932 letter describing *Eight Bells Folly*. "There is a ship foundering—a sun, a moon, two triangular clouds—a bell with an '8' on it—symbolizing eight bells—or noon when he jumped off—and around the bell are a lot of men's eyes—that look up from below to see who the new lodger is to be—on one cloud will be the number 33—Hart's age." You might ask students whether they find this painting an ironic accompaniment to Robertson's journal.

Skill Link

Identifying Correct Verb Forms

Use this activity before you teach the Language Link exercise on p. 459. It will help you assess students' understanding of correct verb forms. For further practice, students can refer to Using Verbs in the Language Handbook (pp. 726–733).

Activity

In each of the following sentences, select the correct form of the verb in parentheses.

1. The sailors should have (known/know) what to do.
2. Dougal quickly (swum/swam) to the dinghy.
3. Have the Robertsons (bring/brought) enough supplies?
4. They might have (run/ran) out of equipment.
5. The book was (wrote/written) by Dougal after the rescue.

A Reading Skills and Strategies

Making Inferences

? What can you infer about Dougal's character from his use of *calmly* here? [Possible responses: He is very brave; he remains calm in emergencies; he is setting an example for his family.]

B Advanced Learners

A famous story about a battle between a man and sharks is Ernest Hemingway's short novel *The Old Man and the Sea*, in which mako sharks devour the fisherman's catch. Encourage students to read the novel and compare Dougal's mental and physical battle with Santiago's.

C Vocabulary Note

Word Origins

Have students read footnote 23 to be sure they understand this sentence. Then, have students use a dictionary to learn the precise definition of *galvanic*. This adjective means "stimulated as if by an electric shock." The word comes from the name of the Italian physician and physicist Luigi Galvani (1737–1798), whose theories spurred research on electrical currents.

D Reading Skills and Strategies

Making Inferences

? Have a volunteer read footnote 26 aloud. What does this reference to British history tell about how Dougal feels? [Possible responses: He feels like a great hero; he is proud of winning the fight.]

E Elements of Literature

Main Idea

? What is the main idea of this paragraph? [Possible responses: Dougal feels proud of winning an important battle; he has not only defeated the "most feared enemy" but is treating the shark as it would have treated him—by making a meal of it.]

breeze throughout the night, with the sea anchor tripped and *Ednamair* making over a knot[20] to the east-northeast. The rising sun guided our daylight progress and the business of survival resumed its daily routine. I had barely started work on my gaff[21] when, looking down into the sea past the flashing blue, green, and gold of the dorado, I spotted the brown shape of a shark. . . . We had caught a flying fish in the night, a very small one, so I put it on the large hook and weighting the line heavily I cast well out to clear the scavenger fish. My baited hook drifted down past the shark and at first I thought he was going to ignore it, but after it came to rest he turned and nosed toward it. Douglas, stretched across the dinghy in my usual place beside the thwart,[22] called: "What're you doing, Dad?" "Catching a shark," I said calmly, watching the shark nose a little closer. "You're bloody mad," Douglas said, sitting up quickly; Robin, too, was sitting up apprehensively, and Lyn said, "You mustn't." "Good old Dad," said Neil and Sandy from the bow. "I'm having him," I said, watching tensely now, as the shark reached the bait; the moment I felt him touch I would have to strike, for if he got the nylon line between his teeth he would bite through it like butter. I was going to try to get the steel shank of the hook between his jaws. He was over it now, I felt the contact with tingling fingers and struck swiftly, the line exploded into action, he was hooked!

He fought with alternate periods of listless acquiescence and galvanic action,[23] twisting and plunging savagely to rid himself of the hook. I was afraid of the line breaking, but I feared more the arrival of a larger shark which would attack the hooked one. Slowly, foot by foot, he came to the surface, the line cutting deep into the heel of my hand. Lyn sat ready in the stern, paddle in hand. The shark broke surface, struggled savagely, and plunged deeply. I had to let him go, he was still too strong, but he was a nice five-footer. A mako shark, Douglas said (he was our shark expert), and I'd hooked him in the eye! Back up he came. "We'll have him this time," I grunted, my hands aching. "Be ready to take the line, Robin . . . I'm going to grab his tail and pull him in that way." Excitement rose high in the dinghy; Robin and Lyn looked a bit uncomfortable at being given the biting end to look after but were determined to do their best. (I knew he would break free if I tried to haul him in head first by the line.)

The shark surfaced again; gingerly Robin took the line from my hand as I quickly leaned over and grabbed the shark's tail. "Trim!"[24] I shouted and Douglas leaned out on the other side of the dinghy. The harsh skin gave me a good grip, and with a quick pull the shark lay over the gunwale.[25] "Lift its head in now!" I kept a firm grip on the tail as Robin lifted the struggling fish inboard with the line. Lyn rammed the paddle into the gaping jaws and they clamped shut on it. Knife in hand I leaned forward and stabbed it through the other eye; the shark struggled, then lay still. Giving Douglas the tail to hold, I stabbed the knife into the slits of the gills behind the head, sawing away at the tough skin until finally the head was severed. "Right, you can let go now!" I felt like Bruce after Bannockburn.[26] We had turned the tables on our most feared enemy; sharks would not eat Robertsons, Robertsons would eat sharks! Quickly I gutted out the liver and heart: a solid thirty-five to forty pounds of fish with

---

20. **knot:** one nautical mile (6,076.12 feet) per hour.
21. **gaff:** strong hook on a pole, used to catch large fish. Robertson was making a gaff out of materials on the dinghy.
22. **thwart:** rower's seat extending across a boat.
23. **he fought . . . action:** The fish went back and forth between lying still, as if it had given up, and jolting into action, as if it had received an electric shock.

24. **trim:** balance a boat by moving the weight around.
25. **gunwale** (gun′əl): upper edge of the side of a boat. Originally, the gunwale supported a ship's guns.
26. **Bruce after Bannockburn:** In 1314, Scotland won independence from England in a battle at the Scottish town of Bannockburn. Robert the Bruce led the Scots against King Edward II's much larger English forces.

Taking a Second Look

Review: Summarizing

Remind students that a summary is a short restatement of the most important events and ideas of a text. The best summaries are complete and concise.

Activity

1. Have students imagine themselves as Dougal on the day the *Lucette* sinks. He wants to keep a journal, but the only available paper is a stack of index cards. He must fit each day's journal entry on one card. Provide each student with three 3-by-5 cards and ask them to choose three entries to summarize.

2. Call on volunteers to read their summaries aloud in class. Encourage listeners to consider if each summary includes all the important information from Robertson's full text.

3. As an extension, students can repeat this exercise with journal entries written for the Advanced Learners activity on p. T446 or the second Choices activity, p. 458.

very little waste apart from the head. We breakfasted on the liver and heart, then Robin chewed the head, watching carefully for the razor-sharp teeth, while I cut strips of white flesh from the almost boneless carcass. It was tougher than the dorado, but juicier, and we chewed the moist strips of shark meat with great relish. . . .

Thirty-eighth Day

. . . The clouds grew thicker as the afternoon advanced; it was going to be a wet night again and perhaps we would be able to fill the water sleeve. Seven gallons of water seemed like wealth beyond measure in our altered sense of values.

I chopped up some dried turtle meat for tea, and Lyn put it with a little wet fish to soak in meat juice. She spread the dry sheets for the twins under the canopy, then prepared their "little supper" as we started to talk of Dougal's Kitchen and if it should have a wine license. As we pondered the delights of Gaelic coffee, my eye, looking past the sail, caught sight of something that wasn't sea. I stopped talking and stared; the others all looked at me. "A ship," I said. "There's a ship and it's coming toward us!" I could hardly believe it but it seemed solid enough. "Keep still now!" In the sudden surge of excitement, everyone wanted to see. "Trim her! We mustn't capsize now!" All sank back to their places.

I felt my voice tremble as I told them that I was going to stand on the thwart and hold a flare above the sail. They trimmed the dinghy as I stood on the thwart. "Right, hand me a flare, and remember what happened with the last ship we saw!" They suddenly fell silent in memory of that terrible despondency when our signals had been unnoticed. "O God!" prayed Lyn, "please let them see us." I could see the ship quite clearly now, a Japanese tuna fisher. Her gray and white paint stood out clearly against the dark cross swell. "Like a

great white bird," Lyn said to the twins, and she would pass within about a mile of us at her nearest approach. I relayed the information as they listened excitedly, the tension of not knowing, of <u>imminent</u> rescue, building like a tangible, touchable, unbearable unreality around me. My eye caught the outlines of two large sharks, a hundred yards to starboard. "Watch the trim," I warned. "We have two man-eating sharks waiting if we capsize!" Then, "I'm going to light the flare now; have the torch ready in case it doesn't work."

I ripped the caps off, pulled out the striker, and struck the primer. The flare smoked, then sparked into life, the red glare illuminating *Ednamair* and the sea around us in the twilight. I could feel my index finger roasting under the heat of the flare and waved it to and fro to escape the searing heat radiating outward in the calm air; then, unable to bear the heat any longer, I dropped my arm, nearly scorching Lyn's face, and threw the flare high in the air. It curved in a brilliant arc and dropped into the sea. "Hand me another, I think she's altered course!" My voice was hoarse with pain and excitement and I felt sick with apprehension that it might only be the ship corkscrewing in the swell, for she had made no signal that she had seen us. The second flare didn't work. I cursed it in frustrated anguish as the priming substance chipped off instead of lighting. "The torch!" I shouted, but it wasn't needed; she had seen us, and was coming toward us.

I flopped down on the thwart. "Our ordeal is over," I said quietly. Lyn and the twins were crying with happiness; Douglas, with tears of joy in his eyes, hugged his mother. Robin laughed and cried at the same time, slapped me on the back, and shouted "Wonderful! We've done it. Oh! Wonderful!" I put my arms

---

WORDS TO OWN
imminent (im′ə·nənt) *adj.*: about to happen.

SURVIVE THE SAVAGE SEA 455

F Reading Skills and Strategies

Adjusting Reading Rate

During this passage of increasing tension and excitement, some students might choose to speed up their reading. Other students might slow down to be sure that they understand each phrase and sentence.

G Elements of Literature

Character

❓ What do his actions and statements tell you about Dougal's character? [Possible responses: He keeps calm in a crisis; the sight of the ship doesn't make him do anything foolish; he doesn't act without thinking.]

Skill Link

Decoding: Consonant Combinations

Discuss with students the following information and strategies for dealing with unusual consonant combinations.

1. A digraph is a two-letter combination. In the digraphs *ch*, *sh*, *th*, and *wh*, each pair of letters stands for a single sound.

2. Analyze words. Does a word have a grammatical suffix like *-ing*? *Corkscrewing* is more manageable when it is broken into parts: *cork* + *screw* + *-ing*.

3. If you're having trouble including a letter sound or if the word sounds strange when you do include it, the letter or letters might be silent: *slightest*.

4. The letter *w* is not always a consonant. It can be part of the spelling for the vowel sound.

Activity

Write the following items on the board. Have students tell which strategies helped them read the underlined words.

1. He <u>thrashed</u> his way through the sea. [The combination *thr* is made up of the digraph *th* and *r*.]

2. Losing the <u>dinghy</u> would be a disaster. [The word can be divided into syllables: *din-ghy*; the *h* is silent.]

3. Exhausted, he <u>sprawled</u> on the floor of the raft. [The *w* is part of the vowel sound.]

4. In the <u>twilight</u>, the flare lit up the sea. [In the combination *ght*, *g* and *h* are silent.]

? Why is Dougal sure he will never again be so contented? [Possible responses: He will never again face such a difficult challenge; future triumphs will seem less wonderful because they will be easier to achieve.]

B **Elements of Literature**

Main Idea

Ask students to explain the main idea of the final sentence. [Possible responses: The Robertsons are grateful for the care the captain and crew gave them—kindness, generosity, and compassion that allowed the family members to regain their physical strength and sense of well-being.]

Resources

Selection Assessment
Formal Assessment
• Selection Test, p. 89
Test Generator
• Selection Test

about Lyn, feeling the tears stinging my own eyes: "We'll get these boys to land after all." As we shared our happiness and watched the fishing boat close with us, death could have taken me quite easily just then, for I knew that I would never experience another such pinnacle of contentment.

In the days that followed we indulged in the luxury of eating and drinking wonderful food, the meals growing in quantity and sophistication. The familiar figure of the cook, Sakae Sasaki, became the symbol around which our whole existence revolved as he bore tray after tray up the foredeck to us. Spinach soup, prawns, fruit juices, fried chicken, roast pork, tinned fruit, fermented rice water, coffee, and, a special treat, lemon-flavored tea; and always in the background of our diet, like the foundation stones of a building, bread and butter. The assault upon our stomachs seemed unending and even when they were full, we still felt hungry—a most frustrating sensation! Our bones and bodies ached in contact with the unyielding deck, luxuriated in the deep hot sea water bath, groaned under the burden of indigestion, relaxed in the cool of the tropical night, and each day we gently exercised our swollen ankles and weakly legs, learning to walk again. . . . In four days Captain Kiyato Suzuki and his wonderful crew brought the milk of human kindness to our tortured spirits and peace to our savage minds.

MEET THE WRITER

"Why Not Indeed?"

Dougal Robertson (1924–1992) was born in Edinburgh, Scotland. After attending Leith Nautical College, Robertson joined the British Merchant Navy. He then took a leave from maritime life to raise a family and work as a dairy farmer.

Robertson and his wife were sitting around the kitchen one day with their four children, listening to a radio broadcast about a yacht race and chatting about their own sailing days. Dougal would long remember what happened next.

66 Suddenly Neil shouted, 'Daddy's a sailor, why can't we go around the world?' Lyn burst out laughing and 'What a lovely idea!' she exclaimed. 'Let's buy a boat and go round the world.' Why not? I looked at Anne [who did not make the trip] and Douglas, both handsome children but the horizons of their minds stunted by the limitations of their environment. In two years they would both have reached school-leaving age, and neither had shown any aptitude for academic study, and the twins, already backward compared with their contemporaries in town, were unlikely to blossom into sudden educational prodigies. In two years' time they would finish their primary school and then . . . Why not indeed? 99

This was the lighthearted beginning of an adventure that eventually took the Robertsons within an inch of their lives.

(Opposite) The rescue, after thirty-eight days adrift.

Assessing Learning

Check Test: Short Answers
1. How many days is the group adrift on the raft? [38]
2. Besides their original stores, what do the castaways eat and drink? [fish, shark, turtle; rainwater, turtle blood]
3. What do they daydream about to lift their spirits? [the food they wish they could eat; a restaurant they could open]
4. What happens after the dinghy breaks away? [Dougal swims to recapture it.]

5. How is the group rescued? [The flare is seen by the crew of a Japanese fishing boat.]

Standardized Test Preparation
For practice with a standardized test format specific to this selection, see
• *Standardized Test Preparation,* p. 68
For practice in proofreading and editing, see
• *Daily Oral Grammar,* Transparency 26

MAKING MEANINGS

First Thoughts

[connect]

1. Complete two of these sentences:
   - I admired . . . because . . .
   - I'd like to talk to . . . about . . .
   - At the end of the story, I felt . . . because . . .

Shaping Interpretations

[synthesize]

2. Get together with two or three classmates, and discuss the words you chose as the most important in the entry called "Thirty-eighth Day." Use your key words to state the **main idea** of that section.

[compare]

3. Look back at the difficult passages you noted as you read. Then, compare your passages with a classmate's. Were any of your choices the same as your partner's? How did you and your partner get through the difficult passages?

[predict]

4. Compare the problems you listed in the chart on page 444 with the ones the Robertsons faced. What physical needs and discomforts did you **predict** correctly? What hazards did you overlook, if any?

[analyze]

5. How did Dougal and the others change as they struggled to survive?

[evaluate]

6. The family would not have made it without the father. What are Dougal's personal qualities? How does Dougal compare with the person you described in your notes for the Quickwrite on page 444?

Extending the Text

[hypothesize]

7. Dougal Robertson has said, "Survival is the hardest school in life; there are no failures." What other true survival stories do you know of? Why do you think some people survive such ordeals while other people perish?

Reading Check

Fill in the graphic organizer below with information you have just learned about the Robertsons' journey.

Main characters
Their problem (conflict)
Event 1
↓
Event 2 (and so on)
↓
Resolution

Reading Check

Main characters—Dougal, Lyn, Neil, Sandy, and Douglas Robertson; Robin (a family friend)
Conflict—to survive until they can reach land or until a ship rescues them
Events—signaling the first ship; the drought; recapturing the dinghy; killing the shark; signaling the second ship
Resolution—the rescue

MAKING MEANINGS

First Thoughts

1. Possible responses: I admired Dougal because he kept his sense of humor; I'd like to talk to Dougal about how he found strength to kill the shark; at the end of the story, I felt happy because the Robertsons had survived.

Shaping Interpretations

2. Possible responses: Because of our *altered sense of values*, even a little increase in our water supply was a relief to us. When we spotted a *ship*, we knew that we *mustn't capsize now.* Our greatest fear was that the ship wouldn't *see us.* We also noticed that *two man-eating sharks were nearby.* Then, we realized that the ship *was coming toward us* and that *our ordeal was over.* I was full of *contentment.*

3. Some students may have discussed passages with a partner or a family member. Others may have reread difficult passages sentence by sentence until they understood them.

4. Students may have mentioned dangerous fish and hunger but may not have thought about the relentless sun.

5. Possible responses: They had no hesitations about eating raw fish or drinking blood—activities that would have horrified them before the shipwreck. They became more aware of their physical surroundings and of the need to avoid danger. They appreciated even minor good fortune.

6. Possible responses: Dougal is calm and practical in an emergency; he does not dwell on difficulties; he tries to keep everyone cheerful.

Extending the Text

7. Students may suggest that survival depends on a combination of luck, strength, intelligence, and will.

Grading Timesaver

Rubrics for each Choices assignment appear on p. 160 in the *Portfolio Management System*.

CHOICES: Building Your Portfolio

1. **Writer's Notebook** Encourage students to write about a person they know rather than choose a celebrity or historical figure.

2. **Creative Writing** Students should keep their journal entries consistent with details in the text. They might prefer to imagine and write about events on days not covered in this excerpt.

3. **Reading/Speaking and Listening** Make sure students clear their literary choices with you before they begin reading. Another story that might interest them is *The Long Winter*, Laura Ingalls Wilder's account of a small Dakota town facing fierce blizzards and starvation during the winter and spring of 1880–1881.

4. **Health** Have students first decide on a specific situation for which they will need the kit, since different climates and environments call for different survival gear. For instance, the hardships that could occur during a car trip through the southwestern desert in July are different from those that could result from climbing the wintry Rocky Mountains. Challenge students to take into account various difficulties they might face.

5. **Informative Report/Science** Students may already know that the North Star (the last star in the "handle" of the Little Dipper) almost never moves when viewed from Earth. This nearly fixed point is an important element in navigating by the stars.

CHOICES: Building Your Portfolio

Writer's Notebook

1. Collecting Ideas for Observational Writing

Dougal Robertson's cheerfulness and determination helped the family survive. Every person has **characteristics** that set him or her apart from others. Picture a person you admire. Have you observed actions and personal qualities that set this person apart from the crowd? Write down all the details you can think of that make this person special in your eyes.

> My friend Lance
> —helps elderly neighbor
> —makes everyone laugh
> —is considerate
> —has great sense of humor

Creative Writing

2. Writing at Sea

Dougal Robertson tells this story, so you don't learn much about the other characters' thoughts and feelings. Write some journal entries that one of the other characters on the raft might have jotted down during the first few hours after the *Lucette* sank. In your entries, cite the date and mention the kind of material the writer is using to write on.

Reading/ Speaking and Listening

3. Against All Odds

If a hiker survives an avalanche by building a snow cave, you're sure to hear about it on TV. Survival stories, whether true or fictional, have been popular ever since people first began to tell stories. Read one famous survival story, such as *Julie of the Wolves, Hatchet, From the Mixed-up Files of Mrs. Basil E. Frankweiler, The Incredible Journey,* or *Kon-Tiki,* and report on it to your class. When you **summarize** the story, focus on problems and solutions. Then, use the story to show why (in your opinion) survival against great odds is a theme that readers can't resist.

Health

4. Survival Kit

Fortunately, the Robertsons had a survival kit on their raft. Describe the contents of a survival kit of your own. Imagine a situation in which you might need such a kit—for example, for your car in case you're stranded in a snowstorm, for your home in case of a blackout, or for a camping trip in case you get lost. You might contact the American Red Cross to request a list of what to include in your kit.

Informative Report/ Science

5. Steering by the Stars

Robertson had no maps, charts, or instruments, yet he was able to steer a course for Costa Rica, a thousand miles away. How did he do it? Write a report about how sailors at sea can use the sun and stars as guides to navigation. Use graphic aids like charts and diagrams to illustrate your report.

458 THIS OLD EARTH

LANGUAGE LINK MINI-LESSON

• Style: Active and Passive Voice

When you want to focus on what is done rather than on who is doing it, use the **passive voice.** Compare these two examples:

ACTIVE VOICE   Dougal <u>made</u> mistakes.

PASSIVE VOICE   Mistakes <u>were made</u>.

The sentence *Mistakes were made* avoids the finger pointing suggested by *Dougal made mistakes.*

When you are unsure who is doing the action, use the passive voice.

PASSIVE VOICE   A ship <u>was spotted</u>.

In most other cases, *avoid* the passive voice. Compare these two sentences:

PASSIVE VOICE   The flare was thrown high in the air by me.

ACTIVE VOICE   I threw the flare high in the air.

As you can see, the **active voice** is more direct, forceful, and concise.

Try It Out

➤ Choose an action-packed passage from "Survive the Savage Sea," perhaps the scene in which Dougal recaptures the drifting dinghy (pages 451–452). Rewrite it in the passive voice. Then, read both the original and the rewritten versions aloud. Which do you like better? Why?

➤ Take out a piece of your own writing, and see how often you've used the passive voice. To check your verbs, circle each one with a highlighter. If you used passive verbs, evaluate them: Would your sentences be stronger in the active voice?

VOCABULARY HOW TO OWN A WORD

WORD BANK	Back to the Story
debris	1. Why were the Robertsons interested in collecting <u>debris</u>?
meager	2. What did the Robertsons regret having in <u>meager</u> amounts? What did they regret having in <u>copious</u> amounts?
tenets	
copious	3. What did the Robertsons do about their <u>scanty</u> food supply?
scanty	4. Why did Dougal say that keeping a steady <u>vigil</u> is one of the <u>tenets</u> of good seamanship?
deteriorating	
testily	5. When and why did Dougal speak <u>testily</u> to his son?
advocates	6. When did the group first realize that rescue was <u>imminent</u>?
vigil	7. Why would Dougal agree with <u>advocates</u> of a never-say-die philosophy?
imminent	
	8. What caused the <u>deteriorating</u> condition of the raft?

SURVIVE THE SAVAGE SEA 459

LANGUAGE LINK

Have students look for examples of the active and passive voice in their own writing. They can rewrite passive-voice sentences to put them in the active voice. Then, have students choose partners and share both the original and the rewritten sentences. Partners may discuss which sentences are more vivid and interesting.

Try It Out

Students need not recast every sentence in this passage. Instead, they can summarize what happens, in their own words, using the passive voice. For example, the beginning of a rewritten version might read: I was told by Douglas that the dinghy was drifting away. I was frightened by the sight of sharks. If the dinghy was not recaptured, we would die.

VOCABULARY
Possible Answers

1. They wanted to retrieve anything that might be useful, even discarded objects.
2. Meager—food, water, flares; copious—miles between them and land.
3. They caught fish and turtles.
4. Keeping watch is an important principle because it warns you of danger.
5. He snapped when Douglas pressed him to predict if it would rain because he felt helpless.
6. They saw the Japanese ship change course and knew it would reach them soon.
7. The supporters of this philosophy refuse to give up.
8. Conditions worsened because of the heat, salt water, and drought.

Resources

Language Link Quick Check

After identifying the voice in the following sentences, rewrite each sentence, changing the voice from passive to active or active to passive.

1. The teddy bear was lost by Neil. [Passive; Neil lost the teddy bear.]
2. Dougal retrieved the dinghy. [Active; The dinghy was retrieved by Dougal.]
3. We might be eaten by the sharks. [Passive; The sharks might eat us.]
4. A ship was spotted by Douglas. [Passive; Douglas spotted a ship.]
5. Dougal caught a shark. [Active; A shark was caught by Dougal.]

T459

OBJECTIVES

1. Read and interpret the poem
2. Analyze exact and slant rhymes
3. Express understanding through observational and creative writing or science

SKILLS

Literary
- Analyze exact and slant rhymes

Writing
- Collect ideas for an observational essay
- Write a poem about a place

Science
- Create a museum display

Planning

- **Traditional Schedule**
  Lesson Plans Including Strategies for English-Language Learners
- **One-Stop Planner**
  CD-ROM with Test Generator

Before You Read

MAGGIE AND MILLY AND MOLLY AND MAY

Make the Connection

By the Sea, You and Me

"Maggie and milly and molly and may" is a poem about water—the most precious element on our planet. What do you associate with the sea? Close your eyes and let sights, sounds, smells, and feelings fill your mind.

Quickwrite

Write down the sensory details you associate with the sea in any "ocean shape" that inspires you, such as a starfish, an octopus, or a series of waves.

salty air

Elements of Literature

Kinds of Rhymes

E. E. Cummings is famous for the ways he plays with sounds and punctuation. This poem is filled with rhyming sounds. Some of the rhymes are **exact** (*may/day, stone/alone, me/sea*),

but some catch us by surprise because they are slightly off. These near rhymes are called **slant rhymes.** *Milly* and *molly,* for example, form a slant rhyme: Their sounds almost rhyme—but not exactly.

> **S**lant rhymes have sounds that are similar but not exactly the same.
>
> *For more on Rhyme, see pages 338–339 and the Handbook of Literary Terms.*

Background

Literature and Language

Editors are probably itching to capitalize the *m*'s in the title of this poem, but they'd better keep their pencils to themselves. E. E. Cummings did not use standard punctuation (or any punctuation, in many cases), and he stopped capitalizing early in his writing career. These quirks of **style** are trademarks of his poetry.

 go.hrw.com
LE0 7-6

460 THIS OLD EARTH

  Resources: Print and Media

Reading
- *Graphic Organizers for Active Reading,* p. 31
- *Audio CD Library*
  Disc 12, Track 2

Assessment
- *Formal Assessment,* p. 91
- *Portfolio Management System,* p. 162
- *Test Generator (One-Stop Planner CD-ROM)*

Internet
- go.hrw.com (keyword LE0 7-6)

maggie and milly and molly and may

E. E. Cummings

maggie and milly and molly and may
went down to the beach(to play one day) **A**

and maggie discovered a shell that sang
so sweetly she couldn't remember her troubles,and

5   milly befriended a stranded star
whose rays five languid° fingers were; **C**

B

and molly was chased by a horrible thing
which raced sideways while blowing bubbles:and

may came home with a smooth round stone
10   as small as a world and as large as alone.

For whatever we lose(like a you or a me)
it's always ourselves we find in the sea **D**

6. **languid:** drooping; weak; slow.

Summary ■■■

Four girls go to a beach one day. Each girl discovers an object that reflects something about herself.

Resources

Listening
Audio CD Library
A reading of this lyric poem is provided in the *Audio CD Library*:
• Disc 12, Track 2
Selection Assessment
Formal Assessment
• Selection Test, p. 91
Test Generator
• Selection Test

Ⓐ Elements of Literature
Alliteration
❓ Ask students to read the first line aloud. What does the poem gain from the repeated *m* sound? [Alliteration makes the line musical, catchy, and easy to remember.] Have students point out and discuss other examples of alliteration as they read the poem.

Ⓑ Critical Thinking
Interpreting
❓ What object does each girl find? [a shell, a starfish, a crab or a breaking wave, a stone]

Ⓒ Elements of Literature
Rhyme
❓ How is the rhyme *star/were* different from the rhyme *may/day*? [*May/day* is an example of exact rhyme; *star/were* is an example of slant rhyme.]

Ⓓ Reading Skills and Strategies
Comparing/Contrasting
❓ How would you describe the girls by what they find? [Possible responses: Maggie is a dreamer; Milly is friendly; Molly is fearful; May is thoughtful.]

Reaching All Students

Struggling Readers
Have each student copy the poem, using conventional capitalization and punctuation. Point out that the poem could contain only two sentences—l. 1–10 and l. 11–12—or it could contain six sentences. Have students reread their versions several times to be sure they grasp each image and idea. Then, have them return to the poem as Cummings wrote it.

English Language Learners
Have students choose partners with whom to read the poem aloud. Partners should take turns reading and listening. Encourage students to help correct each other's pronunciation and understanding of unfamiliar vocabulary. Then, have them repeat the activity, this time concentrating on the alliteration, rhyme, and rhythm.

Partners should share their reactions to both the meaning and the sound. For additional strategies to supplement instruction for these students, see
• *Lesson Plans Including Strategies for English-Language Learners*

MEET THE WRITER

"unknown and unknowable"

E. E. Cummings (1894–1962) started writing poetry as a student at Harvard University. After he read some ancient classical poetry, suddenly, as he put it, "an unknown and unknowable bird started singing." During World War I, Cummings was an ambulance driver in France. He was mistakenly arrested for treason and clapped into detention for three months. That experience was a turning point in his life. In prison, Cummings discovered his passion for freedom and personal growth. Over the next four decades he celebrated these passions. The following quote is from the preface to a book of Cummings's poems. The words appear here just as he wrote them.

> 66 The poems to come are for you and for me and are not for mostpeople
>   —it's no use trying to pretend that mostpeople and ourselves are alike. Mostpeople have less in common with ourselves than the squarerootofminusone. You and I are human beings;mostpeople are snobs. . . .
>
>   you and I are not snobs. We can never be born enough. We are human beings;for whom birth is a supremely welcome mystery,the mystery of growing:the mystery which happens only and whenever we are faithful to ourselves. 99

Student to Student

Student to Student

The Desert

As I walk in the desert,
I see a coral snake passing by,
and the bright sun shines the day.

I hear birds singing on a
5 Ⓐ mesquite tree. I hear animals
crying for food and water.

I feel a strong breeze passing by,
and the animals come to me
so I can touch them.

10 Ⓑ So next time you are in
a desert, like me, see things,
feel things, and hear things.

—Eucario Mendez,
6th grade
Tucson, Arizona

Making the Connections

Connecting to the Theme: "This Old Earth"

After students have read the Cummings poem, discuss the collection theme. What connection does Cummings show between the four girls and the natural world? What does he mean when he says that "it's always ourselves we find in the sea"? [Possible response: Cummings uses specific sensory images to show the connection four young people make with the natural world. Cummings's last line suggests that people seek in nature—and find—reflections of their own characters and personalities.]

Connecting Across Texts

Connecting with "maggie and milly and molly and may"

Ask students what connections they see between "The Desert" and "maggie and milly and molly and may." Are the sea and the desert alike in any way? If so, how? [Possible responses: Both desert and sea are vast natural environments in which humans can find unexpected living and nonliving things. Both poems feature youthful characters who make important, vivid connections with nature.]

MAKING MEANINGS

- [respond]

First Thoughts

1. How do the last lines of the poem strike you? What do they mean to you?

Shaping Interpretations

- [interpret]

2. Cummings writes that "it's always ourselves we find in the sea." How does each girl find herself in the sea?

- [predict]

3. What **exact rhymes** do you hear in the poem? What **slant rhymes** do you hear? What sounds did you *expect* to hear?

Extending the Text

- [hypothesize]

4. What might the girls in Cummings's poem find in the desert described by Eucario Mendez (page 462)? How do you think the speaker of Mendez's poem would feel about the beach?

CHOICES: Building Your Portfolio

Writer's Notebook

1. Collecting Ideas for Observational Writing

Choose a place in nature or a force of nature that arouses a powerful emotion in you—for example, a sunny meadow that makes you feel happy. List your impressions by describing what you see, hear, touch, taste, smell, and feel. Like Mendez, you might say, "As I walk . . . , I see . . . I hear . . . I feel . . .".

Creative Writing

2. Notions of Oceans

Create your own poem about the ocean or another place you've visited, perhaps with a friend. (You might get ideas about the ocean from the notes you made for the Quickwrite on page 460.) Try out any techniques that pleased you in Cummings's poem. You might want to adopt trademarks of Cummings's **style:** no capitalization, not much punctuation, and words run together without space between them.

One writer opened like this:

The beach was clean as milk, the air was sheer as silk, the sun was shining on the shore.

Informative Writing/ Science

3. The Real Thing

Create a museum display that shows the objects maggie, milly, molly, and may find on the beach. Include pictures and scientific information about shells, starfish, crabs (or whatever you think the "horrible thing" is), and stones.

MAGGIE AND MILLY AND MOLLY AND MAY **463**

Assessing Learning

Check Test: True-False

1. Maggie is always cheerful. [False]
2. Molly is fearful at the beach. [True]
3. May discovers a sand castle. [False]
4. The speaker in the poem believes that people can learn important ideas about themselves from the sea. [True]

MAKING MEANINGS

First Thoughts

1. Possible response: We are drawn to natural objects that reflect our personalities in some way. We can also rediscover something about ourselves that we thought we had "lost."

Shaping Interpretations

2. Possible responses: Maggie finds comfort in something that lets her forget; Milly helps a lost creature and thus finds a friend; Molly finds something that makes her fearful and troubled; May finds solitude.
3. Exact: *may/play/day, troubles and/bubbles and, stone/alone, me/sea;* Slant: *milly/molly, star/were, sang/thing.* Students might have expected more exact rhymes because of the poem's simple subject.

Extending the Text

4. The girls might find plants, birds, or animals that would intrigue them. Mendez's speaker seems observant and alert; he or she would probably find much to see, hear, and feel on the beach.

Grading Timesaver

Rubrics for each Choices assignment appear on p. 162 in the *Portfolio Management System.*

CHOICES: Building Your Portfolio

1. **Writer's Notebook** A graphic organizer might help students list details for each of the five senses.
2. **Creative Writing** Since many students may not have visited the ocean, encourage them to write about any setting they like, from a city playground to an apple orchard.
3. **Informative Writing/Science** Challenge students to use the details in l. 8 to determine what Molly's monster might be. [a crab]

OBJECTIVES

I Am of the Earth / Early Song
1. Read and interpret the poems
2. Identify and analyze personification
3. Express understanding through observational and critical writing/cultural connections or paraphrasing

SKILLS

Literary
- Identify and analyze personification

Writing
- Collect ideas for an observational essay
- Analyze and interpret a quotation
- Paraphrase a poem

Viewing/Representing
- Examine Pueblo pottery (ATE)

Planning

- **Block Schedule**
  Block Scheduling Lesson Plans with Pacing Guide
- **Traditional Schedule**
  Lesson Plans Including Strategies for English-Language Learners
- **One-Stop Planner**
  CD-ROM with Test Generator

Speaking and Listening: Appreciating Spoken Language
Play the dramatic readings of these contemporary poems for students (Disc 12, Tracks 3, 4, in the *Audio CD Library*). Ask students to listen for pauses and for emphasis on certain words. Then, ask them to discuss what makes each text appealing.

Before You Read

I AM OF THE EARTH
EARLY SONG

Make the Connection

Mother Earth

Think of all the ways in which you are connected to the earth. To begin, fill in a chart like the one below.

Planet Earth

Gifts we receive from the earth:	Gifts we give back to the earth:

Quickwrite

What is the most important gift the earth gives to you? What is the most important thing you give to the earth? Briefly explain your answers.

Elements of Literature

Personification: Making the World Human

Common sense tells us that a cloud can't cry and a river can't get angry. They can in the imaginations of writers, though.

When writers give human qualities to nonhuman things, they are using **personification.** In "I Am of the Earth," the speaker uses personification to compare the earth to a mother cradling a child.

> **P**ersonification is a kind of metaphor in which a nonhuman thing or quality is talked about as if it were human.
>
> *For more on Personification, see the Handbook of Literary Terms.*

464 THIS OLD EARTH

  — *Resources: Print and Media* —

Reading
- *Graphic Organizers for Active Reading,* p. 32
- *Audio CD Library*
  Disc 12, Tracks 3, 4

Assessment
- *Formal Assessment,* p. 92
- *Portfolio Management System,* p. 163
- *Test Generator (One-Stop Planner CD-ROM)*

I Am of the Earth

Anna Lee Walters

I am of the earth
She is my mother
She bore me with pride
She reared me with love
5   She cradled me each evening
She pushed the wind to make it sing
She built me a house of harmonious colors
She fed me the fruits of her fields
She rewarded me with memories of her smiles
10 She punished me with the passing of time
And at last, when I long to leave
She will embrace me for eternity

Early Song

Gogisgi/Carroll Arnett

As the sun rises
high enough to
warm the frost
off the pine needles,

5   I rise to make
four prayers of
thanksgiving for
this fine clear day,

for this good brown
10 earth, for all
brothers and sisters,
for the dark blood

that runs through me
in a great circle
15 back into this
good brown earth.

Summary ▪

The speaker of "I Am of the Earth" thinks of the earth as a mother: She has raised, fed, and cared for the speaker, and will eventually embrace the speaker in death.

The speaker of "Early Song" gives thanks for a beautiful day, for the people he considers brothers and sisters, for the earth, and for the blood that links humanity to the earth.

Resources ———

Listening
Audio CD Library
Dramatic readings of these poems are provided in the *Audio CD Library:*
• Disc 12, Tracks 3, 4

Ⓐ Elements of Literature
Personification
❓ In "I Am of the Earth," what does the earth do that makes it like a mother? [Possible responses: The earth bears, cares for, nourishes, rewards, punishes, and accepts the speaker.]

Ⓑ Vocabulary Note
Greek Roots
Ask volunteers to define the adjective *harmonious*. [Possible responses: having parts that work well together; having similar ideas, traits, or feelings.] Explain that it is from the Greek word *harmos*, meaning "a fitting" (like the joint connecting two bones). Related words are *harmony*, *harmonic*, and *harmonize*.

Ⓒ Reading Skills and Strategies
Visualizing
❓ What images in "Early Song" help you visualize its setting? [Possible responses: sun rising high, frost, pine needles, fine clear day, good brown earth.] What action words and phrases help you visualize what the speaker does and feels? [Possible responses: rise, make four prayers.]

Ⓓ Critical Thinking
Analyzing Imagery
❓ What beliefs do you think the speaker is conveying by this image? [Possible responses: The speaker comes from, and will return to, the earth; all living things, including the earth, are connected.]

Reaching All Students

English Language Learners
These simple poems provide a good opportunity for students to practice pronunciation and reading aloud. Have each student choose one poem to read aloud to the class. Give students sufficient time to rehearse, and work with them on pronunciation as needed. For additional strategies to supplement instruction for these students, see
• *Lesson Plans Including Strategies for English-Language Learners*

Advanced Learners
Point out the vivid verbs used by the speaker of "I Am of the Earth" to characterize the earth as a mother. First, ask students to choose an object and to decide what kind of person it makes them think of. Students can then write a description (either as a poem or in prose), using vivid verbs to personify the object. Students may decorate their work and post it in the classroom.

Cultural Connections

The four prayers mentioned in l. 6 of "Early Song" (p. 465) are addressed to the north, south, east, and west. Each direction is believed to have specific powers and to offer distinct types of protection to the worshiper.

MEET THE WRITERS

"Words Poured Out..."

Anna Lee Walters (1947–   ) left home at the age of sixteen to attend a boarding school in New Mexico. In the Southwest, Walters began to discover her roots in the Pawnee and Otoe cultures—and in the process unlocked her voice as a writer. She recalls:

❝ Words poured out, page after page. I am still amazed by it, by the torrent of thoughts deposited there.... Today my occupation as a writer is related to what my grandfather and grandmother did when they repeated family history in the manner of their elders, leading the family all over this sacred land, this continent most recently called America in the last five hundred years, in their retelling of the Otoe journey from the dawn of time until they came to rest at Red Rock Creek a little over a century ago. ❞

"What It Feels Like to Be Alive"

Gogisgi/Carroll Arnett (1927–   ), an American of Cherokee descent, was born in Oklahoma City. He has published more than 150 poems and stories in magazines, sometimes under his Cherokee name, Gogisgi.

❝ I write poems because it seems sensible to do so and wasteful not to. A poem has a use insofar as it shows what it feels like to be alive. ❞

466 THIS OLD EARTH

Skill Link

Reading: Describing Mental Images

The concrete images in these poems provide an opportunity for students to write about the mental pictures the words and phrases evoke.

Activity

1. Have students reread both poems and take notes on the pictures that come into their minds. For example, what do students see when they read "She pushed the wind to make it sing"?
2. Have students expand their notes into sentences and paragraphs describing their mental images. Encourage students to use vivid verbs and specific nouns and adjectives to describe what they imagine. If students have difficulty putting their ideas into words, suggest that they first draw the pictures they visualize. Then, they can try writing about the pictures.
3. Volunteers may share their descriptions with classmates. Are the descriptions different, or did some students see similar images?

I AM OF THE EARTH/EARLY SONG

First Thoughts

[speculate]

1. How does each speaker feel about the earth?

Shaping Interpretations

[compare]

2. Walters **personifies** the earth as her mother. What message or feeling about our world does this comparison convey?

[interpret]

3. What does Arnett mean by the "great circle" (line 14)? How does Walters get at the same idea?

Extending the Text

[connect]

4. Are people always grateful children of the earth? How do some people show that their feelings about the earth are very different from the feelings of these two poets?

CHOICES: Building Your Portfolio

Writer's Notebook

1. Collecting Ideas for Observational Writing

Did the earth—or any part of nature—ever feel human to you? What seemed human, and in what way? Check your notes for the Quickwrite on page 464. Can you build on some of those images now?

Critical Writing/Cultural Connections

2. Lessons of the Earth

The following quotations use features of the earth to teach people lessons. Choose one that you like, and write about what it means to you. Include any experiences from your own life that illustrate the lesson.

"Consider the lilies, how they grow; they neither toil or spin; yet I tell you, even Solomon in all his glory was not arrayed like one of these."

—Luke 12:27, the Bible

"There is no hill that never ends."

—Masai proverb

"Do you have the patience to wait till your mud settles and the water is clear?"

—Tao-te Ching

Paraphrasing

3. In Your Own Words

Write a paraphrase of one of the poems you have just read. (When you **paraphrase** something, you put it in your own words, making sure to keep the writer's meaning.) Paraphrasing can help you understand and recall any written work. Follow these rules:

- Read the poem line by line. Rewrite each line or sentence in prose.

- Restate what the poem says as simply and clearly as you can. Don't include your opinions.

First Thoughts

1. Possible response: These speakers consider the earth a family member or a blood relative.

Shaping Interpretations

2. Possible response: The comparison suggests love and respect for the earth, and the power of the earth to nurture, support, and punish.

3. Possible responses: Arnett refers to the cycle of birth and death. Walters speaks of death as the eternal embrace of the mother earth.

Extending the Text

4. Possible response: People who litter, pollute the air and water, and plunder natural resources without restoring them show no respect for the earth.

Grading Timesaver

Rubrics for each Choices assignment appear on p. 163 in the *Portfolio Management System*.

CHOICES: Building Your Portfolio

1. **Writer's Notebook** Suggest that students use vivid verbs as they write about nature's human qualities.

2. **Critical Writing/Cultural Connections** You might explain that the Tao-te Ching is a work of Chinese philosophy written by Lao Tzu in the sixth century B.C.

3. **Paraphrasing** Some students might speak their paraphrases of each idea or line, rather than write them. Students can also audiotape their paraphrases and then transcribe them.

Making the Connections

Connecting to the Theme: "This Old Earth"

After students have read the poems, discuss the collection theme. How do the two speakers view their places in the world? How do they see their relationships to the earth? [Possible responses: The speakers feel connected to, or deeply rooted in, the natural world. Both speakers stress that life comes from and returns to the earth. The first speaker believes, however, that the earth is not always forgiving; it can also punish.]

Assessing Learning

Check Test: True-False

"I Am of the Earth"

1. The speaker calls the earth *she*. [True]
2. The mother is always nurturing. [False]

"Early Song"

3. The speaker is casual about nature. [False]
4. The title refers to dawn. [True]

T467

OBJECTIVES

1. Read and interpret the story
2. Analyze allusion
3. Identify the author's purpose
4. Express understanding through observational and creative writing, speaking and listening, or drama
5. Recognize and appreciate the use of dialect
6. Understand and use new words

SKILLS

Literary
- Analyze allusion

Reading
- Identify the author's purpose

Writing
- Collect ideas for an observational essay
- Write another conclusion to the story

Speaking/Listening
- Have a discussion and make an oral presentation

Language
- Recognize and analyze dialect

Vocabulary
- Understand and use new words

Drama
- Enact tableaux

Viewing/Representing
- Analyze a painting and compare it with the text (ATE)
- Analyze a photograph and compare it with the text (ATE)

Planning

- **Traditional Schedule**
  Lesson Plans Including Strategies for English-Language Learners
- **One-Stop Planner**
  CD-ROM with Test Generator

Before You Read

ANTAEUS

Make the Connection

Home Sweet Home

There's an old saying that goes, "Home is where the heart is." However, people often disagree about what kind of place makes the best home.

Quickwrite

Which do you prefer: the country or the city? Write down some reasons for your choice, or draw a picture of what you think is the perfect home.

Elements of Literature

Allusion

This story centers on an **allusion** to a character from Greek mythology. The reference is in the title—"Antaeus." Antaeus (an·tē′əs) is a giant whose immense strength comes from his mother, the Earth. As long as his feet are on the ground, Antaeus is unbeatable. The superhero Hercules finds out the giant's secret and kills him by simply lifting him off the ground and strangling him. As you read the story, notice the connection between Antaeus and T. J., a modern-day hero.

> **A**n **allusion** is a reference to a statement, a person, a place, or an event from literature, history, religion, mythology, politics, sports, or science.
>
> *For more on Allusion, see the Handbook of Literary Terms.*

Reading Skills and Strategies

Identifying Purpose: Taking Aim

People write with different purposes in mind. People who write political speeches are usually trying to **persuade** us to believe or do something. People who write articles in magazines often want to **inform** us about something. Novelists and short-story writers usually write for other reasons. Some write to **entertain;** some write to **reveal a truth about life** or to **share or re-create an experience.**

Background

Literature and Social Studies

During World War II, the economy of the United States geared up to produce equipment, weapons, and goods to serve the military effort overseas. As industry went into overdrive, many families left their homes in the South so that the adults could work in factories in the North. This is the situation the narrator is referring to as the story opens.

Preteaching Vocabulary

Words to Own

Have students read the ten Words to Own and their definitions listed at the bottom of the selection pages. Have pairs of students use the words in sentences (students can alternate saying words aloud and making up sentences). Then, ask students to find an antonym, in the right-hand column, for each word on the left.

1. ____	resolute [h]	a.	went up
2. ____	desecrated [c]	b.	narrowing
3. ____	sterile [g]	c.	respected
4. ____	esoteric [e]	d.	active
5. ____	contemplate [f]	e.	ordinary
6. ____	descended [a]	f.	consider carelessly
7. ____	dilating [b]	g.	fruitful
8. ____	inert [d]	h.	uncertain

ANTAEUS

Borden Deal

It was a secret place for us, where nobody else could go without our permission.

ANTAEUS 469

Summary ■ ■ ■

The first-person narrator of this story is an unnamed young city boy who hangs out with a group of friends. When T.J. moves into his building from the rural South, the narrator invites him to join the gang. T.J. wants to plant a field in his new home. He and the other boys agree to plant grass in their secret place—an unused flat roof of a neighborhood factory. They haul earth up to the roof and plant stolen seeds. One day, as they look at the sprouting grass, the factory owner discovers them and orders "all that junk" removed. After protesting, the boys follow T.J.'s lead and destroy their garden themselves. T.J. leaves the city; he is found two weeks later, heading home to Alabama. None of the boys ever returns to the roof.

Resources

Viewing and Representing
Videocassette B, Segment 7
The video segment "To Touch the Earth" shows examples of the natural world found in cities. See the *Visual Connections Teacher's Manual.*

Listening
Audio CD Library
A recording of "Antaeus" is provided in the *Audio CD Library:*
• Disc 12, Track 5

Viewing and Representing
Fine Art Transparency
A fine art transparency of William Low's *Street Scene* will help students appreciate the atmosphere of the story.
• Transparency 15
• Worksheet, p. 60

Resources: Print and Media

Reading
• *Reading Skills and Strategies*
  Selection Skill Lesson, p. 130
• *Graphic Organizers for Active Reading,* p. 33
• *Words to Own,* p. 18
• *Spelling and Decoding*
  Worksheet, p. 22
• *Audio CD Library*
  Disc 12, Track 5

Writing and Language
• *Daily Oral Grammar*
  Transparency 27
• *Grammar and Language Links*
  Worksheet, p. 45

Viewing and Representing
• *Viewing and Representing*
  Fine Art Transparency 15
  Fine Art Worksheet, p. 60
• *Visual Connections*
  Videocassette B, Segment 7

Assessment
• *Formal Assessment,* p. 93
• *Portfolio Management System,* p. 164
• *Standardized Test Preparation,* p. 70
• *Test Generator (One-Stop Planner CD-ROM)*

Internet
• go.hrw.com (keyword: LE0 7-6)

A Struggling Readers

Using Context Clues

❓ Students uncertain about the meaning of *stocky* and *robust* can use the context clue "nothing . . . except." If the writer has contrasted the two unfamiliar words with *sissy*, what do they mean? [Possible responses: "short and sturdy"; "strong, healthy, sturdy."]

RESPONDING TO THE ART

In a career that spanned most of the twentieth century, **Georgia O'Keeffe** (1887–1986) emerged as one of the most original and esteemed figures of modern American art. She is best known for intensely observed, close-up views of flowers. Yet her evocations of southwestern deserts (usually focusing on bones, rocks, shells, and clouds) and of northeastern cityscapes are distinctive as well. Point out that the image on these pages shows a detail of the painting on p. 479.

Activity

1. What does this rooftop view reveal that probably couldn't be seen from the street? [Possible responses: details of the rooftops; the density of the city.]

2. How does this painting help the reader understand what the boys' hangout looks like? [Possible response: The painting shows the absence of nature and of open land in a city neighborhood.]

This was during the wartime, when lots of people were coming North for jobs in factories and war industries, when people moved around a lot more than they do now, and sometimes kids were thrown into new groups and new lives that were completely different from anything they had ever known before. I remember this one kid, T. J. his name was, from somewhere down South, whose family moved into our building during that time. They'd come North with everything they owned piled into the back seat of an old-model sedan that you wouldn't expect could make the trip, with T. J. and his three younger sisters riding shakily on top of the load of junk.

Our building was just like all the others there, with families crowded into a few rooms, and I guess there were twenty-five or thirty kids about my age in that one building. Of course, there were a few of us who formed a gang and ran together all the time after school, and I was the one who brought T. J. in and started the whole thing.

The building right next door to us was a factory where they made walking dolls. It was a low building with a flat, tarred roof that had a parapet[1] all around it about head-high, and we'd found out a long time before that no one, not even the watchman, paid any attention to the roof because it was higher than any of the other buildings around. So my gang used the roof as a headquarters. We could get up there by crossing over to the fire escape from our own roof on a plank and then going on up. It was a secret place for us, where nobody else could go without our permission.

I remember the day I first took T. J. up there

---

1. **parapet:** wall or railing.

470 THIS OLD EARTH

---

to meet the gang. He was a stocky, robust kid with a shock of white hair, nothing sissy about him except his voice; he talked in this slow, gentle voice like you never heard before. He talked different from any of us and you noticed it right away. But I liked him anyway, so I told him to come on up.

We climbed up over the parapet and dropped down on the roof. The rest of the gang were already there.

East River from the 30th Story of the Shelton Hotel (detail) by Georgia O'Keeffe. Oil on canvas (30" x 48").

"Hi," I said. I jerked my thumb at T. J. "He just moved into the building yesterday."

He just stood there, not scared or anything, just looking, like the first time you see somebody you're not sure you're going to like.

"Hi," Blackie said. "Where are you from?"

"Marion County," T. J. said.

We laughed. "Marion County?" I said. "Where's that?"

He looked at me for a moment like I was a stranger, too. "It's in Alabama," he said, like I ought to know where it was.

"What's your name?" Charley said.

"T. J.," he said, looking back at him. He had pale blue eyes that looked washed-out, but he looked directly at Charley, waiting for his re-

---

Reaching All Students

Struggling Readers

Identifying the Author's Purpose was introduced on p. 468. For a lesson directly tied to this selection that teaches students to identify purpose by using a strategy called Text Reformulation, see the *Reading Skills and Strategies* binder:
• Selection Skill Lesson, p. 130

English Language Learners

Students may have some difficulty with the dialect in this story. Have them make a two-column chart in which they can list each example of dialect and its counterpart in standard English. Students might complete the Language Link activity on p. 481 before they begin reading. For additional strategies to supplement instruction for these students, see
• *Lesson Plans Including Strategies for English-Language Learners*

Advanced Learners

Before they read Deal's story, have students read a more comprehensive version of the myth of Antaeus. In this story, Hercules, seeking to obtain the golden apples of the Hesperides, meets and fights Antaeus. Ask students to share the story of Hercules and Antaeus with their classmates. Encourage students to look for parallels between the myth and the short story.

action. He'll be all right, I thought. No sissy in him, except that voice. Who ever talked like that?

"T. J.," Blackie said. "That's just initials. What's your real name? Nobody in the world has just initials."

"I do," he said. "And they're T. J. That's all the name I got."

His voice was <u>resolute</u> with the knowledge of his rightness, and for a moment no one had

New Britain Museum of American Art, New Britain, Connecticut. Stephen Lawrence Fund. Photo credit: E. Irving Blomstrann. ©1998 The Georgia O'Keeffe Foundation/Artists Rights Society (ARS), New York.

anything to say. T. J. looked around at the rooftop and down at the black tar under his feet. "Down yonder where I come from," he said, "we played out in the woods. Don't you-all have no woods around here?"

"Naw," Blackie said. "There's the park a few blocks over, but it's full of kids and cops and old women. You can't do a thing."

T. J. kept looking at the tar under his feet. "You mean you ain't got no fields to raise nothing in?—no watermelons or nothing?"

"Naw," I said scornfully. "What do you want to grow something for? The folks can buy everything they need at the store."

He looked at me again with that strange, unknowing look. "In Marion County," he said, "I

had my own acre of cotton and my own acre of corn. It was mine to plant and make ever' year."

He sounded like it was something to be proud of, and in some obscure way it made the rest of us angry. Blackie said, "Who'd want to have their own acre of cotton and corn? That's just work. What can you do with an acre of cotton and corn?"

T. J. looked at him. "Well, you get part of the bale offen your acre," he said seriously. "And I fed my acre of corn to my calf."

We didn't really know what he was talking about, so we were more puzzled than angry; otherwise, I guess, we'd have chased him off the roof and wouldn't let him be part of our gang. But he was strange and different, and we were all attracted by his stolid sense of rightness and belonging, maybe by the strange softness of his voice contrasting our own tones of speech into harshness.

He moved his foot against the black tar. "We could make our own field right here," he said softly, thoughtfully. "Come spring we could raise us what we want to—watermelons and garden truck and no telling what all."

"You'd have to be a good farmer to make these tar roofs grow any watermelons," I said. We all laughed.

But T. J. looked serious. "We could haul us some dirt up here," he said. "And spread it out even and water it, and before you know it, we'd have us a crop in here." He looked at us intently. "Wouldn't that be fun?"

"They wouldn't let us," Blackie said quickly.

"I thought you said this was you-all's roof,"

WORDS TO OWN

resolute (rez'ə·lōōt') *adj.:* firm and purposeful; determined.

ANTAEUS 471

B **Reading Skills and Strategies**
Making Inferences
❓ What does this passage imply about the narrator? [Possible response: He doesn't usually like people who are different from himself.]

C **Elements of Literature**
Character
❓ What does this detail suggest about T.J.? [Possible responses: He is independent and sure of himself; he doesn't care what other people think about him.]

D **Appreciating Language**
Dialect
Explain that *you-all* is an example of dialect—a way of speaking in a particular region or among a particular group (the example is of southern United States dialect). In standard English, *you* can be either singular or plural; *you-all* is always plural. *Down yonder* means "out there."

E **Elements of Literature**
Allusion
❓ How is T.J. similar to the Greek character Antaeus? [Possible response: Antaeus's strength comes from his mother, the Earth; T.J. doesn't feel at home without fields and woods.]

F **Reading Skills and Strategies**
Identifying Purpose
You might pause at this point and ask students to discuss Deal's purpose in writing this story. [Possible responses: to entertain—he has introduced characters, suggested conflict, and aroused the reader's interest in what the characters will do; to reveal a truth about life—he uses the boys' reactions to one another to suggest universal truths about human relations.]

Taking a Second Look

Review: Making Predictions
Remind students that as they read, they make inferences, or guesses, about what will happen next. These predictions are based on what has happened so far and on the reader's own knowledge and experience. Because Deal's story involves anticipation and suspense, it provides a good opportunity for students to practice this skill.

Activity
1. Before students begin Deal's story, make sure they have read the information about Antaeus (p. 468). What do they think Deal's "Antaeus" will be about? Have them write a response to this question in their notebooks.
2. Have students continue making predictions as they read. Start them off with the question

"How will the gang react to T.J.?" (p. 470, top of column 2). After students have finished reading, have them compare their predictions with actual events in the story.
3. As an extension, have students predict what T.J. might do when he is brought back to the city from Nashville. They can use their predictions as springboards for Choices activity 2 (p. 480).

T471

A Struggling Readers
Interpreting Figurative Language
Ask students what they think the phrase "catch fire" refers to here. [Possible response: There is no actual fire, but T.J.'s idea seizes the narrator's imagination as quickly as a fast-spreading fire.]

B Appreciating Language
Dialect
❓ The word *ourn* is modeled on the possessive pronoun *mine*. How would the word be written in standard English? [*ours*] Also, in T.J.'s dialect, a personal pronoun is often inserted between a verb and its direct object, as in "raise us some cotton." What kind of object is *us* here? [indirect object]

C Reading Skills and Strategies
Making Predictions
Ask students whether they think the garden will grow. [Possible responses: Yes, T.J. is knowledgeable and determined that it will grow; no, the other boys won't help him enough.]

D Elements of Literature
Character
❓ What qualities enable T.J. to keep the boys working? [Possible responses: determination; ability to communicate his dreams; shrewdness in getting others to help.]

T. J. said to me. "That you-all could do anything you wanted to up here."

A "They've never bothered us," I said. I felt the idea beginning to catch fire in me. It was a big idea, and it took a while for it to sink in; but the more I thought about it, the better I liked it. "Say," I said to the gang. "He might have something there. Just make us a regular roof garden, with flowers and grass and trees and everything. And all ours, too," I said. "We wouldn't let anybody up here except the ones we wanted to."

"It'd take a while to grow trees," T. J. said quickly, but we weren't paying any attention to him. They were all talking about it suddenly, all excited with the idea after I'd put it in a way they would catch hold of it. Only rich people had roof gardens, we knew, and the idea of our own private <u>domain</u> excited them.

"We could bring it up in sacks and boxes," Blackie said. "We'd have to do it while the folks weren't paying any attention to us, for we'd have to come up to the roof of our building and then cross over with it."

"Where could we get the dirt?" somebody said worriedly.

"Out of those vacant lots over close to school," Blackie said. "Nobody'd notice if we scraped it up."

I slapped T. J. on the shoulder. "Man, you had a wonderful idea," I said, and everybody grinned at him, remembering that he had started it. "Our own private roof garden."

B He grinned back. "It'll be ourn," he said. "All ourn." Then he looked thoughtful again. "Maybe I can lay my hands on some cotton seed, too. You think we could raise us some cotton?"

We'd started big projects before at one time or another, like any gang of kids, but they'd always petered out[2] for lack of organization and

2. **petered out:** gradually disappeared.

direction. But this one didn't; somehow or other T. J. kept it going all through the winter months. He kept talking about the watermelons and the cotton we'd raise, come spring, and when even that wouldn't work, he'd **C** switch around to my idea of flowers and grass and trees, though he was always honest enough to add that it'd take a while to get any trees started. He always had it on his mind, and he'd mention it in school, getting them lined up to carry dirt that afternoon, saying in a casual way that he reckoned a few more weeks ought to see the job through.

Our little area of private earth grew slowly. T. J. was smart enough to start in one corner of the building, heaping up the carried earth two or three feet thick so that we had an immediate result to look at, to <u>contemplate</u> with awe. Some of the evenings T. J. alone was carrying earth up to the building, the rest of the gang distracted by other enterprises or interests, but T. J. kept plugging along on his own, and eventually we'd all come back to him again, and then our own little acre would grow more rapidly.

He was careful about the kind of dirt he'd let us carry up there, and more than once he dumped a sandy load over the parapet into the areaway below because it wasn't good enough. He found out the kinds of earth in all the vacant lots for blocks around. He'd pick it up and feel it and smell it, frozen though it was sometimes, and then he'd say it was good growing soil or it wasn't worth anything, and we'd have to go on somewhere else.

D Thinking about it now, I don't see how he kept us at it. It was hard work, lugging paper sacks and boxes of dirt all the way up the stairs of our own building, keeping out of the way of

----

WORDS TO OWN
domain (dō·mān′) *n.:* territory.
contemplate (kän′təm·plāt′) *v.:* consider; look at or think about carefully.

Using Students' Strengths

Visual Learners
As students read this short story, they might benefit from filling in the graphic organizer provided in the *Graphic Organizers for Active Reading,* p. 33. Students might also locate and study photographs of the rural South and of a large northern city. What are the most striking differences? If students were in T.J.'s place, what would they miss most about Alabama? What might they do to make their big-city home more like the one they left behind?

Naturalist Learners
Have students plan their own rooftop garden. For this activity, they should assume that they have only garden tools and a few dollars to spend and that they must do all the work themselves. What will they plant? How will they get seeds? Have students work together to draw up a plan for their garden. If possible, encourage students to plant an actual garden—either at home, in a community garden, or in pots or windowboxes in the classroom.

the grown-ups so they wouldn't catch on to what we were doing. They probably wouldn't have cared, for they didn't pay much attention to us, but we wanted to keep it secret anyway. Then we had to go through the trapdoor to our roof, teeter over a plank to the fire escape, then climb two or three stories to the parapet, and drop them down onto the roof. All that for a small pile of earth that sometimes didn't seem worth the effort. But T. J. kept the vision bright within us, his words <u>shrewd</u> and calculated toward the fulfillment of his dream; and he worked harder than any of us. He seemed driven toward a goal that we couldn't see, a particular point in time that would be definitely marked by signs and wonders that only he could see.

The laborious earth just lay there during the cold months, <u>inert</u> and lifeless, the clods lumpy and cold under our feet when we walked over it. But one day it rained, and afterward there was a softness in the air, and the earth was live and giving again with moisture and warmth.

That evening T. J. smelled the air, his nostrils <u>dilating</u> with the odor of the earth under his feet. "It's spring," he said, and there was a gladness rising in his voice that filled us all with the same feeling. "It's mighty late for it, but it's spring. I'd just about decided it wasn't never gonna get here at all."

We were all sniffing at the air, too, trying to smell it the way that T. J. did, and I can still remember the sweet odor of the earth under our feet. It was the first time in my life that spring and spring earth had meant anything to me. I looked at T. J. then, knowing in a faint way the hunger within him through the toilsome[3] winter months, knowing the dream that lay behind his plan. He was a new Antaeus, preparing his own bed of strength.

"Planting time," he said. "We'll have to find us some seed."

3. **toilsome:** involving hard work; laborious.

"What do we do?" Blackie said. "How do we do it?"

"First we'll have to break up the clods," T. J. said. "That won't be hard to do. Then we plant the seeds, and after a while they come up. Then you got you a crop." He frowned. "But you ain't got it raised yet. You got to tend it and hoe it and take care of it, and all the time it's growing and growing, while you're awake and while you're asleep. Then you lay it by when it's growed and let it ripen, and then you got you a crop."

"There's those wholesale seed houses over on Sixth," I said. "We could probably swipe some grass seed over there."

T. J. looked at the earth. "You-all seem mighty set on raising some grass," he said. "I ain't never put no effort into that. I spent all my life trying not to raise grass."

"But it's pretty," Blackie said. "We could play on it and take sunbaths on it. Like having our own lawn. Lots of people got lawns."

"Well," T. J. said. He looked at the rest of us, hesitant for the first time. He kept on looking at us for a moment. "I did have it in mind to raise some corn and vegetables. But we'll plant grass."

He was smart. He knew where to give in. And I don't suppose it made any difference to him, really. He just wanted to grow something, even if it was grass.

"Of course," he said, "I do think we ought to plant a row of watermelons. They'd be mighty nice to eat while we was a-laying on that grass."

We all laughed. "All right," I said. "We'll plant us a row of watermelons."

Things went very quickly then. Perhaps half the roof was covered with the earth, the half

---

WORDS TO OWN
shrewd (shrōōd) *adj.:* clever.
inert (in·urt′) *adj.:* inactive.
dilating (dī′lāt·iŋ) *v.* used as *adj.:* becoming wider.

ANTAEUS **473**

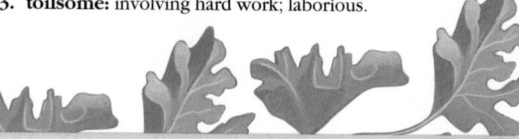

Crossing the Curriculum

Science
Encourage students to investigate the field of horticulture, or gardening. Have students determine what type of soil T.J. is looking for. What other special conditions and equipment would T.J.'s garden need? Have students find out which flowers or vegetables will grow in their local climate. What would these plants require in terms of water, fertilizer, sunlight, and temperature? Students might ask their science teacher for information and advice.

A Critical Thinking

Making Connections

? What is the gang's new understanding about nature? How does this view of nature relate to the view expressed in other selections in this collection? [Possible response: Here and in "The Creation" and "Early Song," nature is seen as a life-giving force. The people of Alaska in "When the Earth Shakes" and the castaways in *Survive the Savage Sea* experience nature's destructiveness.]

B Reading Skills and Strategies

Identifying Purpose

? What can you tell about the group's principles from this passage? [Possible response: Members have learned to respect nature, as shown by the way they treat the fragile grass.] How does this passage suggest that Deal's purpose is to reveal a truth about life? [Possible response: This is a serious passage that describes how the boys have changed since meeting T. J.]

C Reading Skills and Strategies

Making Predictions

? Who are these men? Why have they come to the roof? What do you think will happen, now that these adults have appeared in the story? [Possible responses: The men work in the factory; they are plainclothes detectives. They have heard noise from the roof; neighbors or factory workers have complained about the boys on the roof. Some students may predict that the men will be angry at the boys for bringing the dirt to the roof; other students may predict that the men will be glad that the boys have improved the area.]

D Vocabulary Note

Using Context Clues

Have students use context clues (such as "guilt heavy among us," "tone of voice," and the question just asked by the middle adult) to determine the meaning of *levied*. ["Imposed" or "forced"; the adults' authority imposes guilt on the boys.]

E Critical Thinking

Analyzing Character

? Why does T. J. react differently from the other boys? [He does not realize that a factory roof is considered private property; he is proud of his ability to make plants grow.]

---

that wasn't broken by ventilators,[4] and we swiped pocketfuls of grass seed from the open bins in the wholesale seed house, mingling among the buyers on Saturdays and during the school lunch hour. T. J. showed us how to prepare the earth, breaking up the clods and smoothing it and sowing the grass seed. It looked rich and black now with moisture, receiving of the seed, and it seemed that the grass sprang up overnight, pale green in the early spring.

A We couldn't keep from looking at it, unable to believe that we had created this delicate growth. We looked at T. J. with understanding now, knowing the fulfillment of the plan he had carried along within his mind. We had worked without full understanding of the task, but he had known all the time.

We found that we couldn't walk or play on the delicate blades as we had expected to, but we didn't mind. It was enough just to look at it, to realize that it was the work of our own hands, and each evening, the whole gang was there, trying to measure the growth that had been achieved that day.

B One time a foot was placed on the plot of ground, one time only, Blackie stepping onto it with sudden bravado. Then he looked at the crushed blades and there was shame in his face. He did not do it again. This was his grass, too, and not to be desecrated. No one said anything, for it was not necessary.

T. J. had reserved a small section for watermelons, and he was still trying to find some seed for it. The wholesale house didn't have any watermelon seeds, and we didn't know where we could lay our hands on them. T. J. shaped the earth into mounds ready to receive them, three mounds lying in a straight line along the edge of the grass plot.

We had just about decided that we'd have to buy the seeds if we were to get them. It was

4. **ventilators:** devices used to bring in fresh air.

474 THIS OLD EARTH

a violation of our principles, but we were anxious to get the watermelons started. Somewhere or other, T. J. got his hands on a seed catalog and brought it one evening to our roof garden.

"We can order them now," he said, showing us the catalog. "Look!"

We all crowded around, looking at the fat green watermelons pictured in full color on the pages. Some of them were split open, showing the red, tempting meat, making our mouths water.

"Now we got to scrape up some seed money," T. J. said, looking at us. "I got a quarter. How much you-all got?"

We made up a couple of dollars among us and T. J. nodded his head. "That'll be more than enough. Now we got to decide what kind to get. I think them Kleckley Sweets. What do you-all think?"

He was going into esoteric matters beyond our reach. We hadn't even known there were different kinds of melons. So we just nodded our heads and agreed that yes, we thought the Kleckley Sweets too.

"I'll order them tonight," T. J. said. "We ought to have them in a few days."

C "What are you boys doing up here?" an adult voice said behind us.

It startled us, for no one had ever come up here before in all the time we had been using the roof of the factory. We jerked around and saw three men standing near the trapdoor at the other end of the roof. They weren't policemen or night watchmen but three men in plump business suits, looking at us. They walked toward us.

WORDS TO OWN

desecrated (des′i·krāt′id) *v.*: showed disrespect for (something considered holy).
esoteric (es′ə·ter′ik) *adj.*: specialized; beyond most people's understanding or knowledge.

Skill Link

Activity
Ask students to read the following sentences from p. 476, column 1, of "Antaeus" silently and then aloud. Then, have them identify the words and phrases (italicized) that are not standard English and to rewrite the sentences in standard English. Students might consider the difference in tone between the two versions. (Possible responses are given.)

1. Well, you *wasn't* using the roof. [Well, you weren't using the roof.]
2. We *toted* it up here, and it's our earth. [We hauled it up here, and it's our earth.]
3. You *ain't got no* right! [You don't have any right!]
4. *Can't nobody* touch a man's own land. [Nobody can touch a man's own land.]

Chandler, Mexico (1923), photograph by Edward Weston.

© 1981 Center for Creative Photography, Arizona Board of Regents.

"What are you boys doing up here?" the one in the middle said again.

We stood still, guilt heavy among us, levied by the tone of voice, and looked at the three strangers. **D**

The men stared at the grass flourishing behind us. "What's this?" the man said. "How did this get up here?"

"Sure is growing good, ain't it?" T. J. said conversationally. "We planted it."

The men kept looking at the grass as if they didn't believe it. It was a thick carpet over the earth now, a patch of deep greenness startling in the <u>sterile</u> industrial surroundings.

"Yes, sir," T. J. said proudly. "We toted that earth up here and planted that grass." He fluttered the seed catalog. "And we're just fixing to plant us some watermelon."

The man looked at him then, his eyes strange and faraway. "What do you mean, putting this on the roof of my building?" he said. "Do you want to go to jail?"

T. J. looked shaken. The rest of us were silent, frightened by the authority of his voice. We had grown up aware of adult authority, of policemen and night watchmen and teachers, **E**

WORDS TO OWN
sterile (ster′əl) *adj.:* barren; lacking interest or vitality.

Listening to Music

In a Summer Garden by Frederick Delius

Frederick Delius (1862–1934), one of England's finest composers, learned to play the piano and violin without formal instruction. A world traveler as a young man, Delius for a time owned an orange plantation in Florida, where he heard the African American music that influenced his own work. Eventually he returned to Europe, where he began composing his most significant works, including *A Village Romeo and Juliet, On Hearing the First Cuckoo in Spring,* and *In a Summer Garden.* Left paralyzed and blind by a severe illness in his later years, he continued to create music, dictating his compositions note by note.

Activity
After students have read "Antaeus," have them listen to *In a Summer Garden.* Ask them to make a rough sketch, as they listen, of the kind of garden the music brings to mind. Then, have them compare the garden they sketched with the one described in "Antaeus." The class might also discuss the difference in tone, or mood, between the story and the music.

A **Critical Thinking**

Making Judgments

Ask students who they believe is right and why. [Possible responses: Owner— It is his property that might be damaged; T.J.—No one is using the roof, and the boys have worked hard to create the garden.]

B **Critical Thinking**

Interpreting the Text

❓ What does T.J. mean by having a "right" to the earth? [Possible responses: T.J. believes that using land to grow living things is more important than simply owning the land; for T.J., "earth rights" outweigh property rights.]

C **Reading Skills and Strategies**

Responding to the Text

❓ Is the narrator's assessment of the situation accurate, in your opinion? [Possible responses: Yes, he has a good understanding of the place of children in the world; no, he has merely had an experience with intolerance.]

D **Elements of Literature**

Allusion

❓ How is the Antaeus legend echoed in the comparison of T.J. to "cripples"? [Possible response: When Antaeus is lifted into the air, he loses all his strength.]

E **Reading Skills and Strategies**

Analyzing Motivation

❓ Why do the boys destroy the garden themselves? [Possible responses: T.J. won't let other people destroy what they created; the boys need to release their anger.]

and this man sounded like all the others. But it was a new thing to T. J.

"Well, you wasn't using the roof," T. J. said. He paused a moment and added shrewdly, "So we just thought to pretty it up a little bit."

"And sag it so I'd have to rebuild it," the man said sharply. He started turning away, saying to another man beside him, "See that all that junk is shoveled off by tomorrow."

"Yes, sir," the man said.

T. J. started forward. "You can't do that," he said. "We toted it up here, and it's our earth. We planted it and raised it and toted it up here."

The man stared at him coldly. "But it's my building," he said. "It's to be shoveled off tomorrow."

"It's our earth," T. J. said desperately. "You ain't got no right!"

The men walked on without listening and descended clumsily through the trapdoor. T. J. stood looking after them, his body tense with anger, until they had disappeared. They wouldn't even argue with him, wouldn't let him defend his earth rights.

He turned to us. "We won't let 'em do it," he said fiercely. "We'll stay up here all day tomorrow and the day after that, and we won't let 'em do it."

We just looked at him. We knew there was no stopping it.

He saw it in our faces, and his face wavered for a moment before he gripped it into determination. "They ain't got no right," he said. "It's our earth. It's our land. Can't nobody touch a man's own land."

We kept looking at him, listening to the words but knowing that it was no use. The adult world had descended on us even in our richest dream, and we knew there was no calculating the adult world, no fighting it, no winning against it.

We started moving slowly toward the parapet and the fire escape, avoiding a last look at the green beauty of the earth that T. J. had

planted for us, had planted deeply in our minds as well as in our experience. We filed slowly over the edge and down the steps to the plank, T. J. coming last, and all of us could feel the weight of his grief behind us.

"Wait a minute," he said suddenly, his voice harsh with the effort of calling.

We stopped and turned, held by the tone of his voice, and looked up at him standing above us on the fire escape.

"We can't stop them?" he said, looking down at us, his face strange in the dusky light. "There ain't no way to stop 'em?"

"No," Blackie said with finality. "They own the building."

We stood still for a moment, looking up at T. J., caught into inaction by the decision working in his face. He stared back at us, and his face was pale and mean in the poor light, with a bald nakedness in his skin like cripples have sometimes.

"They ain't gonna touch my earth," he said fiercely. "They ain't gonna lay a hand on it! Come on."

He turned around and started up the fire escape again, almost running against the effort of climbing. We followed more slowly, not knowing what he intended to do. By the time we reached him, he had seized a board and thrust it into the soil, scooping it up and flinging it over the parapet into the areaway below. He straightened and looked at us.

"They can't touch it," he said. "I won't let 'em lay a dirty hand on it!"

We saw it then. He stooped to his labor again, and we followed, the gusts of his anger moving in frenzied labor among us as we scattered along the edge of earth, scooping it and throwing it over the parapet, destroying with anger the growth we had nurtured with such

WORDS TO OWN

descended (dē·send'id) v.: went down.

Getting Students Involved

Cooperative Learning

Debate. Divide students into small groups and designate half the groups as supporters of the roof owner and half as supporters of T.J. and the gang. Then, have all groups brainstorm and plan arguments for a debate. Finally, have pairs of groups debate whether the garden should be allowed to stay on the roof.

Role-Play. Have small groups of students role-play and transcribe a conversation between T.J. and the police officer who finds him in Nashville. What might T.J. say? How might the officer react? One or two students can write down the dialogue as two other students improvise. Students can use this activity as a springboard for Choice 2 (p. 480).

tender care. The soil carried so laboriously upward to the light and the sun cascaded swiftly into the dark areaway, the green blades of grass crumpled and twisted in the falling.

It took less time than you would think; the task of destruction is infinitely easier than that of creation. We stopped at the end, leaving only a scattering of loose soil, and when it was finally over, a stillness stood among the group and over the factory building. We looked down at the bare sterility of black tar, felt the harsh texture of it under the soles of our shoes, and the anger had gone out of us, leaving only a sore aching in our minds, like overstretched muscles.

T. J. stood for a moment, his breathing slowing from anger and effort, caught into the same contemplation of destruction as all of us. He stooped slowly, finally, and picked up a lonely blade of grass left trampled under our feet and put it between his teeth, tasting it, sucking the greenness out of it into his mouth. Then he started walking toward the fire escape, moving before any of us were ready to move, and disappeared over the edge.

We followed him, but he was already halfway down to the ground, going on past the board where we crossed over, climbing down into the areaway. We saw the last section swing down with his weight, and then he stood on the concrete below us, looking at the small pile of anonymous earth scattered by our throwing. Then he walked across the place where we could see him and disappeared toward the street without glancing back, without looking up to see us watching him.

They did not find him for two weeks.

Then the Nashville police caught him just outside the Nashville freight yards. He was walking along the railroad track, still heading South, still heading home.

As for us, who had no remembered home to call us, none of us ever again climbed the escapeway to the roof.

MEET THE WRITER

Keeping the Faith

Like his hero T. J., **Borden Deal** (1922–1985) came from a family of Southern cotton farmers. They knew firsthand the hardships of farm life during the Great Depression. As the following anecdote proves, Deal was just as persistent as T. J.:

66 My short story 'Antaeus' has a strange history. Though it has been reprinted far more often than any other of my nearly one hundred short stories, it took me *ten years* to get it published the first time! True. It was turned down by every quality popular magazine in the country, not once but two or three times. Then, on rereading the story after a year or so, I'd like it all over again, and I'd send it around once more. After ten long years, the story was finally published by one of the country's finest literary magazines, and the next year it was reprinted in the annual collection called *The Best American Short Stories*. Since then, the story has appeared in hundreds of textbooks and anthologies on every level, from grammar school to college. So you see, when you believe in something, it pays to keep the faith and be persistent—just as, in the story, T. J. is persistent in his faith and feeling for the earth. 99

ANTAEUS 477

Connections

This news article about a city's gardening program relates to the selection "Antaeus" and to the theme of the collection.

A Vocabulary Note

Multiple Meanings

? Ask students to look up *olio* in the dictionary. What are its meanings? [a spicy stew; a mixture] Why might the word have been used in the title? [Possible responses: The garden, a mixture of flowers and vegetables, is cared for by 30 gardeners; *olio* is from Spanish *olla*, "pot," and several Spanish words are in the article.]

B Reading Skills and Strategies

Identifying Purpose

? What does this paragraph suggest about the author's purpose? [Possible responses: Since the paragraph gives factual details, the author's main purpose is to inform. Since the paragraph is written in a light and amusing style, her purpose is also to entertain.]

C Appreciating Language

Word Choice

? Why do you think the author has used the expression "roots you tore up to get here"? [Possible responses: She is referring to the difficulty of leaving one's homeland; she is also making a pun (play on words) on *root* of a plant.]

D Critical Thinking

Making Connections

? How does this article relate to other selections in the collection? [Possible responses: It suggests the importance of nature in human life; it shows that in a big city, people create their own natural places (as T.J. tries to do). Unlike the selections that portray nature as cruel, the article depicts it as life-giving (as do "The Creation" and the poems on p. 465).]

Connections
A NEWS ARTICLE

In a Mix of Cultures, an Olio of Plantings

ANNE RAVER

Juan Guerrero grows tomatillos on a scrap of land that used to be a chop shop for stolen cars in the South Bronx. It's his little piece of Mexico.

"He says you cut them up with hot pepper for salsa," said Jose Garcia, who grew up in Puerto Rico. Mr. Guerrero left Puebla, Mexico, four years ago, but he speaks little English, so Mr. Garcia was translating.

He watched Mr. Guerrero peel the papery husk from a hard little green fruit and nodded yes, yes, yes, as his neighbor explained how to dry the fruit for seeds.

"In Puerto Rico," Mr. Garcia said, chuckling, "my father always told me these were poison." Then he politely tasted a pungent leaf that Mr. Guerrero had just picked from a bushy green herb.

"Papalo," Mr. Guerrero said. "Como cilantro."

This 100 by 175 foot piece of earth, on Prospect Avenue between East 181st and 182d Streets, used to grow old car parts, refrigerators, and crack vials. Now it grows zinnias, hollyhocks, eggplants, collard greens, and pear trees. And its thirty gardeners call it "The Garden of Happiness."

Happiness here has little to do with the perfect perennial bed. It's about reclaiming scarred land from drug dealers. And planting a few vegetables and flowers that remind you of the roots you tore up to get here.

Many urban gardeners till city-owned lots leased to them for one dollar a year by Operation Green Thumb, the city's gardening program, which leases more than a thousand lots to 550 community groups. Others just take over garbage-strewn land.

"Gardening takes you back to your roots," said Karen Washington, 37, who took a pickax and shovel to the debris three years ago and now heads the community garden. "My grandparents farmed in North Carolina. If you gave them some store-bought collard greens, they'd look at you like you were crazy."

D —from *The New York Times*

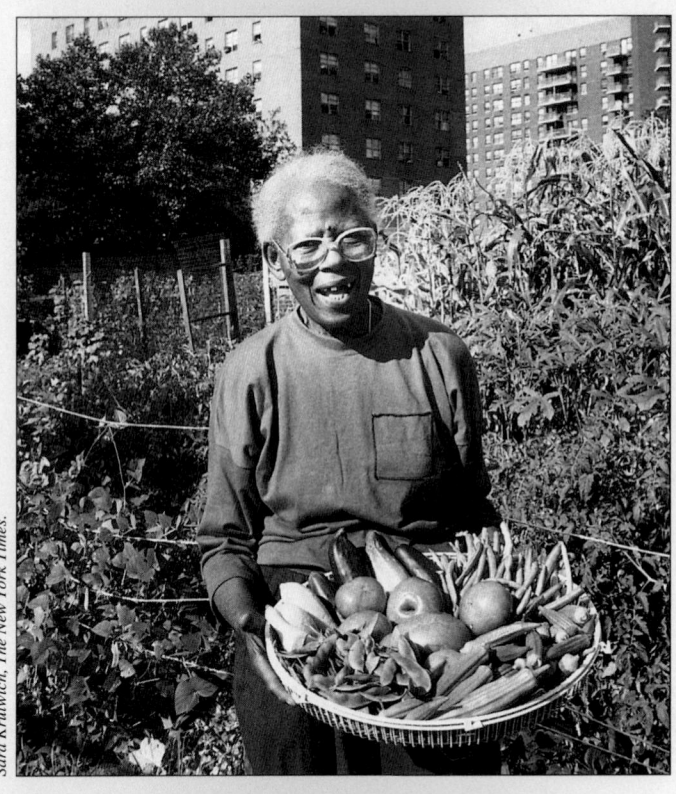

Sara Krulwich, The New York Times.

Urban gardener Annie Vigg with a harvest of squash, tomatoes, beans, peas, and okra.

478 THIS OLD EARTH

Connecting Across Texts

Connecting with "Antaeus"

Have students discuss what the South Bronx gardeners have in common with T.J. [Possible responses: T.J. and the urban gardeners share a deep desire to grow things in the earth. Whereas T.J. has difficulty adapting to life in the city, the South Bronx neighbors have found a way to create a garden that brightens their lives.] Students might imagine themselves as T.J. and write a letter to one of the urban gardeners, to share experiences or ask for advice. Or students might imagine themselves as one of the Bronx gardeners and write a letter to the factory owner, asking that T.J. and his friends be allowed to keep the rooftop garden.

MAKING MEANINGS

[connect]

First Thoughts

1. If you were T. J., what would you do after hearing the words "It's to be shoveled off tomorrow"?

Shaping Interpretations

[evaluate]

2. In your opinion, what's the most important thing the city boys learn from T. J.?

[compare]

3. Find the passage in the story that mentions Antaeus (page 473). Explain the connection between what happens to Antaeus in the myth and what happens to T. J. What do you think the **allusion** adds to the story?

[interpret]

4. Think about the word *escapeway* in the last sentence. In what ways is that passage to the roof an escape for the boys?

[extend]

5. How are the gardeners in the article "In a Mix of Cultures . . ." (see *Connections* on page 478) like T. J.? What other people could be called Antaeus?

[interpret]

6. What do you make of the last line, about the city boys having "no remembered home" to call them? What do you think the word *home* means here?

Connecting with the Text

[compare]

7. Look back at the notes about home that you made for the Quickwrite on page 468. How do your feelings about home compare with T. J.'s?

Reading Check

a. What characteristic makes T. J. seem "different" at first to the narrator?

b. What does T. J. want? What obstacles does he have to overcome to get what he wants?

c. What does the narrator realize for the first time when he smells "the sweet odor of the earth" under his feet (page 473)?

d. How does T. J. react when the boys' project is destroyed?

East River from the 30th Story of the Shelton Hotel by Georgia O'Keeffe. Oil on canvas (30" × 48").

New Britain Museum of American Art, New Britain, Connecticut. Stephen Lawrence Fund. Photo credit: E. Irving Blomstrann. © 1998 The Georgia O'Keeffe Foundation/ Artists Rights Society (ARS), New York.

ANTAEUS 479

MAKING MEANINGS

First Thoughts

1. Possible responses: Argue with the men; destroy the garden; plan a new garden somewhere else; share my anger with friends or family members.

Shaping Interpretations

2. Possible responses: They learn to appreciate the change of seasons and the value of growing something; they learn that persistence can make things happen.

3. Possible responses: When the characters are physically separated from the earth by their opponents, they become physically weak (Antaeus) or feel emotionally incomplete (T.J.). The allusion helps the reader appreciate the heroism of the "ordinary" boy from the rural South.

4. Possible responses: The boys can escape adult authority by going to the roof, where they have space to "hang out."

5. Possible responses: Like T.J., they are city dwellers who want to grow a garden. Like him, too, they are trying to re-create something of the life they left behind. Anyone who tends the earth or draws strength from it can be likened to Antaeus.

6. Possible responses: They have not yet experienced the feeling of love for a particular place, as T.J. has. *Home* refers to the place where a person has family roots.

Connecting with the Text

7. Possible "homes": one's own room; a hangout where one goes with friends; a city street or a country field.

Reading Check

a. He has a gentle and soft voice.

b. He wants to plant a garden on the roof. He has to get the boys to agree to help; they must obtain soil and seeds; they have to carry the soil to the roof secretly.

c. He appreciates nature and has a desire to grow things.

d. He decides to return home to Alabama.

Grading Timesaver

Rubrics for each Choices assignment appear on p. 164 in the *Portfolio Management System*.

CHOICES:
Building Your Portfolio

1. **Writer's Notebook** Encourage students to observe first and begin writing only after several minutes.
2. **Creative Writing** Remind students to keep their new endings consistent with T.J.'s character and the events in the story. Students might work with partners to role-play the scene before they write it. One student can act as T.J. while the partner takes the role of someone offering him guidance.
3. **Speaking and Listening** You might assign one selection to each pair of students.
4. **Drama** Students might present moments not fully shown in the story, like T.J.'s arrival with his family or the boys' arrival on the roof with their first load of soil.

CHOICES: Building Your Portfolio

Writer's Notebook

1. Collecting Ideas for Observational Writing

The city boys in "Antaeus" discover that even a small plot of grass on a tar roof can hold the wonders of nature. Find your own patch of earth to observe: three or four square feet in a back yard or nearby park, a clump of weeds in a vacant lot, even a window box.

Observe your patch carefully for ten to fifteen minutes. Jot down everything you see, smell, feel, and hear.

Dad's rock garden
—violets: purple with white edges
—rocks: like gray-green soldiers
—a whisper of wind

Creative Writing

2. Add a Scene

What happens to T. J.? Write a final scene for the story. Tell it from T. J.'s point of view—let T. J. continue the story, speaking as "I." Before you write, collect your ideas about these details, which should be part of T. J.'s story:

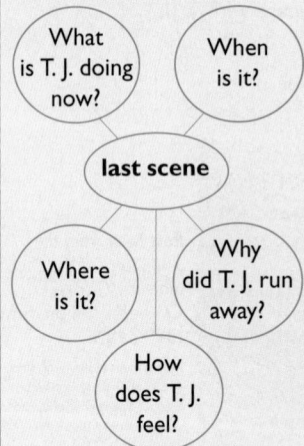

What is T. J. doing now?
When is it?
last scene
Where is it?
Why did T. J. run away?
How does T. J. feel?

Speaking and Listening

3. Literary Round Table

Get together with a partner, and talk about the pieces in this collection. Think about the different **purposes** the writers may have had in mind as they wrote. Did they want to

- inform or explain?
- influence or persuade?
- entertain?
- reveal a truth about our lives?
- share or re-create an experience?

Choose three or four selections, and decide what each writer's purpose was. (Remember that the writer may have had more than one purpose in mind.) Share your findings with the class.

Drama

4. Hold That Thought

Select a dramatic moment from the story and create a tableau of that scene. With a group of classmates, get into and hold the exact pose of characters in the scene. Have another student patrol the tableau and tap different characters to bring them "to life." As soon as someone is tapped, he or she begins to speak, saying what the character might say or might be thinking at that moment. When tapped again, he or she stops talking, and the tapper taps someone else. Afterward, discuss what, if anything, you discovered about the story from creating the tableau.

LANGUAGE LINK [MINI-LESSON]

Handbook of Literary Terms
H E L P

See Dialect.

Style: Dialect—Voices of a Region or a Group

In "Antaeus," T. J. speaks in a way that doesn't sound like standard English. He uses double (even triple) negatives and words like *ourn* for *ours* and *offen* for *from*. Here is an example:

| T. J.'S DIALECT | "You mean you ain't got no fields to raise nothing in?" |
| STANDARD ENGLISH | Do you mean you have no fields in which to raise anything? |

Dialect is a way of speaking that is characteristic of a particular region or group of people. People who study language say that all of us speak one dialect or another. Think of how a British speaker sounds. Think of how a Philadelphian speaks, as compared with a person from Southern California. T. J. speaks one of the dialects of the Deep South. Like all dialects, T. J.'s has a distinctive pronunciation, vocabulary, and grammar. By re-creating T. J.'s dialect, Deal helps us "see" the boy and "hear" his gentle Southern drawl.

> **Try It Out**
> ➤ Do a survey of dialects spoken in your class. Does everyone sound the same, or do you hear varied dialects?
>
> a. Do you say *crick* or *creek* to describe a small stream?
>
> b. Do you say *frying pan*, *skillet*, or *spider* to describe the pan you fry eggs in?
>
> c. How do you pronounce *dear*, *car*, and *water*?
>
> ➤ Listen for a week to hear dialect on TV or on the radio, and write down each instance. Rewrite each expression in the words *you* would use to say the same thing—in your own dialect.

VOCABULARY [HOW TO OWN A WORD]

WORD BANK
resolute
domain
contemplate
shrewd
inert
dilating
desecrated
esoteric
sterile
descended

Back to the Story

1. Describe T. J., using the words *resolute* and *shrewd*.
2. Describe how the city boys feel about the roof garden, using the words *contemplate* and *domain*.
3. Using the words *sterile*, *inert*, and *esoteric*, describe how the boys change the tar roof into a lawn.
4. Write about the owners of the building, using the words *desecrated* and *descended* to describe what they did.
5. Using the word *dilating*, describe the way T. J. responds to the fragrance of the earth.

ANTAEUS 481

LANGUAGE LINK

Have students review their informal and creative writing for examples of dialect. If they have used dialect, ask students to be sure that it fits the purpose of their writing. If they decide that the dialect is not suitable, they can rewrite the passages in standard English.

Try It Out

Have students work with partners to answer the three questions and to discuss their responses with the class. Students can also work in pairs to listen for dialect on the radio or on television. Suggest that partners listen separately to the same programs and compare their revisions afterward.

VOCABULARY
Possible Answers

1. T.J. is too resolute to accept failure and too shrewd to insist on raising only vegetables.
2. The boys contemplate the grass before it is planted. They are proud of this addition to their domain.
3. The roof was inert until the boys began to meet there. With the arrival of T.J. and his esoteric knowledge of gardens, the sterile roof sprouted a small lawn.
4. The owners descended from the roof, having desecrated the garden.
5. With his nostrils dilating, T.J. took a breath of the fresh spring breeze.

Resources ——————

Language
• *Grammar and Language Links*, p. 45

Vocabulary
• *Words to Own*, p. 18

Spelling
For related instruction, see
• *Spelling and Decoding*, p. 22

Language Link Quick Check

Transcribe these examples of dialect into standard English. (Possible responses are given.)

1. "That's all the name I got." [That's my full name.]
2. "Down yonder where I come from, we played out in the woods." [Down South, where I come from, we played in the woods.]
3. "Don't you-all have any woods around here?" [Aren't there any woods near here?]
4. "Come spring we could raise us what we want to." [When spring comes, we could raise anything we like.]
5. "You-all seem mighty set on raising some flowers." [All of you seem determined to raise flowers.]

No Questions Asked

In this brief, lyrical story, the narrator contemplates four trees growing out of a concrete sidewalk. She identifies with their awkward appearance and emulates their strength and persistence as they, and she, struggle to survive in an unfriendly environment.

Ⓐ Reading Skills and Strategies
Responding to the Text
❓ Why does the narrator think she and the trees are the only ones who understand each other? [Possible response: She thinks that she resembles the skinny trees and that, like the trees, she is out of place.]

Ⓑ Reading Skills and Strategies
Finding Details
❓ According to the narrator, what is special about the trees? [Possible responses: They have a will to live; they are angry.]

Ⓒ Reading Skills and Strategies
Responding to the Text
❓ Do you agree that anger can help keep something alive? Explain. [Possible responses: Yes, anger can spur you to correct an unfair situation; no, anger can distract you from trying to improve that situation.]

Ⓓ Critical Thinking
Interpreting
❓ What message do the trees offer the narrator? [Possible response: If the trees can grow in an unfriendly environment, so can she.]

Four Skinny Trees

Sandra Cisneros

Ⓐ They are the only ones who understand me. I am the only one who understands them. Four skinny trees with skinny necks and pointy elbows like mine. Four who do not belong here but are here. Four raggedy excuses planted by the city. From our room we can hear them, but Nenny just sleeps and doesn't appreciate these things.

Ⓑ Their strength is secret. They send ferocious roots beneath the ground. They grow up and they grow down and grab the Ⓒ earth between their hairy toes and bite the sky with violent teeth and never quit their anger. This is how they keep.

Let one forget his reason for being, they'd all droop like tulips in a glass, each with their arms around the other. Keep, keep, keep, trees say when I sleep. They teach.

Ⓓ When I am too sad and too skinny to keep keeping, when I am a tiny thing against so many bricks, then it is I look at trees. When there is nothing left to look at on this street. Four who grew despite concrete. Four who reach and do not forget to reach. Four whose only reason is to be and be.

Crossing the Curriculum

Art
Students might enjoy creating a "four-plex" picture or other artwork. They can choose an object—something from nature, an ordinary household item, or something else that appeals to their imagination—and portray it in four different ways. They might show a tree in the four seasons or a favorite spot at different times of the day. They can depict an item to suggest four different moods—peaceful, angry, excited, and fearful, for example. Another idea is to use different materials to depict the same subject: crayons, folded paper or fancifully cut fabric scraps, clay, felt-tip pens, and so on. A further technique is to locate four different images of a well-known person in magazines, newspapers, and cartoons and to arrange the depictions imaginatively. Students with access to a camera might take several photographs of an intriguing subject. Invite students to share their "four-plexes" with the class.

Cuatro árboles flaquititos

Sandra Cisneros
translated by Elena Poniatowska

Son los únicos que me entienden. Soy la única que los entiende. Cuatro árboles flacos de flacos cuellos y codos puntiagudos como los míos. Cuatro que no pertenecen aquí pero aquí están. Cuatro excusas harapientas plantadas por la ciudad. Desde nuestra recámara podemos oírlos, pero Nenny se duerme y no aprecia estas cosas.

Su fuerza es secreta. Lanzan feroces raíces bajo la tierra. Crecen hacia arriba y hacia abajo y se apoderan de la tierra entre los dedos peludos de sus pies y muerden el cielo con dientes violentos y jamás se detiene su furia. Así se mantienen.

Si alguno olvidara su razón de ser todos se marchitarían como tulipanes en un florero, cada uno con sus brazos alrededor del otro. Sigue, sigue, sigue, dicen los árboles cuando duermo. Ellos enseñan.

Cuando estoy demasiado triste o demasiado flaca para seguir siguiendo, cuando soy una cosita delgada contra tantos ladrillos es cuando miro los árboles. Cuando no hay nada más que ver en esta calle. Cuatro que crecieron a pesar del concreto. Cuatro que luchan y no se olvidan de luchar. Cuatro cuyo única razón es ser y ser.

FOUR SKINNY TREES / CUATRO ÁRBOLES FLAQUITITOS 483

E Appreciating Language
Translation
Encourage students who know Spanish to read the Poniatowska translation aloud. Students who know both languages well can compare the two versions. Explain that writers sometimes use words or phrases from another language in their poems or stories to give the work the flavor of another culture. Invite students to select a word or phrase from the Spanish translation that they think would enrich the English version.

F Vocabulary Note
Word Relatives
? Students who know little or no Spanish can look for Spanish cognates, or relatives, of English words. *Cuatro* means "four." What does the English combining form *quadr-* mean? [four] (*Cuatro* and *quadr-* come from the same Latin word.) What words begin with *quadr-*? [Possible responses: *quadrangle*, *quadruple*; students should use the dictionary to look up any English words they are unfamiliar with.] What word names a four-theater movie house? [*quadruplex*] Challenge students to look for other Spanish words from the story that have English cognates. [Possible responses: *árboles*, English *arbor*; *únicos*, English *unique*; *secreta*, English *secret*; *tierra*, English *terrain*; *mantienen*, English *maintain*; *tulipanes*, English *tulip*; *concreto*, English *concrete*; *razón*, English *reason*.]

Using Students' Strengths

Naturalist Learners
Have students do research to find out what types of trees grow in urban areas. (Some trees that thrive in cities are the ailanthus, the London planetree, and the ginkgo.) What do these trees look like? What special qualities enable these trees to survive in a city? What challenges does a city-sidewalk tree face? What can people do to help these trees? Have students prepare an oral presentation or a poster to share with classmates what they have learned about trees.

Intrapersonal Learners
Point out that Cisneros's narrator identifies strongly with trees. Ask students to write stories, similar to "Four Skinny Trees," about an animal, plant, building, wall, or other object that they feel could be a "best friend." Encourage students to personify this subject, as Cisneros does the trees.

MEET THE WRITER

"A House All My Own"

Sandra Cisneros (1954–   ) was born and raised in Chicago, the only daughter in a working-class family with six sons. The harshness of life in poor neighborhoods made Cisneros shy as a child, so she escaped into the world of books. By the age of ten, she was writing her own poetry.

Cisneros grew up speaking Spanish with her Mexican-born father, but she didn't explore her heritage until she attended the Writer's Workshop at the University of Iowa. There, she began a series of sketches about her old Spanish-speaking neighborhood in Chicago. These sketches grew into her first book, *The House on Mango Street* (1984). In that book, through her narrator, Esperanza, Cisneros speaks of her yearning for a space of her own:

> 66 A house all my own. . . . Only a house quiet as snow, a space for myself to go, clean as paper before the poem. 99

Since then, Cisneros has continued to seek that "house" in poems and stories about an urban world she knows well.

Making the Connections

Connecting to the Theme: "This Old Earth"

After students have read the story, discuss how it relates to the collection theme. Four awkward trees offer Cisneros's narrator a link to the natural world, and they make her feel less alone.

Ask students to compare Cisneros's work with other imaginative pieces in the collection. For instance, Johnson, in his poem, sees nature and humanity as part of divine creation; to Cisneros, sometimes nature and humans must struggle to survive. In "Sky Woman," humans and nature cooperate, especially to overcome evil in the world; the encouragement Cisneros gets from watching the trees also suggests cooperation between human beings and nature. The poem "maggie and milly and molly and may" portrays one aspect of nature, the sea, as a place where humans may experience comfort, companionship, fear, or creativity. For her part, Cisneros's narrator finds herself both reflected in and encouraged by the four trees. The poems "I Am of the Earth" and "Early Song" emphasize the tie between humans and the earth—a theme that T.J., in "Antaeus," represents.

Students may choose to express some of the main ideas of the collection in writing, art work, music, or other creative effort.

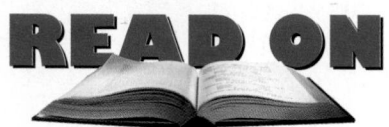
READ ON

Far from the Crowd

Just when Wil Neuton's life in Madison, Wisconsin, seems perfect, his father transplants the family to a lonely backwoods spot in Gary Paulsen's *The Island* (Orchard). Wil learns to like his new life when he finds an island wilderness near his new home and discovers some amazing things about himself and the world.

Listening to the Land

In Jean Craighead George's adventure story *The Talking Earth* (HarperCollins), young Billie Wind, a Seminole, questions her heritage. She doubts that the Seminole legends about the earth are true. To test her beliefs, the Seminole Council sends Billie into the Everglades. In the wilderness, Billie finds she must believe in the old legends if she wants to stay alive.

Sailing, Sailing

Dove (Bantam) is sixteen-year-old Robin Lee Graham's true adventure story of his five-year voyage around the world—alone on a twenty-four-foot sailboat. Along the way, Robin faces fierce storms, suffocating heat, and loneliness. Sail the high seas with him as he finds courage, love, and maturity.

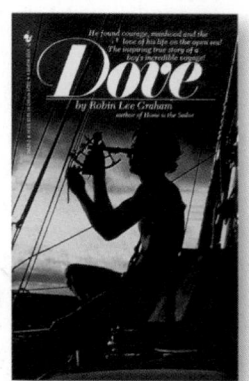

Other Picks

- Kristiana Gregory, *Earthquake at Dawn* (Harcourt Brace). Photographer Edith Irvine and her young assistant, Daisy Valentine, wander San Francisco after a major earthquake and photograph the results of one of nature's most violent acts.

- Laura Ingalls Wilder, *On the Way Home: The Diary of a Trip from South Dakota to Mansfield, Missouri, in 1894* (HarperCollins). The famous author of the *Little House* books describes the beauty of the frontier country she passes through on a journey.

READ ON 485

READ ON
These extended reading suggestions relate to various aspects of the theme "This Old Earth." Each work sheds light on the relationship between humankind and the planet.

Portfolio Assessment Options
The following projects can help you evaluate and assess the reading your students do outside class. Students can add videotapes, audiotapes, transcripts, or slides of completed projects to their portfolios.

- **Create a Time Capsule**
  Have students decide what to include in a time capsule representing Wil Neuton's life in the wilderness. Students should list the items Wil would be likely to include, describe each item, and explain why it is included.

- **Write a Book Review**
  Have students write reviews of the books they choose. Remind the class that a review is not a retelling of the plot but a critique of the book. Start students off with these questions: What did you like or dislike about this book, and why? Would you recommend it? Why or why not? Several students might collect their reviews in one binder for the class to use as a reference.

- **Design a Poster**
  Have students design posters to advertise movie versions of the books they read. Remind them that the poster should capture a central image, event, or theme of the work. The posters might feature a drawing or photograph and a brief caption that arouses other students' interest in the film. Display the posters in the classroom.

Writer's Workshop

MAIN OBJECTIVE
Write an observational essay

MAIN OBJECTIVE
Write an observational essay

PROCESS OBJECTIVES

1. Use appropriate prewriting techniques to identify and develop a topic
2. Create a first draft
3. Use Evaluation Criteria as a basis for determining revision strategies
4. Revise the first draft, incorporating suggestions generated by self- or peer evaluation
5. Proofread and correct errors
6. Create a final draft
7. Choose an appropriate method of publication
8. Reflect on progress as a writer

Planning

- **Block Schedule**
  Block Scheduling Lesson Plans with Pacing Guide
- **One-Stop Planner**
  CD-ROM with Test Generator

Technology HELP

See Writer's Workshop 1 CD-ROM. *Assignment: Observational Writing.*

ASSIGNMENT

Write an essay describing something you've observed.

AIM

To inform; to express yourself.

AUDIENCE

Your teacher and classmates.

DESCRIPTIVE WRITING

OBSERVATIONAL WRITING

In **observational writing,** you use words to paint a picture. You observe your subject closely and write a detailed **description** of what you see.

Professional Model

In this passage from her autobiographical book Cross Creek, *Marjorie Kinnan Rawlings describes chameleons—small lizards capable of changing color—that she observed near her home in Florida.*

The little chameleons are definitely friendly. . . . They watch you for hours with small bright eyes. They enjoy being brought into the house on a bunch of roses, to serve on the dining table for ornament, shading obligingly from their favorite sage-green through taupe to a pinkish mauve, according to their passage over leaf or stem or blossom. . . .

The most ambitious chameleon I have ever seen was swallowing a butterfly twice as wide as he himself was long, the body almost as large as the swallower's. When I first noticed him, he had the butterfly's head in his mouth and the wings stuck out on either side like vast and ferocious moustaches. I stood and laughed at him and he eyed me furiously,

The writer clearly identifies what she is observing.

She describes the subject's appearance.

She describes an action in humorous detail.

486 THIS OLD EARTH

 —*Resources: Print and Media* — —

Writing and Language
- *Portfolio Management System*
  Prewriting, p. 165
  Peer Editing, p. 166
  Assessment Rubric, p. 167
- *Workshop Resources*
  Revision Strategy Teaching Notes, p. 25
  Revision Strategy Transparencies 13, 14
- *Writer's Workshop 1 CD-ROM*
  Observational Writing

(continued)

> switching his tail. I said, "You'll never do it," and went on about my business. An hour later I passed by again and all the butterfly was down except for the wing tips. As I watched, he gulped and the job was done.
>
> —from *Cross Creek* by Marjorie Kinnan Rawlings

She shows how she feels about her subject by quoting what she said to him.

Prewriting

1. Writer's Notebook

WORK IN PROGRESS

Look back at the notes you made in your Writer's Notebook for this collection. Is there a person, place, or thing that you would enjoy observing and describing?

2. Freewriting

For more ideas, freewrite for a minute or two on some of these subjects:

- activities you can observe (someone cooking dinner; a basketball game)
- people you can observe (your older sister; an athlete)
- animals you can observe (your pet; a monkey at the zoo)
- places and things you can observe (the lunchroom; a mall)
- events you can observe (a scientific experiment)

3. Choosing a Subject

To decide on your subject, keep these points in mind:

- You should be able to observe your subject directly or to picture it clearly.
- Your subject should interest you and your readers.

WRITER'S WORKSHOP 487

Introducing the Writer's Workshop

- Read the Professional Model on pp. 486–487 as students follow along. Encourage students to discuss their reactions to Rawlings's descriptions. To which senses do the descriptions appeal? What makes the chameleon come alive for the reader? If students saw the little lizard, would they react to it the same way Rawlings did? Why or why not?

- Be sure that students understand the side notes. Ask class members to identify the two main points that Rawlings makes about the lizards (they are friendly and ambitious) and the details she uses to support her view.

- Discuss with students what makes a good observational essay:
  1. The essay should be based on careful observation of the subject.
  2. It should appeal to the readers' senses (as Rawlings's essay does).
  3. The writer should use vivid, specific verbs, nouns, adjectives, and adverbs.

Teaching the Writer's Workshop

Prewriting

Have students use the techniques suggested on pp. 487–489 (or any others that may be helpful) to come up with ideas. Instead of having students select their own subjects, you can bring some unusual objects to class, such as old photographs, seashells or stones, or inexpensive ornaments. Students should observe an object carefully before they write about it. Some of them might create a word portrait, by closing their eyes, picturing the object, and describing what they "see" and "hear."

Reaching All Students

Struggling Writers

If students have difficulty putting their ideas into words, encourage them to draw pictures or use graphic organizers before they begin writing. Filling in a five-column chart headed *Sight, Hearing, Touch, Smell,* and *Taste* can help students organize sensory details about their subjects. Students might also choose partners with whom to talk about their subjects. Discussing topics can be an effective springboard to writing.

English Language Learners

Point out that simple, everyday words are often the most vivid and specific. Be sure that students understand what sensory words and images are. Students might gain practice by briefly describing objects in the classroom ("the chalky-white, dusty board eraser that makes me sneeze," for example). Then, students should choose essay subjects with which they are familiar.

T487

Have the class read the Student Model on pp. 488–489 aloud. Be sure the students understand the comments in the margin. You can extend the discussion with questions such as the following:

❓ When do you know what the writer's subject is? How does the writer make this subject clear to you?

❓ What vivid verbs does the writer use to describe his observations in the second paragraph? Does he make any unusual or surprising comparisons to help you visualize a detail?

❓ What senses does the writer appeal to in the third paragraph?

❓ How can you tell that the writer observed the subject carefully and thoughtfully?

Strategies for Elaboration

Sensory details: When writing your observation, try to use adjectives that appeal to as many different senses as possible. You'll find visual details easy to include. Challenge yourself to include as well at least one detail of sound, smell, and touch or movement.

Exact words: Exact words sharpen your description. In the Student Model at the right, dragonflies don't just fly; they flutter and glide.

The more sensory details and exact words you include, the more likely you'll be to re-create the scene and to make your readers feel as though they were there.

4. Elaboration: Gathering Details

You've chosen your subject. Now it's time to observe it. How? You observe something by using all of your five senses. Most subjects you can see, hear, and feel; some you can smell or taste as well. Use a chart like the one here to record all the details and events you observe and the impressions they create.

Sensory Details	Events	Impressions
see coconut trees · crickets **hear** airplane · waves **feel** sun · hot air **smell** saltwater **taste** lemon candy	dragonflies flutter and glide · trucks haul tons of dirt · ferries race to Singapore	Patam is just the place for me.

Student Model

THE NATURE OF PATAM

This essay describes a beach scene in Indonesia. How does the writer set the scene? How has he organized his details? What overall impression does he create?

Right now I'm sitting cross-legged on the big gray porch at our Patam beach house. The bright shining sun and hot day make me feel lazy.

The shadowy light-and-dark-green jungle to the left of me has tall, light-brown trunks of trees everywhere. To the right a coconut tree with its palms spread out looks like a parachute. Brown and gray monkeys chatter away as small green crickets sing. Different colored dragonflies flutter and glide so fast in every direction I can't see what color they are!

Lively waves leap to and fro on the pure white beach, while saltwater and rock bash noisily together.

The writer introduces his subject and tells where he is.

Details of sight, sound, and movement create a vivid picture.

Crossing the Curriculum

Science
Research in science demands strong observational skills, and the reports of scientific experiments are like observational essays. Ask a science teacher (or an interested and knowledgeable student) to suggest a simple experiment or demonstration that can be done in the classroom. Have students watch the demonstration and then write down the sensory details they observed.

Art
Encourage students to visualize the details in Benjamin Bethea's essay. Students might then discuss appropriate materials for creating artwork based on their visualizations of the essay. They might choose watercolors, pastels, acrylic paint, or colored pencils. Students who are especially skillful may want to make a diorama of the scene Benjamin describes.

(continued)

An airplane rumbles slowly away. Across the bay trucks rattle loudly as they haul tons of brown dirt dark as chocolate.

Boats are all over the water! About three miles out huge tankers loom above the deep, gigantic, calm blue ocean, with ferries racing past them on their way to Singapore. Another boat, a small abandoned tan-brown sampan, bobs gently up and down in the gold sunlit waters that seem like enormous masses of lemon candy. I think Patam is just the place for me.

The writer moves from the trees near him to the plane, trucks, and boats in the distance.

The writer tells how he feels about this place.

—Benjamin Bethea
Batam Island Christian Home School
Batam, Indonesia

5. Organizing

Here are three ways of organizing ideas:

a. **Chronological order,** arranging details in the order in which they happen. Chronological order works best when you're describing an activity or event.

b. **Spatial order,** describing details by location: near to far, top to bottom, left to right. Spatial order works well when you're describing scenes, people, animals, and objects.

c. **Order of importance,** arranging details from least to most important or from most to least important. Order of importance works well when you're expressing your feelings and when you're describing people, animals, and objects.

Drafting

1. Focusing on the Main Idea

Everything you write needs a focus—a **main idea** that shapes what you put down on paper. To state your main idea clearly, ask yourself: What is my impression of my subject? *or* What is the purpose of my essay?

**Framework
for Observational
Writing**

Introduction (identifies subject, time, and place and gives background information): _____
_____
_____

Observations:
1. _____
Specifics: _____
2. _____
Specifics: _____
3. _____
Specifics: _____
4. _____
Specifics: _____

Conclusion (may include your main impression, your feelings, or your questions about what you observed):
_____
_____
_____

**Language/Grammar Link
H E L P**

Avoiding clichés: page 432. Formal and informal English: page 442. Active and passive voice: page 459. Dialect: page 481.

Drafting

- If you have not yet taught the Student Model, do so before students begin their drafts. Stress the need for students to focus on the main idea they are trying to express. Students might also reread the Professional Model, on pp. 486–487, and state its main idea: Chameleons are fascinating creatures.
- Remind students to use every other line when they write their drafts. They should also leave extra space in the right margin for comments and editing marks.

Getting Students Involved

Cooperative Learning

Word Bank. Some students may need help thinking of words that appeal to the various senses. You can divide the class into five groups (one for each sense) and ask each group to develop a bank of words that apply to its designated sense. The groups can create posters of their words, and the posters can be displayed in the classroom for reference.

Creating Collages. After students have written their essays, have them form small groups. Provide each group with an observational essay written by a student from another group. Invite each group to read the essay aloud and then (using magazines, newspapers, and original artwork) to create a visual collage that represents the images and objects described in the essay.

Evaluating and Revising

Have students use the Evaluation Criteria provided here to review their drafts and determine needed revisions.

Proofreading

Have students proofread their own papers first and then exchange papers with other students. For this assignment, remind students to be particularly careful to vary their sentence structure.

Publishing

Students may want to exchange papers and draw a picture of what a partner has observed. Students can work in small groups to create a bulletin-board display of observational essays and their illustrations.

Reflecting

If students would like to include their observational writing in their portfolios, have them date the work and add a short reflection based on questions such as these:

- Why did I choose this subject?
- Which details do I like best?
- What did I learn from the activity?

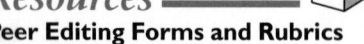

Resources

Peer Editing Forms and Rubrics
- *Portfolio Management System,* p. 166
Revision Transparencies
- *Workshop Resources,* p. 25

Grading Timesaver

Rubrics for this Writer's Workshop assignment appear on p. 167 in the *Portfolio Management System.*

■ *Evaluation Criteria*

Good observational writing

1. *clearly identifies the subject being observed*
2. *uses detailed description to help the reader see, hear, feel, smell, or taste the subject*
3. *organizes details in a clear way*
4. *reveals the writer's feelings about the subject (not necessary in scientific writing)*

Sentence Workshop
H E L P

Using a variety of sentence structures: page 491.

Communications Handbook
H E L P

See Proofreaders' Marks.

Publishing Tip

Draw a picture to illustrate a classmate's observation. Then, with the class, make a bulletin-board display of the essays and drawings.

---

2. Setting the Scene

Whenever you observe something, you view it from a particular place and at a particular time. By telling readers where you are, you give them a place to stand as they observe through your eyes. Wherever you are—nose to nose with your subject, above a lake in a hot-air balloon—make your viewpoint clear.

Evaluating and Revising

1. Peer Review

Exchange papers with a partner, and answer the following questions:

- What did you picture as you were reading?
- Which details stood out? Why?
- Was anything confusing?
- Is there any point on which you would like more information?

Make notes as you listen to your partner's comments.

2. Revising

Review your peer reader's suggestions, and decide on the changes you want to make. Make the changes; then, read your paper again to be sure that they are improvements. When you're satisfied with the content of your paper, you're ready to proofread it.

490 THIS OLD EARTH

Sentence Workshop

USING A VARIETY OF SENTENCE STRUCTURES

The basic pattern of an English sentence is subject-verb-complement (if there is a complement). If you began sentences with the subject all the time, however, your writing would be very boring.

SIMILAR SENTENCE STRUCTURES

Another world was in the sky long ago. It existed before this world. It floated there like a great cloud. No sun was in that world. Light came from the white blossoms of a great tree. The tree grew in the center of the Sky World.

DIFFERENT SENTENCE STRUCTURES

"Long ago, before this world existed, there was another world in the sky. It floated there like a great cloud. In that world there was no sun, but light came from the white blossoms of a great tree that grew in the center of the Sky World."

—Joseph Bruchac, "Sky Woman" (pages 427–428)

To vary your sentences, as Bruchac varied his, try these strategies:

1. Open with a single-word modifier.
2. Open with a phrase or clause.
3. Combine sentences with *and, but,* or *or.*
4. Combine sentences by using subordination.

Try writing a few sentences with the same structure as Bruchac's sentences. Be sure to compare your sentences with those of other students in class.

Writer's Workshop Follow-up: Revision

Exchange your observational writing piece for a classmate's. Where your partner's paper lacks a variety of sentence structures, suggest alternatives. Then, revise your paper, using your classmate's suggestions.

Language Handbook HELP

See Phrases, pages 741–746; Clauses, pages 746–750; Writing Effective Sentences, pages 760–762.

Technology HELP

See Language Workshop CD-ROM. *Key word entry: sentence structures.*

Try It Out

The following paragraph is made up of simple sentences. Change or combine some of them in order to vary the sentence structure.

The earth's mantle is about eighteen hundred miles thick. It is made of rock. It is not familiar rock. The rock is under great pressure. It is deep within the earth. It is also extremely hot. The heat and pressure make the rock behave in certain ways. These ways are strange to us.

Now, go back to any selection you have read in this collection. Copy a sentence you like and divide it into parts. Then, write a sentence of your own with the same structure.

SENTENCE WORKSHOP 491

Resources

Workshop Resources
• Worksheet, p. 47
Language Workshop CD-ROM
• Sentence Structures

Try It Out
Possible Answers
The earth's mantle, which is about eighteen hundred miles thick, is made of unfamiliar rock. Because this rock is deep within the earth, it is very hot and under great pressure. The extreme heat and pressure affect the rock's behavior in strange ways.

Assessing Learning

Quick Check: Rewriting Sentences
Rewrite the following sentences to vary the sentence structure. (Possible responses are given.)

1. "The Creation" is a poem about how God made the world. It is like a sermon. ["The Creation," a poem about how God made the world, is like a sermon.]

2. The Seneca explain how the earth was created. They tell a tale called "Sky Woman." [To explain how the earth was created, the Seneca tell a tale called "Sky Woman."]

3. "When the Earth Shakes" describes what happened during an earthquake. It was an earthquake in Alaska. It happened in 1964. ["When the Earth Shakes" describes what happened during the 1964 earthquake in Alaska.]

4. The Robertsons wanted to sail around the world. They were attacked by killer whales. They survived. [While sailing around the world, the Robertsons survived an attack by killer whales.]

5. T.J. was from the country. His family moved to the city. He made new friends. [T.J., who was from the country, made new friends when his family moved to the city.]

OBJECTIVES

1. Recognize logical arguments
2. Distinguish between inductive and deductive reasoning
3. Analyze and evaluate the organization and presentation of ideas in an editorial or letter to the editor

Using the Strategies

Possible Answers

1. Reba uses mostly inductive reasoning; Bobby uses mostly deductive reasoning.
2. Bobby's argument is more logical than Reba's.
3. Reba's argument is not logical, because she does not support her opinion with facts. "We all like movies better than books" doesn't tell *why*. "Who wouldn't, except maybe somebody with no friends?" seems to be making fun of people who have no friends, and this sentence, too, doesn't support her opinion. Bobby's arguments support his opinion with facts: *Survive the Savage Sea* is well written and convincing; you can reread parts of a book.

Situation

While reading a newspaper, you come across two letters to the editor arguing for two sides of an issue. What strategies can you use to evaluate the issue?

Strategies

Learn what a logical argument is.

When people argue, they try to persuade others to think or act in a certain way. A **logical argument** is based on correct reasoning. When you argue logically, you present opinions backed up by facts. You attack an idea, not the person who has the idea. You try to avoid exaggerations and insults and other language that stirs up strong feelings.

Identify two ways of organizing and presenting information to support arguments.

- In the true story "When the Earth Shakes," people hear rumbling noises. They feel the earth shaking. Buildings fall, and the earth splits open. From evidence around them people conclude that they're in the middle of an earthquake. They're using

492 THIS OLD EARTH

> **Reba Sanchez argues:** "I've seen shark movies. They have terrific special effects. I like to sit in the front so I feel surrounded by the action. I see a movie with friends. We all like movies better than books. Who wouldn't, except maybe somebody with no friends? Seeing a movie is always better than reading a story."

> **Bobby Newton argues:** "Reading a well-written true story is way more exciting than just sitting watching a movie. 'Survive the Savage Sea' is a well-written true story. The descriptions make me feel as if I were right there, getting scared. Reading 'Survive the Savage Sea' is a lot more exciting than seeing a movie. Besides, you can go back and reread the good parts."

inductive reasoning, moving from specific facts or observations to a **conclusion** based on those facts.

- **Deductive reasoning** moves in the opposite direction—from the general to the specific. When you use deductive reasoning, you start with a general idea and present reasons to support it. Here is an example.

    General idea: Sean Riley should be class president.

    Supporting reasons: He's a strong leader and a hard worker, and he has lots of creative ideas.

Using the Strategies

Read the students' arguments in the box above. Then, answer these questions:

1. Which student uses mostly inductive reasoning? Which uses mostly deductive reasoning?
2. Which student presents the better argument—the argument that is more logical? (Set aside your own opinion on the question.)
3. Analyze each argument, using the information on this page. What flaws, if any, can you find in each student's reasoning?

Extending the Strategies

Find an editorial or a letter to the editor in your school paper or a local newspaper. Using the strategies you've just learned, analyze the organization and presentation of ideas. Does the writer use inductive or deductive reasoning? How can you tell?

Reaching All Students

Struggling Readers

Some students may be intimidated by the terms *induction* and *deduction*. After students read a relatively simple editorial or persuasive letter, have them fill in a chart in the shape of a pyramid (or inverted pyramid). They can note the writer's general conclusion at the tip of the pyramid. Then, have students list specific facts and details that support that conclusion; they can write these on horizontal lines leading to the pyramid's base. This graphic organizer

should help students see the "direction" of a persuasive argument.

Advanced Learners

Invite students to analyze and annotate two or three editorials from a local newspaper. Using colored pencils, students can underline each essay's general conclusion, as well as specific facts and observations the writer uses to support that conclusion. Students should then

write one or two brief paragraphs in which they state the topic of each editorial, explain the writer's position on the topic, identify the type of reasoning used, and evaluate the organization and presentation of the ideas.

Learning for Life

Saving Our Planet: Scientific Research

OBJECTIVES
1. Research aspects of an environmental pollution problem
2. Choose and complete a project that presents findings about the problem—its causes, characteristics, and possible solutions

Problem

We all need to be concerned about the problem of environmental pollution. How can you find out more about this problem and about ways to clean up our planet?

Project

Research an environmental pollution problem. Find out how severe the problem is and what can be done to clear it up.

Preparation

1. As a class, discuss the kinds of environmental pollution we have today, such as too much garbage, air pollution, oil spills, and acid rain.

2. Break up into small groups. Each group should pick one environmental pollution problem to research.

Procedure

1. In your group, assign each member a question to research, for example:

   - What causes the problem?

   - How severe is the problem?

   - What steps are being taken to solve it?

   - What else needs to be done?

2. Decide where you can find information on your topic. For example, you might look at science books, magazines, and newspapers. You might also contact the Environmental Protection Agency or other groups concerned with the environment. (They might be listed in the phone book under Environmental Organizations.)

3. Complete your research. Then, meet with your group to discuss the information you found. Organize your notes in clear categories.

4. Figure out how to organize some of your information in a visual format—a chart, graph, diagram, or map, for example.

Presentation

Choose one of these ways to present what you've learned:

1. Earth Day

Hold an Earth Day in your class. Groups should present their environmental topics to the class in oral research reports with visual aids, which could include photographs, diagrams, charts, and maps.

2. Invention

If you're science-minded or creative, come up with your own invention for a "pollution solution"—either a new method or a new product to help clean up the environment. Describe it in detail and make a drawing or diagram.

3. "Save Our Planet" Handbook

Create a "Save Our Planet" handbook. Work as a class, with each group responsible for the section on its environmental problem. Include important facts about the problem, and illustrate your points with diagrams, charts, and maps. Include a list of actions people can take to prevent the problem or to clear it up.

Processing

Write a reflection using this starter: If it were my job to clean up our planet, the first thing I'd do is . . . .

Resources

Viewing and Representing
HRW Multimedia Presentation Maker
Students may wish to use the *Multimedia Presentation Maker* to put together their Earth Day presentations.

Grading Timesaver

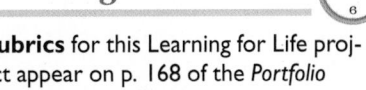

Rubrics for this Learning for Life project appear on p. 168 of the *Portfolio Management System.*

Developing Workplace Competencies

Preparation	Procedure	Presentation
• Analyzing open-ended problems • Determining causes and effects • Processing information • Identifying central issues and problems	• Formulating hypotheses • Classifying data • Predicting consequences	• Stating desired goal • Evaluating actions • Generating related ideas • Formulating alternative solutions • Drawing conclusions

Our Classical Heritage

Theme

Our First Stories *All of the great human stories find expression in the myths of ancient Greece. Here are stories about love, daring, courage, and selfishness. These myths could fit into most thematic connections in this book.*

Reading the Anthology

Reaching Struggling Readers

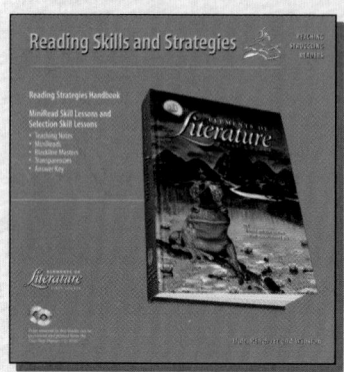

The *Reading Skills and Strategies: Reaching Struggling Readers* binder provides materials coordinated with the Pupil's Edition (see the Collection Planner, p. T493C) to help students who have difficulty reading and comprehending text, or students who are reluctant readers. The binder for seventh grade is organized around eleven individual skill areas and offers the following options:

- **MiniRead** MiniReads are short, easy texts that give students a chance to practice a particular skill and strategy before reading selections in the Pupil's Edition. Each MiniRead Skill Lesson can be taught independently or used in conjunction with a Selection Skill Lesson.

- **Selection Skill Lessons** Selection Skill Lessons allow students to apply skills introduced in the MiniReads. Each Selection Skill Lesson provides reading instruction and practice specific to a particular piece of literature in the Pupil's Edition.

Reading Beyond the Anthology

Read On

Collection Seven includes an annotated bibliography of books suitable for extended reading. The suggested books are related to works in this collection by theme, by author, or by subject. To preview the Read On for Collection Seven, please turn to p. T581.

HRW Library

The *HRW Library* offers novels, plays, and short-story collections for extended reading. Each book in the Library includes one or more major works and thematically or topically related Connections. The Connections are magazine articles, poems, or other pieces of literature. Each book in the *HRW Library* is also accompanied by a Study Guide that provides teaching suggestions and worksheets. For Collection Seven, the following titles are recommended.

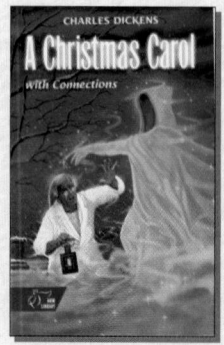

A CHRISTMAS CAROL
Charles Dickens
This nineteenth-century classic looks at greed and its transformation by love. Scrooge's journey through past, present, and future could be compared with the perilous journeys undertaken in myth.

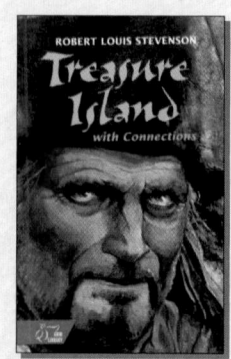

TREASURE ISLAND
Robert Louis Stevenson
Another classic nineteenth-century novel, Stevenson's story also traces a perilous journey. Jim Hawkins's ordeal brings him face to face with greed, treachery, and evil—and a treasure horde at the end.

Skills Focus

Selection or Feature	Reading Skills and Strategies	Elements of Literature	Language/Grammar	Vocabulary/Spelling	Writing	Listening/Speaking	Viewing/Representing
Elements of Literature: The Myths of Greece and Rome (p. 496)		Myths, p. 496 Gods and Goddesses, p. 497					
The Origin of the Seasons (p. 500) Olivia Coolidge	Dialogue with the Text, pp. 500, 509 Draw a Conclusion, p. 509 Identify Causes and Effects, p. 509	Origin Myths, pp. 500, 509, 510	Descriptive Language, p. 511	Prefixes Derived from Greek, p. 511	Write Diary Entries, p. 510 Write an Origin Myth, p. 510 Continue the Story, p. 510		Create a Book Cover, p. 510
Orpheus, the Great Musician (p. 512) Olivia Coolidge	Set a Purpose for Reading, pp. 512, 518 Summarize, p. 518	The Underworld, p. 512	Figurative Language, p. 520 • Simile • Personification	Use Context Clues, p. 520	Write a Song for Orpheus, p. 519 Write a TV News Report, p. 519		Chart Information, p. 518 Map the Underworld, p. 519
Reading Skills and Strategies: Using Context Clues (p. 521)	Context Clues, p. 521			Prefixes and Suffixes, p. 521			Use a Language Chart, p. 521
Echo and Narcissus (p. 522) Roger Lancelyn Green	Use Context Clues, pp. 522, 527 Cite Evidence to Support an Opinion, p. 527	Origin Myth, pp. 522, 527	Words Often Confused, p. 529	Word Roots and Origins, p. 528 Use Context Clues, p. 529	Write in a Character's Point of View, p. 528 Create a Botany Myth, p. 528 Write a Comic Dialogue, p. 528	Dramatize a Dialogue, p. 528	Research and Create a Dictionary of Words with Greek Origins, p. 528
The Flight of Icarus (p. 530) Sally Benson	Make Generalizations, p. 530 Make and Support a Generalization, p. 538	Moral, pp. 530, 537, 538	Adjective vs. Adverb, p. 539	Research Classical Place Names in America, p. 539	Identify and Respond to a Moral, p. 538 Write a Letter from a Character, p. 538 Write an Eye-Witness Account, p. 538	Present a Model or Diagram, p. 538	Create a Diagram or Model, p. 538 Make a Trip Map, p. 538
The Labors of Hercules (p. 540) Rex Warner	Make Connections, pp. 540, 551	The Quest, pp. 540, 551 Tall Tales, p. 551	*Good* and *Well*, p. 553	Create a Glossary, p. 552 Use Words in Context, p. 553	Write an Updated Version of "The Labors of Hercules," p. 552	Present a Biographical Sketch, p. 552	Create a Class Collection of Illustrated Reports, p. 552
King Midas and the Golden Touch (p. 558) Pamela Oldfield	Use Prior Knowledge, pp. 558, 562 Identify a Causal Chain of Events, p. 562	Irony, pp. 558, 562 Metamorphosis, p. 563	Allusions, p. 564	Create Names Based on Mythology, p. 564	Take Notes for an Evaluation, p. 563 Write from a Character's Point of View, p. 563	Dramatize and Perform a Myth, p. 563	Create a Collage Showing a Metamorphosis, p. 563
Elements of Literature: Fables (p. 565)		Fables, p. 565 Moral, p. 565					
Aesop's Fables (p. 566) Aesop	Identify a Text's Purpose, pp. 566, 575	Fable, p. 566 Moral, pp. 566, 575	*Bad* or *Badly?*, p. 577	Similes, p. 577	Write Evaluation Notes, p. 576 Write an Animal Fable, p. 576	Tell a Fable, p. 576	
No Questions Asked: The Dream of Good Fortune (p. 578) Paul Sills	The **No Questions Asked** feature provides students with an unstructured opportunity to practice reading strategies using a selection that extends the theme of the collection.						
Writer's Workshop: Evaluation (p. 582)					Write an Evaluation, pp. 582–586		
Sentence Workshop: Varying Sentence Length (p. 587)			Vary Sentence Length, p. 587		Revise Sentences to Increase Variety, p. 587		
Reading for Life: Reading a Map and a Time Line (p. 588)	Read a Time Line and a Map, p. 588						Make a Time Line, p. 588
Learning for Life: Investigating the Media and Values (p. 589)					Write a Movie Review, p. 589 Write a Dramatic Dialogue, p. 589	Participate in a Debate, p. 589	

Resources for this Collection

Note: All resources for this collection are available for preview on the *One-Stop Planner CD-ROM 2 with Test Generator.* All worksheets and blackline masters may be printed from the CD-ROM.

Internet Resources
go.hrw.com LE0 7-7

Collection Planner

Selection or Feature	Reading and Literary Skills	Language and Grammar
Elements of Literature: The Myths of Greece and Rome (p. 496)	• *Literary Elements,* Transparency 9	
The Origin of the Seasons (p. 500) *retold by* Olivia Coolidge	• *Reading Skills and Strategies: Reaching Struggling Readers* • Selection Skill Lesson, p. 19 • *Graphic Organizers for Active Reading,* Worksheet p. 34 • *Literary Elements:* Transparency 9; Worksheet p. 28	• *Grammar and Language Links:* Descriptive Language, Worksheet p. 47 • *Daily Oral Grammar,* Transparency 28
Orpheus, the Great Musician (p. 512) *retold by* Olivia Coolidge **Connections: The Power of Music from Nadja on My Way** (p. 517) Nadja Salerno-Sonnenberg	• *Reading Skills and Strategies: Reaching Struggling Readers* • Selection Skill Lesson, p. 134 • *Graphic Organizers for Active Reading,* Worksheet p. 35 • *Literary Elements:* Transparency 9; Worksheet p. 28	• *Grammar and Language Links:* Figurative Language, Worksheet p. 49 • *Daily Oral Grammar,* Transparency 29
Echo and Narcissus (p. 522) Roger Lancelyn Green	• *Reading Skills and Strategies: Reaching Struggling Readers* • Selection Skill Lesson, p. 116 • *Graphic Organizers for Active Reading,* Worksheet p. 36 • *Literary Elements:* Transparency 9; Worksheet p. 28	• *Grammar and Language Links:* Confusing Words, Worksheet p. 51 • *Language Workshop CD-ROM,* Possessive Pronouns • *Daily Oral Grammar,* Transparency 30
The Flight of Icarus (p. 530) Sally Benson	• *Reading Skills and Strategies: Reaching Struggling Readers* • Selection Skill Lesson, p. 43 • *Graphic Organizers for Active Reading,* Worksheet p. 37 • *Literary Elements:* Transparency 9; Worksheet p. 28	• *Grammar and Language Links:* Adjectives and Adverbs, Worksheet p. 53 • *Language Workshop CD-ROM,* Adverbs • *Daily Oral Grammar,* Transparency 31
The Labors of Hercules (p. 540) Rex Warner **Connections: The Twelve Tasks of Heracles** (p. 554) *retold by* Marcia Williams	• *Reading Skills and Strategies: Reaching Struggling Readers* • MiniRead Skill Lesson, p. 200 • Selection Skill Lesson, p. 207 • *Graphic Organizers for Active Reading,* Worksheet p. 38 • *Literary Elements:* Transparency 9; Worksheet p. 28	• *Grammar and Language Links:* Good and Well, Worksheet p. 55 • *Language Workshop CD-ROM,* Modifiers • *Daily Oral Grammar,* Transparency 32
King Midas and the Golden Touch (p. 558) *retold by* Pamela Oldfield	• *Reading Skills and Strategies: Reaching Struggling Readers* • Selection Skill Lesson, p. 211 • *Graphic Organizers for Active Reading,* Worksheet p. 39 • *Literary Elements:* Transparency 9; Worksheet p. 28	• *Grammar and Language Links:* Allusions, Worksheet p. 57 • *Daily Oral Grammar,* Transparency 33
Elements of Literature: Fables (p. 565)	• *Literary Elements,* Transparency 10	
Aesop's Fables (p. 566) **Connections: The Boy and the Wolf** (p. 574) Louis Untermeyer	• *Reading Skills and Strategies: Reaching Struggling Readers* • Selection Skill Lesson, p. 138 • *Graphic Organizers for Active Reading,* Worksheet p. 40 • *Literary Elements:* Transparency 10; Worksheet p. 31	• *Grammar and Language Links:* Bad or Badly, Worksheet p. 59 • *Language Workshop CD-ROM,* Bad, Badly • *Daily Oral Grammar,* Transparency 34
No Questions Asked: The Dream of Good Fortune (p. 578) *from* **The Arabian Nights** dramatized by Paul Sills	The **No Questions Asked** feature provides students with an unstructured opportunity to practice reading strategies using a selection that extends the theme of the collection.	
Writer's Workshop: Evaluation (p. 582)		
Sentence Workshop: Varying Sentence Length (p. 587)		• *Workshop Resources,* p. 49
Learning for Life: Investigating the Media and Values (p. 589)		

Collection Resources

- *Cross-Curricular Activities*, p. 47
- *Portfolio Management System:*
  Introduction to Portfolio Assessment, p. 1;
  Parent/Guardian Letters, p. 99
- *Formal Assessment,*
  Reading Application Test, p. 116
- *Test Generator*, Collection Test

Vocabulary, Spelling, and Decoding	Writing	Listening and Speaking, Viewing and Representing	Assessment
			• *Formal Assessment,* Literary Elements Test, p. 113
• *Spelling and Decoding,* Worksheet p. 23	• *Portfolio Management System,* Rubrics for Choices, p. 169	• *Audio CD Library,* Disc 13, Track 2 • *Viewing and Representing:* Fine Art Transparency 16 Worksheet p. 64 • *Portfolio Management System,* p. 169	• *Formal Assessment,* Selection Test, p. 99 • *Standardized Test Preparation,* p. 72, 74 • *Test Generator* (One-Stop Planner CD-ROM)
• *Words to Own,* Worksheet p. 19 • *Spelling and Decoding,* Worksheet p. 24	• *Portfolio Management System,* Rubrics for Choices, p. 171	• *Audio CD Library,* Disc 13, Track 3 • *Portfolio Management System,* Rubrics for Choices, p. 171	• *Formal Assessment,* Selection Test, p. 101 • *Standardized Test Preparation,* p. 76 • *Test Generator* (One-Stop Planner CD-ROM)
• *Words to Own,* Worksheet p. 20 • *Spelling and Decoding,* Worksheet p. 25	• *Portfolio Management System,* Rubrics for Choices, p. 172	• *Audio CD Library,* Disc 13, Track 4 • *Portfolio Management System,* Rubrics for Choices, p. 172	• *Formal Assessment,* Selection Test, p. 103 • *Standardized Test Preparation,* p. 78 • *Test Generator* (One-Stop Planner CD-ROM)
	• *Portfolio Management System,* Rubrics for Choices, p. 174	• *Audio CD Library,* Disc 13, Track 5 • *Viewing and Representing:* Fine Art Transparency 17 Worksheet p. 68 • *Portfolio Management System,* p. 174	• *Formal Assessment,* Selection Test, p. 105 • *Standardized Test Preparation,* p. 80 • *Test Generator* (One-Stop Planner CD-ROM)
• *Words to Own,* Worksheet p. 21 • *Spelling and Decoding,* Worksheet p. 26	• *Portfolio Management System,* Rubrics for Choices, p. 176	• *Visual Connections,* Videocassette B, Segment 8 • *Audio CD Library,* Disc 13, Track 6 • *Portfolio Management System,* Rubrics for Choices, p. 176	• *Formal Assessment,* Selection Test, p. 107 • *Standardized Test Preparation,* p. 82 • *Test Generator* (One-Stop Planner CD-ROM)
	• *Portfolio Management System,* Rubrics for Choices, p. 177	• *Audio CD Library,* Disc 14, Track 2 • *Viewing and Representing:* Fine Art Transparency 18 Worksheet p. 72 • *Portfolio Management System,* p. 177	• *Formal Assessment,* Selection Test, p. 109 • *Standardized Test Preparation,* p. 84 • *Test Generator* (One-Stop Planner CD-ROM)
			• *Formal Assessment,* Literary Elements Test, p. 115
	• *Portfolio Management System,* Rubrics for Choices, p. 178	• *Audio CD Library,* Disc 14, Tracks 3, 4, 5, 6, 7 • *Portfolio Management System,* Rubrics for Choices, p. 178	• *Formal Assessment,* Selection Test, p. 111 • *Test Generator* (One-Stop Planner CD-ROM)
		• *Audio CD Library,* Disc 14, Track 8	
	• *Workshop Resources,* p. 29 • *Writer's Workshop 1* CD-ROM, Evaluation • *Standardized Test Preparation:* Worksheet p. 112 Transparencies 1–6		• *Portfolio Management System* • Prewriting, p. 179 • Peer Editing, p. 180 • Assessment Rubric, p. 181
		• *Viewing and Representing,* HRW Multimedia Presentation Maker	• *Portfolio Management System,* Rubrics, p. 182

 Transparency CD-ROM Video Audio CD

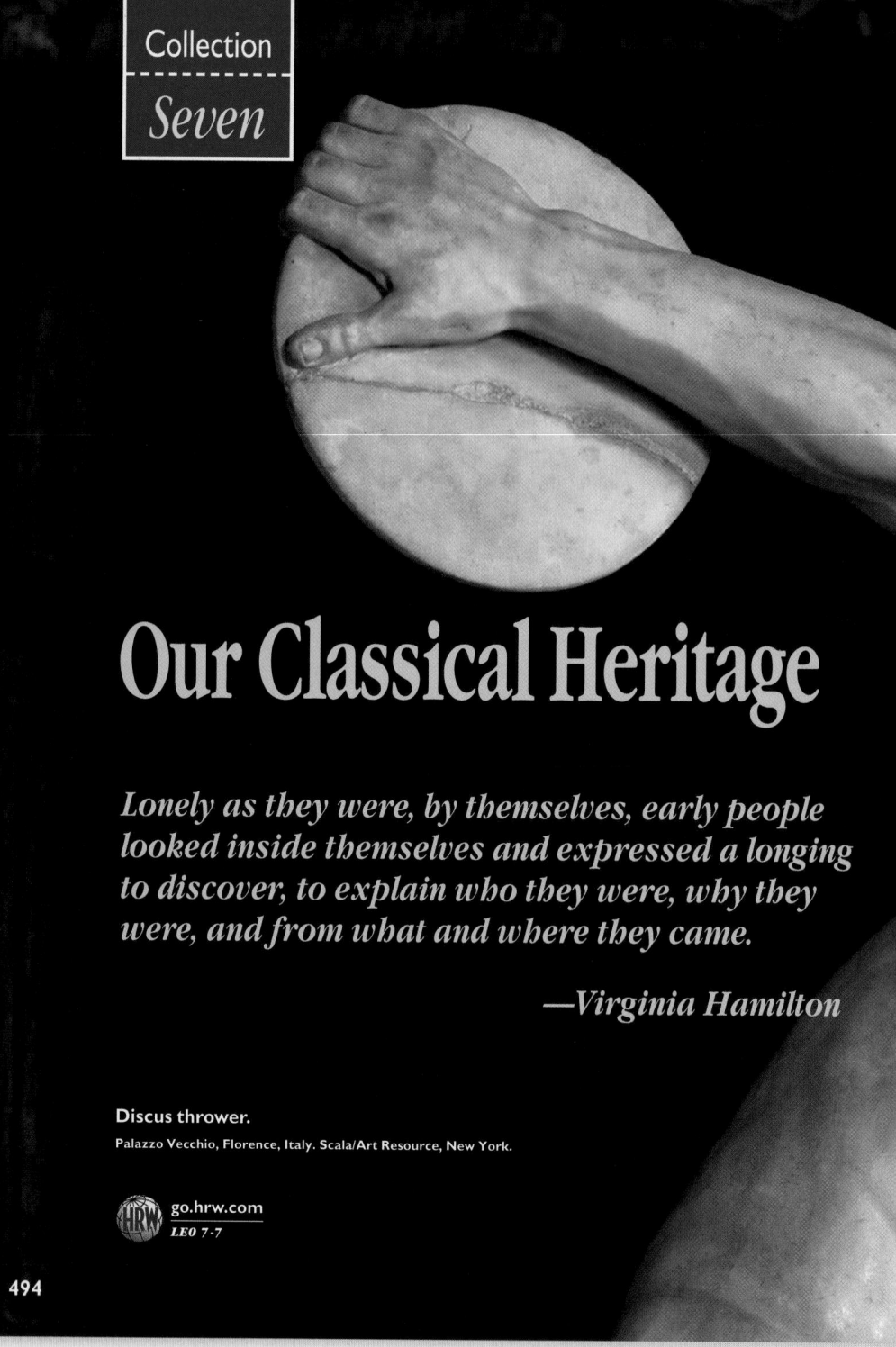

Discus thrower.
Palazzo Vecchio, Florence, Italy. Scala/Art Resource, New York.

go.hrw.com
LEO 7-7

494

Introducing the Theme

Explain to students that the ancient myths in this collection were told by people to explain their history and the natural world around them. Point out that many modern words and ideas have their roots in these stories of ancient gods and goddesses and their interactions with mortals and the natural world. As they read the selections, remind students to look for similarities between these myths and the stories people tell today to explain the modern world.

Responding to the Quotation

Ask students to rephrase the quotation from Virginia Hamilton in their own words. Then, ask them to explain how the mythology of Greece and Rome may connect with the quotation. [Ancient myths often answer the kinds of questions Hamilton mentions.]

Our Classical Heritage

Lonely as they were, by themselves, early people looked inside themselves and expressed a longing to discover, to explain who they were, why they were, and from what and where they came.

—*Virginia Hamilton*

Writing Focus: Evaluation

The following **Work in Progress** assignments build to a culminating **Writer's Workshop** at the end of Collection 7.

- The Origin of the Seasons
- Orpheus, the Great Musician
- Echo and Narcissus
- The Flight of Icarus
- The Labors of Hercules
- King Midas and the Golden Touch
- Aesop's Fables

Take notes for a story evaluation (p. 510)
Compare two mythic characters (p. 519)
Write about standards for an evaluation (p. 528)
Select and evaluate a moral (p. 538)
Make a choice using standards (p. 552)
Make notes on a favorite selection (p. 563)
Record opinions about the fables (p. 576)

Writer's Workshop: Persuasive Writing / Evaluation (p. 582)

Writer's Notebook

Ask students to write a paragraph or two summarizing what they already know about the myths of Greece and Rome. Encourage them to include the names of any gods or goddesses they remember. Have them write a sentence or two explaining why they do or do not enjoy reading myths.

Resources

Portfolio Management System
- Introduction to Portfolio Assessment, p. 1
- Parent/Guardian Letters, p. 99

Formal Assessment
- Reading Application Test, p. 116

Test Generator
- Collection Test

Cross-Curricular Activities
- Teaching Notes, p. 47

Selection Readability

This Annotated Teacher's Edition provides a summary of each selection in the student book. Following each Summary heading, you will find one, two, or three small icons. These icons indicate, in an approximate sense, the reading level of the selection.

■ One icon indicates that the selection is easy.

■ ■ Two icons indicate that the selection is on an intermediate reaading level.

■ ■ ■ Three icons indicate that the selection is challenging.

Resources

Elements of Literature
Words from Mythology
For additional instruction on words from Greek and Roman mythology, see *Literary Elements:*
• Transparency 9

Assessment
Formal Assessment
• Literary Elements Test, p. 113

Elements of Literature

The feature discusses the continuing influence of Greece and Rome in the Western world, reflected even today in architecture, art, literature, science, medicine, monetary systems, and systems of government and law. The essay goes on to describe the origins of myths, to list six uses, or purposes, of myth, and to name some of the major gods and goddesses of Greek and Roman mythology.

Mini-Lesson:
Words from Greek and Roman Mythology
After students have read the essay, ask them to name additional words, images, or expressions from Greek and Roman myths and epics that survive today. [Possible responses: names of planets and months, signs of the zodiac, the figure of Cupid on Valentine's Day cards, and expressions such as "Trojan horse" and "an Achilles' heel."]

THE MYTHS OF GREECE AND ROME

A Writer on Mythology

"Mythology teaches you what's behind literature and the arts; it teaches you about your own life."

—Joseph Campbell

It is hard to imagine what our civilization would be like without the mythology of ancient Greece and Rome. The ancient immortals are still around us in spirit. You might even pass imitations of their "houses" almost every day. Whenever you see a large building with many columns holding up a roof, you are looking at an imitation of a Greek temple.

If you go to any one of the great museums of Europe or America, you will find statues and paintings of classical gods and heroes—as many as you will find of characters and events from history.

If you read poetry in English classes, you will come across references to such ancient places as Troy and Carthage. You will read references to such monsters as the Sirens and the Cyclops, to such gods and heroes as Poseidon, Odysseus (whose Roman name is Ulysses), Athena, and Hercules. These are all names from mythology—names that poets and artists expect us to recognize.

Why Read the Myths?

There is good reason for the continued presence of these strange beings and places in our lives. They are all related to those great classical civilizations of Greece and Rome that were so important to our development as a society. These civilizations gave us much of our astronomy, our mathematics, our philosophy, our architecture, our medicine, our monetary system, and our systems of government and law. We should remember, for instance, that the word *democracy* comes from the Greek word *demokratia*, meaning "rule of the people." This was a kind of government that first flourished in the ancient Greek city-state of Athens.

What Is a Myth?

Myths are stories that are always in some sense religious. Myths represent the deepest wishes and fears of human beings. They helped the ancient people to understand the mysterious and sometimes frightening forces of the universe—forces such as seasonal changes, fire, lightning, drought, floods, and death. Myths probably originated when people began to ask questions about the creation of the world and about their role in it.

Makers of Myths

Most of the myths you will read here originated in the area around the Mediterranean Sea (see the inset of the map on page 498). The early myth makers would not have known how to write. These old myths were passed on orally from generation to generation by the many tribes that traveled through or lived in what is now Greece and western Turkey.

496 OUR CLASSICAL HERITAGE

Reaching All Students

Struggling Readers
Before students read this feature, write the words and names from classical mythology on the board, pronounce them for the class, and ask students to repeat them after you. Also, briefly describe each monster, hero, and god. If possible, show students pictures of any characters who are not already depicted in the illustrations provided in the collection.

English Language Learners
English language learners will also benefit from reading and pronouncing classical names. For additional strategies to supplement instruction for these students, see
• *Lesson Plans Including Strategies for English-Language Learners*

Advanced Learners
Assign each student a different Greek or Roman mythological character. Ask students to research the following information:
• character's special talents
• place(s) associated with the character
• relationship to other mythological characters
Have students share their research by making pocket-sized trading cards with a picture of the character on front and data on the back. Allow class time for students to trade cards.

by David Adams Leeming

By the second century B.C., the Romans had conquered the Greeks and had adopted the Greek myths. The Romans added a new, cynical tone to the old stories. This tone reflected the fact that the Romans were less serious about religion than the Greeks were.

The Uses of Mythology

Great myths are never merely silly or superstitious tales. Like all true art, the great myths give us insights into the nature of our world.

The Greeks and Romans, like all myth makers, used myths for these purposes:

1. to explain the creation of the world
2. to explain natural phenomena
3. to give story form to ancient religious practices
4. to teach moral lessons
5. to explain history
6. to express, as dreams do, the deepest fears and hopes of the human race

A Family Affair: Gods and Goddesses

According to the Greek myths, the divinities lived on Mount Olympus. Many of them traveled down to spend time with ordinary people. To the myth makers, a god or goddess was a powerful being, often identified with a force of nature. The chart below shows some of the divinities and their special powers.

Greek Name	Roman Name	Area of Power
Zeus (zyo͞os)	Jupiter	king of the gods; sky; weather
Apollo (ə·päl′ō)	Apollo	the sun; youth; music; archery; healing; prophecy
Artemis (är′tə·mis)	Diana	twin sister of Apollo; the moon; hunting
Hades (hā′dēz′)	Pluto	king of the underworld
Poseidon (pō·sī′dən)	Neptune	ruler of the seas
Hera (hēr′ə)	Juno	wife of Zeus; queen of gods; women; marriage
Dionysus (dī′ə·nī′səs)	Bacchus	wine; fertility; music
Athena (ə·thē′nə)	Minerva	wisdom; war; crafts
Hephaestus (hē·fes′təs)	Vulcan	craftsman for the gods; fire
Hermes (hʉr′mēz)	Mercury	messenger god; secrets; tricks
Demeter (di·mēt′ər)	Ceres	agriculture; earth; corn
Persephone (pər·sef′ə·nē)	Proserpine	daughter of Demeter; queen of Hades

(continued on next page)

Applying the Element

To help students internalize the purposes of myths, have them plan Myths for Today. Assign students to six small groups. Assign each group a different one of the six "uses of mythology" listed on p. 497. Ask students to provide examples for each purpose.

- Group 1 should specify whose point of view is being presented, for example, a kindergartner's explanation of creation.
- Group 2 should choose a phenomenon, such as a hurricane or a hailstorm.
- Group 3 should choose one custom, such as throwing rice at weddings.
- Group 4 should select a moral or a practical lesson, such as "crime doesn't pay."
- Group 5 should choose a historical event, such as the causes of the Civil War or the story of the first moon landing.
- Group 6 should define the hope or fear to be expressed, such as fear of being alone.

Then, have students brainstorm ideas for creating modern-day myths that illustrate the uses listed on p. 497. When the brainstorming slows down, ask each group to reach consensus on the idea it likes the best. Encourage students to follow up by actually writing new myths.

Using Students' Strengths

Visual Learners
As students read the myths in this collection, have them work in groups to create bumper stickers, comic strips, or posters for mythological characters.

Intrapersonal Learners
Ask students to list in a private place the fears or questions they would like to see answered by a mythological story. Examples might include "Why do good people suffer?" or "Why do I feel alone in a crowd?" Stress that they will not be asked to share these questions with anyone. As they read the myths in this collection, encourage them to note whether ancient storytellers address any of their questions.

Interpersonal Learners
If you have used the teaching idea in Applying the Element, above, these learners may wish to take one of the ideas for a modern myth and improvise a scene to perform for the class.

Mini-Lesson:
The World of Classical Mythology
The literary map on these pages presents the major geographical sites for the myths in this collection. The place names are real, but some of the events or characters that are named exist only in mythology. For example, Lydia, in modern Turkey, is identified as the region where King Midas rules. King Midas is a character in classical mythology, but there was also a real King Midas (see p. T560). Notice that the map also contains two insets. The inset at the lower left on p. 498 shows the island of Sicily, which lies off the toe of Italy's "boot"; the inset identifies Sicily as the mythical home of Persephone. The small inset midway down the right side on p. 499 shows where Greece lies in relation to the rest of the world as represented in world maps today.

The World of Classical Mythology

Crossing the Curriculum

Geography
As students read the myths in this collection, you might have them create their own diorama or relief map of the locale involved in a specific myth. They might use clay or papier-mâché and brightly color their diorama or relief map with tempera or watercolor paints.

Art
Note that the illustration giving the directions north, east, south, and west is called a *compass rose*. Art students might wish to create a compass rose of their own, employing design elements that appeal to their imaginations.

Applying the Element
The feature Reading for Life on p. 588 offers several strategies for using this map. You may wish to have students read the feature now and immediately apply Using the Strategies 3–5 and Extending the Strategies 1.

Propontis

Troy

ASIA MINOR

n

e

w

s

Lesbos

Orpheus buried

Chios

LYDIA
King Midas rules

Greece

Zeus and Hera
married here

SAMOS

Icaria

Icarus drowns

LEBINTHUS

Naxos

Rhodes

King Minos rules

Cnossus

Ida

ad home
Zeus

ELEMENTS OF LITERATURE: THE MYTHS OF GREECE AND ROME 499

OBJECTIVES

1. Read and interpret the myth
2. Identify origin myth and how it explains the changes of seasons
3. Monitor comprehension
4. Express understanding through evaluation and creative writing or art/design
5. Identify descriptive language and use such descriptive language in writing
6. Use a dictionary to understand English prefixes derived from Greek

SKILLS

Literary
- Identify origin myth and how it explains the changes of seasons

Reading
- Monitor comprehension

Writing
- Apply criteria for myth
- Write diary entries as Persephone
- Create a new origin myth
- Write a tale based on the selection

Grammar/Language
- Identify descriptive language and use such descriptive language in writing

Vocabulary
- Use a dictionary to understand English prefixes derived from Greek

Art
- Illustrate a scene

Viewing/Representing
- Relate details of a painting to a myth (ATE)

Before You Read

THE ORIGIN OF THE SEASONS

Make the Connection

Seasons of the Heart

Ancient people looked to myths for answers to questions that they had about nature, just as we look to science today. They wondered, for example, why the growing cycle for crops was linked to the seasons and why there were seasons at all.

Reading Skills and Strategies

Dialogue with the Text

As you read this myth, keep a sheet of paper next to each page so that you can jot down your thoughts and feelings about this explanation of the origin of the seasons. One student's comments appear on the first page of the myth as an example.

Elements of Literature

Origin Myths

The very ancient Greeks did not possess anything like the scientific knowledge we have today. Still, they were just as curious about their natural surroundings as we are about ours. They longed for explanations. Why do we have so many different kinds of flowers? Why is there night and day? Why do the seasons change? For answers to their questions, the ancient people turned to their myth makers. They believed these storytellers were directly in touch with the source of all knowledge—the gods. The myth makers were the guardians of a tradition with the same purpose as science: to provide necessary explanations. These explanations, or **origin myths**, told how something came into being.

> **A**n **origin myth** is an imaginative explanation of how something in the world was created or came to exist.
>
> *For more on Myth, see pages 496–499 and the Handbook of Literary Terms.*

500

As she stretched out her hand, the earth opened in front of her . . .

Planning

- **Traditional Schedule**
  Lesson Plans Including Strategies for English-Language Learners
- **One-Stop Planner**
  CD-ROM with Test Generator

The Origin of the Seasons

retold by **Olivia Coolidge**

D emeter, the great earth mother, was goddess of the harvest. Tall and majestic was her appearance, and her hair was the color of ripe wheat. It was she who filled the ears with grain. In her honor white-robed women brought golden garlands of wheat as first fruits to the altar. Reaping, threshing, winnowing,[1] and the long tables set in the shade for the harvesters' refreshment—all these were hers. Songs and feasting did her honor as the hard-working farmer gathered his abundant fruit. All the laws which the farmer knew came from her: the time for plowing, what land would best bear crops, which was fit for grapes, and which to leave for pasture. She was a goddess whom men called the great mother because of her generosity in giving. Her own special daughter in the family of the gods was named Persephone.

Persephone was the spring maiden, young and full of joy. Sicily was her home, for it is a land where the spring is long and lovely, and where spring flowers are abundant. Here Persephone played with her maidens from day to day till the rocks and valleys rang with the sound of laughter, and gloomy Hades heard it as he sat on his throne in the dark land of the dead. Even his heart of stone was touched by her young beauty, so that he arose in his awful majesty and came up to Olympus to ask Zeus if he might have Persephone to wife. Zeus bowed his head in agreement, and mighty Olympus thundered as he promised.

1. **winnowing:** separating the husks from the grain.

Dialogue with the Text

Demeter is not only a goddess, but she is as pretty as "Snow White."

It's like she's the mother and the farmers are her children. She teaches them everything she knows, as a mother would teach her child.

Persephone seems to represent the spring season.

Even the cruelest can be touched by beauty.

—Rana Jaber
Southwest Middle School
Orlando, Florida

THE ORIGIN OF THE SEASONS 501

Summary ■ ■

This is a modern retelling of an ancient Greek origin myth explaining why the earth has seasons. Demeter is goddess of the harvest. The laughter of her daughter, Persephone, resounds even to the ears of gloomy Hades, who presides over the land of the dead. Hades whisks Persephone away to his bleak domain. Grief-stricken at her daughter's disappearance, Demeter falls into despair. She neglects her harvest duties and the earth is threatened by famine. Zeus sends Hermes to Hades to arrange for Persephone's release. The crafty Hades coaxes Persephone to eat seven pomegranate seeds before she departs. For each seed eaten, Persephone must spend a month of each year in Hades. But during the other five months, the earth rejoices at her presence in verdant splendor.

A Reading Skills and Strategies

Dialogue with the Text

❓ Ask students if their responses to the opening paragraphs of the selection agree with or differ from the comments in Dialogue with the Text. Does the description of Demeter suggest "Snow White"? [Possible response: Demeter is a beautiful, majestic woman whereas Snow White is a beautiful young girl. Some readers may think the comparison inappropriate.] **What is your response to Hades?** [Possible responses: He seems to be sincerely in love; he is touched by the young girl's beauty.]

Resources: Print and Media

Reading
- *Reading Skills and Strategies*
  Selection Skill Lesson, p. 19
- *Graphic Organizers for Active Reading,* p. 34
- *Spelling and Decoding*
  Worksheet, p. 23
- *Audio CD Library*
  Disc 13, Track 2

Elements of Literature
- *Literary Elements*
  Transparency 9
  Worksheet, p. 28

Writing and Language
- *Daily Oral Grammar*
  Transparency 28
- *Grammar and Language Links*
  Worksheet, p. 47

Viewing and Representing
- *Viewing and Representing*
  Fine Art Transparency 16
  Fine Art Worksheet, p. 64

Assessment
- *Formal Assessment,* p. 99
- *Portfolio Management System,* p. 169
- *Standardized Test Preparation,* pp. 72, 74
- *Test Generator (One-Stop Planner CD-ROM)*

Internet
- go.hrw.com (keyword: LE0 7-7)

Thus it came about that as Persephone was gathering flowers with her maidens in the vale of Enna, a marvelous thing happened. Enna was a beautiful valley in whose meadows all the most lovely flowers of the year grew at the same season. There were wild roses, purple crocuses, sweet-scented violets, tall iris, rich narcissus,[2] and white lilies. All these the girl was gathering, yet fair as they were, Persephone herself was fairer far.

As the maidens went picking and calling to one another across the blossoming meadow, it happened that Persephone strayed apart from the rest. Then, as she looked a little ahead in the meadow, she suddenly beheld the marvelous thing. It was a flower so beautiful that none like it had ever been known. It seemed a kind of narcissus, purple and white, but from a single root there sprang a hundred blossoms, and at the sweet scent of it the very heavens and earth appeared to smile for joy. Without calling to the others, Persephone sprang forward to be the first to pick the precious bloom. As she stretched out her hand, the earth opened in front of her, and she found herself caught in a stranger's arms. Persephone shrieked aloud and struggled, while the armful of flowers cascaded down to earth. However, the dark-eyed Hades was far stronger than she. He swept her into his golden chariot, took the reins of his coal-black horses, and was gone amid the rumbling sound of the closing earth before the other girls in the valley could even come in sight of the spot. When they did get there, nobody was visible. Only the roses and lilies of Persephone lay scattered in wild confusion over the grassy turf.

Bitter was the grief of Demeter when she heard the news of her daughter's mysterious fate. Veiling herself with a dark cloud, she sped, swift as a wild bird, over land and ocean for nine days, searching everywhere and asking all she met if they had seen her daughter. Neither gods nor men had seen her. Even the birds could give no tidings, and Demeter in despair turned to Phoebus Apollo, who sees all things from his chariot in the heavens.

"Yes, I have seen your daughter," said the god at last. "Hades has taken her with the consent of Zeus, that she may dwell in the land of mist and gloom as his queen. The girl struggled and was unwilling, but Hades is far stronger than she."

When she heard this, Demeter fell into deep despair, for she knew she could never rescue Persephone if Zeus and Hades had agreed. She did not care any more to enter the palace of Olympus, where the gods live in joy and feasting and where Apollo plays the lyre while the Muses sing. She took on her the form of an old woman, worn but stately, and wandered about the earth, where there is much sorrow to be seen. At first she kept away from the homes of people, since the sight of little children and happy mothers gave her pain. One day, however, as she sat by the side of a well to rest her weary feet, four girls came down to draw water. They were kind hearted and charming as they talked with her and concerned themselves about the fate of the homeless stranger-woman who was sitting at their gates. To account for herself, Demeter told them that she was a woman of good family from Crete, across the sea, who had been captured by pirates and was to have been sold for a slave. She had escaped as they landed once to cook a meal on shore, and now she was wandering to find work.

The four girls listened to this story, much impressed by the stately manner of the strange

---

2. **narcissus** (när·sis′əs): family of lilies including daffodils and jonquils. "Echo and Narcissus" (page 523) gives the ancient Greeks' explanation of how this flower came to be.

La Primavera: Flora (detail) (1477) by Sandro Botticelli.
Uffizi Gallery, Florence, Italy. Erich Lessing/Art Resource, New York.

Reaching All Students

RESPONDING TO THE ART

Sandro Botticelli (1444–1510) of Florence helped to define the Italian Renaissance. Born Alessandro del Filipepi, he came under the early influence of Andrea Verrocchio and Antonio Pollaiuolo. Less concerned with a precise representation of space and perspective than other Italian painters of the period, he created work notable for its boldly imaginative, free-flowing approach. He portrayed subjects drawn from ancient mythology with lush sensuality, as in this detail from *La Primavera: Flora*. Christian motifs predominated in his later, more somber paintings, such as his illustrations for Dante's *Divine Comedy*.

Activity. Have students study the details from Botticelli's work on pp. 503, 505, and 506–507. Ask them to cite specific details relating the painting to "The Origin of the Seasons." [Possible response: The young woman could easily be Persephone, the personification of spring, and the detail showing flowers could be the field from which Hades abducted her.] You might also have students collect other artistic representations of spring, of another season, or of a mythological character, and compare them in terms of content and style with Botticelli's painting.

Resources

Listening
Audio CD Library
A reading of this myth is provided in the *Audio CD Library*:
- Disc 13, Track 2

Selection Assessment
Formal Assessment
- Selection Test, p. 99

Test Generator
- Selection Test

Getting Students Involved

Cooperative Learning

Reader's Theater. Ask students to work in groups of five to write and perform sketches based on scenes from the story. The sketches may be based on passages of dialogue or action. Suggest that the groups choose one member to act as a narrator who introduces and explains the sketch, while the other members take individual or choral parts. Encourage students to include sound effects and background music when they present their reading to the class.

Hot Seat. Divide the class into small groups. Ask each group to choose one character: Demeter, Persephone, or Hades. Ask each student to create a list of the character's main attributes:
- Demeter: grief-stricken, despairing
- Persephone: alone, sad, homesick
- Hades: tricky, unapologetic

Finally, have groups give their members two minutes each on the Hot Seat to respond in character to questions from other members.

woman. At last they said that their mother, Metaneira,[3] was looking for a nurse for their new-born brother, Demophoon.[4] Perhaps the stranger would come and talk with her. Demeter agreed, feeling a great longing to hold a baby once more, even if it were not her own. She went therefore to Metaneira, who was much struck with the quiet dignity of the goddess and glad to give her charge of her little son. For a while thereafter Demeter was nurse to Demophoon, and his smiles and babble consoled her in some part for her own darling daughter. She began to make plans for Demophoon: He should be a great hero; he should become an immortal, so that when he grew up she could keep him with her.

Presently the whole household was amazed at how beautiful Demophoon was growing, the more so as they never saw the nurse feed him anything. Secretly Demeter would anoint him with ambrosia,[5] like the gods, and from her breath, as he lay in her lap, he would draw his nourishment. When the night came, she would linger by the great fireside in the hall, rocking the child in her arms while the embers burned low and the people went off to sleep. Then, when all was still, she would stoop quickly down and put the baby into the fire itself. All night long the child would sleep in the red-hot ashes, while his earthly flesh and blood changed slowly into the substance of the immortals. In the morning when people came, the ashes were cold and dead, and by the hearth sat the stranger-woman, gently rocking and singing to the child.

Presently Metaneira became suspicious of the strangeness of it all. What did she know of this nurse but the story she had heard from her daughters? Perhaps the woman was a witch of some sort who wished to steal or transform the boy. In any case it was wise to be careful. One

3. **Metaneira** (met'ə·nē'rə).
4. **Demophoon** (de·mäf'ō·än').
5. **ambrosia** (am·brō'zhə): food of the gods.

night, therefore, when she went up to her chamber, she set the door ajar and stood there in the crack silently watching the nurse at the fireside crooning over the child. The hall was very dark, so that it was hard to see clearly, but in a little while the mother beheld the dim figure bend forward. A log broke in the fireplace, a little flame shot up, and there clear in the light lay the baby on top of the fire.

Metaneira screamed loudly and lost no time in rushing forward, but it was Demeter who snatched up the baby. "Fool that you are," she said indignantly to Metaneira, "I would have made your son immortal, but that is now impossible. He shall be a great hero, but in the end he will have to die. I, the goddess Demeter, promise it." With that old age fell from her and she grew in stature. Golden hair spread down over her shoulders so that the great hall was filled with light. She turned and went out of the doorway, leaving the baby on the ground and Metaneira too amazed and frightened even to take him up.

All the while that Demeter had been wandering, she had given no thought to her duties as the harvest goddess. Instead she was almost glad that others should suffer because she was suffering. In vain the oxen spent their strength in dragging the heavy plowshare[6] through the soil. In vain did the sower with his bag of grain throw out the even handfuls of white barley in a wide arc as he strode. The greedy birds had a feast off the seed corn that season; or if it started to sprout, sun baked it and rains washed it away. Nothing would grow. As the gods looked down, they saw threatening the earth a famine such as never had been known.

6. **plowshare:** cutting blade of a plow.

La Primavera: Flora (detail) (1477)
by Sandro Botticelli.
Uffizi Gallery, Florence, Italy. Erich Lessing/Art Resource, New York.

Remind students that the illustrations on pp. 503, 505, and 506–507 are details from a larger painting by Sandro Botticelli, titled *La Primavera (Springtime)*. If possible, display a print of the whole painting to help students see how the pieces fit into it. They may be familiar with another of Botticelli's works, *Birth of Venus*.

Activity. Here are some questions you might ask students, in addition to those given in the art note on p. T503.

- Which detail do you like best?
- Does the portrait on p. 503 remind you of any other famous paintings?
- What makes the woman in the detail on p. 503 look as if she represents, or is part of, the natural world? [Possible response: Her neck and face seem to grow out from the background like a plant. The flowers in her hair, around her neck, and on her dress make her seem a part of her surroundings.]

Skill Link

Descriptive Writing

Good descriptive writing evokes images for the reader through concrete, specific nouns (*narcissus*, not *flower*); precise verbs (*cascaded* to earth, not *fell*); and adjectives that appeal to the senses (*white* lilies, *dim* figure, *heavy* plowshare). A discussion of descriptive language appears in the Language Link on p. 511.

Activities

1. As students read the story, ask them to list the descriptive words that catch their eye or ear. After they finish their reading, have them identify the words they found evocative as nouns, verbs, or adjectives. They can check parts of speech in a dictionary, if necessary. Do they find a pattern? Does one part of speech "make" a description come alive for them more than other parts of speech?

2. After students have read the story, divide the class into groups of three. Distribute several travel brochures for exotic destinations, and ask students to read the descriptions in them. Discuss with the class the word choice and style that the descriptions have in common. Ask them to focus on evocative nouns, verbs, and adjectives. Then, ask students to create travel-brochure-style descriptive passages for Enna, for the underworld of Hades, or for Olympus. They should base their descriptions on information provided by the story.

RESPONDING TO THE ART

See the earlier art notes on pp. T503 and T505.

Activity. Ask students what descriptive words and phrases they would use to tell someone about the scenery shown in the detail on these two pages. [Possible responses: bright patches of flowers, growing, alive, thriving, flourishing, jewels on dark velvet.]

Assessing Learning

Observation Assessment

Group Participation. As you observe students participating in any group assignments you make for this selection, note and record individual progress, using the following scale.

M = Mastered   C = Could Improve
P = Problem

_____1. Asks appropriate questions
_____2. Allows others to speak
_____3. Remains focused and on task
_____4. Maintains a positive attitude
_____5. Actively participates

Even the offerings to the gods were neglected by despairing men who could no longer spare anything from their dwindling stores.

At last Zeus sent Iris, the rainbow, to seek out Demeter and appeal to her to save mankind. Dazzling Iris swept down from Olympus swift as a ray of light and found Demeter sitting in her temple, the dark cloak still around her and her head bowed on her hand. Though Iris urged her with the messages of Zeus and offered beautiful gifts or whatever powers among the gods she chose, Demeter would not lift her head or listen. All she said was that she would neither set foot on Olympus nor let fruit grow on the earth until Persephone was restored to her from the kingdom of the dead.

At last Zeus saw that he must send Hermes of the golden sandals to bring back Persephone to the light. The messenger found dark-haired Hades sitting upon his throne with Persephone, pale and sad, beside him. She had neither eaten nor drunk since she had been in the land of the dead. She sprang up with joy at the message of Hermes, while the dark king looked gloomier than ever, for he really loved his queen. Though he could not disobey the command of Zeus, he was crafty, and he pressed Persephone to eat or drink with him as they parted. Now, with joy in her heart, she should not refuse all food. Persephone was eager to be gone, but since the king entreated her, she took a pomegranate[7] from him to avoid argument and delay. Giving in to his pleading, she ate seven of the seeds. Then Hermes took her with him, and she came out into the upper air.

When Demeter saw Hermes with her daughter, she started up, and Persephone too rushed forward with a glad cry and flung her arms

7. **pomegranate** (päm'ə·gran'it): round, red fruit containing many seeds. Pomegranates are pictured on page 509.

La Primavera: Flora (detail) (1477) by Sandro Botticelli.
Uffizi Gallery, Florence, Italy. Erich Lessing/Art Resource, New York.

A Reading Skills and Strategies
Drawing Conclusions
❓ What effect has Demeter's neglect of her duties had on the other gods? [People have stopped making offerings to the gods, so they are probably upset.] Why might Zeus want Demeter to save humanity? [He wishes people to have the grain to resume their customary offerings to the gods.]

B Appreciating Language
Epithets
❓ An **epithet** is a characterizing word or phrase that may accompany or even replace the name of a character—a kind of verbal tag. What phrases are used here to identify, or tag, Hermes and Hades? ["Hermes of the golden sandals," "dark-haired Hades."]

C Critical Thinking
Interpreting Meaning
❓ What clues suggest that Hades has a plan to frustrate Zeus's command? [Possible response: He is called *crafty*, and the story doesn't say that he simply *offers* her the fruit, but that he *entreats* her and *pleads* with her to eat it.]

Making the Connections

Connecting to the Theme:
"Our Classical Heritage"
"The Origin of the Seasons" connects with the theme of the collection by serving as an example of the stories handed down to us.

Cultural Connections
To help students develop further their understanding of origin myths, divide them into small groups. Include both English language learners and English-proficient learners in each group. Instruct each group to choose one aspect of nature and then to recall explanations they have heard for this aspect. A good example might be the cause or origin of thunder. Ask students to compare various stories and then either choose the one they like the best or develop a new explanation about the origin of this phenomenon. Have the groups share their results with the class.

Making Inferences

? Which part of the year does Persephone spend with Hades and which part with her mother, Demeter? [She spends fall and winter in the underworld with Hades and spring and summer on the earth with Demeter.]

B Elements of Literature

Origin Myths

Point out that this myth accounts for the growing cycle of plants. Just as Persephone is trapped in the underworld for part of the year, seeds lie buried underground for a long time before they bring forth new life from the earth.

BROWSING IN THE FILES

About the Author. Olivia Coolidge was born in England and graduated from Oxford University. She taught Latin, Greek, and English in England and in the United States. Besides retelling Greek and Norse myths, she also has written about famous people such as Abraham Lincoln. Her books include *The Maid of Artemis* and *The Apprenticeship of Abraham Lincoln.*

Resources

Viewing and Representing
Fine Art Transparency
After students have read "Origin of the Seasons," "Orpheus," and "Echo and Narcissus," use the transparency of *Autumn* by Giuseppe Arcimboldo to complement all three myths.
• Transparency 16
• Worksheet, p. 64

---

about her mother's neck. For a long time the two caressed each other, but at last Demeter began to question the girl. "Did you eat or drink anything with Hades?" she asked her daughter anxiously, and the girl replied:

"Nothing until Hermes released me. Then in my joy I took a pomegranate and ate seven of its seeds."

"Alas," said the goddess in dismay, "my daughter, what have you done? The Fates have said that if you ate anything in the land of shadow, you must return to Hades and rule with him as his queen. However, you ate not the whole pomegranate, but only seven of the seeds. For seven months of the year, therefore, **A** you must dwell in the underworld, and the remaining five you may live with me."

Thus the Fates had decreed, and even Zeus could not alter their law. For seven months of every year, Persephone is lost to Demeter and rules pale and sad over the dead. At this time Demeter mourns, trees shed their leaves, cold comes, and the earth lies still and dead. But **B** when, in the eighth month, Persephone returns, her mother is glad and the earth rejoices. The wheat springs up, bright, fresh, and green in the plowland. Flowers unfold, birds sing, and young animals are born. Everywhere the heavens smile for joy or weep sudden showers of gladness upon the springing earth.

MEET THE WRITER

"I Write Because . . . I Almost Have To"

Olivia Coolidge (1908–   ), the daughter of an English historian, has used her own storytelling gifts mainly to make mythology and history exciting for young readers. She believes strongly in the power of story:

66 A good book should excite, amuse and interest. It should give a sense of seeing as a movie does. In other words, a good book needs imagination and the gift of a good storyteller. I write because I like writing, because I want to write, and because I almost have to. I have a great many things I want to say, ideas I want to express and pictures I want to convey to other people. **99**

More Gifts from a Good Storyteller

To "see" more myths and ancient stories by Olivia Coolidge, look for *Greek Myths* and *Legends of the North* (both published by Houghton Mifflin). To explore the ancient world from which these stories emerged, check out *The Golden Days of Greece* (Thomas Crowell).

Assessing Learning

Check Test: True-False

1. Zeus gives Hades permission to take Persephone as his wife. [True]
2. Persephone agrees to go to the underworld with Hades. [False]
3. Demeter tries to make Demophoon immortal by placing him in a fire. [True]
4. Demeter allows nothing to grow on earth because she is angry at humanity. [False]
5. Because Persephone eats in the underworld, she has to return for part of each year. [True]

Standardized Test Preparation

For practice with standardized test format specific to this selection, see
• *Standardized Test Preparation*, pp. 72, 74
For practice in proofreading and editing, see
• *Daily Oral Grammar*, Transparency 28

MAKING MEANINGS

First Thoughts

[respond]

1. What are your first impressions of the gods and goddesses in this myth? What do you think of the way they treat one another and the people on earth? Review your reading notes for ideas.

Shaping Interpretations

[infer]

2. How does this story of the kidnapping of a young girl and her mother's grief explain the change of seasons on earth?

[speculate]

3. Why do you think Demeter spends so much time with the baby Demophoon, even planning to make him immortal?

[infer]

4. Demeter is able to force Zeus to change his mind about the marriage of Hades and Persephone. What does this tell you about "the great earth mother"?

[conclude]

5. What **conclusion** can you draw about the power of love over death from this myth?

Connecting with the Text

[connect]

6. Which character in this myth do you feel the most sympathy for? Why?

Extending the Text

[extend]

7. What other accounts do you know of in which someone eats a forbidden food—or breaks a taboo (a rule strictly prohibiting something)—and pays dearly for it?

Reading Check

Many events in this ancient myth are connected by **cause and effect.** On a sheet of paper, describe the effect of each event listed below.

a. Gloomy Hades falls in love with beautiful young Persephone.
Effect:

b. Unhappy about the loss of her daughter, Demeter gives no thought to her duties as the harvest goddess.
Effect:

c. Demeter vows that she will not let fruit grow on the earth until Persephone is returned.
Effect:

d. While in the land of the dead, Persephone eats seven seeds from a piece of fruit.
Effect:

Pomegranates.

THE ORIGIN OF THE SEASONS **509**

MAKING MEANINGS

First Thoughts

1. Possible response: They seem self-centered and spoiled. They are more powerful than humans, but they are not more kind.

Shaping Interpretations

2. Demeter's mood guides the seasons. When Persephone is with her, Demeter's joy brings spring and summer; when Persephone is in the underworld, Demeter's sorrow brings fall and winter.
3. Perhaps because her own child is gone, Demeter may want another child to care for.
4. Possible response: Without her generosity, all people will starve, so even the king of the gods must respect her wishes. She is a powerful force.
5. Demeter's love is powerful enough to bring Persephone back from the world of the dead.

Connecting with the Text

6. Persephone is the most likely choice, because Hades kidnaps her and then tricks her into staying with him in the underworld for more than half of every year.

Extending the Text

7. Possible responses: "Hansel and Gretel," "Goldilocks and the Three Bears," and the story of Adam and Eve from the book of Genesis in the Bible.

Reading Check

a. Hades kidnaps Persephone.
b. Nothing grows, and there is a terrible famine.
c. Zeus sends Hermes to the underworld to arrange for the return of Persephone.
d. Persephone must spend seven months of each year in the underworld.

T509

Grading Timesaver

Rubrics for each Choices assignment appear on p. 169 in the *Portfolio Management System*.

CHOICES: Building Your Portfolio

1. **Writer's Notebook** Call to students' attention the sample chart in the notebook graphic. Students should organize their notes in the same way. Remind them to save their work. They may use it as prewriting for the Writer's Workshop on pp. 582–586.

2. **Creative Writing** Before students begin writing, review the descriptions of Persephone given in the story. Remind students to write the diary entries in character, using the pronoun *I*.

3. **Creative Writing** Before students begin individual work, allow them to brainstorm in groups to come up with reasons for seasonal phenomena such as spring rain, summer heat, winter snow, and the changing colors of leaves in the fall. Provide these guidelines to help students shape their stories to the typical forms of myths.
   - Include supernatural characters with human faults and emotions.
   - Describe the events in the myth as you would describe a dream.

4. **Creative Writing** Remind students that Demeter predicts Demophoon will become a great hero. Read to students accounts of other heroes from mythology, such as Theseus.

5. **Art/Design** Display or distribute books with a variety of cover designs that students may use as models. You may also wish to have students work first in groups of four to create symbols or motifs for Demeter, Persephone, and Hades. Among the possible choices:
   - Demeter: sheaf of wheat, bowl of fruit
   - Persephone: flowers, pomegranate seeds
   - Hades: black horses, gold chariot, throne

Ask students to incorporate the symbols into the scenes they illustrate on the book covers.

CHOICES: Building Your Portfolio

Writer's Notebook

1. Collecting Ideas for an Evaluation

To endure, a myth must tell a good story. A myth must also speak to our deepest wishes and fears. Take some notes about how you think "The Origin of the Seasons" fits these criteria. Does it tell a good story that keeps you interested in what will happen next? Does the story express any universal wishes or any of our worst fears? You might use the chart shown in the notebook.

Evaluation Chart
Suspense:
Good characters:
Interesting theme:
Speaks to our wishes:
Expresses our fears:

Creative Writing

2. Notes from the Underworld

Imagine that you are Persephone. Write diary entries in which you describe your thoughts and feelings about each of the following: picking flowers with your friends in the vale of Enna; being the wife of Hades; returning to your mother and the world of light; eating the pomegranate seeds.

Creative Writing

3. A Myth for All Seasons

Throughout the world, people have told imaginative stories to explain the cycle of seasons. Write your own **origin myth** explaining why the seasons change as they do in your part of the world. If you live in a region where the weather rarely changes, tell why this came to be. Before you begin, decide whether the weather in your region is a punishment or a reward.

Creative Writing

4. The Rest of the Story

What happens to Demophoon? Reread what Demeter says to the mother of the young boy. Then, write a short tale that shows how Demeter's predictions might have come true.

Art/Design

5. Cover Story

The editor of a book of myths for children wants you to design the cover. The illustration on the cover will show a scene from "The Origin of the Seasons." Choose the scene from this myth that you find most dramatic or interesting. Then, illustrate the scene in a way that will make people want to read the myth.

510 OUR CLASSICAL HERITAGE

LANGUAGE LINK `MINI-LESSON`

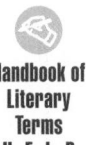

Handbook of Literary Terms

H E L P

See Description.

Style: Descriptive Language

In "The Origin of the Seasons," Hades drives Persephone into a hole in the ground. Here's how Coolidge describes the scene:

> "He swept her into his golden chariot, took the reins of his coal-black horses, and was gone amid the rumbling sound of the closing earth. . . ."

This sentence creates a rich picture because it uses good **descriptive language**. In good descriptive writing you find

1. **concrete, specific nouns:** It isn't just a *vehicle*—it's a *chariot*.
2. **precise verbs:** He didn't just *put* her in—he *swept* her in.
3. **vivid adjectives** that appeal to the senses: The horses are *coal-black*; the earth makes a *rumbling* sound.

Try It Out

Rewrite each of the sentences below, using descriptive language. Remember to use specific nouns, precise verbs, and vivid adjectives.

1. Persephone lived in a perfectly nice place.
2. She went into a valley full of flowers.
3. Some horses went by, making a lot of noise.
4. The cavern was dark.
5. Poor Persephone sat on a throne.

VOCABULARY `HOW TO OWN A WORD`

English Prefixes Derived from Greek

A **prefix** is a word part that is added to the beginning of a word to change the word's meaning. Many prefixes that we use today come from ancient Greek. Some common ones appear in the first column of the chart below. The first row of the chart is filled in for you. Use a dictionary to complete the rest of the chart. Be sure to compare your charts in class.

	Meaning	Example
anti-	*against*	*antidote: something that acts against a poison*
auto-		
hydro-		
meta-		
sym- or *syn-*		

LANGUAGE LINK

Pair students, and ask them to read aloud from their writing. As they read, their partners should ask questions in the form *What kind of _____?* For example, if a student reads the sentence "Persephone lived in a land of abundant flowers," the partner should respond, "What kind of land?" or "What kind of flowers?" The student might then rewrite the sentence as "Persephone lived in a fragrant land of abundant spring flowers such as roses, crocuses, and violets."

Try It Out
Possible Answers
1. Persephone played on a flower-covered island in a blue sea.
2. She gathered flowers in a valley overflowing with roses and lilies.
3. Four black stallions came thundering up out of the earth.
4. The gloomy cavern was pitch black.
5. Sorrowful Persephone slumped on her silver throne.

VOCABULARY
Possible Answers
Auto- means "self"; *autobiography*: a self-told life story.
Hydro- means "water"; *hydroelectricity*: energy from water power.
Meta- means "change"; *metamorphosis*: change in form.
Sym- and *syn-* mean "same"; *synonyms*: words with the same meaning.

Resources ————

Language
• *Grammar and Language Links,* p. 47
Spelling
For related instruction, see
• *Spelling and Decoding,* p. 23

Language Link Quick Check

Replace each of the underlined words in the sentences below with a more specific noun, precise verb, or vivid adjective. [Possible responses appear in brackets.]

1. After she flipped the switch, the rocket went into the air. [blasted, roared]
2. That restaurant serves curry that is really tasty. [spicy]
3. Because she was a queen, she lived in a huge, beautiful house. [palace, mansion]
4. I watched helplessly as the ball broke the window. [shattered]
5. A faint sound surged softly through the crowd when the lights dimmed. [murmuring]

OBJECTIVES
1. Read and interpret the myth
2. Analyze how myth explains the afterlife
3. Set purpose for reading
4. Express understanding through evaluation, creative writing/ music, or research/map making
5. Identify figurative language and use such language in writing
6. Understand and use new words

SKILLS
Literary
- Analyze how myth explains the afterlife

Reading
- Set purpose for reading

Writing
- Evaluate characters
- Prepare a journalistic report

Grammar/Language
- Identify figurative language and use such language in writing

Vocabulary
- Understand and use new words

Music
- Compose a song
- Respond to music (ATE)

Research/Map Making
- Create a map of the underworld

Viewing/Representing
- Identify figures in a relief (ATE)

Before You Read

ORPHEUS, THE GREAT MUSICIAN

Make the Connection

Swept Away by Music

"Music is more important than we will ever know. Great music can pull you right out of your chair. It can make you cry, or laugh, or feel a way you've never felt before."

—Nadja Salerno-Sonnenberg, "The Power of Music" (page 517)

Quickwrite

Think of a time when music touched your life. Write briefly about the experience.

Elements of Literature

The Underworld of Myth

You don't have to read too many myths before you find yourself in that frightful place called the underworld. As you know from "The Origin of the Seasons," the underworld is a dark and gloomy place ruled by the stern god Hades. To reach Hades' home, you cross the River Styx (stiks) on a ferryboat rowed by Charon (ker'ən). Then you pass through gates guarded by Cerberus, a three-headed dog. Normally only the souls of the dead go to Hades. Sometimes, however, living people attempt the dangerous journey, usually to reach someone who has died.

For more on Myth, see pages 496–499 and the Handbook of Literary Terms.

Reading Skills and Strategies

Setting Purposes for Reading: Being Flexible

Journeys to the underworld make exciting stories. Your original **purpose,** or reason, for reading about the dark kingdom may be to **enjoy** the adventure. As you get caught up in the story, however, you may want to **understand** it on a deeper level. Journey with Orpheus to the underworld, and think about what this exciting story says about our fear of death and our desire to overcome it somehow.

Orpheus, Eurydice, and Hermes. Roman copy after Greek original.

Museo Archeologica Nazionale, Naples, Italy.
Erich Lessing/Art Resource, New York.

Planning

- **Block Schedule**
  Block Scheduling Lesson Plans with Pacing Guide
- **Traditional Schedule**
  Lesson Plans Including Strategies for English-Language Learners
- **One-Stop Planner**
  CD-ROM with Test Generator

Preteaching Vocabulary

Words to Own

Have students copy the information on the Words to Own from pp. 515–516. Then direct them to choose from the following list the correct synonym and antonym for each word.

Synonyms	Antonyms
brokenhearted	appealing
horrifying	moved down
moved up	overjoyed
unwillingness	willingness

ORPHEUS, THE GREAT MUSICIAN

RETOLD BY OLIVIA COOLIDGE

HIS LOVE FOR HER WAS HIS INSPIRATION . . .

ORPHEUS, THE GREAT MUSICIAN **513**

RESPONDING TO THE ART

Orpheus, Eurydice, and Hermes, the Roman sculpture shown on this page, is a relief—a form of sculpture in which figures are set off from a flat background. Rome's military conquest of Greece in the second century B.C. was counterbalanced by Greece's cultural conquest of Rome. The educated Greek slaves who filled teaching posts in Roman schools instilled a love for Homer's epics and made the Greek language essential to Roman aristocrats and scholars. Greek influence swept over the arts. Many Roman sculptors churned out precise replicas of Greek classics, like this one.

Activity. After students have read the story of Orpheus, ask them to identify the figures in the relief. They should note facial expressions, gestures, garments, and ornamentation.

Another example of relief appears on p. 514. In high reliefs sculptured figures rise from the background to at least half of their natural depth; shallower forms, like the sculpture of the lyre player are called low reliefs, or bas-reliefs. The lyre was the favorite instrument of the god Apollo, who embodied the virtues of wisdom, harmony, and restraint.

Activity. Have students compare this ancient Greek bas-relief with the Mayan plate on p. 667. What differences do they see in human form and gestures? Which work shows more naturalness and flexibility of form?

  Resources: Print and Media

Reading
- Reading Skills and Strategies
  Selection Skill Lesson, p. 134
- *Graphic Organizers for Active Reading,* p. 35
- *Words to Own,* p. 19
- *Spelling and Decoding*
  Worksheet, p. 24
- *Audio CD Library*
  Disc 13, Track 3

Elements of Literature
- *Literary Elements*
  Transparency 9
  Worksheet, p. 28

Writing and Language
- *Daily Oral Grammar*
  Transparency 29
- *Grammar and Language Links*
  Worksheet, p. 49

Assessment
- *Formal Assessment,* p. 101
- *Portfolio Management System,* p. 171
- *Standardized Test Preparation,* p. 76
- *Test Generator (One-Stop Planner CD-ROM)*

Internet
- go.hrw.com (keyword: LE0 7-7)

Summary ■ ■

In this Greek myth, the hero Orpheus produces music no being can resist. He is madly in love with the nymph Eurydice. On their wedding day, she is bitten by a snake and dies. Grieving, Orpheus descends into Hades to join her. His song so mesmerizes the denizens of the underworld that even Hades is moved. He tells Orpheus to flee the underworld while its guardians remain entranced. Hades will permit Eurydice to follow—unless Orpheus looks back. Orpheus cautiously ascends, torn by inner conflict and worrying about trickery. Just as he approaches daylight, he swirls to look back, and as he reaches for Eurydice, she vanishes in a puff of smoke. He hurries downward again, but the guardians bar his way. For seven days, he grieves in silence on the banks of the River Styx, and then he ascends to earth. Sorrow lends his music even greater power, but he scorns all visitors. At last, infuriated by his contempt and maddened by the god Dionysus, the women of Thrace kill him. His spirit is united with that of Eurydice in the daffodil meadows, where he forever looks back at her.

Resources

Listening
Audio CD Library
A reading of this myth is provided in the *Audio CD Library:*
• Disc 13, Track 3

Selection Assessment
Formal Assessment
• Selection Test, p. 101
Test Generator
• Selection Test

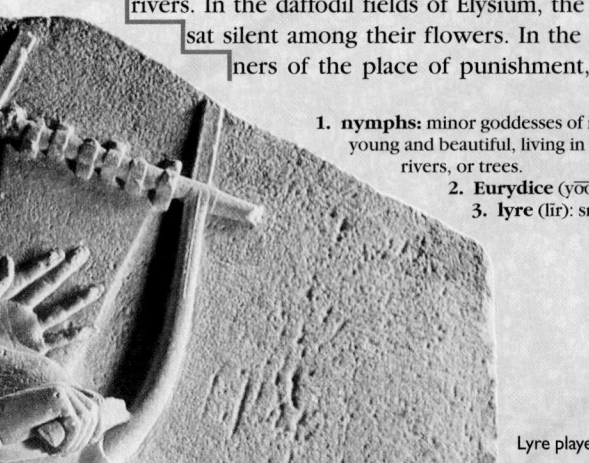

THE EARTH ITSELF SORROWED WITH HIM.

Lyre player. Greece.

A In the legend of Orpheus, the Greek love of music found its fullest expression. Orpheus, it is said, could make such heavenly songs that when he sat down to sing, the trees would crowd around to shade him. The ivy and vine stretched out their tendrils. Great oaks would bend their spreading branches over his head. The very rocks would edge down the mountainsides. Wild beasts crouched harmless by him, and nymphs[1] and woodland gods would listen to him, enchanted.

Orpheus himself, however, had eyes for no one but the nymph Eurydice.[2] His love for her was his inspiration, and his power sprang from the passionate longing that he knew in his own heart. All nature rejoiced with him on his bridal day, but on that very morning, as Eurydice went down to the riverside with her maidens to gather flowers for a bridal garland, she was bitten in the foot by a snake, and she died in spite of all attempts to save her.

Orpheus was <u>inconsolable</u>. All day long he mourned his bride, while birds, beasts, and the earth itself sorrowed with him. When at last the shadows of the sun grew long, Orpheus took his lyre[3] and made his way to the yawning cave which leads down into the underworld, where the soul of dead Eurydice had gone.

B Even gray Charon, the ferryman of the Styx, forgot to ask his passenger for the price of crossing. The dog Cerberus, the three-headed monster who guards Hades' gate, stopped full in his tracks and listened motionless until Orpheus had passed. As he entered the land of Hades, the pale ghosts came after him like great, uncounted flocks of silent birds. All the land lay hushed as that marvelous voice resounded across the mud and marshes of its dreadful rivers. In the daffodil fields of Elysium, the happy dead sat silent among their flowers. In the farthest corners of the place of punishment, the hissing

1. **nymphs:** minor goddesses of nature, usually young and beautiful, living in mountains, rivers, or trees.
2. **Eurydice** (yoo·rid′i·sē′).
3. **lyre** (līr): small harp.

Reaching All Students

Struggling Readers
Setting Purposes for Reading was introduced on p. 512. For a lesson directly tied to this selection that teaches students to set purposes by using a strategy called Story Impressions, see the *Reading Skills and Strategies* binder:
• Selection Skill Lesson, p. 134

English Language Learners
Have students study the layout of the story, examining the illustrations and the brief excerpts from the selection displayed on pp. 513–516. Invite students to reflect on these elements and write questions about them, such as "How will the story involve a lyre?" "Why is the earth sad?" Such reflecting and questioning will give them a head start for understanding the content before they read the myth.

Advanced Learners
As students read the myth, have them copy words and phrases that Coolidge uses to describe Orpheus's music, such as "heavenly song" and "marvelous voice." After they have read the myth, ask them to imagine that they are among the denizens of the underworld who have just heard Orpheus's music for the first time. Direct them to write first-person descriptions of how they feel as the music enters and lightens their dark and dreary world.

flames stood still. Accursed Sisyphus,[4] who toils eternally to push a mighty rock uphill, sat down and knew not he was resting. Tantalus, who strains forever after visions of cool water, forgot his thirst and ceased to clutch at the empty air.

The pillared[5] hall of Hades opened before the hero's song. The ranks of long-dead heroes who sit at Hades' board looked up and turned their eyes away from the pitiless form of Hades and his pale, unhappy queen. Grim and unmoving sat the dark king of the dead on his ebony throne, yet the tears shone on his rigid cheeks in the light of his ghastly torches. Even his hard heart, which knew all misery and cared nothing for it, was touched by the love and longing of the music.

At last the minstrel[6] came to an end, and a long sigh like wind in pine trees was heard from the assembled ghosts. Then the king spoke, and his deep voice echoed through his silent land. "Go back to the light of day," he said. "Go quickly while my monsters are stilled by your song. Climb up the steep road to daylight, and never once turn back. The spirit of Eurydice shall follow, but if you look around at her, she will return to me."

Orpheus turned and strode from the hall of Hades, and the flocks of following ghosts made way for him to pass. In vain he searched their ranks for a sight of his lost Eurydice. In vain he listened for the faintest sound behind. The barge of Charon sank to the very gunwales[7] beneath his weight, but no following passenger pressed it lower down. The way from the land of Hades to the upper world is long and hard, far easier to descend than climb. It was dark and misty, full of strange shapes and noises, yet in many places merely black and silent as the tomb. Here Orpheus would stop and listen, but nothing moved behind him. For all he could hear, he was utterly alone. Then he would wonder if the pitiless Hades were deceiving him. Suppose he came up to the light again and Eurydice was not there! Once he had charmed the ferryman and the dreadful monsters, but now they had heard his song. The second time his spell would be less powerful; he could never go again. Perhaps he had lost Eurydice by his readiness to believe.

---

4. **Sisyphus** (sis′ə·fəs).
5. **pillared:** having pillars (columns).
6. **minstrel:** singer.
7. **gunwales** (gun′əlz): upper edges of the sides of a boat.

WORDS TO OWN
inconsolable (in′kən·sōl′ə·bəl) *adj.:* unable to be comforted; brokenhearted.
ghastly (gast′lē) *adj.:* horrible; ghostlike.

"GO QUICKLY WHILE MY MONSTERS ARE STILLED BY YOUR SONG."

ORPHEUS, THE GREAT MUSICIAN **515**

Listening to Music

"Orpheus" from *Symphonic Poems* by Franz Liszt and *Orpheus* by Igor Stravinsky

Franz Liszt (lĭst) (1811–1886) was one of nineteenth-century Europe's greatest pianists. He was also a talented composer, known for piano pieces such as the *Hungarian Rhapsodies* and for orchestral music such as his twelve symphonic poems, the most famous of which is *Les Préludes*. Writing in a very different style was Russian composer Igor Stravinsky (1882–1971), whose best-known work,

The Rite of Spring, helped usher in the modernist experimentation of the early twentieth century. Many of Stravinsky's works—*Orpheus* among them—originated as ballets.

Activity
Have students listen to the two pieces of music, contrast their styles, and discuss which piece they feel better captures the qualities they associate with Orpheus and his music.

A Reading Skills and Strategies
Setting Purposes for Reading
? What two powerful forces are introduced at the very beginning of the story? [the power of Orpheus's music and the power of his love for the nymph Eurydice] Why do you think the story-teller stresses these two forces? [Possible response: Both must be important to the story.]

B English Language Learners
Appositive Phrases
An appositive phrase consists of an appositive and its modifiers. Commas are used to separate the appositive phrase from the rest of the sentence (see p. 745). Ask students to find the appositive phrases in the first two sentences of this paragraph. [Charon, "the ferryman of the Styx," and Cerberus, "the three-headed monster who guards Hades' gate"] Note that Cerberus itself is an appositive for "the dog."

C Elements of Literature
The Underworld of Myth
? These paragraphs provide a guide to the underworld. What beings and places are mentioned? List and identify each. [*Charon,* ferryman of the Styx; *Cerberus,* monstrous three-headed guard dog; *pale ghosts,* spirits of the dead; *dreadful rivers,* haunt of the ghosts; *daffodil fields of Elysium,* realm of the happy dead; *farthest corners . . . hissing flames,* place of punishment; *Sisyphus,* spirit eternally pushing a rock uphill; *Tantalus,* spirit forever reaching for cool water; *pillared hall,* throne room of King Hades and his queen.]

D Reading Skills and Strategies
Making Predictions
? Remember how Hades tricked Demeter in "The Origin of the Seasons." Do you think Hades will really allow Eurydice to leave the underworld with Orpheus? Explain. [Possible responses: Yes, if Orpheus doesn't look back, because Hades keeps his word. No, even if Orpheus obeys, because Hades will have another trick up his sleeve.]

T515

A Critical Thinking

Speculating

❓ How would the story have turned out if Orpheus had not looked back? [Possible response: Orpheus and Eurydice would have returned from the underworld together and they might have become famous as the couple whose love was so strong that it conquered death.]

B Appreciating Language

Descriptive Language

❓ What are some of the precise verbs, specific nouns, and vivid adjectives that the writer uses in this passage? [Possible responses: Verbs—*shrank, stumbled, mourned*; nouns—*mud banks, wailing, nightingale*; adjectives–*gray, flitting, steep*.]

C Critical Thinking

Challenging the Text

❓ At the end of the story, Orpheus and Eurydice are reunited. Tell why you think this ending does or does not fit with the rest of the story. [Possible responses: The ending fits because their love for each other was so strong that they deserved to be together. The ending does not fit because tragic stories should have sad endings.]

THE SHADE DISSOLVED IN THE CIRCLE OF HIS ARMS LIKE SMOKE.

Every step he took, some instinct told him that he was going farther from his bride. He toiled up the path in <u>reluctance</u> and despair, stopping, listening, sighing, taking a few slow steps, until the dark thinned out into grayness. Up ahead a speck of light showed clearly the entrance to the cavern.

At that final moment Orpheus could bear no more. To go out into the light of day without his love seemed to him impossible. Before he had quite <u>ascended</u>, there was still a moment in which he could go back. Quick in the grayness he turned and saw a dim shade at his heels, as indistinct as the gray mist behind her. But still he could see the look of sadness on her face as he sprung forward saying, "Eurydice!" and threw his arms about her. The shade dissolved in the circle of his arms like smoke. A little whisper seemed to say "Farewell" as she scattered into mist and was gone.

The unfortunate lover hastened back again down the steep, dark path. But all was in vain. This time the ghostly ferryman was deaf to his prayers. The very wildness of his mood made it impossible for him to attain the beauty of his former music. At last, his despair was so great that he could not even sing at all. For seven days he sat huddled together on the gray mud banks, listening to the wailing of the terrible river. The flitting ghosts shrank back in a wide circle from the living man, but he paid them no attention. Only he sat with his eyes on Charon, his ears ringing with the dreadful noise of Styx.

Orpheus arose at last and stumbled back along the steep road he knew so well by now. When he came up to earth again, his song was pitiful but more beautiful than ever. Even the nightingale who mourned all night long would hush her voice to listen as Orpheus sat in some hidden place singing of his lost Eurydice. Men and women he could bear no longer, and when they came to hear him, he drove them away. At last the women of Thrace, maddened by Dionysus and infuriated by Orpheus's contempt, fell upon him and killed him. It is said that as the body was swept down the river Hebrus, the dead lips still moved faintly and the rocks echoed for the last time, "Eurydice." But the poet's eager spirit was already far down the familiar path.

In the daffodil meadows he met the shade of Eurydice, and there they walk together, or where the path is narrow, the shade of Orpheus goes ahead and looks back at his love.

WORDS TO OWN
reluctance (ri·luk′təns) *n.*: unwillingness.
ascended (ə·send′id) *v.*: moved up.

Assessing Learning

Check Test: Short Answer

1. What is Orpheus's great talent? [making beautiful music; or, singing and playing the lyre]
2. How and when does Eurydice die? [She is bitten by a poisonous snake on her wedding day.]
3. After Eurydice dies, where does Orpheus go? [into the underworld]

4. What does Hades tell Orpheus? [Hades says that Orpheus may lead Eurydice out of the underworld if he doesn't look back at her.]
5. Why is Eurydice unable to return to daylight? [Orpheus looks back at the last minute.]

Standardized Test Preparation
For practice with standardized test format specific to this selection, see
• *Standardized Test Preparation*, p. 76
For practice in proofreading and editing, see
• *Daily Oral Grammar*, Transparency 29

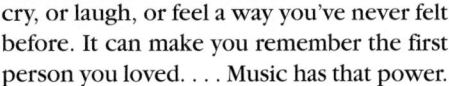

The Power of Music

from **Nadja on My Way**

Nadja Salerno-Sonnenberg

Nadja Salerno-Sonnenberg is a violinist who appears in concert in the United States and throughout the world. She was born in Rome, Italy, and moved to the United States with her family in 1969. She writes about her love of music and her career in her autobiography, Nadja on My Way.

This is something I know for a fact: You have to work hardest for the thing you love most. And when it's music that you love, you're in for the fight of your life.

It starts when your blood fills with music and you know you can't live without it. Every day brings a challenge to learn as much as possible and to play even better than you did the day before.

You may want to achieve fame and glory, or you may want to play for fun. But whenever you fall in love with music, you'll never sit still again.

Music is more important than we will ever know. Great music can pull you right out of your chair. It can make you cry, or laugh, or feel a way you've never felt before. It can make you remember the first person you loved. . . . Music has that power.

Just imagine a world without music. What would you whistle when you walked down the street? How could you make a movie? How could you have a ball game without an organist leading the crowd when you're down by a run in the ninth?

You could be the most successful doctor in the world, but if you never turn on the radio, never go to a concert, never sing in the shower, never see *The King and I*[1]— then you can't be a total, fulfilled human being. It's impossible.

When you realize how vital music is, you realize a musician's fight is quite a noble, heroic endeavor. It didn't always seem that way to me. There was a time, years ago, when I felt discouraged and it seemed selfish to put so much time into music. Being a musician didn't seem as useful to others as being a surgeon, or even a good politician.

But I came to understand that it's a great, great gift to help people forget their everyday life and be uplifted. And better than uplifted, to be inspired; that's what music can do. It's important to us all, and I'm proud to put mind and muscle into recording, concerts, teaching, and studying: into being a musician.

Emotionally, music has brought me an enormous amount of joy and an enormous amount of despair and frustration. Because of music, I have learned what a battle is. I've won most, but not all—not by a long shot.

1. ***The King and I:*** well-known American musical and one of the most widely performed shows in the musical theater. A movie version was made in the 1950s.

ORPHEUS, THE GREAT MUSICIAN 517

Connections

Ⓐ Critical Thinking
Challenging the Text
Ask students if they agree with the writer's statement that you cannot be a "fulfilled human being" without music. Point out that there are many people who are hearing impaired, and discuss other kinds of art, such as films or literature, that might take the place of music for them. Ask students if they respond to other kinds of art as much as they respond to music.

Ⓑ Vocabulary Note
Word History
Point out that the word *vital*, like many English words is indebted to our classical heritage. It comes from *vita*, Latin for "life." By itself, *vital* means "necessary to life." It is used in the medical phrase "vital signs," referring to life signs such as pulse and temperature; and in the sociological phrase "vital statistics," referring to a record of births, deaths, marriages, and patterns of health.

Ⓒ Reading Skills and Strategies
Making Inferences
? What does the writer suggest people experience when they listen to powerful music? [Possible response: Their imaginations are stimulated. They forget their troubles and are uplifted in spirit.] Point out that great art of any kind can sometimes transport people imaginatively to another world.

Ⓓ Reading Skills and Strategies
Drawing Conclusions
? Why does the writer say that music has brought her frustration and despair along with joy? [Possible responses: As a musician, she must sometimes feel the strain that all artists experience when they are struggling to create beauty. She must also wonder if she is measuring up to her own high standards.]

Making the Connections

Connecting to the Theme: "Our Classical Heritage"
"Orpheus, the Great Musician" provides a guide to the classical underworld. Note C on p. T515 instructs students to list the beings and places in the underworld; Choice 3 on p. 519 asks students to use this information in creating an illustrated map of the underworld.

Connecting Across Texts

Connecting with "Orpheus, the Great Musician"
After students have read "The Power of Music" by Nadja Salerno-Sonnenberg on this page, ask them to work in pairs or small groups to write answers to these questions: How does the selection relate to the story of Orpheus? [It also speaks of the power of music.] Which effects of music are mentioned in both the selection and the story of Orpheus? [Possible responses: the power to cause people to forget; the power to make people cry.] What negative aspect of music does Salerno-Sonnenberg mention? [the difficulties and frustrations of learning to play] Call on volunteers to read their responses aloud. Lead a discussion based on the responses, and allow students time to write journal entries reflecting on what they have learned from the selection and the discussion.

First Thoughts

1. Possible responses: Yes, because Hades tricked Persephone; therefore he cannot be trusted. No, even if Hades had lied, there was nothing to be gained by looking back.

Shaping Interpretations

2. The ancient Greeks pictured the afterlife as both sad and happy. Some of the dead are tortured souls; others, who dwell in the fields of Elysium, are happy.

3. Orpheus's love for Eurydice caused him to risk a trip to the underworld, but it also caused him to look back to check for her presence.

4. Possible responses: When Orpheus begins to wonder if Hades is deceiving him; when Orpheus looks back. Have students explain the "deeper level" to which their choice points, such as an understanding of the power of death.

5. Possible responses: Love and death may be at odds. Love is more powerful than death because, in the end, Orpheus and Eurydice are reunited.

6. Possible responses:
   - Mystery of death: Orpheus faces it with music; Demeter forces Hades to let Persephone return.
   - Response of nature: trees, rocks, and animals respond to the joy and grief in Orpheus's music; plants die when Demeter is unhappy and flourish when she is happy.
   - Effect of breaking a taboo: Orpheus loses Eurydice when he looks back; Persephone is forced to spend one month each year in Hades for each pomegranate seed she ate.

7. Possible responses: It can mean that looking back is harmful. It can mean you should set your sights on a goal and stop worrying about anything that is behind you.

Connecting with the Text

8. Possible responses: Yes, Hades made a promise and would have kept it. No, Hades was not fair; he knew Orpheus would look back. If I were a god or goddess, I might let Eurydice go back with Orpheus as a way of thanking him for his beautiful music.

9. Possible responses: My notes, the story, and the selection about music say that music can make people forget their troubles and help them to overcome obstacles.

First Thoughts

[respond]

1. If you were Orpheus, would you have looked back? Why or why not?

Shaping Interpretations

[infer]

2. On the basis of this myth, how do you think the ancient Greeks pictured the afterlife?

[explain]

3. Explain how the same feeling that prompted Orpheus's descent into the underworld also caused him to fail.

[respond]

4. At what point in your reading did you begin to understand this myth on a deeper level?

[conclude]

5. What lessons about love and death does this myth seem to teach? In this story, which is more powerful, love or death? Why?

[compare]

6. Use a chart like the one below to compare this myth with "The Origin of the Seasons."

	"Orpheus"	"The Origin of the Seasons"
How the character faces the mystery of death		
How nature responds to the character's grief or joy		
The effect of breaking a taboo or a rule		

[apply]

7. How does the expression "Never look back" apply to this story?

Connecting with the Text

[evaluate]

8. Do you think Hades was fair to Orpheus and Eurydice in this myth? Tell what you might do to change the outcome if you were a god or goddess.

[synthesize]

9. What does this myth say about the power of music? How does this message compare with your notes for the Quickwrite on page 512 and with Nadja Salerno-Sonnenberg's comments (see *Connections* on page 517)?

Reading Check

Summarize the events of the myth you have just read by filling in a diagram like the one below. Write two or three sentences in each box.

Beginning → Middle → End

Reading Check

- Beginning: Orpheus's music charms all beings. He himself is madly in love with Eurydice, but she dies.
- Middle: Orpheus's music charms everyone in the underworld. Hades tells him that Eurydice may leave while the guardians of Hades are entranced, as long as Orpheus does not look back at her on their way out.
- End: Orpheus distrusts Hades and looks back. Eurydice vanishes. Orpheus's music still charms people, but he scorns them, and the women of Thrace kill him. He joins Eurydice in the daffodil meadows of the underworld.

CHOICES: Building Your Portfolio

Writer's Notebook

1. Collecting Ideas for an Evaluation

In these two myths, Olivia Coolidge presents two characters—Orpheus and Demeter—who almost succeed in conquering death. Which of these tragic characters do you find more interesting? Look back at the myths, and jot down specifics of each character's traits and actions. When you **evaluate,** you make a judgment. How would you judge these two characters?

> Orpheus
> —Traits:
>   musical, loving
> —Actions:
>   bravely enters
>   underworld;
>   foolishly looks
>   back
> —Evaluation:
>   liked him a lot

Creative Writing/Music

2. Odes to Joy and Grief

With a partner, compose one of the songs Orpheus sings in this myth. You might write a song that suggests Orpheus's joy in his love for Eurydice. This song should cause the rocks to "edge down the mountainsides." One partner can work out the basic melody, and the other can write appropriate lyrics.

Zither player between two columns with two roosters (c. 520 B.C.). Black-figured amphora (large storage vase).

Château-Musée, Boulogne-sur-Mer, France. Erich Lessing/Art Resource, New York.

Research/Map Making

3. Where in the (Under) World?

Collect **descriptive details** about the underworld from "Orpheus, the Great Musician," "The Origin of the Seasons," and other Greek myths. ("The Labors of Hercules," page 541, may provide other details.) Draw a **map** of the underworld, using all the sources you can find. Use **labels** to show the location of various characters and landmarks— the River Styx, Cerberus, and Hades' throne room, for example. Draw the characters who populate the shadows.

Creative Writing

4. Orpheus—Live at the Acropolis!

Orpheus has come to town. You're a reporter for a local television station, and you're reporting live from backstage. Tell what the concert is like. Your descriptions of the music should be based on those given in the myth. Your report might include a description of Orpheus and the reaction of the crowd. Be sure to mention any unusual things you see at the concert—for example, does Charon come with Cerberus? Is Eurydice there? How is Orpheus dressed? Does anything magical happen when Orpheus sings?

Grading Timesaver

Rubrics for each Choices assignment appear on p. 171 in the *Portfolio Management System*.

CHOICES: Building Your Portfolio

1. **Writer's Notebook** Have students note that the topic includes Demeter from "The Origin of Seasons" as well as Orpheus. Their notes for Demeter should follow the same pattern shown for Orpheus in the notebook graphic. Remind students to save their work. They may use it as prewriting for the Writer's Workshop on pp. 582–586.
2. **Creative Writing/Music** To plan the lyrics for their music, ask students to review the story and to copy words, phrases, or important passages that they can use or adapt.
3. **Research/Map Making** Distribute or display maps that students may use as models. A simple map showing a three-dimensional view of a local city might make a good example.
4. **Creative Writing** Show students a tape of a live, on-the-spot news report about a cultural or social event. Discuss the reporter's tone and descriptions. Remind students that they will need to include verbal descriptions of any images that a TV camera would normally capture during the report.

> **RESPONDING TO THE ART**
> See Responding to the Art on p. T549 for information on ancient Greek black-figure and red-figure pottery.

Getting Students Involved

Cooperative Learning

In Concert. Before students begin writing their live reports of Orpheus's concert for Choice 4, divide the class into pairs. Tell students to describe to their partners a concert or live performance they have seen. Ask students to use the present tense, as if they were actually attending the concert while describing it. Remind them to include some of the same language when they write about Orpheus's concert.

Sing-Along. If students have difficulty creating melodies for Choice 2, choose an appropriate song that most students already know and ask the whole class to sing it together. Then, ask students to work with partners to write alternate sets of lyrics for the melody they have sung. Allow students to record their songs, and play the tapes for parents during an open house or back-to-school night.

LANGUAGE LINK

Pair students. Have partners exchange pieces of descriptive writing that they have worked on recently. On their partners' papers, students should circle descriptive passages that might be improved by adding figurative language. After their papers are returned to them, students should add any similes or other figures of speech that they think will improve the descriptions.

Try It Out
Answers
1. "birds, beasts, and the earth ... sorrowed"—nonhumans given human characteristics; personification
2. "the pale ghosts ... like great, uncounted flocks of silent birds"—ghosts likened to birds; simile
3. "The shade dissolved ... like smoke"—disappearance of the spirit compared to smoke; simile
Possible responses: Music can warm the world like a sunrise. Music can hide itself in strange places.

VOCABULARY

Possible Answers
1. Rumpelstiltskin had threatened to take her firstborn child away if she could not guess his name.
2. The king saw the ghost of his father.
3. He hates squash, and the main dish was squash casserole.
4. The cloud was high in the sky.

Resources ――――――

Language
• *Grammar and Language Links*, p. 49

Vocabulary
• *Words to Own*, p. 19

Spelling
For related instruction, see
• *Spelling and Decoding*, p. 24

LANGUAGE LINK `MINI-LESSON`

• Style: Figurative Language

Handbook of Literary Terms HELP

See Figure of Speech.

Figurative language describes one thing in terms of another and is not meant to be taken as literally true.

A **simile** is a comparison between two unlike things, using a word such as *like, as, resembles,* or *than.*

EXAMPLE

"... a long sigh <u>like</u> wind in pine trees was heard from the assembled ghosts." [The sigh of the ghosts is compared to the wind in the pines.]

Personification is figurative language in which a nonhuman thing is talked about as if it were human.

EXAMPLE

"... when he sat down to sing, <u>the trees would crowd around to shade him.</u>" [The trees are given the human ability to crowd around someone in order to shade him.]

Try It Out
➤ Find the figurative language in each sentence. Tell what is compared to what. Then, tell if the comparison is a simile or personification.

1. "All day long he mourned his bride, while birds, beasts, and the earth itself sorrowed with him."
2. "As he entered the land of Hades, the pale ghosts came after him like great, uncounted flocks of silent birds."
3. "The shade dissolved in the circle of his arms like smoke."

➤ Write a brief description of how you feel about music. Use simile and personification to help express your feelings.

VOCABULARY `HOW TO OWN A WORD`

WORD BANK
inconsolable
ghastly
reluctance
ascended

Think About It
Each numbered sentence contains a word from the Word Bank. After reading the sentence, make up a reasonable answer to the question that follows. Write your answer.
1. The queen was <u>inconsolable</u>. What just happened to the queen?
2. The king saw a <u>ghastly</u> sight. What did the king see?
3. He ate the meal with some <u>reluctance</u>. What explains his reluctance?
4. The golden cloud <u>ascended</u>. Where was the cloud after it ascended?

Language Link Quick Check

Find the example of figurative language in each sentence, and state whether it is an example of simile or personification.
1. When Orpheus sang a happy song, nature smiled. ["nature smiled"—personification]
2. Orpheus's words poured down on the forest like a soft spring rain. ["words poured ... like a soft spring rain"—simile]
3. As his song grew stronger, the woods began to dance with the breeze. ["woods began to dance with the breeze"—personification]
4. For Tantalus, Orpheus's song was as soothing as a drink of cool water. ["song ... as soothing as a drink of cool water"—simile]
5. Orpheus sang in a voice like sunshine after a storm. ["a voice like sunshine after a storm"—simile]

Reading Skills and Strategies

Booking space on the Net:

READING BETWEEN THE LINES: USING CONTEXT CLUES

Readers often use a word's **context clues**—the surrounding words and sentences—to figure out what the word means. There are two keys to unlocking meaning using context clues. One key unlocks knowledge that is already in your head; the other key unlocks the clues from the text itself.

Clues from Your Head

You may already know something about the word. The more you know about a topic, the more useful context is. To zero in on what you already know, ask yourself these questions:

- What are some words I think of when I look at this word?
- What other words does the word sound like?
- Does the word have any **prefixes** or **suffixes** whose meanings I know?

Clues from the Text

Look at the surrounding text and ask yourself the following:

- What type of text am I reading? What topic might this word relate to?
- Do the surrounding words and sentences give clues to the word's meaning?

- How is the word used in the sentence? What kind of word could I substitute for it? A person, a place, or a thing? A descriptive word?

Putting It Together

Sometimes you can figure out the meaning of an unfamiliar word as you read. Other times it's not so easy. Making a chart like the one below may help you unlock the meanings of difficult words, like *inconsolable*, which appears in "Orpheus, the Great Musician."

Unfamiliar Word	Clues from Your Head	Clues from the Text	Word's Meaning	Dictionary Check
inconsolable	The prefix *in-* means "not." Word looks and sounds like *console*, meaning "to make someone feel better."	Orpheus was inconsolable as he mourned his bride. Therefore, he must have been very sad.	"incapable of being comforted"	Correct!

Apply the strategy on the next page.

Using Students' Strengths

Auditory Learners

Students will recognize context clues more easily if they hear them emphasized during an oral reading. From a myth in this collection, choose three sentences that contain unfamiliar words. Read them aloud, stressing the context clues they contain. Ask students to write definitions for the unfamiliar words based on these clues. Encourage students to look for sentences in "Echo and Narcissus" that provide context clues to unfamiliar words.

Visual Learners

From a myth in this collection, ask students to copy three sentences that contain unfamiliar words. Using the guidelines from the mini-lesson on this page, they should highlight or underline the parts of the sentences that contain context clues. Ask students to choose a different color for each type of clue—blue for synonym clues, yellow for antonym clues, pink for comparison clues, and so on.

OBJECTIVES
1. Use context clues to determine meaning of unfamiliar words
2. Apply prior knowledge and textual clues to unlock meaning

Reading Skills and Strategies

This feature focuses on using context clues to determine the meaning of unfamiliar words. The strategy is emphasized in the next selection, giving students the opportunity to figure out meaning by using different kinds of clues.

Mini-Lesson:
Using Context Clues

List the following types of context clues on the board, and have students copy the list. Suggest that students use these strategies in the next selection they read.

Type: Synonym
Function: Shows that the unfamiliar word is similar to a familiar word
Example: For a beginner, the *novice* played well.

Type: Antonym
Function: Contrasts the unfamiliar word with a familiar word
Example: The speaker was *shrill*, not soft-spoken.

Type: Comparison
Function: Compares the unfamiliar word to a familiar word or phrase
Example: A *salvo* of cheers burst forth like a sudden thunderstorm.

Type: Cause or effect
Function: Shows that the unfamiliar word is a cause or effect of something
Example: Because the game was *curtailed* by a sudden storm, we got home early.

Type: Example
Function: Suggests meaning of the unfamiliar word by providing examples of its use
Example: There are many literary *genres*, including the novel, poem, and short story.

OBJECTIVES

1. Read and interpret the myth
2. Use context clues
3. Express understanding through writing, speaking, or language arts research
4. Identify personal possessive pronouns and contractions
5. Understand and use new words

SKILLS

Reading
- Use context clues

Writing
- List criteria for a myth
- Support an opinion

Writing/Botany
- Write an origin myth

Speaking/Listening
- Create a comic dialogue

Grammar/Language
- Distinguish personal possessive pronouns from contractions

Vocabulary
- Research origins of words
- Understand and use new words

Viewing/Representing
- Compare style and mood of two paintings (ATE)
- Compare the faces of classical figures in two works (ATE)

Planning

- **Block Schedule**
  Block Scheduling Lesson Plans with Pacing Guide
- **Traditional Schedule**
  Lesson Plans Including Strategies for English-Language Learners
- **One-Stop Planner**
  CD-ROM with Test Generator

Before You Read

ECHO AND NARCISSUS

Make the Connection

Dear Me

"Echo and Narcissus" is an **origin myth,** and it is one of several flower myths as well. The myth is also a powerful story about human nature—about what can happen to us when we are absorbed only in ourselves.

Quickwrite

Take a quick survey to find out how your classmates rate the following statements. Each person should rate each statement on a scale from 1 to 5, with 1 meaning you do not agree and 5 meaning total agreement.

1. People judge others by their looks alone.

2. People judge others on more than their looks.

3. Vain, self-centered people are often punished for their behavior.

4. Vain, self-centered people often get away with things.

Which statement do you agree or disagree with most strongly? In your notebook, briefly explain what you think about that statement and why. Share your Quickwrite with the rest of the class.

Reading Skills and Strategies

Using Context Clues

As you read, don't be detained as you struggle vainly to figure out the meaning of a word you don't know. Remember to use the strategies you learned on page 521. (Two vocabulary words from the story appear in these directions. Were you able to figure out their meanings from the **context**?)

"So nothing can stop you talking?"

Preteaching Vocabulary

Words to Own

Have students copy the definitions of the Words to Own from pp. 523–526. Then, ask them to insert the words correctly in the sentences below. Tell them to look for context clues that will help determine the missing word.

detain   intently   parched
unrequited   vainly

1. The nymph chattered on and on in order to _____ Hera so that she could not catch Zeus. [detain]

2. The nymph loved the youth _____, since he spurned her. [vainly]

3. One day, _____ from his day of hunting, the youth went to a mountain pool. [parched]

4. He, too, suffered from _____ love when he fell in love with his own reflection in the water. [unrequited]

5. No matter how _____ the youth stared at his reflection, he never realized he was looking at himself. [intently]

Echo and Narcissus

retold by **Roger Lancelyn Green**

U p on the wild, lonely mountains of Greece lived the Oreades,[1] the nymphs or fairies of the hills, and among them one of the most beautiful was called Echo. She was one of the most talkative, too, and once she talked too much and angered Hera, wife of Zeus, king of the gods.

When Zeus grew tired of the golden halls of Mount Olympus, the home of the immortal gods, he would come down to earth and wander with the nymphs on the mountains. Hera, however, was jealous and often came to see what he was doing. It seemed strange at first that she always met Echo, and that Echo kept her listening for hours on end to her stories and her gossip.

But at last Hera realized that Echo was doing this on purpose to detain her while Zeus went quietly back to Olympus as if he had never really been away.

"So nothing can stop you talking?" exclaimed Hera. "Well, Echo, I do not intend to spoil your pleasure. But from this day

---

1. **Oreades** (ō′rē·ad′ēz).

WORDS TO OWN
detain (dē·tān′) *v.*: hold back; delay.

Summary ▪ ▪

This Greek myth finds Hera on the trail of her husband, Zeus, who often spends time with the Oreades. To distract Hera while Zeus sneaks back to Olympus, Echo, a nymph, chatters on and on. When Hera realizes that Echo is attempting to detain her, she declares that henceforth Echo will be able only to repeat what others say. This irony is compounded by a new conflict when Echo falls in love with the handsome Narcissus, who loves only himself. One day, lost, Narcissus cries for help and hears Echo repeating his shouts. When she hurls herself into his arms, he cruelly rebuffs her. Aphrodite, goddess of love, spares Echo further anguish by letting her die but preserves her voice among rocks and trees. To punish Narcissus, Aphrodite has him fall in love with his own reflection in a mountain pool. He pines away with unrequited passion, and on that spot a new flower blooms, the narcissus.

Resources

Listening
Audio CD Library
A reading of this story is provided in the *Audio CD Library:*
• Disc 13, Track 4

Selection Assessment
Formal Assessment
• Selection Test, p. 103
Test Generator
• Selection Test

A Cultural Connections

❓ What magical beings in forests and mountains have you read or heard about? [Possible responses: elves, trolls, gnomes, leprechauns.]

Resources: Print and Media

Reading
• *Reading Skills and Strategies*
   Selection Skill Lesson, p. 116
• *Graphic Organizers for Active Reading,* p. 36
• *Words to Own,* p. 20
• *Spelling and Decoding*
   Worksheet, p. 25
• *Audio CD Library*
   Disc 13, Track 4

Elements of Literature
• *Literary Elements*
   Transparency 9
   Worksheet, p. 28

Writing and Language
• *Daily Oral Grammar*
   Transparency 30
• *Grammar and Language Links*
   Worksheet, p. 51
• *Language Workshop CD-ROM*

Assessment
• *Formal Assessment,* p. 103
• *Portfolio Management System,* p. 172
• *Standardized Test Preparation,* p. 78
• *Test Generator (One-Stop Planner CD-ROM)*

Internet
• go.hrw.com (keyword: LE0 7-7)

Michelangelo de Merisi, known as **Caravaggio** (1573–1610), broke with the idealism typical of earlier Italian Renaissance art. He created dramatic, intensely naturalistic paintings, using peasants and laborers as models. His use of contrasting light and darkness (chiaroscuro) both shocked and intrigued his contemporaries. The increasingly dark and expressionistic cast of his later work influenced such artists as Rembrandt, Velasquez, and Murillo.

Activity. Ask students to compare Caravaggio's *Narcissus* with Botticelli's *La Primavera: Flora* (pp. 503, 505, 506–507), in terms of style. Ask them how the use of light affects mood in these two paintings.

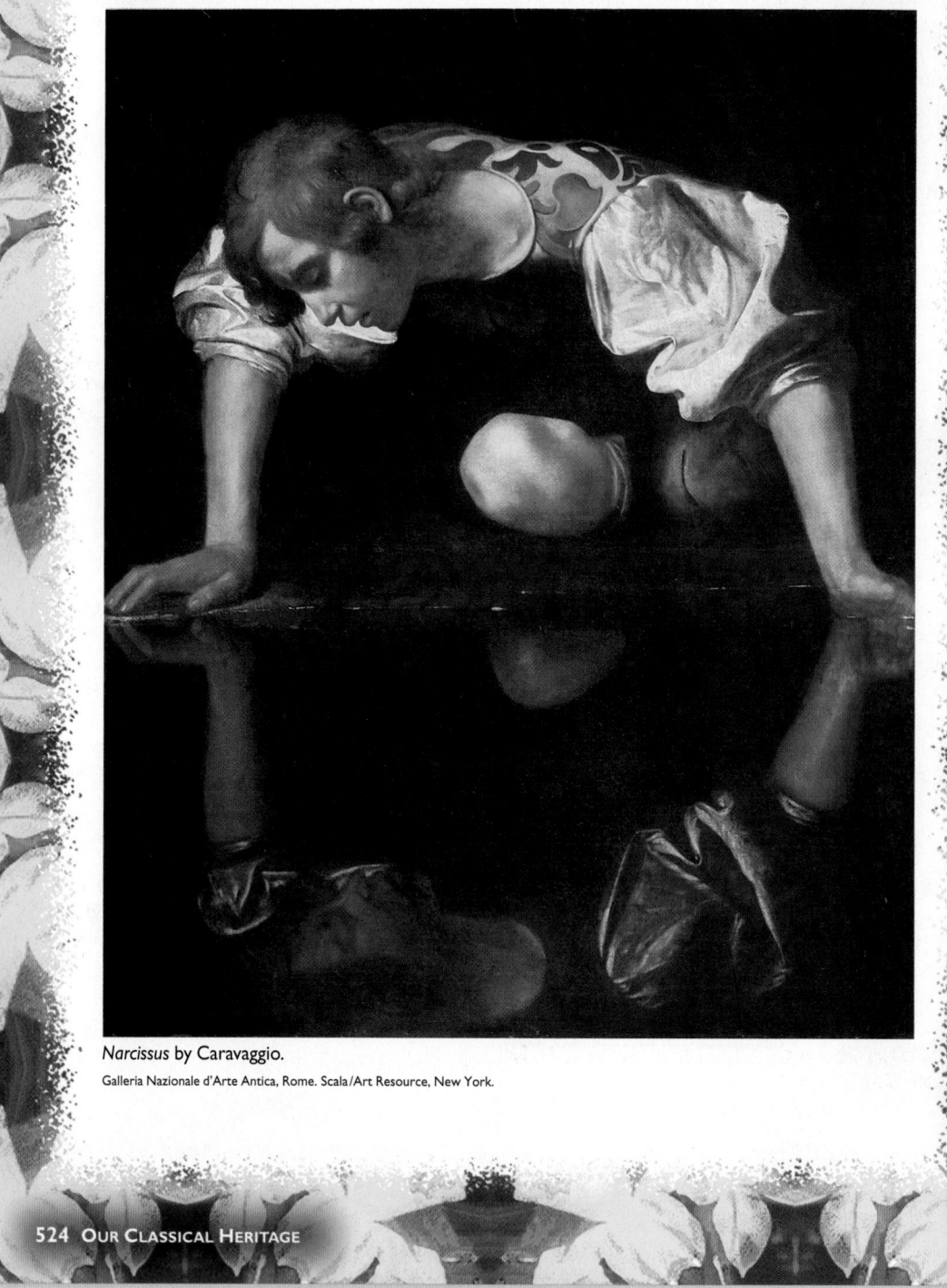

Narcissus by Caravaggio.
Galleria Nazionale d'Arte Antica, Rome. Scala/Art Resource, New York.

Reaching All Students

Struggling Readers
Using Context Clues was introduced on p. 522. For a lesson directly tied to this selection that teaches students to use context clues, see the *Reading Skills and Strategies* binder:
• Selection Skill Lesson, p. 116

English Language Learners
Some English language learners may be unfamiliar with classical mythology. They will appreciate the story more if you tell them about Hera and Aphrodite before they read. Provide information from a handbook of mythology. Explain tactfully that Hera punished women her husband loved and anyone who helped them. Point out that Aphrodite, as the goddess of love, possessed the power to make people fall in love.

Advanced Learners
Challenge advanced students to write a commentary on the Caravaggio painting. Ask them to describe how Narcissus is depicted and how the artist uses light to help create mood.

on, you shall be able only to repeat what other people say—and never speak unless someone else speaks first."

Hera returned to Olympus, well pleased with the punishment she had made for Echo, leaving the poor nymph to weep sadly among the rocks on the mountainside and speak only the words which her sisters and their friends shouted happily to one another.

She grew used to her strange fate after a while, but then a new misfortune befell her.

There was a beautiful youth called Narcissus,[2] who was the son of a nymph and the god of a nearby river. He grew up in the plain of Thebes[3] until he was sixteen years old and then began to hunt on the mountains toward the north where Echo and her sister Oreades lived. **Ⓐ**

As he wandered through the woods and valleys, many a nymph looked upon him and loved him. But Narcissus laughed at them scornfully, for he loved only himself.

Farther up the mountains Echo saw him. And at once her lonely heart was filled with love for the beautiful youth, so that nothing else in the world mattered but to win him.

Now she wished indeed that she could speak to him words of love. But the curse which Hera had placed upon her tied her tongue, and she could only follow wherever he went, hiding behind trees and rocks, and feasting her eyes vainly upon him. **Ⓑ**

One day Narcissus wandered farther up the mountain than usual, and all his friends, the other Theban youths, were left far behind. Only Echo followed him, still hiding among the rocks, her heart heavy with unspoken love. **Ⓒ**

Presently Narcissus realized that he was lost, and hoping to be heard by his companions, or perhaps by some mountain shepherd, he called out loudly:

"Is there anybody here?"

2. **Narcissus** (när·sis′əs).
3. **Thebes** (thēbz).

"Here!" cried Echo.

Narcissus stood still in amazement, looking all around in vain. Then he shouted, even more loudly:

"Whoever you are, come to me!"

"Come to me!" cried Echo eagerly.

Still no one was visible, so Narcissus called again:

"Why are you avoiding me?"

Echo repeated his words, but with a sob in her breath, and Narcissus called once more:

"Come here, I say, and let us meet!"

"Let us meet!" cried Echo, her heart leaping with joy as she spoke the happiest words that had left her lips since the curse of Hera had fallen on her. And to make good her words, she came running out from behind the rocks and tried to clasp her arms about him.

But Narcissus flung the beautiful nymph away from him in scorn.

"Away with these embraces!" he cried angrily, his voice full of cruel contempt. "I would die before I would have you touch me!" **Ⓓ**

"I would have you touch me!" repeated poor Echo.

"Never will I let you kiss me!"

"Kiss me! Kiss me!" murmured Echo, sinking down among the rocks, as Narcissus cast her violently from him and sped down the hillside.

"One touch of those lips would kill me!" he called back furiously over his shoulder.

"Kill me!" begged Echo.

And Aphrodite,[4] the goddess of love, heard her and was kind to her, for she had been a true lover. Quietly and painlessly, Echo pined away and died. But her voice lived on, lingering among the rocks and answering faintly whenever Narcissus or another called.

"He shall not go unpunished for this cruelty,"

4. **Aphrodite** (af′rə·dīt′ē).

WORDS TO OWN
vainly (vān′lē) *adv.:* uselessly; without result.

Ⓐ Reading Skills and Strategies
Responding to the Text
❓ What is your first impression of Narcissus? [Possible responses: He is beautiful, but he is also very stuck-up. He shouldn't laugh at someone who loves him.]

Ⓑ English Language Learners
Idiom
Explain that "tongue-tied" and the question "Cat got your tongue?" are idiomatic expressions meaning that someone is too shy to speak or is otherwise speechless. Ask students to share similar expressions from their first languages.

Ⓒ Reading Skills and Strategies
Making Predictions
❓ What will happen when Echo and Narcissus meet? [Possible responses: Echo will break through Narcissus' absorption with himself. Narcissus will reject Echo.] After students have read the whole story, remind them to compare their predictions with what actually occurs in the story.

Ⓓ Critical Thinking
Interpreting
❓ Why do you think Narcissus is so cruel to Echo? [Possible responses: Narcissus is mean to everyone; he seems to think everyone else is ugly. He loves himself so much that he is unable to love anyone else.]

Crossing the Curriculum

Botany
Point out the illustration of narcissus flowers on p. 526. Have students locate photographs or other illustrations of narcissus flowers and to describe the characteristics of the plant. Ask them to speculate on how the flower received its name. After the class has read the story, have students compare the explanation the story offers with their speculations.

Science
Find a big outdoor wall with a large amount of open space in front of it. Have your class stand about twenty-five feet from the wall and shout "Echo!" together. They probably will not hear an echo. Then, ask them to stand thirty-five feet from the same wall and to shout the word in unison again. This time they should hear a distinct echo. Explain that it is difficult to discern an echo if the distance between the sound and the object reflecting it is less than thirty feet.

Art
Ask students to work in groups of four or five to design memorials to Echo and Narcissus. The memorials should match details from the story and should include epitaphs. Possibilities for Echo include a heart-shaped, sound-reflecting wall inscribed "Her story echoes through the ages." Possibilities for Narcissus include a broken narcissus flower made of clay, in a reflecting pool, inscribed "He spurned love and was shattered by vanity."

OBJECTIVES

1. Read and interpret the myth
2. Identify and interpret the moral
3. Make generalizations
4. Express understanding through writing, science/speaking, or geography/math/art
5. Identify and use modifiers

SKILLS

Literary
- Identify and interpret a moral

Reading
- Make generalizations

Writing
- Evaluate a moral
- Write a letter as Icarus
- Write a generalization about myths
- Write a first-person account

Grammar/Language
- Identify and use modifiers

Science/Speaking
- Report on aircraft

Geography/Math/Art
- Research and draw a map

Music
- Respond to a song (ATE)

Viewing/Representing
- Examine a drawing (ATE)
- Respond to sculptor's art (ATE)

Before You Read

THE FLIGHT OF ICARUS

Make the Connection

Winging It

Long before the invention of the airplane, people yearned to fly. They dreamed of climbing through the air, dipping, floating, plummeting—as free as birds. They wanted to escape the earth and soar above all its problems.

Today, of course, flight is an everyday reality. We travel through the air in everything from helicopters to jumbo jets, from hot-air balloons to space shuttles.

Quickwrite

Complete one of these sentences:

- I long to fly/dread flying like a seagull because . . .

- I had a dream about flying in which . . .

Elements of Literature

Myths with Morals: What's the Message?

When a young bird flies from the nest for the first time, we say that it is "trying its wings." As you read this myth, notice what happens when a young boy tries his wings. If you think about what the boy attempts to do, what he ignores, and what happens to him as a result, you'll find the **morals**—or lessons—in the story.

> **A moral** is a lesson about the right way to behave. The morals in many Greek myths were used to teach children values.
>
> *For more on Myth, see pages 496–499 and the Handbook of Literary Terms.*

Reading Skills and Strategies

Making Generalizations

When you make a **generalization,** you look at evidence and make a broad statement about what it tells you. Someone who says "All stories contain conflicts" is making a generalization from experience with many stories. As you read these myths, think of generalizations you might make about myths and the kinds of stories they tell.

530 OUR CLASSICAL HERITAGE

Resources: Print and Media

Reading
- *Reading Skills and Strategies*
  Selection Skill Lesson, p. 43
- *Graphic Organizers for Active Reading,* p. 37
- *Audio CD Library,*
  Disc 13, Track 5

Elements of Literature
- *Literary Elements*
  Transparency 9
  Worksheet, p. 28

Writing and Language
- *Daily Oral Grammar*
  Transparency 31
- *Grammar and Language Links*
  Worksheet, p. 53
- *Language Workshop CD-ROM*

Viewing and Representing
- *Viewing and Representing*
  Fine Art Transparency 17
  Fine Art Worksheet, p. 68

Assessment
- *Formal Assessment,* p. 105
- *Portfolio Management System,* p. 174
- *Standardized Test Preparation,* p. 80
- *Test Generator (One-Stop Planner CD-ROM)*

Internet
- go.hrw.com (keyword: LE0 7-7)

The Flight of Icarus

retold by **Sally Benson**

Cast of Characters

King Minos (mī′näs′), tyrant of Crete, enemy of Athens.

Theseus (the′sē·əs), hero from Athens held captive by Minos. Daedalus helped him escape from the labyrinth on Crete.

Daedalus (ded′′l·əs), great Athenian architect who built the labyrinth on Crete.

Icarus (ik′ə·rəs), Daedalus's young son.

"Minos may control the land and sea, but he does not control the air."

THE FLIGHT OF ICARUS 531

Summary ■ ■

Minos, king of Crete, locks the designer of his labyrinth, Daedalus, into a tower for helping the Greek hero Theseus escape from the maze. Aided by his son Icarus, Daedalus escapes from the tower and devises a plan to leave the island by air. After Icarus gathers feathers, Daedalus fashions a set of artificial wings. In a cautious test, Daedalus achieves momentary flight. Then he fashions wings for his son, and both of them take to the air. Daedalus warns Icarus not to fly too low, where moisture will damage the wings, nor too high, where the sun will melt the wax holding them together. As the two rise toward freedom, Daedalus is alarmed to see Icarus soaring ever closer to the sun. The story reaches its climax as the wax melts, Icarus's wings disintegrate, and he plunges into the sea. Daedalus buries the boy in a land he names Icaria, in memory of his son. Then, Daedalus flies to Sicily, where he hangs up his own wings as an offering to Apollo. The story of Icarus underscores a moral lesson—the danger of ambition unchecked by caution.

Planning

- **Block Schedule**
  Block Scheduling Lesson Plans with Pacing Guide
- **Traditional Schedule**
  Lesson Plans Including Strategies for English-Language Learners
- **One-Stop Planner**
  CD-ROM with Test Generator

Resources

Listening
Audio CD Library
A reading of this story is provided in the *Audio CD Library*:
- Disc 13, Track 5

Reaching All Students

Struggling Readers

Making Generalizations was introduced on p. 530. For a lesson directly tied to this selection that teaches students to make generalizations by using a strategy called Sketch to Stretch, see the *Reading Skills and Strategies* binder:
- Selection Skill Lesson, p. 43

English Language Learners

Before students read the myth, discuss with them the background information that appears in the Literature and History feature on p. 534. To help them tackle difficult vocabulary, give them this list of words from the story: *ingenious, skirted, misgivings, prowess* (p. 533); *exaltation* (p. 535). Read aloud the sentences from the story in which the words occur. Point out the context clues in sentences and surrounding paragraphs. Discuss each sentence and ask students to write definitions for the words. Finally, ask students to look up dictionary definitions for the words and to compare them with the definitions they wrote. For strategies to supplement instruction for these students, see
- *Lesson Plans Including Strategies for English-Language Learners*

T531

Leonardo da Vinci (1452–1519) is widely celebrated for the universality of his genius. He was not only a great artist but also a brilliant thinker in the fields of geology, botany, astronomy, anatomy, and mechanics. Although many of his inventions, such as flying machines, remained untested conjectures during his lifetime, few people in history can match the breadth and acuity of his work in both art and science. Along with such masters as Raphael and Michaelangelo, he represents the extraordinary achievements of the High Renaissance.

In Florence, Leonardo trained as an apprentice to the painter Andrea del Verrochio. In 1481, he joined the court of Lodovico Sforza, Duke of Milan. He worked in Milan for seventeen years as military engineer, civil engineer, sculptor, and painter. In 1497, he immortalized a wall of the dining hall in the monastery of Santa Maria delle Grazie with his fresco *The Last Supper,* one of the most famous of religious pictures. Leonardo also created what may be the most famous portrait in history—a mysteriously alluring painting of Lisa del Giocondo, wife of a Florentine merchant, popularly known as the *Mona Lisa.*

Activity. Ask students to examine Leonardo's drawing of a flying machine. Encourage them to sketch their own designs for human-powered flying machines.

Drawing of a man operating a flying machine, from a notebook of Leonardo da Vinci (1452–1519). Da Vinci wrote backward and in reverse to keep his notebooks secret; his words can be read by holding the page up to a mirror.

Using Students' Strengths

Kinesthetic Learners
After students have read the story, ask them to work in groups of five to create interpretive dances based on Icarus's flight. One student should dance the part of Icarus, one should dance the part of Daedalus, and the remaining students can choose to act as sun, wind, sea, or some of the farmers or shepherds who observe the flight. Allow students to wear costumes when they perform, and videotape the performance for later review.

Auditory/Visual/Linguistic Learners
Organize students into groups of four to create five-minute musical requiems for Icarus, along with artwork and spoken readings. Groups should divide the following duties: choosing or creating five minutes of music; selecting or drawing images to accompany the music; writing short passages to be read over the music or during breaks in it; and synchronizing the music, images, and readings. Allow students either to perform their requiems live in class or to submit videotapes.

When Theseus escaped from the labyrinth, King Minos flew into a rage with its builder, Daedalus, and ordered him shut up in a high tower that faced the lonely sea. In time, with the help of his young son, Icarus, Daedalus managed to escape from the tower, only to find himself a prisoner on the island. Several times he tried by bribery to stow away on one of the vessels sailing from Crete, but King Minos kept strict watch over them, and no ships were allowed to sail without being carefully searched.

Daedalus was an ingenious artist and was not discouraged by his failures. "Minos may control the land and sea," he said, "but he does not control the air. I will try that way."

He called his son, Icarus, to him and told the boy to gather up all the feathers he could find on the rocky shore. As thousands of gulls soared over the island, Icarus soon collected a huge pile of feathers. Daedalus then melted some wax and made a skeleton in the shape of a bird's wing. The smallest feathers he pressed into the soft wax and the large ones he tied on with thread. Icarus played about on the beach happily while his father worked, chasing the feathers that blew away in the strong wind that swept the island and sometimes taking bits of the wax and working it into strange shapes with his fingers.

It was fun making the wings. The sun shone on the bright feathers; the breezes ruffled them. When they were finished, Daedalus fastened them to his shoulders and found himself lifted upwards, where he hung poised in the air. Filled with excitement, he made another pair for his son. They were smaller than his own, but strong and beautiful.

Finally, one clear, wind-swept morning, the wings were finished, and Daedalus fastened them to Icarus's shoulders and taught him how to fly. He bade him watch the movements of the birds, how they soared and glided overhead. He pointed out the slow, graceful sweep of their wings as they beat the air steadily, without fluttering. Soon Icarus was sure that he, too, could fly and, raising his arms up and down, skirted over the white sand and even out over the waves, letting his feet touch the snowy foam as the water thundered and broke over the sharp rocks. Daedalus watched him proudly but with misgivings. He called Icarus to his side and, putting his arm round the boy's shoulders, said, "Icarus, my son, we are about to make our flight. No human being has ever traveled through the air before, and I want you to listen carefully to my instructions. Keep at a moderate height, for if you fly too low, the fog and spray will clog your wings, and if you fly too high, the heat will melt the wax that holds them together. Keep near me and you will be safe."

He kissed Icarus and fastened the wings more securely to his son's shoulders. Icarus, standing in the bright sun, the shining wings drooping gracefully from his shoulders, his golden hair wet with spray, and his eyes bright and dark with excitement, looked like a lovely bird. Daedalus's eyes filled with tears, and turning away, he soared into the sky, calling to Icarus to follow. From time to time, he looked back to see that the boy was safe and to note how he managed his wings in his flight. As they flew across the land to test their prowess before setting out across the dark wild sea, plowmen below stopped their work and shepherds gazed in wonder, thinking Daedalus and Icarus were gods.

Father and son flew over Samos and Delos, which lay on their left, and Lebinthus,° which lay on their right. Icarus, beating his wings in joy, felt the thrill of the cool wind on his face and the clear air above and below him. He flew higher and higher up into the blue sky until he reached the clouds. His father saw him and

---

° **Samos** (sā′mäs), **Delos** (dē′läs), and **Lebinthus** (lə·bin′thəs): Greek islands in the Aegean Sea.

THE FLIGHT OF ICARUS 533

(A) Vocabulary Note

Using a Dictionary

Some students may be acquainted with modern-day *labyrinths* constructed for entertainment purposes; some may enjoy solving paper-and-pencil mazes. Explain that a *labyrinth* is a maze of intricate passageways and blind alleys. Ask students to look up the definition of *labyrinthine* and to list nouns the word might be used to describe— *argument, logic, bureaucracy,* for example.

(B) Reading Skills and Strategies

Making Generalizations

❓ What impression do you form of Daedalus from the details in the opening paragraphs of the myth? [Possible response: He is not easily discouraged and doesn't waste time feeling sorry for himself.]

(C) Reading Skills and Strategies

Making Predictions

Ask students who are reading the story for the first time to write predictions of what they think Daedalus will do with the feathers. After they have read the story, have them compare their predictions with what actually happens.

(D) Cultural Connections

Ask students who have viewed hang-gliding or hot-air ballooning to relate their experiences to this passage.

(E) Critical Thinking

Interpreting

❓ Why do Daedalus's eyes fill with tears? [Possible response: They are tears of joy at the beauty of his son.]

Getting Students Involved

Cooperative Learning

Partners' Key-Word Review. After students have read "The Flight of Icarus," ask them to skim the text and to make a list of ten words or phrases from the story that they could use to summarize the events. Among the words or phrases they might choose are *escape, prisoner, air, son, feathers, wax, wings, flight, instructions, soared, wind, higher, sun, sea,* and *bitter.* Ask partners to combine lists. Referring to each word or phrase, students should take turns asking their partners "What does the story say about _____?" The partner who is responding should try to answer from memory. Students who are unable to do so should be allowed to respond after rereading the passage in which the word appears. Remind students to ask each other for clarification of any responses they do not fully understand.

LITERATURE AND HISTORY

Some ancient writers credit Daedalus with building, on the island of Sardinia, works known today as *nuraghi*. Nuraghi are towers, some of them fifty feet high, built of massive blocks of volcanic basalt. There are about seven thousand of these conical towers on the island today. It is likely that they were actually built between 1500 and 1100 B.C. by an ancient, advanced group of people from Crete who spread northward and westward throughout the Mediterranean area. Show a picture of a nuraghe to the class, and explain that it is one of the works that many ancient people associated with Daedalus.

Resources

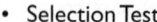

Selection Assessment
Formal Assessment
• *Selection Test*, p. 105
Test Generator
• Selection Test

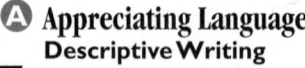

A Appreciating Language
Descriptive Writing
❓ Which words in this passage capture the exhilaration—or the danger—that Icarus experiences? [Possible responses: *soared, glorious, bewitched, blazing, warning, enchanted, frantically.*]

A Creative Genius

Some scholars believe that Daedalus, one of the two main characters in this myth, represents the civilization of Crete, an island in the Mediterranean. In the myths he was a master craftsman and brilliant inventor from Athens who invented sails for ships. Years before this myth opens, Daedalus, in a fit of jealous rage, killed his talented young nephew, who was also an inventor. To escape punishment, Daedalus fled to Crete, which was ruled by King Minos. Today both Crete and Athens are part of Greece, but in the ancient myths they were at war.

Today in Crete you can see ruins of the Palace of Cnossus, where, legend tells us, Daedalus designed a famous labyrinth, or maze, for Minos. There, the king concealed the hideous Minotaur, a creature that was half-bull and half-human. Minos agreed not to wage war with Athens if Athens would send him fourteen young Athenians every year as a tribute. Minos would then feed the young people to the monster. This ritual sacrifice went on for many years, until the Athenian hero Theseus killed the Minotaur and found his way out of the maze. Theseus was able to escape the labyrinth only because Daedalus had revealed to him its secret. Furious at this betrayal, King Minos imprisoned the inventor and his son, Icarus. And that's where the myth of "The Flight of Icarus" begins.

Today on the walls of Minos's palace in Crete, you can see ancient paintings of young maidens and handsome youths leaping over and away from the razor-sharp horns of bulls.

called out in alarm. He tried to follow him, but he was heavier and his wings would not carry him. Up and up Icarus soared, through the soft, moist clouds and out again toward the glorious sun. He was bewitched by a sense of freedom and beat his wings frantically so that they would carry him higher and higher to heaven itself. The blazing sun beat down on the wings and softened the wax. Small feathers fell from the wings and floated softly down, warning Icarus to stay his flight and glide to earth. But the enchanted boy did not notice them until the sun became so hot that the largest feathers dropped off and he began to sink. Frantically he fluttered his arms, but no feathers remained to hold the air. He cried out to his father, but

534 OUR CLASSICAL HERITAGE

Listening to Music

"Flying" by John Lennon, Paul McCartney, George Harrison, and Richard Starkey

Spearheading the British invasion of the American pop charts in the 1960s, the Beatles—John Lennon, Paul McCartney, George Harrison, and Ringo Starr—are often named the greatest rock band ever. The Liverpool-based group, which took the name in 1960 and broke up a decade later, gradually moved from innocuous songs

to more creative ventures, including their innovative 1967 "theme" album *Sgt. Pepper's Lonely Hearts Club Band.* The follow-up, *Magical Mystery Tour,* on which "Flying" first appeared, was written in part for a late 1967 TV film of the same name. "Flying" is atypical of Beatles songs in that it is credited to all four Beatles (Richard Starkey is Ringo Starr's real name) instead of just one or two.

Activity
Have students listen to "Flying" after they have read "The Flight of Icarus." Ask students to jot down words to describe the images and moods the music evokes. Then have them work individually or in groups to change the ending of the song in order to make it reflect the ending of the myth. Have them perform their changed versions in the same humming (or da-dumming) that the Beatles use in "Flying."

his voice was submerged in the blue waters of the sea, which has forever after been called by his name.

Daedalus, crazed by anxiety, called back to him, "Icarus! Icarus, my son, where are you?" At last he saw the feathers floating from the sky, and soon his son plunged through the clouds into the sea. Daedalus hurried to save him, but it was too late. He gathered the boy in his arms and flew to land, the tips of his wings dragging in the water from the double burden they bore. Weeping bitterly, he

buried his small son and called the land Icaria in his memory.

Then, with a flutter of wings, he once more took to the air, but the joy of his flight was gone and his victory over the air was bitter to him. He arrived safely in Sicily, where he built a temple to Apollo and hung up his wings as an offering to the god, and in the wings he pressed a few bright feathers he had found floating on the water where Icarus fell. And he mourned for the birdlike son who had thrown caution to the winds in the exaltation of his freedom from the earth.

MEET THE WRITER

"Stories That Have Rounded Ends"

Sally Benson (1900–1972) never studied writing—she didn't have to: It came naturally. After high school she skipped college and went directly to work, first for a bank and then for newspapers. In 1930, she was reviewing thirty-two movies a month for a daily paper when she got an idea for a short story. She sat down, typed it out, and sold it to *The New Yorker.* Dazed by her good fortune, she stopped writing for nine months. But when her money ran out, she wrote another story and sold that one, too. From then on she poured stories out. Benson published one book of Greek and Roman myths, but most of her stories tell the amusing adventures of a thirteen-year-old girl named Judy Graves.

❝ I like stories that have rounded ends and don't rise to climaxes; that aren't all wrapped up in a package with plot. I like them, that's why I write them. ❞

THE FLIGHT OF ICARUS 535

Assessing Learning

Student to Student

Ⓐ Appreciating Language
Wing Expressions
❓ What is the meaning of these expressions?
- "to take wing" [to leave quickly or to soar mentally]
- "to lend wings to" [to spur the speed of]
- "to clip someone's wings" [to hamper someone's freedom]

Ⓑ Reading Skills and Strategies

Making Generalizations
❓ Based on these lines, what emotions does the speaker feel? [Possible responses: ecstasy; fulfillment.]

Ⓒ Reading Skills and Strategies
Making Inferences
❓ What is the voice that tells the speaker she cannot fly? [Possible responses: the voice of her waking self; the voice of fear.]

Ⓓ Critical Thinking
Making Connections
❓ What word in this line makes the whole line an especially good caption for *The Fall of Icarus* on p. 539? [Possible response: The word *dizzily* captures the out-of-control look of Icarus's body in the engraving.]

Ⓔ Reading Skills and Strategies

Making Generalizations
❓ How might the closing lines be restated to make them apply to people in general? [Possible response: Most people experience only moments of glory—unless they take risks and defy authority or convention.]

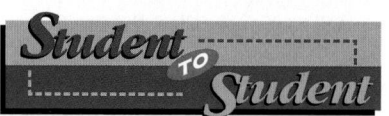

Ⓐ Wings

The same dream again,
   and again,
     and again.
It begins, I sit on a lonely beach.
The waves curl around my feet,
5   sliding through my toes,
And the sea gulls soar overhead.
   The gulls.
I long to be a part of their flight.
I stand and run with the birds,
   leaping, jumping, skipping.
10 Ⓑ Abruptly I come to a cliff.
   I dive.
For one wonderful, fleeting moment
   I glide
on wings of purest gold. A wish come true.
Ⓒ Then comes the Voice . . . echoing.
   "You can't fly . . . can't fly . . . can't fly . . ."
15   The wings are gone.
Ⓓ I plunge dizzily down to the raging sea miles below.
Moments before I splash, I awake, sweating, gasping for air.

I long for the day when I am able to defy the Voice,
Ⓔ to soar, to glide, to join the birds at last.
20 Until then I will hold tight to the single moment of flight that is mine.

—Bronwen Anne Gilbert
Eckstein Middle School
Seattle, Washington

Making the Connections

Connecting to the Theme: "Our Classical Heritage"
"The Flight of Icarus" reflects human preoccupation with freedom—and the lengths to which people will go to achieve it. The moral lesson the myth demonstrates, as well, is that humanity has always struggled with the conflict between setting high goals and knowing when to accept one's limitations.

Connecting Across Texts

Connecting with "The Flight of Icarus"
Divide the class into groups of four, and ask students to discuss these questions:
- How is the poem's speaker like Icarus? [Possible response: Both use wings to fly for a short time; both end up plunging downward toward the sea.]
- How does the experience of the speaker differ from the experience of Icarus? [Possible response: Icarus fails because he tries to fly too high; the speaker fails because she listens to a voice that tells her she cannot really fly.]

After the groups finish their discussions, ask them to share their responses with the rest of the class.

MAKING MEANINGS

First Thoughts

[respond]

1. Look back at the sentences you completed for the Quickwrite on page 530. How might Daedalus and Icarus have completed those sentences?

Shaping Interpretations

[compare]

2. The myths of Persephone and Orpheus include warnings that the characters fail to listen to. How is the story of Icarus like those myths?

[infer]

3. How does Icarus try to be something he is not? What **moral lesson** can you learn from his failure?

[predict]

4. When did you first guess the outcome of the myth? What hints in the story helped you make this prediction?

[identify]

5. Like other myths, this one explains the names of some geographical features in Greece. What are they, and how did they get there?

Connecting with the Text

[connect]

6. How do you feel about Icarus? Do you think teenagers today can identify with him? Why or why not?

Extending the Text

[evaluate]

7. This story seems to suggest that people shouldn't try to "fly too high." We often hear the opposite advice: "Reach for the stars." From your own experience, when do you think taking chances is a good thing? When can it be dangerous?

Reading Check

You're a news reporter on the scene, eager to interview Daedalus when he lands. Write a lead paragraph for the news story, telling what happened, why it happened, whom it happened to, when and where it happened, and how it happened.

Daedalus and Icarus by Antonio Canova.

Museo Correr, Venice, Italy.
Alinari/Art Resource, New York.

THE FLIGHT OF ICARUS 537

RESPONDING TO THE ART

Antonio Canova (1757–1822) incorporated Greek and Roman nobility of form into his portraits of ancient deities and of political leaders of his era such as Napoleon. The son of a northern Italian stonemason, he apprenticed at age eleven to the renowned sculptor Giuseppe Bernardi (Toretti). At age eighteen, he launched his own studio in Venice, and he moved to Rome in his mid-twenties. He was considered the greatest sculptor of his time. **Activity.** Ask students what Daedalus is doing in Canova's statue. [Measuring Icarus for wings.] What is he thinking as he does it? [Possible response: Am I risking my son's life?] What do the gestures of the father and the son reveal about their relationship? [Trust, affection.]

MAKING MEANINGS

First Thoughts

1. Possible response: "I long to fly because I'll be free." Remind students that details of the story must support their ideas.

Shaping Interpretations

2. Icarus also suffers because he forgets or ignores a warning.
3. Icarus tries to be like a bird. The story's moral is that people should know and accept their limits.
4. Some students may have known the myth before they started reading. For others, the most obvious moment of foreshadowing occurs when Daedalus warns Icarus not to fly too low or too high.
5. Icaria is the name of the land where Daedalus buries Icarus, and the sea where he fell is the Icarian Sea. The Greek Island of Icaria still bears that name; the Icarian Sea is an arm of the Aegean Sea between the coast of Asia Minor and the islands of Patmos and Leros.

Connecting with the Text

6. Possible response: Icarus is a lot like teenagers today who take thoughtless risks when they attempt something like a high dive before they really know how. Teenagers can identify with Icarus. Like Icarus, they need to take off on their own.

Reading Check

Sample lead paragraph: *Daedalus, designer of the famed labyrinth in Crete, alit today on Icaria, mourning the death of his son, Icarus. Strapped into the ingenious wings his father had fashioned, Icarus flew so high that the sun melted the wax holding the feathers in place, and the boy plunged into the sea. On landing, Daedalus could only moan, "My son, Icarus! O Icarus, my son!"*

Encourage students to invent an interview with Daedalus and to top their story with a headline, such as *Daring Flight Ends in Tragedy.*

Extending the Text

7. Possible response: Taking a chance is a good thing when one reaches for challenging goals, such as learning a sport or applying to a top college. Taking chances can be dangerous when people are exposed to harm, as in driving during hazardous weather conditions.

Rubrics for each Choices assignment appear on p. 174 in the *Portfolio Management System.*

CHOICES:
Building Your Portfolio

1. **Writer's Notebook** Call students' attention to the notebook graphic. Remind students to save their work; they may use it as prewriting for the Writer's Workshop on pp. 582–586.

2. **Creative Writing** Reach a consensus with the class about Icarus's approximate age. Ask students to write their letters in a style and tone consistent with that age. If students have difficulty getting started, ask them first to make a list of words that Icarus might have used to describe life on Crete with his father. Then, remind students of the gloomy atmosphere of the underworld that is depicted in "The Origin of the Seasons" (p. 501) and "Orpheus, the Great Musician" (p. 513).

3. **Analyzing the Myths** Encourage students to organize their notes in a four-column chart with columns labeled as follows: Story Title, Fantasy Elements, Moral Lessons, and Explanations of Natural Phenomena. Allow them to work with partners or small groups to complete the charts.

4. **Science/Speaking** For this project, students may need extra help and support from a librarian or science teacher. Allow them to work in groups of four to research and design their diagrams or models.

5. **Geography/Math/Art** Review map skills with the class—especially, the use of scales and methods for calculating distance.

6. **Creative Writing** Remind students to write from the point of view of a person who has never seen an airplane or a hot-air balloon. Also, point out that a ground- or sea-level observer would be too far away to be able to tell that the wings were artificially made. Before students begin to write, suggest that they make a storyboard showing what a farmer or fisher would have seen. The sequence of panels might include the following:

CHOICES: Building Your Portfolio

Writer's Notebook

1. Collecting Ideas for an Evaluation

From the three **morals** below, choose the one you think *best* expresses the message of "The Flight of Icarus." Then, jot down your evaluation of the moral. Do you agree or disagree with it? Why?

- Steer a middle course and avoid extremes.
- Listen to your elders.
- If you do not reach too far, you will avoid trouble.

The myth teaches the danger of going to extremes. I partly agree and partly disagree because . . .

Creative Writing

2. Dear Daedalus

Imagine you are Icarus, now in the underworld after your disastrous flight. Write a letter to your father, telling him how you felt during the flight and what it's like in Hades' dark kingdom. (See the myths "The Origin of the Seasons," page 501, and "Orpheus, the Great Musician," page 513, for details about the underworld.)

Analyzing the Myths

3. What Are Myths?

Skim through the myths you have read so far. Take notes on the fantasy elements, moral lessons, and explanations of natural phenomena in the myths. Then, use your notes to make a **generalization** about myths. Open your general statement with the words "Myths are stories that . . .". Support your generalization with details from the myths.

Science/Speaking

4. Winging It

How close is Daedalus to learning the secret of flight? Find out how aircraft today get and remain airborne. Create a diagram or a model to show how one system works, and present it to the class.

Geography/Math/Art

5. Going Places

The myth mentions several places—Crete, Samos, Delos, Lebinthus, Icaria, and Sicily. In a dictionary or an atlas, locate information about these places. Then, find the name of the sea that Icarus and Daedalus cross. Make a large-scale drawing of this area, trace Daedalus's trip from Crete to Sicily, and calculate the distance he travels.

Creative Writing

6. It's a Bird, It's a . . .

Imagine that you are an ancient farmer or fisherman who has just witnessed Icarus's fantastic and tragic flight. Write a first-person account telling what you've seen, or write a poem about your reaction. Look back at the Student to Student poem on page 536 for ideas.

- two winged manlike figures flying together
- the smaller figure breaking away and flying higher
- the smaller figure framed against the sun
- the smaller figure plunging into the ocean
- the larger figure flying off with the body of the smaller one

Ask students to incorporate descriptions of what occurs in each panel into their first-person accounts. Remind them to use the pronoun *I*.

GRAMMAR LINK   MINI-LESSON

• Adjective vs. Adverb

Language Handbook HELP

See The Adverb, page 716.

Many adverbs end in *-ly*. Such adverbs are generally formed by adding the ending *-ly* to adjectives.

EXAMPLES

proud + *ly*: "Daedalus watched him <u>proudly</u> but with misgivings."

secure + *ly*: "He . . . fastened the wings more <u>securely</u> to his son's shoulders."

In some sentences, however, it's hard to know which word to use—the adjective or the adverb.

He arrived <u>safe/safely</u> in Sicily.

To solve this problem, ask yourself which word the modifier describes. An adverb modifies a verb, an adjective, or another adverb.

Technology HELP

See Language Workshop CD-ROM. *Key word entry: adverbs.*

EXAMPLE   "He arrived <u>safely</u> in Sicily. . . ."

An adjective modifies a noun or a pronoun.

EXAMPLE   He had a <u>safe</u> arrival in Sicily.

Try It Out
Choose the correct word from each underlined pair.

1. Daedalus flew <u>rapid/rapidly</u> to lift his son from the sea.

2. The accident had happened so <u>sudden/suddenly</u>.

3. Mourning his son, Daedalus sat <u>listless/listlessly</u> on the sand.

4. Icarus felt <u>confident/confidently</u> that he could fly higher.

VOCABULARY   HOW TO OWN A WORD

Place Names from Greece and Rome

When the first Europeans settled in the land that became the United States, they needed names for their towns and cities. They often looked to ancient Rome and Greece for ideas.

Use the index in an atlas or other geographical reference book to identify the following:

1. the state or states in which the following American cities are located

2. the location of the original Greek or Roman place known by that name

Athens	Delphi	Olympia
Rome	Syracuse	Sparta

The Fall of Icarus (detail). Copper engraving.

The Bettmann Archive.

THE FLIGHT OF ICARUS 539

GRAMMAR LINK

Ask students to select writing assignments they have worked on recently. Ask them to find and circle all of the adjectives and then to hand their papers to partners. The partners should circle any adjectives that were missed and return the papers. Students should then read through their own papers and change into adverbs any adjectives that they have mistakenly used to modify verbs.

Try It Out
Answers
1. rapidly
2. suddenly
3. listlessly
4. confident

VOCABULARY

Answers may vary, depending on sources consulted.

• Athens: 1. Alabama, Georgia, Ohio, Tennessee, Texas. 2. Ancient city-state in Greece, center of Greek culture in 5th century B.C.

• Rome: 1. Georgia, New York. 2. Capital of ancient Roman Empire

• Delphi: 1. Indiana. 2. Home of famous oracle of Apollo in ancient Greece

• Syracuse: 1. Kansas, New York, Utah. 2. Ancient city-state in Sicily

• Olympia: 1. Washington. 2. A plain and sanctuary in Greece, site of ancient festival in honor of Zeus

• Sparta: 1. Georgia, Illinois, Tennessee, Wisconsin. 2. Military city-state in ancient Greece.

Resources —————

Grammar
• *Grammar and Language Links,* p. 53

Grammar Link Quick Check

Choose the correct word from each underlined pair.

1. Icarus thought that flying was <u>wonderful/wonderfully</u>. [wonderful]

2. He felt that he was going <u>unbelievable/unbelievably</u> high. [unbelievably]

3. He flapped his wings more <u>powerful/powerfully</u> to rise even higher. [powerfully]

4. His <u>slow/slowly</u> climb continued. [slow]

5. <u>Final/Finally</u>, he could go no higher; he was losing control. [Finally]

Planning

Before You Read

THE LABORS OF HERCULES

Make the Connection

The Hero Hercules

Hercules (also spelled Heracles) is a mythical Greek hero who performs the most amazing feats of strength in all of mythology. Like other mythic heroes, Hercules is the son of both a god (Zeus, or Jupiter) and a human being and so possesses special qualities. Like many other superheroes, he demonstrates his powers when he is still in his cradle.

Quickwrite

The twelve labors of Hercules include ridding the world of monsters that cause people to suffer. Make a list of at least six tasks a modern superhero or superheroine might accomplish to improve the world.

Elements of Literature

The Quest

A **quest** is a long and perilous journey taken in search of something of great value: a treasure, a person, or a concept, such as peace or freedom. As heroes or heroines pursue their quests, they face trials, tests, and temptations. Heroes and heroines are often helped along the way, sometimes by kindly gods and goddesses, sometimes by loyal friends or even animals. At the end of a quest, the hero or heroine is glorified: crowned the rightful ruler, hailed as the savior of a people, or, as in the story of Hercules, given immortality and a place among the gods. Such honors do not come easily, for the way of the quest is terrifying.

> **A quest** is a perilous journey taken in pursuit of something of great value.

Reading Skills and Strategies

Making Connections: What It Means to Me

Relating ancient myths to your own world can help you understand the stories and give you insights into your life. Myths speak in a universal language—that's why you see so many references to them on television, in newspapers, and in stories (see "Antaeus," page 469, for example). As you read about Hercules' bone-crunching labors, keep in mind the tasks you just listed for today's superhero. How are they similar to or different from the ones Hercules faces?

Hercules fighting Cerberus: one of his twelve labors (575 B.C.). Corinthian hydria (water jar).

Louvre, Paris, France. Erich Lessing/Art Resource, New York.

Preteaching Vocabulary

Have students locate and copy the information on the five Words to Own. Then, give students time to discuss the meanings with a partner. Finally, have them answer these questions about the words.

afflicted   ravaged
pestilential   venomous
pliant

1. Which two verbs tell what a violent monster did to a countryside? [afflicted, ravaged]
2. Which adjective describes the bite of certain snakes and spiders? [venomous]
3. Which adjective describes a rapidly spreading, deadly plague? [pestilential]
4. Which adjective describes a thing or person that bends easily? [pliant]

The Labors of Hercules

retold by Rex Warner

He was
the strongest
of all the
heroes . . .

THE LABORS OF HERCULES **541**

Summary ■ ■ ■

This Greek myth recounts the labors of Hercules, son of Alcmena and Jupiter. Juno, obsessed by hatred and jealousy, afflicts Hercules with a fit of madness in which he kills his wife and children. In stunned grief, he requests a penance from the oracle at Delphi, who prescribes twelve years of service to the cowardly king of Mycenae, Eurystheus. Eurystheus assigns twelve "impossible" jobs, but the hero does them all: (1) He kills and brings back the lion of Nemea. (2) Helped by Iolaus, he destroys the Hydra. (3) He captures a stag sacred to Diana. (4) He brings back a great wild boar and vanquishes a horde of centaurs, including his former teacher, Chiron. (5) He redirects the flow of the river Alpheus to clean the long-neglected stables of Augeus. (6) He destroys the flesh-eating Stymphalian birds. (7) He overcomes a huge bull that has been laying waste to Crete. (8) He kills King Diomedes, who feeds his mares on human flesh, and brings back the horses. (9) He retrieves the belt of Hippolyte, queen of the Amazons. (10) He destroys Geryon, a gigantic monster and brings back his cattle. (11) With Minerva's help, he fetches golden apples from the Hesperides. (12) He brings the watchdog Cerberus up from the underworld.

Resources

Viewing and Representing
Videocassette B, Segment 8
The segment "The Olympic Legacy" illustrates our ongoing connection to ancient Greek culture. See the *Visual Connections Teacher's Manual.*

Listening
Audio CD Library
A reading of this myth is provided in the *Audio CD Library:*
• Disc 13, Track 6

Resources: Print and Media

Reading
• *Reading Skills and Strategies*
    MiniRead Skill Lesson, p. 200
    Selection Skill Lesson, p. 207
• *Graphic Organizers for Active Reading*, p. 38
• *Words to Own*, p. 21
• *Spelling and Decoding*
    Worksheet, p. 26
• *Audio CD Library*
    Disc 13, Track 6

Elements of Literature
• *Literary Elements*
    Transparency 9
    Worksheet, p. 28

Writing and Language
• *Daily Oral Grammar*
    Transparency 32
• *Grammar and Language Links*
    Worksheet, p. 55
• *Language Workshop CD-ROM*

Viewing and Representing
• *Visual Connections*
    Videocassette B, Segment 8

Assessment
• *Formal Assessment*, p. 107
• *Portfolio Management System*, p. 176
• *Standardized Test Preparation*, p. 82
• *Test Generator (One-Stop Planner CD-ROM)*

Internet
• go.hrw.com (keyword: LE0 7-7)

T541

Hercules suffered much during his life, but after his death he became a god. His mother was Alcmena,[1] his father was Jupiter, and he was the strongest of all the heroes who lived in his time.

All through his life he was pursued by the hatred and jealousy of Juno, who tried to destroy him even in his cradle. She sent two great snakes to attack the sleeping baby, but Hercules awoke, grasped their necks in his hands, and strangled them both.

Before he was eighteen, he had done many famous deeds in the country of Thebes, and Creon, the king, gave him his daughter in marriage. But he could not long escape the anger of Juno, who afflicted him with a sudden madness, so that he did not know what he was doing, and in a fit of frenzy killed both his wife and his children. When he came to his senses, in horror and shame at what he had done, he visited the great cliffs of Delphi,[2] where the eagles circle all day and where Apollo's oracle[3] is. There he asked how he could be purified of his sin, and he was told by the oracle that he must go to Mycenae[4] and for twelve years obey all the commands of the cowardly king Eurystheus.[5]

Hercules killing the lion. Black-figured amphora (large storage jar).

Louvre, Paris, France. Erich Lessing/Art Resource, New York.

He found that his arrows had no effect on the tough skin of the lion . . .

his kinsman. It seemed a hard and cruel sentence, but the oracle told him also that at the end of many labors, he would be received among the gods.

Hercules therefore departed to the rocky citadel[6] of Mycenae that looks down upon the blue water of the bay of Argos. He was skilled in the use of every weapon, having been educated, as Jason was, by the wise centaur Chiron.[7] He was tall and immensely powerful. When Eurystheus saw him, he was both terrified of him and jealous of his great powers. He began to devise labors that would seem impossible, yet Hercules accomplished them all.

First he was ordered to destroy and to bring back to Mycenae the lion of Nemea, which for long had ravaged all the countryside to the north. Hercules took his bow and arrows and, in the forest of Nemea, cut himself a great club, so heavy that a man nowadays could hardly lift it. This club he carried ever afterwards as his chief weapon.

He found that his arrows had no effect on the tough skin of the lion, but as the beast

---

1. **Alcmena** (alk·mē′nə).
2. **Delphi** (del′fī).
3. **oracle:** person through whom the gods were consulted. The oracle at Delphi was a woman who would go into a trance and then utter strange sounds. Temple priests interpreted these as words of the god Apollo.
4. **Mycenae** (mī·sē′nē): See map on page 498.
5. **Eurystheus** (yoo·ris′thē·əs).

6. **citadel** (sit′ə·del′): fortress.
7. **centaur** (sen′tôr′) **Chiron** (kī′rän′): A centaur is a mythical creature with the body of a horse and the torso, arms, and head of a human. (**Jason** was another legendary Greek hero.)

WORDS TO OWN
afflicted (ə·flikt′id) *v.*: caused pain or suffering to.
ravaged (rav′ijd) *v.*: ruined; violently destroyed.

Reaching All Students

sprang at him, he half stunned it with his club; then, closing in with it, he seized it by the throat and killed it with his bare hands. They say that when he carried back on his shoulders to Mycenae the body of the huge beast, Eurystheus fled in terror and ordered Hercules never again to enter the gates of the city, but to wait outside until he was told to come in. Eurystheus also built for himself a special strong room of brass into which he would retire if he was ever again frightened by the power and valiance[8] of Hercules. Hercules himself took the skin of the lion and made it into a cloak which he wore ever afterwards, sometimes with the lion's head covering his own head like a cap, sometimes with it slung backwards over his shoulders.

Hercules in lion's skin, menacing Cerberus (575 B.C.). Corinthian hydria (water jar).

Louvre, Paris, France. Erich Lessing/Art Resource, New York.

Hercules himself took the skin of the lion and made it into a cloak which he wore ever afterwards . . .

The next task given to Hercules by Eurystheus was to destroy a huge water snake, called the Hydra, which lived in the marshes of Argos, was filled with poison, and had fifty venomous heads. Hercules, with his friend and companion, the young Iolaus,[9] set out from Mycenae and came to the great cavern, sacred to Pan, which is a holy place in the hills near Argos. Below this cavern a river gushes out of the rock. Willows and plane trees surround the source, and the brilliant green of grass. It is the freshest and most delightful place. But as the river flows downwards to the sea, it becomes wide and shallow, extending

8. **valiance** (val′yəns): courage; determination.
9. **Iolaus** (ī′ō·lā′əs).

into pestilential marshes, the home of stinging flies and mosquitoes. In these marshes they found the Hydra, and Hercules, with his great club, began to crush the beast's heads, afterwards cutting them off with his sword. Yet the more he labored, the more difficult his task became. From the stump of each head that he cut off, two other heads, with forked and hissing tongues, immediately sprang. Faced with an endless and increasing effort, Hercules was at a loss what to do. It seemed to him that heat might prove more powerful than cold steel, and he commanded Iolaus to burn the root of each head with a red-hot iron immediately after it was severed from the neck. This plan was successful. The heads no longer sprouted up again, and soon the dangerous and destructive animal lay dead, though still writhing in the black marsh water among the reeds. Hercules cut its body open and dipped his arrows in the blood. Henceforward these arrows would bring certain death, even if they only grazed the skin, so powerful was the Hydra's poison.

Eurystheus next ordered Hercules to capture and bring back alive a stag[10] sacred to

10. **stag:** full-grown male deer.

WORDS TO OWN
venomous (ven′əm·əs) *adj.*: poisonous; malicious.
pestilential (pes′tə·len′shəl) *adj.*: causing disease; deadly.

THE LABORS OF HERCULES **543**

RESPONDING TO THE ART
See the art note on Greek pottery on p. T549.

F **Critical Thinking**
Hypothesizing
? Why do you think Hercules wears the cloak "ever afterwards"? [Possible responses: He wants people to know that he is the man who killed the lion of Nemea. He wears it as a souvenir of the first labor he completed.]

G **Elements of Literature**
The Quest
? What two elements of a quest are mentioned in this paragraph? [The next task will test the strength and ingenuity of Hercules, and heroes often receive help from others. (See p. 540 in the pupil's edition.)]

H **Reading Skills and Strategies**
Making Inferences
? What do you learn about Hercules from this scene? [Possible responses: He does not give up when it seems that something is too hard to overcome. He shows that he is not only strong but also clever.]

I **Elements of Literature**
The Quest
Point out that this third labor, like the first two, involves a goal, a journey, and a struggle. Point out that each task is a step in a larger quest—Hercules' effort to satisfy the sentence imposed by the oracle of Apollo at Delphi (p. 542).

Getting Students Involved

Cooperative Learning
Reciprocal Teaching. After students have read the first five paragraphs of "The Labors of Hercules," ask a volunteer to help you model a Reciprocal Teaching session for the class. Begin by asking the student to respond to questions such as these:
• (Summarizing) What information does the author provide in the first three paragraphs?

• (Questioning) Why does Hercules go to Delphi?
• (Clarifying) When the oracle sentences Hercules to work for Eurystheus, for whom is she speaking?
• (Predicting) What other labors do you think Eurystheus will give to Hercules? Why?
Switch roles with the student and respond to

questions he or she asks about the next two paragraphs.
Then, divide the class into mixed-ability reading pairs. Ask students to read the rest of the story using Reciprocal Teaching with each other, switching roles often. Encourage them to use each of the four reading comprehension strategies that you modeled.

A Reading Skills and Strategies

Comparing/Contrasting

❓ How does the animal Hercules pursues in his third labor differ from the creatures he sought in his earlier labors? [Possible responses: This animal has done no harm to anyone. This animal is so fast, Hercules must pursue it for a very long time.]

B Struggling Readers

Summarizing

❓ What three labors has Hercules performed so far? [He has killed the lion of Nemea, destroyed the Hydra, and captured a stag sacred to Diana.] What three objects does he wear or carry with him as a result of his first two labors? [The club he used to stun the lion of Nemea, the lion's skin as a cloak, and arrows dipped in the poisonous blood of the Hydra.]

C Appreciating Language

Descriptive Words

❓ Which action words, describing Hercules' battle with the centaurs are especially vivid? [Possible responses: *scattered, driving, dashed, writhing.*]

Diana and famous for its great fleetness of foot, which lived in the waste mountains and forests and never yet had been approached in the chase. For a whole year Hercules pursued this animal, resting for the hours of darkness and pressing on next day in its tracks. For many months he was wholly outdistanced; valleys and forests divided him from his prey. But at the end of the year the stag, weary of the long hunt, could run no longer. Hercules seized it in his strong hands, tied first its forelegs and then its hind legs together, put the body of the beast, with its drooping antlered head, over his neck, and proceeded to return to the palace of King Eurystheus. However, as he was on his way through the woods, he was suddenly aware of a bright light in front of him, and in the middle of the light he saw standing a tall woman or, as he immediately recognized, a goddess, grasping in her hands a bow and staring at him angrily with her shining eyes. He knew at once that this was the archer goddess Diana, she who had once turned Actaeon[11] into a stag and who now was enraged at the loss of this other stag which was sacred to her. Hercules put his prey on the ground and knelt before the goddess. "It was through no desire of my own," he said, "that I have captured this noble animal. What I do is done at the command of my father Jupiter and of the oracle of your brother Apollo at Delphi." The goddess listened to his explanation, smiled kindly on him, and allowed him to go on his way when he had promised that, once the stag had been carried to Eurystheus, it would be set free again in the forests that it loved. So Hercules accomplished this third labor.

He was not, however, to be allowed to rest Eurystheus now commanded him to go out to the mountains of Erymanthus[12] and bring back the great wild boar that for long had terrorized all the neighborhood. So Hercules set out once more, and on his way he passed the country where the centaurs had settled after they had been driven down from the north in the battle that had taken place with the Lapiths at the wedding of Pirithous.[13] In this battle they had already had experience of the hero's strength, but still their manners were rude and rough. When the centaur Pholus offered Hercules some of their best wine to drink, the other centaurs became jealous. Angry words led to blows and soon Hercules was forced to defend himself with his club and with his arrows, the poison of which not only caused death, but also the most extreme pain. Soon he scattered his enemies in all directions, driving them over the plains and rocks. Some he dashed to the ground with his club; others wounded by the poisoned arrows, lay writhing

Cerberus with three heads. Corinthian hydria (water jar).

Louvre, Paris, France. Erich Lessing/Art Resource, New York.

From the stump of each head that he cut off, two other heads, with forked and hissing tongues, immediately sprang.

11. **Actaeon** (ak·tē'ən).

12. **Erymanthus** (er'ə·man'thəs).
13. **Pirithous** (pī·rith'ō·əs).

Using Students' Strengths

Visual/Musical Learners

After students have read the story, ask them to translate one of the battle episodes from "The Labors of Hercules" into a scene for a film script. Tell students to include stage directions or voice-over narration describing the actions of Hercules and his opponent. Suggest that students indicate the musical cues they would use to intensify the mood.

Interpersonal Learners

Divide students into pairs, and ask them to take the roles of Hercules and a news reporter. The reporter will need to prepare questions such as the ones that follow and to take notes on Hercules' responses.

• Which of the labors was the hardest? Why?
• If you had to do it all over again, what would you do differently? Why?

Have the reporters compare notes after they have completed their interviews.

Intrapersonal Learners

Point out that Hercules relies on help from others to complete several of his labors. Remind students that problems a person cannot solve alone can often be solved with help. Ask them to make a two-column chart, using the headings below to record their ideas.

Problem I Could Not Solve [A book I needed to write a report was checked out from library.]
How Someone Could Help [The librarian could suggest other books or resources.]

in agony or kicking their hooves in the air. Some took refuge in the house of the famous centaur Chiron, who had been schoolmaster to Hercules and who, alone among the centaurs, was immortal. As he pursued his enemies to this good centaur's house, shooting arrows at them as he went, Hercules, by an unhappy accident, wounded Chiron himself. Whether it was because of grief that his old pupil had so injured him, or whether it was because of the great pain of the wound, Chiron prayed to Jupiter that his immortality should be taken away from him. Jupiter granted his prayer. The good centaur died, but he was set in Heaven in a constellation of stars which is still called either Sagittarius or else the Centaur.

Hercules mourned the sad death of his old master. Then he went on to Erymanthus. It was winter and he chased the great boar up to the deep snow in the passes of the mountains. The animal's short legs soon grew weary of plowing through the stiff snow and Hercules caught it up when it was exhausted and panting in a snowdrift. He bound it firmly and slung the great body over his back. They say that when he brought it to Mycenae, Eurystheus was so frightened at the sight of the huge tusks and flashing eyes that he hid for two days in the brass hiding place that he had had built for himself.

The next task that Hercules was ordered to do would have seemed to anyone impossible. There was a king of Elis called Augeas,[14] very rich in herds of goats and cattle. His stables, they say, held three thousand oxen, and for ten years these stables had never been cleaned. The dung and muck stood higher than a house, hardened and caked together. The smell was such that even the herdsmen, who were used to it, could scarcely bear to go near. Hercules was now ordered to clean these stables, and going to Elis, he first asked the king to

14. **Augeas** (ô·jē′əs).

promise him the tenth part of his herds if he was successful in his task. The king readily agreed, and Hercules made the great river Alpheus change its course and come foaming and roaring through the filthy stables. In less than a day all the dirt was cleared and rolled away to the sea. The river then went back to its former course, and for the first time in ten years, the stone floors and walls of the enormous stables shone white and clean.

Hercules then asked for his reward, but King Augeas, claiming that he had performed the task not with his own hands but by a trick, refused to give it to him. He even banished his own son, who took the side of Hercules and reproached his father for not keeping his promise. Hercules then made war on the kingdom of Elis, drove King Augeas out, and put his son on the throne. Then, with his rich reward, he returned to Mycenae, ready to undertake whatever new task was given him by Eurystheus.

Again he was ordered to destroy creatures that were harmful to men. This time they were great birds, like cranes or storks, but much more powerful, which devoured human flesh and lived around the black waters of the Stymphalian[15] lake. In the reeds and rocky crags they lived in huge numbers, and Hercules was at a loss how to draw them from their hiding places. It was the goddess Minerva who helped him by giving him a great rattle of brass. The noise of this rattle drove the great birds into the air in throngs. Hercules pursued them with his arrows, which rang upon their horny beaks and legs but stuck firm in the bodies that tumbled one after the other into the lake. The whole brood of these monsters was entirely destroyed, and now only ducks and harmless waterfowl nest along the reedy shores.

Hercules had now accomplished six of his labors. Six more remained. After the killing of

15. **Stymphalian** (stim·fā′lē·ən).

THE LABORS OF HERCULES **545**

Getting Students Involved

T545

Some students may be aware of the connection between the Amazons of myth and Wonder Woman of modern comic books and television. Interested students may wish to research various warrior women characters in the media and explain the connections to the class. They might, for example, explore connections between the Amazons of myth and Xena, the warrior princess of a highly popular TV program.

B Historical Connections

Point out that the two points of land mentioned in the footnote, known since ancient times as the Pillars of Hercules, are the Rock of Gibraltar and the mountain on the coast of Morocco called Jebel Musa.

C Critical Thinking

Analyzing Character

? What does this incident tell you about Hercules? [Possible responses: It shows that he has a reckless side and a temper. He may be angry at Apollo because it was Apollo's oracle at Delphi who told Hercules to perform the labors assigned by Eurystheus.]

the Stymphalian birds, he was commanded to go to Crete and bring back from there alive a huge bull which was laying the whole island waste. Barehanded and alone he grappled with this bull, and, once again, when he brought the animal back into the streets of Mycenae, Eurystheus fled in terror at the sight both of the hero and of the great beast which he had captured.

From the southern sea Hercules was sent to the north to Thrace, over which ruled King Diomedes,[16] a strong and warlike prince who savagely fed his famous mares on human flesh. Hercules conquered the king in battle and gave his body to the very mares which had so often fed upon the bodies of the king's enemies. He brought the mares back to King Eurystheus, who again was terrified at the sight of such fierce and spirited animals. He ordered them to be taken to the heights of Mount Olympus and there be consecrated to Jupiter. But Jupiter had no love for these unnatural creatures, and, on the rocky hillsides, they were devoured by lions, wolves, and bears.

Next, Hercules was commanded to go to the country of the Amazons, the fierce warrior women, and bring back the girdle of their queen Hippolyte.[17] Seas and mountains had to be crossed, battles to be fought; but Hercules in the end accomplished the long journey and the dangerous task. Later, as is well known, Hippolyte became the wife of Theseus of Athens and bore him an ill-fated son, Hippolytus.

Hercules had now traveled in the south, the north, and the east. His tenth labor was to be in the far west, beyond the country of Spain, in an island called Erythia.[18] Here lived the giant Geryon, a great monster with three bodies and three heads. With his herdsman and his two-headed dog, called Orthrus, he looked after

16. **Diomedes** (dī′ə·mē′dēz).
17. **Hippolyte** (hi·päl′i·tē).
18. **Erythia** (er·i·thē′ə).

546 OUR CLASSICAL HERITAGE

huge flocks of oxen, and, at the command of Eurystheus, Hercules came into his land to lift the cattle and to destroy the giant. On his way, at the very entrance to the Atlantic, he set up two great marks, ever afterward to be known by sailors and called the Pillars of Hercules.[19] Later, as he wandered through rocks and over desert land, he turned his anger against the Sun itself, shooting his arrows at the great god Phoebus Apollo. But Phoebus pitied him in his thirst and weariness. He sent him a golden boat, and in this boat Hercules crossed over to the island of Erythia. Here he easily destroyed both watchdog and herdsman, but fought for long with the great three-bodied giant before he slew him, body after body. Then he began to drive the cattle over rivers and mountains and deserts from Spain to Greece. As he was passing through Italy he came near the cave where Cacus, a son of Vulcan, who breathed fire out of his mouth, lived solitary and cruel, since he killed all strangers and nailed their heads, dripping with blood, to the posts at the entrance of his rocky dwelling. While Hercules was resting, with the herds all round him, Cacus came out of his cave and stole eight of the best animals of the whole herd. He dragged them backwards by their tails, so that Hercules should not be able to track them down.

When Hercules awoke from his rest, he searched far and wide for the missing animals, but since they had been driven into the deep recesses of Cacus's cave, he was unable to find them. In the end he began to go on his way with the rest of the herd, and as the stolen animals heard the lowing of the other cattle, they too began to low and bellow in their rocky prison. Hercules stopped still, and soon out of the cave came the fire-breathing giant, prepared to defend the fruits of his robbery and anxious to hang the head of Hercules among

19. **Pillars of Hercules:** two points of lands reaching out into the water on either side of the Strait of Gibraltar.

Professional Notes

Using Cooperative Groups

Students working in cooperative groups may be more productive if you implement the following suggestions:

- Model any speaking and listening activity before students attempt the activity in their groups.

- Quietly observe each group just long enough to make sure that the group is on task, and then move on to briefly observe a different group.

- Try to avoid commenting on group procedures while students are working. Instead, after groups have finished, give students suggestions for improvement that they can use during the next collaborative assignment.

his other disgusting trophies. This, however, was not to be. The huge limbs and terrible fiery breath of Cacus were of no avail against the hero's strength and fortitude. Soon, with a tremendous blow of his club, he stretched out Cacus dead on the ground. Then he drove the great herd on over mountains and plains, through forests and rivers to Mycenae.

Hercules' next labor again took him to the far west. He was commanded by Eurystheus to fetch him some of the golden apples of the Hesperides.[20] These apples grew in a garden west even of the land of Atlas. Here the sun shines continually, but always cool, well-watered trees of every kind give shade. All flowers and fruits that grow on earth grow here, and fruit and flowers are always on the boughs together. In the center of the garden is the orchard, where golden apples gleam among the shining green leaves and the flushed blossom. Three nymphs, the Hesperides, look after this orchard, which was given by Jupiter to Juno as a wedding present. It is guarded also by a great dragon that never sleeps and coils its huge folds around the trees. No one except the gods knows exactly where this beautiful and remote garden is, and it was to this unknown place that Hercules was sent.

He was helped by Minerva and by the nymphs of the broad river Po in Italy. These nymphs told Hercules where to find Nereus,[21] the ancient god of the sea, who knew the past, the present, and the future. "Wait for him," they said, "until you find him asleep on the rocky shore, surrounded by his fifty daughters. Seize hold of him tightly and do not let go until he answers your question. He will, in trying to escape you, put on all kinds of shapes. He will turn to fire, to water, to a wild beast, or to a serpent. You must not lose your courage, but hold him all the tighter, and, in the end, he will

come back to his own shape and will tell you what you want to know."

Hercules followed their advice. As he watched along the sea god's shore he saw, lying on the sand, half in and half out of the sea, with seaweed trailing round his limbs, the old god himself. Around him were his daughters, the Nereids,[22] some riding on the backs of dolphins, some dancing on the shore, some swimming and diving in the deeper water. As Hercules approached, they cried out shrilly at the sight of a man. Those on land leaped back into the sea; those in the sea swam further from the shore. But their cries did not awake their father till Hercules was close to him and able to grip him firmly in his strong hands. As soon as the old god felt the hands upon him, his body seemed to disappear into a running stream of water; but Hercules felt the body that he could not see, and did not relax his grasp. Next it seemed that his hands were buried in a great pillar of fire; but the fire did not scorch the skin, and Hercules could still feel the aged limbs through the fire. Then it was a great lion with wide-open jaws that appeared to be lying and raging on the sands; then a bear, then a dragon. Still Hercules clung firmly to his prisoner, and in the end he saw again the bearded face and seaweed-dripping limbs of old Nereus. The god knew for what purpose Hercules had seized him, and he told him the way to the garden of the Hesperides.

It was a long and difficult journey, but at the end of it Hercules was rewarded. The guardian nymphs (since this was the will of Jupiter) allowed him to pick from the pliant boughs two or three of the golden fruit. The great dragon bowed its head to the ground at their command and left Hercules unmolested. He

22. **Nereids** (nir'ē·idz).

WORDS TO OWN
pliant (plī'ənt) *adj.*: easily bent.

----

20. **Hesperides** (hes·per'i·dēz).
21. **Nereus** (nir'ē·əs).

THE LABORS OF HERCULES **547**

D **Struggling Readers**
Finding Sequence of Events
Check to be sure that students are listing this labor as the eleventh. If their count is off, have them work through the text and their notes with a partner to determine which event they have omitted.

E **Reading Skills and Strategies**
Making Connections
❓ Have you ever visited a particularly beautiful fruit orchard or flower garden? Try to remember what it looked like, how it smelled, and how you felt when you were there. Quickwrite what you remember.

F **Elements of Literature**
The Quest
Point out that Hercules once again receives help on his quest, both from the goddess Minerva and from the nymphs of the river Po. Although their reasons for helping him are never given, it is clear that he would have found his task difficult or impossible without their help.

G **Reading Skills and Strategies**
Making Connections
The various *Star Trek* series are often syndicated on independent television channels. Ask fans of *Star Trek: Deep Space Nine* to compare and contrast Nereus with the character Odo, who is a shape-shifter. The shape-shifter appears in many different mythologies. The character Raven, who appears in American Indian mythology, can transform himself into different shapes. Another character in Greek mythology who is a master of disguise is Proteus.

Crossing the Curriculum

Art
The labors of Hercules were commonly depicted on Greek vases like the one pictured on p. 550. Ask students to find and to bring to class art books containing photographs of painted Greek vases portraying the labors of Hercules. Have students identify the labor depicted on each vase. The class may find that the only labors not commonly depicted are the cleansing of the Augean stables and the capture of the mares of Diomedes.

Geography
Give students a map of ancient Europe, and ask them to mark the locations of as many of Hercules' labors as possible and to explain why they cannot mark the others. Students should deduce that labors 3, 9, 11, and 12 cannot be marked because they occur in unidentified or imaginary locations. Students should be able to find and mark the locations of the other eight labors:
1) Nemea, ancient Argolis; 2) Argos, eastern Pelo-

ponnesus; 4) mountains of Erymanthus, northwest Arcadia; 5) Elis, northwestern Peloponnesus; 6) Lake Stymphalus, northeastern Arcadia; 7) island of Crete; 8) ancient Thrace, east of Macedonia; 10) Erythia (Cadiz), Spanish coast. Although the locations are not given in the text, 3 begins in Argolis and ends in Arcadia, and 9 is in Scythia, near the Black Sea.

The Underworld of Myth

In mythology, the underworld is the world of the dead. Normally, Pluto (Roman name for the Greek god Hades) allows no one who enters it to leave. As the author mentions, of all the mortals who preceded Hercules into the underworld, only one—Orpheus—had returned. Stress that because of the risk of no return, this is the most dangerous labor of all.

B **Critical Thinking**

Hypothesizing

❓ Why do you think Pluto requires that Hercules not use any weapons in capturing Cerberus? [Possible responses: Pluto is the tricky Hades, and he may be trying to snare Hercules in the underworld. Recall Hades' stratagem for keeping Persephone in the land of the dead (p. 501).]

Developing Vocabulary by Listening to Literature Read Aloud

Students acquire vocabulary through listening to selections read aloud. The vocabulary in this myth may challenge some readers. Read aloud the last paragraph on this page. Ask students to jot down unfamiliar words or phrases as they listen. (Students might list *undaunted, writhing,* and *immovably.*) Write some of the words on the board, and ask students to guess at their meanings. Students should draw on their experiences and use the context to figure out a word's meaning. Or have students complete a chart like the one on p. 521 to help uncover the meanings of unfamiliar words.

brought back the apples to Eurystheus, but soon they began to lose that beautiful sheen of gold that had been theirs in the western garden. So Minerva carried them back again to the place from which they came, and then once more they glowed with their own gold among the other golden apples that hung upon the trees.

Now had come the time for the twelfth and last of the labors that Hercules did for his master Eurystheus. This labor would seem to anyone by far the hardest; for the hero was commanded to descend into the lower world and bring back with him from the kingdom of Proserpine[23] the terrible three-headed watchdog Cerberus.

A Hercules took the dark path which before him had been trodden only by Orpheus and Theseus and Pirithous. Orpheus had returned. Theseus and Pirithous, for their wicked attempt, were still imprisoned.

Hercules passed the Furies, undaunted by the frightful eyes beneath the writhing serpents of their hair. He passed the great criminals, Sisyphus,[24] Tantalus, and the rest. He passed by his friend, the unhappy Theseus, who was sitting immovably fixed to a rock, and he came at last into the terrible presence of black Pluto himself, who sat on his dark throne with his young wife Proserpine beside him. To the King and Queen of the Dead, Hercules explained the reason of his coming. "Go," said **B** Pluto, "and, so long as you use no weapon, but only your bare hands, you may take my watchdog Cerberus to the upper air."

23. **Proserpine** (prŏ·sʉr′pi·nē): Roman name for Persephone. (See "The Origin of the Seasons," page 501.)
24. **Sisyphus** (sis′ə·fəs).

Hercules ascending to Olympus.
Red-figured bell crater (bowl).
Kunsthistorisches Museum, Vienna, Austria.
Erich Lessing/Art Resource, New York.

548 OUR CLASSICAL HERITAGE

Skill Link

Using *good* and *well; bad* and *badly*
The correct use of these words is taught in the Grammar Links on pp. 553 and 577.

The words *good* and *bad* are adjectives.
Example (describing the noun *guys*):
In old cowboy movies, the *good* guys wear white hats, and the *bad* guys wear black hats.
Example (describing the pronouns *I* and *you*):
At school today I was *good,* but you were *bad.*

The word *well* can be an adjective or an adverb.

The word *badly* is always an adverb.
Example (describing the verb *play*):
I play the trombone *well,* but I play the piano *badly.*
Example (describing the adjective *rehearsed*):
The play was *well* rehearsed.
Example (describing the adjective *mistaken*):
Jeremy was *badly* mistaken in his answer.
Activity
Use the correct word—*good* or *well, bad* or *badly*— to complete each sentence, and

identify the word that it modifies.
1. Hercules is _____ at conquering monsters. [good, *Hercules*]
2. Hercules performs his labors amazingly _____. [well, *performs*]
3. It is too _____ that Hercules must fight Chiron. [bad, *It*]
4. The centaurs fight _____, but they die _____, writhing in pain from the poisoned arrows. [well, *fight*; badly, *die*]

RESPONDING TO THE ART

Greek pottery. The precise origin of the potter's wheel is lost to history, but no one wielded it with greater mastery than the ancient Greeks. Their exquisitely wrought vessels not only speak volumes about Greek culture and history but also stand as unrivaled specimens of the art of pottery, which was spurred by the encouragement of Solon (c. 640–560 B.C.) and by an abundance of raw red clay. Before 500 B.C., the figures were incised by master potters and then covered in black paint (with occasional touches of dark red) and finished with a brilliant varnish, as in the works shown on pp. 519 and 540–543. This pottery is called black figure. After 500 B.C. the coloring process was reversed. The background scenes were painted black, and the figures stood out in the more natural hue of the jar's reddish clay surface, as in the vessel on pp. 548–549. This work is called red figure.

Activity. Ask students to study carefully the depictions of Hercules' adventures on pp. 540–544 and 548–550. In light of their reading, which picture do they think best evokes an episode of the story? Which picture most closely resembles their own idea of Hercules? Why?

Making the Connections

Connecting to the Theme: "Our Classical Heritage"

The labors of Hercules, like the stories of Samson in the Bible, demonstrate that human beings have always loved stories of derring-do—especially when the hero exhibits cleverness as well as sheer brawn.

Cultural Connections

Ask each student to find and to read a quest story from a culture other than that of ancient Greece or Rome. A starting point might be the book *The Stolen Fire: Legends of Heroes and Rebels from Around the World* by Hans Baumann, translated by Stella Humphries. Encourage students to look for stories that have protagonists who rely more on intelligence and cleverness than on physical strength. Students may read stories with animal heroes or heroines if these fit the criteria for a quest story.

A Critical Thinking

Comparing/Contrasting Myths

❓ How is this journey upward like that of Orpheus and Eurydice? [A hero leads and someone else follows.] How is the outcome different from that of the Orpheus and Eurydice story? [It is implied that both Hercules and Theseus safely achieve the light of day.]

B Critical Thinking

Challenging the Text

❓ Do you think the ending of the story is a good one? Why or why not? [Possible responses: Yes, because Hercules doesn't have to obey Eurystheus any more. No, the final labor turns out to be so easy for Hercules that there's no real climax to the story.]

BROWSING IN THE FILES

About the Author. Rex Warner was well known for his translations of Greek classics. One of his notable works was his translation of the play *Prometheus Bound* by the Greek writer Aeschylus. "The Labors of Hercules" is from *Men and Gods,* one of Warner's collections of myths for young people.

Resources ━━━━━

Selection Assessment

Formal Assessment
• Selection Test, p. 107

Test Generator
• Selection Test

Hercules thanked the dreadful king for giving him the permission which he had asked. Then he made one more request, which was that Theseus, who had sinned only by keeping his promise to his friend, might be allowed to return again to life. This, too, was granted him. Theseus rose to his feet again and accompanied the hero to the entrance of Hell, where the huge dog Cerberus, with his three heads and his three deep baying voices, glared savagely at the intruders. Even this tremendous animal proved no match for Hercules, who with his vise-like grip stifled the breath in two of the shaggy throats and then lifted the beast upon his shoulders and began to ascend again, Theseus following close behind, the path that leads to the world of men. They say that when he carried Cerberus to Mycenae, Eurystheus fled in terror to another city and was now actually glad that Hercules had completed what might seem to have been twelve impossible labors. Cerberus was restored to his place in Hell and never again visited the upper world. Nor did Hercules ever go down to the place of the dead, since, after further trials, he was destined to live among the gods above.

Hercules leading Cerberus to Eurystheus (575 B.C.). Corinthian hydria (water jar).

Louvre, Paris, France. Giraudon/Art Resource, New York.

MEET THE WRITER

Journeys Past and Present

Rex Warner (1905–1986) pursued his dream in many different places around the world. He was born and grew up in England, worked as a teacher in Egypt, ran the British Institute in Greece, taught English in Germany, and finally settled in the United States as an English professor at the University of Connecticut. A respected classical scholar, Warner sought to bring ancient Greece and Rome to life in the modern world.

550 OUR CLASSICAL HERITAGE

Assessing Learning

Self-Reflection

Ask students to use the following scale and list of criteria to rate their own responses on the assignments for this selection.

5 = Strong   4 = Average   3 = Weak
_____ Oral responses during class discussion
_____ Responses during small-group discussion
_____ Written responses (formal or informal)
_____ Other creative responses

Check Test: Short Answer

1. Who is Hercules' father? [Jupiter]
2. What does Hercules wear as a cloak after his first labor? [the skin of the lion of Nemea]
3. How does Hercules clean the Augean stables? [He diverts the course of a river to flow through the stables.]
4. Who helps Hercules? [Iolaus, Minerva, Phoebus, the Po River nymphs, Nereus, the Hesperides, and Pluto]
5. What does Eurystheus do each time Hercules returns from a labor? [He runs and hides.]

Standardized Test Preparation

For practice with standardized test format specific to this selection, see
• *Standardized Test Preparation,* p. 82
For practice in proofreading and editing, see
• *Daily Oral Grammar,* Transparency 32

MAKING MEANINGS

MAKING MEANINGS

First Thoughts

[respond]
1. Hercules has come to be known as a brawny hero, not one with a lot of intelligence. Is this fair? How do you feel about the way he tackles the tasks on his quest?

Shaping Interpretations

[evaluate]
2. Here is a checklist of characteristics for a great **quest** story. How well does "The Labors of Hercules" meet these criteria? Do you know other stories that meet them? The hero
   - is threatened at birth
   - shows early signs of being special
   - is called on to undertake a special quest
   - faces a dangerous journey
   - receives help along the way, including assistance from the gods
   - descends to the underworld
   - is finally rewarded

[explain]
3. Why does Hercules accept his quest?

[explain]
4. Like most myths, this one explains how certain things on earth and in the heavens came to be. Where did the constellation Sagittarius come from? the rocks known as the Pillars of Hercules?

[compare]
5. How is the garden of the Hesperides a kind of paradise? Does it remind you of other paradises? (How is it the opposite of the underworld?)

[contrast]
6. How is Hercules' descent into the underworld unlike the trips made by Orpheus (page 513) and Persephone (page 501)?

[interpret]
7. The challenges Hercules faces are often symbols of challenges we face in life. What do you think each labor stands for?

Extending the Text

[evaluate]
8. Does Hercules remind you of the heroes of any American **tall tales**? In what ways is he similar to larger-than-life heroes like Paul Bunyan, John Henry, and Pecos Bill?

[apply]
9. How is your own life a kind of quest? What can you learn from Hercules' story that might help you reach your goals?

THE LABORS OF HERCULES 551

Reading Check

In a chart with headings like the ones below, write a data sheet about the twelve labors of Hercules.

Twelve Labors of Hercules		
What He Did	For Whom	How It Helped the World

MAKING MEANINGS

First Thoughts

1. Possible response: His planning and cleverness show that he is smart and brave as well as strong.

Shaping Interpretations

2. • threatened by snakes in cradle
   • kills the snakes with his hands
   • takes on twelve labors
   • makes many dangerous journeys
   • receives help from Iolaus, Minerva, nymphs, Phoebus, and Pluto
   • visits underworld, gets Cerberus
   • rewarded with immortality
   The myth meets the criteria for a great quest story.

3. His object is to be purified, after killing his family in a madness that was sent by Juno.

4. Hercules' teacher Chiron is set in the sky as the constellation Sagittarius. The Pillars are marks Hercules sets up at the entrance to the Atlantic.

5. It contains every fruit and flower on earth, growing all year; it is like the Garden of Eden in the Bible. The underworld is dark and gloomy; the garden is bright and pleasant.

6. Unlike Orpheus, Hercules follows Pluto's warning and rescues someone successfully. Unlike Persephone, Hercules is not tricked into returning for parts of the year.

7. Answers will vary, but the most clearly symbolic of the twelve labors is Hercules' journey into the underworld, which can be seen as a journey to conquer death.

Extending the Text

8. Hercules' challenges were more difficult than those of most movie and TV action heroes. Determination and cleverness are as important as strength to many action heroes, just as they were to Hercules.

9. Encourage students to give examples they are willing to share.

Reading Check
What He Did
The Labors of Hercules: (1) Killed Nemean lion, (2) Destroyed Hydra, (3) Captured stag sacred to Diana, (4) Brought back Erymanthian boar, (5) Cleaned Augean stables, (6) Destroyed Stymphalian birds, (7) Overcame Cretan bull, (8) Killed Diomedes and brought back his mares, (9) Retrieved Hippolyte's belt, (10) Destroyed Geryon and brought back his cattle, (11) Fetched apples of the Hesperides, (12) Brought back Cerberus.

For Whom
Hercules performed all twelve labors assigned by Eurystheus to atone for killing his family.
How It Helped the World
Many times he helped the people of a region by ridding them of a harmful menace. Only a few of the labors seem to carry no particular benefit to anyone (3, 9, 11), except insofar as they prove Hercules' ability to carry out the seemingly impossible demands of Eurystheus.

Grading Timesaver

Rubrics for each Choices assignment appear on p. 176 in the *Portfolio Management System*.

CHOICES: Building Your Portfolio

1. **Writer's Notebook** Call to students' attention the sample chart in the notebook graphic; they should organize their notes in the same way. Remind students to save their work. They may use it as prewriting for the Writer's Workshop on p. 582.

2. **Creative Writing/Art** Ask students to model their heroes' or heroines' tasks on Hercules' labors. Remind them that Hercules often had to come up with clever solutions to his problems. Also, point out that even Hercules occasionally had to rely on help from others. You may wish to have students begin by working in groups of four. Ask them to share their lists of tasks with the members of their groups. Then, have the group brainstorm lists of difficulties their heroes or heroines might face during their tasks. After students have completed their lists, distribute copies of a brief story you have written or drawn about a modern hero or heroine, and allow students to use it as a model for their own stories.

3. **Language/Research** Provide dictionaries that students may use as sources for their glossaries. Show the class an illustrated glossary they can use as a model.

4. **Research/Speaking** Provide handbooks, dictionaries of mythology, or addresses of Web sites for students to use as sources. Suggest that students include an epithet for each character. Jason, for example, could be "justice-defending Jason," and Diana could be "Diana, queen of wild things." (See p. T507 for the term *epithet*.) Suggest that students present their biographical sketches to the class as oral stories. Play an audiotape or videotape of an oral rendition of a myth, legend, or other story, and ask the student narrators to use it as a model for their own storytelling performances. Remind students to include both short introductions (giving background information for each of the characters) and dramatic retellings (of one or two of each character's most famous exploits).

CHOICES: Building Your Portfolio

Writer's Notebook

1. Collecting Ideas for an Evaluation

Look back through "The Labors of Hercules," and decide which one of the twelve labors was the most interesting or the most exciting to read about. Base your evaluation on these standards:

- the difficulty and/or importance of the task
- the cleverness of Hercules' solution
- the storyteller's description of the labor

> **Best Labor:**
> Killing the Hydra
> —impossible if he hadn't cleverly thought of heat
> —important since Hercules got his best weapon from it—the poison arrows

Creative Writing/Art

2. Help Wanted: Hero/Heroine

Look back at your notes for the Quickwrite on page 540. What world-improving tasks did you list for your modern-day Hercules? Write a story called "The Five Labors of . . .". Give your superhero or superheroine a name, and explain why his or her fate involves attempting to accomplish these tasks. Then, tell about each labor and the difficulties the hero or heroine overcomes in performing each. Finally, tell how the hero or heroine is rewarded or glorified for successfully completing the work. If you wish, tell your story in the form of a cartoon like "The Twelve Tasks of Heracles" (see *Connections* on page 554).

Language/Research

3. A Labor of Language

From your reading of the myth, what do you suppose a *herculean task* would be? What do you think *Augean* means? Many words in English come from names that appear in the ancient myths.

Using the words below, create an illustrated glossary that you can leave in the classroom for other students to use when they read this myth. First, tell what person or place in mythology the name comes from. Then, draw this person or place. Also, provide a sentence showing how each word is used today.

amazon   herculean
Augean   hydra
Olympian   atlas

Research/Speaking

4. Mythic All-Stars

The characters in "The Labors of Hercules" include some of the greatest names in mythology: Theseus, Hippolyte, Actaeon, Jason, the Amazons, Apollo, Pluto, Diana, Juno. With a group of classmates, do research to find out what these figures are famous for. Deliver to the class a short biographical sketch of each one. Then, compile your reports, along with illustrations, in a class collection of mythic all-stars.

GRAMMAR LINK

Language Handbook HELP

See Glossary of Usage: good, well, *page 786.*

Technology HELP

See Language Workshop CD-ROM. *Key word entry: modifiers.*

• Do a Good Job with *Good* and *Well*

Does choosing between *good* and *well* sometimes seem as hard as the labors of Hercules? Here are a few simple rules to help you get the job done right:

- *Good* is an adjective. Never use it to modify a verb.

- *Well* is usually an adverb. Use it to modify a verb.

NONSTANDARD	Hercules fought good against the Hydra.
STANDARD	Hercules fought well against the Hydra.
STANDARD	Hercules fought a good fight.

Although it is usually an adverb, *well* may be used as an adjective to mean "healthy."

EXAMPLE	The Hydra was not feeling well after its fight with Hercules.

Note: *Feel good* and *feel well* mean different things. *Feel good* means "feel happy or pleased." *Feel well* simply means "feel healthy."

EXAMPLES	Hercules didn't feel good about killing the centaurs.
	Eurystheus didn't feel well when he saw the wild boar's head.

Try It Out

Rewrite each sentence, correcting any usage errors you find.

1. Hercules fought good against the lion of Nemea.

2. Anyone struck by one of Hercules' poison arrows would not feel good about the situation.

3. Hercules found a good way to clean Augeas's stables really good.

4. Juno did not treat Hercules very good, but Diana and Minerva realized he was a good hero.

5. Hercules did well to get the golden apples, although the fruit didn't look as good once it left the garden.

VOCABULARY — HOW TO OWN A WORD

WORD BANK	Vocabulary for the Workplace: At the Movies
afflicted ravaged venomous pestilential pliant	Imagine you're a movie scriptwriter. You have a great idea for a new horror or science fiction film, but you have to persuade the studio bosses to back your project. Write a short persuasive description, or "pitch," of the movie you want to make. Use all five words in the Word Bank to **summarize** the **plot** of the movie.

THE LABORS OF HERCULES 553

GRAMMAR LINK

Ask students to circle each occurrence of the word *good* in an assignment they have recently completed. Have them trade papers with partners, who should underline any of the occurrences of *good* that should be replaced with *well*. Then, ask partners to return the papers so that each student can make the corrections on his or her paper.

Try It Out
Answers
1. well
2. (correct)
3. (correct); well
4. well; (correct)
5. (correct)

VOCABULARY
Sample Answer
This movie features a giant panda who is *afflicted* with a sudden madness that makes him omnivorous and insatiable. He breaks out of the San Diego Zoo and *ravages* southern California, eating everything in his path—people, pets, even UPS trucks. The government tries guns, bombs, and even *venomous* snakes and *pestilential* diseases from the vaults of the Centers for Disease Control, but nothing stops Panda. A hero finally emerges with a *pliant* strategy to solve the crisis.

Before they write their own sentences, encourage students to reexamine the way the words are used in the selection.

Resources ——————

Grammar
- *Grammar and Language Links,* p. 55

Vocabulary
- *Words to Own,* p. 21

Spelling
For related instruction, see
- *Spelling and Decoding,* p. 26

Grammar Link Quick Check

Choose the underlined word that correctly completes each sentence.

1. Hercules' mother must have fed him good/well. [well]

2. Juno tries to kill Hercules when he is in his cradle, but her plot does not work out too good/well. [well]

3. Hercules performs his labors good/well. [well]

4. Hercules wants to make up for his sin by doing good/well deeds. [good]

5. Because Hercules explains himself good/well, Diana forgives him for taking her stag. [well]

Connections

In "The Labors of Hercules," Rex Warner uses the Roman names of three characters. In her clever retelling of the story, Marcia Williams uses the original Greek names. Before students read her cartoon version, write the correlations on the board.

Roman		Greek
Hercules	=	Heracles
Jupiter	=	Zeus
Juno	=	Hera

A Elements of Literature
Conflict

❓ What do you learn here about the Hera/Heracles conflict that is not stated directly in Warner's prose version? [Possible response: Hera was jealous of Heracles' happiness.]

B English Language Learners
Using Graphic Aids

Point out that the cartoon follows certain conventions. Characters' spoken words are shown in balloons with an arrow pointing to the speaker; unspoken thoughts are shown in balloons with scalloped edges. Suggest that students read the comic strip twice to assimilate its humor. First, to get the whole story, they should read only the sentences in the white panels, merely glancing at the pictures above them. Then, they should go back and read the words and thoughts of the cartoon characters.

C Reading Skills and Strategies
Comparing/Contrasting

❓ In the version of the story you read earlier, where did King Eurystheus hide from Hercules? [in his brass room] Why might the cartoonist have made a large pot his hiding place? [Possible response: It's a lot funnier —if he was able to stuff himself into a pot, he must have been very scared.]

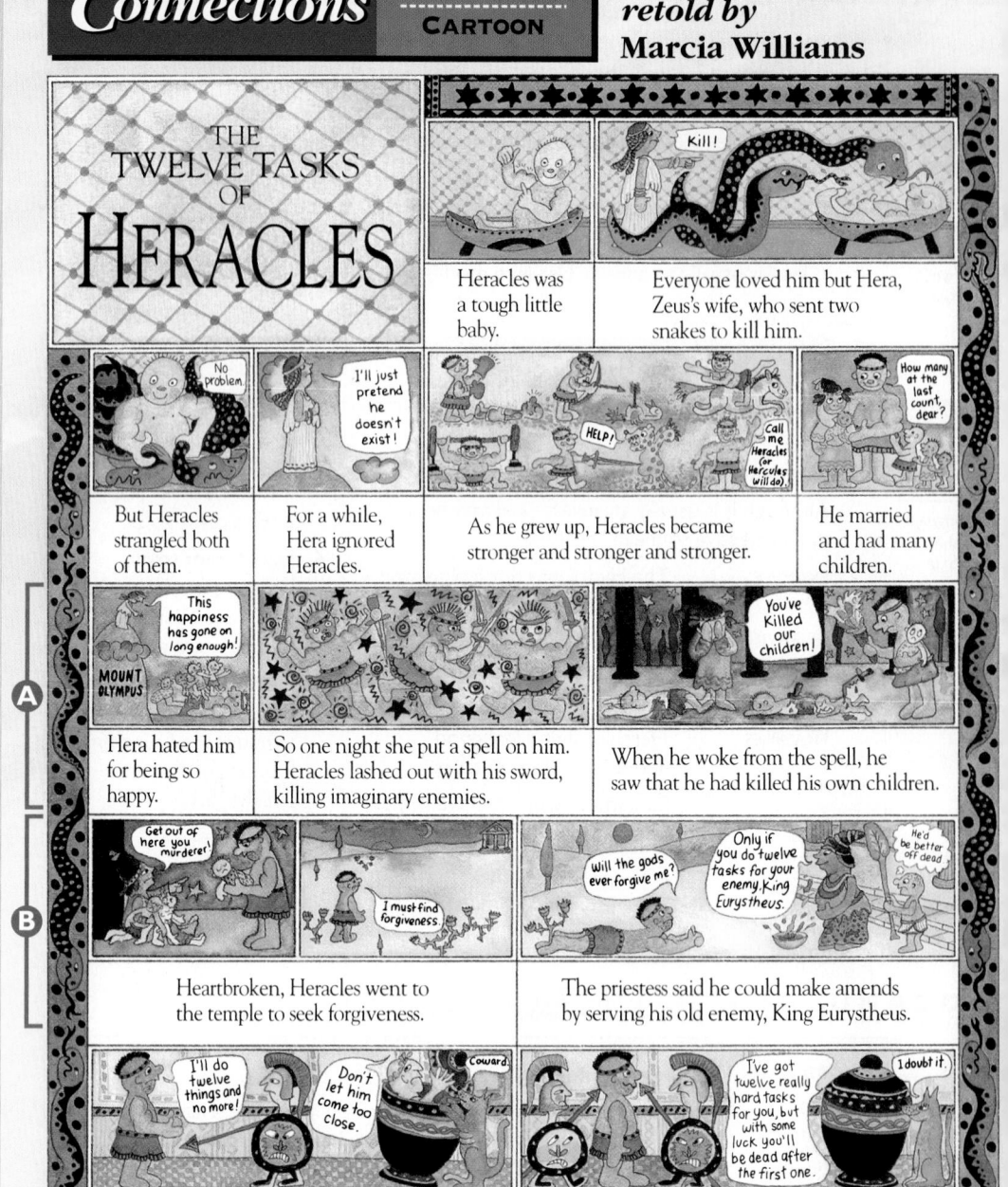

(Pages 554–557) *Heracles* from *Greek Myths for Young Children* ©1991 Marcia Williams.

554 OUR CLASSICAL HERITAGE

Connecting Across Texts

Connecting with "The Labors of Hercules"

Point out that the funniest lines in the comic-strip version of the labors of Hercules are the characters' comments in the word balloons within the panels. After students have read the entire cartoon, take a class vote to select the funniest panel or the funniest comments from a panel. Then, ask students to create a panel, with dialogue in word balloons, that they would like to add somewhere in the strip. Encourage students to create their own comic-strip versions of other myths in this collection.

First, Heracles had to kill the lion of Nemea whose hide was so thick that no sword could penetrate it.

Next, he had to kill the many-headed Hydra, whose very breath could kill man or beast.

Third, he had to capture the sacred, golden-horned deer, an animal as swift as the wind.

The fourth task was to catch a savage boar whose tusks could pierce any armor.

Next, Heracles had to clean out the vast and filthy stables of King Augeas in a single night.

Reprinted by permission of Walker Books, Ltd., London. Published in the US by Candlewick Press, Cambridge, Massachusetts.

(continued on next page)

(continued on next page)

D **Critical Thinking**

Evaluating a Text

? In her condensed version of the story, what details about Hercules and the Hydra does Williams omit? [Possible response: She doesn't mention the Hydra's venom, Hercules' discouragement, or the fact that he dipped his arrows in the venomous blood of the Hydra.]

Assessing Learning

Informal Assessment

Use this list of criteria to evaluate each student's reactions to the comic strip. Use a check mark to indicate that the student has met the objective.

_____ Student's reaction shows an understanding of the humor in the comic strip.

_____ Student's reaction shows an understanding of the connection between the prose selection and the comic strip.

_____ Student's reaction shows an understanding of the humor inherent in the myth.

T555

A Reading Skills and Strategies
Using Prior Knowledge
? According to the prose version, who gave Hercules the rattle? [the goddess Minerva] What is Hercules wearing or carrying that you recognize from the prose version of the story? [the skin of the lion of Nemea, worn as a cloak; the arrows dipped in the venomous blood of the Hydra.]

B Reading Skills and Strategies
Making Inferences
? From the letters that are visible, what does the sign in the second panel most likely say? [Diomedes' Stable—Danger!]

Then he had to to destroy a flock of man-eating birds that hid in a dangerous swamp.

The seventh task was to capture the fire-breathing, marauding bull of Crete.

Next, he had to steal Diomedes's horses, which fed on human flesh.

Then Heracles had to fetch the golden girdle worn by the queen of the Amazon warrior women.

The tenth task was to seize the monster Geryon's cattle, guarded by his two-headed dog.

Making the Connections

Cultural Connections

Quests, which often appear in older literature, are also found in the stories of today. Encourage students to discuss any contemporary books, television series, plays, or movies that tell of a quest. [Plots may include a fugitive's eluding pursuers, week after week; or a group's surmounting obstacle after obstacle as the voyagers attempt to return to their home world.] What similarities do students find between the characters or plots of today's quests and yesterday's?

The eleventh, to collect three golden apples protected by a ferocious dragon.

Heracles's twelfth and last task was the most dangerous of all: to fetch the three-headed guard dog, Cerberus, from Hades itself.

His twelve tasks completed, Heracles returned to King Eurystheus.

The king was dismayed to see him alive, and quickly sent him packing.

Then, to avoid angering the gods, Heracles sent Cerberus back to Hades.

At the temple, Heracles was finally pardoned.

He was content at last, and stronger than ever!

And Hera never bothered Heracles again.

C Elements of Literature

The Underworld of Myth

Help students see that the cartoonist's gray and brown vision of the underworld is consistent with descriptions they have come across in this collection.

D Reading Skills and Strategies

Making Connections

❓ Hercules' labors are said to have occupied him for twelve years. Think about the next twelve years of your life. What are at least four challenging events you expect to face in that span of time? [Possible responses: graduating from high school; choosing a college; finding a career or job; getting married.] Write about one of these challenges and explain any connection you see between the difficulties facing you and those overcome by Hercules.

Getting Students Involved

Cooperative Learning

Big H Clock. Work with the class as a whole to retell the labors of Hercules—or Heracles—in sequential order. On the board or on a transparency, draw a large circle with twelve points, as on the face of a clock. At each point students should name the task that Hercules completed. Work around the clock to create a composite of the twelve labors of Hercules. Have students copy the clock into their own notes for future reference.

Improvisation. Divide students into twelve small groups, and assign each group one of the twelve tasks. Tell students to review their task from both the prose and the comic-strip versions of the myth and then to create an impromptu dramatization of the task. Arrange for the groups to act out their scenes in sequence.

OBJECTIVES

1. Read and interpret the myth
2. Identify irony
3. Use prior knowledge
4. Express understanding through evaluation, creative writing, art, or drama
5. Identify allusion and explain its meaning

SKILLS

Literary
- Identify irony

Reading
- Use prior knowledge

Writing
- Take notes for evaluating a story
- Write a first-person narrative

Grammar/Language
- Identify allusion and explain its meaning

Art
- Create a collage showing metamorphosis

Drama
- Act out the myth

Viewing/Representing
- Collect and identify ornamental objects (ATE)
- Compare artistic representations (ATE)

Before You Read

KING MIDAS AND THE GOLDEN TOUCH

Make the Connection

When Too Much Is Not Enough

Greed is a powerful emotion— it can disrupt friendships, spark wars, and topple empires.

Quickwrite

What happens to people who value money above everything else? Write briefly about a modern-day situation in which greed led to unhappiness or suffering.

Elements of Literature

Irony

Irony is the difference between what you say and what you mean or between what's supposed to happen and what does happen. When you say "Good going" to someone who's just fallen flat on his face, you're using irony. When a firehouse burns down, that's irony. This myth is about an ironic situation: There's a big difference between what Midas *expects* to happen and what does happen.

In general, **irony** is a contrast between expectation and reality.

For more on Irony, see the Handbook of Literary Terms.

Reading Skills and Strategies

Using Prior Knowledge: Building on What You Know

Get together with a group of classmates. Brainstorm to find answers to the questions about greed on the map below. You may want to add questions—and answers—of your own.

> Greed
>
> Definition:
>
> Questions about greed:
>
> What is wrong with it?
>
> What is an example of it?
>
> Who is greedy?
>
> What is its opposite?

(Below) One of a pair of bracelets with ram's-head finials (c. 330–300 B.C.). Greek. Said to be from near Thessaloniki. Gold, rock crystal (8 cm wide x 7.8 cm high).

The Metropolitan Museum of Art, Harris Brisbane Dick Fund, 1937. (37.11.11-.12). Photograph © 1993 The Metropolitan Museum of Art.

558 OUR CLASSICAL HERITAGE

Resources: Print and Media

Reading
- *Reading Skills and Strategies*
   Selection Skill Lesson, p. 211
- *Graphic Organizers for Active Reading*, p. 39
- *Audio CD Library*
   Disc 14, Track 2

Elements of Literature
- *Literary Elements*
   Transparency 9
   Worksheet, p. 28

Writing and Language
- *Daily Oral Grammar*
   Transparency 33
- *Grammar and Language Links*
   Worksheet, p. 57

Viewing and Representing
- *Viewing and Representing*
   Fine Art Transparency 18
   Fine Art Worksheet, p. 72

Assessment
- *Formal Assessment*, p. 109
- *Portfolio Management System*, p. 177
- *Standardized Test Preparation*, p. 84
- *Test Generator (One-Stop Planner CD-ROM)*

Internet
- go.hrw.com (keyword: LE0 7-7)

(Below) Gold oak wreath with a bee and two cicadas.
Copyright British Museum, London.

(Below) Openwork hairnet with framed medallion, decorated with head of a maenad. (c. 250–150 B.C.). Greek. Gold.

The Metropolitan Museum of Art, Gift of Norbert Schimmel, 1987, (1987.220). Photograph © 1983 The Metropolitan Museum of Art, 1993.

KING MIDAS and the Golden Touch

retold by **Pamela Oldfield**

559

Planning

- **Traditional Schedule**
  Lesson Plans Including Strategies for English-Language Learners
- **One-Stop Planner**
  CD-ROM with Test Generator

Summary ■ ■

King Midas of Lydia, already steeped in good fortune, wants to be the most powerful and envied man in the world. One day he finds the satyr Silenus lying drunk in his garden. When Midas returns Silenus to his master, Dionysus, the grateful god offers to grant the king any wish. Midas asks to have anything he touches turn to gold. The granted wish ironically turns into a curse. The desolate king begs Dionysus to repeal the power and follows the god's instruction to bathe in the river Pactolus. Midas emerges relieved to find his golden touch gone.

Resources

Listening
Audio CD Library
A reading of this story is provided in the *Audio CD Library:*
- Disc 14, Track 2

Selection Assessment
Formal Assessment
- Selection Test, p. 109
Test Generator
- Selection Test

Viewing and Representing
Fine Art Transparency
A transparency of the set design for the opera *The Magic Flute* complements the story of King Midas.
- Transparency 18
- Worksheet, p. 72

Reaching All Students

Struggling Readers
Using Prior Knowledge was introduced on p. 558. For a lesson directly tied to this selection that teaches students to use prior knowledge as they read by using a strategy called Anticipation Guides, see the *Reading Skills and Strategies* binder:
- Selection Skill Lesson, p. 211

English Language Learners
Before students read, give them this list of words from the story: *discontented, peered, trespassing* (p. 560), and *jubilant* (p. 561). Read aloud the sentences in which they occur, pointing out context clues. Ask students to write definitions for the words. Then, ask them to compare their definitions with those in a dictionary. For strategies to supplement instruction for these students, see
- *Lesson Plans Including Strategies for English-Language Learners*

Advanced Learners
Invite students to research literary connections—more on the satyr Silenus or the god Dionysus, for example. Or ask them to compare the cure of Midas in the river Pactolus with the cure of Naaman the Syrian in the river Jordan in the Bible (2 Kings 5:1–27). Have students focus on characters, motivations, and resolutions in the two stories. Ask students to comment on the ironic final twist, involving the greed of the character Gehazi, in the Naaman story.

Ⓐ Historical Connections

Tell students there was a real king named Midas who ruled territories in Phrygia, now western Turkey, in the eighth century B.C. Lydia, the kingdom mentioned in this story, was famous for its wealth, and historians believe that the first coins originated there, in the seventh century B.C.

Ⓑ Critical Thinking

Analyzing Character

❓ Does King Midas sound like a bad person? Why or why not? [Possible responses: Yes, the narrator calls him greedy, so he must be bad. No, the narrator comments that he is no better or worse than anyone else; he is just not satisfied with what he has.]

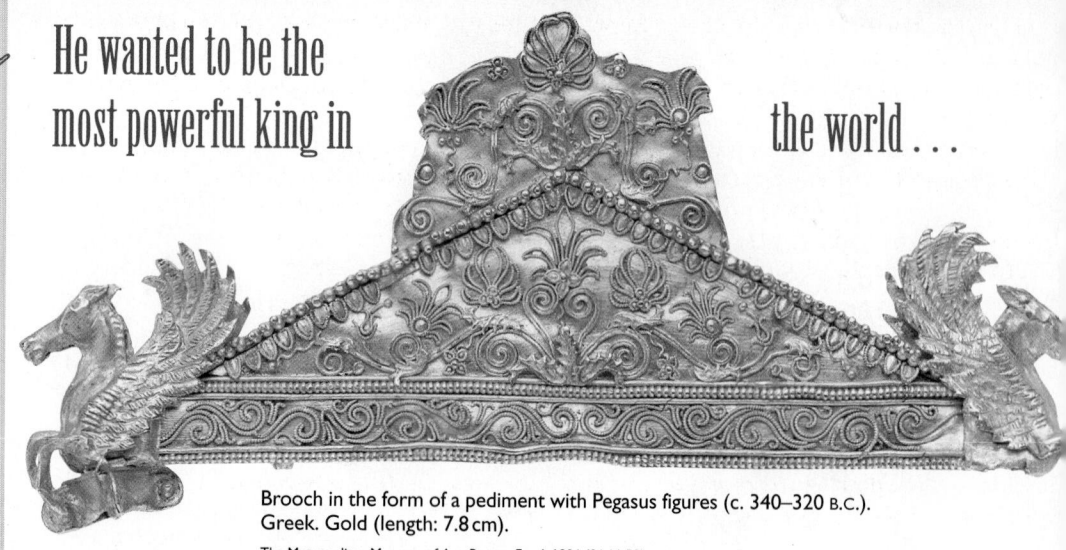

He wanted to be the most powerful king in the world . . .

Brooch in the form of a pediment with Pegasus figures (c. 340–320 B.C.). Greek. Gold (length: 7.8 cm).
The Metropolitan Museum of Art, Rogers Fund, 1906 (06.11.59).
Photograph © 1993 The Metropolitan Museum of Art.

Ⓐ Ⓑ Many years ago in the land of Lydia, there was a beautiful garden. Roses of every shade grew there, and on warm summer nights the air was heavy with their fragrance. The garden belonged to a palace, and the palace was the home of a king whose name was Midas. He was, it is true, rather greedy, but on the whole no better and no worse than any other man. Midas had a loving wife and a daughter he adored, but he was still discontented. He wanted to be the most powerful king in the world; he wanted everyone to envy him.

One day as he was walking through the palace garden, he was startled to see a pair of legs sticking out from beneath his favorite rosebush. The strange thing about these legs was that they had hoofs instead of feet. The king stared at them for a moment and then called for the gardener's boy.

"What do you make of that?" he asked. The boy parted the branches of the rosebush and peered through.

Ⓒ "It's a satyr, Your Majesty," he reported, trying not to laugh. "I think it's Silenus."

The satyrs were strange, mischievous creatures—half man, half beast—who roamed the world in search of adventure. Midas frowned, angry that somebody should be sleeping in his garden.

The boy ran off to fetch the gardener, and between them they dragged Silenus from under the rosebush and pulled him to his feet. Silenus grinned foolishly. He was holding an empty wine jar.

"You are trespassing in my garden," Midas told him severely. "What have you to say for yourself?" The old satyr shrugged.

"I got lost, so I sat down for a drink," he told the king, looking quite unrepentant.

"Disgraceful," said Midas. "I shall send word to your master at once." Silenus began to look worried, for his master was the god Dionysus, who was not only powerful but also quick-tempered.

560 OUR CLASSICAL HERITAGE

Getting Students Involved

Cooperative Learning

Literary Report Card. After students have read all the myths in the collection through the story of Midas, divide them into groups of five and ask them to create Literary Report Cards. The report cards should evaluate nine characters:

- Immortals: Demeter, Hades, Hercules
- Mortals: Orpheus, Echo, Narcissus, Icarus, Daedalus, Midas

In order to create their report cards, each group should follow five steps:

1. Create a list of qualitative criteria, such as courage and goodness, by which the group may judge characters.
2. Evaluate the characters, using the criteria.
3. Assign one A grade to the character who comes closest to meeting the criteria, then two B's, three C's, two D's, and one F.

4. Design and create report-card forms that show the list of criteria, letter grades, and brief comments about each character.
5. Present the group's conclusions to the class orally.

The class does not need to come to a consensus, but encourage groups to argue the merits of the grades they have assigned.

"I beg you not to do that," he cried. "He will be angry with me. Suppose I make a bargain with you? If you will overlook my foolishness, I will entertain you with strange and wonderful tales, better than any you have heard before." **D**

Midas agreed and the satyr stayed on in the palace, delighting the king with wonderful accounts of his adventures. At the end of the week, Midas sent the satyr back to Dionysus. The god was very fond of Silenus, despite his many faults, and was pleased to see him safe and sound. He wanted to thank Midas for taking care of the old satyr and offered the king **E** any gift he cared to name.

Any gift he cared to name! What a marvelous opportunity! He pondered for a whole day and a night and then asked Dionysus if he could make a wish. The god agreed and Midas asked for the power to turn whatever he touched into gold. The god granted his wish, and Midas was jubilant. **F**

"Imagine a king with a golden touch!" he cried. "I shall be the wealthiest and most powerful king in the world."

The king began to experiment with his new gift. He hurried into the garden and touched one of the flowers. At once, the whole bush turned to gold. He went from bush to bush, touching all the blooms, until the entire garden had turned to gold. Then he looked around him. Suddenly Midas felt doubtful. Gone were the colors and the glorious perfume. The garden was still and lifeless.

Inside the palace, the king called for a goblet of wine. As soon as it touched his lips the wine **G** turned to gold and he could not drink.

A terrible thought occurred to him.

"What will happen when I eat?" he wondered. With trembling fingers he reached out to take an apple from a bowl of fruit. As soon as he touched it, the apple turned to gold.

"What have I done?" he whispered. "If I cannot eat or drink I shall die!" He knew that he had made a terrible mistake and decided to beg

Dionysus to take back his gift. "I will go to him at once," he cried, but his decision came too late. At that very moment his daughter ran into the room.

"Stay away from me!" Midas shouted, but she took no notice. She threw her arms around him—and was turned to gold. His daughter was now a gleaming but lifeless statue. The king stared at her in horror.

"What have I done to you?" he cried, kneeling beside her. His grief was so great that nobody could console him. He hurried to the palace of Dionysus and threw himself at the god's feet.

"Forgive my stupid greed!" he begged. "Tell me what I must do to save my child. I will do anything you say."

Dionysus told him to find the river Pactolus and wash himself in its waters. Midas set off at once. He went alone and walked for many miles over rough and stony ground.

When he reached the river he found it flowing deep and strong. Midas waded straight in. He was instantly swept away by the current. When at last he managed to reach the shore, he wondered if the curse had indeed been washed from him. Looking back, he saw that the river now gleamed and sparkled in the sun. On the riverbed tiny nuggets of gold lay among the pebbles. Dionysus had spoken truthfully, and the terrible power had left him. Joyfully Midas made his way home.

As he approached the palace, Midas's daughter ran to greet him. He lifted her into his arms and carried her into the garden. Midas was overjoyed to hear her laughter once again, and he sighed happily as he breathed in the fragrance of the flowers.

"I have learned my lesson," he said softly, **H** "and I am content."

C Elements of Literature
Myth
Point out that unusual creatures play key parts in many myths. Remind students of the important role played by the mythological beasts in "The Labors of Hercules." Point out, however, that mythological creatures may also play helpful or comic roles, as Silenus does in this myth. Explain that satyrs are usually represented in myths and in art as men with small horns, pointed ears, and goat legs with hooved feet.

D Literary Connections
Another famous fictional storyteller is Scheherazade, a woman who postpones her execution by entertaining her husband with suspenseful tales night after night. One of her stories is retold on pp. 578–580. The collection of her tales is called *The Arabian Nights' Entertainment* or *A Thousand and One Nights.*

E Reading Skills and Strategies

Using Prior Knowledge
? Recalling that Midas has been described as greedy, what do you think he will wish for? Record your prediction, and compare it with what happens in the story.

F Cultural Connections
In English, the expression "the Midas touch" refers to the ability to turn any venture into a success.

G Elements of Literature
Irony
? In what ways has the king's wonderful power caused effects far different from what he expected? [He expected wealth and power, and while he is attaining wealth, he is also losing everything of deeper importance to him—the beauty of nature, food to sustain his life, and the life of his beloved daughter.]

H Critical Thinking
Hypothesizing
? Do you think it is possible that the god Dionysus planned Midas's ordeal in order to teach him a lesson? Why or why not? [Possible responses: No, Dionysus could not have predicted the wish Midas would make. Yes, Dionysus may have sent Silenus and granted Midas's wish in order to teach Midas that he should be satisfied with the blessings he already has.]

Assessing Learning

Check Test: Questions and Answers
1. Who entertains King Midas with stories? [the satyr Silenus]
2. Who grants Midas any wish he desires? [the god Dionysus]
3. What is Midas's wish? [that whatever he touches may turn to gold]
4. Why does Midas later want the wish undone? [The effects turn his food and even his daughter into lifeless metal.]

5. How does Midas rid himself of his magic powers? [He washes in the river Pactolus.]

Standardized Test Preparation
For practice with standardized test format specific to this selection, see
- *Standardized Test Preparation,* p. 84

For practice in proofreading and editing, see
- *Daily Oral Grammar,* Transparency 33

MAKING MEANINGS

First Thoughts

1. Possible responses: If I were Midas, I would have thought more before I made a wish. I was surprised when Midas's food turned into gold.

Shaping Interpretations

2. Possible responses: Midas learns that his family is more important than wealth and power. Midas learns to value other things he has taken for granted.

3. Possible response: I wish that if I *want* something to turn to gold, it will change to gold when I touch it.

4. Possible response: The gift Midas sees as a blessing turns out to be a curse that threatens his life and the life of a person he loves.

Connecting with the Text

5. Possible responses: The lesson of the story of Midas is "Think carefully before asking for unnecessary things." The lesson is "Appreciate the good things in life without being greedy for more."

Extending the Text

6. Saying that someone had a "Midas touch" would mean that the person was successful at making money. It would probably be a compliment.

MAKING MEANINGS

[respond]

First Thoughts

1. Finish these sentences:
   - If I were Midas, I . . .
   - I was surprised when . . .

[infer]

Shaping Interpretations

2. At the end of the myth, Midas says, "I have learned my lesson. . . . I am content." What lesson do you think Midas has learned? What makes him feel content?

[synthesize]

3. How would you have worded the wish for the golden touch in order to avoid Midas's problems?

[interpret]

4. In "Echo and Narcissus" (page 523) the fate of Narcissus is ironic because what he loves most—himself—causes his downfall. What **irony** do you see in Midas's story?

Connecting with the Text

[connect]

5. How would you connect the lesson in "King Midas and the Golden Touch" to life today? Look back at your notes for the word map on page 558 for ideas.

Extending the Text

[analyze]

6. What would we mean if we said someone had the "Midas touch"? Would it be a compliment? Look at your notes for the Quickwrite on page 558 for ideas.

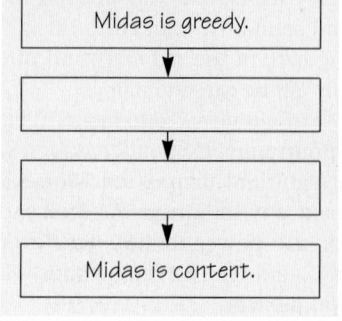

One of a pair of bracelets with ram's-head finials (c. 330–300 B.C.). Greek. Said to be from near Thessaloniki. Gold, rock crystal (8 cm wide x 7.8 cm high).

The Metropolitan Museum of Art, Harris Brisbane Dick Fund, 1937. (37.11.11-.12). Photograph © 1993 The Metropolitan Museum of Art.

Reading Check

The diagram below shows the first **cause** and the final **effect** in the tale of King Midas. Fill in the chain of events that leads from one to the other. Add as many boxes as you need.

Midas is greedy.

↓

↓

↓

Midas is content.

Reading Check
Possible answers:

- Midas is greedy.
- Midas finds the satyr Silenus.
- He returns Silenus to Dionysus.
- Dionysus offers the king "any gift."
- Midas asks Dionysus for the power to change things he touches into gold.
- When his food and drink turn to gold, he cannot eat.
- He decides to ask Dionysus to take back the golden touch.
- He accidentally turns his daughter into a gold statue.
- He begs Dionysus to help him save his daughter.
- He washes in the river Pactolus, as Dionysus tells him to do.
- The golden touch leaves him, and his daughter is restored to life.
- Midas is content.

Making the Connections

Connecting to the Theme: "Our Classical Heritage"

The popularity of the story of Midas shows the universality of its theme. Students should have encountered no difficulty in completing the "greed maps" (see Reading Skills and Strategies on p. 558). Invite students to volunteer examples they may have listed from the myths and legends of other cultures, real life, or popular media.

CHOICES: Building Your Portfolio

Writer's Notebook

1. Collecting Ideas for an Evaluation

Which myth in this collection did you like best? Take notes for an evaluation of the story, noting what you think is best about the myth's story elements—character, setting, suspense, horror, message, or ending.

Favorite Myth
Midas story—
because character
is like people today
who grab at money
and lose touch with
life's simple joys

Creative Writing

2. Solid-Gold Memories

Imagine that you are King Midas's daughter. One moment you're a happy young princess running to greet your dad. The next moment you're solid gold! Focus on what you see and feel as you are frozen into a golden statue. Then, tell how being released from this golden prison affects you. Based on your strange experience, tell what you think of the desire for wealth.

Art

3. Quick-Change Artists

Metamorphosis—a magical change in shape—is a common element in myths. Demeter, Echo, Narcissus, and Midas's daughter all go through metamorphoses. You've probably read other myths with examples of shape changing, too. Create a collage that shows some of these magical transformations. Many collages include words. You might want to add words to yours.

Drama

4. Sharing the Wealth of King Midas

"King Midas and the Golden Touch" is a story rich enough to share with audiences of all ages. Try acting out this myth for a group of younger students in your school or neighborhood. You'll need actors to play the roles of King Midas, Silenus, Midas's daughter, and Dionysus. As you work on the dialogue for your play, think of a dramatic way to show the change from girl to golden statue. After you present the play, you might want to read the myth aloud to the group or hand out a homemade picture book based on the myth.

Illustration from the *Manga* (a book of humorous sketches), vol. 10, by Katsushika Hokusai (1760–1849).

The Metropolitan Museum of Art, Rogers Fund, 1931 (JIB 81.10).

RESPONDING TO THE ART

Katsushika Hokusai (1760–1849) was a master of color woodcut prints; *ukiyoe* (paintings of everyday life); and *manga* (random sketches) like the one of a frog on this page. You can use this artwork, when appropriate, as a segue into "The Frogs Who Wished for a King" (p. 567). **Activity.** Ask students to collect other artistic representations of frogs and compare them with Hokusai's.

Grading Timesaver

Rubrics for each Choices assignment appear on p. 177 in the *Portfolio Management System.*

CHOICES: Building Your Portfolio

1. **Writer's Notebook** Remind students to save their work. They may use it as prewriting for the Writer's Workshop on pp. 582–586.
2. **Creative Writing** Advise students to decide how much background information to provide and to choose the starting point that will create the most interesting story.
3. **Art** Distribute magazines for students to use as sources of photographs for their collages. Allow students to use colored paper and pencils or other materials to enhance the photographs.
4. **Drama** Remind students that the plot and language of their plays should be simple enough for younger children to understand. Suggest that they make audiotapes or videotapes of their performances.

Using Students' Strengths

Visual Learners

As visual learners read the story, ask them to fill in the graphic organizer located in the *Graphic Organizers for Active Reading,* p. 39.

Auditory/Musical Learners

Allow students to create sound effects and music for their dramatizations of the Midas story (Choice 4). Suggest that they create a special sound effect to indicate that something Midas touches has turned to gold, such as a jingling bell. The music should reflect the changes in the king's mood from scene to scene.

LANGUAGE LINK

Ask students to look through recent writing assignments for passages that could be made more clear or more interesting with the addition of allusions. Tell students that their allusions do not have to be only to classical mythology.

Try It Out
Answers

1. Narcissus loved his own appearance; the allusion means Rod is vain.
2. Persephone spends part of every year in Hades; the allusion compares the boarding school to the underworld.
3. The underworld is gloomy and sad; the allusion suggests that the station becomes foreboding.
4. Orpheus could create enchanting music; the allusion suggests that the conductor's skill seems magical.

VOCABULARY
Possible Answers

Students should show knowledge of the special talents of particular characters. Sample responses follow.

1. The Orpheum
2. Neptune's Nets
3. Vulcan's Forge
4. Dear Aphrodite
5. Wings of Mercury
6. Zeus's Bolt
7. Demeter's Choice
8. The Atheneum
9. Pool of Narcissus
10. Dionysus' Vineyard

Resources

Language
- *Grammar and Language Links,* p. 57

LANGUAGE LINK | MINI-LESSON |

Style: Allusions

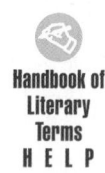

Handbook of Literary Terms HELP

See Allusion.

An **allusion** is a reference to a work of literature or to an actual event, person, or place. When a speaker or writer makes an allusion, he or she expects the audience to recognize the reference and understand its meaning. For example, if you were to say that a stockbroker has "the golden touch," you would expect people to know you are alluding to the Midas myth. If you described cleaning up a flooded basement as "a herculean effort," you would expect people to know you are alluding to those enormous problems Hercules had to tackle. As you can see, a simple allusion can say a great deal in very few words.

Try It Out

For each sentence, identify the allusion to mythology and explain its meaning. Research any allusions you don't recognize.

1. Rod spends thirty minutes combing his hair every morning; he must think he's Narcissus.
2. I feel sorry for Teresa, packed off to boarding school for half the year like poor Persephone.
3. When the power failed, the subway station became a dark and dismal underworld.
4. A modern-day Orpheus, the new conductor coaxes marvelous melodies from the town orchestra.

VOCABULARY | HOW TO OWN A WORD |

Words from Mythology: Making Up Names

People over the ages have often turned to the ancient myths when they've wanted to name something new (such as a planet, a missile, a business, a disease). See if you can use your knowledge of the myths and the chart of gods and goddesses on page 497 to make up imaginative names for these things:

1. a disco
2. a fishery
3. a sheet-metal shop
4. a column written to advise the lovelorn
5. a messenger service
6. a guided missile or bomber
7. a cereal
8. a high school
9. a health club or spa
10. a winery

564 OUR CLASSICAL HERITAGE

Language Link Quick Check

Name a Greek god or goddess with whom each of the people described below could be associated. Use the chart on p. 497, and draw on information from the myths in this collection. You may use the Roman or the Greek name of the god or goddess.

1. A person who loves the ocean. [Neptune, Poseidon]
2. A person who is very powerful. [Jupiter, Zeus]
3. A person who grows her own food. [Ceres, Demeter]
4. A person who relays messages. [Mercury, Hermes]
5. A person who is hardhearted, sad, and gloomy. [Pluto, Hades]

Elements of Literature

OBJECTIVES
1. Read and understand the essay
2. Identify fable and its elements
3. Make connections across cultures

FABLES: Teaching Stories *by* Virginia Hamilton

Very, very brief stories told to teach practical lessons about life are called **fables.** The word comes from the Latin *fabula,* which means "a telling."

The great teller of fables was Aesop, who is thought to have been an African held as a slave in Greece. (According to some authorities, his name comes from the Greek word *ethiope,* meaning "sunburned face.") Aesop lived in the sixth century B.C. He certainly had an extraordinary imagination. Aesop created tales, usually used for political purposes, in which animals behaved like human beings. In Aesop's fables, animals are good and bad, smart and stupid. Some people say that Aesop won his freedom because he provided so many sarcastic stories for his master to use against political opponents.

Aesop told his fables aloud. Other people repeated what they'd heard him tell, and in that way his fables survived over centuries. A version of Aesop's fables was written down by a Greek scribe, but for a thousand years the manuscript was lost. Not until 1844 was a copy found—in a monastery.

The fable's very practical lesson is called a **moral.** Aesop let his listeners guess at his stories' morals, but today the morals are usually written out at the ends of the stories. "Don't count your chickens before they're hatched" is a famous moral that follows the fable "The Maid and the Pail of Milk." In this fable (which does not have animal characters), a girl carrying a pail of milk on her head dreams about all the money and fine clothes she will get from the sale of the milk. She forgets for a moment about the pail, tosses her head, and all the milk spills.

Though Aesop is the most famous fabulist in the West, fables were being told in India and China many years before Aesop's time. Telling teaching stories seems to be part of human nature.

The Crane King eating the frogs who asked for a king, in Aesop's fable of the same name. Wood engraving after Gustave Doré (1832–1883).
The Granger Collection, New York.

ELEMENTS OF LITERATURE: FABLES 565

Resources

Elements of Literature
Fables
For additional instruction on fables, see *Literary Elements:*
• Transparency 10
Assessment
Formal Assessment
• Literary Elements Test, p. 115

Elements of Literature

Up to this point in the collection, students have read myths from ancient Greece and Rome. This feature extends their exploration of our classical heritage to the fables of Aesop.
Mini-Lesson:
Fables
Ask students to name any fables they have already read or heard, and list the titles on the board. Ask the class to state the morals associated with each of the fables, and write the morals next to the titles on the board.
Applying the Element
Ask students to read the titles of the fables on pp. 567–574 and to predict morals for the fables, based on the titles. After students have read the fables, have them return to their notes to compare the morals they predicted with the actual morals at the ends of the fables.

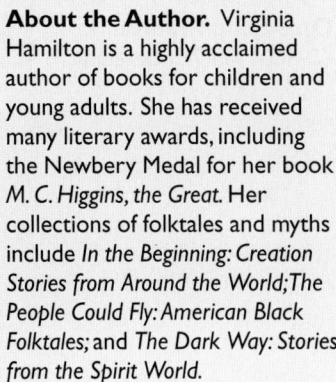

BROWSING IN THE FILES

About the Author. Virginia Hamilton is a highly acclaimed author of books for children and young adults. She has received many literary awards, including the Newbery Medal for her book *M. C. Higgins, the Great.* Her collections of folktales and myths include *In the Beginning: Creation Stories from Around the World; The People Could Fly: American Black Folktales;* and *The Dark Way: Stories from the Spirit World.*

Reaching All Students

Struggling Readers
Help students to recall some of the fables they already know by showing them illustrations of fables by an artist such as Arthur Rackham. Give students a title or moral, and ask them to select the illustration that corresponds to it, or show an illustration, and ask students to guess the title and moral of the fable it depicts.

Advanced Learners
While the tradition of fables in the West begins with Aesop, many equally entertaining fables originated in non-Western cultures or were created by later Western storytellers who followed in the tradition of Aesop. Ask each student to locate a fable by a storyteller other than Aesop, to bring it to class, and to share it by reading it aloud.

OBJECTIVES
Frogs / Fox and Grapes / Town Mouse . . . Country Mouse / Belling the Cat
1. Read and interpret the fables
2. Identify fable and state the moral of each fable
3. Identify purposes of texts
4. Express understanding through evaluation and creative writing or speaking/storytelling
5. Distinguish between *bad* and *badly*
6. Create similes

SKILLS
Literary
- Identify fable and state the moral of each fable

Reading
- Identify purposes of texts

Writing
- Write notes on the usefulness of the fables
- Write a short-short animal fable

Speaking/Listening
- Tell a fable to children

Grammar/Language
- Distinguish between *bad* and *badly*

Viewing/Representing
- Compare illustrations (ATE)
- Interpret expression in an illustration (ATE)

Planning

- **Block Schedule**
  Block Scheduling Lesson Plans with Pacing Guide

- **Traditional Schedule**
  Lesson Plans Including Strategies for English-Language Learners

- **One-Stop Planner**
  CD-ROM with Test Generator

Before You Read

AESOP'S FABLES

Make the Connection

Words to Live By

Deep down people haven't changed much over the years. These next four stories were told more than 2,500 years ago. Even so, the kinds of behavior they warn against will be familiar to you today. For example, can you think of a situation when people

- act jealously and meanly when something good happens to someone else?
- are never satisfied with the simple joys of life?
- always claim to know what should be done but never risk anything to do it?

Quickwrite

Jot down some notes about your experiences with people who behave in one or more of the ways just described. Have you ever found yourself acting like this?

Elements of Literature

Fable

A **fable** is a one-idea story. At the end it gives a single clear **moral,** or lesson, about what to do—or not to do—to succeed in life. Characters in fables are usually animals who act and talk like human beings.

> **A fable** is a brief story in prose or verse that teaches a moral or gives a practical lesson about how to get along in life.
>
> *For more on Fable, see page 565 and the Handbook of Literary Terms.*

Reading Skills and Strategies

Identifying a Text's Purposes: Finding More than One

These short tales have several **purposes:**

- to **entertain,** using animals that talk and act like human beings as characters

- to **inform** by teaching important lessons about life

- to **influence** people or **persuade** them to change their behavior

More than 2,500 years ago, the leaders of ancient Greece used **fables** like the ones here by Aesop to support their ideas in speeches and debates. They hoped that their audiences would relate the messages of the fables to the current political situation.

go.hrw.com
LE0 7-7

566 OUR CLASSICAL HERITAGE

Resources: Print and Media

Reading
- *Reading Skills and Strategies*
  Selection Skill Lesson, p. 138
- *Graphic Organizers for Active Reading,* p. 40
- *Audio CD Library*
  Disc 14, Tracks 3–7

Elements of Literature
- *Literary Elements*
  Transparency 10
  Worksheet, p. 31

Writing and Language
- *Daily Oral Grammar,* Transparency 34
- *Grammar and Language Links,* Worksheet, p. 59
- *Language Workshop CD-ROM*

Assessment
- *Formal Assessment,* p. 111
- *Portfolio Management System,* p. 178
- *Test Generator (One-Stop Planner CD-ROM)*

Internet
- go.hrw.com (keyword: LE0 7-7)

The Frogs Who Wished for a King

Aesop

The Frogs were tired of governing themselves. They had so much freedom that it had spoiled them, and they did nothing but sit around croaking in a bored manner and wishing for a government that could entertain them with the pomp and display of royalty and rule them in a way to make them know they were being ruled. No milk-and-water government for them, they declared. So they sent a petition to Jupiter asking for a king. **(A)**

Jupiter saw what simple and foolish creatures they were, but to keep them quiet and make them think they had a king, he threw down a huge log, which fell into the water with a great splash. The Frogs hid themselves among the reeds and grasses, thinking the new king to be some fearful giant. But they soon discovered how tame and peaceable King Log was. In a short time the younger Frogs were using him for a diving platform, while the older Frogs made him a meeting place, where they complained loudly to Jupiter about the government. **(B)**

To teach the Frogs a lesson, the ruler of the gods now sent a Crane to be king of Frogland. The Crane proved to be a very different sort of king from old King Log. He gobbled up the poor Frogs right and left and they soon saw what fools they had been. In mournful croaks they begged Jupiter to take away the cruel tyrant before they should all be destroyed.

"How now!" cried Jupiter. "Are you not yet content? You have what you asked for, and so you have only yourselves to blame for your misfortunes." **(C)**

Be sure you can better your condition before you seek to change.

AESOP'S FABLES 567

Summary ■

A group of frogs, bored with their freedom, long for a government that imposes order on them. They petition Jupiter for a king. He finds the request foolish but indulges them by hurling down into the water a huge log, which the frogs take as their ruler. At length, finding King Log too placid, they complain again. Jupiter teaches them a lesson by sending as their next ruler a crane who begins to devour them. Besieged by the survivors with pleas for release from this tyrant, Jupiter reminds the frogs that their own discontent caused their woes. **Moral:** *Be sure you can better your condition before you seek to change.*

Resources

Listening
Audio CD Library
A reading of Aesop's fables is provided in the *Audio CD Library*:
• Disc 14, Tracks 3–7

Ⓐ English Language Learners
Interpreting Idiom
Show students how to figure out the meaning of "milk-and-water government" by noting the contrasting context clues in the paragraph. Point out the similarity to the expression *watered down*. Ask students to suggest a one-word synonym for *milk-and-water*. [weak]

Ⓑ Reading Skills and Strategies
Identifying a Text's Purposes
❓ Which purpose is strongest here— to entertain, to inform, or to persuade? [Most students will find the frogs' treatment of King Log and their renewed complaints to Jupiter entertaining.]

Ⓒ Elements of Literature
Fable
❓ How are the frogs in this fable and the lesson they learn similar to King Midas and the lesson he learns? [Both get into trouble by being discontent and asking for something that turns out to be bad for them. Both learn the same lesson: Enjoy what you have.]

Reaching All Students

Struggling Readers
Identifying a Text's Purpose was introduced on p. 566. For a lesson directly tied to this selection that teaches students to identify purpose by using a strategy called Text Reformulation, see the *Reading Skills and Strategies* binder:
• Selection Skill Lesson, p. 138

English Language Learners
Indicate that some fables in the collection illustrate English expressions:
• "Sour grapes" ("The Fox and the Grapes," p. 568)
• "Easier said than done" ("Belling the Cat," p. 572)
• "To cry wolf" ("The Boy and the Wolf," p. 574)
As students read each fable, ask them to write a short explanation of the expression.

Summary ■

A fox spots a bunch of succulent grapes hanging invitingly from a tree. He jumps at them but falls short. After several more futile and increasingly frustrating attempts, the fox stalks off, declaring that the grapes must have been sour anyway. **Moral:** *There are many who pretend to despise and belittle that which is beyond their reach.*

Ⓐ Elements of Literature

Characterization

? What human traits does the fox exhibit? [He is too proud to admit he can't accomplish something. He gives himself a rationale to explain why it wasn't a good idea anyway.]

Ⓑ Elements of Literature

Fable

? Point out that there is no rule saying a fable can have only one moral, and even the same moral may be phrased in many different ways. How might this moral be rephrased? [Possible response: Don't mock what you can't have.] What other morals can you draw from the fable? [Possible responses: Think before you act. Choose realistic goals. Don't attempt the impossible.]

The Fox and the Grapes

Aesop

A Fox one day spied a beautiful bunch of ripe grapes hanging from a vine trained along the branches of a tree. The grapes seemed ready to burst with juice, and the Fox's mouth watered as he gazed longingly at them.

The bunch hung from a high branch, and the Fox had to jump for it. The first time he jumped he missed it by a long way. So he walked off a short distance and took a running leap at it, only to fall short once more. Again and again he tried, but in vain.

Now he sat down and looked at the grapes in disgust.

Ⓐ "What a fool I am," he said. "Here I am wearing myself out to get a bunch of sour grapes that are not worth gaping for."

And off he walked very, very scornfully.

Ⓑ *There are many who pretend to despise and belittle that which is beyond their reach.*

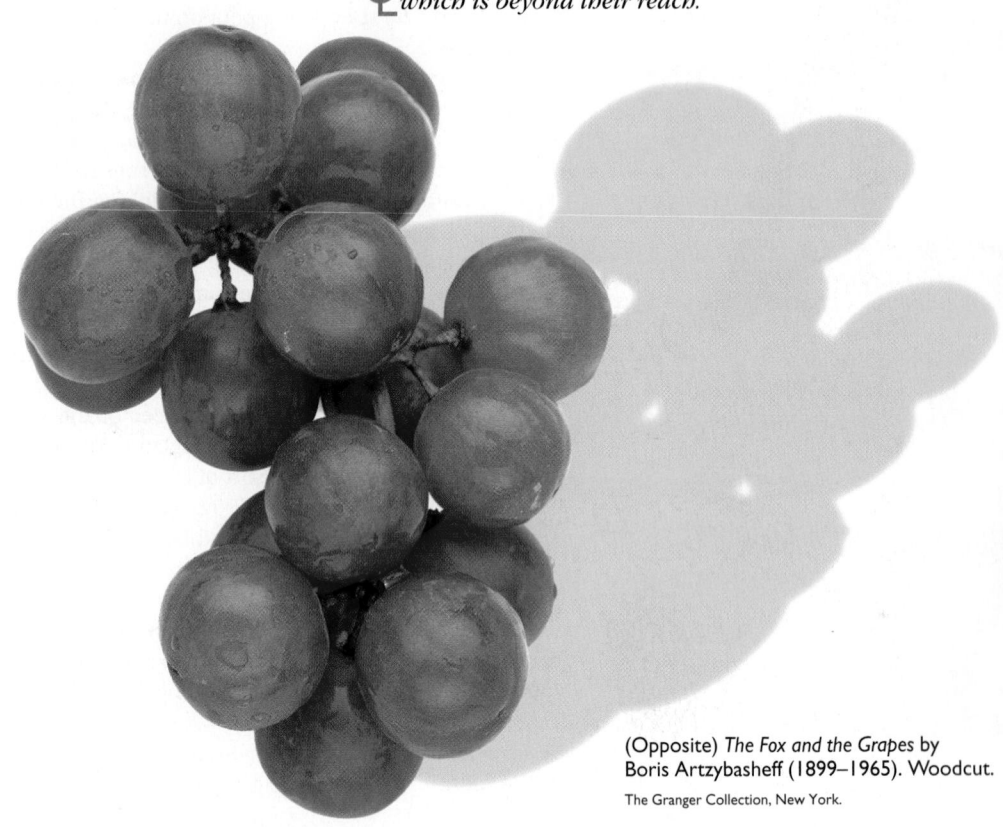

(Opposite) *The Fox and the Grapes* by Boris Artzybasheff (1899–1965). Woodcut.
The Granger Collection, New York.

568 OUR CLASSICAL HERITAGE

Getting Students Involved

Cooperative Learning

Fabulous Theater. The fables in this cluster are rich in images that students can adapt into sound effects and extra dialogue for a Reader's Theater or Radio Drama version of the fable. Divide students into four groups, one for each of Aesop's fables, making sure to include both English language learners and English proficient students in each group. Assign each group one fable. Their task is to create and perform a script, using cues in the story to make notations for sounds or voices to enrich their version. Make sure each student in the group is responsible for some aspect of the production and performance, such as writing, providing sound effects, or serving as one of the voices. Make an audiocassette recorder available so that groups can capture their performance for later sharing with the class.

Using Students' Strengths

Visual Learners
Before students read, ask them to preview the illustrations for all of the fables. Then divide the students into pairs. Give pairs some time to brainstorm ideas for stories based on the illustrations. After they have read the fables, ask them to compare the fables with their own story ideas. Do they feel that their own ideas better fit any of the illustrations? Why?

Verbal Learners
Group students in threes and ask them to choose one of the fables to rewrite as a poem, using "The Boy and the Wolf" on p. 574 as a model. Here is an example:
Some frogs who lived inside a bog
Wanted a king but got a log.
Their words roared upward like a train
Till Jupiter sent them a hungry crane.

Logical/Mathematical Learners
After students have read the fables, ask them to work together to create measured lists of ingredients for a good fable. The ingredients should include such things as "animal characters," "short moral," "humor," and "good title." The quantities should be expressed proportionally as 1, 2, 3, or 4 parts per ingredient. The total "parts" should not exceed twelve. [Possible response: 4 parts animal characters, 4 parts good moral, 2 parts humor, 2 parts good title.]

Summary ▪

A Town Mouse visits her relative, a Country Mouse who lives simply and eats sparingly. Fascinated by the Town Mouse's tales of lavish urban life, the Country Mouse accepts an invitation to visit the city. In the mansion where the Town Mouse resides, an opulent feast is laid out, but before the mice can sample it, a Cat mews menacingly at the door. The mice scurry to a hiding place, and when the Cat is followed by the House Dog, the Country Mouse makes haste to return to her simple rural abode. **Moral:** *Poverty with security is better than plenty in the midst of fear and uncertainty.*

Ⓐ **Reading Skills and Strategies**
Using Context Clues
❓ What context clues suggest the meaning of the word *sparingly*? [The phrase "nibbling a little of this and a little of that" illustrates its meaning.]

Ⓑ **Reading Skills and Strategies**
Drawing Conclusions
❓ Why does the Country Mouse dream about the "delights of city life" after listening to her relative? [Possible response: The Town Mouse describes the city in a way that makes it sound like a beautiful and wondrous place to live.]

The Town Mouse and the Country Mouse

Aesop

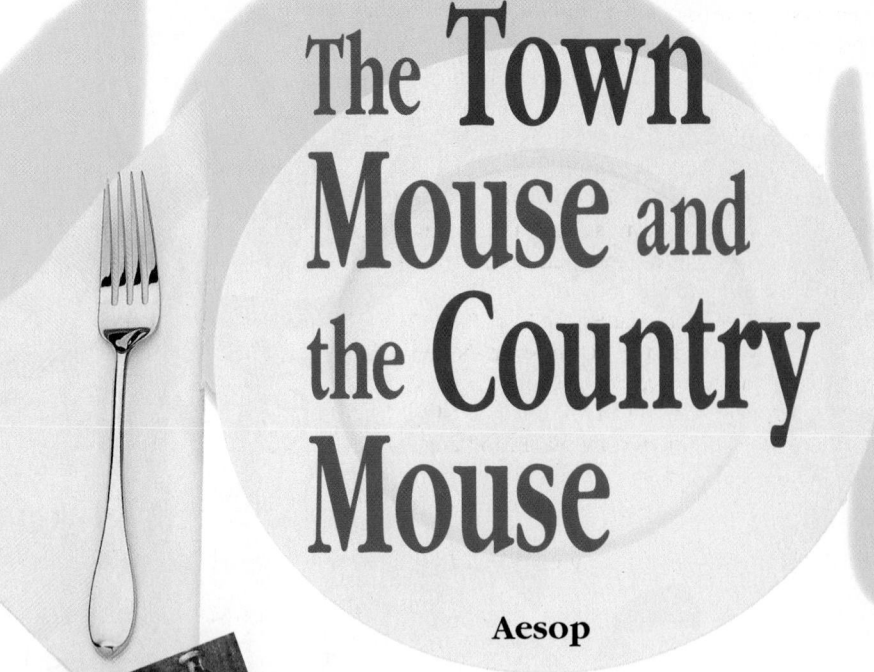

Ⓐ Town Mouse once visited a relative who lived in the country. For lunch the Country Mouse served wheat stalks, roots, and acorns, with a dash of cold water for drink. The Town Mouse ate very sparingly, nibbling a little of this and a little of that, and by her manner making it very plain that she ate the simple food only to be polite.

After the meal the friends had a long talk, or rather the Town Mouse talked about her life in the city while the Country Mouse listened. They then went to bed in a cozy nest in the hedgerow[1] and slept in quiet and comfort until morning. In her sleep the Country Mouse dreamed she was a Town Mouse with all the luxuries and delights of city life that her friend had described for her. So the next day when the Town Mouse asked the Country Mouse to go home with her to the city, she gladly said yes.

1. **hedgerow:** row of bushes forming a hedge.

The Town Mouse and the Country Mouse, illustration by Milo Winter.
The Granger Collection, New York.

570 OUR CLASSICAL HERITAGE

Getting Students Involved

Cooperative Learning
Comic Strips. The brevity of the fables and their use of animal characters make them naturals for translation to comic strips. Divide the class into groups of three to five students, and have each group choose one fable. Ask students to agree on who is responsible for overall planning, who will draw the pictures, and who will write the dialogue for a comic strip based on their fable. Suggest that they review one or more of "The Twelve Tasks of Heracles" on pp. 554–557 as a model, or suggest they consult models from a Sunday newspaper. Display students' finished strips in the classroom.

When they reached the mansion in which the Town Mouse lived, they found on the table in the dining room the leavings of a very fine banquet. There were sweetmeats[2] and jellies, pastries, delicious cheeses—indeed, the most tempting foods that a Mouse can imagine. But just as the Country Mouse was about to nibble a dainty bit of pastry, she heard a Cat mew loudly and scratch at the door. In great fear the Mice scurried to a hiding place, where they lay quite still for a long time, hardly daring to breathe. When at last they ventured back to the feast, the door opened suddenly and in came the servants to clear the table, followed by the House Dog.

The Country Mouse stopped in the Town Mouse's den only long enough to pick up her carpet bag and umbrella.

"You may have luxuries and dainties that I have not," she said as she hurried away, "but I prefer my plain food and simple life in the country with the peace and security that go with it."

Poverty with security is better than plenty in the midst of fear and uncertainty.

2. **sweetmeats:** sweets or candies.

"Should I Never Have Tried to Do Something Risky?"

After you read, decide whether you prefer the lesson taught in the traditional moral for this fable: *Better to have bread and water in peace than a banquet in fear.* Does the fable teach that we should be satisfied with little because of the risks we take if we try for more? Does it mean to say we should never try to get what we want for fear of failure? I myself risked leaving the safety of my Ohio village in order to pursue an uncertain career in New York City. Should I never have tried to do something risky? Could this moral also fit the fable: *Nothing ventured, nothing gained?*

—Virginia Hamilton

The Town Mouse and the Country Mouse, illustration by Charles James Folkard.
The Granger Collection, New York.

C Reading Skills and Strategies

Identifying a Text's Purposes

❓ Which details strike you as amusing? [Possible response: It's funny to imagine the mice scurrying away from their feast, and to see how fast the Country Mouse changes her mind about the delights of the city.] Which detail reminds you of human methods of persuasion? [The City Mouse never mentions the dangerous Cat and Dog. Often when people want to sell you on going somewhere or doing something new, they never mention the drawbacks.]

D Critical Thinking

Extending the Text

❓ Remind the class that even though the Town Mouse thinks the Country Mouse lives in poverty, the Country Mouse actually has everything she needs. Do you think it is better to live a simple life without having to worry about hazards or to live a life of luxury while struggling with constant difficulties? [Responses will vary. Ask students to give the reasons for their opinions.]

Responding to the Quotation

Ask students to read and discuss the boxed quotation by Virginia Hamilton. How do they answer her final question? Have them explain their reasoning.

AESOP'S FABLES **571**

Professional Notes

Enhancing Discussion

To help students feel comfortable when they speak in class, try to start class discussions with prompts that are open-ended. A good open-ended prompt about the fables might be: "If you could make one of the fables into a movie, which one would you choose? Why?" Writing a question on the board before the discussion will ensure that all students have time to think about responses before the discussion begins.

Summary ▪

A group of mice convene to discuss ways of defending themselves against their enemy, the Cat. A young mouse proposes hanging a bell around the cat's neck, an idea that the others endorse enthusiastically until an old mouse calls attention to an insurmountable obstacle: Who will place the bell on the Cat? **Moral:** *It is one thing to say that something should be done, but quite a different matter to do it.*

Ⓐ Critical Thinking
Making Connections
❓ What solution might the Country Mouse from the previous fable suggest to these mice? Remember her personality traits. [Possible response: She would probably suggest that they all move away from the Cat or simplify their lives by avoiding activities that bring them into the Cat's vicinity.]

Ⓑ Critical Thinking
Analyzing Stereotypes
❓ Why do you think the author makes a point of stating that the mouse who suggests the plan is "very young," while the mouse who points out its flaw is "old"? [The author seems to think that young people are foolish and rash and that old people are sensible and wise.] How do you feel about these concepts of youth and age? [Possible responses: On the whole, they are fairly accurate. You can't generalize; some young people are wise, and some old people are foolish.]

Ⓒ Elements of Literature
Fable
❓ What is the more common way of expressing this moral in English? ["Easier said than done."]

Responding to the Quotation

Ask students to read the boxed quotation by Virginia Hamilton and to note her final question. Does the fable remind them of any experiences they are willing to share? Does it connect with any of the comments they jotted down in their Quickwrite (p. 566)?

Belling the Cat

Aesop

(Opposite) *The Favorite Cat* by Nathaniel Currier (1813–1888). Lithograph, hand-colored (12⅛" high x 8¾" wide).

The Metropolitan Museum of Art, Bequest of Adele S. Colgate, 1962. (63.550.159). Photograph © 1983 The Metropolitan Museum of Art.

Ⓐ The Mice once called a meeting to decide on a plan to free themselves of their enemy, the Cat. At least they wished to find some way of knowing when she was coming so they might have time to run away. Indeed, something had to be done, for they lived in such constant fear of her claws that they hardly dared stir from their dens by night or day.

Many plans were discussed, but none of them was thought good enough. At last a very young Mouse got up and said:

"I have a plan that seems very simple, but I know it will be successful. All we have to do is to hang a bell about the Cat's neck. When we hear the bell ringing, we will know imme-Ⓑ diately that our enemy is coming."

All the Mice were much surprised that they had not thought of such a plan before. But in the midst of the rejoicing over their good fortune, an old Mouse arose and said:

"I will say that the plan of the young Mouse is very good. But let me ask one question: Who will bell the Cat?"

Ⓒ *It is one thing to say that something should be done, but quite a different matter to do it.*

"I Thought Belling Was the Name of the Cat"

When I was a child and saw the name of this fable, I thought Belling was the name of the cat. The young mouse of this fable has an idea that is difficult to execute. He reminds me of something to do with my own writing. It takes me no time at all to get an idea for a book. "I'm going to write a mystery!" I once told myself. In less than ten minutes, I had "imagined" the whole story. But it took me more than a year actually to write the mystery novel that came to be entitled *The House of Dies Drear.* I know from experience how hard it is to put words down on paper so that they read well and tell a good story, too. Now when I get an idea, I think of the young mouse of this fable. I think about what I've learned, and a little voice in my ear cautions, "Easier said than done!"

After you read the fable, see if it reminds you of any experiences of your own.

—Virginia Hamilton

Making the Connections

Connecting to the Theme: "Our Classical Heritage"
The fable-telling tradition begun by Aesop continued in the West in succeeding centuries. Interested students may wish to research the role of one of the following in helping to ensure that the tradition continued: Phaedrus, Babrius, Lucian, Marie de France, Christine de Pisan, Geoffrey Chaucer, Jean de La Fontaine, Kenneth Grahame, Beatrix Potter.

Cultural Connections
Suggest that students check school and local libraries for books containing animal stories from other cultures. One good source from India is the *Panchatantra,* a collection of fables that dates back to the second century B.C. or later. Like European fables, these stories can be entertaining as well as instructive. Have students bring in the books they find, and ask them to read passages aloud. Discuss the cross-cultural similarities students find.

THE FAVORITE CAT.

Lith & Pub by N. Currier, 2 Spruce St. N.Y.

Assessing Learning

Observation Assessment

Place check marks on a list like the following to informally assess students' responses to the fables.

_____ Enjoys and becomes involved in fables
_____ Makes personal and extended connections to the fables
_____ Gets beyond the "I like/dislike this story" stage of appreciation
_____ Shows an understanding of possible multiple meanings of fables

Check Test: Short Answer

1. When the frogs want a king, what do they receive as their first king? [a huge log]
2. Why can't the fox get the grapes? [They're too high.]
3. Which mouse, the Town Mouse or the Country Mouse, lives in a mansion? [the Town Mouse]
4. Which mouse asks who is actually going to bell a cat? [an old mouse]

Standardized Test Preparation

For practice in proofreading and editing, see
• *Daily Oral Grammar,* Transparency 34

T573

Connections

Ⓐ Literary Connections

Louis Untermeyer (1885–1977) was an American poet and editor of anthologies such as *Treasury of Great Poems* (1955) and *Treasury of Great Humor* (1972). Explain that Untermeyer based his poem on Aesop's fable "The Boy Who Cried Wolf."

Ⓑ Reading Skills and Strategies

Making Inferences

❓ Why does the boy cry "Wolf!" in ll. 4 and 7? [He hopes that in hunting for the wolves, the neighbors will find his lost lambs.] Why does no one listen to him the evening a wolf really appears? [He has lied too often to be believed.]

Ⓒ Reading Skills and Strategies

Identifying a Text's Purposes

❓ In Untermeyer's rhymed version of Aesop's story, what purposes does he aim to accomplish—entertaining, informing, or influencing? How can you tell? [Possible response: He tries to entertain and to inform by teaching. The rhyme pattern and the archaic word *forsooth* are humorous, but the moral is still a serious lesson about life.]

MEET THE WRITER

A Figure of Fable

Aesop (sixth century B.C.) is said to have been born in Africa, but little is known about his life. Early writers of history agree that he was a slave in Greece and that he was eventually given his freedom. They also say that Aesop met a violent death, perhaps because his sarcastic stories had insulted someone very powerful. Pictures of Aesop show him with a deformed back. Aesop, who became known as one of the Seven Wise Men of Greece, was famous for his clever fables.

Aesop, with figures from his fables. Printed in Augsburg, Bavaria, in 1498 by Johann Schonsperger.

More Fabulous Fables

You can find more of Aesop's fables in many collections, usually titled *Aesop's Fables*.

Connections   A POEM

The Boy and the Wolf

Ⓐ Louis Untermeyer

A boy employed to guard the sheep
Despised his work. He liked to sleep.
And when a lamb was lost, he'd shout,
"Wolf! Wolf! The wolves are all about!"

5 Ⓑ The neighbors searched from noon till nine,
But of the beast there was no sign,
Yet "Wolf!" he cried next morning when
The villagers came out again.

One evening around six o'clock
10 A real wolf fell upon the flock.

"Wolf!" yelled the boy. "A wolf indeed!"
But no one paid him any heed.

Although he screamed to wake the dead,
"He's fooled us every time," they said,
15 And let the hungry wolf enjoy
Ⓒ His feast of mutton, lamb—and boy.

The moral's this: The man who's wise
Does not defend himself with lies.
Liars are not believed, forsooth,°
20 Even when liars tell the truth.

19. forsooth: old-fashioned word meaning "truly."

Connecting Across Texts

Connecting with Aesop's Fables

Read aloud to the class the four morals that conclude the fables on pp. 567–572. Then, divide the class into pairs and ask each set of partners to write a similar message for Untermeyer's poem. After students have finished, ask volunteers to read their morals aloud. Discuss the similarities and differences between students' sentences, and point out the possibility of different interpretations.

After the discussion, allow a few minutes for students to write journal entries reflecting on what they have learned from Untermeyer's poem and from the discussion.

MAKING MEANINGS

First Thoughts

[apply]
1. How could the message in each fable be applied to life today? Refer to your notes for the Quickwrite on page 566 for some ideas.

Shaping Interpretations

[interpret]
2. Suppose you substituted humans for the frogs who wanted a king. What kind of political situation might you be talking about?

[connect]
3. Give an example of someone who shows a "sour grapes" attitude. Your example can be real or made up.

[apply]
4. To what situations in world politics could you apply the moral in "Belling the Cat"?

[analyze]
5. What kinds of situations might the wolf in "The Boy and the Wolf" represent (see **Connections** on page 574)?

Connecting with the Text

[evaluate]
6. In your opinion, which of these fables teaches the most important lesson? Explain your evaluation.

Extending the Text

[apply]
7. Decide which fables might apply in each of these present-day situations. Be ready to give your reasons.

   a. When he doesn't make the team, a boy decides he doesn't like baseball.

   b. Since her parents suspect she is only pretending to be sick again, a girl who actually doesn't feel well is told to go to school.

   c. A family moves into a bigger and better house and then has trouble paying for it.

   d. Bored with his old job, a man finds a new one but soon learns that his boss is hard to please.

Challenging the Text

[evaluate]
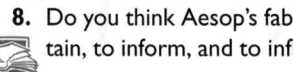
8. Do you think Aesop's fables still fulfill all three **purposes** today—to entertain, to inform, and to influence or persuade?

Reading Check

In your own words, state the **moral** of each fable. State each moral as if you were giving advice to a friend.

a. "The Frogs Who Wished for a King"
Moral:

b. "The Fox and the Grapes"
Moral:

c. "The Town Mouse and the Country Mouse"
Moral:

d. "Belling the Cat"
Moral:

e. "The Boy and the Wolf"
Moral:

MAKING MEANINGS

First Thoughts

1. Student responses should reflect an understanding of the moral of each fable.

Shaping Interpretations

2. Possible response: A democracy that allows a tyrant to take over.
3. Possible response: A child who, after being unable to get a toy to work, decides he or she doesn't want to play with it anyway.
4. The moral could be applied to any situation in which people offer solutions that will not achieve their goal or are impossible to implement, such as selling all of the world's great art to eliminate hunger.
5. Possible responses: The wolf may represent danger; the story could represent any situation in which people have heard false alarms so often that they don't believe a real alarm when they hear it.

Connecting with the Text

6. Remind students that their explanations should include details from the fables they choose.

Extending the Text

7. a. "The Fox and the Grapes"
   b. "The Boy and the Wolf"
   c. "The Town Mouse and the Country Mouse"
   d. "The Frogs Who Wished for a King"

Challenging the Text

8. Possible response: Yes, the fables entertain through funny characters and situations; inform by teaching lessons that are still important; and persuade by showing how foolish a certain attitude or way of behaving really is.

Reading Check
Possible answers:

a. Look before you leap. Think before you speak.
b. Don't say something is worthless just because you can't have it. Don't fool yourself about your desires.
c. A simple, peaceful life is better than a luxurious, dangerous life. Security is more important than adventure.
d. Get real. Easier said than done.
e. If you lie, nobody will trust you when you need someone to listen. Lies backfire.

Rubrics for each Choices assignment appear on p. 178 in the *Portfolio Management System.*

CHOICES:
Building Your Portfolio

1. **Writer's Notebook** Remind students to save their work. They may use it as prewriting for the Writer's Workshop on p. 582.
2. **Creative Writing** Discuss the meaning of each of the lessons with the class before students write their stories. Ask students which animals could be used to illustrate the lessons. It may benefit some students first to meet in threes to brainstorm ideas for completing the chart given in the pupil edition. After they have completed the chart, they can reread the opening sentence of each of the fables, and model their own opening sentence on one of them.
3. **Speaking/Storytelling** Since most of the fables are written in a terse style, allow students to embellish their oral versions with their own comic additions or with modern allusions.

CHOICES: Building Your Portfolio

Writer's Notebook

1. Collecting Ideas for an Evaluation

Write notes on what you think about Aesop's fables. Include your opinions about whether or not the tales are still useful for teaching lessons today.

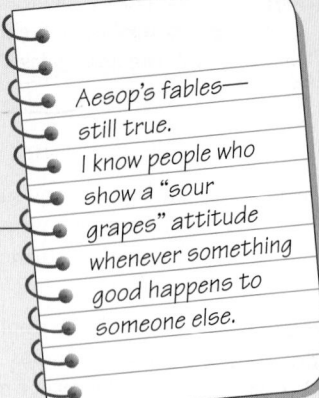

Aesop's fables—still true. I know people who show a "sour grapes" attitude whenever something good happens to someone else.

Creative Writing

2. A Fable for Our Time

Write a short-short animal story that could teach one of these lessons:

- Kindness is never wasted.
- The grass is always greener on the other side of the fence.
- It's best not to want what you can't have.

You might first jot down some ideas in a chart like this one:

Moral	
Animal characters	
Their problem	
What happens	

Speaking/Storytelling

3. A Telling Tale

Aesop's fables weren't meant to be read: Aesop told his stories aloud when they fitted a particular situation. Just like telling a joke, telling a fable requires planning and skill. Pick one of the fables to share. Get to know the fable so well that you can tell it in your own words as if you were making it up on the spot. Tell the fable to a child or a group of children.

FABLE XCIII.

THE FOX AND THE GRAPES.

The Fox and the Grapes (1879), illustration by Herrick. Engraving.

Professional Notes

Storytelling Tips

Give students the following list of suggestions to help them complete the storytelling assignment for Choice 3.

- Wait to begin telling the story until all of your listeners are quiet and looking at you.
- Use pauses to emphasize the parts of the story that you think need to be stressed.
- Adjust the volume of your voice to fit changes in the mood or tone of the story.
- Change your voice to fit the character who is speaking in the story.

GRAMMAR LINK   MINI-LESSON

Language Handbook HELP

See Glossary of Usage: bad, badly, page 785.

Technology HELP

See Language Workshop CD-ROM. Key word entry: bad, badly.

Bad or Badly?

Sometimes writers aren't sure whether to use *bad* or *badly*. *Bad* is an adjective. Use it to modify nouns and pronouns.

> The foolish frogs thought they had a bad government.

Badly is an adverb. Use it to modify verbs.

> The crane king treated the frogs badly.

Verbs that refer to the senses—like *feel, smell, taste,* and *sound*—are often followed by an adjective (not an adverb) that modifies their subject. It is correct to write *feel bad, smell bad,* and so on.

> The fox said that the grapes would taste bad.

> **Try It Out**
>
> Choose the correct word from the underlined pair in each sentence.
>
> 1. The frogs of Frogland misjudged their situation bad/badly.
> 2. The Town Mouse thought her country cousin's food tasted bad/badly.
> 3. For the Country Mouse, living in a house with a cat was a bad/badly idea.
> 4. The young mouse's plan to bell the cat wasn't bad/badly; it was just impractical.
> 5. The boy acted bad/badly when he cried "Wolf" for no reason.

VOCABULARY   HOW TO OWN A WORD

ANIMALS
a bird
a mule
a kitten
a pig
a snail
a peacock
a fox
a bee
a lamb
an owl

Animal Similes

Many familiar similes connect humans with certain animal qualities. (Remember that a **simile** is a comparison between two very different things, using a comparing word such as *like* or *as*.) Which animals in the list on the left connect with which human qualities? (Use each animal just once.) Do you think the similes are fair to the animals?

1. playful as _____
2. free as _____
3. gentle as _____
4. greedy as _____
5. proud as _____
6. busy as _____
7. wise as _____
8. sly as _____
9. stubborn as _____
10. slow as _____

GRAMMAR LINK

Ask students to circle each occurrence of the word *bad* in a writing assignment they have recently completed. Tell them to trade papers with partners, who should underline any occurrences of *bad* that ought to be replaced with *badly*. Then, ask students to return the papers, and have them make corrections on their own papers.

Try It Out
Answers
1. badly
2. bad
3. bad
4. bad
5. badly

VOCABULARY
Answers
1. a kitten
2. a bird
3. a lamb
4. a pig
5. a peacock
6. a bee
7. an owl
8. a fox
9. a mule
10. a snail

Resources ———

Grammar
• *Grammar and Language Links,* p. 59

Grammar Link Quick Check

Choose the word that correctly completes each sentence.

1. The frogs' plan to ask for a king sounds bad/badly. [bad]
2. The fox is embarrassed very bad/badly when he fails to get the grapes. [badly]
3. The Town Mouse wants very bad/badly to go home. [badly]
4. The Country Mouse feels bad/badly when she sees that the Town Mouse does not like the food she serves. [bad]

T577

No Questions Asked

The literature in No Questions Asked gives students the chance to read a selection for enjoyment and enrichment as they further explore the collection theme. Annotated questions in the margins of the Teacher's Edition should be considered optional. No follow-up questions will appear after the selection.

This tale is from *The Arabian Nights*—also called *The Arabian Nights' Entertainment* or *A Thousand and One Nights*. The device that binds the stories together is their narration by Scheherazade. In order to delay her execution, she tells the sultan a new tale each night. The storytelling so intrigues the sultan that he spares her life.

When the story opens, Luqman Ali, a poor man who lives in Baghdad in the alley of the potters, is told by an angel to go to Cairo to seek his fortune. In Cairo he is mistaken for a thief, arrested, and beaten. The Chief of Police tells him that dreams mean nothing; he himself ignored a dream to go to Baghdad, where he would find buried treasure under a stove in a shack in the alley of the potters. Luqman Ali dances home to his shack. He and his wife move the stove, find the treasure, and revel in the jewels.

Resources

Listening
Audio CD Library
A lively recording of this story appears in the *Audio CD Library:*
• Disc 14, Track 8

The Dream of Good Fortune

from **The Arabian Nights,**
dramatized by **Paul Sills**

Characters

Luqman Ali
His Wife
An Angel
The Chief of Police
A Thief
The Lieutenant

578 OUR CLASSICAL HERITAGE

Luq. Luqman Ali, a poor but honest dung sweeper, lived in the alley of the tanners, off the street of the potters, in the heart of the great city of Baghdad.[1]
Wife. He and his wife had nothing in the world but an old iron stove, and barely enough to eat.
Luq. But still they did not despair in the mercy of the Almighty. One night Luqman Ali and his wife lay down to sleep, and he had a dream.
Angel. An angel appeared with a message: "Luqman Ali, alley of the tanners, off the street of the potters, in the city of Baghdad—Dear Luq, Go to Cairo,[2] and there you will find your fortune."
Luq. Luqman Ali awoke his wife and told her of his strange dream.

1. **Baghdad:** ancient Middle Eastern city, the center of Islamic civilization during the period in which many of the *Arabian Nights* stories are set. Today Baghdad is the capital of Iraq.
2. **Cairo** (kī′rō): capital of Egypt.

Listening to Music

Violin solo from *Scheherazade* by Nicholas Rimsky-Korsakov

With Modest Mussorgsky, Alexander Borodin, and two others, Nicholas Rimsky-Korsakov (1844–1908) was a member of the group of composers nicknamed the Russian (or Mighty) Five. The group's aim was to rid classical music of its strong German and French influences and

instead produce compositions of a distinctly Russian nature. Nevertheless, Rimsky-Korsakov's two best-known works draw on other cultures as well: His *Capriccio espagnol* tries to capture the flavor of Spain, and his orchestral suite *Scheherazade* attempts to retell in music four different episodes from *The Arabian Nights*.

Activity
Before students read the selection, play for them the opening portion of *Scheherazade*, which includes the famous violin solo. Explain that the violin music, which recurs throughout, represents Scheherazade spinning her thousand and one tales to the sultan. Ask students to predict the kind of story Scheherazade tells by what the music suggests. Then, have students read the selection to see if their predictions are correct.

Wife. Go back to sleep, my love, it was only a dream.

Angel. Luqman Ali, go to Cairo, and there you will find your fortune.

Luq. Wife, wake up; the angel came again and told me to go to Cairo, to seek my fortune.

Wife. If it happens a third time, you'll have to go.

Angel. Luqman Ali, are you still here? Go to Cairo! Your fortune awaits you there.

Luq. I go! I go! Wife, awaken—I must go to Cairo. And so Luqman Ali set off on the road to Cairo. Through hot desert winds—sandstorms—cold nights. Luqman Ali traveled the road until, weary and sore, in the shimmering heat, he saw the great city of Cairo. Tired and not knowing where to go, he took refuge in the courtyard of a great mosque,³ where he lay down to sleep.

3. **mosque** (mäsk): Moslem house of worship.

Thief. That night, a thief entered the courtyard and broke through the wall of an adjoining house.

[*A woman screams offstage. The* THIEF *returns to the courtyard, hits* LUQ, *and runs off.*]

Luq. Stop, thief! Stop, thief!
Chief of Police. The chief of police . . .
Lieutenant. And his lieutenant . . .
Chief of Police. Arrived at the scene, and they found Luqman Ali, and thinking him to be the thief . . .
Lieutenant. They beat him with their clubs and dragged him off to jail.
Chief of Police. Who are you?
Luq. Luqman Ali.
Chief of Police. Where do you come from?
Luq. Baghdad.
Chief of Police. What brings you to Cairo?
Luq. I had a dream . . .

THE DREAM OF GOOD FORTUNE 579

Ⓐ Critical Thinking
Comparing/Contrasting
❓ Which of the classical Greek myths you read could have had this same title? ["King Midas and the Golden Touch" is the most likely response; accept others if students can explain their reasoning.]

Ⓑ Cultural Connections
❓ What other mythical or magical stories do you know where things come in threes? [Responses may range from "Goldilocks and the Three Bears" to stories from many cultures in which a genie or similar being allows someone three wishes.]

Ⓒ Reading Skills and Strategies
Making Predictions
Pause and ask students to predict what will come of Luqman Ali's dream. [Some will still predict wealth, but may anticipate an outcome like that in the Midas story, where the wealth is harmful. Others may believe that some trickery was involved in the way the angel phrased its directions.] Advise students to save their predictions for comparison with the actual outcome of the story.

Ⓓ Reading Skills and Strategies
Connecting with the Text
Have students consult a map of the Middle East to determine the distance between the two cities of the story, both of which still exist today: Baghdad in Iraq and Cairo in Egypt.

Making the Connections

Connecting to the Theme: "Our Classical Heritage"
While this story does not contain Greek or Roman deities, it does feature a supernatural being—the angel who tells both Luqman Ali and the Chief of Police where to find the fortune. It also employs perennial stock characters, such as the "poor but honest" Luqman Ali, and classic themes, such as the human desire for wealth.

Cultural Connections
In many myths and legends, language that at first seems perfectly clear turns out to be ambiguous or have unexpected significance. In classical Greek mythology, proclamations of the oracle of Apollo at Delphi are notorious for their ambiguity. In Shakespeare's *Macbeth,* the "impossible" predictions of the three Weird Sisters nevertheless come to pass. In Luqman Ali's case, we expect him to find his fortune in Cairo.

Instead he finds the key to a fortune—the words of the Chief of Police. Ask students to recall myths or legends they know, from any culture, that feature promises or predictions made by supernatural beings—gods, genies, angels, tricksters, or spirits. What is misleading or ambiguous about the words themselves or unexpected about the way in which the predictions are fulfilled?

Ⓐ Elements of Literature

Irony

? What is ironic about this speech? [We and Luqman Ali understand something the Police Chief does not. It appears that Luqman had to go far away to discover the treasure that lay under his own stove. The scorn of the rational policeman for "superstitious" people allows Luqman and his wife to benefit from their belief in dreams.]

Ⓑ Reading Skills and Strategies

Connecting with the Text

? How would you state the lesson about life or the moral that the story teaches? Remember that many interpretations are possible, as long as they are supported by the details of the story. [Possible responses: Good fortune begins at home. Believe your dreams. Good things happen to honest people who work for their good fortune.]

[*The* LIEUTENANT *squeezes* LUQ*'s nose, sending him to his knees.*]

Chief of Police. What are you doing in Cairo?
Luq (*rises*). I had a dream . . .

[*The* LIEUTENANT *squeezes his head.*]

Chief of Police (*waving the* LIEUTENANT *away*). What brings you to Cairo?

Luq (*again on his knees*). I had a dream. An angel appeared to me three times in a row and told me to go to Cairo, where I would find my fortune.
Chief of Police. And what did you find?
Luq. I got arrested and beat up.
Chief of Police. It hurts too, doesn't it? Dreams mean nothing. We all have dreams.

You fool! That's the trouble with you people. Superstitious. I had a dream only last night: An angel came to me and told me to go to Baghdad, to the alley of the potters, off the street of the tanners, to a little old shack, and there under an old iron stove I would find a treasure. Did I go? No! I stayed here doing my job. Here, take these dinars[4] and get out of here.

[*So* LUQ *sets off to his home in Baghdad. He "dances" back to Baghdad, calling "Wife, wife." They move the stove, find the treasure, and adorn each other with jewels. She kisses his nose.—"Owww!!!"—Fade Out.*]

---

4. **dinars** (di·närz'): kind of money used in many Middle Eastern countries.

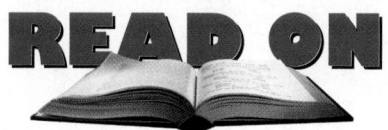

READ ON

Turn On the Light

For centuries the people of Darkness have waged war with the immortal children of Light. Saya, raised by adoptive parents to cherish the light, is given the power to end this war. In *Dragon Sword and Wind Child* (Farrar, Straus & Giroux) by Noriko Ogiwara, this powerful young woman must untangle a puzzling web of good and evil to save the people and land she loves.

Before Superman

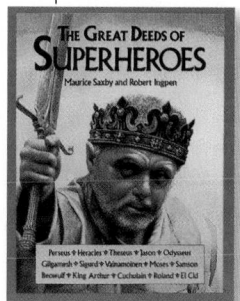

Travel back to ancient times to meet Perseus the Fearless, Heracles the Strong One, Jason the Voyager. These and other superheroes fulfill quests, win contests, and journey to fantastic lands. *The Great Deeds of Superheroes* (Peter Bedrick), retold by Maurice Saxby, contains seventeen action-packed, inspiring tales of some brave, extraordinary heroes.

Wonderful Wonders

A group of eager young listeners gathers at a beautiful country home to hear Eustace Bright tell his famous stories. In Nathaniel Hawthorne's classic *A Wonder Book* (Dutton), the beloved narrator Bright entertains his audience with a mix of Greek myths and tales of his life in the country.

Other Picks

- H. M. Hoover, *The Dawn Palace: The Story of Medea* (Dutton). This unusual retelling of the tragedy of Medea sympathizes with Medea and examines the truth surrounding her horrible deeds.

- Laura C. Stevenson, *The Island and the Ring* (Houghton Mifflin). This mythic fantasy tells of a young woman's quest for justice in an unjust world.

MAIN OBJECTIVE
Write an evaluation of a work

PROCESS OBJECTIVES
1. Use appropriate prewriting techniques to identify and develop a topic
2. Create a first draft
3. Use evaluation criteria as a basis for determining revision strategies
4. Revise the first draft, incorporating suggestions generated by self- or peer evaluation
5. Proofread and correct errors
6. Create a final draft
7. Choose an appropriate method of publication
8. Reflect on progress as a writer

Planning

- **Block Schedule**
  Block Scheduling Lesson Plans with Pacing Guide
- **One-Stop Planner**
  CD-ROM with Test Generator

Technology HELP

See Writer's Workshop 1 CD-ROM. *Assignment: Evaluation.*

ASSIGNMENT

Write an evaluation of a work—such as a story, poem, play, movie, or TV show.

AIM

To persuade; to inform.

AUDIENCE

Your teacher, classmates, or friends.

PERSUASIVE WRITING
EVALUATION

When was the last time a friend asked you, "Have you read any good books lately?" or "What did you think of that movie?" When you answer one of these questions, you are making an **evaluation,** or judgment. You are giving an opinion about whether something is good or bad. Usually you will need to include information and convincing reasons to back up your judgment.

Professional Model

Here is an evaluation of a movie called Ever After, *a new version of the Cinderella story.*

The movie opens with a nineteenth-century French noblewoman who wants to set the record straight on her famous ancestor [Cinderella]. The rousing history she recounts in flashback tells of a young woman whose fiery convictions get her into trouble and whose mind and muscle get her out again. She needs love, but she doesn't need rescuing.

    Cinderella's real name was Danielle. When her beloved father dies, he leaves her to the harsh care of her stepmother. When her stepmother sells off a beloved old servant, Danielle dresses up like a court lady and argues with the prince about human rights until he agrees to

The authors describe the format of the movie (flashback) and the heroine's personality.

They summarize the plot and tell how this version of "Cinderella" is different from the original.

582 OUR CLASSICAL HERITAGE

 Resources: Print and Media

Writing and Language
- *Portfolio Management System*
  Prewriting, p. 179
  Peer Editing, p. 180
  Assessment Rubric, p. 181

- *Workshop Resources*
  Revision Strategy Teaching Notes, p. 29
  Transparencies 15, 16
- *Writer's Workshop 1 CD-ROM*
  Evaluation

Assessment
- *Standardized Test Preparation,* p. 112

The history
of the written
word is rich and
Once upon a tim
Page

(continued)

intervene and release the man.
Love doesn't quite blossom: The
prince is intrigued, but she's
appalled by this restless aristocrat
who admires passion and principle
yet won't act on them.

This complex tale is told with
great buoyancy and wit thanks
to the splendid performances.
"Cinderella" has had hundreds of
variants in dozens of cultures, but
Ever After is the version we've
needed for a long time.

*The authors clearly
state their opinion
of the movie and give
reasons to back up
their judgment.*

—Laura Shapiro and Corie Brown,
from *Newsweek*, August 1998

Works I Have Read	What I Recall Most
"Amigo Brothers" by Piri Thomas	the surprise at the end
"Antaeus" by Borden Deal	the roof garden and how the boys destroy it
Brian's Song by William Blinn	the way the two guys tease each other

Prewriting

1. Writer's Notebook

Review your Writer's Notebook entries for this
collection. If none of those ideas appeal to you, try
the strategy below.

2. What Have You Seen Lately?

Make a list of movies, books, stories, and other forms of entertainment (including music) that you have seen or read or heard
recently. Next to each title, describe what you recall most
vividly about the work. (See the chart at the right.)

3. Decide on Your Standards of Judgment

Whenever you judge the worth of something, you are measuring it against **criteria,** or standards. For a movie, you may have
criteria like these:

WORK IN PROGRESS

Finding Criteria for Judging a Work

"I liked *Raiders of the Lost Ark*."
"Why?"
"Because it was exciting."
"What made it exciting?"
"There were a lot of scary surprises and great escapes."

WRITER'S WORKSHOP 583

Introducing the Writer's Workshop

Read aloud to the class from a newspaper or magazine review of a recent
movie. After students have heard the
review, ask for oral responses to the
following questions:
• How do you decide which movies
  you want to see?
• Why would you want to read a
  movie review? What do you look
  for in a good movie review?
• Would you be satisfied if you read a
  movie review that gave only a summary of the plot? Why or why not?

Teaching the Writer's Workshop

After students have read the Professional Model, ask them to list the
criteria that Shapiro and Brown use to
evaluate *Ever After*. Point out that the
authors never directly state their
standards; they indirectly—but
clearly—suggest them. Remind students to make their own critical standards clear, either directly or indirectly,
in the evaluations they produce for this
workshop.

Prewriting
• Help students work through the
  techniques suggested on pp. 583–
  584. Have them brainstorm additional ideas that may be useful.
• Point out that, although the criteria
  for judging movies will differ somewhat from the criteria for books,
  some qualities can be common to
  both forms—for example, an exciting plot and interesting characters.

Reaching All Students

Struggling Readers
If students choose written works as their subject, first ask them to reread the works and
place stick-on notes next to their favorite passages. They may then go back to match the
marked passages with their evaluation criteria.
Ask students to match each criterion on their
list with a supporting quotation. Similarly, students who choose movies as subjects can use a
VCR to review favorite scenes and transcribe
the dialogue.

English Language Learners
Allow students to use an audiotape recorder in
the prewriting and drafting stages. Students may
record oral prewriting notes, orally try out
parts of their first drafts before writing them, or
compare variations of a particular sentence.
Remind students that they may pause or stop
the recorder at any time to plan their next
words.

T583

Drafting

Remind students to use every other line when they write their drafts. They should also leave extra space in the right margin for comments and editing marks.

- Stress to students that they must provide evidence or examples from their chosen works to support their evaluations.
- Remind students that they will need to consider whether their audience is familiar with the work they are evaluating. If they are writing for an audience that is familiar with the work's plot, characters, and so on, they will not need to explain these elements in detail. An audience unfamiliar with the work will need more background information in order to be able to appreciate the evaluation.

- The action should be exciting.
- The roles should be played by good actors.
- It should be impossible to predict what will happen next.

It's helpful to identify things that matter to you. With a partner, develop a list of criteria for judging a work like the one you're evaluating. Question each other, pushing for more specific answers. (See the dialogue on page 583.)

Take notes on your discussion. Use your notes to write a list of qualities that make a work seem good or bad to you.

Drafting

1. Writing Your First Draft

Sometimes at the end of a movie or a book, you know whether you liked it but you aren't sure why. Discussing it with someone can help you sort out your reasons. A first draft is like one of those conversations—a chance to give shape to your first thoughts. Begin with your reactions, and keep asking "Why?" "Why did I think that, feel that, question that?"

2. Don't Forget Your Audience

Start with a lively quotation, anecdote, or question that your readers can immediately relate to. Give them background information, but leave them curious enough to want to discover the work for themselves.

3. Supporting Your Judgment with Evidence

The body of your evaluation should contain sound reasons for your opinion. Use specific examples from the work or from your personal experience to support your points. You may also want to make comparisons with other works or cite the opinions of authorities.

PEANUTS reprinted by permission United Feature Syndicate, Inc.

Getting Students Involved

Cooperative Learning

Criteria Committees. After students create their lists of criteria, divide the class into groups of four. Ask students to share their lists with one another within their group. Each member should ask at least one specific question about every other member's list. Ask students to focus on helping other members make sure that their criteria are significant and interesting. Students should then individually revise their lists of criteria after considering the questions and comments from their groups.

4. Bringing It to a Close

Tie your thoughts together in an interesting concluding sentence. Restate your case, or offer one more compelling reason in support of your judgment. End with a bang!

Evaluating and Revising

Exchange papers with a classmate, and answer these questions:

- Is the writer's opinion of the work clear? Why or why not?
- Are the reasons for the writer's opinion convincing?
- Does the evaluation seem complete? Why or why not?

Student Model

review of THE LION, THE WITCH, AND THE WARDROBE

Would you like a passport for a most extraordinary excursion into magical lands? If you have never been to Narnia, you can enter this strange, intriguing place by reading C. S. Lewis's *The Lion, the Witch, and the Wardrobe.*

This is the story of four brothers and sisters, Peter, Susan, Lucy, and Edmund Pevensie, who have been sent to visit the country house of Professor Kirk because of the air raids in England during World War II. While they are exploring the house, they enter an old wardrobe and take a fantasy trip to another universe called Narnia. There they meet the great Aslan and help him to defeat the evil White Witch. Aslan is a great lion who has a golden mane, golden eyes, and a face that looks royal, strong, peaceful, and sad. He is described as both "good and terrible at the same time."

The review opens with an intriguing question.

The writer identifies the title and author and evaluates the book as "a most extraordinary excursion into magical lands."

He briefly describes the characters and summarizes the plot.

(continued on next page)

■ *Evaluation Criteria*

A good evaluation

1. *identifies and describes the work*

2. *makes a clear judgment based on specific criteria*

3. *gives reasons and examples to support the judgment*

4. *restates or reinforces the judgment in a strong conclusion*

Language/Grammar Link
HELP

Descriptive language: page 511. Figurative language: page 520. Words often confused: page 529. Adjective vs. adverb: page 539. Good vs. well: page 553. Allusions: page 564. Bad vs. badly: page 577.

Sentence Workshop
HELP

Varying sentence length: page 587.

Using the Model

As class members read the Student Model, be sure they understand the side notes. Ask students to use the following chart to record information from each paragraph in the Student Model. Then, ask students how the Student Model satisfies the Evaluation Criteria on p. 585.

- Students may be impressed by some of the challenging words in the Student Model. Remind students that their own evaluations should include only words whose meanings and connotations they fully understand. If students use a thesaurus, they should choose only synonyms with which they are familiar. Remind the class that one wrong word can ruin a sentence or even a whole paragraph.

The numbers at the left identify the paragraphs in the Student Model.

	Description
1	[introduction/judgment]
2,3	[plot summary]
2,3	[evaluation of characters]
4	[evaluation of setting]
5	[conclusion/judgment]

	Details
1	["magical lands"]
2	[Aslan vs. White Witch; Aslan "good and terrible"]
3	[kids tested by Aslan]
4	[alternate universe]
5	[enjoyable adventure]

Reaching All Students

English Language Learners

To help students integrate quotations into their evaluations, review the rules for using quotation marks with quoted passages. Remind students that the quoted material should fit smoothly into the paragraphs in which they are used. Also ask students to check the punctuation of any titles they have used. Remind them that the titles of novels, movies, and videotapes should be underlined or italicized and that titles of short stories and poems should be in quotation marks.

Evaluating and Revising

Direct students to use the Evaluation Criteria provided here to review their drafts and to determine needed revisions. Ask them to exchange papers with a classmate. The partners should convert the criteria to questions, such as "Does the writer identify and describe the work?" and offer brief written or oral comments.

Publishing

Ask students to show their work to an interested friend or to submit their reviews to the school or local newspaper.

Reflecting

Ask students to name the step of the writing process that was the biggest challenge for them. Invite them to suggest how they can make that step easier on their next assignment.

Proofreading

Have students proofread their own work first and then exchange papers with another student. For this assignment, remind students to be particularly careful of the use of quotation marks when quoting directly from a text or citing an expert's exact words. Remind students that the titles of books, movies, and videotapes call for italic type (or underlining in longhand or on the typewriter) and that titles of short stories and poems require quotation marks.

Resources

Peer Editing Forms and Rubrics
• *Portfolio Management System*, p. 180
Revision Transparencies
• *Workshop Resources*, p. 29

Grading Timesaver

Rubrics for this Writer's Workshop assignment appear on page 181 of the *Portfolio Management System*.

Communications Handbook H E L P

See Listing Sources and Taking Notes.

Proofreading Tips

• When you write a review, pay special attention to the use of quotation marks.

• Be sure to put titles of full-length works in italic type; put titles of shorter works in quotation marks.

Communications Handbook H E L P

See Proofreaders' Marks.

Publishing Tip

Submit your review to your school or local newspaper.

Student Model (continued)

When the children are tested by Aslan, they have to make choices between right and wrong. Aslan encourages the children to make judgments that help them to become mature individuals. Peter is established as the High King and, with the other children, rules Narnia for many years. One day, they find their way back to the wardrobe and discover that, although years have passed in Narnia, only moments have gone by in their own world.

Time travel provides a convenient way of moving the characters into settings that are surreal and exciting. The unusual environment makes it possible for Lewis to introduce strange powers and creatures, such as animals that talk and have the power to tell the difference between right and wrong. Lewis's Narnia provides an alternate universe, where mundane laws are suspended, and unusual characters and settings become the norm.

Here, the writer backs up his evaluation with examples of ways in which Narnia is extraordinary and magical.

If you enjoy *The Lion, the Witch, and the Wardrobe*, you're really in luck because Lewis wrote six sequels to this adventure. These perilous journeys into the magical land of Narnia should keep you entertained for a good, long time!

—John Belletti
Manhasset Middle School
Manhasset, New York

The review ends with an enthusiastic reference to other works by the same author.

First appeared in *Merlyn's Pen: The National Magazines of Student Writing.*

Assessing Learning

Standardized Test Preparation

For practice with standardized test prompts and formats, see
• *Standardized Test Preparation*, p. 112

Sentence Workshop

VARYING SENTENCE LENGTH

In other Sentence Workshops you've learned the importance of varying sentence length. You've learned that you can vary sentence length by combining sentences or by using a variety of structures. When you get good at varying sentence length, you can just feel that your paragraph has the right rhythm. You can also check your sentences by counting words. If the tally shows that the sentences in your paragraph are of different lengths, you're probably on your way to a style that grabs the eye and catches the ear.

An interesting paragraph is made up of sentences of varied lengths—some medium, some long, some short.

"Persephone was the spring maiden, young and full of joy [**10 words**]. Sicily was her home, for it is a land where the spring is long and lovely, and where spring flowers are abundant [**22 words**]. Here Persephone played with her maidens from day to day till the rocks and valleys rang with the sound of laughter, and gloomy Hades heard it as he sat on his throne in the dark land of the dead [**39 words**]."

—Olivia Coolidge, "The Origin of the Seasons" (page 501)

"Hercules had now accomplished six of his labors [**8 words**]. Six more remained [**3 words**]. After the killing of the Stymphalian birds, he was commanded to go to Crete and bring back from there alive a huge bull which was laying the whole island waste [**30 words**]."

—Rex Warner, "The Labors of Hercules" (pages 545–546)

Writer's Workshop Follow-up: Revision

Exchange your evaluation for a classmate's. Count the words in each sentence. If most of the sentences are about the same length, suggest ways to vary their length. Exchange papers again, and review your classmate's suggestions.

Language Handbook HELP

See Writing Effective Sentences, pages 760-762.

Try It Out

Edit the following paragraph. Change some of the sentences in order to vary their length.

The journey from the depths of Hades to the upper world was long and hard. It was much easier to go down the path to the underworld than to climb it. The path was dark and misty. It was also full of strange shapes and noises. In many places it was merely black and silent. Orpheus would stop and listen. Nothing moved behind him.

SENTENCE WORKSHOP 587

Resources

Workshop Resources
• Worksheet, p. 49

Try It Out
Possible Answer
The journey from the depths of Hades to the upper world was long and hard. Going down the path to the underworld was much easier than climbing it. The dark and misty path was sometimes full of strange shapes and noises, but in many places it was merely black and silent. Orpheus would stop and listen. Nothing moved behind him.

Assessing Learning

Quick Check: Varying Sentence Length

Revise the following paragraph by combining sentences to create variety.

Aesop wrote many fables. Fables are short animal stories. They teach moral lessons. These fables have become well loved. Many storytellers have imitated them. Storytellers imitate them because they are entertaining. They are instructional. They are fun to write and to tell. Almost anyone can enjoy a fable.

[Possible response: Aesop wrote many fables, animal stories that teach moral lessons. These fables have become well loved. Many storytellers have imitated them because they are entertaining, instructional, and fun to write and to tell. Almost anyone can enjoy a fable.]

OBJECTIVES

1. Read and interpret a map and its insets
2. Read and interpret a time line
3. Compare and contrast maps
4. Make a time line

Using the Strategies

Answers

1. During the 700s B.C. myths are written down and the first Olympics are held.
2. Grandpa was twenty when he came to the United States.
3. Hades kidnaps Persephone.
4. Hercules is born in Thebes.
5. The inset at the lower left shows the island of Sicily and part of the coast of north Africa. Or the inset on the right at the middle of the page shows where Greece lies in relation to the rest of the world.

Extending the Strategies

Possible Answers

1. Ionian Sea, Aegean Sea, Gulf of Corinth, Sparta, Athens, Mount Olympus, Mount Parnassos
2. Responses will vary. Encourage students to use as models Grandpa's Time Line on this page and the map on pp. 498–499.

Situation

Imagine that your grandfather was born in Greece. You show him the map on pages 498–499. "You won't find a drawing of me there," he says. "People made up those myths thousands of years before I was born. Get me a pencil. I'll show you." Then Grandpa draws a time line like the one on this page.

Strategies

Both maps and time lines present information in a graphic way, like a diagram.

Use a time line to find out when events happened.

- A time line may show a vast span of time, such as thousands or millions of years.
- Events on a time line are listed in chronological order, with long-ago events at one end and more recent events at the other. The approximate date (year or century) of each event appears either above or below the line.

Use a map to find places.

- Some maps show natural features, such as oceans, bodies of land, mountains, even stars and planets. Many maps show structures made by people, such as cities, streets, and parks.
- Maps show direction. You can read a map to see how to get from one place to another. On page 499 you'll find a symbol called a *compass rose,* which tells you where north, south, east, and west are located.
- A map's *scale* tells you how size on the map compares with actual size or distance in real life. One inch on a map may equal one, ten, or fifty miles or more.

Using the Strategies

1. Look at the time line on this page. Which two events in ancient Greece might have happened within one person's lifetime?
2. How old was Grandpa when he came to the United States?
3. Find Sicily on the map on pages 498–499. Can you tell what mythic event takes place there?
4. Where is Hercules born?
5. Find the two small maps set into the main map. Pick one of these inset maps, and tell what it shows.

Extending the Strategies

- Find a map of modern Greece. Which of the old place names are still in use?
- Make a time line showing important events that happened to you.

588 OUR CLASSICAL HERITAGE

Using Students' Strengths

Visual Learners/Kinesthetic Learners
Invite students to bring in maps that they have found interesting to use and easy to understand. Supplement their maps by bringing in maps of various types and sizes, particularly relief maps and illustrated maps that present prominent features of an area three-dimensionally.

Logical/Mathematical Learners
Assign proficient math students to give a brief chalkboard demonstration of how to make a scale for a map.

Learning for Life

Investigating the Media and Values

OBJECTIVES

1. Identify messages about behavior expressed in recent movies
2. Conduct research in newspapers and magazines
3. Choose and complete a project (writing a movie review, writing a dramatic dialogue, debating a given question)

Problem

The myths and fables you've just read presented lessons in behavior for people of ancient times. Today movies and TV give us models of behavior. What messages about behavior do today's popular media suggest? How can we learn to think more critically about those messages?

Project

Analyze a movie, and interpret its messages about behavior. Discuss how people may be affected by the attitudes and values expressed in the movie.

Preparation

1. With a group of classmates, choose a movie to discuss. The film can be a current one or one released in the last few years. Be sure to get permission from your parents and teacher to see the movie.

2. Before you watch the movie, look at ads for it and read some reviews. Then, jot down ideas about the attitudes and values you expect the film to show. Think about questions like these:

   - Who are the heroes and the villains? How are they portrayed?
   - What role does violence play? What role does kindness or helping others play?
   - Does the movie paint a dark picture of life or a hopeful one?

Procedure

1. Watch the movie and write your reactions right away.

2. Reflect on the ideas you had before watching the movie. Have they changed?

3. Work with your group to create the following:

   - a description of the values and attitudes expressed by the characters
   - a description of the main characters and their roles

Presentation

Present your findings in one of the following ways:

1. Movie Review

Write a review of the movie for your school newspaper. Focus on the movie's message about behavior.

2. Dramatic Dialogue

Write a dialogue between the hero of a myth and the main character of the movie you watched. Have the two characters compare their experiences and views of the world.

3. Debate

Debate this question with another group of students: Do the attitudes and values expressed in the media influence people's behavior, or do the media simply reflect the attitudes found in our society?

Processing

Write a reflection on what you learned from this project.

Resources

Viewing and Representing
HRW Multimedia Presentation Maker
Students may wish to use the *Multimedia Presentation Maker* to create visuals to accompany their debates.

Grating Timesaver

Rubrics for this Learning for Life project appear on p. 182 of the *Portfolio Management System.*

BEETLE BAILEY.   Reprinted with special permission of King Features Syndicate.

Developing Workplace Competencies

Preparation	Procedure	Presentation
• Working on a team	• Making judgments	• Thinking creatively
• Identifying central issues	• Recognizing relationships	• Synthesizing information
• Acquiring information	• Evaluating information	• Communicating ideas
• Processing information	• Interpreting information	• Reasoning effectively

900 Cinderellas: Our World Heritage in Folklore

Theme

Follow That Pumpkin! *Folk tales are told throughout the world, and their purpose is twofold: to instruct and to entertain listeners. Though the stories may differ from culture to culture, they always reveal a world in which the good are rewarded, the wicked are punished, and magical transformations occur as part of everyday life.*

Reading the Anthology

Reaching Struggling Readers

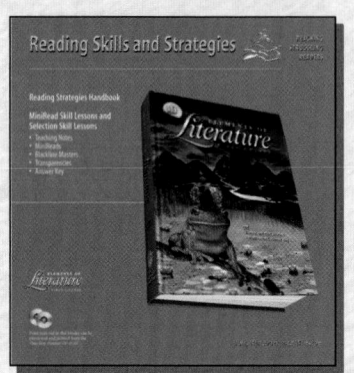

The *Reading Skills and Strategies: Reaching Struggling Readers* binder provides materials coordinated with the Pupil's Edition (see the Collection Planner, p. T589C) to help students who have difficulty reading and comprehending text, or students who are reluctant readers. The binder for seventh grade is organized around eleven individual skill areas and offers the following options:

- **Mini Read** MiniReads are short, easy texts that give students a chance to practice a particular skill and strategy before reading selections in the Pupil's Edition. Each MiniRead Skill Lesson can be taught independently or used in conjunction with a Selection Skill Lesson.

- **Selection Skill Lessons** Selection Skill Lessons allow students to apply skills introduced in the MiniReads. Each Selection Skill Lesson provides reading instruction and practice specific to a particular piece of literature in the Pupil's Edition.

Reading Beyond the Anthology

Read On Collection Eight includes an annotated bibliography of books suitable for extended reading. The suggested books are related to works in this collection by theme, by author, or by subject. To preview the Read On for Collection Eight, please turn to p. T669.

HRW Library The *HRW Library* offers novels, plays, and short-story collections for extended reading. Each book in the Library includes one or more major works and thematically or topically related Connections. The Connections are magazine articles, poems, or other pieces of literature. Each book in the *HRW Library* is also accompanied by a Study Guide that provides teaching suggestions and worksheets. For Collection Eight, the following titles are recommended.

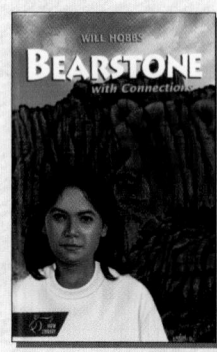

BEARSTONE
Will Hobbs
A young Native American comes of age with the help of an elderly farmer and a love of nature. The central figure, Cloyd Atcitty, is a kind of Cinderella — an outcast without parents.

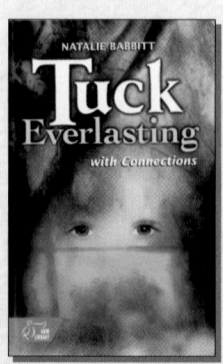

TUCK EVERLASTING
Natalie Babbitt
Like many folk tales, this story centers on a magic spring that brings everlasting life to those who drink from it.

Skills Focus

Selection or Feature	Reading Skills and Strategies	Elements of Literature	Language/ Grammar	Vocabulary/ Spelling	Writing	Listening/ Speaking	Viewing/ Representing
Aschenputtel (p. 592) *German, retold by Jakob and Wilhelm Grimm, translated by Lucy Crane*	Identify the Main Idea, pp. 592, 604, 605	Motif, pp. 592, 604 Character, p. 605 Setting, p. 605 Plot, p. 605	*All Right, A Lot, Should Have,* and *Would Have,* p. 606	Write Definitions of New Words, p. 606	Take Notes for a News Article, p. 605 Create a New Version of "Cinderella," p. 605 Write a New Story Ending, p. 605	Retell "Cinderella," p. 605 Dramatize a New "Cinderella," p. 605	Illustrate a Folk Tale, p. 605
The Algonquin Cinderella (p. 607) *Algonquin, retold by M. R. Cox* **Yeh-Shen** (p. 615) *Chinese, retold by Ai-Ling Louie*	Compare Texts, pp. 607, 622	Character Types, pp. 607, 622 Metamorphosis, p. 622	*Two, To,* and *Too,* p. 624	Spelling: When to Double the Final Consonant Before a Suffix Beginning with a Vowel, p. 624	Identify the Known and Unknown, p. 623 Story Swap, p. 623 Identify Questions for Research, p. 623	Participate in a Group Discussion, p. 623	Use a Graphic Organizer to Compare Texts, p. 607 Use a Graphic Organizer to Compare Characters, p. 622
Elements of Literature: Folk Tales (p. 625)		Folk Tales, p. 625 Motifs, p. 625 Escape Stories, p. 626 Storytelling, p. 626					
Reading Skills and Strategies: Summarizing (p. 627)	Summarize, p. 627 Make a Story Map, p. 627		Transitions, p. 627				Use a Story Map, p. 627
Oni and the Great Bird (p. 628) *Abayomi Fuja*	Summarize, pp. 628, 636	Character, p. 635 Motif, p. 635 Hero, p. 636 Setting, p. 636 Conflict, p. 636	*They're, Their, There,* p. 637	Use New Words in a Work Context, p. 637	Research a Topic, p. 636 Write a Folk Tale, p. 636 Write a Summary, p. 636		Design a Book Jacket, p. 636
Master Frog (p. 638) *Vietnamese, retold by Lynette Dyer Vuong*	Make Predictions, pp. 638, 646 Summarize, p. 646	Metamorphosis, pp. 638, 646 Character, p. 646 Motif, p. 646	Use Specific Words, p. 648	Use Words in Context, p. 648	Freewrite About Talent, p. 647 Rewrite the Beginning of a Story, p. 647 Compare Themes, p. 647	Audiotape a Story, p. 647	
Sealskin, Soulskin (p. 649) *Inuit, retold by Clarissa Pinkola Estés*	Summarize a Story for a Specific Audience, p. 659	Fantasy, pp. 649, 659 Title, p. 659	Oral Storytelling, p. 661	Use New Words, p. 661	Write a Modern Legend, p. 660 Write a Short Story, p. 660	Stage a Debate, p. 660 Tell an Interactive Tale, p. 660	Use a Chart, p. 660
No Questions Asked: The Hummingbird King (p. 662) *Argentina Palacios*	The **No Questions Asked** feature provides students with an unstructured opportunity to practice reading strategies using a selection that extends the theme of the collection.						
Speaking and Listening Workshop: Speaking to Inform (p. 670)						Prepare and Deliver a Formal Speech, p. 671	
Writer's Workshop: Informative Report (p. 672)		Organization, p. 674 Main Point, p. 674			Research and Write a Report, pp. 672–676 Document Sources, p. 676		
Sentence Workshop: Parallel Structure (p. 677)			Parallel Structure, p. 677		Proofread Sentences for Parallel Structure, p. 677		
Reading for Life: Searching the Internet (p. 678)	Key Words, p. 678 Use a Directory, p. 678				Research an Author, p. 678		
Learning for Life: Researching Our Heritage: Comparing Cultures (p. 679)					Research Another Culture, p. 679	Plan a Folk-Tale Festival, p. 679	Present a Multimedia Report, p. 679 Create an On-Line Guide, p. 679

Skills Focus

Resources for this Collection

Note: All resources for this collection are available for preview on the *One-Stop Planner CD-ROM 2 with Test Generator.* All worksheets and blackline masters may be printed from the CD-ROM.

Internet Resources
go.hrw.com LE0 7-8

Selection or Feature	Reading and Literary Skills	Language and Grammar
Aschenputtel (p. 592) *German, retold by* Jakob and Wilhelm Grimm *translated by* Lucy Crane **Connections: . . . And Then the Prince Knelt Down and Tried to Put the Glass Slipper on Cinderella's Foot** (p. 601) Judith Viorst **In Search of Cinderella** (p. 601) Shel Silverstein	• *Reading Skills and Strategies: Reaching Struggling Readers* • Selection Skill Lesson, p. 91 • *Graphic Organizers for Active Reading,* Worksheet p. 41	• *Grammar and Language Links: All Right, A Lot, Should Have, and Would Have,* Worksheet p. 61 • *Language Workshop CD-ROM,* Usage • *Daily Oral Grammar,* Transparency 35
The Algonquin Cinderella (p. 607) *Algonquin, retold by* M. R. Cox **Connections: Dinorella** (p. 612) Pamela Duncan Edwards **Yeh-Shen** (p. 615) *Chinese, retold by* Ai-Ling Louie **Connections:** *from* **Ashpet** (p. 621) *Appalachian, retold by* Granny Shores	• *Reading Skills and Strategies: Reaching Struggling Readers* • Selection Skill Lesson, p. 156 • *Graphic Organizers for Active Reading,* Worksheet p. 42	• *Grammar and Language Links: Two, To and Too,* Worksheet p. 63 • *Language Workshop CD-ROM,* Homonyms • *Daily Oral Grammar,* Transparencies 36, 37
Elements of Literature: Folk Tales (p. 625)	• *Literary Elements,* Transparency 11	

Oni and the Great Bird (p. 628)
 Yoruban, retold by Abayomi Fuja
	• *Reading Skills and Strategies: Reaching Struggling Readers*
	  • MiniRead Skill Lesson, p. 190
	  • Selection Skill Lesson, p. 196
	 • *Graphic Organizers for Active Reading,* Worksheet p. 43
		• *Grammar and Language Links: They're, Their, There,* Worksheet p. 65
		 • *Language Workshop CD-ROM,* Their, They're, There
		 • *Daily Oral Grammar,* Transparency 38

Master Frog (p. 638) *Vietnamese, retold by* Lynette Dyer Vuong	• *Reading Skills and Strategies: Reaching Struggling Readers* • Selection Skill Lesson, p. 61 • *Graphic Organizers for Active Reading,* Worksheet p. 44	• *Grammar and Language Links: Using Specific Words,* Worksheet p. 67 • *Daily Oral Grammar,* Transparency 39
Sealskin, Soulskin (p. 649) *Inuit, retold by* Clarissa Pinkola Estés **Connections: Oral Storytelling: Making the Winter Shorter** (p. 657) Joan Burditt	• *Graphic Organizers for Active Reading,* Worksheet p. 45	• *Grammar and Language Links: Oral Storytelling,* Worksheet p. 69 • *Daily Oral Grammar,* Transparency 40
No Questions Asked: The Hummingbird King (p. 662) Argentina Palacios **Connections: The Search Goes On** (p. 666) Carolyn Meyer and Charles Gallenkamp	The **No Questions Asked** feature provides students with an unstructured opportunity to practice reading strategies using a selection that extends the theme of the collection.	
Speaking and Listening Workshop: Speaking to Inform (p. 670)		
Writer's Workshop: Informative Report (p. 672)		
Sentence Workshop: Parallel Structure (p. 677)		• *Workshop Resources,* p. 51
Learning for Life: Researching Our Cultural Heritage (p. 679)		

Collection Resources

- *Cross-Curricular Activities,* p. 61
- *Portfolio Management System:*
  Introduction to Portfolio Assessment, p. 1;
  Parent/Guardian Letters, p. 101
- *Literary Elements:*
  Transparency 11; Worksheet p. 34
- *Formal Assessment,*
  Reading Application Test, p. 132
- *Test Generator,* Collection Test

Vocabulary, Spelling, and Decoding	Writing	Listening and Speaking, Viewing and Representing	Assessment
• *Words to Own,* Worksheet p. 22 • *Spelling and Decoding,* Worksheet p. 27	• *Portfolio Management System,* Rubrics for Choices, p. 183	• *Audio CD Library,* Disc 15, Track 2 • *Portfolio Management System,* Rubrics for Choices, p. 183	• *Formal Assessment,* Selection Test, p. 120 • *Standardized Test Preparation,* pp. 86, 88 • *Test Generator* (One-Stop Planner CD-ROM)
• *Spelling and Decoding,* Worksheet p. 28	• *Portfolio Management System,* Rubrics for Choices, p. 184	• *Audio CD Library,* Disc 15, Tracks 3, 4 • *Viewing and Representing:* Fine Art Transparency 19 Worksheet p. 76 • *Portfolio Management System,* Rubrics for Choices, p. 184	• *Formal Assessment,* Selection Test, p. 122 • *Standardized Test Preparation,* p. 90 • *Test Generator* (One-Stop Planner CD-ROM)
			• *Formal Assessment,* Literary Elements Test, p. 130
• *Words to Own,* Worksheet p. 23 • *Spelling and Decoding,* Worksheet p. 29	• *Portfolio Management System,* Rubrics for Choices, p. 185	• *Audio CD Library,* Disc 16, Track 2 • *Portfolio Management System,* Rubrics for Choices, p. 185	• *Formal Assessment,* Selection Test, p. 124 • *Standardized Test Preparation,* p. 92 • *Test Generator* (One-Stop Planner CD-ROM)
• *Words to Own,* Worksheet p. 24 • *Spelling and Decoding,* Worksheet p. 30	• *Portfolio Management System,* Rubrics for Choices, p. 186	• *Visual Connections,* Videocassette B, Segment 9 • *Audio CD Library,* Disc 16, Track 3 • *Portfolio Management System,* Rubrics for Choices, p. 186	• *Formal Assessment,* Selection Test, p. 126 • *Standardized Test Preparation,* p. 94 • *Test Generator* (One-Stop Planner CD-ROM)
• *Words to Own,* Worksheet p. 25 • *Spelling and Decoding,* Worksheet p. 31	• *Portfolio Management System,* Rubrics for Choices, p. 187	• *Viewing and Representing:* Fine Art Transparency 20 Worksheet p. 80 • *Portfolio Management System,* Rubrics for Choices, p. 187	• *Formal Assessment,* Selection Test, p. 128 • *Standardized Test Preparation,* p. 96 • *Test Generator* (One-Stop Planner CD-ROM)
		• *Audio CD Library,* Disc, 16, Track 4	
			• *Portfolio Management System,* p. 189
	• *Workshop Resources,* p. 33 • *Standardized Test Preparation:* Worksheet p. 120 Transparencies 7–12 • *Writer's Workshop I CD-ROM,* Report of Information		• *Portfolio Management System* • Prewriting, p. 190 • Peer Editing, p. 191 • Assessment Rubric, p. 192
		• *Viewing and Representing,* HRW Multimedia Presentation Maker	• *Portfolio Management System,* Rubrics, p. 193

Transparency CD-ROM Video Audio CD

T589D

Collection Planner

OBJECTIVES

1. Read literature on the theme "900 Cinderellas: Our World Heritage in Folklore"
2. Interpret literary elements used in the literature with special emphasis on the folk-tale tradition
3. Apply a variety of reading strategies, particularly summarizing
4. Respond to the literature in a variety of modes
5. Learn and use new words
6. Develop skill in formal speaking
7. Plan, draft, revise, proof, and publish an informative report
8. Demonstrate the ability to use the Internet as a research tool
9. Explore, through a variety of projects, ways to compare different cultures from around the world

Introducing the Theme

"Cinderella" has been described as the world's best-known folk tale, because versions of the Cinderella story exist in the literature of cultures around the world. As students read the folk tales in this collection, encourage them to think about the cultures that shaped the various versions of familiar tales—and about how they might learn more about those cultures.

go.hrw.com
LEO 7-8

Writing Focus: Informative Report

WORK IN PROGRESS

The following **Work in Progress** assignments in this collection build to a culminating **Writer's Workshop** at the end of Collection 8.

• Aschenputtel	Take notes for a news article using *5W-How* questions (p. 605)
• The Algonquin Cinderella / Yeh-Shen	Discuss knowledge of Appalachia (p. 623)
• Oni and the Great Bird	Research facts about Yoruban culture (p. 636)
• Master Frog	Explain a personal talent (p. 647)
• Sealskin, Soulskin	List topics about Inuit culture (p. 660)

Writer's Workshop: Expository Writing / Informative Report (p. 672)

> *These are the
> stories that never,
> never die, that are
> carried like seed
> into a new country,
> are told to you and
> me and make in us
> new and lasting
> strengths.*
>
> —*Meridel Le Sueur*

900 Cinderellas: Our World Heritage in Folklore

591

Responding to the Quotation

Meridel Le Sueur (1900–1996) is best remembered as a journalist and activist. During the Great Depression, she wrote powerfully about the hardships of the poor. Later, she turned to experimental prose, novels, and poetry. Her books for children, which deal with real and legendary American figures, combine history with regional lore.

? Ask students to explain Le Sueur's statement that some stories never die. [Possible responses: People keep retelling favorite stories, and over the years the stories may change and grow; these stories live in the minds of people who have heard them.] **What story do you know that you think will never die?** [Responses will vary but may include stories from the folk-tale tradition.]

Writer's Notebook

Have students jot down some notes about (or possibly an outline of) a story that they think deserves to live forever. The story may be one that they have read or seen on film, or it may be an original story that they would like to tell themselves.

Resources

Portfolio Management System
- Introduction to Portfolio Assessment, p. 1
- Parent/Guardian Letters, p. 101

Formal Assessment
- Reading Application Test, p. 132

Test Generator
- Collection Test

Cross-Curricular Activities
- Teaching Notes, p. 61

Selection Readability

This Annotated Teacher's Edition provides a summary of each selection in the student book. Following each Summary heading, you will find one, two or three small icons. These icons indicate, in an approximate sense, the reading level of the selection.

- ■ One icon indicates that the selection is easy.
- ■ ■ Two icons indicate that the selection is on an intermediate reading level.
- ■ ■ ■ Three icons indicate that the selection is challenging.

OBJECTIVES

1. Read and interpret the folk tale
2. Identify motif in storytelling
3. Find the main idea
4. Express understanding through informative and creative writing or speaking and listening
5. Identify and correct errors in spelling usage
6. Understand and use new words

SKILLS

Literary
- Identify motif and explain its function in a story

Reading
- Find the main idea

Writing
- Collect ideas for an informative report
- Write an alternative version of a folk tale
- Write a new ending for a tale

Speaking/Listening
- Dramatize a folk tale

Grammar/Language
- Spell and use the words *all right, a lot, should have,* and *would have* correctly

Vocabulary
- Understand and use new words

Planning

- **Block Schedule**
  Block Scheduling Lesson Plans with Pacing Guide
- **Traditional Schedule**
  Lesson Plans Including Strategies for English-Language Learners
- **One-Stop Planner**
  CD-ROM with Test Generator

Before You Read

ASCHENPUTTEL

Make the Connection

A Story to Tell

What popular story features these characters?

- a hard-working girl
- a wicked stepmother
- a woman with a magic wand
- a prince of a fellow

You probably know these characters from the fairy tale "Cinderella." "Cinderella" and "Aschenputtel" are two versions of the same story, about a "little ash girl" (or "cinder girl") whose dream comes true.

Round robin. In a small group, talk about why you think the story of "Cinderella" is such a favorite. What do people like about this story? What deep human wishes do you think this story expresses? As you read this German folk tale, keep a sheet of paper handy so that you can jot down your reactions. Look at the student's comments on page 594 as an example, but keep your own notes.

Elements of Literature

Motifs in Folk Tales: The Number Three

In "Aschenputtel," as in much European folklore, three is a charmed number. For example, the three sisters take turns trying on the golden slipper. This repetition of events in threes builds suspense: We know that if something happens once, it will probably happen two more times. Like other repeated elements in storytelling, the frequent use of the number three is called a **motif** (mō·tēf').

> **A** motif is a repeated element in storytelling.

Background

Literature and Literary History

People around the world have been telling the Cinderella story for ages. There are more than nine hundred versions of this popular tale. Scholars have traced the oldest version back more than a thousand years, to China. The version that you probably know best was collected in the 1600s by a French writer named Charles Perrault. His is the only version to include a fairy godmother and a midnight curfew. "Aschenputtel" is the German version of the Cinderella story.

Reading Skills and Strategies

Main Idea: It's the Message

The **main idea** is the message, insight, or lesson that is the focus of a piece of writing. You can find the main idea if you pay attention to important details as you read. One way to find the main idea of "Aschenputtel" is to ask yourself what wishes and fears this story expresses.

592   900 CINDERELLAS: OUR WORLD HERITAGE IN FOLKLORE

Preteaching Vocabulary

Words to Own

Discuss the definitions of the Words to Own listed at the bottom of the selection pages. Encourage students to think of other sentences in which these words might appear. Then, have students choose the word that best completes each of the following sentences.

1. At the movies, one child _____ in her whining until her father bought her some popcorn. [persisted]

2. That individual is a fraud; I doubt that he has a(n) _____ bone in his whole body. [pious]

3. Could this bush be _____ because the soil here is poor? [stunted]

4. Despite the paramedics' efforts, the accident victim _____ at the scene. [expired]

5. Among the ancient Medes and Persians, once a law was _____, not even a king could change it. [ordained]

Aschenputtel

German, retold by
Jakob *and* **Wilhelm Grimm**,
translated by Lucy Crane

*"Is the stupid
creature to sit
in the same
room with
us?"*

ASCHENPUTTEL **593**

Summary ■ ■ ■

A rich widower, the father of a virtuous girl, remarries. The girl's stepmother and stepsisters ridicule her and consign her to menial chores. Forcing her to rest among the cinders of the hearth, they call her Aschenputtel ("Cinder-fool"). When her father gives her a twig, Aschenputtel plants it at her mother's grave. A hazel tree springs up; from it, a white bird rises and promises to grant her wishes.

The king declares a festival at which his son will choose a bride. When her stepmother devises a chore to keep her at home, Aschenputtel calls upon the birds to fulfill the woman's demand. The tree then provides the girl with clothes so fine that the prince stays by her side all evening. He attempts to follow her home, but she eludes him. These events are repeated the following two nights. At the end of the third evening, Aschenputtel loses a shoe as she runs off. The prince vows to marry the girl whom the shoe fits. Despite cutting off parts of their feet, the stepsisters fail the test. Aschenputtel stuns them when the shoe fits and she rides off with the prince. At the wedding, pigeons peck out the stepsisters' eyes.

Resources

Listening
Audio CD Library
You can find an elegant recording of this story in the *Audio CD Library*:
• Disc 15, Track 2

Resources: Print and Media

Reading
• *Reading Skills and Strategies*
  Selection Skill Lesson, p. 91
• *Graphic Organizers for Active Reading*, p. 41
• *Words to Own*, p. 22
• *Spelling and Decoding*
  Worksheet, p. 27
• *Audio CD Library*
  Disc 15, Track 2

Elements of Literature
• *Literary Elements*
  Transparency 11
  Worksheet, p. 34

Writing and Language
• *Daily Oral Grammar*
  Transparency 35
• *Grammar and Language Links*
  Worksheet, p. 61
• *Language Workshop CD-ROM*

Assessment
• *Formal Assessment*, p. 120
• *Portfolio Management System*, p. 183
• *Standardized Test Preparation*, pp. 86, 88
• *Test Generator (One-Stop Planner CD-ROM)*

Internet
• go.hrw.com (keyword: LE0 7-8)

T593

A **Reading Skills and Strategies**

Making Predictions

? What prediction can be made from the mother's words? [Possible response: After her mother's death, Aschenputtel may face problems that will make it hard for her to remain "pious and good."]

B **Reading Skills and Strategies**

Finding the Main Idea

? The stepsisters are described as beautiful in appearance but wicked and ugly at heart. What is the story saying about appearance and reality? [Possible responses: People can't be judged by the way they look; beautiful people can be vain and mean; what a person is like on the inside can't be assumed from external appearances.]

C **Critical Thinking**

Speculating

? Why do you think the only character who is given a name is Aschenputtel? [Possible response: In folk tales, character types are more important than individuals, because what is emphasized is a fixed pattern of behavior.]

There was once a rich man whose wife lay sick, and when she felt her end drawing near, she called to her only daughter to come near her bed and said,

A "Dear child, be <u>pious</u> and good, and God will always take care of you, and I will look down upon you from heaven and will be with you."

And then she closed her eyes and <u>expired</u>. The maiden went every day to her mother's grave and wept and was always pious and good. When the winter came, the snow covered the grave with a white covering, and when the sun came in the early spring and melted it away, the man took to himself another wife.

B The new wife brought two daughters home with her and they were beautiful and fair in appearance but at heart were wicked and ugly. And then began very evil times for the poor stepdaughter.

"Is the stupid creature to sit in the same room with us?" said they. "Those who eat food must earn it. Out with the kitchen maid!"

They took away her pretty dresses and put on her an old gray kirtle[1] and gave her wooden shoes to wear.

"Just look now at the proud princess, how she is decked out!" cried they, laughing, and then they sent her into the kitchen. There she was obliged to do heavy work from morning to night, get up early in the morning, draw water, make the fires, cook, and wash. Besides that, the sisters did their utmost to torment her—mocking her and strewing peas and lentils among the ashes and setting her to pick them up. In the evenings, when she was quite tired out with her hard day's work, she had no bed to lie on but was obliged to rest on the hearth among the cinders. And as she always looked **C** dusty and dirty, they named her Aschenputtel.

It happened one day that the father went to the fair, and he asked his two stepdaughters what he should bring back for them.

"Fine clothes!" said one.

---

1. **kirtle:** old-fashioned word for "dress."

WORDS TO OWN

pious (pī′əs) *adj.*: deeply religious.
expired (ek·spīrd′) *v.*: died. In Latin, *exspirare* means "to breathe out"; *to breathe out one's last breath* is to die.

Reaching All Students

Struggling Readers
Main Idea was introduced on p. 592. For a lesson directly tied to this story that teaches students to identify main idea by using a strategy called Most Important Word, see the *Reading Skills and Strategies* binder:
• Selection Skill Lesson, p. 91

English Language Learners
Students may be confused by the mix of poetry and prose in "Aschenputtel." For each example of poetry, discuss what is being asked or announced. Students should see that the poetry is reserved for the birds and the tree that help Aschenputtel. For additional strategies to supplement instruction for these students, see
• *Lesson Plans Including Strategies for English-Language Learners*

Advanced Learners
Most students will be familiar with the version of "Cinderella" told by Charles Perrault, a French writer. Have a group of students prepare a diagram that takes common elements of two versions (the evil stepfamily, magical helpers, the prince, the search for the owner of the shoe, and so on) and demonstrates how the Grimm and Perrault versions treat those elements.

"Pearls and jewels!" said the other.

"But what will you have, Aschenputtel?" said he.

"The first twig, Father, that strikes against your hat on the way home; this is what I should like you to bring me."

So he bought for the two stepdaughters fine clothes, pearls, and jewels, and on his way back, as he rode through a green lane, a hazel twig struck against his hat; and he broke it off and carried it home with him. And when he reached home, he gave to the stepdaughters what they had wished for, and to Aschenputtel he gave the hazel twig. She thanked him and went to her mother's grave, and planted this twig there, weeping so bitterly that the tears fell upon it and watered it, and it flourished and became a fine tree. Aschenputtel went to see it three times a day and wept and prayed, and each time a white bird rose up from the tree, and, if she uttered any wish, the bird brought her whatever she had wished for.

Now it came to pass that the king ordained a festival that should last for three days and to which all the beautiful young women of that country were bidden so that the king's son might choose a bride from among them. When the two stepdaughters heard that they too were bidden to appear, they felt very pleased, and they called Aschenputtel and said,

"Comb our hair, brush our shoes, and make our buckles fast, we are going to the wedding feast at the king's castle."

Aschenputtel, when she heard this, could not help crying, for she too would have liked to go to the dance, and she begged her stepmother to allow her.

"What, you Aschenputtel!" said she. "In all your dust and dirt, you want to go to the festival! You that have no dress and no shoes! You want to dance!"

But since she persisted in asking, at last the stepmother said,

"I have scattered a dish full of lentils in the ashes, and if you can pick them all up again in two hours, you may go with us."

Then the maiden went to the back door that led into the garden and called out,

> O gentle doves, O turtledoves,
> And all the birds that be,
> The lentils that in ashes lie
> Come and pick up for me!
>   The good must be put in the dish,
>   The bad you may eat if you wish.

Then there came to the kitchen window two white doves, and after them some turtledoves, and at last a crowd of all the birds under heaven, chirping and fluttering, and they alighted among the ashes; and the doves nodded with their heads and began to pick, peck, pick, peck, and then all the others began to pick, peck, pick, peck and put all the good grains into the dish. Before an hour was over, all was done, and they flew away. Then the maiden brought the dish to her stepmother, feeling joyful and thinking that now she should go to the feast; but the stepmother said,

"No, Aschenputtel, you have no proper clothes, and you do not know how to dance, and you would be laughed at!"

And when Aschenputtel cried for disappointment, she added,

"If you can pick two dishfuls of lentils out of the ashes, nice and clean, you shall go with us," thinking to herself, "for that is not possible." When she had strewed two dishfuls of lentils among the ashes, the maiden went through the back door into the garden and cried,

> O gentle doves, O turtledoves,
> And all the birds that be,
> The lentils that in ashes lie

WORDS TO OWN
ordained (ôr·dānd') v.: ordered or decreed.
persisted (pər·sist'id) v.: continued firmly or steadily.

ASCHENPUTTEL 595

D Elements of Literature
Motif
? How long is the festival supposed to last? [three days] How do the stepsisters' demands show that "three is a charmed number"—that is, a motif in this story? [The stepsisters require Aschenputtel to do three things to help them get ready for the festival.]

E Cultural Connections
Animal Symbolism
Point out that Aschenputtel describes these doves as gentle and that in many cultures, doves symbolize peace. (They also may symbolize the mother's soul, at peace in Heaven.) Invite students to explain how various birds are viewed in their cultural backgrounds (as symbols of wisdom or strength, for example, or as omens of trouble).

F Elements of Literature
Onomatopoeia
? What other words associated with birds, such as pick and peck, have sounds that suggest their meanings? [Possible responses: cheep, chirp, squawk, tweet, twitter, flutter.]

G Struggling Readers
Questioning
? If you met Aschenputtel in the garden at this moment, what questions would you ask her? [Possible responses: Why are your stepmother and stepsisters so mean? Why doesn't your father help you? Do you think that the birds will come back? Did you let your stepmother trick you again, or do you have a plan?]

Getting Students Involved

Cooperative Learning
The Problem Patrol. Aschenputtel is given tasks that seem impossible to accomplish; fortunately, she has the doves to help her. Students may never face a situation like hers, but they face other challenges and problems on a daily basis. Ask students, working in groups of three or four, to form a "Problem Patrol" and determine how they would handle a difficult task. Here is one possible situation that students might consider, along with a problem-solution chart that they might use in their groups:

Before you are allowed to go to the movies, you must complete your chores. The movie begins in one hour, but it will take you at least two hours to finish your chores. What will you do?

Problem	Solution
[How to complete chores and still see the movie?]	[Ask for help; try to see a later movie.]

A ⓐ English Language Learners
Breaking Down Difficult Text
Long sentences like this, in which thoughts are connected by a series of *ands*, appear frequently in this story. Have students rephrase this sentence into at least three shorter ones. [Possible response: So there came to the kitchen two white doves. Then some turtledoves came, followed by a crowd of all the other birds under heaven, chirping and fluttering. They alighted among the ashes. The doves nodded with their heads and began to pick, peck, pick, peck. Then the other birds joined in and put all the good grains into the dish.]

B ⓑ Vocabulary Note
Multiple Meanings
❓ What does the stepmother mean by "proper clothes"? What else can *proper* mean? [Possible responses: Here, *proper* means "suitable"—in this case, elegant and formal. Other meanings of *proper* include "conforming to genteel behavior" and "belonging to a specific individual."]

C ⓒ Elements of Literature
Motif
❓ How does the number three show up in Aschenputtel's problem—and in its solution? [Aschenputtel's stepmother rejects the girl's request to go to the festival three times; three times, the girl leaves the house to ask for help (from the doves and then from the hazel bush).]

D ⓓ Reading Skills and Strategies

Finding the Main Idea
❓ Why do the stepmother and stepsisters fail to recognize Aschenputtel at the festival? [Possible response: Because they are impressed only by appearances, they have never considered the beauty of the girl covered with dust and dirt and dressed in shabby clothes.]

Come and pick up for me!
    The good must be put in the dish,
    The bad you may eat if you wish.

ⓐ So there came to the kitchen window two white doves, and then some turtledoves, and at last a crowd of all the other birds under heaven, chirping and fluttering, and they alighted among the ashes, and the doves nodded with their heads and began to pick, peck, pick, peck, and then all the others began to pick, peck, pick, peck and put all the good grains into the dish. And before half an hour was over, it was all done, and they flew away. Then the maiden took the dishes to the stepmother, feeling joyful and thinking that now she should go with them to the feast. But her stepmother said, "All this is of no good to you; you cannot come with us, for you have no proper clothes and cannot dance; you would ⓑ put us to shame."

Then she turned her back on poor Aschenputtel and made haste to set out with her two proud daughters.

And as there was no one left in the house, ⓒ Aschenputtel went to her mother's grave, under the hazel bush, and cried,

    Little tree, little tree, shake over me,
    That silver and gold may come down
        and cover me.

Then the bird threw down a dress of gold and silver and a pair of slippers embroidered with silk and silver. And in all haste she put on the dress and went to the festival. But her stepmother and sisters did not know her and thought she must be a foreign princess, she ⓓ looked so beautiful in her golden dress. Of Aschenputtel they never thought at all and supposed that she was sitting at home, picking the lentils out of the ashes. The King's son came to meet her and took her by the hand and danced with her, and he refused to stand up with anyone else so that he might not be obliged to let

go her hand; and when anyone came to claim it, he answered,

    "She is my partner."

And when the evening came, she wanted to go home, but the prince said he would go with her to take care of her, for he wanted to see where the beautiful maiden lived. But she escaped him and jumped up into the pigeon house. Then the prince waited until her father came along, and told him that the strange maiden had jumped into the pigeon house. The father thought to himself, "It cannot surely be Aschenputtel" and called for axes and hatchets and had the pigeon house cut down, but there was no one in it. And when they entered the house, there sat Aschenputtel in her dirty clothes among the cinders, and a little oil lamp burnt dimly in the chimney; for Aschenputtel had been very quick and had jumped out of the pigeon house again and had run to the hazel bush; and there she had taken off her beautiful dress and had laid it on the grave, and the bird had carried it away again, and then she had put on her little gray kirtle again and had sat down in the kitchen among the cinders.

The next day, when the festival began anew, and the parents and stepsisters had gone to it, Aschenputtel went to the hazel bush and cried,

    Little tree, little tree, shake over me,
    That silver and gold may come down
        and cover me.

Then the bird cast down a still more splendid dress than on the day before. And when she appeared in it among the guests, everyone was astonished at her beauty. The prince had been waiting until she came, and he took her hand and danced with her alone. And when anyone else came to invite her, he said,

    "She is my partner."

And when the evening came, she wanted to go home, and the prince followed her, for he wanted to see to what house she belonged; but she broke away from him and ran into the gar-

---

Listening to Music

Cinderella, the musical by Richard Rodgers (1902–1979), composer, and Oscar Hammerstein II (1895–1960), lyricist

Rodgers and Hammerstein together created a string of memorable musicals, including *Oklahoma!, Carousel, South Pacific, The King and I,* and *The Sound of Music.* Somewhat lesser known is their musical version of the Cinderella story. *Cinderella* was well received as a 1957 television production and was remade successfully in 1965

and 1997. (For a photograph from a different musical version, see p. 605.)

Activities
• After students have read "Aschenputtel," play a few songs from *Cinderella*—for example, "In My Own Little Corner," "The Prince Is Giving a Ball," and "Ten Minutes Ago." Ask students how well they think these songs capture the story as the Grimms told it. (You might point

out that the musical is based on Perrault's version, not on that of the Grimm brothers.)
• Have students work in pairs (like Rodgers and Hammerstein) to write a song based on "Aschenputtel" or another Cinderella tale in Collection Eight. Students may fit new words to a familiar melody or create a song that is wholly their own. Invite volunteers to perform their songs.

"Aschen Poodle"—A Modern Furry Tale

You know the story of Cinderella—but have you ever seen a Cinderella with a furry coat and a big wet nose? For William Wegman, a photographer known for his unusual pictures of his famous Weimaraner dogs, the story of Cinderella has gone to the dogs.

In Wegman's version of the Cinderella story, his dog Battina is the beautiful Cinderella, while her real-life mother, named Fay Wray, plays her wicked stepmother. Wegman's *Cinderella* is complete with cruel Weimaraner stepsisters, a Weimaraner fairy godmother, and a Weimaraner prince.

Wegman's dogs look so comfortable in their roles that after reading his *Cinderella,* you probably wouldn't be at all surprised to see the lovely Weimaraner Cinderella shyly appear at your next party.

Copyright William Wegman, Courtesy PaceWildenstein-MacGill, New York.

LITERATURE AND ART

Students can probably think of many ways animals are used to mimic human beings: animal acts at the circus; TV commercials that have talking animals; calendars that show animals aping people, and the like. Have students think about all kinds of animals and their personalities. Then invite students to suggest other animals that could be used to represent Cinderella/Aschenputtel and to explain their choices.

E **Elements of Literature**
Motif
? Does this time period have anything to do with the motif? Explain. [This is another example of the "charmed" number three; it is the third day of the festival.]

---

den at the back of the house. There stood a fine large tree, bearing splendid pears; she leapt as lightly as a squirrel among the branches, and the prince did not know what had become of her. So he waited until her father came along, and then he told him that the strange maiden had rushed from him, and that he thought she had gone up into the pear tree. The father thought to himself,

"It cannot surely be Aschenputtel" and

called for an axe and felled the tree, but there was no one in it. And when they went into the kitchen, there sat Aschenputtel among the cinders, as usual, for she had got down the other side of the tree and had taken back her beautiful clothes to the bird on the hazel bush and had put on her old gray kirtle again.

On the third day, when the parents and the stepchildren had set off, Aschenputtel went again to her mother's grave and said to the tree, **E**

ASCHENPUTTEL 597

Using Students' Strengths

Auditory/Musical Learners
Have students summarize "Aschenputtel" in a story-round, either as they read the tale or after they have finished. To guide their comments, ask students to answer the questions "What happened?" and "What happened next?" Have them keep repeating the question until the story has been retold completely and accurately.

Verbal Learners
Have students assume the persona of a character in "Aschenputtel" and then write a letter to one of the other characters. Remind students to use thoughts and language consistent with their chosen characters. Invite students to exchange letters.

Visual Learners
Ask students to illustrate their favorite scene from "Aschenputtel" and to take a caption for their illustration from the story. Work with students to create a "gallery walk" of the finished illustrations, which your class and others can enjoy. As students show their displays (arranged by scene), they can explain why they chose that particular scene and method of depiction.

Little tree, little tree, shake over me,
That silver and gold may come down
  and cover me.

A Then the bird cast down a dress the likes of which had never been seen for splendor and brilliancy, and slippers that were of gold.

And when she appeared in this dress at the feast, nobody knew what to say for wonderment. The prince danced with her alone, and if anyone else asked her, he answered,

"She is my partner."

And when it was evening, Aschenputtel wanted to go home, and the prince was about to go with her when she ran past him so **B** quickly that he could not follow her. But he had laid a plan and had caused all the steps to be spread with pitch,[2] so that as she rushed down them, her left shoe remained sticking in it. The prince picked it up and saw that it was of gold and very small and slender. The next morning he went to the father and told him that none should be his bride save the one whose foot the golden shoe should fit. Then the two sisters were very glad, because they had pretty feet. The eldest went to her room to try on the shoe, and her mother stood by. But she could not get her great toe into it, for the shoe was too small; then her mother handed her a knife, and said,

"Cut the toe off, for when you are queen, you will never have to go on foot." So the girl **C** cut her toe off, squeezed her foot into the shoe, concealed the pain, and went down to the prince. Then he took her with him on his horse as his bride and rode off. They had to pass by the grave, and there sat the two pigeons on the hazel bush and cried,

There they go, there they go!
There is blood on her shoe;
The shoe is too small,
—Not the right bride at all!

2. **pitch:** here, black, sticky tar.

Then the prince looked at her shoe and saw the blood flowing. And he turned his horse round and took the false bride home again, saying she was not the right one and that the other sister must try on the shoe. So she went into her room to do so and got her toes comfortably in, but her heel was too large. Then her mother handed her the knife, saying, "Cut a piece off your heel; when you are queen, you will never have to go on foot."

So the girl cut a piece off her heel and thrust her foot into the shoe, concealed the pain, and went down to the prince, who took his bride before him on his horse and rode off. When they passed by the hazel bush, the two pigeons sat there and cried,

There they go, there they go!
There is blood on her shoe;
The shoe is too small,
—Not the right bride at all!

Then the prince looked at her foot and saw how the blood was flowing from the shoe and staining the white stocking. And he turned his horse round and brought the false bride home again.

"This is not the right one," said he. "Have you no other daughter?"

"No," said the man, "only my dead wife left behind her a little <u>stunted</u> Aschenputtel; it is impossible that she can be the bride." But the King's son ordered her to be sent for, but the mother said,

"Oh, no! She is much too dirty; I could not let her be seen."

But he would have her fetched, and so Aschenputtel had to appear.

First she washed her face and hands quite clean and went in and curtseyed to the prince,

- -

WORDS TO OWN

stunted (stunt'id) *v.* used as *adj.:* not properly grown.

- -

Crossing the Curriculum

Social Studies

Ask students to research and report on festivals in Europe during the Middle Ages. (Students may work independently or collaborate on a report in a panel discussion or multimedia presentation.) Students should discuss the types of entertainment and competitions held, food, dress, and other elements of a festival.

Art

What kind of home might Aschenputtel hope to have with the prince? To help students consider her possible future, have them assemble a collection of pictures and drawings of medieval castles. The collection should include a brief description of each castle, as well as information on the daily lives of those who lived and worked in the castle.

Assessing Learning

Observation Assessment: Group Work

While students work on a group activity, observe their discussions and evaluate observations such as the following with 1=Often, 2=Sometimes, or 3 =Rarely:

- Acquires data
- Thinks creatively
- Evaluates data
- Works well with people from diverse backgrounds
- Demonstrates individual responsibility

who held out to her the golden shoe. Then she sat down on a stool, drew her foot out of the heavy wooden shoe, and slipped it into the golden one, which fitted it perfectly. And when she stood up and the prince looked in her face, he knew again the beautiful maiden that had danced with him, and he cried,

"This is the right bride!"

The stepmother and the two sisters were thunderstruck and grew pale with anger, but the prince put Aschenputtel before him on his horse and rode off. And as they passed the hazel bush, the two white pigeons cried,

> There they go, there they go!
> No blood on her shoe;
> The shoe's not too small,
> The right bride is she after all.

ASCHENPUTTEL 599

And when they had thus cried, they came flying after and perched on Aschenputtel's shoulders, one on the right, the other on the left, and so remained.

And when her wedding with the prince was appointed to be held, the false sisters came, hoping to curry favor[3] and to take part in the festivities. So as the bridal procession went to the church, the eldest walked on the right side and the younger on the left, and the pigeons picked out an eye of each of them. And as they returned, the elder was on the left side and the younger on the right, and the pigeons picked out the other eye of each of them. And so they were condemned for the rest of their days because of their wickedness and falsehood.

3. **curry favor:** try to win approval by flattering and fawning.

D **Elements of Literature**
Motif
? How do the pigeons' cries illustrate the motif of "threes" in this story? [The pigeons cry out three times before the prince and Aschenputtel come together.]

D **Elements of Literature**
Motif
? How do the pigeons' cries illustrate the motif of "threes" in this story? [The pigeons cry out three times before the prince and Aschenputtel come together.]

E **Reading Skills and Strategies**

Finding the Main Idea
? The stepsisters are "condemned ... because of their wickedness and falsehood." Why is Aschenputtel rewarded? [Possible response: She is just the opposite. She finds love because she has remained "pious and good," despite her problems.]

Making the Connections

Connecting to the Theme:
"900 Cinderellas: Our World Heritage in Folklore"

As students may assume from the title of Collection Eight, folk tales are a part of cultures around the world, and elements of the Cinderella story are found in many of those folk tales. Students may not make the connection at first when they read "Aschenputtel." When they consider the main idea of this story, however, they may begin to see how that idea would appeal to people from many parts of the world. Have students suggest other ideas from the story that appear in many folk tales and list these on the chalkboard. [Examples include surviving the death of a parent, learning to fend for yourself, and falling in love with royalty.] Challenge students to read on to see if any other folk tales in Collection Eight pick up on these ideas.

Cultural Connections

Several details in the Grimm brothers' telling of this story might be handled differently by a storyteller from another culture. Invite students to research and report on how some other cultures might address these matters:

- the status of a widower's children when the widower remarries
- respect for siblings
- romance between members of different social classes

BROWSING IN THE FILES

About the Authors. Jakob and Wilhelm Grimm lived in an era during which the German states were struggling to achieve a unified constitutional government. The brothers supported this movement by gathering stories from a heritage common to people throughout Germany and by preparing a massive dictionary of the German language. Jakob was the bolder and more experimental of the two, and he was good with words. Within the family, he kept rigidly to his work schedule but also could take time to be a lovable uncle. Wilhelm was the gentler, more poetic brother, and he had a gift for popular speech.

A Critic's Comment. The Grimms have been criticized for reworking the material that they collected into "literary" stories. As Bruno Bettelheim notes, however, "It is not that the brothers did not take some liberties with the tales when they published them. They often tightened the plot or clarified it to obtain a more closely knit tale. It was their genius that out of several versions of the same tale they wove one which in the end was truer to the spirit of the folktale.... Thanks to the brothers' poetic and historic genius they recognized what in the versions they were told was the product of the imagination of the person who told the story and what was the essential tale that lay behind it, and this they created or rather re-created by the small changes they introduced into the tale they had been told."

The Granger Collection, New York.

MEET THE WRITERS

Two Brothers with a Dream

Before the 1800s, most fairy tales were not written down. They existed only in the memories of people who had heard them from their elders. **Jakob** (1785–1863) and **Wilhelm** (1786–1859) **Grimm** decided that the traditional stories of Germany ought to be written down in one book before they were forgotten. Jakob wrote:

66 It is high time that these old traditions were collected and rescued before they perish like dew in the hot sun or fire in a stream and fall silent forever in the unrest of our days. 99

The two brothers wandered from farm to village, looking for good storytellers who knew the old tales. They listened patiently and wrote the stories down. By the time the last edition of their stories was published, in 1857, the brothers had collected about two hundred tales. Some of the best-known ones are "Little Red Riding Hood," "Rumpelstiltskin," "Hansel and Gretel," "Sleeping Beauty," and, of course, "Aschenputtel," or "Cinderella."

More Grimm Stories

If you browse through *The Complete Grimm's Fairy Tales* (Pantheon), you will find some truly grim stories. These German tales are filled with acts of cruelty and murder. In the United States, retellers of the tales have sometimes toned them down, producing storybook versions that are much less terrifying.

600   900 CINDERELLAS: OUR WORLD HERITAGE IN FOLKLORE

Assessing Learning

Check Test: Short Answer

1. With whom does Aschenputtel live, and why? [She lives with her father, her stepmother, and her two stepsisters because her own mother has died.]
2. What happens to the twig that Aschenputtel plants? [It grows into a tree that is the home for a magic bird.]
3. How is Aschenputtel able to go to the festival?

[The white bird in the tree brings her lovely clothes.]

4. After she first meets the prince, where does Aschenputtel go? [She jumps up into a pigeon house.]
5. What do the stepsisters do to try to convince the prince that they are the true brides? [They cut off part of their feet so the shoe will fit.]

Standardized Test Preparation

For practice with standardized test format specific to this selection, see
• *Standardized Test Preparation*, p. 88
For practice in proofreading and editing, see
• *Daily Oral Grammar*, Transparency 35

...And Then the Prince Knelt Down and Tried to Put the Glass Slipper on Cinderella's Foot

Judith Viorst

I really didn't notice that he had a funny nose.
And he certainly looked better all dressed up in fancy clothes.
He's not nearly as attractive as he seemed the other night.
So I think I'll just pretend that this glass slipper feels too tight.

(A)

In Search of Cinderella

Shel Silverstein

From dusk to dawn
From town to town,
Without a single clue,
I seek the tender, slender foot **(B)**
To fit this crystal shoe.
From dusk to dawn,
I try it on **(C)**
Each damsel that I meet.
And I still love her so, but oh,
I've started hating feet.

ASCHENPUTTEL 601

(A) **Elements of Literature**
Point of View
? How is the point of view of this poem different from the point of view of "Aschenputtel"? [Viorst's poem is told from the point of view of the speaker (Cinderella herself); "Aschenputtel" is told from this omniscient third-person point of view.]

(B) **Reading Skills and Strategies**
Comparing and Contrasting
? How is this poem similar to the story of "Aschenputtel"? [Possible response: Both refer to a man who is interested in the girl whose foot fits the shoe.]

(C) **Reading Skills and Strategies**
Making Inferences
? Who is the speaker in this poem? [The prince is the speaker.]

Connecting Across Texts

Connecting with "Aschenputtel"
Ask students to compare the characters of Aschenputtel and the prince with the speakers in the poems by Viorst and Silverstein. Help students create a chart that will allow them to see the differences between the Grimm brothers' characters and the modern characters presented by the poets. In one column, students should list adjectives that describe Aschenputtel; then, adjectives that describe the character in Viorst's poem. Have them fill in characteristics for the two versions of the prince.

Aschenputtel	[considerate]
Viorst's Cinderella	[observant]
Grimm's prince	[determined]
Silverstein's prince	[realistic]

Ⓐ Critical Thinking
Making Connections
❓ How is the beginning of this story similar to and yet different from "Aschenputtel"? [Possible responses: It is similar because there is a child who faces a difficult task (cutting the lawn with scissors) and who has two siblings who are unpleasant people. It is different because the characters are teenage boys rather than young women and because the story is set in modern times.]

Ⓑ Appreciating Language
Formal and Informal Dialogue
To make the characters more realistic, the authors have them speak in an informal style, peppering their dialogue with expressions such as "No way, man!" and "I dunno." You might challenge students to express some of the same dialogue more formally (for example, "You're wrong" and "I don't know") and comment on the differences.

Ⓒ Reading Skills and Strategies
Responding to the Text
❓ What do you think of the fact that Chris's getaway involves no magical helpers? [Some students may miss that familiar element of the Cinderella story. Other students may feel that Chris's getaway is more true to life.]

> **FROM THE EDITOR'S DESK**
> Hamburgers, French fries, pencils, and paper were all that four girls needed to write this story. They sat at the kitchen table and created this modern-day version of "Cinderella." Johnny Depp was in the first draft but didn't make the revision.

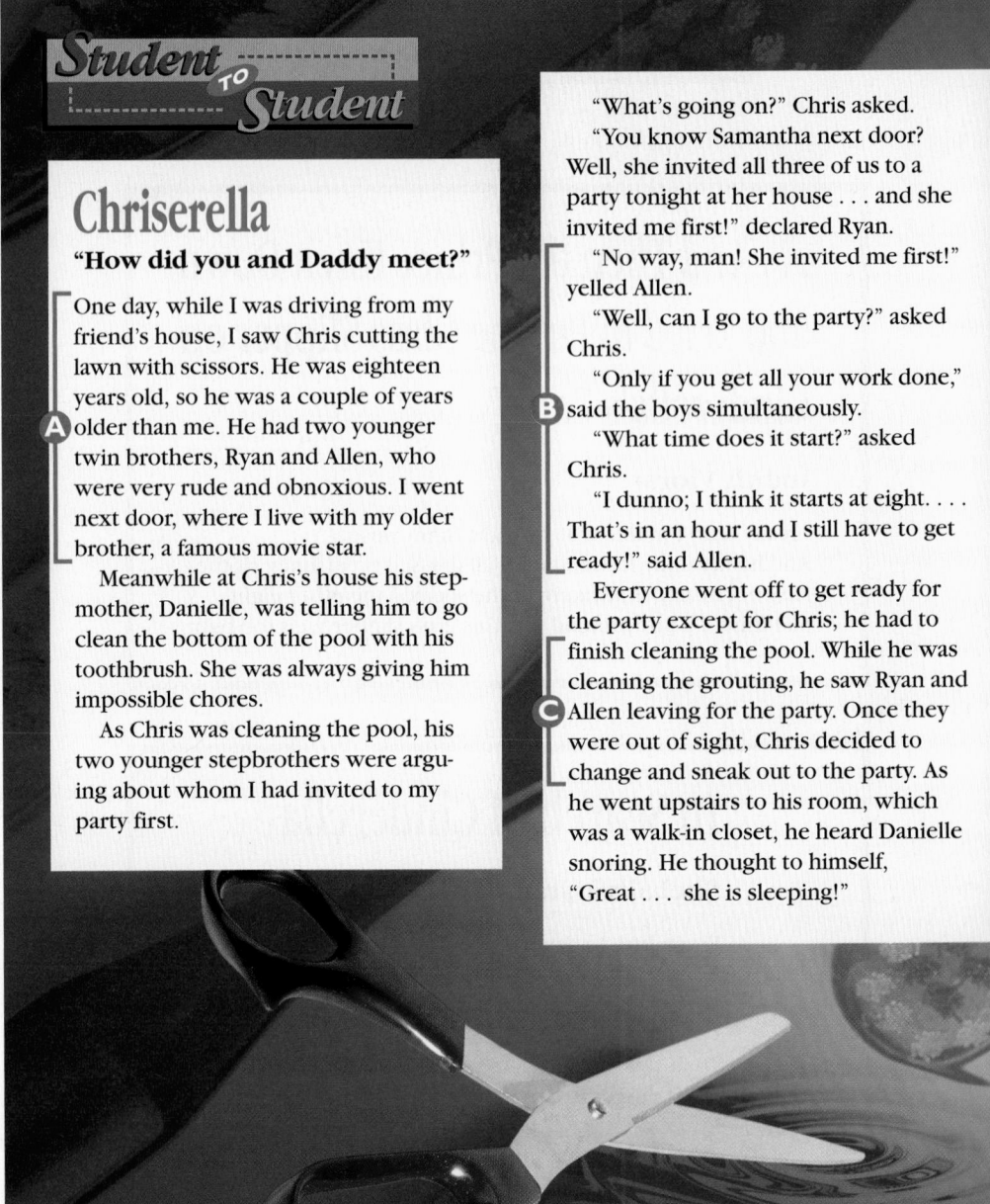

Student to Student

Chriserella

"How did you and Daddy meet?"

Ⓐ One day, while I was driving from my friend's house, I saw Chris cutting the lawn with scissors. He was eighteen years old, so he was a couple of years older than me. He had two younger twin brothers, Ryan and Allen, who were very rude and obnoxious. I went next door, where I live with my older brother, a famous movie star.

Meanwhile at Chris's house his stepmother, Danielle, was telling him to go clean the bottom of the pool with his toothbrush. She was always giving him impossible chores.

As Chris was cleaning the pool, his two younger stepbrothers were arguing about whom I had invited to my party first.

"What's going on?" Chris asked.

"You know Samantha next door? Well, she invited all three of us to a party tonight at her house . . . and she invited me first!" declared Ryan.

"No way, man! She invited me first!" yelled Allen.

"Well, can I go to the party?" asked Chris.

"Only if you get all your work done," Ⓑ said the boys simultaneously.

"What time does it start?" asked Chris.

"I dunno; I think it starts at eight. . . . That's in an hour and I still have to get ready!" said Allen.

Everyone went off to get ready for the party except for Chris; he had to finish cleaning the pool. While he was cleaning the grouting, he saw Ryan and Ⓒ Allen leaving for the party. Once they were out of sight, Chris decided to change and sneak out to the party. As he went upstairs to his room, which was a walk-in closet, he heard Danielle snoring. He thought to himself, "Great . . . she is sleeping!"

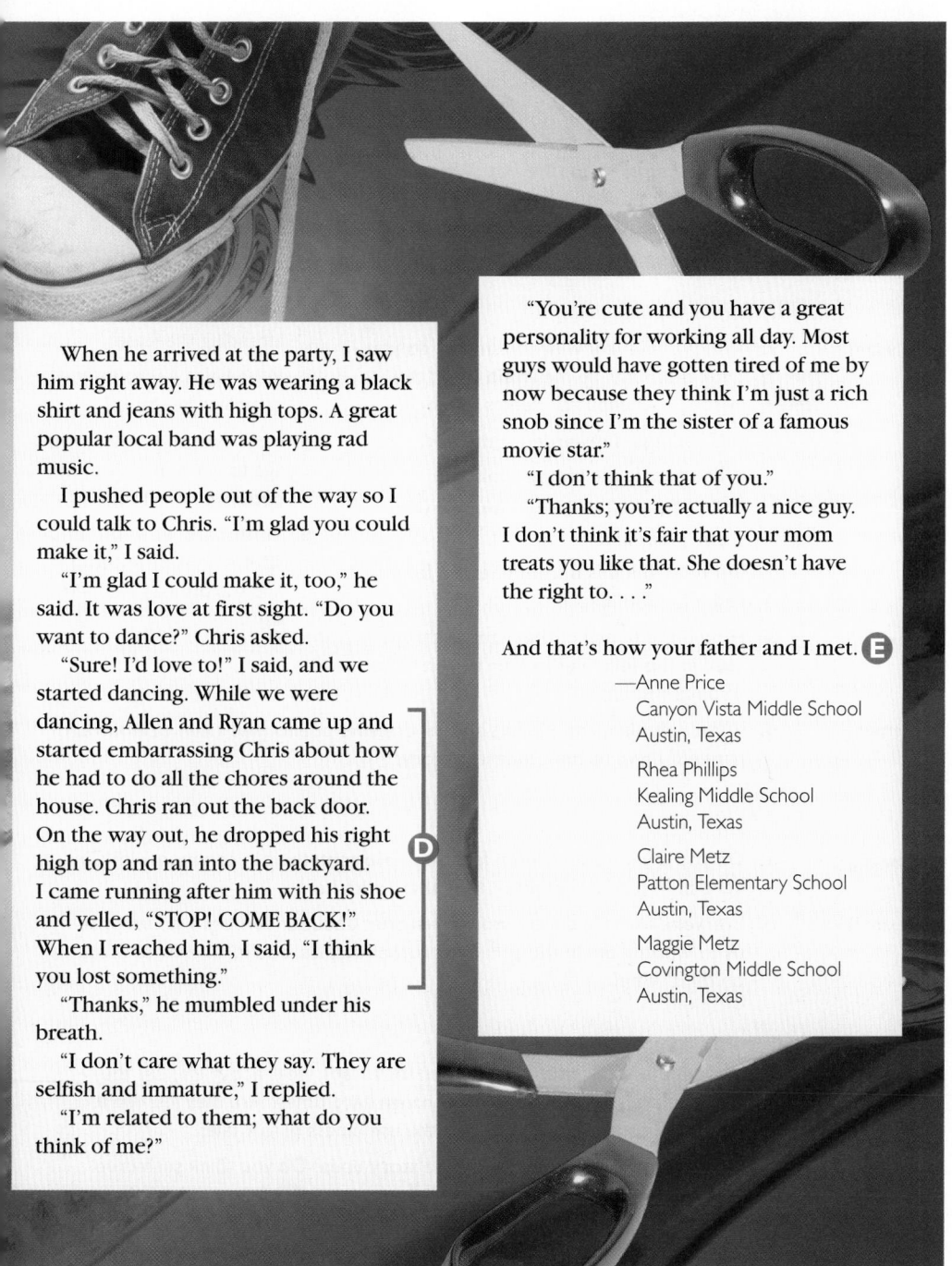

When he arrived at the party, I saw him right away. He was wearing a black shirt and jeans with high tops. A great popular local band was playing rad music.

I pushed people out of the way so I could talk to Chris. "I'm glad you could make it," I said.

"I'm glad I could make it, too," he said. It was love at first sight. "Do you want to dance?" Chris asked.

"Sure! I'd love to!" I said, and we started dancing. While we were dancing, Allen and Ryan came up and started embarrassing Chris about how he had to do all the chores around the house. Chris ran out the back door. On the way out, he dropped his right high top and ran into the backyard. I came running after him with his shoe and yelled, "STOP! COME BACK!" When I reached him, I said, "I think you lost something."

"Thanks," he mumbled under his breath.

"I don't care what they say. They are selfish and immature," I replied.

"I'm related to them; what do you think of me?"

"You're cute and you have a great personality for working all day. Most guys would have gotten tired of me by now because they think I'm just a rich snob since I'm the sister of a famous movie star."

"I don't think that of you."

"Thanks; you're actually a nice guy. I don't think it's fair that your mom treats you like that. She doesn't have the right to. . . ."

And that's how your father and I met. **E**

—Anne Price
Canyon Vista Middle School
Austin, Texas

Rhea Phillips
Kealing Middle School
Austin, Texas

Claire Metz
Patton Elementary School
Austin, Texas

Maggie Metz
Covington Middle School
Austin, Texas

ASCHENPUTTEL **603**

D Elements of Literature
Climax
As the speaker picks up the high top and chases after Chris, the story builds to its point of greatest tension and excitement. Students may find it helpful to sketch a story map, showing how events have led up to this climax.

E Critical Thinking
Extending the Text
? In your opinion, does this story represent the way that most young people feel about relationships? Explain. [Possible responses: Yes; many people feel that it is very easy to meet the people whom they will love forever. No; this story is very much like the fairy tale, and real life is quite different.]

Resources ————
Assessment
• *Standardized Test Preparation*, p. 86

Connecting Across Texts

Connecting with "Aschenputtel"
Have students work in groups to complete a comparison chart similar to the one shown. In the first column, students should list characteristics of the stories that serve as points of comparison; in the second and third columns, they should mark (and jot down a comment or two, if they wish) which story or stories illustrate each characteristic.

Characteristics	Aschenputtel	Chriserella
[Main character is bothered by stepbrothers.]		X
[Main character is bothered by stepsisters.]	X	
[Main character is bothered by stepmother.]	X	X

MAKING MEANINGS

First Thoughts

1. Possible response: The story expresses our deep desires to find love and happiness, to be rescued from a horrible situation, to be rewarded for being good, to see evil punished, to see miracles happen. The story may be about our fear of losing a parent or of not being part of the family; Aschenputtel's problems begin only after her mother's death.

Shaping Interpretations

2. Answers to this questions will vary, and students should be encouraged to argue for their choices. Probably the best answer is "Goodness is rewarded in the end," since the good Aschenputtel is eventually rewarded with marriage to the prince and escape from her horrible situation. See also the father's words to Aschenputtel at the start of the story. The second lesson could also be justified: The bad stepsisters and step-mother are punished severely.

3. The stepmother sets three impossible tasks, the festival lasts three days, Aschenputtel asks for three dresses and escapes from the prince three times, and three sisters try on the slipper. The motif helps build suspense because the reader wants to know how the third time will be different.

4. Viorst takes a feminist viewpoint, imagining that the prince doesn't look as good to Cinderella in daylight; Cin-derella therefore decides to pretend the slipper is too tight. Silverstein is comical, telling the incident from the point of view of the prince, who has come to hate feet.

Extending the Text

5. Yes, even in happy families, children sometimes feel they are treated unfairly by parents or siblings; like Aschenputtel, such children might hope to have someone befriend and help them.

6. Answers will vary. Possible novels include *The Secret Garden* and *Hatchet*.

Challenging the Text

7. Folk tales may give unrealistic ideas about life. Good does not always pre-vail, nor is evil always discovered or punished. Nevertheless, folk tales can give children courage to get through hard times because such stories pro-vide hope of a brighter future. Some psychologists believe that fairy tales

MAKING MEANINGS

First Thoughts

[respond]

1. Think about the round robin discussion you had before you read this story. Which of our deepest wishes do you think this story expresses? Do you think it is also about some of our fears? Explain.

Shaping Interpretations

[synthesize]

2. Which of the following statements do you think best sums up the **main idea,** the lesson "Aschenputtel" seems to teach?

   - Goodness is rewarded in the end.
   - Bad people are always punished.
   - True love means being loved for who you really are.

   Do you think this is a good lesson for today's world? Explain.

[explain]

3. How is the **motif** of the number three used in this folk tale? Explain how it helps to build suspense.

[interpret]

4. What new slants do Viorst's and Silverstein's poems (see *Connections* on page 601) give to the Cinderella story?

Extending the Text

[connect]

5. Do you think most children feel they have something in common with Cin-derella? What feelings might they share with her?

[extend]

6. Everyone likes Cinderella stories—stories about underdogs who surprise us by winning out in the end. What other stories, books, or movies focus on this theme?

Challenging the Text

[analyze]

7. Do you think folk tales give children unrealistic ideas about life? Do they give children the courage to get through hard times? Are they just fun to read? Talk about your opinions of the usefulness of folk tales.

[evaluate]

8. How do you feel about the way the story ends? Do you think such cruel details *should* be removed from children's stories? Talk about your response to the stepsisters' punishment.

---

actually help young children deal with their fears by leading them to experi-ence, in their imaginations, a fearful situation and its resolution.

8. Possible responses: The story ends cruelly for some characters. These details should be removed for little children, who will not enjoy or learn from a story if it scares them. These details should *not* be removed; chil-dren know that the story is a fan-tasy. Students' responses should include their opinions about the stepsisters' punishment.

Reading Check

a. What does Aschenputtel do with the twig her father gives her?

b. What does the step-mother do to stop Aschenputtel from attending the feast?

c. Who helps Aschenputtel complete her tasks?

d. How does the prince man-age to get one of Aschen-puttel's golden slippers?

e. What happens to the step-sisters on Aschenputtel and the prince's wedding day?

Reading Check

a. Aschenputtel plants the twig on her mother's grave, where it grows into a hazel tree.

b. Aschenputtel's stepmother makes her ashamed of her appearance and has her separate lentils from the ashes.

c. All the birds in the area help Aschenputtel complete her tasks.

d. The prince has the steps coated with pitch so her shoe will stick as she runs away.

e. The stepsisters' eyes are plucked out by the pigeons.

CHOICES: Building Your Portfolio

Writer's Notebook

1. Collecting Ideas for an Informative Report

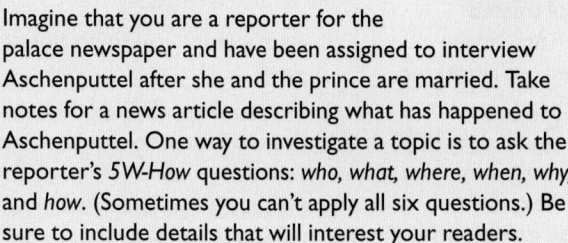

Imagine that you are a reporter for the palace newspaper and have been assigned to interview Aschenputtel after she and the prince are married. Take notes for a news article describing what has happened to Aschenputtel. One way to investigate a topic is to ask the reporter's *5W-How* questions: *who, what, where, when, why,* and *how.* (Sometimes you can't apply all six questions.) Be sure to include details that will interest your readers.

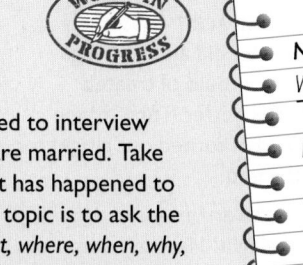

News Story
Whom is the story about?
New princess.
What happened to her?
Mistreated girl rescued by prince.
Etc.

Creative Writing/ Speaking

2. Role Reversal

What might happen if a princess rescued an under-dog boy from a life of drudgery? One version of this story is told in the Student to Student on page 602. Create your own version of "Cinderella." Decide on your **characters, setting,** and **plot,** and then write the story. You can stick closely to the story of "Aschenputtel" or come up with a totally new plot, but try to use the **motif** of three. Illustrate your story, and read it aloud to a group of younger children.

Creative Writing

3. If the Shoe Fits . . .

Write a new ending for "Aschenputtel," describing how the characters might react if Aschenputtel pre-tended that the golden slip-per was too tight or if the prince got sick of the sight of all those feet. Look back at the *Connections* poems (page 601) for inspiration.

Poster for Walt Disney's *Cinderella* (1950).

Speaking and Listening

4. A Real Cinderella Story

Imagine a Cinderella story set today in your own com-munity. Who would the underdog be? Who or what would hold the underdog back? Who would rescue the underdog, and how would this happen? With a group of classmates, brain-storm to come up with some ideas. Then, plot out your story. You could act out your modern Cin-derella story or videotape the production for your class.

Rubrics for each Choices assignment appear on p. 183 in the *Portfolio Management System.*

CHOICES: Building Your Portfolio

1. **Writer's Notebook** You might begin by having students suggest *5W-How?* questions that relate to current classroom work in other subject areas. Remind students to save their work for possible use in the Writer's Workshop on pp. 672–676.
2. **Creative Writing/Speaking** Students might work together to brainstorm these questions:
   - When and where will the story take place?
   - Who will the main characters be?
   - Will the boy be weak and helpless or strong and courageous?
   - Will the princess be shy or bold?
   - How will you use the motif of three?
3. **Creative Writing** To generate ideas for a new ending, have each student describe in one sentence a possible ending. Collect the sen-tences and distribute them at ran-dom. Explain that students need not use the ending that they receive but that they may use it if they wish.
4. **Speaking and Listening** Discuss with students the concept of the underdog. Have students determine their own definition of *underdog* before they develop the plot of a new story.

Using Compiled Information to Raise Additional Questions

Sometimes when students write informative reports, such as the one they will write for the Writer's Workshop on p. 672, their research will raise new questions. For example, a student compiling information on Yoruban culture may become interested in rites of passage in his or her own culture. Encourage students to use their research as a springboard for pursuing related topics.

GRAMMAR LINK

Challenge students to choose some work from their portfolios and to look for examples of these pairs of words. Suggest that they write the first of each pair of words in red and the second in blue. Using contrasting colors makes the distinction between the words in each pair highly visible to students.

Try It Out
Answers
1. Aschenputtel had to do <u>a lot</u> of work.
2. Do you think it's <u>all right</u> for children to hear stories with violent endings?
3. I think Aschenputtel <u>should have</u> spoken up for herself more.

Students' summaries should include plot details as well as the incorrect use of the troublesome words.

VOCABULARY
Possible Answers
1. *Pious* means "very religious."
2. A plant might expire because of a lack of sunlight or water or because of disease.
3. The event ordained by the king was a three-day festival.
4. You might admire a person who persisted by sticking to a difficult task instead of giving up, but you might be annoyed by a person who persisted in asking for favors.
5. A stunted plant might be found in a place that lacked sunlight or water.

Resources ——————

Grammar
• *Grammar and Language Links*, p. 61

Vocabulary
• *Words to Own*, p. 22

Spelling
For related spelling instruction, see
• *Spelling and Decoding*, p. 27

GRAMMAR LINK MINI-LESSON

All Right, A Lot, Should Have, and *Would Have*

Langugage Handbook HELP

See Glossary of Usage: all right, a lot, *and* could of, *pages 785 and 786.*

Technology HELP

See Language Workshop CD-ROM. *Key word entry:* usage.

Read the following paragraph. Can you spot the errors in spelling and usage?

SPELLING-CHECKER ALERT

The stepsisters did alot of things wrong. They should of treated Aschenputtel better. Then maybe things would of turned out alright for them in the end.

Did you spot the errors—*alot, should of, would of,* and *alright*? Here are some tips to help you remember the correct spelling or usage of these expressions:

1. The expressions *a lot* and *all right* each consist of two words. Don't run the two words together into one word. (Remember that *all right* is like *all wrong.*)

2. Remember to pronounce the helping verbs *should have* and *would have* correctly. *Of* is not a verb and never follows *could, should,* or *would.*

Try It Out
➤ Find the misused or misspelled word in each sentence. Then, write the sentence correctly.

1. Aschenputtel had to do alot of work.

2. Do you think it's alright for children to hear stories with violent endings?

3. I think Aschenputtel should of spoken up for herself more.

➤ Do a survey of another class to see how many students have trouble with these words. To carry out your survey, write a summary of Aschenputtel's story in which you misuse or misspell each of these four phrases at least once. See how many students can spot the errors. Report your findings to your class.

VOCABULARY HOW TO OWN A WORD

WORD BANK	Write About It
pious expired ordained persisted stunted	1. Write a definition of *pious* that a fourth-grader could understand. 2. Suppose a plant <u>expired</u>. What could cause this? 3. What events in the story of Aschenputtel were <u>ordained</u> by a king or a prince? 4. When would you admire someone who <u>persisted</u>? When would you be annoyed by such a person? 5. Where would you expect to find a plant that was <u>stunted</u>?

Grammar Link Quick Check

Proofread the following sentences by finding the misspelled or incorrect words.

1. The sisters should of been kind to Aschenputtel. [The sisters <u>should have</u> been kind to Aschenputtel.]

2. Alot of birds picked the lentils from the ashes. [<u>A lot</u> of birds picked the lentils from the ashes.]

3. Everything turned out alright, didn't it? [Everything turned out <u>all right</u>, didn't it?]

4. "Aschenputtel" and "Cinderella" have alot of things in common, including two sisters who should of been nicer to other people. ["Aschenputtel" and "Cinderella" have <u>a lot</u> of things in common, including two sisters who <u>should have</u> been nicer to other people.]

Before You Read

THE ALGONQUIN CINDERELLA
YEH-SHEN

Make the Connection

Universal Truths

Many stories told in different parts of the world are surprisingly similar. No one is sure why this is so. Some people think it is because certain real-life wishes and fears are so powerful and so universal that people the world over want to express them in story form. One of the things we learn from all these tales is that despite their many cultural differences, people around the world have a lot in common.

Quickwrite

Pick a statement that you strongly agree or disagree with from the list below. Freewrite for a few minutes about why you feel as you do.

- It's easy to tell who's good and who's bad.

- Good always wins out over bad in the end.

- People can be cruel or jealous.

- People sometimes value wealth above love.

- People learn from their mistakes.

Elements of Literature

Character Types

In "The Algonquin Cinderella" and "Yeh-Shen" you will find some familiar folk-tale characters: the wicked stepmother, the cruel sisters, the handsome prince. Such characters are either all good or all bad. Unlike most people in real life, these **character types** do not grow, change, or learn from their unusual experiences.

> The characters in folk tales are **character types**—recognizable, unchanging figures whom we meet over and over again in one tale after another.
>
> *For more on Character, see the Handbook of Literary Terms.*

Reading Skills and Strategies

Comparing Texts: Looking for Likenesses

Read these stories once just for fun. Then, read them a second time, keeping a piece of paper handy. On the paper, make a chart like the one below. Fill it in with similarities you see in these stories and "Aschenputtel." Are you surprised at how similar these stories are—one Algonquin, one Chinese, and one German?

	Story 1	Story 2	Story 3
Wicked stepmother			
Cruel sisters			
Handsome prince			
Special helpers			
Magical events			
Wishes come true			

607

Summary ▪ ▪

In a Micmac village, a being known as the Invisible One plans to marry the first woman who can see him. Each evening, his sister tests a different village girl, but no one can answer her questions about his appearance. Like other women of the village, two daughters of an old widower try but fail to see the Invisible One. Their younger sister, Oochigeaskw—badly scarred from her oldest sister's abuse and shabbily dressed—also tries. She can see the Invisible One, and she answers his sister's questions correctly. Transformed into a beauty by a bath from the Invisible One's sister, Oochigeaskw becomes the wife of the Invisible One.

Resources

Listening
Audio CD Library
You will find an engrossing recording of this story in the *Audio CD Library:*
• Disc 15, Track 3

A The Algonquin Cinderella

Algonquin, retold by **M. R. Cox**

> The poor little girl in her strange clothes with her face all scarred, was an awful sight...

(Inset) A Micmac mother and son (1854).
National Anthropological Archives 56.827, Smithsonian Institution, © Smithsonian Institution.

608

Resources: Print and Media

Reading
• *Reading Skills and Strategies*
  Selection Skill Lesson, p. 156
• *Graphic Organizers for Active Reading*, p. 42
• *Spelling and Decoding*
  Worksheet, p. 28
• *Audio CD Library*
  Disc 15, Tracks 3, 4

Elements of Literature
• *Literary Elements*
  Transparency 11

Worksheet, p. 34

Writing and Language
• *Daily Oral Grammar*
  Transparencies 36, 37
• *Grammar and Language Links*
  Worksheet, p. 63
• *Language Workshop CD-ROM*

Viewing and Representing
• *Viewing and Representing*
  Fine Art Transparency 19
  Fine Art Worksheet, p. 76

Assessment
• *Formal Assessment*, p. 122
• *Portfolio Management System*, p. 184
• *Standardized Test Preparation*, p. 90
• *Test Generator (One-Stop Planner CD-ROM)*

Internet
• go.hrw.com (keyword: LE0 7-8)

There was once a large village belonging to the Micmac Indians of the Eastern Algonquins, built beside a lake. At the far end of the settlement stood a lodge, and in it lived a being who was always invisible. He had a sister who looked after him, and everyone knew that the girl who could see him might marry him. There were very few girls who did not try to marry him, but it was very long before anyone succeeded.

This is the way in which the test of sight was carried out. At evening time, when the Invisible One was due to return home, his sister would walk with any girl who might come down to the lakeshore. She, of course, could see her brother, since he was always visible to her. As soon as she saw him coming, she would say to the girls:

"Do you see my brother?"

"Yes," they would generally reply—though some of them did say "No."

To those who said that they could indeed see him, the sister would ask, "What is his shoulder strap made of?"

Or, some people say that she would inquire, "What is his moose-runner's haul?" or "What does he draw his sled with?"

And they would answer, "A strip of rawhide," or "A green flexible branch," or something like that.

Then the sister, knowing that they had not told the truth, would say, "Very well, let us return to the wigwam!"

When they went in, she would tell the girls not to sit in a certain place, because it belonged to the Invisible One. Then, after they had helped to cook the supper, they would

Re-creation of an Eastern Woodland Indian wigwam.

THE ALGONQUIN CINDERELLA **609**

Ⓐ Historical Connection
The Micmacs
The translator of this legend, which was collected in the late 1800s, calls it "An Algonquin Cinderella," but strictly speaking the story is about a Micmac Cinderella. The Micmac belong to a widespread group of people who speak dialects of the Algonquin language. Algonquin dialects were or are spoken in Canada, New England, the Atlantic coastal region southward to North Carolina, and the Great Lakes region westward to the Rocky Mountains. Algonquin speakers include the Algonquin, Micmac, Cree, Ojibwa, Blackfoot, Cheyenne, and Arapaho.

Ⓑ Reading Skills and Strategies

Comparing Texts
❓ How does the wooing of the Invisible One differ from the wooing of the prince in "Aschenputtel"? [Possible response: Potential wives visit the Invisible One one by one; all those pursuing the prince see him at once, at a festival.]

Ⓒ Elements of Literature
Character Types
❓ How would you describe these women, as a group of characters? [Possible response: They are liars, who do not deserve the Invisible One.] Who in "Aschenputtel" is like them? Explain. [They are similar to the stepsisters, who "lie" by cutting off parts of their feet so that they can fit into the shoe.]

Reaching All Students

Struggling Readers
Comparing Texts was introduced on p. 607. For a lesson directly tied to these selections that teaches students to compare the two texts by using a strategy called Comparison Grid, see the *Reading Skills and Strategies* binder:
• Selection Skill Lesson, p. 156

English Language Learners
Before students read "Yeh-Shen" (p. 615), tell them that in Chinese culture, age is revered and that it is a common Eastern belief that the spirits of dead relatives or ancestors are manifested in animals. Urge students to note or highlight each interchange between Yeh-Shen and her fish. For additional strategies to supplement instruction for these students, see
• *Lesson Plans Including Strategies for English-Language Learners*

Advanced Learners
After students read "Yeh-Shen" (p. 615), have them rewrite one of the stories from the perspective of a character other than Oochigeaskw or Yeh-Shen. For example, "The Algonquin Cinderella" could be told by the Invisible One, or "Yeh-Shen" could be told by the stepmother. Encourage students to compare their stories and perhaps compile them for a class anthology.

A **Reading Skills and Strategies**

Comparing Texts

❓ What details here remind you of other folk tales that you have read? What details are different? [Possible response: The father is a widower; there are three unmarried daughters, the third of whom is disliked by the others. The difference here is that the third daughter is unattractive, not beautiful.]

B **Elements of Literature**

Character Types

❓ How are the characters in this story typical of characters in folk tales? [Possible response: One sister is cruel; the father is kind but seemingly unaware of his daughter's mistreatment; the youngest sister does not complain to her father about the mistreatment.]

C **Advanced Learners**

Interpreting

❓ What do you think the sister of the Invisible One understands? [Possible responses: As the sister of an invisible man, she knows that people cannot always see things that are valuable. She knows that a person's external appearance does not necessarily reveal the person's true self.]

D **Reading Skills and Strategies**

Visualizing

Ask students to imagine the transformation of Oochigeaskw as it might be portrayed on film. Call on volunteers to describe what they "see." [Responses will vary but may suggest the "morphing" techniques that are available through computer-generated imaging.]

---

wait with great curiosity to see him eat. They could be sure that he was a real person, for when he took off his moccasins they became visible, and his sister hung them up. But beyond this, they saw nothing of him, not even when they stayed in the place all night, as many of them did.

Now there lived in the village an old man who was a widower, and his three daughters. The youngest girl was very small, weak, and often ill. And yet her sisters, especially the elder, treated her cruelly. The second daughter was kinder and sometimes took her side. But the wicked sister would burn the younger girl's hands and feet with hot cinders. The girl was covered with scars from this treatment. She was so marked that people called her Oochigeaskw, the Rough-Faced Girl.

When her father came home and asked why the youngest girl had such burns, the bad sister would say at once that it was the girl's own fault, for she had disobeyed orders and gone near the fire and fallen into it.

These two elder sisters decided one day to try their luck at seeing the Invisible One. So they dressed themselves in their finest clothes and tried to look their prettiest. They found the Invisible One's sister and took the usual walk by the water.

When the brother came, and when they were asked if they could see him, they answered, "Of course." And when asked about the shoulder strap or sled cord, they answered, "A piece of rawhide."

But of course they were lying like the others, and they got nothing for their pains.

The next afternoon, when the father returned home, he brought with him many of the pretty little shells from which wampum was made, and the sisters set to work to string them.

That day, poor little Oochigeaskw, who had always gone barefoot, got a pair of her father's moccasins, old ones, and put them into water to soften them so that she could wear them. Then she begged her sisters for a few wampum shells. The elder called her a little pest, but the younger one gave her some. Now, since she had no clothes other than her usual rags, the poor little thing went into the woods and got herself some sheets of birch bark. From these, she made a dress and put marks on it for decoration, in the style of long ago. She also made a petticoat and a loose gown, a cap, leggings, and a handkerchief. She put on her father's large old moccasins, which were far too big for her, and went forth to try her luck. She would try, she thought, to see the Invisible One.

She did not begin very well. As she set off, her sisters shouted and hooted, hissed and yelled, and tried to make her stay. And the loafers around the village, seeing the strange little creature, called out "Shame!"

The poor little girl in her strange clothes, with her face all scarred, was an awful sight, but she was kindly received by the sister of the Invisible One. And this was, of course, because this noble lady understood far more about things than simply the mere outside which all the rest of the world knows. As the brown of the evening sky turned to black, the lady took the girl down to the lake.

"Do you see him?" the Invisible One's sister asked.

"I do, indeed—and he is wonderful!" said Oochigeaskw.

The sister asked, "And what is his sled string?"

The little girl said, "It is the Rainbow."

"And, my sister, what is his bow string?"

"It is the Spirit's Road—the Milky Way."

"So you *have* seen him," said his sister. She took the girl home with her and bathed her. As she did so, all the scars disappeared from the girl's body. Her hair grew again, as it was combed, long, like a blackbird's wing. Her eyes were now like stars: In all the world there was no other such beauty. Then, from her trea-

---

Taking a Second Look

Review: Analyzing Cause and Effect

Explain that oral storytellers knew the importance of showing why certain events happened as they did and what outcomes arose from certain actions. For example, this teller makes it clear that it is the sister's understanding about "more . . . than the mere outside" that leads her to welcome Oochigeaskw kindly.

Activities

1. Have students list ways to complete this sentence: At first, Oochigeaskw seems an unlikely bride for the Invisible One because _____.

2. Have students improvise a scene in which the Invisible One's sister announces that the Invisible One has been "found out" and that he now will marry. How would the news affect the rest of the village?

sures, the lady gave her a wedding garment and adorned her.

Then she told Oochigeaskw to take the *wife's* seat in the wigwam, the one next to where the Invisible One sat, beside the entrance. And when he came in, terrible and **E** beautiful, he smiled and said:

"So we are found out!" **F**

"Yes," said his sister. And so Oochigeaskw became his wife.

The Indian village of Pomeiooc. Watercolor by John White (c. 1585).
The Granger Collection, New York.

THE ALGONQUIN CINDERELLA **611**

E Vocabulary Note
Multiple Meanings
Explain that *terrible,* in addition to its more common meanings, sometimes is used as a synonym for "awesome." Discuss which meaning is intended here. [Students probably will suggest "awesome," for the Invisible One has not demonstrated a frightening or evil character.]

F Reading Skills and Strategies
Drawing Conclusions
❓ What is the Invisible One's secret, which now has been found out? [The secret is that he is not human but a creature of the sky.]

RESPONDING TO THE ART

In this illustration, a group of dwellings called wigwams makes up a village like the one in the story. A wigwam is a long, narrow hut with a cylindrical roof. Its framework is constructed of slender poles that are stuck into the ground and curved over at the top to form a roof. Woven mats, pressed bark, or animal skins cover the roof. Whereas tepees were used in the West, wigwams were found in the eastern part of North America from Quebec to the Carolinas.

Getting Students Involved

Cooperative Learning
Talk Show. After students have read the selections in this lesson, have them conduct interviews with the different Cinderellas. Divide the class into groups of six—one moderator, three different Cinderellas, and two other guests (such as stepparents or husbands). Group members should discuss the moderator's questions and the characters' responses and interaction with each other. Ask a volunteer group to practice and present its talk show.

Crossing the Curriculum

Geography
Distribute a world map to each student. Use a globe or large world map, and call on volunteers to locate Germany, the Appalachian region of the United States, the Ottawa River region of Canada, and China. Have students label and color these areas on their own maps. In the bottom margin, have students write the names of the stories in Collection Eight read thus far and the origin of each. Have students keep their maps and add information as they read more stories from the world folklore tradition.

Connections

In prehistoric times, the "dainty and dependable" Dinorella suffers abuse from her stepsisters Dora and Doris. When they receive an invitation to a dance at the den of Duke Dudley, the stepsisters ridicule Dinorella's appearance and lack of dinosaur jewels. Left alone, Dinorella is visited by Fairydactyl, who provides her with dinosaur jewels. As she approaches the site of the dance, Dinorella sees a deinonychus carrying off the duke for his next meal. Summoning up her courage, Dinorella hurls insults and dirt balls at the deinonychus. The predator, thinking that the flashing of Dinorella's jewels are the eyes of a demon, is frightened; and when Dinorella throws one of her diamonds at him, he drops the duke and runs away. Duke Dudley vows to marry the dinosaur to whom the jewel belongs. As Doris and Dora clamor for his attention, Fairydactyl summons Dinorella, who has the matching jewel. The duke declares his love, and the happy pair dance off.

A Elements of Literature
Alliteration
❓ Alliteration can help establish a mood or emphasize words. What is the effect of the alliteration in the first sentence? [Possible response: The repetition adds to the humor of the story by emphasizing funny names ("Dinorella") and images ("dinosaur den").]

B Elements of Literature
Character Types
Call on volunteers to describe how Dora and Doris fit the character type of the "wicked stepsisters." [Like other examples that students already have met, these two are demanding and insulting. They enjoy tormenting their stepsister.]

Dinorella
Pamela Duncan Edwards

A Dora, Doris, and Dinorella lived down in the sand dunes in a dinosaur den.

Dora and Doris did nothing all day. They dumped debris around the den. They never did the dusting or the dishes. Dinorella was dainty and dependable. Dora and Doris were dreadful to Dinorella. All day they demanded . . .

B "**DINORELLA**, dig the garden."
"**DINORELLA**, fetch us drinks."
"**DINORELLA**, start the dinner."
"She's a dingbat," sniggered Dora.
"She's a dumbhead," giggled Doris.

One day a card was delivered to the den:

> *Dinosaur Dance*
> *Duke Dudley's Den*
> *At Dusk*
> *Hors d'oeuvres, Dandelion Cola*
> *Dancing Until Dawn*

Duke Dudley was the most dashing dinosaur in the dunes.

"I would die for a date with the duke," said Dora, decorating herself with dinosaur jewels.

"Definitely," sighed Doris, dolling up for the dance.

C "A dance," said Dinorella diffidently. "How divine."

"**YOU** can't go to the dance," said Doris. "**YOU'RE** too dowdy."

"**YOU'RE** too dull," agreed Dora. "And **YOU** don't have decent dinosaur jewels. Of course **YOU** can't go to the dance."

Poor Dinorella felt down in the dumps as she watched her stepsisters depart.

Suddenly, Dinorella heard a droning noise.

"Don't be dismal," cried Fairydactyl. "You **SHALL** go to the dance."

"But I'm so drab," said Dinorella, "and I don't have decent dinosaur jewels."

"I'll soon deal with that," declared

Getting Students Involved

Cooperative Learning
What's So Funny? "Dinorella" is a spoof of the Cinderella tale. Have students hold a panel discussion on the function of humor in this story. For example, does humor help make a familiar tale seem fresher, or does it mock the tradition of the tale? Do the lessons that the tale offers still come across when laughter is involved?

Enrichment Activity
Writing Across Time. After students have finished reading this lesson's selections, challenge them to adopt the persona of Aschenputtel, Oochigeaskw, Dinorella, Yeh-Shen, or Ashpet. Have students then write letters, in character, to one of these other protagonists. Students may assume that the correspondents know each other's stories and that they are writing to share thoughts about their similar situations. Also allow students to move beyond this point,

if they wish, to ask questions of the other character, to share thoughts about matters not directly covered in the stories, and so on. Work with students to prepare a format for sharing the completed letters, and encourage students to tell how completing this activity helped them understand the two characters (the writer and the recipient of the letter) better.

Fairydactyl. "These will outdazzle all other dinosaur jewels."

"**DARLING** Fairydactyl!" exclaimed Dinorella in delight. With her diamonds dangling, she set out for the dance.

Dusk had fallen when Dinorella heard a deafening disturbance coming from the direction of Duke Dudley's Den.

A DASTARDLY DEED WAS TAKING PLACE!

A deinonychus was dragging off the duke.

"**I'M DONE FOR!**" cried the

duke. "He will **DEVOUR** me!"

"Indeed I will!" laughed the deinonychus. "I'll be digesting you by daybreak."

Dinorella was not a daring dinosaur, but something drastic had to be done.

"I may become dessert, but I'm determined to drive away that dreaded carnivore."

Dinorella climbed to the top of the dune.

"**YOU DISGUSTING DUMMY,**" she roared. "**DROP THE DUKE!**"

Dinorella began to hurl dirtballs at the deinonychus.

The dumbfounded deinonychus stopped in disbelief. "Who called me a dummy?" he demanded.

The moon's light caught Dinorella's dangling diamonds. Dots and dabs of light darted toward the deinonychus.

"**A DEVIL!**" cried the deinonychus. "See its dreadful demon eyes!"

Dinorella detached a diamond and directed it toward the deinonychus.

The diamond hit the deinonychus **HARD** in his dentures.

"The devil will destroy me with its deadly eyes," bellowed the distraught deinonychus. He dumped Duke Dudley and departed double-quick. **E**

A Reading Skills and Strategies
Responding to the Text
❓ What do you think of the dinosaurs' panicked response? [The image of dinosaurs, usually depicted as fierce and lumbering, "dashing about in distress" is incongruous and funny.] What do you think of Duke Dudley's response? [Students may admire his "cool"—his calm and clear-headedness.]

B Appreciating Language
Word Choice
❓ Words can have suggested meanings (connotations) as well as actual meanings (denotations). What connotations are suggested by *delirious*? [Possible response: The female dinosaurs are wildly excited and behave as though they are feverish.] by *bellowed*? [Possible response: A bull bellows so the sound Dora makes is powerful, loud, and ridiculous.] What other words might you use in their place? [Possible responses, respectively: thrilled, excited; shouted, yelled.]

C Elements of Literature
Character Types
❓ Judging from these comments, which type of "prince" do you think Duke Dudley resembles more—the prince in "Aschenputtel," or the Invisible One from "The Algonquin Cinderella"? Explain. [Possible response: He is more like the prince in "Aschenputtel," for both are interested in the Cinderella character's physical beauty.]

The den was dense with dinosaurs dashing about in distress. "A demon," they cried. **"WE'RE DOOMED."**

"DIMWITS!" roared Duke Dudley through the din. "Demons don't throw diamonds. It was a damsel who defended me with her dazzling dinosaur jewel.

"When I discover her, I shall ask her to be my darling."

All the dinosaur dames were delirious.

"The jewel is mine!" they each declared.

"MINE!" cried Doris.

"NO, DEFINITELY MINE," bellowed Dora, giving Doris a dig. "I am the damsel you desire."

"I DOUBT IT," declared Duke Dudley. "Your dinosaur jewels don't match."

Just then, Fairydactyl arrived at the dance. She quickly saw the dilemma. **"WHERE IS DINORELLA?"** she demanded.

"Dinorella!" scoffed Dora, "that dopey domestic."

"Dinorella!" laughed Doris. "She's back at the den."

But Fairydactyl spied Dinorella dodging behind the dune.

"DINORELLA," she directed, "come down."

So down came Dinorella, looking distracted.

Cried the duke, "She wears but one dazzling jewel!

"Dinorella, you are adorable. You're definitely quite a dish. I beg you to be my dearest."

"DREAMY!" said Dinorella as they danced off into the dawn.

"DRAT!" said Dora and Doris.

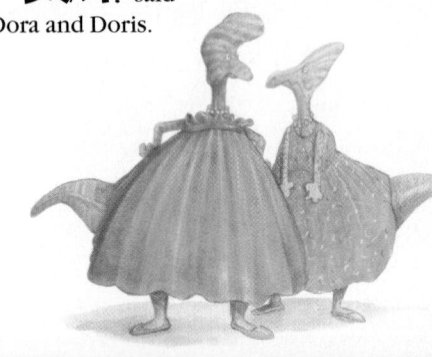

Connecting Across Texts

Connecting with "The Algonquin Cinderella"
After students have read "Dinorella," point out the importance of jewels—in particular, Dinorella's diamond—to this story. Explain that sometimes a person with admirable qualities is called a "jewel," as well. Ask students to draw jewel-shaped outlines and fill in the outlines with words, ideas, or images that they think show Dinorella to be a "jewel" of a character. Then have them review their responses, circling and perhaps annotating any responses that they think apply to Oochigeaskw of "The Algonquin Cinderella."

Carp (1848) by Taito.
Courtesy of the Board of Trustees of the Victoria and Albert Museum, London.

YEH-SHEN

Chinese, retold by
Ai-Ling Louie

THE ONLY FRIEND THAT YEH-SHEN HAD WAS A FISH . . .

In the dim past, even before the Ch'in and the Han dynasties, there lived a cave chief of southern China by the name of Wu. As was the custom in those days, Chief Wu had taken two wives. Each wife in her turn had presented Wu with a baby daughter. But one of the wives sickened and died, and not too many days after that Chief Wu took to his bed and died too.

Summary ■ ■

The orphaned daughter of Chief Wu is mistreated by her stepmother and has only one friend: a fish whom she feeds every day. The girl is devastated when her stepmother eats this fish, but a mysterious old man tells her that the bones of the fish have power to help her. For some time, Yeh-Shen depends upon the bones to provide food; but when the spring festival comes, the girl asks for decent clothes. The spirit of the bones provides a wondrous outfit and warns her not to lose the golden shoes. At the festival, her beauty inspires wonder. Fearing recognition, she flees, losing a shoe—and, with it, communication with the spirit of the bones. The king of T'o Han comes into possession of the lost shoe and places it on public display in hopes of finding its owner. No one can wedge her foot into the tiny shoe but Yeh-Shen; and when she does, she is transformed. The king marries her, but her stepmother and stepsister are left at their cave dwelling, where they die in a shower of flying stones.

Background

"Yeh-Shen" was probably told for centuries before it was first recorded (see Meet the Writer, p. 620). Ask students how the fact that this story is so old affects their view of "Cinderella" as a "world folk tale."

Resources

Listening
Audio CD Library
An affecting recording of this folk tale is included in the *Audio CD Library*:
• Disc 15, Track 4

Viewing and Representing
Fine Art Transparency
You may wish to use the fine art transparency of *A Chinese Cinderella,* by Lo Koon-chiu, to introduce this lesson and provide prereading motivation.
• Transparency 19
• Worksheet, p. 76

Writing and Language
• *Daily Oral Grammar*
   Transparency 37

A Reading Skills and Strategies

Comparing Texts

? From what you know so far, how is Yeh-Shen's life similar to that of Aschenputtel, Oochigeaskw, and Dinorella? [All of them are treated unfairly and are given hard, unpleasant work to do.] How is it different? [There is no mention of a stepmother for Oochigeaskw or Dinorella, and Oochigeaskw is not beautiful.]

B Reading Skills and Strategies

Making Predictions

Ask students what they think will happen to Yeh-Shen and her fish. Remind them to return to and check those predictions later.

C Critical Thinking

Speculating

? Who do you think has sent the old man that Yeh-Shen calls "uncle"? [Possible responses: The spirit of the dead fish has sent him; the spirit of Yeh-Shen's father has sent him.]

Resources

Selection Assessment
Formal Assessment
• Selection Test, p. 122
Test Generator
• Selection Test

IT WAS A BEAUTIFUL FISH WITH GOLDEN EYES.

A Yeh-Shen, the little orphan, grew to girlhood in her stepmother's home. She was a bright child and lovely too, with skin as smooth as ivory and dark pools for eyes. Her stepmother was jealous of all this beauty and goodness, for her own daughter was not pretty at all. So in her displeasure, she gave poor Yeh-Shen the heaviest and most unpleasant chores.

The only friend that Yeh-Shen had to her name was a fish she had caught and raised. It was a beautiful fish with golden eyes, and every day it would come out of the water and rest its head on the bank of the pond, waiting for Yeh-Shen to feed it. Stepmother gave Yeh-Shen little enough food for herself, but the orphan child always found something to share with her fish, which grew to enormous size.

B Somehow the stepmother heard of this. She was terribly angry to discover that Yeh-Shen had kept a secret from her. She hurried down to the pond, but she was unable to see the fish, for Yeh-Shen's pet wisely hid itself. The stepmother, however, was a crafty woman, and she soon thought of a plan. She walked home and called out, "Yeh-Shen, go and collect some firewood. But wait! The neighbors might see you. Leave your filthy coat here!" The minute the girl was out of sight, her stepmother slipped on the coat herself and went down again to the pond. This time the big fish saw Yeh-Shen's familiar jacket and heaved itself onto the bank, expecting to be fed. But the stepmother, having hidden a dagger in her sleeve, stabbed the fish, wrapped it in her garments, and took it home to cook for dinner.

When Yeh-Shen came to the pond that evening, she found her pet had disappeared. Overcome with grief, the girl collapsed on the ground and dropped her tears into the still waters of the pond.

C "Ah, poor child!" a voice said.

Yeh-Shen sat up to find a very old man looking down at her. He wore the coarsest of clothes, and his hair flowed down over his shoulders.

"Kind uncle, who may you be?" Yeh-Shen asked.

"That is not important, my child. All you must know is that I have been sent to tell you of the wondrous powers of your fish."

616   900 CINDERELLAS: OUR WORLD HERITAGE IN FOLKLORE

Professional Notes

China and the Chinese

The name *China* is derived from the Ch'in Dynasty (221–206 B.C.), under whose rule the country was united as an empire. The Ch'in Dynasty also undertook the building of the Great Wall, which remains one of the best-known symbols of China. The Ch'in Dynasty was succeeded by the Han Dynasty, which ruled for more than four centuries. Both dynasties were important in Chinese history and cul-

ture; both are mentioned in this story's opening.

We use the word *Chinese* broadly to refer to the inhabitants of China or to the various languages spoken by its people. In general, the people of China refer to themselves as "Han" (as in the Han Dynasty) or "sons of Han," and they accept the Chinese system of cultural values. Several small minority groups, however, view themselves as non-Chinese and do not accept

the Han values. Rather, these are groups that speak a common language, occupy a common area, and share a common sense of social values. Most of them live in sparsely populated areas along China's frontiers. They have cultural relationships with minority groups in neighboring countries, such as Kazakhstan, Kyrgyzstan, Russia, North Korea, Mongolia, Thailand, and Myanmar.

"My fish, but sir . . ." The girl's eyes filled with tears, and she could not go on.

The old man sighed and said, "Yes, my child, your fish is no longer alive, and I must tell you that your step-mother is once more the cause of your sorrow." Yeh-Shen gasped in horror, but the old man went on. "Let us not dwell on things that are past," he said, "for I have come bringing you a gift. Now you must listen carefully to this: The bones of your fish are filled with a powerful spirit. Whenever you are in serious need, you must kneel before them and let them know your heart's desire. But do not waste their gifts."

Yeh-Shen wanted to ask the old sage many more questions, but he rose to the sky before she could utter another word. With heavy heart, Yeh-Shen made her way to the dung heap to gather the remains of her friend.

Time went by, and Yeh-Shen, who was often left alone, took comfort in speaking to the bones of her fish. When she was hungry, which happened quite often, Yeh-Shen asked the bones for food. In this way, Yeh-Shen managed to live from day to day, but she lived in dread that her stepmother would discover her secret and take even that away from her.

So the time passed and spring came. Festival time was approaching: It was the busiest time of the year. Such cooking and cleaning and sewing there was to be done! Yeh-Shen had hardly a moment's rest. At the spring festival young men and young women from the village hoped to meet and to choose whom they would marry. How Yeh-Shen longed to go! But her stepmother had other plans. She hoped to find a husband for her own daughter and did not want any man to see the beauteous Yeh-Shen first. When finally the holiday arrived, the stepmother and her daughter dressed themselves in their finery and filled their baskets with sweetmeats. "You must remain at home now and watch to see that no one steals fruit from our trees," her stepmother told Yeh-Shen, and then she departed for the banquet with her own daughter.

As soon as she was alone, Yeh-Shen went to speak to the bones of her fish. "Oh, dear friend," she said, kneeling before the precious bones, "I long to go to the festival, but I cannot show myself in these rags. Is there some-

"THE BONES OF YOUR FISH ARE FILLED WITH A POWERFUL SPIRIT."

YEH-SHEN 617

Carp with Bogbean by Sadatora (nineteenth century).

British Library, London/Bridgeman Art Library, London.

where I could borrow clothes fit to wear to the feast?" At once she found herself dressed in a gown of azure[1] blue, with a cloak of kingfisher feathers draped around her shoulders. Best of all, on her tiny feet were the most beautiful slippers she had ever seen. They were woven of golden threads, in a pattern like the scales of a fish, and the glistening soles were made of solid gold. There was magic in the shoes, for they should have been quite heavy, yet when Yeh-Shen walked, her feet felt as light as air.

"Be sure you do not lose your golden shoes," said the spirit of the bones. Yeh-Shen promised to be careful. Delighted with her transformation, she bid a fond farewell to the bones of her fish as she slipped off to join in the merrymaking.

That day Yeh-Shen turned many a head as she appeared at the feast. All around her people whispered, "Look at that beautiful girl! Who can she be?"

But above this, Stepsister was heard to say, "Mother, does she not resemble our Yeh-Shen?"

Upon hearing this, Yeh-Shen jumped up and ran off before her stepsister could look closely at her. She raced down the mountainside, and in doing so, she lost one of her golden slippers. No sooner had the shoe fallen from her foot than all her fine clothes turned back to rags. Only one thing remained—a tiny golden shoe. Yeh-Shen hurried to the bones of her fish and returned the slipper, promising to find its mate. But now the bones were silent. Sadly Yeh-Shen realized that she had lost her only friend. She hid the little shoe in her bedstraw and went outside to cry. Leaning against a fruit tree, she sobbed and sobbed until she fell asleep.

The stepmother left the gathering to check on Yeh-Shen, but when she returned home, she found the girl sound asleep, with her arms wrapped around a fruit tree. So, thinking no more of her, the stepmother rejoined the party. Meantime, a villager had found the shoe. Recognizing its worth, he sold it to a merchant, who presented it in turn to the king of the island kingdom of T'o Han.

The king was more than happy to accept the slipper as a gift. He was entranced by the tiny thing, which was shaped of the most precious of metals, yet which made

1. **azure** (azh′ər): like the color of the sky.

Crossing the Curriculum

no sound when touched to stone. The more he marveled at its beauty, the more determined he became to find the woman to whom the shoe belonged. A search was begun among the ladies of his own kingdom, but all who tried on the sandal found it impossibly small. Undaunted, the king ordered the search widened to include the cave women from the countryside where the slipper had been found. Since he realized it would take many years for every woman to come to his island and test her foot in the slipper, the king thought of a way to get the right woman to come forward. He ordered the sandal placed in a pavilion[2] by the side of the road near where it had been found, and his herald[3] announced that the shoe was to be returned to its original owner. Then, from a nearby hiding place, the king and his men settled down to watch and wait for a woman with tiny feet to come and claim her slipper. **E**

All that day the pavilion was crowded with cave women who had come to test a foot in the shoe. Yeh-Shen's stepmother and stepsister were among them, but not Yeh-Shen—they had told her to stay home. By day's end, although many women had eagerly tried to put on the slipper, it still had not been worn. Wearily, the king continued his vigil into the night. **F**

It wasn't until the blackest part of night, while the moon hid behind a cloud, that Yeh-Shen dared to show her face at the pavilion, and even then she tiptoed timidly across the wide floor. Sinking down to her knees, the girl in rags examined the tiny shoe. Only when she was sure **G** that this was the missing mate to her own golden slipper did she dare pick it up. At last she could return both little shoes to the fish bones. Surely then her beloved spirit would speak to her again.

Now the king's first thought, on seeing Yeh-Shen take the precious slipper, was to throw the girl into prison as a thief. But when she turned to leave, he caught a glimpse of her face. At once the king was struck by the sweet harmony of her features, which seemed so out of keeping with the rags she wore. It was then that he took a closer

2. **pavilion:** large tent or shelter, often highly decorated.
3. **herald:** the person in a king's court who makes official announcements.

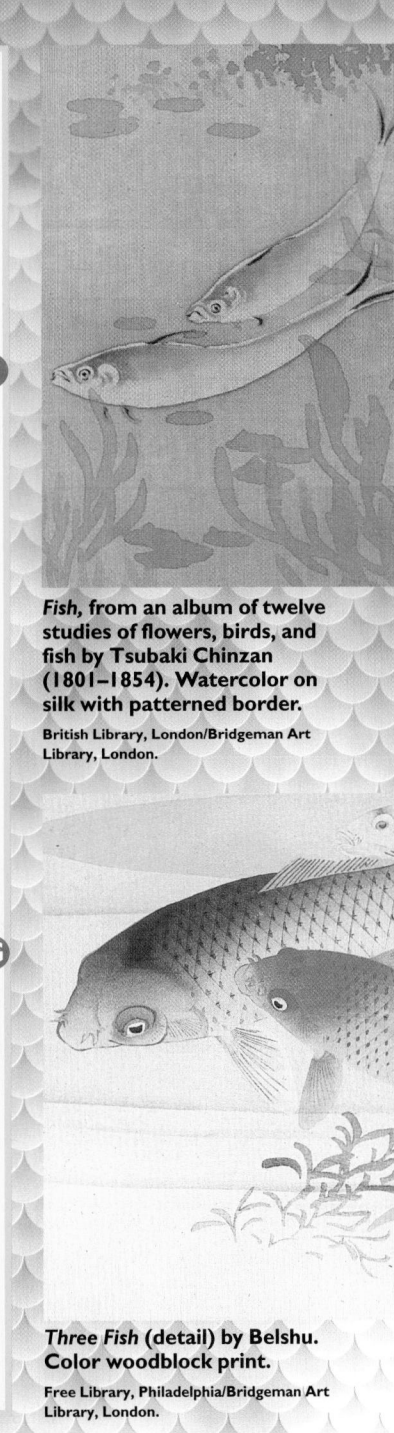

Fish, from an album of twelve studies of flowers, birds, and fish by Tsubaki Chinzan (1801–1854). Watercolor on silk with patterned border.
British Library, London/Bridgeman Art Library, London.

Three Fish (detail) by Belshu. Color woodblock print.
Free Library, Philadelphia/Bridgeman Art Library, London.

YEH-SHEN 619

Making the Connections

Connecting to the Theme: "900 Cinderellas: Our World Heritage in Folklore"
Ask students whether they would pair "Yeh-Shen" with "The Algonquin Cinderella" (as has been done in this collection) or with "Aschenputtel." Invite explanations. [Possible responses: The present match is good because both stories come from non-European cultures. "Yeh-Shen" should be matched with "Aschenputtel," for Oochigeaskw does not need magic to change her situation.]

Cultural Connections
Yeh-Shen's story may be the oldest of the "900 Cinderellas," for the Chinese recording (see p. 620) was set down about 700 years before the first printed Cinderella story appeared in Europe. Its heroine was named Sheh Hsien, but the basic details were what students have just read. Most folklorists did not look far beyond Europe for the source of the Cinderella story until R. D. Jameson lectured on the connection in 1932.

Assessing Learning

A Cultural Connections
Foot-Binding

In the story, the narrator comments a number of times on the tininess of Yeh-Shen's feet, apparently considered one attribute of a beautiful woman. For hundreds of years in Chinese culture, many women had tiny feet—3 or 4 inches long—as the result of foot-binding. In this practice, feet were wrapped so tightly that bones were broken and the feet compressed, virtually crippling these women. Foot-binding was outlawed in China early in the twentieth century.

B Critical Thinking
Interpreting

❓ What lesson is to be learned from this story? [Possible responses: Evil will be punished and good rewarded. A good friendship can help a person through difficult times.]

BROWSING IN THE FILES

About the Author. "When I was a girl," recalls Ai-Ling Louie (1949–), "it seemed I always had my nose in a book. I remember walking down the crowded, noisy hallway of my junior high school and reading all the while. I could even climb three flights of stairs and never miss a word." Writing was a long-time interest of hers; as she says, however, "My desire to be a writer didn't come into full bloom until I became an elementary school teacher. I found myself fascinated by the books my school children were reading. I used to love to write stories to tell the children. *Yeh-Shen* was written for my class to hear."

A Critic's Comment. R. D. Jameson, who was largely responsible for bringing Yeh-Shen's story to the West, wrote, "Popular tales are literary creations. Cinderella, *Hamlet* and the *Aeneid* are words put together by human beings, symbols of human thought and feeling controlled by tradition and communicated to other human beings. But popular art is more transparent than sophisticated art, and by a comparison of many treatments of the same popular theme we can frequently get a glimpse of the strange processes of literary creation."

HER LOVELINESS MADE HER SEEM A HEAVENLY BEING.

A look and noticed that she walked upon the tiniest feet he had ever seen.

With a wave of his hand, the king signaled that this tattered creature was to be allowed to depart with the golden slipper. Quietly, the king's men slipped off and followed her home.

All this time, Yeh-Shen was unaware of the excitement she had caused. She had made her way home and was about to hide both sandals in her bedding when there was a pounding at the door. Yeh-Shen went to see who it was—and found a king at her doorstep. She was very frightened at first, but the king spoke to her in a kind voice and asked her to try the golden slippers on her feet. The maiden did as she was told, and as she stood in her golden shoes, her rags were transformed once more into the feathered cloak and beautiful azure gown.

Her loveliness made her seem a heavenly being, and the king suddenly knew in his heart that he had found his true love.

B Not long after this, Yeh-Shen was married to the king. But fate was not so gentle with her stepmother and stepsister. Since they had been unkind to his beloved, the king would not permit Yeh-Shen to bring them to his palace. They remained in their cave home, where one day, it is said, they were crushed to death in a shower of flying stones.

MEET THE WRITER
It Runs in the Family

Ai-Ling Louie remembers hearing the story "Yeh-Shen," the Chinese version of "Cinderella," from her grandmother. Louie became curious about the origins of this story, which had been told in her family for three generations, so she did some research. She learned that the tale was first written down by Tuan Cheng-shi in an ancient Chinese manuscript during the Tang dynasty (A.D. 618–906) and had probably been handed down orally for centuries before that.

620 900 CINDERELLAS: OUR WORLD HERITAGE IN FOLKLORE

Assessing Learning

Check Test: Short Answer

1. Where and when do "The Algonquin Cinderella" and "Yeh-Shen" take place? ["The Algonquin Cinderella" takes place in Canada around 200 years ago; "Yeh-Shen" takes place in China centuries ago.]
2. How is Oochigeaskw treated? [Her oldest sister burns her with hot cinders.]
3. What happens to Yeh-Shen's pet? [Her stepmother kills it.]
4. How does the Invisible One's sister know that the other village girls are lying? [Their descriptions of her brother are incorrect.]
5. What happens when Yeh-Shen loses her shoe? [Her clothes turn back into rags.]

Standardized Test Preparation

For practice with standardized test format specific to this selection, see
• *Standardized Test Preparation*, p. 90
For practice in proofreading and editing, see
• *Daily Oral Grammar*, Transparencies 36, 37

from Ashpet

Appalachian, retold by **Granny Shores,** *collected by* **Richard Chase**

One time there was a woman had two daughters, and they kept a hired girl. They treated this girl mean. She was bound out to 'em, had to do all the hard work, little as she was. They wouldn't buy her any pretty clothes or nothin', made her sleep right up against the fireplace and the ashes got all over her, so they called her Ashpet.

Well, one day they were all fixin' to go to church meetin'. They never let Ashpet go anywhere. They knew she was prettier than the old woman's two girls, and if anybody came to the house, they always shoved Ashpet under a washtub. That day, just when they were tryin' to get fixed up to go to meetin', their fire went out, so they had to borrow fire. Now there was an old woman lived over the gap in the mountain. These rich folks, they wouldn't have nothin' to do with this old woman, but they had to have fire so they sent the oldest one of the girls over there to borrow some fire. The oldest girl she went traipsin' on over the gap. She thought herself so good she didn't go in the house, just stuck her hand through a crack in the logs.

"I come after fire."

"Come in and comb my hair and I'll give ye some."

"I'll not put my pretty clean hands on your old cat comb!"

"You'll get no fire."

The old woman she sent the next oldest. She went a-swishin' up the hill and through the gap. She was so nice! She ran her hand through that crack.

"I want some fire."

"Come in and comb my hair."

"Me? Put my nice white hands on your old cat comb?"

"Put off, then. You'll get no fire."

Then the old woman hollered for Ashpet. And Ashpet she went on up through the gap, ran down the holler, and went right on in the house.

"Good evenin', Auntie."

"Good evenin', Ashpet."

"I want to borry a coal of fire, please, ma'm."

"Comb my hair and you can have it."

Ashpet combed her hair for her, and then the old woman gave her some fire: put it in an old dried toadstool.

"You goin' to meetin', Ashpet?"

"Law, no! They never let me go anywhere at all. I got to wash the dishes and scour the pots. I'll not get done till meetin's plumb over."

"You want to go?"

"Why, yes, I'd like that the best in the world!"

"Time they all get good and gone, I'll be up there to see you." . . . [*And Granny's story goes on.*]

Connecting Across Texts

Connecting with "Yeh-Shen"
You might use one or both of the following activities to help students connect these two folk tales.
- Have the class work together to complete a combined story map of "Ashpet" and "Yeh-Shen." The diagram should indicate characters, settings, conflicts, plot events, and outcomes. Have students refer to the map as they compare and contrast the tales.
- Point out the element of jealousy that is common to both of these stories. Then ask pairs of students to think of a real-life situation that causes jealousy. Have them summarize the problem on a sheet of paper. Below the summary, have them brainstorm possible courses of action, choose a likely solution, anticipate stumbling blocks, and propose arguments while writing in favor of a proposed solution. Call on volunteers to share their problems and solutions; in particular, encourage them to explain whether or not their solutions might have helped resolve the jealousy directed toward Yeh-Shen or Ashpet.

MAKING MEANINGS

First Thoughts

1. The basic human wishes answered in the Cinderella stories are that one should be loved for who one is and that goodness should be rewarded.

Shaping Interpretations

2. Students should recognize that there is a wicked stepmother (an actual stepmother or stepmother type) in all of the stories except "The Algonquin Cinderella" and "Dinorella" and that all of the stories feature cruel sisters or stepsisters (again, actual siblings or sibling types). Students should list other character types, such as the father or the prince. Students may feel that these character types seem very one-sided.

3. At the beginning of the story, the fish is Yeh-Shen's only friend. Later, it is the spirit of the fish's bones that has the power to grant Yeh-Shen's wishes.

4. Most students will feel that Oochigeaskw's metamorphosis is more miraculous because her scars are washed away, her hair grows long, and her eyes become like stars. In "Yeh-Shen," the main character has ragged clothes, but she does not need to be transformed since she is already beautiful.

5. Differences include the homes in which the main characters live and the kinds of help that the main characters receive from others. Students also may say that the stories teach the values of the cultures from which they arose.

MAKING MEANINGS

THE ALGONQUIN CINDERELLA
YEH-SHEN

[summarize]

First Thoughts

1. The Cinderella story appears in many cultures all over the world. What fears and wishes are expressed in these Cinderella stories from two very different cultures? (Be sure to check your Quickwrite notes.)

Shaping Interpretations

[analyze]

2. The cruel stepmother is a **character type** in "Yeh-Shen." What other character types appear in Cinderella stories? Work together with a partner to fill in a chart like the one below. After you've filled in your chart, discuss these character types. Do you think some of them are unfair?

Reading Check

a. Who gives Oochigeaskw a hard time? Why?

b. Who gives Yeh-Shen a hard time? Why?

c. Who helps Oochigeaskw in her troubles? Who helps Yeh-Shen?

d. How does Oochigeaskw prove she can see the Invisible One?

e. How does the king find Yeh-Shen?

Story	Character Types			
	Wicked Stepmother	Cruel Stepsisters	Handsome Prince	Helpers
"Aschenputtel"				
"The Algonquin Cinderella"				
"Dinorella"				
"Yeh-Shen"				
"Ashpet"				

[recall]

3. What part does an animal play in Yeh-Shen's story?

[evaluate]

4. Which **metamorphosis,** Yeh-Shen's or Oochigeaskw's, seems more miraculous to you? Explain why.

[connect]

5. You've considered the common elements of Cinderella stories from four cultures: German, Algonquin, Chinese, and Appalachian. You've also read "Dinorella," a "prehistoric" fairy tale (see *Connections* on page 612). What important variations, or differences, do you notice from story to story? Do all the stories teach the same values? Talk it over.

622   900 CINDERELLAS: OUR WORLD HERITAGE IN FOLKLORE

Reading Check

a. Her two older sisters give her a hard time. They may enjoy bullying her because she is small and weak.

b. Yeh-Shen's stepmother gives her a hard time because she is jealous of Yeh-Shen's beauty and goodness.

c. The Invisible One's sister helps Oochigeaskw.

Yeh-Shen receives help from an elderly "kind uncle" and from the wondrous powers of the spirit in the bones of her fish.

d. She identifies his sled string as the Rainbow and his bow string as the Milky Way.

e. The king waits for a woman with tiny feet to come and claim her slipper.

CHOICES: Building Your Portfolio

Writer's Notebook

1. Collecting Ideas for an Informative Report

How much do you know about the culture and geography of Appalachia? With a partner, discuss what you know about Appalachia and what questions occur to you as you think about "Ashpet" (see *Connections* on page 621). Be sure you can locate Appalachia on a map.

What we know:
—People live in mountains of West Virginia and Kentucky.
—Lots of coal mining

What we wonder:
—Was Lincoln born there?
—Is the soil poor?

Creative Writing

2. Story Swap

Get together with a partner, and choose two similar characters from two different Cinderella stories. Take the role of one of these characters and let your partner take the role of the other. One character writes a message to the other, and the second character then writes a message back. If you are the stepmothers in "Aschenputtel" and "Yeh-Shen," for example, you might explain to each other why you treated your stepdaughter as you did. If you are a prince or a king, you might describe your lonely life before you met your Cinderella or your great joy after meeting her.

Cultural Connections

3. Fact and Fiction

Skim either "Yeh-Shen" or "The Algonquin Cinderella," looking for details about food, clothing, homes, families, and customs that are different from your own. Make a list of questions suggested by these cultural details that you might like to research.

Critical Thinking/ Speaking

4. Unhappily Ever After

Horrible punishments are common in folk tales: Remember the stepsisters in "Aschenputtel," their eyes pecked out by pigeons, or the stepmother and stepsister in "Yeh-Shen," crushed to death by flying stones. These violent punishments are often "cleaned up" or softened when the stories are retold to children today. Do you think this is a good idea? In a group, discuss this question of violence in fairy tales and folk tales told to children.

Rubrics for each Choices assignment appear on p. 184 in the *Portfolio Management System*.

CHOICES: Building Your Portfolio

1. **Writer's Notebook** Individuals could be invited to answer questions for the whole class. Remind students to save their work. They may use it as prewriting for the Writer's Workshop on pp. 672–676.

2. **Creative Writing** Suggest that before partners begin role-playing, they summarize each character's role and its importance to the story.

3. **Cultural Connections** Have students work in groups of three. Each group member should choose one or two different topics to investigate. Suggest that students share their notes and brainstorm together to develop questions to research.

4. **Critical Thinking/Speaking** Invite the school counselor, principal, or nurse to visit the class and respond to the comments and decisions made by students concerning this issue.

GRAMMAR LINK

Have a supply of recent newspapers and magazines available for class use. Ask each student to choose a few pages from one of the periodicals and skim it, looking for examples of *two, to,* and *too.* Invite students to share examples of these homophones and to explain why the choice in print is correct (or, in the rare case of an error, why it is incorrect).

Try It Out
Answers
1. two
2. too
3. to

Students' reviews should demonstrate—either through corrections or verification that original choices were correct—an understanding of the use of the homophones *two, to,* and *too.*

SPELLING

Answers
1. preferred
2. clapping
3. whispered
4. sobbing
5. bedded
6. scarred

Resources ———————
Grammar
• *Grammar and Language Links,* p. 63
Spelling
For related spelling instruction, see
• *Spelling and Decoding,* p. 28

GRAMMAR LINK   MINI-LESSON

Technology HELP

See Language Workshop CD-ROM. *Key word entry: homonyms.*

• *Two, To, and Too*

Notice how the words *two, to,* and *too* are used in the following paragraph:

> Oochigeaskw has two sisters, while Yeh-Shen has just one stepsister. Oochigeaskw goes to the home of a powerful being and becomes his wife. Yeh-Shen marries someone powerful, too.

To use these sound-alike words correctly, remember these tips:

two (the number): *Two* contains a *w.* Turn the *w* to the left and you have the numeral *3.*

to ("toward"): *To* + ward.

too ("also"; "more than enough"): *Too* has "more than enough" *o*'s.

Try It Out
➤ In each sentence, choose the correct word from the underlined pair.

1. Which to/two Cinderella stories are your favorites?
2. Do you think the Cinderella stories are too/to unrealistic?
3. I went to/two the library to look for facts about the Algonquins.

➤ Take out something you have written, and circle each usage of *two, to,* and *too.* Review the rules on this page and correct each word you have used incorrectly.

SPELLING   HOW TO OWN A WORD

Language Handbook HELP

See Adding Prefixes and Suffixes, page 781.

Spelling Strategies

Can you tell which of these words is misspelled?

   occured   tailored

If you chose "occured," you're right—or lucky. Not knowing when to double the final consonant before a suffix beginning with a vowel (*-ing, -er, -ed,* or *-en*) is a common spelling problem. To figure it out, just follow the simple rule below—your suffixes will then fit onto the ends of words as precisely as the shoe slipped onto Cinderella's foot.

The final consonant is doubled before a suffix if *both* of these conditions are present:

1. The word has only one syllable or the accent is on the last syllable.
2. The word ends in a single consonant preceded by a single vowel.

For example, *bid* becomes *bidding* because it contains only one syllable. *Marvel* becomes *marveled*—no doubling of the final consonant—because the accent is not on the final syllable. Try the rule out on these words:

1. prefer + ed
2. clap + ing
3. whisper + ed
4. sob + ing
5. bed + ed
6. scar + ed

Grammar Link Quick Check

Choose the word that correctly completes each sentence.
1. Too/Two many people think that folk tales are just for little children. [Too]
2. In fact, these stories relate to/too the adult world in many ways. [to]
3. Isn't it fascinating that similar stories can emerge from two/too very different cultures? [two]
4. Some people think that reading folk tales takes to/too much time. [too]
5. There are more than two/too versions of many folk tales. [two]

Elements of Literature

OBJECTIVES
1. Recognize the universal nature and appeal of folk tales
2. Identify some common elements of folk tales
3. Explain how folk tales provide a sense of community among readers and listeners

FOLK TALES: Telling Tales *by* Virginia Hamilton

Who tells stories where you live? Is it your mother or father? Is it your uncle or aunt? your cousin or your friend? Is it you?

"Nobody I know tells stories," I answered when my English teacher asked that question. "At my house, everybody just talks."

Now I realize that both my father and mother were storytellers. I simply did not recognize that what they were "talking" were stories. My four brothers and sisters and I, and our parents, talked about everything, all the time. We had only the radio for entertainment—there wasn't television until I was twelve—and we got used to hearing talking. It was natural for us to listen to stories and then do some telling ourselves.

Mother would begin a story with "That reminds me" or "I remember when." Once she began, "That reminds me of the time all of the Boston ivy fell from Mrs. Pinton's house."

"All of it? All at once—when did that happen?" my oldest sister, Nina, asked. And

Mother was off and running with the tale about "the day the ivy fell." It is a story, part true, part fiction, and part tragic, that found its way into my novel *Sweet Whispers, Brother Rush.*

My mom and dad loved telling stories and remembering their pasts. We don't know for certain, but perhaps folk tales—"tells"—began in a similar way.

How Folk Tales Grow

Folk tales are stories passed on by word of mouth, often over many centuries. Each time the tale is told, it is changed a bit because no two people tell a story exactly the same way.

Some of these folk tales travel; that is, as they are told and retold, they move out of their original environments into other times and other places. Although traditional folk tales reflect the particular culture and people that created them, common features, called **motifs**, can be found in folk stories from many parts of the world. You'll find that

many folk tales include motifs like grateful beasts; tests of the hero; magic; false parents; fairy godmothers; and brave youngest sons and daughters.

Handed down from generation to generation, told over and over again, these "tells" become familiar stories— "They say the people could fly . . ."; "Once upon a time . . .". They have become tales of the folks.

American Folk Tales: Keeping Cultures Alive

When the first Europeans came with their folk tales, the Native Americans already had an elaborate and rich folklore tradition. Other folk tales traveled to the New World from other countries. For example, Africans who were brought to America as slaves carried with them their unique "folk-telling" traditions. Over generations they passed on tales about their lives on the plantations and about their relationships with the white men and women who held them as slaves.

(continued on next page)

Resources

Elements of Literature
Folk Tales: Identifying Character Types
For more instruction on character types in folk tales, see *Literary Elements:*
• Transparency 11
Selection Assessment
Formal Assessment
• Literary Elements Tests, p. 130

Elements of Literature

In this feature, Virginia Hamilton—a folklorist and a skilled writer of original stories—uses recollections of folk-tale storytelling in her family to explore folk tales as "self-portraits" of their tellers and as a global vehicle for sharing dreams, frustrations, and values.
Mini-Lesson:
Folk Tales
Arrange to have a storyteller come to class, secure an audiotape (or, preferably, a videotape) of a storytelling session, or prepare to perform your favorite tale for the class. After students have read this feature, allow them to experience the pleasure of being the audience of a storyteller. Suggest that students take notes on the performance and see if they can find evidence of any of the elements, such as motifs or metamorphoses, that Hamilton mentions. Follow up with a class discussion, inviting students to name their favorite aspects of the experience and to share other comments.

Using Students' Strengths

Auditory Learners
How is a story that is *heard* different from a story that is *read*? Ask students to reflect upon one or more "told" stories (possibly in conjunction with the mini-lesson on this page). Then have them prepare a "Storyteller's Checklist," identifying vocal qualities that make a "told" story more enjoyable (for example, differentiating characters' voices, assuming a hushed tone for suspense, and so on).

Logical/Mathematical Learners
Ask students to give the stories' characters both a number rating and a letter rating, as follows:

1 = very bad	A = very weak
2 = bad	B = weak
3 = neither good nor bad	C = neither weak nor powerful
4 = good	D = powerful
5 = very good	E = very powerful

Have students rate these characters: Oochigeaskw, her sisters, her father, the Invisible One, his sister; Dinorella, her stepsisters, Fairy-dactyl, Duke Dudley; Yeh-Shen, her stepmother, the bone spirit, the king; Ashpet, her employer's daughters, the old woman. Encourage students to meet in groups to compare, discuss, and report on their ratings.

Applying the Element

Use "Folk Tales: Telling Tales" to help students review some elements of folk tales. Ask the following questions:

- According to Hamilton, what is a "tell," or folk tale? [It is a story that is passed along by word of mouth, often over generations.]
- Name two motifs that are common in folk tales. [Possible answers: grateful beasts, heroic tests, magic, false parents, fairy godmothers, brave youngest children.] Why, then, are stories with the same motif not the same in every way? [As folk tales traveled beyond their places of origin, they changed to reflect and meet the needs of new listeners. Storytellers also might change other elements of the tales to satisfy their own desire for creativity.]
- What two types of folk tales were associated with enslaved African Americans? [Animal tales and escape stories are linked with that experience.] Why were such stories told? [Escape stories captured the people's desire to get away from the conditions of slavery. Animal tales helped symbolize the interaction of people in the plantation community.]
- What does Hamilton mean when she says, "Folk tales are our self-portraits"? [Folk tales capture who we are; they show what we care about, what we fear, what we aspire to be, and so on.]

As students review the collection selections read thus far, and as they read more selections, have them look for the folk-tale elements that Hamilton mentions and consider in what sense each tale is a "self-portrait."

(continued from previous page)

In fact, the African American storyteller developed the animal tale into a highly individual form. In this animal tale the social order of the plantation is broken down into animal elements, which symbolize the people in the plantation community. The African folk-tale tellers who were slaves fantasized about freedom and so developed another kind of folk tale, an **escape story**, about flying away from slavery.

In America, people from Ireland, Denmark, Germany, France, Italy, Poland, Turkey, the Middle East, Russia, China, Japan, Korea, Vietnam, Cambodia, the Philippines, Brazil, Haiti, Puerto Rico, Nigeria, Jamaica, and practically everywhere else have told their children folk tales from their old homelands. These stories, as well as their dances, songs, and folk art, help these people stay together and keep their beliefs and cultures alive.

Folk Tales and Community

Some folk tales are simple stories and others are com-plex. But the basic situation of the tale teller weaving his or her magic for a community of listeners is found everywhere, in every society.

For generation after generation, folk tales keep alive and close what we regard as important. They reveal who we are. As they instruct us in living, they show us our weaknesses and strengths, our fears and joys, our nightmares and wishes. Folk tales are our self-portraits.

"Tells" and Tale Givers

All over America there are folk-tale-telling festivals, in which tale tellers stand up and give "tells" to the listeners. In New London, Connecticut, the National Congress on Storytelling is held every June at Connecticut College. Festivals take place in Michigan, Ohio, Kentucky, and other states. The National Association for the Preservation and Perpetuation of Storytelling is based in Tennessee.

Storytelling is an ancient and wonderful custom. I have grown out of the tale-giving tradition and so, perhaps, have some of you. As you read these folk tales and fables from around the world, think about those early folk-tale tellers who committed tales to memory in order to tell them aloud. Try to picture what those early tellings must have been like—imagine the smoky underground kivas of the Pueblos, the dusty village squares in Nigeria.

Sitting or standing there, surrounded by the community of listeners, the teller calls softly, "Time was when the animals could talk . . ." The listeners respond. They lean forward, absolutely quiet now, eager to hear, to be entertained, to learn.

Reaching All Students

Struggling Readers

Students may find it helpful to have a set of questions upon which to focus as they read. Preview the questions in Applying the Element, or turn the subheadings in the feature into questions: How do folk tales grow? How have American folk tales kept cultures alive? What do folk tales have to do with a sense of "community"? Why are "tells" and storytellers important?

English Language Learners

This feature offers culturally diverse students many opportunities to participate. Call on volunteers to describe occasions when old stories are told within the family and to comment about how those stories are family "self-portraits." Ask other volunteers to summarize a tale that they think reflects their cultural background; then have the class discuss elements from Hamilton's essay that apply to it.

Advanced Learners

Some of Virginia Hamilton's "tells" appear in *The People Could Fly: American Black Folktales* (Knopf, 1985). Have students read stories in that collection (or listen to them read by James Earl Jones on the audiocassette edition), summarize them for the class, and explain how Hamilton puts into practice the things that she notes in this feature.

Reading Skills and Strategies

Booking space on the Net:

OBJECTIVES
1. Identify the characteristics of an effective summary
2. Recognize the value of transition expressions in summaries
3. Use a story map to take notes on a story before summarizing it

SUMMARIZING: HITTING THE HIGHLIGHTS

Have you ever heard someone say "Don't tell me about all the details—just cut to the chase"? Summarizing is a way of cutting to the chase. A **summary** is a short restatement of the main events and essential ideas of a text. When you summarize a story, you tell about its most important characters and events. You tell what causes the events and

you tell how the events are connected, one to the other. A summary highlights major details and leaves out unimportant ones. It is shorter than the original story and is written in your own words.

Knowing how to summarize helps you understand and remember what you read and also helps you share what you have read with others. If you were to summarize a story (or movie) for a friend, you would tell who the main characters are, what their conflict is, what the major events are, and how the story ends. If the story's setting is important, you'd describe that, too. You would use **transition expressions** like *then, after, as a result,* and *finally* to show when and where events happened and how the events are connected.

While you're reading a story, take notes in the form of a story map like the one

Story Map

Characters:
Conflict:
Time and place:
Main event:
Main event:
Main event:
Resolution:

above. Your story-map notes will give you most of the information you need to write a summary. All you need to add are transition words.

The character in the story you are about to read has great powers. After you read the story, you'll have a chance to try out your powers of summarizing.

Reading Skills and Strategies

This feature focuses on the importance of summarizing and the characteristics of an effective summary. Whether they are retelling a story or reviewing material for a test, students will find that summarizing is a valuable learning skill. The strategy of summarizing will be applied in the selection that follows.
Mini-Lesson: Summarizing
After students have read this feature, create a model of the story map on the chalkboard or overhead projector. Have the class choose an episode of a favorite television program with which the majority of the class is familiar. Call on volunteers to help you complete a model for that program.

Apply the strategy on the next page.

Reaching All Students

Struggling Readers
Remind students that a conflict—some sort of struggle or clash—is a major element in a story. Urge students to concentrate on the conflict in the stories that they want to summarize—who is clashing with whom (or what), where that clash leads, and how it is resolved (if at all). You might model this method using one of the Cinderella stories that students already have read.

English Language Learners
Expand on the discussion of transition words and phrases, noting the relationships that they indicate. You might begin with these examples:

to show the next step in the plot: *at first, before long, next, soon, suddenly*

to show a cause or effect: *as a result, if, since*

to emphasize a key detail: *certainly, in fact, of course, perhaps*

Advanced Learners
Have groups of students summarize the plots of favorite stories (in print or on film) in two ways: a one-sentence summary and a one-paragraph summary. Then have groups challenge each other to name the stories as the summaries are read aloud. Award five points for successful identification of each one-paragraph summary and ten points for successful identification of each one-sentence summary.

OBJECTIVES

1. Read and interpret the folk tale
2. Summarize the story
3. Express understanding through informative and creative writing, summarizing, or art/design
4. Identify and use homophones correctly
5. Understand and use new words

SKILLS

Reading
• Summarize the story

Writing
• Collect ideas for an informative report
• Write an original folk tale
• Write a summary of the story

Grammar/Language
• Identify and use correctly the homophones *they're, their,* and *there*

Vocabulary
• Use new words in a summary of a superhero's adventure

Art
• Design a book jacket

Viewing/Representing
• Describe the impression made by a piece of folk art (ATE)

Planning

• **Block Schedule**
  Block Scheduling Lesson Plans with Pacing Guide
• **Traditional Schedule**
  Lesson Plans Including Strategies for English-Language Learners
• **One-Stop Planner**
  CD-ROM with Test Generator

Before You Read

ONI AND THE GREAT BIRD

Make the Connection

Heroes

Superman, Wonder Woman, and Batman are popular action heroes. What makes these larger-than-life characters superheroes? How are they different from real-life heroes? To compare the two, think about the superheroes you've met in books, in movies, and on television. Then, copy the chart below, and complete it by putting a check mark in each box where the answer would be yes.

Quickwrite

Write briefly about what you think makes someone a hero.

Reading Skills and Strategies

Summarizing

A lot happens in the next story. After you read it, you'll be asked to "cut to the chase" and create a **summary.** It may help you to take a separate sheet of paper and make a story map, like the one on page 627. As you read, fill in your map.

Background

Literature and Music

"Oni and the Great Bird" is a folk tale of the Yoruba, a West African people known for their storytelling and musical talents. In the tale, short songs, or chants, are set off from the rest of the story. When Yoruban stories are told at ritual gatherings, these lines are chanted to the accompaniment of drums called gangans. These drums are used to imitate the sounds and patterns of Yoruban speech.

	Real-Life Hero	Superhero
1. shows courage?		
2. is sometimes fearful?		
3. makes mistakes?		
4. is mortal?		
5. relies on others?		
6. has special powers?		

Preteaching Vocabulary

Words to Own

Have students, either in pairs or individually, read the definitions of the Words to Own listed at the bottom of the selection pages. To check their mastery, ask them to explain their answers to the following questions.

1. "I **implored** Mom to let me go with you," your friend says, "but she wouldn't give in." How hard did your friend try?

2. If a vehicle **hovered,** what was it doing? Which vehicles can hover?

3. What would you do if you discovered an **impostor**?

4. You entered the concert hall as the program **commenced.** How late were you?

5. Would you want to undertake a dangerous expedition with someone who thought he was **invincible**? Why or why not?

Oni and the Great Bird

Yoruban, retold by Abayomi Fuja

Yoruban water-spirit mask (early twentieth century).
Ijebu region, Nigeria.

The Fine Arts Museum of San Francisco, Museum exchange, 76.12.1.

ONI AND THE GREAT BIRD **629**

Summary ■ ■

Oni is born wearing boots that grow as he grows. The boots later prove to make him invulnerable to enemy arrows. Oni's peers fear him, however, and have him banished. Oni comes to the village of Ajo, where he offers to help its people by vanquishing Anodo, a giant eagle that menaces the village. Oni kills the monstrous bird but is trapped beneath a cotton tree that Anodo uproots when it crashes to earth. Oni wriggles free, leaving one of his magic boots behind. The next day, when a local warrior takes credit for the kill, Oni asserts his claim. The boot is retrieved, Oni shows that it fits only his own foot, and he receives half of the kingdom as his reward.

Resources

Listening
Audio CD Library
You can find a compelling recording of this tale in the *Audio CD Library*:
• Disc 16, Track 2

RESPONDING TO THE ART
Nigerian art is characterized by diverse styles. One prevalent artistic tradition is the mask. Some masks are carved from wood and boast bold figures, others resemble skulls and human heads, and still others depict animal features and geometric shapes. Call on volunteers to name adjectives that they think describe this mask. [Possible responses: *detailed, noble, mysterious.*]

Resources: Print and Media

Reading
• *Reading Skills and Strategies*
    MiniRead Skill Lesson, p. 190
    Selection Skill Lesson, p. 196
• *Graphic Organizers for Active Reading*, p. 43
• *Words to Own*, p. 23
• *Spelling and Decoding*
    Worksheet, p. 29
• *Audio CD Library*
    Disc 16, Track 2

Elements of Literature
• *Literary Elements*
    Transparency 11
    Worksheet, p. 34

Writing and Language
• *Daily Oral Grammar*
    Transparency 38
• *Grammar and Language Links*
    Worksheet, p. 65
• *Language Workshop CD-ROM*

Assessment
• *Formal Assessment*, p. 124
• *Portfolio Management System*, p. 185
• *Standardized Test Preparation*, p. 92
• *Test Generator (One-Stop Planner CD-ROM)*

Internet
• go.hrw.com (keyword: LE0 7-8)

A Critical Thinking

Recognizing Bias

❓ Why do Oni's fellow villagers not accept him? [Oni is thought to be strange because he was born wearing boots; he is not harmed when enemy arrows strike him. The other villagers fear him.]

B Reading Skills and Strategies

Summarizing

After students have read the first paragraph, challenge them to recap Oni's biography, up to his banishment, in no more than two sentences. [Possible response: Oni, who was born wearing magical boots, is invulnerable to enemy arrows. Because they fear his strangeness, some villagers make a false charge against him and have him banished.] Students might save their summaries for the summary activity on p. 636.

C Cultural Connections

One Land, Many Peoples

The Yoruba, who live chiefly in southwestern Nigeria, are one of more than 250 tribal groups in Nigeria. The name *Yoruba* identifies both the people and one of Nigeria's regional languages. When Oni left his village, it is quite possible that he met a group of people with a different language and set of customs.

Yoruban mounted-warrior veranda post, carved by Olowe of Ise (twentieth century).

New Orleans Museum of Art: Museum Purchase: Ella West Freeman Foundation Matching Fund.

The other young men were afraid to have him near them.

There was once a strange boy called Oni who was born wearing a pair of boots. As Oni grew, the boots grew also. When he was a boy of eighteen years of age, war broke out between his people and another village. It was during the battle that Oni made a second discovery about himself, which separated him from his fellow men and made him different. The enemy arrows did not seem to harm him. Many pierced his body, which in the ordinary course of events should have slain him. The other young men noticed this too. They already regarded Oni as strange because of his wonderful boots, but when they discovered that he could not be killed, they were afraid to have him near them. When he returned from the war, several people tried to kill him in various ways but without any success. Finding this did not work, it was decided to find an excuse to banish him. He was accused of setting a house on fire in the village, and although Oni had nothing to do with the fire, he was found guilty and banished.

Oni wandered alone on foot for a long time. One afternoon he came to the banks of a great river, and finding an empty canoe and feeling tired of walking, he got into the boat and made his way downstream. Towards evening, when it was growing dark, Oni reached a town and

630   900 Cinderellas: Our World Heritage in Folklore

Reaching All Students

Struggling Readers

Summarizing was introduced on p. 628. For a lesson directly tied to this story that teaches students to summarize by using a strategy called Somebody Wanted but So, see the *Reading Skills and Strategies* binder:
• MiniRead Skill Lesson, p. 190
• Selection Skill Lesson, p. 196

English Language Learners

After students have read the account of Oni's battle against the fearsome Anodo (p. 632), invite them to share stories from their own cultural traditions about heroes who confront monstrous beings. For additional strategies to supplement instruction for these students, see
• *Lesson Plans Including Strategies for English-Language Learners*

Advanced Learners

When students have completed the story, ask why Oni was feared and ultimately banished from his own village but accepted and ultimately honored by strangers. Challenge students to suggest a response in a format of their own choosing—for example, in an essay, in hypothetical interviews with people from the two villages, or in a panel discussion. You might have students decide which three responses are most likely and which of the three is the strongest.

decided to pull into the bank and spend the night there. There were the sounds of many bells being rung and people seemed to be in a hurry. Oni tied up the canoe and climbed the bank, and as he did so, he met an old man. "Good evening, my friend. My name is Oni. I am a stranger to your town and have nowhere to spend the night. Will you take me to your house?" Oni asked the old man.

"Yes, certainly, come along with me, but we must go quickly because the bells are ringing and it is growing dusk," replied the old man.

"What is the name of your town and why do your people ring bells on the approach of darkness?" asked Oni.

"People call this place Ajo, but hurry up, we must get indoors. I will explain the bells to you when we are inside," replied the old man.

When they reached the old man's house, they found his people waiting anxiously for him at the door. The bells had now stopped ringing and they were hurried inside and the door was securely fastened.

"Now," said the old man, "sit down and eat with us and I will explain. For many years now we, the people of Ajo, have been troubled by the nightly arrival of a giant eagle. We call it Anodo. It always appears on the approach of darkness and stays until the approach of dawn. Anybody who is unfortunate enough to be out of doors at the time of its appearance is sure to be killed by it. You were very fortunate, young man, to reach Ajo before darkness. Our king has ordered the ringing of bells to warn the people to return to their homes and lock the doors. None of us knows where the eagle comes from or where it goes when it leaves us at dawn. It is a terrible curse, and in the past it has killed many of our people."

The old man had hardly finished speaking when Oni heard the sound of great wings flapping over the house. It sounded like a great wind, and the windows and doors shook in their frames.

"It must be a very great bird," remarked Oni. After Oni had fed, the old man gave him a mat and a cloth and he lay down to sleep in the corner of the room. Sleep would not come to Oni, however, for he heard the constant noise of the great eagle's wings as it flew to and fro over Ajo.

When morning had come and the eagle had departed, Oni thanked the old man for his kindness and set out to find the king of Ajo and to ask for an audience.[1] It was granted.

"My name is Oni and I am a stranger to your town. I have come to offer my services in helping to rid this town of the eagle Anodo," said Oni.

"And what makes you think you will succeed where so many others have tried and failed?" asked the king.

"I have certain powers and juju,"[2] said Oni.

"So had the others. One by one all my hunters have tried and have been killed or carried off by Anodo. Strangers have come from time to time to offer their services, but they too have perished. It is some time now since anybody has tried to kill Anodo, and I have issued orders to my remaining hunters not to try, as enough of them have been killed already," said the king.

"Have you ever offered a reward to anybody who could succeed in killing the bird?" asked Oni.

"Indeed, yes. The man who succeeds will have half my kingdom. I made that offer long ago," replied the king.

"Then I will try tonight," answered Oni, and he paid his respects to the king and departed.

Oni returned to the old man's house and told him what had happened and of his intention to challenge Anodo. The old man was very

1. **audience:** here, formal interview with a person of high rank.
2. **juju:** magic charms used by some West African tribes; the magic of such charms.

D Elements of Literature
Suspense
? How do the ringing bells and hurrying people create a feeling of suspense about the village of Ajo? [Possible response: The fact that people are running about while bells are ringing suggests that the bells are an alarm. The reader wonders what would warrant such an alarm.]

E Struggling Readers
Finding Details
Point out that the speaker is giving background information. Ask students to list the important details that are presented. [Possible responses: The village has been troubled for years by a giant eagle. The bird arrives at dusk and stays until dawn. It kills anyone who is not safely indoors. The bells are rung as a warning to villagers to return home. No one knows where the eagle comes from or where it goes when it leaves at dawn.]

F English Language Learners
Interpreting Idioms
From time to time is an idiom meaning "occasionally" or "once in a while." Invite students to share expressions from languages other than English with a similar meaning or to use *from time to time* in original sentences.

G Reading Skills and Strategies
Responding to the Text
? Do you think Oni would have offered to kill the eagle if there were no reward? Why or why not? [Possible responses: Yes, he would have taken the challenge because he wanted to help the people and/or because he felt that the eagle could not harm him. No, without the reward, he might not have wanted to take the risk.]

Using Students' Strengths

Auditory/Musical Learners
Ask students to listen for sounds in the story, such as boots walking, a canoe gliding downstream, or the flapping of gigantic wings. Have students tape-record simulations of the sounds, perhaps using classroom objects. As students share the recordings, invite them to speculate about how an oral storyteller might have expressed the sounds.

Naturalist Learners
Students with a sensitivity to the workings of the natural world might compare the actions of Anodo with the activities of real eagles in the wild. Students might explore such matters as eagles' hunting behaviors and diet; students also might read about and be prepared to explain how much of a threat wild eagles pose to humans.

Crossing the Curriculum

Geography
Ask students to find Nigeria on a map and to locate a river along which Oni could have traveled to find the village of Ajo. Next, provide them with pages from an almanac that contain information on the country (or have them find such information on their own), and ask them to create a travel brochure using facts about the Yoruba people or Nigeria.

A Reading Skills and Strategies
Identifying Cause and Effect
❓The villagers obviously are afraid of the eagle. Why, then, are they so upset about Oni's attempt to kill it? [Possible response: They probably doubt that Oni will succeed. They may fear that Anodo will retaliate, taking out his vengeance on them.]

B Elements of Literature
Figurative Language
❓What does Oni mean when he sings about "the knives of nature and man"? [The "knives of nature" are Anodo's sharp talons; the "knives of man" are Oni's weapons.]

C Appreciating Language
Action Verbs
Have students identify the action verbs (or verb forms) in this sentence [*threw, swooped, seizing, drew*] and discuss how they help set the battle in vivid motion. Ask students to find and comment on other action verbs in the account of the battle. [Examples include *pecked, buried, beat, rolled, swept,* and *plunged.*]

D Reading Skills and Strategies

Summarizing
Newspaper headlines are a type of summary. Challenge students to create newspaper headlines that summarize the battle in an interesting but accurate way. [Possible responses: Booted Stranger Beats Monster Bird; Anodo Falls to Oni's Arrow.]

---

frightened and <u>implored</u> him to give up the idea, for he would only perish and perhaps all those in the house too. But Oni was not frightened. He took his bow and arrows and knives and examined them carefully.

It seemed ages to Oni before he heard the bells ringing. Never had he known a longer day in his life. The old man was uneasy and his people were almost hostile towards Oni. When they heard the bells ringing at last, they lost no time in fastening the doors and windows and ordered Oni to lie down on his mat and keep quiet.

Presently they heard the noise of a great wind, which heralded the approach of Anodo. Soon the great wings were above the house. Oni waited till the great bird was overhead and then he <u>commenced</u> to sing:

> Tonight Oni will be at war with Anodo,
> The eagle whose talons are sharper than knives,
> For now the knives of nature and man will meet.
> Oni is <u>invincible</u>; his knife is sharp.

Anodo heard the challenge as he <u>hovered</u> over the house, and circling slowly round, he came back and sang:

> Ah, fortune, I have found a victim tonight,
> I have lived many months without a kill,
> Will the singer come out and feel the sharpness
> Of my talons and of my beak? It will take me
> A moment to tear him to pieces. Come out.

All the people in the house were terrified. They seized Oni and threw him out of the house, fearing the vengeance of Anodo on them all.

As they threw Oni out into the road, Anodo swooped down and, seizing him in his talons, drew him upwards. Oni slashed the eagle in the chest with his knife and the eagle dropped him with a scream. Oni fell to the ground,

dazed. He picked himself up as the huge bird descended once again. He had time to use his bow and discharge an arrow into Anodo before the wounded bird beat him to the ground with his great wings and pecked him severely. Again Oni's knife tore at the eagle, and he buried it twice in Anodo. Slowly the eagle beat his great wings and rose slowly into the air; then he hovered for a last terrible dive on Oni. Oni watched him and, putting an arrow in his bow, took aim. The great bird hovered; then with a terrible noise he tore down on the boy, gathering speed as he came. There was a great roar of wind as he came down. Oni discharged a second arrow, then another and another in quick succession, but still the bird came on. A moment later it had hit Oni and knocked him over. The boy rolled over, a thousand lights dancing before his eyes; then all went blank, and he felt himself sinking down and down into a bottomless pit. He was knocked unconscious and had not seen that the great bird was already dead before it struck him. Its great wings swept the boy to one side, and it plunged on into a cotton tree, which snapped like a twig and came crashing down to bury the eagle and Oni under a mass of leaves.

When Oni recovered, he felt very weak, and it was all he could do to free himself from the great wing of the dead Anodo and the cotton tree leaves. As he struggled, one of his magic boots came off and remained stuck beneath the dead bird. He was very weak and with great difficulty staggered along till he reached the edge of the river; then Oni fainted again.

Early next morning the people came out to see the dead Anodo lying in the broken cotton

---

WORDS TO OWN
implored (im·plôrd′) *v.*: asked or begged.
commenced (kə·menst′) *v.*: began.
invincible (in·vin′sə·bəl) *adj.*: unbeatable.
hovered (huv′ərd) *v.*: hung in the air.

---

632   900 CINDERELLAS: OUR WORLD HERITAGE IN FOLKLORE

Skill Link

Decoding: Words with *ie*
Point out that there's a mnemonic to help people remember whether a word is spelled with *ie* or *ei:*

> *I* before *e* except after *c*
> And when sounded like *a*
> As in *neighbor* and *weigh.*

When one is reading, however, the problem is how to pronounce *ie.* These words from the selection illustrate some of the possibilities:

a. In *pierce, ie* stands for short *i.*
b. In *pieces* and *chiefs, ie* stands for long *e.*
c. In *view, ie* is followed by *w,* producing a long *u.*
d. In *quiet, ie* stands for two vowel sounds: long *i* and the unstressed vowel sound schwa.
e. In *audience, ie* also stands for two different vowel sounds, but in this word the sounds are long *e* and schwa.

Activity
Have students determine the sound of *ie* in each of these words and identify the type of sound, using the lettered list on the right.

1. field	[b]	**a.** short *i*	
2. client	[d]	**b.** long *e*	
3. fierce	[a]	**c.** long *u*	
4. obedient	[e]	**d.** long *i* and schwa	
5. siege	[b]	**e.** long *e* and schwa	
6. review	[c]		

LITERATURE AND ORAL STORYTELLING

Spreading the Word

Since the beginning of time, folks have always wanted to spread the word. The ones who can spread the word the most effectively have the ability to "talk dat talk" and "walk dat walk." In other words, they can grab the imagination of the listener and hold on to it for as long as they like, conjuring up images of the good and the bad, the weak and the strong, and the trickster and the fool. They have the ability to make you laugh until you cry, cry until you laugh, stand up and shout, or stare in amazement at their gestures and characterizations.

In the African American culture, past and present, these folks have gone by many names. Today they are called preachers, healers, teachers, comedians, blues singers, poets, dancers, rappers, liars, painters, and historians. In a performance all storytellers will use whatever it takes to get the story across. To hear them is to hear the drum, the heartbeat of Africa. To see them tell the story is to experience the highlights of African ritual, at its best, a total theatrical performance.

—Linda Goss and Marian E. Barnes
(Linda Goss tells "The Frog Who Wanted to Be a Singer" on page 172.)

Epa cult mask.
Founders Society Purchase, Friends of African Art Fund. Photograph © 1995 The Detroit Institute of Arts.

tree. There was great rejoicing and drumming and the king soon appeared with his chiefs to view the wonderful sight. "Who is the great man who killed Anodo?" he asked. One of his hunters stepped forward and, prostrating[3]

3. **prostrating** (präs′trāt′iŋ): throwing oneself on the ground to show humility and submission; a traditional gesture of respect toward rulers in many cultures.

ONI AND THE GREAT BIRD 633

LITERATURE AND ORAL STORYTELLING

In West Africa the word *griot* (grē′ ō) is the name for a person who is an expert in oral performance. In Africa today a griot may be a professional storyteller, singer, or entertainer. In the past the griot's role was chiefly that of preserving tradition. Griots were skilled at creating and transmitting the many forms of African oral literature. Many also memorized their nation's histories and laws. Rather than consulting books or libraries, people in Africa's kingdoms consulted griots. Elsewhere on the African continent, storytellers, bards, town criers, and oral historians also preserved and continued the oral traditions.

Resources

Selection Assessment
Formal Assessment
• Selection Test, p. 124
Test Generator
• Selection Test

Making the Connections

Connecting to the Theme:
000 Cinderellas:
ur World Heritage in Folklore"
ter students have finished reading the selec-
n, review the fact that in many Cinderella
es, footwear is a key part of the hero's iden-
y. Challenge students to compare the impor-
nce of Oni's boots with that of Aschenputtel's
Yeh-Shen's slippers.

Cultural Connections
Drum talking is used for leading tribal dances and for sending messages. The Yoruba people use a cylinder-shaped drum with strings that, when squeezed, produce a wide range of notes. A drummer uses a curved drumstick to change the pitch and rhythm of sounds to "talk" in a special drum language based on the Yoruba spoken language.

Assessing Learning

Self-Assessment: Rating Responses
Ask students to use the following scale and list of criteria to rate their responses on the assignments for this selection.
3=Strong   2=Average   1=Weak
____ Oral responses during class discussion
____ Responses during small-group discussion
____ Creative responses (other than writing)
____ Written responses (formal or informal)
Work with students to plan strategies for improvement in each "weak" category.

❓ How is Oni's situation similar to the situation of Aschenputtel? [Possible response: Oni loses his boot and must prove his identity by showing that he is the only one who can fit into it, just as Aschenputtel has to prove her identity by fitting into the slipper that she lost.]

B **Reading Skills and Strategies**
Responding to the Text

❓ Suppose that the people of Oni's village learn about this story. What might they think of him now? [Possible responses: Now that he owns half the kingdom, they might want to be friends with him. Some of them may still fear him because of his magical powers.]

BROWSING IN THE FILES

About the Author. In his stories, Abayomi Fuja attempts to maintain the spirit of Yoruban storytelling by including many phrases that traditionally are chanted in the form of free verse. The Yoruba, who live mainly in Nigeria, are estimated to number more than five million. For centuries they have been known for their drum-based story- and speech-making talents.

A Critic's Comment. In her introduction to Fuja's collection of tales, Anne Pellowski points out that stories like that of Oni "may be told for the sheer enjoyment . . . , or as one African way of explaining the actions of men and beasts, or to teach a moral in the Yoruba manner. When one can tell them with the perfect fusion of all three purposes, one is close to being a Yoruba storyteller."

---

himself on the ground, claimed that he was responsible for the deed.

"Then you will be rewarded generously, for I have promised to give half my kingdom to the man who killed Anodo and it is yours," replied the king.

There was great rejoicing and dancing and the hunter was carried to the king's palace and feasted. A very bedraggled figure then appeared; his clothes were torn and one of his boots was missing. It was Oni.

"Ah," said the king, "here is the stranger who calls himself Oni and who came yesterday to announce his intention of killing the eagle. You come too late, my friend, I fear."

"I killed Anodo. This man is an <u>impostor</u> and a liar," said Oni.

There was whispering between the king and his chiefs. At last he said, "Very well, you claim to have killed Anodo. What proof have you got to offer?"

"You see my condition," replied Oni, "but if you require further proof, send your men out to clear away the dead eagle and the broken cotton tree. Somewhere underneath you will find one of my boots."

The king ordered his men to go at once and search for the boot. After some little time the men returned. They carried Oni's magic boot. "We found it underneath the dead eagle's wing," they announced to the king.

A "Now if you are still undecided and disbelieve my story, will you ask everybody to try on the boot and see if it fits," said Oni.

The king ordered everybody to try to see if they could fit the boot to their feet. Strange to relate, although it looked a perfectly normal boot, nobody could manage to put it on. When they had all tried without success, the boot was placed before the king and Oni stepped forward and said:

Boot from Heaven—boot from Heaven,
Go on to your master's foot.

Immediately, the boot started to move from before the king and fitted itself onto Oni's foot of its own accord. The people and the king were convinced of the truth of Oni's claims and marveled greatly and were very delighted and grateful for his brave deed. The dishonest hunter was taken out and executed, and Oni received the promised reward.

B That night, for the first time for many years, the bells of Ajo did not sound the curfew. Instead, the streets were full of happy, dancing people.

WORDS TO OWN
impostor (im·päs′tər) n.: person who pretends to be someone or something that he or she is not.

MEET THE WRITER
At Home in Two Worlds

Abayomi Fuja, a Yoruban, was born in Nigeria. When he was growing up, Fuja was taught by British missionaries, so he learned English and studied European stories at school. As an adult he decided to celebrate his Yoruban heritage by collecting the traditional folk tales of his people. He devoted six years to recording tales like "Oni and the Great Bird." Though written in English, they remain true to the style and spirit of the original Yoruban folk tales. By retelling these traditional African stories in English, Fuja brings together the two worlds in which he grew up.

More Tales from the Yoruba

If you liked "Oni and the Great Bird," you might want to explore the other stories in *Fourteen Hundred Cowries* (Oxford University Press), the book it's taken from. (A cowrie is a glossy shell that the Yoruba use to signal certain ideas. For instance, two shells placed together means friendship; two shells placed apart means hostility.)

Assessing Learning

Check Test: Short Answer

1. What was strange about Oni's birth? [He was born wearing boots.]
2. Why do people fear him? [He cannot be harmed by enemy arrows in battle.]
3. In the town of Ajo, why does the bell ring? [to warn people to get indoors before darkness and the arrival of Anodo]

4. What weapons does Oni use to kill the bird? [a knife and a bow and arrow]
5. What is Oni's reward for killing the bird? [half of the kingdom]

Standardized Test Preparation

For practice with standardized test format specific to this selection, see
• *Standardized Test Preparation*, p. 92
For practice in proofreading and editing, see
• *Daily Oral Grammar*, Transparency 38

MAKING MEANINGS

MAKING MEANINGS

First Thoughts

[respond]

1. Do you think Oni is a hero? Be sure to check your Quickwrite notes.

Shaping Interpretations

[analyze]
2. Look back at Oni's song to Anodo before the fight (page 632). What do you think the song shows about Oni's **character**?

[infer]
3. The magic boots set Oni apart, making him "strange" and "different." What lesson might this tale teach Yoruban children about how to behave toward people who are different from them?

[interpret]
4. Think about what happened to the hunter who tried to take credit for killing Anodo. What does his fate tell you about the beliefs of the Yoruba?

[synthesize]
5. What **motifs** does "Oni and the Great Bird" share with the Cinderella stories?

Extending the Text

[connect]
6. In this story, Oni saves the people from the threat of a giant eagle. If the story were set in modern times, what dangerous force might Oni have to save the people from?

[apply]
7. Oni was an outsider—even among his own people. Do you think that heroes in real life are usually outsiders, or are they usually part of the group? Give examples to support your point of view.

Challenging the Text

[evaluate]
8. At the beginning of the story, you learn that Oni cannot be killed. Does this ruin the suspense of the story? Why or why not?

Reading Check

a. Why must Oni leave his village?

b. How does the king of Ajo react to Oni's offer to fight Anodo?

c. What happens when Oni fights Anodo?

d. How does Oni prove that the hunter who claims to have killed Anodo is an impostor?

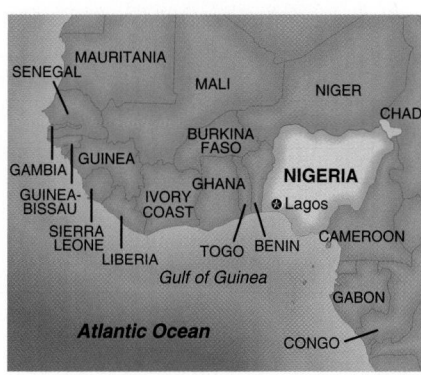

ONI AND THE GREAT BIRD 635

MAKING MEANINGS

First Thoughts

1. Possible response: Oni's superior strength makes him seem heroic, as does the fact that he cannot be killed. Most important, though, is his heroic goal to do good (in this case, to protect people who are in danger).

Shaping Interpretations

2. The song reveals Oni's confidence and belief in his own power.

3. Yoruban children might learn to respect differences in people and to understand that some differences actually may be good.

4. The execution of the dishonest hunter suggests that the Yoruba disapprove of lying.

5. One motif shared with Cinderella stories is the number three: Oni stabs the eagle three times before it dies, and the eagle attacks him three times. Other motifs include the hero's being an outcast, fitting into a special shoe, and singing special songs.

Extending the Text

6. Responses might include such natural disasters as a hurricane, earthquake, or tornado.

7. Responses will vary. Students may suggest that fictional heroes such as Superman often are outsiders but that real-life heroes, such as Mohandas Gandhi or Abraham Lincoln, usually are supported and praised by most of the people whom they attempt to help.

Challenging the Text

8. No, knowing that Oni cannot be killed does not stop the reader from wanting to know what happens to him.

Reading Check

a. Oni is banished after being declared guilty of setting a villager's house on fire—a false accusation made by villagers who fear him.

b. The king seems doubtful, for he tells Oni that many others have tried but failed to kill Anodo.

c. In a fierce battle, Oni shoots Anodo from the sky. As the bird crashes to the ground, it plunges into a cotton tree, which buries both Anodo and Oni.

d. While freeing himself, Oni has lost one of his boots. It is found beneath Anodo's body. Oni invites everyone to try it on, but it fits only his foot.

Rubrics for each Choices assignment appear on p. 185 in the *Portfolio Management System.*

CHOICES:
Building Your Portfolio

1. **Writer's Notebook** You might compile a master list of topics for students. Remind students to save their work. They may use it as prewriting for the Writer's Workshop on pp. 672–676.
2. **Creative Writing** To help students begin, tell them to think of a threatening problem that they believe needs to be solved. Suggest that students consider current problems in health, science, or society.
3. **Writing a Summary** Have students work in groups of four, with each group member thinking of one part of the story and discussing it with the others. Groups then can work together to condense the story into several sentences.
4. **Art/Design** The children's section of a local public library or bookstore can be a rich resource for students who need help generating ideas for their book jackets. Encourage students to browse, looking at covers of bestsellers, classic books, and other books that catch their eye.

CHOICES: Building Your Portfolio

Writer's Notebook

1. Collecting Ideas for an Informative Report

Like most folk tales from other cultures, the Yoruban tale "Oni and the Great Bird" suggests many topics for further investigation. Choose one of the following topics about Yoruban culture or another topic that your teacher approves:

- Yoruban art   • Yoruban music   • Yoruban literature
- women's roles in Yoruban culture
- men's roles in Yoruban culture

Research your topic, and write down the four most interesting facts you learn about it.

Women in Yoruban culture
—do not farm
—control sale of goods in marketplace
—weave baskets
—spin and dye cotton

Creative Writing

2. Homemade Hero

Using "Oni and the Great Bird" as a model, write your own folk tale about a superhero. First, decide **where** and **when** your story will take place. Second, think about your **characters.** What human and superhuman qualities does the **hero** have? Next, decide what **conflict,** or problem, your hero will face. Finally, decide how the hero will solve the problem and bring the story to an end. You can use a chart like the one below to **outline** your story.

Writing a Summary

3. Summing Up Oni

Writing a **summary** is a way to sum up the most important events of a story. Refer to the notes you took while you read, and write a summary of the story. Tell about each major event in a complete sentence. Use words like *then, after,* and *as a result* to indicate when and where events happened.

Art/Design

4. Judge a Book by Its Cover

Imagine that you are creating a picture-book version of this story. Design a book jacket for the story. Be sure your design displays the title and the name of the reteller in an appealing script or typeface.

	"Oni and the Great Bird"	My Folk Tale
setting	Yoruban village	
hero	Oni: Because of magic boots, he can't be killed.	
conflict, or problem	Giant eagle threatens town.	
conclusion	Oni kills eagle, saves town.	

GRAMMAR LINK MINI-LESSON

Language Handbook HELP

See Personal Pronouns, pages 710 and 734; Apostrophes, page 777.

Technology HELP

See Language Workshop CD-ROM. Key word entry: their, they're, there.

• They're, Their, There

Many words in English sound like other words but have very different meanings and functions. Three words often confused are *they're*, *their*, and *there*:

they're: a contraction of "they are."

their: a personal possessive pronoun.

there: a word that means "at that place" or that begins a sentence such as "There was once a strange boy called Oni who was born wearing a pair of boots."

EXAMPLES

When the people of the town hear the bells, they're very frightened. [They are very frightened.]

" 'Our king has ordered the ringing of bells to warn the people to return to their homes and lock the doors.' " [*Their* is a possessive pronoun modifying *homes.*]

Tonight there will be much celebrating in the town.

When you find one of these confusing words in your writing, ask yourself:

1. Can I substitute the words *they are*? If so, *they're* is OK.

2. Does the word answer the question *whose*? If so, *their* is OK.

Try It Out

Be a test maker. Write five sentences that ask for a choice between *there, their,* and *they're.* Exchange tests with a partner, and then grade your partner's paper. Does making a test on the *there/their/they're* problem help you see the differences between the words?

VOCABULARY   HOW TO OWN A WORD

WORD BANK

implored
commenced
invincible
hovered
impostor

Vocabulary for the Workplace: Lights, Action, Script

Imagine that you work for an animation production company that is launching a cartoon about a new superhero. Use the words in the Word Bank to write a summary of the cartoon superhero's first adventure. (You may make the verbs any tense you wish.)

(Left) Spiderman.
(Right) Superman.

ONI AND THE GREAT BIRD 637

GRAMMAR LINK

Ask students to choose a piece of writing from their portfolios and to circle the words *they're, their,* or *there* wherever they appear. Have students exchange papers; then have partners check the papers that they receive, evaluating the correctness of the circled words.

Try It Out
Answers

Invite students to comment upon what they learn from preparing a test such as the following:
Directions: Fill in the blank with *there, their,* or *they're.*

1. Are you going _____ tomorrow? [there]
2. Do you know if _____ going, too? [they're]
3. Please put _____ books on the desk for me. [their]
4. _____ going to the movie with me Saturday. [They're]
5. _____ supposed to hang _____ coats _____. [They're, their, there]

VOCABULARY

Students should demonstrate their knowledge of the meanings of the Words to Own as defined on pp. 632–634.

Resources ———

Grammar
• *Grammar and Language Links,* p. 65

Vocabulary
• *Words to Own,* p. 23

Spelling
For related spelling instruction, see
• *Spelling and Decoding,* p. 29

Grammar Link Quick Check

Choose the word that correctly completes each sentence.

1. They're/There were many people who wanted to try on Oni's boot. [There]
2. Oni thought, "These people—they're/there all impostors." [they're]
3. "There/Their attempts will fail." [Their]
4. "There/Their is my boot, and now I will prove that their/they're liars." [There, they're]
5. Soon the people of Ajo were dancing they're/there around the fire, singing the praises of their/there new hero. [there, their]

OBJECTIVES

1. Read and interpret the folk tale
2. Analyze the element of metamorphosis in stories
3. Make predictions while reading
4. Express understanding through informative and creative writing or speaking and listening
5. Identify specific words in a text and use specific words in one's own writing
6. Understand and use new words

SKILLS

Literary
- Analyze metamorphosis and its function in the story

Reading
- Make predictions

Writing
- Collect ideas for an informative report
- Write the beginning of an original tale featuring an animal character
- Write a report that compares and contrasts two literary works

Speaking/Listening
- Tape-record a reading of the story, including sound effects

Grammar/Language
- Identify specific words in a text and use specific words in one's own writing

Vocabulary
- Understand and use new words

Planning

- **Traditional Schedule**
  Lesson Plans Including Strategies for English-Language Learners
- **One-Stop Planner**
  CD-ROM with Test Generator

Before You Read

MASTER FROG

Make the Connection

Beauty Is Only Skin Deep

The main character of this Vietnamese folk tale is just like other boys except for his unusual appearance. People who judge him only by his looks are missing all the special qualities and talents that lie beneath the surface.

Quickwrite

There's more to all of us than what appears on the surface. What are your special qualities and talents? List some of the things you're good at, and then write a few sentences about the one that is your favorite.

Elements of Literature

Metamorphosis: Changing Skins

When you talk about this story, you'll probably use the word *metamorphosis*. **Metamorphosis** means a marvelous transformation, or change, from one shape to another. You might already know about metamorphosis from ancient myths and fairy tales. In many folk tales a warty frog with bulgy eyes becomes a handsome prince when someone else loves

> **A** metamorphosis is a marvelous change from one shape or form to another one.
>
> *For more on Metamorphosis, see the Handbook of Literary Terms.*

it, and the lovers usually live happily ever after. In this story, however, the metamorphosis has an unusual twist.

Reading Skills and Strategies

Making Predictions: Guessing What's Ahead

"Master Frog" is a good story to use for **making predictions,** or guessing what's going to happen next. Warning: There are many twists and turns ahead. *Before you read,* follow these steps:

- Preview the quotations on pages 639–643.
- Remember what you've learned about **metamorphosis.**
- Think about your prior experience with fairy tales.
- Write a sentence predicting what will happen in this story.

While you read, follow these steps:

- Modify your original prediction.
- Write a new prediction before you begin each page.

Did you guess correctly—or were you totally surprised?

One of a pair of belt buckles. Eastern Inner Mongolia.
Asian Art Museum of San Francisco, The Avery Brundage Collection, B60B1082/1083.

Preteaching Vocabulary

Words to Own

As students consider the definitions of the Words to Own, which appear at the bottom of the selection pages, ask them to think about the intensity of each word. Have pairs or small groups of students suggest at least two synonyms or near-synonyms for each word (using a thesaurus, if they wish) and explain how the similar words compare in intensity.
Possible responses:
admonished: cautioned (less intense), advised (more intense), scolded (more intense)
entreaties: wishes (less intense), petitions (less intense), demands (more intense)
charade: make-believe (less intense), trickery (more intense), deceit (more intense)
presumptuous: confident (less intense), egotistical (more intense), audacious (more intense)
cowered: quailed (less intense), cringed (less intense), groveled (more intense)

Master Frog

Vietnamese, retold by
Lynette Dyer Vuong

Except for his strange appearance, Master Frog was really quite an ordinary boy . . .

G iang Dung[1] was a plain girl, so plain in fact that all the townspeople marveled when her parents finally found her a husband. Then they nodded their heads knowingly and whispered to one another that the young man must have been after her father's money. He had plenty of it, it was true, and Giang Dung was his only child. The day of the wedding came and passed, and the people found more interesting things to gossip about until a few months later, when Giang Dung's husband died.

1. **Giang Dung** (zäng′ zōōm′): Vietnamese for "pretty face," an ironic name for a plain girl.

MASTER FROG **639**

Summary ■■■

After her husband dies, Giang Dung gives birth to a frog. The creature grows up as a clever, affectionate boy. When he asks to marry the king's daughter, the astonished king curtly dismisses him; Master Frog counters by causing a magical stampede of wild animals in the palace. Princess Kien Tien offers to marry him, and the pair soon settle into a happy marriage. One day Kien Tien is horrified to find the frog dead. Her mourning is interrupted by the appearance of a handsome young man. It is the new incarnation of Master Frog, a prince of Fairyland, who had come to earth in search of adventure. The prince warns his bride that his frog skin must be preserved or he will have to return to Fairyland. When Kien Tien's jealous sisters destroy the skin, Master Frog dies. The sisters then drug Kien Tien, throw her into the sea, and tell their father that the princess has committed suicide. Returning to earth, Master Frog dashes to the watery depths to rescue his beloved, and they live happily ever after.

Resources ———

Viewing and Representing
Videocassette B, Segment 9
This *Visual Connections* segment, "Jackie Torrence: Be True to Yourself," is an interview with author Torrence. It includes Torrence's sharing of a folk tale. You may wish to use this segment with "Master Frog." See the *Visual Connections: Teacher's Manual.*

Listening
Audio CD Library
A winning recording of this story is included in the *Audio CD Library:*
• Disc 16, Track 3

Resources: Print and Media ———

Reading
• *Reading Skills and Strategies*
   Selection Skill Lesson, p. 61
• *Graphic Organizers for Active Reading,* p. 44
• *Words to Own,* p. 24
• *Spelling and Decoding*
   Worksheet, p. 30
• *Audio CD Library*
   Disc 16, Track 3

Elements of Literature
• *Literary Elements*
   Transparency 11
   Worksheet, p. 34

Writing and Language
• *Daily Oral Grammar*
   Transparency 39
• *Grammar and Language Links*
   Worksheet, p. 67

Viewing and Representing
• *Visual Connections*
   Videocassette B, Segment 9

Assessment
• *Formal Assessment,* p. 126
• *Portfolio Management System,* p. 186
• *Standardized Test Preparation,* p. 94
• *Test Generator (One-Stop Planner CD-ROM)*

Internet
• go.hrw.com (keyword: LE0 7-8)

FROM THE EDITOR'S DESK

"Master Frog" has much to recommend it; for example, it shows an "outsider" beating the odds, and it offers a glimpse into a culture with which students may be unfamiliar. One reason that we included it, however, is that we knew something about its origin—namely, that Lynette Dyer Vuong discovered it while visiting a bookstore in Saigon. We hope that as you share this tidbit, students might take a greater interest in browsing through libraries and bookstores on their own. Who knows—they, too, might want to write about what they find!

A Reading Skills and Strategies
Drawing Conclusions

? How do these townspeople seem to feel about physical beauty? Explain. [Possible response: They seem to value it highly. They gossip about why anyone would marry a girl as plain as Giang Dung and speculate that when she is widowed, she will not find another husband.]

B English Language Learners
Context Clues

If students are not familiar with the word *laughingstock*, ask if they can figure out its meaning from context. [an object of ridicule]

C Critical Thinking
Analyzing Character

? What do Giang Dung's attitude toward her son and her actions on his behalf reveal about her character? [Possible response: She is a loving and attentive mother who accepts the child as he is.]

"It's fortunate that she's expecting a child," one person said, and the rest agreed. "At least she'll have someone to look after her in her old age. It's certain she'll never find anyone else to marry her."

A But when the child was born, instead of being a boy to carry on her husband's name or at least a girl to give her some comfort and companionship, it was only a frog. And the people's tongues wagged again until they tired of the subject. "What would you expect? Giang Dung almost looks like a frog herself, she's so ugly."

Poor Giang Dung cried for days until she had no tears left. Then she resigned herself to her fate and determined to raise the frog as well as she could. If she was being punished for some unknown evil she had committed, she would have to make the best of it and serve her sentence. But on the other hand, Heaven sometimes worked in mysterious ways, and it was just possible that some great destiny lay ahead for her son.

But as the years passed, Giang Dung forgot both of these theories. Except for his strange appearance, Master Frog was really quite an ordinary boy—now mischievous, now helpful, but always affectionate. He followed her around the house as she went about her daily tasks, helping her to care for the silkworms.[2] He gathered mulberry leaves for her to chop and place in their trays; he watched them as they began to spin their cocoons, fascinated at the way they swung their heads down and round and then up again to surround themselves with the fine strands. He often perched beside her as she sat at the loom and thought it great fun to take the shuttle in his mouth and wriggle his small body in and out among the warp threads. Sometimes, as she

2. **silkworms:** moth caterpillars that produce cocoons of silk fiber. Some silkworms are grown and cultivated as the source of silk.

was cooking, he would hop up on the stove to stir the soup, or if he was sure she was not watching him, to snap up some tasty tidbit with his long, sticky tongue. But, like other children, he was often bored with being indoors and went out to play hide-and-seek and hopscotch with the boys of the neighborhood. All in all, he was both a good-natured and an intelligent little fellow, and his mother decided at last that something must be done about his education.

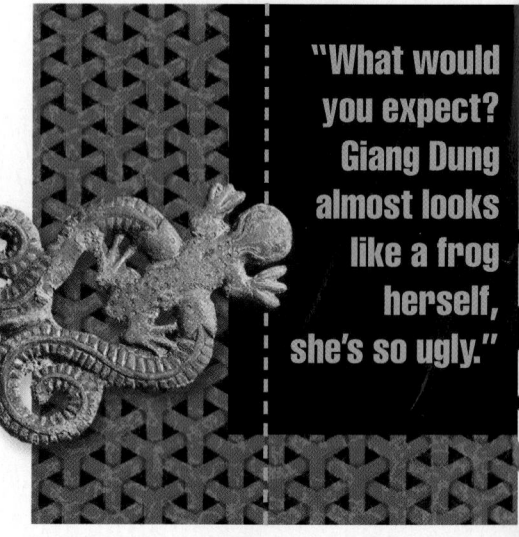

"What would you expect? Giang Dung almost looks like a frog herself, she's so ugly."

"A frog? In my class?" the teacher demanded when Giang Dung brought him to the school. **B** "Impossible! I would be the laughingstock of the town."

C "Then at least let him sit at the back and listen," she pleaded with him. "I promise you he won't cause you any trouble."

As the weeks went by, Master Frog proved himself such a model student that at last the teacher moved him up to the head of the class and often admonished the others to follow his

---

WORDS TO OWN
admonished (ad·män′isht) v.: warned or urged.

Reaching All Students

Struggling Readers
Making Predictions was introduced on p. 638. For a lesson directly tied to this story that teaches students to make predictions by using a strategy called Probable Passage, see the *Reading Skills and Strategies* binder:
• Selection Skill Lesson, p. 61

English Language Learners
Although "Master Frog" is an old story, Vuong uses modern dialogue in telling it. As you discuss passages of dialogue in the story, invite students to contrast various characters' manners of speaking (the king's daughters, for example). For additional strategies to supplement instruction for these students, see
• *Lesson Plans Including Strategies for English-Language Learners*

Advanced Learners
In her introduction to *The Brocaded Slipper*, from which this tale comes, Lynette Dyer Vuong says that for Master Frog, "winning the princess did not automatically rid him of his ugly skin. In Vietnamese fairy tales one usually must work hard to deserve to 'live happily ever after.'" Challenge students to support Vuong's comment by citing specific details from the story.

example. At first he had tried to grasp the brush with his front feet but later found that he could form more graceful characters if he held it in his mouth. Generally he was the first to commit a passage to memory, and if none of the others could correctly interpret a line of the reading, the teacher would call on Master Frog. Finally, Master Frog completed his education and grew to young froghood.

"It's time to think of learning some trade," Giang Dung suggested to him one day. "Tomorrow I will go to town and talk to some of the craftsmen. Perhaps one of them would be willing to take you on as an apprentice."

But Master Frog shook his head. "Mother, first I would like to get married."

"G . . . get married!" she stammered, almost unable to believe her ears. "I . . . is there any particular girl you have in mind?"

"Yes, Mother. Princess Kien Tien,[3] the king's youngest daughter."

Giang Dung drew back in alarm. "Son, you must be out of your mind! How could you ever hope to marry the king's daughter?"

"Nevertheless I shall marry her." Master Frog planted all four feet on the table in a stance of determination. "Tomorrow I shall go to the king to ask for her hand."

All Giang Dung's protests—all her entreaties —were in vain. Master Frog had made up his mind, and nothing could change it. And so the next morning he and Giang Dung set off for the palace.

Giang Dung set him down as they entered the audience hall, and he hopped straight up to the king, bowing respectfully as he neared the throne. The king stared at him in astonishment as he made his request and then burst out laughing.

"So you want to marry my daughter," he said. "Well, I have three daughters. Which one is it you want? But don't be in a hurry to make up

3. **Kien Tien** (kē·'n' tē·en').

your mind." His lips twisted in amusement as he motioned to one of the courtiers.[4] "Bring their royal highnesses here."

"Come here, my dears," he beckoned to them as they entered the hall. "A suitor has presented himself to request the hand of one of you." With a grand sweep of his forearm he indicated Master Frog at the foot of the throne. "He has not yet told me the extent of his kingdom or the number of vassals[5] who pay him tribute, but does he not have a noble air?" He turned back to Master Frog. "Allow me to introduce my daughters to your highness: Kim Chau,"[6] he pointed to the first, who cast a contemptuous glance in Master Frog's direction, then gave her head such a violent toss that one of her pearl hairpins slipped from its place and fell to the floor; "Bich Ngoc,"[7] he indicated the second, who made a face at him and stuck out her tongue; "and Kien Tien," he presented the last of the three, who had stood the whole time, her hands folded in her long sleeves and her eyes on the floor. "Now would you please tell me which of the three pleases you?"

Kim Chau's chin rose a trifle higher. "I won't marry him, Father."

"I'll kill myself if you force me to marry him," Bich Ngoc declared with a stamp of her foot.

"Your Majesty," Master Frog interrupted them, "it is Kien Tien whose hand I have come to seek."

"Enough of this charade." The king's face had grown angry. "We have carried this joke far enough." He motioned to the guards. "Take this

4. **courtiers** (kôrt'ē·ərz): royal attendants.
5. **vassals:** subjects.
6. **Kim Chau** (kim' chō'): *Kim* is Vietnamese for "gold" and *chau* for "pearl or precious stone."
7. **Bich Ngoc** (bik' näp'): *Ngoc* is Vietnamese for "emerald."

WORDS TO OWN
entreaties (en·trēt'ēz) *n.*: earnest requests.
charade (shə·rād') *n.*: obvious pretense or act.

MASTER FROG 641

Crossing the Curriculum

Professional Notes

presumptuous creature out of my sight at once and execute him."

As the king finished speaking, Master Frog croaked in a loud voice. Suddenly the building began to shake as lightning flashed and thunder roared. On all sides the doors flew open, and the guards cowered in terror as wild beasts of every description burst into the hall. Elephants trumpeted as they stampeded in, tigers roared, leopards and panthers growled as they sprang from one corner to another.

"A few minutes ago Your Majesty inquired about my vassals," Master Frog's croak rose above the uproar. "They have come. I will leave them here to answer any questions you may have about the extent of my kingdom. Until we meet again, Your Majesty." Master Frog turned and hopped toward the exit.

"Wait! Wait!" the king shouted after him as a tiger leapt over his throne, pursuing a panther in a game of tag. "You can't leave us like this, surrounded by all these wild beasts." But Master Frog only hopped over their backs, one after another, as he made his way to the door. "Daughters, what shall we do?"

"I wouldn't marry a frog if he were the son of Jade Emperor!" Kim Chau's voice was as haughty as ever, though she winced[8] as a leopard brushed past her.

Bich Ngoc covered her face as a bear lumbered toward her. "I'd rather be torn limb from limb!" she screeched.

"Father, I'll marry him." Kien Tien squeezed between two elephants to the king's side. "It's not right for us to think only of ourselves when the whole kingdom may be in danger. And the frog cannot be such a bad sort. He's obviously an individual of great power, yet he does not appear to be cruel. With all these beasts surrounding us, not one of us has been harmed."

As she finished speaking, the uproar ceased, and one by one the beasts filed from the hall.

Master Frog stood alone before the king.

"I will send the engagement gifts tomorrow," he said as he, too, turned and hopped from the room.

A few days later the wedding was celebrated with great pomp and ceremony. Kings and dignitaries[9] of all the surrounding countries came to pay their respects, and no one dared to laugh at Master Frog or the princess, for the tales of his great power had spread far and wide.

During the weeks that followed, Master Frog and Kien Tien lived together happily as the two came to understand each other better and to care for each other more deeply. In spite of his ugliness, Kien Tien found him such an intelligent and such a pleasant companion that as the days went by, she grew genuinely fond of him. Then one morning she awoke to find the frog lying dead on the pillow beside her.

With a cry she lifted her husband's body to her lips, kissing it again and again as her tears wet the mottled[10] green skin. Someone called her name, and she looked up to see a handsome young man standing next to the bed, his arms outstretched as if to embrace her.

She backed away from him, crying out in alarm. "How dare you come here?" she demanded. "Can't you see my husband is dead and I am mourning him?" Suddenly her eyes narrowed. "Or was it you who killed him, you miserable creature!" She burst into fresh tears. "You shall surely die for your crime!"

The man smiled. "No, Kien Tien. I am Master Frog. What you are holding there is only my skin, which I shed during the night." He sat down beside her. "I am a fairy, a heavenly mandarin,[11] one of the sons of Jade Emperor. I was

---

8. **winced** (winst): drew back in fear, making a face.

9. **dignitaries:** people holding high, dignified positions.
10. **mottled** (mät′ 'ld): spotted or streaked.
11. **mandarin:** member of any powerful group.

WORDS TO OWN

presumptuous (prē·zump′chōō·əs) adj.: too bold; arrogant.
cowered (kou′ərd) v.: crouched and trembled in fear.

bored with the life in Fairyland and wanted to seek adventure in the world below. But when I asked my father's permission, he was angry with me. He said he would grant my request but that I must be born as a frog. Only if I could succeed in that form would I be able to resume my true shape. Now I have proved myself and am allowed to shed the frog's skin. But you must put the skin away carefully where no harm can come to it because if it should ever be destroyed, I would have to return immediately to Jade Emperor's palace."

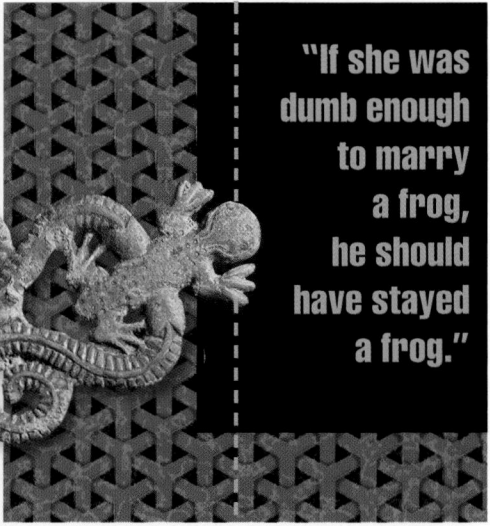

"If she was dumb enough to marry a frog, he should have stayed a frog."

Overjoyed at her good fortune, Kien Tien did as he said. The days that followed were full of joy for the newlyweds. The king was filled with pride at the handsomeness and intelligence of his son-in-law, which matched so well the beauty and talent of his youngest daughter. He took them wherever he went to show them off. On every trip that he made to the surrounding countries, they accompanied him in his golden palanquin,[12] and when he rode

12. **palanquin** (pal′ən·kēn′): covered structure enclosing a couch. A palanquin is carried by long poles resting on the shoulders of two or more men.

through the streets of the capital, they sat beside him on the back of his white elephant, cheered by all who watched them pass.

"Why didn't he tell us who he was in the first place?" Kim Chau grumbled to her sister as they watched the parade from the palace balcony. "Was it fair to come in that ugly old frog skin and then change into a handsome prince after he'd married Kien Tien?"

"If she was dumb enough to marry a frog, he should have stayed a frog," Bich Ngoc grunted in agreement.

"He should be punished for his deception. What right did he have to ask for Kien Tien anyway? I'm the oldest."

"Kien Tien says he's a son of Jade Emperor, but I don't believe it. He's probably nothing but an ordinary frog. Why don't we see if we can find his skin and have a look at it?"

The sisters went to Kien Tien's room, searching through chest after chest and shelf after shelf till at last, among a pile of her most precious silks, they found what they were looking for.

"She hid it well enough," Kim Chau sniffed. "No wonder. It's an ugly old thing, isn't it?"

Bich Ngoc reached for it, turning it over in her hands. "It certainly is. And just as I thought, nothing but an ordinary frog skin." She squinted her eyes thoughtfully. "Who knows but what, if we caught a couple of frogs for ourselves, they might shed their skins for us? There might be a handsome prince in any one of them if we could just get him to come out." She stuffed Master Frog's skin into her sash as the two of them hurried out to the pond.

Day by day Kim Chau and Bich Ngoc watched their chosen frogs, waiting for the hoped-for transformation. They fed them on the most delicious foods; petted them; cooed endearments and whispered promises of fame, fortune, and riches in their ears. And each night they gently laid them on the pillow next to them, certain that the coming morning

F Vocabulary Note
Word Origins
A white elephant was a prized possession, often worshipped in southeastern Asia. The term *white elephant* also refers to a possession no longer wanted by its owner. This definition refers to a custom of the kings of Siam, who would express displeasure with a member of the court by giving him a white elephant. The expense of the elephant's upkeep would bring the courtier to financial ruin.

G Reading Skills and Strategies
Making Inferences
? Why is Bich Ngoc so interested in seeing the frog skin? [Possible responses: She wants to see if perhaps Master Frog is still a frog and the prince is a hoax; she wants to harm the frog skin because she is jealous.]

H Appreciating Language
Specific Words
? What are some of the specific words that help us imagine Bich Ngoc and her plan? [Specific words include *squinted, caught, stuffed,* and *sash*.]

Taking a Second Look

Review: Recognizing Comparison and Contrast
Have students verify that "Master Frog" can be described basically as the story of an underdog (or underfrog) and how he wins, loses, and regains his true love. Point out that one characteristic that enriches the folk tale is the undercurrent of comparison and contrast among the characters.

Activities
1. Have students create a chart, Venn diagram, or other graphic organizer in which they can note similarities and differences among characters — for example, Giang Dung and Tien Kien; Tien Kien and her sisters; the king and Jade Emperor. As students share their work, ask them to explain how what they learn from studying the characters in this way

enriches their understanding of the tale's main ideas.

2. Invite pairs of students to improvise dramatic monologues in which characters that they want to compare and contrast talk about their lives and their feelings about the events in "Master Frog." Follow up with a class discussion.

A Reading Skills and Strategies

Making Predictions

❓ What do you think the sisters are going to do next? [Possible response: They seem desperate to keep their sister from finding out why her husband has died—so desperate, perhaps, that they may try to kill her.]

B **Elements of Literature**

Metamorphosis

❓ In what sense has Master Frog undergone another metamorphosis? [He has come back to life.]

C **Reading Skills and Strategies**

Drawing Inferences

❓ How does Bich Ngoc try to deceive her brother-in-law and hide her guilt? [Possible response: She weeps false tears of grief, repeats to him the lie about Kien Tien's suicide, and offers to help in any way she can.]

D **Literary Connections**

The Crystal Palace

In Vietnamese mythology, the Crystal Palace was the underwater home of the Dragon King (Hai Long Vuong), ruler of the seas. "Master Frog" presents the Dragon King as the brother of Jade Emperor.

Resources

Selection Assessment

Formal Assessment
• Selection Test, p. 126

Test Generator
• Selection Test

---

would bring the answer to their dreams. But nothing happened; both frogs remained as they were when they had fished them from the pond.

"There has to be a prince in there!" Bich Ngoc cried one morning in exasperation. "And I'm not going to wait any longer to find him." She picked up a knife and began to skin the poor creature alive.

Kim Chau snatched up her own frog and followed her example. But before they were finished, it was plain that no prince was to be found. In disgust the sisters threw the corpses into the fireplace.

Bich Ngoc jerked Master Frog's skin from her belt. "I don't know what I'm still carrying this around for," she grunted as she tossed it into the fire.

Meanwhile in Kien Tien's room, she and Master Frog were just getting out of bed. Suddenly he gave a cry of pain.

"My chest, my arms, my legs are burning!" he cried. "My whole body is on fire."

As Kien Tien rushed to his side, he fell to the floor, writhing in agony. Moments later he lay lifeless in her arms. Kien Tien pressed him close to her, weeping bitterly.

"It must be because you burned his old frog skin," Kim Chau whispered to Bich Ngoc when they heard what had happened. "What are we going to do? Sooner or later she'll discover the skin is missing, and if she finds out we took it and tells Father . . ."

Bich Ngoc clapped her hand over her sister's mouth. "We aren't going to sit around and wait for that to happen!"

Together they went to Kien Tien's room, where she lay on the bed weeping. They sat down beside her, stroking her hair to comfort her.

"Come, little sister, it's a terrible tragedy, but you mustn't spend the whole day lying here crying." Bich Ngoc poured some tea from the teapot on the table, dropping a little sleeping

powder into the cup as she carried it back to the bed. "Here, drink something warm. It'll make you feel better."

Kien Tien raised her head, sipping the hot liquid as Bich Ngoc held it to her lips. Then she lay down again and was soon fast asleep.

Quickly the sisters lifted her and carried her outside to the carriage. As fast as they could make the horses go, they rode out of town to the seaside. Then, making sure that no one was around, they shoved their sister out of the carriage, watching with satisfaction as she hit the surface of the water and sank beneath the waves. Then they rushed home to tell their father that Kien Tien had committed suicide.

"We tried to stop her," Bich Ngoc sobbed into her handkerchief. "But she wouldn't listen to us. She was so miserable at the thought of never seeing Master Frog again that she threw herself into the sea. The waves carried her away before we could call for help."

Suddenly gasps rose throughout the audience hall. Master Frog had entered the room.

He approached the throne, bowing respectfully. "Jade Emperor has allowed me to return to the earth to complete my lifetime," he told the king. "But why is everyone crying? What has happened?" He gazed from one person to another, seeking an answer.

"Dear brother-in-law, our sister is dead." Bich Ngoc wiped the tears from her eyes as she spoke. "She was so overcome with sorrow at losing you that she threw herself into the sea." She stepped closer to him, laying her hand on his arm. "I know what a shock it is for you. But Kim Chau and I will do everything we can to help. Either one of us would be willing to take our sister's place."

But Master Frog was already running toward the door. At his order a horse was saddled, and he leapt on its back, riding at top speed toward the sea. Fearlessly he dove in, letting his body sink to the bottom. Swiftly he ran across the ocean floor to the Crystal Palace and, bursting

---

Assessing Learning

Cooperative Learning: Grading Options

Here are some grading suggestions to show students the importance of their individual efforts in cooperative learning situations:

• Individual score plus bonus points if all members of a group reach certain criteria
• Individual score plus group average
• Totaling members' individual scores
• Group score on a single product

Making the Connections

Connecting to the Theme: "900 Cinderellas: Our World Heritage in Folklore"

Explain that Vuong herself relates "Master Frog" to "The Frog Prince" rather than to "Cinderella"; summarize "The Frog Prince" as necessary. Have students review "Cinderella" elements in Vuong's tale. [Possible responses: Master Frog is treated with contempt by siblings (of his wife); he undergoes a magical transformation; he and his love live happily ever after.]

through the gates, prostrated himself before the Dragon King of the Waters.

The Dragon King gazed down at him kindly. "Stand up, nephew. What you are seeking may be behind you."

As Master Frog rose, a company of shrimps and turtles entered the hall. One of them bore Kien Tien in his arms.

"My soldiers have found your wife," the Dragon King told him. "I would have let her live here in my palace, but since you've come for her, you may take her home with you."

Master Frog rushed toward her joyfully. As he lifted her from the turtle-soldier's arms, she opened her eyes and smiled up at him. Then both of them fell at the Dragon King's feet to thank him for his mercy.

Master Frog led Kien Tien out of the Crystal Palace and up through the water to the shore, where his horse was waiting. Together they rode back to the palace.

Kim Chau glanced down from her balcony to see Master Frog reining his horse below. She drew back in alarm and called to her sister.

"We're done for," she trembled, grabbing Bich Ngoc's arm and pulling her after her. "Kien Tien will tell Father everything."

The two of them raced down the stairs and out a back way. "We'll hide in the forest," Bich Ngoc decided. No one will find us there."

And the two were never seen or heard of again. But as for Kien Tien and Master Frog, they lived happily ever after, loved and respected by all for their kind deeds. Before many days had passed, they had Giang Dung brought to the palace, where she lived in comfort and happiness to a ripe old age. In due time Master Frog became king and, with Kien Tien as his queen, ruled their people in peace and prosperity for many long years.

E Reading Skills and Strategies
Connecting with the Text
❓ How does the ending of this tale remind you of other stories in this collection? [Possible response: The main characters live happily ever after, while the troublemakers suffer the consequences of their evil deeds.]

BROWSING IN THE FILES

About the Author. Vuong's interest in Vietnamese folklore was sparked by her work on *The Brocaded Slipper*. She went on to publish other collections—*The Golden Carp* and *Sky Legends of Vietnam*.

A Critic's Comment. The *Booklist* review of *The Brocaded Slipper* calls Vuong's storytelling style "modern and smooth." It recommends the book as an "excellent and unusual addition to folklore collections."

Writers on Writing. When Lynette Dyer Vuong was seven years old, her father built her an area that she thought of as a castle; there, she began composing and illustrating fantasy stories of adventure. At the age of ten, she wrote her first historical novel—a fifty-page tale that taught her the importance of research. Often invited to speak to young people about writing, Vuong explains that for her, the reward of writing comes from sharing her thoughts and ideas with her readers.

MEET THE WRITER

Taking a Chance on Love

Lynette Dyer Vuong (1938–) believes in love at first sight because that's what happened when she met a young Vietnamese man who was studying in the United States. Love led her to follow him back to Vietnam, marry him, and stay there with him for thirteen years—the country was then in the midst of the Vietnam War.

As Vuong learned Vietnamese, she began to follow another love—the world of folklore and fairy tales. She was amazed to discover that Vietnam has its own versions of five stories she loved as a child—"Cinderella," "Thumbelina," "The Frog Prince," "Rip Van Winkle," and "Goose Girl." She remembers:

66 Five familiar faces in an unfamiliar land; it is fascinating that similar ideas have arisen and then developed into different stories under the influence of two such diverse cultures as East and West. Perhaps it is a testimony to the fact that we are each uniquely individual, . . . yet bound together by a common humanity. 99

Vuong fled Vietnam with her husband and children in 1975. She continues to work on retelling the fairy tales she had grown to love.

More Tales Linked by Common Humanity

If you'd like to read the other fairy tales Vuong discovered during her stay in Vietnam, look for her book *The Brocaded Slipper* (J. B. Lippincott).

Assessing Learning

Check Test: Short Answer
1. What do people think about Master Frog's mother? [They find her plain and ugly.]
2. Whom does Master Frog want to marry? [He wants to marry Princess Kien Tien, the king's youngest daughter.]
3. Why does Master Frog have to protect his frog skin after he becomes human? [If something happens to it, he will have to return to Jade Emperor's palace.]
4. What causes the prince to die? [Bich Ngoc throws his skin into the fire.]
5. Where do the prince and Kien Tien find each other again? [They are reunited at the Crystal Palace, on the ocean floor.]

Standardized Test Preparation
For practice with standardized test format specific to this selection, see
• *Standardized Test Preparation,* p. 94
For practice in proofreading and editing, see
• *Daily Oral Grammar,* Transparency 39

MAKING MEANINGS

First Thoughts

1. Responses will vary but may include the appearance of wild animals in the king's hall or the lovers' reunion in the Crystal Palace.

Shaping Interpretations

2. Kim Chau and Bich Ngoc show their disgust in their faces; Kien Tien, however, reacts politely to Master Frog. This behavior shows the youngest sister's generous character and the shallowness of her sisters' characters.

3. Kien Tien finds Master Frog to be an intelligent, pleasant companion.

4. The sisters feel that Master Frog is a very handsome prince and are angry that he has fooled them. They are jealous of their sister, as well. Their change of heart shows the selfishness of these two young women.

5. There is no wicked stepmother in "Master Frog," but there are two cruel sisters and a handsome prince (Master Frog, after his metamorphosis). The Dragon King and several sea creatures help reunite Master Frog with his wife. The tale is full of magical events—Master Frog's birth and youthful intellect, his metamorphosis, Kien Tien's rescue, and the lovers' reunion.

6. One of the most important lessons that this story teaches is that what a person is like on the inside is more important than what he or she looks like.

Extending the Text

7. Possible responses: In "Rumpelstiltskin," straw turns into gold; Rumpelstiltskin causes the transformation. In "The Algonquin Cinderella," a scarred face turns beautiful; the Invisible One's sister uses water to cause the transformation.

8. Responses will vary and should be based on students' own experiences, stories that they have read, or films or television programs that they have seen.

Challenging the Text

9. Students may or may not have been surprised to see that the princess survives being thrown into the ocean. They may suggest that the twist improves the story by letting it end happily; indeed, they may have predicted some sort of "happily ever after" ending themselves.

MAKING MEANINGS

First Thoughts

[respond]
1. Which scene in the story do you remember most vividly? Why?

Shaping Interpretations

[analyze]
2. What is different about the ways Kien Tien, Kim Chau, and Bich Ngoc first react to Master Frog? What does this tell you about each girl's **character**?

[interpret]
3. What qualities does Kien Tien admire in Master Frog even before she realizes that he is a prince?

[interpret]
4. How do Kim Chau's and Bich Ngoc's feelings about Master Frog change after his **metamorphosis**? What does their sudden change of heart tell you about them?

[synthesize]
5. Earlier (see page 607) you filled in a chart with the fairy tale **motifs** you found in three Cinderella stories. Which motifs do you see in Master Frog's story? Think of such motifs as the wicked stepmother, the cruel sisters, the handsome prince, special helpers, magical events, and wishes come true.

[interpret]
6. What lessons do you think this story teaches?

Extending the Text

[connect]
7. What other stories do you know in which a **metamorphosis** takes place? In each case, what causes the metamorphosis?

[apply]
8. Kien Tien can look beyond Master Frog's appearance and see the person within, but her sisters can't. Do you think most people are like Kien Tien, or are they like her sisters? Why do you think so?

Challenging the Text

[evaluate]

9. Think about the **predictions** you made as you read "Master Frog." Were you surprised by the twist this story takes at the end? Did you prefer any of your predicted endings?

> ### Reading Check
> Use a story map like the one on page 627 to **summarize** what happens in this story. Be sure to compare your maps in class.

CHINA
Hanoi
LAOS
Gulf of Tonkin
Vientiane
South China Sea
THAILAND
Bangkok
CAMBODIA
Phnom Penh
Gulf of Thailand
VIETNAM

> ### Reading Check
> Story-map summaries should include the characters (especially Master Frog, the king, Kien Tien, Kim Chau, and Bich Ngoc), the conflict (primarily Master Frog's wooing of the princess, followed by the sisters' jealousy when he changes into human form), the time and place (Vietnam in some indefinite past), the main events (Master Frog's birth, his suit for the princess, his metamorphosis, the betrayal by his sisters-in-law), and the resolution (his reunion with his wife and taking of the throne).

CHOICES: Building Your Portfolio

Writer's Notebook

1. Collecting Ideas for an Informative Report

In your notes for the Quickwrite on page 638, you named at least one of your own special talents. Freewrite now for a few minutes about that talent. Think of what you would like to tell other people about your skill and why it is important to you.

What I Do Well

Swimming

—The best part is teaching swimming at the pool.

—I like to help kids get over their fear of putting their heads underwater. Here's how I do it:

Creative Writing

2. Would You Rather Be a Bee?

What if the Jade Emperor had decided that his son should be born a spider? a bee? or a pig? Reread the beginning of "Master Frog," and look for details that describe froggy behavior. Then, choose another animal and write the beginning of a story about it. Use vivid details to describe the animal's behavior.

Speaking and Listening

3. Frog on Tape

Record on tape a reading of this story. You'll have to figure out ways to create sound effects that will help your listeners imagine details from the story: Master Frog's hopping and croaking, the sounds of the wild animals that appear at the king's court, thunder, galloping horses, the ocean, and so on. Play your finished tape for the class.

Comparing Themes

4. Books About Looks

As you probably know, "Master Frog" isn't the only story that shows how looks can be deceiving. Other folk tales with this theme include "Beauty and the Beast," "The Ugly Duckling," and "The Frog Prince." *The Snow Goose*, by Paul Gallico, is a modern novel with the same theme. Read one of these works, and write a report comparing and contrasting its characters, conflicts, and theme with those of "Master Frog."

From *Beauty and the Beast* (1991).
© Disney Enterprises, Inc./Photofest.

MASTER FROG 647

Grading Timesaver

Rubrics for each Choices assignment appear on p. 186 in the *Portfolio Management System*.

CHOICES: Building Your Portfolio

1. **Writer's Notebook** Remind students to save their work. They may use it as prewriting for the Writer's Workshop on pp. 672–676.
2. **Creative Writing** Use the chalkboard to develop a character cluster for Master Frog. Students may then refer to his traits and apply them to the animals that they choose to use in rewriting the story.
3. **Speaking and Listening** Organize students into groups of three. One student will decide what sound effects will be used, another student will perform them, and a third student will operate the tape recorder.
4. **Comparing Themes** You might encourage students to retell stories from their own or other cultures. Suggest that students use a note-taking system, such as a story ladder, to record the story elements. An attribute web for each character will simplify comparisons later.

LANGUAGE LINK

Ask students to find a passage from a novel or other type of reading that they have enjoyed recently. Have them evaluate the use of specific words in the passage, citing nouns, verbs, adjectives, and adverbs that strike them as particularly effective.

Try It Out
Possible Answers
1. emerald, jade
2. stared, glared
3. flew, bounded
Peer evaluation should demonstrate— either through suggestions for change or verification that original choices help readers "see" the subject of the writing—an understanding of the power of specific words.

VOCABULARY
Possible Answers
1. After her mother <u>admonished</u> them for being so late, the twins made several <u>entreaties</u> that they be allowed to go to the game.
2. Fellow seventh-graders, we must not <u>cower</u> under this rule. It is not <u>presumptuous</u> to challenge a rule that we think is unfair. We may be <u>admonished</u> for our views, but let's stand up for our rights.

Resources ——————

Language
• *Grammar and Language Links,* p. 67
Vocabulary
• *Words to Own,* p. 24
Spelling
For related instruction, see
• *Spelling and Decoding,* p. 30

LANGUAGE LINK `MINI-LESSON`

Style: Using Specific Words

No two words have exactly the same meaning. Some words, like *sit,* have a general meaning but do not paint a vivid picture. Other words, like *perch* or *settle,* describe specific kinds of sitting. Each paints a different picture.

The author of "Master Frog" helps us imagine the creature's froggy behavior by using specific words to describe him. For example, she says that he *perched* beside his mother as she sat at the loom and would *wriggle* his body in and out of the threads on the loom.

B.C.   By permission of Johnny Hart and Creators Syndicate, Inc.

Try It Out
➤ Rewrite the following sentences, replacing the underlined words with more exact ones. Be sure to compare your revisions in class.

1. Kien Tien's tears wet the <u>greenish</u> skin of her dead husband's body.
2. When Master Frog said he wanted to marry the king's daughter, the king <u>looked</u> at him.
3. When Master Frog croaked, tigers, leopards, and panthers <u>came</u> into the room.

➤ To make sure your writing helps readers "see" exactly what you mean, ask a classmate to read a piece of your writing and point out any parts that could be improved by using more specific words.

VOCABULARY `HOW TO OWN A WORD`

WORD BANK	
admonished	## Vocabulary for Hard Times
entreaties	1. Use two words from the Word Bank to write a statement about a student who's been grounded for two weeks.
charade	
presumptuous	2. Use three words from the Word Bank to write a few sentences urging students to challenge an unfair rule.
cowered	

648   900 CINDERELLAS: OUR WORLD HERITAGE IN FOLKLORE

Language Link Quick Check

Rewrite the following sentences, replacing the underlined words with more specific ones.
[Possible replacements for the underlined words are shown.]
1. People thought that it was <u>good</u> that Giang Dung had a child so that someone would look after her when she was older. [fortunate]

2. Master Frog and his wife lived together <u>well</u>. [blissfully]
3. What <u>mean</u> sisters Kim Chau and Bich Ngoc were! [malicious]
4. Kien Tien <u>walked</u> slowly through the woods, <u>sad</u> for her lost love. [wandered; grieving]
5. At last, the young <u>people</u> left the Crystal Palace and <u>went</u> home. [lovers; galloped]

Before You Read

SEALSKIN, SOULSKIN

Make the Connection

Talk to the Animals

Have you ever looked into an animal's eyes and wanted to talk to it? Have you ever felt that an animal understood you when no one else did? If the answer is yes, you're not alone. Part of the reason folk tales are so popular is that in these simple stories, people and animals often share relationships in which they communicate complex feelings and thoughts.

Quickwrite

If you could have a conversation with an animal, what animal would you pick? What wisdom could you gain from such a conversation? Think about the characteristics of different kinds of animals before answering this question. Then, write down what kind of animal you wish to communicate with and what you think you would learn from it.

Elements of Literature

The Fantastic

Many folk tales contain elements of **fantasy**. That is, things happen in them that could not happen in real life, which is governed by the laws of nature. As you read "Sealskin, Soulskin," notice how the tale blends realistic descriptions of human conflicts with events that are pure fantasy.

OBJECTIVES

1. Read and interpret the folk tale
2. Identify fantasy
3. Express understanding through writing, speaking and listening, or debate
4. Identify stylistic techniques of good storytelling and prepare a short passage for oral telling
5. Understand and use new words

SKILLS

Literary
- Identify fantasy

Writing
- Collect ideas for an informative report
- Write an original legend
- Write an original short short story featuring a talking animal

Speaking/Listening
- Participate in the group telling of an interactive tale
- Participate in a debate

Grammar/Language
- Identify oral storytelling techniques and prepare a reading

Vocabulary
- Understand and use new words

Viewing/Representing
- Compare and contrast folk art from different cultures (ATE)
- Make inferences about people's lives from a photograph (ATE)

Planning

- **Block Schedule**
  Block Scheduling Lesson Plans with Pacing Guide

- **Traditional Schedule**
  Lesson Plans Including Strategies for English-Language Learners

- **One-Stop Planner**
  CD-ROM with Test Generator

SEALSKIN, SOULSKIN **649**

Preteaching Vocabulary

Words to Own

Have students read the definitions of the Words to Own at the bottom of the selection pages. Use the following activity to reinforce students' understanding of the words.

- Show how to use a dictionary to research the etymology of a word. Explain that dictionaries may differ in the etymologies they provide. Also explain the symbols and abbreviations used. A typical etymology uses the less-than symbol (<) to mean "derived from."

(A guide to all symbols and abbreviations is generally provided in a dictionary's introduction.) The Modern English word *bereave* comes from the Middle English *bireven,* which in turn is derived from the Old English *bereafian* [*be-,* "cause to be" + *reafian,* "to rob"]. To bereave a person is to rob him or her or to cause the person to feel robbed or deprived.

- Have pairs of students look up the derivation of the Words to Own and relate the etymology of each word to its present usage.

Summary ■ ■

A lonely hunter sees a group of seal women dancing atop a great rock and impulsively steals one of their sealskins. He proposes marriage to its owner, promising to return the sealskin after seven summers, at which time she will be free to leave. The seal woman agrees and, in time, bears him a son, Ooruk. At the end of the seven years, she claims her skin, but her husband refuses to return it. Ooruk is led to the water's edge by the voice of the wind; there he sees an old silver seal and finds his mother's sealskin. When he gives it to her, she carries him to the ocean depths, where the old silver seal—Ooruk's grandfather—greets them. After a week's stay, Ooruk is taken back to land by his mother and grandfather. They kiss him and depart, with the mother's promise to remain with him in spirit. The boy grows into a great bard; his mother, now a holy seal, retains the wise and loving look of a human.

Resources

Selection Assessment
Formal Assessment
• Selection Test, p. 128
Test Generator
• Selection Test

Viewing and Representing
Fine Art Transparency
A fine art transparency of *Shape changers*, by an unknown artist, can provide a focus for class discussion and other postreading activities connected to this lesson.
• Transparency 20
• Worksheet, p. 80

Sealskin, Soulskin

Inuit, retold by
Clarissa Pinkola Estés

"I cannot be wife, for I am of the other . . ."

(Above) Mask from western Alaska showing symbols of the Moon, Air, Cosmos, and Stars.
Smithsonian Institution, Washington, D.C.
Werner Forman/Art Resource, New York.

Resources: Print and Media

Reading
• *Graphic Organizers for Active Reading*, p. 45
• *Words to Own*, p. 25
• *Spelling and Decoding*
    Worksheet, p. 31

Elements of Literature
• *Literary Elements*
    Transparency 11
    Worksheet, p. 34

Writing and Language
• *Daily Oral Grammar*
    Transparency 40
• *Grammar and Language Links*
    Worksheet, p. 69

Viewing and Representing
• *Viewing and Representing*
    Fine Art Transparency 20
    Fine Art Worksheet, p. 80

Assessment
• *Formal Assessment*, p. 128
• *Portfolio Management System*, p. 187
• *Standardized Test Preparation*, p. 96
• *Test Generator (One-Stop Planner CD-ROM)*

Internet
• go.hrw.com (keyword: LE0 7-8)

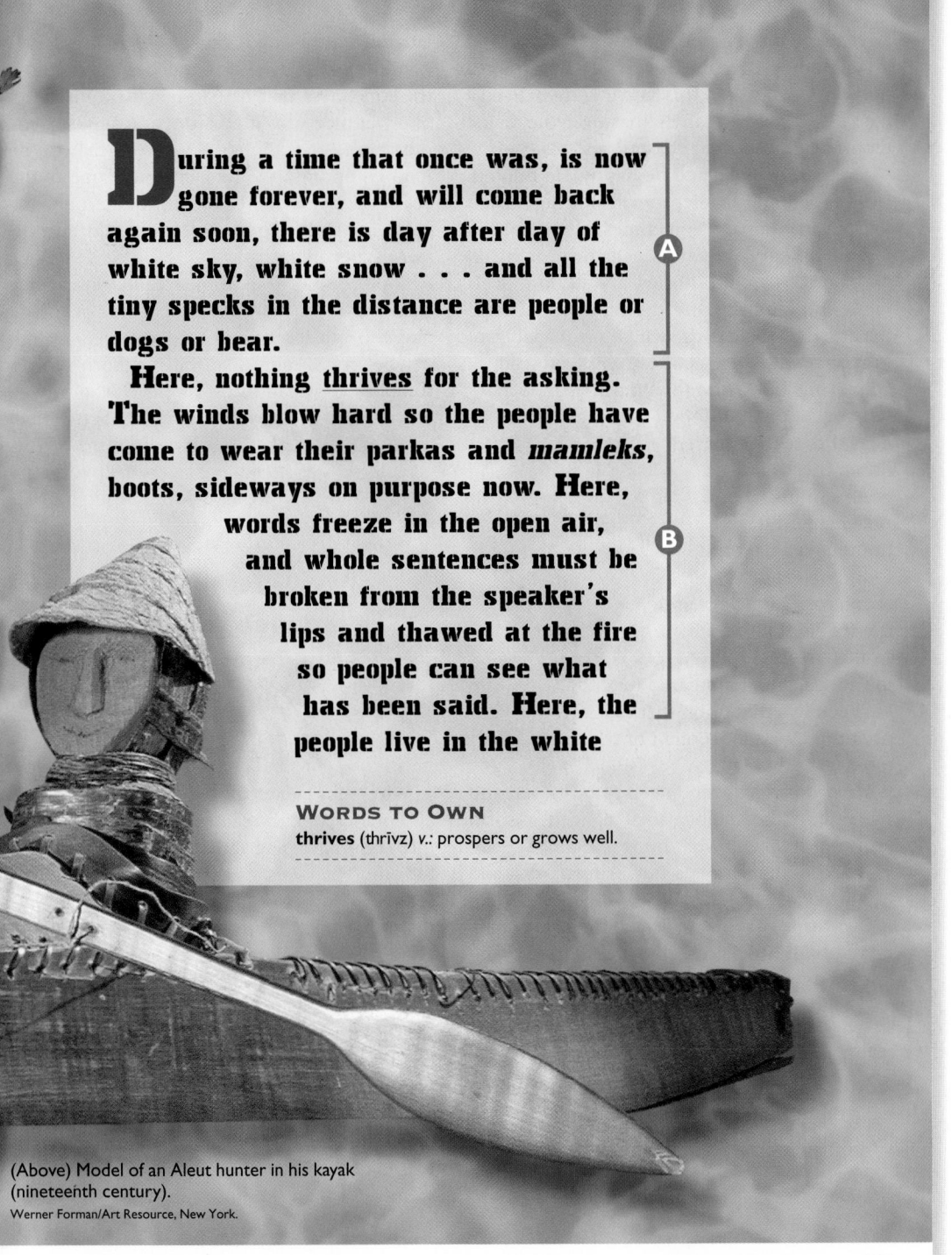

During a time that once was, is now gone forever, and will come back again soon, there is day after day of white sky, white snow . . . and all the tiny specks in the distance are people or dogs or bear.

Here, nothing <u>thrives</u> for the asking. The winds blow hard so the people have come to wear their parkas and *mamleks*, boots, sideways on purpose now. Here, words freeze in the open air, and whole sentences must be broken from the speaker's lips and thawed at the fire so people can see what has been said. Here, the people live in the white

---

WORDS TO OWN
thrives (thrīvz) *v.*: prospers or grows well.

(Above) Model of an Aleut hunter in his kayak (nineteenth century).
Werner Forman/Art Resource, New York.

SEALSKIN, SOULSKIN **651**

RESPONDING TO THE ART
Carved masks and figurines are part of the folk art of many cultures. Encourage students to compare and contrast the Eskimo folk art on pp. 650–651 with the Yoruban folk art on pp. 628–629, 630, and 633.

A Reading Skills and Strategies
Making Inferences
❓ Where do you think this place is, and who lives there? [Possible responses: It is some northern land, inhabited by Arctic peoples. It could be a fantasy kingdom where imaginary creatures live.]

B Elements of Literature
Fantasy
The storyteller says that "words freeze in the open air." Have students find other examples of fantasy in the opening paragraphs. [On this page, it is fantastic to think of sentences that must be thawed before they can be heard. On the next page, fantastic details include living in the hair of Annuluk and having tears carve a chasm into a man's cheeks.]

Reaching All Students

Struggling Readers
Students will encounter a constant interplay between factual and fantastic details as they read this story. Ask them to name some stories or films that blend factual and fantastic details and then have them distinguish the realistic elements or facts from the fantasy.

English Language Learners
Explain that many of the statements in the story cannot be taken literally. Encourage students to question any phrases or sentences that puzzle them. Help them to paraphrase or restate these ideas in their own words. For additional strategies to supplement instruction for these students, see
• *Lesson Plans Including Strategies for English-Language Learners*

Advanced Learners
The end of this tale notes the adult Ooruk's skill as a "singer and maker of stories." Invite students, working individually or collaboratively, to write a song or story that they think Ooruk might create. As students present the results, encourage them to explain the role that Ooruk's childhood experiences with "the great seal spirits" might have taken in shaping the song or story.

Critical Thinking

Extending the Text

? Do you think it is possible to live alone happily without other humans for company? [Possible response: No; people need to communicate with their own kind. Yes; people can live alone for a long time, but not forever.]

B Reading Skills and Strategies

Identifying Cause and Effect

? What is it about the seals that makes the man feel his loneliness? [Possible response: Their eyes have a human quality, reminding the man of the human company that he does not have.]

C Elements of Literature

Fantasy

? What details suggest that these dancers are not human? [Humans could not survive in such a setting—dancing bare-skinned on a rock in the sea. The skin of the dancers shimmers like the skin of fish.] How much farther must you read before you know for sure that these are beings of fantasy? [At the end of the page, one dancer confesses to the man that she is "of the other" and that she lives beneath the waves.]

D Appreciating Language

Elliptical Style

Point out the ellipses in this paragraph, noting that they suggest pauses or fragmented thinking. Help students see how the use of ellipses makes the flow of thought more natural. Have them read the paragraph aloud and then comment upon the conversational quality that the ellipses foster.

---

and abundant hair of old Annuluk, the old grandmother, the old sorceress who is Earth herself. And it was in this land that there lived a man . . . a man so lonely that over the years, tears had carved great chasms[1] into his cheeks.

He tried to smile and be happy. He hunted. He trapped and he slept well. But he wished for human company. Sometimes out in the shallows in his kayak when a seal came near, he remembered the old stories about how seals were once human, and the only reminder of that time is their eyes, which are capable of portraying those looks, those wise and wild and loving looks. And sometimes then he felt such a pang of loneliness that tears coursed down the well-used cracks in his face.

One night he hunted past dark but found nothing. As the moon rose in the sky and the ice floes glistened, he came to a great spotted rock in the sea, and it appeared to his keen eye that upon that old rock there was movement of the most graceful kind.

He paddled slow and deep to be closer, and there atop the mighty rock danced a small group of women. Well, he was a lonely man, with no human friends but in memory—and he stayed and watched. The women were like beings made of moon milk, and their skin shimmered with little silver dots like those on the salmon in springtime, and the women's feet and hands were long and graceful.

So beautiful were they that the man sat stunned in his boat, the water lapping, taking him closer and closer to the rock. He could hear the magnificent women laughing . . . at least they seemed to laugh, or was it the water

1. **chasms** (kaz′əmz): deep cracks or gaps.

laughing at the edge of the rock? The man was confused, for he was so dazzled. But somehow the loneliness that had weighed on his chest like wet hide was lifted away, and almost without thinking, as though he were meant to, he jumped up onto the rock and stole one of the sealskins laying there. He hid behind an outcropping and he pushed the sealskin into his *qutnguq*, parka.

Soon, one of the women called in a voice that was the most beautiful he'd ever heard . . . like the whales calling at dawn . . . or no, maybe it was more like the newborn wolves tumbling down in the spring . . . or, but, well no, it was something better than that, but it did not matter because . . . what were the women doing now?

At least they seemed to laugh, or was it the water laughing at the edge of the rock?

Why, they were putting on their sealskins, and one by one the seal women were slipping into the sea, yelping and crying happily. Except for one. The tallest of them searched high and searched low for her sealskin, but it was nowhere to be found. The man felt emboldened—by what, he did not know. He stepped from the rock, appealing to her, "Woman . . . be . . . my . . . wife. I am . . . a lonely . . . man."

"Oh, I cannot be wife," she said, "for I am of the other, the ones who live *temequanek*, beneath."

"Be . . . my . . . wife," insisted the man. "In seven summers, I will return your sealskin to you, and you may stay or you may go as you wish."

Professional Notes

Who's an Eskimo?

The name *Eskimo* is applied to the groups of people who inhabit the coastal areas of the arctic and subarctic regions of North America through the northeastern tip of Siberia. The Algonquian people of eastern Canada used the name *Eskimo* because of the animal-skin clothing that those in the colder climate wore. Those who were called *Eskimo* refer to themselves as *Inuit*, meaning "people."

Getting Students Involved

Cooperative Learning

Puppet Theater. Have students work in groups of four to create and perform "Sealskin, Soulskin" in puppet-theater form. Students might make puppets from gloves, socks, yarn, or other materials of their choice. Students should organize their groups by discussing who will make the puppets, how they will be made, who will act each part, who will provide backdrops and props, and so on. If possible, videotape groups' performances.

Creating a Found Poem. After students have finished reading this folk tale, have them create a found poem based on lines of text from the story. For a simple activity, ask students to choose four to six lines and to arrange the lines in an order that pleases them. For more of a challenge, have students create such an arrangement for each episode of the tale. Work with students to create a format for sharing the poems.

The young seal woman looked long into his face with eyes that but for her true origins seemed human. Reluctantly she said, "I will go with you. After seven summers, it shall be decided."

So in time they had a child, whom they named Ooruk. And the child was <u>lithe</u> and fat. In winter the mother told Ooruk tales of the creatures that lived beneath the sea while the father whittled a bear in whitestone with his long knife. When his mother carried the child Ooruk to bed, she pointed out through the smoke hole to the clouds and all their shapes. Except instead of recounting the shapes of raven and bear and wolf, she recounted the stories of walrus, whale, seal, and salmon . . . for those were the creatures she knew.

But as time went on, her flesh began to dry out. First it flaked, then it cracked. The skin of her eyelids began to peel. The hairs of her head began to drop to the ground. She became *naluaq*, palest white. Her plumpness began to wither. She tried to conceal her limp. Each day her eyes, without her willing it so, became more dull. She began to put out her hand in order to find her way, for her sight was darkening.

And so it went until one night when the child Ooruk was awakened by shouting and sat upright in his sleeping skins. He heard a roar like a bear that was his father <u>berating</u> his mother. He heard a crying like silver rung on stone that was his mother.

"You hid my sealskin seven long years ago, and now the eighth winter comes. I want what I am made of returned to me," cried the seal woman.

"And you, woman, would leave me if I gave it to you," boomed the husband.

"I do not know what I would do. I only know I must have what I belong to."

"And you would leave me wifeless, and the boy motherless. You are bad."

And with that her husband tore the hide flap of the door aside and disappeared into the night.

The boy loved his mother much. He feared losing her and so cried himself to sleep . . . only to be awakened by the wind. A strange wind . . . It seemed to call to him, "Oooruk, Ooorukkkk."

And out of bed he climbed, so hastily that he put his parka on upside down and pulled his mukluks[2] only halfway up. Hearing his name called over and over, he dashed out into the starry, starry night.

"Oooooooorukkk."

The child ran out to the cliff overlooking the water, and there, far out in the windy sea, was a huge shaggy silver seal. . . . Its head was enormous, its whiskers drooped to its chest, its eyes were deep yellow.

"Oooooooorukkk."

The boy scrambled down the cliff and stumbled at the bottom over a stone—no, a bundle—that had rolled out of a cleft[3] in the rock. The boy's hair lashed at his face like a thousand reins of ice.

"Oooooooorukkk."

The boy scratched open the bundle and shook it out—it was his mother's sealskin. Oh, and he could smell her all through it. And as he hugged the sealskin to his face and inhaled her scent, her soul slammed through him like a sudden summer wind.

"Ohhh," he cried with pain and joy, and lifted the skin again to his face and again her soul passed through his. "Ohhh," he cried again, for he was being filled with the unending love of his mother.

And the old silver seal way out . . . sank slowly beneath the water.

2. **mukluks** (muk′luks′): boots made of sealskin.
3. **cleft**: crack.

WORDS TO OWN
lithe (līth) *adj.*: flexible and graceful.
berating (be·rāt′iŋ) *v.* used as *adj.*: scolding.

SEALSKIN, SOULSKIN **653**

E **Struggling Readers**
Monitoring Comprehension
Much information is compressed into these two paragraphs. To help students keep on track, model reading this passage aloud. Talk about its imagery, remark on confusing words or phrases, and explain how you adjust your thinking as you read. You then might have student pairs read the story together, taking turns using such monitoring strategies.

F **Critical Thinking**
Making Judgments
? Is the man selfish? Why or why not? [Possible responses: Yes; it is selfish to insist that she remain, especially given the physical toll that doing so is taking on her. No; the man needs her company, and Ooruk needs his mother.]

G **Advanced Learners**
Analyzing a Turning Point
At this magical moment, Ooruk comes to a new understanding of his mother's power. Ask students to locate and comment upon the ways that Estés describes what Ooruk takes into himself at this moment. [He inhales her scent, twice feels her soul slamming through him, and is filled with her love.] At the story's end, review this moment, pointing out its importance in making Ooruk a powerful storyteller and songsmith.

H **Reading Skills and Strategies**
Drawing Conclusions
? What does the old seal have to do with Ooruk's finding the sealskin? [Possible response: He probably is the one calling Ooruk outside to find the sealskin.]

Taking a Second Look

Review: Using Prior Knowledge
Students may never have visited Arctic lands, and no student ever met a shape-shifter. Nevertheless, students may be surprised at the knowledge that they bring to this story—and how it helps them make meaning as they read it.
Activities
1. Have students name stories (in print or on film) that include a shape-shifter (for example, a werewolf or an alien). Ask students to write and share brief, informal essays about what happens to that shape-shifter when he or she interacts with "normal" people. Discuss how those people's feelings toward the shape-shifter are similar to or different from the husband's or the son's feelings toward the seal woman, as well as how the shape-shifter's fate compares with that of the seal woman.

2. Have students brainstorm a list of words, phrases, and images that come to mind when they hear the word *Arctic*. After they have read the story, ask them to review their lists. Invite comments about how their notes showed that they understood something about the lives of Arctic peoples or had misconceptions about these people.

Crossing the Curriculum

Geography
Ask students to find out where the Inuit live
today and to pinpoint the locations on a map.
Have them do research to find out various cultural characteristics of this group; then discuss
how the Inuit people's way of life is influenced
by their physical environment.

Using Students' Strengths

Visual Learners
After the story has been read, have students
work in small groups to create a story map. Ask
them to identify major events in the story and
then draw pictures of the events on a large
piece of paper, following the order in which they
happened. Display the story maps in the classroom so students can compare their work.

Kinesthetic Learners
Have pairs of students mirror each other to act
out this story as it is being read aloud. One student should be the actor; the other should copy
the movements of the actor as closely as possible. Ask students to reverse roles at least once
as the story unfolds; afterward, invite them to
describe how this activity helped them to
understand this story, its conflicts, or its
elements of fantasy better.

The boy climbed the cliff and ran toward home with the sealskin flying behind him, and into the house he fell. His mother swept him and the skin up and closed her eyes in gratitude for the safety of both.

She pulled on her sealskin. "Oh, mother, no!" cried the child.

She scooped up the child, tucked him under her arm, and half ran and half stumbled toward the roaring sea.

"Oh, mother, don't leave me!" Ooruk cried.

And at once you could tell she wanted to stay with her child, she *wanted* to, but something called her, something older than she, older than he, older than time.

"Oh, mother, no, no, no," cried the child. She turned to him with a look of dreadful love in her eyes. She took the boy's face in her hands, and breathed her sweet breath into his lungs, once, twice, three times. Then, with him under her arm like a precious bundle, she dove into the sea, down, and down, and down, and still deeper down, and the seal woman and her child breathed easily under water.

And they swam deep and strong till they entered the underwater cove of seals, where all manner of creatures were dining and singing, dancing and speaking, and the great silver seal that had called to Ooruk from the night sea embraced the child and called him grandson.

"How fare you up there, daughter?" asked the great silver seal.

The seal woman looked away and said, "I hurt a human . . . a man who gave his all to

Mother and child (1928). Nunivak, Alaska.
The Anchorage Museum of History and Art, Anchorage.

have me. But I cannot return to him, for I shall be a prisoner if I do."

"And the boy?" asked the old seal. "My grandchild?" He said it so proudly his voice shook.

"He must go back, father. He cannot stay. His time is not yet to be here with us." And she wept. And together they wept.

And so some days and nights passed, seven to be exact, during which time the luster came back to the seal woman's hair and eyes. She turned a beautiful dark color, her sight was restored, her body regained its plumpness, and she swam uncrippled. Yet it came time

"He must go back, father. He cannot stay. His time is not yet to be here with us."

to return the boy to land. On that night, the old grandfather seal and the boy's beautiful mother swam with the child between them. Back they went, back up and up and up to the topside world. There they gently placed Ooruk on the stony shore in the moonlight.

His mother assured him, "I am always with you. Only touch what I have touched, my fire sticks, my *ulu*, knife, my stone carvings of otters and seal, and I will breathe into your lungs a wind for the singing of your songs."

The old silver seal and his daughter kissed the child many times. At last, they tore themselves away and swam out to sea, and with one last look at the boy, they disappeared beneath the waters. And Ooruk, because it was not his time, stayed.

As time went on, he grew to be a mighty drummer and singer and a maker of stories, and it was said this all came to be because as a

SEALSKIN, SOULSKIN 655

A **Elements of Literature**
Conflict
? What struggle is going on in the woman's mind? [Possible response: She loves her son and does not want to leave him, but she cannot fight the overwhelming need to return to her home in the sea.]

B **Vocabulary Note**
Context Clues
Dreadful often is used as a synonym for *horrible*. Ask students to use context clues to determine its meaning at this moment in the story. [Possible response: Ooruk never has seen his mother like this, and he is scared that she is leaving him. The look in her eyes probably fills him with fear. *Dreadful* also must mean "frightening."]

C **English Language Learners**
Word Order
Students may have difficulty with the inverted word order in this line. Substitute the words "How do you fare up there" and ask them to supply a more conversational expression, such as "How are you doing?"

D **Elements of Literature**
Fantasy
? What is fantastic about the objects that the woman leaves behind for Ooruk? [Possible response: They are magical. Whenever Ooruk touches them, he will be filled with a special ability, from his mother, to sing his songs.]

Making the Connections

Connecting to the Theme:
"900 Cinderellas:
Our World Heritage in Folklore"
While students read this story, ask them to keep a two-column dialectical journal in which they can record important quotations from the story and their reactions to the quotations. After students have finished reading, have them review their comments. Call on volunteers to share comments that they think apply to other stories in the collection or to Cinderella-type tales, in general.

Cultural Connections
Seal people are also prominent in Irish and Scottish folklore, where they are known as Roane or as Selkies. In general they are considered to be fairy creatures. They wear their skins to travel through the sea and remove them to take on human form. Many tales of these people resemble "Sealskin, Soulskin" (as suggested in Question 7, p. 659).

Assessing Learning

Peer Assessment: Evaluating Someone's Contributions
Give students the following checklist and scale for evaluating the contribution of a partner or fellow group member.

1=Always	2=Sometimes	3=Never

_____ Stays focused on the topic and task
_____ Contributes original ideas
_____ Expands upon others' ideas
_____ Follows through with responsibilities

Critical Thinking

Challenging the Text

❓ Do you like the way that this story ends? Why or why not? [Possible responses: It is sad that Ooruk and his father are left alone. Although the ending is somewhat sad, Ooruk grows through the experience, and he still sees his mother at times.]

BROWSING IN THE FILES

Writers on Writing. Clarissa Pinkola Estés says that she "can't remember a time" when she wasn't telling stories. But why use fairy tales to convey her ideas about psychology? Estés notes that "people have always told tales to penetrate past the ego to the spirit. My grandmother used to say tales have the ability to travel deep into a person, which is why we called them medicine."

child he had survived being carried out to sea by the great seal spirits. Now, in the gray mists of morning, sometimes he can still be seen, with his kayak <u>tethered</u>, kneeling upon a certain rock in the sea, seeming to speak to a certain female seal who often comes near the shore. Though many have tried to hunt her, time after time they have failed. She is known as *Tan qigcaq*, the bright one, the holy one, and it is said that though she be a seal, her eyes are capable of portraying those human looks, those wise and wild and loving looks.

WORDS TO OWN

tethered (teth′ərd) v. used as *adj.*: tied.

Seal-oil lamp with a seal.
Werner Forman/Art Resource, New York.

MEET THE WRITER

Trading Stories

Clarissa Pinkola Estés feels a special bond with storytellers everywhere. Born to Mexican parents and then adopted by a family of Hungarians, she remembers the European and Mexican immigrant storytellers from her childhood. She says:

66 I've traded stories at kitchen tables and under grape arbors, in henhouses and dairy barns, and while patting tortillas, tracking wildlife, and sewing the millionth cross-stitch. 99

More Stories to Trade

Some of the many stories Estés has written or collected were published in her best-selling book *Women Who Run with the Wolves* (Ballantine).

656   900 CINDERELLAS: OUR WORLD HERITAGE IN FOLKLORE

Assessing Learning

Check Test: Short Answer

1. Why is the man so unhappy before he meets the seal woman? [He has no human company.]
2. Why does the woman say she cannot be the man's wife? [She is a seal woman, and the sea is her home.]
3. After Ooruk finds his mother's sealskin, what does he do with it? [He gives it to his mother.]

4. Why must Ooruk leave the underwater cove of seal people? [It is not his time to be there.]
5. How does Ooruk keep in touch with his mother? [He talks to her while kneeling on a rock in the sea. He also feels a connection with her when he touches the objects that she has left for him.]

Standardized Test Preparation

For practice with standardized test format specific to this selection, see
• *Standardized Test Preparation*, p. 96
For practice in proofreading and editing, see
• *Daily Oral Grammar*, Transparency 40

Connections
AN ESSAY

Oral Storytelling: Making the Winter Shorter

Picture this: One night you pick up the remote to turn on the television to watch your favorite show. The set refuses to come on. You give it a little nudge. Suddenly the screen bursts open and out walk the actors—in person.

If you lived in an Inuit hamlet long ago, you would hear stories, lots of them, and the storyteller would be right in front of you, not on an electronic screen in a plastic box. You would be sitting spellbound along with other children and adults in a kashim, a big snow house, watching and listening to the performer. The only sounds in the room would be the howling of the winds outside and the whispers and shouts of the storyteller.

Like people everywhere, the Inuit used stories for entertainment, but their stories also had another purpose. The children may not have realized that they were learning important lessons as they sat with their eyes glued to the performers who were shouting, making faces, and flinging their arms about. The lessons might have been about treating people kindly or showing respect for animals. These stories were not like the quiet bedtime stories you might remember from your childhood. They were often spine-tingling, roller-coaster, spinning-out-of-control tales.

Storytelling was especially popular in the wintertime. Imagine the sun disappearing totally from the end of November until the middle of January. Even then the sun barely emerges—turning the sky from inky black to gray. In the darkness, people gather at the kashim and enter through a short tunnel. There they beat the snow off their clothes with a stick. If they don't do this, they will have to sit all evening feeling the dampness of the melting snow on their skin. A faint light comes

SEALSKIN, SOULSKIN **657**

Connections

In this essay, Joan Burditt discusses the purposes and power of storytelling among the Inuit. She encourages readers to imagine themselves in a kashim (snow house), listening to an Inuit storyteller and learning the lessons of the tales while outside the winter passes.

Ⓐ Reading Skills and Strategies
Finding the Main Idea
❓ Why do you think the writer begins by describing a situation that could never take place in reality? [Possible response: She wants to establish her main idea early—namely, that a skilled storyteller can bring a tale "to life."]

Ⓑ Critical Thinking
Making Connections
❓ If Inuit tales teach lessons, what do you think is the lesson of "Sealskin, Soulskin"? [Possible responses: Every being should be free to be itself. Artistic skill comes from supernatural inspiration.] Do you think that "Sealskin, Soulskin" is a "spine-tingling, roller-coaster, spinning-out-of-control" tale? [Responses will vary. Students may suggest that this description fits moments within the story but not the story as a whole.]

Ⓒ Cultural Connections
Seasonal Influences
You might point out that just as arctic winters are marked by extended darkness, arctic summers have long periods of daylight. Discuss how such long periods of darkness and light might affect the way in which a people live.

Reaching All Students

English Language Learners
Among the Inuit, storytelling is an important vehicle for teaching lessons about life and proper behavior. Ask students to think about how they have learned the lessons about life and behavior that are important to their culture (ethnic, national, religious, and so on). Students may keep a journal and enter their thoughts about this question and then, if they wish, share them during class discussion.

Using Students' Strengths

Verbal Learners
Although much of a storyteller's skill lies in nonverbal cues, the words of the story are not unimportant. Challenge students to skim through "Sealskin, Soulskin," noting words and expressions that "pop out" at them from a storytelling perspective. Call on volunteers to comment upon ways in which a storyteller might build upon such language to create a memorable "tell" of this Inuit tale.

Assessing Learning

Observation Assessment: Looking for Mastery
As you observe students working on assignments for this essay and the story that it follows, note their progress on the following points with an M (Mastery) or a C (Could Improve)
- Asks appropriate questions
- Stays on task unreminded
- Completes work on time
- Maintains positive attitude
- Participates actively

OBJECTIVES
1. Read and enjoy the story
2. Connect the story to the collection theme

No Questions Asked

The literature in No Questions Asked gives students the chance to read a selection for enjoyment and enrichment as they further explore the collection theme. Annotated questions in the margins of the Teacher's Edition should be considered optional. No follow-up questions will appear after the selection.

At the opening of the story, the wife of a chief gives birth to a son. When an extraordinarily large and colorful hummingbird attends the birth, the high priest determines that the baby, too, will be extraordinary. He gives the baby boy a bright red feather as a protective charm; the boy is named Kukul, after the feather. Kukul grows to be handsome and clever, and he is invulnerable in battle. He has an enemy, however—Chirumá, his uncle, who would have become chief if Kukul had not been born. When Chirumá fails to undermine Kukul's claim as chief, he steals Kukul's charm and then kills him. Kukul's body, however, is transformed into a beautiful, wise bird—a quetzal. The people make the quetzal their symbol of freedom.

Resources

Listening
Audio CD Library
A recording of this story is provided in the *Audio CD Library*:
• Disc 16, Track 4

Ⓐ Historical Connections
The Mayan People
The Maya civilization of Mexico and parts of Central America flourished from around 250 to 900. It remained in existence until 1697, when the last Maya kingdom, Taytasal, was conquered by the Spanish. Only three manuscripts survived the years of conquest. Known as codices, these manuscripts are written like a picture album; they were made by gluing together pieces of paper into a single long strip and folding it accordion-style.

NO Questions ASKED

THE HUMMINGBIRD KING

Mayan, retold by **Argentina Palacios**

© Justin Kerr

Ⓐ yramids, palaces, and temples of stone stand silent and abandoned, hidden by dense rain forests. But that was not always so. Long, long ago, great cities built by the Mayan people were centers of activity.

In one of those cities—one whose name has long been forgotten—there lived an old *halac uinic*, or chief. Since he had no son to succeed[1] him, he knew that his younger brother, Chirumá, would one day take his place.

Ⓑ But the chief's wife wanted a child. Each day, she prayed with all her heart. And, one day, her prayers were answered. She gave birth to a son. The child was born on the thirteenth day of the month, a lucky day. For the number thirteen reminded the Mayan people of their thirteen heavens.

Just as the baby was being born, another sign appeared. A beautiful hummingbird perched on a tree branch in front of the stately residence. It was not an ordinary bird, but the largest and most brightly colored hummingbird anyone had ever seen. No one had ever remembered a bird of its kind standing still for so long.

The high priest determined that this was an omen. "The messenger of the gods has come," he said. "He is telling us that this child will be extraordinary, just like this hummingbird."

In the days that followed, a special naming ceremony took place. The high priest gave the chief and his wife a bright red feather he'd found beneath the tree branch where the hummingbird perched.

"We shall name our son Kukul," the chief's wife proclaimed. "That name means 'beautiful feather.'"

"And so shall this feather protect the boy as long as he carries it with him," the priest said.

Ⓒ A great celebration took place in the public plaza. Everyone joined the festivities. Everyone was happy, except Chirumá. He knew that, because of this child, he would never become *halac uinic*.

Ⓚ ukul grew into a handsome young man with jet-black hair and skin the color of cinnamon. He was quick of mind and excelled at any task he was given. As a young boy, he spent long hours with his father. Together, they would study the stars.

Like all Mayan boys, Kukul learned the art of

---

1. **succeed:** follow into a position (here, the position is that of *halac uinic,* or chief).

Making the Connections

Connecting to the Theme: "900 Cinderellas: Our World Heritage in Folklore"
The setting of this folk tale differs from others in this collection; furthermore, only "Oni and the Great Bird" matches this tale in its focus upon conflicts between men. Nevertheless, students will see the "900 Cinderellas" theme of personal action or reward repeated in Kukul's story.

Work with students to make a summary chart of the "hero" characters from the stories in this collection. Have them chart the rewards each character receives (if known). Use these notes as a springboard to a discussion about such topics as the following:
• the difference between external and internal beauty
• the nature of heroism
• the ways in which folk tales can help teach readers about the actions and characters that are valued in a particular culture

"THIS CHILD WILL BE EXTRAORDINARY, JUST LIKE THIS HUMMINGBIRD."

warfare from his elders. He made his own spears, bows, and arrows—straight and strong as the boy himself.

Soon the time came for Kukul to take his place among the men of his nation. A nomad[2] tribe was attempting a raid. Kukul, Chirumá, and the others went to war. Showers of spears and arrows rained down. Kukul fought bravely, at times at the very front. But wherever he was, not a single weapon fell on him.

Chirumá observed this. "The gods must watch out for Kukul," he thought to himself.

All at once, Kukul saw an arrow flying straight toward Chirumá, and Kukul positioned himself like a shield in front of his uncle. The arrow changed its course and fell to the ground without harming anyone. The enemy fled in astonishment and Kukul turned toward the wounded.

"How could it be that Kukul never gets hurt?" Chirumá wondered. "He must have a strong charm. I will find out."

That night, as Kukul slept on his straw mat, Chirumá came upon him. He carefully searched Kukul's sleeping body but found nothing. Then he saw it—a large red feather barely sticking out of the straw mat.

"His charm!" Chirumá said cheerfully to himself, as he carefully lifted the feather from its hiding place.

When Kukul awoke, he saw that the feather was gone. He searched everywhere, but he

2. **nomad:** wandering, with no permanent home. Nomadic peoples move about constantly in search of food, pasture, and so on.

could not find it. Nor could he remember the words of the priest on the day he was born. Without realizing it, Kukul had lost the charm and all the protection it provided.

It came to pass that the old chief went to the afterlife. Upon his death, all the high priests prepared to meet in council to choose a new chief. Chirumá knew that the priests would favor his nephew. He looked for the youngest priest, the one he knew could be easily swayed.

"Kukul is not a hero," he said. "Arrows never fall where he places himself. He is afraid to fight."

"No, he is not," said the priest. "Kukul is using his intelligence to win."

Chirumá would find any opportunity to talk to that priest about Kukul. Another day, he told him, "Kukul is reckless. He stops to take care of the wounded and puts his men in danger."

"Kukul is compassionate," replied the priest.

"He is inexperienced," countered Chirumá, as he sowed the seeds of doubt.

Now according to custom, a new *halac uinic* could be anyone in the departed chief's family. The high priests met.

"It should be Kukul, without a doubt," said the oldest priest.

"It should be Kukul," the second priest chimed in.

"Yes, without a doubt," the third priest added.

There was silence. "It should be Chirumá," said the youngest. "Kukul is too young and inexperienced."

They argued about the merits of each man. In the end, no one changed his vote and Kukul was chosen as *halac uinic.*

Under his rule, there was peace throughout the land. In time, even Chirumá's friend came to appreciate that Kukul had been a good choice.

Kukul spent much time studying the stars. He made mathematical calculations. He could tell the farmers the best times to plant to reap

THE HUMMINGBIRD KING 663

B **Reading Skills and Strategies**
Identifying Cause and Effect
? Why might people decide that this baby is no ordinary child? [Possible response: He is born on a lucky day (the thirteenth), and a large and colorful hummingbird appears at his birth.]

C **Elements of Literature**
Foreshadowing
? Reread what is said about the red feather and about Chirumá. How might this information foreshadow what is to come later in the story? [Possible response: Kukul may come to need the feather's protection—perhaps protection from Chirumá.]

D **Critical Thinking**
Comparing
? How is Kukul like Oni in "Oni and the Great Bird"? [Possible response: Both have a power that protects them from their enemies—and both have enemies.]

E **Reading Skills and Strategies**
Making Inferences
? Why does Chirumá say such things about his nephew? [Possible responses: Chirumá is jealous of Kukul and wants to make Kukul look bad in front of the people who admire him. Chirumá wants the priest to choose him as the new chief.]

F **Critical Thinking**
Speculating
? Do you think that the young priest's opinion will have much influence? Why or why not? [Possible response: Probably not; he is the youngest and perhaps the least experienced of the priests, and the other priests want Kukul to become the chief.]

Taking a Second Look

Review: Previewing the Text
Before students begin reading the story, remind them that they often can focus their reading by setting a "let's find out" goal for themselves. Encourage students to do so by taking a few moments to reflect and build upon clues that this story provides.

Activity
Ask students to write their own prereading

questions and predictions for "The Hummingbird King," based on the title of the story and on the quotation at the top of p. 663. [Responses might resemble the following:
• Questions: Who is the hummingbird king? What's so unusual about the hummingbird that someone is talking about?
• Predictions: A man, not a woman, will be the

hero of this story. The story will feature a bird character or a person who becomes ruler of the birds.]

After students have finished the story, ask them to compare their questions and predictions with the events described in the story; invite comments.

Invite students to comment on the artifacts shown on pp. 664–665. In particular, encourage students to talk or write about the sense of determination in the figures—and how an evil determination helps drive the plot of "The Hummingbird King."

Ⓐ Elements of Literature

Onomatopoeia

❓ Why are words like *rustling, flurry,* and *fluttered* effective in describing this moment? [Possible response: They sound like the sounds that they name—and that makes the description very vivid.]

Ⓑ Reading Skills and Strategies

Drawing Conclusions

❓ About whom is the hummingbird warning Kukul? Explain. [Possible response: He is probably warning Kukul about Chirumá. Chirumá has cause to resent Kukul; he also has tried already to undermine the choice of Kukul as chief and has gained possession of the charm that protects Kukul.]

Ⓒ Elements of Literature

Fantasy

Students have witnessed several amazing transformations while reading the stories in this collection. Discuss students' thoughts about this one, especially as it occurs after Kukul dies. [Possible response: It is sad that Kukul dies before the transformation takes place; nevertheless, he changes into something extremely beautiful, and in his new form he becomes a symbol of one of his culture's highest values.]

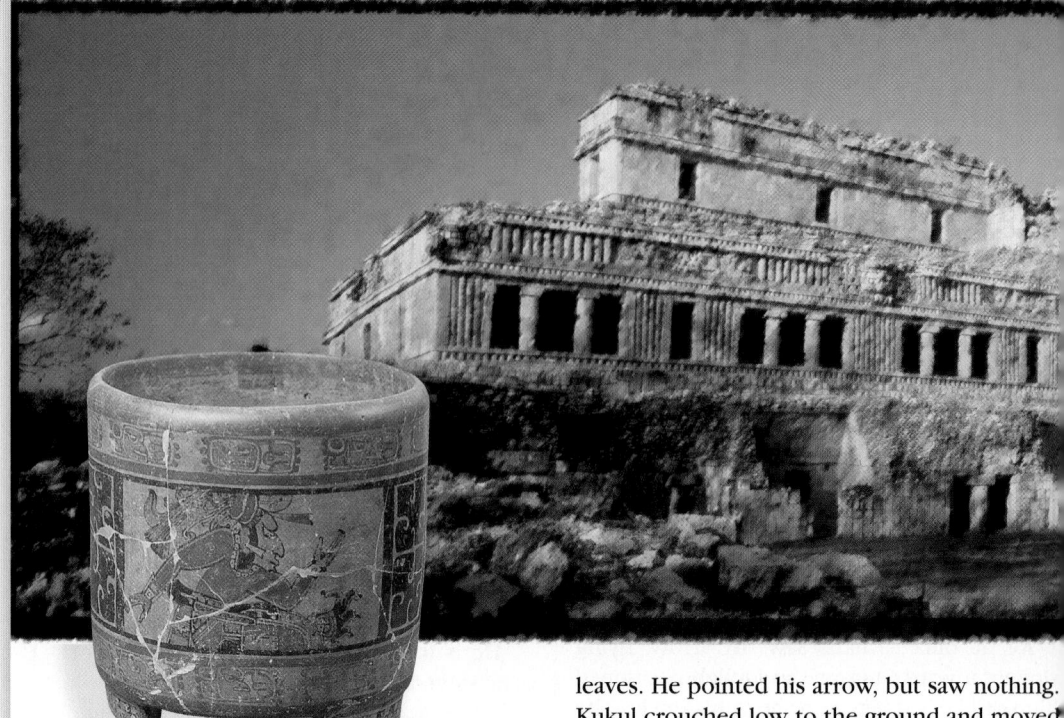

Mayan tripod vase from the Valley of Ulúa (tenth century).
Musée d'ethnographie, Geneva, Switzerland. Scala/Art Resource, New York.

the richest crops. Everybody was happy with Kukul, except Chirumá.

One day, Kukul was hunting in the forest. He heard the rustling of leaves and raised his bow and arrow. With a flurry, a magnificent hummingbird, larger than any hummingbird Kukul had ever seen, fluttered next to him. The hummingbird spoke these words, "I am your guardian, Kukul. My job is to warn you. Beware. Death is circling you. Beware of a man."

"Magnificent hummingbird, my guardian, what man should I beware of?" asked Kukul.

"Someone very close to you. Be careful, Kukul," said the bird. Then it flew away.

Kukul walked on through the forest. As he came to a thicket, he heard the faint rustling of leaves. He pointed his arrow, but saw nothing. Kukul crouched low to the ground and moved slowly. He had not gone far when . . . *sssss* . . . it came. An arrow pierced his chest.

In pain, Kukul pulled out the arrow and headed for the river to wash his wound. "Surely, it is not deep," he tried to convince himself, but his strength began to fade as his chest turned scarlet with blood.

A few more steps and Kukul had to lean against a tree. "It is so dark," he moaned. He fell onto a sea of emerald grass and there he died. Alone. Betrayed.

Then, something extraordinary happened. Slowly, Kukul's body changed to the color of the grass, but his chest remained scarlet. His skin became feathers, and his hair a gorgeous crest.

By the time Chirumá came out of the thicket, Kukul's arms had turned into wings. All Chirumá could see was a glowing green bird with a scarlet chest and a long,

Connecting Across Texts

Comparing Kukul to the Classics

Like "The Hummingbird King," many classical Greek myths tell of humans who are transformed into animals or objects from the natural world. Challenge students to read about any of the following characters from Greek mythology and to compare their fates with that of Kukul.

- Arachne
- Daphne
- Ceyx and Alcyone
- Callisto
- Baucis and Philemon

Getting Students Involved

Cooperative Learning

"Hummingbird" Hot Seat. After students have read the story, divide the class into groups of five. Have each group choose a character—either Kukul or Chirumá—and make a list of his traits. [Possible responses: Kukul—clever, brave, wise; Chirumá—jealous, plotting, manipulative.]

Have the groups that represent one character brainstorm questions to ask the other character. Then, give a student from each group two minutes on the Hot Seat to respond in character to questions from the other groups.

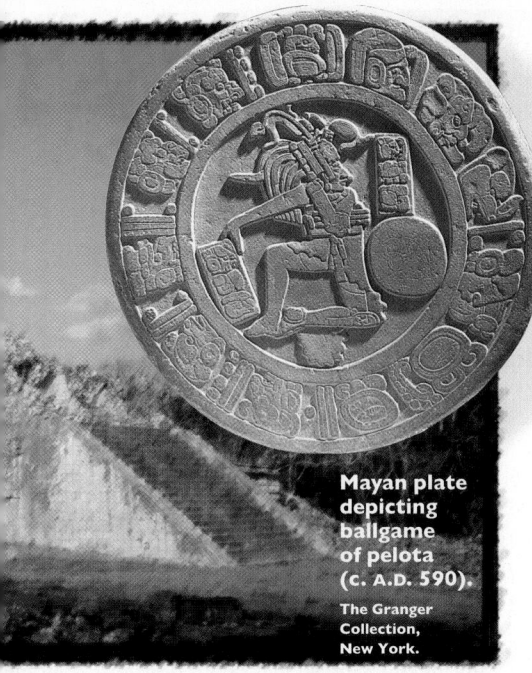

Mayan plate depicting ballgame of pelota (c. A.D. 590).
The Granger Collection, New York.

long tail, flying off into the sunlight.

The people mourned the loss of Kukul, but after a time, Chirumá was chosen to be the new chief. Chirumá was a cruel and warlike king, and soon after, enemies again attacked the city and in fierce battle took Chirumá prisoner. Everybody watched while his body was painted black and white, the colors of a slave. He was taken away from the city, never to be seen again.

Today, a most beautiful green bird with a scarlet chest, a long, long tail, and a gorgeous crest perches high up on the trees in the deep, cool cloud forest, watching everything and listening for the rustling of leaves.

The Mayan of old called this bird *kukul*. They carved its image into stone and placed it on their temples and palaces. Today this wise and peaceful bird—a symbol of freedom to all its people—is known as the *quetzal*.

MEET THE WRITER
Quetzal Tales

Argentina Palacios grew up in Panama. As an adult living in Texas, Palacios at first became a teacher, like her mother. Little by little, though, she discovered the rewards of writing and telling stories. "The Hummingbird King" is one of the stories she tells children and adults at schools, museums, zoos, and even jails around the country.

"The Hummingbird King" tells the story of the origin of the quetzal (ket·säl′). The quetzal is a brilliantly colored bird found only in the cloud forests of the highlands of Guatemala. The bird's head and back are emerald green; its chest is bright red. There is a wide crest of gold-and-green hairlike feathers on its head. The upper tail feathers are very large—up to three feet long.

Palacios says:

66 Legends say the quetzal loves its freedom so much that it will die in captivity. But the cloud forests that are its natural habitat are disappearing from the earth. Happily, scientists have had some success breeding the quetzal in zoos and nature parks, preserving the Mayan ideal of people living in harmony with nature. 99

Mayan seated figure of a priest or nobleman. Hardwood.
The Granger Collection, New York.

Connections

To make the point that the world still holds undiscovered treasures—and mysteries—Meyer and Gallencamp recount a 1984 discovery at Río Azul, the ruins of an ancient Maya town. The authors describe the finding of the ruins and the later surprise of discovering a mysterious, untouched tomb there. Along the way, they also note how archaeological sites have been looted and the measures that the United States has taken to stop the trade in stolen national treasures.

A Appreciating Language
Parallelism

Urge students to savor this opening paragraph; then, point out ways in which the authors use parallel structure (with an example in each of the four sentences) to connect ideas and add interest to the reading. Encourage students to look for other examples of parallelism as they continue to read.

B Reading Skills and Strategies
Connecting with the Text

? Did you know that archaeology could be this exciting—or this dangerous? If you were thinking about a career in archaeology, would this information make you more eager about it—or less? Explain. [The possibility of danger might prove a discouragement to some and an incentive to others.]

C Critical Thinking
Hypothesizing

? Why do you think that some people might want to have private collections of illegal artifacts? [Possible responses: They take pride in having something that other people do not have. They experience a thrill from being involved in an illegal activity.]

Connections

A HISTORY

The Search Goes On
from *The Mystery of the Ancient Maya*

Carolyn Meyer and Charles Gallenkamp

Brilliant achievements, exciting revelations, and countless unsolved mysteries—this is the legacy left by the ancient Maya. Huge areas remain to be explored, dozens of key sites to be investigated. There are hieroglyphic inscriptions[1] to decipher[2] and mountains of data to analyze. And so there are always new projects, new digs, new studies—and new breakthroughs.

In 1962 a geologist prospecting for an oil company in the jungle of Guatemala came across a cluster of ruins. He got in touch with Richard E. W. Adams, a young archaeologist who was on a dig in another part of the country. At that time all the two could do was to map the Río Azul site, named for a river nearby. There was no money then to excavate[3] the ruins they had found.

Over the next twenty years thieves dug trenches around the pyramids, tunneled into them, and even split them open to get at the treasures inside. The looters ransacked[4] at least twenty-eight tombs in this and the surrounding area, smuggling jewelry and other priceless objects into the United States, where they were sold to art collectors for huge sums of money. When Adams returned to Río Azul in 1981, he heard about the looting and saw the deep trenches and the scattered rubble. On one occasion he and another scientist surprised armed looters at work. Shots were fired and one of the thieves was wounded, but they all got away. After the incident Guatemalan government troops swept the area, and guards with automatic weapons have remained on duty ever since to prevent further looting.

There are tragic consequences to looting: When artifacts[5] are stolen and sold, all the valuable information they could provide is lost forever. The whole historical and archaeological context of each piece of remarkable pottery and exquisite jade jewelry is destroyed. A stolen artifact becomes merely a prized object in a private collection that is often kept secret or shared with only a few connoisseurs.[6]

But unscrupulous[7] collectors are willing to pay enormous sums for treasures for their private collections. The possibility of such profit

---

1. **hieroglyphic** (hī′ər·ō′glif′ik) **inscriptions:** engraved hieroglyphics (writing in which pictures, rather than letters, are used).
2. **decipher** (dē·sī′fər): interpret; find the meaning of.
3. **excavate** (eks′kə·vāt′): uncover by digging.
4. **ransacked:** looted; robbed.
5. **artifacts:** objects made by people or adapted for human use.
6. **connoisseurs** (kän′ə·sʉrz′): people who are experts on something, especially something in the arts.
7. **unscrupulous** (un·skroo′pyə·ləs): dishonest.

666   900 CINDERELLAS: OUR WORLD HERITAGE IN FOLKLORE

Professional Notes

Protecting the Past

Posting guards at archaeological sites is just one way in which Guatemala is trying to avert the theft of Maya artifacts. Looters often are willing to risk an armed confrontation with such guards, however, because dealing in this stolen treasure is very profitable. In fact, it is estimated that this "business" earns its participants about $120 million each year.

Reaching All Students

Struggling Readers

Students may find the reading level of this feature somewhat challenging. Before you begin, therefore, ask students to think of action-adventure movies about finding a treasure. (The opening sequence of *Raiders of the Lost Ark* may be an ideal discussion starter.) Have students draw upon their knowledge of such films as they offer comments about various kinds of treasure and the lengths to which treasure hunters might go to reach their goals. Work with students to make a master list of scenes that they might expect in a film about treasure hunting. As they read "The Search Goes On," ask them to make notes about any details that remind them of such scenes. Invite comments, filling in any important details that may have been missed.

T666

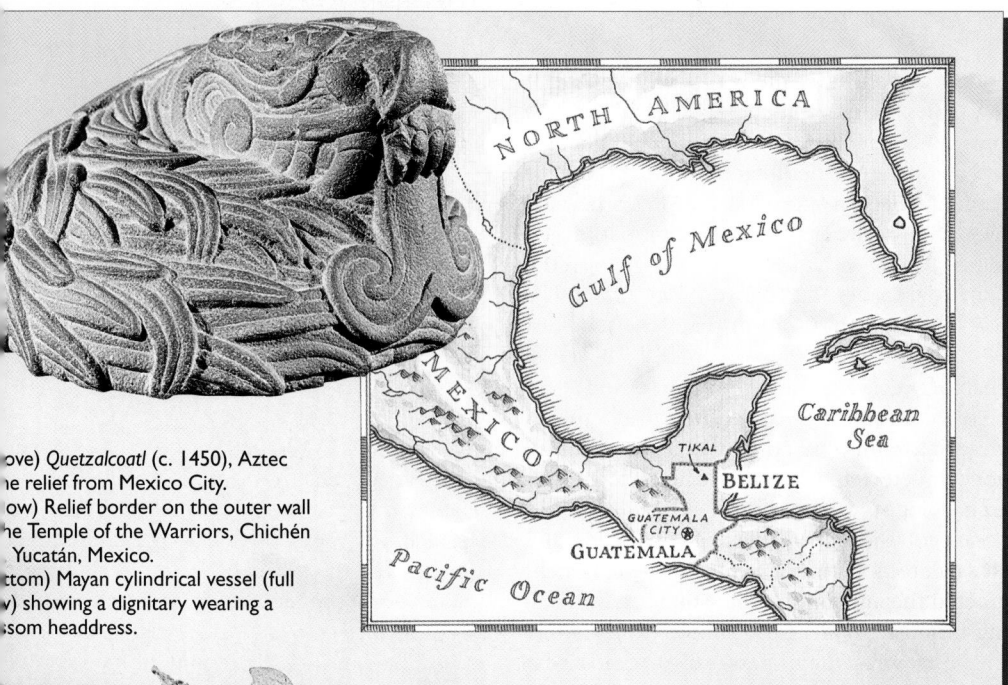

(above) *Quetzalcoatl* (c. 1450), Aztec stone relief from Mexico City.

(below) Relief border on the outer wall of the Temple of the Warriors, Chichén Itzá, Yucatán, Mexico.

(bottom) Mayan cylindrical vessel (full view) showing a dignitary wearing a blossom headdress.

D Cultural Connections
Quetzalcoatl
Quetzalcoatl, the Feathered Serpent, was an important god of the Aztecs, the people who dominated Mexico after the decline of the Mayas. The Mayas did not worship Quetzalcoatl, but they did worship a closely related god whom they called Kukulcan.

E Reading Skills and Strategies
Making Inferences
? Why do you think the United States has committed itself so strongly to stopping archaeological looting? [Possible responses: The United States holds that a country has a right to the national treasures found within its borders. The United States appreciates the importance of allowing historians and scientists, as well as collectors, access to such artifacts.]

drives looters to search out and plunder[8] as-yet undiscovered sites. Once they've taken what they want, the looters use smuggling networks to get the ancient jars and jewels out of the jungle and into the hands of collectors all over the world.

Adams and other archaeologists used the incident at Río Azul to convince Congress to pass a law to stop national treasures looted in other countries from being brought into the United States. In addition, the United States signed an agreement that commits this country to recover and return stolen cultural and archaeological objects from Mexico and Central America.

Meanwhile, Adams raised the money to begin excavating the ruin in a race against the looters. The ancient city of Río Azul was probably a small center

E

8. **plunder:** loot.

Crossing the Curriculum

Architecture
From the mention of the city of Tikal and the photograph on p. 668, students should realize that the Mayas were master architects. Have interested students or groups of students research and report on Maya architecture—for example, different kinds of buildings; use of stone, mortar, and wood; features such as windows and the use of color.

Social Studies
The descendants of the ancient Mayas are an important cultural group in Guatemala today. Challenge students to find out about the lives and concerns of the modern Mayas. Then, have them present their findings to the class.

Getting Students Involved

Cooperative Learning
A Tribute for *Great Son*. At the end of this feature, students learn a little about a nobleman buried at the Río Azul site. Who is he, and what does the inscription *great son* have to do with him? Could he possibly be Kukul? Invite students to respond by creating a tribute to this nobleman in a format of their own choosing (for example, a fictitious obituary or a portrait). Have students share and discuss their tributes.

A Reading Skills and Strategies

Identifying Cause and Effect

? How do the workers know they have found a tomb before they reach its entrance? [Possible response: The workers discover that there is a secret chamber cut into the rock below the ground surface. The fact that it is painted suggests that it is a tomb containing valuable artifacts.]

B Elements of Literature

Irony

? What is ironic about the workers' entry into the tomb? [Possible response: Instead of using high-tech gear to lower themselves into the chambers, they make a ladder that probably was much like one the Maya themselves might have used.]

C Critical Thinking

Interpreting

? At the beginning of this feature, the authors say that the Maya have left "countless unsolved mysteries." How does the information at the end of the feature support this statement? [Possible response: The authors share what little is known of the occupant of Tomb 19—that he seems to have been a nobleman and that perhaps he has something to do with an inscription that reads *great son*. His actual identity is, for now, a mystery.]

under the control of the bigger city of Tikal, a few miles to the south. It covers about 470 acres and contains four major temple pyramids and adjoining smaller buildings. Adams and his team had been working on the site for several weeks in the spring of 1984, hoping to get as much accomplished as possible before the rainy season began. Then on May fifteenth a workman's leg plunged through rock-and-dirt fill and down through the roof of a secret chamber, a cave cut into the rock some 13 feet below the surface of the ground. Hidden by a wing of a temple built on top of it, the cave had gone undetected by looters—and until then by archaeologists as well.

One of the expedition leaders peered in. "It's painted!" he yelled; whoops of excitement greeted the announcement. They began working furiously to clear the rubble from the entrance to what they knew was a tomb. Next they lowered a miniature video camera into the opening. And finally, using vines and saplings from the jungle—traditional Maya building materials—they climbed down into the chamber.

The skeleton of a nobleman in his thirties, his shroud nothing more than dust, lay on a wooden bier.[9] Elaborate and mysterious wall paintings and fifteen pieces of pottery surrounded his body. One of the pieces was a beautifully made jar with an unusual screw-top lid. On top of the skeleton lay a stingray spine used in bloodletting rituals. Parrots chattered overhead and Guatemalan government guards with rifles and machetes stood by as the contents of Tomb 19, as it was now designated, were recorded and labeled and then transported to the National Museum of Anthropology in Guatemala City.

9. **bier** (bir): platform on which a corpse is placed.

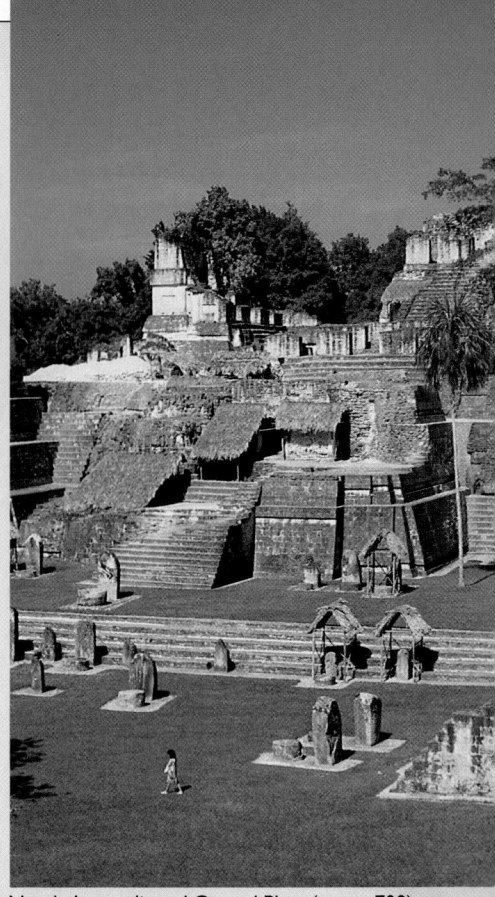

North Acropolis and Central Plaza (c. A.D. 700), Mayan ruins, Tikal, Guatemala.

The date of the tomb is about A.D. 420 to 470, the height of the Classic period.[10] Adams, who calls it "a moment frozen in time," believes that the tomb was built for a relative of a ruler buried in a large pyramid nearby, already looted and stripped of its wall paintings. All that could be read of the hieroglyphics on the walls and pottery were the words *great son*.

10. **Classic period:** the period, from around A.D. 250 to around 900, during which Mayan civilization reached its peak.

Connecting Across Texts

Connecting with "The Hummingbird King"

"The Search Goes On" makes it quite clear that ancient pottery, jewelry, carvings, and the like are very valuable. What about ancient stories—how valuable are they? Ask students to make a checklist, noting characteristics that they think create value in an ancient artifact. The following example may help them get started (although students may choose to omit some of these points in their checklists):

_____1. Provides clues to the daily lives of ancient people

_____2. Reveals what ancient people loved or thought important

_____3. Is beautiful, regardless of who made it, or when

_____4. Supplies historical information not known before now

Have students apply their checklists to "The Hummingbird King," seeing which criteria the story meets and noting any new criteria that it suggests. In a follow-up discussion, invite students to share their comments. If you wish, extend the discussion by having students apply the same criteria to other folk tales in this collection and share the results.

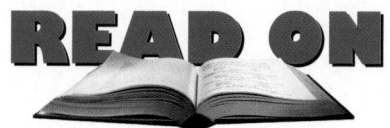

READ ON

Good Folks

Let the appealing and simply told stories in *The Magic Listening Cap* (Creative Arts) by Yoshiko Uchida carry you off to the Japanese countryside. These fourteen folk tales are full of humor, wisdom, and the ring of universal truth.

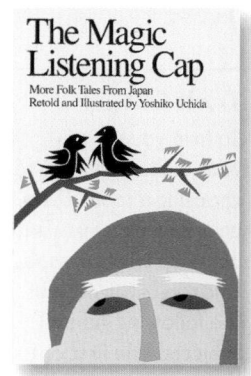

High Tones

Listen to the powerful and inspiring language of drums. Experience the different rhythms of drumming for protection, freedom, and transformation. The ten tales of *Patakin: World Tales of Drums and Drummers* (Henry Holt) by Nina Jaffe celebrate a variety of drums and their special roles in storytelling.

Fairy Friendly

All the best-loved fairy tales are in Andrew Lang's *Blue Fairy Book* (Puffin), first published more than a hundred years ago. Cinderella, Rumpelstiltskin, and Aladdin keep company with many other favorites. You'll also find plenty of less familiar characters who are sure to win your heart in this classic book.

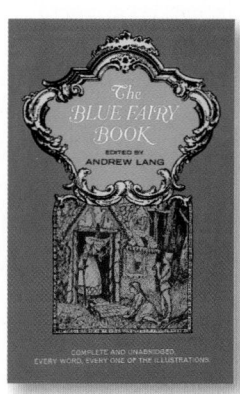

Other Picks

- Laurence Yep, *Tongues of Jade* (HarperCollins). Seventeen ancient Chinese folk tales tell of mystery, magic, and the simple truths of human relationships.

- Julius Lester, *The Tales of Uncle Remus: The Adventures of Brer Rabbit* (Dial). The hilarious trickster Brer Rabbit is up to his ears in mischief in this classic collection of folk tales.

READ ON

Portfolio Assessment Options
The following projects can help you evaluate and assess your students' reading accomplishments outside the class. Videotapes or audiotapes of completed projects may be included in students' portfolios.

- **Collect Story Reviews** Students who choose *The Magic Listening Cap* may write evaluations of the stories (covering all fourteen, if possible). A collection of reviews, kept in the classroom library, can encourage other students to explore Uchida's stories for themselves.

- **Compare Folk Tales** Students should remember that "talking drums" are part of the Yoruban storytelling tradition. Students may enjoy reading the tales in *Patakin: World Tales of Drums and Drummers* and reporting on comparisons between any of its tales and "Oni and the Great Bird," the Yoruban folk tale in this collection.

- **Videotape a Scene** Students with a director's eye can organize a troupe of players to rehearse, act out, and videotape a scene from the *Blue Fairy Book*. If possible, have them shoot "on location" at an appropriate site, using simple costumes such as hats or masks. Wrap up by hosting a class film festival.

- **Create Nonsense Art** Some unlikely creatures and crises beg for illustrations. Artists may sketch, paint, or sculpt scenes, characters, or creatures of their choice for either *Tongues of Jade* or *The Tales of Uncle Remus: The Adventures of Brer Rabbit*. Ask students to display their works and to explain the choices that they made in their art.

Resources

Performance Rubric
- *Portfolio Management System*, p. 189

Introducing the Speaking and Listening Workshop

- Explain that much of the fear that people sometimes have about giving speeches can be resolved through efficient planning.
- Emphasize the importance of choosing an effective topic and a clear focus. With a good topic and coverage plan, students will have confidence in their work even before they start rehearsing their speeches.
- Share examples of effective presentations that you have witnessed. Call on volunteers to do the same.

Try It Out
Possible Responses
movies:
a. [how to budget for a film]
b. [the difference between a director and a producer]
first aid:
a. [common household first aid]
b. [the contents of a well-stocked first-aid kit]
guitars:
a. [how to choose a guitar]
b. [great rock-and-roll guitarists]
baseball:
a. [how baseball teams choose their players]
b. [baseball as "big business"]
Italian cooking:
a. [how different types of pasta are made]
b. [the history of pizza]

Try It Out

To help you narrow your focus when you're choosing a topic, team up with a classmate and come up with two specific topics for each of the following general subjects. The first one has been done for you.

General Topic	Specific Topic
mountain climbing	**a.** how to rappel off a cliff **b.** how to rescue a climber in trouble
movies	**a.** **b.**
first aid	**a.** **b.**
guitars	**a.** **b.**
baseball	**a.** **b.**
Italian cooking	**a.** **b.**

SPEAKING TO INFORM

You're nervous. Your Scout leader has asked you to talk to the troop about winter camping. It's your first try at **formal speaking**—talking to an audience about a specific topic. How do you give your speech without falling apart? Some suggestions follow.

Choosing Your Topic

If you need to select the topic for an informative speech, ask yourself these questions:

1. **What is my purpose?** People give speeches for different reasons: to inform (an astronomer explains how stars are born), to persuade (an activist explains how to save the spotted owl), to entertain (a comedian tells what happened when he tried in-line skating).

   As you plan your speech, keep in mind what you hope to accomplish. Do you want your listeners to learn something about black holes, for instance, or how to pitch a tent on snow? to change their opinion? or simply to be amused?

2. **Who is my audience?** To decide if your topic is right for your audience, ask yourself, "Is this audience interested in my topic?" If the answer is yes, you're on the right track. A speech about new ways to pull teeth may fascinate dentists but bore the high school varsity.

   Ask yourself, "Does my audience know something about my topic?" Your listeners don't have to be experts to enjoy your speech. Keep in mind, though, that you must tailor the speech to your audience's level of knowledge. If you describe a new computer system to engineers, they'll understand what you mean by *mouse, boot,* and *window.* Use the same technical words in a talk to preschoolers, though, and they'll probably get a very different picture.

Getting Students Involved

Cooperative Learning
Student Knowledge Survey. The question "Does my audience know something about my topic?" is an important guide to the content of a planned speech. To give students a taste of this kind of evaluation, have them take a class survey, giving the same list of topics to everyone and asking each student to rate each topic. Topics can come from a master list of students' answers to the Try It Out activity or from a master list of possible topics. Students should rate each topic as follows:

A = Know nothing about it and am/am not interested in learning about it. (Circle one)
B = Know a little about it and would like to learn more
C = Know a lot about it and am/am not interested in learning more. (Circle one)

Organizing Your Speech

Even a joke won't work if you're so scatterbrained that you give away the punch line. As you plan your speech, consider these suggestions:

- Sharpen your focus. A speech on how chimps learn language is more manageable than a speech on primates in general.

- Organize your main ideas. Here are three approaches:

  1. Organize by **topic.** Break down a general subject into three or four categories. If your subject is airplanes, for instance, you might talk about jets, propeller planes, and gliders.

  2. Organize by **chronology.** Describe a series of events in time order, or explain how to do something step by step.

  3. Organize by **comparison and contrast.** Persuade listeners to do something by telling what will happen if they do it and what will happen if they don't.

- Write each main idea on a note card, and number the cards.

- Begin with a hook. Open with a question, an anecdote, or a surprising fact that will hook listeners from the start.

- End with a punch. Wrap up with a vivid image, a question, a quotation, or a strong statement of opinion.

Giving Your Speech

Rehearse at least once, preferably in the room where you'll give the speech. If you can, bring along a friend to give you feedback. Keep in mind that the image you project is almost as important as your subject. Here are some hints for giving your speech:

- Look at your audience. Don't read your speech word for word. Try to make eye contact with someone.

- Pronounce your words carefully, and speak loudly enough for everyone to hear. Speak neither too slowly nor too quickly.

- Pause briefly after an important point or before a new topic. You may also pause to answer questions from the audience. Some speakers, though, prefer to limit questions to the end.

SPEAKING AND LISTENING WORKSHOP 671

Try It Out

Before giving a persuasive speech—like "Having Ferrets as Pets Should Be Outlawed"— try arguing for the opposing viewpoint. Ask a friend to listen and say which argument is more convincing. Arguing for both sides will give you a firmer grasp of your subject.

Peanuts reprinted by permission of UFS, Inc.

Teaching the Speaking and Listening Workshop

- To supplement this feature, show a few video clips of professionally produced informative presentations— for example, newscasts, science programs, infomercials, and "how-to" programs.
- After students have watched the clips, have them identify and rate the effectiveness of the following:
  1. The purpose of the presentation
  2. The target audience
  3. The techniques that the presenter uses to hold the audience's attention
- Ask students to use their ratings to develop a list of criteria that they can use when planning their own presentations.

Try It Out
Students might work in pairs on this activity, with partners role-playing the opposing side. Urge students to develop several points for their arguments and to experiment with arranging those points in various orders until they find the sequence that they consider most effective.

Speaking and Listening: Determining Purpose
Before students listen to an informative speech, be sure that they have clarified their purpose in listening: Do they wish to learn something, solve a problem, or find the answer to some question? Should they bring a notebook to the presentation?

Speaking and Listening: Comparing Perceptions
After listening to the speech and taking notes on it, students should compare their perceptions of the speech and the speaker with those of other listeners. Do they agree on the speaker's message? How did the speaker affect each listener?

Reaching All Students

Struggling Learners
For some students, the hardest part of formal speechmaking is choosing a focused topic and planning the coverage of the speech. Try pairing these students with peers (one-person "test audiences") on whom they can try out ideas for topics and then possible introductions, organizations, and conclusions. Urge students to evaluate their partner's effectiveness and the overall value of peer guidance.

Advanced Learners
Students who are comfortable with the basics of speechmaking might focus on ways to supplement the text of a speech. Working individually or collaboratively, have them list aids that a speaker might use (for example, pie charts, transparency outlines, prints of fine art or historic photographs, audio and video clips, and the like). Other students may wish to consult these lists as they plan their own speeches.

MAIN OBJECTIVE
Write an informative report

PROCESS OBJECTIVES
1. Use appropriate prewriting techniques to identify and develop a topic
2. Create a first draft
3. Use Evaluation Criteria as a basis for determining revision strategies
4. Revise the first draft, incorporating suggestions generated by self- or peer evaluation
5. Proofread and correct errors
6. Create a final draft
7. Choose an appropriate method of publication
8. Reflect on progress as a writer

Planning

- **Block Schedule**
  Block Scheduling Lesson Plans with Pacing Guide
- **One-Stop Planner**
  CD-ROM with Test Generator

Technology HELP

See Writer's Workshop 1 CD-ROM. *Key word entry: Report of Information.*

ASSIGNMENT

Write a report in which you present information on a topic.

AIM

To inform.

AUDIENCE

Your teacher and classmates.

BUILDING YOUR PORTFOLIO

Writer's Workshop

EXPOSITORY WRITING

INFORMATIVE REPORT

For your informative report, you'll do some detective work. You'll find, organize, and present facts that add to your readers' knowledge of your topic.

Professional Model

Africa is big. It's the second largest of the seven continents, with 11.5 million square miles of dancing grasslands, mysterious mountains, devouring forests, lazy rivers, watchful coastlines, and angry deserts. . . .

Africa is a continent of extremes—sometimes lovely and serene, other times grotesque and full of rage, many times both at once. After all, Africa is home to some of nature's most unusual creations—hippopotamus, elephant, zebra, giraffe, crocodile, cobra, falcon, leopard, and lion—but not the Asiatic tiger! Africa is also the breeding place of the malaria-carrying *Anopheles* mosquito; the tsetse fly, which infects its victims with the deadly "sleeping disease"; and the insatiable ten-year locust.

Understanding Africa's massive and diverse land is the first step in trying to comprehend the peoples who carved out civilizations within its geographical extremes.

—from "Africa in 1492"
by Patricia and Fredrick McKissack

The writers start with a clear and forceful statement and back it up with facts.

In this paragraph the writers present more facts to support their main idea.

The last sentence supports the main idea and provides a strong conclusion.

 — *Resources: Print and Media* —

Writing and Language
- *Portfolio Management System*
  - Prewriting, p. 190
  - Peer Editing, p. 191
  - Assessment Rubric, p. 192
- *Workshop Resources*
  - Revision Strategy Teaching Notes, p. 33
  - Revision Strategy Transparencies 17, 18
- *Writer's Workshop 1 CD-ROM*
  - Report of Information

Assessment
- *Standardized Test Preparation*, p. 120

The history of the written word is rich and *Once upon a tim*

Prewriting

1. Writer's Notebook

If you have Writer's Notebook entries for this collection, review them. Look for ideas on which you can build a report.

2. Listing and Brainstorming

For more ideas, consider the following:

- List what you know—and want to know—about other lands and cultures mentioned in this collection—for example, those of Germany, Vietnam, China, or West Africa.
- List aspects of your own culture that interest you—for example, music, dance, sports, art, handicrafts, foods, or traditions.
- List topics about which you have a great deal of knowledge you'd like to share with other people.

3. Choosing and Narrowing Your Topic

Choose a topic you're really interested in. To be sure it's narrow enough, check an encyclopedia or another general source. If the encyclopedia article goes on for many pages, your topic is probably too broad for a brief report.

4. Researching Your Topic

a. Finding Information

Most informative reports are based on several sources of information (it's a good idea to have at least three). Do research in the library. Use the Internet and conduct interviews with experts if you can.

b. Taking Notes

- Write your notes on 3- × 5-inch note cards. On each card, write the source of the information.
- Write your notes in your own words. It's fine to use abbreviations and fragments. If you copy anything word for word, be sure to put quotation marks around it.

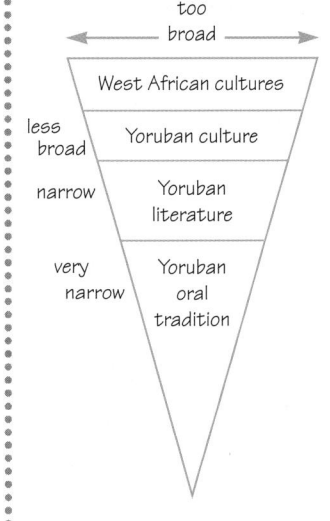

	too broad
less broad	West African cultures
narrow	Yoruban culture
	Yoruban literature
very narrow	Yoruban oral tradition

Communications Handbook HELP

See Evaluating Sources; Listing Sources and Taking Notes.

Introducing the Writer's Workshop

- Lead students in a brainstorming session on how reporters for television news shows get their information. After listing their ideas on the board, point out that reporters use research skills to gather information. Reporters must listen, observe, and read to gather their data, as students will have to do for their papers.
- Call on volunteers to read aloud the Professional Model on p. 672. Discuss the sidenotes; in particular, have students identify specific factual details that support the main idea. Encourage students to use these sidenotes as goals for their own writing.
- Be sure that students understand that the purpose of their writing is not just to provide information on an interesting topic but also to make a "point" with that information.

Teaching the Writer's Workshop

Prewriting

- Have students use the techniques suggested on pp. 673–674 (or any others that may be helpful to them) to come up with ideas, a research plan, and an outline.
- Prepare to offer advice, as needed, especially while students take notes and consider their outline. You may wish to require students to submit sample note cards and the draft of an outline for your review.

Reaching All Students

Struggling Writers

The task of preparing an informative report may seem overwhelming to some students. Encourage students to break the task into smaller components; work with them, as necessary, to create a checklist through which they can track their progress. You also might point out that students can change their minds during the writing process; for example, if they feel the need to add more information or brainstorm

for new ideas, they can go back and do more prewriting.

Also urge students to appreciate the need for clarity; in particular, encourage them to present facts and statistics in terms that their readers can understand. For example, the Professional Model mentions that the size of Africa is 11.5 million square miles. How might students help their readers imagine how big that is?

English Language Learners

An informative report is a perfect place for students to explore an aspect of their family history or cultural background (as Lay Yan does in the Student Model on p. 675). You might have students make a list of possible topics based on the 5W-H? questions (for example, *What do my parents mean when they talk about . . . ? Why do we celebrate . . . in our family?*).

Organizing and Outlining Information from Multiple Sources

Students may have difficulty organizing information they have collected from a variety of sources. Suggest that they sort through their notes and organize them into groups or sets that cover the same ideas. For example, for a report on the beginning of baseball, a student might come up with one set of notes that tell about the inventor of baseball. Another set might cover the earliest rules of the game.

In the next step of organizing information—the outline—each set of notes becomes a main heading. Have students take these steps before they outline:

- Decide how to order the main ideas, and then write them on a piece of paper.
- Go through the notes in each set, and put them in an order that makes sense. The main facts in each set are the outline's subheadings. Write the subheadings under the appropriate main headings.

Drafting

- If you have not already taught the Student Model, do so before students begin their drafts.
- Discuss the Framework for an Informative Report. You may wish to name a topic with which students are familiar and with them brainstorm interesting ways to introduce and conclude a report on that topic.
- Emphasize the importance of crediting quotations (or paraphrases of quotations). If possible, model some ways of identifying the source of such information.
- Remind students to double-space their drafts. They also should leave extra space in the right margin for comments and editing marks.

Outline:
A Typical Day in a Cambodian Village
Organization: time order
I. Morning
   A. Rooster instead of alarm clock
   B. Go outside to wash
      1. Brush teeth with finger and sand
      2. Water in barrel
   C. Breakfast not customary
II. Daytime
   A. Long walk to school . . .

Main point: Customs are different in Cambodia.

Framework for an Informative Report

Introduction (a surprising or dramatic bit of information, plus a clear statement of the main topic):_____
_____

Body (topics arranged in an order that makes sense, developed with facts, examples, statistics, or explanations):
1. Topic: _____
  Details: _____
2. Topic: _____
  Details: _____
3. Topic: _____
  Details: _____

Conclusion (statement or restatement of main point): _____
_____

---

5. Making an Outline

Making an outline is a good way to plan and to organize the information you'll put in your report.

- **Organization.** Decide how you will organize your information. For example, you might use order of importance or time order. Notice that the Student Model on page 675 uses time order, discussing a typical day from morning to night.
- **Support.** Decide which facts and examples from your notes you will use to support each part of your report. Make an outline, and then arrange your note cards in the order of the points in your outline.
- **The main point.** At the end of your outline, write a sentence that sums up the main point of your report.

Drafting
1. Getting Started

Your draft will have three parts. You may find it easier to write the introduction after you have drafted the body.

- **Introduction.** To capture your readers' attention, offer an unusual piece of information or set a surprising scene. Make your topic clear, perhaps by stating your main point.
- **Body.** Write at least one paragraph for each main heading in your outline. Use facts, statistics, and examples from your note cards to develop each paragraph. As you're writing, be alert for places where you need to do more research.
- **Conclusion.** Bring your report to a definite close. If you haven't already stated your main point, do so now. If you have, refer to it again. You might add a summary or a reflection.

2. Tips for Drafting

- As you write, you may get good ideas that aren't in your outline. If they help to illustrate your main point, include them. Also, don't hesitate to depart from your outline if you discover a better way of arranging your report.
- From your note cards, take facts and examples that support your points. Work them into your report. If you need more information, it's fine to go back to a source.
- If you use a quotation, be sure to name the writer or speaker. Using someone else's words without crediting him or her is *plagiarism,* and it is a form of stealing.

Using Students' Strengths

Auditory/Musical Learners
Most students will benefit from additional practice in taking notes. Have students bring to class one of the sources for their reports. In small groups, one student will read a paragraph from one source; then, listeners will give an oral summary of what they have just heard and write the information on note cards. Have group members check each other's notes for clarity and meaning.

Getting Students Involved

Cooperative Learning
Revision Groups. Collect and photocopy students' drafts (enough copies so that each member of a particular group can have one). Then, divide the class into groups of three or four and distribute the copies. Assign group members the following duties: discussion leader (keeps the discussion going), time-keeper (makes sure that all papers are discussed in the allotted time), moderator (keeps the group on task), and recorder (takes notes).

Then, ask students to evaluate the drafts. First, have students comment upon one strong aspect of each draft; then, have them suggest revisions for one paper at a time, using the Evaluating and Revising questions on p. 676 plus any other criteria that they choose as a group. Return the copies to the writers, assuring writers that the final decisions about changes should be their own.

A TYPICAL DAY IN A CAMBODIAN VILLAGE

In the morning there is no clock to awaken us. The rooster crows to wake us up. We go outside to wash our face and wash our teeth with our fingers. Sometimes we use salt or sand or shaved charcoal to wash our teeth. We don't have indoor plumbing in the house; that's why we have to go outside to the rain barrel or near the stream to wash.

I go back inside the house and I put on a sarong (my school uniform) to go to school. It isn't a custom to eat breakfast in Cambodia.

The school is far from my house. I have to walk a long way to get to the school. In school there is no indoor plumbing or electricity. We have to use cloth put in the oil can and a match to light it if it's a dark day. If it's a sunny day we open the window. When it's time to go to recess we go home and eat rice and come back to school. We stay in school until five o'clock in the evening. When we get out of school we have to walk home again.

At night my family of seven people sleeps on two mats. We don't have beds to sleep on, that's why we have to sleep on the mat. In Cambodia when we go to sleep we have to clean our feet first before we go to sleep. That's our culture. We don't have to wash our face or hands or teeth but we must wash our feet.

My house has only two rooms. One room's for cooking and eating and the other room is for sleeping. We don't have any furniture in our house—no table, no chairs, just mats and a small wood-burning stove to cook on. My mother also has cooking utensils like pots, pans, eight dishes and eight spoons, chopsticks but no forks. It is the custom to sit in a circle on the floor to eat our meals in Cambodia.

We don't wear pajamas to sleep. Mother, father, and girls wear sarongs, and boys wear shorts.

—Lay Yan
Moody Middle School
Lowell, Massachusetts

The writer uses the title to make her topic clear.

The report is organized in chronological order, beginning with the morning.

The writer uses facts and examples to share her knowledge with us.

The writer repeatedly supports her main point—that customs are different in Cambodia.

The writer uses details that show that she knows her subject well.

WRITER'S WORKSHOP 675

As class members read the Student Model, make sure that they understand the sidenotes. You can extend the discussion by having students focus on questions like these:

? Compare the Student Model to the outline in the margin of this page. What part of Lay Yan's report does the outline cover?

? How does the writer set a scene to introduce her report?

? What information does the writer provide about daytime activities in the Cambodian village? About nighttime activities?

? Can you find three details in the report that suggest that Cambodian customs are different from American customs? Name them.

? Think about the information that Lay Yan presents. If you were presenting this information, how else might you organize it? Why would you—or wouldn't you—organize it differently?

Drawing Conclusions from Information Drawn from Multiple Sources

Weighing and assessing information from a variety of sources is a difficult step for students. Caution them not to draw conclusions based on a single source. Before they draw a conclusion, tell them to be sure that each source

- is directly relevant to their topic
- is as recent as possible
- is accurate and reliable
- presents representative viewpoints on the topic (if there are multiple opinions on an issue)

Choosing Reference Materials and Resources for Writing, Revising, and Editing

As students write, revise, and edit their reports, they should consult specific reference materials. For example, in writing their report, they might want to look in a book of synonyms, such as *Roget's International Thesaurus* or *Webster's New Dictionary of Synonyms,* if they are looking for just the right words to describe their topic. In revising, they may decide to consult *Collier's Encyclopedia* or *The World Book 1999 Multimedia Encyclopedia* if they need additional information on their topic. And in editing, they might want to check the *MLA Handbook for Writers of Research Papers* to be sure that they have cited their sources correctly.

Reaching All Students

Advanced Learners

You might want to use one or both of these activities with students who have mastered the fundamentals of report writing.

- Have students focus on the tone and diction of their reports. Explain that students may choose a conversational tone for an informational report but that they probably would want to avoid slang and jargon, which might confuse readers. Have students read their drafts aloud to a small group; have group members respond with feedback about the suitability of the tone and diction.

- After students have finished their reports, show a short, informational documentary video. Have students listen for elements that parallel elements in their reports—for example, clear indication of topic, points in an order that makes sense, types of details that support the topic, and a satisfactory conclusion. Pause the video occasionally so that students can discuss the elements that they identify.

Evaluating and Revising

Before students revise their papers, discuss the Revision Model with them. Then, ask students to use the Evaluation Criteria provided here to review their drafts and determine needed revisions.

Proofreading

Have students proofread their own papers first and then exchange with another student. For this assignment, remind students to be particularly careful to punctuate compound and complex sentences correctly.

If time permits, the final copy should be put aside for at least a day before it is proofread for the final time by the author.

Publishing

Students may want to give their reports in the form of multimedia presentations. If so, be prepared to offer guidance about locating and using visuals, audio materials, and so on. Alternatively, students might gather their reports into a class binder and store the binder in the classroom library as a future reference source.

Reflecting

Urge students to write a short reflection on the process of preparing an informative report and to consider including it in their writing portfolios. Students might start by completing one of these statements:

- The biggest challenge in preparing this report was . . .
- The part of this report that I like best is . . . because . . .
- The most interesting fact that I found during my research was this: . . .
- The most interesting thing that I learned about myself during this assignment was this: . . .

Resources

Peer Editing Forms and Rubrics
- *Portfolio Management System*, p. 191

Revision Transparencies
- *Workshop Resources*, p. 33

Technology HELP

See Writer's Workshop 1 CD-ROM. *Key word entry: Report of Information. See Bibliography Maker.*

■ *Evaluation Criteria*

A good informative report

1. *centers on one topic that is supported by explanations and facts*

2. *presents information with authority*

3. *organizes information in a way that makes sense*

4. *documents any outside sources used*

Language/Grammar Link HELP

Common usage problems: pages 606, 624, and 637. Using specific words: page 648. Oral storytelling: page 661.

Communications Handbook HELP

See Listing Sources and Taking Notes.

Sentence Workshop HELP

Parallel structure: page 677.

Revision Model

In the morning there is no clock

to awaken us. The rooster crows

to wake us up. We go outside to   *Can you make parts of the third sentence parallel?*

wash
wash our face and ~~washing~~ our
                          ∧

teeth with our fingers. Some-   *This is confusing. I need to know more.*
              or sand or shaved charcoal
                 to wash our teeth
times we use salt. We don't have
                      ∧

indoor plumbing in the house;

that's why we have to go

to the rain barrel or near the stream   *Can you add some specifics?*
outside to wash.
       ∧

3. Listing Sources

On a page at the end of your report, list any outside sources you used. Put them in alphabetical order by author's last name (or by title if no author is named). Follow the guidelines in the Communications Handbook or a style guide your teacher selects. Look carefully at the punctuation, capitalization, and order of information in the guide you use. Follow it exactly.

Evaluating and Revising

On a sheet of paper, write the following questions. Leave space between them for responses. Then, attach the paper to your draft, and trade drafts with a classmate.

- What is the main point of this report?
- What new things did I learn from this report?
- Are any parts confusing? How might the writer make them clearer?
- What, if anything, might make the first paragraph stronger?

Use your partner's responses to improve your draft.

Grading Timesaver

Rubrics for this Writer's Workshop assignment appear on p. 192 of the *Portfolio Management System.*

Assessing Learning

Standardized Test Preparation
For practice with standardized test prompts and formats, see
- *Standardized Test Preparation*, p. 120

Sentence Workshop

PARALLEL STRUCTURE

What is wrong with this sentence?

The daughters liked fine clothes and money and to go to parties.

The items listed are not **parallel**—they're not in the same grammatical form. Two are nouns (*clothes* and *money*), and one is a phrase (*to go to parties*). To correct the sentence, make the items in the list parallel. In sentences with parallel structure, nouns are balanced with nouns, phrases with phrases, clauses with clauses.

PARALLEL   The daughters liked fine clothes and money and parties. [three nouns]

PARALLEL   The daughters liked to wear fine clothes, to have money, and to go to parties. [three phrases]

Below are two more sentences with errors in parallelism, along with a corrected version of each.

NOT PARALLEL   Cinderella didn't have time to read books, go for walks, or talking with friends. [three phrases with different structures]

PARALLEL   Cinderella didn't have time to read books, go for walks, or talk with friends. [three phrases with the same structure]

NOT PARALLEL   The fairy godmother knew that Cinderella was miserable and her sad life. [a clause and a noun with modifiers]

PARALLEL   The fairy godmother knew that Cinderella was miserable and that she had a sad life. [two clauses]

Writer's Workshop Follow-up: Revision

Take out your informative report, and exchange papers with a classmate. Look for parallel structure in sentences where your partner has joined elements with *and, but,* or *or.* Suggest revisions for sentences that are out of balance.

Try It Out

The following sentences are out of balance: They do not use parallel structure. Edit them to put the ideas in parallel form. Be sure to exchange papers with a classmate. Can any sentence be rewritten in more than one way?

1. The king saw trumpeting elephants, roaring tigers, and the panthers growling.
2. The weather was cold, rainy, and there was wind.
3. The guests at the ball sang, laughed, and there was dancing.
4. He liked to play the lute, ride horses, and singing.

Resources

Workshop Resources
- Worksheet, p. 51

Try It Out
Possible Response
1. The king saw trumpeting elephants, roaring tigers, and growling panthers.
2. The weather was cold, rainy, and windy.
3. The guests at the ball sang, laughed, and danced.
4. He liked to play the lute, ride horses, and sing songs.

Assessing Learning

Quick Check: Parallel Structure
Revise the following sentences to make them parallel. (Possible responses are given.)

1. Aschenputtel was gentle, beautiful, and obeyed her stepmother. [Aschenputtel was gentle, beautiful, and obedient to her stepmother.]
2. Yeh-Shen searched for her shoe, sad, hopelessly, and worried. [Yeh-Shen searched for her shoe, feeling sad, hopeless, and worried.]
3. The eagle stopped and plunged, focusing and attacking Oni. [The eagle stopped, plunged, focused, and attacked Oni.]
4. Master Frog was unusual and ugly in appearance but showing intelligence and courage. [Master Frog was unusual and ugly in appearance, but he showed intelligence and courage.]
5. The Mayas fought fierce and determinedly. [The Mayas fought fiercely and determinedly.]

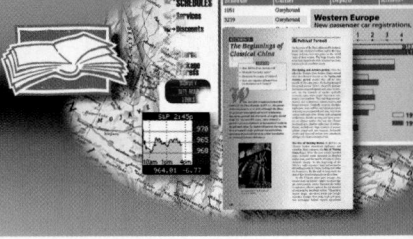

Reading for Life

Searching the Internet

Situation

Your teacher wants you to use the Internet to find information for research reports. You've been assigned to write a report on a topic of your choice about world folklore. You decide to write about Cinderella stories. Use these strategies to narrow your search.

Strategies

Use key words.

Try using more than one key word. If you try the key word *Cinderella*, you'll get thousands of "hits" (sites), many of which have nothing to do with the fairy tale. To limit your list, try using two key words. If you use the key words *Cinderella* and *stories* together, for example, you'll be more likely to get a list of sites that discuss your subject.

Use directories.

A **directory** is an index of selected sites grouped by subject.

• Yahooligans is a directory designed especially for kids. It sorts sites into broad subject areas like Entertainment and Science. Start by clicking

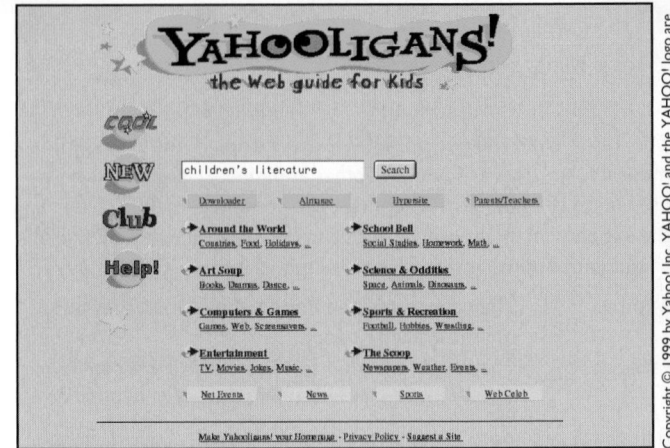

on a listed subject that you think might include the information you want. If nothing seems to fit, come up with a general subject and type it in the *Search* box. If *Cinderella Stories, Folklore,* and *Folk Tales* don't produce any sites, try *Children's Literature.*

For smoother surfing:

• Check out sites in the order in which they're listed. The better ones usually appear at the beginning.

• To evaluate a site, read the brief description provided.

• If you come up with too many hits or you find no useful ones in the first ten,

try these strategies: Use synonyms for your key word; try using an additional key word; check your spelling; click on the help function.

Using the Strategies

1. Which key words produced the most useful list of sites?

2. Which of the strategies described do you find easiest to use? Why?

Extending the Strategies

Use the Web to find information on your favorite author. If you don't have a favorite, see what you can find on Jakob and Wilhelm Grimm or on Virginia Hamilton.

Reaching All Students

Struggling Readers

Unless they already frequent the Internet, students may struggle with differences between reading an interactive Web page and a static printed page of text. Work with these students, either individually or in small groups, at a computer with Internet access. Point out Web site features that they should find familiar—for example, titles, subheads, and lists—and then move to distinctive online features, such as hypertext links and the ability to enlarge visuals.

English Language Learners

Invite students for whom English is a second language to explore Web resources that may be available in their first languages and to report on the results. Students might begin by accessing Yahoo! (http://www.yahoo.com) and using one of the links under its list of World Yahoo!s. (If the desired language does not use a Roman alphabet, Yahoo! will explain how to make its alphabet accessible.)

OBJECTIVES

1. Gain familiarity in using the Internet
2. Use keywords and directories to locate information about a given topic
3. Evaluate strategies for locating information and the usefulness of particular Web sites

Learning for Life

Researching Our Heritage: Comparing Cultures

OBJECTIVES

1. Identify questions about another culture and then use those questions to choose topics for research
2. Develop an individual or collaborative plan for research
3. Locate and organize information about a topic
4. Choose a format for presenting the research and then present the information to the class

Problem

Cultures from all over the world come together in the United States. How much do you know about your own or another culture? What would you like to know?

Project

Research some questions about another culture. Then, compare that culture with your own. Organize your findings and present them to the class.

Preparation

1. Jot down what you know about the culture you've chosen.

2. With a few classmates, come up with a list of research questions about the following areas that you might compare:

   • oral traditions

   • art, crafts, music, dance

   • foods

   • geographical or regional characteristics

   • discoveries, inventions

3. From your group's questions, select a few topics that you want to find out more about.

Procedure

1. In your group, talk about how to research the topics you're interested in. You might consult your librarian, conduct interviews, read books or encyclopedia articles, or listen to music.

2. Are other students in your class interested in the same culture that you are researching? If so, consider working as a research team, with each of you doing a specific job.

3. Do the research and organize your information.

Presentation

Present your findings in one of the following ways:

1. Multimedia Report

Use a variety of media to present your report. You might include maps, drawings, photographs, voice or music recordings, videotape, costumes and foods, or demonstrations of dances. Make your report clear, informative, and entertaining.

2. Folk-Tale Festival

Plan a folk-tale festival for your class or grade. Individuals or small groups can present a folk tale or legend. The presentation—including different voices, sound effects, and music—can be videotaped or performed live. Make the presentation as dramatic as possible. Afterward, hold a class discussion to compare the cultures represented.

3. On-line Culture Guide

Using a computer, create a guide to the countries or regions your class has researched. Include sections covering, for example, folklore, the arts (such as painting, music, and dance), important cities, places of interest, and customs (such as traditions, foods, and clothing). Make sure your information is carefully organized and can be located in several different categories.

Processing

To reflect on what you have learned, complete this starter: I'd like to continue exploring cultures by . . . .

Resources

Viewing and Representing
HRW Multimedia Presentation Maker
Students may wish to use the *Multimedia Presentation Maker* to present the information gathered during their research.

Grading Timesaver

Rubrics for this Learning for Life project appear on p. 193 of the Portfolio Management System.

Developing Workplace Competencies

Preparation	Procedure	Presentation
• Making inferences • Generating different ideas • Making decisions	• Recognizing relationships • Classifying data • Determining relevant information	• Solving insight problems • Comparing similarities and differences • Working with others

more information about a topic, turn to the
(s) in this book indicated on a separate line at
end of the entries. To learn more about *Allusion*,
example, turn to pages 468 and 564.

On another line are cross-references to entries
is Handbook that provide closely related infor-
on. For instance, at the end of *Autobiography* is a
s-reference to *Biography*.

ITERATION **The repetition of the same or
similar consonant sounds in words that are
together.** Though alliteration usually occurs
e beginning of words, it can also occur within or
e end of words. Among other things, alliteration
help establish a mood, emphasize words, and
e as a memory aid. In the following example the
und is repeated at the beginning of the words
n and *sad* and within the words *uncertain* and
ng:

> And the silken sad uncertain rustling of each
> purple curtain
>
> — Edgar Allan Poe, from "The Raven"

See pages 338–339, 349.

USION **A reference to a statement, a per-
, a place, or an event from literature, history,
gion, mythology, politics, sports, or science.**
sions enrich the reading experience. Writers ex-
: readers to recognize an allusion and to think, al-
t at the same time, about the literary work and
person, place, or event that it refers to. The fol-
ing lines, describing a tunnel in the snow, contain
llusion to Aladdin, a character in *The Thousand
One Nights:*

> With mittened hands, and caps drawn low,
> To guard our necks and ears from snow,
> We cut the solid whiteness through.
> And, where the drift was deepest, made
> A tunnel walled and overlaid
> With dazzling crystal: we had read

> Of rare Aladdin's wondrous cave,
> And to our own his name we gave.
>
> —John Greenleaf Whittier,
> from "Snow-Bound"

The cave in the tale contains a magic lamp that helps
Aladdin discover vast riches. By alluding to Aladdin's
cave, Whittier makes us see the icy tunnel in the
snow as a magical, fairy-tale place.

The cartoon below makes an allusion to a popular fairy tale.

See pages 468, 479, 564.

*"Now, this policy will cover your home for fire, theft,
flood and huffing and puffing."*

Reprinted from The Saturday Evening Post © 1993.

ATMOSPHERE **The overall mood or emotion
of a work of literature.** A work's atmosphere can
often be described with one or two adjectives, such
as *scary, dreamy, happy, sad,* or *nostalgic.* A writer creates atmosphere by using images, sounds, and descriptions that convey a particular feeling.

See also *Mood.*

AUTOBIOGRAPHY **The story of a person's
life, written or told by that person.** Jean Fritz
wrote a popular autobiography called *Homesick: My
Own Story* (page 105) about her early life in China.
Another well-known autobiographical work is Maya
Angelou's *I Know Why the Caged Bird Sings.*

See page 121.
See also *Biography.*

BIOGRAPHY **The story of a real person's life, written or told by another person.** Jean Fritz has written biographies of many famous American figures, including Paul Revere, Benjamin Franklin, and Pocahontas. Frequent subjects of biographies are movie stars, television personalities, politicians, sports figures, self-made millionaires, even underworld figures. Biographies are among the most popular forms of contemporary literature.

See pages 121, 122.
See also *Autobiography*.

CHARACTER **A person or animal who takes part in the action of a story, play, or other literary work.** In some works, such as Aesop's fables, a character is an animal. In myths and legends a character may be a god or a superhero, like Jupiter or Hercules in "The Labors of Hercules" (page 541). Most often a character is an ordinary human being, such as Kevin in "User Friendly" (page 357).

The process of revealing the personality of a character in a story is called **characterization.** A writer can reveal a character in the following ways:

1. by letting the reader hear the character speak
2. by describing how the character looks and dresses
3. by letting the reader listen to the character's inner thoughts and feelings
4. by revealing what other people in the story think or say about the character
5. by showing the reader what the character does—how he or she acts
6. by telling the reader directly what the character's personality is like (cruel, kind, sneaky, brave, and so on)

When a writer uses the first five ways to reveal a character, the reader must make an inference, based on the evidence the writer provides, to decide what the character is like. When a writer uses the sixth method, however, the reader doesn't make a decision but is told directly what kind of person the character is.

Characters can be classified as static or dynamic. A **static character** is one who does not change much in the course of a work. The father in "A Day's

Wait" (page 81) is a static character. By contras[t] **dynamic character** changes as a result of [a] story's events. Roger Clark in "Miss Awful" (p[age] 369) is a dynamic character.

A character's **motivation** is any force t[hat] drives or moves the character to behave in a [par]ticular way. Many characters are motivated by [the] force of fear or love or ambition.

See pages 80, 85, 356, 365, 386,
605, 607, 635, 636,

CONFLICT **A struggle or clash between opp[os]ing characters or opposing forces.** In an **exter[nal] conflict** a character struggles against some outs[ide] force. This outside force may be another chara[cter] or society as a whole or a storm or a grizzly bea[r] even a machine. In "Three Skeleton Key" (page [   ]) the characters have an external conflict wit[h a] swarm of sea rats. An **internal conflict,** on [the] other hand, takes place within a character's min[d. It] is a struggle between opposing needs, desires [or] emotions. In "After Twenty Years" (page 193), [Offi]cer Wells must resolve an internal conflict: Shoul[d he] arrest an old friend or let him go?

See pages 2, 19, 22, 61, 118, 199, 244,
270–271, 300, 322, 349, 457,

CONNOTATION **The feelings and asso[cia]tions that a word suggests.** For example, [small,] *cramped,* and *compact* all have about the same dic[tio]nary definition, or **denotation,** but they have dif[fer]ent connotations. A manufacturer of small c[ars] would not describe its product as tiny or cramp[ed.] Instead, the company might say that its cars are c[om]pact. To grasp a writer's full meaning, the rea[der] must pay attention not only to the literal definit[ion] of words but also to their connotations. Conn[ota]tions can be especially important in poetry.

See page

DENOTATION **The literal, dictionary de[fini]tion of a word.**

See page
See also *Connota[tion.]*

SCRIPTION **The kind of writing that cre-**
s a clear image of something, usually by using
ails that appeal to one or more of the senses:
ht, hearing, smell, taste, and touch. Writers
description in all forms of fiction, nonfiction, and
try. In "Fish Cheeks" (page 135), Amy Tan vividly
cribes the colors, sounds, and tastes of her fam-
Christmas celebration.

See pages 134, 141, 511.

ALECT **A way of speaking that is characteris-**
of a particular region or group of people. A
ect may have a distinct vocabulary, pronunciation
tem, and grammar. In a sense, we all speak a
lect. One dialect usually becomes dominant in a
ntry or culture and is accepted as the standard
y of speaking. In the United States, for example,
formal written language is known as standard
lish. This is the dialect used in most newspapers
magazines.

Writers often reproduce regional dialects, or
ech that reveals a character's economic or social
ss, in order to give a story local color. Mr. Baumer
'Bargain" (page 231) speaks in a dialect that re-
ls that his first language is German. The poem
adam and the Rent Man" (page 227) is written in a
ect spoken in some urban African American
mmunities in the northeastern United States.

See page 481.

ALOGUE **A conversation between two or**
re characters.** Most stage dramas consist en-
ely of dialogue together with stage directions.
reenplays and television dramas sometimes in-
de an unseen narrator.) The dialogue in a drama,
h as *Brian's Song* (page 274), must move the plot
ng and reveal character almost single-handedly.
alogue is also an important element in most sto-
s and novels as well as in some poems and nonfic-
n. It is one of the most effective ways for a writer
show what a character is like. It can also add real-
and humor.

In the written form of a play, dialogue appears
hout quotation marks. In prose or poetry, how-
r, dialogue is usually enclosed in quotation marks.

A **monologue** is a part of a drama in which one
character speaks alone.

See pages 78, 96, 270.

DRAMA **A story written to be acted in front of**
an audience. (A drama can be appreciated and enjoyed in written form, however.) In a drama, such as
Brian's Song (page 274), the action is usually driven by
a character who wants something very much and
takes steps to get it. The related events that take
place within a drama are often separated into **acts.**
Each act is often made up of shorter sections, or
scenes. Most plays have three acts, but there are
many, many variations. The elements of a drama are
often described as **introduction** or **exposition,**
complications, conflict, climax, and **resolution.**

See pages 270–271, 273.

FABLE **A brief story in prose or verse that**
teaches a moral or gives a practical lesson about
how to get along in life. The characters of most
fables are animals that behave and speak like human
beings. Some of the most popular fables are attrib-
uted to Aesop, who is thought to have been a slave in
ancient Greece. The poem "The Boy and the Wolf"
(page 574) is a retelling in verse of one of Aesop's
fables.

See pages 565, 566.
See also *Folk Tale, Myth.*

FICTION **A prose account that is made up**
rather than true. The term *fiction* usually refers to
novels and short stories. Fiction may be based on a
writer's experiences or on historical events, but
characters, events, and other details are altered or
added by the writer to create a desired effect. "The
No-Guitar Blues" (page 217) is a fictional account
based on an episode in the writer's childhood.

See also *Nonfiction.*

FIGURE OF SPEECH **A word or phrase that**
describes one thing in terms of something else
and is not literally true. Figures of speech always involve some sort of imaginative comparison

HANDBOOK OF LITERARY TERMS 683

between seemingly unlike things. The most common forms are **simile** ("The stars were like diamonds"), **metaphor** ("My soul is an enchanted boat"), and **personification** ("The sun smiled down on the emerald-green fields").

See pages 168, 397.
See also *Metaphor, Personification, Simile.*

FLASHBACK **An interruption in the action of a plot to tell what happened at an earlier time.** A flashback breaks the usual movement of the narrative by going back in time. It usually gives background information that helps the reader understand the present situation. "A Mason-Dixon Memory" (page 206) contains a long flashback.

A break in the unfolding of a plot to an episode in the future is known as a **flash-forward.**

See pages 206, 213.

FOLK TALE **A story, with no known author, that originally was passed on from one generation to another by word of mouth.** Most folk tales reflect the values of the society that preserved them. "Master Frog" (page 639) is a folk tale about the importance of who we are on the inside. Folk tales often contain **fantastic** elements, or events that could not happen in the world as we know it.

See pages 625–626.
See also *Fable, Myth, Tall Tale.*

FORESHADOWING **The use of clues to suggest events that will happen later in the plot.** Foreshadowing is used to build suspense or create anxiety. In a drama a gun found in a bureau drawer in Act One is likely to foreshadow violence later in the play. In *Brian's Song* (page 274), Brian Piccolo's weight loss foreshadows his illness and death later in the play.

See pages 64, 77, 192, 199, 241, 322.
See also *Suspense.*

FREE VERSE **Poetry without a regular meter or a rhyme scheme.** Poets writing in free verse try to capture the natural rhythms of ordinary speech.

To create their music, poets writing in free ve[rse] may use internal rhyme, repetition, alliteration, [and] onomatopoeia. Free verse also frequently makes [use] of vivid imagery. The following poem in free verse [ef]fectively uses images and the repetition of words [to] describe the effects of a family's eviction for not p[ay]ing rent:

> **The 1st**
> What I remember about that day
> is boxes stacked across the walk
> and couch springs curling through the air
> and drawers and tables balanced on the curb
> and us, hollering,
> leaping up and around
> happy to have a playground;
>
> nothing about the emptied rooms
> nothing about the emptied family
>
> —Lucille Clifto[n]

See pages 338, 398, 4[ ]
See also *Poetry, Rhyme, Rhyt*[hm]

IMAGERY **Language that appeals to the sens**[es.] Most images are visual—that is, they create pictu[res] in the reader's mind by appealing to the sense [of] sight. Images can also appeal to the sense of hear[ing,] touch, taste, or smell or to several senses at on[ce.] The sensory images in "The Highwayman" (pa[ge] 341) add greatly to the enjoyment of the poe[m.] Though imagery is an element in all types of writ[ing,] it is especially important in poetry.

See page 3[ ]
See also *Poe*[try.]

IRONY **In general, a contrast between expec**[ta]tion and reality. Irony can create powerful effe[cts,] from humor to strong emotion. There are thr[ee] common types of irony:

1. **Verbal irony** involves a contrast betwe[en] what is said or written and what is meant[. If] you were to call someone who failed a m[ath] test Einstein, you would be using ver[bal] irony.

2. **Situational irony** occurs when what happens is very different from what is expected to happen. The surprise ending of "After Twenty Years" (page 193) involves situational irony.

3. **Dramatic irony** occurs when the audience or the reader knows something a character does not know. Near the conclusion of *Brian's Song* (page 274), the reader feels an anxious sense of irony when Mr. Eberle asks Brian Piccolo to give his permission for another operation. Although Brian doesn't yet know it, we know that Brian's cancer has spread.

See pages 558, 562.

MERICK A humorous five-line verse that s a regular meter and the rhyme scheme *ba. Limericks often have place names in their mes. The following limerick was published in Ed-'d Lear's *Book of Nonsense* in 1846, when limericks 'e at the height of their popularity:

> There was an old man with a beard,
> Who said, "It is just as I feared!
> Two owls and a hen,
> Four larks and a wren
> Have *all* built their nests in my beard!"

See pages 338–339.

AIN IDEA The most important idea ex-essed in a paragraph or in an entire essay. e main idea may be directly stated in a **topic ntence,** or the reader may have to look at all details in the paragraph and make an **inference,** educated guess, about its main idea.

See pages 144, 149, 443, 444.

TAMORPHOSIS A marvelous change from e shape or form to another one. In myths the nge is usually from human to animal, from animal to human, or from human to plant. Greek and Roman myths contain many examples of metamorphosis. The myth of Echo and Narcissus (page 523) tells how the vain youth Narcissus pines away for love of his own reflection until he is changed into a flower.

See pages 638, 646.
See also *Myth.*

METAPHOR An imaginative comparison between two unlike things in which one thing is said to be another thing. A metaphor is an important type of figurative language. Metaphors are used in all forms of writing and are common in ordinary speech. If you were to say someone has a heart of gold, you would not mean that the person's heart is actually made of metal. You would mean, instead, that the person is warm and caring. You would be speaking metaphorically.

Metaphors differ from similes, which use specific words (notably *like, as, than,* and *resembles*) to state comparisons. William Wordsworth's famous comparison "I wandered lonely as a cloud" is a simile because it uses *as.* If Wordsworth had written "I was a lonely, wandering cloud," he would have been using a metaphor.

See pages 131, 168, 171, 397, 403.
See also *Figure of Speech, Personification, Simile.*

PEANUTS reprinted by permission of United Feature Syndicate, Inc.

MOOD **The overall emotion created by a work of literature.** A work of literature can often be described with one or more adjectives: *sad, scary, hopeful, exciting,* and so on. These are descriptions of the work's mood—its emotional atmosphere. For example, the mood of "Annabel Lee" (pages 351–352) could be described as haunting or romantic. That mood has a lingering effect on its readers.

See page 393.
See also *Atmosphere.*

MOTIVATION See *Character.*

MYTH **A story that explains something about the world and typically involves gods or other superhuman beings.** Myths, which at one time were believed to be true, reflect the traditions of the culture that produced them. Almost every culture has **origin myths** (or **creation myths**), stories that explain how something in the world (perhaps the world itself) came to be. Myths may also explain many other aspects of nature. The ancient Greek myth of Demeter and Persephone (page 501), for example, explains the change of seasons. Most myths are very old and were handed down orally long before being put in written form. In some of the world's greatest myths, a hero or even a god embarks on a **quest,** a perilous journey taken in pursuit of something of great value.

See pages 426, 430, 496–499, 500, 510, 527.
See also *Fable, Folk Tale.*

NONFICTION **Prose writing that deals with real people, events, and places without changing any facts.** Popular forms of nonfiction are the **autobiography,** the **biography,** and the **essay.** Other examples of nonfiction include newspaper stories, magazine articles, historical writing, scientific reports, and even personal diaries and letters.

Nonfiction writing can be subjective or objective. **Subjective writing** expresses the feelings and opinions of the writer. **Objective writing** conveys

the facts without introducing any emotion or p[er]sonal bias.

See pages 104, 121–[
See also *Autobiography, Biography, Fic[tion]*

NOVEL **A fictional story that is usually [be]tween one hundred and five hundred bo[ok] pages long.** A novel uses all the elements of sto[ry]telling—plot, character, setting, theme, and poin[t of] view. A novel, because of its length, usually has m[ore] characters, settings, and themes and a more c[om]plex plot than a short story. Modern writers so[me]times do not pay much attention to one or mor[e of] the novel's traditional elements. Some novels to[day] are basically character studies that include only [the] barest story lines. Other novels don't look much [be]yond the surface of their characters and concentr[ate] instead on plot and setting. A novel can deal with [al]most any topic. Many of the books recommende[d in] the Read On sections of this text are novels.

ONOMATOPOEIA **The use of words w[ith] sounds that echo their sense.** Onomatopo[eia] (än′ō·mat′ō·pē′ə) is so natural to us that we us[e it] at a very early age. *Buzz, rustle, boom, ticktock, tw[eet],* and *bark* are all examples of onomatopoeia. O[no]matopoeia is an important element in creating [the] music of poetry. In the following lines the poet c[re]ates a frenzied mood by choosing words that imi[tate] the sounds of alarm bells:

> Oh, the bells, bells, bells!
> What a tale their terror tells
> Of Despair!
> How they clang, and clash, and roar!
> What a horror they outpour
> On the bosom of the palpitating air!
> Yet the ear, it fully knows
> By the twanging
> And the clanging
> How the danger ebbs and flows.
>
> —Edgar Allan Poe, from "The Bells[

See page 3[
See also *Alliterat[ion]*

PERSONIFICATION **A figure of speech in which a nonhuman thing or quality is talked about as if it were human.** In the following lines, sleep is spoken of as a human weaver:

The soft gray hands of sleep
Toiled all night long
To spin a beautiful garment
Of dreams

—Edward Silvera, from "Forgotten Dreams"

See pages 464, 467, 520.
See also *Figure of Speech, Metaphor, Simile.*

PLOT **The series of related events that make up a story.** Plot is "what happens" in a short story, novel, play, or narrative poem. Most plots are built on these bare bones: An **introduction,** or **exposition,** tells us who the characters are and what their **conflict** is. **Complications** arise as the characters take steps to resolve the conflict. The plot reaches a **climax,** the most emotional or suspenseful moment in the story, when the outcome is decided one way or another. The last part of a story is the **resolution,** when the characters' problems are solved and the story ends.

Not all works of fiction or drama have this traditional plot structure. Some modern writers experiment, often eliminating parts of a traditional plot in order to focus on elements such as character, point of view, or mood.

See pages 22–23, 61, 96, 270–271, 349, 605.
See also *Conflict.*

POETRY **A kind of rhythmic, compressed language that uses figures of speech and imagery designed to appeal to emotion and imagination.** We know poetry when we see it because it is usually arranged in a particular way on the page. Traditional poetry often has a regular pattern of rhythm (meter) and may have a regular **rhyme scheme.** **Free verse** is poetry that has no regular rhythm or rhyme. The major forms of poetry are the **lyric** (a songlike poem that expresses a speaker's feelings) and the **narrative** (a poem that tells a story). Two popular narrative forms are the **epic** and the **ballad.**

See pages 24, 338–339, 355, 397.
See also *Figure of Speech, Free Verse, Imagery, Refrain, Rhyme, Rhythm, Speaker, Stanza.*

POINT OF VIEW **The vantage point from which a story is told.** The most common points of view are the **omniscient,** the **third-person limited,** and the **first person.**

1. In the **omniscient,** or all-knowing, **point of view** the narrator knows everything about the characters and their problems. This all-knowing narrator can tell about the characters' past, present, and future. This kind of narrator can even tell what the characters are thinking or what is happening in other places. This narrator is not in the story. Instead, he or she stands above the action, like a god. The omniscient is a very familiar point of view; we have heard it in fairy tales since we were very young. "Aschenputtel" (page 593) is told from the omniscient point of view: "And when the evening came, she wanted to go home, and the prince followed her, for he wanted to see to what house she belonged. . . ."

2. In the **third-person limited point of view,** the narrator focuses on the thoughts and feelings of only one character. From this point of view, readers observe the action through the eyes and feelings of only one character in the story. "The Smallest Dragonboy" (page 47) is told from the third-person limited point of view: "There was such a lot to know and understand about being a dragonrider that sometimes Keevan was overwhelmed. How would he ever be able to remember everything he ought to know at the right moment?"

3. In the **first-person point of view,** one of the characters, using the personal pronoun *I,* is telling the story. The reader becomes very familiar with this narrator but can know only

HANDBOOK OF LITERARY TERMS 687

what he or she knows and can observe only what he or she observes. All information about the story must come from this character. In some cases the information is incorrect. "A Day's Wait" (page 81) is told from the first-person point of view of the boy's father. He does not know what is worrying his son: "I sat at the foot of the bed and read to myself while I waited for it to be time to give another capsule. It would have been natural for him to go to sleep, but when I looked up he was looking at the foot of the bed, looking very strangely."

See pages 202–203, 216, 224, 230, 241.

REFRAIN **A group of words repeated at intervals in a poem, song, or speech.** Refrains are usually associated with songs and poems, but they are also used in speeches and other forms of literature. Refrains are most often used to create rhythm, but they may also provide emphasis or commentary, create suspense, or help hold a work together. Refrains may be repeated with small variations in a work in order to fit a particular context or to create a special effect. The first six lines are used as a refrain in the song "A Place in the Choir" (page 178).

See pages 420, 425.

RHYME **The repetition of accented vowel sounds and all sounds following them in words close together in a poem.** *Mean* and *screen* are rhymes, as are *crumble* and *tumble*. Rhyme has many purposes in poetry: It creates rhythm, lends a song-like quality, emphasizes ideas, organizes the poem (for instance, into stanzas or couplets), provides humor or delight for the reader, and makes the poem memorable.

Many poems—for example, "The Runaway" (page 25)—use **end rhymes,** rhymes at the end of a line. In the following stanza, *walls/calls/falls* form end rhymes, as do *hands/sands:*

> Darkness settles on roofs and walls,
> But the sea, the sea in the darkness calls;
> The little waves, with their soft, white hands,

> Efface the footprints in the sands,
> And the tide rises, the tide falls.
>
> —Henry Wadsworth Longfellow,
> from "The Tide Rises, the Tide Falls"

Internal rhymes are rhymes within lines. T[he] following line has an internal rhyme (*turning/burnin[g]*):

> Back into the chamber turning, all my soul
> within me burning
>
> —Edgar Allan Poe, from "The Raven"

Rhyming sounds need not be spelled the sa[me] way; for instance, *gear/here* forms a rhyme. Rhym[es] can involve more than one syllable or more th[an] one word; *poet/know it* is an example. Rhymes [in]volving sounds that are similar but not exactly t[he] same are called **slant rhymes** (or **near rhymes** [or] **approximate rhymes**). *Leave/live* is an example [of] a slant rhyme. Poets writing in English often u[se] slant rhymes because English is not a very rhymab[le] language. It has many words that rhyme with [no] other word (*orange*) or with only one other wo[rd] (*mountain/fountain*). Poets interested in how a poe[m] looks on the printed page sometimes use e[ye] **rhymes,** or **visual rhymes**—rhymes involvi[ng] words that are spelled similarly but are pronounc[ed] differently. *Tough/cough* is an eye rhyme. (*Tough/rou[gh]* is a "real" rhyme.)

The pattern of end rhymes in a poem is calle[d a] **rhyme scheme.** To indicate the rhyme scheme [of] a poem, use a separate letter of the alphabet f[or] each rhyme. For example, the rhyme scheme [of] Longfellow's stanza at the left is *aabba.*

See pages 24, 27, 338, 447, 4[..]
See also *Free Verse, Poetry, Rhyth[m]*

RHYTHM **A musical quality produced by t[he] repetition of stressed and unstressed syllab[les] or by the repetition of certain other sound p[at]terns.** Rhythm occurs in all language—written a[nd] spoken—but is particularly important in poetry.

The most obvious kind of rhythm is the regul[ar] pattern of stressed and unstressed syllables that

nd in some poetry. This pattern is called **meter.**
he following lines describing a cavalry charge,
rhythm echoes the galloping of the attackers'
ses:

> ˘ ˘ ′ ˘ ˘ ′ ˘ ˘ ′ ˘ ˘
> The Assyrian came down like the wolf on the
> ⠀⠀′
> ⠀⠀fold,
> ˘ ˘ ′ ˘ ˘ ′ ˘ ˘ ′ ˘ ˘
> And his cohorts were gleaming in purple and
> ⠀⠀′
> ⠀⠀gold;
> ˘ ˘ ′ ˘ ˘ ′ ˘ ˘ ′ ˘
> And the sheen of their spears was like stars on
> ⠀⠀˘ ′
> ⠀⠀the sea,
> ˘ ˘ ′ ˘ ˘ ′ ˘ ˘ ′
> When the blue wave rolls nightly on deep
> ⠀⠀˘ ˘ ′
> ⠀⠀Galilee.
>
> —George Gordon, Lord Byron,
> ⠀⠀from "The Destruction of Sennacherib"

king the stressed (′) and unstressed (˘) syllables
line is called **scanning** the line. Lord Byron's
ned lines show a rhythmic pattern in which two
tressed syllables are followed by a stressed syl-
e. Read the lines aloud and listen to this rhythmic
tern. Also, notice how the poem's end rhymes
create the rhythm.

⠀Writers can also create rhythm by repeating
rds and phrases or even by repeating whole lines
sentences.

> See pages 338, 348, 349.
> See also *Free Verse, Poetry, Rhyme.*

TTING **The time and place in which the
ents of a work of literature take place.** Most
en the setting of a narrative is described early in
story. Setting often contributes to a story's emo-
nal effect. In "Song of the Trees" (page 29), the
est setting helps create a soothing (yet mysteri-
s) mood. Setting frequently plays an important
e in a story's plot, especially one that centers on a
flict between a character and nature. In "Survive
Savage Sea" (page 445), for example, the ship-
ecked Robertson family struggles against the sea.
ne stories are closely tied to particular settings,
it is difficult to imagine them taking place else-

where. By contrast, other stories could easily take
place in a variety of settings.

> See pages 96, 152, 165, 270,
> 273, 348, 605.

SHORT STORY **A fictional prose narrative
that is usually ten to twenty book pages long.**
Short stories were first written in the nineteenth
century. Early short-story writers include Sir Walter
Scott and Edgar Allan Poe. Short stories are usually
built on a plot that consists of at least these bare
bones: the **introduction** or **exposition, conflict,
complications, climax,** and **resolution.** Short
stories are more limited than novels. They usually
have only one or two major characters and one important setting.

> See pages 22–23.
> See also *Conflict, Fiction, Plot.*

SIMILE **A comparison between two unlike
things, using a word such as *like, as, than,* or *resembles.*** The simile is an important type of figure of
speech. In the following lines, a simile creates a clear
image of moths in the evening air:

> When the last bus leaves, moths stream
> ⠀⠀toward lights like litter in wind.
>
> ⠀⠀—Roberta Hill, from "Depot in Rapid City"

This example shows that similes can generate a
strong emotional impact. By choosing to compare
the moths to litter, the poet not only creates a picture in the reader's mind but also establishes a lonely,
dreary mood.

> See pages 168, 171, 520.
> See also *Figure of Speech, Metaphor.*

SPEAKER **The voice talking in a poem.** Sometimes the speaker is identical to the poet, but often
the speaker and the poet are not the same. The poet
may be speaking as a child, a woman, a man, an animal, or even an object.

> See also *Poetry.*

HANDBOOK OF LITERARY TERMS 689

STANZA **In a poem, a group of consecutive lines that forms a single unit.** A stanza in a poem is something like a paragraph in prose; it often expresses a unit of thought. A stanza may consist of any number of lines. "I'm Nobody!" (page 169) consists of two four-line stanzas, each expressing a separate idea. In some poems each stanza has the same rhyme scheme.

See also *Poetry, Rhyme.*

SUSPENSE **The uncertainty or anxiety the reader feels about what will happen next in a story.** In "Three Skeleton Key" (page 65), the narrator hooks the reader's curiosity in the first sentences when he says he is about to describe his "most terrifying experience."

See pages 22, 64, 77, 440.
See also *Foreshadowing.*

SYMBOL **A person, a place, a thing, or an event that has its own meaning *and* stands for something beyond itself as well.** Examples of symbols are all around us—in music, on television, and in everyday conversation. The skull and crossbones, for example, is a symbol of danger; the dove is a symbol of peace; and the red rose stands for true love. In literature, symbols are often more personal. For example, in "Names/Nombres" (page 145), Julia Alvarez's name is a symbol of her cultural identity.

See pages 24, 27.

TALL TALE **An exaggerated, fanciful story that gets "taller and taller," more and more far-fetched, the more it is told and retold.** The tall tale is an American story form. Two famous tall-tale characters are Pecos Bill and Paul Bunyan. Here is a short tall tale:

This artist was so talented that when he painted a dog it bit him. But he should have known better. Earlier he had painted a snowstorm and caught cold.

See also *Folk*

THEME **The idea about life revealed in a w of literature.** A theme is not the same as a sub The subject of a work can usually be expressed word or two: *love, childhood, death.* The theme is idea that the writer wishes to convey about a pa ular subject. The theme must be expressed in at one sentence. For example, the subject of "Pa Parrot" (page 404) is a boy's relationship with hi ther. The story's theme might be this: It is impor to spend time with the people you love.

A story can have several themes, but one often stand out from the others. A work's the are usually not stated directly. The reader ha think about all the elements of the work and them to make an **inference,** or educated gu about what the themes are.

It is not likely that two readers will ever sta theme in exactly the same way. Sometimes rea even differ greatly in their interpretations of the A work of literature can mean different things to ferent people.

See pages 23, 28.

TONE **The attitude that a writer takes tow the audience, a subject, or a character.** Ton conveyed through the writer's choice of words details. The poem "Sarah Cynthia Sylvia St Would Not Take the Garbage Out" (page 257 light and humorous in tone. By contrast, the po "As I Gaze upon My Father" (page 402) is seriou tone.

See pages 226,

PUTTING TOGETHER A MULTIMEDIA PRESENTATION

When people talk about **media,** they mean both print and nonprint ways of communicating. Newspapers, magazines, advertisements, TV, radio, photographs, music videos, movies, and the World Wide Web are just a few of the many media.

The computer industry uses the word **multimedia** to refer to a combination of two or more of the following media:

text: letters and numbers

sound: music; speeches; readings of stories, poems, and plays; sound effects, such as thunder

graphics: drawings, paintings, photographs, charts, maps, patterns, color

video: sections clipped, or copied, from professionally made full-length movies or from videos made with a handheld camcorder

animation: movement of objects and figures on screen

interactivity: constant exchange of information between the computer and the user

People find new ways of working with media all the time. Don't worry if you don't have the latest software and equipment. You can learn a lot by working on both low-tech and high-tech media and multimedia projects. Follow these steps:

1. **Get together with others in a group.** When several students combine their talents and skills, they can often come up with a better product than a student working alone. You can learn a lot about yourself and other people by working with others. Besides, it's often more fun than working by yourself.

2. **Decide what you want to do.** Keep in mind

   • group members' interests and strengths

   • your equipment, tools, software, and hardware

3. **Design the project.** Use a word processing program to make a plan and a schedule. Keep a record of who is supposed to do what and of when each job has to be done.

4. **Create the content.** If you're doing skits based on Greek myths, write a script, make costumes, and find props. If you're doing a multimedia presentation, create or find the text, graphics, and

High Tech

For a **high-tech presentation** including sound, you'll need a computer with a sound card and speakers. Find out if your school has the software you'll need to

• create and edit graphics, video, and sound

• combine all the media you want to include

• make your presentation interactive

Low Tech

Equipment for a **low-tech presentation** might include the following items:

• recorders
• musical instruments
• a copy machine
• an overhead projector
• cameras
• camcorders
• a VCR

sounds you'll need. Check multimedia "galleries" (or graph archives) of paintings on-line and on CD-ROM disk to see if you find scenes from Greek myths. You may be able to find a clip fro performance of Greek folk music. Better yet, if someone in y group plays an instrument, tape the music and use it as backgro for your presentation.

5. **Put it all together.** If you're doing a reading of Native Ameri poems with background music, for example, you may need to h several rehearsals. Try reading the poems in different sequences see which you like best. Ask another group to give you feedback fore you perform in front of the class. If your group would rat not perform live, you could videotape your work. With the r technology, you can turn a live performance into a multimedia p sentation. Just add some graphics and text, and make your progr interactive.

Scanning, Clipping, and Creating

If you have access to a scanner, you can scan photos, artwork, and map well as handwritten and printed material from books, newspapers, magazines. A scanner stores images in a digital format so that they can used on a computer.

You can also find lots of material on the Internet and on CD-RC disks. Multimedia programs give you access to graphics, video, and sou "galleries" from all over the world. If the program allows you to use much material as you want, clip whatever you need.

It may be impossible for you to create certain kinds of material, such nature scenes or news coverage of a historical event. Still, try to cre your own text, graphics, sound, and video whenever you can. You can CD-ROMs of actors reading stories, but why not do your own readin You can find and download text about Virginia Hamilton, but you'll le more about writing if you read two or three articles about her and wr your own text.

Making an Interactive Program

Multimedia or authoring programs show you how to create interact links. You can set up your presentation in either of these ways:

- The user moves from one screen to the next along a path you've out.

- The user has choices about where to go next.

To plan your presentation, try making a flowchart, a map show what's on each screen. Draw a rectangle for each screen and arro showing the paths the user can follow.

esenting Edgar Allan Poe. Suppose your teacher has assigned the
ss to do a project on an American writer. Your group decides to do a
ltimedia presentation on Edgar Allan Poe. The group chooses to in-
de the information laid out in this flowchart, which shows the paths a
er might follow.

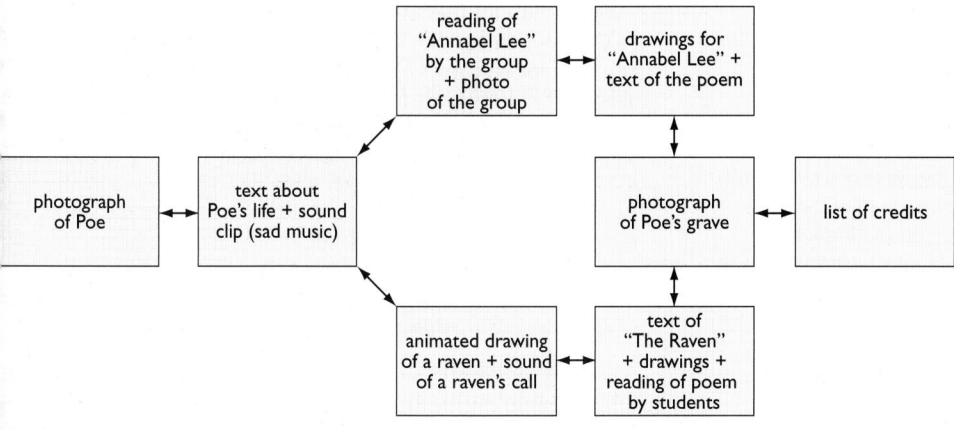

Word Processing

e word processing programs to

create schedules and assignment sheets for your project

type original text, scripts, and programs

correct errors and revise your writing

There's no substitute for peer editing. Spelling checkers and grammar
eckers pick up only certain kinds of errors. Give everyone in the group a
ance to edit your writing. Leave room for comments and questions by
ble-spacing drafts, and make a copy for each group member. Have every-
e put comments on his or her own copy or on screen. Make sure all the
up members are in agreement before you create the final text.

Word processing programs offer many formatting options. You can
oose from a number of type styles and sizes to create different effects.
r example, you may want to use large type for headlines. If you have a
awing program, you can even design your own letters. Word processing
ograms also let you change the margins for parts of your text. For ex-
ple, you may want to leave extra space around an important section.
u can also use lines, boxes, and bullets, or dots, to separate items and
ke them easier to read.

Giving Credit Where It's Due

It's important to give credit
to anyone who contributed
in any way to your presentation. Even if the owner of
the material gave it to you,
you should credit the person who created it. Avoid
plagiarizing (plā′jə·rīz·iŋ),
or passing off others' work
as your own.

You may want to print a
separate page or screen of
credits at the end of your
presentation. See pages
697–698 for information on
writing credits.

The Reference Section

Every library has materials you can use only in the library. These materials include encyclopedias; biographical, scientific, and other types of dictionaries; almanacs; atlases; bibliographies; and **indices** (in′di·sēz′), comprehensive lists of books, magazines, or newspapers arranged by author, title, and subject. These resources often appear in both print and electronic form.

Using a Media Center or Library

To find a book, tape, film, or video in the library, start by looking in t catalog. Most libraries use an **on-line,** or computer, **catalog.**

On-line catalogs vary from library to library. With some you be searching for resources by **title, author,** or **subject.** With others y simply enter **keywords** for the subject you're researching. With eit system, you enter information into the computer and a new screen show you a list of materials or subject headings relating to your reque When you find an item you want, write down the title, author, and **c number,** the code of numbers and letters that shows you where to f the item on the library's shelves.

Some libraries still use card catalogs. A **card catalog** is a collection index cards arranged in alphabetical order by title and author. Nonfict is also cataloged by subject.

Electronic Databases. Electronic databases are collections of inf mation you can access by computer. You can use these databases to f such resources as encyclopedias, almanacs, and museum art collections

There are two kinds of electronic databases. **On-line databases** accessed at a computer terminal connected to a modem. The modem lows the computer to communicate with other computers over telepho lines. **Portable databases** are available on magnetic tape, diskette, CD-ROM.

A **CD-ROM** (compact disk-read only memory) is played on a co puter equipped with a CD-ROM player. If you were to look up *Amy Tan* a CD-ROM guide to literature, for example, you could hear passages fr her books and read critical analyses of her work.

Periodicals. Most libraries have a collection of magazines and news pers. To find up-to-date magazine or newspaper articles on a topic, us computerized index, such as *InfoTrac* or *EBSCO.* Some of these indices p vide a summary of each article. Others provide the entire text, which can read on screen or print out. The *Readers' Guide to Periodical Literatur* a print index of articles that have appeared in hundreds of magazines.

Using the Internet

The **Internet** is a huge network of computers. Libraries, news servic government agencies, researchers, and organizations communicate a share information on the Net. The Net also lets you chat on-line with s dents around the world. For help in using the Internet to do research or communicate with someone by computer, explore the following options

e World Wide Web

easiest way to do research on the Internet is on the World Wide
. On the Web, information is stored in colorful, easy-to-access files
d **Web pages.** Web pages usually have text, graphics, images, sound,
even video clips.

ing a Web Browser

look at Web pages with a **Web browser,** a program for accessing in-
ation on the Web. Every page on the Web has its own address, called
RL, or Uniform Resource Locator. If you know the address of a Web
you want to go to, just enter it in the location field on your browser.
undreds of millions of Web pages are connected by **hyperlinks,**
h let you jump from one page to another. These links are usually un-
ined or colored words or images, or both, on your computer screen.
h hundreds of millions of linked Web pages, how can you find the
rmation you want?

ing a Web Directory

u're just beginning to look for a research topic, click on a **Web direc-**
y, a list of topics and subtopics created by experts to help users find
sites. Think of the directory as a giant index. Start by choosing a
d category, such as Literature. Then, work your way down through
subtopics, perhaps from Poetry to Poets. Under Poets, choose a Web
that looks interesting, perhaps one on Robert Frost.

ing a Search Engine

u already have a topic and need information about it, try using a
rch engine, a software tool that finds information on the Web. To use
arch engine, just go to an on-line search form and enter a **search**
n, or keyword. The search engine will return a list of Web pages con-

taining your search term.
The list will also show you
the first few lines of each
page. A search term such as
Frost may produce thou-
sands of results, or **hits,** including weather data on
frost. If you're doing a search
on the poet Robert Frost,
most of these thousands of
hits will be of no use. To find
useful material, you have to
narrow your search.

"On the Internet, nobody knows you're a dog."

You've Got Mail!

E-mail is an elec-
tronic message sent
over a computer network.
On the Internet you can
use e-mail to reach institutions, businesses, and individuals. When you e-mail
places like museums, you
may be able to ask **experts**
about a topic you're re-
searching. You can also use
e-mail to chat with students
around the country and
around the world.

Internet forums, or
newsgroups, let you discuss
and debate lots of subjects
with other computer users.
You can write and send a
question to a forum and
get an answer from some-
one who may (or may not)
know something about
your topic.

Techno Tip

- If you get too few hits,
use a more general word
as your search term.

- If you get too many hits,
use a more specific word
as your search term.

COMMON SEARCH OPERATORS AND WHAT THEY DO	
AND	Demands that both terms appear on the page; narrows search
+	Demands that both terms appear on the page; narrows search
OR	Yields pages that contain either term; widens search
NOT	Excludes a word from consideration; narrows search
–	Excludes a word from consideration; narrows search
NEAR	Demands that two words be close together; narrows search
ADJ	Demands that two words be close together; narrows search
" "	Demands an exact phrase; narrows search

Techno Tip

To evaluate a Web source, look at the top-level domain in the URL. Here is a sample URL with the top-level domain—a government agency—labeled.

top-level domain

http://www.loc.gov

Refining a Keyword Search

To focus your research, use **search operators,** such as the w AND or NOT, to create a string of keywords. If you're looking material on Robert Frost and his life in Vermont, for example, might enter the following:

Frost AND Vermont NOT weather

The more focused search term yields pages that contain both *F* and *Vermont* and nothing about weather. The chart on the left plains how several search operators work.

Evaluating Sources

Since anyone—even you—can publish a Web page, it's impor to evaluate your sources. Use these criteria to evaluate a sourc

Authority

Who is the author? What is his or her knowledge or experie Trust respected sources, such as the Smithsonian Institution, n person's newsletter or Web page.

Accuracy

How trustworthy is the information? Does the author give his or sources? Check information from one site against information fror least two other sites or print sources.

Objectivity

What is the author's **perspective,** or point of view? Find out whether information provider has a bias or hidden purpose.

Currency

Is the information up-to-date? For a print source, check the copyr date. For a Web source, look for the date on which the page was cre or revised. (This date appears at the bottom of the site's home page.)

Coverage

How well does the source cover the topic? Could you find better infor tion in a book? Compare the source with several others.

sting Sources and Taking Notes

hen you write a research paper, you must **document,** or iden-
, your sources so that readers will know where you found your
terial. You must avoid **plagiarism,** or presenting another
ter's words or ideas as if they were your own.

sting Sources

 each source, and give it a number. (You'll use these source
mbers later, when you take notes.) Here's where to find the pub-
ation information (such as the name of the publisher and the
pyright date) you'll need for different types of sources:

Print sources. Look at the title and copyright pages of the
book or periodical.

On-line sources. Look at the beginning or end of the document or in a separate electronic file. For a Web page, look for a
link containing the word *About*.

Portable electronic databases. Look at the start-up screen,
the packaging, or the disc itself.

ere are several ways to list sources. The chart on page 698
ows the style created by the Modern Language Association.

king Notes

re are some tips for taking notes.

Put notes from different sources on separate index cards, sheets of
paper, or computer files.

At the top of each card, sheet of paper, or file, write a label telling what
that note is about.

At the bottom, write the numbers of the pages on
which you found the information.

Use short phrases, and make lists of details and ideas.
You don't have to write full sentences.

Use your own words unless you find material you want
to quote. If you quote an author's exact words, put
quotation marks around them.

e sample note card at the right shows how to take notes.

eparing a List of Sources

 your source cards to make a **works cited** list, which should appear at
 end of your report. At the top of a sheet of paper, type and center the

COMMON TOP-LEVEL DOMAINS AND WHAT THEY STAND FOR	
.edu	Educational institution. Site may publish scholarly work or the work of elementary or high school students.
.gov	Government body. Information is generally reliable.
.org	Usually a nonprofit organiza-tion. If the organization pro-motes culture (as a museum does), information is generally reliable; if it advocates a cause, information may be biased.
.com	Commercial enterprise. Infor-mation should be evaluated carefully.
.net	Organization offering Internet services. Information is gener-ally reliable.

Sample Note Card

Poe's Childhood and Youth	1
—Parents were actors—father deserted family, mother died before Poe's 3rd birthday	
—Raised by Frances and John Allan	
—Published first poems at age 18	p. 20

Penmanship: Writing Legibly
Remind students to keep notes cards
legible by printing instead of using cursive writing.

heading *Works Cited.* Below it, list your sources in alphabetical order. F
low the MLA guidelines for citing sources (see the chart below). The sa
ple works cited list below shows you how to do this.

Sample Works Cited List

Anderson, M. K. Edgar Allan Poe: A Mystery. New York: Franklin Watts
    1993.
"The Life of a Poet." Edgar Allan Poe Historic Site Home Page. 1997.
    15 Dec. 1997 <http://www.nps.gov/edal/brochure.htm>.
"Poe, Edgar Allan." The World Book Encyclopedia. 1996 ed.

The chart below shows citations of print, audiovisual, and electronic sourc

MLA GUIDELINES FOR CITING SOURCES	
Books	Give the author, title, city of publication, publisher, and copyright year. Anderson, M. K. Edgar Allan Poe: A Mystery. New York: Franklin Watts, 1993.
Magazine and newspaper articles	Give the author (if named), title of the article, name of the magazine or newspaper, date, and page numbers. "Did Rabies Fell Edgar Allan Poe?" Science News 2 Nov. 1996: 282.
Encyclopedia articles	Give the author (if named), title of the article, name of the encyclopedia, and edition (year). "Poe, Edgar Allan." The World Book Encyclopedia. 1996 ed.
Interviews	Give the expert's name, the words *Personal interview* or *Telephone interview,* and the date. M. K. Anderson. Telephone interview. 12 Jan. 1998.
Films, videotapes, and audiotapes	Give the title; producer, director, or developer; medium; distributor; and year of release. Edgar Allan Poe: Terror of the Soul. Prod. Film Odyssey. Videocassette. PBS Home Video, 1995.
Electronic materials, including CD-ROMs and on-line sources	Give the author (if named); title; title of project, database, periodical, or site; electronic posting date (on-line); type of source (CD-ROMs); city (CD-ROMs); distributor (CD-ROMs); publication date (CD-ROMs) or access date; and Internet address (if any). "Poe, Edgar Allan." Grolier Multimedia Encyclopedia. CD-ROM. Danbury: Grolier Interactive, 1993. "The Life of a Poet." Edgar Allan Poe Historic Home Site Page. 1997. 15 Dec. 199 <http://www.nps.gov/edal/brochure.htm>.

READING STRATEGIES

Using Word Parts

Many English words can be divided into parts. If you know the meaning
various word parts, you can often determine the meanings of words.

A word part added to the beginning of a word or root is called a **prefix**. A word part added to the end of a word or root is called a **suffix**. Prefixes and suffixes can't stand alone. They must be added to words or other word parts.

A **base word** can stand alone. It is a complete word all by itself, although other word parts may be added to it to make new words.

Prefix	Base Word	Suffix	New Word
il–	legal	–ly	illegally
re–	arrange	–ment	rearrangement

Roots, like prefixes and suffixes, usually can't stand alone. Roots can combine with one or more word parts to form words.

Word Root	Meaning	Examples
–aud–	to hear	audition, auditorium
–port–	to carry	portable, transport
–pend–	to hang	depend, pendulum

COMMONLY USED PREFIXES		
Prefix	**Meaning**	**Examples of Prefix + Base Words**
anti–	against, opposing	antifreeze, antibiotic
bi–	two	biplane, biweekly
co–	with, together	cooperate, coauthor
dis–	away, expel from, opposing	dislocate, disagreement
in–	not	incredible, independent
inter–	between, among	international, interchangeable
mis–	badly, not, wrongly	misbehave, misuse
non–	not	nonprofit, nonsensical
post–	after, following	postgraduate, postwar
pre–	before	precaution, prefix
re–	back, again	review, rewind
semi–	half, partly	semicircle, semifinal
sub–	under, beneath	submarine, subway
trans–	across, beyond	transaction, transatlantic
un–	not, reverse of	unsure, untie

Understanding Influences of Other Languages on the Spelling of English

In addition to knowing the meaning of these prefixes, students should understand that their spelling can also often offer clues to meaning and that they should learn to look for **spelling-meaning relationships.** For example, *in–*, a prefix that comes from Latin, means "not." This prefix takes other forms or spellings depending on the consonant that it precedes. However, its meaning remains the same. Explain to students that *in–* becomes *il–* before *l* (*illogical, illegal*), *im–* before *m* and *p* (*immortal, impure*), and *ir–* before *r* (*irregular, irrational*). In each case, regardless of spelling, the meaning is "not." Ask students to check a dictionary for several more words that have absorbed the prefix *in–* into the base word (*illegible, illiterate, immature, improper, irreverence, irreversible*).

Using Structural Analysis to Identify Words: Greek Suffixes

A knowledge of common Greek suffixes can help students unlock the meaning of a variety of words. Students will frequently encounter these Greek suffixes:

Suffix	Meaning	Example
–ician	specialist in	beautician
–ine	chemical substance	chlorine
–oid	resembling	humanoid
–phobia	fear of	claustrophobia

Ask students to think of at least one more word using each suffix.

Organizing Information

Remind students to use outlining, para-phrasing, and summarizing as means of organizing and assimilating information. Outlining can help them clarify the relationship between ideas. Paraphrasing can help them break down and organize complicated ideas. Summarizing allows them to condense information and make decisions about what is important.

STORY MAP
Basic situation:
Setting:
Main character:
His or her problem:
Main events or complications:
Climax:
Resolution:

COMMONLY USED SUFFIXES		
Suffix	**Meaning**	**Examples of Base Words + Suffix**
–able	able, tending to, worthy of	dependable, laughable
–ate	become, cause to be	domesticate, motivate
–dom	state, condition	boredom, wisdom
–en	become, cause to be	deepen, awaken
–ful	full of, characterized by	thankful, beautiful
–hood	condition, quality	brotherhood, neighborhood
–ion	action, condition	celebration, education
–ize	become, make, cause to be	civilize, legalize
–ly	in a certain way	timely, quickly
–ment	result, action	punishment, enjoyment
–ness	quality, state	happiness, selfishness
–or	one who	director, liberator
–ous	characterized by	dangerous, glorious
–ship	condition, state	ownership, relationship
–y	full of, characterized by, tending to	sandy, easy, sleepy

Summarizing, Paraphrasing, and Outlining

When you finish reading a text, check your understanding by writing **summary,** a short restatement of the important ideas and details work. There are many ways to summarize; use the one that works bes the type of text you've read. For a short story, use a **story map** like one shown at the left.

For a poem, try writing a **paraphrase.** In a paraphrase you exp every idea, line by line, in your own words. Here is a paraphrase of a p by Emily Dickinson:

Poem	Paraphrase
Fame is a bee. It has a song— It has a sting— Ah, too, it has a wing.	Fame is like a bee because it ha its joy, like the happy buzzing of bee (the bee's "song"); it can hu other people, the way a bee sti can hurt; and it can disappear, j as a bee can fly off.

or a work of nonfiction, make an **outline** showing the **main ideas**
supporting details:

Main idea
A. Supporting detail
  1. Supporting detail
    a. Supporting detail

STUDY SKILLS

...ing a Dictionary

...can use a print or electronic dictionary to find the precise meaning
...usage of words. The elements of a typical entry are explained below.

- **Entry word.** The entry word shows how a word is spelled and how it is divided into syllables. It may also show capitalization and alternative spellings.

- **Pronunciation.** Phonetic symbols and **diacritical marks** (symbols added to letters) show how to pronounce the entry word. A key to these symbols usually appears on every other page.

- **Part-of-speech label.** This label shows how the entry word is used in a sentence. Some words may function as more than one part of speech. For words like these, a part-of-speech label is provided before each set of definitions.

- **Other forms.** The spellings of plural forms of nouns, the principal parts of verbs, and the comparative and superlative forms of adjectives and adverbs are shown.

- **Word origin.** A word's origin, or **etymology** (et′ə·mäl′ə·jē), is its history. It tells how the word or its parts entered the English language. In the example shown, the etymology traces the word *escape* from Middle English (ME), Norman French (NormFr), and Vulgar, or everyday, Latin (VL) to its origins in the Latin (L) word part *ex–* (out of) and the Late Latin (LL) word *cappa* (cloak).

Sample Dictionary Entry

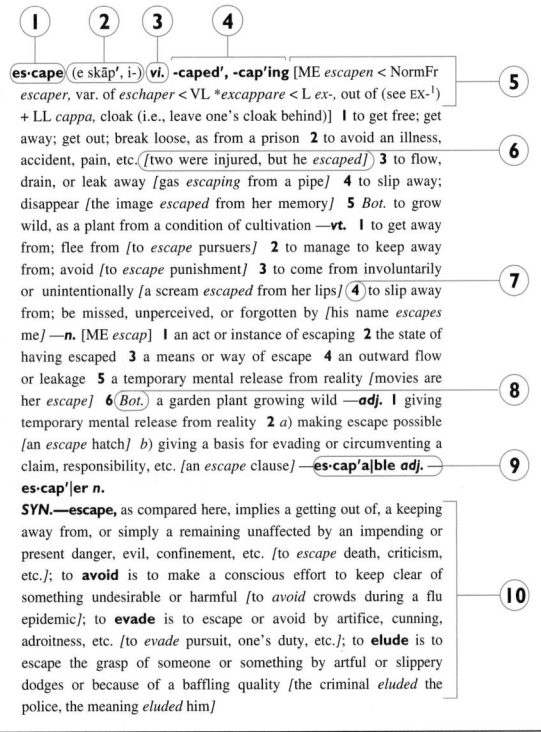

©1994 *Webster's New World Dictionary of American English,* Third College Edition.

Using the Glossary to Find Pronunciations

Have students turn to the guide to pronunciation symbols that appears at the bottom of each right-hand Glossary page, starting on p. 789. Have them practice using the guide's phonetic symbols and diacritical marks to sound out several Glossary words that they know how to pronounce. Then, tell them that the guide's words and symbols will help them decode unfamiliar words. Suggest an unfamiliar word, and have students work as a class to sound it out using the guide's pronunciation symbols.

6. **Examples.** Phrases or sentences show how the word is used.

7. **Definitions.** If a word has more than one meaning, the mea[n]
   are numbered or lettered.

8. **Special-usage labels.** These labels identify special meaning[s]
   special uses of the word.

9. **Related word forms.** These are other forms of the entry w[ord]
   usually created by the addition of suffixes.

10. **Synonyms and antonyms.** Synonyms (words similar in mea[ning])
    and antonyms (words opposite in meaning) may appear at the [end]
    of an entry.

Using a Thesaurus

A **thesaurus** is a collection of synonyms. You use a thesaurus when y[ou]
looking for a word that expresses a specific meaning. There are two k[inds]
of thesauruses. One kind, developed by Peter Mark Roget, groups w[ords]
according to meaning. Here's how to use it:

- In the index, look up the word that conveys your general mea[ning]
  Under FREE, for example, you might find *escape, freedom, liberty,*
  will. Each of these subentries is followed by a number.

- Choose the subentry whose meaning is closest to what you ha[ve]
  mind. In this case, suppose you choose *escape.*

- In the body of the text, find the number that follows the sube[ntry]
  escape in the index. Then, look under this number to find synonym[s]
  escape.

The second kind of thesaurus lists words in alphabetical order, as in a [dic]
tionary. See the sample entry below.

Sample Thesaurus Entry

---

shun, *v.* —*SYN.* dodge, evade, keep away from, ignore, neglect; see also
avoid. —*ANT.* accept, ADOPT, take advantage of.

©1997 *Webster's New World Thesaurus,* Third Edition.

ading Maps, Charts, and Graphs

pes of Maps

ysical maps show the natural landscape of an area. In these maps, ding is often used to show physical features like mountains, hills, and eys; colors are often used to show **elevation** (height above or below level). **Political maps** show political units, such as states and nations. y usually show borders and capitals. The map of Canada, the United tes, and Mexico shown here is a political map. **Special-purpose maps** used to present information such as the routes of explorers. The liter-map on pages 498–499 is a special-purpose map.

w to Read a Map

. **Identify the map's focus.** The map's title and labels tell you its focus—its subject and the geographical area it covers.

. **Study the legend.** The **legend,** or **key,** explains the symbols, lines, colors, and shading used in the map. (The map on this page has a legend.)

. **Check directions and distances.** Maps often include a **compass rose,** a diagram that shows north, south, east, and west. If you're looking at a map that doesn't have one, assume that north is at the top, west is to the left, and so on. Many maps also include a **scale** to help you relate distances on the map to actual distances. Note the compass rose and scale on the map on this page.

. **Look at the larger context.** The **absolute location** of any place on earth is given by its **latitude** (the number of degrees north or south of the equator) and **longitude** (the number of degrees east or west of the **prime meridian,** or 0 degrees longitude). Some maps also include **locator maps,** which show the area depicted in relation to a larger area. Notice the locator map in the upper right corner of the map shown here.

Penmanship: Writing Legibly

If students create their own graphs for reports or presentations, remind them that their visual aids will be more legible if they print instead of using cursive writing.

Line Graph

People in My Town Speaking Two or More Languages Fluently

Bar Graph

Venomous Snakes

Pie Graph

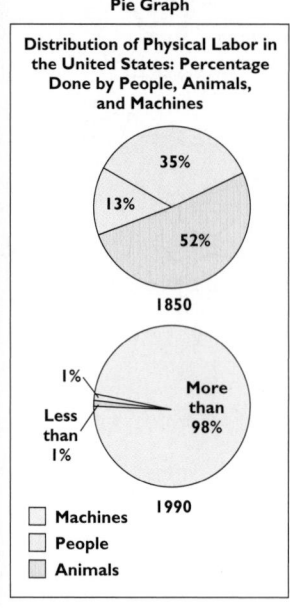

Distribution of Physical Labor in the United States: Percentage Done by People, Animals, and Machines

35%
13%
52%

1850

1%
Less than 1%
More than 98%

1990

☐ Machines
☐ People
☐ Animals

Types of Charts and Graphs

A **flowchart** shows a **sequence** of events or the steps in a process. F[...] charts are often used to show cause-and-effect relationships. The sequ[...]ing chart on page 433 is an example of a flowchart. A **time line** sh[...] events in **chronological order** (the order in which they happened).

| | Langston Hughes born 1902 | | Julia Alvarez born 1950 |

1825

1830 Emily Dickinson born

1899 Ernest Hemingway born

1905 Ernesto Galarza born

195[...] An[...] Ta[...] bor[...]

A **table** presents categorized facts arranged in rows and column[...] make them easy to understand and compare. The table on page 497, [...] example, shows the Greek and Roman names of mythological gods [...] goddesses and their areas of power.

Line graphs usually show changes in quantity over time. In line gra[...] dots showing the quantity at different times are connected to create a [...] **Bar graphs** generally compare quantities within categories. **Pie gra**[...] or **circle graphs,** show proportions. A pie graph is a circle divided [...] different-sized sections, like slices of a pie.

How to Read a Chart or a Graph

1. **Read the title.** The title tells you the subject and purpose of [...] chart or graph.

2. **Read the labels.** The labels tell you what type of informatio[...] presented.

3. **Analyze the details.** Read numbers carefully. Note increase[...] decreases. Look for the direction or order of events and for tre[...] and relationships.

STRATEGIES FOR TAKING TESTS

When you begin a test, **scan** it quickly and count the items. Then, de[...] how to spend your time. Here are some sample test questions and spe[...] strategies for answering four kinds of test questions.

True/false questions ask you to determine whether a given stateme[...] true or false. For example:

1. T F   Ernesto Galarza was born in Mexico but moved to [...] United States as a young boy.

HOW TO ANSWER TRUE/FALSE QUESTIONS

Read the statement carefully. The whole statement is false if any part of it is false.

Look for words like *always* and *never*. A statement is true only if it is always true.

Multiple-choice questions ask you to select a correct answer from several choices. For example:

1. The theme of a story is its

   A subject   **C** conflict
   B message   **D** setting

HOW TO ANSWER MULTIPLE-CHOICE QUESTIONS

Make sure you understand the question or statement before you look at the choices.

Look for words such as *not* and *always,* which may help you eliminate some choices.

Read all the choices before selecting an answer. Eliminate choices that you know are incorrect.

Think carefully about the remaining choices. Pick the one that makes the most sense.

Matching questions ask you to match the items in one list with the items in another list. For example:

Directions: Match each item in the left-hand column with its definition in the right-hand column.

__ **1.** setting   **A** story of a person's life

__ **2.** biography   **B** language that appeals to the senses

__ **3.** metaphor   **C** time and place of a literary work

__ **4.** imagery   **D** comparison between unlike things

HOW TO ANSWER MATCHING QUESTIONS

Read the directions carefully. Not all the items in one column may be used, and items may be used more than once.

Scan the columns. First, match items you are sure of. Then, match items you are less sure of.

For the rest of the items, make your best guess.

Analogy questions ask you to figure out the relationship betw[een]
two words and then identify another pair with a similar relationship.
example:

Directions: Select the best pair of words that best completes the ana[logy.]

SENTENCE : PARAGRAPH : : _____

A noun : verb   **C** essay : paragraph
B paragraph : essay   **D** poetry : nonfiction

HOW TO ANSWER ANALOGY QUESTIONS

- Figure out the relationship between the words in the first pair. (In the example, a sentence is part of a paragraph.)

- Express the analogy in a statement or question. (A sentence is part of [a] paragraph. In what other pair is the first item part of the second item?[)]

- Select the pair of words with the same relationship as the first pair. (A paragraph is part of an essay.)

Essay questions in a test ask you to think critically about things you [have]
learned and to express your understanding in a paragraph or more.

ESSAY QUESTIONS

Key Verb	Task	Sample Question
analyze	Take something apart to see how it works.	Analyze the character of Cassie in "Song of the Trees."
compare	Discuss likenesses. (Sometimes *compare* means "compare *and* contrast.")	Compare the theme of "A Mason-Dixon Memory" with that of *Brian's Song*.
contrast	Discuss differences.	Contrast the fairy tale "Cinderella" with the German folk tale "Aschenputtel."
define	Give specific details that make something unique.	Define the term *onomatopoeia*.
describe	Give a picture in words.	Describe the setting of "Bargain."
discuss	Examine in detail.	Discuss the theme of "Amigo Brothers."
explain	Give reasons for something.	Explain why foreshadowing creates suspense.
identify	Discuss specific characteristics.	Identify the rhyme scheme of "The Runaway."
list (*also* outline *or* trace)	Give all steps in order or certain details about a subject.	List the main parts of a plot.
summarize	Briefly review the main points.	Summarize the plot of "Rikki-tikki-tavi."

WRITING FOR LIFE

Writing Business Letters

To request information from someone who is far away or difficult to reach, write a business letter. Follow these guidelines:

1. **Write in formal English.** Avoid slang. The tone of your letter should be polite and respectful.

2. **Be clear.** Explain why you are writing. Include important information, and be as brief as possible.

3. **Make the letter look professional.** Type, print, or write your letter on unlined 8½- × 11-inch paper. Follow the **block form** (shown below).

Sample Business Letter

794 South Hillside Avenue
Glendale, MO 63122

November 14, 1999

Ms. Pilar Lopez
Executive Director
Glendale Chamber of Commerce
192 Claymore Street
Glendale, MO 63123

Dear Ms. Lopez:

I am researching the history of our town. I would like to know who first settled the town and why they chose this location.

Please send me any information that might help me with my research. I have enclosed a self-addressed, stamped envelope for your reply.

Sincerely,

Douglas Davidson

Douglas Davidson

1 Heading
Your street address
Your city, state, and ZIP code
The date you write the letter

2 Inside Address
The name and address of the person you are writing to. Use a title like *Mr., Ms.,* or *Mrs.* or a professional title, such as *Dr.* or *Professor,* before the person's name. Put the person's business title after the name.

3 Salutation (greeting)
End the salutation with a colon.

4 Body
Your message. If the body is more than one paragraph long, leave an extra line between paragraphs.

5 Closing
Use *Yours truly* or *Sincerely,* followed by a comma.

6 Signature
Type or print your name, leaving space for your signature. Sign your name in ink below the closing.

Reading to Take Action: Filling Out Forms

After students have read about how to fill out a form, ask them to bring to class a variety of forms to complete. For example, they might bring in subscription forms for newspapers and magazines, job applications from the local employment office, or an application for a library card. Have students work in small groups to fill out the forms. You might also want to have students practice filling out the form below.

INFORMATION FORM

NAME _____

NICKNAME _____

PHONE # _____

ADDRESS _____

_____

PARENT OR GUARDIAN _____

_____

Filling Out Forms

When you fill out a form, your purpose is to give clear, complete infor‍mation. Follow these guidelines whenever you complete forms.

1. Look over the entire form before you begin.

2. Look for and follow special instructions (such as *Type or print or a pencil*).

3. Read each item carefully.

4. Supply all the information requested. If a question does not apply you, write *does not apply,* or use a dash or the abbreviation N (meaning "not applicable").

5. When you're finished, make sure nothing is left blank. Also, ch for errors and correct them neatly.

6. Mail the form to the correct address or give it to the right perso

PROOFREADERS' MARKS

Symbol	Example	Meaning
≡	Fifty-first street	Capitalize lowercase letter.
/	Sally's Aunt	Lowercase capital letter.
∧	the capital *of* Maine	Insert.
⌒	What's the the deal?	Delete.
⌒	a broken flower pot	Close up space.
∿	believe	Change order (of letters or words
¶	¶"Goodbye," she said.	Begin a new paragraph.
⊙	Stay well⊙	Add a period.
⋏	Of course⋏you may be wrong.	Add a comma.

THE PARTS OF SPEECH

THE NOUN

A *noun* is a word used to name a person, a place, a thing, or an idea.

PERSONS	giant, Miss Nettie Hopley, baby sitter, immigrant
PLACES	pasture, Italy, Sutter's Fort, Crocker Art Gallery
THINGS	quilt, key, frog, desk, Newbery Medal, *Voyager 2*
IDEAS	knowledge, friendliness, success, love, self-esteem

Compound Nouns

A *compound noun* is two or more words used together as a single noun. The parts of a compound noun may be written as one word, as separate words, or as a hyphenated word.

ONE WORD	butterfly, playground, Passover, classroom
SEPARATE WORDS	Golden Age, compact disc, post office
HYPHENATED WORD	self-control, bull's-eye, six-year-old

TIPS FOR SPELLING

Compound words may be written as one word, as separate words, or as a hyphenated word. To be sure you are spelling a compound word correctly, always use a current dictionary.

Collective Nouns

A *collective noun* is a word that names a group.

EXAMPLES   class   family   choir   herd   jury

Common Nouns and Proper Nouns

A *common noun* is a general name for a person, a place, a thing, or an idea. A *proper noun* names a particular person, place, thing, or idea. Proper nouns always begin with a capital letter. Common nouns begin with a capital letter in titles and when they begin sentences.

COMMON NOUNS	poem	nation	day
PROPER NOUNS	"The Runaway"	Japan	Friday

QUICK CHECK 1

Identify the nouns in the following sentences. Classify each noun as common or proper. Also label any *compound* or *collective* nouns.

EXAMPLE   1. "Rikki-tikki-tavi" is a short story by Rudyard Kipling.
1. *"Rikki-tikki-tavi"—compound, proper; short story— compound, common; Rudyard Kipling—compound, proper*

Resources
- *Language Handbook Worksheets,* pp. 1–14
- *Language Workshop CD-ROM,* Chapter 1: Parts of Speech

LANGUAGE HANDBOOK

1. Rikki-tikki-tavi—compound, proper; pet—common; family—collective, common; India—proper
2. mongoose—common; Rikki-tikki—compound, proper; fear—common
3. teeth—common; person—common
4. cobra—common; bathroom—compound, common
5. lives—common; Teddy—proper; family—common

Try It Out: Possible Answers

1. As Cinderella wept under a willow tree, a fairy godmother suddenly appeared.
2. She waved a magic wand.
3. A pumpkin turned into a coach.
4. With another wave of the fairy godmother's wand, Cinderella's torn rags turned into a beautiful gown.
5. Overjoyed, Cinderella thanked the fairy godmother and rode to the ball at the castle.

Try It Out ✎

In the following paragraph, replace the vague nouns with exact, specific nouns.

[1] As a girl wept under a tree, a woman suddenly appeared. [2] She waved a magic stick. [3] A vegetable turned into a vehicle. [4] With another movement of the woman's stick, the girl's torn clothing turned into a beautiful dress. [5] Overjoyed, the girl thanked the woman and rode to the party at the building.

> **NOTE** Some authorities prefer to call possessive forms of pronouns (such as *my, his,* and *their*) *possessive adjectives.* Follow your teacher's instructions regarding possessive forms.

---

1. Rikki-tikki-tavi is the brave pet of a family in India.
2. A fierce little mongoose, Rikki-tikki knows no fear.
3. Although his teeth are sharp, he would never bite a person.
4. Instead, he kills a deadly cobra in the bathroom.
5. He saves the lives of Teddy and his family.

Using Specific Nouns

Whenever possible, use specific, exact nouns. Using specific nouns will make your writing more accurate as well as more interesting.

NONSPECIFIC   Animals drank from the water.
SPECIFIC   Horses, cattle, and burros drank from the creek.

THE PRONOUN

1b.   A *pronoun* is a word used in place of one or more nouns pronouns.

EXAMPLES   Emily Dickinson took few trips; Dickinson spent most of Dickinson's time at Amherst.
Emily Dickinson took few trips; **she** spent most of **her** time at Amherst.

The word that a pronoun stands for is called its *antecedent.* The antecedent is not always stated.

STATED   Dickinson wrote many **poems** and hid **them** in her room.
UNSTATED   **Who** edited *The Poems of Emily Dickinson?*

Personal Pronouns

A *personal pronoun* refers to the one speaking (*first person*), the one spoken to (*second person*), or the one spoken about (*third person*).

PERSONAL PRONOUNS		
	SINGULAR	**PLURAL**
First Person	I, me, my, mine	we, us, our, ours
Second Person	you, your, yours	you, your, yours
Third Person	he, him, his, she, her, hers, it, its	they, them, their, theirs

flexive and Intensive Pronouns

flexive pronoun refers to the subject and directs the action of the **·** back to the subject. An *intensive pronoun* emphasizes a noun or **ther** pronoun. Reflexive and intensive pronouns have the same form.

FIRST PERSON   myself, ourselves

:OND PERSON   yourself, yourselves

HIRD PERSON   himself, herself, itself, themselves

LEXIVE   Emily Dickinson wrote **herself** notes on the backs of recipes.

ENSIVE   She did all the baking **herself.**

·monstrative Pronouns

·emonstrative pronoun (*this, that, these, those*) points out a person, a **·e**, a thing, or an idea.

·AMPLE   **This** is a collection of her poems.

·errogative Pronouns

·interrogative pronoun (*what, which, who, whom, whose*) introduces a **·stion.**

·AMPLE   **What** were Dickinson's household duties?

·lative Pronouns

·elative pronoun (*that, what, which, who, whom, whose*) introduces a **·ordinate** clause.

·AMPLE   Dickinson wrote of thoughts and feelings **that** she had.

·definite Pronouns

·indefinite pronoun refers to a person, a place, or a thing that is not **·cifically** named. Many indefinite pronouns can also serve as adjectives.

Common Indefinite Pronouns				
all	each	few	no one	several
any	either	many	nobody	some
both	everything	none	one	somebody

·ONOUN   **Neither** of Emily's sisters was aware of the poems.

·JECTIVE   **Neither** sister was aware of the poems.

QUICK CHECK 2

·ntify each of the pronouns in the following sentences as *personal,*
·exive, intensive, demonstrative, interrogative, relative,* or *indefinite.*

☞ *This, that, these,* and *those* can also be used as adjectives. See page 713.

☞ See pages 746–750 for more on subordinate clauses.

Quick Check 2: Answers

1. you—personal
2. herself—intensive; that—relative; she—personal
3. who—interrogative; her—personal
4. you—personal; this—demonstrative; your—personal; some—indefinite; her—personal
5. You—personal; yourself—reflexive; someone—indefinite; them—personal

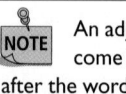

NOTE An adjective may come before or after the word it modifies.

EXAMPLES **Each one** of the guests ate **steamed fish.** [The adjective *each* modifies *one.* The adjective *steamed* modifies *fish.*]
The **minister, proper and dignified,** was also **courteous.** [The adjectives *proper, dignified,* and *courteous* modify *minister.*]

EXAMPLE 1. I wonder about anyone who is famous.
    1. *I—personal; anyone—indefinite; who—relative*

1. Are you famous or important?
2. Emily Dickinson herself declared that she wasn't.
3. Yet, who doesn't recognize her name today?
4. If you don't, this is your chance to read some of her poems.
5. You can decide for yourself if someone important wrote them.

THE ADJECTIVE

1c. An *adjective* is a word used to modify a noun or a pronoun.

To **modify** a word means to describe the word or to make its meaning more definite. An adjective modifies a word by telling *what kind, which one, how much,* or *how many.*

WHAT KIND?	WHICH ONE?	HOW MUCH? or HOW MANY?
noisy relatives	*those* days	*many* years
proper manners	*another* skirt	*more* guests
Mexican food	*next* lesson	*one* mistake

Articles

The most frequently used adjectives are *a, an,* and *the.* These adjectives are called **articles.** The adjectives *a* and *an* are **indefinite articles.** Each one indicates that the noun refers to someone or something in general. *A* is used before a word beginning with a consonant sound. *An* is used before a word beginning with a vowel sound.

EXAMPLES **An** early gift later caused Tan **an** embarrassing moment.
    Her mother gave her **a** miniskirt.
    It took him **an** hour to find **a** uniform that fit.

The adjective *the* is a **definite article.** It indicates that the noun refers to someone or something in particular.

EXAMPLE **The** minister's son attended **the** potluck dinner.

Proper Adjectives

A *proper adjective* is formed from a proper noun and begins with a capital letter.

PROPER NOUNS	PROPER ADJECTIVES
China	**Chinese** customs
America	**American** manners
Buddhist	**Buddhist** monk
Christmas	**Christmas** dinner

> NOTE Some proper nouns, such as *Buddhist,* do not change spelling when they are used as adjectives.

Demonstrative Adjectives

This, that, these, and *those* can be used as adjectives and as pronouns. When these words modify a noun or a pronoun, they are called **demonstrative adjectives.** When used alone, these words are called **demonstrative pronouns.**

DEMONSTRATIVE ADJECTIVES	Is **this** story more interesting than **that** one? **Those** dishes are considered a delicacy.
DEMONSTRATIVE PRONOUNS	**That** is the way to hold chopsticks. Are **these** typical foods in China?

☞ For more about demonstrative pronouns, see page 711.

Nouns Used as Adjectives

When a noun modifies another noun or a pronoun, it is considered an adjective. Most compound nouns can be used as adjectives.

NOUNS	NOUNS USED AS ADJECTIVES
fish	**fish** scales
holiday	**holiday** menu
bicycle	**bicycle** tires
Christmas Eve	**Christmas Eve** celebration

QUICK CHECK 3

Identify each adjective in the following sentences. Then, give the word the adjective modifies. Do not include the articles *a, an,* and *the.*

EXAMPLE 1. That name sounds strange to me.
   1. *That—name; strange—name*

Having an unusual name can be a problem for anyone. That problem plagued Julia Alvarez all through school. As a girl, she was known by many names—Judy, Jules, and even Alcatraz—but her family pronounced *Julia* "Hoo-lee-ah." Those neighbors with a New York City accent said "Joo-lee-ah." Family members told her to keep writing and her name would be famous.

Quick Check 3: Answers
1. unusual—name
2. That—problem
3. many—names; her—family
4. Those—neighbors; New York City—accent
5. Family—members; her—name; famous—name

1d. A *verb* is a word used to express action or a state of bei◼

EXAMPLES   Gary Soto **wrote** "The No-Guitar Blues."
                Soto's stories **seem** realistic to me.

Every sentence must have a subject and a verb. The verb says something about the subject.

Action Verbs

1e. An *action verb* may express physical action or mental
action.

PHYSICAL ACTION   lean, watch, hop, say, push, toss, pull
MENTAL ACTION   want, hope, regret, wonder, forget, dream

Transitive and Intransitive Verbs

(1) A *transitive verb* is an action verb that expresses an action
directed toward a person or thing.

EXAMPLE   He **held** a guitar. [The action of *held* is directed toward
               guitar.]

With transitive verbs, the action passes from the doer (the subject)
the receiver of the action. Words that receive the action of a transitive
verb are called *objects*.

EXAMPLES   She called **him**. [*Him* is the object of the verb *called.*
             The boy told the **villagers** a **lie**. [Both *villagers* and *l*◼
             are objects of the verb *told.*]

(2) An *intransitive verb* expresses action (or tells something
about the subject) without passing the action to a receive◼

EXAMPLE   Fausto **waited** hopefully for a reward. [The action of
               waited is not directed toward a receiver. The verb
               waited does not have an object.]

Linking Verbs

1f. A *linking verb* links, or connects, the subject with a noun
pronoun, or an adjective in the predicate.

EXAMPLES   The dog's name **was** Roger. [name = Roger]
             Los Lobos **became** Fausto's role models. [Los Lobos =
             role models]

☞ For more about subjects and verbs, see pages 720–723 and 751–753.

☞ For more information about objects, see page 755.

 A verb may be transitive in one sentence and intransitive in another.

TRANSITIVE He **smelled** his grandfather's aftershave.

INTRANSITIVE Grandfather **smelled** good.

intransitive verbs, linking verbs never take direct objects.

Linking Verbs Formed from the Verb Be			
am	were	should have been	was being
are	be	will have been	can be
being	been	has been	must be
is	may be	have been	might be
was	would be	will be	could be

her Linking Verbs appear, grow, seem, stay, become, look,
ll, taste, feel, remain, sound, turn

lping Verbs

A *helping verb (auxiliary verb)* helps the main verb to
express an action or a state of being.

MPLES **could** be **may have** asked **might have been** caught

COMMONLY USED HELPING VERBS	
orms of *Be*	am, be, being, was, are, been, is, were
orms of *Do*	do, does, did
orms of *Have*	have, has, had
Other Helping Verbs	can, may, must, should, would, could, might, shall, will

A *verb phrase* consists of a main verb and at least one helping verb.

AMPLE Fausto **could have kept** the money. [The main verb is
kept.]

QUICK CHECK 4

ntify the italicized verb in each of the following sentences as an *action*
, a *linking verb,* or a *helping verb.* Then, for each action verb, tell
ether the verb is *transitive* or *intransitive.*

AMPLE 1. Have you *read* other poems by Shel Silverstein?
    1. *action verb, transitive*

Sarah Cynthia Sylvia Stout would not *take* the trash out.
It *smelled* bad.
She *did*n't care about that or about her family or friends.
Finally, she *was* alone with her garbage.
That huge pile of garbage *reached* to another state.

☞ See pages 756–757
for more information
about linking verbs.

 NOTE Some words may
be either action
verbs or linking verbs, depending on how they are
used.

LINKING The dog
looked hungry.

ACTION The dog
looked for another
orange peel.

 NOTE Sometimes the
verb phrase is in-
terrupted by other words.

EXAMPLES **Will** you
please **explain** the
theme of this story?
Fausto **did** not [*or* **did**n't]
tell the dog's owners
the truth.

☞ For more informa-
tion about verb phrases,
see pages 720, 741, and
752.

Quick Check 4: Answers
1. action verb, transitive
2. linking verb
3. helping verb
4. linking verb
5. action verb, intransitive

Quick Check 5: Answers
1. sadly—cried
2. Too—soon; soon—sailed
3. not—would yield; most—desperate
4. harder—tried
5. Eventually—rescued

Try It Out: Possible Answers
1. wonderfully
2. refreshingly
3. completely
4. Rather
5. truly

 NOTE Adverbs may come before, after, or between the words they modify.

EXAMPLES **Slowly**, the shark was circling.

The shark was **slowly** circling.

The shark was circling **slowly.**

☞ For more on modifiers in general, see Part 5: Using Modifiers.

Try It Out ✎

For each use of *very* below, substitute another adverb. You may wish to revise the sentence.

1. For entertainment, they imagined *very* delicious foods.
2. Douglas dreamed of a *very* cold honeydew melon.
3. At night on the sea, they felt *very* alone.
4. *Very* quickly, they pulled the sea turtle aboard.
5. After their rescue, a *very* fine cook helped them back to health.

THE ADVERB

1h. An *adverb* is a word used to modify a verb, an adjective, another adverb.

MODIFYING A VERB	They could **not** radio for help.
MODIFYING AN ADJECTIVE	The sun was **extremely** hot.
MODIFYING ANOTHER ADVERB	**Quite** bravely, they landed a sha

An adverb tells *where, when, how,* or *to what extent* (*how much* or *how long*).

WHERE?	Killer whales are common **here.**
HOW?	The accident occurred **suddenly.**
WHEN?	**Then** the survivors depended on their wits.
TO WHAT EXTENT?	They were **exceptionally** careful with thei supplies.

The word *not* is an adverb. When *not* is part of a contraction like *hadn't,* the *–n't* is an adverb.

✓ QUICK CHECK 5

Identify the adverb or adverbs in each of the following sentences. Then give the word or phrase each adverb modifies.

EXAMPLE 1. Have you ever wondered about being shipwrecked?
1. *ever—Have wondered*

1. Neil cried sadly for their lost ship.
2. Too soon, a cargo vessel sailed into the distance.
3. Dougal Robertson would not yield to his most desperate fears.
4. He steeled himself and tried harder.
5. Eventually, a Japanese tuna fisher rescued them.

 TIPS FOR WRITERS

Using Descriptive Adverbs

The adverb *very* is overused. In your wri ing, try to replace *very* with more descri tive adverbs, or revise the sentence so that other words carry more of the descriptive meaning.

EXAMPLE Their ordeal at sea lasted a very long time

REVISED Their ordeal at sea lasted an **extremely** long time.

or

Their ordeal at sea lasted **thirty-eight day**

THE PREPOSITION

i. A *preposition* is a word used to show the relationship of a noun or a pronoun to another word in the sentence.

Notice how a change in the preposition changes the relationship between *waves* and *rocks* in each of the following examples.

The waves crashed **under** the rocks.
The waves crashed **on** the rocks.
The waves crashed **against** the rocks.
The waves crashed **in front of** the rocks.

Commonly Used Prepositions

aboard	before	in	over
about	behind	in addition to	past
above	below	in front of	since
according to	beneath	inside	through
across	beside	in spite of	throughout
against	between	into	under
around	from	out of	without

The Prepositional Phrase

A preposition is usually followed by a noun or a pronoun. This noun or pronoun is called the **object of the preposition.** All together, the preposition, its object, and any modifiers of the object are called a **prepositional phrase.**

EXAMPLE The family went **to beautiful Cocoa Beach.**

A preposition may have more than one object.

EXAMPLE Tiffany sat **with David, Susan, and Amber.**

 QUICK CHECK 6

Identify the preposition or prepositions in each of the following sentences. Then, give the object of each preposition.

EXAMPLE 1. Do you know any stories about the sea?
   1. *about—sea*

1. Elizabeth told a sad story about her youth.
2. She had loved a man of the sea.
3. She never said the words to him.
4. One day, he didn't return from a fishing trip.
5. Still, according to Elizabeth, he is always with her.

NOTE Some words may be used as either prepositions or adverbs. To tell an adverb from a preposition, remember that a preposition is always followed by a noun or pronoun object.

NOTE Do not confuse a prepositional phrase that begins with *to* (*to town*) with a verb form that begins with *to* (*to run*).

☞ For more about prepositional phrases, see pages 735, 740, and 741–742.

Quick Check 6: Answers
1. about—youth
2. of—sea
3. to—him
4. from—trip
5. according to—Elizabeth; with—her

THE CONJUNCTION

1j. A *conjunction* is a word used to join words or groups of words.

(1) *Coordinating conjunctions* connect words or groups of words used in the same way.

Coordinating Conjunctions						
and	but	or	nor	for	so	yet

EXAMPLES Echo **or** Narcissus [two proper nouns]
down from Olympus **and** to the mountains [two prepositional phrases]
Echo angered Hera, **so** Hera punished her. [two independent clauses]

(2) *Correlative conjunctions* are pairs of conjunctions that connect words or groups of words used in the same way.

Correlative Conjunctions		
both . . . and	either . . . or	neither . . . nor
not only . . . but also	whether . . . or	

EXAMPLES **Both** the nymphs **and** Echo were loyal to Zeus. [two nouns]
She **not only** delayed Hera **but also** detained her. [two verbs with objects]
Either Echo would have love, **or** she would die. [two complete ideas]

THE INTERJECTION

1k. An *interjection* is a word used to express emotion. An interjection does not have a grammatical relation to other words in the sentence. Usually an interjection is followed by an exclamation point. Sometimes an interjection is set off by a comma.

EXAMPLES **Oh!** You surprised me.
Why, I've heard this story before.
Wow! What a story that was.
Well, Hera certainly isn't someone to cross!

NOTE When *for* is used as a conjunction, it connects groups of words that are sentences, and it is preceded by a comma. On all other occasions, *for* is used as a preposition.

CONJUNCTION The team forfeited the game, **for** they refused to play.
PREPOSITION Outraged, people shouted **for** fair play.

Coordinating conjunctions that join independent clauses are preceded by a comma. See page 769.

Common Interjections			
aha	hooray	ouch	wow
aw	oh	well	yikes
goodness	oops	whew	yippee

QUICK CHECK 7

Identify the *conjunctions* and *interjections* in the following sentences.

EXAMPLE 1. Well, Echo was either unwise or unlucky.
  1. *Well*—interjection; *either . . . or*—conjunction

1. Echo not only answered Narcissus but also ran to and embraced him.
2. Oh! Why did Narcissus scoff and shove Echo away?
3. Goodness! Narcissus was a handsome but self-centered person.
4. Both Echo and Narcissus suffered because of his selfishness.
5. They were doomed, yet he lives on in the narcissus flower.

DETERMINING PARTS OF SPEECH

The part of speech of a word is determined by the way the word is used in a sentence. Many words can be used as more than one part of speech.

EXAMPLES This **well** belongs to the golf course. [noun]
    Well, Dondré was quite disappointed. [interjection]
    He has always played **well.** [adverb]

    Clifton Davis suddenly remembered an event from his **past.** [noun]
    Didn't his team drive **past** the Lincoln Memorial? [preposition]
    As they rode along, the lights of the city flew **past.** [adverb]

QUICK CHECK 8

Identify the part of speech of the italicized word in each sentence.

EXAMPLE 1. *For* Dondré Green, it was a blessing in disguise.
  1. *preposition*

1. *Any* of the boys might have objected, but no one did.
2. They all would *back* him.
3. And they never looked *back*.
4. *Support* like that can make a man proud.
5. I wish everyone would *support* each other as those boys did!

LANGUAGE HANDBOOK 719

LANGUAGE HANDBOOK

Quick Check 7: Answers
1. not only . . . but also—conjunction; and—conjunction
2. Oh—interjection; and—conjunction
3. Goodness—interjection; but—conjunction
4. Both . . . and—conjunction
5. yet—conjunction

Quick Check 8: Answers
1. Any—pronoun
2. back—verb
3. back—adverb
4. Support—noun
5. support—verb

T719

• *Language Handbook Worksheets,*
  pp. 15–26
• *Language Workshop CD-ROM,*
  Chapter 2: Agreement

2 AGREEMENT

NUMBER

Number is the form of a word that indicates whether the word is singular or plural.

2a. When a word refers to one person, place, thing, or idea, the word is *singular* in number. When a word refers to more than one, it is *plural* in number.

SINGULAR	house	drum	wife	I	he	each
PLURAL	houses	drums	wives	we	they	all

For more about plurals, see pages 783–784.

AGREEMENT OF SUBJECT AND VERB

2b. A verb agrees with its subject in number.

A subject and verb *agree* when they have the same number.

(1) Singular subjects take singular verbs.

EXAMPLE A **messenger gives** the king's orders.

(2) Plural subjects take plural verbs.

EXAMPLE Many **wives weep** after their husbands' departures during the war.

The first auxiliary (helping) verb in a verb phrase must agree with its subject.

EXAMPLES **He is** marching to war.
They are marching to war.

Generally, nouns ending in *s* are plural (*candles, ideas, neighbors, horses*), and verbs ending in *s* are singular (*sees, writes, speaks, carries*). However, verbs used with the singular pronouns *I* and *you* generally do not end in *s*.

For more information about verb phrases, see pages 715, 741, and 752.

✓ QUICK CHECK I

For each of the following sentences, choose the correct form of the verb in parentheses.

EXAMPLE 1. (*Do, Does*) you like folk tales like this one?
   1. *Do*

1. A tree spirit (*take, takes*) the shape of the absent husband.
2. Many days (*pass, passes*).
3. Then the husband (*return, returns*).
4. Dogs (*bark, barks*) at him.
5. The judge (*has, have*) suggested a solution.

Quick Check I: Answers
1. takes
2. pass
3. returns
4. bark
5. has

Problems in Agreement

Prepositional Phrases Between Subjects and Verbs

2c. The number of a subject is not changed by a prepositional phrase following the subject.

NONSTANDARD One of the strongest heroes are Hercules.

STANDARD One of the strongest heroes **is** Hercules.

Indefinite Pronouns

Some pronouns do not refer to a definite person, place, thing, or idea and are therefore called *indefinite pronouns.*

2d. The following indefinite pronouns are singular: *anybody, anyone, each, either, everybody, everyone, neither, nobody, no one, one, somebody, someone.*

EXAMPLE **Neither** of these offers **relieves** him of his task.

2e. The following indefinite pronouns are plural: *both, few, many, several.*

EXAMPLE **Both** of the wild boar's tusks **frighten** Eurystheus.

2f. The following indefinite pronouns may be either singular or plural: *all, any, most, none, some.*

The number of these pronouns is often determined by the object in a prepositional phrase that follows the pronoun. If the pronoun refers to a singular object, the subject is singular. If the pronoun refers to a plural object, the subject is plural.

EXAMPLES **All** of the stable **needs** cleaning. [*All* refers to *stable.*]
All of the stalls **need** cleaning. [*All* refers to *stalls.*]

Compound Subjects

2g. Subjects joined by *and* usually take a plural verb.

EXAMPLE **Augeas** and **Eurystheus rule** kingdoms.

2h. When subjects are joined by *or* or *nor*, the verb agrees with the subject nearer the verb.

EXAMPLES Neither the **Hydra** nor Juno's huge **snakes defeat** Hercules.
Neither Juno's huge **snakes** nor the **Hydra defeats** Hercules.

COMPUTER NOTE You may want to create an indefinite-pronoun guide to help you use these pronouns correctly. First, summarize the information in rules 2d–2f and 2p–2r. Then, choose several examples to illustrate the rules. Using a computer, you can create a "Help" file in which to store this information. Call up your "Help" file whenever you run into difficulty with indefinite pronouns in your writing. If you don't use a computer, keep a writing notebook.

NOTE A compound subject that names only one person or thing takes a singular verb.

EXAMPLES The **friend** and **teacher** of Hercules **is** Chiron.
Law and **order suffers** when monsters roam the land.

Other Problems in Agreement

2i. **Collective nouns may be either singular or plural.**

A collective noun takes a singular verb when the noun refers to the gro[up] as a unit. A collective noun takes a plural verb when the noun refers to the individual parts or members of the group.

EXAMPLES An oxen **herd goes** with Hercules. [The herd as a uni[t] goes.]

The **herd call** to the stolen cattle. [The members of t[he] herd individually call.]

2j. **When the subject follows the verb, find the subject, and make sure the verb agrees with it. The subject usually follows the verb in sentences beginning with *here* or *ther[e]* and in questions.**

EXAMPLES There **is Centaurus**, and there **are** its **stars**.
Does the **fox** really not **want** the grapes?

The contractions *here's, there's,* and *where's* contain the verb *is* and should be used only with singular subjects.

NONSTANDARD There's the constellations Hydra and Leo.
STANDARD There **are** the **constellations** Hydra and Leo.
STANDARD There's the **constellation** Hydra.

2k. **The contractions *don't* and *doesn't* must agree with thei[r] subjects.**

Use *don't* with plural subjects and with the pronouns *I* and *you*. Use *doesn't* with other singular subjects.

EXAMPLES **They don't** like movies about Hercules, and **I don't** either.
This **film doesn't** seem realistic, but **that doesn't** matter to me.

2l. **Words stating amounts are usually singular.**

A word or phrase stating a weight, a measurement, or an amount of money or time is usually considered a single item. Such a word or phras[e] takes a singular verb.

EXAMPLE Five **dollars is** too much for a movie ticket.

2m. **The title of a book or the name of an organization or country, even when plural in form, usually takes a singul[ar] verb.**

EXAMPLES *Aesop's Fables* **is** on our reading list.
Has the **United States** signed the treaty?

NOTE When the subject of a sentence follows the verb, the word order is said to be *inverted*. To find the subject of a sentence with inverted order, restate the sentence in normal word order.

INVERTED There **goes Hercules**.
NORMAL **Hercules goes** there.

INVERTED Into the clearing **stepped** the mighty **Hercules**.
NORMAL The mighty **Hercules stepped** into the clearing.

. **A few nouns, though plural in form, are singular and take singular verbs.**

AMPLES   news, measles, mathematics, civics, mumps, physics

QUICK CHECK 2

the following sentences, correct each error in agreement.

AMPLE   1. There's many interesting stories about heroes.
        1. *There are many interesting stories about heroes.*

A flock of monstrous birds hover over the Stymphalian lake.
Doesn't the arrows of Hercules strike each bird in turn?
Neither Nereus nor his daughters foils Hercules.
The god of the oceans don't escape Hercules.
Some of the ancient myths seeks to explain actual geological or botanical facts.

AGREEMENT OF PRONOUN AND ANTECEDENT

. **A pronoun agrees with its antecedent in number and gender.**

antecedent is the word the pronoun refers to. Some singular per-
al pronouns have forms that indicate gender. Masculine pronouns
er to males. Feminine pronouns refer to females. Neuter pronouns
er to things (neither male nor female) and sometimes to animals.

FEMININE	she	her	hers
MASCULINE	he	him	his
NEUTER	it	it	its

AMPLES   The **speaker** in "Annabel Lee" lost **his** bride.
         Annabel Lee had given **her** heart to him.
         Heaven sent **its** angels for Annabel Lee.

The antecedent of a personal pronoun can be another kind of pro-
un, such as *each, neither,* or *one.* To determine the gender of a personal
onoun that refers to one of these other pronouns, look in the phrase
t follows the antecedent.

AMPLES   **Each** of these **men** left **his** mark on the development
            of the American short story.
         Neither of the **women** got what **she** wanted.

NOTE When an antece-
dent may be either
masculine or feminine, use
both the masculine and the
feminine forms.

EXAMPLES No one
ever gave **his or her**
approval of Poe's
criticisms.
Everybody wanted **his
or her** writing in Poe's
magazine.

Quick Check 2: Answers
1. hovers
2. Don't
3. foil
4. doesn't
5. seek

Problems in Agreement of Pronoun and Antecedent

Indefinite Pronouns

2p. A singular pronoun is used to refer to *anybody, anyone,* *each, either, everybody, everyone, neither, nobody, no one,* *one, someone,* and *somebody.*

EXAMPLE **Each** of these countries has **its** own Cinderella story.

2q. A plural pronoun is used to refer to *both, few, many,* an*d* *several.*

EXAMPLES **Both** of these stories take **their** characters from lege*n*
Many of these versions are similar, but **they** all diffe*r*

2r. Either a singular or a plural pronoun may be used to re*fer* to *all, any, most, none,* and *some.*

The number of the pronouns *all, any, most, none,* and *some* is determine*d* by the object in the prepositional phrase following the pronoun.

EXAMPLES **Some** of the story may come from the culture telling*.*
[*Some* refers to the singular noun *story.*]
Some of the sisters are punished for **their** cruelty.
[*Some* refers to the plural noun *sisters.*]

Compound Subjects

2s. A plural pronoun is used to refer to two or more antecedents joined by *and.*

EXAMPLE The **sisters and their mother** never share **their** fine clothing.

2t. A singular pronoun is used to refer to two or more singular antecedents joined by *or* or *nor.*

EXAMPLE Neither **the mother nor a sister** shared **her** clothes.

Other Problems in Pronoun-Antecedent Agreement

2u. Either a singular or a plural pronoun may be used with *a* collective noun.

EXAMPLES The royal **family** was preparing **its** celebration.
The royal **family** are greeting **their** new princess.

2v. Words stating amounts usually take singular pronouns.

EXAMPLE Admission costs five **dollars.** Maybe I can earn **it** in ti*me*

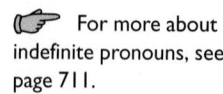 For more about indefinite pronouns, see page 711.

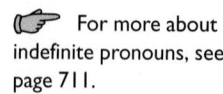 For more information about collective nouns, see page 709.

V. The title of a book or the name of an organization or a country, even when plural in form, usually takes a singular pronoun.

EXAMPLES   I read *Folktales Around the World,* and **it** was great.
The **United Nations** can revise **its** charter.

W. A few nouns, though plural in form, are singular and take singular pronouns.

EXAMPLE   **Physics** is important, but **it** has nothing to do with folk tales.

 See page 723 for a list of singular nouns that are plural in form.

QUICK CHECK 3

For each blank in the following sentences, give a pronoun that will complete the meaning of the sentence. Then, identify the antecedent or antecedents of that pronoun.

EXAMPLE   1. Kari or Leah will bring _____ copy of *The Glass Slipper.*
1. *her—Kari or Leah*

1. Aschenputtel and Cinderella got _____ names from ashes.
2. One of the stories features pigeons in _____ ending.
3. Many of the stories reward _____ heroes, but some don't.
4. The court cheered the prince and her and gave _____ a grand wedding.
5. Neither the prince nor the Pharaoh married the young woman _____ expected.

Using Compound Antecedents

Sentences with singular antecedents joined by *or* or *nor* can sound awkward if the antecedents are of different genders. If the sentence sounds awkward, revise it to avoid the problem.

AWKWARD   Ana or Ed will read her or his version of *Cinderella.*

REVISED   **Ana** will read **her** version of *Cinderella,* or **Ed** will read **his.**

Similarly, a singular and a plural antecedent joined by *or* or *nor* can create an awkward or a confusing sentence. Revise such a sentence to avoid the problem.

AWKWARD   Either my cousins or Mary will bring their video of *Cinderella.*

REVISED   Either **my cousins** will bring **their** video of *Cinderella,* or **Mary** will bring **hers.**

Try It Out ✎

Revise each of the following sentences to eliminate awkward pronoun usage.

1. Neither her mother nor her sisters recognized that the girl was their own Aschenputtel.
2. Either birds or a fish help the heroine in their own way.
3. Did a fish or a falcon lend their help to Yeh-Shen?
4. Neither Yeh-Shen nor the king could have guessed her or his fate.
5. Joey or Linda will read his or her report on "Sealskin, Soulskin."

LANGUAGE HANDBOOK   725

Quick Check 3: Answers
1. their—Aschenputtel and Cinderella
2. its—One
3. their—Many
4. them—prince and her
5. he—prince nor Pharaoh

Try It Out: Possible Answers
1. The mother and the sisters did not recognize that the girl was their own Aschenputtel.
2. Either birds help the heroine in their own way, or a fish does in its own way.
3. Did a fish or a falcon help Yeh-Shen?
4. Yeh-Shen and the king could not have guessed their fate.
5. Either Joey will read his report on "Sealskin, Soulskin," or Linda will read hers.

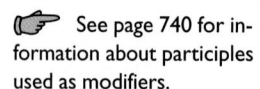

3 USING VERBS

THE PRINCIPAL PARTS OF A VERB

The four basic forms of a verb are called the **principal parts** of the ve[rb]

3a. The principal parts of a verb are the *base form,* the *pres[ent] participle,* the *past,* and the *past participle.*

BASE FORM	PRESENT PARTICIPLE	PAST	PAST PARTICIPL[E]
work	(is) working	worked	(have) worke[d]
sing	(is) singing	sang	(have) sung

The principal parts of a verb are used to express the time that an action occurs.

PRESENT TIME	I **sing** rhythm and blues now. We **are singing** along with the frog.
PAST TIME	The frog **sang** at the Big Time Weekly Concert. We **have sung** there before.
FUTURE TIME	The audience **will sing** along with the frog. By 8:00 P.M., we **will have sung** two numbers.

Regular Verbs

3b. A *regular verb* forms its past and past participle by addi[ng] *–d* or *–ed* to the base form.

BASE FORM	PRESENT PARTICIPLE	PAST	PAST PARTICIPL[E]
use	(is) using	used	(have) used
attack	(is) attacking	attacked	(have) attacke[d]

Avoid the following common errors when forming the past or past participle of regular verbs:

1. leaving off the *–d* or *–ed* ending

NONSTANDARD	We use to think the frog couldn't sing.
STANDARD	We **used** to think the frog couldn't sing.

2. adding unnecessary letters

NONSTANDARD	The audience of animals attackted him.
STANDARD	The audience of animals **attacked** him.

NOTE Notice that the present participle and the past participle require helping verbs (forms of *be* and *have*).

☞ See page 740 for information about participles used as modifiers.

QUICK CHECK I

each of the following sentences, supply the correct past or past participle form of the verb given in italics.

AMPLE   **I.** *discover*   Frog has _____ his singing talent.
       I. *discovered*

cross   He _____ over to the other side of the pond.
visit   He has _____ his friends to tell them of his wish to sing.
join   The birds already have _____ together to form a group.
use   Fox let Frog sing but also _____ a trick to fool Frog.
leap   When Frog was introduced, he _____ out on stage.

regular Verbs

An *irregular verb* forms its past and past participle in some other way than by adding *–d* or *–ed* to the base form.

irregular verb forms its past and past participle by

hanging vowels *or* consonants

Base Form	Past	Past Participle
AMPLE ring	rang	(have) rung

hanging vowels *and* consonants

Base Form	Past	Past Participle
AMPLE go	went	(have) gone

aking no changes

Base Form	Past	Past Participle
AMPLE spread	spread	(have) spread

Avoid the following common errors when forming the past or past ticiple of irregular verbs:

using the past form with a helping verb

NSTANDARD   Frog has went to the Big Time Weekly Concert.
   STANDARD   Frog **went** to the Big Time Weekly Concert.
                or
   STANDARD   Frog **has gone** to the Big Time Weekly Concert.

using the past participle form without a helping verb

NSTANDARD   I seen all of his shows.
   STANDARD   I **have seen** all of his shows.

adding *–d* or *–ed* to the base form

NSTANDARD   The elephant throwed a pineapple at the frog.
   STANDARD   The elephant **threw** a pineapple at the frog.

When you are not sure how to spell the principal parts of an irregular verb, look in a dictionary.

LANGUAGE HANDBOOK 727

LANGUAGE HANDBOOK (vertical sidebar)

Quick Check I: Answers
1. crossed
2. visited
3. joined
4. used
5. leaped or leapt

COMMON IRREGULAR VERBS

GROUP I: Each of these irregular verbs has the same form for its past and past participle.

BASE FORM	PRESENT PARTICIPLE	PAST	PAST PARTICIPL
bring	(is) bringing	brought	(have) brough
build	(is) building	built	(have) built
catch	(is) catching	caught	(have) caught
hold	(is) holding	held	(have) held
lay	(is) laying	laid	(have) laid
lead	(is) leading	led	(have) led
say	(is) saying	said	(have) said
send	(is) sending	sent	(have) sent
spin	(is) spinning	spun	(have) spun
swing	(is) swinging	swung	(have) swung

Quick Check 2: Answers

1. brought
2. laid
3. led
4. built
5. caught

 QUICK CHECK 2

For each of the following sentences, give the correct past or past participle form of the verb in parentheses.

EXAMPLE 1. Joey (*say*) he had the blues.
1. *said*

1. Frog has (*bring*) rhythm and blues to the world.
2. Since then, many a guitarist has (*lay*) down a blues riff.
3. Many blues singers (*lead*) listeners to recall sad times.
4. Some musicians have (*build*) that sound using only a harmonica
5. Others (*catch*) the beat with only their voice.

COMMON IRREGULAR VERBS

GROUP II: Each of these irregular verbs has a different form for its p and past participle.

BASE FORM	PRESENT PARTICIPLE	PAST	PAST PARTICIPL
begin	(is) beginning	began	(have) begun
choose	(is) choosing	chose	(have) chose
do	(is) doing	did	(have) done
draw	(is) drawing	drew	(have) drawn
go	(is) going	went	(have) gone
know	(is) knowing	knew	(have) know
run	(is) running	ran	(have) run
shake	(is) shaking	shook	(have) shake
sing	(is) singing	sang	(have) sung
swim	(is) swimming	swam	(have) swum

QUICK CHECK 3

each of the following sentences, give the correct past or past partici-
form of the verb in parentheses.

AMPLE   **1.** Louis Armstrong really (*know*) how to play jazz on his
trumpet.
   1. *knew*

Some say rhythm and blues (*begin*) in the 1940s.
Like the frog, the legendary Muddy Waters (*draw*) crowds.
Who has (*sing*) with him?
Have you ever (*do*) the bump or the mashed potato?
In the story, the lion (*shake*) to the twist.

COMMON IRREGULAR VERBS			

GROUP III: Each of these irregular verbs has the same form for its base
form, past, and past participle.

BASE FORM	PRESENT PARTICIPLE	PAST	PAST PARTICIPLE
burst	(is) bursting	burst	(have) burst
cost	(is) costing	cost	(have) cost
cut	(is) cutting	cut	(have) cut
hit	(is) hitting	hit	(have) hit
hurt	(is) hurting	hurt	(have) hurt
let	(is) letting	let	(have) let
put	(is) putting	put	(have) put
read	(is) reading	read	(have) read
set	(is) setting	set	(have) set
spread	(is) spreading	spread	(have) spread

QUICK CHECK 4

each of the following sentences, give the correct past or past partici-
form of the verb in italics.

AMPLE   **1.** How many people have been (*hurt*) by misunderstandings
with others?
   1. *hurt*

cost   Slade and others like him have _____ Mr. Baumer a lot of
money.
hit   Once, Slade _____ Mr. Baumer.
let   Yet, Mr. Baumer _____ Slade work for him.
set   Secretly, Mr. Baumer has _____ a trap for Slade.
read   Unlike Slade, Mr. Baumer _____ the warning.

Quick Check 3: Answers
1. began
2. drew
3. sung
4. done
5. shook

Quick Check 4: Answers
1. cost
2. hit
3. let
4. set
5. read

Try It Out

Revise each of the following sentences to sound natural in a dialogue.

1. Butch replied, "I must say, old friend, that I cannot quite believe you."
2. "Gracious, what a marvelous party that was!" beamed Tanya when the group met Monday morning at school.
3. "Please accept our congratulations on a job well done," cried Jim's teammates, slapping him on the back after the game.
4. "I beg your pardon, but you are sitting in my seat," said the sergeant to the recruit.
5. "What an unfaithful friend you are to have spoken against me behind my back," exclaimed Angela to her classmate.

Using Nonstandard Verb For[m]

Using standard verb forms is importa[nt] almost all the writing that you do for school. Your readers expect standard usage in essays an[d] reports. On the other hand, readers expect the dialogue[in] plays and short stories to sound natural. For dialogue to sound natural, it must reflect the speech patterns of rea[l] people, and real people speak in all sorts of nonstandar[d] ways. Look at the following example from the short sto[ry] "Bargain."

> "I think he hate me," Mr. Baumer went on. "Tha[t's] the thing. He hate me for coming not from this co[un]try. I come here, sixteen years old, and learn to re[ad] and write, and I make a business, and so I think he hate me."

How might you translate this passage into standard E[ng]lish? How would that affect your impression of Mr. Baum[er]?

You may want to discuss the use of nonstandard verb forms with yo[ur] teacher. Together you can decide how you can use such forms in your writing.

VERB TENSE

3d. The *tense* of a verb indicates the time of the action or state of being that is expressed by the verb.

Every verb has six tenses.

Present	Past	Future
Present Perfect	Past Perfect	Future Perfect

This time line shows how the six tenses are related to one another.

Past	*Present*	*Future*
existing or happening in the past	existing or happening now	existing [or] happenin[g in] the futur[e]

Past Perfect	*Present Perfect*	*Future Perfect*
existing or happening before a specific time in the past	existing or happening sometime before now or starting in the past and continuing now	existing or happenin[g] before a specific tim[e] in the future

Listing all forms of a verb in the six tenses is called *conjugating* a verb[.]

CONJUGATION OF THE VERB *WRITE*

PRESENT TENSE

SINGULAR	*PLURAL*
I write	we write
you write	you write
he, she, *or* it writes	they write

PAST TENSE

SINGULAR	*PLURAL*
I wrote	we wrote
you wrote	you wrote
he, she, *or* it wrote	they wrote

FUTURE TENSE

SINGULAR	*PLURAL*
I will write	we will write
you will write	you will write
he, she, *or* it will write	they will write

PRESENT PERFECT TENSE

SINGULAR	*PLURAL*
I have written	we have written
you have written	you have written
he, she, *or* it has written	they have written

PAST PERFECT TENSE

SINGULAR	*PLURAL*
I had written	we had written
you had written	you had written
he, she, *or* it had written	they had written

FUTURE PERFECT TENSE

SINGULAR	*PLURAL*
I will have written	we will have written
you will have written	you will have written
he, she, *or* it will have written	they will have written

NOTE In the future tense and in the future perfect tense, the helping verb *shall* is sometimes used in place of *will*.

onsistency of Tense

e. **Do not change needlessly from one tense to another.**

hen writing about events in the present, use verbs in the present tense.
hen writing about events in the past, use verbs in the past tense.

CONSISTENT When they were satisfied, they begin planting.

CONSISTENT When they **are** satisfied, they **begin** planting.

CONSISTENT When they **were** satisfied, they **began** planting.

QUICK CHECK 5

Read the following paragraph, and decide whether it should be rewritten in the present or past tense. Then, change the verb forms to make the verb tense consistent.

EXAMPLE [1] These city boys enjoyed gardening when they get the chance.

1. These city boys enjoyed gardening when they got the chance.

or

1. These city boys enjoy gardening when they get the chance.

[1] No one tells them no, so they started to work. [2] It is hard, too; over and over, they carried dozens of sacks of dirt up the stairs. [3] None of the neighbors noticed them, or maybe they don't mind. [4] At last, almost before they know it, the rooftop is ready. [5] The rich, black earth waits for seeds.

> **COMPUTER NOTE**
>
> Most word processors can help you check your writing to be sure that you've used verbs correctly. Spelling checkers will highlight misspelled verb forms such as *drownded* or *costed*. Style-checking software can point out inconsistent verb tenses and may also highlight questionable uses of problem verb pairs such as *lie/lay* or *rise/raise*.

SPECIAL PROBLEMS WITH VERBS

Sit and Set

(1) The verb *sit* means "rest in an upright, seated position." *Sit* seldom takes an object.

(2) The verb *set* means "put (something) in a place." *Set* usually takes an object.

BASE FORM	PRESENT PARTICIPLE	PAST	PAST PARTICIPLE
sit (rest)	(is) sitting	sat	(have) sat
set (put)	(is) setting	set	(have) set

EXAMPLES Let's **sit** in the shade. [no object]
Let's **set** the buckets here. [Let's set what? *Buckets* is the object.]

Lie and Lay

(1) The verb *lie* means "rest," "recline," or "be in a place." *Lie* never takes an object.

(2) The verb *lay* means "put (something) in a place." *Lay* usually takes an object.

BASE FORM	PRESENT PARTICIPLE	PAST	PAST PARTICIPLE
lie (rest)	(is) lying	lay	(have) lain
lay (put)	(is) laying	laid	(have) laid

AMPLES   In the photograph, juicy, red watermelons **lay** on rich earth. [no object]

They **laid** dirt on the roof. [They laid what? *Dirt* is the object.]

e and Raise

The verb *rise* means "go up" or "get up." *Rise* never takes an object.

The verb *raise* means "lift up" or "cause (something) to rise." *Raise* usually takes an object.

BASE FORM	PRESENT PARTICIPLE	PAST	PAST PARTICIPLE
rise (go up)	(is) rising	rose	(have) risen
raise (lift up)	(is) raising	raised	(have) raised

AMPLES   My next-door neighbors **rise** very early in the morning. [no object]

They **raise** the blinds at dawn. [They raise what? *Blinds* is the object.]

QUICK CHECK 6

each of the following sentences, choose the correct verb form in entheses.

AMPLE   1. Our garden (*lies, lays*) in the sunniest corner of our backyard.

   1. *lies*

uan Guerrero (*raises, rises*) the bag containing the tomatillos he aas grown.

Like Juan, other people also (*sat, set*) out their own plants each pring.

He will not just (*sit, set*) and remain idle.

Avoiding the heat of the day, Mr. Garcia also (*raises, rises*) early to end his plot.

Once, only junk and trash (*lay, laid*) there, but now there is a eautiful garden.

Quick Check 6: Answers
1. raises
2. set
3. sit
4. rises
5. lay

Resources

- *Language Handbook Worksheets,* pp. 39–46
- *Language Workshop CD-ROM,* Chapter 4: Using Pronouns Correctly

NOTE Possessive pronouns (such as *my, your,* and *our*) are also sometimes called **possessive adjectives.**

For more about possessive pronouns, see pages 710 and 777.

NOTE To choose the correct pronoun in a compound subject, try each form of the pronoun separately.

EXAMPLE: Beterli and (*he, him*) quarreled. [*He* quarreled. *Him* quarreled.]

ANSWER: Beterli and **he** quarreled.

For more about predicate nominatives, see page 756.

734 LANGUAGE HANDBOOK

4 USING PRONOUNS

CASE

Case is the form of a noun or a pronoun that shows how it is used. There are three cases: *nominative, objective,* and *possessive.* The form of a noun is the same for both the nominative and objective cases. A noun changes its form for the possessive case, usually by the addition of an apostrophe and an *s.*

Most personal pronouns have different forms for all three cases.

PERSONAL PRONOUNS		
SINGULAR		
NOMINATIVE CASE	**OBJECTIVE CASE**	**POSSESSIVE CASE**
I	me	my, mine
you	you	your, yours
he, she, it	him, her, it	his, her, hers, its
PLURAL		
NOMINATIVE CASE	**OBJECTIVE CASE**	**POSSESSIVE CASE**
we	us	our, ours
you	you	your, yours
they	them	their, theirs

The Nominative Case

4a. A subject of a verb is in the nominative case.

EXAMPLES **I** enjoy Anne McCaffrey's writing style. [*I* is the subject of *enjoy.*]

He and **she** were still at home. [*He* and *she* are the subjects of *were.*]

4b. A *predicate nominative* is in the nominative case.

A **predicate nominative** follows a linking verb and explains or identifies the subject of the verb. A personal pronoun used as a predicate nominative follows a form of the verb *be* (*am, is, are, was, were, be,* or *been*).

EXAMPLES The last one to arrive there was **he.** [*He* identifies the subject *one.*]

Could it be **she**? [*She* identifies the subject *it.*]

e Objective Case

A *direct object* **is in the objective case.**

rect object follows an action verb and tells *who* or *what* receives the **on** of the verb.

MPLES   The bronze dragon's choice amazed **us.** [*Us* tells *who*
         was amazed.]
         Heth moved his wings and dried **them.** [*Them* tells
         what Heth dried.]

An *indirect object* **is in the objective case.**

ndirect object comes between an action verb and a direct object and
to *whom* or *to what* or *for whom* or *for what.*

MPLES   Heth asked **him** a question. [*Him* tells *to whom* Heth
         asked a question.]
         The dragon and his rider taught **them** a lesson. [*Them*
         tells *to whom* they taught a lesson.]

An *object of a preposition* **is in the objective case.**

repositional phrase contains a preposition, a noun or pronoun called
object of the preposition, and any modifiers of that object.

MPLES   like a **hero**   near **us**
         next to **Dr. Chang**   without **you** and **me**

pronoun used as the object of a preposition should always be in the
ctive case.

MPLES   A great honor had been bestowed on **him.**
         We went with **her** to the mall.

QUICK CHECK I

each of the following sentences, identify the correct personal
oun in parentheses.

MPLE   **1.** Rikki's gentleness surprised (*she, her*).
         1. *her*

ikki had almost drowned, but an English boy named Teddy
escued (*he, him*).
ould a mongoose live with (*they, them*) happily?
eddy's mother wasn't sure whether a mongoose would make a
ood pet, but Rikki gave (*she, her*) a surprise.
idn't (*he, him*) save their lives?
The winner of this battle will be (*I, me*)!" he vowed.

  👉   For more about
direct objects, see page
755.

  👉   For more about
indirect objects, see page
755.

  👉   For a list of prepositions, see page 717. For
more about prepositional
phrases, see pages 717,
740, and 741–742.

Quick Check I: Answers
1. him
2. them
3. her
4. he
5. I

Try It Out: Answers

1. The other candidates and we dashed to the Impression.
2. "Save a good place for my friends and me," someone called.
3. I wondered who would be first and thought, "Maybe it'll be I!"
4. When K'last asked me who Keevan was, I answered, "That's he."
5. Keevan was the smallest, yet it was he who impressed the bronze dragon.

Try It Out

Revise each of the following sentences to show standard and polite usage of pronouns.

1. We and the other candidates dashed to the Impression.
2. "Save a good place for me and my friends," someone called.
3. I wondered who would be first and thought, "Maybe it'll be me!"
4. When K'last asked me who Keevan was, I answered, "That's him."
5. Keevan was the smallest, yet it was him who impressed the bronze dragon.

NOTE In spoken English, the use of *whom* is becoming less common. In fact, when you are speaking, you may correctly begin any question with *who* regardless of the grammar of the sentence. In written English, however, you should distinguish between *who* and *whom.*

Improving Pronoun Usage

Expressions such as *It's me, That's her,* and *It was the*▮ are accepted in everyday speaking. In writing, howe▮ such expressions are generally considered nonstand▮ and should be avoided.

STANDARD   It is **I.**   That is **she.**   It was **they**▮

Additionally, remember that it is considered polite to put first-person pronouns (*I, me, mine, we, us, ours*) last ▮ compound constructions.

EXAMPLE   **The dragonriders and we** arrived at th▮ Hatching Ground.

SPECIAL PRONOUN PROBLEMS

Who and Whom

The pronoun *who* has different forms in the nominative ▮ objective cases. *Who* is the nominative form; *whom* is th▮ objective form.

When deciding whether to use *who* or *whom* in a question, follow these steps:

STEP 1:   Rephrase the question as a statement.
STEP 2:   Decide how the pronoun is used in the statement—as subject, predicate nominative, object of the verb, or obje▮ of a preposition.
STEP 3:   Determine the case of the pronoun according to the rule▮ standard English.
STEP 4:   Select the correct form of the pronoun.

EXAMPLE: (*Who, Whom*) did Jerry see?
STEP 1:   The statement is *Jerry did see* (*who, whom*).
STEP 2:   The subject of the verb is *Jerry,* the verb is *did see,* an▮ the pronoun is the direct object.
STEP 3:   A pronoun used as a direct object should be in the obj▮ tive case.
STEP 4:   The objective form is *whom.*
ANSWER: **Whom** did Jerry see?

Pronouns with Appositives

Sometimes a pronoun is followed directly by a noun that identifies the▮ pronoun. Such a noun is called an **appositive.** To choose which prono▮ to use before an appositive, omit the appositive, and try each form of▮ pronoun separately.

MPLE: (*We, Us*) boys live in the Carolinas. [*Boys* is the appositive.] *We* live in the Carolinas. *Us* live in the Carolinas.

WER: **We** boys live in the Carolinas.

 For more about
appositives, see page 745.

flexive Pronouns

exive pronouns (such as *myself*, *himself*, and *yourselves*) can be used as
ects. Do not use the nonstandard forms *hisself* and *theirself* or *their-*
es in place of *himself* and *themselves*.

NSTANDARD   Jerry prepared a fire for hisself.
STANDARD   Jerry prepared a fire for **himself.**

 For more about
reflexive pronouns, see
page 711.

QUICK CHECK 2

each of the following sentences, choose the correct pronoun in
entheses.

AMPLE   **1.** May (*we, us*) students read aloud?
   1. *we*

For (*who, whom*) did the boy work?
Jerry did not often play with (*we, us*) in the neighborhood.
(Who, Whom) wrote *The Yearling*?
He promised (*hisself, himself*) that he would do a good job.
They seemed pleased with (*theirselves, themselves*).

USING MODIFIERS

COMPARISON OF MODIFIERS

odifier is a word, a phrase, or a clause that describes or limits the
ning of another word. Two kinds of modifiers—*adjectives* and
erbs—may be used to compare things.

The three degrees of comparison of modifiers are
positive, comparative, and *superlative*.

POSITIVE	cold	loud	politely
MPARATIVE	colder	louder	more politely
JPERLATIVE	coldest	loudest	most politely

gular Comparison

Most one-syllable modifiers form their comparative and
superlative degrees by adding *–er* and *–est*.

POSITIVE	sharp	calm	cold
MPARATIVE	sharper	calmer	colder
JPERLATIVE	sharpest	calmest	coldest

NOTE To show decreas-
ing comparisons,
all modifiers form their
comparative and superla-
tive degrees with *less* and
least.

POSITIVE
  calm
  rapidly
COMPARATIVE
  less calm
  less rapidly
SUPERLATIVE
  least calm
  least rapidly

(2) Some two-syllable modifiers form their comparative and superlative degrees by adding *–er* and *–est*. Others form th[] comparative and superlative degrees by using *more* and *m*[]

POSITIVE	simple	sudden	quietly
COMPARATIVE	simpler	more sudden	more quietly
SUPERLATIVE	simplest	most sudden	most quietly

(3) Modifiers that have three or more syllables form their com[] parative and superlative degrees by using *more* and *most*.

POSITIVE	luxurious	fearfully	curious
COMPARATIVE	more luxurious	more fearfully	more curi[]
SUPERLATIVE	most luxurious	most fearfully	most curi[]

Irregular Comparison

Some modifiers do not form their comparative and superlative degree[] using the regular methods.

POSITIVE	bad	far	good	well	many	much
COMPARATIVE	worse	farther	better	better	more	more
SUPERLATIVE	worst	farthest	best	best	most	most

 QUICK CHECK 1

Give the forms for the comparative and superlative degr[] of the following modifiers.

EXAMPLE 1. colorful
1. *more (less) colorful, most (least) colorful*

1. fine	5. daring	9. well
2. cautiously	6. comfortable	10. dainty
3. gladly	7. much	
4. thankful	8. cozy	

Drop the final silent e before a suffix beginning with a vowel.

EXAMPLES   safe + er = safer
ripe + est = ripest
gentle + er = gentler

Uses of Comparative and Superlative Forms

5b. Use the comparative degree when comparing two thin[] Use the superlative degree when comparing more than two.

COMPARATIVE   This mouse is **safer** than the Town Mouse.
She sleeps **more soundly** than the Town Mouse[]

SUPERLATIVE   This mouse is the **safest** one in the world.
Of the three animals, the cat slept **most soundl**[]

5c. Use *good* to modify a noun or a pronoun. Use *well* to modify a verb.

EXAMPLE   The Town Mouse enjoyed **good food.** She **ate well.**

738 LANGUAGE HANDBOOK

Quick Check 1: Answers

1. finer (less fine), finest (least fine)
2. more (less) cautiously, most (least) cautiously
3. more (less) gladly, most (least) gladly
4. more (less) thankful, most (least) thankful
5. more (less) daring, most (least) daring
6. more (less) comfortable, most (least) comfortable
7. more (less), most (least)
8. cozier (less cozy), coziest (least cozy)
9. better (less well), best (least well)
10. daintier (less dainty), daintiest (least dainty)

Use adjectives, not adverbs, after linking verbs.

EXAMPLE   The Town Mouse's life seemed **wonderful.** [*not* wonderfully]

Avoid using double comparisons.

A *double comparison* is the use of both *–er* and *more* (*less*) or both *–est* and *most* (*least*) to form a comparison. A comparison should be formed in only one of these two ways, not both.

EXAMPLE   The Country Mouse is **safer** [*not* more safer] than the Town Mouse.

A *double negative* is the use of two negative words to express one negative idea.

Common Negative Words			
barely	never	none	nothing
hardly	no	no one	nowhere
neither	nobody	not (–n't)	scarcely

NONSTANDARD   She hasn't never liked cats.

STANDARD   She hasn't ever [*or* has never] liked cats.

QUICK CHECK 2

The following sentences contain incorrect forms of comparison. Revise each sentence, using the correct form.

EXAMPLE   1. The acorns were the more delicious of all the foods.
    1. *The acorns were the most delicious of all the foods.*

1. Of course, the Town Mouse had the more finer foods.
2. However, the Country Mouse couldn't hardly enjoy those foods.
3. To the mice, was the cat most dangerous than the dog?
4. The Town Mouse ate worst on her visit to the country.
5. Of the two mice, which is the safest?

PLACEMENT OF MODIFIERS

Place modifying words, phrases, and clauses as close as possible to the words they modify.

Notice how the meaning of the following sentence changes when the position of the phrase *from the country* changes.

Quick Check 2: Answers
1. Of couse, the Town Mouse had the finer foods.
2. However, the Country Mouse could hardly enjoy those foods.
3. To the mice, was the cat more dangerous than the dog?
4. The Town Mouse did not eat well on her visit to the country.
5. Of the two mice, which is the safer?

The mouse **from the country** saw a cat. [The phrase modif
mouse.]

The mouse saw a cat **from the country.** [The phrase modif
cat.]

Prepositional Phrases

A **prepositional phrase** consists of a preposition, a noun or a pronou
called the *object of the preposition,* and any modifiers of that object. A
prepositional phrase used as an adjective should be placed directly afte
the word it modifies.

MISPLACED   A cat would not be dangerous to the mice with a bel

CLEAR   A cat **with a bell** would not be dangerous to the mic

A prepositional phrase used as an adverb should be placed near the
word it modifies.

MISPLACED   The mice had a meeting about the cat **in fear.**

CLEAR   **In fear,** the mice had a meeting about the cat.

Avoid placing a prepositional phrase in a position where it can modi
either of two words. Place the phrase so that it clearly modifies the wo
you intend it to modify.

MISPLACED   The mouse said in the morning she would go. [Does
the phrase modify *said* or *would go?*]

CLEAR   The mouse said she would go **in the morning.**

or

CLEAR   **In the morning,** the mouse said she would go.

Participial Phrases

A **participial phrase** consists of a verb form—either a present partici
or a past participle—and its related words. A participial phrase modifie
noun or a pronoun. Like a prepositional phrase, a participial phrase
should be placed as close as possible to the word it modifies.

MISPLACED   The mice hid from the cat scurrying fearfully.

CLEAR   **Scurrying fearfully,** the mice hid from the cat.

A participial phrase that does not clearly and sensibly modify any wo
in the sentence is a **dangling participial phrase.** To correct a dangling
phrase, supply a word that the phrase can modify, or add a subject, a ve
or both to the dangling modifier.

DANGLING   Worried constantly, a plan was needed.

CLEAR   Worried constantly, **the mice** needed a plan.

or

CLEAR   The mice needed a plan **because they worried**
constantly.

☞ For more about
prepositions and preposi-
tional phrases, see pages
717, 735, and 741–742.

☞ For more about
participial phrases, see
page 743.

auses

clause is a group of words that contains a verb and its subject and that used as a part of a sentence. An ***adjective clause*** modifies a noun or a pronoun. Most adjective clauses begin with a relative pronoun, such as *t, which, who, whom,* or *whose.* An ***adverb clause*** modifies a verb, an ective, or another adverb. Most adverb clauses begin with a subordi-ting conjunction, such as *although, while, if,* or *because.*

Like phrases, clauses should be placed as close as possible to the rds they modify.

SPLACED   The fable was written by Aesop that we read today.

CLEAR   The fable **that we read today** was written by Aesop.

☞ For more about clauses, see Part 7: Clauses.

QUICK CHECK 3

ch of the following sentences contains a misplaced or dangling modifier. vise each sentence so that it is clear and correct.

AMPLE   **1.** A cat was frightening the mice with sharp claws and teeth.

        1. *A cat with sharp claws and teeth was frightening the mice.*

The mice complained about the cat at the meeting.

A bell could protect the mice on the cat.

Ringing loudly with each step, the mice could run away.

The plan had a flaw that he was suggesting.

An old mouse questioned the young mouse shaking his head sadly.

COMPUTER NOTE

A computer can help you find and correct nonstandard forms of modifiers such as *baddest, expensiver,* and *mostest.* However, the computer cannot help you make sure that a modifier is not misplaced or dangling. You will need to check the placement of your modifiers yourself.

PHRASES

a. A *phrase* is a group of related words that is used as a single part of speech and does not contain a verb and its subject.

VERB PHRASE   should have been stabled

EPOSITIONAL PHRASE   with a shudder and whitened eyes

☞ For more information about verb phrases, see pages 715, 720, and 752.

THE PREPOSITIONAL PHRASE

b. A *prepositional phrase* includes a preposition, a noun or pronoun called the *object of the preposition,* and any modifiers of that object.

AMPLES   The runaway was filled **with confusion and fear.**

         The colt **in front of them** climbed **up the wall.**

☞ For a list of commonly used prepositions, see page 717.

Quick Check 3: Possible Answers

1. At the meeting, the mice complained about the cat.
2. A bell on the cat could protect the mice.
3. Ringing loudly with each step, a bell would warn the mice to run away.
4. The plan that he was suggesting had a flaw.
5. Shaking his head sadly, an old mouse questioned the young mouse.

Resources ———

- *Language Handbook Worksheets,* pp. 57–69
- *Language Workshop CD-ROM,* Lessons 23–25: Phrases

NOTE An adjective phrase always follows the word it modifies. That word may be the object of another prepositional phrase.

EXAMPLE "The Runaway" is a poem **about a colt in the snow.**

[The phrase *about a colt* modifies the predicate nominative *poem.* The phrase *in the snow* modifies the object *colt.*]

 NOTE An adverb phrase may come either before or after the word it modifies.

EXAMPLES **Before that time,** Frost had published little.
Frost had published little **before that time.**

The Adjective Phrase

6c. An *adjective phrase* is a prepositional phrase that modifie
a noun or a pronoun.

An adjective phrase tells *what kind* or *which one.*

EXAMPLES Robert Frost was a poet **of nature.** [What kind?]
"The Runaway" is the one **about a colt.** [Which one?]

More than one adjective phrase may modify the same word.

EXAMPLE A pasture **of snow on a mountain** upsets him. [The
phrases *of snow* and *on a mountain* modify *pasture.*]

The Adverb Phrase

6d. An *adverb phrase* is a prepositional phrase that modifies
verb, an adjective, or an adverb.

An adverb phrase tells *how, when, where, why,* or *to what extent* (that is, *how long, how many,* or *how far*).

EXAMPLES The colt bolted **with a nervous snort.** [How?]
The colt seemed uneasy **because of the snow.** [Why
The poem takes place late **in the day.** [When?]
Frost had written poetry **for many years.** [How long

More than one adverb phrase may modify the same word or words.

EXAMPLE **At the Kennedy Inauguration,** Frost read **to the
American people.**

An adverb phrase may be modified by an adjective phrase.

EXAMPLE **In his poem about the runaway,** Frost uses several
verbals. [The adverb phrase modifies the verb *uses.* Th
adjective phrase modifies *poem.*]

✓ QUICK CHECK 1

Identify the prepositional phrase or phrases in each numbered sentence
in the following paragraph. Then, label each phrase as an *adjective phrase*
or an *adverb phrase.* Give the word the phrase modifies.

EXAMPLE [1] They make judgments about the colt and its care.
1. *about the colt and its care—adjective phrase—judgments*

[1] Many of Robert Frost's poems contain imagery from nature.
[2] These images say much about people and human nature. [3] "The
Runaway" focuses on a colt's experiences during its first winter. [4] I
the poem Frost shows observers' reactions to the colt. [5] The colt, t
subject of conversation between the observers, is important to them

Quick Check 1: Answers

1. of Robert Frost's poems—adjective phrase—many; from nature—adjective phrase—imagery
2. about people and human nature—adjective phrase—much
3. on a colt's experiences—adverb phrase—focuses; during its first winter—adjective phrase—experiences
4. In the poem—adverb phrase—shows; to the colt—adjective phrase—reactions
5. of conversation—adjective phrase—subject; between the observers—adjective phrase—conversation; to them—adverb phrase—important

742 LANGUAGE HANDBOOK

VERBALS AND VERBAL PHRASES

A *verbal* is a form of a verb that is used as a noun, an adjective, or an adverb. There are three kinds of verbals: the *participle*, the *gerund*, and the *infinitive*.

Participles and Participial Phrases

1. **A *participle* is a verb form that can be used as an adjective.**

There are two kinds of participles—*present participles* and *past participles*.

Present participles **end in –ing.**

EXAMPLE   The rats **swimming** ashore alarmed them. [*Swimming,* a form of the verb *swim,* modifies *rats.*]

Most *past participles* **end in –d or –ed. Others are irregularly formed.**

EXAMPLES   No one was on the **abandoned** ship. [*Abandoned,* a form of the verb *abandon,* modifies *ship.*]

The rats, **known** for their ferocity, swam toward the sailors. [*Known,* a form of the verb *know,* modifies *rats.*]

2. **A *participial phrase* consists of a participle and all the words related to the participle. The entire phrase is used as an adjective.**

EXAMPLES   **Seeing a ship nearby,** scores of rats dove into the sea. [The participial phrase modifies the noun *scores.* The noun *ship* is the direct object of the present participle *seeing.*]

We could see the sharks **feasting hungrily on the swarms of rats.** [The participial phrase modifies the noun *sharks.* The adverb *hungrily* and the adverb phrase *on the swarms of rats* modify the present participle *feasting.*]

☞ For information on placement of participial phrases, see page 740.

Gerunds and Gerund Phrases

3. **A *gerund* is a verb form ending in –ing that is used as a noun.**

SUBJECT	**Singing** can be fun.
PREDICATE NOMINATIVE	My favorite pastime is **singing.**
OBJECT OF PREPOSITION	I warm up before **singing.**
DIRECT OBJECT	Do you enjoy **singing**?

6h. A *gerund phrase* consists of a gerund and all the words related to the gerund.

EXAMPLE **Counting the innumerable rats on the lighthouse** calmed the men. [The gerund phrase is the subject of sentence. The noun *rats* is the direct object of the gerund *counting*.]

Infinitives and Infinitive Phrases

6i. An *infinitive* is a verb form that can be used as a noun, a adjective, or an adverb. Infinitives usually begin with *to*.

NOUNS **To escape** was their sole desire. [subject]
Was the sailors' fate **to become** dinner? [predicate nominative]
They had **to signal** but not **to let** the rats in. [direct objects]

ADJECTIVES The time **to signal** was now. [*To signal* modifies *time.*]
Who was the first man **to crack** under the pressure [*To crack* modifies *man.*]

ADVERBS Rescuers were quick **to answer.** [*To answer* modif *quick.*]
They came to the island **to tend** the light. [*To tend* modifies *came.*]

6j. An *infinitive phrase* consists of an infinitive and its modifiers and complements. The entire infinitive phrase ma act as an adjective, an adverb, or a noun.

EXAMPLES Lighthouses are one way **to warn ships away from rocks.** [adjective]
The men were grateful **to see the ship.** [adverb]
To be rescued was their only hope. [noun]

✓ QUICK CHECK 2

Identify each italicized phrase in the following sentences as *participial, gerund,* or *infinitive.*

EXAMPLE 1. *Swimming in the sea* was easy for the rats.
1. *gerund*

1. The rats, *lured by the scent,* approached the lighthouse.
2. *Seeing the laughing men* enraged the frenzied rats.
3. They tried *to get in through the windows and door.*
4. *Clawing and biting the metal, glass, and stone,* they succeeded
5. What happened to the horrified men left *to fend for themselves*

NOTE *To* plus a noun or a pronoun (*to class, to them, to the dance*) is a prepositional phrase, not an infinitive. Be careful not to confuse infinitives with prepositional phrases beginning with *to.*

INFINITIVE I want **to go.**
PREPOSITIONAL PHRASE I want to go **to sea.**

Quick Check 2: Answers
1. participial
2. gerund
3. infinitive
4. participial
5. infinitive

APPOSITIVES AND APPOSITIVE PHRASES

‹. An *appositive* is a noun or a pronoun placed beside another noun or pronoun to identify or explain it.

positives are often set off from the rest of the sentence by commas or hes. However, when an appositive is necessary to the meaning of the tence or when it is closely related to the word it refers to, no commas necessary.

AMPLES   The author **George G. Toudouze** wrote the story "Three Skeleton Key." [The noun *George G. Toudouze* identifies the noun *author*.]

The men saw a strange ship, **one** with Dutch lines and three masts. [The pronoun *one* refers to the noun *ship*.]

Their victims—the **captain** and **crew**—had vanished. [The nouns *captain* and *crew* explain who were the victims.]

I. An *appositive phrase* consists of an appositive and its modifiers.

AMPLES   Le Gleo, **one of the lighthouse keepers,** had horrible nightmares. [The adjective phrase *of the lighthouse keepers* modifies the appositive *one*.]

Rats, **the foul scourge of sailing ships,** pressed for entrance. [The article *the,* the adjective *foul,* and the adjective phrase *of sailing ships* modify the appositive *scourge*.]

☞ For information on the use of commas with appositives and appositive phrases, see page 770.

QUICK CHECK 3

ntify the appositives or appositive phrases in the following sentences. e the word or words each appositive or appositive phrase identifies or lains.

AMPLE   **I.** The rats, a huge and hardy breed, swarmed the decks.
      I. *a huge and hardy breed—rats*

Three men—the narrator, Le Gleo, and Itchoua—stared in horror at the rats.

The entire crew would likely have perished but for the engineer, a brave man.

Terriers, dogs bred for hunting, were certainly no match for these vicious rats.

The supply boat, the last one of the month, would be no help because it would arrive too late.

His friend Le Gleo was never the same again.

Quick Check 3: Answers
1. the narrator, Le Gleo, and Itchoua— men
2. a brave man—engineer
3. dogs bred for hunting—Terriers
4. the last one of the month—supply boat
5. Le Gleo—friend

Try It Out: Possible Answers

1. Three Skeleton Key was a small rock about twenty miles offshore.
2. Three convicts, in hiding after escaping from prison, had died there.
3. People said that the dead men's skeletons danced at night.
4. To save money, he volunteered for the lighthouse job.
5. Having smooth, slick surfaces, the rocks were dangerous.

Resources ————

- *Language Handbook Worksheets,* pp. 70–77
- *Language Workshop CD-ROM,* Lessons 26–28: Clauses

Try It Out

For each of the following items, use phrases to combine the short, choppy sentences into one smooth sentence.

1. Three Skeleton Key was a small rock. It was about twenty miles offshore.
2. Three convicts had died there. They were in hiding after escaping from prison.
3. People said that the dead men's skeletons danced. They danced at night.
4. He wanted to save money. He volunteered for the lighthouse job.
5. The rocks had smooth, slick surfaces. They were dangerous.

TIPS FOR WRITERS

Using Phrases to Combine Sentences

Knowing how to use different kinds of phrases can help you improve your writing. For example, revise a series of choppy sentences, combine them by turning at least one sentence into a phrase.

CHOPPY	A beautiful ship approached. The ship was a Dutch three-master.
APPOSITIVE PHRASE	A beautiful ship, **a Dutch three-master,** approached.
PARTICIPIAL PHRASE	A beautiful Dutch ship **having three masts** approached.
INFINITIVE PHRASE	A beautiful Dutch three-master continued **to approach us.**

7 CLAUSES

7a. A *clause* is a group of words that contains a verb and its subject and that is used as a part of a sentence.

Every clause has a subject and a verb. However, not every clause expresses a complete thought.

COMPLETE THOUGHT   **Wagons delivered** milk daily.

INCOMPLETE THOUGHT   before **cars were invented**

The two kinds of clauses are the *independent clause* and the *subordinate clause.*

THE INDEPENDENT CLAUSE

7b. An *independent* (or *main*) *clause* expresses a complete thought and can stand by itself as a sentence.

                              S   V
INDEPENDENT CLAUSE   Joseph pulled the wagon.

THE SUBORDINATE CLAUSE

7c. A *subordinate* (or *dependent*) *clause* does not express a complete thought and cannot stand alone as a sentence.

                              S   V
SUBORDINATE CLAUSE   that Pierre drove

The meaning of a subordinate clause is complete only when the clause attached to an independent clause.

AMPLE   Joseph pulled the wagon **that Pierre drove.**

QUICK CHECK I

ntify each of the following groups of words as an *independent clause* or *bordinate clause.*

AMPLE   1. because Pierre was growing old
         1. *subordinate clause*

although Pierre did not read or write
everyone liked him
although he arrived early each day to get his wagon
when he spoke to his horse
Joseph knew every stop on the route

he Adjective Clause

An *adjective clause* is a subordinate clause that modifies a noun or a pronoun.

adjective clause usually follows the word it modifies and tells *which one what kind.*

AMPLES   Joseph knew every house **that they served.** [Which house?]

         Pierre was a man **who loved his job.** [What kind of man?]

An adjective clause is usually introduced by a *relative pronoun.*

Relative Pronouns				
that	which	who	whom	whose

A *relative pronoun* relates an adjective clause to the word that the use modifies.

AMPLES   After work, Pierre, **who had seemed fit,** limped slowly. [The relative pronoun *who* relates the clause to the noun *Pierre.*]

         St. Joseph, **whose name the horse bore,** was also kind and faithful. [The relative pronoun *whose* relates the clause to the noun *St. Joseph.*]

Sometimes a relative pronoun is preceded by a preposition that is part the adjective clause.

AMPLE   The character **to whom I am referring** is Jacques.

☞ For information on when to set off adjective clauses with commas, see rule 13i(1) on page 770.

NOTE   The relative pronouns *who* and *whom* are used to refer to people only. The relative pronoun *that* is used to refer both to people and to things. The relative pronoun *which* is used to refer to things only.

Quick Check I: Answers
1. subordinate clause
2. independent clause
3. subordinate clause
4. subordinate clause
5. independent clause

✓ **QUICK CHECK 2**

Identify the adjective clause in each of the following sentences. Give the relative pronoun and the word that the relative pronoun refers to.

EXAMPLE 1. Jacques, who was the foreman, seemed kind.
       1. *who was the foreman, who—Jacques*

1. Pierre Dupin worked for a milk company that was in Montreal.
2. The wagon that he drove carried milk to St. Catherine Street.
3. Pierre relied on his horse, whom he had named Joseph.
4. Joseph, whose coat was white, was large and reliable.
5. Pierre was offered a pension, which is a regular payment to a re- tired person.

The Adverb Clause

7e. An *adverb clause* is a subordinate clause that modifies a verb, an adjective, or an adverb.

An adverb clause tells *where, when, how, why, to what exten[t]* or *under what condition.*

EXAMPLES   They live **where it never gets cold.**
       [Where?]
       When he left, I cried. [When?]
       Grover's room seems **as if it will never be the same.** [How?]
       Because the weather was hot, the co[ol] water felt good. [Why?]
       My parents still miss him **as much as I do.** [To what extent?]
       If I keep tickling him, he won't fall asleep. [Under what condition?]

An adverb clause is introduced by a **subordinating co[n]junction**—a word that shows the relationship between the adverb clau[se] and the word or words that the clause modifies.

COMPUTER NOTE

A computer can help you proofread your writing. Use the computer's "Search" function to locate any use of the words *after, as, before, since,* and *until.* Examine the use of such words at the beginnings of sentences. Determine whether the word begins a prepositional phrase or a subordinate clause. In most cases, an introductory prepositional phrase is not set off by a comma. An introductory adverb clause, however, should be followed by a comma.

NOTE Some subordinating conjunctions, such as *after, as, before, since,* and *until,* are also used as prepositions.

Common Subordinating Conjunctions			
after	as though	since	when
although	because	so that	whenever
as	before	than	where
as if	how	though	wherever
as long as	if	unless	whether
as soon as	in order that	until	while

n adverb clause does not always follow the word it modifies. When
dverb clause begins a sentence, the clause is followed by a comma.

MPLE   Whenever King Midas touched something, it turned to
         gold.

Placement of Adverb Clauses

In most cases, the decision of where to place an adverb clause is a matter of , not correctness. Both of the following sentences are ect.

lthough she was almost unknown during her lifetime, Emily Dickinson is now considered a major American poet.

mily Dickinson is now considered a major American poet **although she was almost unknown during her lifetime.**

ch sentence might you use in a paper on Emily kinson? The sentence to choose would be the one looks and sounds better in the **context**—the rest of paragraph to which the sentence belongs.

QUICK CHECK 3

tify the adverb clause in each of the following sentences. For each se, circle the subordinating conjunction, and underline the subject e and the verb twice.

MPLE   1. Many things change as you grow older.
         1. (as) you grow older

Grover worked on the computer whenever he could.
He packed all his things before he left.
Because he needed the computer, he took it too.
Although the room has been painted, it reminds me of him.
t won't be the same as long as he is gone.

e Noun Clause

A *noun clause* is a subordinate clause used as a noun.

un clause may be used as a subject, a complement (predicate nomi-ve, indirect object, or direct object), or an object of a preposition.

SUBJECT	**What Mama promises** is tomorrow.
DICATE NOMINATIVE	She is **who makes us happy.**
INDIRECT OBJECT	She bids **whoever is sleeping** good morning.

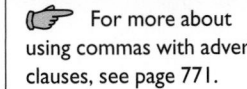

For more about using commas with adverb clauses, see page 771.

Try It Out ✎

Each of the following sentences contains an adverb clause. Decide whether you think each adverb clause is placed where it would read best in context. If the clause could be better placed, revise the sentence. If the clause reads best where it is, write *No change.*

[1] "The Highwayman" was an inevitable reading assignment when I was in school. [2] I now enjoy the poem although I laughed at it then. [3] Because it was remote in time and place, I did not relate to it. [4] The vocabulary and content seemed false because they were unfamiliar. [5] However, I discovered that this poem is filled with lively images when I read it carefully!

Try It Out: Possible Answers

1. When I was in school, "The High-wayman" was an inevitable reading assignment.
2. Although I laughed at it then, I now enjoy the poem.
3. I did not relate to it because it was remote in time and place.
4. No change.
5. However, when I read it carefully, I discovered that this poem is filled with lively images!

Quick Check 3: Answers

1. (whenever) he could
2. (before) he left
3. (Because) he needed the computer
4. (Although) the room has been painted
5. (as long as) he is gone

DIRECT OBJECT   Choose **whichever you need mo**

OBJECT OF A PREPOSITION   A poem can be about **whatever ye** **think is important.**

Common Introductory Words for Noun Clauses

how	what	whatever	which
who	whoever	when	whichever
whom	whomever	where	that

 QUICK CHECK 4

Identify the noun clause in each of the following sentences. Tell wheth the noun clause is a *subject*, a *predicate nominative*, a *direct object*, an *ind object*, or an *object of a preposition*.

EXAMPLE   1. Whatever we do affects our whole family.
           1. *Whatever we do—subject*

1. What Evelyn Tooley Hunt is talking about is a mother's effect or her family.
2. This mother gives whoever is near warmth and brightness.
3. Similarly, she puts love into whatever she is cooking.
4. Notice that Hunt compares her warmth to grits and gravy.
5. A bright future is what her constant love promises.

8 SENTENCES

8a.   A *sentence* is a group of words that has a subject and a verb and expresses a complete thought.

A sentence begins with a capital letter and ends with a period, a quest mark, or an exclamation point.

EXAMPLES   Sandra Cisneros wrote "Four Skinny Trees**.**"
             Have you read any of her work**?**
             What surprising rhythms she uses**!**

SENTENCE OR SENTENCE FRAGMENT?

A *sentence fragment* is a group of words that either does not have a subject and verb or does not express a complete thought.

SENTENCE FRAGMENT   The rhythms in this story. [What about rhythms in this story?]

SENTENCE   The rhythms in this story are based on repetition.

☞ For guidelines on using *who* and *whom* correctly, see page 736. The same guidelines apply to *whoever* and *whomever*.

Quick Check 4: Answers
1. What Evelyn Tooley Hunt is talking about—subject
2. whoever is near—indirect object
3. whatever she is cooking—object of a preposition
4. that Hunt compares her warmth to grits and gravy—direct object
5. what her constant love promises—predicate nominative

Resources ━━━━━
- *Language Handbook Worksheets,* pp. 78–87
- *Language Workshop CD-ROM,* Lessons 29 and 30: Sentences

TENCE FRAGMENT After reading her story. [Who read her story? What happened then?]

SENTENCE After reading her story, I looked at trees differently.

QUICK CHECK 1

whether each group of words is a *sentence* or a *sen-* [*fragment*]. If the word group is a sentence, correct it [a]dding a capital letter and end punctuation. If the word [gro]up is a sentence fragment, correct it by adding words [to m]ake a complete sentence, and also capitalize and [pun]ctuate it correctly.

[EX]AMPLE 1. one of my favorite writers
1. *sentence fragment—One of my favorite writ-ers is Sandra Cisneros.*

[L]et me recommend this story
[i]n front of her house grow four skinny trees
[g]rowing in the midst of concrete
[w]here they don't belong
[d]o you see a part of yourself in nature

THE SUBJECT AND THE PREDICATE

[se]ntence consists of two parts: a *subject* and a *predicate*.

A *subject* **tells whom or what the sentence is about. The** *predicate* **tells something about the subject.**

```
       subj.              pred.
```
[EX]AMPLE Helen Callaghan played professional baseball.

[Fin]ding the Subject

[Usu]ally, the subject comes before the predicate. Sometimes, however, the [subj]ect may appear elsewhere in the sentence. To find the subject of a [sen]tence, ask *Who?* or *What?* before the predicate. In sentences that [beg]in with *here*, *there*, or *where*, ask *Here* (or *There* or *Where*) before the [pre]dicate, followed by *who?* or *what?* after the predicate.

[EXA]MPLES In the old photograph was a **woman at bat.** [Who was? A woman was.]

By the way, **her son** plays for the Astros. [Who plays? Her son does.]

Do **you** play baseball? [Who does play? You do play.]

Where is **my notebook?** [Where is what? Where is my notebook.]

If sentence fragments are a problem in your writing, a computer may be able to help you. Some style-checking programs can identify and highlight sentence fragments. Such programs are useful, but they aren't perfect. The best way to eliminate fragments from your writing is still to check each sentence yourself. Be sure that each expresses a complete thought and has a subject and a verb.

NOTE The subject of a sentence is *never* part of a prepositional phrase.

EXAMPLE **Many** of the women in the league at-tended the reunion. [Who attended? You might be tempted to say *women*, but *women* is part of the prepositional phrase *of the women. Many* attended.]

LANGUAGE HANDBOOK 751

Quick Check 1: Answers
1. sentence—Let me recommend this story.
2. sentence—In front of her house grow four skinny trees.
3. sentence fragment—They are growing in the midst of concrete.
4. sentence fragment—They survive where they don't belong.
5. sentence—Do you see a part of yourself in nature?

T751

The Simple Subject

8c. A *simple subject* is the main word or group of words in t[he] complete subject.

EXAMPLES   Her **mother** still had that old fire. [The complete sub[j]ect is *her mother.*]

          "The No-Guitar Blues" by Gary Soto is on the test. [The complete subject is *"The No-Guitar Blues" b*[y] *Gary Soto.*]

The Simple Predicate, or Verb

8d. A *simple predicate,* or *verb,* is the main word or group o[f] words in the complete predicate.

A **complete predicate** consists of a verb and all the words that descr[ibe] the verb and complete its meaning. Usually, the complete predicate follows the subject in a sentence. Sometimes, however, the complete predicate appears at the beginning of a sentence. Other times, part of [the] predicate may appear on one side of the subject and the rest on the o[ther] side.

EXAMPLES   **In the darkness of a doorway stood** a stranger.
          On this night, he **had a meeting with an old frie**[nd.]
          Would his friend **appear**?

A simple predicate may be a one-word verb, or it may be a verb phrase. A **verb phrase** consists of a main verb and its helping verbs.

EXAMPLES   O. Henry's stories often **end** with a twist.
          "After Twenty Years" **does** not **have** a happy ending[.]

✓ QUICK CHECK 2

Identify the *complete subject* and *simple subject* and the *complete predica*[te] and *simple predicate* in each of the following sentences.

EXAMPLE   **1.** On the mantel was an old baseball.
          1. *an old baseball—complete subject; baseball—simple sub*[ject;]
          on the mantel was—complete predicate; was—simple predicate

1. The All-American Girls Professional Baseball League was started [by] Philip K. Wrigley.
2. It enjoyed ten years of popularity.
3. Have you seen the movie about the Rockford Peaches?
4. The famous Rockford Peaches was only one of nine teams.
5. At the league's reunion many years later was a much older Callaghan.

NOTE In this book, the term *subject* refers to the simple subject unless otherwise indicated.

NOTE In this book, the term *verb* refers to the simple predicate unless otherwise indicated.

☞ For more about verb phrases, see pages 715, 720, and 741.

Quick Check 2: Answers

1. The All-American Girls Professional Baseball League—complete subject; All-American Girls Professional Baseball League—simple subject; was started by Philip K. Wrigley—complete predicate; was started—simple predicate
2. It—complete subject and simple subject; enjoyed ten years of popularity—complete predicate; enjoyed—simple predicate
3. you—complete subject and simple subject; Have seen the movie about the Rockford Peaches—complete predicate; Have seen—simple predicate
4. The famous Rockford Peaches—complete subject; Rockford Peaches—simple subject; was only one of nine teams—complete predicate; was—simple predicate
5. a much older Callaghan—complete subject; Callaghan—simple subject; At the league's reunion many years later was—complete predicate; was—simple predicate

e Compound Subject

A *compound subject* consists of two or more connected subjects that have the same verb. The usual connecting word is *and* or *or*.

AMPLES   Neither **Daedalus** nor **Icarus** escaped the king's anger.
Among Daedalus's gifts were **creativity, ingenuity,**
and **skill.**

e Compound Verb

A *compound verb* consists of two or more verbs that have the same subject.

nnecting word—usually *and, or,* or *but*—is used between the verbs.

MPLE   He **flew** upward, **turned,** and **called** to his son.

oth the subject and the verb of a sentence may be compound.

```
        S           S      V              V
```
MPLE   **Icarus** and his **father put** on the wings and **took** off.
[Icarus put on the wings and took off. His father put on
the wings and took off.]

QUICK CHECK 3

tify the *subjects* and the *verbs* in the following sentences.

AMPLE   1. Myths and fairy tales sometimes hide their meanings.
1. *Myths, fairy tales—subjects; hide—verb*

The myth of Icarus tells about creativity and warns of its dangers.
n this story, Daedalus and his son suffer a tragic fate.
Yet, did they not also create wings and fly?
You and I can read the story, learn, and avoid their
mistakes.
Echo and Narcissus" and this classic story can teach
us much.

Using Compound Subjects and Verbs

Using compound subjects and verbs, you
combine ideas and reduce wordiness in your writing.
npare the examples below.

RDY   With his wings, Daedalus escaped. Icarus
escaped also.

ISED   With their wings, **Daedalus and Icarus
escaped.**

Try It Out block

Try It Out ✎

Using compound subjects and verbs, combine the following pairs of sentences.

1. Daedalus angered King Minos. Daedalus was imprisoned by King Minos.
2. Clouds sailed through the skies. Birds sailed through the skies.
3. Daedalus melted wax. Daedalus shaped a skeleton of a wing.
4. Daedalus flew close to his son, Icarus. Icarus flew close to his father.
5. Delos rushed by beneath them. Samos rushed by beneath them.

Quick Check 3: Answers

1. myth—subject; tells, warns—verbs
2. Daedalus, son—subjects; suffer—verb
3. they—subject; did create, fly—verbs
4. you, I—subjects; can read, learn, avoid—verbs
5. "Echo and Narcissus," story—subjects; can teach—verb

Try It Out: Possible Answers

1. Daedalus angered King Minos and was imprisoned by him.
2. Clouds and birds sailed through the skies.
3. Daedalus melted wax and shaped a skeleton of a wing.
4. Daedalus and his son, Icarus, flew close to each other.
5. Delos and Samos rushed by beneath them.

9 COMPLEMENTS

9a. A *complement* is a word or a group of words that completes the meaning of a verb.

Every sentence has a subject and a verb. Often a verb also needs a complement to complete the meaning of the verb. A complement may be noun, a pronoun, or an adjective. Each of the following subjects and ve needs a complement to make a complete sentence.

	S V
INCOMPLETE	James Weldon Johnson became [what?]

	S V C
COMPLETE	James Weldon Johnson became **a poet.**

	S V
INCOMPLETE	Johnson's poetry is [what?]

	S V C
COMPLETE	Johnson's poetry is **wonderful.**

	S V
INCOMPLETE	Tamisha showed [what? to whom?]

	S V C C
COMPLETE	Tamisha showed **me** her **poem.**

As you can see, a complement may be a noun, a pronoun, or an adjective. An adverb is never a complement.

ADVERB He writes **powerfully.** [*Powerfully* tells how he writes.]

COMPLEMENT His writing is **powerful.** [The adjective *powerfu* modifies the subject *writing.*]

A complement is never in a prepositional phrase.

OBJECT OF A PREPOSITION The whole world was in **darkness**

COMPLEMENT The whole world was **darkness.**

☞ For more information about prepositional phrases, see pages 717, 735, 740, and 741–742.

✓ QUICK CHECK I

Identify the *subjects, verbs,* and *complements* in the sentences in the follo paragraph. [Remember: A complement is never in a prepositional phras

EXAMPLE [1] Will you read "The Creation" aloud?
  1. *you—subject; will read—verb; "The Creation"—complen*

[1] With his deep voice, James Earl Jones is a marvelous speaker [2] Only his rich voice can do justice to a poem like "The Creation. [3] With lingering pauses and startling changes of volume, Jones's performance is awe-inspiring. [4] Can you find us a recording of hi recitation? [5] No one will speak or move a muscle during the who performance.

Quick Check I: Answers
1. James Earl Jones—subject; is—verb; speaker—complement
2. voice—subject; can do—verb; justice—complement
3. performance—subject; is—verb; awe-inspiring—complement
4. you—subject; Can find—verb; us, recording—complements
5. No one—subject; will speak, move—verbs; muscle—complement

DIRECT OBJECTS

A *direct object* is a noun or a pronoun that receives the action of the verb or that shows the result of the action. A direct object tells *what* or *whom* after a transitive verb.

EXAMPLE In this poem, God creates **light, animals,** and all **things.** [The nouns *light, animals,* and *things* receive the action of the transitive verb *creates* and tell *what.*]

A direct object can never follow a linking verb because a linking verb does not express action.

LINKING VERB People **became** living souls. [The verb *became* does not express action; therefore, it does not have a direct object.]

A direct object is never part of a prepositional phrase.

OBJECT OF A PREPOSITION Humans gazed at the **moon.** [*Moon* is not the direct object of the verb *gazed; moon* is the object of the preposition *at.*]

INDIRECT OBJECTS

Like a direct object, an *indirect object* helps to complete the meaning of a transitive verb. If a sentence has an indirect object, it always has a direct object also.

An *indirect object* is a noun or a pronoun that comes between the verb and the direct object and tells *to what* or *to whom* or *for what* or *for whom* the action of the verb is done.

EXAMPLE In the last stanza, God gives **man** life. [The noun *man* tells *to whom* God has given life.]

Linking verbs do not have indirect objects. Also, an indirect object, like a direct object, is never in a prepositional phrase.

LINKING VERB The cypress **is** a type of evergreen tree. [The linking verb *is* does not express action, so it cannot have an indirect object.]

DIRECT OBJECT Cypress trees give **swamps** deep shade. [The noun *swamps* shows *to what* cypress trees give shade.]

OBJECT OF A PREPOSITION They give deep shade to the **swamps.** [The noun *swamps* is the object of the preposition *to.*]

☞ For more about transitive verbs, see page 714.

☞ For more about linking verbs, see pages 714–715 and 756. For more about prepositional phrases, see pages 717, 735, 740, and 741–742.

 NOTE Like a direct object, an indirect object may be compound.

EXAMPLE Cypresses give **swamps** and **creeks** deep shade.

Identify the *direct objects* and the *indirect objects* in the following senten
[Note: Not every sentence has an indirect object.]

EXAMPLE 1. Johnson's God has physical presence.

    1. *presence—direct object*

1. This poem delivers a strong characterization of God.
2. With the muscle of a worker, this God makes the world.
3. For Johnson, all the earth shows us His footsteps.
4. Not God's intellect but His body literally gives humans breath.
5. After all, God shaped humans in His own image.

SUBJECT COMPLEMENTS

A *subject complement* completes the meaning of a linking verb and identifies or describes the subject.

		Common Linking Verbs			
appear	become	grow	remain	smell	stay
be	feel	look	seem	sound	taste

EXAMPLES   This unfortunate person became **Sky Woman**. [*Sky Woman* identifies the subject *person.*]

     The story of Sky Woman is **sad**. [*Sad* describes the subject *story.*]

There are two kinds of subject complements—the *predicate nomina* and the *predicate adjective*.

Predicate Nominatives

9d.   A *predicate nominative* is a noun or a pronoun that follow a linking verb and identifies the subject or refers to it.

EXAMPLE   Sky Woman became the **Great Earth Mother**. [The co pound noun *Great Earth Mother* is a predicate nomina tive that identifies the subject *Sky Woman.*]

Like subjects and objects, predicate nominatives never appear in prepositional phrases.

EXAMPLE   The world was only a few **bits** of earth on a turtle. [Th word *bits* is a predicate nominative that identifies the subject *world. Earth* is the object of the preposition *of* and *turtle* is the object of the preposition *on.*]

---

1. characterization—direct object
2. world—direct object
3. footsteps—direct object; us—indirect object
4. breath—direct object; humans—indirect object
5. humans—direct object

 For information about linking verbs, see pages 714–715 and 755.

 NOTE   Expressions such as "It is I" and "That was he" sound awkward even though they are correct. In conversation, you would likely say "It's me" and "That was him." Such nonstandard expressions may one day become acceptable in writing as well as in speech. For now, however, it is best to follow the rules of standard English in your writing.

 NOTE   A predicate nominative may be compound.

EXAMPLE   Her helpers were **birds**, a **muskrat**, a **toad**, and a **turtle**.

756   LANGUAGE HANDBOOK

edicate Adjectives

A *predicate adjective* is an adjective that follows a linking verb and describes the subject.

AMPLE Sky Woman was **young** and **beautiful.** [The words *young* and *beautiful* are predicate adjectives that describe the subject *Sky Woman*.]

Some verbs, such as *look*, *grow*, and *feel*, may be used as either linking bs or action verbs.

KING VERB The Chief of Heaven **looked** angry. [*Looked* is a linking verb because it links the adjective *angry* to the subject *Chief of Heaven*.]

TION VERB Sky Woman **looked** through the hole in the floor of Heaven. [*Looked* is an action verb because it expresses Sky Woman's action.]

QUICK CHECK 3

ntify the subject complement in each of the following tences. Then, label each as a *predicate nominative* or a dicate adjective.

AMPLE 1. Traditional stories are one way of understanding nature.

1. *way—predicate nominative*

These stories may seem simple but may be quite complex.
After all, their theme is the whole world.
Sky Woman's misfortune was our good fortune.
With her fall, the world became possible.
Is anything, even luck, permanent?

Using Action Verbs

Overusing the linking verb *be* can make writing dull and lifeless. As you evaluate r writing, you may get the feeling that nothing is *happen-* that nobody is *doing* anything. That feeling may be an ication that your writing contains too many *be* verbs. erever possible, replace a dull *be* verb with a verb that resses action.

BE VERB "Sky Woman" **is** a traditional Seneca story.

TION VERB Traditionally, the Seneca people **tell** the story of Sky Woman.

COMPUTER NOTE

The overuse of *be* verbs is a problem that a computer can help you eliminate. Use the computer's "Search" function to locate and highlight each occurrence of *am, are, is, was, were, be, been,* and *being.* In each case, determine whether the *be* verb is necessary or whether it could be replaced with an action verb for greater impact.

Try It Out ✎

Revise each of the following sentences by substituting an interesting action verb for the dull *be* verb.

1. The Chief of Heaven was angry at Sky Woman.
2. Paradise was the home of the Chief of Heaven, Sky Woman, and many animals and plants.
3. Animals of all kinds were her friends.
4. The shell of that turtle is now the earth.
5. Many things from the sky are now on earth.

LANGUAGE HANDBOOK 757

Quick Check 3: Answers

1. simple, complex—predicate adjectives
2. world—predicate nominative
3. fortune—predicate nominative
4. possible—predicate adjective
5. permanent—predicate adjective

Try It Out: Possible Answers

1. The Chief of Heaven burned with anger at Sky Woman.
2. The Chief of Heaven, Sky Woman, and many animals and plants lived in paradise.
3. Animals of all kinds befriended her.
4. The shell of that turtle changed into the earth.
5. Many things from the sky now flourish on earth.

Resources ———

- *Language Handbook Worksheets,* pp. 95–102
- *Language Workshop CD-ROM,* Lesson 34: Sentence Structure; Lesson 35: Sentence Purpose

SENTENCES CLASSIFIED BY STRUCTURE

One way that sentences are classified is by **structure**—the kinds of clauses and the number of clauses the sentences contain.

The Simple Sentence

10a. A *simple sentence* **has one independent clause and no subordinate clauses.**

EXAMPLE   Jean Fritz and her parents discussed her problem and
                                         found a clever solution to it.

Notice in the example above that a simple sentence may have a compound subject, a compound verb, or both.

> For more about compound subjects and compound verbs, see pages 721 and 753.

The Compound Sentence

10b. A *compound sentence* **has two or more independent clauses but no subordinate clauses.**

The independent clauses are usually joined by a coordinating conjunction *and, but, for, nor, or, so,* or *yet.* The independent clauses in a compound sentence may also be joined by a semicolon.

EXAMPLES   Jared read *Old Yeller,* and then he saw the movie.

               Anne McCaffrey has written many stories about drag-
                                         ons; in fact, she has contributed to their popularity.

> For more about using commas in compound sentences, see page 769. For more about using semicolons, see pages 771–772.

The Complex Sentence

10c. A *complex sentence* **has one independent clause and at least one subordinate clause.**

EXAMPLE   When I read one of Anne McCaffrey's stories, I want to ride a dragon.

Independent Clause   I want to ride a dragon

Subordinate Clause   When I read one of Anne McCaffrey's stories

QUICK CHECK I

...tify each of the following sentences as *simple, compound,* ...omplex.

...MPLE   1. *Homesick* was interesting to me because I
              once lived abroad.

           1. *complex*

...Boys and girls ran and played on the playground.
...ean Fritz did not feel like part of their world at the
...British school.

...They sang "God Save the King," but she didn't.

...Her problem disappeared after she spoke to her
...father.

...She told her amah that *sewing machine* meant "hello."

Using Varied Sentence Structure

Variety is the spice of life. It's also the spice of writing. By varying the length and ...structure of your sentences, you can make your writing ...rer and more interesting to read.

...imple sentences are best used to express single ideas. ...escribe more complicated ideas and to show relation-...s between them, use compound and complex sentences.

SENTENCES CLASSIFIED BY PURPOSE

...ddition to being classified by structure, a sentence is also classified ac-...ding to its purpose. The four kinds of sentences are *declarative, inter-*...*tive, imperative,* and *exclamatory.*

...**d.**   A *declarative sentence* makes a statement. It is followed by
       a period.

...MPLE   I can guess what that is.

...**e.**   An *interrogative sentence* asks a question. It is followed by
       a question mark.

...MPLE   What was the matter with Ted's bike?

...**f.**   An *imperative sentence* gives a command or makes a
       request. It is followed by a period. A strong command is
       followed by an exclamation point.

...MPLES   Please open the door, Theo.
           Look out!

A computer can help you analyze your writing for sentence length and structure. Programs are available that will tell you the average number of words in your sentences and the number of each kind of sentence you used. In this way, you can easily see which sentence structures you've mastered and which ones you'll need to work on.

Try It Out

Read each of the following items containing short sentences. Decide what type of sentence structure would best express the ideas in each item. Then, rewrite the item.

1. Commas seemed complicated. Andrea Hull knew how to use them.
2. Andrea Hull knew more than young Jean. Andrea taught her many things.
3. Embroidery is beautiful. It can be tedious.
4. She stretched the cloth. She marked her pattern. She began stitching.
5. A design is finished. Everyone can enjoy it.

NOTE   If an imperative sentence does not have a subject, the "understood" subject is always *you.*

EXAMPLE
(You) Do it now!

LANGUAGE HANDBOOK 759

Quick Check I: Answers
1. simple
2. simple
3. compound
4. complex
5. complex

Try It Out: Possible Answers
1. Though commas seemed complicated, Andrea Hull knew how to use them.
2. Andrea Hull, who knew more than young Jean, taught Jean many things.
3. Embroidery is beautiful, but it can be tedious.
4. After she stretched the cloth, she marked her pattern and began stitching.
5. After a design is finished, everyone can enjoy it.

☞ For more on the different end marks of punctuation, see page 768.

10g. An *exclamatory sentence* shows excitement or express strong feeling. An exclamatory sentence is followed by exclamation point.

EXAMPLES   What a bargain this is**!**
We won regionals**!**

✓ QUICK CHECK 2

Classify each of the following sentences according to its purpose— *declarative, interrogative, imperative,* or *exclamatory.*

EXAMPLE   1. Explain the theme of this story, Andy.
1. *imperative*

1. Have you ever lived in a foreign country?
2. As a child, Jean Fritz attended a British school in China.
3. How wonderful the Yangtze River was!
4. Please take me there.
5. Read *Homesick,* and see for yourself.

11 WRITING EFFECTIVE SENTENCES

Combining Sentences

11a. Improve short, choppy sentences by combining them in longer, smoother sentences.

There are many ways to combine sentences. Here are a few examples.

(1) Insert words and phrases.

CHOPPY   The pan was hot. The pan was made of iron.
COMBINED   The **iron** pan was hot.

CHOPPY   Cook the steak. Cook it for five minutes.
COMBINED   Cook the steak **for five minutes.**

(2) Use coordinating conjunctions.

CHOPPY   Father likes steak. Mother does too.
COMBINED   Father **and** Mother like steak.

CHOPPY   The preparation was Chinese. The food was not.
COMBINED   The preparation was Chinese, **but** the food was not.

(3) Use subordinate clauses.

CHOPPY   Be careful. It is easy to be burned.
COMBINED   Be careful **because it is easy to be burned.**

CHOPPY   I sliced the meat. It was already cooked.

COMBINED   I sliced the meat **that was already cooked.**

QUICK CHECK 1

Use the methods you've learned in this section to combine some of the choppy sentences in the following paragraph.

EXAMPLE   [1] He is Chinese. [2] He is American.
   1. *He is Chinese and American.*

[1] "T-Bone Steak" is a poem about identity. [2] It was written by Wing Tek Lum. [3] The poet describes an ordinary moment. [4] This ordinary moment is filled with meaning. [5] The meaning is complex. [6] It includes self-assertion, rebellion, respect, and self-acceptance. [7] Preparing the meal is almost a ritual for the family. [8] It is a ritual that asserts their individuality. [9] The meal draws from Chinese and American customs. [10] Elements of both cultures contribute to the family's identity.

Revising Run-on Sentences

11b.   Avoid using run-on sentences.

If you run together two complete sentences as if they were one sentence, you get a *run-on sentence.*

RUN-ON   This poet values individuality, he also respects tradition.

Here are two of the ways you can revise run-on sentences.

You can make two sentences.

REVISED   This poet values individuality**.** **He** also respects tradition.

You can use a comma and the coordinating conjunction *and, but,* or *or.*

REVISED   This poet values individuality**,** **but** he also respects tradition.

Revising Stringy Sentences and Wordy Sentences

11c.   Improve *stringy* and *wordy sentences* by making them shorter and more precise.

Stringy sentences have too many independent clauses strung together with words like *and* or *but.*

STRINGY   The Hummingbird King was betrayed, and an enemy betrayed him, and Kukul turned into a hummingbird, for the hummingbird symbolizes freedom for the Maya, and even today he watches everything.

> **NOTE**   A *comma splice* is a kind of run-on sentence in which a comma is used without a coordinating conjunction to join independent clauses. The sample run-on sentence given under rule 11b is a comma splice.

LANGUAGE HANDBOOK   761

LANGUAGE HANDBOOK

Quick Check 1: Possible Answers

Written by Wing Tek Lum, "T-Bone Steak" is a poem about identity. The poet descries an ordinary moment filled with complex meaning, which includes self-assertion, rebellion, respect, and self-acceptance. Preparing the meal is almost a ritual that asserts the family's individuality. The meal draws from Chinese and American customs, because elements of both cultures contribute to the family's identity.

T761

To fix a stringy sentence, you can break the sentence into two or m[ore]
sentences. You can also turn some of the independent clauses into
phrases or subordinate clauses.

REVISED   When the Hummingbird King was betrayed by an enem[y,]
Kukul turned into a hummingbird, the symbol of freedo[m]
for the Maya. Even today, he watches everything.

You can revise wordy sentences in three different ways.

1. Replace a group of words with one word.

WORDY   With great sorrow, they mourned their king.

REVISED   **Sorrowfully,** they mourned their king.

2. Replace a clause with a phrase.

WORDY   When Kukul's life ended, he turned into a hummingbird[.]

REVISED   **After his death,** Kukul turned into a hummingbird.

3. Take out a whole group of unnecessary words.

WORDY   What I mean to say is that Kukul is known as the *quetza[l.]*

REVISED   Kukul is known as the *quetzal.*

 QUICK CHECK 2

The following paragraph contains run-on, stringy, and wordy sentences[.]
Revise them to improve the style of the paragraph.

EXAMPLE   [1] We know little about many ancient cultures due to th[e]
fact that records have been lost.
     1. *We know little about many ancient cultures because recor[ds]*
have been lost.

[1] Many people all over the world have legends,
these legends tell of people being turned into animals[.]
[2] It seems evident that people must feel a great kins[hip]
with the animals. [3] Many of these legends feature an
animal, and the animal was once a person, and that
person had special powers. [4] The fact is that many
animals have powers that people do not have. [5] Perhaps these legends are expressive of the idea that peo[ple]
sometimes have envy for animals.

Revising Wordy Sentences

Extra words and phrases tend to make
writing sound awkward and unnatural.
As you revise your writing, read your sentences aloud to
check for wordiness or a stringy style. If you run out of
breath before the end of a sentence, it is likely stringy,
wordy, or both.

Quick Check 2: Possible Answers

1. The world over, many legends tell of people being turned into animals.
2. Evidently, people feel a great kinship with animals.
3. Many of these legends feature an animal that was once a person with special powers.
4. Many animals do have powers that people do not have.
5. Perhaps these legends show that people sometimes envy animals.

Try It Out: Possible Answers

1. Many legends, myths, and fairy tales have survived for centuries because they address something important in people.
2. Their impossibility continually surprises and delights readers.
3. People have long told stories that explain both human behavior and natural forces.
4. Children and their parents read these stories or view them on film.
5. The needs of a culture, the details of a story, and its ending may change, but the readers remain.

Try It Out

Revise each of the following sentences to eliminate wordiness and stringy style.

1. The reason that many legends, myths, and fairy tales have survived for centuries is that they address something important in people.
2. They continually surprise and delight readers due to the fact of their impossibility.
3. People have long told stories that explain human behavior and ones that explain natural forces in the world.
4. Children read these stories or view them on film, and so do their parents.
5. The needs of a culture change, and details of the story change, and the ending may change, but the readers remain.

2 CAPITAL LETTERS

Capitalize the first word in every sentence.

EXAMPLE   Who gets a place in the choir?

The first word of a sentence that is a direct quotation is capitalized only if the quotation begins within a sentence.

EXAMPLE   Francis Bacon states, "**K**nowledge is power."

Traditionally, the first word in a line of poetry is capitalized. However, some modern poets and writers do not follow this style. When you are quoting, follow the capitalization used in the source of the quotation.

EXAMPLE   **I**t was many and many a year ago,
        In a kingdom by the sea,
      That a maiden there lived whom you may know
        By the name of Annabel Lee;
      And this maiden she lived with no other thought
        Than to love and be loved by me.
            —Edgar Allan Poe, "Annabel Lee"

Capitalize the pronoun *I*.

EXAMPLE   **I** enjoyed the book, but **I** didn't like the film.

Capitalize the interjection *O*.

The interjection *O* is most often used on solemn or formal occasions. It is usually followed by a word in direct address.

EXAMPLE   Protect us in the battle, **O** great Athena!

QUICK CHECK 1

Most of the following sentences contain errors in capitalization. If a sentence is correct, write *C*. If there are errors in the use of capitals, correct the word or words that should be changed.

EXAMPLE   **1.** William says that *i* am his best friend.
        1. *I*

1. If i need a ride, i will give you a call.
2. Loretta is in Maine, but Oh, how she would like to visit Paris.
3. oh no, I left my backpack on the bus!
4. Please accept these gifts, o Lord.
5. The poem ends with a question.

Capitalize proper nouns.

A *common noun* is a general name for a person, a place, a thing, or an idea. A *proper noun* names a particular person, place, thing, or idea.

> ☞ For more about using capital letters in quotations, see page 774.

> **NOTE**   The interjection *oh* requires a capital letter only at the beginning of a sentence. Otherwise, *oh* is not capitalized.
>
> **EXAMPLES**   **Oh**, look at the sunset!
> We felt tired but, **oh**, so victorious.

Quick Check 1: Answers
1. I, I
2. oh
3. Oh
4. O
5. C

You may be able to use your spelling checker to help you capitalize names correctly. Make a list of the names you write most often. Be sure that you have spelled and capitalized each name correctly. Then, add this list to your computer's dictionary or spelling checker.

A common noun is capitalized only when it begins a sentence or is part of a title. A proper noun is always capitalized. Some proper nouns consist of more than one word. In these names, short prepositions (those of fewer than five letters) and articles (*a, an, the*) are not capitalized.

COMMON NOUNS	statue	man
PROPER NOUNS	Statue of Liberty	Eric the R

(1) Capitalize the names of persons and animal

EXAMPLES Franklin Chang-Díaz, Alice Walker, Lassie, Shamu

(2) Capitalize geographical names.

TYPE OF NAME	EXAMPLES
Towns, Cities	San Diego, Jamestown
Islands	Isle of Wight, Wake Island
Counties, States	Cook County, New Hampshire
Countries	New Zealand, Germany
Bodies of Water	Gulf of Mexico, Indian Ocean
Forests, Parks	Sherwood Forest, Yellowstone National Par
Streets, Highways	Route 44, West Fourth Street
Mountains	Mount Washington, Big Horn Mountain
Continents	South America, Asia
Regions	the West Coast, the Great Plains

NOTE In a hyphenated street number, the second part of the number is not capitalized.

EXAMPLE Seventy-eighth Street

NOTE Words such as *north, east,* and *southwest* are not capitalized when they indicate direction, but they are capitalized when they are part of a proper name.

EXAMPLES go south for the winter
northeast of Atlanta
East End Cafe
Old West Jamboree

(3) Capitalize the names of planets, stars, and other heavenly bodies.

EXAMPLES Jupiter   Sirius   Milky Way
Big Dipper   North Star

(4) Capitalize the names of teams, organizations, businesses, institutions, and government bodies.

TYPE OF NAME	EXAMPLES
Teams	Detroit Pistons, Seattle Seahawks
Organizations	Girl Scouts, African Studies Association
Businesses	Wilson's Vacuum World, Seaside Cycle Shop
Institutions	Cary Memorial Hospital, Hilltop High School
Government Bodies	Air National Guard, Department of Agricultur

NOTE The word *earth* is not capitalized unless it is used along with the names of other heavenly bodies that are capitalized. The words *sun* and *moon* are not capitalized.

● Capitalize the names of historical events and periods, special events, and calendar items.

TYPE OF NAME	EXAMPLES
Historical Events	**B**attle of **B**unker **H**ill, **Y**alta **C**onference
Historical Periods	**G**reat **D**epression, **M**iddle **A**ges
Special Events	**O**klahoma **S**tate **F**air, **C**annes **F**ilm **F**estival
Calendar Items	**F**riday, **F**ourth of **J**uly

● Capitalize the names of nationalities, races, and peoples.

EXAMPLES Greek, Asian, Caucasian, Hispanic, Shawnee

● Capitalize the names of religions and their followers, holy days, sacred writings, and specific deities.

TYPE OF NAME	EXAMPLES
Religions and Followers	**Z**en **B**uddhism, **C**hristianity, **M**uslim
Holy Days	**P**assover, **L**ent, **R**amadan
Sacred Writings	**T**ao **T**e **C**hing, **B**ible, **T**almud, **K**oran
Specific Deities	**H**oly **S**pirit, **B**rahma, **A**llah, **J**ehovah

● Capitalize the names of buildings and other structures.

EXAMPLES World Trade Center, Golden Gate Bridge, Ritz Theater

● Capitalize the names of monuments and awards.

TYPE OF NAME	EXAMPLES
Monuments	**V**ietnam **V**eterans **M**emorial, **S**tatue of **L**iberty
Awards	**N**ewbery **M**edal, **P**urple **H**eart

10) Capitalize the names of trains, ships, aircraft, and spacecraft.

TYPE OF NAME	EXAMPLES
Trains	*Silver Rocket, Orient Express*
Ships	*Nimitz, Santa Maria*
Aircraft	*Spirit of St. Louis, Air Force One*
Spacecraft	*Apollo 11, Columbia*

NOTE The name of a season is not capitalized unless it is part of a proper name.

EXAMPLES the last day of summer, the Oak Ridge Winter Carnival

NOTE The word *god* is not capitalized when it refers to a mythological god. The names of specific gods, however, are capitalized.

EXAMPLE The king of Greek gods was Zeus.

EXAMPLES Nike shoes, Buick station wagon, Wrangler jeans

 QUICK CHECK 2

Correct each of the following expressions, using capital letters as needed

EXAMPLE 1. the stone age
1. *the Stone Age*

1. decisions of the united states supreme court
2. three skeleton key, an island off guiana
3. pictures of saturn sent by *voyager 2*
4. the apaches of the southwest
5. the tomb of the unknown soldier

12e. Capitalize proper adjectives.

A *proper adjective* is formed from a proper noun and is almost always capitalized.

PROPER NOUN   Rome, Islam, King Arthur
PROPER ADJECTIVE   Roman army, Islamic culture, Arthurian legen

**12f. Do *not* capitalize the names of school subjects, except la
guage classes and course names followed by a number.**

EXAMPLES I have tests in English, math, and Art II.

12g. Capitalize titles.

(1) **Capitalize the title of a person when it comes before a nam**

EXAMPLES Does Ms. Tam know Dr. Politi or Governor Halsey?

(2) **Capitalize a title used alone or following a person's name only when you want to emphasize
the position of someone holding a high office.**

EXAMPLES We grew quiet as the Rabbi rose to speak
Is he the rabbi at the new synagogue?

A title used alone in direct address is often capitalized.

EXAMPLES Is the patient resting comfortably, Nurse?
What is your name, Sir [*or* sir]?

(3) **Capitalize a word showing a family relationship
when the word is used before or in place of a
person's name.**

EXAMPLES Hey, Mom, I received a letter from Aunt
Christina and Uncle Garth.

Quick Check 2: Answers
1. decisions of the United States Supreme Court
2. Three Skeleton Key, an island off Guiana
3. pictures of Saturn sent by *Voyager 2*
4. the Apaches of the Southwest
5. the Tomb of the Unknown Soldier

☞ For more about proper nouns and proper adjectives, see pages 709 and 712–713.

 Remember that correct capitalization of abbrevia-tions is part of proper spelling. You may notice that certain abbreviations are capitalized.

EXAMPLES Mr. Ms. U.S. TV Fla.
NAACP

However, some abbreviations, especially those for measurements, are not capitalized.

EXAMPLES in. ft lb cc ml

Consult a dictionary for the correct capi-talization of an abbreviation.

---

766 LANGUAGE HANDBOOK

Do not capitalize a word showing a family relationship when a posses-
comes before the word.

AMPLES Angela's **m**other and my **g**randmother Daphne coach the
softball team.

**Capitalize the first and last words and all important words
in titles of books, magazines, newspapers, poems, short
stories, historical documents, movies, television programs,
works of art, and musical compositions.**

mportant words in titles include

prepositions of fewer than five letters (such as *at, of, for, from, with*)

pordinating conjunctions (*and, but, for, nor, or, so, yet*)

rticles (*a, an, the*)

TYPE OF NAME	EXAMPLES
ooks	*The Old Man and the Sea, Dust Tracks on a Road*
Magazines	*Sports Illustrated, Woman's Day*
Newspapers	*San Francisco Examiner, The Miami Herald*
Poems	"My Father Is a Simple Man," "Annabel Lee"
hort Stories	"The Naming of Names," "A Day's Wait"
Historical Documents	Bill of Rights, Emancipation Proclamation
Movies	*Stand and Deliver, Jurassic Park*
elevision Programs	*FBI: The Untold Stories, A Different World*
Works of Art	*Birth of Venus, The Old Guitarist*
Musical Compositions	*The Marriage of Figaro,* "In the Pines"

QUICK CHECK 3

e capital or lowercase letters to correct each error in capitalization in
following sentences.

AMPLE 1. Did you know that dr. Santos subscribes to *field and
stream*?
1. *Did you know that Dr. Santos subscribes to* <u>Field and Stream</u>?

When my Aunt Rose and I went to Mexico, she introduced me to
grandmother Villa.
Try looking up that word in *the american heritage dictionary.*
Did you hear commissioner of education boylan's speech?
Did the treasurer review the club's budget, senator?
When I get older, I hope I will be like the father in "My Father Is A
Simple Man."

NOTE The article *the* before a title is not
capitalized unless it is the
first word of the title.

EXAMPLES Is that the
late edition of the
Chicago Sun-Times?
I read an interesting story
in *The New Yorker.*

If you are not sure
whether *the* is part of a
magazine's title, look for
the official title in the magazine's masthead or on the
table-of-contents page. For
a newspaper, look on the
editorial page. For a book,
look on the title page.

☞ For information on
when to italicize (under-
line) a title, see page 773.
For information on using
quotation marks for titles,
see page 776.

Quick Check 3: Answers

1. When my Aunt Rose and I went to
   Mexico, she introduced me to
   Grandmother Villa.
2. Try looking up that word in *The
   American Heritage Dictionary.*
3. Did you hear Commissioner of
   Education Boylan's speech?
4. Did the treasurer review the club's
   budget, Senator?
5. When I get older, I hope I will be like
   the father in "My Father Is a Simple
   Man."

NOTE A two-letter state abbreviation without periods is used only when it is followed by a ZIP Code.

EXAMPLE
Austin, **TX** 78741

 NOTE Some widely used abbreviations are written without periods.

EXAMPLES UN, FBI, PTA, NAACP, PBS, CNN, YMCA, VHF

 NOTE Abbreviations for most units of measure are written without periods.

EXAMPLES cm, kg, ml, ft, lb, mi, oz, qt

The abbreviation for *inch* (*in.*) is written with a period to prevent confusion with the word *in.* If you're not sure whether to use periods with abbreviations, look in a dictionary.

13 PUNCTUATION

END MARKS

An **end mark** is a mark of punctuation placed at the end of a sentence. The three kinds of end marks are the *period*, the *question mark*, and the *exclamation point.*

13a. Use a period at the end of a statement.

EXAMPLE Kristi Yamaguchi is a world-champion figure skater.

13b. Use a question mark at the end of a question.

EXAMPLE Did Gordon Parks write *The Learning Tree*?

13c. Use an exclamation point at the end of an exclamation.

EXAMPLES Wow! What a view!

13d. Use a period or an exclamation point at the end of a request or a command.

EXAMPLES Please give me the scissors. [a request]
Give me the scissors! [a command]

13e. Use a period after most abbreviations.

TYPES OF ABBREVIATIONS	EXAMPLES			
Personal Names	Pearl S. Buck		W.E.B. Du Boi	
Titles Used with Names	Mr.	Ms.	Jr.	Sr.	Dr
States	Ky.	Fla.	Tenn.	Cali
Addresses	St.	Blvd.	P.O. Box	
Organizations and Companies	Co.	Inc.	Corp.	Assr
Times	A.M.	P.M.	B.C.	A.D.

Place A.D. before the number and B.C. after the number. For centuries expressed in words, place both A.D. and B.C. after the century.

EXAMPLES A.D. 540   31 B.C.   sixth century B.C.   third century A

When an abbreviation with a period ends a sentence, another period is not needed. However, a question mark or an exclamation point is use as needed.

EXAMPLES This is my friend J. R.
Have you met Nguyen, J. R.?

QUICK CHECK I

d end marks where they are needed in the following sentences.

AMPLE   I. Japanese haiku are very short poems
           I. *Japanese haiku are very short poems.*

Have you ever heard of Little Tokyo

It's a Japanese neighborhood in Los Angeles, Calif, bordered by First St, Third St, Alameda St, and Los Angeles St

Some friends of ours who live in Los Angeles, Mr and Mrs Cook, Sr, and their son, Al, Jr, introduced us to the area

They met our 11:30 AM flight from Atlanta, Ga, and took us to lunch at a restaurant in the Japanese Plaza Village

What a great afternoon we had with our friends

COMMAS

ems in a Series

f. **Use commas to separate items in a series.**

ords, phrases, and clauses in a series are separated by commas to show e reader where one item in the series ends and the next item begins. mmas are always needed with three or more items in a series. Two ms often do not need a comma.

VORDS IN A SERIES   *Hammock, canoe,* and *moccasin* are Native American words.

IRASES IN A SERIES   Seaweed was in the water, on the beach, and in our shoes.

AUSES IN A SERIES   Tell us who was there, what happened, and why it happened.

If all items in a series are joined by *and* or *or,* commas are not needed.

AMPLE   I voted for Corey **and** Mona **and** Ethan.

g. **Use a comma to separate two or more adjectives that come before a noun.**

AMPLE   An Arabian horse is a fast, beautiful animal.

ompound Sentences

h. **Use a comma before *and, but, or, nor, for, so,* or *yet* when it joins independent clauses.**

AMPLE   I enjoyed *The King and I,* **but** *Oklahoma!* is still my favorite musical.

You may omit the comma before *and, but, or,* or *nor* if the clauses e very short and there is no chance of misunderstanding.

LANGUAGE HANDBOOK 769

Quick Check I: Answers

I. Have you ever heard of Little Tokyo?

2. It's a Japanese neighborhood in Los Angeles, Calif., bordered by First St., Third St., Alameda St., and Los Angeles St.

3. Some friends of ours who live in Los Angeles, Mr. and Mrs. Cook, Sr., and their son Al, Jr., introduced us to the area.

4. They met our 11:30 A.M. flight from Atlanta, Ga., and took us to lunch at a restaurant in the Japanese Plaza Village.

5. What a great afternoon we had with our friends!

LANGUAGE HANDBOOK

T769

Interrupters

13i. Use commas to set off an expression that interrupts a sentence.

Two commas are needed if the expression comes in the middle of the sentence. One comma is needed if the expression comes at the beginning or the end of the sentence.

EXAMPLES   Yes, my favorite gospel singers, BeBe and CeCe Winar were on TV, Ed.

(1) Use commas to set off a *nonessential* participial phrase or a *nonessential* subordinate clause.

A *nonessential* (or *nonrestrictive*) phrase or clause adds information the sentence but can be omitted without changing the main idea of the sentence.

NONESSENTIAL PHRASE   Orpheus, **mourning his bride,** entere Hades.

NONESSENTIAL CLAUSE   Orpheus, **who was a musician,** met a cruel fate.

(2) Use commas to set off an appositive or an appositive phras that is nonessential.

APPOSITIVE   The gray ferryman, **Charon,** did not charge him any fare.

APPOSITIVE PHRASE   Even Cerberus, **the dog at the gate,** listene

(3) Use commas to set off words used in direct address.

EXAMPLE   Do you know, **Elena,** when the next bus is due?

(4) Use commas to set off a parenthetical expression.

A *parenthetical expression* is a side remark that either adds information or relates ideas in a sentence. Some of these expressions are not always used as interrupters. Use commas only when the expressions are parenthetical.

EXAMPLES   What, **in your opinion,** is the best solution to this problem? [parenthetical]
I have faith **in your opinion.** [not parenthetical]

Introductory Words, Phrases, and Clauses

13j. Use a comma after certain introductory elements.

(1) Use a comma after *yes*, *no*, or any mild exclamation such a *well* or *why* at the beginning of a sentence.

 NOTE   Do not set off an *essential* (or *restrictive*) phrase or clause. It cannot be omitted without changing the meaning of the sentence.

ESSENTIAL PHRASE   All the spirits **toiling in Hades** stopped and listened.

ESSENTIAL CLAUSE   The song **that Orpheus sang** charmed the king of Hades.

AMPLE   Yes, King Midas had been foolish.

Use a comma after an introductory prepositional phrase if the phrase is long or if two or more phrases appear together.

AMPLES   **Long ago in a land called Lydia,** King Midas lived.
In the garden of his palace, he met Silenus.

Use a comma after a participial phrase or an infinitive phrase that introduces a sentence.

RTICIPIAL PHRASE   **Threatened by Midas,** the satyr struck a bargain.

NFINITIVE PHRASE   **To reward Midas,** Dionysus offered a gift.

Use a comma after an introductory adverb clause.

AMPLE   **When his daughter arrived,** he warned her to stay away.

nventional Situations

Use commas in certain conventional situations.

Use commas to separate items in dates and addresses.

AMPLES   They met on June 17, 1965, in Erie, Pennsylvania.
My address is 520 Cocoa Lane, Orlando, FL 32804.

Use a comma after the salutation of a friendly letter and after the closing of any letter.

AMPLES   Dear Aunt Margaret,   Sincerely yours,

QUICK CHECK 2

ert commas where they are needed in the following sentences.

AMPLE   1. This story the tale of King Midas warns us about greed.
1. *This story, the tale of King Midas, warns us about greed.*

Horrified by the sight of his daughter Midas wept.
Well Midas left the palace went to Dionysus and begged relief.
Dionysus sometimes a merciful god told him to go to Pactolus.
In the deep strong waters of the river Midas washed himself.
My friend do not make Midas's error or you may not find mercy.

:micolons

Use a semicolon instead of a comma between independent clauses when they are not joined by *and, but, or, nor, for, so,* or *yet.*

AMPLE   Our parents settled our dispute; they gave us each half.

NOTE Use a semicolon rather than a period between independent clauses only when the ideas in the clauses are closely related.

EXAMPLE I called Leon; he will be here in ten minutes.

Quick Check 2: Answers

1. Horrified by the sight of his daughter, Midas wept.
2. Well, Midas left the palace, went to Dionysus, and begged relief.
3. Dionysus, sometimes a merciful god, told him to go to Pactolus.
4. In the deep, strong waters of the river, Midas washed himself.
5. My friend, do not make Midas's error, or you may not find mercy.

Try It Out: Possible Answers

1. The frogs wanted a king who could amuse them with royal customs. A strong ruler would be exciting, they thought.
2. Jupiter heard their request, and though he granted it, he felt they were foolish.
3. Jupiter threw down a large log, and it landed next to the frogs.
4. Was this strange, new king fearsome, or was he peaceful?
5. Strangely enough, these spoiled, bored frogs were not grateful. They petitioned Jupiter, who again granted their wish.

Quick Check 3: Answers

1. Some reptiles like a dry climate; others prefer a wet climate.
2. The first lunch period begins at 11:00 A.M.
3. Icarus flew too high; his wings melted.
4. In Ruth 1:16, Ruth pledges her loyalty to Naomi.
5. The frogs wanted a king; they got one.

Try It Out ✎

Decide whether each of the following sentences is better expressed as a single sentence or as two or more sentences. Then, write the sentence accordingly. Revise the sentence for style and clarity as well.

1. The frogs wanted a king, one who could amuse them with royal customs; they thought a strong ruler would be exciting.
2. Jupiter heard their request; he granted it; he felt they were foolish.
3. Jupiter threw down a large log; the log landed next to the frogs.
4. Was this strange, new king fearsome; was he peaceful?
5. Strangely enough, these spoiled, bored frogs were not grateful; they petitioned Jupiter, who again granted their wish.

NOTE Never use a colon directly after a verb or a preposition. Omit the colon, or reword the sentence.

INCORRECT My stepsister's favorite sports are: basketball, tennis, swimming, and bowling.

CORRECT My stepsister's favorite sports are basketball, tennis, swimming, and bowling.

NOTE Use a colon between chapter and verse in referring to passages from the Bible.

EXAMPLES John 3:16
Matthew 6:9-13

Using Semicolons

Semicolons are most effective when they are not overused. Sometimes it is better to separate a compound sentence or a heavily punctuated sentence into two sentences rather than to use a semicolon.

ACCEPTABLE In the jungles of South America, it rain every day, sometimes all day; the vegetation there, some of which is found nowhere else in the world, is lush, dense, and fast-growing.

BETTER In the jungles of South America, it rain practically every day, sometimes all day The vegetation there, some of which is found nowhere else in the world, is lu dense, and fast-growing.

Colons

13m. Use a colon before a list of items, especially after expressions like *as follows* or *the following*.

EXAMPLE Minimum equipment for camping include the following: bedroll, utensils for eating, warm clothing, and rope.

13n. Use a colon in certain conventional situations.

(1) Use a colon between the hour and the minute.

EXAMPLES 11:30 P.M.   4:08 A.M.

(2) Use a colon after the salutation of a business letter.

EXAMPLES Dear Ms. Gonzalez: To Whom It May Concern:

✓ QUICK CHECK 3

Insert a colon or semicolon wherever one is needed in each sentence.

EXAMPLE 1. Daedalus made Minos the following furniture, weapons and armor.
1. *Daedalus made Minos the following: furniture, weapons, a armor.*

1. Some reptiles like a dry climate others prefer a wet climate.
2. The first lunch period begins at 11 00 A.M.
3. Icarus flew too high his wings melted.
4. In Ruth 1 16, Ruth pledges her loyalty to Naomi.
5. The frogs wanted a king they got one.

UNDERLINING (ITALICS)

...cs are printed letters that lean to the right, such as *the ...rs in these words*. In handwritten or typewritten work, ...cate italics by underlining.

TYPED   <u>Born Free</u> is the story of a lion that became a pet.

...BLISHED   *Born Free* is the story of a lion that became a pet.

COMPUTER NOTE If you use a computer, you may be able to set words in italics yourself. Most word-processing software and many printers are capable of producing italic type.

a. Use underlining (italics) for titles of books, plays, periodicals, works of art, films, television programs, recordings, long musical compositions, trains, ships, aircraft, and spacecraft.

TYPE OF TITLE	EXAMPLES	
Books	*Barrio Boy*	*House Made of Dawn*
Plays	*Macbeth*	*Visit to a Small Planet*
Periodicals	*Hispanic*	*The New York Times*
Works of Art	*The Thinker*	*American Gothic*
Films	*Stand and Deliver*	*Jurassic Park*
Television Programs	*Home Improvement*	*Wall Street Week*
Recordings	*Unforgettable*	*Man of Steel*
Long Musical Compositions	*Don Giovanni*	*The Four Seasons*
Ships	*Calypso*	*USS Nimitz*
Trains	*Orient Express*	*City of New Orleans*
Aircraft	*Enola Gay*	*Spirit of St. Louis*
Spacecraft	*Apollo 12*	*USS Enterprise*

NOTE The article *the* before the title of a magazine or a newspaper is usually neither italicized nor capitalized when it is written within a sentence. Some periodicals do include *the* in their titles.

EXAMPLES My parents subscribe to the *San Francisco Chronicle.* On Sundays, we all share *The New York Times.*

☞ For examples of titles that are not italicized but enclosed in quotation marks, see page 776.

b. Use underlining (italics) for words, letters, and figures referred to as such.

...AMPLES What is the difference between the words *affect* and *effect*?
Don't forget to drop the final *e* before you add *–ing* to that word.
Is the last number a *5* or an *8*?

Resources ————

- *Language Handbook Worksheets,* pp. 135–139
- *Language Workshop CD-ROM,* Lessons 49 and 50: Punctuating Titles and Quotations

LANGUAGE HANDBOOK

Quick Check 1: Answers

1. Sometimes I forget the <u>r</u> in the word <u>friend</u> and write <u>fiend</u>.
2. Pablo Picasso's famous painting <u>Guernica</u> is named for a Spanish town that was bombed during the Spanish Civil War.
3. My father reads the <u>Washington Post</u> because he likes Carl Rowan's column.
4. The movie <u>My Left Foot</u> celebrates the accomplishments of a writer and artist who has serious disabilities.
5. Janice finally found her mistake; she had written the <u>4</u> in the wrong column.

NOTE Do not use quotation marks for an *indirect quotation,* which is a rewording of a direct quotation.

DIRECT QUOTATION
Kaya asked, "What is your interpretation of the poem?"

INDIRECT QUOTATION
Kaya asked what my interpretation of the poem was.

✓ *QUICK CHECK 1*

Underline the words that should be italicized in each of the following sentences.

EXAMPLE 1. Who will play the lead in Brian's Song?
1. *Who will play the lead in <u>Brian's Song</u>?*

1. Sometimes I forget the r in the word friend and write fiend.
2. Pablo Picasso's famous painting Guernica is named for a Spanish town that was bombed during the Spanish Civil War.
3. My father reads the Washington Post because he likes Carl Rowan's column.
4. The movie My Left Foot celebrates the accomplishments of a writer and artist who has serious disabilities.
5. Janice finally found her mistake; she had written the 4 in the wrong column.

QUOTATION MARKS

14c. Use quotation marks to enclose a *direct quotation*—a person's exact words.

EXAMPLE "Here is Eric's drawing of the runaway," said Ms. Rios.

14d. A direct quotation begins with a capital letter.

EXAMPLE Brandon shouted, "Let's get busy!"

14e. When the expression identifying the speaker interrupts a quoted sentence, the second part of the quotation begins with a small letter.

EXAMPLE "Gee," Angelo added, "the boy in 'A Day's Wait' is a lot like my brother."

When the second part of a divided quotation is a separate sentence, it begins with a capital letter.

EXAMPLE "Travel is exciting," said Mrs. Ash. "Space travel is no exception."

14f. A direct quotation is set off from the rest of the sentence by a comma, a question mark, or an exclamation point, but not by a period.

Set off means "separated." If a quotation appears at the beginning of a sentence, place a comma after it. If a quotation falls at the end of a sentence, place a comma before it. If a quoted sentence is interrupted, place a comma after the first part and before the second part.

AMPLES "I just read a story by Amy Tan**,**" Alyssa said.

Mark said**,** "I've read a couple of her stories, too."

"Alyssa**,**" asked Janet**,** "what story did you read?"

When a quotation ends with a question mark or an exclamation point, comma is needed.

AMPLE "Have you seen my brother**?**" Alicia asked.

g. A period or a comma is always placed inside the closing quotation marks.

AMPLES Ramón said, "My little brother loves Shel Silverstein's poems**."**

"My sister does too**,"** Paula responded.

h. A question mark or an exclamation point is placed inside the closing quotation marks when the quotation itself is a question or exclamation. Otherwise, it is placed outside.

AMPLES "Is the time difference between Los Angeles and Chicago two hours**?"** asked Ken. [The quotation is a question.]

Linda exclaimed, "I thought everyone knew that**!"** [The quotation is an exclamation.]

What did Sandra Cisneros mean in her story "Four Skinny Trees" when she wrote "Keep, keep, keep, trees say when I sleep**"?** [The sentence, not the quotation, is a question.]

I can't believe that Mom said, "I'm not planning to raise your allowance until next year**"!** [The sentence, not the quotation, is an exclamation.]

When both the sentence and the quotation at the end of the sentence questions (or exclamations), only one question mark (or exclamation nt) is used. It is placed inside the closing quotation marks.

AMPLE Who wrote the poem that begins "How do I love thee**?"**

ii. When you write dialogue (conversation), begin a new paragraph each time you change speakers.

AMPLE "Frog, how may we help you?"

"Uh, well, uh, you see," says Frog, "I would like to become a part of your group."

"That's wonderful," says the head bird.

"Yes, wonderful," echo the other birds.

"Frog, you may help us carry our worms," says the head bird.

"That's not what I had in mind," says Frog.

—Linda Goss, "The Frog Who Wanted to Be a Singer"

LANGUAGE HANDBOOK 775

14j. When a quotation consists of several sentences, place quotation marks at the beginning and at the end of the whole quotation.

EXAMPLE   "Take the garbage out. Clean your room. Have fun!" said Dad.

14k. Use single quotation marks to enclose a quotation with a quotation.

EXAMPLES   "I said, 'The quiz will be this Friday,'" repeated Mr. Allyn.
"What poem begins with the words 'I'm Nobody'?" Carol asked.

14l. Use quotation marks to enclose titles of short works such as short stories, poems, articles, songs, episodes of television programs, and chapters and other parts of books.

TYPE OF TITLE	EXAMPLES	
Short Stories	"Papa's Parrot"	"Amigo Brothers"
Poems	"Early Song"	"The Runaway"
Articles	"Free Speech and Free Air" "How to Sharpen Your Wit"	
Songs	"La Bamba"	"Amazing Grace"
Episodes of Television Programs	"Heart of a Champion" "The Trouble with Tribbles"	
Chapters and Other Parts of Books	"Learning About Reptiles" "English: Origins and Uses"	

☞ For examples of titles that are italicized, see page 773.

✓ **QUICK CHECK 2**

Revise the following sentences by adding commas, end marks, quotation marks, and paragraph breaks where necessary.

[1] Gordon, do you ever think about pencils Annie asked [2] I'm always wondering where I lost mine Gordon replied [3] Well said Annie let me tell you some of the things I learned about pencils [4] Sure Gordon said I love trivia [5] People have used some form of pencils for a long time Annie began [6] The ancient Greeks and Romans used lead pencils [7] However, pencils as we know them weren't developed until the 1500s, when people began using graphite [8] What's graphite asked Gordon [9] Graphite is a soft form of carbon Annie explained that leaves a mark when it's drawn over most surfaces [10] Thanks for the information, Annie Gordon said Now, do you have a pencil I can borrow?

Quick Check 2: Answers
[1] "Gordon, do you ever think about pencils?" Annie asked. [2] "I'm always wondering where I lost mine," Gordon replied. [3] "Well," said Annie, "let me tell you some of the things I learned about pencils." [4] "Sure," Gordon said, "I love trivia." [5] "People have used some form of pencils for a long time," Annie began. [6] "The ancient Greeks and Romans used lead pencils. [7] However, pencils as we know them weren't developed until the 1500s, when people started using graphite." [8] "What's graphite?" asked Gordon. [9] "Graphite is a soft form of carbon," Annie explained, "that leaves a mark when it's drawn over most surfaces." [10] "Thanks for the information, Annie," Gordon said. "Now, do you have a pencil I can borrow?"

APOSTROPHES

a. The *possessive case* of a noun or a pronoun shows ownership or relationship.

To form the possessive case of a singular noun, add an apostrophe and an *s*.

AMPLES a dog's collar   Cinderella's slipper

To form the possessive case of a plural noun ending in *s*, add only the apostrophe.

AMPLES doctors' opinions   hosts' invitations

To form the possessive case of a plural noun that does not end in *s*, add an apostrophe and an *s*.

AMPLES women's suits   geese's noise

To form the possessive case of some indefinite pronouns, add an apostrophe and an *s*.

AMPLES someone's opinion   no one's fault

b. To form a contraction, use an apostrophe to show where letters have been left out.

ontraction is a shortened form of a word, figure, or group of words.

AMPLES
I am ....I'm	they had ....they'd
1996 ....'96	where is ....where's
let us ....let's	of the clock ....o'clock

The word *not* can be shortened to *–n't* and added to a verb, usually 'hout changing the spelling of the verb.

EXAMPLES
is not ....isn't	had not ....hadn't
do not ....don't	should not ...shouldn't

CEPTIONS will not ....**won't**   cannot ....**can't**

Do not confuse contractions with possessive pronouns.

CONTRACTIONS	POSSESSIVE PRONOUNS
t's snowing. [*It is*]	**Its** front tire is flat.
Who's Clifton Davis? [*Who is*]	**Whose** idea was it?
There's only one answer. [*There is*]	This trophy is **theirs**.
They're not here. [*They are*]	**Their** dog is barking.

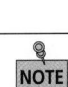 **NOTE** A proper name ending in *s* may take only an apostrophe to form the possessive case if the addition of 's would make the name awkward to pronounce.

EXAMPLES
Ms. Masters' class
Hercules' feats

 NOTE Do not use an apostrophe with possessive personal pronouns.

EXAMPLES **His** pantomime was good, but **hers** was better.

LANGUAGE HANDBOOK 777

LANGUAGE HANDBOOK

Resources
• *Language Handbook Worksheets,* pp. 140–146
• *Language Workshop CD-ROM,* Lessons 47 and 48: Punctuating Possessives, Contractions, and Plurals; Lesson 52: Hyphens, Italics, Parentheses, and Dashes

Quick Check 1: Answers

1. My cousin Dorothy, everybody's favorite, usually gets all A's.
2. It isn't correct to use &'s in your compositions.
3. Many of my friends' scores were in the 80's and 90's
4. They'll meet us later, if it's not raining where we're going.
5. Who's signed up to try out for a part in "Antaeus"?

15c. Use an apostrophe and an *s* to form the plurals of letter numerals, and signs, and of words referred to as words.

EXAMPLES   Your *2*'s look like *5*'s.
              Don't use &'s in place of *and*'s.

✓ *QUICK CHECK 1*

Add an apostrophe wherever one is needed in the following sentences

EXAMPLE   1. Who wrote "A Days Wait," class?
              1. *Who wrote "A Day's Wait," class?*

1. My cousin Dorothy, everybodys favorite, usually gets all As.
2. It isnt correct to use &s in your compositions.
3. Many of my friends scores were in the 80s and 90s.
4. Theyll meet us later, if its not raining where were going.
5. Whos signed up to try out for a part in *Antaeus*?

HYPHENS

15d. Use a hyphen to divide a word at the end of a line.

(1) Divide a word only between syllables.

INCORRECT   Didn't Carrie write her science report on the tyrann osaurs, the largest meat-eating dinosaurs?

CORRECT   Didn't Carrie write her science report on the tyran-nosaurs, the largest meat-eating dinosaurs?

(2) Divide an already hyphenated word at a hyphen.

INCORRECT   I went to the state fair with my sister and my broth-er-in-law.

CORRECT   I went to the state fair with my sister and my brothe in-law.

(3) Do not divide a word so that one letter stand alone.

INCORRECT   On our last class trip, all of us stayed o-vernight in a hotel.

CORRECT   On our last class trip, all of us stayed overnight in a hotel.

15e. Use a hyphen with compound numbers fro *twenty-one* to *ninety-nine* and with fraction used as adjectives.

EXAMPLES   thirty-five   one-half   forty-eighth

TIPS FOR SPELLING

Hyphens are used in some compound names. In such cases, the hyphen is part of the name's spelling.

PEOPLE   Daniel Day-Lewis
            Orlando Hines-Smith
PLACES   Wilkes-Barre [city]
            Stratford-on-Avon [borough]

If you are not sure whether a name is hyphenated, consult a reference source.

---

778 LANGUAGE HANDBOOK

PARENTHESES

6f. Use parentheses to enclose material that is added to a sentence but is not considered of major importance.

EXAMPLES Mohandas K. Gandhi **(1869–1948)** led India's struggle for independence.

Ms. Matsuo served us the sushi **(sōō′shē)**.

Fill in the order form carefully. **(Do not use a pencil.)**

My great-uncle Chester **(he's Grandma's brother)** will stay with us.

DASHES

6g. Use a dash to indicate an abrupt break in thought or speech.

EXAMPLES Ms. Alonzo—she just left—will be one of the judges.

"You'll find it—oh, excuse me, Sir—over here," said the librarian.

QUICK CHECK 2

For each of the following sentences, insert hyphens, parentheses, or dashes where they are needed.

EXAMPLE 1. My grandfather, who is seventy five, can recite "The High wayman."

1. *My grandfather, who is seventy-five, can recite "The High-wayman."*

On Fifty third Street, there is a restaurant called The Highwayman.

The restaurant founded in 1925 draws half of its cus tomers from tourists.

I painted its one hundred thirty one chairs a tedious job, to say the least.

Last night, the restaurant was oh, hi, Ed about one quarter full.

It's decorated like an inn my restaurant won't be.

TIPS FOR WRITERS

Punctuating Parenthetical Information

Too many parenthetical expressions in a piece of writing can distract readers from the main idea. Keep your meaning clear by limiting the number of parenthetical expressions you use.

NOTE Many words and phrases are used *parenthetically;* that is, they break into the main thought of a sentence. Most parenthetical elements are set off by commas or parentheses. Sometimes, parenthetical elements demand stronger emphasis. In such instances, a dash is used.

Try It Out

Revise the following sentences to eliminate the parentheses. If you think the sentence is best written with parentheses, write *C.*

1. *Survive the Savage Sea* (true stories are my favorites) is about people on a raft.
2. Yellowstone National Park (established in 1872) covers territory in Wyoming, Idaho, and Montana.
3. The writer Langston Hughes (1902–1967) is best known for his poetry.
4. Alligators use their feet and tails to dig holes (called "gator holes") in marshy fields.
5. On the Sabbath we eat braided bread called challah (pronounced khä′ lə).

Quick Check 2: Possible Answers

1. On Fifty-third Street, there is a restaurant called the Highwayman.
2. The restaurant (founded in 1925) draws half of its cus-tomers from tourists.
3. I painted its one hundred thirty-one chairs—a tedious job, to say the least.
4. Last night, the restaurant was —oh, hi, Ed—about one-quarter full.
5. It's decorated like an inn (my restaurant won't be).

Try It Out: Possible Answers

1. *Survive the Savage Sea* is about peo-ple on a raft. True stories are my favorites.
2. Established in 1872, Yellowstone National Park covers territory in Wyoming, Idaho, and Montana.
3. C
4. Alligators use their feet and tails to dig holes, called "gator holes," in marshy fields.
5. C

Resources

- *Language Handbook Worksheets,* pp. 147–153
- *Language Workshop CD-ROM,* Lessons 55 and 56: Rules of Spelling

16 SPELLING

USING WORD PARTS

Many English words are made up of various word parts. Learning to sp‹ the most frequently used parts can help you spell many words correctl‹

Roots

16a. The *root* of a word is the part that carries the word's co‹ meaning.

WORD ROOT	MEANING	EXAMPLES
–dict–	speak	dictation, dictionary
–duc–, –duct–	lead	educate, conductor
–ject–	throw	eject, reject
–ped–	foot	pedal, biped
–vid–, –vis–	see	videotape, invisible

Prefixes

16b. A *prefix* is one or more letters or syllables added to the beginning of a word or a word part to create a new wor‹

PREFIX	MEANING	EXAMPLES
anti–	against, opposing	antiwar, anticlimax
co–	with, together	coexist, codependent
in–	not	inaccurate, ineffective
re–	back, again	reclaim, rebuild
trans–	across, beyond	transport, translate

Suffixes

16c. A *suffix* is one or more letters or syllables added to the end of a word or a word part to create a new word.

SUFFIX	MEANING	EXAMPLES
–able	able, likely	readable, perishable
–ance, –ancy	act, quality	admittance, constancy
–ate	become, cause	captivate, activate
–ize	make, cause to be	socialize, motorize
–ness	quality, state	peacefulness, sadness

780 LANGUAGE HANDBOOK

...and *ei*

... Except after *c*, write *ie* when the sound is long *e*.

XAMPLES achieve believe chief field piece
ceiling conceit deceit deceive receive

:EPTIONS either protein neither seize weird

.. Write *ei* when the sound is not long *e*, especially when the sound is long *a*.

XAMPLES foreign forfeit height heir their
freight neighbor reign veil weigh

:EPTIONS ancient conscience patient friend efficient

QUICK CHECK I

...the letters *ie* or *ei* to spell each of the following words correctly.

AMPLE **1.** bel . . . ve
1. *believe*

:r . . . f	**5.** . . . ght	**9.** r . . . ndeer
' . . . n	**6.** perc . . . ve	**10.** p . . . rce
ı . . . ce	**7.** pat . . . nce	
:h . . . ld	**8.** th . . . f	

...*de*, –*ceed*, and –*sede*

:. The only English word ending in –*sede* is *supersede*. The only words ending in –*ceed* are *exceed*, *proceed*, and *succeed*. Most other words with this sound end in –*cede*.

AMPLES concede intercede precede recede secede

...ding Prefixes and Suffixes

:. When adding a prefix to a word, do not change the spelling of the word itself.

AMPLES mis + spell = **mis**spell il + logical = **il**logical

. When adding the suffix –*ly* or –*ness* to a word, do not change the spelling of the word itself.

XAMPLES slow + ly = slow**ly** dark + ness = dark**ness**

:EPTIONS For words that end in *y* and have more than one syllable, change the *y* to *i* before adding -*ly* or -*ness*.
happy + ly = happ**ily** lazy + ness = laz**iness**

NOTE This time-tested verse may help you remember the *ie* rule.

I before *e*
Except after *c*
Or when sounded like *a*,
As in *neighbor* and *weigh*.

The rhyme above and rules 16d and 16e apply only when the *i* and the *e* are in the same syllable.

Quick Check I: Answers
1. grief
2. vein
3. niece
4. shield
5. eight
6. perceive
7. patience
8. thief
9. reindeer
10. pierce

NOTE When adding *–ing* to words that end in *ie*, drop the e and change the *i* to *y*.

EXAMPLES
lie + ing = **lying**
die + ing = d**ying**

16i. **Drop the final silent e before a suffix beginning with a vowel.**

EXAMPLES line + ing = lin**ing**   desire + able = desirable

EXCEPTIONS Keep the final silent *e* in a word ending in *ce* or *ge* before a suffix beginning with *a* or *o*.
notice + able = notic**eable**
courage + ous = courag**eous**

16j. **Keep the final silent e before a suffix beginning with a consonant.**

EXAMPLES hope + less = hope**less**   care + ful = care**ful**

EXCEPTIONS nine + th = nin**th**   argue + ment = argum━

16k. **For words ending in y preceded by a consonant, chang━ the y to i before any suffix that does not begin with i.**

EXAMPLES try + ed = tr**ied**   duty + ful = dut**iful**

16l. **For words ending in y preceded by a vowel, keep the y when adding a suffix.**

EXAMPLES pray + ing = pray**ing**   pay + ment = paymen━

EXCEPTIONS day—da**ily**   lay—la**id**   pay—pa**id**   say—sai━

16m. **Double the final consonant before a suffix beginning w━ a vowel if the word**

(1) **has only one syllable or has the accent on the last syllable**

and

(2) **ends in a single consonant preceded by a single vow━**

EXAMPLES sit + ing = sit**ting**   begin + er = begin**ner**

EXCEPTIONS Do not double the final consonant in words endin━ in *w* or *x*.
mow + ing = mo**wing**   wax + ed = wa**xed**

NOTE In some cases, the final consonant either may or may not be doubled.

EXAMPLE
cancel + ed = cance**led**
or cance**lled**

Otherwise, the final consonant is usually not doubled before a suff━ beginning with a vowel.

EXAMPLES sing + er = sin**ger**   final + ist = final**ist**

 QUICK CHECK 2

Add the given prefix or suffix to each word listed at the top of the ne━ page.

EXAMPLE **1.** display + ed
1. *displayed*

m + migrate   **5.** semi + circle   **9.** carry + ed

e + settle   **6.** trace + able   **10.** advantage + ous

n + certain   **7.** jog + er

ucky + ly   **8.** dry + ness

rming the Plurals of Nouns

For most nouns, add –s.

AMPLES   desks   ideas   shoes   friends   cameras   Wilsons

For nouns ending in s, x, z, ch, or sh, add –es.

AMPLES   gases   foxes   waltzes   inches   dishes   Suarezes

For nouns ending in y preceded by a vowel, add –s.

AMPLES   decoys   highways   alleys   Rileys

For nouns ending in y preceded by a consonant, change the y to i and add –es.

XAMPLES   armies   countries   cities   ponies   allies   daisies

CEPTIONS   For proper nouns ending in *y,* just add *–s.*
     Brady—Bradys   Murphy—Murphys

For some nouns ending in f or fe, add –s. For others, change the f or fe to v and add –es.

AMPLES   beliefs   thieves   sheriffs   knives
     giraffes   leaves   roofs   calves

For nouns ending in o preceded by a vowel, add –s.

AMPLES   radios   patios   stereos   igloos
     Matteos

For nouns ending in o preceded by a consonant, add –es.

XAMPLES   tomatoes   potatoes   echoes   heroes

CEPTIONS   For musical terms and proper nouns, add *–s.*
     alto—altos   soprano—sopranos
     Blanco—Blancos   Nakamoto—Nakamotos

The plural of a few nouns is formed in irregular ways.

AMPLES   oxen   geese   feet   teeth   women   mice

For most compound nouns, form the plural of the last word in the compound.

AMPLES   bookshelves   push-ups   sea gulls   ten-year-olds

TIPS FOR SPELLING

In some names, marks that show pronunciation are just as important as the letters themselves.

PEOPLE   Alemán   Böll   Ibáñez
     Khayyám   Janáček   Eugène
PLACES   Açores   Bogotá   Camagüey
     Gîza   Köln   Sainte-Thérèse

If you're not sure about the spelling of a name, ask the person whose name it is, or check in a reference source.

Quick Check 2: Answers
  1. immigrate
  2. resettle
  3. uncertain
  4. luckily
  5. semicircle
  6. traceable
  7. jogger
  8. dryness
  9. carried
10. advantageous

Quick Check 3: Answers

1. cargoes
2. diaries
3. Gómezes
4. sit-ups
5. children
6. videos
7. hooves
8. Japanese
9. *M's*
10. *10's*

Resources

- *Language Handbook Worksheets,* pp. 154–157
- *Language Workshop CD-ROM,* Chapter 10: Usage

 When you use numbers in your writing, follow these guidelines:

- Spell out a number that begins a sentence.

EXAMPLE   **Fifty** people received free tickets.

- Within a sentence, spell out numbers that can be written in one or two words.

EXAMPLE   In all, **fifty-two** people worked on our play.

- If you use several numbers, some short and some long, write them all the same way. Usually, it is better to write them all as numerals.

EXAMPLE   We sold **86** tickets today and **121** yesterday.

- Spell out numbers used to indicate order.

EXAMPLE   Our team came in **third** [*not* 3rd] in the track meet.

16w. For compound nouns in which one of the words is modified by the other word or words, form the plural of the word modifie

EXAMPLES   brothers-in-law   maids of honor
eighth-graders   boy scouts

16x. For some nouns, the singular and the plura forms are the same.

SINGULAR AND PLURAL   Sioux   trout   sheep
deer   moose   series

16y. For numerals, letters, symbols, and words used as words, add an apostrophe and –s.

EXAMPLES   *4*'s   *s*'s   *$*'s   *and*'s

 QUICK CHECK 3

Spell the plural form of each of the following items. [No
An item may have more than one correct plural form. Y
only need to give one.]

EXAMPLE 1. &
1. &'s

1. cargo
2. diary
3. Gómez
4. sit-up
5. child
6. video
7. hoof
8. Japanese
9. *M*
10. *10*

17 GLOSSARY OF USAGE

This Glossary of Usage is an alphabetical list of words and expressions that are commonly misused in English. Throughout this section some examples are labeled *standard* or *nonstandard*. **Standard English** is the most widely accepted form of English. It is used in *formal* situations, su as in speeches and writing for school, and in *informal* situations, such a in conversation and everyday writing. **Nonstandard English** is languag that does not follow the rules and guidelines of standard English.

---

all ready, already   *All ready* means "completely prepared." *Already* means "before a certain point in time."

EXAMPLES   Everyone was **all ready** for the show.
That bill has **already** been paid.

ight Used as an adjective, *all right* means "unhurt" or "satisfactory." d as an adverb, *all right* means "well enough." *All right* should always be ten as two words.

AMPLES   Linda fell off the horse, but she is **all right.** [adjective]
       Does this suit look **all right** on me? [adjective]
       You did **all right** at the track meet. [adverb]

t   *A lot* should always be written as two words.

AMPLE   She knows **a lot** about computer software.

wheres, everywheres, nowheres, somewheres   Use these ds without the final *s*.

AMPLE   I didn't go **anywhere** [*not* anywheres] yesterday.

Do not use *at* after *where*.

AMPLE   Where is it? [*not* Where is it at?]

, badly   *Bad* is an adjective. *Badly* is an adverb.

AMPLES   The raw celery did not taste **bad.** [*Bad* modifies the
       noun *celery.*]
       One little boy behaved **badly.** [*Badly* modifies the verb
       behaved.]

ween, among   Use *between* when referring to two things at a time, n though they may be part of a group containing more than two.

AMPLES   In homeroom, Carlos sits **between** Bob and me.
       Some players practice **between** innings. [Although a
       game has more than two innings, the practice occurs
       only *between* any two of them.]

Use *among* to refer to a group rather than separate individuals.

AMPLES   We saved ten dollars **among** the three of us. [As a
       group, the three saved ten dollars.]
       There was disagreement **among** the fans about the
       coach's decision. [The fans are thought of as a group.]

t, busted   Avoid using these words as verbs. Use a form of either t or *break.*

AMPLES   The door **burst** [*not* busted] open and rats teemed in.
       What would happen if the window **broke** [*not* busted]?

ose, chose   *Choose* is the present tense form of the verb *choose.* It mes with *whose* and means "select." *Chose* is the past tense form of ose. It rhymes with *grows* and means "selected."

AMPLES   Did you **choose** "Fish Cheeks" for your report?
       Sara **chose** "Miss Awful."

NOTE   Many writers overuse *a lot.* Whenever you run across *a lot* as you revise your own writing, try to replace it with a more exact word or phrase.

☞ **among**   See **between, among.**
as   See **like, as.**
as if   See **like, as if, as though.**

☞ **because**   See **reason . . . because.**

👉 doesn't, don't
See page 722.

could of Do not write *of* with the helping verb *could*. Write *could ha*
Also avoid *had of, ought to of, should of, would of, might of,* and *must of.*

EXAMPLE All of Emily Dickinson's poems **could have** [*not* coul*
of*] been lost.

fewer, less *Fewer* is used with plural words. *Less* is used with singula*
words. *Fewer* tells "how many"; *less* tells "how much."

EXAMPLES We sold **fewer** [*not* less] tickets than they did.
These plants require **less** water than those do.

good, well *Good* is always an adjective. Never use *good* as an adverb
Instead, use *well.*

EXAMPLE Nancy sang **well** [*not* good] at the audition.

Well may also be used as an adjective to mean "healthy."

EXAMPLE He didn't look **well** after eating the entire pizza.

👉 had of See
could of.

had ought, hadn't ought *Had* should not be used with *ought.*

EXAMPLE Eric **ought** [*not* had ought] to help us; he **oughtn't** [*n*
hadn't ought] to have missed our meeting yesterday.

he, she, they Avoid using a pronoun along with its antecedent as th*
subject of a verb. This error is called the **double subject.**

NONSTANDARD Linda Goss she is a famous writer.
STANDARD Linda Goss is a famous writer.

hisself *Hisself* is nonstandard English. Use *himself.*

EXAMPLE Ira bought **himself** [*not* hisself] a polka-dot tie.

how come In informal situations, *how come* is often used instead of *
why. In formal situations, *why* should always be used.

INFORMAL I don't know how come she didn't take the garbage o*
FORMAL I don't know **why** she didn't take the garbage out.

👉 its, it's See page
777.

kind of, sort of In informal situations, *kind of* and *sort of* are often us*
to mean "somewhat" or "rather." In formal English, *somewhat* or *rather*
preferred.

INFORMAL He seemed kind of embarrassed by our applause.
FORMAL He seemed **somewhat** embarrassed by our applause.

✓ *QUICK CHECK 1*

Revise each of the following sentences to correct any error in usage.

EXAMPLE 1. The author she had lived in China.
1. *The author had lived in China.*

Alot of stars and planets have names from mythology.
Icarus had ought to have listened to his father.
If he had listened, he could of survived.
I wonder how come he didn't listen.
Surely, Daedalus's heart was busted by the death of his son.

rn, teach   *Learn* means "gain knowledge." *Teach* means "instruct" or
ow how."

AMPLES   He is **learning** how to play the guitar.
His grandfather is **teaching** him how to play.

e, as   In informal situations, the preposition *like* is often used instead
he conjunction *as* to introduce a clause. In formal situations, *as* is
ferred.

AMPLE   Look in the dictionary, **as** [*not* like] the teacher suggests.

e, as if, as though   In informal situations, the preposition *like* is
en used for the compound conjunctions *as if* or *as though.* In formal
ations, *as if* or *as though* is preferred.

AMPLES   They acted **as if** [*not* like] they hadn't heard him.
You looked **as though** [*not* like] you knew the answer.

Do not use *of* with other prepositions such as *inside, off,* and *outside.*

AMPLE   Did anyone fall **off** [*not* off of] the raft?

Revising Adverbs in Sentences

In informal situations, the adjective *real*
is often used as an adverb meaning
ry" or "extremely." In formal situations, *extremely* or
ther adverb is preferred.

ORMAL   I'm expecting a real important telephone
call.

ORMAL   I'm expecting an **extremely** important
telephone call.

ason . . . because   In informal situations, *reason . . .
ause* is often used instead of *reason . . . that.* In formal
ations, use *reason . . . that,* or revise your sentence.

FORMAL   The reason I did well on the test was because I had
studied hard.

FORMAL   The **reason** I did well on the test was **that** I had studied
hard.

me, somewhat   Do not use *some* for *somewhat* as an adverb.

AMPLE   My writing has improved **somewhat** [*not* some].

less   See **fewer, less.**

lie, lay   See pages 732–733.

might of, must of   See **could of.**

ought to of   See **could of.**

Try It Out ✎

Revise the following sentences by substituting another adverb for the word *real.* Use a variety of adverbs.

1. Hercules was real strong.
2. He accomplished many tasks that were real hard.
3. Stories of his labors are real interesting.
4. They have endured a real long time.
5. Even today, real young children know his story from television shows.

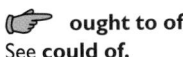
should of   See **could of.**

somewheres   See **anywheres,** etc.

Quick Check I: Answers

1. A lot of stars and planets have names from mythology.
2. Icarus ought to have listened to his father.
3. If he had listened, he could have survived.
4. I wonder why he didn't listen.
5. Surely, Daedalus's heart was broken by the death of his son.

Try It Out: Possible Answers

1. Hercules was extremely strong.
2. He accomplished many tasks that were amazingly hard.
3. Stories of his labors are very interesting.
4. They have endured an exceptionally long time.
5. Even today, very young children know his story from television shows.

sort of See **kind of, sort of.**

NOTE Here's an easy way to remember the difference between *stationary* and *stationery:*

You write a lett**er** on stationery.

 who's, whose See page 777.

 would of See **could of.**

stationary, stationery The adjective *stationary* means "in a fixed position." The noun *stationery* means "writing paper."

EXAMPLES Furnishings in a space capsule must be **stationary.**
I need a new box of **stationery.**

them *Them* should not be used as an adjective. Use *those.*

EXAMPLE The fox couldn't get **those** [*not* them] grapes.

way, ways Use *way,* not *ways,* in referring to a distance.

EXAMPLE They still had a long **way** [*not* ways] to go.

when, where Do not use *when* or *where* incorrectly in a definition.

NONSTANDARD In bowling, a "turkey" is when a person makes three strikes in a row.

STANDARD In bowling, a "turkey" is making three strikes in a row.

where Do not use *where* for *that.*

EXAMPLE I read **that** [*not* where] Pete Sampras won the match.

who, which, that The relative pronoun *who* refers to people only; *which* refers to things only; *that* refers to either people or things.

EXAMPLES Kim is the only one **who** got the right answer. [perso
My bike, **which** has ten speeds, is for sale. [thing]
He is the one person **that** can help you. [person]
This is the ring **that** I want to buy. [thing]

without, unless Do not use the preposition *without* in place of the conjunction *unless.*

EXAMPLE My mother said I can't go **unless** [*not* without] I finish
my homework first.

 QUICK CHECK 2

Revise the following sentences to correct any error in usage.

EXAMPLE 1. The team forfeited the game like they had agreed to.
1. *The team forfeited the game as they had agreed to.*

1. The reason they forfeited was because Dondré couldn't play ther
2. What was going on inside of their heads?
3. They would not play without their teammate could play, too.
4. That story learned me something about loyalty.
5. True friendship is where people value each other as much as themselves.

Quick Check 2: Possible Answers
1. They forfeited because Dondré couldn't play there.
2. What was going on inside their heads?
3. They would not play unless their teammate could play, too.
4. That story taught me something about loyalty.
5. True friendship means that people value each other as much as themselves.

e glossary below is an alphabetical list of words
nd in the selections in this book. Use this glossary
t as you use a dictionary—to find out the meanings
unfamiliar words. (Some technical, foreign, and more
scure words in this book are not listed here but in-
ad are defined for you in the footnotes that accom-
ay many of the selections.)

Many words in the English language have more than
e meaning. This glossary gives the meanings that
ly to the words as they are used in the selections in
s book. Words closely related in form and meaning
e usually listed together in one entry (for instance,
orehensive and apprehensively), and the definition is
en for the first form.

The following abbreviations are used:

adj.	adjective
adv.	adverb
n.	noun
v.	verb

Each word's pronunciation is given in parentheses. A
de to the pronunciation symbols appears at the bot-
m of each right-hand glossary page.

For more information about the words in this glos-
y, or for information about words not listed here,
nsult a dictionary.

stracted (ab·strak′tid) *adj.*: absent-minded.

cord (ə·kôrd′) *v.*: give; grant. —*n.*: agreement.

cordance (ə·kôrd′′ns) *n.*: agreement; harmony.

aptation (ad′əp·tā′shən) *n.*: change that improves
the chance of survival.

monish (ad·män′ish) *v.*: warn or urge.

o (ə·dōō′) *n.*: fuss; trouble.

vocate (ad′və·kit) *n.*: person who speaks or writes
in support of something.

ict (ə·flikt′) *v.*: cause pain or suffering to.

ape (ə·gāp′) *adv.*: with the mouth wide open in surprise or wonder. —*adj.*: wide open.

ony (ag′ə·nē) *n.*: intense physical pain.

alleviate (ə·lē′vē·āt′) *v.*: relieve; reduce.

alter (ôl′tər) *v.*: modify; change. —**altered** *v.* used as
adj.

amble (am′bəl) *v.*: walk easily, without hurrying.

amiss (ə·mis′) *adj.*: wrong; improper.

anachronism (ə·nak′rə·niz′əm) *n.*: something out of
its proper time in history, like a television in the
Middle Ages or penicillin in ancient Rome.

anchorage (aŋ′kər·ij) *n.*: place that gives or seems to
give stability or security.

anguish (aŋ′gwish) *n.*: suffering; pain.

anomalous (ə·näm′ə·ləs) *adj.*: abnormal; strange.

appalling (ə·pôl′iŋ) *adj.*: shocking; horrifying.

appoint (ə·point′) *v.*: set; decide upon. —**appointed**
v. used as *adj.*

apprehensive (ap′rē·hen′siv) *adj.*: anxious; uneasy.
—**apprehensively** *adv.*

apt (apt) *adj.*: quick to learn.

artful (ärt′fəl) *adj.*: skillful.

ascend (ə·send′) *v.*: move up.

ashen (ash′ən) *adj.*: pale.

assertion (ə·sʉr′shən) *n.*: statement; declaration.

assure (ə·shoor′) *v.*: guarantee; promise confidently.

astound (ə·stound′) *v.*: amaze; surprise.

atrocious (ə·trō′shəs) *adj.*: very bad.

attend (ə·tend′) *v.*: pay attention; wait on.

awe (ô) *n.*: mixed feeling of respect, wonder, and fear.

baleful (bāl′fəl) *adj.*: wicked or threatening. —**bale-
fully** *adv.*

ballad (bal′əd) *n.*: song that tells a story.

banish (ban′ish) *v.*: send into exile; get rid of.

barrage (bə·räzh′) *n.*: heavy, prolonged attack.

baton (bə·tän′) *n.*: slender stick used by a conductor
to direct an orchestra or choir.

beam (bēm) *v.*: smile warmly. —**beaming** *v.* used as
adj.

bear (ber) *v.*: carry. —**bore** (bôr), **borne** (bôrn)

belated (bē·lāt′id) *adj.*: late or delayed.

berate (be·rāt′) *v.*: scold. —**berating** *v.* used as *adj.*

billow (bil′ō) *v.*: surge; rise.

āte, cär; ten, ēve; is, īce; gō, hôrn, look, tool; oil, out; up, fʉr; ə *for unstressed vowels, as* a *in* ago, u *in* focus; ′ *as in*
in (lat′′n); chin; she; zh *as in* azure (azh′ər); thin, *the;* ŋ *as in* ring (riŋ)

---

blasé (blä·zā′) *adj.*: bored or unimpressed; not easily excited.

blissful (blis′fəl) *adj.*: having great joy or happiness. —**blissfully** *adv.*

bluff (bluf) *n.*: steep cliff.

blunt (blunt) *adj.*: plain-spoken and abrupt.

blurt (blʉrt) *v.*: say suddenly, without stopping to think.

bore (bôr) *v.*: See *bear.*

bout (bout) *n.*: match; contest.

brace (brās) *v.*: make ready for impact.

bravado (brə·vä′dō) *n.*: pretended courage.

breach (brēch) *n.*: 1. break in a wall. 2. breaking of a law or promise.

brigade (bri·gād′) *n.*: group of people organized to function as a unit.

buckle (buk′əl) *v.*: collapse (usually under pressure).

calisthenics (kal′is·then′iks) *n.*: exercises to develop a strong, trim body.

canister (kan′is·tər) *n.*: small can.

capsize (kap′sīz′) *v.*: overturn (usually said of a boat).

cascade (kas·kād′) *v.*: fall like a waterfall.

cease (sēs) *v.*: stop.

cement (sə·ment′) *v.*: confirm; unite.

chaotic (kā·ät′ik) *adj.*: confused; disordered.

chaperone (shap′ər·ōn′) *n.*: person who accompanies young people to supervise their behavior.

charade (shə·rād′) *n.*: obvious pretense or act.

chink (chiŋk) *n.*: narrow opening.

churn (chʉrn) *v.*: shake or stir violently, as when milk is made into butter in a churn.

civic (siv′ik) *adj.*: of a city or citizenship.

clamor (klam′ər) *n.*: loud, confused noise.

clannish (klan′ish) *adj.*: very loyal to one's group and hostile to outsiders.

clarity (klar′ə·tē) *n.*: clearness.

clench (klench) *v.*: close firmly. —**clenched** *v.* used as *adj.*

coarse (kôrs) *adj.*: of poor quality; rough or harsh in texture.

commence (kə·mens′) *v.*: begin.

communion (kə·myōōn′yən) *n.*: deep understanding; communication of thoughts without speaking.

comparable (käm′pə·rə·bəl) *adj.*: similar.

compatible (kəm·pat′ə·bəl) *adj.*: in agreement; in harmony.

compliance (kəm·plī′əns) *n.*: giving in to a request or demand.

condemn (kən·dem′) *v.*: disapprove strongly of.

condescending (kän′di·sen′diŋ) *adj.*: proud; haughty.

confrontation (kän′frən·tā′shən) *n.*: face-to-f meeting between opposing sides.

congregate (käŋ′grə·gāt′) *v.*: gather into a crowd.

conjure (kän′jər) *v.*: call upon, as by a magic spell.

consensus (kən·sen′səs) *n.*: opinion of all or most.

consign (kən·sīn′) *v.*: send; deliver.

console (kən·sōl′) *v.*: make less sad; comfort.

consolation (kän′sə·lā′shən) *n.*: comfort.

consternation (kän′stər·nā′shən) *n.*: fear or sho that causes helplessness or confusion.

constriction (kən·strik′shən) *n.*: limitation.

consultation (kän′səl·tā′shən) *n.*: meeting to discu decide, or plan something.

contemplate (kän′təm·plāt′) *v.*: consider; look at think about carefully.

contraption (kən·trap′shən) *n.*: strange machine gadget.

convivial (kən·viv′ē·əl) *adj.*: sociable or friendly.

convoluted (kän′və·lōōt′id) *adj.*: very complicated.

copious (kō′pē·əs) *adj.*: plentiful.

cosset (käs′it) *v.*: pamper.

counter (kount′ər) *v.*: say in defense.

cower (kou′ər) *v.*: crouch and tremble in fear.

critique (kri·tēk′) *v.*: evaluate and criticize.

crow (krō) *v.*: boast in triumph.

cultivated (kul′tə·vāt′id) *adj.*: prepared and used growing crops.

curt (kʉrt) *adj.*: rude and with few words. —**cur** *adv.*

dash (dash) *v.*: knock; strike with violence.

debris (də·brē′) *n.*: rough, broken bits of litter.

defiance (dē·fī′əns) *n.*: open, bold resistance to thority; opposition.

deign (dān) *v.*: consider it appropriate to one's digni

delve (delv) *v.*: search.

derange (dē·rānj′) *v.*: unsettle; make disorde —**deranged** *v.* used as *adj.*

derisive (di·rī′siv) *adj.*: scornful and ridiculing.

descend (dē·send′) *v.*: go down.

desecrate (des′i·krāt′) *v.*: show disrespect for sor thing (considered holy).

desolation (des′ə·lā′shən) *n.*: lonely grief; misery.

despondency (di·spän′dən·sē) *n.*: loss of hope.

detached (dē·tacht′) *adj.*: not involved emotiona indifferent.

detain (dē·tān′) *v.*: hold back; delay.

deteriorate (dē·tir′ē·ə·rāt′) *v.*: get worse.

detract (dē·trakt′) *v.*: take away.

nitary (dig'nə·ter'ē') *n.*: person holding high, dignified position or office.

ate (dī'lāt') *v.*: become wider. **—dilating** *v.* used as
adj.

inution (dim'ə·nōō'shən) *n.*: lessening.

contented (dis'kən·tent'id) *adj.*: not satisfied.

crimination (di·skrim'i·nā'·shən) *n.*: showing of
prejudice; actions or policies meant to treat minor-
ty groups unfairly.

hearten (dis·härt''n) *v.*: discourage. **—disheartened** *v.* used as *adj.*

lodge (dis·läj') *v.*: drive out; force from a position
or place.

mal (diz'məl) *adj.*: miserable; gloomy. **—dismally**
adv.

may (dis·mā') *n.*: loss of confidence in the face of
trouble or danger.

parage (di·spar'ij) *v.*: show disrespect for; "put
down."

pel (di·spel') *v.*: drive away. **—dispelled**

perse (di·spʉrs') *v.*: scatter; move in different directions. **—dispersing** *v.* used as *adj.*

pute (di·spyōōt') *n.*: argument. **—***v.*: argue; debate.

sipate (dis'ə·pāt') *v.*: scatter and disappear.

tract (di·strakt') *v.*: draw attention away; divert.
—distracted *adj.*

tress (di·stres') *n.*: sorrow; pain.

main (dō·mān') *n.*: territory.

ur (dʊr) *adj.*: gloomy; sullen.

one (drōn) *v.*: talk on and on in a dull way.

plicate (dōō'pli·kāt') *v.*: make double.

tiful (dōōt'i·fəl) *adj.*: obedient. **—dutifully** *adv.*

indle (dwin'dəl) *v.*: shrink.

se (ēz) *v.*: move carefully.

stasy (ek'stə·sē) *n.*: delight; state of absolute joy.

ible (ed'ə·bəl) *adj.*: fit to be eaten.

rie (ir'ē) *adj.*: mysterious; weird in a frightening way.

otism (ē'gō·tiz'əm) *n.*: conceit; talking about oneself too much.

mination (ē·lim'ə·nā'shən) *n.*: removal from competition.

ide (ē·lōōd') *v.*: escape by quickness or cleverness.

ber (em'bər) *n.*: glowing piece of coal or wood
from a fire.

embolden (em·bōl'dən) *v.*: give courage; make bold.

emerge (ē·mʉrj') *v.*: come forth into view.

enervate (en'ər·vāt') *v.*: exhaust; weaken. **—enervated** *v.* used as *adj.*

enigmatic (en'ig·mat'ik) *adj.*: mysterious; like a riddle.

ensue (en·sōō') *v.*: come after; follow immediately.

entitle (en·tīt''l) *v.*: qualify.

entreaty (en·trēt'ē) *n.*: earnest request.

epic (ep'ik) *adj.*: grand; heroic.

erode (ē·rōd') *v.*: wear away.

erupt (ē·rupt') *v.*: explode or burst forth.

esoteric (es'ə·ter'ik) *adj.*: specialized; beyond most
people's understanding or knowledge.

ethnicity (eth·nis'ə·tē) *n.*: membership in a group
with a common cultural background.

evade (ē·vād') *v.*: avoid. **—evading** *v.* used as *adj.*

evict (ē·vikt') *v.*: remove from a rented apartment by
legal means. **—evicted** *v.* used as *adj.*

exaltation (eg'zôl·tā'shən) *n.*: feeling of great joy.

exasperate (eg·zas'pər·āt') *v.*: irritate. **—exasperated** *v.* used as *adj.*

exceedingly (ek·sēd'iŋ·lē) *adv.*: extremely; very.

excessive (ek·ses'iv) *adj.*: too great; not moderate.
—excessively *adv.*

exertion (eg·zʉr'shən) *n.*: effort; activity.

exhalation (eks'hə·lā'shən) *n.*: breathing out.

expand (ek·spand') *v.*: develop in detail.

expire (ek·spīr') *v.*: die. In Latin, *exspirare* means "to
breathe out"; *to breathe out one's last breath is "to die."*

extensive (ek·sten'siv) *adj.*: covering a large area; vast.
—extensively *adv.*

exuberant (eg·zōō'bər·ənt) *adj.*: in high spirits. **—exuberantly** *adv.*

facade (fə·säd') *n.*: literally, the front part of a building;
a "front" put up to hide real feelings.

facility (fə·sil'ə·tē) *n.*: building that makes possible
some activity.

falter (fôl'tər) *v.*: speak hesitantly; stumble in speech.

fathom (fath'əm) *v.*: understand completely.

fawn (fôn) *v.*: flatter or lower oneself to make friends.
—fawning *v.* used as *n.*

festoon (fes·tōōn') *v.*: adorn with flowers, papers, or
other decorations.

fetid (fet'id) *adj.*: stinking like something rotten.

āte, cär; ten, ēve; is, īce; gō, hôrn, look, tōōl; oil, out; up, fʉr; ə *for unstressed vowels, as* a *in* ago, u *in* focus; ' *as in*
in (lat''n); chin; she; zh *as in* azure (azh'ər); thin, *the;* ŋ *as in* ring (riŋ)

---

finesse (fə·nes′) *n.*: skill; cunning.

finicky (fin′ik·ē) *adj.*: fussy and extremely careful.

flail (flāl) *v.*: move wildly or excitedly. —**flailing** *v.* used as *adj.*

flank (flaŋk) *v.*: surround on either side.

flare (fler) *v.*: burst out suddenly in anger.

flat (flat) *n.*: low-lying marsh.

fledgling (flej′liŋ) *n.*: young bird.

flimsy (flim′zē) *adj.*: poorly made; easily broken or damaged.

fling (fliŋ) *v.*: throw with force; hurl. —**flung** *v.*

flourish (flʉr′ish) *v.*: thrive; grow well.

fluidity (floo′id·ə·tē) *n.*: grace of movement.

flung (fluŋ) *v.*: See **fling**.

fluster (flus′tər) *v.*: confuse; upset. —**flustered** *v.* used as *adj.*

footage (foot′ij) *n.*: length of film that has been shot.

forlorn (fôr·lôrn′) *adj.*: hopeless. *Forlorn* may also mean "deserted" or "abandoned."

formidable (fôr′mə·də·bəl) *adj.*: awe-inspiring; impressive.

frenzied (fren′zēd) *adj.*: wild.

frolicsome (fräl′ik·səm) *adj.*: playful; merry.

fumble (fum′bəl) *v.*: search awkwardly.

furrow (fʉr′ō) *n.*: narrow groove.

gait (gāt) *n.*: way of walking or running.

gape (gāp) *v.*: stare with the mouth open, in wonder or surprise.

garland (gär′lənd) *n.*: wreath or woven chain.

garment (gär′mənt) *n.*: article of clothing.

ghastly (gast′lē) *adj.*: horrible; ghostlike.

gingerly (jin′jər·lē) *adv.*: carefully; cautiously.

glint (glint) *v.*: glitter; shine.

glower (glou′ər) *v.*: stare angrily; scowl. —**glowering** *v.* used as *adj.*

goad (gōd) *v.*: push or drive. A goad is a stick with a sharp point used to herd oxen.

grave (grāv) *adj.*: serious; somber.

grim (grim) *adj.*: stern; harsh. —**grimly** *adv.*

habitual (hə·bich′oo·əl) *adj.*: done or fixed by habit; customary.

haggle (hag′əl) *v.*: argue about price; bargain.

harry (har′ē) *v.*: cause worry; torment. —**harried** *v.* used as *adj.*

heave (hēv) *v.*: raise or lift with effort. —**heaved, hove** (hōv) —*n.*: the act of heaving.

heretical (hə·ret′i·kəl) *adj.*: against established view

horde (hôrd) *n.*: large, moving crowd.

hover (huv′ər) *v.*: **1.** hang in the air. **2.** linger; wait.

idiocy (id′ē·ə·sē) *n.*: stupidity; foolishness.

ignominious (ig′nə·min′ē·əs) *adj.*: shameful.

immense (im·mens′) *adj.*: enormous. —**immens** *adv.*

imminent (im′ə·nənt) *adj.*: about to happen.

impart (im·pärt′) *v.*: make known.

impassive (im·pas′iv) *adj.*: not showing emotion.

impel (im·pel′) *v.*: drive. —**impelled, impelling**

imperative (im·per′ə·tiv) *adj.*: absolutely necessar

implore (im·plôr′) *v.*: ask or beg.

imposing (im·pō′ziŋ) *adj.*: impressive; grand.

impostor (im·päs′tər) *n.*: person who pretends to someone or something that he or she is not.

impresario (im′prə·sä′rē·ō′) *n.*: director or mana of a theater, opera, or ballet.

inadequate (in·ad′i·kwət) *adj.*: not sufficient; equal to what is required.

incessant (in·ses′ənt) *adj.*: endless; constant. —**inc santly** *adv.*

incision (in·sizh′ən) *n.*: cut (usually in reference surgery).

inclined (in·klīnd′) *adj.*: willing; likely to do.

inconsolable (in′kən·sōl′ə·bəl) *adj.*: unable to comforted; brokenhearted.

incredulous (in·krej′oo·ləs) *adj.*: unbelievi —**incredulously** *adv.*

indifferent (in·dif′ər·ənt) *adj.*: uninterested; unco cerned.

indulgent (in·dul′jənt) *adj.*: kind or lenient, often excess.

industrious (in·dus′trē·əs) *adj.*: hard-working.

inert (in·ʉrt′) *adj.*: inactive.

infiltrate (in·fil′trāt) *v.*: gradually enter or sneak int

inhabit (in·hab′it) *v.*: live in; occupy.

inkling (iŋk′liŋ) *n.*: hint; slight indication.

innumerable (in·noo′mer·ə·bəl) *adj.*: too many be counted.

insolent (in′sə·lənt) *adj.*: boldly disrespectful.

install (in·stôl′) *v.*: settle; establish in a place.

instinctive (in·stiŋk′tiv) *adj.*: natural; inborn.

integrity (in·teg′rə·tē) *n.*: literally, completeness. people, *integrity* usually refers to honor and sincer

intent (in·tent′) *adj.*: having great concentration. — **tently** *adv.*

interior (in·tir′ē·ər) *n.*: inside.

erweave (in′tər·wēv′) v.: connect closely; blend. **—interwove, interwoven**

erwoven (in′tər·wō′vən) v.: See *interweave.*

ricate (in′tri·kit) adj.: complicated; full of detail.

incible (in·vin′sə·bəl) adj.: unbeatable.

everence (i·rev′ər·əns) n.: disrespect.

lation (ī′sə·lā′shən) n.: state of being alone; solitude.

(jär) v.: jolt; shock.

tle (jäs′əl) v.: shove; bump. **—jostling** v. used as *adj.*

ilant (jōō′bə·lənt) adj.: joyful; triumphant.

en (kēn) adj.: sharp and quick in seeing; acute.

ead (nēd) v.: form by mixing and working, usually with the hands.

orious (lə·bôr′ē·əs) adj.: involving hard work.

itude (lat′ə·tōōd′) n.: region determined by distance north or south from the equator.

nch (lônch) v.: rush; plunge.

r (lir) v.: look at slyly and knowingly. **—leering** v. used as *adj.*

islation (lej′is·lā′shən) n.: laws; the making of laws.

e (līth) adj.: flexible and graceful.

ch (lurch) v.: roll or pitch suddenly forward or to one side.

id (loor′id) adj.: sensational; shocking.

e (lōōt) n.: old stringed instrument related to the guitar.

jestic (mə·jes′tik) adj.: dignified; grand.

neuver (mə·nōō′vər) v.: move skillfully.

ngle (maŋ′gəl) v.: tear and crush; ruin. **—mangled** v. used as *adj.*

aniacal (mə·nī′ə·kəl) adj.: wildly insane; raging.

antle (man′təl) n.: cloak or cover.

aritime (mar′i·tīm′) adj.: having to do with the sea or ships.

artial (mär′shəl) adj.: military.

aw (mô) n.: mouth (jaw, throat) of a hungry animal. *Maw* suggests a huge, threatening mouth.

meager (mē′gər) adj.: literally, very thin; not enough.

meddlesome (med′'l·səm) adj.: interfering.

mercantile (mur′kən·tīl′) adj.: related to trade (the buying and selling of goods).

mill (mil) v.: move in a circular or random motion, like cattle or a crowd of people.

misgiving (mis·giv′iŋ) n.: doubt; uneasy feeling.

mobilize (mō′bə·līz′) v.: make ready for motion.

molten (mōl′tən) adj.: melted by heat.

monotonous (mə·nät′'n·əs) adj.: having little variety; boring.

morose (mə·rōs′) adj.: gloomy.

mortify (môrt′ə·fī′) v.: cause to feel ashamed and hurt. **—mortified** v. used as *adj.*

mottled (mät′'ld) adj.: blotchy, streaked, and spotted.

multitude (mul′tə·tōōd′) n.: mass; large number.

muster (mus′tər) v.: call forth.

namesake (nām′sāk′) n.: person with the same name as someone else.

notable (nōt′ə·bəl) adj.: remarkable; outstanding.

nurture (nur′chər) v.: nourish; raise.

objective (əb·jek′tiv) n.: aim; goal.

obscure (əb·skyoor′) adj.: unclear; not easily understood. **—v.:** hide; conceal.

observatory (əb·zurv′ə·tôr′ē) n.: building equipped for scientific observation.

officious (ə·fish′əs) adj.: tending to interfere; bossy, as if in charge. **—officiously** adv.

ominous (äm′ə·nəs) adj.: threatening, like a bad sign; warning of something bad.

ordain (ôr·dān′) v.: order or decree.

ordeal (ôr·dēl′) n.: difficult and painful experience.

organism (ôr′gə·niz′əm) n.: individual plant or animal.

pallid (pal′id) adj.: pale.

parched (pärcht) adj.: very hot and dry.

particle (pärt′i·kəl) n.: tiny piece.

paunch (pônch) n.: potbelly.

peer (pir) v.: look closely.

peevish (pēv′ish) adj.: irritable; ill-humored.

āte, cär; ten, ēve; is, īce; gō, hôrn, look, tōōl; oil, out; up, fur; ə *for unstressed vowels, as* a *in* ago, u *in* focus; ′ *as in* in (lat′'n); chin; she; zh *as in* azure (azh′ər); thin, *the;* ŋ *as in* ring (riŋ)

---

pensive (pen′siv) *adj.*: thoughtful. —**pensively** *adv.*

perish (per′ish) *v.*: die.

permissive (pər·mis′iv) *adj.*: allowing freedom; tolerant of behavior disapproved of by others.

persist (pər·sist′) *v.*: continue firmly or steadily.

perturb (pər·tʉrb′) *v.*: disturb; trouble. —**perturbed** *v.* used as *adj.*

pestilential (pes′tə·len′shəl) *adj.*: causing disease; deadly.

phonetic (fō·net′ik) *adj.*: having to do with speech sounds.

pious (pī′əs) *adj.*: deeply religious.

pivot (piv′ət) *v.*: rotate; turn around as if on an axis.

plait (plāt) *n.*: braid of hair.

pliant (plī′ənt) *adj.*: easily bent.

poise (poiz) *v.*: balance.

pomp (pämp) *n.*: showy display; splendor.

ponder (pän′dər) *v.*: think deeply about.

portent (pôr′tent′) *n.*: omen; warning.

predecessor (pred′ə·ses′ər) *n.*: person who precedes (goes before) someone else.

predicament (prē·dik′ə·mənt) *n.*: difficult and unpleasant situation; problem.

predicate (pred′i·kāt′) *v.*: affirm or base on something. —**predicated** *v.* used as *adj.*

predominant (prē·däm′ə·nənt) *adj.*: main. —**predominantly** *adv.*

predominate (prē·däm′ə·nāt′) *v.*: have authority or influence; prevail.

presumptuous (prē·zump′choo·əs) *adj.*: too bold; arrogant.

proceed (prō·sēd′) *v.*: move along; advance.

prod (präd) *v.*: urge or stir into action.

prodigy (präd′ə·jē) *n.*: child genius.

promenade (präm′ə·nād′) *n.*: public place for a leisurely walk.

prop (präp) *v.*: support or hold in place with a support.

proposition (präp′ə·zish′ən) *n.*: something put up for consideration.

prospect (prä′spekt′) *n.*: something hoped for or expected.

prostrate (präs′trāt′) *v.*: throw oneself on the ground to show humbleness.

provisions (prō·vizh′ənz) *n.*: stock of food and other supplies stored for future need.

provoke (prō·vōk′) *v.*: cause action or feeling, usually anger or annoyance.

prow (prou) *n.*: forward part of a ship or boat.

prowess (prou′is) *n.*: ability; skill.

pungent (pun′jənt) *adj.*: here, sharp smelling; a sharp tasting. Spicy foods are pungent.

quaver (kwā′vər) *v.*: tremble.

query (kwir′ē) *n.*: question.

radiant (rā′dē·ənt) *adj.*: 1. bright; filled with lig 2. showing well-being.

ramshackle (ram′shak′əl) *adj.*: likely to fall to piece

rank (raŋk) *adj.*: 1. in bad taste. 2. coarse and ov grown.

raspish (rasp′ish) *adj.*: rough; grating.

ravage (rav′ij) *v.*: ruin; violently destroy.

reassure (rē′ə·shoor′) *v.*: comfort; give hope or c fidence; from the Latin word *securus*, meaning " cure." Compare with *assure*. —**reassuring** *v.* us as *adj.*

recede (ri·sēd′) *v.*: 1. withdraw; become more dista 2. move back. —**receding** *v.* used as *adj.*

recitation (res′ə·tā′shən) *n.*: saying aloud in pub something memorized.

reconvene (rē′kən·vēn′) *v.*: reassemble.

reluctance (ri·luk′təns) *n.*: unwillingness.

remnant (rem′nənt) *n.*: what is left over; remain part.

render (ren′dər) *v.*: make; give, hand over, or prese

replenish (ri·plen′ish) *v.*: make full or complete agai

reprehensible (rep′ri·hen′sə·bəl) *adj.*: deserv blame.

reproachful (ri·prōch′fəl) *adj.*: expressing blame; cusing. —**reproachfully** *adv.*

resolute (rez′ə·loot′) *adj.*: firm and purposeful; det mined.

resolve (ri·zälv′) *v.*: decide; make a formal statemen

resound (ri·zound′) *v.*: echo loudly; fill with sound.

respiration (res′pə·rā′shən) *n.*: breathing.

resume (ri·zoom′) *v.*: go on again after interruption

retort (ri·tôrt′) *v.*: answer in a sharp, quick manner.

retrieve (ri·trēv′) *v.*: get back.

rickety (rik′it·ē) *adj.*: weak and shaky.

rigid (rij′id) *adj.*: hard and firmly fixed.

rigor (rig′ər) *n.*: hardship; difficulty.

robust (rō·bust′) *adj.*: strong and healthy.

rollick (räl′ik) *v.*: play in a lively, carefree way; ro —**rollicking** *v.* used as *adj.*

roster (räs′tər) *n.*: list of names.

rouse (rouz) *v.*: stir up, usually to anger or acti wake.

eful (rōō′fəl) *adj.*: having sorrow or pity; regretful. —**ruefully** *adv.*

mple (rum′pəl) *v.*: wrinkle; make untidy. —**rum-pled** *v.* used as *adj.*

t (rut) *n.*: set, routine process, usually viewed as dull.

ge (sāj) *n.*: wise person, especially an elder.

vage (sal′vij) *v.*: save or rescue cargo, goods, prop-erty, and so on. *Salvage* is used especially to mean "save things from a shipwreck." —**salvaged** *v.* used as *adj.*

nter (sôn′tər) *v.*: stroll; walk in an unhurried way.

vor (sā′vər) *v.*: enjoy with appreciation.

ld (skôld) *v.*: burn or injure with hot liquid or steam.

anty (skan′tē) *adj.*: not enough. *Scanty* and *meager* are synonyms; *scanty* and *copious* are antonyms.

athing (skā′thiŋ) *adj.*: harsh.

rawl (skrôl) *v.*: write quickly and sloppily.

rutiny (skrōōt′n·ē) *n.*: close examination.

attle (skut′l) *v.*: run or move quickly; scurry.

ar (sir) *v.*: burn the surface of. —**searing** *v.* used as *adj.*

ep (sēp) *v.*: flow out slowly through small holes; leak.

ethe (sēth) *v.*: be violently angry or disturbed. —**seething** *v.* used as *adj.*

ntry (sen′trē) *n.*: guard.

rewd (shrōōd) *adj.*: clever.

lle (sīd′l) *v.*: move sideways in a sly way.

multaneously (sī′məl·tā′nē·əs) *adj.*: at the same time. —**simultaneously** *adv.*

ge (sinj) *v.*: slightly burn.

ewer (skyōō′ər) *v.*: pierce and hold with a long pin. —**skewered** *v.* used as *adj.*

irt (skʉrt) *v.*: narrowly avoid.

itter (skit′ər) *v.*: skip along quickly and lightly.

ack (slak) *adj.*: loose.

oth (slôth) *n.*: laziness.

ber (sō′bər) *adj.*: serious; calm; thoughtful. —**soberly** *adv.*

lemn (säl′əm) *adj.*: formal and serious.

mber (säm′bər) *adj.*: serious.

w (sō) *v.*: plant seed for growing. —**sowed, sown**

wn (sōn) *v.*: See *sow.*

aring (sper′iŋ) *adj.*: careful in spending or using. —**sparingly** *adv.*

spate (spāt) *n.*: outpouring. In Britain, a *spate* is a flash flood.

specify (spes′ə·fī′) *v.*: describe in detail.

spectacles (spek′tə·kəlz) *n.*: eyeglasses.

squander (skwän′dər) *v.*: waste.

stalwart (stôl′wərt) *adj.*: strong and sturdy.

stamina (stam′ə·nə) *n.*: endurance; ability to resist fatigue.

stately (stāt′lē) *adj.*: dignified; grand.

staunch (stônch) *adj.*: firm; loyal.

sterile (ster′əl) *adj.*: barren; lacking interest or vitality.

stir (stʉr) *v.*: move or change position, especially only slightly.

stoic (stō′ik) *adj.*: not showing or complaining about pain. Stoics were philosophers of ancient Greece who tried not to let pleasure or pain affect them.

stolid (stäl′id) *adj.*: unemotional.

stride (strīd) *v.*: walk with long steps; walk vigorously. —**strode** (strōd), **stridden** (strid′′n)

strode (strōd) *v.*: See *stride.*

stunt (stunt) *v.*: cause to grow improperly. —**stunted** *v.* used as *adj.*

subdue (səb·dōō′) *v.*: soften; reduce. —**subdued** *v.* used as *adj.*

submerge (səb·mʉrj′) *v.*: sink; cover with liquid. —**submerged** *v.* used as *adj.*

substantial (səb·stan′shəl) *adj.*: considerable; strong.

subterfuge (sub′tər·fyōōj′) *n.*: sneaky strategy; trick used to deceive others.

subtle (sut′′l) *adj.*: not open or direct; crafty. —**subtly** *adv.*

suffice (sə·fīs′) *v.*: be enough.

sufficient (sə·fish′ənt) *adj.*: enough.

suffuse (sə·fyōōz′) *v.*: fill with a glow. —**suffused** *v.* used as *adj.*

suppress (sə·pres′) *v.*: keep back; restrain or put down.

surge (sʉrj) *v.*: move in a heavy, swelling motion.

surly (sʉr′lē) *adj.*: bad-tempered, rude, and hostile.

surname (sʉr′nām′) *n.*: last name.

survey (sər·vā′) *v.*: examine; consider carefully.

sustain (sə·stān′) *v.*: support; strengthen. —**sustaining** *v.* used as *adj.*

swagger (swag′ər) *n.*: bold, arrogant stride; strut.

āte, cär; ten, ēve; is, īce; gō, hôrn, look, tōōl; oil, out; up, fʉr; ə *for unstressed vowels, as* a *in* ago, u *in* focus; ′ *as in* tin (lat′′n); chin; she; zh *as in* azure (azh′ər); thin, the; ŋ *as in* ring (riŋ)

---

tangible (tan′jə·bəl) *adj.*: capable of being touched or felt.

taunt (tônt) *v.*: mock; jeer at.

taut (tôt) *adj.*: tense; showing strain.

teeter (tēt′ər) *v.*: wobble.

tempo (tem′pō) *n.*: pace.

tenement (ten′ə·mənt) *n.*: apartment. Tenement buildings are often cheaply built and poorly maintained.

tenet (ten′it) *n.*: belief of a group; doctrine.

testy (tes′tē) *adj.*: irritable. —**testily** *adv.*

tether (teth′ər) *v.*: tie. —**tethered** *v.* used as *adj.*

theorist (thē′ə·rist) *n.*: person having knowledge of, rather than practicing, the principles and methods of an art or a science.

thrive (thrīv) *v.*: prosper or grow well.

throng (thrôŋ) *n.*: crowd.

tidings (tīd′iŋz) *n.*: news.

tier (tir) *n.*: layer; row.

torpor (tôr′pər) *n.*: sluggishness.

torrent (tôr′ənt) *n.*: flood or rush.

trajectory (trə·jek′tə·rē) *n.*: curved path of something thrown or passing through space.

tramp (tramp) *v.*: step on firmly and heavily.

transform (trans·fôrm′) *v.*: change the form or outward appearance of.

treacherous (trech′ər·əs) *adj.*: dangerous; untrustworthy. —**treacherously** *adv.*

trespass (tres′pəs) *v.*: go on another's land or property without permission.

trifle (trī′fəl) *n.*: bit; small amount.

trigger (trig′ər) *v.*: set off.

trundle (trun′dəl) *v.*: roll along.

tuft (tuft) *n.*: bunch or clump of things (such as grass or hair) growing close together.

tyrant (tī′rənt) *n.*: cruel, oppressive ruler.

unbidden (un·bid′'n) *adj.*: not invited; unasked.

unceasing (un·sēs′iŋ) *adj.*: endless; not stopping. —**unceasingly** *adv.*

uncomprehending (un′käm·prə·hend′iŋ) *adj.*: without understanding. —**uncomprehendingly** *adv.*

undaunted (un·dônt′id) *adj.*: not discouraged; not shocked.

undulation (un′dyōō·lā′shən) *n.*: wavy movement.

unison (yōōn′ə·sən) *n.*: harmony; unity. When peo[ple] speak in unison, they are saying the same thing at t[he] same time.

unrequited (un′ri·kwīt′id) *v.* used as *adj.*: not [re]turned in kind.

unwieldy (un·wēl′dē) *adj.*: heavy and awkward; ha[rd] to manage.

upend (up·end′) *v.*: set on end; topple.

usher (ush′ər) *v.*: bring in.

utter (ut′ər) *v.*: speak.

vacate (vā′kāt′) *v.*: cause to be unoccupied; leave.

vain (vān) *adj.*: useless; without result. —**vainly** *adv.*

valiant (val′yənt) *adj.*: brave and determined.

vengeful (venj′fəl) *adj.*: seeking to cause injury in [re]turn for an injury; seeking revenge.

venomous (ven′əm·əs) *adj.*: poisonous; malicious.

vermilion (vər·mil′yən) *adj.*: bright red; scarlet.

vicinity (və·sin′ə·tē) *n.*: neighborhood.

vigil (vij′əl) *n.*: watch; guard.

vigor (vig′ər) *n.*: active physical force; energy.

visualize (vizh′ōō·əl·īz′) *v.*: picture.

wallow (wäl′ō) *v.*: move heavily and clumsily.

waver (wā′vər) *v.*: become unsteady; show doubt [or] indecision.

weary (wir′ē) *v.*: make or become tired or worn o[ut]. —**wearied** *v.* used as *adj.*

wedge (wej) *n.*: piece that is thick at one end and na[r]rows to a thin edge.

whimsical (hwim′zi·kəl) *adj.*: full of silly, fanciful ide[as].

whittle (hwit′əl) *v.*: cut thin pieces from wood with[a] knife; carve.

wholehearted (hōl′härt′id) *adj.*: hearty; since[re]. —**wholeheartedly** *adv.*

wisp (wisp) *n.*: thin, light piece.

wither (with′ər) *v.*: shrivel; dry up. —**withering** [v.] used as *adj.*

woeful (wō′fəl) *adj.*: sad; mournful. —**woefully** *adv.*

writhe (rīth) *v.*: twist and squirm.

zest (zest) *n.*: excitement; keenness.

r permission to use copyrighted material, grateful acknowledg-
ent is made to the following sources:

merican Library Association: From Newbery Award Acceptance
eech by Mildred D. Taylor, 1977.

arroll Arnett: "Early Song" by Gogisgi/Carroll Arnett from *South
ne.* Copyright © 1979 by Gogisgi/Carroll Arnett. Published by Eliza-
th Press.

te Público Press: "Immigrants" from *Borders* by Pat Mora. Copy-
ght © 1986 by Pat Mora. Published by Arte Público Press–Univer-
y of Houston, Houston, TX, 1986. "My Father Is a Simple Man"
om *The Sadness of Days: Selected and New Poems* by Luis Omar Sali-
s. Copyright © 1987 by Luis Omar Salinas. Published by Arte
blico Press–University of Houston, Houston, TX, 1987.

he Associated Press: "Buddies Bare Their Affection for Ill Class-
ate" by Associated Press from *Austin American-Statesman,* March 19,
94. Copyright © 1994 by The Associated Press.

**theneum Books for Young Readers, an imprint of Simon &
huster Children's Publishing Division:** ". . . And Then the Prince
elt Down and Tried to Put the Glass Slipper on Cinderella's Foot"
om *If I Were in Charge of the World and Other Worries* by Judith
orst. Text copyright © 1981 by Judith Viorst.

arma Bene Bambara: Quote by Toni Cade Bambara about writing
ort stories.

san Bergholz Literary Services, New York: "Names/Nombres"
Julia Alvarez. Copyright © 1985 by Julia Alvarez. First published in
uestro, March 1985. All rights reserved. "Cuatro árboles flaquititos"
om *La casa en Mango Street* by Sandra Cisneros, translated by Elena
oniatowska. Copyright © 1984 by Sandra Cisneros; translation
pyright © 1994 by Elena Poniatowska. Published by Vintage Es-
ñol, a division of Random House, Inc. All rights reserved. "Four
inny Trees" from *The House on Mango Street* by Sandra Cisneros.
opyright © 1984 by Sandra Cisneros. Published by Vintage Books, a
vision of Random House, Inc., New York, and in hardcover by Al-
ed A. Knopf, Inc., New York, in 1994. All rights reserved.

OA Editions, Ltd., 260 East Ave., Rochester, NY 14604: From
reaklight" and "the 1st" from *good woman: poems and a memoir
969–1980* by Lucille Clifton. Copyright © 1987 by Lucille Clifton.

seph Bruchac: "Sky Woman" by Joseph Bruchac. Copyright
1997 by Joseph Bruchac.

rthur Cavanaugh: "Miss Awful" by Arthur Cavanaugh from
cCall's, April 1969. Copyright © 1969 by Arthur Cavanaugh.

**hildren's Better Health Institute, Benjamin Franklin Literary &
Medical Society, Inc., Indianapolis, Indiana:** From "Kachinas: Sa-
ed Drama of the Hopis" by Lonnie Dyer from *Young World.* Copy-
ght © 1976 by Review Publishing Company.

olumbia TriStar Television: Slightly adapted from *Brian's Song* by
Villiam Blinn. Copyright © 1971 by Screen Gems, a division of Co-
mbia Pictures.

on Congdon Associates, Inc.: "The Naming of Names" by Ray
radbury from *Thrilling Wonder Stories.* Copyright © 1949 by Standard
Magazines, Inc.; copyright renewed © 1976 by Ray Bradbury.

RICKET Magazine: "Wings" by Bronwen Anne Gilbert from
RICKET, vol. 18, no. 11, July 1991. Copyright © 1991 by Carus Pub-
shing Company. "Sir Kensley the Brave" by Megan Washam from
RICKET, vol. 19, no. 1, September 1991. Copyright © 1991 by Carus
ublishing Company.

rown Publishers, Inc.: "Overture" (retitled "The Power of Music")
om *Nadja on My Way* by Nadja Salerno-Sonnenberg. Copyright
1989 by Nadja Salerno-Sonnenberg.

elacorte Press, a division of Random House, Inc.: "User
riendly" by T. Ernesto Bethancourt from *Connections: Short Stories,*
dited by Donald R. Gallo. Copyright © 1989 by T. Ernesto
ethancourt.

**ial Books for Young Readers, a division of Penguin Putnam
c.:** "The Flight of Icarus" from *Stories of the Gods and Heroes* by Sally

Benson. Copyright 1940 and renewed © 1968 by Sally Benson. *Song
of the Trees* by Mildred D. Taylor. Copyright © 1975 by Mildred
Taylor.

Doubleday, a division of Random House, Inc.: Excerpt (retitled
"The Only Girl in the World for Me") from *Love & Marriage* by Bill
Cosby. Copyright © 1989 by Bill Cosby. "King Midas and the Golden
Touch" from *Tales from Ancient Greece* by Pamela Oldfield. Copyright
© 1988 by Grisewood and Dempsey, Ltd.

Esquire Magazine: "Three Skeleton Key" by George G. Toudouze
from *Esquire,* January 1937. Copyright 1937 by Hearst Communications, Inc. All rights reserved. Esquire is a trademark of Hearst Magazines Property, Inc.

**Dr. Clarissa Pinkola Estés and Ballantine Books, a division of
Random House, Inc.:** From "Sealskin, Soulskin" from *Women Who
Run with the Wolves* by Clarissa Pinkola Estés, Ph.D. Copyright
© 1991, 1992, 1995 by Clarissa Pinkola Estés, Ph.D. All performance,
derivative, adaptation, musical, audio and recording, illustrative, theatrical, film, pictorial, electronic, and all other rights reserved.

Firebrand Books, Ithaca, New York: From "World View" from
Talking Indian: Reflections on Survival and Writing by Anna Lee Walters.
Copyright © 1992 by Anna Lee Walters.

Samuel French, Inc.: From "The Dream of Good Fortune: Arabian
Nights" from *More from Story Theatre,* by Paul Sills. Copyright © 1981
by Paul Sills. CAUTION: Professionals and amateurs are hereby
warned that *More from Story Theatre,* being fully protected under the
copyright laws of the United States of America, the British Common-
wealth countries, including Canada, and the other countries of the
Copyright Union, is subject to a royalty. All rights, including professional, amateur, motion picture, recitation, public reading, radio, television and cable broadcasting, and the rights of translation into
foreign languages, are strictly reserved. Any inquiry regarding the
availability of performance rights, or the purchase of individual copies
of the authorized acting edition, must be directed to Samuel French,
Inc., 45 West 25th Street, NY, NY 10010 with other locations in
Hollywood and Toronto, Canada.

Jean Fritz c/o Refna Wilkin: From "American Bicentennial Reading," prepared by Jean Fritz for The Children's Book Council, Inc.
Copyright © 1975 by Jean Fritz. From "George Washington, My Father, and Walt Disney" by Jean Fritz (given on June 6, 1975, at the
Sixth Annual Spring Festival of the New England Round Table of Children's Librarians at Kennebunkport, Maine) from *The Horn Book,* vol.
LII, no. 2, April 1976. Copyright © 1976 by Jean Fritz.

Gale Research Inc.: Quote by Olivia Coolidge from "Olivia
Coolidge" from *Something About the Author,* vol. 1, edited by Anne
Commire. Copyright © 1971 by Gale Research Inc. Quotes by Anne
McCaffrey from "Anne McCaffrey" from *Something About the Author,*
vol. 8, edited by Anne Commire. Copyright © 1976 by Gale Research
Inc. Quotes by Patricia Lauber from "Patricia Lauber" from *Something
About the Author,* vol. 33, edited by Anne Commire. Copyright © 1983
by Gale Research Inc.

Brooke Garner: Letter to Holt, Rinehart and Winston from Brooke
Garner, November 12, 1991. Copyright © 1997 by Brooke Garner.

Glamour: From "Forum: 'To Help the Handicapped, Talk to Them'"
by Itzhak Perlman from *Glamour,* vol. 85, no. 3, March 1987. Copyright © 1987 by Condé Nast Publications, Inc.

Linda Goss: From "The Frog Who Wanted to Be a Singer" by Linda
Goss from *Talk That Talk: An Anthology of African-American Storytelling*
by Linda Goss and Marian E. Barnes. Copyright © 1983 by Linda
Goss.

Harcourt Brace & Company: From "A Note from the Author"
from *In the Beginning* by Virginia Hamilton. Copyright © 1988 by
Virginia Hamilton. Illustration by Thomas Locker for "Gold" by Pat
Mora from *Home: A Journey Through America,* edited by Thomas
Locker and Candace Christiansen. Copyright © 1998 by Thomas
Locker. "The Algonquin Cinderella," retold by M. R. Cox, from *World
Tales: The Extraordinary Coincidence of Stories Told in All Times, in All*

ilomel Books: *Yeh-Shen: A Cinderella Story from China,* retold by Ling Louie. Text copyright © 1982 by Ai-Ling Louie.

ablishers Weekly: From "Shel Silverstein," an interview by Jean rcier from *Publishers Weekly,* February 24, 1975. Copyright © 1975 Publishers Weekly.

P. Putnam's Sons, a division of Penguin Putnam Inc.: From *mesick* by Jean Fritz. Copyright © 1982 by Jean Fritz.

ndom House UK Ltd.: "Narcissus" (retitled "Echo and Narcis-") from *Tales the Muses Told* by Roger Lancelyn Green. Copyright 1965 by Don Bolognese. Published by The Bodley Head.

tate of Dougal Robertson: Slightly adapted from *Survive the vage Sea* by Dougal Robertson. Copyright © 1975 by Dougal bertson. In memory of the indomitable spirit of Dougal and Lyn bertson and the courage of their family.

t Mora, www.patmora.com: "Gold" by Pat Mora. Copyright © 98 by Pat Mora. Originally published by Harcourt Brace in *Home: A urney Through America* by Thomas Locker and Candace Chrisnsen.

ie Saturday Review: "The Dinner Party" by Mona Gardner from e *Saturday Review of Literature,* vol. 25, no. 5, January 31, 1941. opyright © 1979 by General Media Communications, Inc.

holastic Inc.: From *The Last Dinosaur* by Jim Murphy. Copyright 1988 by Jim Murphy.

ribner, a division of Simon & Schuster: "A Day's Wait" from *inner Take Nothing* by Ernest Hemingway. Copyright 1933 by arles Scribner's Sons; copyright renewed © 1961 by Mary Heming-y.

arold Shaw Publishers, Wheaton, IL 60189: From *Walking on ater* by Madeleine L'Engle. Copyright © 1980 by Crosswicks.

olonel John D. Silvera, Executor of the Estate of Edward Silra: From "Forgotten Dreams" by Edward Silvera from *The Poetry the Negro, 1746–1970,* edited by Langston Hughes and Arna ntemps.

mon & Schuster: From preface to *Talk That Talk: An Anthology of rican-American Storytelling,* edited by Linda Goss and Marian E. rnes. Copyright © 1989 by Linda Goss and Marian E. Barnes. From Peck of Salt" from *Family: A Celebration* by Jane Howard. Copyright 1978 by Jane Howard.

mon & Schuster Books for Young Readers, an imprint of Simon Schuster Children's Publishing Division: From *The Winter Hero* James Lincoln Collier and Christopher Collier. Copyright © 1978 James Lincoln Collier and Christopher Collier. "Papa's Parrot" om *Every Living Thing* by Cynthia Rylant. Text copyright © 1985 by ynthia Rylant.

ary Soto: Comment on "No-Guitar Blues" by Gary Soto.

ll Staines/Mineral River Music: "A Place in the Choir" from *If I ere a Word, Then I'd Be a Song* by Bill Staines. Copyright © 1980 by lk-Legacy Records, Inc.

aniels Associates: "The Hummingbird King" from *The Humming-d King: A Guatemalan Legend,* written and adapted by Argentina lacios. Copyright © 1993 by Troll Associates.

Stone Soup, the magazine by children: From "Being Different" by Amy Yustein, 13 years old, from *Stone Soup, the magazine by children,* September/October 1989. Copyright © 1989 by the Children's Art Foundation. "The Day the Butterfly Came" by Kristen Sparks, 12 years old, from *Stone Soup, the magazine by children,* November/December 1989. Copyright © 1989 by the Children's Art Foundation. "The Pitch That Didn't Work" by Michael Levitin, 13 years old, "An Immigrant in the United States" by Ponn Pet, 11 years old, and "A Typical Day in a Cambodian Village" by Lay Yan, 13 years old, from *Stone Soup, the magazine by children,* vol. 18, no. 3, January/February 1990. Copyright © 1990 by the Children's Art Foundation. "The Nature of Patam" by Benjamin Bethea, 9 years old, from *Stone Soup, the magazine by children,* vol. 21, no. 5, May/June 1993. Copyright © 1993 by the Children's Art Foundation.

Amy Tan and Sandra Dijkstra Literary Agency: "Fish Cheeks" by Amy Tan. Copyright © 1987 by Amy Tan. Originally appeared in *Seventeen Magazine,* December 1987.

Piri Thomas: "Amigo Brothers" from *Stories from El Barrio* by Piri Thomas. Copyright © 1978 by Piri Thomas.

Transafrica Press: Proverb from *Edeno Oo Lmaasai: Wisdom of Maasai* by A. ol'Oloisolo Massek and J. O. Sidai. Copyright © 1974 by Transafrica Publishers.

University of Arizona Press: Quotes by Joseph Bruchac from *Survival This Way: Interviews with American Indian Poets* by Joseph Bruchac. Copyright © 1987 by The Arizona Board of Regents.

University of Notre Dame Press: From *Barrio Boy* by Ernesto Galarza. Copyright © 1971 by University of Notre Dame Press.

Viking Penguin, a division of Penguin Putnam Inc.: "The Creation" from *God's Trombones* by James Weldon Johnson. Copyright 1927 by The Viking Press, Inc.; copyright renewed © 1955 by Grace Nail Johnson.

Anna Lee Walters: "I Am of the Earth" by Anna Walters from *Voices of the Rainbow: Contemporary Poetry by American Indians,* edited by Kenneth Rosen. Copyright © 1975 by Anna Lee Walters.

Mel White: "A Mason-Dixon Memory" by Clifton Davis, slightly adapted from *Reader's Digest,* March 1993. Copyright © 1993 by Mel White.

Roberta Hill Whiteman: From "Depot in Rapid City" by Roberta Hill from *A Book of Women Poets: From Antiquity to Now,* edited by Aliki Barnstone and Willis Barnstone.

T. J. Wilson: "Kids Should Be Paid for Chores" by T. J. Wilson from *Young Writers Literary Magazine,* June 1993. Copyright © 1993 by T. J. Wilson. Published by Atlantic Middle School, North Quincy, MA.

YAHOO!: "YAHOOLIGANS!" title screen, December 18, 1998. Online, World Wide Web. Copyright © 1998 by YAHOO!, Inc. Available at www.yahooligans.com. All rights reserved. YAHOOLIGANS! and the YAHOOLIGANS! logo are trademarks of YAHOO!, Inc.

Joseph D. Younger: From "The Joy Luck Writer," an interview with Amy Tan by Joseph D. Younger from *Amtrak Express Magazine,* vol. 13, no. 4, July/August 1993.

PICTURE CREDITS

he illustrations on the Contents pages are picked up from pages in e textbook. Credits for those illustrations can be found either on e textbook page on which they appear or in the listing below.

age xx–1, Lori Adamski Peek/Tony Stone Images, (inset) Marc uench/Tony Stone Images; 3, Joe McDonald/DRK Photo; 4, Dindia/Omni-Photo Communications; 7, Renee Lynn/Animals Animals; Michael Fogden/Photo Researchers; 9, Dr. E. R. Degginger; 10, nset) Victoria McCormick/Photo Researchers, (background) Dr. R. Degginger; 12, Krupaker Senani/Oxford Scientific Films/Animals nimals; 14, Ingrid Jeske/Animals Animals; 15, A. W. Ambler/Photo esearchers; 16, Corbis; 17, 18, Joyce Photographics/Photo Re-searchers; 18, Dover Publications, Inc.; 25, Ralph A. Reinhold/Animals Animals; 26, Ivan Massar/Black Star; 41, Jack Ackerman/Penguin USA; 65, Ken Biggs/Photo Researchers; 69, Stephen Dalton/Photo Researchers; 70, Tom McHugh/Photo Researchers; 72, Robin Smith/Tony Stone Images; 75, Stephen Dalton/Photo Researchers; 81, Jack Parsons/Omni-Photo Communications; 82, Turnsek/Tony Stone Images; 83, Michael Quackenbush/The Image Bank, (inset) Jack Parsons/Omni-Photo Communications; 84, (inset) J. Bryson/SYGMA, Michael Quackenbush/The Image Bank; 101, F. Cruz/SuperStock; 102–103, Ryuichi Sato/Photonica; 104, © PhotoDisc, Inc. 1998; 105, © 1993 Tom Van Sant/The Geosphere Project/The Stock Market;

VOCABULARY AND SPELLING

NDEX OF ART

NE ART